Special Edition Using MS-DOS 6.22

Third Edition

Jim Cooper

Contributors to previous editions:
Allen L Wyatt, Sr.
Bruce Hallberg
Ed Tiley
Jon Paisley

201 W. 103rd Street
Indianapolis, Indiana 46290

Contents

I

1. DOS and the Personal Computer 11
2. Starting DOS 23
3. Using DOS Commands 41
4. Using the DOS Shell 57

II Files and Directories

5. Understanding Files and Directories 99
6. Understanding Disks and Disk Drives 127
7. Preparing and Maintaining Disks 149
8. Managing Your Files 191
9. Protecting and Recovering Your Data 231

III Controlling DOS

10. Working with System Information 275
11. Controlling Your Environment 293
12. Using Peripherals 307
13. Controlling Devices 317
14. Understanding the International Features of DOS 339

IV Maximizing DOS

15. Using the DOS Editor 361
16. Understanding Batch Files 389
17. Understanding ANSI.SYS 415
18. Mastering DOSKEY and Macros 431
19. Configuring Your Computer 441
20. Networking DOS 471
21. Connecting to the Internet 483
22. Third-Party Utilities 493

V Appendixes

A. Files Supplied with MS-DOS 6.22 503
B. DOS Environment Variables 519
C. DOS Messages 529
D. DOS and DOS Utility Programs' Keyboard Commands 563
E. ASCII and Extended ASCII Codes 573
F. Command Reference 583
G. Glossary 959

Index 965

Special Edition Using MS-DOS 6.22, Third Edition

Copyright © 2002 by Que

All rights reserved. No part of this book shall be reproduced, stored in a retrieval system, or transmitted by any means, electronic, mechanical, photocopying, recording, or otherwise, without written permission from the publisher. No patent liability is assumed with respect to the use of the information contained herein. Although every precaution has been taken in the preparation of this book, the publisher and author assume no responsibility for errors or omissions. Nor is any liability assumed for damages resulting from the use of the information contained herein.

International Standard Book Number: 0-7897-2573-8

Library of Congress Catalog Card Number: 2001087888

Printed in the United States of America

First Printing: May 2001

04   03   02   01   4   3   2   1

Trademarks

All terms mentioned in this book that are known to be trademarks or service marks have been appropriately capitalized. Que cannot attest to the accuracy of this information. Use of a term in this book should not be regarded as affecting the validity of any trademark or service mark.

Warning and Disclaimer

Every effort has been made to make this book as complete and as accurate as possible, but no warranty or fitness is implied. The information provided is on an "as is" basis. The author and the publisher shall have neither liability nor responsibility to any person or entity with respect to any loss or damages arising from the information contained in this book.

Associate Publisher
Dean Miller

Acquisitions Editor
Michelle Newcomb

Development Editor
Maureen McDaniel

Managing Editor
Thomas F. Hayes

Project Editor
Heather McNeill

Copy Editor
Chuck Hutchinson

Indexer
Chris Barrick

Proofreader
Maribeth Echard

Technical Editor
James A. Glocke

Team Coordinator
Cindy Teeters

Interior Designer
Ruth Harvey

Cover Designers
Dan Armstrong
Ruth Harvey

Page Layout
Heather Hiatt Miller
Stacey Richwine-DeRome

CYNTHIA STENSETH

Table of Contents

Introduction 1

Who Should Read This Book? 2

What Hardware Do You Need? 2

What Versions Are Covered? 2

What Is Not Covered? 3

How Is This Book Organized? 3
    Part I: DOS Fundamentals 3
    Part II: Files and Directories 4
    Part III: Controlling DOS 5
    Part IV: Maximizing DOS 5
    Appendixes 6

Conventions Used in This Book 7

I DOS Fundamentals

1 DOS and the Personal Computer 11

DOS, Windows, and the PC 12

Other Flavors of DOS 12

PC Hardware 12
    The PC Architecture 13
    Computer Memory 13
    Peripheral Devices 14

What Happens When the Power Is Turned On? 15

DOS and Random Access Memory 17
    Conventional Memory 18
    Expanded Memory 19
    Extended Memory 20

DOS and Disks 20

2 Starting DOS 23

Booting Your Computer 24
    Understanding the Boot Disk 24
    Creating a Floppy Boot Disk 25

System Configuration 26
    `CONFIG.SYS` 27
    `AUTOEXEC.BAT` 30

Creating Multiple Configurations 32
    Creating a Default Configuration 34
    Displaying Color Menus 34
    Using the Configuration Menu As a System Menu 36

Project: Controlling the Boot Process 38

3 Using DOS Commands 41

Understanding DOS Commands 42
    Internal Versus External 42

Understanding the Elements of a DOS Command 42
    The Command Syntax 43
    The Command-Line Parameters 45
    The Optional Switches 45

Getting Help 46
    Using the Command-Line Help Switch 46
    Using the Online Help System 47

Issuing DOS Commands 51
    Editing and Canceling Commands 52
    Using Scroll Control 54
    Using Wildcards in DOS Commands 54

Troubleshooting 55

4 Using the DOS Shell 57

What Is the DOS Shell? 58

Starting the DOS Shell 59
    Using the Shell Interface 60
    Selecting an Area 62
    Moving Around an Area 63

Using the DOS Shell Menus 64
  Using the Menu Bar 64
  Using Pull-Down Menus 64
  Using Keystroke Commands 66
  Using Dialog Boxes 67
  Modifying the View 70

Using the Shell Screen Modes 75

Using the Program List 77
  Working with Program Groups 78
  Working with Program Items 81

Working with Directories 83
  Expanding and Collapsing Branches 84
  Creating Directories 86

Working with Files 87
  Selecting a Single File 87
  Selecting Multiple Files 87
  Selecting All Files 89
  Deselecting All Files 89
  Selecting Files Across Directories 89
  Copying Files in the Shell 89
  Moving a File in the Shell 91
  Using the Shell to View a File 91
  Associating Files with Programs 92

Using the Task Swapper 93

Project: Using the Help System 94

II Files and Directories

5 Understanding Files and Directories 99

Introducing the DOS File System 100
  Understanding Files 100
  Understanding Filenames 101
  Observing File-Naming Conventions 104
  Understanding File Attributes 107

Understanding the Role of Directories 110

Expanding the File System Through Subdirectories 113
  Understanding Pathname Expressions 115
  Creating Directories with MKDIR (MD) 117
  Changing the Current Directory with CHDIR (CD) 119
  Deleting Directories with RMDIR (RD) 120
  Using DELTREE to Delete Directories 120
  Renaming Directories 121

Helping DOS Find Files with PATH 122

Listing Directories with TREE 123

Using a Temporary Directory 124

Troubleshooting 125

6 Understanding Disks and Disk Drives 127

Understanding the Disk's Magnetic Storage Technique 128

Understanding Disk Drives 129
  Hard Disk Drives 130
  Floppy Disk Drives 131
  Write-Protecting a Floppy Disk 132

Understanding the Dynamics of the Disk Drive 133
  Disk Drive Heads 133
  Disk Tracks 134
  Disk Cylinders 134
  Disk Sectors 136

Understanding Disk Formats 137
  Floppy Disk Formats 138
  Raw Capacity and Usable Capacity 139
  Hard Disk Drive Formats 139

Understanding DoubleSpace   140
  Installing DoubleSpace   141
  Controlling the Operation of
  DoubleSpace   142
  Displaying Compressed Drive
  Information   142
  Changing the Size of a Compressed
  Drive   143
  Changing the Compression
  Ratio   143
  Formatting a Compressed Drive   145
  Deleting a Compressed Drive   145
  Creating a New Compressed
  Drive   145
  Using Other DoubleSpace
  Features   146

Case Study: Adjusting for Drift   148

7 Preparing and Maintaining Disks   149

Understanding Disk Preparation   150

Preparing Floppy Disks with the
FORMAT Command   151
  Formatting Floppy Disks   152
  FORMAT's Other Tasks   154
  Using FORMAT's Switches   156

Preparing the Hard Disk   158
  Dividing a Hard Disk with
  FDISK   159
  Partitioning a Drive   164
  Formatting a Hard Disk   166

Disk Commands   166
  Naming Disks with LABEL   166
  Examining Volume Labels with
  VOL   167
  Using SYS to Transfer the DOS
  System   167

Getting the Most Speed from Your Hard
Disk   168
  Using a Disk Cache
  (SMARTDrive)   169
  Using FASTOPEN   173

Using a RAM Disk   174
Defragmenting Your Disk   177

Getting the Most Space from Your Hard
Disk   181
  Deleting Unnecessary Files   182
  Using File Compression   183
  Archiving Files   183

Projects   184
  Analyzing a Disk with CHKDSK   184
  Analyzing a Disk with the SCANDISK
  Utility   188

8 Managing Your Files   191

Using DOS to Work with Files   192

Listing Files with the DIR
Command   193
  Issuing the DIR Command   193
  Understanding the Operation of the
  DIR Command   194
  Displaying a Screen of Information
  with the DIR Command   195
  Searching for Files with the DIR
  Command   198
  Customizing the DIR Command   199

Viewing Files   199
  Understanding Types of Files   200
  Using the TYPE Command to View
  Files   200

Copying Files   202
  Using the COPY Command   202
  Using the XCOPY Command   206
  Copying Entire Disks with
  DISKCOPY   210

Moving Files   212
  Moving Directories and Files   213
  Renaming Directories with
  MOVE   214

Setting Defaults for COPY, XCOPY, and
MOVE   214

Renaming Files 214

Comparing Files 215
    Comparing Files with FC 215
    Comparing Disks with DISKCOMP 219

Deleting Files 221
    Understanding the Delete Operation 221
    Deleting Files from the Command Line 222
    Deleting Unwanted Files 222

Using Interlnk to Share Another Computer's Resources 222
    Setting Up Interlnk 223
    Loading INTERLNK.EXE 225
    Loading the Server 226
    Establishing the Interlnk Connection 227
    Using Interlnk to Transfer Files 228
    Using a Remote Printer 228
    Installing Interlnk Remotely 228
    Running Programs Remotely 229

Case Study: Editing Files with Multiple Data Formats 229

9 Protecting Your Data 231

Avoiding Data Loss 232

Understanding Microsoft Backup 233
    Configuring the Backup Programs 235
    Understanding Microsoft Backup Functions 236
    Backup Types 238
    Issuing the MSBACKUP Command 239

Using Microsoft Backup 239
    Performing a Full Backup 239
    Performing Intermediate Backups 242
    Special-Purpose Backups 243
    Using Other Backup Options 247
    Restoring Backup Files 248

Understanding Computer Viruses 252
    Understanding How Viruses Spread 252
    Fighting Viruses with Microsoft Anti-Virus 253
    Using the Windows Version of Microsoft Anti-Virus 256
    Guarding Against Infection 257

Unformatting a Disk 257
    Recovering from an Accidental Format 258
    Recovering from an Accidental Format Without a MIRROR Image File 259
    Rebuilding a Partition Table 261

Recovering Deleted Files with UNDELETE 262
    Using UNDELETE from the Command Line 262
    Recovering Files with UNDELETE 264
    Using the DOS Directory to Recover a File 266

Using the Microsoft Undelete Program for Windows 3.x 267
    Configuring Microsoft Undelete 267
    Selecting Files to Recover 268
    Recovering Files 269
    Using Other Options 270

Project: Developing a Backup Policy 270

III Controlling DOS

10 Working with System Information 275

Changing the Date and Time 276
    Issuing the DATE Command 277
    Issuing the TIME Command 278

Displaying the Version Using the VER Command 279

Setting the Version Using the SETVER Command 280

Displaying Memory Statistics 283
    Issuing the MEM Command 283
    Understanding the Operation of MEM 283

Loading a Secondary Command Processor 288
    Issuing the COMMAND Command 288
    Understanding the Operation of COMMAND.COM 289
    Using EXIT to Leave the Current Copy of the Command Processor 290
    Uses for a Secondary Command Processor 290

11 Controlling Your Environment 293

Changing DOS Variables 294
    Issuing the SET Command 294
    Changing Environment Variables with SET 294
    Defining Your Own Environmental Variables with SET 295

Changing the User Interface 295
    Changing the Command Prompt with PROMPT 295
    Altering the Look of the Screen with MODE 298

Changing Disk Drives 301
    The ASSIGN Command 302
    The JOIN Command 302
    The SUBST Command 302
    Using the COMSPEC Variable 304

12 Using Peripherals 307

Understanding Device Drivers 308
    Understanding Hardware Interrupts 309
    Understanding Direct Memory Access (DMA) Channels 311
    Understanding Memory Input/Output Addresses 312

Setting Up Device Drivers 312

Troubleshooting Device Drivers 314

13 Controlling Devices 317

Device Commands 318

The CLS Command 319

The GRAPHICS Command 319
    Issuing the GRAPHICS Command 319
    Using GRAPHICS to Print a Screen Image 321

The PRINT Command 322
    Issuing the PRINT Command 322
    Using PRINT to Print Several Files 324
    General Rules for Using PRINT 324

The CTTY Command 325

The MODE Command 326
    Using MODE to Change Parallel Port Settings 326
    Using MODE to Change Serial Port Settings 328
    Using MODE to Redirect a Parallel Port to a Serial Port 330
    Using MODE to Change the Typematic Rate 331

Using Redirection Commands 332
    Issuing the Redirection Operators 332
    General Rules for Using Redirection 334

The MORE Filter 334
    Issuing the MORE Filter 334
    Using MORE to Pause the
    Screen 334
    General Rules for Using MORE 335

The FIND Filter 335
    Issuing the FIND Filter 335
    Using FIND to Find Files on
    Disk 336
    General Rules for Using FIND 337

The SORT Filter 337
    Issuing the SORT Filter 337
    Using SORT to Sort Subdirectory
    Listings 338
    General Rules for Using SORT 338

14 Understanding the International Features of DOS 339

Internationalization 340

Understanding COUNTRY.SYS 340

Understanding KEYB.COM 342

Understanding Code Page
Switching 344
    Checking Your Hardware for Code
    Page Switching 345
    Installing Code Page Switching 346
    Loading the Code Page Tables 348
    Switching the Code Page 349
    Exploring More Uses for MODE and
    CODEPAGE 350
    Considering Keyboard
    Remappings 351
    Using Dead Keys 352
    Using Foreign-Language
    Commands 354

International Country Codes 354

IV Maximizing DOS

15 Using the DOS Editor 361

Understanding the DOS Editor 362
    Uses for the DOS Editor 362
    Files Required to Run the DOS
    Editor 362
    Using the DOS Editor from a
    Floppy Disk 363
    Starting the DOS Editor 363
    Getting Acquainted with the Initial
    Editor Screen 364

Navigating the DOS Editor 364
    Understanding the Menu System 365
    Understanding Dialog Boxes 365
    Using Shortcut Keys 366
    Using a Mouse 367

Mastering Fundamental Editing
Techniques 368
    Moving the Cursor 369
    Scrolling 370
    Inserting Text into a Line 370
    Deleting Text from a Line 370
    Splitting and Joining Lines 371
    Inserting and Deleting an Entire
    Line 371
    Overtyping 371

Learning Special Editing
Techniques 371
    Using Automatic Indent 372
    Using Tab 372
    Using Place Markers 373

Block Editing 373
    Selecting Text 373
    Understanding the Clipboard 374
    Working with Text Blocks 374

Searching and Replacing 376
    Using the Find Command 377
    Using the Change Command 378

Managing Files 379
   Introducing the File Menu 379
   Saving a File 380
   Using the Open Command to Load a File 382
   Loading a File When You First Start the DOS Editor 383
   Using the New Command 383
   Printing a File 383
   Exiting the DOS Editor 384

Starting the DOS Editor with Optional Switches 384

Project: Customizing the DOS Editor Screen 385
   Changing Colors and Removing Scrollbars 385
   Saving Customized Settings 386
   Using the Help System 387

16 Understanding Batch Files 389

Introducing Batch Files 390

Understanding the Contents of Batch Files 391

Creating a Simple Batch File 392

Understanding Replaceable Parameters 393

Using Batch File Commands 397
   Displaying Messages and Inserting Comments 398
   Branching with GOTO 398
   Using the IF Command 399

Pausing for Input in a Batch File 404
   Making a Two-Way Choice 405
   Creating a Simple Menu 405
   Creating a Simple Display Menu 406

Using FOR..IN..DO 407
   Using a FOR..IN..DO Batch File 408

Using FOR..IN..DO at the DOS Prompt 409
Using FOR..IN..DO with Other Commands 409

Moving Parameters with SHIFT 409

Running Batch Files from Other Batch Files 411
   Shifting Control Permanently to Another Batch File 411
   Calling a Batch File and Returning Using CALL 411
   Using COMMAND.COM to Execute a Batch File 412

17 Understanding ANSI.SYS 415

What Is ANSI.SYS? 416

Installing ANSI.SYS 416

Using ANSI.SYS 416
   Issuing ANSI.SYS Codes in Batch Files 417
   Issuing ANSI.SYS Codes in Text Files 418
   Issuing ANSI.SYS Codes with the PROMPT Command 419

Controlling Your Screen with ANSI.SYS 419
   Cursor Movement 420
   Cursor Positioning 420
   Setting the Screen Mode 421
   Setting the Text Attributes 421
   Screen Control 423

Customizing Your Keyboard with ANSI.SYS 423
   Reassigning Character Keys 424

ANSI Control Codes 425
   ANSI Set and Reset Display Mode Control Codes 425
   ANSI Display Color and Attribute Control Codes 425
   ANSI Cursor Control Codes 426

ANSI Miscellaneous Display Control Codes   427
ANSI Keyboard Layout Control Codes   427

18 Mastering DOSKEY and Macros   431

Using DOSKEY   432
   Loading DOSKEY   432
   Editing the Command Line   433
   Reusing Commands   434

Creating and Using Macros   436
   Creating Macros   437
   Running Macros   439
   Deleting Macros   440

19 Configuring Your Computer   441

Getting the Most from Your Computer Resources   442

Understanding Device Drivers   443

Optimizing Your Computer's Memory   445
   Using Extended Memory and HIMEM.SYS   445
   Understanding HIMEM.SYS   445
   Loading DOS into High Memory   448
   Using Expanded Memory and EMM386.EXE   449
   Loading Device Drivers and TSRs into Upper Memory   451
   Displaying the Amount of Free and Used Memory   453
   Configuring Memory with MemMaker   455

Providing Memory for Your Applications   460

Increasing Hard Disk Performance   461

Fine-Tuning Your Computer with CONFIG.SYS and AUTOEXEC.BAT   463

Accessing Files through FCBS   463
Using the FILES Command   463
Using LASTDRIVE to Change the Number of Disk Drives   464
Using the SHELL Command   464
Using the INSTALL Command   466
Using the REM Command   467
Using the SWITCHES Command   467
Telling DOS When to Break   468
Using the DOS Pretender Commands   468
Using Other Device Control Commands   469

20 Networking DOS   471

Common Networks for DOS-Based Computers   472

Learning Preinstallation Items   472

Installing the Novell NetWare Client Software   473

Installing the Microsoft Network Client   478

Using the Network   481

Project: Network Client Setup Tips   482

21 Connecting to the Internet   483

Internet Connection Options for DOS-Based Computers   484

Connecting to Your ISP   484

Using Internet Tools   485

A Sample FTP Session   489

Project: Common Problems with DOS Internet Tools   491

22 Third-Party Utilities   493

Enhancing Your Computer with Utility Programs   494

Understanding Freeware, Shareware, and Demoware 494

PKWare's PKZIP and PKUNZIP 495

McAfee VirusScan 496

4DOS 497

V Appendixes

A Files Supplied with MS-DOS 6.22 503

About MS-DOS Files 504

MS-DOS 6.22 Files 504

MS-DOS 6.22 Supplemental Disk Files 512

MS-DOS Utility File Extensions by Version 515

B DOS Environment Variables 519

Understanding the DOS Environment 520

APPEND 520

COMSPEC 521

CONFIG 522

COPYCMD 522

DIRCMD 522

MSDOSDATA 523

PATH 524

PROMPT 525

TEMP and TMP 525

windir 526

WINPMT 526

C DOS Messages 529

General DOS Messages 530

DOS Device Error Messages 557

D DOS and DOS Utility Programs' Keyboard Commands 563

DOS Startup Control Keys 564

ROM BIOS Control Keys 564

DOS Control Keys 565

Command-Line Editing Keys Without DOSKEY 565

Command-Line Editing Keys with DOSKEY 567

Edit Keystroke Commands 568

DOS Shell Keystroke Commands 569

E ASCII and Extended ASCII Codes 573

F Command Reference 583

DOS Commands by Function 583
   Batch File Commands 584
   CONFIG.SYS Commands 584
   CONFIG.SYS DEVICE= Drivers 585
   Directory Commands 586
   Disk Commands 586
   File Commands 587
   DOS Applications 587
   Help Commands 588
   International Commands and Device Drivers 588
   Memory and System Performance Commands 589
   Miscellaneous Commands 589
   Windows Applications 590

Conventions Used in This Command Reference 590
   Icons Used in This Command Reference 592
   Filenames and Pathnames 593

Legal Filename Characters 593
DOS Reserved Names 594

?, *   1.0 and later—Internal 594
Using the ? Wildcard Character in a Filename or Extension 595
Using the * Wildcard Character in a Filename or Extension 595
Examples 595
See Also 595

> and >>   2.0 and later—Internal 596
See Also 596

<   2.0 and later—Internal 596
See Also 597

| 2.0 and later—Internal 597
See Also 598

:label   1.0 and later—Internal 598
Syntax 598
Notes 598
Examples 598
Messages 598
See Also 599

%n   1.0 and later—Internal 599
Syntax 599
Notes 599
Examples 600
See Also 600

%envir%   4.0 and later—Internal 600
Syntax 600
Notes 600
Examples 601
See Also 602

@   4.0 and later—Internal 602
Syntax 602
Notes 603
See Also 603

;   6.0 and later—Internal 603
Syntax 603
Notes 603
Examples 604
See Also 604

?   6.0 and later—Internal 604
Syntax 604
Parameters and Switches 604
Notes 604
Examples 605
Messages 605
See Also 605

[blockname]   6.0 and later—Internal 606
Syntax 606
Notes 606
Examples 607
See Also 608

ANSI.SYS (device driver)   2.0 and later—External 608
Syntax 608
Parameters and Switches 609
Notes 609
Examples 610
See Also 610

APPEND   3.3 and later—External 610
Syntax 610
Parameters and Switches 611
Notes 611
Examples 612
Messages 612
See Also 613

ASSIGN   2.0 to 5.0—External 613
Using SUBST Instead of ASSIGN 613
See Also 613

ATTRIB   3.0 and later—External 613
Syntax 614
Parameters and Switches 614
Notes 614
Examples 615
Messages 615
See Also 615

BACKUP   2.0 to 5.0—External 616
See Also 616

BREAK   2.0 and later—Internal
BREAK=   2.0 and later—Internal   616
　Syntax   616
　Parameters and Switches   616
　Notes   616
　See Also   617

BUFFERS=   2.0 and later—Internal   617
　Syntax   617
　Parameters and Switches   617
　Notes   618
　See Also   618

CALL   3.3 and later—Internal   619
　Syntax   619
　Parameters and Switches   619
　Notes   619
　Examples   620
　Messages   621
　See Also   621

CD or CHDIR   2.0 and later—Internal   621
　Syntax   621
　Parameters and Switches   622
　Notes   622
　Examples   622
　Messages   623
　See Also   624

CHAIN   624
　Syntax   624
　Parameters and Switches   624

CHCP   3.3 and later—Internal   624
　Syntax   624
　Parameters and Switches   624
　Notes   624
　Messages   625
　See Also   625

CHDIR (see CD)   626

CHECK   626
　Syntax   626
　Parameters and Switches   626
　Remarks   626

CHKDSK   1.0 and later—External   626
　Syntax   626
　Parameters and Switches   626
　Exit Codes   627
　Rules   627
　Notes   627
　Messages   628
　See Also   630

CHKSTATE.SYS (see MEMMAKER)   631
　See Also   631

CHOICE   6.0 and later—External   631
　Syntax   631
　Parameters and Switches   631
　Exit Codes   632
　Notes   632
　Examples   632
　See Also   633

CLS   2.0 and later—Internal   633
　Syntax   633
　Notes   633
　See Also   634

CMOSCLK.SYS   634
　Syntax   634
　Parameters and Switches   634
　Notes   634

CNFIGNAM.EXE   634
　Syntax   634
　Parameters and Switches   634
　Notes   635

COMMAND   2.0 and later—External   635
　Syntax   635
　Parameters and Switches   635
　Rules   636
　Notes   636
　See Also   636

COMP   1.0 to 5.0—External   636
　Syntax   637
　Parameters and Switches   637

Notes 637
Messages 637
See Also 638

CONFIG 638
Syntax 638
Parameters and Switches 638

COPY 1.0 and later—Internal 639
Syntax 639
Parameters and Switches 639
Rules 640
Notes 641
Messages 642
See Also 642

COUNTRY= 3.0 and later—Internal 642
Syntax 643
Parameters and Switches 643
Notes 643
Examples 644
See Also 644

COUNTRY.SYS (see COUNTRY=) 644
See Also 645

CPBACKUP 645
Syntax 645
Parameters and Switches 645
Notes 647
See Also 647

CPBDIR 647
Syntax 647
Parameters and Switches 647
See Also 647

CPSCHED 647
Syntax 647
Parameters and Switches 648
See Also 648

CRC 648
Syntax 648
Parameters and Switches 648

CREATE 648
Syntax 648
Parameters and Switches 648
See Also 649

CSCRIPT 649
Syntax 649
Parameters and Switches 649
Notes 650

CTTY 2.0 and later—Internal 650
Syntax 650
Parameters and Switches 650
Notes 650
See Also 651

CURSOR.EXE 651
Syntax 651
Parameters and Switches 651

CVT.EXE 651
Syntax 651
Parameters and Switches 651
Notes 651

DATAMON 652
Syntax 652
Parameters and Switches 652
Notes 652

DATE 1.0 and later—Internal 653
Syntax 653
Parameters and Switches 653
Notes 653
See Also 653

DBLSPACE 6.0 and later—External 654
Syntax 654
Notes 654
See Also 655

DBLSPACE/AUTOMOUNT 6.2—External 655
Syntax 655
Parameters and Switches 655
Notes 655

Examples 655
See Also 655

DBLSPACE/CHKDSK 6.0 only—
External 656
    Syntax 656
    Parameters and Switches 656
    Notes 656
    See Also 656

DBLSPACE/COMPRESS 6.0 and later—
External 656
    Syntax 656
    Parameters and Switches 656
    Notes 657
    Examples 657
    See Also 657

DBLSPACE/CREATE 6.0 and later—
External 657
    Syntax 658
    Parameters and Switches 658
    Notes 658
    Examples 659
    See Also 659

DBLSPACE/DEFRAGMENT 6.0 and later—
External 659
    Syntax 659
    Parameters and Switches 659
    Notes 659
    See Also 660

DBLSPACE/DELETE 6.0 and later—
External 660
    Syntax 660
    Parameters and Switches 660
    Notes 660
    See Also 661

DBLSPACE/DOUBLEGUARD 6.2—
External 661
    Syntax 661
    Parameters and Switches 661
    Notes 661
    Examples 661
    See Also 661

DBLSPACE/FORMAT 6.0 and later—
External 661
    Syntax 662
    Parameters and Switches 662
    Notes 662
    See Also 662

DBLSPACE/INFO 6.0 and later—
External 662
    Syntax 662
    Parameters and Switches 662
    See Also 663

DBLSPACE/LIST 6.0 and later—
External 663
    Syntax 663
    See Also 663

DBLSPACE/MOUNT 6.0 and later—
External 663
    Syntax 663
    Parameters and Switches 664
    Notes 664
    Examples 664
    See Also 664

DBLSPACE/RATIO 6.0 and later—
External 664
    Syntax 665
    Parameters and Switches 665
    Notes 665
    Examples 665
    See Also 665

DBLSPACE/SIZE 6.0 and later—
External 665
    Syntax 666
    Parameters and Switches 666
    Examples 666
    See Also 666

DBLSPACE/UNCOMPRESS 6.2—
External 666
    Syntax 666
    Parameters and Switches 667
    Notes 667
    See Also 667

DBLSPACE/UNMOUNT   6.0 and later—
External   667
   Syntax   667
   Parameters and Switches   667
   Notes   668
   See Also   668

DBLSPACE.SYS (device driver)
6.0 and later—External   668
   Syntax   668
   Parameters and Switches   668
   Notes   669
   Examples   670
   See Also   670

DCONVERT   671
   Syntax   671
   Parameters and Switches   671
   Notes   671
   See Also   671

DEBUG   1.0 and later—External   671
   Syntax   671
   Parameters and Switches   672
   Notes   672
   Examples   672

DEFRAG   6.0 and later—External   672
   Syntax   672
   Parameters and Switches   673
   Exit Codes   674
   Notes   674
   See Also   675

DEL or ERASE   1.0 and later—
Internal   675
   Syntax   675
   Parameters and Switches   675
   Notes   675
   Messages   676
   See Also   676

DELOLDOS   5.0 and later—
External   676
   Syntax   676
   Parameters and Switches   676
   Notes   676
   See Also   676

DELPURGE.EXE   677
   Syntax   677
   Parameters and Switches   677

DELWATCH.EXE   677
   Syntax   677
   Parameters and Switches   677
   See Also   678

DELQ or ERAQ   678
   Syntax   678
   Parameters and Switches   678

DELTREE   6.0 and later—
External   679
   Syntax   679
   Parameters and Switches   679
   Exit Codes   679
   Notes   679
   See Also   679

DEVICE=   2.0 and later—Internal   679
   Syntax   680
   Parameters and Switches   680
   Notes   680
   Examples   681
   Messages   681
   See Also   682

DEVICEHIGH=   5.0 and later—
Internal   682
   Syntax   682
   Parameters and Switches   683
   Notes   683
   Examples   685
   Messages   686
   See Also   686

DEVLOAD   687
   Syntax   687
   Parameters and Switches   687

DIR   1.0 and later—Internal   687
   Syntax   687
   Parameters and Switches   687
   Notes   689
   See Also   689

DISKCOMP 1.0 and later—
External 690
   Syntax 690
   Parameters and Switches 690
   Exit Codes 690
   Notes 690
   Messages 691
   See Also 691

DISKCOPY 1.0 and later—
External 692
   Syntax 692
   Parameters and Switches 692
   Exit Codes 692
   Notes 692
   Messages 693
   See Also 694

DISKMAP.EXE 694
   Syntax 694
   Parameters and Switches 694

DISKOPT.EXE 694
   Syntax 694
   Parameters and Switches 695

DISPLAY.SYS (device driver)
3.3 and later—External 695
   Syntax 695
   Parameters and Switches 696
   Notes 697
   Examples 697
   See Also 698

DOS= 5.0 and later—Internal 698
   Syntax 698
   Parameters and Switches 698
   Notes 698
   Examples 699
   Messages 700
   See Also 700

DOSBOOK 700
   Syntax 700
   Parameters and Switches 700

DOSDATA 701
   Syntax 701
   Parameters and Switches 701

DOSDOCK 701
   Syntax 701
   Parameters and Switches 701

DOSKEY 5.0 and later—External 701
   Syntax 701
   Parameters and Switches 702
   Notes 702
   Examples 703
   Messages 704
   See Also 704

DOSSHELL 4.0 to 6.0—External 704
   Syntax 704
   Parameters and Switches 704
   Notes 705
   Examples 706
   Messages 706
   See Also 707

DPMI 707
   Syntax 707
   Parameters and Switches 707

DPMS.EXE 707
   Syntax 707
   Parameters and Switches 708
   Notes 708

DRIVER.SYS (device driver)
3.2 and later—External 708
   Syntax 708
   Parameters and Switches 708
   Notes 710
   Examples 711
   Messages 711
   See Also 711

DRIVPARM= 3.2 and later—
Internal 711
   Syntax 711
   Parameters and Switches 711

Notes 712
Examples 713
See Also 714

DRMOUSE 714
Syntax 714
Parameters and Switches 714

DRVLOCK 714
Syntax 714
Parameters and Switches 714

DYNALOAD 715
Syntax 715
Parameters and Switches 715
Notes 715

E 715
Syntax 715
Parameters and Switches 716
Notes 716

ECHO 2.0 and later—Internal 716
Syntax 716
Parameters and Switches 717
Notes 717
Examples 718
See Also 719

EDIT 5.0 and later—External 719
Syntax 719
Parameters and Switches 719
See Also 720

EDLIN 1.0 to 5.0—External 720
See Also 720

EGA.SYS (device driver) 5.0 and later—External 720
Syntax 720
Parameters and Switches 720
Notes 720
Examples 721
See Also 721

EJECT 721
Syntax 721
Parameters and Switches 721
Remarks 721

EMM386 5.0 and later—External 721
Syntax 722
Parameters and Switches 722
Notes 722
See Also 722

EMM386.EXE (device driver) 5.0 and later—External 722
Syntax 722
Parameters and Switches 723
Notes 726
See Also 726

ERASE (see DEL) 726

ERAQ (see DELQ) 726

EXE2BIN 1.1 to 5.0—External 727
Syntax 727
Parameters and Switches 727
Notes 727

EXIT 2.0 and later—Internal 727
Syntax 727
Notes 728
See Also 728

EXPAND 5.0 and later—External 728
Syntax 728
Parameters and Switches 728
Rules 728
Notes 729
Examples 729
Messages 729
See Also 729

EXTRACT 730
Syntax 730
Parameters and Switches 730

FASTHELP 6.0 and later—External 730
Syntax 730
Parameters and Switches 730
Notes 731
See Also 731

FASTOPEN 3.3 and later—External 731
   Syntax 731
   Parameters and Switches 731
   Rules 731
   Notes 732
   See Also 732

FC 3.3 and later—External 732
   Syntax 732
   Parameters and Switches 733
   Notes 733
   Examples 734
   See Also 734

FCBS= 3.1 and later—Internal 734
   Syntax 734
   Parameters and Switches 734
   Notes 734
   See Also 735

FDISK 2.0 and later—External 735
   Syntax 735
   Parameters and Switches 735
   Rules 735
   Notes 736
   See Also 736

FILELINK 736

FILES= 2.0 and later—Internal 737
   Syntax 737
   Parameters and Switches 737
   Notes 737
   Examples 737
   See Also 738

FILEUP 738
   Syntax 738
   Parameters and Switches 738
   Notes 738
   See Also 738

FIND 2.0 and later—External 738
   Syntax 738
   Parameters and Switches 738
   Exit Codes 739
   Rules 739
   Notes 739
   Examples 739
   See Also 740

FOR 2.0 and later—Internal 740
   Syntax 740
   Parameters and Switches 740
   Notes 741
   Examples 742
   See Also 742

FORMAT 1.0 and later—External 743
   Syntax 743
   Parameters and Switches 743
   Exit Codes 744
   Rules 744
   Notes 745
   Messages 746
   See Also 746

GOTO 2.0 and later—Internal 747
   Syntax 747
   Parameters and Switches 747
   Notes 747
   See Also 747

GRAFTABL 3.0 to 5.0—External 747
   Syntax 747
   Parameters and Switches 748
   Exit Codes 748
   Notes 748
   See Also 748

GRAPHICS 2.0 and later—External 748
   Syntax 748
   Parameters and Switches 749
   See Also 750

HCONVERT 750
   Syntax 750
   Parameters and Switches 750
   Remarks 750

HELP 5.0 and later—External 750
    Syntax 751
    Parameters and Switches 751
    Notes 751
    See Also 751

HIINSTALL or INSTALLHIGH 751
    Syntax 751
    Parameters and Switches 752

HILOAD (see LOADHIGH) 752

HIMEM.SYS (device driver)
4.0 and later—External 752
    Syntax 752
    Parameters and Switches 752
    Notes 756
    Examples 757
    Messages 757
    See Also 759

IBMAVD 759
    Syntax 759

IBMAVSP 759
    Syntax 759
    Parameters and Switches 760

IEXTRACT 761
    Syntax 761
    Parameters and Switches 761

IF 2.0 and later—Internal 761
    Syntax 761
    Parameters and Switches 761
    Notes 762
    Examples 764
    See Also 765

INCLUDE= 6.0 and later—Internal 765
    Syntax 766
    Parameters and Switches 766
    Notes 766
    Examples 767
    See Also 768

INSTALL= 4.0 and later—Internal 768
    Syntax 768
    Parameters and Switches 768
    Notes 768
    Examples 769
    Messages 769
    See Also 769

INSTALLHIGH (see HIINSTALL) 769

INTERLNK 6.0 and later—
External 770
    Syntax 770
    Parameters and Switches 770
    Notes 770
    Examples 772
    Messages 773
    See Also 774

INTERLNK.EXE (device driver)
6.0 and later—External 774
    Syntax 774
    Parameters and Switches 774
    Notes 776
    Examples 778
    Messages 779
    See Also 781

INTERSVR 6.0 and later—External 781
    Syntax 781
    Parameters and Switches 781
    Notes 782
    Examples 784
    Messages 784
    See Also 786

JOIN 3.1 to 5.0—External 786
    Syntax 786
    Parameters and Switches 786
    Rules 787
    Notes 787
    Messages 788
    See Also 788

KBDBUF.SYS (device driver) External 788
　Syntax 788
　Parameters and Switches 788
　Notes 789
　Examples 789
　Messages 789
　See Also 789

KEYB 3.3 and later—External 790
　Syntax 790
　Parameters and Switches 790
　Exit Codes 790
　Notes 791
　Messages 791
　See Also 792

KEYBOARD.SYS (see KEYB) 792
　See Also 793

LABEL 3.0 and later—Internal 793
　Syntax 793
　Parameters and Switches 793
　Rules 793
　Notes 794
　Messages 794
　See Also 794

LASTDRIVE= 3.0 and later—Internal 795
　Syntax 795
　Parameters and Switches 795
　Notes 795
　Examples 795
　Messages 796
　See Also 796

LH (see LOADHIGH) 796

LOADER 796
　Syntax 796
　Parameters and Switches 797

LOADFIX 5.0 and later—External 797
　Syntax 797
　Parameters and Switches 798
　Notes 798

LOADHIGH or LH 5.0 and later—Internal 798
　Syntax 798
　Parameters and Switches 798
　Notes 799
　Rules 799
　Examples 799
　See Also 800

MD or MKDIR 2.0 and later—Internal 800
　Syntax 800
　Parameters and Switches 800
　Notes 800
　Messages 801
　See Also 801

MEM 4.0 and later—External 802
　Syntax 802
　Parameters and Switches 802
　Rules 803
　Notes 803
　See Also 803

MEMMAKER 6.0 and later—External 803
　Syntax 804
　Parameters and Switches 804
　See Also 804

MEMMAX 805
　Syntax 805
　Parameters and Switches 805

MENUCOLOR= 6.0 and later—Internal 805
　Syntax 805
　Parameters and Switches 805
　Notes 806
　Examples 807
　See Also 807

MENUDEFAULT= 6.0 and later—Internal 807
　Syntax 807
　Parameters and Switches 807
　Notes 808
　Examples 808
　See Also 809

MENUITEM= 6.0 and later—Internal 809
    Syntax 809
    Parameters and Switches 809
    Notes 809
    Examples 810
    See Also 811

MIRROR 5.0—External 811
    Syntax 811
    Parameters and Switches 811
    Rules 812
    Notes 812
    Messages 813
    See Also 813

MKDIR (see MD) 813

MODE 1.1 and later—External 813
    Display Device Status
    Information 814
    Parameters and Switches 814
    Notes 814
    Messages 814
    See Also 815

MODE COM# 1.1 and later—External 815
    Syntax 815
    Parameters and Switches 815
    Notes 816
    See Also 816

MODE CON 4.0 and later—External 817
    Syntax 817
    Parameters and Switches 817
    Notes 817
    Examples 818
    Messages 818
    See Also 818

MODE *device* CP 3.3 and later—
External 818
    Syntax 818
    Parameters and Switches 819
    Notes 820
    Examples 821
    See Also 821

MODE *display* 2.0 and later—
External 821
    Syntax 822
    Parameters and Switches 822
    Notes 823
    Examples 823
    Messages 823
    See Also 824

MODE LPT# 3.2 and later—
External 824
    Syntax 824
    Parameters and Switches 824
    Rules 825
    Notes 825
    See Also 826

MONOUMB.386 6.0 and later—
Windows 826
    Syntax 826
    Parameters and Switches 826
    Notes 827
    See Also 827

MORE 2.0 and later—External 827
    Syntax 827
    Parameters and Switches 827
    Rules 827
    Notes 828
    See Also 828

MOVE 6.0 and later—External 828
    Syntax 828
    Parameters and Switches 828
    Exit Codes 829
    Notes 829
    Examples 830
    See Also 830

MSAV 6.0 and later—External 830
    Syntax 830
    Parameters and Switches 831
    Exit Codes 832
    Notes 832
    See Also 833

MSBACKUP 6.0 and later—External 833
    Syntax 833
    Parameters and Switches 833
    Rules 833
    Notes 834
    See Also 834

MSCDEX 6.0 and later—External 835
    Syntax 835
    Parameters and Switches 835
    Notes 835
    Examples 836
    See Also 836

MSD 6.0 and later—External 836
    Syntax 836
    Parameters and Switches 836
    Notes 837
    See Also 837

MSHERC 5.0—External 837
    Syntax 837
    Parameters and Switches 837
    Notes 837

MWAV 6.0 and later—Windows 838
    See Also 838

MWAVTSR 6.0 and later—Windows 838
    See Also 838

MWBACKUP 6.0 and later—Windows 838
    See Also 839

MWUNDEL 6.0 and later—Windows 839
    See Also 839

NLSFUNC 3.3 and later—External 840
    Syntax 840
    Parameters and Switches 840
    Notes 840
    See Also 840

NUMLOCK= 6.0 and later—Internal 840
    Syntax 841
    Notes 841
    Examples 841

NWCACHE 842
    Syntax for Loading NWCACHE 842
    Parameters for Loading NWCACHE 842
    Syntax for NWCACHE After It Is Loaded 843
    Parameters for NWCACHE After It Is Loaded 843

NWCDEX 843
    Syntax 843
    Parameters and Switches 843
    Notes 844
    See Also 844

PASSWD 844
    Syntax 844
    Parameters and Switches 844
    Notes 844

PASSWORD 844
    Syntax 844
    Parameters and Switches 845
    Notes 845

PATH 2.0 and later—Internal 845
    Syntax 845
    Parameters and Switches 846
    Notes 846
    Messages 846
    See Also 847

PAUSE 1.0 and later—Internal 847
    Syntax 847
    Notes 847
    Examples 848
    Messages 848
    See Also 849

PCM 849
    Syntax 849
    Notes 849

PCMATA.SYS 849

PCMCS 849

PCMDINST 849
    Syntax 849

PCMFDISK 850
    Syntax 850
    Notes 850

PCMRMAN (Standalone Utility) 850
    Syntax 850
    Notes 850

PCMRMAN (Command-Line Utility) 850
    Syntax 850
    Parameters and Switches 850
    Notes 851

PCMSCD 851
    Syntax 851
    Notes 851

PCMSETUP 851
    Syntax 851

POWER 6.0 and later—External 852
    Syntax 852
    Parameters and Switches 852
    Notes 852
    Examples 854
    Messages 854
    See Also 854

POWER.EXE (device driver) 6.0 and later—External 854
    Syntax 854
    Parameters and Switches 855
    Notes 855
    Examples 856
    Messages 857
    See Also 857

PRINT 2.0 and later—External 857
    Syntax 857
    Parameters and Switches 857
    Rules 858
    Notes 859
    Messages 859
    See Also 860

PRINTER.SYS (device driver) 3.3 to 5.0—External 860
    Syntax 860
    Parameters and Switches 860
    Notes 861
    Examples 862
    See Also 862

PROMPT 2.0 and later—Internal 862
    Syntax 862
    Parameters and Switches 862
    Notes 862
    Examples 864
    See Also 864

QBASIC 5.0 and later—External 864
    Syntax 864
    Parameters and Switches 864
    Notes 865

QCONFIG 865
    Syntax 865
    Parameters and Switches 865

RAMBOOST 866
    Syntax 866
    Parameters and Switches 866

RAMBOOST.EXE 867
    Syntax 867
    Parameters and Switches 867
    Notes 867

RAMDRIVE.SYS (device driver) 3.2 and later—External 867
    Syntax 867
    Parameters and Switches 868
    Notes 868

Examples **870**
Messages **870**
See Also **871**

RAMSETUP **871**
Syntax **871**
Parameters and Switches **871**
Notes **872**
See Also **872**

RD or **RMDIR** 2.0 and later—Internal **872**
Syntax **872**
Parameters and Switches **872**
Notes **872**
Messages **873**
See Also **873**

RECOVER 2.0–5.0—External **873**
See Also **874**

REM 1.0 and later—Internal **874**
Syntax **874**
Parameters and Switches **874**
Notes **874**
Examples **875**
See Also **875**

REMOVDRV **875**
Syntax **875**
Parameters and Switches **875**
Notes **876**

REN or **RENAME** 1.0 and later—Internal **876**
Syntax **876**
Parameters and Switches **876**
Notes **876**
Messages **876**
See Also **876**

RENDIR **877**
Syntax **877**
Parameters and Switches **877**

REPLACE 3.2 and later—External **877**
Syntax **877**
Parameters and Switches **877**
Exit Codes **878**
Rules **878**
Notes **878**
Messages **879**
See Also **880**

REPORT **880**
Syntax **880**
Parameters and Switches **880**
See Also **880**

RESIZE **880**
Syntax **880**
Parameters and Switches **880**

RESTORE 2.0 and later—External **881**
Syntax **881**
Parameters and Switches **881**
Exit Codes **882**
Rules **882**
Notes **882**
Messages **883**

RMDIR (see **RD**) **884**

SCANDISK 6.22—External **884**
Syntax **884**
Parameters and Switches **884**
Exit Codes **886**
Notes **886**
Examples **887**
Messages **888**
See Also **888**

SCANREG **888**
Syntax **888**
Parameters and Switches **888**
Notes **889**

SCHEDULE **889**
Syntax **889**
Parameters and Switches **889**
See Also **890**

SCREATE.SYS 890
   Syntax 890
   Parameters and Switches 890
   See Also 890

SCRIPT 890
   Syntax 891
   Parameters and Switches 891
   Notes 891

SDEFRAG 891
   Syntax 891
   Parameters and Switches 891

SDIR 892
   Syntax 893
   Parameters and Switches 893
   See Also 894

SET 2.0 and later—Internal 894
   Syntax 894
   Parameters and Switches 894
   Notes 894
   Examples 896
   Messages 897
   See Also 897

SETUP (Stacker) 897
   Syntax 897
   Parameters and Switches 897

SETVER 5.0 and later—External 898
   Syntax 898
   Parameters and Switches 898
   Exit Codes 899
   Notes 899
   Examples 901
   Messages 901
   See Also 903

SETVER.EXE (device driver)
5.0 and later—External 904
   Syntax 904
   Parameters and Switches 904
   Notes 904
   Examples 906
   Messages 906
   See Also 906

SHARE 3.0 and later—External 906
   Syntax 906
   Parameters and Switches 906
   Rules 906
   Notes 907
   See Also 907

SHELL= 2.0 and later—Internal 907
   Syntax 908
   Parameters and Switches 908
   Notes 908
   Examples 909
   Messages 909
   See Also 909

SHIFT 2.0 and later—Internal 910
   Syntax 910
   Notes 910
   See Also 910

SIZER (see MEMMAKER) 910
   See Also 910

SMARTDRV 6.0 and later—External 911
   Syntax 911
   Parameters and Switches 911
   Notes 913
   Examples 913
   See Also 913

SMARTDRV.EXE (device driver)
6.0 and later—External 914
   Syntax 914
   Parameters and Switches 914
   Notes 914
   Examples 914
   See Also 914

SMARTMON 6.0 and later—
Windows 914
   See Also 915

SORT 2.0 and later—External 915
   Syntax 915
   Parameters and Switches 915
   Notes 916
   Examples 916
   See Also 916

SSETUP 917
   Syntax 917
   Parameters and Switches 917

STAC 917
   Syntax 917
   Parameters and Switches 917

STACHIGH.SYS 917
   Syntax 917
   Parameters and Switches 917

STACKER 918
   Syntax 918
   Parameters and Switches 918

STACKS= 3.2 and later—Internal 918
   Syntax 918
   Parameters and Switches 918
   Notes 919
   Examples 919
   Messages 919

SUBMENU= 6.0 and later—Internal 920
   Syntax 920
   Parameters and Switches 920
   Notes 920
   Examples 921
   See Also 922

SUBST 3.1 and later—External 922
   Syntax 922
   Parameters and Switches 922
   Notes 922
   Messages 923
   See Also 924

SWITCH 924
   Syntax 924
   Parameters and Switches 924

SWITCHES= 5.0 and later—Internal 924
   Syntax 924
   Parameters and Switches 924
   Notes 924
   Examples 926
   Messages 926
   See Also 926

SYS 1.0 and later—External 926
   Syntax 927
   Parameters and Switches 927
   Notes 927
   Messages 927
   See Also 928

SYSINFO 928
   Syntax 929
   Parameters and Switches 929

TASKMGR 929
   Syntax 929
   Parameters and Switches 929
   Notes 930

TIME 1.0 and later—Internal 930
   Syntax 930
   Parameters and Switches 930
   Notes 930
   See Also 931

TIMEOUT 931
   Syntax 931
   Parameters and Switches 931
   See Also 931

TOUCH 931
   Syntax 931
   Parameters and Switches 931

TREE 2.0 and later—External 932
   Syntax 932
   Parameters and Switches 932
   See Also 932

TUNER 933
   Syntax 933
   Parameters and Switches 933

TYPE 1.0 and later—Internal 933
   Syntax 933
   Parameters and Switches 933
   Notes 933
   Examples 934
   See Also 934

UMBCGA.SYS 934
    Syntax 934
    Parameters and Switches 934
    Notes 934

UMBEMS.SYS 934
    Syntax 934
    Parameters and Switches 934

UMBHERC.SYS 935
    Syntax 935
    Parameters and Switches 935
    Notes 935

UMBMONO.SYS 935
    Syntax 935
    Parameters and Switches 935
    Notes 935

UNCOMP 936
    Syntax 936
    Parameters and Switches 936

UNDELETE 5.0 and later—External 936
    Syntax 936
    Parameters and Switches 936
    Rules 938
    Notes 938
    Examples 939
    See Also 939

UNFORMAT 5.0 and later—External 939
    Syntax 939
    Parameters and Switches 939
    Rules 940
    Notes 940
    See Also 940

UNINSTALL 940
    Syntax 941
    Parameters and Switches 941

UNPACK2 941
    Syntax 941
    Parameters and Switches 941
    Notes 941

UNSTACK 942
    Syntax 942
    Parameters and Switches 942

VER 2.0 and later—Internal 942
    Syntax 942
    Notes 942
    Examples 942
    See Also 943

VERIFY 2.0 and later—Internal 943
    Syntax 943
    Parameters and Switches 943
    Notes 943
    Examples 944
    Messages 944

VFINTD.386 6.0 and later—
Windows 944
    Syntax 944
    Parameters and Switches 944
    Notes 945
    Examples 945

VIEW 945
    Syntax 945
    Parameters and Switches 946

VOL 2.0 and later—Internal 946
    Syntax 946
    Parameters and Switches 946
    Notes 946
    Examples 946
    Messages 947
    See Also 947

VSAFE 6.0 and later—External 947
    Syntax 947
    Parameters and Switches 947
    Rules 948
    Notes 948
    Examples 948
    See Also 949

WINA20.386   5.0 and later—Windows   949
   Syntax   949
   Parameters and Switches   949
   Notes   949
   Examples   950
   Messages   950
   See Also   950

XCOPY   3.2 and later—External   950
   Syntax   950
   Parameters and Switches   950
   Exit Codes   951
   Rules   952
   Notes   952
   Messages   953
   See Also   954

XCOPY32   954

XDEL   955
   Syntax   955
   Parameters and Switches   955

XDF   955
   Syntax   955
   Parameters and Switches   955
   Notes   955

XDFCOPY   956
   Syntax   956
   Parameters and Switches   956

XDIR   956
   Syntax   956
   Parameters and Switches   956
   See Also   957

Glossary   959

Index   965

About the Author

Jim Cooper is a Senior Systems Engineer currently working for a services and infrastructure provider in Charlotte, North Carolina. He has worked in the information technology field for more than 12 years and holds numerous certifications, including MCSE+I and MCT. He has contributed chapters to numerous other books for Pearson Technology Group.

Tell Us What You Think!

As the reader of this book, *you* are our most important critic and commentator. We value your opinion and want to know what we're doing right, what we could do better, what areas you'd like to see us publish in, and any other words of wisdom you're willing to pass our way.

As an Associate Publisher for Que, I welcome your comments. You can fax, e-mail, or write me directly to let me know what you did or didn't like about this book—as well as what we can do to make our books stronger.

Please note that I cannot help you with technical problems related to the topic of this book, and that due to the high volume of mail I receive, I might not be able to reply to every message.

When you write, please be sure to include this book's title and author as well as your name and phone or fax number. I will carefully review your comments and share them with the author and editors who worked on the book.

Fax: 317-581-4666

E-Mail: feedback@quepublishing.com

Mail: Dean Miller
Que
201 West 103rd Street
Indianapolis, IN 46290 USA

INTRODUCTION

In this introduction

Who Should Read This Book?   2

What Hardware Do You Need?   2

What Versions Are Covered?   2

What Is Not Covered?   3

How Is This Book Organized?   3

Conventions Used in This Book   7

After its introduction in 1981, MS-DOS was the most widely used operating system in the world. Hundreds of thousands of programs have been written for MS-DOS.

Special Edition Using MS-DOS 6.22, Third Edition represents Que Corporation's continuing commitment to provide the best computer books in the industry. Over the years, this book has evolved as DOS has evolved, culminating in what you are reading right now. Keeping pace with technology and explaining it clearly, simply, and completely has been Que's goal. This book, which is a comprehensive learning tool and reference volume for users of MS-DOS, reflects the maturity of DOS and the far-reaching impact that DOS has had on the computing industry. Even the most popular operating system today, Windows 95/98/ME, is still based on an upgraded version of DOS.

Special Edition Using MS-DOS 6.22, Third Edition offers DOS users a comprehensive source of information that can help them organize their work with the PC more effectively and make their hardware respond more efficiently.

Who Should Read This Book?

This book is written and organized to meet the needs of a large group of readers. It is suited for readers who have a basic familiarity with DOS but need more information to increase their knowledge and sharpen their skills. *Special Edition Using MS-DOS 6.22, Third Edition* is also a comprehensive reference on DOS for the more advanced user.

Maybe you have just learned to use your PC and are looking to move beyond the basics. Perhaps you have upgraded your hardware to a more powerful PC, with more memory and disk capacity. Or maybe you have upgraded your version of DOS and want to take advantage of its new or expanded features. If you find that you fit into any of these categories, this comprehensive edition is a "must have" volume.

What Hardware Do You Need?

This book applies to the family of personal computers with Intel x86-based processors. There are literally thousands of manufacturers today making PCs, too numerous to list here. MS-DOS will run on virtually any model available today, although you might encounter problems locating drivers for newer hardware components, such as sound and network cards.

What Versions Are Covered?

We have discovered that the vast majority of readers are using MS-DOS version 6.x. This book is focused on DOS version 6.22, although limited information is available for those using an older DOS version. (The best advice we can offer is that you upgrade your system. If you are using a version of DOS older than 6.0, upgrade right away; you will find it well worth the time and effort.) Throughout this book, specific versions of DOS are indicated.

When a particular reference applies to both DOS 6.0 and 6.22, however, the more generic *DOS 6* designation is used.

What Is Not Covered?

This book does not include the DEBUG or LINK commands, nor does it include a technical reference to the applications programming interface that DOS provides for programmers.

For information on how to install or upgrade your version of DOS, you should refer to a separate book—your MS-DOS manual. *Special Edition Using MS-DOS 6.22, Third Edition* assumes that you already have DOS installed and are using it.

Also not included in this book are computer-specific setup or configuration commands. Although these commands often are distributed with the same disks as DOS, they are too variable to be covered adequately here. Your computer-supplied manual and your PC dealer are the best sources of information about these machine-specific features.

How Is This Book Organized?

You can flip quickly through this book to get a feeling for its organization. *Special Edition Using MS-DOS 6.22, Third Edition* approaches DOS in a logical, functionally defined way. The material in this book is arranged in four main parts and a set of appendixes that include a Command Reference, and a glossary.

Part I: DOS Fundamentals

Part I, "DOS Fundamentals," is devoted to explaining the fundamental role of DOS in a working PC:

- Chapter 1, "DOS and the Personal Computer," looks at today's PCs. The chapter explores the major components of the PC and addresses the use of system and peripheral hardware. In this chapter, you get a feel not only for your system but also for systems with different keyboards, displays, and peripherals. You also learn the role of DOS in relation to your system.

- Chapter 2, "Starting DOS," steps through the process of booting DOS and explains important concepts along the way. You also learn how you can control the booting process through setting up multiple configurations.

- Chapter 3, "Using DOS Commands," introduces and explains how to use DOS commands. You learn the concepts behind issuing commands at the DOS command line. The chapter explains syntax, parameters, and switches in an easy-to-learn fashion. Important keys and various examples of the DOS command are also covered, along with information on how to access the DOS built-in help system.

- Chapter 4, "Using the DOS Shell," gets you up and running with the DOS Shell. This chapter explores the DOS Shell screen and discusses aspects of the Shell common to all its commands.

PART II: FILES AND DIRECTORIES

Part II, "Files and Directories," covers everything you need to know about the heart of DOS—working with disks and the files stored on them:

- Chapter 5, "Understanding Files and Directories," recognizes the important job DOS performs in managing your files. This chapter defines files and clearly explains file-naming conventions. Also explored is the tree-structured directory system used by DOS to organize your files. You learn how to use commands that create, change, remove, and display directories.

- Chapter 6, "Understanding Disks and Disk Drives," provides the framework you need to better understand how DOS stores information on your disk. You discover what disks are, how information is recorded on them, and some of the technological issues related to disks. Additionally, you explore the use of DoubleSpace, the DOS program that enables you to virtually double the amount of information you can store on your disk drives.

- Chapter 7, "Preparing and Maintaining Disks," builds on the information presented in Chapter 6. Here, you learn what formatting does and how DOS uses formatted disks to store your files. This chapter describes SMARTDrive, a disk cache that increases the speed with which you can access data on your hard disk, and Microsoft Defrag, a utility that keeps your files in proper order. You also learn how to partition a hard disk into sections that DOS can use as logical disks. Also presented are two DOS commands, CHKDSK and SCANDISK, that analyze disks for damage.

- Chapter 8, "Managing Your Files," is devoted to managing your files and illuminating the file-level DOS commands. Here, you learn how to examine directory listings, view the contents of files, and use the INTERLNK program to transfer files between a laptop and your desktop computer. Because you probably spend most of your time with DOS working with files, this chapter also offers an in-depth view of the file-level commands. Each command includes examples that help you appreciate the full power of these important commands.

- Chapter 9, "Protecting and Recovering Your Data," covers the important issues involved with safeguarding the most important part of your computer system—your computer data. You learn common-sense solutions to data protection, as well as how to use the backup programs supplied with DOS. This chapter also discusses how you can recover from catastrophic errors or events. You learn how to undelete files, unformat a drive, and recover data on your hard disk. When you find yourself in a situation that requires this information, you'll probably agree that this chapter alone is worth the price of this book. Finally, this chapter also discusses computer viruses and how to protect your computer against them.

Part III: Controlling DOS

Part III, "Controlling DOS," covers the DOS commands and concepts that enable you to change how DOS does its work. The information covered in Part III lets you use DOS effectively to reflect the way you do your work:

- Chapter 10, "Working with System Information," covers the commands that set and retrieve system information in your DOS-based computer. These commands often are neglected, but they key you into the control panel of DOS. These commands are helpful whether you oversee one PC or help other users with their PCs.

- Chapter 11, "Controlling Your Environment," discusses how you can set system variables and change the DOS prompt. You also learn how you can use the MODE command to change how DOS displays information on your screen, as well as how you can use DOS to change your disk drive configuration.

- Chapter 12, "Using Peripherals," explains device drivers and covers what you need to know to correctly install them. You learn how to set hardware interrupts and what the difference is between hardware and software interrupts.

- Chapter 13, "Controlling Devices," explains the DOS commands that control the behavior of logical DOS devices. By using these commands, you can control the way DOS sees your system's drives and directories. You learn how to use your printer while doing other computer work, and you see how to use the DOS pipes and filters effectively.

- Chapter 14, "Understanding the International Features of DOS," steps you through the complicated, but sometimes necessary, configuration of a PC to various international language standards.

Part IV: Maximizing DOS

Part IV, "Maximizing DOS," provides the information you need to tap the expanded power available with DOS. This part of the book helps you use the many features provided with DOS and helps you customize your computer system:

- Chapter 15, "Using the DOS Editor," provides a tutorial approach to the built-in text-file editor that comes with DOS. The examples developed in this chapter show you how to use the DOS Editor as a day-to-day utility. With the careful attention given to the Editor's practical use, you learn the skills needed to quickly compose a text file. Practical examples, using the DOS Editor to create memos and batch files, also are presented.

- Chapter 16, "Understanding Batch Files," guides you through the process of creating batch files and keystroke macros. The commands related to batch files are explained in a tutorial style. Useful examples make it easier to master the basics of batch files.

- Chapter 17, "Understanding ANSI.SYS," shows you how to make DOS screens look colorful and controlled. The details of the ANSI.SYS driver are presented in workshop fashion. You learn how to reassign keys, control the cursor's position onscreen, display the date and time, and more. This chapter also describes the ANSI commands that you can use with the ANSI.SYS device driver provided by DOS. ANSI commands enable you to control how information is displayed on your screen.

- Chapter 18, "Mastering DOSKEY and Macros," covers an alternative to batch files. You can use the DOSKEY program to create simple macros that quickly accomplish a series of tasks. You learn how to use DOSKEY to make entering DOS commands easier and faster, as well as how to record commonly used commands as macros.

- Chapter 19, "Configuring Your Computer," is a comprehensive collection of DOS commands and directives that can help you get the best performance from your PC. In this chapter, you learn to use Microsoft MemMaker, a utility that automatically and optimally configures the way your PC uses RAM. You also learn how to set up your CONFIG.SYS and AUTOEXEC.BAT files to provide the best overall system configuration.

- Chapter 20, "Networking DOS," discusses the Novell and Microsoft clients for DOS and shows you how to install and configure each. You also learn how to identify and fix various common network problems.

- Chapter 21, "Connecting to the Internet," covers your options for connecting to the Internet and explains the fundamentals of shell accounts. You learn how to use Telnet and FTP to download files and how to troubleshoot problems you might encounter with these tools.

- Chapter 22, "Third-Party Utilities," covers the basics of freeware, shareware, and demoware and shows you how you can enhance your computer with this class of software. You learn about several powerful shareware utility programs that can help you get the most out of your DOS system.

Appendixes

Special Edition Using MS-DOS 6.22, Third Edition, also includes seven appendixes containing useful information:

- Appendix A, "Files Supplied with MS-DOS 6.22," lists the files that are provided with MS-DOS 6.22 and includes a brief description of what each file is used for. The information in this appendix can help you determine whether you can safely remove some of the files installed by DOS.

- Appendix B, "DOS Environment Variables," describes the environment variables used by DOS and its utility programs, which you can use to control the way DOS operates on your computer.

- Appendix C, "DOS Messages," lists and explains screen messages you might see while you are using DOS.

- Appendix D, "DOS and DOS Utility Programs' Keyboard Commands," lists the various keyboard commands available at the DOS prompt or when you are using utility programs such as EDIT and DOSSHELL.

- Appendix E, "ASCII and Extended ASCII Codes," This appendix lists the 256 characters defined by the American Standard Code for Information Interchange (ASCII), which is the character set that DOS uses on PC-compatible computers.
- Appendix F, "Command Reference," lists in alphabetical order all the commands that DOS provides for use at the DOS prompt or in your `CONFIG.SYS` file. For each command, the purpose, proper syntax, and notes concerning its use are provided. In many cases, examples and error messages are included to help you use the command correctly. If you are unsure of how to use a particular DOS command, or if you would like to know more about it, check the entry for the command in this section. The "Command Reference" is a complete, easy-to-use, quickly accessed resource on the proper use of DOS commands.
- This book wraps up with Appendix G, "Glossary" which offers definitions for many of the new terms you were introduced to in this book.

Conventions Used in This Book

Certain conventions are followed in this edition to help you more easily understand the discussions:

- UPPERCASE letters are used to distinguish filenames and DOS commands. Please note, however, that although uppercase letters are used in the examples, you can type commands in either upper- or lowercase letters.
- In most cases, keys are represented as they appear on your keyboard, and key combinations are connected by plus signs. For example, Ctrl+Break indicates that you press and hold the Ctrl key while you press the Break key. Other key combinations, such as Ctrl+Z or Alt+F1, are activated in the same manner.
- Words or phrases defined for the first time appear in *italic*.
- Words or phrases that you are asked to type appear in `monospace`. Screen displays and onscreen messages also appear in a special `monospace` typeface.
- Throughout the chapters of this book, syntax lines appear in `monospace` type and use the conventions shown in the following example:
  `dc:pathc\CHKDSK filename.ext /V /F /?`

  In any syntax line, not all elements can be represented in a literal manner. For example, `filename.ext` can represent any filename with any extension. It also can represent any filename with no extension at all. However, command names (such as `CHKDSK`) and switches (such as `/V`, `/F`, and `/?`) are represented in a literal way.

  To activate the command `CHKDSK.EXE`, you first must type the command name `CHKDSK`. Any literal text (text you type letter for letter) in a syntax line appears in UPPERCASE letters. Any variable text (text that acts as a placeholder for other text) is shown in *lowercase italic* letters.

> **Note**
>
> The conventions used for syntax lines in the "Command Reference" are slightly different from those used in the chapters of this book. Refer to the section "The Conventions Used in This Command Reference" near the beginning of Appendix F for more information on how syntax lines are presented in that section.

PART 1

DOS Fundamentals

1 DOS and the Personal Computer 11

2 Starting DOS 23

3 Using DOS Commands 41

4 Using the DOS Shell 57

CHAPTER 1

DOS AND THE PERSONAL COMPUTER

In this chapter

DOS, Windows, and the PC   12

Other Flavors of DOS   12

PC Hardware   12

What Happens When the Power Is Turned On?   15

DOS and Random Access Memory   17

DOS and Disks   20

DOS, Windows, and the PC

You might find it hard to believe, but the personal computer is now more than 20 years old, and so is the MS-DOS operating system. At one time, more than 95% of all the tens of millions of personal computers sold used MS-DOS as the operating system. Nowadays, almost all systems use a variation of the Windows operating system, although DOS compatibility is still provided through DOS subsystems. Previously, in Windows 95/98, you could boot into an MS-DOS command prompt, bypassing the Windows user interface. With the release of Windows ME, this capability is no longer available.

The objective of this chapter is to familiarize those of you who are less experienced computer users with the inner workings of your system. If you are an old hand and already familiar with the way your computer and DOS interact, you might want to skim through this chapter on your way to Chapter 2, "Starting DOS."

For those readers who have been using computers only a short time or who have never checked out the inner workings of a PC, this chapter provides a quick introduction that gives you the basics. Knowing this information enables you to better exploit the features of DOS and gives you more control over your computing environment.

Other Flavors of DOS

Although MS-DOS is by far the most prevalent variant of the DOS family, one other version from IBM needs to be mentioned. Now that Microsoft has quit developing MS-DOS as a standalone product, this version is the only alternative for someone wanting new and advanced features of the operating system.

IBM has continued to develop the initial DOS product since its inception. It has released upgraded versions containing many of the same features of the upgraded MS-DOS versions.

The latest version is called PC DOS 2000. Some of the new features include Y2K compliance, support for the REXX programming language, PCMCIA cards, unattended scheduling, and remote installation.

PC Hardware

In 1981, IBM introduced the IBM PC, which became the worldwide standard for personal computers. This standard endures to this day—even through all the subsequent upgrades in technology.

In the early 1980s, IBM manufactured and sold more than half of all the personal computers sold. As the decade wore on, however, IBM's grip on computer sales weakened and scores of manufacturers introduced models of their own. All these manufacturers adopted the basic hardware architecture that made the original IBM computers a de facto standard.

THE PC ARCHITECTURE

The heart and soul of any personal computer is its *central processing unit* (*CPU*). The CPU is a microprocessor chip capable of receiving input, processing data, and producing the results as output. DOS-compatible personal computers have long been based on the Intel family of microprocessors and their clones.

Everything in your computer is designed around the needs of the CPU. The CPU is plugged or soldered into the main circuit board of your system, which is where the term *motherboard* comes from. The motherboard also contains the core group of components needed to build a complete computer system.

The CPU communicates to the rest of the system via the system bus. The system bus provides a communications highway where the CPU can "talk to" memory chips, as well as to peripheral devices installed in the expansion slots along the bus.

> **Note**
> The word *peripheral* comes from the Greek language and means *around the center*. As it is used in computer jargon today, a peripheral is any device that is connected to your computer's CPU, either by an expansion slot card or plugged into a port.

In your system, DOS plays the role of the traffic cop, organizing the flow of data in the computer and offering services that programs can use. DOS directs the activities of your system's CPU and helps the CPU to communicate instructions and receive information from other parts of the system. In other words, DOS makes all the separate components inside your computer system work together as if they were all one single machine.

When you install a video card or a modem into an expansion slot in your computer, it must conform to certain standards. These standards ensure that both DOS and the CPU know how to interface with the device.

It is not unusual for some peripheral devices, such as parallel and serial communications ports, to be built directly onto the motherboard of the computer. These devices also must conform to the standards that allow DOS and the CPU to control them.

COMPUTER MEMORY

To perform operations, your computer uses binary numbers to represent both data and program instructions. Binary numbers use the binary digits 0 and 1 in various combinations to represent everything you do with your computer. Binary digits are usually called *bits*, which is an abbreviation of *binary digits*.

Computer memory is nothing more than thousands—or millions—of individual switches that can have one of two states: on or off. The binary digit 0 represents off, whereas 1 represents the on condition. Eight bits arranged together form a *byte*; the arrangement of bits within the byte can produce one of 256 (2^8) possible values.

Each one of the 256 possible values of a byte is arranged into an extension of the ASCII (American Standard Code for Information Interchange) code. The original ASCII code used seven bits to represent 128 different characters. After the eighth bit was added, ASCII could represent up to 256 characters. Officially, this set is called the *PC 8 Symbol Set* but has come to be known—somewhat inaccurately—by computerists all over the world as the *ASCII Extended character set*.

The first 32 ASCII codes represent common commands used by the CPU and peripherals for such activities as making the speaker beep, telling a printer to use compressed print, controlling data transmissions, and so on. The rest of the ASCII codes represent letters, numerals, and graphic characters. Therefore, a method is needed to store this information and make it available to the CPU.

To store information, your computer typically uses three kinds of memory:

- Random access memory (RAM)
- Read-only memory (ROM)
- Disk-based storage

Each type of memory plays a different role in your system.

Random access memory, or RAM for short, is a volatile form of memory. *Volatile* means that it can hold information only when electrically powered. If you turn off the power, all the information stored in RAM chips is lost. Think of RAM as an electronic chalkboard where information can be written and erased at will. When you turn off the computer, RAM is erased automatically. As you will see later in this chapter, RAM is broken down into three categories, determined by the way the computer addresses memory.

Read-only memory, or ROM for short, is a close cousin to RAM, with one important exception: The information stored on ROM is nonvolatile. ROM information is permanently recorded on the circuits of the chip during manufacturing and cannot be erased. When you turn off the computer's power, this information is not lost. When you turn the computer on again, the information stored in ROM is once again available to the CPU and to DOS. Your computer uses ROM to store instructions and programming, as you will see later in this chapter.

The third type of computer memory is disk storage. If you have the typical computer system, you can use both floppy disks and a hard disk (often called a hard drive) to store information while the computer is turned off. Disk storage uses metal or plastic disks coated with a magnetic material to record and play back information in much the same way as a stereo system uses magnetic tapes to record and play back music. Disk storage comes in a sometimes bewildering array of formats. Later in this chapter, you will find the information you need to demystify disk storage.

PERIPHERAL DEVICES

Although you might think of your computer system as a single machine, it actually is made up of many discrete peripheral devices. Strictly speaking, your computer is the CPU and its attached RAM. By themselves, the CPU and RAM can do nothing useful because there is no way to provide input for the CPU to work with, and no way for the CPU to provide output in a form you can understand and use. Without peripheral devices, a computer is worthless. Without an operating system such as DOS, your computer would be the modern equivalent of the Tower of Babel.

Every part of your computer except the CPU and memory is a peripheral device. Keyboards, disk drives, printers, and monitors are all examples of peripheral devices. One of the most basic jobs DOS performs for you is to provide the standards and programming necessary to add peripheral devices to your system so that you can get some work done.

Back in the wild and woolly days of personal computers, before the IBM PC, each computer maker employed its own standards and peripheral devices. If you had an Apple II computer, you couldn't share disks with anyone who didn't have an Apple II. If the keyboard for your TRS-80 broke, you couldn't replace it with a keyboard from any other type of machine. Worst of all, if you went from an Apple II to another kind of computer, you had to learn a whole new set of commands.

One of the ancestors of DOS was an operating system called CP/M (Control Program for Microcomputers). CP/M standardized the commands necessary for using a computer, many of which are still used in DOS, but each different computer manufacturer still used different standards for peripheral devices and disk formats. According to legend, IBM investigated using CP/M as its operating system for the first PCs. As the rumor goes, there were differences in time frames, engineering, and personalities, so IBM turned to a small upstart company called Microsoft. If things had gone differently, this book might have been titled *Special Edition Using CP/M*!

The simultaneous introduction of the IBM Personal Computer and DOS changed the computing world forever. For the first time, because of standardization, users could walk into a computer store and buy disk drives, video cards, keyboards, and other peripherals made by other companies to put into their IBM or compatible computers.

Peripherals that are sold today for personal computers adhere to two standards: hardware and software. The hardware standards ensure that peripherals can fit into your system without doing damage and that they can communicate with the CPU. The software standards imposed by DOS ensure that the peripheral becomes an integral, functioning part of your computer system.

WHAT HAPPENS WHEN THE POWER IS TURNED ON?

When you flip the power switch on your computer system, you set into motion a series of steps that must occur before you can see the DOS prompt, which signals that your computer is ready for use. No doubt you have seen these steps performed, possibly without realizing their significance. This set of steps is called *booting the computer*. This phrase refers to the old saying "pull yourself up by the bootstraps," meaning to make something of yourself from nothing. That's exactly what booting does; it makes that expensive paperweight on your desk into a fully functional computer.

The first of these steps is the activation of the Power On Self Test (POST). The Power On Self Test is a program that has been recorded on a ROM chip located on the motherboard of your system. This program gets the ball rolling. First, it loads instructions into RAM for the CPU to follow. These instructions tell the computer to perform a quick self-diagnostic check of the hardware. One of the first things you see when you turn on the computer, therefore, is the system counting and testing the installed RAM.

Next, the POST checks to see that the system setup is still valid. Your system contains a special kind of chip called a Complementary Metal-Oxide Semiconductor, or CMOS, that stores information about your system's configuration. CMOS chips are used because they need only a trickle of power, which can be supplied by a battery, to retain the stored information for several years. Your system's date and time settings are stored on this chip, along with information about installed floppy disk drives, hard disk configuration, and other system configuration information that can vary from manufacturer to manufacturer. If the system setup is okay, the POST passes on to the next step: loading the operating system.

When the self test is satisfied that everything about your system is in order, it is time to load DOS using another program found on your system's ROM chips—the bootstrap loader. This program's job is simple and to the point: Find the operating system's loader on the disk and make it run. By default, the first place it searches is drive A, to see whether you have a bootable floppy disk inserted into the drive. If the program fails to find a disk in drive A, it next looks to your hard disk. When the loader finds a valid operating system (in this case DOS), it starts the program found on the boot sectors of the disk. Most computers today will allow you to specify in the BIOS where you want the computer to look for the operating system loader—for example, going straight to the hard drive and bypassing searching the floppy drive.

Completely describing all the steps involved in booting DOS might take several pages and bore you to tears, so the following description is somewhat simplified. When the ROM bootstrap loader finds a disk with a bootable copy of DOS, it transfers control to that disk's boot sectors, where the DOS loading program takes over.

The first file loaded is IO.SYS. IO.SYS places into memory the basic input/output services DOS provides. After this file is loaded, the second file, MSDOS.SYS, is loaded. Between these two files, DOS sets up the many services it offers to programs, such as file handling, printer handling, and so on.

IO.SYS **and** MSDOS.SYS

If you look at a directory of your boot disk, you normally do not see the IO.SYS and MSDOS.SYS files listed. Both of these files have the hidden attribute, which prevents the DIR command from listing them in the directory.

Also, because hardware manufacturers sometimes alter portions of DOS to meet specific hardware needs, these files might have slightly different names. IBMIO.SYS and IBMDOS.SYS are common variations, for example.

`MSDOS.SYS` completes the foundation for providing DOS services to your system. After it is loaded, it checks the disk's boot directory (normally `C:\`) to see whether a file named `CONFIG.SYS` is present. If this file is found, it is loaded into memory, converted to all uppercase letters, and interpreted. Each line of `CONFIG.SYS` specifies some type of configuration information, such as a device driver to be loaded or a system setting to be made. After these settings are established, `COMMAND.COM` is loaded.

`COMMAND.COM` is the user interface to DOS. Its job is to evaluate whether commands presented to DOS from the keyboard or from batch files are legal. If the commands are legal, they are run. If a command is not legal, `COMMAND.COM` is responsible for issuing one of those error messages that can prove so frustrating to new users.

Just before `COMMAND.COM` turns the computer over to you, the user, it checks to see whether a file called `AUTOEXEC.BAT` is present in the boot directory. `AUTOEXEC.BAT` is a standard batch file that usually contains commands to customize your DOS installation. The only thing special about `AUTOEXEC.BAT` is that it gets run automatically during bootup.

DOS AND RANDOM ACCESS MEMORY

To understand the memory issues that surround DOS and your computer system, you first need to know a bit of history. When Intel designed the 8088 and 8086 processors on which the first generation of DOS computers (PCs and XTs) was based, Intel thought that no user would ever need more than one megabyte (1MB) of memory. Most of the computers then in use had only 64 kilobytes (64KB) of memory, so this speculation might have been reasonable at the time. The problem is that this speculation was wrong—very wrong.

Real Mode Versus Protected Mode

When Intel developed the 80286 processor, it created a new mode of operation that allowed the CPU to address memory of more than 1MB. Additionally, more than one program could run at the same time, with each program protected from the actions of other programs. This mode of operation was called *protected mode*.

To differentiate this new capability from the limited capabilities of the 8088 and 8086 processors, the term *real mode* was coined. Not until the release of the 80386 generation of processors did protected mode software begin to appear.

Shortly after the release of the IBM PC, Lotus released a hot new spreadsheet program called 1-2-3. Soon businesses were buying PCs by the carload just to run Lotus 1-2-3. It wasn't long before users found they could build large spreadsheets that exceeded the memory limits of their computers.

A few years later, IBM introduced the PC-AT, based on Intel's 80286 processor. The AT's processor was faster than those used in PC and XT machines, and it had the capability to access up to 16MB of memory using a new processor feature called *protected mode*. Unfortunately, DOS was never enhanced to take advantage of this capability, so software developers never used the full capabilities of the 80286 chip. Many ATs lived and died without ever running protected-mode software.

Later still, Intel developed 80386 and 80486 chips that addressed up to 4 gigabytes (4GB) of memory. Until Windows 3.0 came on the scene, precious little software was able to run the computer's protected mode. Instead, users simply used these machines as fast PCs. Users who needed more memory than the original 1MB had to rely on a memory scheme called *expanded memory*, which was created collectively by Lotus, Intel, and Microsoft.

Today, the current family of Intel chips is the Pentium group. They include the Pentium, Pentium MMX, Pentium II, Pentium III, and Pentium IV CPUs. Also, other companies, such as AMD, now are making Intel-based CPUs that are in direct competition with the Pentiums. The Pentium-based CPUs can address more than 4GB of memory, depending on the operating system and CPU version.

RAM is classified in three ways: conventional memory, expanded memory, and extended memory. Understanding the distinctions can be quite useful.

Conventional Memory

As you've already learned, the generation of personal computers that preceded DOS and the IBM PC used, at most, 64KB of random access memory. The Intel 8088 processor addressed up to 1MB—which was, at the time, a significant advance. Of this 1MB, 640KB was made available for DOS and applications programs to use. The remaining 384KB was reserved for system use. Figure 1.1 shows the way conventional memory is used under DOS.

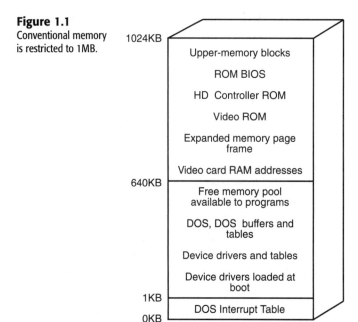

Figure 1.1
Conventional memory is restricted to 1MB.

As you can see in the figure, DOS places a table of available services into memory, beginning at byte 0. When DOS loads the rest of itself into memory, it occupies memory addresses beginning at 1KB. The space from 1KB to 640KB is reserved for DOS and whatever programs you might run. Addresses of more than 640KB (the infamous 640KB barrier) are reserved for addresses for ROMs and for accessing video card memory.

In DOS, memory addresses use a *segment:offset* notation to pinpoint an exact location where data or program instructions can be stored. These address locations are always specified using the hexadecimal number system. Each segment is 64KB in length, but each segment begins only 16 bytes up from its neighbor. The offset portion of the address specifies how many bytes the address is from the beginning of the segment.

Programmers soon discovered that an extra block of usable memory can be gained by specifying the last possible segment in the 1MB area in the segment portion of the address. Using this trick opens up an extra 64KB (minus the 16 bytes that fall below the 1MB line) of memory, more than 1MB that can be addressed without sending DOS and the processor into never-never land. Thus, the *high memory area* was born.

This newly discovered high memory area was almost immediately grabbed by network designers. They saw this area as a safe place to put their data buffers, which didn't take RAM away from running programs that were already beginning to feel the squeeze of the 640KB barrier.

Beginning with the release of DOS 5.0, users could employ unused addresses between 640KB and 1MB to run DOS, programs, and device drivers by using HIMEM.SYS and EMM386.EXE to make this space available. You use the LOADHIGH and DEVICEHIGH DOS commands to place programs, device drivers, and even portions of DOS itself into the *upper memory area*.

→ For more information about using upper memory blocks, **see** Chapter 19, "Configuring Your Computer," **p. 441**.

EXPANDED MEMORY

When Lotus 1-2-3 users and others began demanding a way to access more than the 640KB memory provided by the conventional memory scheme, Lotus, Intel, and Microsoft worked together to come up with the Expanded Memory Specification (EMS), also known as the LIM 3.2 specification. This specification was adopted before the Intel 80286 processor hit the market. EMS was an immediate hit, which in part accounts for the fact that few software companies even tried to exploit the enhanced memory addressing capabilities of the 80286 processor. Programs that needed more than 640KB memory could easily be modified to adhere to the EMS system, so there was no great push for DOS to use the chip's protected mode, which could address up to 16MB of RAM.

The Expanded Memory Specification makes more memory available to processors running in *real mode*, the name given to the mode of operation that mimics the original 8088 processor used in PCs and XTs. The LIM specifications reserve a 64KB area of memory in the upper memory block (the area between 640KB and 1MB) for use as a page frame.

Shortly after the EMS specification was adopted, several companies—including AST Research, at the time the largest seller of add-on memory boards—came up with an

Enhanced Expanded Memory Specification (EEMS). This new expanded memory scheme used a backfilling technique that eliminated the need for the page frame in upper memory and allowed expanded memory to reside inside the 640KB range. In fact, some early EEMS products required users to remove any RAM in their system above the 256KB mark, which provided 384KB of expanded RAM to be situated within conventional memory addresses.

The Expanded Memory Specification has always been, and will always be, a kludge. Life today would be much simpler for those folks who support computer users if the hardware and software manufacturers had taken a "bite-the-bullet" attitude when the 80286 processor became available and built systems to use extended memory.

The DOS Expanded Memory Manager (EMM386) made old-fashioned EMS boards obsolete because it simulated expanded memory using the extended memory.

Extended Memory

The Extended Memory Specification (XMS) is a simpler way of making memory addresses of more than 1MB available to your programs. Extended memory is simply an extension of conventional memory addresses. The 384KB system memory area is still present under XMS, so programs can use the conventional 640KB memory area and addresses greater than 1MB.

To implement extended memory, the protected mode operations of the processor (80286, 80386, 80486, or higher) are turned on. DOS accomplishes this task by loading HIMEM.SYS at bootup from the CONFIG.SYS file. HIMEM, which is an extended memory manager, enables DOS to address memory above the conventional 1MB mark.

Few DOS programs take advantage of the availability of extended memory. Windows and Windows programs, however, routinely use extended memory.

DOS and Disks

RAM is volatile storage. As soon as the power goes off, RAM goes to sleep. ROM provides a permanent storage medium, but you can't write files to ROM. What is needed is a third method of storing data and programs. DOS stands for *disk operating system*, so if you get the notion that disks are used for permanent storage of data and programs, give yourself the afternoon off.

One of the major functions of DOS is to facilitate the reading and writing of data stored on disks. Disks are circular platters of plastic or metal coated with a magnetic emulsion similar to that used to produce cassette or video tapes.

By offering standardized disk services, DOS saves programmers countless hours of work because their programs can simply ask DOS to read or write a disk. The programmer is spared the task of writing code to store data. These DOS file services also provide an added benefit to computer users: Because DOS takes care of placing files onto disks, any file created by a DOS program can reside on the same disk as any other DOS file.

When a program writes to a disk, DOS ensures that the data is stored as a named collection of information called a *file*. DOS rules determine naming conventions. A legal DOS filename can be from one to eight characters, followed by an optional period and a one- to three-character extension. A filename's extension is most often used to indicate the type of file being stored.

> **Note**
>
> In the case of Windows 95/98/ME, you can use long filenames in Windows, but when you are looking at the files from DOS, the filenames are shortened to the standard 8.3 format. The name is shortened by taking the first six characters of the filename and then adding a tilde (~) followed by an incrementing value, starting with 1.
>
> Windows NT/2000 shows the long filename for files and directories in the command prompt window.
>
> For more information on this and other DOS file operations, see Chapter 8, "Managing Your Files."

Floppy disks are wafer-thin plastic disks coated with a magnetic emulsion and encased within a protective sleeve. The original IBM PC used floppy disks measuring 5 1/4 inches across. Today, 3 1/2-inch floppies have become the industry standard. The advantages of the 3 1/2-inch format are the greater data density (the disks hold considerably more information than the physically larger 5 1/4-inch disks) and the hard plastic sleeve that better protects the disks from damage.

Floppy disks are most commonly used to store data to be archived or transferred to another computer. The biggest disadvantages of floppy disks are that reading and writing on floppies is relatively slow, and they do not hold enough information to accommodate today's larger programs and data files.

Hard disks are nonremovable, high-capacity, rigid platters sealed inside a dust-free casing. For increased storage capacity, several platters can be stacked within a single hard disk drive where multiple pickup heads are used to read and write the stored information. You can find more detailed information about magnetic disks in Chapter 7, "Preparing and Maintaining Disks."

Another storage technology finding wider use today is removable media. This technology uses cartridges that can hold anywhere from 100MB to 2GB of data. The most popular brand is Iomega, with the Zip (100MB–250MB) and Jaz (1GB–2GB) disks and drives. Another newer option is the LS-120 floppy disk, which uses a special 3 1/2-inch floppy disk and drive and can hold up to 120MB of data. The best thing about this solution is that the LS-120 drive can still read standard floppies, which eliminates the need for an additional drive.

CHAPTER 2

STARTING DOS

In this chapter

    Booting Your Computer   24

    System Configuration   26

    Creating Multiple Configurations   32

    Project: Controlling the Boot Process   38

Booting Your Computer

In Chapter 1, "DOS and the Personal Computer," you read a description of the steps taken when you boot up your computer. In fact, two types of booting are available. The first is known as a *cold boot*. This term comes from the fact that the computer's power is off and the unit is not yet warm. As you might guess, the second type of boot is the *warm boot*.

A cold boot occurs when you turn on the power switch to your system. Some systems also have a reset button. Pressing this button also triggers a cold boot. The difference between a cold and warm boot is simple. A cold boot begins at the absolute beginning, using the Power On Self Test (POST) to check the condition of the system's major components and RAM.

A warm boot, on the other hand, bypasses the preliminary self test, moving directly to the loading of the operating system. A warm boot is triggered when you press the Ctrl+Alt+Del keys all at the same time. This combination of keys was chosen because on most keyboards it is almost impossible to press these three keys simultaneously by accident.

> **Note**
> Although the general population might believe differently, computer users have a tremendous sense of humor. This sense of humor has introduced two slang terms to distinguish between cold and warm boots. Because early PCs had a large red power switch on the side of the case, cold booting has been dubbed "Big Red Button Time," or BRB for short. A BRB is usually necessary only when your system is so thoroughly hung up and confused that it fails to respond to the Ctrl+Alt+Del key combination. Pressing these three keys normally triggers a warm boot, so some anonymous wag named a warm boot "the three-finger salute."

> **Note**
> Using the Ctrl+Alt+Del combination for a warm reboot works only when you are booted straight into DOS. If you are using Windows 9x, using Ctrl+Alt+Del first brings up a task list. From there, you have the option of shutting down or canceling. Microsoft provided this extra step to encourage users to shut down Windows instead of just warm-booting the machine.

The net effect of either a cold or warm boot is to wipe the slate clean and start the computer out fresh. Being the sophisticated computer user that you are, of course, you should realize that rebooting the computer on a whim could be a dangerous proposition. Triggering a boot when a file is open and you're in the process of editing can cause you to lose valuable data because you don't have an opportunity to save the file to disk before the boot takes place.

Understanding the Boot Disk

In the preceding chapter, you learned that during the booting process three files are loaded into memory: IO.SYS, MSDOS.SYS, and COMMAND.COM. You also learned that two other files—`CONFIG.SYS` and `AUTOEXEC.BAT`—are used in the boot process as well. The reason for calling this information to your attention again is to point out that DOS is not a monolithic creation. Rather, DOS is composed of many modular components working together.

DOS is not, however, a mind reader, so you are required to specially prepare bootable disks capable of starting your computer. You can create bootable disks in two ways: You can use the `FORMAT` command, with the `/S` switch, or you can use the `SYS` command.

When you use the `FORMAT` command to create a bootable disk, using the `/S` switch causes the newly formatted disk to contain the disk portion of the bootstrap loader in the boot sector, `IO.SYS`, `MSDOS.SYS`, and `COMMAND.COM`. If any of these four conditions is not satisfied, you cannot use the disk to start DOS.

Using the `SYS` command to make a disk bootable requires you to know a few undocumented facts about the way boot disks are constructed. For a disk to be bootable, the following conditions must be met:

- `IO.SYS` must be the first directory entry in the root directory of the disk.
- `MSDOS.SYS` must be the second entry in the root directory.
- `IO.SYS` must be the first physical file on the disk.

Knowing these three rules, you now can understand more readily why the `SYS` command so often reports the `No Room for System on Destination Disk` error message even though the disk has plenty of free space. If files already are written on the disk, chances are that the first directory entry in the root is taken.

Many years ago, when DOS was well on the way to becoming the number one bootlegged software of all time, the DOS development team came up with the `/B` switch to the `FORMAT` command. Sending someone a bootable disk is a violation of your DOS software license because that disk enables the person to start up a computer with software for which he or she hasn't paid. The idea behind the `/B` switch is to reserve space on the disk so that you can use the `SYS` command later to make the disk bootable.

In practice, the `/B` switch of the `FORMAT` command simply copies `IO.SYS` and `MSDOS.SYS` to the newly formatted disk, leaving off `COMMAND.COM` and the bootstrap loader. This restriction ensures that the `SYS` command can come along later and finish the job of making the disk bootable. You might need the `/B` switch only once every five years, but it can come in handy.

Creating a Floppy Boot Disk

These days, finding a computer system lacking a hard drive is unusual, if not impossible. The single major exception to this rule is a network workstation where the file server provides all the hard drive storage needed (at one time this was very common in Novell-based networks). Because the boot process must be local to the workstation on a standard PC, booting from a floppy in this case is a no-brainer.

Booting from the computer's hard drive is, in general, more efficient. Hard drives are faster than floppy drives, so booting from the hard drive gets you to a DOS prompt more quickly.

In some cases, though, you need to have a floppy disk to boot from. One scenario would be where COMMAND.COM on the hard drive has been damaged. To recover from this damage, you would need to boot from a floppy and copy the system files back to your hard drive using the SYS.COM command.

Follow these steps to create a boot floppy:

1. Format a floppy disk in drive A using the /S (System) switch to make it a bootable disk. If you have compressed your drive with DoubleSpace, FORMAT automatically copies DBLSPACE.BIN to the new floppy as a hidden system file.
2. Copy AUTOEXEC.BAT and CONFIG.SYS to the new boot disk.
3. Copy all the files you need for a clean boot to the floppy. Include DBLSPACE.SYS if you have compressed disks. If you are going to be using the disk as an emergency backup to repair system files on a hard drive, you should also copy the SYS.COM file over.

> **Note**
>
> I have found it is also very useful to use a DOS boot disk along with a DOS CD-ROM driver to load new systems where I want to copy the source files without adding CONFIG.SYS or AUTOEXEC.BAT to the hard drive. You can do the same by creating a boot disk with all the files that are necessary to prepare a hard drive, such as FDISK, FORMAT, and SYS, along with the MCSDEX command for the CD-ROM. Using driver device files is discussed further in Chapter 13, "Controlling Devices."

→ For a detailed description of the boot process, **see** "What Happens When the Power Is Turned On" in Chapter 1, "DOS and the Personal Computer," **p. 15**.

System Configuration

If you are not a long-time computer user, or if you have always had someone else maintain your system configurations for you, you might not be familiar with the roles played by two important files during startup. The CONFIG.SYS and AUTOEXEC.BAT files customize the way your computer is configured. These files load drivers, set options, and tweak the DOS environment.

> **Note**
>
> The *DOS environment* is a space in memory reserved for creating variables that can be looked at by programs running on your system. The default size of the DOS environment is only 256 bytes in length. Some programs make extensive use of the DOS environment to store customization settings. You can use the SHELL command to increase the size of the environment.

→ For a detailed description of the syntax and usage of the SHELL command, **see** Appendix F, "Command Reference," **p. 583**.

CONFIG.SYS

During the boot process, as soon as IO.SYS and MSDOS.SYS are loaded into memory and before COMMAND.COM is loaded, a search is made of the root directory of the boot disk to see whether the CONFIG.SYS file exists. On 99% of the computers in use today, the file is available.

When CONFIG.SYS is found, its contents are read into memory, and the file is acted on line by line. Each line in CONFIG.SYS contains a DOS command that tells DOS to enhance the DOS configuration.

A number of DOS commands are valid in CONFIG.SYS. Table 2.1 gives a quick rundown of those commands. For detailed information, refer to Appendix F, "Command Reference."

TABLE 2.1   COMMANDS OFTEN USED IN CONFIG.SYS

Command	Meaning
BREAK	Determines how DOS reacts to the Ctrl+Break or Ctrl+C keystrokes.
BUFFERS	Sets the number of file buffers DOS uses in transferring data to and from disk.
COUNTRY	Configures language-dependent features.
DEVICE	Loads a device driver (special software to control your computer's configuration) in conventional memory.
DEVICEHIGH	Loads a device driver into upper memory (above 640KB).
DOS	Determines whether DOS is loaded into the high memory area and whether DOS maintains links to upper memory blocks.
DRIVPARM	Modifies the parameters for an existing drive by specifying information about tracks, sectors, heads, and so on.
FCBS	Determines the number of file control blocks that can be open simultaneously. Needed only for ancient software compatibility.
FILE	Sets the number of files that can be open simultaneously.
INCLUDE	Includes the contents of a configuration block.
INSTALL	Loads a memory-resident (TSR) program.
LASTDRIVE	Specifies the highest valid disk drive letter.
MENUCOLOR	Defines a startup menu's text and background colors.
MENUDEFAULT	Specifies the default configuration block and a timeout value.
MENUITEM	Identifies items on the startup menu.
NUMLOCK	Specifies the initial setting of the NUMLOCK key.
REM	Creates a remark. Nothing following REM on the same line is acted on by DOS during booting.
SET	Creates and sets values for environment variables.
SHELL	Informs DOS what command processor should be used. SHELL also is used to increase the default size of the DOS environment.

Chapter 2 Starting DOS

Table 2.1 Continued

Command	Meaning
STACKS	Sets the number and size of stacks used to process hardware interrupts.
SUBMENU	Provides the capability to add a second level of menus.
SWITCHES	Specifies special DOS options.

Figure 2.1 shows the contents of a typical `CONFIG.SYS` file. In all likelihood, the DOS installation program either created or modified your `CONFIG.SYS` file.

Figure 2.1
A typical `CONFIG.SYS` file.

```
DEVICE=C:\DOS\HIMEM.SYS
DEVICE=C:\DOS\EMM386.EXE NOEMS HIGHSCAN NOVCPI WIN=B500-B7FF
WIN=B200-
ÂB4FF
DOS=UMB, HIGH
BUFFERS=15, 0
FILES=49
LASTDRIVE=N
STACKS=9, 256
SWITCHES=/k /f
SHELL=C:\DOS\COMMAND.COM C:\DOS\ /e:512 /P
DEVICEHIGH /L:2,12048 =C:\DOS\SETVER.EXE
DEVICEHIGH /L:2,10928 =C:\DOS\SBPCD.SYS /D:MSCD001 /P:220
DEVICEHIGH /L:2,44784 =C:\DOS\DBLSPACE.SYS /MOVE
```

As you can see in this figure, a great deal is going on. Table 2.2 provides a quick play-by-play of each line of the `CONFIG.SYS` file shown in Figure 2.1. If you want more in-depth information about one of the commands discussed here, see the "Command Reference."

Table 2.2 Play-by-Play of a Typical `CONFIG.SYS` File

Command	Meaning
`DEVICE=C:\DOS\HIMEM.SYS`	Uses the `DEVICE` command to load `HIMEM.SYS`, the Extended Memory Manager. `HIMEM.SYS` accesses memory addresses above 1MB, including the high memory area from 1024KB to 1088KB. This file must be loaded before `EMM386`.
`DEVICE=C:\DOS\EMM386.EXE NOEMS HISCAN NOVCPI WIN=B500-B7FF WIN=B200-B4FF`	Uses `DEVICE` to load `EMM386.EXE`, the Expanded Memory Manager. The parameters shown on this line (from left to right) specify no EMS memory, check availability of upper memory blocks, disable VCPI support, and areas in upper reserve memory for Windows. You must load `EMM386.EXE` to get access to upper memory (640KB to 1024KB).

System Configuration

TABLE 2.2 CONTINUED

Command	Meaning
`DOS=UMB, HIGH`	Uses the `DOS` command to specify that upper memory be used and to load portions of DOS into the high memory area (1024KB to 1088KB).
`BUFFERS=15, 0`	Sets up 15 buffers for transferring files, with 0 secondary cache buffers created.
`FILES=49`	Specifies that DOS make 49 file handles available so that many files can be open at a time.
`LASTDRIVE=N`	Specifies that drive N is the highest drive present in the system. This setting should include drives created by DoubleSpace and any drives used by your network if you are connected to one.
`STACKS=9, 256`	Specifies that nine stacks of 256 bytes each are used to handle hardware interrupts.
`SWITCHES=/k /f`	The `/k` switch disables extended keyboard support, and the `/f` switch dispenses with the default two-second delay after the `Starting MS-DOS...` message appears during bootup.
`SHELL=C:\DOS\COMMAND.COM C:\DOS\ /e:512 /F`	Increases the size of the DOS environment to 512 bytes. Don't forget to use the `/P` switch if you use this command; otherwise, DOS ignores `AUTOEXEC.BAT` at boot time.
`DEVICEHIGH /L:2,12048 = C:\DOS\SETVER.EXE`	Loads the SETVER driver into upper memory.
`DEVICEHIGH /L:2,10928 = C:\DOS\SBPCD.SYS /D:MSCD01 /P:220`	Loads a CD-ROM driver into upper memory and specifies MSCD01 as the device name.
`DEVICEHIGH /L:2,44784 = C:\DOS\DBLSPACE.SYS /MOVE`	Loads the DoubleSpace driver into upper memory.

If upper memory is not available when you use the `DEVICEHIGH` command, DOS loads drivers into conventional memory as though the `DEVICE` command were used.

You easily can customize your `CONFIG.SYS` file by using the `EDIT` command. Exercise caution, however, because you accidentally can alter commands that screw up your configuration. Using the following command to make a backup of the file before editing is always a good idea:

`COPY CONFIG.SYS CONFIG.OLD`

That way, you can restore the old settings if something goes wrong.

> **Note**
> When modifying any file, it is a good idea to not remove any lines, but rather add REM to the beginning of the line. This causes the file to ignore that line, because it is seen as a remark, not a command.

AUTOEXEC.BAT

After COMMAND.COM is loaded into memory during the boot process, the system is ready for you to use. The last task the boot process performs is to look in the boot directory for the AUTOEXEC.BAT file. If an AUTOEXEC.BAT file is found, it is then fed to COMMAND.COM's batch-file processor.

AUTOEXEC.BAT can contain almost any legal DOS command, except those commands such as DEVICE and SHELL, which are reserved for use in CONFIG.SYS. AUTOEXEC.BAT is used mostly to run commands that further configure the DOS session and to run those commands that need to be run only once when the computer is started up.

Although DOS now enables you to use the SET command in either CONFIG.SYS or AUTOEXEC.BAT, traditionally you found these SET commands exclusively in AUTOEXEC.BAT or in batch files run later for special purposes. There is one good reason to continue this practice. If you have your initial SET commands split between CONFIG.SYS and AUTOEXEC.BAT, you possibly can create the same variable twice by using different values. If CONFIG.SYS contains the line SET TEMP=C:\TEMP and AUTOEXEC.BAT contains the line SET TEMP=C:\MYTEMP, for example, the value of the TEMP variable is MYTEMP after AUTOEXEC.BAT is run.

In effect, AUTOEXEC.BAT is nothing but a regular batch file. Two things make it special, however. The first (and most important item) is that it is executed automatically each time your computer is booted. The second is that because AUTOEXEC.BAT is considered part of the booting process, DOS 6.2 enables you to step interactively through each command in AUTOEXEC.BAT, just as you can through CONFIG.SYS. This capability is discussed in more detail in the next section.

→ For a better understanding of batch files, **see** Chapter 16, "Understanding Batch Files," **p. 389**.

To better understand your AUTOEXEC.BAT file, check out Figure 2.2. It lists the contents of a typical AUTOEXEC.BAT file.

Figure 2.2
A sample AUTOEXEC.BAT file.

```
@ECHO OFF
CLS
PROMPT $P$G
PATH C:\DOS;D:\WINDOWS;C:\;C:\NU
SET PCPLUS-F:\PROCOMM
SET TEMP=C:\TEMP
SET BLASTER=A220 I5 D1 T2
SET SOUND=G:\SBPRO
LH /L:0;1,42432 /S C:\DOS\SMARTDRV.EXE
LH /L:1,56928 C:\DOS\MOUSE.COM /Y
LH /L:1,13984 C:\DOS\SHARE /L:500
LH /L:1,6400 C:\DOS\DOSKEY.COM
LH /L:1,46576 C:\DOS\MSCDEX /d:MSCD001 /M:15 /V
SET WINPMT=Running Windows $P$G
WIN
```

Table 2.3 provides a quick play-by-play of each line of the AUTOEXEC.BAT file shown in Figure 2.2.

TABLE 2.3 PLAY-BY-PLAY OF A TYPICAL AUTOEXEC.BAT FILE

Command	Meaning
@ECHO OFF	Suppresses the display of the commands as they are processed. (The @ symbol at the beginning of the line suppresses display of the command line.)
CLS	Clears the screen.
PROMPT PG	Alters the way the DOS prompt is displayed. The PG portion of the line causes the prompt to show the currently logged drive and path, followed by a greater-than sign (>). You can use the PROMPT command to turn the DOS prompt into anything you want it to be.
	To learn how to change the look of the command prompt, see "Changing the Command Prompt with PROMPT" in Chapter 11, p. 295, and "Issuing ANSI.SYS Codes with the PROMPT Command" in Chapter 17, p. 419. Also, see "PROMPT" in the "Command Reference."
PATH C:\DOS;D:\WINDOWS;C:\;C:\NU	Specifies where and in what order DOS should search directories when a command is entered at the DOS prompt or in a batch file. DOS looks in these directories for a COM, EXE, or BAT file having the same name as the command. Only after these directories have been searched does DOS return the dreaded Bad Command or File Name error message.
	For detailed information about error and other messages, see Appendix C, "DOS Messages."
SET PCPLUS=F:\PROCOMM SET TEMP=C:\TEMP SET BLASTER=A220 I5 D1 T2 SET SOUND=G:\SOUNDPRO	These four lines use the SET command to place variables in the DOS environment. Environment variables can contain character strings, which programs can use to determine parameters. The SET BLASTER variable, for example, documents the Sound Blaster Pro card's installation parameters. Programs that play sounds routinely rely on this variable to provide information they need.
LH /L:0;1,42432 /S C:\DOS\SMARTDRV.EXE	Loads the SMARTDRV.EXE utility into upper memory.
LH /L:1,56928 C:\DOS\MOUSE.COM /Y	Loads the DOS mouse driver into upper memory.
LH /L:1,13984 C:\DOS\SHARE /L:500	Loads the SHARE.EXE utility into upper memory.

Table 2.3 Continued

Command	Meaning
`LH /L:1,6400 C:\DOS\DOSKEY.COM`	Loads the `DOSKEY` utility into upper memory.
`LH /L:1,46576 C:\DOS\MSCDEX /d:MSCD001 /M:15 /V`	Loads the `MSCDEX` utility, which assigns a drive letter to a CD-ROM drive that has been loaded in `CONFIG.SYS`. The `/d` switch specifies the drive name that was provided in `CONFIG.SYS`.
`SET WINPMT=Running Windows $P$G`	Creates an environment variable that specifies how the DOS prompt should be displayed when you're running a DOS session under Windows.
`WIN`	Automatically launches Windows every time the computer boots.

Remember, nothing is sacred or untouchable about `AUTOEXEC.BAT`; it's simply another batch file. Use the `EDIT` command to add and delete entries to create the exact startup configuration you want to have each time you use your computer. Creating a backup of the file before you edit it is always a good idea, of course. Use the following:

`COPY AUTOEXEC.BAT AUTOEXEC.OLD`

By creating a backup, you can restore the previous version if you accidentally mess up your configuration.

→ For more information about the `EDIT` command, **see** Chapter 15, "Using the DOS Editor," **p. 361**.

→ For more detailed information, **see** "Fine-Tuning Your Computer with `CONFIG.SYS` and `AUTOEXEC.BAT`" in Chapter 19, "Configuring Your Computer," **p. 463**.

Creating Multiple Configurations

Being able to boot your computer into one of several configurations is often handy. You might run a DOS program that requires expanded memory, for example, but nothing else you do requires EMS. If you run Windows and Windows programs most of the time, the 64KB page frame in expanded memory (EMS), also called upper memory, can be a drag on performance, so doing without the EMS is better. Maybe you have reason to log in to a network several times a day, but some of your programs object to having the network shell take up memory that they want to use. You might have any number of reasons to want different configurations at different times.

With earlier versions of DOS, you had to jump through hoops if you needed to have more than one standard configuration. A common trick was to have two or more versions of `CONFIG.SYS` tucked away in subdirectories or written in the boot directory with alternative names. When you needed a configuration different from your normal working environment, you had to copy one of these alternative `CONFIG.SYS` files into the boot directory and reboot. Changing back to your normal configuration was just as complex. No more!

A new DOS feature enables you to create multiple configurations within your CONFIG.SYS file and display a menu of the available options. To create a boot menu, all you have to do is divide your CONFIG.SYS files into sections by naming each section. A section name consists of a word inside brackets, as in [menu]. Two section names have special meanings.

The [menu] creates the menu of options displayed at boot time. Each menu item is created with a line similar to the following:

```
menuitem=Normal,Everyday Configuration
```

The word to the right of the equal sign is the name of the section you want to use for your configuration, and the words following the comma make up the menu prompt. If you omit the description, the section name is used as the menu prompt.

The [common] section enters lines that should be used in all your various configurations. You can have more than one section named [common]. DOS executes these sections in the order in which they appear in the file.

Microsoft recommends that multiple configuration CONFIG.SYS files end with a [common] section, even if it is empty. You end the file with a [common] section to accommodate programs that create entries in CONFIG.SYS. Usually, programs append their entries to the end of CONFIG.SYS. By having a [common] section at the end of your file, you ensure that new entries are always executed.

Figure 2.3 shows a multiple configuration CONFIG.SYS file. When the computer on which this CONFIG.SYS file resides boots up, a menu appears offering you two different configurations. If you select Work, the network and mouse drivers are loaded. If you select Games, no network or mouse driver is loaded. Instead, the ANSI.SYS driver is loaded. In all other respects, the configurations are the same because those aspects of the DOS session are controlled by the entries in the [common] sections.

Figure 2.3
A multiple configuration CONFIG.SYS file.

```
[menu]
menuitem=Work
menuitem=Games

[common]
DEVICE=C:\DOS\HIMEM.SYS
DEVICE=C:\DOS\EMM386.EXE NOEMS
BUFFERS =15,0
FILES=49
DOS=UMB,HIGH

[work]
DEVICE=C:\DOS\NET.SYS
DEVICE=C:\DOS\MOUSE.SYS

[games]
DEVICE=C:\DOS\ANSI.SYS

[common]
```

Creating a Default Configuration

You can include a line in the [menu] section of CONFIG.SYS to create a default configuration that is used if a selection is not made from the menu within a specified number of seconds. Here's an example:

```
menudefault=work,5
```

Placing this line in the [menu] section causes DOS to default to the work configuration if a menu selection is not made within five seconds after the menu is displayed.

Displaying Color Menus

Another command enables you to specify screen colors for displaying the boot menu. Here's an example:

```
menucolor=15,1
```

Placing this line in the [menu] section of CONFIG.SYS causes DOS to display the menu using bright white letters on a blue background. The first parameter supplies the color code for the foreground color; the second parameter, which is optional, specifies the background color. If you do not specify the background color, the default value of 0 (black) is used. Table 2.4 shows the valid color codes you can use.

TABLE 2.4   CONFIG.SYS MENU COLORS

Number	Color
0	Black
1	Blue
2	Green
3	Cyan
4	Red
5	Magenta
6	Brown
7	White
8	Gray
9	Bright Blue
10	Bright Green
11	Bright Cyan
12	Bright Red
13	Bright Magenta

Creating Multiple Configurations

Table 2.4	Continued
Number	**Color**
14	Yellow
15	Bright White

Tip

You can pull an undocumented trick when you're specifying menu colors. Most video cards are not capable of displaying bright colors (9 through 15) as the background color. If you specify a bright background color on most video cards, the foreground color is set to blink. Thus, the following line produces a blinking yellow foreground on a standard blue background:

`menucolor=14,9`

Figure 2.4 shows how you can edit the sample CONFIG.SYS file in Figure 2.3 to display a menu in color. The foreground is yellow and the background is blue. Descriptive menu prompts and a default configuration also have been added.

Figure 2.4
Displaying a configuration menu in color with descriptive prompts and a default configuration.

```
[menu]
menuitem=work,Normal Configuration
menuitem=games,Let's Play Games
menucolor=14,1
menudefault=work,10

[common]
DEVICE=C:\DOS\HIMEM.SYS
DEVICE=C:\DOS\EMM386.EXE NOEMS
BUFFERS =15,0
FILES=49
DOS=UMB,HIGH

[work]
DEVICE=C:\DOS\NET.SYS
DEVICE=C:\DOS\MOUSE.SYS

[games]
DEVICE=C:\DOS\ANSI.SYS

[common]
```

The CONFIG.SYS file shown in Figure 2.4 renders the menu shown in Figure 2.5. Notice that DOS precedes each menu choice with a number. You can select a menu prompt in one of two ways. The first method is to press the number key corresponding to the prompt you want to select. The second method is to highlight the desired prompt and press Enter.

Figure 2.5
The DOS 6.2 startup menu.

```
MS-DOS 6.2 Startup Menu
=========================

   1. Normal Configuration
   2. Let's Play Games

Enter a choice: 1        Time remaining: 10




F5=Bypass startup files F8=Confirm each line of CONFIG.SYS
and AUTOEXEC.BAT [N]
```

USING THE CONFIGURATION MENU AS A SYSTEM MENU

Almost everyone who is computer literate knows someone who just will never get the hang of working with computers. These same people are the ones you give the exact syntax of the COPY command letter by letter every time they call you with a problem. These users figure out just enough about one or two programs to get their work done and to be dangerous. Sadly, even DOSSHELL is a mystery to them.

You can employ a trick using DOS environment variables to turn the CONFIG.SYS configuration menu into a system menu that runs a particular program each time the computer is booted. When a particular configuration is chosen, DOS automatically creates an environment variable named CONFIG. As its value, this variable is given the name of the configuration section chosen. If you choose to have a section called [net] as your configuration, for example, the value of CONFIG is net.

You can use the value of CONFIG to branch off within the AUTOEXEC.BAT file to run commands specific to that configuration. Assume that CONFIG.SYS contains three sections that offer you a choice in the configuration menu between Windows, WordPerfect, and Lotus 1-2-3. Also, assume that these sections are named WINDOWS, WP, and LOTUS.

In batch files, you can create sections similar to the sections that you can create in CONFIG.SYS. In batch files, however, you name sections by using the colon (:), as in the following:

:labelname

You can execute a specific section of commands by using the GOTO command inside the batch file. Because AUTOEXEC.BAT is a batch file like any other, you can use the value of the CONFIG variable to branch off in AUTOEXEC.BAT. Figure 2.6 shows how you might construct such an AUTOEXEC.BAT file.

Figure 2.6
Use the CONFIG variable to run configuration-specific commands.

```
ECHO OFF
CLS
PROMPT $P$G
PATH C:\DOS;D:\WINDOWS;C:\;C:\NU
SET PCPLUS-F:\PROCOMM
SET TEMP=C:\TEMP
SET BLASTER=A220 I5 D1 T2
SET SOUND=G:\SBPRO
LH /L:0;1,42432 /S C:\DOS\SMARTDRV.EXE
LH /L:1,56928 C:\DOS\MOUSE.COM /Y
LH /L:1,13984 C:\DOS\SHARE /L:500
LH /L:1,6400 C:\DOS\DOSKEY.COM
REM  Commands above are common to all configurations.
GOTO %CONFIG%

:WINDOWS
SET WINPMT=Running Windows $P$G
WIN
GOTO END

:WP
C:\WP\WP
GOTO END

:LOTUS
CD 123
123
GOTO END

:END
REM Check once in a while to make sure you haven't
REM installed any programs that put lines here that
REM need to be moved to the common lines at the top.
```

As you can see in the figure, AUTOEXEC.BAT is divided into five sections. The first section contains all the commands common to all configurations. This section isn't named because DOS begins executing lines at the top. The last line of this section uses GOTO to branch directly to one of the three choices on the CONFIG.SYS menu.

Three named sections occupy the middle of the file. Because they each finish with a GOTO command that directs the batch file to the :END section, only those commands in the chosen section execute.

The :END section is necessary to let DOS skip over the sections that haven't been chosen and to let any commands added by software installation take effect. The problem is that commands in the :END section do not take effect until you exit from whatever program is called by one of the named sections above :END. When you install new software, always check AUTOEXEC.BAT if you use this technique because you might have to move entries up into the first section of commands common to all configurations.

A drawback to using this technique is that when you exit the program, you don't have any way to loop back into the menu except to reboot the computer. Also, the startup menu always advertises the availability of the F5 and F8 keys.

Make sure not to simply reboot the computer while you're still in an application program; otherwise, you lose data. Similarly, avoid using the F5 or F8 keys, or you might think the menu is broken.

Project: Controlling the Boot Process

Users who practice safe computing should make sure that they have a floppy-based boot disk before messing with either `CONFIG.SYS` or `AUTOEXEC.BAT`. Fortunately, the DOS development team has made this practice less necessary. A new feature introduced in DOS 6.0 enables you to use function keys to exercise control over the boot.

Imagine, for example, that you have just edited `AUTOEXEC.BAT` to load a program during bootup. For whatever reason, this program is incompatible with your system, and the computer simply freezes each time the command is run. You can never get to a DOS prompt to edit the file because the machine hangs every time. You can boot off your floppy boot disk, of course, but now you have an easier way.

When the `Starting MS-DOS...` message appears onscreen during the boot process, you know that `IO.SYS` and `MSDOS.SYS` are about to be loaded. At this point, you can press two keys or key combinations that modify the boot process. If you use DOS 6.0, you can use the F5 and F8 keys; with DOS 6.2, you can use these two keys or Ctrl+F5 or Ctrl+F8.

If you press the F5 key when the message appears, DOS bypasses loading and processing both `CONFIG.SYS` and `AUTOEXEC.BAT`. You boot up as if you had a floppy boot disk that didn't contain these files.

If you have installed DoubleSpace, you also can press Ctrl+F5. This key combination not only skips `CONFIG.SYS` and `AUTOEXEC.BAT`, but also skips the loading of DoubleSpace. This practice is great if you have programs (such as the latest high-performance games) that do not work with disk-compression programs such as DoubleSpace.

If you press the F8 key when the `Starting MS-DOS...` message appears, DOS displays the following message:

```
MS-DOS will prompt you to confirm each CONFIG.SYS command.
```

Each line in `CONFIG.SYS` then is displayed along with a `[Y,N]` prompt. To execute the displayed command, press either `Y` or Enter (not both). To bypass the command, press `N`.

After you have dealt with all the lines in `CONFIG.SYS`, you see the following message:

```
Process AUTOEXEC.BAT [Y,N]?
```

DOS is giving you the option of bypassing the execution of AUTOEXEC.BAT. Answer this query as you did the earlier ones. If you press N, the AUTOEXEC.BAT file is skipped entirely. If you are using DOS 6.2 and you press Y, each line in your AUTOEXEC.BAT file is displayed, in turn, and you can choose whether you want it executed.

The final key combination you can use to modify the boot process is Ctrl+F8. If you press this combination, you can process CONFIG.SYS and AUTOEXEC.BAT interactively, but DoubleSpace is not loaded. Understand that if you choose this option, drivers or programs that you attempt to load (which are normally stored on a compressed drive) are not accessible.

After you have broken through to the DOS prompt, you then can use the EDIT command to rectify whatever problem keeps your system from successfully booting.

By default, who a two-second delay occurs between the time the Starting MS-DOS... message appears and the loading of DOS system files begins. If you eliminate this delay by using the SWITCHES=/F command in CONFIG.SYS, DOS still can recognize the F5, Ctrl+F5, F8, or Ctrl+F8 keystrokes. Even on a fast hard drive, IO.SYS and MSDOS.SYS take a second or two to load. You should be able to break in with a keystroke before CONFIG.SYS is processed.

CHAPTER 3

USING DOS COMMANDS

In this chapter

Understanding DOS Commands   42

Understanding the Elements of a DOS Command   42

Getting Help   46

Issuing DOS Commands   51

Troubleshooting   55

Understanding DOS Commands

When you want your computer to perform an action, you communicate this request for service by entering commands at the DOS prompt. All DOS commands begin with a word, sometimes called a *keyword*, that identifies the action you want to take. Most DOS commands can accept parameters that refine the scope of the command. The DIR command, for example, tells DOS to show you a list of files written on a disk. Adding parameters to this command enables you to specify exactly the files you want listed.

Internal Versus External

DOS recognizes and responds to more than 80 commands. The programming to provide the most commonly used commands is contained within the DOS command interpreter, COMMAND.COM. You use commands such as DIR and COPY so frequently that making them available on demand whenever the computer is displaying a DOS prompt saves time. Because DOS does not have to *launch* (start) any program to provide the service, the commands provided by COMMAND.COM are called *internal commands*. You can tell which commands are internal by looking in the directory where DOS is installed. You never find COPY.COM or COPY.EXE, so you know that the COPY command is internal.

Other commands are stored as utility programs in a directory on your hard disk. Because these commands are not built into the command processor, they are called *external commands*. When you type a command that COMMAND.COM does not recognize as one of its internal commands, COMMAND.COM responds by looking on disk for a program file having the same name as the command. The FORMAT command, for example, is provided by programming found in the file FORMAT.COM, which is located in the DOS directory.

Whether internal or external, all DOS commands conform to rules that provide a grammar or syntax that is consistent throughout DOS. As a user, you need to make sure only that DOS can find the program files for external commands.

Understanding the Elements of a DOS Command

To begin to understand DOS commands, you first need to know a few fundamental facts:

- DOS requires that you use a specific set of rules, or *syntax*, when you issue commands.
- All DOS commands begin with a keyword that identifies the action you want performed.
- *Parameters*, which are a part of a command's syntax, refine the way a command is executed.

Syntax is the order in which you type the elements of the DOS command—its grammar. If you say, "Ball red the choose I," people probably will not understand that you are trying to say, "I choose the red ball." Some people might understand what you are trying to say, but not many. A computer, on the other hand, has no intelligence or imagination; it can interpret commands only according to its programming. Programming several optional syntaxes for commands requires using a great deal of extra memory and disk space, which cuts down on the resources available to do real work. That's why you have to supply the intelligence and imagination and why you must enter DOS commands precisely according to the rules of command syntax.

You can think of the command keyword as the action part, or verb, of a DOS command. In addition to the keyword, many commands require or allow further directions. You supply these directions as parameters and switches. Parameters tell DOS what action to take or how to apply the action. Using DOS commands is easy as long as you follow the rules of order and use the correct parameters. After you know the basic rules, you often can figure out parameters for commands that you don't use on a regular basis.

> **Note**
> You run applications software—such as word processors or drawing programs—by entering a command at the DOS prompt. The command you use to start an application is the name of the program file (COM or EXE) in which the programming for the software is stored.

Most applications software incorporates the issuing of commands as part of the software's operation. The commands discussed in this book are DOS commands. Be sure that you know the difference between DOS commands, which you issue at the DOS command line, and the commands you learn to use with your applications software.

If you are unsure whether a command you have been taught to use is part of DOS, look in Appendix F, "Command Reference." If that command is not listed, it is an application program command, not a DOS command.

The Command Syntax

The syntax for most DOS commands can be boiled down to one of the following two simple formats:

```
KEYWORD Drive\Files Switches
```

```
KEYWORD SourceFiles TargetFiles Switches
```

A DOS command always begins with the keyword, which is the name of the command, followed by a space. If you use the language metaphor, the keyword is the verb that specifies the action to be taken.

The first example shows the common form for DOS commands that don't change files in some way. The *Drive\Files* portion of the example is a parameter that specifies what drive or files on which the command is supposed to act. This parameter is analogous to a noun in English. In other words, the parameter is the thing on which the verb acts. This portion of the syntax is in *italic* to show that the parameter is optional. The parameter also can be followed by command-line switches. To extend the language metaphor, switches are like adverbs; they modify the verb. They change the action to be done.

The second example here is typical of the syntax for most DOS commands that operate on groups of files. The keyword, of course, specifies the action, followed by two parameters that indicate the disk or files that provide the data source for the action. The second parameter indicates the target disk or files. To copy a group of files from one disk or directory to another, for example, you can use the following command:

```
COPY A:Myfile.TXT B:Yourfile.TXT
```

This command copies a file having the name MYFILE.TXT on drive A into the memory of your computer and then writes the contents of the file onto drive B using the name YOURFILE.TXT.

> **Note**
>
> Some parameters or switches are optional, meaning that some parts of the command syntax, such as the keyword, are mandatory. When you enter only the mandatory command elements, DOS (in most cases) uses default parameters for other elements.
>
> A good example is the COPY command. If the following is the command, the default target is the currently logged disk and directory:
>
> ```
> COPY A:MyFile.TXT
> ```
>
> If you're in C:\TEMP, the file is copied to that directory, and the current filename, MYFILE.TXT, is the target filename as well.
>
> As you can see, having defaults makes commands easier to use and shorter, and gives you fewer opportunities to make mistakes.

Because many DOS commands have several parameters, switches, and defaults, different forms of these commands might be correct. You seldom, if ever, use all the optional syntax for any command. Some switches actually are mutually exclusive. You cannot format a floppy disk as both high density and low density, for example.

To find out what options are available for any given command, you should look up the command in the "Command Reference" later in this book. The first time you look up a complex command, don't let the sheer volume of optional parameters and switches throw you for a loop. Even the simplest of DOS commands has several options.

The way the syntax is presented often is called the *paradigm*. Even the simple DOS commands have an imposing paradigm. A good example is the DIR command, a real workhorse of a command. Its paradigm looks something like the following:

```
DIR filespec /P /W /S /B /L /C /CH /O:sortorder /A:attributes
```

You use the DIR command to display a directory of one or more files stored on a disk. This command might look formidable, but it is much easier to understand if you break down the individual components.

→ For a description of the DIR command and its options, **see** "Listing Files with the DIR Command" in Chapter 8, "Managing Your Files", **p. 193**.

THE COMMAND-LINE PARAMETERS

In addition to the command's name, a DOS command contains syntax elements known as *parameters*. Parameters (sometimes called *arguments*) are the parts of a command line that provide DOS with the objects of the command's action. The objects might be files, system settings, or hardware devices.

In the DIR example in the preceding section, *filespec* is the complete filename, including any drive, path, and wildcards that you want the DIR command to use. In some commands, you might see the *filespec* spelled out, as in the following:

```
d:path\filename.ext
```

Don't be confused by this formal rendering of the *filespec*; it simply states that the *filespec* can contain a drive letter, a pathname, a filename, and an extension.

> **Note**
>
> Many new users are confused about the way slashes and backslashes are used in commands. In actuality, their uses are stated simply in two rules:
>
> - Backslashes (\) are used as separators (delimiters) when specifying directory and file information.
> - Slashes (/), sometimes called *forward slashes*, are used as signals to DOS that the next character is a command-line switch.
>
> A good memory association to use is that a backslash connects one name back to the name that comes before it, whereas a slash connects to the character in front of it.

THE OPTIONAL SWITCHES

A *switch* is a parameter that turns on an optional function of a command. Switches are special parameters because they usually are not the objects of a command's action; rather, switches modify the command's action. You can use the /W switch with the DIR command, for example, to display a wide directory of files instead of the usual single-column list. Switches can make a basic command more versatile and powerful. In the DIR example, /P, /W, /S, /B, /L, /O, /C, /CH, and /A are switches.

Usually, you can use a command's switches in any order or any combination. Not all DOS commands have switches, however. Also, the letter used for a switch in one DOS command might have a different meaning in another DOS command. In addition, some switches require a parameter. You usually attach switch parameters to the switch by using a colon (:), as in the following example:

```
FORMAT A: /F:360 /S
```

In this example, the /F switch specifies that a 360KB floppy disk be formatted in a disk drive that normally uses high-density (1.2MB) disks.

Getting Help

These days, the manuals supplied with DOS don't provide all the information they did in previous versions. They no longer contain a complete printed reference for all the DOS commands. To get the official Microsoft syntax for every DOS command, you have to pony up extra dollars to buy the *MS-DOS Technical Reference*. Because you already have *this* book, you probably don't want or need the *Technical Reference*. Appendix F, "Command Reference," contains a wealth of information about undocumented switches and parameters.

In place of the printed manual that used to come with DOS, Microsoft has opted instead to supply an online command reference. It falls short of the reference in the back of this book, of course, because it doesn't include the undocumented information; but most of the time, you will find the online reference to be adequate and handy.

To access online help for the use of a particular command, use one of the following procedures from the DOS prompt:

- Type the DOS command, followed by the switch /?.
- Type HELP, followed by the DOS command.

The following sections describe each method in detail.

Using the Command-Line Help Switch

One DOS command-line switch is never documented in the syntax examples, but you can use this switch with any DOS command. The /? switch is universal to all DOS commands.

After you enter a DOS command followed by the /? switch, DOS prints to the screen a summary of the command syntax. In some cases, the sample syntax is simplified by omitting options not available to you at the command line. A good example is the EMM386 command. Usually, EMM386 is loaded via CONFIG.SYS. After DOS is running, only those parts of the command that are accessible during a DOS session are displayed, omitting the parameters that can be given only at boot time.

The handy thing about using the /? switch is that it gives you a short summary of the command, leaving enough room onscreen for a DOS prompt. This way, you can refer to the syntax and type the command without taking your attention away from the screen.

To get a command summary of the DIR command, for example, type the following command and then press Enter:

```
DIR /?
```

DOS displays the command summary help screen shown in Figure 3.1.

Figure 3.1
Using the DOS command summary help.

```
Displays a list of files and subdirectories in a directory.
DIR [drive:][path][filename]        Specifies drive, directory, and/or files
to list.
/P        Pauses after each screenful of information.
/W        Uses wide list format.
/A        Displays files with specified attributes
attribs   D  Directories     R  Read-only files H  Hidden files
          S  System files    A  Files ready to archive   -  Prefix meaning
"not"
O/    List by files in sorted order.
sortord   N  By name (alphabetic)      S  By size (smallest first)
          E  By extension (alphabetic)       D  By date & time (earliest
first)
          G  Group directories first  -  Prefix to reverse order
          C  By compression ratio (smallest first)
/S        Displays files in specified directory and all subdirectories.
/B        Uses bare format (no heading information or summary).
/L        Uses lowercase.
/C[H]     Displays file compression ratio; /CH uses host allocation unit size.
Switches may be preset in the DIRCMD environment variable.  Override
preset switches by prefixing any switch with - (hyphen) -- for example, /-W.
```

USING THE ONLINE HELP SYSTEM

The second method for obtaining help is to use HELP, followed by the keyword you want information about. If you don't know the keyword you are looking for, just type HELP and you are presented with a list of command keywords from which to choose.

The online help system displays a detailed description of the command's function, correct syntax, available switches, and a detailed explanation of the effect of each switch.

The online help system also contains special notes and examples related to each command, which enables you to view information on related commands or topics by using only a few keystrokes. If you have a mouse, using the online help system is a snap. You even can print information on selected commands.

To get the complete online help for the DIR command, for example, type the following and then press Enter:

HELP DIR

DOS displays the online help screen shown in Figure 3.2.

NAVIGATING THE HELP SYSTEM

The online help system contains a great deal of information and provides several ways for you to locate, view, and print topics of interest to you. You can use either a mouse or the keyboard to issue commands in the online help system; this section describes both methods. Most of the keystrokes and mouse movements are the same for the help system as they are for the DOS Shell program.

→ For more detailed information about moving around a window, **see** Chapter 4, "Using the DOS Shell," **p. 57**.

Figure 3.2
The DOS online help facility shows syntax, notes, and examples about each DOS command.

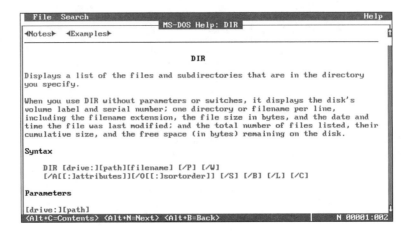

Because the HELP command provides such complete information, information about a topic or command usually requires more than one screen. To view all the information about a topic, you must scroll the display forward and backward.

To scroll through the text one line at a time, use one of the following methods:

- Click the downward-pointing scroll arrow in the scrollbar at the right edge of the screen to move forward one line. To move backward, click the upward-pointing scroll arrow.
- Press the Ctrl+down arrow key combination to move forward; press the Ctrl+up arrow key combination to move backward.

To scroll through the text one screen at a time, use one of these methods:

- Click the scrollbar below the scroll box to move forward one screen; click above the scroll box to move backward.
- Press the PgDn key to move forward one whole screen; press the PgUp key to move backward.

In Figure 3.2, notice the words *Notes* and *Examples* near the top-left corner of the screen. Each word is enclosed within solid, triangular characters. Each of these specially marked words is a *jump*. A jump provides a link to additional information on the currently selected topic or to related topics.

Jumps in the body of the help system's text are marked with angle brackets (<>). The brackets are colored to help you more easily see them if your video card and monitor support color. Although not shown in Figure 3.2, the word <TREE> at the end of the DIR help text is another example of a jump.

When you select a jump, the online help system displays the text related to the topic named by the jump word. To select a jump, use one of the following methods:

- Click the jump with the mouse.
- Move the cursor over the jump and then press Enter.

If you select the <Examples> jump shown in Figure 3.2, the help system displays a screen containing examples of the DIR command and explanations of each example. Selecting a jump such as <TREE> causes the help system to display the help for the TREE command.

In Figure 3.2, the solid bar across the top of the screen with the words *File* and *Search* is the help system's menu bar. You use the help system's pull-down menus in the same way you use the pull-down menus in the DOS Shell.

→ If you are unfamiliar with using pull-down menus, **see** Chapter 4, "Using the DOS Shell," **p. 57**.

The choices on the File menu enable you to print a topic or exit the online help system. The choices on the Search menu enable you to search for a topic, word, or phrase and repeat the last search.

Another solid bar appears at the bottom of the screen (refer again to Figure 3.2). The bottom-right corner of this area of the help screen displays numbers indicating the current line and column number of the cursor. In Figure 3.2, the cursor is at line 1, column 2 of the help text for the DIR command.

At the left edge of this area, three keystroke combinations and their functions are displayed:

<Alt+C=Contents> <Alt+N=Next> <Alt+B=Back>

Each label enclosed in brackets also doubles as a command button if you have a mouse. You can click the command button or press the key command, Alt+C, causes the online help system to display its table of contents. Each item in the table of contents is a jump. The Next command, Alt+N, causes the online help system to display the next topic. The Back command, Alt+B, causes the online help system to display the last topic you looked at.

Table 3.1 summarizes the command keys, and their actions, available in the online help system.

TABLE 3.1 ONLINE HELP COMMAND KEYS

Key	Action
Alt	Activates the help system menu
Alt+B	Returns to the last topic you viewed
Alt+C	Displays the list of topics covered in the help system
Alt+F	Opens the File menu
Alt+S	Opens the Search menu
Alt+N	Moves to the next topic
Ctrl+down arrow	Scrolls the screen down one line
Ctrl+up arrow	Scrolls the screen up one line

Table 3.1 Continued

Key	Action
Ctrl+Home	Moves to the beginning of the current topic
Ctrl+End	Moves to the end of the current topic
Enter	Selects a menu command or selects the jump under the cursor (the DOS help system displays the text for the jump topic)
Esc	Cancels a command; closes a menu or dialog box without making a selection or carrying out the action
F1	Displays context-sensitive help on using the online help system
F3	Repeats the last search
A–Z	Moves to the next jump beginning with the letter pressed
Shift+*letter*	Moves to the previous jump beginning with the letter pressed
PgUp	Scrolls the text up one screen
PgDn	Scrolls the text down one screen
Shift+Ctrl+F1	Moves to the preceding topic
Tab	Moves clockwise to the next jump
Shift+Tab	Moves counterclockwise to the next jump

Printing a Topic

The online help system enables you to print the text for the currently displayed topic. You may optionally send the output to a file on your disk instead of to the printer. The Print command is located on the File menu.

When the help system displays the File menu, click the Print command. The help system opens the Print dialog box shown in Figure 3.3.

→ For information on using dialog boxes, option buttons, text boxes, and command buttons, **see** Chapter 4, "Using the DOS Shell," **p. 57**.

Figure 3.3
The online help system's Print dialog box.

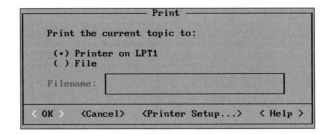

To print the current topic on your printer, simply press Enter or click the OK command button. To send the text for the current topic to a disk file, select the File option button;

then, in the text box, enter the name of the file to which you want to send the output. Finally, press Enter or click the OK command button.

Searching for a Topic

You use the Find command to search for a specific topic, word, or phrase. The Find command is located on the Search menu.

When the help system opens the Find dialog box, you see a screen similar to the one shown in Figure 3.4.

Figure 3.4
The online help system's Find dialog box.

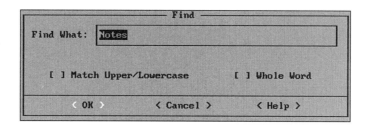

When the Find dialog box first opens, the Find What text box contains the word that the cursor was on when you selected the Find command. In Figure 3.4, the cursor was on the word *Notes* when the Find command was selected, so the Find What text box contains the word *Notes*.

Enter the topic, word, or phrase that you want to search for in the Find What text box, or use the word already in the text box. Then, select which of the two Find options you want to use. You can use one, both, or neither of these options.

If you check the Match Upper/Lowercase option check box, the search is case sensitive. If you check the Whole Word option check box, it is assumed that you are searching for a whole word; partial word matches will be ignored.

You can repeat any search by selecting the Repeat Last Find command on the Search menu or by pressing F3.

Exiting the Help System

To exit the online help system using the mouse, pull down the File menu and click Exit. To exit the help system using the keyboard, press Alt+F, followed by X.

Issuing DOS Commands

When you enter a DOS command, two sets of parameters determine how the command is carried out. Any parameters or switches that you explicitly type take precedence, of course, but unless you override them, the default values for a command are used.

Throughout this chapter, you've seen the DIR command used as an example. Here's one more:

DIR /P

When you issue the DIR command to see the files on a disk, the currently logged directory is used unless you specify otherwise. Also, all the files in the directory are shown unless you somehow override the default by explicitly specifying a file or group of files. By default, the display of files scrolls to the end without stopping. In the preceding example, the display of all files in the current directory (the default) is used, but the /P switch, which makes the listing pause after each page of filenames, overrides the default behavior of scrolling to the end of the list without stopping.

Figure 3.5 breaks down the different elements that make up the DIR command. As you can see, only two of the switches (/P and /W) are illustrated.

Figure 3.5
The syntax of the DIR command.

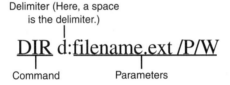

Figure 3.6 is a diagram of the DIR command as you might use it. If you are unfamiliar with the anatomy of a command, the following sections explain each of the different parts.

Editing and Canceling Commands

You occasionally might make a mistake when you are entering a command. Because DOS does not act on the command until you press Enter, you can correct a mistake by using the arrow keys or the Backspace key to reposition the cursor and type over your entry. If you need to insert characters into the command line, press the Ins key to turn on the insert mode. After you press Enter, DOS automatically returns to the overtype mode.

If, however, you have gotten way off track and want to cancel what you have and start over, you can press the Esc key, Ctrl+C, or Ctrl+Break.

DOS stores keystrokes that have not yet been displayed in a type-ahead buffer. The idea of the type-ahead buffer is to keep keystrokes from being lost when entered by fast typists, or when a prolonged operation takes the computer's focus away from the keyboard for a moment. If the type-ahead buffer gets filled with keystrokes, your PC beeps when you press an additional keystroke, warning you that you are losing keystrokes. The buffer storage areas also give DOS some special editing capabilities.

Each time you complete a command by pressing Enter, the command is stored in another buffer, the last command buffer. Using the DOS editing keystrokes, you can recall the last command, or you can pull the preceding command line from the buffer and use it again. This feature is helpful when you want to issue a command that is similar to the last command you used or when you mistyped a parameter. Table 3.2 lists the keys you use to edit the input buffer.

Figure 3.6
Issuing the DIR command.

DIR	An internal DOS command that lists the contents of a disk directory
d:	A symbolic way to indicate a disk drive name
filename.ext	A symbolic way to show a filename and its extension
/P	A switch that displays the directory one screen at a time
/W	A switch that displays a directory in five columns

To issue the DIR command, follow these steps:

1. Type **DIR**. (Use upper- or lowercase.) Press the spacebar.
2. Type the disk name, followed by a colon if necessary–A:, B:, or C:.
3. Type the name of the files if you want to see the directory listing for a specific file.
4. Type **/P** to *pause* the directory 23 lines at a time.
5. Type **/W** for a *wide* directory.
6. Press Enter.

TABLE 3.2 DOS COMMAND-LINE EDITING KEYS

Key	Action
Tab	Moves the cursor to the next tab stop
Esc	Cancels the current line and does not change the last command buffer
Ins	Enables you to insert characters into the line
Del	Deletes a character from the line
F1 or right arrow	Copies the next single character from the last command buffer
F2	Copies all characters from the last command buffer up to, but not including, the next character you type
F3	Copies all remaining characters from the preceding command line

Table 3.2	Continued
Key	Action
F4	Deletes all characters from the last command buffer up to and including the next character typed (opposite of F2)
F5	Moves the current line into the buffer but does not allow DOS to execute the line
F6	Produces an end-of-file marker (^Z) when you copy from the console to a disk file

These editing keystrokes come from the earliest versions of DOS. Beginning with version 5.0, there is a better way. The DOSKEY command, usually entered via AUTOEXEC.BAT, loads into memory a program that creates a much larger buffer to store previous command lines. (Refer to the "Command Reference" for the DOSKEY listing.) You can recall these commands by pressing the up-arrow key. The DOSKEY buffer is 512 bytes by default, which is enough on average to store the last 20 commands executed.

→ For a complete reference source for DOS editing keystrokes, **see** Appendix D, "DOS and DOS Utility Programs' Keyboard Commands," **p. 563**.

Using Scroll Control

The term *scrolling* describes what happens as a DOS screen fills with information. When DOS displays text in response to your typing or as a result of a DOS command, the text fills the screen from left to right and top to bottom. As the screen fills, information scrolls off the top of the display. To stop a scrolling screen, press Ctrl+S (hold down the Ctrl key and then press S). Press any key to restart the scrolling. On enhanced keyboards, press the Pause key to stop scrolling.

Using Wildcards in DOS Commands

Almost everyone has at one time played a game, such as poker, that employs wildcards. If you hear the dealer say "Deuces are wild!" you know that cards having the number 2 printed on the face can be substituted for any other card in the deck.

DOS uses wildcards, too. When you're entering DOS commands, you can use wildcards to specify groups of files. DOS recognizes two wildcard characters: the question mark (?) and the asterisk (*), also called star ("star dot star" means *.*).

In DOS commands, the ? represents any single character. The following command produces a directory listing of any files in the currently logged directory that have a filename beginning with the letters *LTR* followed by up to three characters:

```
DIR LTR???.TXT
```

Also, only those files bearing the extension .TXT match and are listed. Thus, LTR.TXT, LTR0.TXT, LTR01.TXT, LTR001.TXT, LTRMOM.TXT, LTR_32.TXT, and LTR999.TXT are listed, but LTRPOPS.TXT or LTR1001.TXT are not.

The * represents any string of characters. For example, *.* represents all filenames with any extension, the default scope of the DIR command. The following command lists all files in the currently logged directory having the extension .DOC:

DIR *.DOC

The following command lists all the files listed by the DIR LTR???.TXT example, as well as filenames not matched by that form of the command:

DIR LTR*.TXT

You should look out for one thing when you're using the * wildcard, however. The following command does *not* produce the result you might expect:

DIR *LTR.TXT

This example does not list all the .TXT files whose names end in *LTR*. Rather, it lists all the files having the extension .TXT. The reason is deceptively simple. Because the * can represent up to eight characters in a filename, any string of characters matches *LTR.

After you get the hang of using wildcards to refine the scope of command parameters that supply filenames, you will find that you are well on your way to becoming a DOS power user.

TROUBLESHOOTING

My program won't run from the C:\ prompt!

When you install DOS on your system, by default, the program files for external commands are written to a directory named DOS on the drive letter that your computer boots from. Because most systems boot from drive C, most of the time you'll find that the DOS directory is called C:\DOS.

If you look into the AUTOEXEC.BAT file, you'll probably find a command line that begins with PATH, followed by a list of directories. This command tells DOS where to search for program files when it is trying to run a command. If your DOS directory is listed in the PATH command line, COMMAND.COM can find the program files for external commands no matter what disk drive or directory you are logged on to. A PATH statement looks like this:

Path=c:\; c:\DOS; c:\windows

If you install a program to a new directory without adding that directory to the PATH statement, that program will run only if you change directories to where it resides. When you add the program's home directory to the PATH statement, you can execute any file in that directory, no matter what directory you are currently in.

CHAPTER 4

Using the DOS Shell

In this chapter

- What Is the DOS Shell? 58
- Starting the DOS Shell 59
- Using the DOS Shell Menus 64
- Using the Shell Screen Modes 75
- Using the Program List 77
- Working with Directories 83
- Working with Files 87
- Using the Task Swapper 93
- Project: Using the Help System 94

What Is the DOS Shell?

The DOS Shell program is a visually oriented user interface that replaces the DOS command line with easy-to-use and easy-to-understand menus. It enables you to use a mouse (or other pointing device) to perform many common DOS tasks.

Introduced with DOS 4.0, the DOS Shell is no longer a primary part of DOS. With the advent of DOS 6.2, it has been relegated to the status of a supplemental program and is thus included on the Supplemental Disk. If you are upgrading from an earlier version of DOS, however, the earlier version of the DOS Shell will remain on your disk.

The DOS Shell is a mildly controversial feature of DOS. Although it is praised by some as a kinder and gentler way of using DOS, others deride it as a crutch and a crippled imitation of Windows. In fact, there is truth to both opinions.

The DOS Shell has features that are strikingly familiar to Windows users. The point-and-click interface, disks and directories displayed in tree format, the capability to associate file-name extensions with the program that produced them so that selecting a file also starts the program—these features are all hallmarks of the popular Windows operating environment. In fact, if your video card permits (EGA and higher), you can run the Shell in graphics mode.

Still, to perform complex tasks, you often are required to enter command lines using the Run option of the File menu. For anything but the most rudimentary tasks, you still are required to know the syntax of DOS commands.

Unlike Windows, which was built from the ground up to be used as a graphical interface, the DOS Shell is mostly text based. Using the extended ASCII drawing characters, the DOS Shell simulates a *graphical user interface* (*GUI*). Even when it's run in graphics mode, the interface changes only slightly.

Many longtime DOS users find the DOS Shell to be restrictive, even though many tasks are easier and quicker when you use the Shell. On the other side of the coin, many new computer users, especially those with less than one year's experience, find the Shell easier to work with than the bare DOS prompt.

Most users who begin their computer careers working with the DOS Shell usually end up doing one of two things. They either discard the Shell, like a worn-out pair of training wheels, or they move on to the Windows environment.

In practice, the DOS Shell has become a tool used by PC support specialists when training newer users. Many MIS departments and support consultants find that if they teach new users the ins and outs of the DOS Shell, they end up fielding fewer support calls from inexperienced users.

It is assumed that many of the readers of this book fall into the category of support specialist or office computer guru. Although you might not want to use the DOS Shell in your own work, you might want to use it as training wheels for users that you must support.

With the DOS Shell, you can select many commands from a menu instead of typing the commands on the DOS command line. More significantly, with the DOS Shell, many tasks are greatly simplified. You can search quickly through directories or an entire hard disk for files or groups of files. Using a mouse, you can select and copy files between directories or between disks using a Windows-like drag-and-drop feature.

The DOS Shell also provides features not available at the DOS prompt. You can start one applications program, for example, and then switch to a second application without exiting from the first. Unlike other environments, such as those provided by Windows, QEMM, or 386MAX, however, programs in the background cannot remain active.

The DOS Shell enables you to view the contents of files in ASCII or hexadecimal formats without opening applications programs. Another feature associates specific filename extensions with a particular applications program so that selecting a file causes DOS to start the associated program.

> **Note**
>
> To use the DOS Shell effectively, you must have a mouse and mouse driver present on the system. Although you can stumble through the Shell using keystrokes, using a mouse can reduce frustration and save time.
>
> For the mouse to be available, the mouse device driver must be loaded into memory before you run the DOS Shell. DOS 6.0 and later include a generic mouse device driver called MOUSE.COM, which can usually be found in the DOS directory. The mouse driver usually is loaded with a line in the AUTOEXEC.BAT file using the LOAD or LOADHIGH command.
>
> Remember that some mouse devices are not Microsoft mouse-compatible and might not work properly with the generic DOS mouse driver. Manufacturers of such mouse devices normally include a special mouse driver for you to use. See the mouse manual for details.

STARTING THE DOS SHELL

After installing the DOS Shell from the Supplemental Programs disk, you can start it by typing the following at the DOS prompt to load the DOS Shell into memory:

DOSSHELL

The DOS Shell first displays a copyright notice and then displays the full-screen DOS Shell window.

When the Shell first loads, it also displays a message box in the center of the screen containing the message Reading Disk Information. The Shell scans the currently logged drive for the directory structure and file information. After the drive is scanned, the Shell creates a display similar to the one shown in Figure 4.1.

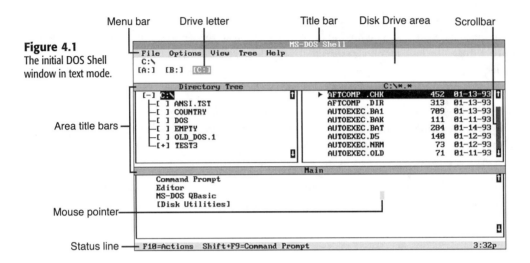

Figure 4.1
The initial DOS Shell window in text mode.

Using the Shell Interface

When you start the DOS Shell, the top line of the screen, the *title bar*, displays the program name, MS-DOS Shell. The second line of the screen, the *menu bar*, lists the names of available menus. You can choose all DOS Shell commands from menus that pull down from the menu bar.

Just below the menu bar, the available disk drives are listed, along with a prompt showing the current drive and directory. All types of drives, including CD-ROMs and DoubleSpace drives, are listed.

Initially, the DOS Shell window appears in text mode, as shown in Figure 4.1. See "Using the Shell Screen Modes," later in this chapter, for information on switching to graphics mode. Figure 4.2 shows the 34-line graphics mode available for VGA displays.

Note that the bitmap icons used to indicate drives also indicate drive types. The icons for a hard disk differ from the icons used to indicate a floppy disk or CD-ROM.

The last line of the DOS Shell window is the *status line*. The status line usually displays two messages: F10=Actions and Shift+F9=Command Prompt. At the right side of the status line, the Shell displays the current time. Occasionally, the status line also displays other messages related to the command you are executing.

> **Caution**
>
> Using Shift+F9 to get a DOS prompt is completely safe when you are working only in DOS. If, however, you want to run the DOS Shell in a DOS session launched under Windows, do not use Shift+F9 to get to a command prompt; otherwise, you can corrupt memory.
>
> The terminology can be confusing, but many programs enable you to "shell out to DOS" or "launch a DOS Shell." These terms have been in use since early versions of DOS that did not include the DOSSHELL program. DOSSHELL uses different terminology, but the effect is the same.

> Programs that shell out to a DOS prompt do so by launching COMMAND.COM as a second application. Launching COMMAND.COM in this fashion is dangerous under Windows because the normal safeguards Windows uses to ensure memory integrity are bypassed.
>
> Programs that are run under this second COMMAND.COM in a Windows DOS session can allocate memory that is never reclaimed after the program terminates. Worse, programs might try to use memory already in use by Windows or a Windows application. These conditions can cause the computer to hang and unsaved data to be lost.
>
> If you need a DOS prompt while you're working in Windows, always launch a separate DOS session from the Windows Program Manager.

Figure 4.2
The DOS Shell window displayed in graphics screen mode.

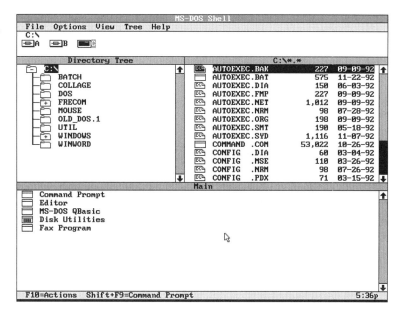

Between the drive area and status line, the DOS Shell divides the screen into rectangular windows, each of which is headed by an *area title bar*. When there is more information than can be displayed in the window, you can scroll up and down using either the keyboard or mouse.

When a window is active, at least one item is highlighted for selection. At the right edge of these windows you find *scrollbars*. If you press the arrow keys or the PgUp/PgDn keys to move the active highlight bar, the scrollbars are relegated simply to showing you the relative position (top to bottom) of the currently highlighted area. Using the mouse is quicker and more efficient. See the section "Moving Around an Area," later in this chapter, for details about using the mouse interface.

Drive informationis displayed in a pair of windows. The left window displays the directory structure of the disk, and the right window displays the files found in the currently highlighted directory.

Using the View menu, you can choose to view two disk drive windows, or you can choose to view Program/File Lists. In this view, the bottom window of the display serves as a menu for starting DOS applications and for accessing DOS utility programs. This area lists a group of programs, called a *program group*. The name of the currently listed program group appears in the area title bar. In text mode, group names are shown enclosed in brackets (refer to Figure 4.1). In graphics mode, icons indicate single programs and groups. Notice how the icon for Disk Utilities differs from the other icons shown in Figure 4.2. To switch to a group, double-click its icon or highlight the group using the arrow keys and press Enter.

When you choose Enable Task Swapper from the Options menu, a fourth area, the *task list area*, is displayed in the DOS Shell window. The active task list area displays the names of DOS applications you have activated through the DOS 6.0 task swapper. Figure 4.3 shows the DOS Shell window with the active task list displayed.

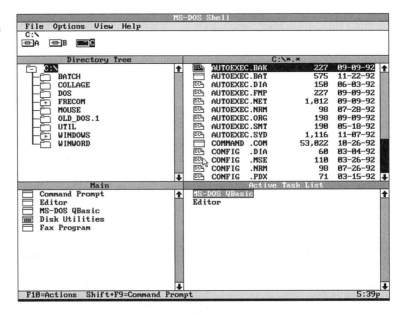

Figure 4.3
The DOS Shell window with the active task list displayed.

SELECTING AN AREA

Although several windows can be displayed in the DOS Shell, at any given moment only one area is *selected* (active) at a time. The selected area is indicated by a highlighted area title bar. An area must be selected before you can perform any operation in that area.

You can use either of the following methods to select an area in the Shell window:

- Move the mouse pointer into the area you want to activate and click the left button. The Shell highlights the area's title bar.

- Press the Tab key to cycle through the areas that are currently displayed in the window.

Moving Around an Area

After you select an area, the Shell highlights one of the items listed in the area. This highlight is called the *selection cursor*. To move the selection cursor within the selected area, use one of the following methods:

- Use the cursor-movement keys on the keyboard. Press the up- or down-arrow key to move up or down one item at a time. Press PgUp or PgDn to move up or down one page at a time. Press Home or End to go to the beginning or end of the list.

- Use the mouse and scrollbar to scroll up or down (see Figure 4.4). You learn how to use the scrollbars in the following paragraphs.

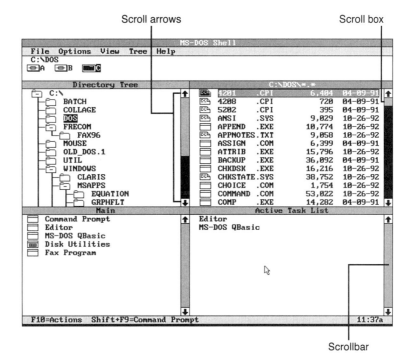

Figure 4.4
Scrollbars are located on the right side of each area of the Shell window.

The scrollbar has the following components:

- A scroll arrow is located at the top and bottom of the bar. By clicking the scroll arrow, you scroll text up or down one line at a time. Click the scroll arrow and hold down the mouse button to scroll continuously in the direction of the arrow.

- A scroll box, sometimes called a *thumb*, is located on the scrollbar between the up-scroll arrow and the down-scroll arrow. The position of the box on the scrollbar indicates the relative position of the selection cursor with respect to the entire list of items in the selected area.

Click the scrollbar above the scroll box to move the selection cursor up one page at a time. Click below the scroll box to move down one page at a time.

You can scroll quickly through the list in either direction by clicking the scroll box, holding down the left mouse button, and dragging the box in the direction you want the selection cursor to move.

Using the DOS Shell Menus

You can initiate virtually every DOS Shell operation by choosing options from menus. These DOS Shell menus fall into two categories: the menu bar and pull-down menus.

Using the Menu Bar

When the disk drive area, directory tree area, or file list area is active, the menu bar lists five menu names: File, Options, View, Tree, and Help. The Tree menu name does not appear when the program list or active task list is the active area. Choosing a menu name displays a pull-down menu.

You can choose a menu option from the menu bar in one of three ways:

- Move the mouse pointer to an option and click the left button.
- Press the F10 key or Alt key to activate the menu bar. The Shell underlines one letter in each menu name and places a selection cursor on the menu name File at the left end of the menu bar. Press the key that corresponds to the underlined letter in the menu name you want to choose. To choose View from the menu bar, for example, press F10 or Alt and then press V.
- Press F10 or Alt to activate the menu bar, use the right- or left-arrow key to move the selection cursor to your choice, and press Enter. This method is sometimes called the *point-and-shoot method*.

Even after you choose a menu name, you still can choose another menu name by clicking the name or by using the right- or left-arrow key.

Using Pull-Down Menus

When you choose a menu name from the menu bar, the Shell displays a pull-down menu, which displays a list of items below the menu bar. If you choose File, for example, while the file list is the active area, the Shell displays the File pull-down menu shown in Figure 4.5. The items listed in the menu depend on which area is active.

To choose an item from a pull-down menu, use one of the following methods:

- Move the mouse pointer to a menu item and click the left button.
- The Shell underlines one letter in each menu item. Press the key that corresponds to the underlined letter in the item you want to choose. To choose View File Contents from the File menu in Figure 4.5, for example, press V.

Figure 4.5
The File pull-down menu displayed when the file list area is active.

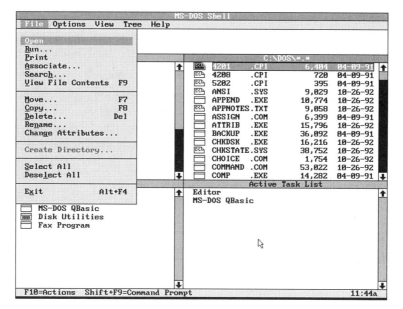

- The Shell places the selection cursor on the first item at the top of the pull-down menu. Use the up- or down-arrow keys to move the selection cursor to your choice and then press Enter.

When a menu is pulled down, you can display an adjacent menu by pressing the left- or right-arrow key. To cancel a pull-down menu without making a selection, click the menu name, click an area outside the menu, or press Esc. The Shell returns to the preceding window display. You also can press Alt or F10 to cancel a pull-down menu while maintaining an active menu bar so that you can choose another menu name. The DOS Shell uses the following conventions when it lists menu items:

- A menu item that displays a dialog box, which is discussed later in this chapter, ends with an ellipsis (...).

- A menu item that is dimmed, such as the Create Directory item shown in Figure 4.5, is not a valid option in the current context.

- Some menu items toggle between two states—on or off. A menu item that is toggled on displays a small diamond to the left of the item name. The diamond is absent when the item is turned off.

- Some commands that you can select through menu items have shortcuts in the form of key combinations or keystroke commands. When a keystroke command shortcut is available for a command, the Shell lists the keystroke in the menu, to the right of the command. Five of the commands in the File menu, for example, list shortcut keystroke commands (refer to Figure 4.5).

Using Keystroke Commands

The DOS Shell provides many *hotkeys*. Many of these commands are listed in pull-down menus. Two such commands, F10 and Shift+F9, are listed in the Shell window status line.

Table 4.1 lists all DOS Shell hotkey commands for DOS 6. After you learn these keystroke commands, you might find them quicker to use than any equivalent menu items. Using menus requires that you use multiple keystrokes or that you take one hand from the keyboard to use the mouse. To perform a command by using the hotkeys, you press a single keystroke or keystroke combination. Windows users will find many of these hotkeys familiar.

TABLE 4.1 DOS SHELL SHORTCUT COMMANDS

Key	Function
F1	Displays context-sensitive help
F3	Exits the DOS Shell, returns to the command line, and removes the DOS Shell from memory (same as Alt+F4)
Alt+F4	Exits the DOS Shell, returns to the command line, and removes the DOS Shell from memory (same as F3)
F5	Refreshes the file list(s)
Shift+F5	Repaints the screen
F7	Moves selected file(s)
F8	Copies selected file(s)
Shift+F8	Extends selection in Add mode
F9	Views file contents
Shift+F9	Accesses the command line without removing the DOS Shell from memory (do not use under Windows!)
F10	Activates the menu bar (same as Alt)
Alt	Activates the menu bar (same as F10)
Del	Deletes selected file(s)
+	Expands one level of the current branch in the directory tree
*	Expands all levels of the current branch in the directory tree
Ctrl+*	Expands all branches in the directory tree
– (hyphen)	Collapses the current branch in the directory tree
Alt+Tab	Cycles through active tasks, if Task Switching is enabled
Alt+Esc	Switches between the active task and the DOS Shell, if Task Switching is enabled
Shift+up arrow	Extends selection up
Shift+down arrow	Extends selection down

Using the DOS Shell Menus

Table 4.1 Continued

Key	Function
Shift+left arrow	Extends selection left
Shift+right arrow	Extends selection right
Esc	Cancels the current function
Tab	Cycles forward through areas (left to right, top to bottom)
Shift+Tab	Cycles backward through areas (right to left, bottom to top)
Ctrl+/	Selects all files in the selected directory
Ctrl+F5	Refreshes the selected directory
Ctrl+\	Cancels file selections

Using Dialog Boxes

As you work with the DOS Shell, the program routinely displays messages and prompts in pop-up boxes, called *dialog boxes*, onscreen. Any menu item that ends with an ellipsis displays a dialog box when you choose the item. When you choose Copy from the File menu, for example, the Copy File dialog box appears (see Figure 4.6).

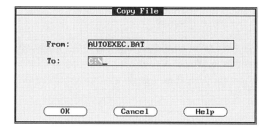

Figure 4.6
The Copy File dialog box.

Dialog boxes fall into two general categories: those that request information and those that provide information. The Copy File dialog box in Figure 4.6 is an example of a dialog box that requests information. Pressing F1, by contrast, displays a dialog box that provides information and is titled MS-DOS Shell Help (see Figure 4.7). This help screen assists you in learning the Shell.

All dialog boxes are built from a standard set of elements: text boxes, list boxes, option buttons, option check boxes, and command buttons. The following sections explain how to use each element.

Using a Text Box

When you need to type information in a dialog box, the Shell includes one or more rectangular fields known as *text boxes*. The Copy File dialog box shown in Figure 4.6 contains two text boxes, one labeled From and one labeled To.

Figure 4.7
The MS-DOS Shell Help dialog box.

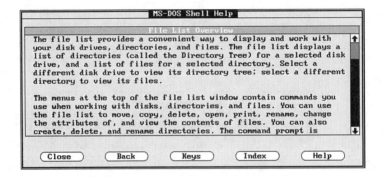

To make an entry in a text box, you first highlight the box. Using the mouse, move the mouse pointer to the box and click the left button. Alternatively, you can press Tab or Shift+Tab repeatedly until the text box is highlighted.

Often, the Shell provides a default value in each text box. The text boxes in Figure 4.6, for example, include the default values AUTOEXEC.BAT and C:\. When you select a text box, the Shell highlights any default contained in that text box. Typing new text in the text box replaces the default value.

Sometimes you don't want to replace the entire default value in a text box. When you want to edit the value, press the right- or left-arrow key to cause the Shell to remove the highlighting. You then can edit the existing entry.

After you make the desired entry or change the value in the text box, press Enter to accept the value that is displayed in the text box. When you press Enter, the Shell also closes the dialog box and executes the command, if any, with which the dialog box is associated.

USING A LIST BOX

Some dialog boxes contain information or a list of choices displayed in a rectangular area, referred to in this book as a *list box*. A title bar appears at the top of each list box, as well as a scrollbar on the right side of the list box. Refer to Figure 4.7, which shows a help dialog box containing a list box titled File List Overview.

Often the text or list is too long to fit in the list box, so the Shell enables you to scroll vertically through the contents of the box. To scroll through a list box, use your mouse and the scrollbar, or use the cursor-movement keys.

USING OPTION BUTTONS

Some dialog boxes require that you use *option buttons* (also called radio buttons) to select command settings. Each option button is a circle (a pair of parentheses if your screen is in text mode) followed by a command setting. Option buttons always occur in groups—never alone. The buttons in each group are mutually exclusive; only one button can be selected at a time.

The File Display Options dialog box shown in Figure 4.8, for example, contains option buttons listed on the right side of the dialog box, beneath the label Sort By. Displayed filenames can be sorted by name, extension, date, size, or disk order, but the Shell does not sort files by more than one of these parameters at a time.

Figure 4.8
The File Display Options dialog box.

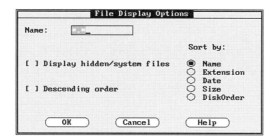

> **Tip**
>
> You can execute the command associated with a dialog box by pressing Enter, even though the cursor is not in the OK command button (as long as the cursor is not on one of the other command buttons).

To select a different option button, use the mouse to click the desired option button. Alternatively, press Tab or Shift+Tab to move the underscore (cursor) to the group of option buttons. Then, use the up- or down-arrow key to move the dot to the desired button. Press the spacebar to select the new option. Press Enter to close the dialog box and execute the command, if any, with which the dialog box is associated.

Using Option Check Boxes

Some Shell dialog boxes enable you to select the desired command settings by "checking" the appropriate *option check boxes*. An option check box is a pair of brackets followed by a command setting. The File Display Options dialog box in Figure 4.8, for example, contains the following check boxes:

- Display Hidden/System Files
- Descending Order

An option check box turns a command setting on or off. The setting is checked (or on) when an X appears between the brackets. The setting is off when the space between the brackets is blank. To toggle the setting on or off, use the mouse to click between the brackets. Alternatively, press Tab or Shift+Tab to move the cursor to the option check box and then press the spacebar. Each time you click the box or press the spacebar, the option toggles on or off.

Using Command Buttons

After you make any desired entries in text boxes, select appropriate option buttons, and check the correct check boxes, you are ready to execute the DOS Shell command. To do so, choose one of the *command buttons*. Most dialog boxes in the DOS Shell contain three command buttons: OK, Cancel, and Help (refer to Figure 4.8). The OK command button activates the choices you made in the dialog box and executes the command, if any, with which the dialog box is associated. The Cancel command button aborts any changes you made in the dialog box and returns to the DOS Shell window. The Help command button accesses the Shell's online help facility.

To execute a command button, use one of the following methods:

- Move the mouse pointer to the desired command button and click the left mouse button.
- Press Tab or Shift+Tab to move the cursor to the desired command button and press Enter.

Modifying the View

The DOS Shell is quite flexible. In the directory tree area and file list area, you can display directories and filenames from any of your computer's disk drives, including directories and filenames from two disks at one time. You also can display just the program list, change the entire screen to a graphics mode, and show as many as 60 lines of information on a single screen (depending on the capability of your computer's monitor).

The following sections describe how to modify the display to list directories and files from other disks, to display files from two disks at one time, and to change the amount of information displayed about each file. In addition, the following sections show you how to display the program list full-screen and how to change the number of lines that appear onscreen.

Logging On to a Different Disk

As you learned in Chapter 2, "Starting DOS," each time you turn on your computer, the operating system (DOS) is loaded from one of your computer's disks. This disk is the boot disk. If your system is configured to start the DOS Shell immediately after your computer boots up, the Shell window lists directories and filenames found on the boot disk. Often, you might need to display the directories and filenames on a disk other than the boot disk. Figure 4.2, for example, shows three drive letters: A, B, and C. Drive C is the boot disk; therefore, the directories found in drive C are shown in the directory tree. Drive C's icon is highlighted, indicating that C is the currently selected disk drive.

To display the directories found on another disk, move the mouse pointer to the drive icon of the desired disk and click the left mouse button. Alternatively, press the left- or right-arrow key until the Shell highlights the drive letter you want and then press Enter.

The Shell displays a message that it is reading the disk information and then displays in the directory tree and file list areas of the DOS Shell window the directories and filenames from the target disk. Figure 4.9, for example, shows filenames from a disk in drive B.

Figure 4.9
Displaying the directories and filenames from the disk in drive B.

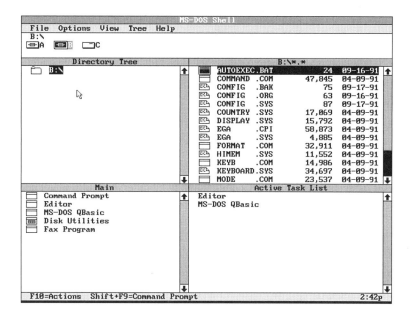

Because the DOS Shell enables you to start other programs that can create, modify, or delete files on your disk, the list of files in the DOS Shell window might at times be inaccurate. If you suspect that the directory tree area or file list area does not reflect the actual contents of the disk, use the Shell's Refresh command. To refresh the file list, press F5 or choose Refresh from the View menu (see Figure 4.10).

> **Note**
> When DOS Shell is run in text mode, there is no visual differentiation between file types. Running the Shell using one of the graphics modes, however, causes file lists to show icons to the left of the listed files. These icons differentiate between executable files and document files. If you look closely at the icons in Figure 4.9, you see that document files are represented as dog-eared pages and that executable files (.EXE, .COM, and .BAT) have a rectangular icon that represents a running program.

The Shell displays the message Reading Disk Information and then returns to the DOS Shell window and displays the updated list of directories and files in the directory tree and file list areas.

Figure 4.10
The View menu.

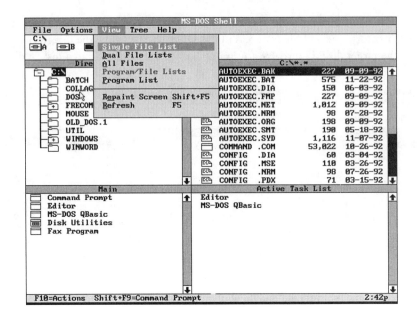

Switching Between Dual and Single File Lists

From time to time, you might want the convenience of seeing lists of directories and files from two disks simultaneously. Perhaps you want to copy a file from one disk to another, or maybe you want to compare the list of files on one disk to the list of files on another disk.

The DOS Shell enables you to display two file lists on the same screen. To do so, choose Dual File Lists from the View menu (refer to Figure 4.10).

The Shell replaces the program list area, at the bottom of the window, with a second disk drive area, directory tree area, and file list area showing the directory tree and file list from the current disk drive (see Figure 4.11). This view is called a *dual file list*.

Even though the initial display of the second file list is a duplicate of the top window, each file list is independent of the other. Note that each file list has its own set of disk drive icons. To select a second disk drive in the bottom portion of the window, click the icon in the bottom disk drive area for the drive for which you want to list directories and files.

Alternatively, press Tab or Alt+Tab to cycle the selection cursor until it highlights the drive icon of the currently selected drive in the bottom disk drive area. Then use the left- or right-arrow key to highlight the desired drive icon and press Enter.

The Shell lists directories and filenames from the second disk in the lower set of directory tree and file list areas (see Figure 4.12). You can switch between the two lists by using the mouse or the Tab key.

Figure 4.11
A dual file list.

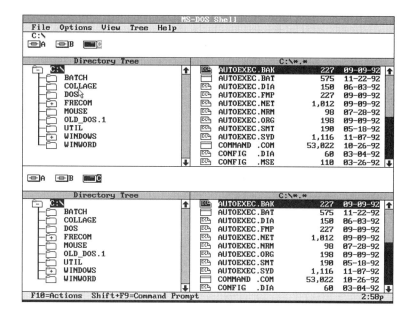

Figure 4.12
Viewing directories and filenames from two disks at one time.

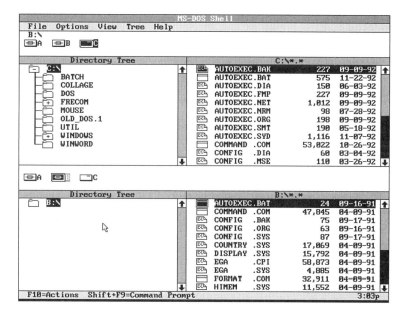

At times, especially when a directory contains many files, you need a single full-screen file list. Choose Single File List from the View menu to see a list, called a *single file list*, similar to the one shown in Figure 4.13.

Figure 4.13
Viewing a single file list.

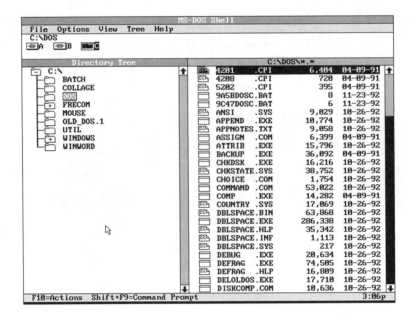

> **Note**
> When you exit from the DOS Shell, it remembers the changes you made using the View menu. The next time you start the Shell, it will have the same appearance.

DISPLAYING ALL FILES

Occasionally, you might want the Shell window to display all files on a disk, regardless of the directory. To display all files in a single list, choose All Files from the View menu.

In the All Files view, the Shell displays a window on the right side of the screen listing the names of all files on the disk in alphabetical order (see Figure 4.14). To the left of this window is an area that displays information about the currently highlighted file.

SWITCHING BETWEEN THE PROGRAM LIST AND THE PROGRAM/FILE LISTS

The first time you start the DOS Shell, the DOS Shell window displays the directory tree area, file list area, and program list area. Some users prefer to use the DOS Shell primarily as a menu for starting applications programs and thus don't want to view the directory tree and file list every time. The DOS Shell, therefore, provides a view that displays only the program list. To select this view, shown in Figure 4.15, choose Program List from the View menu.

If you decide later that you want to display the directory tree and file list areas onscreen along with the program list area, you need only choose Program/File Lists from the View menu. The DOS Shell then returns to the original view, with the disk drive area, directory tree area, and file list area in the top half of the screen and program list area in the bottom half of the screen.

Figure 4.14
The All Files view.

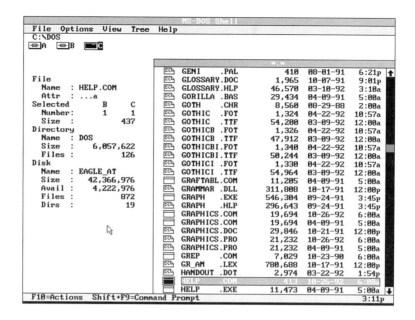

Figure 4.15
The full-screen program list area.

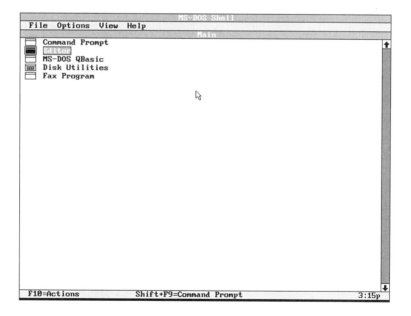

Using the Shell Screen Modes

As you learned previously in this chapter, the DOS Shell window can be displayed as a text representation of a GUI (graphical user interface) or in graphics mode. The number of available screen modes depends on the type of display adapter and monitor you have.

When you launch DOSSHELL the first time, the Shell window appears in the default 25-line low-resolution text mode. If your video card permits, and most modern ones do, you can choose Display from the Options menu to select from a variety of modes.

If you have a system with video cards that can support more text and graphic modes, you can choose from an array of modes ranging from the default 25-line text mode up to high-resolution graphics modes that display 60 lines of information onscreen. Table 4.2 shows the full list of display modes available.

TABLE 4.2	AVAILABLE VIDEO MODES IN THE DOS SHELL	
Text	25 lines	Low Resolution
Text	43 lines	High Resolution 1
Text	50 lines	High Resolution 2
Graphics	25 lines	Low Resolution
Graphics	30 lines	Medium Resolution 1
Graphics	34 lines	Medium Resolution 2
Graphics	43 lines	High Resolution 1
Graphics	60 lines	High Resolution 2

To change the screen mode, first select the Options menu (see Figure 4.16) and then choose Display. The Screen Display Mode dialog box appears (see Figure 4.17). Next, highlight a choice in the dialog box, and click OK or press Enter. If you are unsure about your video card's support for a particular mode, you can choose the Preview button to see what results from that choice.

Figure 4.16
The Options menu.

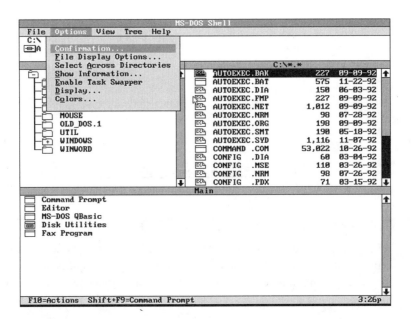

Figure 4.17
The Screen Display Mode dialog box.

Using the Program List

In addition to providing an alternative DOS interface to the command line, the DOS Shell also provides a convenient method for running all the other programs stored in your computer. A program that performs this function is sometimes called a *menuing program*. The Shell's program list area provides menuing capability.

Items listed in the program area of the DOS Shell window fall into two categories: program items and program groups. A *program item* starts a specific software application on your hard disk; a *program group* is a collection of program items or other program groups.

Program groups enable you to group your applications programs by category. You can create a Word Processing group, a Database group, and a Spreadsheet group, for example. By default, the initial list of program items, which you see when you first start the DOS Shell, are in the Main program group. The Main group includes another program group named Disk Utilities, which includes program items that perform disk-related DOS commands.

You can easily tell whether an option listed in the program list area is a program item or a program group. When the DOS Shell window is in text screen mode, program group names are enclosed in brackets. For example, the Disk Utilities program group appears as [Disk Utilities] when the screen is in text mode.

In graphics mode, the Shell uses special icons to distinguish between program items and program groups. The following icon appears to the left of program item names:

The following icon appears to the left of program group names:

When you first install the DOS Shell, the program list area lists the program group Main. This group includes the program items Command Prompt, Editor, and MS-DOS QBasic. Selecting a program item starts the selected program. Also included in the Main program group is the program group Disk Utilities. Selecting Disk Utilities causes the Shell to display another group of program items, the Disk Utilities group, which consists of DOS utility programs that enable you to copy, back up, restore, format, and undelete disks (see Figure 4.18). You can press Esc to return to the preceding program group or select the Main program group, which appears at the top of the program list.

Figure 4.18
Disk Utilities program items.

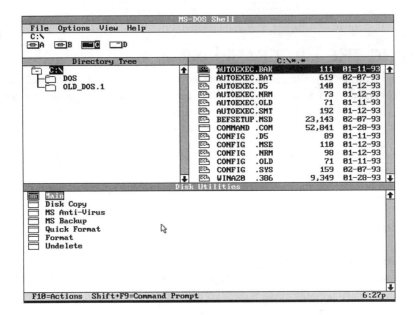

To run a program item or select an alternative program group, highlight your choice and press Enter, or simply double-click your choice. If you choose to run a program, you are returned to the DOS Shell when that program terminates.

Working with Program Groups

Now that you know what program groups are, you need to learn how you can work with them. The following sections teach you how to add, modify, and delete program groups.

Adding a Program Group

To add a new program group, make the program list area the active area of the DOS Shell window and display the program group to which the new group is to be added. If you want to add a new program group to the Main program group, for example, press Esc until the title bar of the program list area displays the title Main. When you want to add a program group to a different program group, use the mouse or cursor-movement keys to select the intended "parent" group in the program list area.

When the program group you want is displayed, complete the following steps:

1. Choose New from the File menu. The New Program Object dialog box appears (see Figure 4.19). This dialog box contains two option buttons: Program Group and Program Item.

Figure 4.19
The New Program Object dialog box.

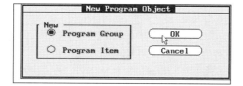

2. Click the Program Group option button, and then click the OK command button or press Enter. The Add Group dialog box appears (see Figure 4.20). This dialog box contains three text boxes: Title, Help Text, and Password. You must type an entry in the Title text box to supply the group name. Entries in the Help Text and Password text boxes are optional.

Figure 4.20
The Add Group dialog box.

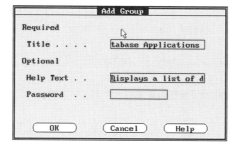

3. Type a program group title in the Title text box. (You can use up to 23 characters, including spaces.) This title will be the name, or menu option, that appears in the program list area when the parent program group is displayed.

   If you are creating a program group for your database applications, for example, you might type Database Applications in the Title text box. This title appears not only in the program list area, but also in that area's title bar when a program group is activated.

4. Type a help message, if you choose, in the Help Text text box. (The message can be up to 255 characters long, even though the Shell can display only 20 characters at a time in the text box; the text in the text box scrolls to the left as you type past the 20th character.)

   For a Database Applications group, for example, you might type the help message Displays list of database applications. Afterward, whenever you press F1 while the Database Applications item is highlighted, the help message appears.

The Shell displays help messages in the Shell Help dialog box and formats the help message to fit in the dialog box. If you want a line to break at a particular point, type the characters ^m (or ^M) at that point. Any following text starts on the next line when the help message is displayed in the Help dialog box.

5. Type a password, if you choose, in the Password text box. (The password can be up to 20 characters long, including spaces.)

> **Caution**
> Using a password to limit access to a DOS Shell program group provides only minimal security. Any user with access to your computer easily can bypass the Shell and start programs from the DOS command line instead.

6. Click the OK command button or press Enter. The Shell adds the new program group to the selected program group. Now, if you select the new program group, the Shell opens an empty file list area so that you can add program items.

Modifying Program Group Properties

After you create a program group, you can change the parameters that define it—its *properties*—through the Shell File menu. To change a program group's properties, highlight the group's name in the file list area and choose Properties from the File menu. The Program Group Properties dialog box appears (see Figure 4.21).

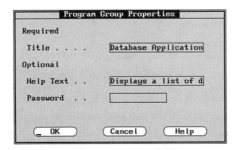

Figure 4.21
The Program Group Properties dialog box.

This dialog box essentially is a copy of the Add Group dialog box, except that the title, help message, and password (if you supplied one) for the selected group already appear in the text boxes. Make any changes you want, and then click OK or press Enter. Clicking Cancel returns you to the Shell window without changing any of the program group's properties.

Deleting a Program Group

Through the File menu, you also can remove a program group. Before you delete a program group, make sure that all items in the group are deleted (see the section "Deleting a Program Item" later in this chapter).

To delete a program group, select the group name and choose Delete from the File menu or press the Del key. The Delete Item dialog box appears (see Figure 4.22). Select Delete This Item, and click OK or press Enter.

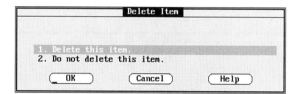

Figure 4.22
The Delete Item dialog box.

> **Note**
> If you attempt to delete a program group before it is empty, the Shell displays an error message box.

CHANGING THE ORDER OF A GROUP'S LISTINGS

Placing the groups that you use most frequently near the top of the group listing is convenient, enabling you to find these groups quickly. You can place groups in any order you want. To move a group from one place to another in the menu list, follow these steps:

1. Move the selection bar to the group that you want to move.
2. Choose Reorder from the File menu. The Shell displays the following message in the status line:
   ```
   Select location to move to, then press Enter. Esc to cancel.
   ```
3. Use the cursor-movement keys to move the selection bar to the desired new location for the selected group and then press Enter. The Shell moves the group to the new position.

You can repeat these steps as often as necessary to produce the order you want for your groups.

WORKING WITH PROGRAM ITEMS

After you create program groups, you next will want to add program items. The following sections describe how to add program items, as well as how to modify and delete existing program items in the program group. (To reorder program items, follow the procedure described in the preceding section.)

ADDING A PROGRAM ITEM

Adding a program item is similar to adding a program group. When you want to add a program item to a particular group, make the program list area the active area of the DOS Shell window and then display the program group to which you want to add the program item. If you want to add a program item to the Database Applications program group, for example, press Esc until Main appears in the title bar of the program list area and then use the mouse or cursor-movement keys to highlight Database Applications.

After you've selected the program group, choose New from the File menu and select Program Item from the dialog box. The Add Program dialog box appears (see Figure 4.23).

Figure 4.23
The Add Program dialog box.

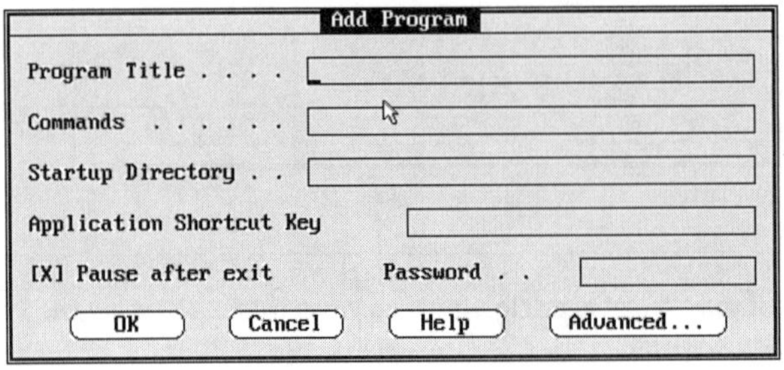

This dialog box contains five text boxes: Program Title, Commands, Startup Directory, Application Shortcut Key, and Password. You must type entries in the Program Title and Commands text boxes, but entries in the Startup Directory, Application Shortcut Key, and Password text boxes are optional. All entries in the Add Program dialog box are referred to collectively as the program item's *properties*.

You also can click the Advanced command button to add a help message, specify special memory or video requirements, or select other advanced options.

Modifying Program Items

Modifying the properties of a program item is fairly easy and straightforward. To modify properties, follow these steps:

1. Activate the program list area. If the group that contains the program item that you want to modify is not included in the selected group, select the program group that includes the item.
2. Use the mouse or cursor-movement keys to move the selection bar to the name of the program item that contains the properties you want to modify.
3. Choose Properties from the File menu. The Program Item Properties dialog box appears.
4. Make the desired changes in the values in the text boxes. Then click OK or press Enter to confirm your choices.

Deleting a Program Item

You might want to delete a program item that you no longer use. The program itself is not deleted—only the program item. To remove a program from your computer, you must delete that program's files from the disk.

To delete a program item, follow these steps:

1. Move the selection bar to the name of the item that you want to delete.
2. Choose Delete from the File menu or press Del. The Delete Item dialog box appears.
3. Select 1. Delete this item. Then click OK or press Enter. The Shell deletes the program item from the selected program group list.

Using Shortcut Keys

You can specify shortcut keys to start applications. When you specify these key combinations, the Shell displays them in the Application Shortcut Key text box in the Add Program dialog box. If you press and hold down Ctrl and Alt simultaneously and then press P, for example, the Shell displays ALT+CTRL+P in the text box.

A specified shortcut-key combination starts the program only if the following three conditions are met:

- The DOS 6.0 task swapper is enabled.
- You started the program through the DOS Shell's program list area.
- You used one of the task-swapper keystrokes (Alt+Tab, Alt+Esc, or Ctrl+Esc) to switch to another program or back to the Shell.

Suppose that you first enable the DOS Shell task swapper and then start Paradox from the program item in the Database Applications program group. You then switch back to the Shell by pressing Alt+Tab and start WordStar. To return to Paradox quickly, you simply press the shortcut key you defined (for example, Ctrl+Alt+P). The task swapper quickly swaps WordStar to disk and displays the Paradox screen.

> **Caution**
> When creating shortcut keys, make sure that you are not using key combinations that are already used by DOS Shell.

When you return to the DOS Shell window while the program you were using earlier is swapped out to disk, the Shell lists the shortcut in parentheses to the right of the program item title in the active task list area.

Working with Directories

DOS manages files on your disks by maintaining file information in a hierarchical directory structure. The directory tree area, in the upper-left quadrant of the window, graphically depicts this directory structure. At the top of this area, the root directory of the logged disk is shown as a folder-shaped icon or as a pair of brackets ([]) if the DOS Shell is in text mode. All other directories are shown as folder-shaped icons (or pairs of brackets). These other directories are listed below the root icon and connected to the root icon by a vertical line. The name of each directory is listed to the right of its icon.

At any time during a session with the DOS Shell, one directory name is highlighted. This highlighted directory is referred to as the *selected directory*. When you first start the Shell, the directory that is current when you start the program is the selected directory (usually the root directory of the boot disk). The file list area of the DOS Shell window, in the upper-right quadrant of the screen, lists the filenames in the selected directory.

Expanding and Collapsing Branches

As you know, the DOS directory structure is treelike. The root directory is like the trunk of a tree, with all other directories growing out like branches of a tree. The DOS Shell graphically represents this treelike nature in the directory tree area of the DOS Shell window as an upside-down tree.

The DOS directory structure can have multiple levels, but initially the Shell shows only the first level of the tree. Each first-level directory—a directory attached directly to the root—is depicted as a branch of the tree. Just as branches of a real tree can have offshoot branches, each DOS directory can contain offshoot directories. The Shell indicates that a directory contains other directories by placing a plus sign (+) in the directory icon. Figure 4.24 shows plus signs in the directory icon for the following first-level directories:

- DV
- OLD_DOS.1
- OPTQEMM

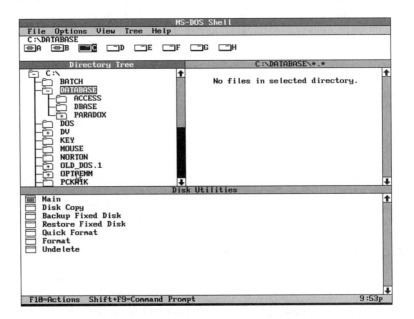

Figure 4.24
Expanding a directory tree branch.

To *expand* (show the directories subordinate to) by one level a directory tree branch that shows a + in its directory icon, click the + in the directory icon or do the following:

1. Select the directory tree area that contains the target directory icon.
2. Move the selection cursor to the directory name.
3. Press the + key, or choose Expand One Level from the Tree menu.

The Shell then shows the next level of directories beneath the selected directory. Figure 4.25, for example, shows the expanded DATABASE directory containing three second-level directories: ACCESS, DBASE, and PARADOX.

Offshoot directories can contain more offshoots. The relationship among directory levels is analogous to a family tree—child, parent, grandparent, and so on. When a second-level directory contains one or more third-level directories, the Shell shows a plus sign (+) in the second-level directory icon. The directory icon of the PARADOX directory shown in Figure 4.25, for example, indicates that this branch of the DATABASE directory also contains at least one directory. To expand one level of the PARADOX branch, follow the procedure you used to expand one level of the DATABASE branch.

If you do not remember precisely where a directory is located in the directory tree, expanding branches one level at a time can become tedious. When you want to expand all levels beneath a particular directory branch, use the following procedure:

1. Use the mouse to click the directory name or use the arrow keys to move the selection cursor to the directory name.
2. Press the * key, or choose Expand All from the Tree menu.

The Shell expands all levels of the tree below the currently selected directory. Figure 4.25, for example, shows the fully expanded DATABASE branch of drive C's directory tree.

Figure 4.25
The fully expanded DATABASE branch.

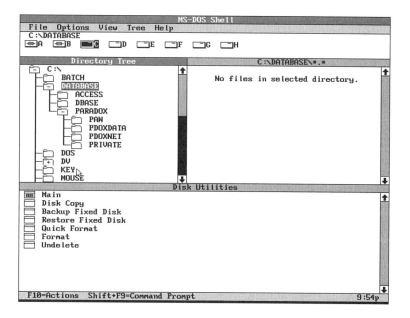

The opposite of expanding a directory branch in the directory tree area is *collapsing* a branch. When you first start the DOS Shell, you might notice that a root directory's icon contains a minus sign (–). After you expand a directory branch, the icon for the expanded branch also contains a minus sign. These minus signs are a reminder that you can collapse the branch. To collapse a branch whose icon contains a minus sign, click the directory icon with your mouse or use the following procedure:

1. Select the directory name.
2. Press the – (hyphen) key or choose Collapse Branch from the Tree menu.

To collapse the entire tree, click the root directory icon or do the following:

1. Select the root directory name at the top of the directory tree.
2. Press the – (hyphen) key or choose Collapse Branch from the Tree menu.

The Shell collapses the entire tree down to the root level and places a + in the root directory icon.

CREATING DIRECTORIES

Because the only automatically available directory on a DOS disk is the root, you must add any additional directories. Even after you establish a workable directory structure for your computer, you occasionally need to create new directories on your disks. DOS enables you to add directories to a disk through the DOS Shell, instead of having to exit to a command prompt to add directories.

To create a new directory using the DOS Shell, do the following:

1. Select the directory tree area of the DOS Shell window.
2. Select the directory to be the parent of the new directory.
3. Select File from the menu bar to display the File menu.
4. Choose Create Directory from the File menu.

   The Shell displays the Create Directory dialog box shown in Figure 4.26. This dialog box indicates the name of the parent directory, C:\SPREADSH.

Figure 4.26
The Create Directory dialog box.

5. Type the name of the new directory, and press Enter or click OK.

The Shell creates the new directory and returns to the directory tree area of the DOS Shell window. The Shell also adds to the tree an icon for the new directory.

Working with Files

In the DOS Shell, you perform file-management operations primarily through the File menu. The active menu options displayed in the File menu, however, vary according to which area of the window is active. Although the menu options displayed when the directory tree is active are the same as the options displayed when the file list is active, many of these menu options are dimmed (not valid) when the directory tree is active.

The DOS Shell's file-management commands operate on all selected files. At any time, you can select any number of files. The Shell displays both the name and file-list icon of each selected file in reverse video. Selected files need not be from the same directory.

Selecting a Single File

To select a single file, follow these steps:

1. Activate the directory tree area.
2. Use the mouse and scrollbar or the cursor-movement keys to scroll through the directory tree until the name of the directory containing the files you want to select appears.
3. Use the mouse or arrow keys to move the selection cursor to the target directory.
4. Activate the file list area.
5. Use the mouse and scrollbar or the cursor-movement keys to scroll the file list until the name of the file you want to select appears.
6. Click the name of the file to be selected (the target file). Alternatively, use the cursor-movement keys to move the selection cursor to the target file and then press the spacebar.

To indicate that a file is selected, DOS displays the filename and file list icon in reverse video.

> **Note**
> A file is not selected until the icon is displayed in reverse video. Simply highlighting the filename with the selection cursor is not sufficient to select the file.

Selecting Multiple Files

If you want to apply a DOS Shell command to several files, applying the command simultaneously to all the files is more efficient than applying it to one file at a time. After you select the first file, you can select the other files in either of the following ways (this procedure is referred to in the DOS Shell as *extending the selection*):

CHAPTER 4 USING THE DOS SHELL

- Hold down the Ctrl key and click the name of the file that you want to select.
- Press Shift+F8. When the message ADD appears in the status bar, move the selection cursor to the name of the file you want to select and then press the spacebar. Press Shift+F8 again to turn off the ADD message.

The icon and filename of each selected file appear in reverse video (see Figure 4.27).

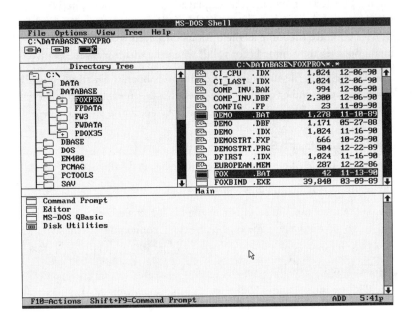

Figure 4.27
Selecting several files in the DOS Shell.

Frequently, you might want the Shell to work on several files that are listed one after the other in the list area. To select contiguous files, you can select each file individually, using the previously discussed method. But the Shell provides an easier way to select files as a group.

To select contiguous files in the DOS Shell, follow these steps:

1. Select the first file.
2. Use one of the following procedures to select the remaining files:
   - Use the mouse to position the pointer on the last file you want to select, press the Shift key, and click the left mouse button.
   - While holding the Shift key, use the cursor-movement keys to move the selection bar to the last file.

The Shell selects all the files. To indicate that these files are selected, the Shell displays the filenames and their icons in reverse video.

Selecting All Files

To select all the files in a directory, follow these steps:

1. Select the directory in the directory tree area.
2. Activate the file list area.
3. Press Ctrl+/, or choose Select All from the File menu.

Deselecting All Files

After you select files, you might decide that you don't want to perform a DOS Shell operation on that group of files. Perhaps you want to start a fresh selection process by *deselecting* all selected files. Normally, selecting a different directory also deselects all selected files.

You also can deselect all selected files in one procedure. Use the mouse to click anywhere in the file area or press the spacebar. Alternatively, choose Deselect All from the File menu.

Selecting Files Across Directories

By default, the DOS Shell enables you to select files in only one directory at a time. By selecting a different directory, you deselect all selected files. Occasionally, however, you might want to perform a file-management operation on files from several directories. You might want to copy to a floppy disk, for example, one file from each of three directories on your hard disk.

Before you can select files in several directories, you must choose Select Across Directories in the Options menu.

To copy files from three directories to a floppy disk in one procedure, you must first select the directories and then the files, one at a time. Then, choose the Copy command from the File menu to copy all the selected files to the floppy disk.

Copying Files in the Shell

With the DOS Shell, you can copy one or more files in a directory, between directories, or between disks, using any of several approaches. The approach described in this section—the dual file list method—is the quickest and easiest to learn and use.

To perform the copy operation using the dual file list method, you first must select the source and target drive and directory and create a dual file list. Complete the following steps:

1. Select the source drive and directory (those that contain the files you want to copy).
2. Choose Dual File Lists from the View menu to switch to the dual file list.

> **Note**
> Under certain specific circumstances, you can skip step 2. For example, you can drag selected files to another directory on the same disk without opening a dual file list. Completing this step, however, always produces the result that you want.

3. Use the mouse or the cursor-movement keys to select the target drive and directory in the second directory tree.
4. Use the mouse or keyboard to select, in the first (upper) file list, the files that you want to copy.

The remaining steps for completing the copy operation differ, depending on whether you want to use the mouse or the keyboard. If you use a mouse, complete the following steps:

1. Position the mouse pointer on a selected file in the upper file list. Hold down the Ctrl key while you press and hold the left mouse button. While holding down both the Ctrl key and the mouse button, drag the mouse pointer to the target drive letter in the lower drive area or, alternatively, to the target directory's name in the lower directory tree.

   When you begin to drag the mouse, the pointer changes from an arrow (or a block, in text mode) to a circle (or two exclamation-point symbols, in text mode). When the pointer enters the second directory tree, the circle becomes a file icon (or a diamond, in text mode). If you are copying several files, the file icon resembles a stack of three papers. Figure 4.28 shows how you should have the dual file lists set up before dragging the filenames to copy them to the target disk.

Figure 4.28
Using the dual file list display to copy files.

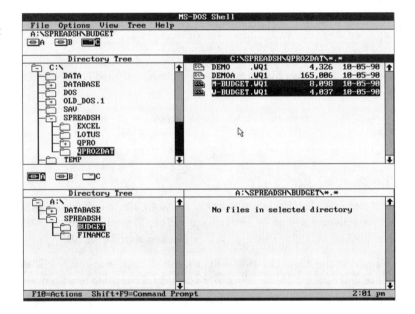

Note

When you are copying files to a different disk, you don't have to hold down the Ctrl key; holding down the mouse button is enough. If you drag files to another directory on the same disk without holding down the Ctrl key, however, the Shell assumes that you want to *move* the files rather than *copy* them.

Depending on the selections you have made in the Confirmations Item dialog box, which can be accessed from the Options menu, you might be asked to confirm the copy operation.

2. To confirm that the copy should take place, click Yes.

To copy files using the keyboard only, complete the copy procedure by following these steps:

1. Choose Copy from the File menu or press F8. The Shell displays the Copy File dialog box. This dialog box contains the From and To text boxes. The Shell lists the source files in the From text box and the source directory in the To text box.
2. Type the target drive and directory name in the To text box and then press Enter. The Shell copies the files to the target directory and displays a message to that effect in the center of the screen.

MOVING A FILE IN THE SHELL

When the DOS Shell moves a file, the program copies the file from one storage location to another and then deletes the file from its original location. Therefore, the steps for moving one or more files with the DOS Shell are nearly the same as those for copying files. When you want to move one or more files, select the files to be moved just as you do if you are going to copy them.

If you are using a mouse, position the mouse pointer on one of the selected files in the upper file list. Hold down the Alt key while you press and hold down the left mouse button. While holding both the Alt key and the mouse button, drag the mouse pointer to the target drive letter in the lower drive area or to the target directory's name in the lower directory tree.

To move files using only the keyboard, follow these steps:

1. Choose Move from the File menu or press F7. The Shell displays the Move File dialog box. This dialog box contains the From and To text boxes. The Shell lists the source files in the From text box and the source directory in the To text box.
2. Type the target drive and directory name in the To text box, and then click OK or press Enter. The Shell moves the files to the target directory and displays a message to that effect in the center of the screen.

USING THE SHELL TO VIEW A FILE

When you want to view the contents of a file from within the DOS Shell, follow these steps:

1. Select the target file in the file list area.
2. Choose View File Contents from the File menu.

When the file you want to view contains only ASCII characters, the Shell displays the ASCII file viewer. One of the files distributed with DOS 6.0, for example, is named APPNOTES.TXT and contains only ASCII text. To view the contents of APPNOTES.TXT, select its name in the file list area and then choose View File Contents from the File menu. The Shell displays the file in the ASCII viewer (see Figure 4.29).

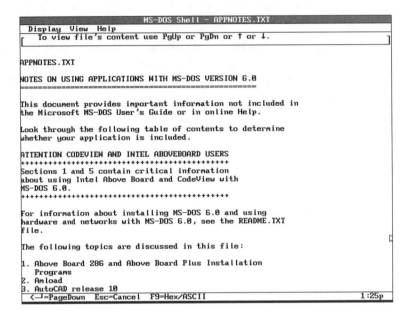

Figure 4.29
The ASCII viewer.

To scroll through the file, use the cursor-movement keys or use the mouse to click the labels PgUp, PgDn, ↑, or ↓, which are displayed near the top of the window.

When the file you want to view contains data other than ASCII characters, the DOS Shell uses the hexadecimal (base 16, often referred to as *hex*) viewer. If you select the DOS command processor file, COMMAND.COM, and press F9, for example, it displays the contents of the file as four columns of hexadecimal codes and one column of ASCII characters. (This information normally has meaning only to programmers and to the computer.) As in the ASCII viewer, you can scroll through the file by using the cursor-movement keys or the mouse.

Associating Files with Programs

Many programs create and work with files that have distinctive filename extensions. The DOS Shell enables you to associate particular extensions with a specific program so that you can start the program and load a file with an associated extension in one step.

The easiest method of associating a file extension with a program is to follow these steps:

1. In the file list area, select a file whose extension you want the Shell to associate with a specific program.

2. Choose Associate from the File menu. The Shell displays the Associate File dialog box, containing a text box in which you can type the program's directory path and filename. If the current file extension already is associated with a program, the Shell displays the program's path and filename in the text box.

3. In the text box, type the program's complete filename, including the extension. If the file is in a directory that's not included in the PATH statement, type the directory path as well as the filename.

4. Click OK or press Enter.

> **Note**
>
> Program associations are stored in an ASCII file called DOSSHELL.INI. You can use any text editor, including the DOS Editor, to edit this file.

USING THE TASK SWAPPER

The DOS Shell also has the capability to load more than one program at a time. DOS accomplishes this feat through a technique called *task swapping*. To activate this feature, choose Enable Task Swapper from the Options menu. The Shell adds an active task list area to the window (see Figure 4.30). Initially, nothing is listed in this area because no program (other than the Shell) is active.

Figure 4.30
The DOS Shell window with an active task list area.

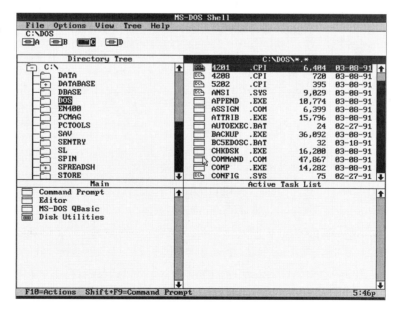

With the task swapper enabled, you still start programs by using any of the methods described earlier in this chapter. But after you start a program, you can jump back to the DOS Shell instantly without exiting the program. Simply press Alt+Esc or Alt+Tab, and the screen returns to the DOS Shell window, where the program (or associated data file) is listed in the active task list area. DOS has swapped the contents of memory (RAM) to disk, freeing space in memory so that you can run another program.

The fastest way to switch between active tasks is to hold down the Alt key and tap the Tab key. *Do not release the Alt key.* The Shell displays the name of the task at the top of the screen. Still holding down the Alt key, press the Tab key again to see the name of the next task. Repeat this keystroke until the target task name appears. Finally, release the Alt key. The Shell switches to the target task.

PROJECT: USING THE HELP SYSTEM

At any time during a DOS Shell session, pressing the F1 key causes a help window to appear. Online help assists you with the current selection or action so that you can make an informed selection.

The help system is *contextual*, meaning that DOS looks at the menu item currently highlighted and provides information about that selection. You can go from that help screen to other help screens to get help on additional topics. Figure 4.31 shows a typical help screen.

Figure 4.31
The Changing Colors help screen.

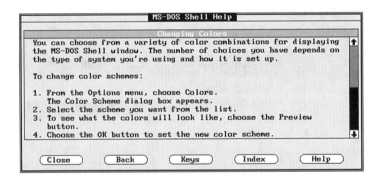

Five command buttons appear at the bottom of a help screen:

- **Close** returns you to the screen from which you pressed F1.
- **Back** returns to the preceding help screen.
- **Keys** displays an index of help information on keystroke commands.
- **Index** displays the DOS Shell help index, a list of topics on which you can receive help.
- **Help** displays information on how to use the help system. Use the mouse and scrollbar or the cursor-movement keys to display the information in which you are interested.

Additional related topics are listed in a different color on the help screen. Use the Tab key to highlight the related topic and press Enter, or click the topic. The Shell displays another help screen.

Choose the Close command button or press Esc to return to the screen from which you pressed F1.

Operating techniques are fairly consistent throughout the DOS Shell, and because the Help information is quite thorough, you should be able to learn what isn't covered by selecting the menu items and using the Help feature to guide you.

PART II

FILES AND DIRECTORIES

5 Understanding Files and Directories   99

6 Understanding Disks and Disk Drives   127

7 Preparing and Maintaining Disks   149

8 Managing Your Files   191

9 Protecting and Recovering Your Data   231

CHAPTER 5

UNDERSTANDING FILES AND DIRECTORIES

In this chapter

Introducing the DOS File System   100

Understanding the Role of Directories   110

Expanding the File System Through Subdirectories   113

Helping DOS Find Files with PATH   122

Listing Directories with TREE   123

Using a Temporary Directory   124

Troubleshooting   125

Introducing the DOS File System

Two primary roles of a disk operating system are storing and retrieving data. This chapter introduces you to the fundamental ways in which DOS handles these roles. To provide data storage and retrieval, the operating system must provide a common method for file storage and retrieval so that any software package can access information easily and quickly. It is also important that DOS provide these services without your having to know the internal details of how the disk works and why.

DOS generally insulates you from the technical details involved in storing and retrieving data on your computer. You must, however, prepare disks by formatting them, and you might occasionally have to repair them. In this chapter, you learn information about the most basic part of DOS—the file and directory system. After you've mastered this information, you will have a firm footing for understanding DOS completely.

Ask almost any non–computer user what a file is, and he or she almost invariably describes a collection of papers wrapped in a manila folder. Such files are typically stored in file cabinets.

On a computer, a *file system* is an organized collection of files that has a direct parallel to the old, familiar file cabinet. The hard disk and floppy disks you use to store data electronically use many of the same conventions. Each file on a disk has a unique name, just as each file folder in a file cabinet is labeled for identification. Files are arranged on your disks in directories (discussed later in this chapter) to make them easier to find, just as sections in a file cabinet are organized into group file folders that have a common purpose.

Understanding Files

A *file* is a variable-length collection of related information that is referenced by a name. Just as a file folder can be filled with various papers that contain information in the form of writing, an electronic file can contain various pieces of related information wrapped up in an electronic file folder referenced by the file's name.

Files written to disk can serve many purposes. A word processor file might hold all the sentences in a letter or book chapter. A database file might contain the names and addresses of all the members of a club or all the invoices for a store. Just as a good secretary uses color-coded labels and different markings on file folders to indicate the type of information in a file, DOS filenames most often indicate what kind of information they hold.

Often the way data is written in a file depends on the software that creates it. You can type the same letter, using all the same words and punctuation, using Microsoft Word and WordPerfect. When printed, the letters are identical, yet the format of the files created by these two programs is very different. You can, with a little work, use Microsoft Excel or Lotus 1-2-3 to store the same letter in yet another file format.

Although many programs recognize one another's file formats and convert them for you, DOS cares little about the format of a file's content. DOS doesn't bother trying to decipher the contents of a file. Its job is to wrap the information in a file folder (the file's name) and put it where you can find it later. Your job is to know what the file contains and which program you need to use to access correctly the data contained in the file.

In a computer setting, a file can contain data (information), programs (instructions that guide computer tasks), or both. A file can exist on a disk, on magnetic tape, on CD-ROMs, or even in a computer's memory. Files are made up of elements of data or programs. The individual elements can be stored as patterns of holes in a paper tape, as patterns of magnetic fields on the surface of a disk, and in many other ways.

Fortunately, unless you write programs for a living, you usually can ignore the technical aspects of how a file is stored. After all, you don't have to know how a fuel injector works to drive a fuel-injected car.

Physical storage techniques for files vary greatly, but on PCs a few file storage methods dominate. On PCs, floppy disks are used primarily for distributing files to other computers. Hard disks provide long-term and working storage. CD-ROMs often are used for storing files that do not need to be edited or altered, and tape drives and floppy disks are used to make backup copies of files for safekeeping.

Regardless of the actual media (floppy, hard disk, tape, and so on), DOS uses *filenames* to identify files. As you might remember from an earlier chapter, a full filename consists of one to eight characters followed by a period (.) and up to three characters called the *extension*. The period and extension are optional but are used almost universally.

The *name* portion of a filename (before the period) usually provides a mental picture or description of the contents of the file. Extensions, on the other hand, traditionally describe the *type* of file—its format.

If you're using a word processing application to write a memo, you might use as the name portion of a filename the name (or a close approximation) of the person who will receive the memo. You then can use the extension .MEM to indicate that the file is a memo. You can call a memo to Mr. Fleenor, for example, FLEENOR.MEM. Similarly, you can use the extension .DOC for office-policy document files. A monthly policy statement for January can be named JAN.DOC.

DOS enables you to use a wide variety of filenames. You are free to develop your own file-naming conventions, provided that you stay within the character limits imposed by DOS and the requirements of the software you use to create the file. Although most software packages are lenient in the filenames they can use, many programs require a file to have a specific extension before they recognize the file as one of their own

UNDERSTANDING FILENAMES

DOS ensures that every one of your files has a name. In fact, DOS does not provide a way to put file data on a disk without a filename. When a file is created, either by your software or a DOS file service routine, information about the physical location of the file is stored in a *File Allocation Table* (*FAT*), which is similar to a book's table of contents. DOS places the name of each file and its attributes in a special structure called a *directory*, which you can think of as the chapter headings of a book. Using this analogy, you can think of files as the pages in each chapter.

For now, however, you need only concern yourself with the names of files. You learn more about the other parts of the DOS file system later in this chapter. Keep in mind that a directory is a special structure used to store filenames and files. Later in this chapter, you learn more information about the directory.

CREATING FILENAMES

The characters you see on your computer screen are the ASCII code representations of bytes of data. One character is stored in one byte. In a disk directory, each slot where a filename can be stored reserves a space 11 bytes long (8 for the first part of the filename plus 3 for the extension). DOS accepts for filenames most characters that you use for "everyday" names. You can use the uppercase and lowercase letters *A* through *Z*; DOS automatically stores letters in uppercase in a directory entry. You also can use the numeric characters *0* through *9* and many punctuation characters not used as separators in the file system.

Following are the rules for creating legal filenames:

- Each filename on a disk must be unique.
- Filenames, even though they are not always expressed that way, include the drive letter and directory path of the file. In practical terms, this naming convention means that each file in a directory must have a unique name because the difference in directory names adds to a filename's uniqueness.
- A filename consists of the following items:
  - A name of one to eight characters
  - An optional extension of one to three characters
  - A period between the name and the extension (if an extension is used)
- The following characters are allowed in a filename:
  - The letters *A* through *Z* (lowercase letters are transformed into uppercase automatically)
  - The numerals 0 through 9
  - The following special characters and punctuation marks:
    $ # & @ ! ( ) - { } ' _ ~ ^ '
- DOS reserves certain ASCII codes for other uses and does not let them be a part of the filename. The following characters are not allowed in a filename:
  - Any control character (ASCII codes used as commands)
  - The space character
  - The following special characters and punctuation symbols:
    = / [ ] " : ; , ? * \ < > |

To understand why DOS disallows the use of some characters in filenames, you must look below the surface of DOS. Certain characters are not allowed because DOS does not pass those characters from the keyboard to the command or external command program that controls a file's name. You cannot, for example, use the Ctrl+G (^G) character in a filename because Ctrl+G tells an input device to sound the computer's bell or beep signal. DOS does not accept the Escape character, produced by the Esc key, as part of a filename because DOS interprets the Esc key as your request to cancel the command line and start again.

Another example of an unacceptable character is Ctrl+S (^S), which DOS and other operating systems use to stop the flow of characters from the input device to the output device. Ctrl+S stops screen scrolling, for example. If you press Ctrl+S while entering a filename, DOS assumes that you are entering an input-stopping character, not part of a filename.

You cannot use in a filename any characters that COMMAND.COM and external command programs use to divide the parameters and switches from the command in a command line. Because DOS must *parse* (distinguish the various components of) the command line, certain characters are seen as delimiters of parameters or as parts of a parameter. The backslash character (\), for example, separates directory names in a path specifier. DOS always reads a backslash in a command line as part of a path.

Avoiding Reserved Names

One of the ways in which DOS is able to control so many different types of devices is by using a *logical device*. It is important to understand that each of these devices has a name that is reserved and cannot be used for other purposes.

In theory, DOS treats all the input and output devices it controls as if they were made out of software. Such devices include almost everything you think of as belonging to a computer system—disks, printers, keyboards, screens, and modems.

The PC manufacturers are responsible for accepting and generating data in a fashion that conforms to DOS standards. The actual control over the actions of a device (print heads, disk drive motors and heads, and so on) is left to programming contained on ROM chips incorporated into the devices. Thus, DOS needs to know only that a printer exists and that the printer is connected to the system in a specific way, normally via a parallel or serial port.

To you, a parallel port is a hardware connector where you plug in a cable. To DOS, the parallel port is simply an address in memory where it sends and receives data. Each of these addresses is called a *logical device* and is given a name. By default, DOS expects to see a printer connected to the first parallel port, which it calls LPT1.

The first available disk is A:. By convention, B: is reserved for the second floppy disk, and C: is reserved for the first hard disk volume. The keyboard and video card are combined to create a logical device named CON:.

Notice that all these logical device names end with the colon (:). The colon signifies that something is a DOS logical device. In some contexts, however, the colon is omitted, as in this example:

```
COPY CON SUMFILE.TXT
```

This variation of the COPY command tells DOS to take input from the console (CON:) and save it to the currently logged drive and directory as a file having the name SUMFILE.TXT.

What does all this talk of logical devices have to do with filenames? Simply, DOS's internal routines treat logical devices like files in many ways. That's why when you try to name a file with a name for a logical device, DOS gets confused and weird things can happen, such as losing data or sending a file to a printer.

For this reason, DOS reserves names for its logical devices. DOS can treat some of these logical PC devices in a high-level way by accepting their names as input or output parameters in a command line, as in the preceding example. Before it uses the filename parameters in a command line to look for a file, DOS checks to see whether the filename is a device name. Table 5.1 lists the major logical DOS input and output device names and their purposes.

TABLE 5.1 DOS DEVICE NAMES

Device Name	Purpose
COM*x* or AUX	Identifies a serial communication port (*x* can be the number 1, 2, 3, or 4).
LPT*x* or PRN	Identifies a parallel printer port (*x* can be the number 1, 2, 3, or 4).
CON	Identifies the screen and keyboard.
NUL	Identifies the "do nothing" device, also called a *bit bucket*. Output sent to NUL is not displayed, stored, or acted on in any way.
CLOCK$	Provides date and time services.

Never attempt to write a disk file with a name that is the same as one of the device names listed in Table 5.1. DOS intercepts the device name, even if you add an extension, and tries to use the device—not the file you intend—to complete the command. Use a device name only as a device parameter in a command.

OBSERVING FILE-NAMING CONVENTIONS

A *convention* is an informal rule that is not explicitly enforced. DOS filenames often follow certain conventions. Although you can use any filename that follows DOS's character and device-name rules, observe DOS file-naming conventions whenever possible. You can, for example, name a memo file and give it a BAT extension, but this extension has a special meaning to DOS because all batch files have the extension BAT. As long as you do not try to execute the memo as a batch file, DOS is happy. If you try to execute the memo file, however, DOS sees the BAT extension and tries to execute it. Of course, the memo cannot be executed because it probably isn't made up of legal DOS commands.

You can name an EXE file with a COM extension. Although both files are executable, they have internal differences. DOS does not take the extension's name to mean that the file is indeed an EXE or COM file; DOS inspects a key part of the file before deciding how to load and execute the program file. If you name a spreadsheet file as an EXE or COM file, for example, DOS is not fooled into executing the nonprogram file. In all likelihood, your system simply will lock up, and you will have to perform a warm boot to begin again.

Many software manufacturers use certain extensions for special file formats created by their applications. To avoid confusion about the contents of a file, avoid using those extensions. Table 5.2 lists some conventional filename extensions and their meanings. Multiple programs can use the same extensions in their file-naming conventions.

TABLE 5.2   COMMON FILENAME EXTENSIONS

Extension	Common Use
ARC	Archive (compressed file)
ASC	ASCII text file
ASM	Assembler source file
BAK	Backup file
BAS	BASIC program file
BAT	DOS batch file
BGI	Borland Graphics Interface file (Quattro, Paradox)
BIN	Binary program file
BMP	Windows bitmap file
C	C source file
CPP	C++ source file
CBL	COBOL source file
CFG	Program configuration information
CHP	Chapter file (Ventura Publisher)
CHR	Character file (Quattro, Paradox)
CNF	Program configuration information
COM	Program file
CPI	Code page information file (DOS)
DAT	Data file
DB	Database file (Paradox)
DBF	Database file (dBASE)
DCT	Dictionary file
DEV	Program device driver file
DIF	Data Interchange Format file
DIR	A program data file used as a directory
DLL	Windows dynamic link library

Table 5.2 Continued

Extension	Common Use
DOC	Document file (used by many word processors)
DOT	Word for Windows template file
DRV	Program device driver file
DTA	Data file
EPS	Encapsulated PostScript file
EXE	Executable program file
FNT	Font file
GIF	Graphics Interchange Format file (CompuServe)
GRP	Windows Program Group
H	A header file for a C program
HLP	Help file
IDX	Index file (Q&A)
IMG	GEM image (graphics) file
INF	Information file
INI	Initialization files (Windows and other programs)
LET	Letter
LHA	Compressed file (LHARC)
LIB	Program library file
LOG	File logging actions
LST	Listing of a program (in a file)
MAK	A programmer's make file
MAP	Linker map file
MSG	Program message file
NDX	Index file (dBASE)
OBJ	Intermediate object code (program) file
OLD	Backup file
OVL	Program overlay file
OVR	Program overlay file
PAK	Packed (archive) file
PAS	Pascal source file
PCX	Picture file for PC Paintbrush
PIF	Program Information File (TopView/Windows)

TABLE 5.2 CONTINUED

Extension	Common Use
PM4	PageMaker 4 data file
PM5	PageMaker 5 data file
PRN	Program listing for printing
PRO	Profile (configuration file)
PS	PostScript program file
RFT	Revisable Form Text (Document Content Architecture)
RPT	A report file
RTF	Rich Text Format, a Microsoft document exchange format
SAM	Ami Pro document
SAV	Backup file
STY	Style sheet (Ventura Publisher, Microsoft Word)
SYS	System or device driver file
TIF	Picture file in Tagged Image File Format (TIFF)
TMP	Temporary file
TST	Test file
TXT	Text file
WK1	Worksheet file (Lotus 1-2-3 Release 2)
WK2	Quattro Pro 5.0 spreadsheet file
WK3	Worksheet file (Lotus 1-2-3 Release 3)
WKQ	Quattro spreadsheet file
WKS	Worksheet file (Lotus 1-2-3, Releases 1 and 1A)
WQ1	Quattro Pro spreadsheet file
XLM	Excel macro file
XLS	Excel spreadsheet file
ZIP	Compressed file (PKZIP)

UNDERSTANDING FILE ATTRIBUTES

As you will learn later in this chapter, DOS tracks each file on a disk through a *directory entry*. This entry maintains critical information about the file and where it is stored on disk. One of the pieces of information maintained in the directory entry is called the *file attribute field*. This one-byte field stores a number of characteristics about each file but is not displayed in a normal directory listing. Each characteristic stored in the file attribute field is called a *file attribute*, and each file can have more than one file attribute. Each file attribute is represented in the attribute byte by a single bit, often called an *attribute bit*. Table 5.3 lists the attributes and their purposes in DOS. You can view and modify most attribute bits by using the ATTRIB command; DOS manages some attribute bits directly.

TABLE 5.3   FILE ATTRIBUTES AND THEIR MEANINGS

Attribute Bit	Meaning
Archive	When DOS writes to a file, it sets the Archive attribute on. Some DOS commands such as MSBACKUP and XCOPY remove this attribute from files. Files having the Archive attribute have been altered or created since the last time they were archived.
Hidden	This file is bypassed by most DOS file-managementcommands and does not appear in a directory listing. Hidden files, however, are listed by the DOS Shell in the file list area.
Read-only	This file can be accessed for information but cannot be erased or modified. (Note that you can erase a read-only file by using the DOS Shell.)
Subdirectory	This attribute identifies the entry as a directory rather than a standard file.
System	This file is a DOS system file.
Volume Label	This entry is the volume label for a disk. The entry does not identify an actual file.

The Archive attribute works with DOS file-management commands to determine which files the commands process. The MSBACKUP command resets the Archive attribute of any file it copies to disk. As you work with the files on your disk, each file on which DOS performs a write operation gets flagged with the Archive attribute, which signals that the file has changed since it was last archived. If you have a recent full-disk backup, you can create a backup of only the files that have changed since the last backup by telling MSBACKUP that you want to copy only files having the Archive attribute.

A file entry with the Hidden attribute turned on is "invisible" determineto most DOS file-management commands. Hidden files have filenames and extensions like normal user files but are not processed by the DIR and COPY commands. The two DOS system files on the boot disk are examples, as are the files that manage a DoubleSpace drive.

You can detect the presence of hidden files by using the ATTRIB or CHKDSK command. Using ATTRIB, you also can list hidden files. CHKDSK merely indicates the number of hidden files on the disk.

The Subdirectory attribute indicates to DOS that the entry is not intended for a user file but for an additional directory called a subdirectory. When it carries out file-management commands, DOS knows to bypass a file with the Subdirectory attribute turned on.

The System attribute indicates that a file is an operating system file. The two DOS system files have this attribute in addition to the Hidden attribute. You need not worry about the System attribute; it does not affect your DOS work.

The Volume Label attribute indicates that the directory entry involved is to be used as the name of the volume, not as a filename. DOS then combines the filename and extension fields to provide an 11-character volume label for the disk. Only a Volume Label entry can have this attribute set (turned on).

The Archive, Hidden, Read-only, and System attributes are the only attributes you can change directly through DOS. DOS controls the other attributes without your intervention.

Changing File Attributes with the ATTRIB Command

DOS's ATTRIB command provides the means to change the settings of the Archive, Read-only, Hidden, and System attributes. The syntax of the ATTRIB command is

ATTRIB [+R|-R] [+A|-A] [+S|-S] [+H|-H] *filespec* [/S]

If you issue the ATTRIB command with no parameters, you get a list of all the files in the current directory, along with a display of their attribute status. Figure 5.1 shows a typical result.

Figure 5.1
The ATTRIB display when no parameters are given.

```
H:\TEST>ATTRIB
     A              H:\TEST\CONFIG.MEM
     A              H:\TEST\FM_LETS.DBF
     A              H:\TEST\FM_LETS.DBT
     A       R      H:\TEST\GROUND.DBF
     A       R      H:\TEST\GROUP.DBF
     A       R      H:\TEST\GUEST.DBF
     A       R      H:\TEST\GUEST.LBL
     A              H:\TEST\HOTEL.DBF
     A              H:\TEST\HOT_COMM.DBF
     A              H:\TEST\LIST.DBF
     A              H:\TEST\PASSW.DBF
     A              H:\TEST\PAYMTS.DBF
     A              H:\TEST\PAY_VEND.DBF
     A       R      H:\TEST\RES_AIR.DBF
     A       R      H:\TEST\RES_CAR.DBF
     A       R      H:\TEST\RES_GROU.DBF
     A       R      H:\TEST\RES_HOT.DBF
     A       R      H:\TEST\RES_TOUR.DBF
     A              H:\TEST\SEMI_4.DBF
     A              H:\TEST\TOUR.DBF
     A              H:\TEST\TRANS.MEM

H:\TEST>
```

As you can see in the figure, all the files have the Archive attribute set on. Also, all the files whose names begin with the letters R and G are marked as Read-only.

To change the attributes of files, use the first letter of each attribute's name and a plus (+) sign to set the attributes on or a minus (–) sign to set the attributes off. You can have any logical combination on one command line, such as the following:

ATTRIB -A +R

The preceding example turns off the Archive attribute and turns on the Read-only attribute for every file in the current directory. You can narrow the scope of the ATTRIB command by specifying a pathname expression (drive, path, and wildcards are honored) on the command line, as in the following:

```
ATTRIB -R G*.*
```

This example removes the Read-only attribute from only those files whose names begin with G. (You get a heavy dose of pathname expressions later in this chapter.)

You also can widen the scope of the ATTRIB command by using the /S switch. If you give ATTRIB a pathname expression as a parameter, by default the actions are limited only to the specified path. Giving no pathname expression to ATTRIB limits its action to the currently logged directory. Using the /S switch widens the scope of the ATTRIB command to include any directories under the directory where ATTRIB begins its actions.

Establishing Read-Only Files

The ATTRIB command gives you control over file attributes. In particular, the Read-only attribute makes DOS unable to overwrite a file. DOS commands such as EDIT, COPY, DEL, and XCOPY are capable of changing the data contained in a file. Files with the Read-only attribute cause a message to appear, telling you that the command you have tried to use cannot provide the service you are wanting.

In practice, however, the Read-only attribute has become little more than a confirmation flag to many modern programs. Both the DOS Shell and Windows File Manager can erase files having the Read-only attribute, for example, but only after you confirm that it is okay.

To give files the Read-only attribute, use the +R parameter, as in the following:

```
ATTRIB +R F:\WSTAR\*.TXT
```

Using the -R parameter has exactly the opposite effect, that of removing the Read-only flag.

> **Caution**
>
> The FDISK and FORMAT commands command do not observe the read-only status of a file. FDISK and FORMAT are disk-level commands; therefore, they don't look at disk directories when they are doing their jobs. Don't rely on the Read-only attribute of a file to protect the file from a disk-level command. Use the disk's write-protect tab to prevent floppies from being destroyed with FDISK and FORMAT.

Understanding the Role of Directories

To this point in the chapter, you have read many references to the directory. These references, although necessary for the explanations of files at the time, do not provide a great deal of information about directories. Now that you know all about files, however, it is time to turn your attention to the method used by DOS to organize files—directories.

In many homes, flatware is stored in a drawer in the kitchen. In some homes, the forks and knives and spoons are laid in a jumble, all mixed up. In other homes, a plastic tray that has compartments for each type of utensil is used. Forks stay with forks, salad forks have their own compartment, and so on. The capacity of the drawer to store flatware is not affected, but the drawer stays more organized. So it is with directories. DOS directories have the same purpose: They keep your files organized.

The *root directory* is an important table created by the FORMAT command on every disk it touches. It is called the root directory because it is the root, or beginning, of the disk's file system. DOS uses the directory as a kind of index system for finding files. The filenames and subdirectory names in this index system are called *directory entries*. DOS allows for a fixed number of directory entries in the root directory. This number is the same for disks with the same format but varies with different formats. Disks with larger capacities allow for more root directory entries. Although limited, the number of entries is generous. If you properly organize your disks, you will never even come close to this limit.

The DIR command is a window into the structure of a DOS directory. The DIR command accesses and displays selected parts of directory entries, as in this example:

```
C:\>dir ??.bat

 Volume in drive C is DATA-TRAIN
 Volume Serial Number is 1A9A-BEDA
 Directory of C:\

D4           BAT         39  09-18-90  12:51a
EE           BAT         34  04-23-92   4:05p
G            BAT         31  05-03-92   3:35a
HJ           BAT         28  12-10-92   6:34p
SK           BAT         26  08-27-90   3:23p
T            BAT         53  06-04-92   1:01a
W            BAT        128  05-25-92  10:49a
WP           BAT         16  08-27-91   3:46a
WS           BAT         35  12-05-90   2:40p
DP           BAT         37  09-06-91  10:37a
       10 file(s)            427 bytes
                      16,437,248 bytes free

C:\>
```

As you can see, DIR lists the filenames, extensions, the number of bytes in the file, the date it was last written to disk, and the time of the last write. The DIR command, however, does not display all the elements of a directory entry. Table 5.4 lists the components of a directory entry.

TABLE 5.4 THE MAIN FEATURES OF DOS DIRECTORIES

Feature	Example	What Is Stored
Filename	THANKYOU	Eight-character file prefix
Filename extension	DOC	Three-character file suffix
File attributes	R (read-only)	Special status information about this file used by DOS

Table 5.4 Continued

Feature	Example	What Is Stored
Time	10:22	The time of creation or last modification
Date	11-14-91	The date of creation or last modification
Starting cluster	576	The number of the first cluster allocated to this file by DOS in the FAT
File size	1024 bytes	The number of bytes in this file

You undoubtedly recognize the filename, extension, time, and date components of a directory entry as the ones displayed by the DIR command. DIR also displays the file size. These components, or fields, of a directory entry contain information useful to you as well as to DOS (see Figure 5.2). DIR displays this information to assist your file-management activities.

Figure 5.2
The fields of a directory entry.

| Filename | Extension | Attributes | Reserved | Time | Date | Starting Cluster | Size |

> **Note**
>
> The easiest way to cause DOS to display the names of the current drive and directory is to place the following line in your AUTOEXEC.BAT file:
>
> PROMPT pg
>
> This line alters the default DOS prompt to show you the current pathname expression. For more information about PROMPT, see Chapter 11, "Controlling Your Environment."

> **Note**
>
> DOS also stores volume labels in directory entries, using the combined filename and extension fields to form an 11-byte (11-character) field just like a filename. DOS knows that the directory entry is a volume label—not a filename—because the Volume Label attribute for the entry is set.

The starting cluster and file attribute fields, shown in Table 5.4 and in Figure 5.2, are not included in the DIR command's displayed output. The starting cluster field contains the cluster number of the first cluster DOS has allocated for a particular file's storage.

Chaining Through a File

The starting cluster field of a file's directory entry is the key to the file's storage allocation as tracked in the FAT. You recall that DOS creates a FAT for each disk during formatting. The FAT indicates whether each cluster on the disk is allocated to a file. Much as a restaurant hostess looks at a table chart for a place to seat you, DOS looks at the FAT for available clusters when a file is created or enlarged. When you arrive early at a restaurant, it is nearly empty, and the hostess seats you in the general vicinity of other guests, leaving other sections of the restaurant unused. When DOS allocates files on a freshly formatted disk, DOS uses the first cluster and sequences through a connected series of clusters, leaving many clusters unused at the end of the

FAT. When you leave the restaurant, the hostess marks your table as being available. Likewise, when you erase or shorten a file, DOS marks the released clusters in the FAT as being available to store another file.

You might have had a dining experience in which the hostess did not have enough adjacent tables to seat your entire party. Your group is fragmented across two or more tables, with other parties seated at tables between the parts of your group. Your group is fragmented, but you can remain connected as a group by telling the waiter, "We're with those people over there," as you point to the other table.

When a DOS command or applications program asks DOS to store a file on the disk, DOS checks the FAT, finds the next available cluster, and stores a portion of the file there. If that cluster cannot accommodate the entire file, DOS finds the next available cluster and stores part of the file there. DOS does not look for the largest available block of clusters, so the entire file might not fit in the first group of available clusters. starting As with the large party in the restaurant, your file becomes fragmented across the disk.

In Chapter 7, "Preparing and Maintaining Disks," you learn more about fragmentation. There, you also learn how you can correct this condition and improve your disk performance.

Expanding the File System Through Subdirectories

Earlier in this chapter, disk directories were likened to the plastic trays that many households use to organize eating utensils. The metaphor is not outlandish. This plastic tray separates similar utensils to make them easier to find; takes up very little room; and generally simplifies the storage of forks, spoons, knives, and so on. The DOS directory structure simplifies the storage of program and data files and makes them easier to find when needed.

When you use FORMAT to prepare a disk, it creates a root directory structure. The number of entries that this directory can contain is limited. On most floppy disk formats, the number of entries is limited to 512. On hard disks, the capacity is proportional to the size of the volume (logical disk) being created. There is very little chance that you will ever exceed the capacity, unless you try to store all the files on your hard disk in the root directory.

Imagine what chaos might reign if all your files were lumped together in one single directory. You would never be able to tell what files belonged with what program. Your data files from your word processor would all be scrambled up with files created by other programs, and every time you wanted to locate a file, the directory listing would go on for screen after screen.

To avoid these problems, DOS employs a method of creating *subdirectories* that branch off from the root directory. Subdirectories can in turn branch off into subordinate subdirectories. Figure 5.3 shows part of the display generated by the TREE command, which is used to represent the directory of a disk graphically.

Figure 5.3 shows the directory structure of a working disk drive. At the top of the tree, the E: represents the root directory. The vertical line that aligns with the E: shows the first level of directories, those that appear in the root directory. Two subdirectories, BRIEF and CLIPPER5, branch off from the root. The BRIEF directory in turn branches off four times to create four subdirectories to hold files associated with Brief, a programmer's editor. One of these subordinate directories contains Help files, another contains macro files, and so on. If you want to find a file containing a Brief macro, you use the DIR file to generate a listing, as in the following:

DIR E:\BRIEF\MACROS

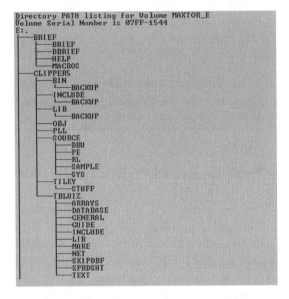

Figure 5.3
Directories are used to organize the files on a disk.

It is unlikely that a Brief macro can work its way into the CLIPPER5\LIB directory, so you can see that, by creating and maintaining directories, you can pinpoint easily the files you need to work with. In Chapter 13, "Controlling Devices," you learn about the FIND command, which helps track down files that are not stored where you think they should be stored.

A good general system for creating directory structures is to have each application you install on your hard disk be contained within its own directory. The directory should have a name that tells you immediately what program resides in the directory. A good name for a WordPerfect directory is WP, for instance.

Installation programs for software applications often install files into directory structures created during installation. The Clipper programming language automatically creates a directory called CLIPPER5 and then places library, object, and binary files into subdirectories called LIB, OBJ, and BIN. It also creates other directories, but you get the idea.

Files associated with the main application can be made to reside in subdirectories that hold groups of files of the same types. The Clipper installation routine puts all the library files into the LIB directory. If later you create or buy other libraries from another source, you can copy them into the library directory, or you can create a directory that branches off the LIB directory to hold these files. You should do whatever makes them easiest for you and your software to find them.

Understanding Pathname Expressions

A *pathname expression* indicates the path that DOS must traverse to find a specified file or group of files. A pathname expression has three components: drive, directories, and files.

The drive component identifies the disk drive used to store the files. It is made up of three characters: the drive letter, followed by a colon (:) and a backslash (\), as in the following example:

`C:\`

DOS uses the backslash character to separate the directories within a pathname expression. The preceding example is a pathname expression that indicates the root directory of drive C because the backslash immediately follows the colon.

The directory component of the pathname expression is a list of all the directories that must be traversed to reach the last named directory or the file component. The following is an example:

`C:\WINDOWS\SYSTEM\GAMES`

In this example, the pathname expression tells DOS to look for files by starting at the root directory of C:, moving into the WINDOWS directory, through the SYSTEM directory that branches from the WINDOWS directory, and then into the GAMES directory. Simply stated, a pathname expression gives DOS directions to directories, just like you might give a friend directions to your house.

The third portion of a pathname expression specifies a single file explicitly, or it uses wildcards to specify a group of files, as in the following two examples:

`C:\WINDOWS\SYSTEM\GAMES\SOL.EXE`

`C:\DOS\*.COM`

The first example specifies a single file in the GAMES directory, whereas the second example specifies a group of files using a wildcard. Pathname expressions can use ?, *, ., and .. as valid wildcard characters.

DOS requires each file on a disk to have a unique name. For this reason, DOS considers a file's full name to be the pathname expression that explicitly identifies that one file. For example, the name

`C:\DOS\GO.BAT`

is not the same as the following:

`C:\TEMP\GO.BAT`

Yes, two files have the name GO.BAT, but they are in different directories, so both files have a unique name.

If you issue the following command, which file's contents are displayed depends on what directory you are currently logged in to:

`TYPE GO.BAT`

If you are logged in to either the DOS or TEMP directories of drive C, you see the contents of the file named GO.BAT found in that directory. If you are logged in to the GRAPHIC directory, you might get a `file not found` message.

The trick to using pathname expressions effectively is knowing when to use the full formal pathname and when to use a less specific pathname expression.

People, like files, can be called either by a formal title, such as George W. Bush, President of the United States, or by a less formal form of address, such as President George Bush. Mr. Bush and George are other examples of names that identify the President. Pathname expressions can likewise be formal or informal.

New Directories

Newcomers to DOS often are puzzled to see directory listings that contain filenames that look like periods. Many people, afraid to appear silly, never ask what the periods mean.

When you create a new directory in DOS, it adds two entries to the new directory. The name of the first entry is always . (called *dot*). The second entry is always named . . (called *dot-dot*). The dot entry in a directory refers, or points, to the directory that contains it. You can think of the dot entry as an alias for the current directory's name, analogous to the pronoun *me*. Although no DOS manual documents this fact, you also can use the dot as a wildcard character in most commands. For example, the following

    DEL .

is the same as

    DEL *.*

DOS uses the dot-dot entry to point to the parent of the current directory. This entry is an alias for the parent directory's name and is analogous to the names *Mom* or *Dad*. The following command, for example, lists all the files in the current directory's parent directory:

    DIR ..

In the root directory, . . has no meaning because the root directory has no parent.

The full formal pathname expression for a file expresses the location of a file or group of files explicitly without regard to the currently logged directory. This type of pathname expression is sometimes called an *absolute path*. The following is an example:

TYPE C:\AUTOEXEC.BAT

This command displays the contents of your AUTOEXEC.BAT file onscreen no matter what drive or directory is currently logged. If, however, you currently are logged in to the root directory of C:, typing the C:\ portion of the pathname expression becomes optional because DOS always looks for a specified file in the current directory. Therefore, the following finds the proper file if you are logged in to C:\:

TYPE AUTOEXEC.BAT

This pathname formal expression uses a *relative path* to locate the file. Specifying a relative path involves giving directions to DOS, based on its currently logged directory. Each of the following three examples uses a relative path as its pathname expression:

```
DIR ..
DIR C:
DIR SAMPLES\*.DOC
```

The first uses .. to cause DIR to show all files in the directory from which the current directory branches out. The second example lists all files in whatever directory is currently logged on drive C. The third example lists all the .DOC files in the SAMPLES directory, which branches off from the current directory.

Pathname expressions can range from the very simple to the very complex. Keep in mind two rules when you're creating directories on your system:

- DOS pathname expressions cannot exceed 63 characters in length, including the implicit backslash DOS adds internally.
- Typing long strings of directory names is both a pain in the neck and an invitation to typing errors.

If you really understand the second rule, you will never have a problem with the first rule. When you're creating directory structures on hard disks, keep the depth of directories to a minimum. When you are tempted to create a pathname that exceeds three directories deep, stop and think. At least half the time, you can come up with a better way to arrange directories so that you don't end up typing pathname expressions that sprawl across half the screen.

As complex as pathname expressions can become, most new users are surprised to find that they need learn only three simple commands to create and maintain DOS directories. The following sections provide a rundown of each command.

CREATING DIRECTORIES WITH MKDIR (MD)

DOS provides the internal MKDIR command to create directories. You can abbreviate the name of the command as MD for convenience. Because MD, or *make directory*, is easier to remember, this form is used in this chapter. Anywhere you see a reference to the MD command, you can substitute MKDIR.

The syntax for the MD command is as follows:

```
MD d:\path\dirname
```

The command uses a pathname to explicitly describe the drive and pathway to the new directory to be created. You learn more about pathnames in the following paragraphs. For now, consider the following line:

```
MD E:\BRIEF\MACROS\OLDMACS
```

This example creates the OLDMACS directory branching from the BRIEF\MACROS directory. Subdirectory names are just directory entries in the parent directory. MACROS, for example, is just an entry in the BRIEF directory. What differentiates a subdirectory name from a filename is the Directory attribute. The starting cluster associated with the directory name is the first cluster on the disk where that directory's entries are written.

DOS naming rules allow a directory name to be up to 11 characters long. You can create a directory named STUFF.OLD, but by convention, DOS users have largely agreed to keep directory names to eight characters or fewer. When the DIR command lists a directory, subdirectories are marked with a <DIR> in the column where the size of a file is normally shown. Figure 5.4 illustrates how directory names are listed by DIR.

Figure 5.4
Directory names are marked with <DIR> to show that they are not files.

```
E:\>dir

 Volume in drive E is MAXTOR_E
 Volume Serial Number is 07FF-1544
 Directory of E:\

BRIEF         <DIR>        03-31-92   10:09a
CLIPPER5      <DIR>        06-26-93    3:20a
FAST    TXT         809    07-30-93    1:03a
ME            <DIR>        03-10-93    4:37p
WAV           <DIR>        03-31-92   10:11a
WINWORD       <DIR>        03-31-92   10:13a
WORD          <DIR>        03-31-92   10:11a
SLOW    TXT         878    07-30-93    1:03a
MEDIUM  TXT         793    07-29-93   11:57p
        9 file(s)         2480 bytes
                    14,737,408 bytes free

E:\>
```

Tip
You also can use the MOVE command in certain circumstances to create new directories. Information about MOVE is presented later in this chapter and in Chapter 8, "Managing Your Files."

As you can see, the DIR listing shows the directory structure for the root directory of E:. It contains several entries for subdirectories as well as three text files.

When you use the MD command, follow these guidelines:

- The specified or implied parent directory of the intended directory must exist. If the JILL directory doesn't exist, MD JILL\JACK fails.
- MD cannot make more than one directory at a time.
- MD does not change the current directory to the new directory. To change to the new directory, you must use CHDIR (CD).

If, for example, your current directory is \DOS and you want to add the directory \DOS\DRIVERS, you can issue the following command:

MD DRIVERS

Notice that no backslash appears in front of the new directory name. DOS interprets this path to be a relative path, and it adds the current directory path to the pathname expression on the command line.

Changing the Current Directory with CHDIR (CD)

As you work with drives and files in DOS, you can consider each directory to be a location and the pathname expression of the directory to be its map. DOS keeps in memory your current location on each drive of your machine.

Use the CHDIR command to change from one directory to another. The short form of CHDIR is CD, meaning *change directory*. If you are in the WINDOWS directory and you want to work in the SYSTEM directory that branches off the WINDOWS directory, issue the following command:

```
CD SYSTEM
```

The WINDOWS\SYSTEM directory then becomes your currently logged directory. DOS remembers which directory is current for each drive in your system. When you switch to another drive, DOS automatically retains a memory of where you were working last. Consider this example:

```
C:
CD \DOS\UTILS
F:
COPY *.BAT C:
```

In this example, you move onto drive C and change directories to the DOS\UTILS directory. The next command moves you to drive F and copies all the batch files in the current directory of F: to the current directory of C:. In this case, the files are copied to C:\DOS\UTILS.

> **Note**
> To change directly to the root directory of the currently logged disk from any directory on the disk, issue the following command:
> ```
> CD \
> ```
> Also, if you are not sure what directory you are currently in, issuing the CD command with no pathname expression causes DOS to display the full pathname expression for the current directory.
>
> You can also issue the following command to return to the directory above your current one (for example to move from C:\DATA\DOCS to C:\DATA):
> ```
> CD ..
> ```

You can use either a relative path or an absolute path to specify what directory to change into. Assume you are currently logged in to C:\DOS\UTILS, for example, and issue the following command:

```
CD ..\STUFF
```

This example uses a relative path to log you in to the C:\DOS\STUFF directory. You also can log in to the same directory by issuing this command:

```
CD \DOS\STUFF
```

When you're using the CD command, follow these guidelines:

- The drive and path parameters in the command line must be valid.
- If the path parameter begins with \, CD assumes that the directory specified in the path is absolute—from the root.
- If the path parameter does not begin with \, CD assumes that the directory given in the path is relative to the current directory.
- When you specify a drive parameter but no path parameter, CD reports the current working directory for the specified disk.
- When you omit the path parameter and the drive parameter from the command line, CD reports the current working directory of the currently logged drive.

Deleting Directories with RMDIR (RD)

Just as you occasionally need to add a directory to a disk, you might need to delete a directory. DOS enables you to remove empty directories at the end of a directory branch in the directory tree with the RMDIR command, RD for short.

When you're working with the RD command, remember that RD can delete only empty directories. If a directory contains files or has another directory branching from it, RD fails. To delete a directory using RD, use a command similar to the following:

```
RD \COLD\HOT\WARM
```

If the WARM directory is empty, RD removes it from the directory tree.

Using DELTREE to Delete Directories

The DELTREE command, new in DOS 6.0, makes the RD command obsolete. DELTREE enables you to delete directories that contain files—even complete branches of a directory tree. This command removes the directory you specify and everything in it—subdirectories, files, and files in subdirectories. In addition, attributes of files in the subdirectories are ignored. You do not need to use ATTRIB to clear attributes such as Read-only or Hidden before you delete them.

The syntax for DELTREE is as follows:

```
DELTREE /Y d:path
```

The optional d: parameter specifies the disk that contains the directory branch to be removed. If you omit d: from the command line, DOS assumes that the current (logged) disk holds the directory to be removed.

The required pathname expression specifies the topmost level of the directory branch to be removed. If the path begins with a backslash (\), DOS assumes that the path to the directory name is absolute from the root. If the *path* parameter does not begin with a backslash, DOS assumes that the path to the directory name is relative from the current directory of d:.

The /Y parameter is optional. Because DELTREE is a potentially dangerous command, capable of wiping out hundreds of files at a time, DOS normally displays the following message:

```
Delete d:path and all its subdirectories? [Y/N]
```

If you type Y and press Enter, the command proceeds; if you type N and press Enter, the operation stops. If you use the /Y parameter, however, the message does not appear, and DELTREE proceeds as though you had typed Y.

> **Caution**
>
> DELTREE deletes everything in its path. As with anything in computing, a feature that gives you a great deal of power also gives you the ability to shoot yourself in the foot. Be sure you no longer need anything in any of the directories subordinate to the one you name before proceeding. To make sure, first issue the DIR command (with the /S parameter) or the TREE command, which is discussed later in this chapter.

Assume, for example, that your hard disk has a string of directories branching off from the root directory of C:. The pathname expression that specifies the lowest level directory is C:\HOT\COLD\WARM\TEPID\ICY. If you issue this command, all the files and directories in the WARM directory are deleted regardless of file attributes:

```
DELTREE /Y C:\HOT\COLD\WARM
```

Any directories that may branch off from WARM, TEPID, or ICY are also deleted, along with any files they contain.

As you can see, DELTREE is a powerful command. Always double-check your command line for errors before you press Enter to activate the command.

Remember, too, that you can use wildcards in the pathname expression of the command line, but use them only with caution. If a wildcard in a pathname expression matches both directory names and filenames, both are deleted. It is often a good idea to use the DIR command first to see what files the pathname expression affects before using that pathname expression with DELTREE.

RENAMING DIRECTORIES

Having to change the name of a directory is not uncommon. This need might arise because you misspell the name of the directory during creation or because you have upgraded software and want the upgrade to be reflected in the directory name.

The MOVE command enables you to rename directories from the command line and also moves files from one directory to another. The syntax of the MOVE command for renaming directories is as follows:

```
MOVE d:oldpath d:newpath
```

The optional *d:* parameter specifies the disk that contains the directory branch to be removed. If you omit *d:* from the command line, DOS assumes that the current (logged) disk holds the directory to be removed.

This command requires two pathname expressions. The first specifies the directory you want to move or rename. The second pathname expression specifies the new name of the target directory or the name of a directory to be created as a result of the command's actions. If the directory does not exist, MOVE prompts you to ask whether the directory should be created. Answer Y, and the new directory is created.

To rename a directory, use the MOVE command as in the following example:

```
MOVE C:\TEMP\BAK C:\TEMP\BACKUP
```

Helping DOS Find Files with PATH

When you issue a DOS command, COMMAND.COM, the command interpreter, looks first to see whether the command is internal to DOS. If the command is not internal, DOS looks on the disk for a filename having the same name as the command.

In this regard, both external DOS commands and other executable files have equal status. Files having the extensions .EXE, .COM, and .BAT are all considered by DOS to be executable program files. DOS simply looks for any executable file having the same name as the command-line keyword. It then runs the first file it finds.

> **Note**
> The DOS search path works only with executable files. If a program uses auxiliary files such as overlays and data files, an error can occur unless the program is written to search its own directory, not just the currently logged directory.
>
> None of DOS's external commands use auxiliary files, so you never have a "file not found" problem as long as the DOS directory is included in the search path. To run applications that use auxiliary files, you should log in to the directory where the application is written to disk to ensure error-free operation.

You have three ways to make sure DOS finds an external program file. You can do any of the following:

- Log in to the disk and directory that contains the command
- Supply the path in the command line
- Establish a DOS search path to the command's directory

The PATH command places a path search string in the DOS environment. DOS uses the contents of this environment variable to determine where on the system it should look for program files.

Normally, the PATH command is included as a statement in the AUTOEXEC.BAT file, so it takes effect even before the first DOS prompt is displayed. Using the PATH command, however, is not restricted to lines in AUTOEXEC.BAT. You can type a new search string at any DOS prompt. Whether it is in a batch file or typed at a DOS prompt, the PATH command is used the same way, as in the following example:

PATH C:\;C:\DOS;D:\WINDOWS;E:\BRIEF

If you enter a command at the DOS prompt and COMMAND.COM does not recognize it as an internal DOS command, DOS always looks first in the currently logged directory. If the file cannot be found there, DOS uses the PATH information to first search the root directory of drive C, then the \DOS directory of C:, then the WINDOWS directory on D:, and finally the BRIEF directory on E:. Only after searching all five directories for an executable file, and not finding it, does DOS give you the dread Bad command or file name message.

The directories you want searched are listed on the command line separated by semicolons (;). The order in which the directories are listed is the order in which they are searched. For this reason, it is prudent to keep the DOS directory and other frequently used directories at the front of the search string.

In the preceding sample PATH command, DOS is directed to first look in the root directory of drive C. This directory is traditionally a favorite repository for batch files that automate the launching of applications. The second directory specified is the DOS directory. The DOS directory should always be at or near the beginning of the search path because files in this directory are constantly being called on. Having the DOS directory at the head of the search path cuts down on the time spent searching for external DOS commands. Exceedingly long search paths can dramatically slow down your computer's response time.

The order of the search path is important for another reason as well. If two directories have executable programs with the same names, the program that is run is the one whose directory is specified closer to the beginning of the search path.

Although the maximum length of the search path is 127 characters, avoid creating long search paths. Traditionally, search paths are used mainly to allow DOS to find often-used utilities without having to change logged drives or directories. Having too many directories in the search path slows down system performance because it takes DOS longer to determine whether a command is valid. Some software applications, such as Windows, require an entry in the search path for efficient operation, however. In general, if you seldom use the executable files in a directory, it is better to leave that directory out of the search path.

LISTING DIRECTORIES WITH TREE

DOS provides an external command, TREE, that lists all the directories of a disk as a tree structure similar to the DOS Shell's directory display. Figure 5.4 shows the TREE command's output. The TREE command also can list the files in the directories. TREE is especially useful when you're working with hard disks because it visually maps out the directory structures of disks.

The TREE command syntax is as follows:

TREE *d:path* /F /A

d: is an optional parameter that indicates the drive whose directories you want to list. If you omit *d:*, TREE lists the directories on the current disk drive.

The *path* expression names the directory where TREE is to start processing the listing. If you omit this parameter, TREE begins processing from the root directory.

TREE accepts two switches. The /F switch instructs TREE to display the files contained within directories as part of the visual tree. The /A switch instructs TREE to use printable characters instead of the line-drawing characters normally used to indicate branching of directories. Use the /A switch when you're directing output to an older printer that cannot print graphics characters or when using a text-only video adapter.

Using a Temporary Directory

Many programs and some DOS operations use a directory as a temporary location to store scratchpad files. A *scratchpad file* is a file that is created as a buffer to store information temporarily before a permanent file is created. A good example of a program that uses temporary storage space is Windows. Windows creates .TMP files in the temporary directory to hold swapping information. Also, the Windows Print Manager uses the temporary directory to create files to hold print jobs. Other programs use temporary space as a place to store sorting information, backup copies of files being processed, and so on.

Traditionally, DOS users have created a directory called TEMP that branches off the root directory of C:. In fact, if this directory doesn't exist when you install DOS 6.22 using the Setup program, it is created for you automatically.

The SET command, which creates DOS environment variables, normally is used in AUTOEXEC.BAT to create a variable called TEMP, as shown in this example:

```
SET TEMP=C:\TEMP
```

Redirecting Your Output

Like DIR and TYPE, TREE is one of those DOS commands that can produce many pages of output. DOS offers two features to enable you to capture screen output in a more usable form.

You can use the MORE command to capture screen output from other commands and present the screens one at a time, pausing for a keystroke as each screen is displayed. MORE is unusual because you enter it on the command line of another command using the pipe (|) symbol, which you can find on the same key as the backslash on most keyboards. Check out the following command example:

```
TREE /F | MORE
```

The preceding command captures the output of the TREE command and passes it to the MORE command. The MORE command breaks up the output into single screen portions. As each single screenful of the output is displayed, MORE waits for you to press a key before it displays the next screenful.

The problem with MORE is that you cannot go backward. When a screenful of output has been replaced with another, the first screenful is lost. To see it again, you must repeat the command that called MORE.

You also can use the DOS redirection feature to capture long output to a file or send it directly to a printer by using the output redirection symbol (>), as in the following two examples:

```
TREE /F >TREE.TXT
```

```
TREE /F >PRN
```

The first example directs the output to be saved in a file named TREE.TXT. You then can use an editor to view the output of the TREE command. If your editor has problems displaying graphic characters, use the /A switch to get readable output.

The second example directs the output of the TREE command to the printer. Make sure the printer is online and ready before you put the TREE command into action.

For more information on DOS's redirection features, see Chapter 13.

When DOS or another program needs to create temporary files, it looks in the environment to see whether a TEMP variable exists. This way, you can direct DOS to use a specific directory. If you don't have a TEMP directory, most software uses the currently logged directory to create scratchpad files. You should always make sure that the TEMP directory resides on a disk with plenty of free space. Lack of scratchpad space can make programs run much more slowly than normal or display an error message.

> **Caution**
>
> Most programs that create scratch files do a good job of cleaning up after themselves by deleting any files they might create when the files are no longer needed.
>
> It is a good idea to check the TEMP directory every few days just to make sure that no scratchpad files have been orphaned by a power failure or untimely reboot. If you find files in the TEMP directory, you should delete them.
>
> Be careful, however, not to delete files in the TEMP directory while you're running Windows or when you're shelled out to a DOS session from within a running application. Under these circumstances, the files still might be active and in use. Never delete files from the TEMP directory unless you are at a DOS prompt with no other programs running.

TROUBLESHOOTING

What happened to my filenames?

Modern operating systems, such as Windows 95/98/ME and Windows NT/2000, enable you to have filenames up to 256 characters. A common problem occurs when a user copies files with long filenames to a DOS machine that supports only the 8.3 filename format. DOS renames a long filename by truncating it and adding a tilde (~) and a numeric character.

If you copy the file CONVERTIBLE.EXE to a DOS machine, for example, you end up with a file called CONVER~1.EXE.

If you try to name a file with an illegal character or with too many characters in the extension, you encounter other errors. The following example uses the COPY command to show what can happen:

```
COPY TEST.TXT 123456789.1234
```

Notice that both the filename and extension given for the destination filename contain an extra character: The filename has the extra character 9, and the extension has the extra character 4. You might predict that DOS will issue a message warning that the filename and extension are too long. No such luck! DOS simply truncates the filename to eight characters and the extension to three characters to create a legal filename (12345678.123), and then it completes the COPY operation.

Illegal characters in a filename can prevent DOS from carrying out a command. Here's an example:

```
COPY 12345678.123 1[3.123
```

This command causes DOS to display the following message:

```
File creation error
```

Few experienced DOS users purposely use illegal characters in a filename, but typos easily can creep into your DOS commands and introduce illegal characters into filename parameters. Type commands carefully, remembering that DOS's reaction to an illegal filename isn't always predictable.

CHAPTER 6

UNDERSTANDING DISKS AND DISK DRIVES

In this chapter

Understanding the Disk's Magnetic Storage Technique   128

Understanding Disk Drives   129

Understanding the Dynamics of the Disk Drive   133

Understanding Disk Formats   137

Understanding DoubleSpace   140

Case Study: Adjusting for Drift   148

Understanding the Disk's Magnetic Storage Technique

Early computer hobbyists used everything from discarded paper tape drives to cassette tapes to store files. For a while, Radio Shack sold cassette tapes that didn't have the normal plastic leader at the head of the tape so that computer users didn't have to wind tapes past the leader by hand.

Fortunately, the fastest advances in computer science have revolved around memory and storage. The original IBM PC had two single-sided 5 1/4-inch (160KB) floppy disk drives, period. Hard drives weren't supported by the IBM PC BIOS until the 10MB hard disk became the standard in the early XTs.

Floppy disks have evolved to the point where four standard formats are in common use. A fifth format—Extra High Density—is available, but few manufacturers support it yet. You learn more about these sizes later in this chapter.

Hard disks have changed the most. A number of technology standards have come and gone as hard disks have steadily grown larger and faster. Drives that are capable of storing more than twenty gigabytes (approximately two billion bytes) now cost less than $200.

CD-ROM drives, which can hold more than 640MB of data, are widely available in today's systems and have become the standard for software. Also, with the advent of both write-once (CD-R) and rewritable (CD-RW) CD-ROM media, CDs now have many more uses, such as backups and custom software distribution. Another format that has recently come on the scene is DVD-ROM, which is a new CD-style format that can hold more than 17GB of information. The main drawback of DVD-ROM drives at this time is their relatively slow speed. Although some CD-ROM drives are as fast as 72x speed, the best DVD-ROM drive is currently around 16x speed. With regard to creating your own DVD-ROMs, DVD-ROM recorders are—at the time of this writing— expensive (more than $800 a drive) compared to CD-R and CD-RW; eventually, this format will probably surpass the current CD-R standard.

Magnetic media come in two basic flavors: floppy and hard. The following sections give you the technical background on how disks work.

Although this material doesn't make using the COPY or FORMAT commands any more or less effective, knowing this information can save your data. Magnetic disks, like humans, are mortal; they sometimes suddenly drop dead. Usually, users make mistakes that wreck disks, but sometimes disks just give up the ghost unexpectedly or get trapped in a lightning zap. Disks are generally prone to hazard. This, of course, is why backups are so important. Highly specialized disk-editing software such as Norton Disk Doctor and others of its ilk can help you to revive and resurrect lost data, but only if you know how disks are formatted and how data is stored.

Almost everyone is familiar with the way audio tape recorders work. Because tape recorders and computer disks use similar technologies, take a moment to review the form of the technology you are probably most familiar with.

In a cassette tape, a long thin ribbon of plastic is coated with an emulsion of ferrous oxides (magnetic coatings), enclosed in a protective plastic case, and passed through a tape transport. The transport mechanism pulls the ribbon of tape through at a controlled speed and brings the tape into contact with three magnetic tape heads.

Most tape recorders use an erase head, a record head, and a playback head. On some inexpensive tape recorders, a single head is used for both playback and recording. This setup doesn't, by itself, lower sound quality; it means only that you can't listen to the tape as it is recorded.

When you're recording a tape, the erase head randomizes the magnetic particles in the oxide emulsion, effectively erasing any previously stored information (sound).

The stereo record head actually has two heads: one for the left channel and one for the right. Sounds are converted into electrical fields. As the tape passes across the record head, it passes through these fields, and the random magnetic particles align into replicas of the field through which it passes.

When the tape passes over the playback head, the magnetic patterns on the tape are picked up much like a microphone's diaphragm picks up sound waves. The magnetic images create electrical fields that then can be turned back into sound waves with a speaker.

A standard stereo cassette tape has four tracks of sound information, two in each playback direction. The ribbon of tape has four discrete stripes of magnetic information.

Now imagine that you make a cassette tape several inches in width. Cut circular discs out of the tape, enclose them in a plastic casing, and build a machine that locks onto the center of the disc and rotates it like a potter's wheel. To the machine, add a magnetic tape head mounted on an arm that can float over the surface of the disc. As the magnetic disc rotates, the head can be positioned to create magnetic stripes in concentric rings, just like the rings in a tree trunk, except that they are symmetrical and evenly spaced.

Voilà! You have just invented the *floppy disk*!

Understanding Disk Drives

Actually, you must complete a few steps before you have a *floppy disk drive*. First, discard the record head. Because you are recording only the ones and zeros of binary numbers (the bits in a byte), you can simply record over previously recorded information. Because there are only two possible signals rather than varying shades of musical nuance, when you write a one or a zero, it effectively overwrites the previous character. You need only a single read/write head for each side of the disk, so your floppy disk needs two head assembly units to be double-sided.

You also need to record a formatting track to parallel or interweave with the data tracks so that a computer can say, "Record this group of bytes in this location and then read the bytes on that other location." Provide internal programming on a ROM chip so that DOS only needs to send instructions to the disk drive to read and write data from any location at any time. Oh, yes, and hide all this complexity from computer users. Now you have invented the usable floppy disk!

Take it one step further. Coat a stack of ceramic or metal disks with a much denser magnetic material, mount them on a spindle, and spin them much faster than before. Then, mount multiple high-density read/write heads, one for each platter side. Beef up the response times and speeds for all the moving components. Seal all these components into a dust-free can; now you have invented the *hard disk*, also called a *fixed disk* because the platters cannot be removed without the user damaging them.

The mechanical parts and electrical circuits of disk drives are complex. Although a disk drive is part of a PC system, the drive is a machine in its own right. DOS relies on the driver programs of the BIOS (the basic input/output system, found on ROMs inside your computer) and on ROMs within the drive to handle the low-level control of the drive's mechanical components.

All disk drives have certain common components: read/write heads, head-positioner mechanisms, and disk-spinning motors. All disk drives record on disks. Some disks are removable, and some are built into the drive. Both fixed disks and removable disks spin on a center spindle within the disk drive.

Today, most PCs incorporate both fixed disks and removable disks. The BIOS extensions of DOS make provisions for both types of drives. Even with their common features, fixed and floppy disk drives have some important differences, which are described in the following sections. Knowing these distinctions can help you understand how each type of drive operates in your system.

Hard Disk Drives

Drives with built-in disks are called *fixed disk drives* or, because their disks are made of rigid material, *hard disk drives*. You can shorten these terms to *fixed disk* and *hard disk*.

A hard disk drive can contain more than one hard disk, or *platter*. Multiple platters are arranged in a stack, with space between the individual platters. Hard disk drives have great storage capacity; these drives can hold anywhere from a few million to a few billion bytes of data.

Figure 6.1 shows a cutaway view of a typical older hard disk. The platters are the drive's magnetic disks. A head-positioner arm holds the read/write heads above and below each surface of each platter. When the drive leaves the factory, the components are not exposed, as they are in this figure; the drive is sealed to keep dust, hair, dirt, smoke, and other contaminants out of the delicate mechanical parts.

These parts are delicate because the read/write heads must float very close to the surface of the platter without actually touching them. A single hair on the surface produces a reaction similar to driving the family car over a fallen tree trunk.

Figure 6.1
An inside view of the main components of a hard disk.

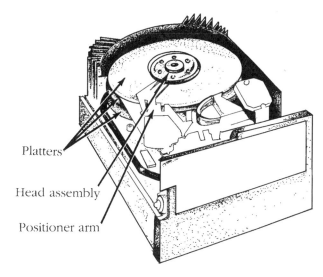

Hard disks have the advantages of quick operation, high reliability, and large storage capacity. Hard disks have the disadvantage of tying the data stored on the disk to the PC in which the drive is installed. Because the hard disk's platters cannot be removed, the data is tied to the drive. Moving an entire hard disk to another computer simply to use the hard disk's data is impractical.

One way of sharing files among many computers is to run wire or fiber-optic cables between machines and allow a single computer to offer file services for all the connected workstations. Within this idea, you find the genesis of computer networking.

FLOPPY DISK DRIVES

In a PC system, the disadvantage of tying data to the hard disk is counterbalanced by the PC's floppy disk drive. Floppy disks are protected by a permanent jacket, which encloses the flexible disk. The flexible disk inside the jacket is made of Mylar and is coated with sensitive magnetic film.

The first floppy disks were eight inches in diameter. By today's standards, the early 8-inch floppy disks didn't store much data.

A smaller version of the 8-inch floppy—the 5 1/4-inch mini-floppy—quickly became the floppy of choice for PC designers because of its smaller size. The 3 1/2-inch microfloppy is yet another departure from its larger, older cousins because it incorporates a rigid plastic case (its jacket) as a protective cover. The 3 1/2-inch Mylar disk inside the microfloppy disk is flexible, like the media in 8-inch and 5 1/4-inch floppies.

Not surprisingly, given the history of computer development, each new generation of floppy has gotten smaller in physical size. What does surprise many new users is that the physically smaller disks each have greater storage capacity than did their larger ancestors. If some hardware manufacturers have their way, a very high-capacity 2-inch floppy disk is in your future.

The original IBM PCs used a single-sided 5 1/4-inch floppy disk that stored only 160KB of data. Later drive mechanisms in PCs, XTs, and their clones added a second read/write head assembly to access the other side, and the double-sided, double-density 5 1/4-inch floppy disk that had the capacity to store 360KB was born. Further advances in drive technology enabled IBM to introduce the double-sided, high-density 5 1/4-inch floppy with the AT generation of computers. These new disks had the capacity to store 1.2MB, almost quadruple the storage of the double-sided variety.

When IBM introduced the PS/2 computer models, it used a disk drive type that had been pioneered on the Apple Macintosh. A 3 1/2-inch floppy disk that was capable of storing 720KB of data was the standard drive on early PS/2s. Because 720KB was a step down from the 1.2MB available on 5 1/4-inch disks, the development of a 3 1/2-inch high-density format was accelerated. Most of today's 3 1/2-inch drives are high density but, like their 5 1/4-inch cousins, they also can read and write double-density disks. Figure 6.2 shows the 3 1/2-inch disk drive.

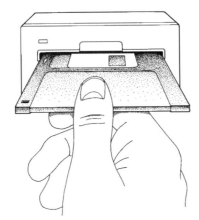

Figure 6.2
Insert the metal shutter on a 3 1/2-inch disk first.

WRITE-PROTECTING A FLOPPY DISK

You often store data on floppy disks that should not be erased. To ensure that the files on a floppy disk do not get erased accidentally, you can write-protect the disk.

To write-protect a 3 1/2-inch disk, locate the plastic write-protect shutter and slide it so that the window is open (see Figure 6.3).

When a disk is write-protected, the drive cannot write new information on the disk, even if you inadvertently issue a command that attempts to write data to the disk.

Figure 6.3
A 3 1/2-inch floppy disk showing a built-in write-protect shutter.

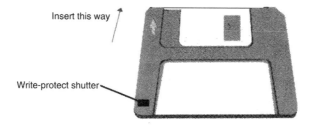

Understanding the Dynamics of the Disk Drive

Thus far, the discussion of the mechanics of magnetic disk technology has centered on the physical. The following sections of this chapter introduce you to the logical aspects of how drives are constructed and used.

Disk Drive Heads

The read/write heads used in magnetic disk drives bear little resemblance to the heads in a tape recorder because they must be mounted in such a way that they can cover the entire radius of a disk. Figure 6.4 shows the hardware for read/write heads.

Figure 6.4
Typical disk drive head assemblies.

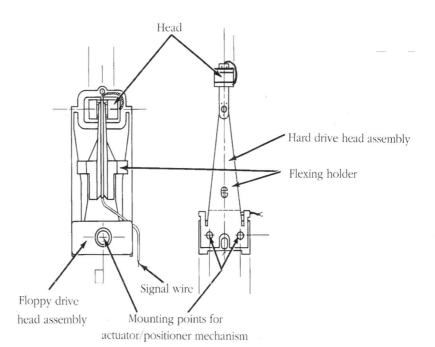

As you can see, the heads are held in place on flexible metal assemblies. Wires that carry electrical signals connect to a flexible ribbon cable. The ribbon cable absorbs wire movements when the head assembly moves back and forth from track to track.

DISK TRACKS

Regardless of the type of disk drive, all disks spin on a center axis, just like a CD spins in your stereo system. A floppy disk spins at 360 revolutions per minute; the rotational speed of a hard disk is 10 times greater (approximately 3,600rpm). The heads, which are positioned above the spinning surface of the disk, are held and moved in distinct steps by an actuator arm and head positioner.

The actuator arm and positioner move the heads over the tracks, which are thin stripes of magnetically recorded information. Magnetic disk tracks are concentric circles, not a spiraling groove. Each track is broken up into areas called *sectors*. As you can see in Figure 6.5, sectors are all the same size physically. At the inside track, the sectors are very close together, but at the outermost track, the edges of the sectors are farther apart.

Figure 6.5
Concentric tracks on a disk's surface; each track is segmented into areas called sectors.

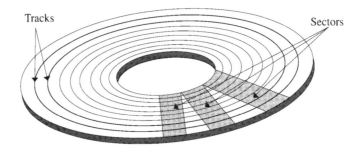

DISK CYLINDERS

A disk drive's multiple heads are affixed to a single positioner mechanism, which can move only in a straight line. When one head moves one track in or out on its side of a platter (or floppy), the other heads all move one track on their respective sides of their respective platters.

If the disk has more than one platter—and most hard disks do—all the heads are positioned on the same track on each of the platters. This alignment of heads on the same track position on different sides of the platters is called a *cylinder*, a term derived from the imaginary shape of the stacked circular tracks at any one stopping point of the positioner mechanism (see Figure 6.6).

On most drives, only one head can be active at one time; the drive must activate all its heads in sequence to write (or read) all tracks across the platters at a particular cylinder position. To fill a cylinder, a four-head drive writes a track with Head 1, Head 2, Head 3, and finally Head 4. The head positioner moves one cylinder, and the sequence repeats. Processing all tracks of a cylinder before moving to the next cylinder is efficient because all the heads are already in new track positions. As you can see, the data for a file is spread across all the platters of a hard disk and on both sides of a floppy.

Another factor that spreads files across disks is *sector interleaving*. Hard disks spin quickly—so quickly that some hard disk mechanisms cannot write a sector and be ready to write the next sector as it spins under the head. If the drive waits for a full revolution of the platter, however, too much time is wasted. For this reason, hard disks use an interleave; that is, they write a sector and then skip two before writing to the third. Interleaves are expressed in ratios, so a hard disk that writes one and skips two has a 1:3 interleave. Some fast drives do not have to wait; they can easily write to the next sector, giving the drive a 1:1 ratio.

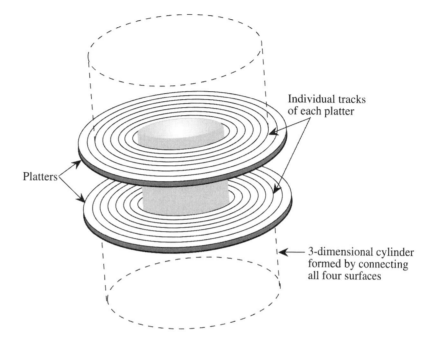

Figure 6.6
Tracks, platters, and cylinder.

When you create files, DOS writes to all the empty sectors on a cylinder and then moves to the closest cylinder with empty sectors. As you use a disk over a period of time, you naturally create and destroy many files.

DOS creates, on the outer tracks of a disk, a table called the *file allocation table* (*FAT*). When you delete a file, DOS simply changes the FAT to mark as vacant the tracks and sectors that the file occupied; the file's directory information is similarly voided. Remember, drives do not have an erase head, so even "erased" files are still present on the disk until you write over them. If you erase a file accidentally, you can use the UNDELETE command or a commercial program such as PC Tools or the Norton Utilities to get it back. Just make sure that nothing writes to the drive before you unerase the file; otherwise, the empty sectors can be used for another file.

→ For more information on UNDELETE, **see** Chapter 8, "Managing Your Files," **p. 191.**

Imagine for a moment that you create a bunch of files on a disk; some are small and some are large. Use the DOS DEL command to delete only the smallest files, and you can free up enough room to store another large file. The empty spaces on the disk are distributed across the disk much like the holes in a slice of Swiss cheese. When you tell DOS to create a new large file, the first cylinder to be written to is the one closest to the head position that currently has available sectors.

When all the sectors on that cylinder are full, the drive moves the heads to another track and fills all the available space on that cylinder. The process continues until all the data in a file is written. The FAT is updated to show the locations of the data. This process of writing data on widely dispersed cylinders is called *file fragmentation*.

File fragmentation is not a dangerous condition, but the constant repositioning of the heads slows the operations of the drive and puts extra strain on the actuator mechanism. For these reasons, DOS offers the DEFRAG command, which rearranges files on the disk so that they are contiguous.

→ For more information on improving your system's performance with DEFRAG, **see** "Defragmenting Your Disk," **p. 177**.

Disk Sectors

When a disk is blank, as it is when it comes from the factory, the disk contains no tracks and, therefore, no information. DOS has to prepare the disk to accept data. This preparation process is known as *formatting*.

As its name implies, formatting places a uniform pattern of format information in all tracks of the disk. The format information in each track enables DOS to slice each track into smaller, more manageable components of fixed size. These components are called *sectors*.

Figure 6.7 shows the sectors of a floppy disk, represented as slices of a disk's surface. The figure shows the boundaries for every other sector. The concentric arcs between the indicated sectors are the disk's tracks. Notice that each track has the same number of sector boundaries (and, therefore, sectors).

Figure 6.7
A visual representation of sectors.

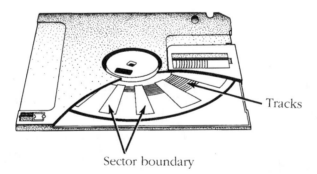

As you can see in Figure 6.7 and previously in Figure 6.5, the arrangement of sectors creates V-shaped areas of the disk that remain unused; these areas are *sector boundaries*. Although you might think that this construction is a waste, it makes the mechanics of drives easier to work with because the sectors are all a uniform size. Having a uniform size for sectors provides DOS with a standard unit of data transmission.

DOS reads and writes disk data one sector at a time. Some of DOS's internal file-system bookkeeping is performed by sectors. To DOS, a sector is the disk's most manageable block of data. By default, DOS uses 512-byte sectors.

The number of sectors formatted into each track is tied to the data density the drive uses when reading or writing data. The more dense the recording in a track and the more tracks on a disk, the more sectors DOS can format. Designers keep reliability in mind when selecting the number of tracks and number of sectors per track. Floppy disk drives are designed with more margin for error than are hard disk drives. You can easily see why some margin for error is desirable for a drive that must ensure the mechanical alignment of disks that users simply shove into the drive door. Floppy disk drives must also be able to read disks that might have been stored in a place where magnetic fields weakened the disk's magnetic imprint.

Despite the protective disk jacket, the magnetic-coated surfaces of many floppy disks can be contaminated by smoke, dust, or fingerprints. A drive must be able to tolerate some disk contamination and still perform without errors. Clearly, no disk drive can avoid errors if the disks it uses are abused. Drive heads cannot read through liquid spills, for example, or through dents made by a ballpoint pen.

Hard disk drives have greater data-storage capacity than do their floppy cousins. This capacity is due in large part to the precision with which the drive's critical components work with the special oxides that magnetically coat the platters. In addition, the working parts of the drive are sealed at the factory in a way that protects the platters, positioners, and heads from contamination. With outside influence on these critical components sealed out, a hard disk drive can offer more tracks and sectors in the same space that a floppy drive occupies. When you consider the fact that most hard disks have more than one platter, each of which is capable of two-sided operation and each of which provides more tracks than a floppy disk can, you begin to understand how hard disks have such large storage capacities.

Understanding Disk Formats

Disk drives have a universal way of dividing a disk's available physical space: The number of platters, number of sides, number of tracks, number of bytes per sector, and number of sectors per track are the specific details that factor into this logical division of disk space. The specification for a disk's use of its physical space is called the disk's *format*.

PCs use a variety of disk drive sizes and formats. Some older PCs, for example, have both 5 1/4-inch and 3 1/2-inch floppy drives that can handle both double-density and high-density disks, while newer PCs only have a 3 1/2-inch floppy.

Most PC users and software manuals differentiate one format from other formats by using the byte-capacity figure for the desired format. Each new version of DOS has maintained support for the disk formats that were supported by its predecessors. This support ensures that disks made with older drive formats can be used with current versions of DOS.

Floppy Disk Formats

The first DOS-supported disk drives allowed for twice as many tracks on a 5 1/4-inch floppy disk as the standard 5 1/4-inch disk formats of the time could accommodate. These DOS formats were called *double-density* formats. The original PC disk size and format was 5 1/4-inch, single-sided, 40 tracks, with eight sectors per track and 512 bytes per sector. These disks are called *single-sided, double-density* (SSDD) disks. The capacity of this 8-sector, single-sided format is 160KB (KB equals 1,024 bytes).

> **Note**
>
> Computers generally store data in groups of eight *bits*. An 8-bit group of data is called a *byte*. By design, digital computers are most efficient when working with numbers as some power of 2. Numbers that are powers of 2 can be represented directly in binary notation.
>
> Computer programmers and designers apply this power-of-2 convention to the expression of a quantity of bytes. A kilobyte, for example, is 1,024 bytes; 2 kilobytes is 2,048 bytes, or 2KB. A megabyte, or 1MB, equals 1,024KB. A gigabyte, or 1GB, is 1,024MB.
>
> You don't have to know about the use of numbers in the power of 2, except to note that capacity expressed in kilobytes, megabytes, or gigabytes uses 1,024 as the multiplier rather than 1,000 because a byte has eight bits, and 1,000 is not evenly divisible by eight. For scaling purposes, however, you can think of 1KB as representing approximately 1,000 bytes.
>
> The capacity of disk drives is stated in kilobytes, megabytes, or gigabytes. The storage capacity of a modern hard disk drive is usually anywhere from 2GB to 80GB. The typical capacity of floppies ranges from hundreds of thousands of bytes to more than 2MB, so a floppy drive's capacity can be described in either kilobytes or megabytes.

As you learned earlier, the two types of 5 1/4-inch floppies have different storage capacities (either 360KB or 1.2MB). Similarly, a 3 1/2-inch disk can store either 720KB or 1.44MB. Still another standard format for 3 1/2-inch disks was introduced a few years ago, offering 2.88MB of storage. To date, this format has not widely caught on because you must have a floppy disk drive and disks manufactured specifically to achieve 2.88MB storage capacity.

Table 6.1 summarizes the common floppy disk formats.

TABLE 6.1   DOS Floppy Disk Formats

Format	Tracks	Sectors/Track	Total Sectors	Usable Capacity
SSDD	40	8	320	160KB
DSDD	40	8	640	320KB
SSDD-9	40	9	360	180KB
DSDD-9	40	9	720	360KB
DSDD-9	80	9	1420	720KB*

Table 6.1 Continued

Format	Tracks	Sectors/Track	Total Sectors	Usable Capacity
DSHD-15	80	15	2400	1.2MB
DSHD-18	80	18	2880	1.44MB*
HD-36	80	36	5760	2.88MB**

*3 1/2-inch formats
**Requires special disk and disk drive

Raw Capacity and Usable Capacity

The process of formatting a blank disk places on the disk some data that is not part of the disk's total capacity. A 1.44MB disk, for example, actually holds more than 1.44MB of information. You cannot use this extra space, however; the space is reserved for sector-identification and error-checking information. If you buy disks for a 1.44MB drive, the identification label might say that the disks have 2MB capacity; disks for a 720KB drive might indicate 1MB capacity. To understand this apparent discrepancy, you need to understand the difference between total, or *raw*, capacity and usable, or *formatted*, capacity. The larger of the two numbers for the same disk is considered to be the *raw capacity* of the disk.

Raw capacity includes the space that the formatting information occupies. The smaller of the two numbers for the same disk is the *usable capacity* of the disk. This number of bytes is available for storing files after the formatting information has been put on the disk.

Hard disk manufacturers sometimes advertise the raw capacity of their drives instead of the usable capacity. Your 80MB drive, therefore, might give you only 78MB when formatted. Fortunately, most manufacturers of hard disks state the capacity of their drives as formatted capacity. Hard disks also lose some overhead space. If you have any doubt as to the meaning of a hard disk's stated capacity, ask the dealer whether the capacity is determined before or after formatting. In this book, disk capacity refers to usable capacity after formatting.

Hard Disk Drive Formats

Formats for hard disks nearly always employ 512-byte sectors, usually with 17 sectors per track. There is an alphabet soup of hard drive types: MFM, IDE, RLL, ESDI, SCSI, and so on. Each type of hard disk uses different numbers of sectors per track. You have to worry about these differences only when you are installing a hard disk drive. The manufacturer of the drive provides you with head, sector, and track information specific to your drive.

You can understand the concept of hard disk capacity by remembering the concept of cylinders. Hard disks, you might recall, have two or more heads. Remember that a cylinder is the alignment of all the heads on the same track on both sides of each platter. A disk with 306 tracks on one side of one platter has 306 cylinders. The total number of tracks on the disk is the number of cylinders times the number of heads. The disk's capacity in bytes is the number of tracks times the number of sectors per track times the number of bytes per sector. To obtain the capacity in kilobytes, divide the result by 1,024. To obtain the capacity in megabytes, divide the kilobyte total by 1,024. For approximations of capacity in megabytes, you can divide by a rounded 1,000.

DOS does not provide low-level format data for a hard disk as it does for a floppy disk. Hard disks normally are given a low-level format at the factory, so you seldom need to initiate a low-level format on a hard disk. DOS uses the low-level format as a base upon which to perform its high-level format.

In a discussion of hard disk formatting, the term *format* refers to the high-level format initiated by the DOS FORMAT command. During the formatting of a hard disk, DOS initializes its bookkeeping tables and then writes dummy data into the disk's tracks. From your point of view, formatting a hard disk is the same basic operation as formatting a floppy. DOS keeps the details of the low-level format hidden and out of your way.

Understanding DoubleSpace

Beginning with DOS 6.0, Microsoft decided to include a disk-compression program called DoubleSpace. The decision to include it was apparently prompted by the popularity and success of third-party disk compression programs such as Stacker. Microsoft refined and improved DoubleSpace in DOS 6.2.

DoubleSpace enables DOS to compress data automatically when you store the data on disk and to uncompress the data when you use it. DoubleSpace works transparently; you have no indication that the program is compressing your files, except that your disk can hold more data than before. You can select which drives use compression and which do not. You might decide, for example, to compress drive C, but not drive D, which contains OS/2.

> **Caution**
> Only if the DoubleSpace driver is loaded can you read a compressed drive. If you use another operating system in addition to DOS—such as OS/2, Unix, Xenix, or Windows NT—you cannot access a compressed drive while you are running that other system.

Using DoubleSpace provides one major advantage: The amount of data you can store on your hard disk is roughly doubled because DoubleSpace is analyzing your data and squeezing more information into less space. DoubleSpace uses a compression algorithm similar to that used in compression programs such as WinZip. The exact amount of additional data you can store varies, depending on the characteristics of the data itself, because different data can be compressed different amounts. Text files and some graphics files (such as TIF files), for instance, can be compressed quite a bit. Other files, such as WAV files (used for sound) or GIF files (used for graphics), are already compressed and do not benefit from DoubleSpace.

Using DoubleSpace also has the following minor disadvantages:

- DoubleSpace must perform extra work to compress and uncompress data each time you access your disk. This extra work takes time and slows your computer slightly. If you have a 386 or 486 computer, for example, the slowdown is so insignificant that you almost certainly will never notice the difference. On slower computers, however, you might notice that operations involving a lot of disk access seem to run a bit more slowly than before.
- DoubleSpace requires some conventional memory—about 50KB if you load DoubleSpace high (into upper memory) by using `DEVICEHIGH`.
- Without the DoubleSpace device driver, a system cannot access a hard disk on which the files are compressed with DoubleSpace. This restriction is not likely to cause problems, but if your computer breaks, you cannot remove your hard disk and use it in a computer that has an earlier version of DOS.
- You cannot use DoubleSpace with some disk-intensive programs. This is primarily evident with some game programs that swap screens and sound between memory and disk.

> **Caution**
> A drive might contain files that cannot or should not be compressed. The Windows swap file, for example, must remain uncompressed.

When you apply compression to a drive, DoubleSpace makes the drive appear as though it were two drives, with two distinct drive letters. DoubleSpace divides the disk into a compressed drive and an uncompressed drive so that you still can store some of your files in an uncompressed format.

You can decide how much of the disk to allocate for each area. If you don't expect to store any files in an uncompressed format, make the uncompressed drive small (a fraction of a megabyte) and allocate the rest to the compressed drive. Conversely, if you expect to store the Windows swap file on the uncompressed drive, allocate several megabytes to that drive.

DOS assigns a new drive letter to one of the areas so that you can access either area by using the appropriate drive letter. If you apply compression to drive C, for example, DoubleSpace might tell you that from now on C refers to the uncompressed portion of the disk and J refers to the compressed portion.

Installing DoubleSpace

To install DoubleSpace, type the following command at the DOS prompt:

DBLSPACE

You must not have any other programs running when you first issue this command. In particular, you must not be running Windows or the DOS Shell.

DoubleSpace first asks whether you want an Express or Custom Setup; the default is Express. If you choose Express, DoubleSpace compresses the existing files on drive C.

Choose Custom Setup if you want to select the drive to compress. DBLSPACE then installs the DoubleSpace driver in the DOS kernel and reboots your machine.

DoubleSpace also might add a line to your CONFIG.SYS file, such as the following:

DEVICEHIGH=C:\DOS\DBLSPACE.SYS /MOVE

This line does not load the DoubleSpace device driver; the DOS kernel loads the driver automatically when you install DoubleSpace. Instead, the line moves the driver into upper memory (if you have upper memory blocks available). If you remove this line from CONFIG.SYS, you still load the DoubleSpace driver, just not into upper memory.

Controlling the Operation of DoubleSpace

You can run DoubleSpace at any time to get information about compression on your disks or to control various facets of DoubleSpace's operation. You run DoubleSpace simply by typing the following command:

DBLSPACE

When DoubleSpace starts, it lists all the available drives that employ compression. For each drive, DoubleSpace shows the total amount of space and current free space available.

Many DoubleSpace operations require you to select a drive, either by using the arrow keys to position the selection bar on one of the drives or by clicking a drive.

Displaying Compressed Drive Information

To display information about a compressed drive, select the compressed drive, choose Drive from the menu bar, and then choose Info from the resulting menu. (If you do not have a mouse, press Alt+D, and then position the cursor on Info and press Enter.) For a shortcut, you can also double-click or simply press Enter when the drive is first selected.

Figure 6.8 shows the information display for a small compressed drive. In this example, notice that most of the disk is allocated for compressed files and is accessed as drive I; about 2MB is uncompressed and is accessed as drive D.

Figure 6.8
DoubleSpace can provide an estimate of free space on a drive based on the current compression ratio of the files.

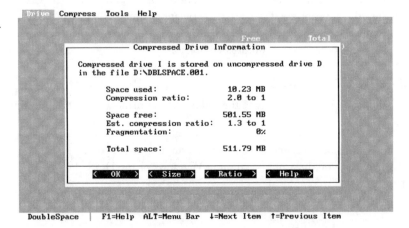

This figure also tells you that the estimate of 501.55MB free is based on a compression ratio of 1.3 to 1, but the compression ratio that DoubleSpace actually has achieved on the data stored so far is 2 to 1. Therefore, if the rest of the drive is used for the same type of data, you actually are capable of storing more data than DoubleSpace's estimate of 501MB leads you to expect.

Clicking the Size and Ratio buttons enables you to change the size of the compressed area and the estimating ratio, respectively. The following sections discuss both methods.

Changing the Size of a Compressed Drive

On each compressed disk, DoubleSpace reserves some room for uncompressed files. To change the size of the uncompressed area (thereby changing the size of the compressed area correspondingly), perform one of the following actions:

- While displaying the Compressed Drive Information dialog box, click the Size button.
- On the main screen, select Drive and then Change Size.

When you perform either action, the Change Size dialog box appears (see Figure 6.9).

Figure 6.9
The Change Size dialog box will appear whenever you modify the size settings of the DoubleSpace drive.

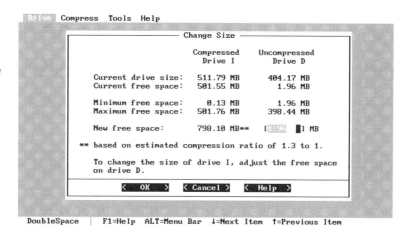

In this dialog box, you can change the amount of space that DoubleSpace reserves for the uncompressed area.

Changing the Compression Ratio

After you use a compressed drive for a time, you might discover that the actual compression ratio achieved by DoubleSpace is different from the ratio it uses to predict free space. You can ask DoubleSpace to use a different ratio to estimate free space by performing one of the following:

- While displaying the Compressed Drive Information dialog box, click the Ratio button.
- On the main screen, choose Drive and then Change Ratio.

DoubleSpace displays the current ratio that it is using for estimates and the actual ratio that it has been able to achieve in compressing your files so far. If the files you previously stored in this drive are typical of the files that you expect to store in the future, you should change the new ratio to match the ratio for stored files.

In the Change Compression Ratio dialog box shown in Figure 6.10, DoubleSpace is using a 1.3-to-1 ratio to estimate free space but has achieved a 2-to-1 ratio for existing files.

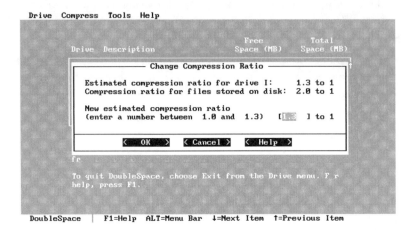

Figure 6.10
You can also modify the compression ration of a DoubleSpace drive.

The amounts of total space and free space that DoubleSpace displays are estimates that depend on the type of data you store on the disk. In predicting free space, DoubleSpace takes into account the size and actual free space of the compressed volume and then determines an estimated compression ratio. The general rule is that the larger the amount of free space on your compressed volume, the lower the compression ratio used by DoubleSpace. Thus, the large compressed volume used as an example in this chapter has a low 1.3-to-1 compression ratio.

If you have a smaller compressed volume, DoubleSpace uses a higher compression ratio, closer to 2 to 1. In other words, if DoubleSpace has 10MB of physical disk space free, the program predicts that it can compress 20MB of your data into that space.

The estimates used by DoubleSpace are necessarily off—sometimes way off. As you work with your compressed volume, you can adjust the compression ratio used by DoubleSpace for its estimates.

> **Note**
> Changing the compression ratio does not change the amount of compression that DoubleSpace can squeeze out of any specific file, only the ratio that DoubleSpace uses to estimate future compression.

Formatting a Compressed Drive

You do not need to format a compressed drive in the same sense that you format other drives to prepare them for use. When you use DoubleSpace to create a compressed drive, you must have already formatted that drive in the usual way. On the other hand, people often format an existing drive as a simple way of erasing all data on a drive, and you can format a compressed drive if you want to erase all the data stored on that drive. However, you cannot use the standard DOS format on a compressed drive.

To format a compressed drive, select the drive you want to format from the list of compressed drives, and then choose Drive and Format. DoubleSpace displays an alert box that asks whether you're sure you want to format the drive. If you click OK, DoubleSpace erases all data stored in that drive.

> **Caution**
> You cannot unformat a compressed drive. After you choose Format and click OK, your data is gone forever.

Deleting a Compressed Drive

If you no longer want to use a compressed drive, you can delete that drive. To do so, select the drive that you want to delete from the list of compressed drives. Next, choose Drive and then Delete. DoubleSpace displays a dialog box warning that you will permanently destroy the contents of the compressed drive and asks you for confirmation. If you click OK, DoubleSpace deletes the drive and all the data in the drive. The space that was allocated to the compressed drive returns to the corresponding uncompressed drive.

> **Caution**
> Make sure you copy all the data from your compressed drive to a backup device or to an uncompressed drive before you delete a compressed drive. You also can use the Uncompress feature, discussed later in this chapter.

Creating a New Compressed Drive

You can create a new compressed drive by choosing an option from the Compress menu. DoubleSpace displays a menu from which you can select either of two ways to compress the disk.

To compress an existing disk and all the data stored on it, follow this procedure:

1. From the Compress menu, choose Existing Drive. DoubleSpace displays a dialog box listing existing uncompressed drives, along with their current and projected free space.

2. Select the drive you want to compress. DoubleSpace displays a dialog box showing the drive letter that it assigns to the uncompressed drive and the amount of space it allocates to that drive. DoubleSpace allocates the rest of the space to the compressed drive.

You must allocate at least 0.14MB to the uncompressed drive; use this value if you do not expect to need any uncompressed space. If you want to change either of these values, select the value that you want to change.

When you are ready to proceed, choose Continue or press Enter.

3. DoubleSpace displays a screen informing you that it is ready to compress the drive. DoubleSpace then prompts you to press C. If you press C, the program creates the compressed drive and compresses existing files in that drive. The new compressed drive uses the original drive letter, and the uncompressed drive receives the new drive letter.

If you want to leave existing files in the uncompressed drive and create a new compressed drive from the free portion of the existing drive, follow this procedure:

1. From the Compress menu, choose Create New Drive. DoubleSpace displays a dialog box listing existing uncompressed drives, along with their current and projected free space.

2. Select the drive to which you want to apply compression. DoubleSpace displays the drive letter it will assign to the compressed drive, the compression ratio it will use to estimate free space, and the amount of free space it will leave in the uncompressed drive, in addition to the space already used by existing files. The program allocates the rest of the space to the compressed drive.

   You must leave at least 0.14MB of free space in the uncompressed drive; use this value if you do not expect to need any more uncompressed space. If you want to change any of these values, click the value you want to change.

   When you are ready to proceed, click Continue or press Enter.

3. DoubleSpace tells you how much time the program requires to create the drive and prompts you to press C to continue. The program then creates the compressed drive, which is empty. All existing files remain in the uncompressed drive. The uncompressed drive retains the original drive letter, and the compressed drive receives the new drive letter.

Using Other DoubleSpace Features

You can choose two other useful features from the Tools menu: Defragment and Uncompress. A Chkdsk option also is available from the Tools menu, but it just displays information indicating that the Chkdsk function has been replaced by the SCANDISK command.

→ To find out more about SCANDISK, **see** "Analyzing a Disk with the SCANDISK Utility," **p. 188**.

The Defragment option enables you to defragment a compressed volume. You can use either this option or the standard DEFRAG command (from the DOS prompt). If you choose to use this option, DoubleSpace displays a dialog box asking whether you want to defragment the disk. If you choose Yes, DoubleSpace performs the defragmentation. Note that defragmenting a compressed disk does not significantly increase the speed with which you can access the disk (as DEFRAG does for a regular disk), but it sometimes does enable you to store a bit more data on the compressed disk.

Beginning with DOS 6.2, DoubleSpace enables you to uncompress a previously compressed drive. You do so by copying the data on a compressed portion of a drive to the uncompressed portion. Before you choose this option, do the following:

- Make sure you reduce the size of the compressed drive as far as possible by using the Size feature previously discussed. Conversely, this action increases the size of the uncompressed portion of the disk.
- Make a backup of your compressed volume.

→ For more information about the MSBACKUP program, **see** "Issuing the MSBACKUP Command," **p. 239**.

> **Caution**
> Uncompressing a DoubleSpace volume can take up to several hours. Make sure you allocate enough free time to complete the procedure.

After you reduce the size of the compressed drive and back it up, choose Uncompress from the Tools menu. DoubleSpace displays a dialog box indicating that it is going to uncompress files and copy them to the uncompressed portion of the hard drive; it also reminds you to make a backup of your compressed data. When you choose Yes, the drive uncompression begins. DoubleSpace then performs the following steps:

1. It performs a surface scan using SCANDISK to determine the reliability of the destination (uncompressed) disk drive.
2. It performs other SCANDISK tests to verify the integrity of the compressed volume.
3. It performs another surface scan, this time on the source (compressed) disk drive.
4. It uncompresses the files on the source drive, moving them to the destination drive.
5. It deletes the compressed drive.
6. If the compressed drive being deleted is the last one in your system, DoubleSpace removes all references to DoubleSpace from CONFIG.SYS and marks the DoubleSpace kernel so that it doesn't load when DOS is booted.
7. It reboots the computer.

After the computer reboots, the uncompression is complete. Check your data to make sure that it all appears intact; then, you can use your system as normal.

> **Tip**
>
> If you have programs that do not work with DoubleSpace, but you still want to enjoy the benefits of disk compression, place the programs on an uncompressed volume. Then, when you need to use those programs, reboot your computer and use the Ctrl+F5 or Ctrl+F8 keys to control whether DoubleSpace capability is loaded.

→ For information on using multiple boot configurations, **see** "Creating Multiple Configurations," **p. 32**.

CASE STUDY: ADJUSTING FOR DRIFT

Drift occurs when the alignment of a hard drive's read/write heads drift slightly after continual use of the drive. Drift also can be detected when you remount the drive or stand the computer on its side like a tower. This drifting does not affect the information that has been written to the disk, but the heads might have difficulty locating the information because the low-level format identification information, which is needed to find the data, is no longer aligned beneath the heads. You can eliminate this problem by performing a low-level format of the disk to align the low-level disk tracks with the current location of the heads. Also, magnetic signals that are recorded on disks lose strength over the years, so the manufacturer's low-level format might fade to a point where the heads cannot reliably read format information.

Normally, a low-level format of your hard disk erases all existing data. Certain types of third-party software, however, can perform a low-level format without data loss.

CHAPTER 7

PREPARING AND MAINTAINING DISKS

In this chapter

Understanding Disk Preparation   150

Preparing Floppy Disks with the FORMAT Command   151

Preparing the Hard Disk   158

Disk Commands   166

Getting the Most Speed from Your Hard Disk   168

Getting the Most Space from Your Hard Disk   181

Projects   184

Understanding Disk Preparation

Both floppy disks and audiocassette tapes use magnetic media to store information, but they're different in other ways. You cannot just drop a blank disk into a drive and use the disk in the same way that you can use a blank tape to record.

Why? The disk's recorded areas (sectors) can be accessed in any order, randomly. The tape, however, is sequential. As it plays, the tape recorder doesn't jump around from place to place—unless, of course, it is being operated by a teenager.

To implement random access on a disk, you first must lay down information that can be used to find small sections of the disk quickly. In some ways, this process is like drawing the lines on a sheet of notebook paper to show where the writing should be done. This preparation process is called *formatting*. The DOS FORMAT command performs this process for disks; you do nothing more than enter the command. FORMAT analyzes a disk for defects, generates a root directory, sets up a storage table, and makes other technical modifications.

When you format a disk, DOS creates data-storage divisions on the disk's surface. As you learned in Chapter 6, "Understanding Disks and Disk Drives," these divisions are concentric circles called *tracks* (see Figure 7.1). DOS decides what type of drive you have and then positions the tracks accordingly.

Figure 7.1
Anatomy of a floppy disk.

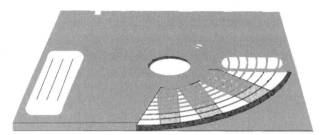

You probably already know that with computers, items that are numbered often begin with 0 rather than 1. It's the same way with tracks on the disk; they're numbered beginning with track 0. DOS uses this first track (track 0) to record vital information about the disk's format. Later, by checking this information on track 0, DOS quickly can determine how to work with the disk.

As you can see in Figure 7.1, each track is divided into segments called *sectors*, which are the smallest divisions of a disk. When you issue the FORMAT command, DOS creates a special disk table called the *file allocation table* (*FAT*). The FAT, which is always located on track 0, monitors every sector on a disk as groups of clusters. DOS stores data in the clusters and uses the track and cluster numbers to retrieve the data.

A *cluster* is the smallest unit of storage that DOS allocates for file storage at one time, unless you are using DoubleSpace or a similar file-compression utility. DoubleSpace drives have storage allocated in smaller units, but this doesn't affect the way DOS views the disk. DOS hands data to be written to DoubleSpace in the standard way.

In the preceding chapter, you learned about cylinders. A cylinder is formed by stacking tracks on top of one another. A cylinder on a floppy disk, for example, is made by stacking two tracks: the front and back of the disk. The two read/write heads in the floppy drive are positioned over two tracks. Tracks are broken up into sectors, so the read/write heads are positioned over two sectors.

DOS does not write one file on the front sector and one file on the back sector because doing so creates a situation in which the read/write heads have to move around too much, slowing operations. To prevent this problem, DOS looks at the two sectors under the floppy drive's heads as a single unit—a cluster. Therefore, if you write a file containing only six bytes onto a floppy disk, DOS reserves a cluster (two 512-byte sectors) for the file to reside in.

On hard disks, the number of sectors in a cluster also is equal to the number of read/write heads. Therefore, a disk with four platters would group eight sectors into a cluster, so writing a six-byte file would actually take 4KB of free space.

At first, all this unused space might seem wasted, but look at any disk and see how many files are only six bytes long. Data files are seldom static because information constantly is being added or removed. Chances are that the file won't remain six bytes long. Also, when you think that most files are thousands or hundreds of thousands of bytes long, a few unused sectors represent a very small percentage of total used disk space.

All DOS commands use tracks and clusters as road maps that enable them to carry out their operations. When a disk is formatted, DOS creates a FAT and root directory that are suited to the capacity of the disk.

Preparing Floppy Disks with the FORMAT Command

The FORMAT command prepares disks for use. All disks to be used by DOS must be formatted by DOS to be treated as valid DOS disks. Both floppies and hard disks must be formatted before they can be used. If you try to use a disk that has not been formatted, DOS reports a General failure, which sounds cataclysmic. All it really means is that the disk you are trying to read does not have valid format information. If the disk you are trying to read has been formatted and you know that it has been formatted, a problem exists. If that drive is your C: drive, you do have a cataclysmic experience to endure. Most of the time, however, a General failure just means that somebody has handed you an unformatted disk.

> **Caution**
>
> When you issue the FORMAT command with its required parameters, DOS presents you with a prompt, requiring that you answer a question before the command actually begins its work. In the case of a floppy, DOS prompts you to insert the proper disk into the drive. On a hard disk, DOS reminds you that you are about to wipe out everything on the disk.
>
> In either case, the tendency of experienced users is just to hit the key and go. *Don't!* Take a deep breath and read the prompt. You might have accidentally specified C: when you really meant B:. Take a moment to be sure; the data you save might be your own.

Reformatting an old disk also can be an efficient way to delete the contents without the hassle of dealing with individual files and directories. Before DOS 5.0, reformatting a disk in effect erased the data stored on the disk and left you with no way of getting it back. Starting with DOS 5.0, however, the FORMAT command first determines whether the disk contains data. If the disk contains data, FORMAT saves a copy of the boot sector, FAT, and root directory in a safe place on the disk. Then UNFORMAT can find the information if you need to unformat the disk. You can unformat a disk only if you have not created or copied other files onto the disk.

In DOS 5.0 (or later), the FORMAT command clears the disk's FAT and the first character of each filename in the root directory but does not erase any data. The program also scans the entire disk for bad sectors. FORMAT then saves the first letter of each filename in a safe place on the disk.

> **Caution**
>
> FORMAT is a DOS command that can quickly wipe out the contents of a disk. This command is safer than it used to be, but before you use it, make sure that you are familiar with its syntax and the way it works. FORMAT issues warning messages onscreen and prompts you for verification before formatting a hard disk. Take care when you use FORMAT, read the screen prompts, and, most importantly, keep good backups of your data.
>
> Also, the FORMAT command cannot format a disk that has been write-protected. If the command fails for this reason, determine what the disk contains before simply unprotecting the disk and proceeding with the format.

Formatting Floppy Disks

Most disks you buy today come preformatted. If not, then they must first be formatted by DOS before using them. Some commands, such as DISKCOPY and BACKUP, stop and format disks if they're given unformatted disks to work with, but few DOS commands are so accommodating.

The syntax for the FORMAT command is as follows:

FORMAT d: /Q /V:label /F:size /S /B /C /U /1 /4 /8 /N:sectors /T:tracks

This syntax shows all the switches available with the FORMAT command, but you normally use only a few of them at a time. (All the FORMAT switches are discussed in the section "Using FORMAT's Switches," later in this chapter.)

You use the simplest version of the FORMAT command when you are formatting a floppy disk that has the maximum capacity of which the drive is capable, as in the following example:

FORMAT A:

This command formats a nonbootable disk in the A: drive. If you are formatting a 360KB disk in a drive whose maximum capacity is 360KB, or if you are formatting a 1.2MB floppy in a high-density drive, fine. If, however, you are formatting a 360KB disk in a 1.2MB drive, you have to give the FORMAT command that information. To tell the FORMAT command the desired format size of the disk, use the /F switch. The /F switch is followed by a colon (:) and the size of the disk to be formatted, as in the following line:

```
FORMAT A: /F:360
```

This command formats a double-density 5 1/4-inch disk in a high-density drive. Similarly, the following formats a double-density 3 1/2-inch disk in a high-density drive:

```
FORMAT A: /F:720
```

Remember, if you are formatting a high-density disk in a high-density drive, you do not have to give FORMAT the /F switch. Table 7.1 provides the valid values you can enter as part of the /F switch.

TABLE 7.1   ACCEPTABLE /F SWITCH SETTINGS FOR FLOPPY DISKS OF VARIOUS CAPACITIES

Size	Can Be Entered As (Select One)					
160KB	160	160K	160KB			
180KB	180	180K	180KB			
320KB	320	320K	320KB			
360KB	360	360K	360KB			
720KB	720	720K	720KB			
1.20MB	1200	1200K	1200KB	1.2	1.2M	1.2MB
1.44MB	1440	1440K	1440KB	1.44	1.44M	1.44MB
2.88MB	2880	2880K	2880KB	2.88	2.88M	2.88MB

Telling the Capacity of Disks by Sight
With 5 1/4-inch disks, you easily can tell the difference between 360KB disks and 1.2MB high-density disks: The 360KB disks have a plastic reinforcement ring around the large hole in the center of the disk, whereas high-density disks do not have a hub ring. Other than that small difference, however, they look the same.

When looking at 3 1/2-inch disks, you can easily identify 1.44MB high-density disks because they have a second square hole on the edge opposite the write-protect tab's hole. A 720KB double-density disk has only one hole, for the write-protect tab.

You cannot arbitrarily decide to format a double-density disk as a high-density disk. If you try to format a 720KB disk as a high-density 1.44MB disk, DOS tells you how to proceed, as shown here:

```
D:\>FORMAT B: /F:1440
Insert new diskette for drive B:
and press ENTER when ready...

Checking existing disk format.
Existing format differs from that specified.
This disk cannot be unformatted.
```

```
Proceed with Format (Y/N)?y
Formatting 1.44M
Invalid media or Track 0 bad - disk unusable.
Format terminated.
Format another (Y/N)?
```

As you can see, DOS asks whether you want to format another disk. Just make sure it is a disk with a capacity matching the /F switch's value.

Similarly, you cannot format a 2.88MB disk if your floppy drive doesn't support it, even if you have a 2.88MB disk in hand. If you attempt this action, you see the following messages:

```
D:\>FORMAT B: /F:2880
Insert new diskette for drive B:
and press ENTER when ready...

Checking existing disk format.
Existing format differs from that specified.
This disk cannot be unformatted.
Proceed with Format (Y/N)?y
Formatting 2.88M
Parameters not supported by drive.
```

Other switches can be added to the command line to provide other formatting services. You can use the following command line, for example, to format a bootable 720KB disk in a 1.44MB drive:

```
FORMAT B: /F:720 /S
```

When you add the /S (System) switch, FORMAT creates a bootable disk.

FORMAT'S OTHER TASKS

The primary task of the FORMAT command is to divide the disk into logical storage sectors, but this task is not the command's only purpose. FORMAT gives each disk a unique serial number and prompts you for a volume label (name) for the disk. As the formatting proceeds, FORMAT continually updates what percentage of the disk has been formatted.

Assume for the moment that you have issued the command in the preceding section to format a 720KB bootable disk. The following lines show the FORMAT dialog from start to finish:

```
C:\>FORMAT B: /F:720 /S
Insert new diskette for drive B:
and press ENTER when ready...

Checking existing disk format.
Formatting 720K
Format complete.
System transferred

Volume label (11 characters, ENTER for none)? bootable

     730,112 bytes total disk space
     199,680 bytes used by system
     530,432 bytes available on disk
```

```
          1,024 bytes in each allocation unit.
             518 allocation units available on disk.

Volume Serial Number is 1F44-0EE0

Format another (Y/N)?
```

When you press Enter to begin formatting, FORMAT first displays a two-line prompt, telling you to enter a disk in drive B. Always make sure that this is what you intend. Next, FORMAT must perform several steps.

The first of these steps is to check the disk format and preserve the FAT and directory structures in case you need to use the UNFORMAT command. Formatting then begins, and FORMAT ticks off the percentage of completion until the format is finished. You are told that the format is complete and nominally error free. If you use the /S switch, the boot sector is prepared, and the DOS system files are transferred to the disk.

You then are prompted to provide a volume label. Most users simply press Enter to bypass this option, but you can use the volume label to your advantage in creating a cataloging system for your disks. You might want to name floppy disks according to categories such as budget, correspondence, backups, and so on.

When you press Enter to leave the Volume label prompt, FORMAT displays some relevant numbers about the disk. The first line shows the total capacity of the disk. If you create a bootable disk, the second line shows the amount of space taken up by the DOS system files. You also are shown the amount of remaining free space on the disk.

> **Caution**
> As you can tell by examining the information provided by FORMAT, the DOS system files take up almost 200KB of space on a newly formatted disk. Don't use the /S switch carelessly. This switch is intended only for the disks with which you plan to start the computer. Making disks bootable unnecessarily is a major waste of space.

FORMAT then provides you with numerical data on what it calls *allocation units*. In this context, saying *allocation units* is just a fancy way of saying *clusters*. Each sector is 512 bytes, and a floppy disk has two read/write heads; therefore, a cluster is 1,024 bytes in length. The second line tells you that 518 clusters are available. Multiply 518 and 1,024, and you get 530,432, exactly the amount of free space shown by FORMAT.

> **Note**
> As reliable as floppy disks are, they sometimes have flaws. If you hear an unusual grinding or churning noise while formatting a disk, the disk is probably damaged or has an excessive number of flaws. Any bad sectors found by FORMAT are reported as part of the numerical data.
> Depending on the number of flaws that are found, you might want to reformat the disk, throw it away, or use it only for noncritical storage.

> **Cleanliness Is Next to Godliness**
>
> Just as you must occasionally clean the heads in a cassette deck or VCR, you should clean the read/write heads in your floppy drives every once in a while. How often depends on whether you are getting errors on the drive, on the environment your computer lives in, and on how much you use the floppy drive.
>
> Problems with reading a nearly full disk almost always indicate the need to clean the drive. Sectors near the hub are much closer together than the sectors of Track 1, and they are the first to display errors related to unclean heads.
>
> Computer retailers sell various disk drive cleaning products. Most have a cleaning pad encased in a floppy disk jacket. You squeeze a few drops of an alcohol-based cleaning fluid onto the cleaning pad and insert the disk into the drive. To begin cleaning, you issue a command such as `DIR A:` that causes DOS to try to read the disk, and the heads are scraped clean. Check with your computer supply vendor for more information on floppy drive cleaning.
>
> Because your hard disk is sealed at the factory, you *never* have to clean its heads. Don't even think about it.

The last thing the FORMAT routine does is to assign a serial number to the disk. The purpose of a serial number is to enable programs to determine whether you have switched disks. The serial number, which is assigned automatically during formatting, uses the time and date of the format to create a hexadecimal number to be used as the serial number. No two disks from the same machine should ever have the same serial number, assuming that the system clock is properly set.

Finally, FORMAT offers to process another disk. By choosing this option, you can format more than one disk at a time. If you answer yes to the prompt by pressing Y and then Enter, FORMAT prompts you to place another disk in the drive. Any subsequently formatted disks will have the same attributes as the command-line parameters you entered to start the command. Only the serial numbers will be different.

Using FORMAT's Switches

The FORMAT command responds to several switches that modify its behavior. Table 7.2 provides a list of the available switches in the FORMAT syntax. Detailed information also is available in Appendix F, "Command Reference."

> **A True Story**
>
> Computer retailers have many wonderful stories to tell. This incident happened in Florida.
>
> A woman called the computer store and asked to speak to the manager. She was connected to the owner, who asked how he could help her. The following conversation ensued:
>
> "I was just in a different store and bought a box of floppy disks."
>
> "Yes, ma'am."
>
> "Well, the salesman there suggested that I format all the disks in the box so that they would all be formatted when I need one."
>
> "That's not a bad idea. Is there a problem?"
>
> "Well, I don't know. I barely got the third one in. I can't imagine getting the fourth one in; it's too tight, and there are 10 disks in the box."

"Can you hold on?"

Somehow the owner of the store managed to get the phone on hold before rolling out of his chair to the floor in a laughing fit. Needless to say, all activity in the store stopped as employees and customers gathered around the owner to hear the resolution.

In the end, a service technician was dispatched to her place of business. The mangled disks were successfully removed without damaging the drive, and the owner charged her only half the normal service charge out of pity.

The moral of this story is that when you read that you can format more than one disk at a time, don't take this advice literally.

TABLE 7.2 COMMONLY USED FORMAT SWITCHES

Switch	Action
/B	Allocates space on the formatted disk for system files by creating hidden files of the same name and size on track 0. Used to create disks that can be made bootable with DOS 4.01 and earlier versions.
/F:size	Specifies the size of the floppy disk to be formatted (such as 160, 180, 320, 360, 720, 1.2, 1.44, and 2.88). You can specify kilobytes or megabytes if you prefer, but doing so is not necessary because DOS understands all the parameters shown here.
/Q	Performs a quick format on a previously formatted disk. This switch effectively and quickly erases the contents of a disk so that it can be used again.
/S	Copies the system files and COMMAND.COM to the formatted disk, creating a bootable disk.
/U	Performs an unconditional format so that the disk cannot be unformatted with UNFORMAT.
/N:sectors	Enables you to specify the number of sectors per track (between 1 and 99). This switch now is obsolete and has been replaced with the /F:size switch.
/T:tracks	Specifies the number of tracks per disk side (between 1 and 999). This switch now is obsolete and has been replaced with the /F:size switch.
/V:label	Enables you to specify the volume label without waiting for a prompt.
/C	Retests a block previously marked as bad.
/1	Creates single-sided disks. This switch now is obsolete.
/4	Provides a shortcut for formatting a 5 1/4-inch 360KB floppy disk in a high-density drive. This switch does the same thing as specifying /F:360.
/8	Creates disks that are compatible with early versions of DOS that used 8 sectors per track rather than the 9 or 15 used today. This switch now is obsolete.

The following sections describe some of the ways in which you can use the FORMAT command's switches.

PERFORMING A QUICK FORMAT (/Q)

One way to clear all data from a disk is to format the disk. Because the formatting procedure can be relatively slow, the Quick Format feature was introduced.

Using a Quick Format saves you the hassle of changing the attributes of read-only files so that they can be deleted. A Quick Format also gets rid of directories without the laborious process of deleting all subordinate files and directories.

To clear data from a disk, type the command FORMAT /Q and then press Enter. If FORMAT cannot give a disk a Quick Format, a prompt appears, asking whether you want to do a regular format.

Performing an Unconditional Format (/U)

Unless you use the /U switch, the FORMAT command performs a safe format of previously formatted disks. FORMAT first determines whether a disk has been formatted. If the disk has been formatted, FORMAT clears the FAT, boot record, and root directory but does not erase any data. FORMAT then scans the entire disk for bad sectors and saves a copy of the FAT, boot record, and root directory to a MIRROR image file where the UNFORMAT command can find them. If the disk has not been formatted previously, FORMAT overwrites every data byte with the hexadecimal value F6.

If you want DOS to overwrite all data on a previously formatted floppy disk (a procedure called *unconditional formatting*), use the /U switch. The following command, for example, unconditionally formats a disk in drive A:

FORMAT A: /U

Adding System Files (/S)

If you want to use a disk to start your computer, the disk must contain hidden DOS system files as well as the command processor (COMMAND.COM). One way to install these system files on a disk is to use the /S switch during the formatting procedure. The /S switch reduces the disk's available storage capacity by about 185KB.

→ For details on the /S switch, **see** Chapter 2, "Starting DOS," **p. 23**.

> **Caution**
> Don't use the /S switch with FORMAT unless you plan to create a disk from which you can boot. Having at least one bootable system disk as a backup is important in case the disk that contains your working copy of DOS fails or your hard drive develops errors.

Preparing the Hard Disk

Quite apart from the normal formatting that must be done to any DOS disk, hard disks require a little bit of extra work to get them ready for use. DOS provides the FDISK command to prepare a hard disk to be formatted.

The following sections explain how DOS divides and formats a hard disk. If you are relatively inexperienced, be sure to heed all warnings and read all explanations carefully. You are moving into potentially dangerous territory when you start playing around with FDISK.

However, if you are determined to experiment with FDISK, make sure that you have a good backup of everything on the disk.

> **Caution**
>
> Many computer dealers preinstall DOS, Windows, and other programs you purchase. In all cases, you should have copies of these programs on their original floppy disks, or more common nowadays, CD-ROM. Without such disks, you do not have a legal copy of the program. If your dealer has installed an application, such as a word processing program, do not format the hard disk unless you also have a copy of the program on CD-ROM or floppy disks. If you reformat your hard disk, all programs and data will be erased.

Dividing a Hard Disk with FDISK

Before you can format a hard disk, you must partition it—that is, divide the hard disk logically into one or more areas called *partitions*. A partition is simply a section of the storage area of a hard disk. Many operating systems, including DOS, can use disk partitions, and most systems have some utility program that creates and manages partitions. In DOS, that utility program is the external command FDISK.

> **Note**
>
> Many computer dealers use FDISK on a system's hard disk before delivering the system to the user. In addition, FDISK is executed automatically by the DOS 6.22 Setup command during installation. If your hard disk contains files, it has already been partitioned with FDISK and formatted. If you have any questions about your hard disk's preparation, consult your dealer.

Most hard disk users choose a DOS partition size that encompasses the entire hard disk. In other words, the one physical hard disk appears to DOS to be one logical hard disk. In this day of rapid growth in the size of the ordinary hard disk, you might want to rethink the idea of making a single volume out of a disk that might span many thousands of megabytes. You might find it more manageable to have several partitions of smaller sizes.

DOS uses a partition table to store information on how the space on a hard disk is arranged. FDISK is the command that manipulates the information in the table.

Some PC users want to have both DOS and another operating system on their hard disk. Different operating systems use file systems that might not be compatible with DOS. Some operating systems, for example, can use file systems that are compatible with DOS-OS/2 and Windows NT. Some operating systems that have DOS-compatible file structures can use multiboot routines that give the user the opportunity to select which operating system to boot. The incompatibility comes into play only when you are using totally foreign operating systems that must reside in different partitions. FDISK, however, only can create DOS partitions and reserve spaces on the disk; another operating system's equivalent utility can be used to prepare the partition for its own file scheme.

The partition table can be arranged so that DOS uses one partitioned section while another operating system, such as Unix, uses the other partitioned section. Through separation, each operating system sees its partition as its own hard disk. Only one of these partitions, however, can be bootable. To use a partition with another operating system, you have to boot from a floppy when using the other operating system.

Fortunately, DOS installations that require a second operating system are rare. The rest of this chapter pertains to the 99.9% of installations in which DOS is the only operating system in use.

As you probably remember from an earlier chapter, DOS looks at disk drives as logical devices. A byproduct of this arrangement is the fact that you can use FDISK to carve up a single large hard disk into smaller, more manageable volumes. Each volume has its own drive letter and, for all practical purposes, becomes a separate hard disk.

> **Note**
>
> Although making a large hard disk into a single logical drive might seem tempting, doing so might create some disadvantages. If your hard drive is especially large, any command that scans the entire drive, such as DIR or CHKDSK, might take an inordinately long time to complete execution. Files might become harder to find due to their sheer numbers. Unless you work with very large data files, you might prefer to limit your logical drives to 120MB or smaller.

The FDISK command has no parameters. To start this utility, you simply type FDISK and press Enter.

In DOS 3.3 and later versions, you can use FDISK to create more than one DOS partition. After you create a primary DOS partition (or boot disk) with FDISK, you can create an extended DOS partition, which you can divide into one or more logical drives.

After you have created your partitions, you must use the FORMAT command to format all DOS partitions and logical drives before you can use them.

> **Caution**
>
> You can use the FDISK command to delete an existing partition from the disk partition table. If you delete an existing partition, you lose all data in the files contained in that partition. Be sure that you have backed up or copied any data from a partition that you want to delete. FDISK is not a command to experiment with unless your hard disk contains no data.

There are two types of partitions: the *primary* partition, from which the computer can boot, and an *extended* partition, which you can divide into logical drives. The primary DOS partition is normally assigned the drive name C. The extended partition can be used to create drives D, E, F, and so on.

After you partition the hard disk, DOS treats the logical drives as separate drives and creates a file system for each when the drive is formatted. Figure 7.2 shows the opening screen that appears when you run `FDISK`.

Figure 7.2
`FDISK` partitions your hard disk so that DOS can use it efficiently.

```
                        MS-DOS Version 6.2
                      Fixed Disk Setup Program
                   Copyright Microsoft Corp. 1983 - 1993

                            FDISK Options

Current fixed disk drive: 1

Choose one of the following:

1. Create DOS partition or Logical DOS Drive
2. Set active partition
3. Delete partition or Logical DOS Drive
4. Display partition information
5. Change current fixed disk drive


Enter choice: [1]




Press Esc to exit FDISK
```

As you can see, the Create option is the offered default; the number for this option appears within the brackets following the `Enter choice` prompt. You won't destroy the data on your disk if you accidentally choose this option; `FDISK` will simply beep and inform you that you have already created partitions.

Caution
The third choice enables you to delete partitions. Unless something is wrong with your system or you are deliberately reconfiguring a drive, leave this one alone! Deleting partitions results in data loss.

To see how your hard disk is partitioned, press 4 to select Display Partition Information and then press Enter. `FDISK` presents a screen similar to the one shown in Figure 7.3. The information shown by your computer, of course, will be different.

Figure 7.3 shows the `FDISK` display output for the hard disk that was used in writing this chapter. Note that this disk has two partitions, both dedicated to DOS format. The first acts as the C: drive. The A under status indicates that it is the active partition and that it can be used for booting. This drive—drive C—is 32MB in size, uses the standard DOS FAT 16-bit architecture, and takes up only 10% of the hard disk's available space.

Figure 7.3
Partition information as displayed by FDISK.

```
                    Display Partition Information

Current fixed disk drive: 1

Partition  Status   Type      Volume Label   Mbytes   System    Usage
  C: 1       A      PRI DOS   DATA-TRAIN       32     FAT16      10%
     2              EXT DOS                   289                90%



Total disk space is  321 Mbytes (1 Mbyte = 1048576 bytes)


The Extended DOS Partition contains Logical DOS Drives.
Do you want to display the logical drive information (Y/N)......?[Y]




Press Esc to return to FDISK Options
```

Figure 7.3 also shows that an extended partition of 289MB takes up the rest of the drive. As the bottom of the FDISK display indicates, this partition is used to create logical drives. To see what logical drives have been created in the extended partition, you only have to press Enter because Y, the default value, is already displayed. To return to the main FDISK screen, press Esc. Figure 7.4 shows the makeup of the extended DOS partition.

Figure 7.4
Extended partitions can be used to carve the hard disk into logical drives.

```
                 Display Logical DOS Drive Information

Drv  Volume Label   Mbytes   System   Usage
 D:  MAXTOR_D        100     FAT16     35%
 E:  MAXTOR_E         50     FAT16     17%
 F:  MAXTOR_F         50     FAT16     17%
 G:  MAXTOR_G         50     FAT16     17%
 H:  MAXTOR_H         38     FAT16     13%




Total Extended DOS Partition size is  289 Mbytes (1 MByte = 1048576 bytes)



Press Esc to continue
```

The logical drive information shown in Figure 7.4 indicates that the 289MB contained in the partition is divided into five logical drives, D: through H:. The size of each of the logical drives is shown and marked as having the standard DOS file allocation table. The Usage column indicates the relative sizes in relation to the partition, not the disk as a whole. Sharp-eyed readers will notice that the usage numbers add up to only 99%; FDISK rounds off fractional percentages.

By examining the information in Figures 7.3 and 7.4, you can tell that the drive has 321MB of usable capacity broken into six drive letters, C: through H:. The rationale behind these settings and the relative sizes of the drives is as follows.

Drive C takes the biggest pounding. Because it is the boot drive, almost every commercial software package you install tries to make changes or install drivers on the C: drive. C: also is the traditional home of the DOS directory in which DOS's external command program files are written and of directories used to store utility programs such as Norton Utilities and PC Tools. Plus, C: usually houses a TEMP directory, where many software packages look for disk resources to use as a scratch pad. Windows Print Manager, for example, uses the TEMP directory to spool printing jobs into a file so that it can send data to the printer in the background. The drive is just large enough to accommodate all these uses and provide space to install software for testing, yet it's small enough to back up easily. Unproven software sometimes eats the disk it's installed on, so easy restoration of backup files is a key factor in the size of the C: drive.

Drive D on the hard disk is the Windows drive. Windows software tends to be large, as is Windows itself. When you use DoubleSpace, the 100MB of reported space becomes closer to 200MB—almost enough to do the job. Drives E and F store applications and the overflow from drive D. On drives E and F, you find word processors, programming editors, communications programs, and so on. Drive G is given over to graphics programs and files. Drive H is a programming disk where source code to programs is written. *Source code* is the term used for the files that contain programming language statements compiled into working EXE and COM files.

As you can see, the partitions of this hard disk have been thought out in advance. Utilizing disk space effectively is the first step in optimizing DOS's efficiency. Before you partition a hard disk, analyze the ways in which you use a computer. If you do desktop publishing, use Windows; if you do database work on large files, you might want to partition the disk into fewer drives with larger capacities. One key point to keep in mind is that partitions should be small enough to enable you to make backups easily.

Checking Partition Status

You can check the status of your partition table by using the FDISK command's /STATUS switch as follows:

FDISK /STATUS

FDISK shows a table of your hard disk's partition information without starting the FDISK program (see Figure 7.5).

Figure 7.5
Displaying disk partition information.

```
Fixed Disk Drive Status
Disk   Drv    Mbytes    Free    Usage
  1                321       0     100%
        C:       32
        D:      100
        E:       50
        F:       50
        G:       50
        H:       38




        (1 MByte = 1048576 bytes)  C:\>chkdsk
```

> **Caution** The next section of this chapter contains specific information about creating partitions with FDISK. Performing the steps given in the example will destroy the data on your hard disk. Do not practice these steps unless you have reliable backups of all the data on all the drives of your hard disk. If you can, practice first on a hard disk that is not currently loaded with data.

PARTITIONING A DRIVE

The steps required for partitioning a hard disk for the first time and those required for repartitioning a drive to change the structures of the logical drives are very similar.

If you are repartitioning an existing hard disk structure, make sure that you have a rock-solid backup of all the files on the disk. If you plan to change the sizes of logical drives, back up individual directories rather than perform a whole-drive backup.

The actions shown in this section should be performed only by experienced users of DOS. Not knowing what you are doing can cost you all the files on your hard disk. After you have your backups safely stored away and have a bootable floppy containing FDISK and FORMAT, follow these steps to repartition your hard disk:

1. **Plan the partitions.** Decide how you want the partitioning to be done. Create a chart on paper and apportion the available disk space among the partitions you want to create.
2. **Start FDISK.** If you are repartitioning a drive that is currently partitioned, choose to delete existing partitions from the main FDISK menu. After the existing partitions have been deleted, the drive will be unusable until you repartition and reformat.

3. **Create the primary partition.** Select Create DOS Partition from the FDISK main screen. If the drive does not have any existing partitions, a menu appears. Choose 1 to create the partition to act as drive C. By default, FDISK offers the entire disk capacity for the primary partition. If you want to break the hard drive into multiple logical drives, answer N to the confirmation prompt and press Enter.

   FDISK enables you to enter capacities for partitions as megabytes or as a percentage. Choose one method or the other, and then assign the amount of space you want C: to have and return to the main FDISK menu.

4. **Make the primary partition the active partition.** Choose Set Active Partition from the FDISK main menu to make C: the active partition to be made bootable.

5. **Create the extended partition.** Again, choose Create from the main menu, but this time choose to Create Extended DOS partition. Again, FDISK offers to make the remaining disk space the size of the partition. If you want just C: and D:, accept the default. If you want to create more than one logical drive, reject the default and follow the prompts to specify the size of the partition to be used for D:.

6. **Create logical drives.** If you finish creating a partition and disk sectors still are not assigned to a partition, FDISK loops around to create another logical drive. It offers to use all remaining space for the logical drive. If you want to break the remaining space into more than one drive, answer N to reject the default and enter a value manually. When you create the last logical drive, accept the default to make sure that no usable cylinders are left out of the partition table.

7. **Format each logical drive.** After you have set up the partitions the way you want them, exit FDISK and save the partition table. Reboot the computer using your bootable floppy and then format each of the logical drives you have created. Remember to format C: using the /S switch to make it bootable.

8. **Reboot and check the drives.** After you have formatted each of the logical drives, reboot the computer from the hard disk and run directories of all the logical drives to make sure that they were created the way you intended and that they are recognized as valid DOS drives.

9. **Install files.** If you are repartitioning a drive or installing a new hard disk on an existing system, restore all the backups you made, including the DOS files on the boot drive and the files in the DOS directory.

   If you are installing a new system, install DOS and then begin installing any software packages that have to reside on the hard disk of the computer.

10. **Test, test, test.** Before you pronounce the job finished, reboot from the hard disk, test all the software that you installed, and make sure that all configuration files, drivers, and so on are actually written at the locations specified by entries in CONFIG.SYS and AUTOEXEC.BAT.

Formatting a Hard Disk

Simply stated, you format a hard disk or logical drive just like you format a floppy disk.

Assume that the hard disk (or logical disk) you are going to format is drive C. (If you are formatting another drive, use its drive letter in place of C in the example.) If your drive is not the primary DOS partition, you don't have to use the /S switch; DOS boots only from the primary DOS partition. To format drive C, follow these steps:

1. Insert your working copy of the DOS Startup disk—or any bootable disk that contains FORMAT.COM—into drive A.
2. Switch to that drive by typing A: and pressing Enter.
3. Type the following command and press Enter:
   FORMAT C:/S

   FORMAT issues the following warning message and confirmation prompt:
   ```
   WARNING, ALL DATA ON NON-REMOVABLE DISK
   DRIVE C: WILL BE LOST!
   Proceed with Format (Y/N)?
   ```

   This prompt is extremely important. When the prompt appears onscreen, examine it carefully to confirm the disk-drive name (letter) before you press Y. If you make a habit of pressing Y in response to the confirmation prompts of less dangerous commands, you might make a serious mistake with this final FORMAT confirmation prompt.

4. If the specified drive is the one you want to format, press Y; if not, press N to terminate FORMAT. If you press Y, FORMAT updates the display with progress reports on the formatting operation. Depending on the size of the disk that is being formatted, the process can take from just a few minutes to more than half an hour. The greater a disk's capacity, the longer the process takes.

All the normal Format complete and System transferred messages that you see when formatting floppies also are presented when you are formatting a hard disk.

Disk Commands

Several useful DOS commands can help you prepare and maintain disks. The following sections are devoted to these commands.

Naming Disks with Label

The external command LABEL adds, modifies, or changes a disk's volume label. In DOS, a volume label is a name given to a physical or logical disk.

If a disk's volume label is blank (if you or another user pressed Enter when FORMAT or LABEL prompted for the label), you can use the LABEL command to add a volume label or change the current volume label.

DOS displays the volume label when you issue commands such as VOL, CHKDSK, DIR, and TREE. Giving each disk—physical or logical—a volume label is a good idea. A disk with a unique volume label is easier to identify than one that doesn't have a label.

The syntax for the LABEL command is as follows:

LABEL *d*:*label*

d: is the name of the drive that holds the disk you want to label.

label, the optional label text that you supply as the new volume label, can include up to 11 characters. DOS immediately updates the specified or default drive's label with no warning prompt. If you do not supply the *label* parameter, LABEL automatically goes into an interactive mode that prompts you for a new label.

Keep in mind this special restriction: You cannot use the LABEL command in a networked drive.

Examining Volume Labels with VOL

The internal command VOL is convenient when you want to view a disk's volume label or verify that a label exists. VOL accesses the disk's volume label from the root directory and then displays the label that was created during the disk's formatting or modified by a subsequent LABEL command.

You can use VOL freely because it is a display-only command; it does not change any files or the label name.

The syntax of the VOL command is simple:

VOL *d*:

d: is the optional name of the drive whose volume label you want to see. If you omit a value for *d*:, DOS displays the label for the default drive.

Using SYS to Transfer the DOS System

All DOS disks have a DOS file system, but only disks with the DOS system files and COMMAND.COM can be used to start the computer. The external command SYS transfers (copies) the hidden system files necessary to make a disk bootable.

As you learned earlier in this chapter, you can make a disk bootable by using the /S switch with the FORMAT command. You can use the SYS command when you need to make an already formatted disk bootable. The disk must have room for the system files that SYS intends to transfer, and those system files must be compatible with your version of DOS.

To use SYS successfully, observe the following rules:

- The destination disk must be formatted.
- The destination disk must contain sufficient free space for the two hidden system files and COMMAND.COM (just more than 133KB for DOS 6.22 system files; more than 197KB if

you use DoubleSpace), it must already contain earlier versions of the system files, or it must have been formatted with the /B switch.

- You cannot use SYS in a networked drive. If you want to use SYS in a networked drive, you must log off the network or pause your drive. (For the exact restrictions, consult your system's network documentation.)

- You must include the destination-drive parameter in the SYS command. SYS does not transfer a copy of the system to the current drive; the destination must be a different drive.

The syntax for the SYS command is as follows:

SYS *ds: dd:*

dd: is the target, or destination, drive for the system files. You must specify a drive name (letter) for drive *dd:*. The drive specified by *ds:* is the drive used for the source of the system files.

Suppose that you are using DOS 6.22 with a hard disk and have an empty disk that you want to make bootable for use with another computer. To do so, follow these steps:

1. Insert the formatted disk (the one you want to transfer system files onto) into drive A.
2. Type the following command:

    SYS C: A:

SYS replies with the message System transferred. The system files now are on the disk in drive A. Now you can use this disk to boot your computer.

> **Note** The C: in step 2 is optional, depending on whether drive C is current. If you are logged on to drive C, C: is already the default source for the system files; therefore, you don't have to add it to the command line.

GETTING THE MOST SPEED FROM YOUR HARD DISK

Your hard disk just might be the most important component of your computer. Many aspects of your computer's performance are strongly influenced by the characteristics of your disk. These characteristics include the following:

- **Speed**—The speed of your hard disk influences the speed of your system. Even if your computer's processor is super fast, a slow disk can make your computer perform like a snail.

- **Space**—The amount of space on your disk determines what you can do with your computer. No matter how fast and powerful your processor is, if you have only 20MB of space on your disk, you cannot run much Windows software.

The most dramatic way to increase your computer's performance is to purchase a larger, faster hard disk. As an alternative to buying another hard disk, you often can increase your computer's performance simply by making the best use of your current hard disk. In the following sections, you learn how to get the most speed and most space from your hard disk. The safety issue is covered thoroughly in Chapter 9, "Protecting Your Data."

The programs you use on your computer frequently must access data on disk. The speed at which your computer can retrieve that information is one of the most significant factors that determine how fast the computer operates. You can buy faster disk drives (which are expensive), or you can use DOS, which provides several techniques you can use to increase the speed at which your programs access information without actually increasing the speed of your disk. The following sections explain those techniques.

Using a Disk Cache (SMARTDrive)

Perhaps the most significant way to enhance the performance of your hard disk is to use a disk-caching program. Disk caching takes advantage of the fact that during the course of normal work, most users access the same programs and data repeatedly within a short period. You might list the contents of a file, edit the file, and then print it; or you might run the same program several times in a row. Even if you don't access programs or data repeatedly, the programs you use probably do.

If you have a disk-caching program installed, that program allocates some of your memory for temporary data storage on disk. When you access data, the disk-caching program saves that data in its memory area, on the assumption that you are likely to use the same data—or related data stored with it—in the near future (within a few seconds, perhaps). If you (or your program) do try to read the same data again soon, the disk-caching program intercepts the disk access and gives the program the data stored in memory. You (or your program) receive the data immediately because DOS doesn't actually read the data from disk; instead, the disk-caching program finds the data in its cache buffer. If your program never requests the same information again, the caching program eventually realizes that you are not likely to use that data soon and deletes the data from memory.

The disk-caching program that comes with DOS is named SMARTDRV.EXE, or simply *SMARTDrive*. SMARTDrive builds its buffer area in XMS or EMS memory, using very little conventional memory. When DOS reads information from the disk, it places that information in the cache and sends specifically requested information to the program that requested it. SMARTDrive, however, reads more information than the program requests and stores this information in memory. If the program later requests information that is already in memory, the cache can supply the information faster than DOS can if DOS has to read the disk again.

SMARTDrive eliminates redundant disk writing by putting information on disk only when the data differs from data already stored. The program also accumulates information, writing out data only when a certain amount has accumulated. Write-caching operations decrease the amount of time that your programs spend writing to disk, but write caching also forces you to shut down your computer by issuing a special SMARTDrive command (explained later in this section) or by making sure you return to the DOS prompt.

> **Caution**
>
> You might not want to use write caching in an area with unreliable electrical power. If the power fails while SMARTDrive is accumulating data, you lose the data that it has not yet written to disk. This risk of data loss is of little concern if you own an uninterruptible power supply (UPS), which keeps your computer running during a power failure. There is no equivalent danger in the case of read caching.

A disk-caching program such as SMARTDrive remembers which sections of the disk you have used most frequently. When the cache must be recycled, the program retains the data in the most frequently used areas and discards the data in the less frequently used areas. In a random disk-access operation in which program and data files are scattered uniformly across the disk, the cache method of recycling the least frequently used area is more efficient than the buffer method of recycling the oldest area. A cache tends to keep in memory the most heavily used areas of the disk.

To start SMARTDrive, enter a command with the following syntax in your AUTOEXEC.BAT file:

```
SMARTDRV drive+ | drive-... /E:elementsize initcachesize wincachesize
    /B:buffersize /C /R /F /N /L /Q /S /U /V /X
```

The SMARTDRV command is followed by the drives for which you want caching used. This notation takes the form of a drive letter, followed optionally by a plus (+) or minus (–) sign, as in the following examples:

C	Specifies that drive C will be cached for reads but not for writes
C+	Specifies that drive C will be cached for reads and writes
C–	Specifies that drive C will not be cached

If you don't specify any drive letters in your SMARTDRV command, floppy disk drives are read cached but not write cached, and hard disks are read cached and write cached. If you are using the version of SMARTDrive supplied with DOS 6.22, you also can cache your CD-ROM drives. Other kinds of drives—such as network drives and compressed drives—are not cached.

As an alternative to specifying every drive you want read cached but not write cached, you can use the /X switch. SMARTDrive then enables only read caching; write caching for all drives is automatically disabled. The /X switch is used automatically when you install DOS 6.22 (unless you were using SMARTDrive with different switches in an existing AUTOEXEC.BAT file).

The /E:elementsize parameter specifies the number of bytes that SMARTDrive reads or writes at a time: 1,024; 2,048; 4,096; or 8,192 (the default value). The larger the value, the more conventional memory SMARTDrive uses, but the fewer disk accesses you are likely to need.

The *initcachesize* parameter is a number that specifies the size (in kilobytes) of the cache when SMARTDrive starts. The larger the cache, the more likely that SMARTDrive can find information required by programs in the cache. The larger the cache, however, the more memory SMARTDrive requires. If you do not specify *initcachesize*, SMARTDrive selects a value based on the amount of memory in your system.

The *wincachesize* parameter specifies the size (in kilobytes) to which DOS can reduce the cache when you start Windows so that Windows can use the memory for other purposes. The philosophy behind this parameter is that if SMARTDrive uses too much of your memory, Windows runs too slowly. Therefore, even though SMARTDrive becomes less efficient by giving up some of its memory, Windows can run faster. When you exit Windows, SMARTDrive recovers the memory it gave up for Windows. Table 7.3 shows the default values for *initcachesize* and *wincachesize*.

TABLE 7.3 DEFAULT SMARTDRIVE MEMORY VALUES

Size of Extended Memory	Default Value for *initcachesize*	Default Value for *wincachesize*
Up to 1MB	All XMS	Zero (no caching)
Up to 2MB	1MB	256KB
Up to 4MB	1MB	512KB
Up to 6MB	2MB	1MB
6MB or more	2MB	2MB

The /B:*buffersize* parameter tells SMARTDrive how much additional information to read when DOS executes a disk read. Because programs often read sequentially through files, SMARTDrive anticipates that the next data request will be for the area following the current area. The default size of the read-ahead buffer is 16KB; this value can be any multiple of *elementsize*. The larger the value of *buffersize*, the more conventional memory SMARTDrive uses.

The /L switch prevents SMARTDrive from loading into your upper memory area (UMA). This option might be useful if other programs need to use the UMA.

Normally, the DOS 6.22 version of SMARTDrive enables read caching for CD-ROM drives. If you do not want this feature enabled, you can use the /U switch.

The /Q switch tells SMARTDrive to be "quiet" while installing itself rather than displaying the usual status messages. This is the opposite of the /V switch, which turns on "verbose" mode and shows the status messages.

You also can run SMARTDrive as a command from the DOS prompt. Several special switches that provide important features are available from the command line. The first is the /S switch. You determine the status of SMARTDrive by using this switch. Following is an example of typical output:

```
Microsoft SMARTDrive Disk Cache version 5.0
Copyright 1991,1993 Microsoft Corp.

Room for    256 elements of   8,192 bytes each
There have been    3,251 cache hits
     and     524 cache misses

Cache size: 2,097,152 bytes
Cache size while running Windows:  2,097,152 bytes

             Disk Caching Status
drive   read cache   write cache   buffering
----------------------
  A:       yes          no           no
  B:       yes          no           no
  C:       yes          yes          no
  D        yes          yes          no
  I*       yes          yes          no

* DoubleSpace drive cached via host drive.
Write behind data will be committed before command prompt returns.


For help, type "Smartdrv /?".
```

Perhaps the most interesting information in this output is the speed that SMARTDrive achieves. In the preceding example (which was generated after a session with a word processing program), for 3,251 disk accesses, SMARTDrive already had the data in its cache. For only 524 attempted disk accesses did SMARTDrive actually have to access the disk. In other words, because of SMARTDrive, the computer didn't have to perform 80% of attempted disk accesses.

The /C switch is important if you use write caching. Remember that write caching causes SMARTDrive to accumulate data that is destined for the disk until a certain amount accumulates. If you are getting ready to turn off your computer, you must tell SMARTDrive that no more data is to be written to disk and instruct the program to finish writing whatever data it has accumulated. You can perform this operation (called *flushing* in technical circles) by typing the following command:

SMARTDRV /C

You do not need to execute this command if you are rebooting by pressing Ctrl+Alt+Del. But if you have enabled write caching, be sure to use this command when you reset or turn off your computer.

If you are using DOS 6.22, the precaution of using the /C switch is not necessary. Instead, SMARTDrive automatically flushes the write buffer to disk whenever you return to the DOS prompt. This assumes, of course, that you have not disabled the feature by using the /N switch. (Typically, you should disable this feature only if you are doing extensive batch file operations and don't want the continual buffer flushing to degrade the performance of your batch files.) If you turn off this feature by using the /N switch, you can turn it on later by using the /F switch.

USING FASTOPEN

Another way to improve hard disk performance is to use the FASTOPEN program. FASTOPEN is not a device driver per se, but an executable program that you can include in AUTOEXEC.BAT. You also can load the program through CONFIG.SYS by using the special INSTALL command.

→ For more information on using the INSTALL command, **see** "Using the INSTALL Command," **p. 466**.

You can use FASTOPEN only with hard drives. FASTOPEN caches directory information, holding in memory the locations of frequently used files and directories.

A directory is a type of file that you cannot access through regular means. DOS reads and writes directories in a manner similar to the way it handles other files. Part of the directory entry for a file or subdirectory holds the starting point for the file in the file allocation table. Because DOS typically holds the FAT in the disk buffers, FASTOPEN was developed to hold directory entries in memory.

FASTOPEN is not a complex command, but you must do a little work before you can use it effectively. The syntax for FASTOPEN is as follows:

FASTOPEN.EXE *d:* = *n* /X

The *d:* parameter is the name of the first hard drive that you want FASTOPEN to track. (You can specify up to 24 hard disks or hard disk partitions at one time.) The /X switch, which is similar to the /X switches of other commands, enables FASTOPEN information to reside in EMS. By default, FASTOPEN uses conventional memory.

The *n* parameter is the number of directory entries that FASTOPEN is to cache. Each file or subdirectory requires one directory entry. You can enter a value ranging from 10 to 999. If you do not specify a value for *n*, DOS uses a default value of 48.

You can use FASTOPEN on as many disks as you want. Be aware, however, that the total number of directory entries or fragmented entries FASTOPEN can handle is 999. If you issue the command for several disk drives, the sum of the *n* values cannot exceed 999. The practical limit of *n* is between 100 and 200 per disk. If you specify a value much higher, DOS wades through the internal directory entries more slowly than it reads information from disk. Additionally, each directory entry stored in memory takes 48 bytes. Considering this trade-off of speed and memory, the 100-to-200-disk limit yields adequate performance.

Using too small a number for *n* also can be a disadvantage. When directory entries are recycled, FASTOPEN discards the least recently used entry when it needs space for a new entry. If the *n* value is too small, DOS discards entries that it still might need. The objective is to have enough entries in memory so that FASTOPEN operates efficiently, but not so many entries that FASTOPEN wastes time wading through directory entries.

To load FASTOPEN as part of your regular configuration, use the INSTALL command in your CONFIG.SYS file as follows:

INSTALL = FASTOPEN.EXE C:

To load FASTOPEN into upper memory, use LOADHIGH in AUTOEXEC.BAT. The following command, for example, loads FASTOPEN into upper memory and tracks filenames and directories on drive C:

LOADHIGH C:\DOS\FASTOPEN C:

> **Note**
> Keep in mind the following points regarding the use of FASTOPEN:
> - Do not use FASTOPEN if you are using Windows.
> - Do not run a disk-defragmenting program, such as DEFRAG, while FASTOPEN is running.

USING A RAM DISK

Another way to speed disk operation doesn't involve a disk at all. A RAM disk is a device driver that uses a portion of your computer's memory to emulate a disk drive. You use a RAM drive as you use any other disk drive. Because this "imitation," or virtual, disk is located in RAM, a RAM disk is extremely fast compared with a real disk drive. You must, however, give up a significant amount of memory to create a useful RAM disk. Worse, you cannot store anything in that disk permanently; the contents of the RAM disk disappear when you turn off or reboot your computer.

As a general rule, a disk-caching program such as SMARTDrive provides better overall performance gains than a RAM disk. You generally use RAM disks to enhance the performance of one or two specific programs that read and write to the disk frequently or that use overlays. A disk cache, on the other hand, improves the performance of all programs that read and write to disk.

> **Tip**
> If your computer's memory resources are limited, give more consideration to a disk cache rather than to a RAM disk.

Overlays and RAM Disks

Some programs are too large to fit in your PC's memory. These programs load a core part into memory and access additional parts from overlay files as necessary. When a new section of the program is needed, the appropriate overlay for that section is read from the disk into the area occupied by the current overlay.

The term *overlay* comes from this process of overlaying sections of program space in memory with new sections. RAM disks facilitate rapid switching of active overlays because the overlay disk files actually are in memory, not on disk. You must copy any needed overlay files to the RAM disk before starting the program. You also must configure the program to look for its overlays on the RAM disk.

The RAM disk driver that comes with DOS is named RAMDRIVE.SYS. To install RAMDRIVE and create a virtual disk, include RAMDRIVE.SYS as a device driver in CONFIG.SYS. The syntax for including RAMDRIVE.SYS is as follows:

```
DEVICE = RAMDRIVE.SYS disksize sectorsize entries /E /A
```

The *disksize* parameter indicates the size of the RAM disk (in kilobytes). This number can range from 16 to 32,767 (equivalent to 32MB). The default value is 64.

The *sectorsize* parameter represents the size of the sectors used in the virtual disk. You can specify one of three sector sizes: 128, 256, or 512 (the default) bytes. Normally, you do not change this parameter; if you do, however, you also must specify the *disksize* parameter.

The *entries* parameter determines the maximum number of directory entries permitted in the RAM disk's root directory. This parameter can be a value ranging from 2 to 1,024. The default value is 64. You normally don't need to change this parameter. If you do specify the entries parameter, you also must enter the *disksize* and *sectorsize* parameters. Set the number of directories based on the size of the RAM disk and the number of files you are storing.

By default, DOS creates a RAM disk in conventional memory. You can, however, include the /E switch to cause the RAM disk to be created in XMS memory. Even with this switch, however, RAMDRIVE uses some conventional memory, so you might want to try loading the RAMDRIVE.SYS device driver into upper memory. The following command creates a 1,024KB RAM disk in XMS memory and loads the device driver into upper memory:

```
DEVICEHIGH=C:\DOS\RAMDRIVE.SYS 1024 /E
```

> **Caution**
> If you want your RAM disk to use extended memory, it must follow the CONFIG.SYS commands that load HIMEM.SYS or a different memory manager.

The /A switch creates the RAM disk in EMS memory. To use this switch, you must load an expanded memory manager (such as EMM386.EXE) before loading RAMDRIVE.SYS. You cannot use the /A and /E switches for the same RAM disk. You can create different RAM disks, however, some using EMS memory and others using XMS memory. Given a choice, use XMS memory.

After you insert the DEVICE=RAMDRIVE.SYS command into CONFIG.SYS and reboot your computer, DOS displays a message similar to the following during initialization of your computer:

```
Microsoft RAMDrive version 3.07 virtual disk D:
  Disk size: 64k
  Sector size: 512 bytes
  Allocation unit: 1 sectors
  Directory entries: 64
```

Most importantly, this message tells you that this RAM disk is accessed as drive D. The message also shows the disk size, sector size, allocation-unit (cluster) size, and maximum number of root directory entries.

The amount of RAM in your computer, the programs you use, and the convenience of a RAM disk help determine what size RAM disk you use and even whether you need to use a RAM disk at all.

Drive Letters and Block Devices

The logical disk drive names (the drive letters) that DOS assigns to disks created by RAMDRIVE.SYS and DRIVER.SYS (see the "Command Reference") depend on the placement of the commands in the CONFIG.SYS file. You might try to use the wrong disk drive name if you do not know how DOS assigns drive names. When DOS encounters a block device driver (that is, any device that transfers data in blocks rather than in bytes), DOS assigns the next highest drive letter to that device. The order is first come, first assigned.

The potential for confusion comes when several block device drivers are loaded. The order of loading, based on the order of the commands in the CONFIG.SYS file, determines the names assigned by DOS. If you load RAMDRIVE.SYS first and DRIVER.SYS second, the RAM disk might be named D and the DRIVER.SYS disk one letter higher. If you switch the lines so that DRIVER.SYS loads first, the disk drive names also switch; the DRIVER.SYS disk is D, and the RAM disk is E.

> **Tip**
> One excellent way to use a RAM disk is to assign the TEMP environment variable to this virtual drive. Certain programs use an environment variable named TEMP to determine where to create various temporary files. These temporary files usually are written and read frequently during the operation of the program; their temporary nature makes them good candidates for storage in a RAM disk.

To assign TEMP to a RAM disk, you first have to determine a name for the virtual disk and then use the SET command (see the "Command Reference"). Assign the TEMP variable to a subdirectory rather than to the RAM disk's root directory to avoid the 64-filename limit. Assuming that the RAM disk becomes drive D, use the following commands in AUTOEXEC.BAT to create a directory on the virtual disk and to cause temporary files to be written to that directory:

```
MD D:\TEMPDATA
SET TEMP = D:\TEMPDATA
```

Some programs use an environment variable named TMP instead of TEMP for the same purpose. In such a case, substitute TMP for TEMP in the preceding command.

> **Caution**
> Because RAM disks are memory-based devices, you lose their contents when you reboot or turn off your PC. To prevent data loss, you must copy the contents of a RAM disk to a conventional disk file before rebooting or turning off the power. If you (or your program) are creating or modifying RAM disk files, copy the files to an actual disk regularly in case a power failure occurs.

Defragmenting Your Disk

If all you ever did with your hard disk was add files, the space available on your disk would be used very efficiently. DOS would add one file and then another to your disk, with each file being stored entirely within a contiguous area, followed by another contiguous file, an arrangement that enables DOS to access your files very efficiently.

Nobody, however, only adds new files to a disk. As you use your disk, you add new files, delete existing files, and add new data to existing files. Over time, data becomes scattered over the disk, and even the data within a single file might reside in chunks throughout the disk. This scattering of data is called *fragmentation*. The following sections discuss fragmentation in detail.

Understanding the Effects of Fragmentation

The more fragmented your disk, the slower your computer runs. Suppose that a third of your hard disk is currently full and that all the used space is at the front of the disk so that you have no fragmentation. Whenever you request data from the disk, the disk heads do not have to move very far and can access your data quickly.

If the same data is spread across the disk, however, the disk heads might have to move across the entire disk to access data. The longer movement requires more time, and you might notice the difference. Moreover, the disk might require more time to access each individual file. When you run a program (at least, a program that doesn't use overlays), DOS must read the program from disk into memory. That operation is much faster if the entire program is in successive locations on the disk and much slower if the disk heads must move to widely separated locations on the disk.

Fragmentation, which is almost inevitable, tends to increase the longer you use your disk. Programs that defragment your disk—that is, move all the data to the beginning of the disk and store each file's data in the same place—have long been available from third-party software vendors. The following section discusses DOS's built-in defragmentation program.

Understanding the Basic Operation of DEFRAG

DOS 6.0 was the first version of DOS to come with a defragmentation program, called DEFRAG. You execute DEFRAG by typing the following at the DOS prompt:

DEFRAG

A dialog box appears, asking which drive you want to defragment (see Figure 7.6).

Figure 7.6
The DEFRAG disk selection dialog box.

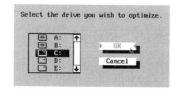

Select a drive by clicking a drive letter. Alternatively, use the arrow keys to move to the desired drive and then press Enter. DEFRAG scans the selected drive and displays a map of the used and unused portions. You need not understand the map to use DEFRAG effectively, but if you're interested in understanding DEFRAG's analysis of your disk, study the legend at the bottom-right corner of the screen; it explains the symbols in the disk map.

After displaying the map, DEFRAG suggests one of the following courses of action:

- **Do Nothing**—If the disk is not fragmented, DEFRAG tells you that you don't need to perform any operation.
- **Defragment Files Only**—If most of the data in the used area of the disk is stored together but the individual files are scattered throughout that area, DEFRAG recommends that you defragment the files. After DEFRAG completes this operation, the same area of the disk is in use, but the data in that area is rearranged so that the data for each file is stored together. DEFRAG usually recommends this operation for disks that are mostly full.
- **Full Optimization**—If the used area of the disk is scattered across the disk, DEFRAG recommends that you perform a full optimization, meaning that you defragment the entire disk. DEFRAG rearranges the used areas on the disk so that all the used portion of the disk is at the beginning of the disk and the data for each file is stored contiguously.

Figure 7.7 shows a typical recommendation from DEFRAG.

Figure 7.7
Viewing the DEFRAG command's analysis and recommendation.

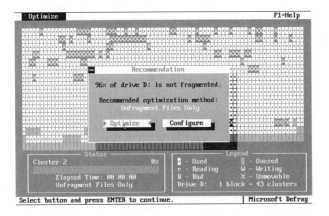

If you choose Optimize, DEFRAG reorganizes your disk using the suggested method. Be prepared to wait. Although DEFRAG does its work quickly, it still might take a long time on a large, heavily fragmented disk.

When DEFRAG suggests a particular type of defragmentation, you do not have to accept its recommendation. When it recommends that only the files be defragmented, for example, it is telling you that the extra efficiency you gain by performing a disk defragmentation is not worth the time required by DEFRAG. However, you might be willing to allow DEFRAG the extra time to perform the more complete disk defragmentation.

As Figure 7.7 shows, when DEFRAG makes a recommendation, you can click Configure to select various options that control how DEFRAG works. When you click Configure, DEFRAG presents the Optimize menu, which includes more operations than just configuration; the first item tells DEFRAG to begin the defragmentation procedure. Table 7.4 lists the functions available in the Optimize menu.

TABLE 7.4   THE DEFRAG OPTIMIZE (CONFIGURATION) MENU

Selection	Meaning
Begin Optimization	Begins optimization of your hard disk, using any configuration options you have selected
Drive	Enables you to choose the drive you want to optimize
Optimization Method	Enables you to choose full optimization or file only (might leave empty space between files)
File Sort	Enables you to choose how files are sorted within directories, if at all
Map Legend	Displays a legend of the symbols DEFRAG uses to show disk usage
About Defrag	Displays information about the DEFRAG program
Exit	Exits DEFRAG

If you want to change the type of defragmentation that DEFRAG performs, choose Optimization Method. This option presents a dialog box in which you can specify whether DEFRAG defragments only files or completely defragments the disk. After you make a selection, you can choose Begin Optimization from the Optimize menu; DEFRAG then performs the optimization you selected.

Normally, DOS doesn't store filenames in a directory in any particular order. As you create and delete files, DOS removes old names and inserts new names wherever empty space occurs. The result is that when you use DIR to list the contents of a directory, often the files appear to be listed in random order. You can overcome this disorganized appearance by using the sorting switches available with the DIR command or by using some application programs, such as WordPerfect, which sort a directory each time they display it. This is not a permanent solution, however. The directory information is still stored on disk in a disorganized manner.

While DEFRAG reorganizes your disk, you can tell it to organize the names of the files within the directories in one of five ways:

- **Unsorted**—This option, which is the default, tells DEFRAG to leave the names in their current order.
- **Name**—DEFRAG organizes the directory alphabetically by filename. This option is probably the one you will find most useful.
- **Extension**—DEFRAG organizes the directory by extension name; for example, all the COM files appear together, all the EXE files appear together, and so on.

- **Date & Time**—DEFRAG sorts the directory by the date and time the files were last modified. This option enables you to tell at a glance which files have and have not been modified recently.
- **Size**—DEFRAG organizes files by the amount of disk space they consume.

You also can specify that the sort be in ascending or descending order—that is, that values get larger or smaller as the directory listing proceeds. Usually, you want an ascending sort for names so that the list starts with the beginning of the alphabet and proceeds through the end of the alphabet. If you're sorting by size, however, you might want a descending sort so that the biggest files are listed first and the smallest files last.

You can specify how DEFRAG sorts directories from the DEFRAG Optimize menu by choosing File Sort. Figure 7.8 shows the File Sort menu. Alternatively, you can provide command-line arguments, discussed in the next section, to specify file sort type.

Figure 7.8
The DEFRAG File Sort menu.

When you use DEFRAG, you usually start it simply by typing DEFRAG. Like most DOS commands, however, DEFRAG has a number of startup options available. The complete syntax for DEFRAG is as follows:

DEFRAG d: /F /U /S:order /B /SKIPHIGH /LCD /BW /G0 /H

Normally, DEFRAG asks which drive you want to defragment. If you specify the d: parameter, DEFRAG uses it as the drive you want to defragment.

Typically, DEFRAG recommends the type of defragmentation you need to perform. The /F parameter tells DEFRAG to defragment the disk (leaving no empty spaces between files); the /U parameter tells DEFRAG to defragment files (possibly leaving empty space between files). If you specify one of these parameters, DEFRAG does not make a recommendation, but it immediately carries out the type of defragmentation you specify.

You can control whether DEFRAG sorts directory entries by using the /S switch. /S is optionally followed by a colon and one or more characters that specify how you want the entries sorted within each directory. Valid letters are listed in the following:

N Alphabetical order by name

E Alphabetical order by extension

D	By date and time, with the oldest dates (that is, files that were last modified farthest in the past) listed first
S	By size, with the smallest files listed first

The following command, for example, defragments drive C and sorts files in alphabetical order by name:

```
DEFRAG C: /SN
```

You also can place a minus sign (–) after a sort letter to specify a descending sort instead of ascending. Consider these two commands:

```
DEFRAG C: /SS
DEFRAG C: /SS-
```

The first (without the minus sign) lists the smallest files first; the second (with the minus sign) lists the largest files first.

The /B switch tells DEFRAG to reboot your computer after the defragmentation process is complete.

The /SKIPHIGH switch tells DEFRAG to load itself into conventional memory. Otherwise, DEFRAG uses upper memory, if available.

The /LCD switch uses a color scheme that is likely to be more readable if you are using a laptop or notebook computer with an LCD screen.

The /BW switch tells DEFRAG to use a black-and-white color scheme, which is likely to be more pleasing if you have a monochrome monitor.

The /G0 switch disables the mouse and graphics character set. Use this switch if DEFRAG displays strange characters on your monitor.

Normally, DEFRAG does not reorganize hidden files. You can use the /H switch to tell DEFRAG to move hidden files.

> **Note**
> When you use DEFRAG, keep in mind the following restrictions:
> - You cannot use DEFRAG to defragment drives over a network.
> - You cannot run DEFRAG from Windows.
> - Disk statistics reported by DEFRAG and CHKDSK or SCANDISK differ slightly. When listing the number of directories, for example, DEFRAG counts the root directory, but CHKDSK does not.

Getting the Most Space from Your Hard Disk

Since the introduction of PCs in 1981, the amount of disk storage space available to the average user has increased steadily. The original PCs used cassette tapes for mass storage and offered, as an option, floppy disks with only 160KB of storage space. Today, many PCs are sold with hard disks that are thousands of times larger, usually 10GB and higher. It is important to discuss other options, though, because many older PCs that are still running are quite capable of running DOS, but they have only 100MB to 500MB hard drives. Upgrading these machines is not cost effective, so other ways to increase space are needed.

A decade ago, few software vendors wrote software that required several megabytes of disk storage because they knew that few of their potential customers' systems had that kind of storage capability. Now vendors rarely think twice about releasing software that requires more than 40MB of disk storage; they expect that most people have that much space to spare. Some newer programs, especially games, can require up to 400MB of space to load completely.

Although you cannot increase the physical capacity of your disk without buying a larger disk, you might be able to increase the amount of data you can store on your disk by using the techniques discussed in the next couple of sections. First, you learn about manual methods of freeing disk space; then you learn about DoubleSpace, which provides full-time disk compression.

The two most popular methods of freeing disk space are to delete files you no longer need and to compress computer files. You also can archive files that you no longer need on floppy disks or tape backups.

Deleting Unnecessary Files

Much of the software available today is very complex, offering many features that you probably will never use. As a result, many of the files copied to your hard disk when you install a software program are files that you never open. You might be able to find and delete some of these files, thereby freeing some of your hard disk space.

> **Tip**
> Some programs, such as Microsoft Word for Windows, ask which features you expect to use and install only the files that are appropriate for you. If you later change your mind, you can install the missing pieces then.

> **Caution**
> Be sure to use the installation routine for programs such as Word to remove files. Never delete program files directly, unless you are sure there will be no adverse harm to the program.

When you install DOS, dozens of programs are installed on your hard disk. If you are short on disk space, you might want to browse through these programs and delete the ones that are not important to you. Consider the following examples:

- DOS includes many files that enable it to work with foreign-language character sets, including German, Swedish, and French. If you expect to use your computer only in the United States, you can delete these files to free disk space.
- Some DOS utilities might duplicate functions that are available in other programs installed in your system. If you use a backup program (such as Norton Backup or FastBack), for example, you can delete the DOS backup program, MSBACKUP.

→ To determine which files supplied with DOS you can safely remove, **see** Appendix F, "Command Reference," **p. 583**.

Another side effect of upgrading your version of DOS is that the old DOS files (from the previous version) are stored in a directory that begins with the letters OLD_DOS. After the upgrade is complete and you are sure that you want to continue using the new version of DOS, you can safely delete this directory and everything within it. The program DELOLDDOS, provided with DOS, can take care of this deletion for you.

USING FILE COMPRESSION

If you examine the file that contains the text for this chapter, you find that many words—such as *DOS* and *the*—are repeated frequently. Most data includes such repetition—patterns that occur over and over within a file, whether the file contains text, customer data, or machine instructions.

Many programmers have written programs that analyze these patterns and squeeze a file's data into a smaller space by converting the data into a kind of shorthand notation. (PKZip and LHArc are examples of such programs.) This process is known as *compression*. In special cases, the compressed data might require as little as 10% of the original space, although 50% is more typical.

If you are interested in acquiring a good compression program, check out an online download site, such as http://www.downloads.com or http://www.zdnet.com. File compression software is used extensively in telecommunications because the smaller files transfer faster and with less cost.

ARCHIVING FILES

Over time, you probably use your computer to perform many different tasks and complete a multitude of projects. When you complete a project, a good plan of action is to compress the files using compression software discussed in the preceding section.

You can move compressed files easily to high-density floppy disks or to a backup tape. You then can store these disks or tapes for long periods of time in case you need the information again.

Take a look at your hard drive and the dates of the data files contained on it. You might find that you have many files that you have not accessed for a long time. Such files are prime candidates for archiving.

Projects

The following two projects will walk you through using the CHKDSK and SCANDISK utilities. These utilities are very important in analyzing hard drives and determining whether there might be a problem. CHKDSK can be used on uncompressed drives, whereas SCANDISK is required to check compressed drives.

Analyzing a Disk with CHKDSK

The external command CHKDSK analyzes a floppy or hard disk. CHKDSK checks a disk's FAT, directories, and—if you want—the fragmentation of the files on the disk.

CHKDSK is DOS's self-test command. It makes sure that the internal tables that keep files in control are in order.

Although the technical details of how CHKDSK performs its analysis are beyond the interest of most casual DOS users, the better you understand CHKDSK, the more comfortable you will be when the command uncovers problems. Just because you don't understand exactly how CHKDSK works doesn't mean that you must avoid using it.

CHKDSK checks for the following problems in the FAT:

- Unlinked cluster chains (lost clusters)
- Multiply linked clusters (cross-linked files)
- Invalid next-cluster-in-chain values (invalid cluster numbers)
- Defective sectors where the FAT is stored

CHKDSK checks for the following problems in the directory system:

- Invalid cluster numbers (out of range)
- Invalid file attributes in entries (attribute values that DOS does not recognize)
- Damage to subdirectory entries (CHKDSK cannot process them)
- Damage to a directory's integrity (its files cannot be accessed)

> **Note**
> CHKDSK is meant to work with normal DOS volumes; it does not work with DoubleSpace disk volumes. If you want to analyze both DOS and DoubleSpace volumes, use the SCANDISK command, which is discussed later in this chapter.

Optionally, CHKDSK repairs problems in the FAT that are caused by lost clusters, and it writes the contents of the lost clusters to files. CHKDSK also can display all files and their paths. (Paths are discussed in Chapter 5, "Understanding Files and Directories.")

> **Note**
>
> Running CHKDSK periodically on your hard disk and on important floppies is good practice. Because the FAT and hierarchical directory system work together to track filenames and locations, a problem in the FAT or one of the directories is always serious. In all likelihood, CHKDSK can find and correct most problems in a disk's internal bookkeeping tables.

The CHKDSK command uses the following syntax:

CHKDSK *filespec* /F/V

The optional *filespec* parameter is the drive, path, and filename of the file to be analyzed for fragmentation. If you don't include a *filespec*, CHKDSK does not check for fragmentation.

/F is the optional fix switch, which instructs CHKDSK to repair any problems it encounters.

/V is the verbose switch, which instructs CHKDSK to provide filenames onscreen as it analyzes the files.

When the process is complete, CHKDSK displays a screen report of its findings. This report summarizes disk and system memory usage. Figures 7.9 and 7.10 show typical CHKDSK reports.

Figure 7.9
A typical report produced by CHKDSK with no parameters.

```
Volume DCI 3         created 09-13-1993 5:30a
Volume Serial Number is 1B2B-392C

 340,746,240 bytes total disk space
  21,094,400 bytes in 6 hidden files
     884,736 bytes in 107 directories
 199,917,568 bytes in 3,195 user files
 118,849,536 bytes available on disk

       8,192 bytes in each allocation unit
      41,595 total allocation units on disk
      14,508 available allocation units on disk

     655,360 total bytes memory
     570,528 bytes free

Instead of using CHKDSK, try using SCANDISK.  SCANDISK can reliably detect
and fix a much wider range of disk problems.  For more information,
type HELP SCANDISK from the command prompt.
```

Figure 7.10
The report produced when CHKDSK is issued with a path.

```
C:\>chkdsk \umsd\*.doc

Volume DCI 3        created 09-13-1993 5:30a
Volume Serial Number is 1B2B-392C

 340,746,240 bytes total disk space
  21,094,400 bytes in 6 hidden files
     851,968 bytes in 103 directories
 199,409,664 bytes in 3,188 user files
 119,390,208 bytes available on disk

       8,192 bytes in each allocation unit
      41,595 total allocation units on disk
      14,574 available allocation units on disk

     655,360 total bytes memory
     570,528 bytes free

C:\UMSD\UMD03.DOC Contains 3 non-contiguous blocks

Instead of using CHKDSK, try using SCANDISK.  SCANDISK can reliably detect
and fix a much wider range of disk problems.  For more information,
type HELP SCANDISK from the command prompt.
```

> **Note**
> Take advantage of the CHKDSK command's capability to make a "dry run" of its checking routines. You can use this feature to assess reported problems. Before issuing CHKDSK with the /F switch, for example, issue the command without the switch. CHKDSK without /F prompts you if the command finds a problem (as though you had used the /F switch). After you have assessed the findings of CHKDSK and have taken remedial actions, you can issue CHKDSK with the /F switch so that the command can fix the problems it finds.

DOS stores every file as a chain of clusters. Each cluster is a group of sectors; clusters are also referred to as allocation units. Each entry in the disk's directory points to the entry in the FAT that contains the list of clusters allocated to a file.

> **Caution**
> Use CHKDSK /F only when you are running at the DOS prompt. You do not want to have other programs running because CHKDSK expects the DOS file system to be dormant while CHKDSK does its work. If you are shelled out to a DOS prompt from within an application or are running a DOS session under Windows, CHKDSK can damage your files.

CHKDSK processes each directory, starting at the root and following each subdirectory. It checks the cluster chain by using the directory entry's FAT pointer and then compares the size of the file (in bytes) with the size of the FAT's allocation (in clusters). CHKDSK expects to find enough chained clusters in the FAT to accommodate the file, but not more than are necessary. If CHKDSK finds too many clusters, it displays the following message:

```
Allocation error,
size adjusted
```

The file is truncated—excess clusters are deallocated—if you use the /F switch.

CHKDSK makes sure that each of the FAT's clusters is allocated only once. In rare circumstances—for example, if power problems or hardware failures occur—DOS can give the same cluster to two different files. By checking each cluster chain for cross-linked files, CHKDSK can report mixed-up files. Each time you see that the message filename is cross-linked on cluster *nnnnn*, copy the file reported in *filename* to another disk. When CHKDSK reports another file with the same message, copy the second file to another disk also. Chances are that the contents of the two files are mixed up, but you have a better chance of recovering the files if you save them to another disk before CHKDSK "fixes" the problem.

CHKDSK expects every cluster in the FAT to be available for allocation, part of a legitimate directory-based cluster chain, or a marked bad cluster. If CHKDSK encounters any clusters or cluster chains that are not pointed to by a directory entry, CHKDSK issues the message lost clusters in *XXX* chains. CHKDSK then asks the following:

```
Convert lost chains to files (Y/N)?
```

This message appears even if you didn't use the /F switch.

If you used the /F switch and you press Y, CHKDSK turns each cluster chain into a file in the root directory. Each file that is created has the name FILE*nnnn*.CHK. (*nnnn* is a number, starting with 0000, that increments by 1 for each file created by CHKDSK.) If you did not use the /F switch and you press Y, nothing happens. CHKDSK, however, does tell you what it would have done had you used the /F switch.

> **Note**
> You can use the TYPE command to examine the contents of a text file, and you might be able to use the DOS EDIT command to put the text back into its original file. The TYPE or EDIT commands don't do you any good, however, for a binary (program or data) file. If the problem is with a program file, you might have to use the DOS COMP or FC command to compare your disk's binary files with their counterparts from your master disks.

Of course, the disk does not physically lose any sectors. A lost cluster report does not indicate that the clusters are bad; lost clusters indicate only that DOS made a bookkeeping error in the FAT, which makes some clusters appear to DOS to be lost. The clusters are not tied to a directory entry, but they're marked as being in use.

The lost cluster problem is most likely to occur when a program you are running crashes because of an error while files are being manipulated.

Remember that CHKDSK reports problems found during operation, but it does not repair the problems unless you include the /F switch in the command line. Running CHKDSK at least once a week is a good idea. Run CHKDSK daily during periods of extreme file activity.

ANALYZING A DISK WITH THE SCANDISK UTILITY

You might already know a bit about DoubleSpace, which was introduced with DOS 6.0. DoubleSpace enables you to virtually double the amount of information that can be stored on your disk. To accomplish this compression, however, information must be stored in a nonstandard manner. This means that CHKDSK cannot provide correct information about a disk volume that uses DoubleSpace.

Beginning with DOS 6.2, however, there is a solution: the SCANDISK command. This command works with either regular or DoubleSpace disk volumes, and it provides greater functionality than did the older CHKDSK command. In fact, whenever you use CHKDSK, you see this message at the bottom of any display:

```
Instead of using CHKDSK, try using SCANDISK.  SCANDISK can reliably detect
and fix a much wider range of disk problems.  For more information, type
HELP SCANDISK from the command prompt.
```

SCANDISK can detect and resolve all the problems that can be handled by CHKDSK. In addition, it can detect and correct the following problems:

- MS-DOS boot sector errors
- Defective clusters
- Problems in a DoubleSpace volume header
- Structure problems in the file structures of a DoubleSpace volume
- Errors in the DoubleSpace compression structure
- Errors in DoubleSpace volume signatures

The SCANDISK command has two possible syntaxes. If you want it to check a file or group of files, use the following syntax:

SCANDISK /FRAGMENT *filespec*

If you want SCANDISK to analyze an entire drive, use the following syntax:

SCANDISK *switches d:*

In this syntax, *d:* is the drive you want to check; if you do not supply a drive, SCANDISK assumes that you want to check the current drive. Many more switches can be used with SCANDISK than with CHKDSK. These switches are detailed in Table 7.5.

Table 7.5 Possible Switches for Use with SCANDISK

Switch	Meaning
/ALL	Checks all local drives.
/AUTOFIX	Fixes any problems that are encountered without asking first.
/CHECKONLY	Analyzes the disk but does not fix any problems.
/CUSTOM	Uses the SCANDISK settings contained in the file SCANDISK.INI.
/FRAGMENT	Checks a file for fragmentation. You must specify the full filename after the switch.
/MONO	Forces display settings for a monochrome monitor.
/NOSAVE	Doesn't save lost cluster chains into files; simply frees them (used only with /AUTOFIX).
/NOSUMMARY	Indicates that SCANDISK should not stop at summary screens (used only with /AUTOFIX or /CHECKONLY).
/SURFACE	Performs a surface scan.
/UNDO	Undoes previous repairs. You must have an undo disk, and you must specify the drive on the command line.

> **Caution**
> Use SCANDISK only at the DOS prompt. SCANDISK does not work properly if you are operating under a multitasking shell such as DESQview, Windows, or the DOS Shell. Exit these programs before you attempt to use SCANDISK.

You might have already noted, from the information in Table 7.5, that you can store your SCANDISK parameters in the file SCANDISK.INI. This file, which is stored in the DOS directory, specifies how you want SCANDISK to operate. For more information on this file, use a text editor to load the file. It contains extensive comments on how you can modify the file to change the behavior of SCANDISK.

As an example of how SCANDISK operates, enter SCANDISK at the DOS prompt. You see a screen similar to the one shown in Figure 7.11.

Each of the five listed areas is in turn analyzed by SCANDISK. The first four areas are processed very quickly. The final area takes more time; therefore, you are prompted before SCANDISK actually performs a surface test. On a 340MB hard drive, for example, a surface scan can take up to 35 minutes to complete. This amount of time is necessary because every sector on the disk is read and analyzed to make sure that it is correct.

Figure 7.11
The SCANDISK screen.

```
Microsoft ScanDisk
---------------------------------

ScanDisk is now checking the following areas of drive C:

        Media descriptor
        File allocation tables
    »   Directory structure
        File system
        Surface scan




    < Pause >    < More Info >    < Exit >

---------------------------------
```

CHAPTER 8

MANAGING YOUR FILES

In this chapter

Using DOS to Work with Files   192

Listing Files with the DIR Command   193

Viewing Files   199

Copying Files   202

Moving Files   212

Setting Defaults for COPY, XCOPY, and MOVE   214

Renaming Files   214

Comparing Files   215

Deleting Files   221

Using Interlnk to Share Another Computer's Resources   222

Case Study: Editing Files with Multiple Data Formats   229

Using DOS to Work with Files

After you have installed DOS on your computer, created your directories, and installed programs, in a sense you have set up housekeeping on your PC.

Most programs generate files as you work with them. You begin to accumulate files on your computer's disks in much the same way that you accumulate possessions in your home or office. Fortunately, DOS provides useful file-management commands that help you keep file clutter to a minimum. This chapter covers file-management techniques.

One of the most difficult things to do in this age of multiple-gigabyte hard drives is to keep track of all the information stored on your hard drive. By creating a directory structure that segregates groups of files according to their uses, you can keep the files on your computer's hard disk organized and cataloged. The adage "a place for everything and everything in its place" is never more true than when you're storing files on a large hard disk.

It is important that you understand the distinction between utility programs and applications when devising a strategy to manage files using DOS. A *utility* is generally regarded as a single-purpose program that performs one specific task and then gets out of your way. An *application* generally provides a working environment capable of providing all the services required to perform general tasks such as word processing and creating pictures.

DOS's external commands are perfect examples of utilities. Each external command serves a specific purpose, such as sorting lists or formatting disks. You usually run a utility program by typing a command line at the DOS prompt. It does its work and then terminates, giving you another DOS prompt to work from. Utilities usually have all their programming contained in a single EXE or COM file, and they seldom use auxiliary files. It therefore is most often convenient to place utility programs into directories that are part of the search path so that they are available no matter what directory you are logged in to. By default, most utilities act on files in the currently logged directory.

Applications, even though they might be dedicated to a single activity such as word processing or database management, have a much broader scope. Unlike utilities, which do their job and terminate to a DOS prompt, applications create a working environment in which users can access the features of the applications. Only when you exit an application do you receive another DOS prompt.

Applications usually are installed into a directory of their own. They often use auxiliary files such as *overlays*—a special type of file that contains the programming code necessary to provide a subset of the application's features. These auxiliary files often make it necessary or convenient to log in to an application's home directory before running the application. This isn't a hard-and-fast rule because some utilities also create files. The most notable feature of an application, in the context of this discussion, is that it most often creates files having a specific format unique to the application. WordPerfect creates WordPerfect files, Lotus 1-2-3 creates 1-2-3 files, and so on.

In terms of working with files, the distinction between utilities and applications is simple. Utilities most often work with files in place—that is, in the location (directory) where they were created. Applications, on the other hand, usually work with files in specific directories created to store files that have the native format particular to that application.

> **Tip**
>
> When you're creating directory structures on your hard disk, it is usually a good idea to create dedicated directories for your applications where those applications can store the files you create. Doing so enables you to find a particular file more easily when you need it.

LISTING FILES WITH THE DIR COMMAND

The DIR command is one of the first commands most DOS users learn. It also is the most-used command in the DOS inventory. The command quickly gives you a list of your files, along with the date and time you created them, and the file sizes. If you type only DIR, you are using only a fraction of the command's full power. The following sections help you unlock the power of the DIR command.

> **Note**
>
> By default, many applications create files in their home directories when installed. Many of these applications have dozens of auxiliary files (overlays, printer drivers, video drivers, and so on). For this reason, it is a good idea to create one or more directories—branching off an application's home directory—where files created by the application are stored.
>
> Many applications have settings that can specify which directory newly created files should be written in. Check the documentation for your applications to find out how to set up default directories for newly created files.

ISSUING THE DIR COMMAND

DIR is an internal command. All the programming for this command is contained in COMMAND.COM, so you will never find DIR.EXE in your DOS directory. The syntax of the DIR command is as follows:

DIR *FileNameExp* /P /W /A:*attributes* /O:*order* /S /B /L

FileNameExp is a filename expression that can contain the drive, path, and file specification. Of course, the filename expression can include wildcards.

The DIR command also uses several switches. These switches and their definitions are shown in Table 8.1.

Table 8.1 DIR Switches

Switch	Action
/P	Displays one screen of information and then pauses. Pressing any key causes DIR to continue the listing.
/W	Displays only the filenames, without the size, date, or modification time of the files. Files are listed in columns across the screen rather than one filename per line.
/A:attributes	Displays only files that have, or lack, file attributes you specify, such as read-only, hidden, or system files.
/O:order	Lists files in a different sorted order, such as alphabetical order by name.
/S	Lists the contents of subdirectories.
/B	Lists filenames only, one per line.
/L	Lists all filenames in lowercase.
/C	Displays the file compression ratio.
/CH	Displays the file compression ratio using the host allocation unit size.

When you issue the DIR command with parameters missing, DOS uses default values. If you omit the filename expression, DIR uses the currently logged directory. Unless you use the /O switch, files and directories are listed in their regular, unsorted order.

Understanding the Operation of the DIR Command

When you issue the DIR command, the volume label and serial number of the disk are displayed along with a filename expression that specifies what directory is being displayed. Files and subdirectories are then displayed in the following format unless you specify the /W switch:

```
CIS      ZIP    55,029 08-01-01  11:47p
DISCPASS     <DIR>       06-16-01   3:10a
```

The first line of the example shows the standard format for files. Directory information is divided into five columns. From left to right, they are as follows:

- Filename
- Extension
- Size of the file in bytes
- The last date the file was edited
- The time of day the file was last edited

The second line of the example shows how directories are displayed. The <DIR> symbol indicates that the entry is a directory and thus doesn't have a byte count.

The information displayed by DIR includes most of the data stored in the directory table. The file attributes do not appear, but DOS uses them to determine whether to display a file. By default, hidden files are not included in this list. The location of the first cluster in the file allocation table (FAT) for the file also is not displayed because knowing the file's starting cluster is of little use to you as a user.

At the end of the listing, DOS indicates the total number of files in the directory, the total number of bytes used by the listed files, and the total number of bytes free on the current disk. The DIR report for C:\DOS, for example, might show the following information:

```
157 file(s)     6,455,328 bytes
              119,504,896 bytes free
```

If you add the size of each of the listed files on the disk and subtract the result from the total disk capacity, that number and the number of free bytes shown in the directory listing probably do not match, but the directory listing is correct. Remember that hidden files are not shown; more importantly, the size of the file is not necessarily the same as the amount of disk space it occupies.

You might remember from earlier chapters that a *cluster* is the smallest possible chunk of disk space that can be allocated. When you create a file, no matter how small, DOS allocates at least one cluster to store the file. The directory listing shows the length of the data stored in bytes and calculates the free space, based on the number of free clusters on the disk. These free clusters are the remaining positions on the disk, not yet allocated to another file.

The free space reported by DIR is the number of unallocated clusters (also called allocation units) multiplied by the size of a cluster (1,024 bytes on most hard disks). You also can use CHKDSK to get a report of the total number of allocation units available on the disk.

Displaying a Screen of Information with the DIR Command

If you add the /P switch to the DIR command, DOS pauses the scrolling of the screen at the end of each screen of information. Pressing any key displays the next page of information.

To see more filenames, use the /W switch. When you use this switch, a directory listing like the one shown in Figure 8.1 appears.

With hierarchical directories, your directory listing includes subdirectory names and files. In the wide listing, directory names are enclosed in brackets ([ ]). Because the filenames are grouped so closely together, a wide listing can be useful when you want to see the types of files in a directory.

Using the Attributes Switch (/A)

When you specify the /A switch, only those files having the attributes you include on the command line are listed in the DIR display. The /A switch uses one or more of the following codes for the *attributes* parameter:

D	Directory attribute
R	Read-only attribute
H	Hidden attribute
A	Archive attribute
S	System attribute

Figure 8.1
Using the /W switch to see filenames presented in wide format.

```
Volume in drive C is DCI 3
Volume Serial Number is 1B2B-392C
Directory of C:\DOS

[.]            [..]           CHOICE.COM     COUNTRY.SYS    GORILLA.BAS
MONEY.BAS      NIBBLES.BAS    REMLINE.BAS    DBLSPACE.BIN   ASSIGN.COM
KEYB.COM       KEYBOARD.SYS   MSD.EXE        NLSFUNC.EXE    README.TXT
DOSSHELL.COM   SCANDISK.EXE   ATTRIB.EXE     GRAFTABL.COM   CHKDSK.EXE
DEBUG.EXE      DEFRAG.EXE     DEFRAG.HLP     MIRROR.COM     EMM386.EXE
SCANFIX.EXE    EXPAND.EXE     MSHERC.COM     FDISK.EXE      FORMAT.COM
HELP.COM       MEM.EXE        4201.CPI       4208.CPI       5202.CPI
MORE.COM       LCD.CPI        SCANDISK.INI   SYS.COM        XCOPY.EXE
ANSI.SYS       APPEND.EXE     DBLWIN.HLP     DELTREE.EXE    DISKCOMP.COM
DISKCOPY.COM   DISPLAY.SYS    DOSHELP.HLP    DOSKEY.COM     DRIVER.SYS
FASTHELP.EXE   FASTOPEN.EXE   COMP.EXE       FC.EXE         FIND.EXE
SCANFIX.INI    WHATSNEW.TXT   GRAPHICS.COM   DOSSHELL.EXE   DOSSWAP.EXE
EDLIN.EXE      HIMEM.SYS      EXE2BIN.EXE    INTERLNK.EXE   INTERSVR.EXE
MOUSE.COM      MOVE.EXE       POWER.EXE      SMARTMON.EXE   SMARTMON.HLP
VFINTD.386     JOIN.EXE       CHKSTATE.SYS   DBLSPACE.EXE   DBLSPACE.HLP
DBLSPACE.INF   DBLSPACE.SYS   MEMMAKER.EXE   MEMMAKER.HLP   MEMMAKER.INF
RAMDRIVE.SYS   SIZER.EXE      SMARTDRV.EXE   MWBACKUP.EXE   EDIT.COM
EDIT.HLP       MWBACKF.DLL    MWBACKR.DLL    RECOVER.EXE    NETWORKS.TXT
OS2.TXT        QBASIC.EXE     QBASIC.HLP     HELP.HLP       MWBACKUP.HLP
EGA.SYS        WNTOOLS.GRP    LOADFIX.COM    MODE.COM       MSTOOLS.DLL
DOSSHELL.GRB   PRINT.EXE      SHARE.EXE      SUBST.EXE      MSBACKDB.OVL
MSBACKDR.OVL   DOSSHELL.HLP   MSBACKFB.OVL   MSBACKFR.OVL   MSBACKUP.HLP
MSBACKUP.EXE   MSBACKUP.OVL   MSBCONFG.HLP   MSBCONFG.OVL   MONOUMB.386
MWGRAFIC.DLL   MWUNDEL.EXE    MWUNDEL.HLP    SORT.EXE       UNDELETE.EXE
DOSSHELL.INI   MOUSE.INI      MSAV.INI       MSAV.EXE       PACKING.LST
CHKLIST.MS     MSAV.HLP       MSAVHELP.OVL   MSAVIRUS.LST   MWAV.EXE
MWAV.HLP       MWAVABSI.DLL   MWAVDLG.DLL    MWAVDOSL.DLL   MWAVDRVL.DLL
MWAVMGR.DLL    MWAVSCAN.DLL   MWAVSOS.DLL    MWAVTSR.EXE    DELOLDOS.EXE
EGA.CPI        EGA2.CPI       GRAPHICS.PRO   PRINTER.SYS    KEYBRD2.SYS
SMARTDRV.SYS   APPNOTES.TXT   LABEL.EXE      MSCDEX.EXE     REPLACE.EXE
DOSSHELL.VID   RESTORE.EXE    SETVER.EXE     TREE.COM       UNFORMAT.COM
VSAFE.COM      COMMAND.COM
       157 file(s)    6,455,328 bytes
                    119,504,896 bytes free
```

If you include the /A switch with no *attributes* parameter, DOS lists all filenames—even the filenames of hidden and system files—regardless of file attribute. To see only a listing of all hidden files in the current directory, enter the following command and press Enter:

DIR /AH

You can use attribute codes in any combination and in any order. You can list all filenames with the read-only and archive attributes, for example, by issuing the following command:

DIR /ARA

DOS lists only filenames that have both attributes.

To list only filenames that do not have a certain attribute, insert a minus sign (–) before the attribute code. To see all files that are not directories and that don't have the archive bit, for example, type the following command at the command line and press Enter:

DIR /A-A-D

Using the Order Switch (/O)

As mentioned earlier, the /O switch enables you to choose the order in which DOS lists filenames. When you want DOS to sort the file list in a particular order, use the /O switch with the following sort codes:

C	Sorts files by compression ratio
D	Sorts files chronologically by date and time
E	Sorts files alphabetically by file extension
G	Groups directories first before showing files
N	Sorts files alphabetically by name
S	Sorts files numerically by file size

You can include sort codes in any combination. The order of the sort codes determines the final sorted order. /ONE, for example, sorts the filenames first by name and then by extension. The command DIR /OEN sorts files by extension (for example, grouping all .COM files together and all .EXE files together) and then sorts the files by name. If you include the /O switch in a DIR command without specifying a sort code, DOS sorts the files alphabetically by name.

DOS assumes that all sorting is to be done in ascending order—A through Z, smallest to largest, earliest to latest. DOS uses these criteria (the default setting) unless you precede your sort codes with a minus sign (–) to force the sort into reverse order—Z through A, largest to smallest, latest to earliest.

Using the /B and /L Switches

You can use the /B switch to display a "bare" file list—a list of filenames without information about file size and the date and time the file was last changed. The following is an example:

DIR A: /B

DOS lists all filenames of the files in the current directory of the floppy disk in drive A. For this example, DOS does not list file size or file date and time.

> **Tip**
>
> Another way to view directory listings, especially for extremely long listings, is to *pipe* the information to a text file for later viewing or printing. To do so, you use the > symbol after the DIR command and then specify a filename as follows:
>
> DIR > dirlist.txt
>
> This technique is especially helpful if you want to use the information in another program, such as Word, because you can cut and paste from the text file.

If you want to capture the file list to a file, issue a command similar to this:

DIR A: /B >FILES.TXT

You can use the /L switch with the DIR command if you want the filenames to appear in lowercase letters.

Searching for Files with the DIR Command

No matter how carefully you construct your directory structures, occasionally you lose a file. Most of the time you simply forget where you put a particular file. Sometimes, however, you lose the file because you have mistyped a filename expression. When you look in the directory in which you think a file should reside, it is missing. Other times, you simply forget the exact name of the file you're looking for.

The DIR command is an effective tool for finding "lost" files when you use the /S switch. Entering the following command causes DOS to display every file written to drive C:

```
DIR C:\ /S
```

You can, of course, use filename expressions and other DIR switches to narrow the scope of the search. The following example lists all the .DOC files in WordPerfect's directory as well as all the directories that branch off the WP directory:

```
DIR C:\WP\*.DOC /S
```

Assume for the moment that you have created budget spreadsheets using your spreadsheet software and that you have saved these spreadsheets on your hard disk. You want to make a copy of the budget spreadsheet files, but you cannot remember the directory in which they are located. However, you do remember that all the filenames start with the letters *BUDG*. You can use the DIR command to search the hard disk for the location of the files. To do so, change to the root directory of your hard disk and then type the following command:

```
DIR BUDG*.* /S
```

When you press Enter, DOS displays a listing similar to this:

```
 Volume in drive C is DCI 3
 Volume Serial Number is 1B2B-392C

 Directory of C:\SPREADSH\QPRO4DAT

BUDGET     WQ1       4,037 10-05-01   2:00a
        1 files(s)        4,037 bytes

 Directory of C:\WORD_PRO\ENDATA

BUDGET     WK1       5,120 04-07-01   8:51p
        1 files(s)        5,120 bytes

Total files listed:
        2 files(s)        9,157 bytes
                    119,504,896 bytes free
```

> **Note**
>
> As you have seen, you can use the DIR command to locate files if you know something about their filenames. But what do you use if you know only that the file contains the text "Meet me in St. Louis, Louie," and that the string is to be found in one of three files? In this case, you use the FIND command. Because FIND is useful in various situations, it is covered in detail in Chapter 13, "Controlling Devices."

Customizing the DIR Command

If you find that you continually use one or more of the several switches with the DIR command, you can avoid typing them repeatedly by creating an environment variable named DIRCMD using the following command:

SET DIRCMD=*switches*

For the *switches* parameter, substitute the switch or switches you want DOS to use automatically. If, for example, you want DOS to sort filenames alphabetically and pause scrolling after each screenful of information, include the following command in your AUTOEXEC.BAT file:

SET DIRCMD=/ON/P

Then, reboot the computer. DOS creates the environment variable DIRCMD and gives it the value /ON/P. Each time you issue the DIR command, DOS adds these two switches automatically.

You can override a switch that is recorded in DIRCMD by preceding the switch with a minus sign (–). To override the /P switch currently recorded in DIRCMD, for example, so that DOS lists all filenames without pausing at the end of each screen of information, issue the DIR command shown here:

DIR /-P

Viewing Files

After you find a file, you often need to peek into it to find out what it contains. Knowing what a file contains is crucial to knowing how to best work with the file. DOS provides tools to enable you to look into files.

Previously, you learned that DOS stores files on disks in binary format—using zeros and ones. You learned that these binary digits, grouped in bundles of eight, form bytes. You also read that each byte can form one of 256 values called the ASCII code, which represents letters, numbers, computer commands, and so on. That description is fine as far as it goes, but it is a simplistic view that doesn't present the whole picture.

→ For more information on how DOS stores data, **see** Chapter 6, "Understanding Disks and Disk Drives," **p. 127**.

A computer uses bits and bytes in many ways. The microprocessor in your computer is designed to use binary digits in groups of eight, true. But those binary digits can be used in different contexts. Each bit in a byte might be used to indicate the status of a condition, with 1 meaning on and 0 meaning off. Large numeric values, such as a spreadsheet might use, might be stored in two or four bytes, which are translated into decimal numbers that users understand. Bytes also are used to deliver instructions (program code) to your computer's microprocessor.

Understanding these contexts isn't at all important for you to be able to work with your computer, but knowing that these contexts exist makes it much easier to work with files. When you need to view the contents of files, having this knowledge is essential.

Understanding Types of Files

From a user's point of view, files fall into two categories: binary and ASCII. Binary files are not understandable by humans. When you try to look into them, they appear to be gibberish. Strings of smiley faces, hearts, and a slew of weird-looking symbols are interspersed with letters and numbers to produce an unintelligible display. When you see this kind of display, you know you have opened a binary file.

ASCII files use bytes to represent the symbols you use to communicate every day: letters, numerals, punctuation marks, and so on. An ASCII file is the simplest file format used by DOS. When DOS displays or prints an ASCII file, the groupings of binary digits are directly translated into a human-readable format. ASCII files also are referred to as *DOS text files*, or simply *text files*.

Unless you are programming, binary files are of little interest to you. DOS *does* provide the DEBUG command to view and edit binary files, but you had better know what you are doing. The DEBUG command is documented in Appendix F, "Command Reference," for the sake of completeness, but its use is far beyond the scope of this book. It is enough for you to know that if you open a binary file, you can look all you want, but under no circumstances do you want to change anything or do a disk save on the file, even by accident. Changing even one byte in an executable file can render a program useless and can even be dangerous to your data.

→ DOS provides two commands for viewing the contents of ASCII files: EDIT and TYPE. The EDIT command enables you to view and edit files. For complete information on EDIT, **see** Chapter 15, "Using the DOS Editor," **p. 361**.

Using the TYPE Command to View Files

When you need to see the contents of an ASCII text file, you can use the TYPE command. By redirecting the output of TYPE, you can print a hard copy of the file.

The syntax for the TYPE command is as follows:

TYPE *filename.ext*

Replace *filename.ext* with the name of the file you want DOS to display. (Remember to include a disk drive and pathname, if necessary.) A filename is not optional. Wildcard characters are not permitted because TYPE can display the contents of only one file at a time.

TYPE is designed to display the contents of a text file that contains ASCII characters. When you issue a TYPE command, DOS opens the specified file and sends the file's contents to the screen as ASCII characters. When DOS encounters a Ctrl+Z character (ASCII decimal 26; the end-of-file character), it stops displaying the contents of the file and returns to the command prompt.

When you use TYPE to view a text file, the file's contents can fill and begin to scroll off the screen faster than you can read the text. You can press Ctrl+S or the Pause key (available only on the Enhanced Keyboard) to stop scrolling, but the text you want to see might already have scrolled off the screen. The MORE filter displays a screenful of a command's output and then pauses until you press a key. You can use MORE with the TYPE command as follows:

TYPE AUTOEXEC.BAT | MORE

The | character in this command is the DOS pipe character, which instructs DOS to send a command's output to the filter that follows the pipe character. Piping to MORE causes DOS to pause the scrolling of the screen when the screen fills. You can press any key to display the next screenful.

→ For detailed information on DOS redirection and MORE, **see** Chapter 13, "Controlling Devices," **p. 317**.

> **Tip**
> An even easier way to display an ASCII file one screen at a time is to redirect a file into the MORE command without using the TYPE command. To do so, use the following syntax:
> MORE < d:path\filename.ext
> The < symbol causes DOS to use the specified file parameter as input to the MORE filter. DOS displays the file, one page at a time, displaying the message -More- at the end of each page. To display a file in the C:\DOS directory, for example, type the following command (replacing filename.ext with the filename and extension of the file you want to view), and press Enter:
> MORE < C:\DOS\filename.ext

If you want a simple printed copy of the contents of a text file, you can redirect the output of the TYPE command to the printer by using the special redirection character, the greater-than sign (>). To print the contents of the README.TXT file, for example, make sure that your printer is online and then issue the following command:

TYPE README.TXT >PRN

Your printer prints the file. (Because TYPE does not format the text into pages, the printed output might not break at page boundaries.)

When you use the TYPE command, remember the following guidelines:

- The output of TYPE stops when the command encounters the first Ctrl+Z in the file.
- Because TYPE does not accept wildcards in the filename parameter, use of the command is limited to one file at a time.
- TYPE tries to interpret any file as an ASCII text file, even if the file contains non-ASCII data. If you use a binary file (such as a COM or EXE file) as the file parameter, the TYPE command's output might produce graphical characters, control-character sequences, and beeps. Its output might even lock up your computer, forcing you to reboot.
- You can pause the TYPE command's output by pressing Ctrl+S or Pause. Press any key to resume scrolling.
- You can terminate the TYPE command's output by pressing Ctrl+C or Ctrl+Break.

Copying Files

Probably the most common file-related function is copying files from one disk or directory to another, a fundamental job for disk operating systems. MS-DOS provides the internal COPY command for use at the command line. Copying files via the DOS Shell is covered in Chapter 4, "Using the DOS Shell."

The DOS COPY command enables you to copy files as well as data to and from logical devices. Figure 8.2 diagrams the copy operation used with several possible inputs and two possible outputs. Three of the possible inputs consist of more than one file or logical device. DOS can join two or more inputs into one output in a process called *combining*. You might never need to use all these inputs and outputs, but they're available.

Figure 8.2
Possible inputs and outputs in a copy operation.

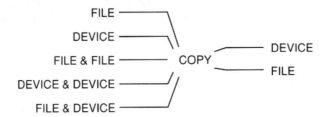

Using the COPY Command

You can create a COPY command line in various ways. All the variations say the same thing to DOS: "COPY THIS THERE." The THIS represents the source—the files to be copied. The THERE represents the target—the disk location or device you want the files to be copied to.

When you perform a copy operation, remember the following guidelines:

- The source parameter must contain at least one of the following parameters: path, file, or device.

- If the file specification portion of a filename expression is omitted, all files in the specified directory and drive are copied. This situation is equivalent to supplying *.* as the source-file parameter.

- You can specify additional source-file parameters by using the + operator to combine the files.

- If the source-file parameter contains a wildcard and the destination parameter is a filename, the destination file is the combination of source files that match the source-file parameter.

- If COPY detects an attempt to copy a single source file to itself (same drive, directory, filename, and extension), the copy operation is aborted.

- The optional destination parameter consists of a combination of drive, path, and filename parameters. If you don't provide a drive or path, DOS uses the current drive or path for the destination. If you don't specify a destination filename, DOS uses the source file's name as the destination parameter.

- COPY is definitely a versatile file-management workhorse, but you do have to be careful. An incorrect COPY operation can do nearly as much damage as an incorrect DEL command because the destination file's entries in the FAT and in the directory are not saved as they were, making file recovery all but impossible. Be sure to treat COPY with respect. Many programs include warning messages as part of their internal file copying commands. The COPY command gives no warning when it is about to overwrite existing files.

In a COPY command, the order of the parameter requirements always moves from the source to the destination, or target. The full syntax for the COPY command is as follows:

COPY *SourceExpression* *TargetExpression* /V /A /B /Y

The *SourceExpression* and *TargetExpression* parameters specify either a filename expression that specifies one or more files or a DOS device, as in the following example:

COPY STUFF.TXT PRN

In this example, the file STUFF.TXT (an ASCII text file) is copied to the printer to produce a hard copy of the file's contents. Use COPY to print ASCII files only because files containing word processor codes, graphics, or file headers don't result in clean reproductions of the file's content.

For combining files, the source expression can be two or more filename expressions that specify a single file, joined with the + symbol, as in this example:

COPY MEMO1.TXT + B:\MEMOS\MEMO2.TXT   H:\MYMEMO.TXT

In this example, the file MEMO1.TXT, located in the currently logged directory, will be combined with a file located in the MEMOS directory of drive B to create a file having the name MYMEMO.TXT on drive H.

As you can see, you can use four switches with the COPY command: /V, /A, /B, and /Y. The /A and /B switches can be applied to individual filename expressions in both the source and target expressions. The following list details the uses of the COPY switches:

- The /V switch verifies that the copy has been recorded correctly.
- When /A is used in *SourceExpression*, files are treated as ASCII; that is, COPY copies all the information in the file up to, but not including, the first end-of-file marker (ASCII decimal 26). DOS ignores anything after the end-of-file marker.
- When /A is used in *TargetExpression*, an end-of-file marker is added to the end of the ASCII file after it is copied.
- When /B is used in *SourceExpression*, COPY copies the entire file (based on its size, as listed in the directory) as though the copied file were a program file (binary). Any end-of-file markers are copied.
- When /B is used in *TargetExpression*, it does not add the end-of-file marker to the end of the copied data.
- The /Y switch indicates whether you want COPY to overwrite files with the same name without prompting. You can use the /-Y switch to indicate that you want to be prompted.

Copying Groups of Files

Suppose that you have 20 files you want to copy to a floppy disk or to another directory on your hard disk. You can use wildcards in the filename expression to specify a subset of the files in a directory, as in this example:

`COPY C:\ROCCANTI\*.TXT B:`

This example finds all the .TXT files in the ROCCANTI directory and copies them onto the floppy disk in drive B. You do, of course, have to make sure that the disk in drive B has enough room to receive the files. Use the DIR command to find out how many bytes the files to be copied require and to make sure that at least that much space is available on drive B.

If you want to copy all the files in a directory to another disk or another directory, use a command similar to this:

`COPY E:\CLIPPER5\INVNTRY\*.* H:\TEST`

In this example, the *.* wildcard expression specifies that all files in the INVNTRY directory are to be copied to the TEST directory on drive H.

> **Tip**
>
> Some older keyboards do not have a conveniently placed key for the asterisk. You might want to use the . wildcard to specify all files in the directory, as in this line:
> `COPY E:\CLIPPER5\INVNTRY\. H:\TEST`
> This command is functionally equivalent to the preceding example using the *.

Combining Text Files

Although you can use COPY to combine any files, the combine operation is most effective when the files are ASCII text files. In most cases, combining binary files results in an unusable destination file.

For the following examples, assume that the current directory contains three text files, all with .TXT extensions. The files and their contents are listed here:

File	Contents
INTRO.TXT	Combining is
BODY.TXT	the joining of files
ENDING.TXT	into a new file.

To join the three files into a fourth file, type the following command:

`COPY INTRO.TXT+BODY.TXT+ENDING.TXT ALL.TXT`

The resulting file, ALL.TXT, contains the text from the three source files. To verify ALL.TXT, issue the following command:

`TYPE ALL.TXT`

TYPE sends the contents of ALL.TXT to the screen. DOS displays the following output:

```
Combining is the joining of files into a new file.
```

> **Note:** If you omit the target expression, or specify only drive and path information in the filename expression, the file created by combining files has the same name as the first filename specified in the source expression.

RENAMING FILES WITH COPY

As you might guess from the examples in the preceding section, you can change the name of a file or group of files by using COPY. Consider this example:

```
COPY *.TXT *.ASC
```

This example copies all the files in the current directory having the extension TXT. Each TXT file is copied to an ASC file. The ASC files have the same names as the original TXT files. The contents are the same and the names are the same—only the extensions are altered.

COPYING FROM A DEVICE TO A FILE

A common and handy use of the COPY command is copying to a file keystrokes entered from the keyboard or console device. (CON is the device name for console, a device constructed using your keyboard and monitor.) You can use the resulting text file as a batch file, a configuration file, a memo, and so on.

To practice copying from the keyboard to a file, you can create a simple batch file that changes the current directory to \123R3 and starts Lotus 1-2-3 Release 3. The command that creates the batch file is shown here:

```
COPY CON C:\DOS\RUN123.BAT
```

When you press Enter, DOS displays the cursor on the next line, but the DOS prompt does not appear. You can type the file by following these steps:

1. Type C: and press Enter. The cursor drops to the next line.
2. Type CD\123R3 and press Enter. The cursor drops to the next line.
3. Type LOTUS and press Enter. The cursor drops to the next line.
4. Press the F6 function key or Ctrl+Z to indicate the end of the file. DOS displays the end-of-file marker (^Z).
5. Press Enter. The ^Z code indicates to DOS that you are finished entering data into the file. DOS responds with the message 1 file(s) copied.

To confirm that the new file appears the way you want it, you can use the TYPE command to review its contents.

> **Note:** If you try this example on your system, be sure to use the appropriate directory names for DOS and Lotus 1-2-3.

Knowing how to use COPY CON can be both a lifesaver and a pain in the neck. It can be a lifesaver because COPY CON enables you to create a text file on any DOS system. It also can be a pain in the neck because after you have pressed Enter to go to the next line, you cannot go back and edit previous lines. If you make a mistake, you must start over again.

If the DOS EDIT command—found only in version 5.0 and later—is available, or if some other ASCII editor is available, use it. You are much better off using the editor instead of the COPY command because you can more easily correct any typos you find.

USING THE XCOPY COMMAND

The external command XCOPY is an enhanced version of COPY that, among other capabilities, can copy whole directories and their subdirectories while creating directories on the destination disk.

Using XCOPY, you can exercise much more control over the files to be copied. You can copy only those files with the archive attribute set, for example, or only those files with a date stamp on or after a specified date.

The syntax of XCOPY is similar to that of COPY, but the switches are more complex. The XCOPY syntax is as follows:

```
XCOPY SourceExpression TargetExpression /V /P /W /S /E /A /M /Y /D:date
```

Just like the COPY command, XCOPY takes filename expressions to specify the source files and the target files for the operation. Unlike COPY, XCOPY has several switches that enable you to finely control how the copy is performed. Following is a rundown of the available switches:

- /V verifies the accuracy of the copy operation by comparing each file as it is written to the original file.
- /P displays a prompt to confirm whether you want to create each destination file. Using /P, you can specify a group of files with a wildcard and then decide which files you actually want to copy. If, for example, you want to copy several files in a directory but don't want to enter five separate COPY commands, you can use the following:
  ```
  XCOPY *.TXT B: /P
  ```
  As each file is about to be copied, XCOPY prompts you to see whether that file is to be copied. Answer Y and the file is copied; answer N and it is skipped.
- /W causes XCOPY to pause before copying any files, displaying the prompt `Press any key to begin copying file(s)`. You can pause to change disks.
- /S causes XCOPY to copy the files located in any directories that branch off from the source directory. Empty directories are ignored.
- /E causes XCOPY to copy even empty directories.

- /A causes XCOPY to copy only files with the archive attribute set without modifying the file's attributes.
- /M causes XCOPY to remove the archive bit from any files copied.
- The /Y switch indicates whether you want XCOPY to overwrite files with the same name without prompting. You also can use the /-Y switch to indicate that you want to be prompted.
- /D enables you to specify a date parameter. XCOPY copies only files with a date attribute on or after the specified date. Which date format you use depends on the country setting you use.

In an XCOPY operation, DOS might not always recognize whether a particular parameter refers to a file or to a directory. When ambiguity arises, XCOPY asks whether the destination is a filename or pathname.

> **Note** All files created by XCOPY have the archive attribute set automatically, even if the original source file does not have the archive attribute.

Consider the following command:

```
XCOPY C:\WORDS\*.* A:\WORDS
```

If no directory named WORDS exists on the destination disk, DOS cannot determine whether you intend to create a file or a directory named WORDS on the A disk.

XCOPY displays the following message:

```
Does WORDS specify a file name
or directory name on the target
(F = file, D = directory)?
```

Press F when the destination (target) is a filename or D when the destination is a directory. Unlike COPY, XCOPY creates directories on the destination disk as needed.

If you append a backslash to the name of the target directory, XCOPY automatically assumes that the target is a directory, not a file. Continuing the preceding example, if you use the following command instead, you do not have to specify that the target is a directory:

```
XCOPY C:\WORDS\*.* A:\WORDS\
```

XCOPY creates the \WORDS directory if it does not exist.

Understanding the Operation of XCOPY

XCOPY is best described as a hybrid between COPY and BACKUP/RESTORE. XCOPY and COPY duplicate files between directories and disks. Unlike COPY, however, XCOPY does not copy files to a nondisk device, such as the printer (PRN) or console (CON). Like BACKUP and RESTORE, XCOPY can copy files selectively and traverse the directory tree to copy files from more than one directory. XCOPY also can make a destination directory when one does not exist. This directory capability makes XCOPY useful for duplicating a directory branch onto another disk.

Like COPY but unlike BACKUP, XCOPY copies files that are directly usable. (You cannot use files processed by BACKUP until you have processed them with RESTORE.)

When using the XCOPY command, consider the following guidelines:

- XCOPY cannot copy hidden source files.
- XCOPY does not overwrite read-only destination files.
- If a file parameter is omitted in the XCOPY syntax, XCOPY assumes the *.* full wildcard pattern as the default file parameter.
- If you include the /D switch, you must enter the date parameter in the format of the system's DATE command or in the format indicated by the latest COUNTRY command.
- The /V switch performs the same read-after-write checking as the SET VERIFY ON global verify flag.

To use XCOPY to copy empty source subdirectories, you must specify both the /S and /E switches.

> **Tip**
>
> The XCOPY command is one of the most useful DOS file commands available. To copy the source files of an entire program (such as Windows 95) to the hard drive, for example, it is much easier to use the XCOPY command with wildcards and the /S switch (to copy subdirectories) than to attempt to drill down and copy each directory by itself with the COPY command.

Using XCOPY Effectively

Using XCOPY, you can control by date or archive attribute the files copied, you can copy complete subdirectory trees, and you can confirm which files to copy. The command has several ideal uses: copying files selectively between disks or directories, performing a quick hard disk backup (backing up only a few critical files in several subdirectories), and keeping the directories of two or more computers synchronized.

With COPY, your control is limited. COPY duplicates all files that match the given name—an all-or-nothing approach. If you use the /P switch with XCOPY, however, DOS asks whether you want to copy each file.

Using XCOPY is practical if you want to make backup copies of something less than a disk full of files from several directories. Rather than BACKUP, you might prefer to use the command XCOPY /A to select files that have changed since the last backup.

> **Tip**
>
> Keep the following points in mind when you use XCOPY to back up a disk:
> - If you suspect that the files cannot fit on one disk, be sure to use the /M switch. As XCOPY copies each file, the command resets the file's archive attribute bit. When the destination disk is full, XCOPY stops. At this point, you can change disks and restart the XCOPY command, again using the /M switch. XCOPY copies the files whose archive bit has not yet been reset.
> - XCOPY cannot break a large source file between destination disks. If you need to back up a file that doesn't fit on a single floppy disk, you must use BACKUP.
> - A favorite use of XCOPY is to synchronize the contents of the hard disks of two computers. Many people have one computer at work and another at home. If both computers have hard disks, keeping the copies of programs and data files current is a major task. Which files did you change today? Which machine has the more current version?
> - When you want to keep separate hard disks synchronized, you might find the XCOPY command's /A, /D:*date*, and /S switches especially useful. The /S switch forces XCOPY to traverse your disk's directory structure, playing a hunting game for source files. Whether you use /A or /D depends on how often you copy files between the machines. If you copy files between the machines frequently, you might prefer the /A switch. If you allow many days to pass between synchronizing your computers' contents, you might find that the /D switch works better. Use /D if you have run BACKUP on the source machine since you last used XCOPY. BACKUP resets the archive attribute so that the command's /A switch does not catch all files changed between XCOPY backups.

→ For more information on backing up files, **see** "Understanding Microsoft Backup," **p. 233**.

Duplicating Disks with XCOPY

The XCOPY command can be used to create duplicate floppy disks, even when the disks are different sizes or formats. You can't make a disk hold more than its capacity, of course, so you can't use XCOPY to copy a full 1.44MB floppy disk onto a 720KB disk. You can, however, transfer the contents and directory structures of a 1.2MB 5 1/4-inch disk to a 1.44MB 3 1/2-inch disk, or a 720KB 3 1/2-inch disk to a 1.2MB or 1.44MB disk. Assume that you have a 720KB disk with several levels of directories in drive B, for example, and you want to copy it to a 1.2MB disk in drive A. To do so, you issue the following command:

```
XCOPY B: A: /S
```

Duplicating a Directory Branch

For this example, assume that your hard disk has a subdirectory named \WPFILES that contains a few word processing files. \WPFILES also has two subdirectories. The first, \WPFILES\MEMOS, contains your current memos; the second, \WPFILES\DOCS, contains your document files. You want to keep a current set of the files in these three directories stored on a floppy disk. To copy all the files in this directory branch to the floppy disk, issue the following command:

```
XCOPY C:\WPFILES A:\WPFILES\ /S
```

XCOPY immediately begins to read the source directories. DOS displays the following messages:

```
Reading source file(s)...
C:\WPFILES\LET9_1.WP
C:\WPFILES\LET9_2.WP
C:\WPFILES\LET9_3.WP
C:\WPFILES\LET9_4.WP
C:\WPFILES\LET9_5.WP
C:\WPFILES\DOCS\SCHEDULE.DOC
C:\WPFILES\MEMOS\SALES.MEM
     7 File(s) copied
```

Because you included the /S switch, XCOPY copied the files in C:\WPFILES, C:\WPFILES\MEMOS, and C:\WPFILES\DOCS. The A:\WPFILES path parameter causes XCOPY to ask whether the name specifies a directory or a file. \WPFILES conceivably can be a user file in the root directory. The full pathname of each file is echoed to the screen as the file is copied to drive A. When the command finishes, the \WPFILES directory branch has been copied to drive A.

As another example, assume that your PC experiences a hardware failure and needs to go to the shop for repairs. You want to use your floppy disk that contains the \WPFILES directory branch to place that directory branch on a second computer's hard disk. To do so, enter the following command:

```
XCOPY A: C: /S
```

XCOPY reverses the copy process described in the preceding paragraphs by copying all the files on drive A to corresponding subdirectory locations on drive C.

COPYING ENTIRE DISKS WITH DISKCOPY

The external DISKCOPY command makes exact duplicates of a disk. Duplication is so complete that even file fragmentation is preserved. If the target disk has not yet been formatted, DISKCOPY automatically formats it before performing the duplication.

DISKCOPY does have one major limitation. You can copy only like media to like media. A 1.2MB disk, for example, can be successfully copied only to another 1.2MB disk. You cannot use DISKCOPY to duplicate a 720KB floppy disk on a 1.44MB disk. See the section on using XCOPY to duplicate disks earlier in this chapter for information on duplicating unlike disks.

The syntax for DISKCOPY is as follows:

```
DISKCOPY SourceDisk TargetDisk /1 /V /M
```

The source disk is the drive letter that holds the original disk to be duplicated. The target disk is the optional name of the drive that holds the disk to receive the copy. This destination drive is sometimes called the target drive. If you don't specify a drive name for the target, DOS assumes that you want to use the current drive and prompts you to insert and remove source and destination disks as necessary.

Only three switches are recognized by DISKCOPY. The /1 switch causes DOS to copy only the first side of a double-sided disk. This switch, which is a holdover from old versions of DOS, enables you to copy single-sided disks. Chances are, you will never need the /1 switch.

The /V switch instructs DOS to verify that the copy and original are identical. This switch slows down operations by adding the extra comparison step. You use this switch only when you are working with disks that you will never have an opportunity to copy again and you need to make absolutely sure you got a clean copy.

The /M switch forces DISKCOPY to work in memory only. Using this switch means that DISKCOPY does not use temporary files on your hard disk to aid in duplication. Instead, all operations are performed in memory. This method of operation effectively forces you to swap disks during the copy, as was required in older versions of DOS.

> **Note**
>
> If you leave out the drive names in the DISKCOPY command line, DOS uses the current drive as the specifier. If you have a system with only one disk drive or if the second disk drive supports only different formats, you can simply issue this command:
>
> DISKCOPY
>
> Remember to log on to the drive you want to use before issuing the command. DOS prompts you to insert the source disk and target disk at the appropriate times.

The following is the classic example of the DISKCOPY command:

DISKCOPY A: B:

This example assumes that both drive A and drive B contain disks having the same capacity. After you issue the DISKCOPY command, DOS prompts you to insert the disks into the proper drives. Make sure that you insert the disks into the correct drives. Write-protect the source disk to safeguard its contents in case of a disk mix-up.

When the disks are in place, you are ready to continue. Press any key to start the DISKCOPY process. When the process is complete, DOS asks whether you want to make another copy. Press Y to copy another disk or N to exit the command (see Figure 8.3). If the drives or disks are not compatible, an error message appears, and nothing is copied (see Figure 8.4).

Figure 8.3
A typical DISKCOPY command sequence and messages from DOS.

```
C:\>DISKCOPY A: B:
Insert SOURCE diskette in drive A:
Insert TARGET diskette in drive B:
Press any key to continue . . .
Copying 80 tracks
9 sectors per track, 2 side(s)
Volume Serial Number is 1EEA-0431
Copy another diskette (Y/N)? N
C:\>
```

Figure 8.4
An error message produced by the DISKCOPY command.

```
C:\>diskcopy a: b:
Insert SOURCE diskette in drive A:
Insert TARGET diskette in drive B:
Press any key to continue . . .
Drive types or diskette types
not compatible
Copy process ended
Copy another diskette (Y/N)?
```

Moving Files

In early versions of DOS, if you wanted to move a file from one place to another, you had to first copy the file and then delete the original. Now DOS enables you to move files from one location to another using the MOVE command.

The MOVE command's syntax is similar to the syntax for COPY. In effect, the syntax of the MOVE command says, "MOVE THIS THERE."

In a MOVE command, the order of the parameter requirements always moves from the source to the destination, or target. The full syntax for the MOVE command is as follows:

MOVE *SourceExpression*(s) *TargetExpression* /Y

> **Caution**
> If you omit a path parameter from both the source and target, you either copy or rename the source file, depending on whether the specified target filename exists. If the name exists, you copy the source file over the target file, eliminating the target file. If the name does not exist, you rename the source file.

If your source parameter includes only one file, you can rename the file as you move it by specifying a new filename or extension as part or all of the target parameter. If your source parameter includes more than one file, you cannot use a filename and extension parameter as part of the target parameter. If you do so, however, DOS assumes that you want the target file to be the target for all the files to be moved, and the message `Cannot move multiple files to a single file` appears. You must, however, specify either a drive or directory as the target.

The /Y switch indicates whether you want MOVE to overwrite files with the same name without prompting. You also can use the /-Y switch to indicate that you want to be prompted.

As an example of how to use MOVE, suppose you want to move a file called BUDGET01.WQ1 from a directory called C:\SPREADSH\QPRO4DAT to a directory called D:\OLDFILES (assuming neither directory is current). In this case, you enter this command:

MOVE C:\SPREADSH\QPRO4DAT\BUDGET01.WQ1 D:\OLDFILES

If the move is successful, DOS displays the following message:

c:\spreadsh\qpro4dat\budget01.wq1 => d:\oldfiles\budget.wq1 [ok]

> **Caution**
> If the source and target parameters represent the same file, DOS erases the file without warning you.

Moving Directories and Files

You can use MOVE to move files from one directory to another. If the target directory doesn't exist, the MOVE command creates it. Figure 8.5 shows the MOVE command moving all the files in H:\TEST to a new TEST directory on drive G.

Figure 8.5
Moving all the files in a directory.

```
H:\>rd g:\test

H:\>move h:\test\*.* g:\test
Make directory "g:\test"? [yn] y
h:\test\ground.dbf => g:\test\ground.dbf [ok]
h:\test\group.dbf => g:\test\group.dbf [ok]
h:\test\guest.dbf => g:\test\guest.dbf [ok]
h:\test\passw.dbf => g:\test\passw.dbf [ok]
h:\test\paymts.dbf => g:\test\paymts.dbf [ok]
h:\test\pay_vend.dbf => g:\test\pay_vend.dbf [ok]
h:\test\res_air.dbf => g:\test\res_air.dbf [ok]
h:\test\res_car.dbf => g:\test\res_car.dbf [ok]
h:\test\res_grou.dbf => g:\test\res_grou.dbf [ok]
h:\test\res_hot.dbf => g:\test\res_hot.dbf [ok]
h:\test\res_tour.dbf => g:\test\res_tour.dbf [ok]
h:\test\semi_4.dbf => g:\test\semi_4.dbf [ok]
h:\test\tour.dbf => g:\test\tour.dbf [ok]
h:\test\trans.mem => g:\test\trans.mem [ok]

H:\>
```

As you can see in the figure, the source expression specifies that all the files in the TEST directory on drive H are to be moved to a directory called TEST on drive G. Because the directory doesn't exist on drive G, MOVE prompts you to make sure that you intend to create a new directory to hold the moved files. As each file is moved, MOVE displays the original name, a => symbol, and the new name of each file.

The MOVE command has no effect on H:\TEST other than to remove the files from the directory. The source directory is not deleted from drive H. Also, the MOVE command pays no attention to the read-only file attribute. Even files marked read-only are moved.

Renaming Directories with MOVE

Another use for the MOVE command is to rename a directory, as shown in the following example:

MOVE C:\MEMOS   C:\LETTERS

The effect of the sample command is to rename the MEMOS directory as LETTERS without affecting the files contained in the directory.

Setting Defaults for COPY, XCOPY, and MOVE

If you are using DOS 6.22, you can use a new environment variable to specify how you want all three file-management commands—COPY, XCOPY, and MOVE—to work. The COPYCMD environment variable is similar to the DIRCMD environment variable discussed in the section "Customizing the DIR Command" earlier in this chapter; it sets default switches that DOS uses whenever you issue the COPY, XCOPY, or MOVE commands.

The command to set the COPYCMD environment variable is as follows:

SET COPYCMD=switches

For the *switches* parameter, substitute the switch or switches you want DOS to use automatically. If, for example, you do not want DOS to prompt you when it is about to overwrite a destination file, include the following command in your AUTOEXEC.BAT file:

SET COPYCMD=/Y

Then reboot the computer. DOS creates the environment variable COPYCMD and gives it the value /Y. Each time you issue the DIR command, DOS adds this switch automatically.

You can override a switch that is recorded in COPYCMD by preceding the switch with a minus sign (–). To override the /Y switch that is currently recorded in COPYCMD (so that DOS tells you when it will overwrite a file), for example, issue the COPY command as shown here:

COPY / -Y

Renaming Files

If copying files is the most common file-related function of DOS, renaming files probably follows close on its heels. The reasons for renaming a file are many. You might want to use the current filename for another file, or perhaps you want to create a name that better describes the contents of the current file. Whatever the reason, DOS enables you to rename a file using the internal command RENAME. Like some other DOS commands, RENAME also has a short form, REN. Which form you use depends on how you feel about typing three extra letters.

The DOS rename operation changes the name in a file's directory entry, but the file and its physical location on the disk remain unchanged. Because two files in the same directory cannot have the same name, DOS does not change a filename if the new filename already exists.

The syntax for RENAME is either of the following:

RENAME OldExpression NewExpression

REN OldExpression NewExpression

The REN command requires two parameters. *OldExpression* is a filename expression that specifies the files to be renamed. *NewExpression* is a filename expression that specifies what the new names of the files will be. Consider this example:

REN MEMO.TXT MEMO12.TXT

This example renames the file MEMO.TXT as MEMO12.TXT.

You also can use wildcards to specify groups of files to be renamed. Suppose, for example, that you have a group of files named MEMO1.TXT, MEMO2.TXT, and so on in your directory. To rename them, you can issue this command:

REN MEMO?.TXT LTR?.DOC

The result is that MEMO1.TXT is renamed as LTR1.DOC, MEMO2.TXT becomes LTR2.DOC, and so on.

When you use RENAME, remember the following guidelines:

- You can use the commands REN and RENAME interchangeably at the command line. Both commands produce identical results.
- You must supply both an old filename and a new filename. The filenames can contain wildcards for DOS to use in pattern matching.
- You cannot use the RENAME operation to move a file from one directory or disk to another directory or disk.

Note If you are not sure which files a wildcard parameter will match, issue the DIR command, using the wildcard pattern that you plan to use in the filename parameter. DIR lists the matching filenames. Study these names carefully to see whether using the wildcard pattern with the RENAME command will produce the result you expect.

COMPARING FILES

MS-DOS 6.22 contains a program called FC that allows you to compare files to verify their integrity. For example, if you have your entire company's budget in a file and you wanted to make a copy of it to store offsite, using the FC command to verify that the copied file is exactly the same would provide an additional verification that it is a valid copy. The following sections will describe how to use the FC command effectively.

COMPARING FILES WITH FC

The external command FC (meaning file comparison) compares two files or two sets of files to find differences in the files. Any differences are reported onscreen. When a copied file is extremely important, you can use FC to compare the file with the original. If differences are found, you know that a problem might exist with the copy. Normally, DOS detects data integrity errors while reading and writing files, but if you want to be sure that two files are the same, you can ease your mind by using FC.

> **Note**
>
> PC DOS versions 1.0 through 5.0 and MS-DOS versions 3.3 through 5.0 include a simpler file comparison command, COMP. This command, however, is less versatile than FC, provides less information, has fewer options, and cannot compare files of different lengths.

The FC command has two general syntax forms. One form uses the /B switch for a forced binary comparison; the other form uses the remaining switches in an ASCII comparison. The two forms of syntax are as follows:

FC /B *SourceExpression TargetExpression*

FC /A /C /L /LB*n* /N /*nnnn* /T /W *SourceExpression TargetExpression*

The source expression specifies the originals of the files to be compared. If you use wildcard characters in this parameter, all files matching this parameter are compared with the second file.

The target expression specifies the files to be compared to the originals. Usually, you need to specify only the drive and directory part of a filename expression. FC compares those files specified in the source expression that can be found in the target directory.

> **Note**
>
> If you use wildcard characters in both the source and target expressions, FC compares the files as sets. That is, only those files whose names match in other respects are compared.
>
> If you use the command FC *.WK1 *.BAK, for example, FC compares each worksheet file having the extension .WK1 with the worksheet file having the same base name and the extension .BAK. AUGSEPT.WK1, for example, is compared with AUGSEPT.BAK. FC does not compare every worksheet file with every backup file.

The switches used by FC enable you to control the operations of the command more tightly. The switches used are as follows:

- /A instructs FC to abbreviate its output (DOS 3.2 and later versions), displaying only the first and last lines of each set of differences separated by an ellipsis (…).
- /B performs a binary (byte-by-byte) comparison, showing the hexadecimal address and value of every differing byte.
- /C causes FC to ignore the case of alphabetic characters when making comparisons; thus, c = C.
- /L instructs FC to compare the files in ASCII mode, even when the files have EXE, COM, SYS, OBJ, LIB, or BIN extensions (DOS 3.2 and later versions).

- /LB*n* sets the number of lines in the FC command's buffer to *n*. The default number is 100 (DOS 3.2 and later versions). If the number of consecutive nonmatching lines exceeds the buffer size, FC aborts the compare operation.
- /N instructs FC to include the line numbers of lines reported in the output (DOS 3.2 and later versions).
- /*nnnn* establishes the number of lines that must match after a difference in order to resynchronize FC.
- /T instructs FC to view tab characters as literal characters rather than tab-expanded spaces (DOS 3.2 and later versions).
- /W instructs FC to compress whitespace—tabs, empty lines, and spaces—into a single space for purposes of file comparison.

Understanding the Operation of FC

FC works in two modes: ASCII and binary. It defaults to ASCII mode comparison when the files to be compared do not have extensions (EXE, COM, SYS, OBJ, LIB, or BIN) that traditionally indicate binary files.

In ASCII mode, FC compares two files line-by-line. Lines from both files are held in a line buffer. FC uses the lines in the buffer to compare the first file to the second.

If FC detects a difference, it displays the first filename followed by the last matching line and the mismatching line or lines from the first file. It then displays the next line to match in both files.

After displaying mismatch information about file 1, FC repeats the same sequence for file 2. The file 2 name is displayed first, followed by the last matching line and the mismatching lines from file 2, ending on the next line that matches in both files, thus synchronizing the two files.

FC can help you determine whether the contents of two files are different by showing you the extent and location of any mismatch it finds. You can use this output as an alternative to a side-by-side comparison of the file contents.

> **Tip**
> If you are comparing two files that are not the same, you can quickly stop the reporting of differences by pressing Ctrl+C or Ctrl+Break.

In binary mode, FC compares two files byte-for-byte. At the first difference, the byte offset position in the first file is reported along with the value of the two files' bytes at that position. The offset and byte values are reported in hexadecimal (base 16) form. This form of FC is essentially equivalent to the older COMP command.

In binary mode, FC does not attempt to resynchronize the two files by finding an adjusted point of byte agreement. If one file has an additional byte at one place in the file, FC reports the additional byte and all subsequent bytes of the file as mismatches.

If one file is longer than its comparison file, the binary mode compares as many bytes as are present and then reports that one file is longer. When a binary file comparison results in a long listing of differences, you might want to stop the FC operation by pressing Ctrl+C or Ctrl+Break.

Only one switch is available in the binary mode. The /B switch causes the comparison to be binary even if file extensions indicate that the files are not binary. You use the /B switch to compare two text files in binary mode. You might find situations in which you prefer to have the binary-mode output format of FC than the ASCII mode format. Binary mode format reports differences as pairs of hexadecimal values. You then can see the values of characters, such as Ctrl+G (bell), that do not produce printed output.

When you use FC, keep in mind that the default number of lines that must match in an ASCII comparison after a difference has ended is two. The files are then considered resynchronized. Using the /*nnnn* switch, you can change the number of "must match" lines by setting *nnnn* to the desired value.

USING FC TO COMPARE A COPIED FILE TO ITS ORIGINAL

Suppose that you are copying the ANSI.SYS file from your hard disk to a floppy disk to use for an important demonstration on another PC. When the copy is complete, you set the disk on the edge of your desk and go to the break room to get coffee. When you return, you notice that the disk has fallen off your desk and landed against the small transformer that runs your cassette recorder. You are worried that the magnetic field from the transformer has damaged ANSI.SYS. To verify that the copied ANSI.SYS file is good, you can compare it to the original by using the following command:

```
FC A:ANSI.SYS C:\DOS\DRIVERS\ANSI.SYS
```

After a few seconds, FC reports FC: No differences encountered. The copy of ANSI.SYS seems to be good.

COMPARING TWO TEXT FILES

Suppose that two similar text files, ORIGINAL.TXT and ANOTHER.TXT, are located in the default directory of the current drive. ORIGINAL.TXT contains the following text:

```
This is the first line.
This is the second line.
1
2
3
4
5
This is the last line.
```

ANOTHER.TXT contains the following text:

```
This is the first line.
This is not the third line.
1
2
```

```
3
4
5
6
7
8
9
This is the last line.
```

Note that ANOTHER.TXT has four more lines than ORIGINAL.TXT and that the second lines of the files contain differing text. These simple files illustrate how FC reports differences. You can use the principles illustrated here to understand the result of comparisons of more complex files. If, for example, you want to compare the two files that are in the same directory, you issue the following command:

```
FC ORIGINAL.TXT ANOTHER.TXT
```

FC makes the following report:

```
Comparing files ORIGINAL.TXT and ANOTHER.TXT ***** ORIGINAL.TXT
This is the first line.
This is the second line.
1
***** ANOTHER.TXT
This is the first line.
This is not the third line.
1
*****


***** ORIGINAL.TXT
5
This is the last line.
***** ANOTHER.TXT
5
6
7
8
9
This is the last line.
*****
```

FC displays the lines before and after the mismatched line, if any exist. It also finds mismatches that are not on equivalent lines so that it can match text even when one file contains material not found in the other. The second report concerning ANOTHER.TXT shows all the lines between the one containing the numeral 5 and the one containing the text This is the last line. Only these two matching lines appear in the report concerning ORIGINAL.TXT.

Comparing Disks with DISKCOMP

You can confirm that two disks are identical by using the external command DISKCOMP, which compares each track of one disk to each track of another disk sector-by-sector. Like DISKCOPY, DISKCOMP is a floppy-only command; you cannot use DISKCOMP to compare two hard disks. Furthermore, the disk types and capacities must be the same for both disks in the comparison; any difference in disks made with DISKCOPY is a sign of a problem disk.

One practical use of DISKCOMP is comparing a master disk included with a software package to a working copy of that disk. DISKCOMP confirms whether the working copy is good.

Normally, you use DISKCOMP to test disks that were made from originals with the DISKCOPY command. Because DISKCOMP doesn't write any information to either disk, both disks can be write-protected. If the disks are identical, DOS displays the message Compare OK.

The syntax for DISKCOMP is similar to that for DISKCOPY. The syntax for DISKCOMP is as follows:

DISKCOMP *SourceDisk TargetDisk* /1 /8

The source disk is the original, and the target disk is the copy. DISKCOMP recognizes only two switches. The /1 switch causes DOS to compare only the first sides of the disks. The /8 switch compares only the first eight sectors of each track on the disks. Both of these switches provide backward compatibility for testing floppy disks made with very old versions of DOS.

An example of the DISKCOMP command is as follows:

DISKCOMP A: B:

When the first DISKCOMP operation is complete, DOS asks whether you want to compare another disk.

In the sequence shown in Figure 8.6, a working copy of a master disk is being compared to the original master. Notice the comparison errors. The working copy no longer is reliable, or other files have been added to the disk since DISKCOPY was used to make a working copy from the master. The best way to solve the problem is to make a new working copy.

Figure 8.6
Comparing a working copy of a master disk to the original disk.

```
C:\>DISKCOMP A: B:
Insert FIRST diskette in drive A:
Insert SECOND diskette in drive B:
Press any key to continue . . .
Comparing 80 tracks
9 sectors per track, 2 side(s)
Compare error on
side 0, track 0
Compare error on
side 0, track 22
Copy another diskette (Y/N)? N
C:\>
```

If you issue the DISKCOMP command with no drive parameters, DOS uses only one drive to carry out the comparison and prompts you to insert the first and second disks alternately. Depending on your system's memory, you swap disks once or several times. By entering DISKCOMP alone, without parameters, you tell DOS to use the current floppy drive even if your system has two floppy drives. Make sure that you don't mix up the disks when you're swapping them. If you don't keep track of which disk DOS wants in the drive, you might end up comparing part of a disk to itself.

DELETING FILES

Because no disk has unlimited storage space and because nearly every file eventually becomes obsolete, DOS provides a way for you to erase or delete files from your disks. The internal ERASE command enables you to delete files you no longer need.

Unlike other DOS commands' short forms, the ERASE command's short form is not simply an abbreviation of the keyword. The short form of ERASE is DEL. Because the short form is shorter, thus quicker to type, it is generally used rather than ERASE.

When you delete a file, DOS locates that file in the directory and marks the directory entry with a special internal indicator. DOS considers this space to be available for reassignment when a new file is added to the directory. By reclaiming a deleted file's directory entry, DOS can control the expansion of a subdirectory or reclaim one of the limited root directory entries.

Understanding the Delete Operation

The delete operation does not affect the contents of a file's allocated clusters. Deleting a file does not record over the file's data in the way erasing a cassette tape records over existing audio. Rather, DOS alters its bookkeeping records in the directory and in the file allocation table. The directory entry for the file is "deleted" by changing the first character of the filename to an unprintable character (E5 hex), and the FAT cluster chain for the file is deallocated. DOS marks the file's clusters as being "free."

The DOS bookkeeping records for the deleted file remain relatively intact until another file is added to the directory or until another file is expanded or added in any directory. The UNDELETE utility (discussed in Chapter 9, "Protecting Your Data,") takes advantage of the fact that DOS does not erase a file's content when you delete the file. UNDELETE "fixes" the deleted file's directory entry and reconstructs the deleted file's cluster chain. If another file has been added, however, the UNDELETE command might not be capable of recovering the deleted file because DOS might have reallocated some or all of the storage space assigned to the deleted file.

The syntax for deleting files is either of the following:

DEL *FileNameExpression* /P

ERASE *FileNameExpression* /P

The filename expression specifies the drive, the directory, and/or the name of the files to be deleted. You can use wildcards to specify multiple files.

Using the optional /P switch causes DEL (or ERASE) to prompt you for confirmation before DOS deletes each file. Press Y to instruct DOS to delete a file or press N to skip the file without erasing it.

When you are executing a delete operation, remember the following guidelines:

- At the command line, the DEL (or ERASE) command does not erase files marked with the read-only, hidden, or system attribute.

- The delete operation does not remove a directory, erase a volume label, or erase a hidden or system file.
- If you specify a directory name as the filename expression on the DEL command line, DOS tries to delete all the files in the specified subdirectory.

DELETING FILES FROM THE COMMAND LINE

The internal DEL and ERASE commands remove files from the disk, returning to the disk the space occupied by the deleted files. When you use DEL or ERASE to erase a file, DOS no longer can access the file. The erased file's directory entry and storage space become available to DOS for storage of another file.

> **Caution**
> Because DEL (or ERASE) deletes files from your disk, use the command with caution. DEL accepts wildcards in the file parameter. A momentary lapse of your attention while you are using DEL can wipe out important data in the blink of an eye.

DELETING UNWANTED FILES

Suppose that you have completed and delivered a series of memos composed in your word processing program. That program automatically creates in the C:\WP directory a backup file, with a BAK extension, for each memo. You want to keep the memo files on disk so that you can refer to them, but after the memos are safely delivered, you do not need the BAK files. You can erase the files with BAK extensions one at a time, or you can issue the DEL command as follows:

```
DEL C:\WP\*.BAK
```

In this command line, the *.BAK filename parameter instructs DOS to delete all the files with the BAK extension. When the DEL command completes its work, all files with BAK extensions are removed from the directory. Because this command line includes drive and path parameters, you can issue the command from any logged disk and current directory and still erase the BAK files in C:\WP.

USING INTERLNK TO SHARE ANOTHER COMPUTER'S RESOURCES

More and more users now have come to own more than one computer. Often they have a desktop machine in the office and a notebook or laptop computer they use when they travel. Although having two computers extends your computing power to places other than your office, having two computers also can make it difficult to keep data in both places up-to-date. Furthermore, it is not uncommon for two users in an office to need to share files, and maybe even a printer, at times.

The DOS feature called Interlnk enables you to access drives and printers on a remote computer as though they were part of your computer. You can use this feature to transfer files from a laptop or notebook computer to your desktop computer, to print files from your portable computer on a printer attached to your desktop computer, and even to run programs directly from the remote computer.

When you use Interlnk, one computer—the server—becomes the completely passive "slave" of the other. Before you start, decide which computer you want to work on. The server should be the computer with the resources—files or printers—that you want to use remotely.

Setting Up Interlnk

Interlnk uses two executable files. `INTERLNK.EXE` makes a machine the client. You must load this file into the computer by using the `DEVICE` command in `CONFIG.SYS`. After the Interlnk client software is loaded, it remains in memory as a terminate-and-stay-resident (TSR) application that responds to a set of commands not normally available in DOS.

`INTERSVR` is a command run from the DOS prompt. It completely takes over the system to act as an extension to the client computer running `INTERLNK.EXE`. You can run `INTERSVR.EXE` in a Windows-hosted DOS session, but while it's running, all multitasking activities in Windows are suspended.

> **Note**
> *Interlnk* is the name given to the features provided by `INTERLNK.EXE` and `INTERSVR.EXE`. `INTERLNK` and `INTERSVR` are commands provided by Interlnk. You can tell by the capitalization and the computer font whether the following sections are speaking of Interlnk features or the `INTERLNK` command.

→ Use DOS's multiple configuration feature to enable your computer to boot with or without `INTERLNK.EXE` loaded. For information on multiple configurations, **see** Chapter 2, "Starting DOS," **p. 23**.

You need to have a special cable built for use with Interlnk. The cable connects one machine to the other and can use either a serial or parallel connection. You cannot use a standard printer cable because the connector pins of an Interlnk cable must follow the configuration shown in Table 8.2.

TABLE 8.2   CABLE CONFIGURATIONS FOR USE WITH INTERLNK

Pin Connections for Serial Port Connections

9 Pin	25 Pin		25 Pin	9 Pin
5	7	↔	7	5*
3	2	↔	3	2
7	4	↔	5	8

Table 8.2 Continued

Pin Connections for Serial Port Connections

9 Pin	25 Pin		25 Pin	9 Pin
6	6	↔	20	4
2	3	↔	2	3
8	5	↔	4	7
4	20	↔	6	6

Pin Connections for Parallel Port Connections

25 Pin		25 Pin
2	↔	15
3	↔	13
4	↔	12
5	↔	10

Pin Connections for Parallel Port Connections

25 Pin		25 Pin
6	↔	11
15	↔	2
13	↔	3
12	↔	4
10	↔	5
11	↔	6
25	↔	25

* Ground wire

> **Tip**
>
> You can use either a serial or parallel connection to wire the two computers together, but only a serial connection using all seven wires is capable of using the /RCOPY switch of INTERSVR. The /RCOPY switch enables you to connect to computers that do not have InterInk already installed by copying INTERSVR.EXE to the remote computer and running it.
>
> If you have only a 3-wire, or NULL modem, serial cable, or parallel cable, you need to carry floppy disks to put INTERSVR.EXE on the slave machine.

Loading INTERLNK.EXE

Interlnk uses a *client/server* metaphor to divide the responsibilities of the software. INTERLNK.EXE provides the client portion of Interlnk. The client module takes complete control of the server machine. Disks on the server appear to the client as though they are part of the client machine. Printers on the server are likewise made to appear as though they are attached to the client. INTERLNK.EXE is loaded at boot time via CONFIG.SYS. The syntax to load the Interlnk client portion, INTERLNK.EXE, is as follows:

```
DEVICE=d:path\INTERLNK.EXE /DRIVES:n /NOPRINTER /COM:n | address
   /LPT:n| address /AUTO /NOSCAN /LOW /BAUD:rate /V
```

The filename expression *d:path* indicates the drive and directory where INTERLNK.EXE is written to disk. The other parameters are as follows:

- /DRIVES:*n* specifies the number of redirected drives. The default is 3.

- /NOPRINTER specifies that printers are not to be redirected. By default, all printers are redirected.

- /COM:*n* |*address* specifies a serial port to be used for data transfer. The port can be specified as *n*, the port number, or the *address* of the port. If you specify the /COM switch without an accompanying /LPT switch, no parallel port is used. By default, Interlnk scans all available serial ports and uses the first port it finds connected to the server.

- /LPT:*n* | *address* specifies a parallel port to be used for data transfer. The port can be specified as *n*, the port number, or the *address* of the port. By default, the first port found connected to the server is used. If you specify the /LPT switch without an accompanying /COM switch, no serial port is used. By default, all COM and LPT ports are scanned.

- /AUTO causes Interlnk to be loaded only when a connection is detected. By default, Interlnk is loaded even when no client/server connection is detected.

- /NOSCAN causes Interlnk to be loaded into memory but not activated until you issue the INTERLNK command. DOS does not recognize the INTERLNK command, however, unless the device driver has been loaded.

- /LOW specifies that Interlnk is to be installed in conventional memory. By default, Interlnk is loaded into an upper memory block (UMB) if space is available.

- /BAUD:*rate* is used only in serial communications to set the speed at which the two computers communicate through the serial cable. Valid rates are 9600, 19200, 38400, 57600, and the default, 115200. If you find serial communications unreliable, try lowering the baud rate to eliminate transmission errors.

- /V is used for serial communications to prevent conflicts with the computer's timer. If one of the computers hangs up when you try to communicate, try the /V switch.

Normally, Interlnk scans all your drives and all your ports when this device driver loads. If you have a serial mouse and plan to run Microsoft Windows, add a parameter that tells

Interlnk which port is connected to the remote computer. If you are using a second printer port for your connection, for example, type the following line:

```
DEVICE=C:\DOS\INTERLNK.EXE /LPT2
```

This command prevents Interlnk from examining all your serial and parallel ports (and from disrupting your mouse operations in the process).

LOADING THE SERVER

INTERSVR is an executable file, loaded from the command line, that suspends all the operations of the computer and gives control over the computer's resources to INTERLNK, running on the client computer. You do not have to load INTERLNK.EXE on the server to make an Interlnk connection.

If you load INTERSVR on a machine that is running a multitasking system such as Windows or QEMM, all background operations are suspended until you exit INTERSVR. The syntax to load the server portion of Interlnk, INTERSVR.EXE, is as follows:

```
INTERSVR.EXE /X=drives /COM:n | address /LPT:n| address
    /BAUD:rate /B /V /RCOPY
```

- /X specifies the letter or letters of drives to be excluded from redirection. By default, all drives are redirected. If /X is used, any listed drives are unavailable to the client.

- /COM:n | address specifies a serial port to be used for data transfer. The port can be specified as n, the port number, or the address of the port. If you specify the /COM switch without an accompanying /LPT switch, no parallel port is used. By default, Interlnk scans all available serial ports and uses the first port it finds connected to the client.

- /LPT:n | address specifies a parallel port to be used for data transfer. The port can be specified as n, the port number, or the address of the port. By default, the first port found connected to the client is used. If you specify the /LPT switch without an accompanying /COM switch, no serial port is used. By default, all COM and LPT ports are scanned.

- /BAUD:rate is used only in serial communications to set the speed at which the two computers communicate through the serial cable. Valid rates are 9600, 19200, 38400, 57600, and the default, 115200. If you find serial communications unreliable, try lowering the baud rate to eliminate transmission errors.

- /B causes the Interlnk screen to be displayed in monochrome.

- /V is used for serial communications to prevent conflicts with the computer's timer. If one of the computers hangs up when you try to communicate, try the /V switch.

- /RCOPY is used to copy the Interlnk files from one computer to another. You must be using a fully pinned serial cable, and the MODE and CTTY commands must be available on the computer where Interlnk is being installed.

Establishing the Interlnk Connection

After you load INTERLNK on the client machine, all you have to do is load INTERSVR on the server machine, and you're in business. When you issue the INTERSVR command on the server, you see a screen similar to the one shown in Figure 8.7.

Figure 8.7
INTERSVR, activated and waiting for INTERLNK.

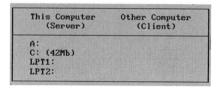

> **Caution**
> You can use InterInk for occasional resource sharing. If you constantly interrupt another user's work, however, to use his or her printer, consider investing in a printer-sharing device or installing a small network.

After you have INTERSVR working on the server, return to the client machine and issue the following command:

INTERLNK

This command activates the connection. A message similar to the one shown in Figure 8.8 appears, telling you how you can access the server's resources.

Figure 8.8
Establishing the InterInk connection.

```
Scanning

Port=LPT2

This Computer        Other Computer
   (Client)             (Server)
------------         ------------------------
D:           equals   A:
E:           equals   C:(42Mb)
LPT1:        equals   LPT2:
```

This message tells you that drive A of the remote computer now is available to you as drive D of your local computer, and drive C of the remote computer now is drive E of your local computer.

Using Interlnk to Transfer Files

After you have Interlnk running on both computers, you can use standard DOS commands to gain access to the server's resources.

Using the values shown in Figure 8.8, if you want to see a directory on drive C of the remote computer, type the following command:

```
DIR E:
```

To copy files from one computer to the other, issue a COPY (or XCOPY) command, with a drive of one computer as the source and a drive of the other computer as the target. To copy C:\SPREADSH\BUDGET.WQ1 from your local computer to the server, for example, you issue a command such as this:

```
COPY C:\SPREADSH\BUDGET.WQ1 E:\SPREADSH
```

Using a Remote Printer

Suppose that your remote computer is connected to a laser printer and your local computer isn't. The status report indicates that LPT1 of your computer is linked to LPT2 of the remote computer. Assuming that the laser printer is attached to LPT2 on that computer, you install your program to print its file to LPT2. Interlnk takes care of redirecting the print job to the server.

Installing Interlnk Remotely

If one of your computers is running DOS 6.22 and the other is running a version of DOS older than DOS 6.0, Interlnk will not be installed. Interlnk can install itself on the remote computer, however, if it is running on the local computer and if the computers are connected via a serial cable using all seven pins. A parallel cable does not suffice. Also, the MODE command must be available on the remote unit. On the local computer, issue the following command:

```
INTERLNK /RCOPY
```

You are prompted to select the serial port to be used. After you indicate that port, go to the remote computer and type the following commands:

```
MODE COMn:2400,N,8,1,P
CTTY COMn:
```

In these commands, *n* represents the number of the serial port you are using on the remote computer. This parameter forces the remote computer to accept input from the specified serial port. When you finish typing these commands, return to the computer on which Interlnk is installed and press Enter. Messages on both computers tell you that INTERLNK.EXE and INTERSVR.EXE are being copied. On the receiving computer, the message looks like the following example:

```
Loading bootstrap

Receiving INTERSVR.EXE (37266) 100%

Receiving INTERLNK.EXE (17133) 100%
```

The files are placed in the current directory of the receiving computer. Both computers then return to DOS. You can use either computer as the client or the server, provided that you install the device driver in the server's CONFIG.SYS file. If the remote computer is running an early version of DOS, however (3.3 or earlier, for example), you might not be able to access files on the server that were created under a version of DOS later than DOS 5.0, especially if those files are larger than 32MB.

Running Programs Remotely

After you are linked to another computer by Interlnk, you can use that computer's drives as though they were part of your local computer. Thus, you can run a program on the remote computer from the command line as you run one on your local computer.

Because programs on the remote computer do not appear on your local computer's path, you must either log on to the drive and directory where the program resides or enter a PATH command to extend the client's path to a remote directory on the server.

Which technique is appropriate depends on how the program works. If, for example, the program must be run from its home directory when it is not on the path, use the first option. Otherwise, you can use the second technique.

The preceding techniques actually just load the program from the remote computer and run it on your local computer. Consequently, you might encounter problems if the program is set up to use specific aspects of the remote computer's hardware that the local computer lacks. Suppose, for example, that the two computers have different types of screens. The program might be set up to display text and graphics on the remote computer's screen and might be unable to display anything on your local computer.

Another problem occurs if the program expects to find specific files on a particular drive but cannot access the drive because the drive names have been changed. Drive C still is drive C of your local computer, but drive C of the remote computer now is known to DOS as drive E of your local computer. If the program needs to find certain files in drive C, it cannot find those files unless they also exist in the same directory of your local computer. (In such a case, don't run the program from the remote computer; use the version on your local computer instead.)

Case Study: Editing Files with Multiple Data Formats

One problem you commonly encounter when attempting to edit files is multiple data formats. Some files contain a mixture of binary and ASCII data. Almost all modern applications store data and documents in proprietary file formats that contain binary elements. Many of these proprietary formats use a binary header. A *header* is a block of information at the beginning of a file that is used by a program as a map to the contents of the file.

Editing this type of file with a tool other than the program that created it can be dangerous. You can change the file so that the parent program no longer recognizes the file as being in the proper format.

If you know that a file was created by a specific application, use that application to view and edit the file. The parent application usually has a method of turning data into ASCII format, either with a conversion utility or by a special file save feature built into the application. See your application's documentation for details.

CHAPTER 9

PROTECTING YOUR DATA

In this chapter

Avoiding Data Loss   232

Understanding Microsoft Backup   233

Using Microsoft Backup   239

Understanding Computer Viruses   252

Unformatting a Disk   257

Recovering Deleted Files with UNDELETE   262

Using the Microsoft Undelete Program for Windows 3.x   267

Project: Developing a Backup Policy   270

Avoiding Data Loss

Desktop personal computers store information on hard disk drives. These days drives average 4GB–20GB in size, with drives in newer high-end systems hitting as much as 40 or 60GB. (Older systems, however, might have hard drives of only 500MB, and possibly smaller.) The hard drive stores the operating system and application files installed on the system. It typically also includes all the personal and business data that has been loaded or created on that system. The software and data represent a significant investment in money and effort that would be lost if your hard disk were damaged or erased.

Today's personal computers are reliable and economical data processing machines. Like all other machines, however, computers are subject to failures and operator errors. Table 9.1 lists some hardware and software problems discussed in this chapter and suggests ways to prevent these problems.

TABLE 9.1 HARDWARE AND SOFTWARE PROBLEMS AND PREVENTION TECHNIQUES

Problem	Prevention
Static electricity	Use antistatic liquid or floor mat; place a "touch pad" on desk.
Overheating	Clean clogged air vents; remove objects that block vents; use air-conditioned room during the summer.
Damaged floppy disks	Don't leave floppy disks to be warped by the sun; avoid spilling liquids on them; store disks in a safe place; avoid magnetic fields from appliances (televisions, microwave ovens, and so on); if you're using 5.25-inch floppies, do not use a ballpoint pen to write on the disk labels.
Data loss	Keep current backups of your hard disk and any floppy disks that contain important data; scan for viruses; use delete-tracking.
Viruses	Always scan a questionable disk for viruses before copying any files from it to your hard disk.

Always be cautious about your computer's environment. With the low cost of surge suppressors and desktop UPS systems, you would be wise to use one of them. If lightning or another sort of power surge destroys your brand-new Pentium III system, you will regret not spending $60 on an uninterruptible power supply (UPS)/surge suppressor.

Your computer might perform erratically when it is too hot. Because circuits are unreliable when they overheat, you might get jumbled data. Make sure that your computer has room to breathe by cleaning the air vents and allowing plenty of space for air to circulate.

You generate static electricity on your body when humidity is low, when you wear synthetic fabrics, or when you walk on carpet. Just by touching your keyboard while carrying a static charge, you can send an electrical shudder through your computer, causing a data jumble or circuit failure. Fortunately, you can avoid static problems by touching your grounded system cabinet before touching the keyboard. If static electricity is a serious problem for you, ask your dealer about antistatic products, which are inexpensive and easy to use.

Finally, be sure to keep your computer clean and free of dust. It is usually a good idea to use a can of compressed air to blow out the dust that accumulates over time. Take special care to keep the fan outlet on the power supply clean and free of anything that will impede airflow.

Understanding Microsoft Backup

Compared to floppy disks, hard disks have many advantages. Hard disks are faster, have larger storage capacities and root directories, support multiple partitions, and never require a disk swap. A file on a hard disk can be many times the size of a file on a floppy disk. Commands such as COPY and XCOPY enable you to keep a few duplicate files on a floppy for backup purposes, but DOS provides a pair of special programs specifically designed for the big jobs: Microsoft Backup (MSBACKUP.EXE) and Microsoft Backup for Windows 3.x (MWBACKUP.EXE).

> **Note**
> Starting with Windows 95, Microsoft has moved to a graphical backup program. The version of DOS that is installed with Windows 9x does not include the command-prompt backup utility.
>
> For more information on using the Windows 95/98/ME backup utility, see Que's *Special Edition Using Windows 95*, *Special Edition Using Windows 98*, or *Special Edition Using Windows Millennium*.

By default, the Setup program installed one of these programs when you installed DOS on your computer. If your system has Microsoft Windows 3.1, however, you have the option of installing both programs. As you might expect, Microsoft Backup for Windows can be used only within Microsoft Windows. The DOS version, however, can be used either at a command prompt or in a DOS window within Microsoft Windows.

> **Note**
> If you do not now use Microsoft Windows but plan to add that operating environment to your system later, you must reinstall DOS to install the Windows version of the backup program.

Both backup programs are full-featured programs that enable you to perform the following tasks:

- Copy files from a hard disk to another disk, usually a floppy disk.
- Restore the copied files to their original location or to another disk of your choice.
- Compare files on your backup copies with the originals to ensure their validity.

Both programs have several types of menus and many options to enable you to copy only those files you want to copy and to ease the process of making backups regularly. Because the programs are similar, this chapter focuses on MSBACKUP. Relevant differences in the Windows version are noted.

> **Tip**
>
> The files copied to the backup disk do not have the same format as files on your hard disk or files copied with the COPY or XCOPY commands. The directories of disks written by the backup programs show only one file per disk, taking all the available space, as in the following example:
>
> ```
> Volume in drive A is DEFAULT FUL
> Directory of A:\
>
> CC30914A 001    1,457,664 09-14-93   6:02a
>         1 file(s)      1,457,664 bytes
>                               0 bytes free
> ```
>
> These files might actually contain the data that originally appeared in many files on your hard disk, along with information about their original location. Before you can use these files, you must restore them by using the Restore portion of one of the Backup programs.

Both versions of the Backup program can read backup disks created by the other version. You need not worry, therefore, about losing access to backup data if you switch from one version of the program to the other.

Backup disks contain not only special copies of files but also directory information about each file. This information enables the programs to copy the backup files to their original locations in the directory tree.

The Backup programs can spread a single file across more than one floppy disk. This capability enables you to copy to multiple disks files that are too big to fit on a single disk. If a backup operation uses more than one disk, each disk is linked internally to the next disk to form a backup set.

During the backup operation, each disk in a set is filled to capacity before the next disk is requested. If a file is only partially written to a backup disk when the disk reaches full capacity, the remainder of the file is written to the next disk in the set.

Like XCOPY, the Backup programs can copy files selectively. You can specify a directory or branch of directories, a filename, a filename patterned after a wildcard, and additional selection switches. By taking advantage of the programs' selectivity, you can maintain more than one set of backup disks, each set having its own logical purpose.

You can, for example, keep one backup set that contains every file on your hard disk. This set is insurance against data loss resulting from a hard disk failure or crash. You might have another backup set that contains only the files that have their archive attributes turned on. With an archive set for each day of the week, you can recover a week's worth of data between complete backups. When your hard disk fails, you replace it, restore using the full set, and then update with the daily sets.

You can lose the data on your hard disk in many ways. If you have not replicated the data, you might be forced to re-create the data and suffer the consequences of permanent data loss if you cannot re-create the data.

Configuring the Backup Programs

Before you can create backups of your data with either backup program, you must first test the program for compatibility. The test is performed automatically the first time you run the program. A special program runs through some of the backup program's menus, making selections as though you were running the program yourself. This program tests your floppy disk drives and the speed of your processor chip and hard disk. Periodically, dialog boxes appear and ask you for permission to continue. You respond by selecting "buttons" similar to those you might have seen in dialog boxes in the DOS Shell and the DOS Editor. You select options in the same way: by pressing the highlighted letter, by moving the highlight to the desired button with the Tab or Shift+Tab key, or by clicking the desired button. In the DOS version, a highlighted button has pointers at its left and right ends and is a different color from the other buttons. In the Windows version, the highlighted button is simply a different color.

The program then displays a dialog box that gives you the option of choosing the drive and medium you want to use for the compatibility test (see Figure 9.1). To select a different capacity disk, move the highlight to the appropriate entry with the cursor keys; then press the spacebar. Choose OK when the setting conforms to your choice. (If you have only one low-density drive, this option is not available.) If you have two drives of the same type, the program uses both, alternating backup disks between the drives.

Figure 9.1
Choosing a disk drive and capacity for backups.

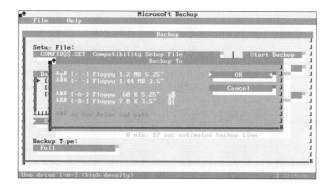

The program then selects a group of files to back up and completes a backup. This procedure requires two floppy disks of the type you selected. Make sure that they do not contain any data you want to save because the disks will be erased completely. The program instructs you when to insert the disks. When the backup is complete, the program compares the data on the backup disks with the source files to verify that the backup is accurate.

> **Note**
> Even after you configure one of the backup programs, you still have to configure the second program. However, the backup files that either program creates can be read by the other program.

Your computer will probably pass the compatibility test. If it does, you can proceed to make backups with the program. However, the program might display the following warning message:

```
DMA Buffer size too small. You will not be able to perform a backup,
compare, or restore until the DMA buffer size is increased. See
'Troubleshooting' in your MS-DOS manual.
```

If this message appears, and you have an 80386 or 80486 microprocessor, use the DEVICE command to load the memory manager EMM386.EXE in your CONFIG.SYS file. Add the parameter D=64 to the command, as shown in the following line:

```
DEVICE:C:\DOS\EMM386.EXE D=64
```

If you have an 8088 or 80286 microprocessor and do not use an expanded memory manager, you will not encounter this problem; but the program might still fail the compatibility test. (See Chapter 19, "Configuring Your Computer," for details on EMM386.EXE and the CONFIG.SYS file.)

When you finish running the tests, the programs save your configuration information to disk so that it can be used whenever you run the backup program again.

Understanding Microsoft Backup Functions

Both the DOS and Windows backup programs have five basic functions: Backup, Compare, Restore, Configure, and Quit. In the DOS version, the dialog box shown in Figure 9.2 contains buttons representing each function. In the Windows version, the functions are represented by a series of icons near the top of the screen (see Figure 9.3).

Figure 9.2
The opening DOS Backup dialog box.

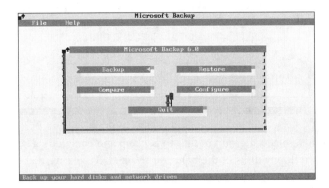

The functions are listed here:

- **Backup** duplicates all or selected files from your hard disk onto floppy disks.
- **Compare** compares the files in a set of backup floppy disks to their source on the hard disk to verify that the copies are accurate.
- **Restore** copies the files on your backup floppy disks to the hard disk, in either their original location or a new location, or to another floppy disk in usable form.

- **Configure** enables you to select default settings for the program. In the DOS version, you can choose the following actions:
    - Change the number of rows of text shown on the screen
    - Switch to a display using normal text characters rather than the graphics characters shown in the illustrations here
    - Adjust the way your mouse behaves
    - Change the screen colors
- **Quit** enables you to exit the program.

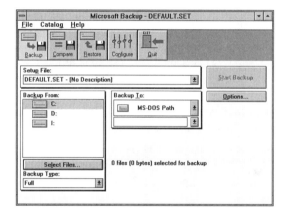

Figure 9.3
The opening Backup for Windows screen.

The Configure options, which appear in Figure 9.4, are similar to the options found on the DOS Shell's Options menu. You can also select a different drive or disk capacity for your backups or send your backups to a DOS path—that is, a directory on your hard disk.

→ For more information on using DOS Shell, **see** Chapter 4, "Using the DOS Shell," **p. 57**.

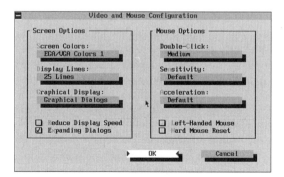

Figure 9.4
Changing DOS Backup's display and mouse options.

Both programs have pull-down menus at the top of the screen. The File menu enables you to load and save setup files—files that contain all the settings you will use for a particular type of backup or restore. The File menu also enables you to print catalog files containing a list of the files that have been backed up. Both backup programs have a Help menu as well, which explains techniques and procedures. The Windows Backup program has a third menu, a Catalog menu, which enables you to select catalog files for restoration or comparison. This menu does not appear in the DOS version; however, you can select catalog files after you have chosen to perform a restore or compare.

Backup Types

Depending on your backup requirements, the following three specific types of backups can be performed using MSBACKUP:

- A *full backup* copies every file on your hard disk. Keep at least two full backup sets so that you can re-create your system if your hard disk is destroyed; you need not make both copies at the same time.

- An *incremental backup* copies only new files or files that have been changed since the last full or incremental backup was performed. You use an additional set of disks for the incremental backup set. You might complete several backups between full backups, depending on how many files you work with and how large the files are. Each time you perform an incremental backup, you add any files that are new or have been modified since the previous new or incremental backup.

- A *differential backup* copies only files that are new or have been changed since the last full backup and requires a separate set of disks from the full backups. With a differential backup, however, you reuse the same floppy disks for each backup until you perform your next full backup.

The distinction between incremental and differential backups lies with the archive bit. When you perform a full backup, the backup programs turn off the archive attribute for any file that is backed up. When you modify or create a file, DOS turns on the new or modified file's archive attribute.

When you perform an incremental backup, the backup programs turn off the archive bit so that each incremental backup includes only files created or modified since the previous incremental backup. When you perform a differential backup, however, the backup programs do not turn off the archive bit. Therefore, every file modified or created since the previous full backup is copied. The differential backup is appropriate if you work with the same few files daily and do not need several generations of each file.

You can perform a full backup weekly, monthly, or at some other interval. The intervening (incremental or differential) backup intervals reduce your risk of data loss between full backups. The time between performing intermediate backups depends on the amount of risk to your data you are willing to take. In a business setting, you might reduce your risk to an acceptable level by performing an intermediate backup every other day. If your PC activity level is high, you might have to perform an incremental backup daily. If your PC activity is minimal, a differential backup once every two weeks might be frequent enough to reduce your risk to a manageable level.

In addition to these three types of backups, you can create backup sets for special purposes. You can select files to include in, or exclude from, the backup. You can select these files individually, by directory, according to a wildcard pattern, by date, or by attribute, and save the selections in a setup file. You learn how to select files for backups later in this chapter.

ISSUING THE MSBACKUP COMMAND

The syntax for the MSBACKUP command is shown in the following line:

MSBACKUP *filename* /*video*

Both switches are optional. *filename* is the name of a setup file. If you created setup files for different types of backups, you can load one automatically by specifying the file on the command line. If you do not specify a setup file, MSBACKUP loads DEFAULT.SET and applies the settings to the drive specified in that file. If no drive is specified, MSBACKUP applies the settings to the default drive.

/*video* specifies the type of video display to be used. Use /LCD for laptops or other LCD screens, /BW for black and white, or /MDA for monochrome displays, including those attached to Hercules-type adapters. Do not specify a video type for a color display.

By default, MSBACKUP uses the path contained in the MSDOSDATA environment variable to determine where to look for configuration information. If this environment variable does not exist, the program searches the directory from which MSBACKUP was started. If it is not located there, MSBACKUP uses default values and creates a configuration information file in that directory. To add this environment variable, add the following line to your AUTOEXEC.BAT file:

SET MSDOSDATA=C:\DOS

You can change the path to the right of the equal sign to any other valid directory you want to use for your backup configuration information.

USING MICROSOFT BACKUP

Now that you understand how Microsoft Backup (MSBACKUP.EXE) and Microsoft Backup for Windows 3.x (MWBACKUP.EXE) work, it is time to see how to use them to perform your backup procedures. The following sections explain how to perform these tasks.

PERFORMING A FULL BACKUP

In this section, you learn how to complete a full backup. First, you learn how to use MSBACKUP and then Microsoft Backup for Windows.

PERFORMING A FULL BACKUP WITH MSBACKUP

To perform a full backup in DOS, follow these steps:

1. Enter the following command:
   MSBACKUP

The program scans drive C (unless you specified a different drive and saved the information in the default setup file, DEFAULT.SET), reads its directories, and then presents its opening screen.

2. Choose the Backup button. As shown in Figure 9.5, the default setup file is loaded, and the selected backup type is Full. To perform a full backup, select the drive to back up from the Backup From list by double-clicking the appropriate drive, or by using the cursor-movement keys to move the highlight to the drive and pressing the spacebar. You might choose more than one drive. Each time you choose a drive, Backup scans the drive and adds the selected files to the totals.

Figure 9.5
The Backup screen.

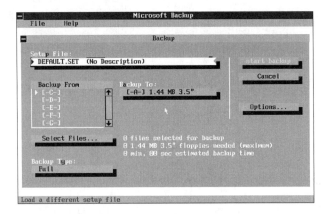

As you select files to back up, the Backup screen shows you exactly what is required. A message similar to this one appears:

```
1,316 files (with catalog) selected for backup
24 1.44 MB 3.5" floppies needed (maximum)
15 min, 50 sec estimated backup time
```

Backup formats any target disks that are not formatted and compresses the data on the backup disks so that the capacity of the disks required might be less than the amount of data you need to back up.

> **Note**
> The Windows Backup program indicates how many bytes of data are selected for backup and compresses the files so that fewer backup disks and less time are required to complete a backup.

3. Choose Start Backup. The program begins by creating a backup catalog, listing the files to be backed up and the options chosen. The following message appears:
   `Insert diskette #1 in drive A:`

   As the backup progresses, a display similar to Figure 9.6 appears.

4. When the disk is full, the program prompts you to insert the next disk, and so on until the backup is complete.

Figure 9.6
Viewing the progress of a backup.

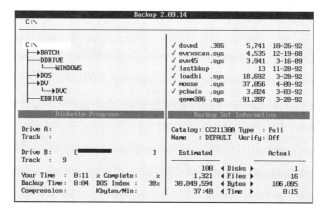

As you remove each disk, label it "Full Backup #*nn*," in which *nn* is the number of the disk in the series. Date the label, also. When the backup is complete, the opening screen reappears.

COMPARING THE BACKUP TO THE ORIGINAL FILES

The first time you use a series of disks for a backup, compare the backups to the originals to verify that the disks are readable and accurate. You don't want to discover that your backup is unusable when you want to use it to recover a hard disk!

To perform a compare, follow these steps:

1. Choose Compare. A screen similar to the main Backup screen appears.
2. Choose Backup Set Catalog, and select the setup file you used for the backup. (If you haven't saved any setup files, it will be DEFAULT.SET.)
3. Select the drive or drives from the Compare From list; the number of files to compare changes from 0 to the number of files you backed up.
4. The program prompts you to insert each disk in turn, and a progress screen keeps you apprised of events.

At the end of the process, the dialog box indicating that no errors were found or that the errors were corrected will probably appear. If this is not the case, you might want to discard the disks that contain the errors, replace them with new ones, and repeat the backup.

> **Tip**
>
> When you quit the program, you might be told that you have not saved your changes in the DEFAULT.SET setup file. In this case, you are asked whether you want to save your changes or discard them. You might find it more helpful to save your settings explicitly to other files that you can load either from within the program or from the command line. To save a backup setup, choose Save As from the File menu, and specify a filename and, optionally, a drive and directory where the setup file should be stored. The program automatically supplies the extension .SET.

Performing a Full Backup in Windows 3.x

The procedure for performing a full backup in Windows is essentially the same as for DOS. The primary difference is the appearance of the screen. When the program loads, you see a message warning you not to use your disk drives while a backup, restore, or compare operation is in progress. You can prevent this message from reappearing each time you load the program by checking the Disable This Message box. Otherwise, you proceed the same way you would in DOS. You can work in other programs while the backup is proceeding. A beep informs you when you must change disks.

Performing Intermediate Backups

Two types of intermediate backups are possible: incremental and differential. The difference depends on the status of the archive bit for selecting files. The incremental backup resets the archive bit after completion, and the differential backup does not reset it.

Performing an Incremental Backup

To perform an incremental backup, choose Backup Type and then choose Incremental from the dialog box. The backup proceeds in the same way as the full backup. Mark each disk in the set with the number and date belonging to the increment for this backup.

You might perform an incremental backup every Tuesday and Friday, for example, and run a full backup every two weeks. Under this plan, you accumulate four incremental backup sets before you have to repeat the backup cycle and reuse the disks.

> **Note**
>
> No matter what type of backup you perform, the backup programs erase the target disks; therefore, each incremental backup must start on a new target disk. You cannot add backup files to disks that have been used as part of a set. By default, the backup programs warn you when the disk you are using is part of an existing backup set and give you the options of overwriting the disk, placing a different disk in the drive, or canceling the backup.

Performing a Differential Backup

If you use the differential backup method, you have just one intermediate backup set. The first time you do an intermediate backup in a backup cycle after a full backup, start with disk number 01 in your intermediate backup set. You might need more than one disk to complete the backup. Because the differential method does not reset the archive bit, the next intermediate backup set includes all the files included in the first intermediate backup set. Consequently, you can reuse the same backup disks for each intermediate backup set. To perform a differential backup, select Differential from the Backup Type dialog box and proceed as you would with a full backup.

The differential method has the advantage of using fewer backup disks than the incremental method. On the other hand, you retain only one intermediate copy of your files that have been modified or created since the previous full backup. If you think you might need to examine successive iterations of a file, use the incremental method.

Special-Purpose Backups

You are not limited to full and intermediate backups of entire disks. You can specify any file or group of files to be included in a backup. When you complete a project, for example, you might want to back up all the files associated with that project in a special series for archival purposes. Or you might want to back up such files daily in a series of incremental or differential backups. Both backup programs provide the means to make any number of special-purpose backups.

To select a group of files for a special backup, first make sure that your backup type is Full. Otherwise, you cannot include files that do not have their archive bit set. Next, choose Select Files. The backup program scans the default (or selected) drive to see how many files and directories are on it and displays a screen similar to the DOS Shell, with drives at the top, directories at the left, and files at the right (see Figure 9.7). The status line displays the following message:

```
Select entire directories with right mouse button or Spacebar
```

Figure 9.7
Selecting files to back up.

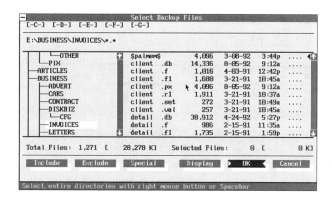

You also see a series of buttons at the bottom of the screen. The Shell-like window and buttons provide two different (although complementary) ways to select files for backing up. These procedures differ somewhat in the two backup programs.

Selecting Files Manually

When you choose Select Files and go to the selection screen, you see that the root directory of the current drive is highlighted. To select an entire directory, move the highlight to it; then double-click, press the spacebar, or click once with the right mouse button. A pointer appears next to the root directory, and check marks appear next to the filenames. To select only some of the files in a directory, select the files individually in the file window, or select the directory containing them and then deselect the files you want to exclude. To select or deselect a file, follow the same procedure you use to select a directory.

When only some of the files in a directory are selected, the pointer next to the directory name changes to the > symbol.

Press Alt+N to select the Include button and then choose OK. This action selects all the files in all the subdirectories of the root directory—that is, the entire drive. Choose OK; the Backup screen reappears.

You select files and directories for backup in Microsoft Backup for Windows 3.x the same way as in MSBACKUP. The main difference is the manner in which selection information is displayed. A series of symbols lets you know in detail which directories have some or all files selected and whether some or all of the selected files will be backed up. (Files might be selected and not backed up if you have chosen an intermediate type of backup, or if you have given the program explicit instructions not to back up some of the selected files, as described in the next section.) Choosing the Legend button displays the description of the symbols, as shown in Figure 9.8.

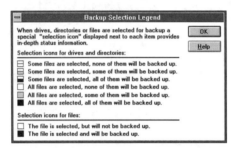

Figure 9.8
File selection legend in Microsoft Backup for Windows 3.x.

If you want to reuse the selections you have made, be sure to save the selections in a setup file; if you don't do so, your selections are saved in the DEFAULT.SET file. To save your selections in a setup file, choose Save Setup As from the File menu. The Save Setup File dialog box appears, enabling you to give the backup set a name and description (see Figure 9.9). You can optionally choose a different drive and directory for the setup file. (The default is C:\DOS.) Figure 9.9 shows the Windows version of the dialog box, but the DOS version is similar.

Figure 9.9
The Save Setup File dialog box.

The next time you want to perform a backup of this type, load the setup file. In the DOS version, you can load the setup file from the command line or by choosing Open Setup from the File menu. In the Windows version, you can load the setup file from within the program using the same command. (The Open Setup File dialog box is similar to the Save

Setup File dialog box.) Under some mysterious circumstances, you sometimes have to choose the appropriate drive from the Backup From list to activate your selections; usually, however, you do not.

CHOOSING FILES USING SELECTION CRITERIA

The buttons at the bottom of the file selection screen give you many ways to select files to include in or exclude from a backup. These buttons also control other aspects of the program:

- **Include** and **Exclude** enable you to specify a path to include or exclude, and a filename. The filename might include a wildcard pattern. You can optionally check a box to include all subdirectories of the specified path.

  In addition to selecting files to include, you might want to exclude the following types of files, even from a full backup:
    - Configuration files that are regenerated or updated every time you use an applications program
    - Backup files created by applications programs (usually having the extension .BAK, or some other extension including the characters *B* and *K*)
    - Temporary files (usually having the extension .TMP or an extension including the $ sign)

- **Special** enables you to exclude read-only, hidden, system, or copy-protected files, or select files by date.
- **Display** enables you to determine whether the files appear in the file window sorted by name, extension, size, date, or attribute, and whether selected files appear before unselected files when the screen is refreshed.

  The Display button in Microsoft Backup for Windows 3.x, in addition to the functions available in MSBACKUP, enables you to determine which of the directory data appears in the file window. You can selectively exclude the file date, file time, file size, and file attributes. You can also rearrange the display so that the directory window appears above the file window rather than to its left.

Microsoft Backup for Windows includes two other buttons:

- **Legend** displays the Backup Selection Legend window (refer to Figure 9.8).
- **Print** enables you to print a list of the files selected for backup, either to the printer or to a file. (You can print the contents of the setup file from either program by choosing Print from the File menu.)

EDITING THE INCLUDE/EXCLUDE LIST IN MSBACKUP

When you choose Include or Exclude, the dialog box contains a button labeled Edit Include/Exclude List. Choosing this button produces the dialog box shown in Figure 9.10. You can select an entry to copy, delete, or edit.

Figure 9.10
The MSBACKUP Edit Include/Exclude List.

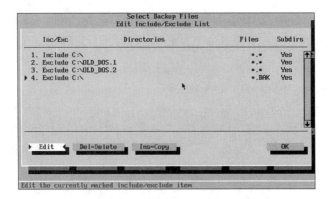

To edit a selection, choose Edit. This command displays the Edit dialog box (see Figure 9.11). In this dialog box, you can specify a drive, path, and filename, including wildcard patterns. You can choose whether to include or exclude the specified files and whether to apply the selection to subdirectories of the current directory.

Figure 9.11
Editing file specifications.

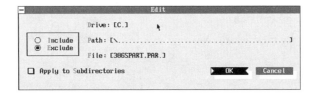

To use the Edit dialog box effectively, you first must copy an existing specification in the Edit Include/Exclude List dialog box (refer to Figure 9.10). Then select one of the copies and choose Edit. After you reach the Edit dialog box, you can enter any specifications you want.

In MSBACKUP, you need not include a drive name in a specification for inclusion or exclusion. By not specifying a drive name, you can apply the same specifications to any or all drives and select the drives from the Backup From list. In Microsoft Backup for Windows 3.x, you must include a drive name. However, you can load a setup file created by MSBACKUP in Microsoft Backup for Windows.

Editing the Include/Exclude List in Microsoft Backup for Windows 3.x

In Microsoft Backup for Windows 3.x, a single dialog box contains the list of included and excluded file specifications and the fields for editing specifications (see Figure 9.12). You do not have to edit existing specifications. You can just enter your criteria (which must include a drive name) and choose Add.

Figure 9.12
Including and excluding files in Microsoft Backup for Windows.

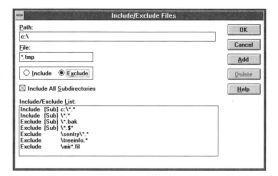

Using Other Backup Options

Both backup programs give you additional options concerning their behavior. To view or change these options, use the Options button on the Backup screen. Figure 9.13 shows the resulting dialog box in Microsoft Backup for Windows 3.x, with the default options selected. The options—and the defaults—are the same in MSBACKUP.

Figure 9.13
The Backup Options dialog box.

The Backup Options dialog box contains the following options:

- **Verify Backup Data** forces the backup program to read the file from the backup disk after it is written and compare it to the original file. This process ensures that the backup is safe and accurate. When you use this option, however, the backup takes nearly twice as long.

- **Compress Backup Data** causes the program to compress the data before writing it to the backup disk. Compression results in the backup requiring fewer disks and might reduce the time required.

- **Prompt Before Overwriting Used Diskettes** causes the program to display a warning before writing backup data on a used disk. You can then choose to overwrite the files on the backup disk or use a different disk.

- **Always Format Diskettes** forces the program to format every backup disk before writing to it so that the backup programs always format an unformatted disk or a badly formatted disk. Choosing this option increases the time required for a backup.

- **Use Error Correction** adds special coding to each backup disk to make recovering the data easier if the backup disks become damaged or worn out. This option decreases the amount of data you can fit on each backup disk, but the extra margin of safety is worth the loss.

- **Keep Old Backup Catalogs** prevents the programs from erasing the previous catalog when you perform a full backup. If, as suggested, you have two separate full backup series, leave this option selected so that you can use the catalogs to locate files to be restored.

- **Audible Prompts (Beep)** causes the computer to beep every time a prompt appears.

- **Quit After Backup** automatically closes the program when your backup procedure is complete. This option is useful when you are running MSBACKUP from a batch file or running Microsoft Backup for Windows in the background.

- **Password Protection** enables you to enter a password, which will thereafter be required to access the backup data or catalog.

Restoring Backup Files

Performing a backup operation is akin to buying an insurance policy. You hope you never have to use it, but if disaster strikes, you have a way to replace the loss. To reinstate lost data onto your hard disk, choose the Restore button in either program.

> **Note**
> The DOS backup programs can restore only data backed up with one of these programs or with one of the Norton backup programs, published by Symantec Corporation. DOS includes an external RESTORE command, which is the only command that can read files copied to a backup set by the BACKUP command from earlier versions of DOS. Consult the "Command Reference" later in this book for details on the use of this command.

The Restore option enables you to restore an individual file, selected files, or an entire hard disk.

Both backup programs provide the same facilities when restoring files, but they're arranged somewhat differently. When you choose Restore, the program loads the most recent backup set catalog and displays the Restore screen shown in Figure 9.14. The catalog's name appears in the Backup Set Catalog field. The drive and capacity used for the backup appear in the Restore From field, and Original Locations appears in the Restore To field.

Figure 9.14
The Restore screen.

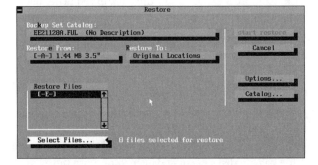

To choose another backup set for restore, select Backup Set Catalog and choose one of the other files listed. If the file is not in the default catalog directory (`C:\DOS`), choose Catalog and then choose Load; then select the drive and directory from the appropriate list before choosing the catalog file.

If your hard disk contains no catalog file for the backup series from which you want to restore, choose Catalog and then Retrieve. The program asks you to place the last disk of the backup series in your drive, and the backup program reads the catalog from the disk. If the program cannot read the catalog, the catalog is missing, or the disk is damaged, choose Catalog and then Rebuild. The program asks you to insert each backup disk from the series beginning with disk 01. The backup program reconstructs the catalog from the data on the backup disks.

> **Note**
> The Catalog command appears on a button in MSBACKUP and on the menu bar in Microsoft Backup for Windows 3.x.

By default, the programs restore files to their original locations. If the file's original directory is no longer on the destination disk, the program creates the directory before restoring the file. The programs make directory entries for files that are no longer on the destination disk and allocate the next available space in the FAT for the restored file's allocation.

You can restore to other drives or other directories. To do so, choose Restore To, and select Other Drives or Other Directories. You might want to use this option to restore an older version of a file without destroying your current version. By default, the programs automatically overwrite existing files of the same name in the same location. If you choose either of the alternative locations, you have a chance to enter both a drive name and directory path after you begin the restore.

You can restore all or only some of the files in a backup set. To restore all the files, select the drive or drives in the Restore Files list. This action selects all the files in the backup set that were originally on the selected drive.

To select individual files to restore, choose Select Files. You again see a screen similar to the DOS Shell screen. However, only those drives included in the backup appear on the drive bar, and no filenames appear in the file window if the current directory did not include any files that were backed up. In Microsoft Backup for Windows 3.x, directories that contain no files in the backup set appear in light gray. You select files and directories to restore in the same way you selected files and directories for backup.

When the correct entries appear in all fields of the Restore screen, choose Start Restore. Like the Backup module, the Restore module prompts you for the disks of the backup set.

> **Note**
> Restoring a full backup set to a freshly formatted disk eliminates any file fragmentation that might have existed on the disk when you backed up the files. Restoring an incremental backup set, however, might result in fragmented destination files. As you might recall, fragmentation doesn't affect the file's integrity, but it might slow disk performance slightly.

When you restore files, keep the following guidelines in mind:

- The destination disk must already be formatted. The restore operation, unlike the backup operation, has no provision to format the destination disk.
- Files restored to a freshly formatted disk are not fragmented.

RESTORING FILES AFTER A DISK FAILURE

This section presents an example of restoring files. Assume that you are using a backup policy that includes a weekly full backup on Friday and an incremental backup each Wednesday. You have two backup sets. The first set from Friday contains all files. The second set contains only files modified or created after Friday, but before Thursday.

> **Caution**
>
> If you have copy-protected files on your hard disk when you do a backup, they might not restore properly to a destination disk. Ideally, you uninstall copy-protected software using the manufacturer's suggested procedure before you perform the backup; then you reinstall the copy-protected programs after the restore operation. This practice might not be practical, however. Keep in mind that you might have to reinstall copy-protected software after restoring a complete disk.

Now suppose that you are saving a worksheet file on Thursday morning when a worker begins to use a large drill next door. DOS reports the following message:

```
General Failure on drive C:
```

You abort the spreadsheet session and run CHKDSK or SCANDISK to ensure that your FAT and directory system are in order. (Chapter 7, "Preparing and Maintaining Disks," covers the operation of both CHKDSK and SCANDISK.) DOS reports hundreds of lost clusters.

You have had an electrical noise–induced hard disk failure. You have no choice but to reformat your hard disk and then fall back to your backup disks. This process requires the steps discussed in the following paragraphs.

You first have to reboot your computer with a DOS startup disk in drive A because the DOS utilities on your hard disk might be corrupt. After you format your hard disk, copy the external DOS commands back to the hard disk from the DOS master disks. You must use MSBACKUP for the restore because you have not yet restored Windows. Use the PATH command to set a search path to the DOS directory so that DOS can locate the MSBACKUP command.

In case of total disk failure, restore your backup sets in chronological order. Restore your latest full backup set first. Locate the disks from your full backup set and put them in their proper order. Then, issue the MSBACKUP command. You probably will have to configure the program all over again. After you have completed this process, choose Restore.

Put the last disk into drive A, and choose Catalog and then Retrieve. Select the appropriate drive or drives in the Restore Files list. Choose Start Restore.

DOS lists the full path and filenames of the files being restored on the progress screen. When all the files from the first disk are restored to the hard disk, DOS prompts you for the next disk in the backup set. This cycle repeats until you have completed the restore operation.

After restoring the full backup set, you must restore the incremental backup set. Because you want to restore all the files in the incremental backup set, you use the same procedures you used to restore the full backup set. The operation proceeds in the same fashion.

After both backup sets are restored, run CHKDSK or SCANDISK to ensure that the hard disk is in order. Keep both backup sets intact until you have determined that your hard disk is performing correctly. Run CHKDSK or SCANDISK several times during the day. If all is in order, perform a full backup at the end of the day.

Performing a Selective Restore

This section discusses how to perform a selective restore operation. Assume that last week you accidentally deleted the database file CLIENT.DB from your INVOICES directory. You discovered the error today and have already tried, unsuccessfully, to use the UNDELETE command. Luckily, an up-to-date version of the CLIENT.DB file is on your most recent backup set.

To restore only the \BUSINESS\INVOICES\CLIENT.DB file from the backup set, load the backup program you use, choose Restore, select the appropriate backup set, and choose Select Files.

You again see a tree and file window, as shown in Figure 9.15. Select the file from the file window.

Figure 9.15
Selecting a file to restore.

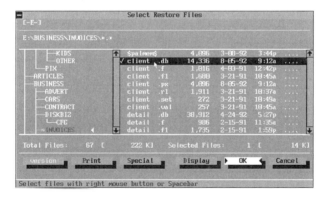

As in the complete restore example, RESTORE prompts you to insert the first disk. You can insert the first disk, or if you know the disk number that holds the CLIENT.DB file, you can insert that disk. RESTORE bypasses any files on the source disk that are not included in the destination parameter you gave in the command. When RESTORE encounters the file \BUSINESS\INVOICES\CLIENT.DB, the program lists the filename on the progress screen and copies the file to the destination disk.

Understanding Computer Viruses

In working with computers, you probably have encountered situations in which the computer didn't do what you wanted it to do. Frustrating as these situations can be, they simply represent a misunderstanding between you and your computer.

Computer viruses are quite different; viruses are supposed to do harm to your computer. Viruses are programs, written by unscrupulous programmers, designed to make copies of themselves and spread from one computer to another, just as a biological virus spreads in people. Usually, viruses also damage your computer by destroying legitimate data and programs. Creating a virus is against the law, but depraved programmers still spread viruses for the same reason that vandals throw bricks through windows—to cause senseless damage.

To protect yourself, you must understand how viruses work. The following sections explain computer viruses in detail.

Understanding How Viruses Spread

Computer viruses come in thousands of variations, each of which works a little differently. How viruses spread from one computer to another, and the damage they do, depends on how the virus is written.

A virus begins in the hands of an experienced but morally corrupt programmer who is either malicious or insensitive to the damage caused. The programmer usually starts with an existing program (anything from a game to a word processing program) and adds a few carefully crafted instructions that modify the workings of the program. This person then distributes the altered program to other users, either on a floppy disk or through an electronic bulletin board.

When the unsuspecting recipient runs the altered software, the program might appear to work correctly, but the added code—the virus—performs some type of operation that the victim doesn't want. This operation might delete important files or erase the hard disk entirely. The virus also might display a taunting message. The most dangerous viruses, however, do no immediate damage; they might alter the operating system by planting a kind of time bomb. Days, weeks, or months after the original infected program ran, the operating system might suddenly go wild, deleting files and destroying data.

Worse, most viruses are designed to spread to other computers. Between the time when a virus infects a computer and the time when it begins to damage that computer, the virus might copy itself onto every floppy that the victim inserts into the computer. Because the victim is unaware that the computer is infected until the virus begins to do damage, he or she might unwittingly spread hundreds of copies to friends.

Strange as it might seem, more than 10,000 viruses exist today. You should be concerned about computer viruses, and you should be serious about protecting your system. However, you might derive some comfort from knowing that your computer can become infected in only one of two ways:

- Loading and running infected software. Your chance of infecting your computer decreases greatly if you get software only from reputable software companies. When you load software from bulletin boards or from an illegal source, your chances of encountering a virus increase.
- Booting from an infected floppy disk. Many viruses spread when a computer boots from a floppy disk that carries the virus. Beware of disks that weren't formatted by you or by someone you trust.

FIGHTING VIRUSES WITH MICROSOFT ANTI-VIRUS

Your best defense against viruses is a virus-scanning program. Such a program can scan files and disks, looking for telltale sequences of instructions that have been identified as parts of known viruses. Used correctly, a good virus program can protect you against the vast majority of known viruses before they damage your computer.

DOS includes two programs—Microsoft Anti-Virus (MSAV) and Microsoft Anti-Virus for Windows (MWAV)—that can scan your memory and disk for hundreds of known viruses. You can use these programs to detect and destroy viruses.

Note Windows 9x and the accompanying version of DOS no longer include the Microsoft Anti-Virus program. I recommend that you purchase a third-party application, such as Symantec's Norton Antivirus. You can find more information about it at http://www.symantec.com/.

Caution Although the Microsoft Anti-Virus program is included with DOS 6.22, I highly recommended that you use a new third-party program that has updated signature files for all the new viruses that are cropping up every day.

In its simplest use, you can start MSAV simply by typing MSAV at the DOS prompt. You can select the functions you want to perform from MSAV's menu. Figure 9.16 shows the main MSAV menu.

Figure 9.16
The Microsoft Anti-Virus main menu.

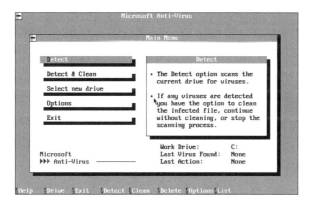

The following list describes the options in this menu:

- **Detect** looks for viruses and tells you what it finds, but it does not destroy viruses.
- **Detect & Clean** looks for viruses and destroys any it finds.
- **Select New Drive** enables you to specify the drive on which Detect or Detect & Clean runs.
- **Options** enables you to configure various options that determine how MSAV works.
- **Exit** terminates MSAV.

The most common operation you will perform is scanning for viruses. To scan the currently logged drive for viruses, select Detect (or press F4). MSAV scans the current drive for viruses and reports on how many files it searched and how many viruses it found (none, you hope). Figure 9.17 shows a sample report after MSAV has done its work.

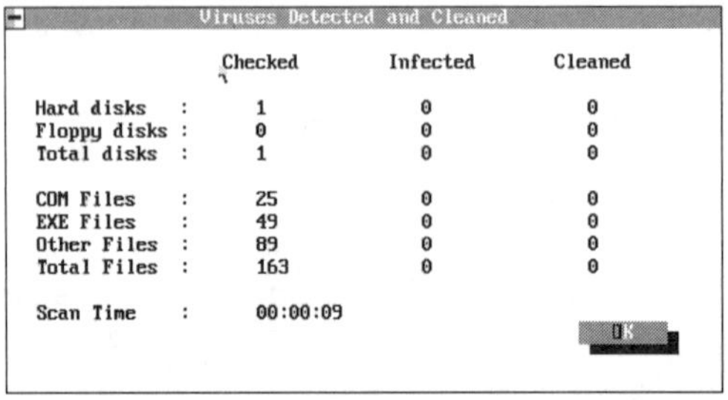

Figure 9.17
Typical MSAV report after a virus scan is completed.

```
            Viruses Detected and Cleaned
                  Checked      Infected      Cleaned
Hard disks    :      1            0            0
Floppy disks :      0            0            0
Total disks  :      1            0            0

COM Files    :     25            0            0
EXE Files    :     49            0            0
Other Files  :     89            0            0
Total Files  :    163            0            0

Scan Time    :  00:00:09
                                          [ OK ]
```

With luck, you will never face the unpleasant prospect of finding a virus on your system. However, if MSAV finds a virus during its scan, it displays a dialog box telling you which virus it found and which file contained the virus, and asking what you want to do. If you select Continue, MSAV keeps looking for more viruses. If you select Clean, MSAV destroys the virus and then continues searching.

If you want to tell MSAV to scan your disk and clean any viruses it finds, select Detect & Clean. MSAV cleans any viruses it finds.

If you want to scan a different drive, choose Select New Drive (or press F2) and select the drive you want to scan.

The complete command-line syntax of the DOS version of Microsoft Anti-Virus is shown here:

MSAV *drive*: /S /C /R /A /L /N /P /F videoswitches /VIDEO

If you specify the *drive* parameter, MSAV scans the indicated drive; otherwise, it scans the currently logged drive.

The /S switch tells MSAV to immediately invoke the Detect function, causing it to scan the specified drive. However, with this option, MSAV doesn't remove any viruses it finds. The /C switch tells it to scan and remove the viruses it finds.

The /R switch tells MSAV to create a scan report. MSAV creates a file called MSAV.RPT, which lists the number of files MSAV scanned, the number of viruses detected, and the number of viruses removed. MSAV.RPT is always created in the drive's root directory.

The /A switch causes MSAV to scan all drives except A and B. The /L switch causes MSAV to scan all hard disks on your computer, but not drives on a network.

The /N switch causes MSAV to run without using the graphical user interface. If it detects a virus, it returns a special exit code (86). This switch is useful when you're scanning for viruses within a batch file.

The /P switch runs MSAV with a command-line interface rather than a graphical user interface. Normally, MSAV displays filenames as it scans. The /F switch tells MSAV not to display filenames. Use this switch only with the /N or /P switch.

MSAV also recognizes many switches that control how it uses the screen. These switches are shown in Table 9.2. You can use the /VIDEO switch to display all these options.

TABLE 9.2 MSAV OPTIONS FOR CONTROLLING DISPLAY

Switch	Meaning
/25	Sets the screen to 25 lines (default)
/28	Sets the screen to 28 lines (VGA only)
/43	Sets the screen to 43 lines (EGA or VGA)
/50	Sets the screen to 50 lines (VGA only)
/60	Sets the screen to 60 lines (Video 7 display adapters only)
/BF	Uses the computer's BIOS for video display
/BT	Enables a graphics mouse in Windows
/BW	Uses a black-and-white scheme
/FF	Uses screen updating that works especially fast on CGA displays
/IN	Uses a color scheme
/LCD	Uses a scheme that works well on LCD screens
/LE	Reverses left and right mouse buttons
/MONO	Uses a monochromatic color scheme
/NF	Disables alternative fonts
/NGM	Uses the default mouse character rather than the graphics mouse pointer
/PS2	Resets the mouse if the mouse pointer disappears

UNDERSTANDING CHECKLISTS

After you have used MSAV to scan a drive, you might notice that each directory contains a file called CHKLIST.MS. This file contains identifying information (called *checksums*) about the files in that directory. Each time MSAV scans the files in that directory again, it can compare the current status of the file against information in the CHKLIST.MS file. If a file has become infected since the CHKLIST.MS file was created, the checksums indicate that a change has occurred.

The CHKLIST.MS files don't require much disk space, but if you want to free some disk space, you can start MSAV and press F7 to tell MSAV to delete all CHKLIST.MS files.

If you don't want MSAV to create CHKLIST.MS files in the future, start MSAV and select Options (or press F8), and turn off Create New Checksums.

LISTING VIRUSES

If you are interested in learning about the viruses known to MSAV, you can use MSAV's List feature to access its list of viruses. Start MSAV and press F9 to see MSAV's virus list.

You can use the scrollbars to scan through the list of known viruses, or you can search for a particular virus by entering its name in the blue box and selecting Find Next.

When you find a virus about which you would like more information, click the virus's name. MSAV displays information about the virus, such as the sample shown in Figure 9.18.

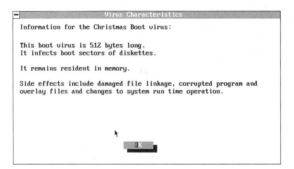

Figure 9.18
Sample information about a virus.

USING THE WINDOWS VERSION OF MICROSOFT ANTI-VIRUS

The Windows version of Microsoft Anti-Virus, MWAV, is almost identical in its operation to the DOS version. When you invoke MWAV, you see the dialog box shown in Figure 9.19. Select the drive you want to scan, and then click Detect to scan without removing viruses, or Detect and Clean to scan for viruses and remove any viruses found.

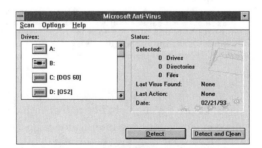

Figure 9.19
Microsoft Anti-Virus for Windows main dialog box.

By selecting the Scan menu, you can access most of the other options described with MSAV in the preceding section. This menu includes Delete CHKLIST Files, which deletes all the CHKLIST.MS files on your disk, and Virus List, which enables you to access MWAV's virus list.

GUARDING AGAINST INFECTION

Most users can protect themselves against viruses by following these steps:

1. Before you load any software from floppy disks, scan all the disks with MSAV or MWAV. Click Select New Drive, select your floppy disk drive, and execute Detect for each disk.
2. After you install new software and before you run it, run MSAV or MWAV on your hard disk.
3. If you download software from bulletin boards, run MSAV or MWAV on your hard disk before you run that software.
4. Never boot from a floppy disk that you have not scanned for viruses (with MSAV or MWAV) or that you did not format yourself.

UNFORMATTING A DISK

Sooner or later, virtually all PC users format a disk accidentally. The UNFORMAT command provides you with your best chance to undo the damage. UNFORMAT is designed to restore the previous format of hard and floppy disks. It also can help you recover from accidental change or damage to a hard disk's partition table.

UNFORMAT is one of those DOS commands that was originally part of commercial products. Microsoft has licensed the code for the UNFORMAT command from Central Point Software. UNFORMAT came to the DOS package from Central Point's PC Tools.

UNFORMAT has two primary uses:

- To recover files after an accidental format
- To rebuild a damaged partition table on your hard disk

Because UNFORMAT completely rebuilds a disk's FAT, root directory, and boot record, you should use this command only as a last resort. The degree of success you have in recovering all files depends on which version of DOS you used to format the disk, what switches you used, and what you have done to the disk since you reformatted it.

> **Caution**
> If the disk that you accidentally formatted is a hard disk, do not install DOS on it because the DOS files will overwrite files you want to recover. Do not copy or save files of any kind to the reformatted hard disk. If you have to reboot the computer, use a bootable floppy disk.

> **Note**
>
> The FORMAT command creates a MIRROR image file during the safe format procedure. The MIRROR image file contains a copy of the disk's FAT, root directory, and boot record. It saves this information in a normally unused portion of the disk. At the same time, FORMAT creates a hidden file named MIRORSAV.FIL, which contains information required by DOS to locate the MIRROR image file. The MIRORSAV.FIL file is given the hidden attribute, so it is not "visible" by the DIR command unless you use the /AH switch. If you use the /U switch with FORMAT, however, no MIRROR image file is created, and UNFORMAT does not work.

When you want to use UNFORMAT after an accidental format, use the following syntax:

UNFORMAT d: /J /L /P /TEST /U

d: is the drive that contains the disk to be unformatted.

/J causes UNFORMAT to verify that the MIRROR image file accurately reflects the current disk information.

/L searches a formatted disk and lists the file and directory names found.

/P sends all output to a printer.

/TEST provides a test run to indicate whether UNFORMAT can unformat a disk successfully.

/U attempts to unformat a disk without the benefit of a MIRROR image file.

When you want to use UNFORMAT to rebuild a hard disk partition table, use the following syntax:

UNFORMAT /PARTN /L /P

/PARTN causes the command to try to rebuild the hard disk partition tables.

/L displays the current partition table.

/P sends all output to a printer.

Recovering from an Accidental Format

Suppose that you just accidentally formatted a hard disk (or used the DOS RECOVER command incorrectly—see Appendix F, "Command Reference," for a discussion of RECOVER). In this case, you need to use UNFORMAT, which uses the information stored in the MIRROR image file to restore the FAT, root directory, and boot record to their preformatting condition.

To unformat a disk that was safe-formatted, type the following command at the DOS prompt:

UNFORMAT d:

(Remember to replace the d: with the letter of the drive that contains the disk you want to unformat.) UNFORMAT first tells you to insert a disk into the specified drive and press Enter.

When you follow these instructions, the computer beeps and displays a screen similar to this:

```
Restores the system area of your disk with
the image file created by MIRROR

WARNING!            WARNING!

This should be used ONLY to recover from the inadvertent use
of the DOS FORMAT command or the DOS RECOVER command.
Any other use of UNFORMAT may cause you to lose data!
Files modified since the MIRROR file was created may be lost.
```

As you can see, UNFORMAT first tries to scare you by giving you messages such as WARNING! Then, it settles down and searches the disk for the MIRROR file created the last time the disk was formatted. It then displays a message similar to the following:

```
The last time MIRROR was used was at hh:mm on mm-dd-yy.
```

For the *hh:mm* and *mm-dd-yy* information in this message, UNFORMAT substitutes the time and date at which MIRROR.FIL was created. UNFORMAT again causes your computer to beep and then displays the following message, substituting the correct drive letter for *d*:

```
The MIRROR image file has been validated.

Are you SURE you want to update the SYSTEM area
of your drive d (Y/N)?
```

If you choose to use the MIRROR information, UNFORMAT restores the FAT, root directory, and boot record stored in the MIRROR file. Unfortunately, UNFORMAT might have problems fully restoring fragmented files. If UNFORMAT cannot restore a file due to fragmentation, it displays a prompt asking whether you want the file erased or truncated. This incapability to deal with file fragmentation severely limits the usefulness of UNFORMAT. Hard disks begin to fragment files from the first day you start using them.

Don't think of the UNFORMAT command as a magic bullet that will keep you and your disks from peril. Rather, think of it as a last-ditch chance to save you from a mistake that has only a 50/50 chance of being totally successful. Nothing will save you from data losses better than a rigorously applied system of disk backups.

Recovering from an Accidental Format Without a mirror Image File

Even if a MIRROR image file is not available for a formatted disk, the UNFORMAT command might be able to recover most of the data. This process takes more time than if a MIRROR image file were available, however, and it does not recover files that were in the disk's root directory.

To use UNFORMAT to unformat a hard disk on which no current MIRROR image file exists, use the following syntax:

```
UNFORMAT d: /U /L /TEST /P
```

Replace *d:* with the letter of the drive that contains the accidentally formatted disk.

The /U switch stands for "unformat" and tells UNFORMAT that you are not using a MIRROR image file created by FORMAT.

The optional /L parameter causes UNFORMAT to list all files and directories found during the UNFORMAT operation. Similarly, /P causes UNFORMAT to send the entire UNFORMAT process to your printer.

Use the /TEST option to run a simulation of the process so that you can see which files UNFORMAT can recover before any changes are written to the hard disk.

After you execute the command, UNFORMAT displays the following message:

```
CAUTION !!

This attempts to recover all files lost after a
FORMAT, assuming you've NOT been using MIRROR. This
method cannot guarantee complete recovery of your files.

The search-phase is safe: nothing is altered on the disk.
You will be prompted again before changes are written to
the disk.
Using drive d:
Are you SURE you want to do this?
If so, type Y; to cancel the operation, press any other key.
```

To continue with the unformat operation, press Y and then press Enter. Press any other key to cancel the process. While searching the disk, UNFORMAT displays the following message:

```
Searching disk
pp% searched, mm subdirectories found.
Files found in the root: 0
Subdirectories found in the root: mm
```

UNFORMAT does not find any root-level files, but it substitutes for *mm* the number of root-level subdirectories it finds. (Refer to Chapter 5, "Understanding Files and Directories," for a discussion of files and the root directory.) As UNFORMAT searches the disk, the command continually updates the last message, substituting the percentage of the disk read for *pp* and the number of subdirectories found for *mm*.

After UNFORMAT completes its search of the disk's data, the command lists the subdirectories found. Depending on which version of the FORMAT command you used, UNFORMAT might or might not be able to recover the names of subdirectories. If it cannot, UNFORMAT gives each subdirectory a name in the format SUBDIR.*nnn*, with *nnn* representing a number ranging from 1 to 512. If UNFORMAT can find the subdirectory names, it displays them and then displays a message similar to this one:

```
Walking the directory tree to locate all files_

Path=D:\
Path=D:\DIRNAME\
Path=D:\
```

In this message, D is the drive name, and DIRNAME is the subdirectory name. This message is repeated for each subdirectory found. UNFORMAT then lists the number of files found, including subdirectories, and displays the following warning:

```
Files found: nn
Warning!  The next step writes changes to disk.
Are you sure you want to do this?

If so, type Y; to cancel the operation, press any other key.
```

To proceed with the unformat operation, press Y and then Enter. Again, UNFORMAT has problems dealing with fragmented files, so you have to decide whether to truncate or delete fragmented files.

Rebuilding a Partition Table

UNFORMAT also enables you to recover from a corrupted hard disk partition table. Such an error normally generates this DOS message:

```
Invalid drive specification
```

To recover from this problem, you first must issue the UNFORMAT command with the /PARTN switch and then use UNFORMAT without this parameter to restore the FAT, root directory, and boot sector.

To recover from a corrupted hard disk partition table, follow these steps:

1. Boot your computer (with a floppy disk, if necessary) and display the DOS prompt.
2. Change to a drive that contains the UNFORMAT file, UNFORMAT.COM. If your only hard disk is inaccessible because of partition-table corruption, use a copy of DOS on a floppy disk. (You can find UNFORMAT.COM on the startup disk, one of the disks used during DOS installation.)
3. Type the following command at the DOS prompt:
   UNFORMAT /PARTN

   UNFORMAT prompts you to insert the disk containing the file PARTNSAV.FIL and to type the name of that disk drive.
4. Insert the disk that contains the copy of the partition table created by MIRROR.
5. Type the letter of this drive and press Enter. MIRROR rebuilds the partition table from the file PARTNSAV.FIL found on the floppy disk. After UNFORMAT rebuilds the partition table, the program prompts you to insert a master DOS disk into drive A and press Enter. To complete this process, you need a bootable backup disk that contains your system files and the UNFORMAT command.
6. Insert a bootable DOS disk into drive A and then press Enter. UNFORMAT causes your computer to reboot.
7. Use the copy of UNFORMAT on the floppy to restore the FAT, root directory, and boot record, following the steps described in "Recovering from an Accidental Format" earlier in this chapter.

Recovering Deleted Files with UNDELETE

Because of the way DOS deletes files, reversing the process is relatively easy, but only if you act promptly. When DOS deletes a file, it changes the first character in the filename recorded in the directory area of the disk so that the target file no longer is listed. As far as DOS is concerned, the file is gone. DOS does not erase the filename entry completely, or overwrite any data in the file, until it needs the space for another file.

Eventually, as you add new files to the disk, DOS reallocates the disk space assigned to the deleted file, causing new data to overwrite the old data. Soon, the file and its data are gone permanently. But if you use the UNDELETE command before DOS has a chance to overwrite a deleted file's data, you can reverse the DELETE operation.

> **Note**
> If you discover that you accidentally deleted a file, immediately try to recover it. The longer you wait, the less likely you are to recover the file completely by using the UNDELETE command.

Using UNDELETE from the Command Line

UNDELETE provides three levels of protection against losing accidentally deleted files: delete sentry, delete tracking, and standard. Both the delete sentry and delete tracker options require you to load the memory-resident portion of UNDELETE, which requires just over 13KB of memory.

Delete sentry gives you the highest level of protection by creating a hidden subdirectory called SENTRY. As files are deleted, the memory-resident portion of UNDELETE moves copies of the files into this directory without changing the FAT entry for the file. UNDELETE regulates the amount of disk space that can be taken up by files stored in the SENTRY directory to about 7% of the disk's total space. As files are deleted and the SENTRY directory fills up, the oldest files in the directory are deleted for real to make room for recent additions.

Delete tracker's protection is one step down from the sentry. It uses a hidden file named PCTRACKER.DEL to record information about deleted files. When files are deleted, the delete tracker feature releases the file's FAT entry, making the disk space available to another file. You can undelete the file as long as no other file has been written to that location. Using delete tracker makes undelete operations easier because it stores the file's original names but does nothing to protect the file's location on the disk from being overwritten. Delete tracker, however, uses much less disk space.

The standard level of protection depends on a deleted file's directory entry and disk location remaining intact. If neither location has been overwritten, the standard undelete protection simply restores the directory entry as being no longer deleted. Despite the standard method's relative lack of protection, most DOS users rely on the standard method because memory is not lost due to loading the memory-resident version of UNDELETE, and disk space is not used to store deleted files or information about deleted files.

The UNDELETE command has the following two syntactical forms:

UNDELETE `FileNameExpression` /DS|/DT|/DOS

UNDELETE /LIST|/ALL|/PURGE[`drive`]|/STATUS|/LOAD|/UNLOAD |/S[`drive`] T`drive`[`-entries`]]

The `FileNameExpression` of the first form specifies the file or files to be undeleted. You can use wildcards to indicate multiple files. By default, if you do not specify a filename, DOS attempts to undelete all deleted files in the current directory. If you do not specify a method using the three switches of the first form, DOS attempts to use delete sentry if available, then tracking if available, and then DOS standard if neither of the other methods is available.

The /DS switch tells DOS to use the delete sentry method, recovering only files stored in the SENTRY directory. You are prompted to confirm undeletion of each file.

The /DT switch instructs DOS to use the delete tracking method of recovering the specified files. You are prompted to confirm undeletion of each file.

/DOS causes DOS, in its attempt to undelete files, to rely on the information still stored in the DOS directory instead of using one of the other more protective methods.

/LIST displays a list of the files that can be recovered without attempting to recover them.

The /ALL switch attempts to recover all deleted files without a confirmation prompt for each file. When used with this switch, UNDELETE first attempts to use the delete sentry method if available, then tries the delete tracking method, and finally if neither of these methods is available, uses information directly from the DOS directory.

/LOAD causes UNDELETE to install itself in memory. If no UNDELETE.INI file is found, it is created.

/UNLOAD removes the memory-resident portion of UNDELETE from your system's memory, disabling the delete sentry and delete tracking methods of file recovery.

/PURGE deletes the contents of the SENTRY directory on the specified drive. If no drive is specified, UNDELETE searches the current drive for the directory.

/STATUS lists the type of delete protection in effect for each of the drives currently protected with sentry or tracking.

/S enables delete sentry protection on the specified drives using the information found in UNDELETE.INI. If this file is not found, it is created. Normally, you establish delete sentry protection by adding a line in AUTOEXEC.BAT.

/T enables the delete tracking protection on the specified drives using information from UNDELETE.INI. If this file is not found, it is created. The `-entries` portion of this parameter specifies the maximum number of files that can be tracked. Valid values range between 1 and 999. Normally, you establish delete tracking protection by adding a line in AUTOEXEC.BAT.

Recovering Files with UNDELETE

To install delete sentry or delete tracking, you ideally put a command line in your AUTOEXEC.BAT file to load the UNDELETE command with its deletion tracking or delete sentry option. These options load a memory-resident portion of the regular UNDELETE command. You specify which option you want to use by including in the command-line switches that load UNDELETE as a resident program.

Suppose that you want to recover a file and have installed UNDELETE with the delete sentry option. Change to the directory that contains the deleted file and then type the following command:

UNDELETE filename.ext

Be sure to substitute the name of the file that you want to recover for *filename.ext*. When you press Enter, DOS displays a message similar to this one:

```
UNDELETE - A delete protection facility

Copyright  1987-1993 Central Point Software, Inc.
All rights reserved.

Directory: C:\SPREADSH\QPRODAT
File Specifications: filename.ext
   Searching Delete Sentry control file...
    Delete Sentry control file contains     1 deleted files.
   Searching deletion-tracking file....
    Deletion-tracking file contains     0 deleted files.

   Of those,        0 files have all clusters available,
                    0 files have some clusters available,
                    0 files have no clusters available.

   MS-DOS directory contains     0 deleted files.
   Of those,        0 files may be recovered.

Using the Delete Sentry method.
   Searching Delete Sentry control file....
    filename.ext    4037    11-29-01    4:58p   ...A Deleted 12-5-01 1:32a

This file can be 100% undeleted. Undelete (Y/N)?n
```

This message indicates, in place of *filename.ext*, the name of the file you specified. The message then indicates the total number of deleted files by this name listed in the Delete Sentry directory; the total number of files by this name in the deletion tracking file; the number of files by this name that have all clusters available and, therefore, are recoverable; the number of partially recoverable files; and the number of files that are not recoverable.

Next, the DELETE command's message might indicate that the deleted file still is listed in the MS-DOS directory. Such a file might have been deleted when UNDELETE was not resident in memory as well as when delete tracking was active.

Finally, the UNDELETE message lists the first file matching *filename.ext* that DOS found in the Delete Sentry directory. If this file is recoverable (that is, if the file's clusters have not yet been reallocated to another file), DOS asks whether you want to undelete the file. To recover the file, press Y. DOS recovers the file and displays the following message:

```
File successfully undeleted.
```

The UNDELETE message also lists any other files with the same name in the Delete Sentry directory. The files are listed one by one, starting with the most recently deleted files. For each file, UNDELETE asks whether you want to recover the file. If additional files with the same name are listed in the deletion tracking file, UNDELETE repeats the procedure for each of these files.

If recovering a file creates a duplicate filename in the directory, UNDELETE displays the following message:

```
The filename already exists. Enter a different filename.

Press "F5" to bypass this file.

If you want to recover this file, type a unique filename (one that
does not already exist in the current directory). Otherwise, press F5
to skip this file.
```

> **Note**
> You might have created and deleted same-named files in a particular directory more than once. (In fact, every time you save a file on which you are working, you delete the preceding version and create a new one.) So, don't be alarmed or confused if UNDELETE asks more than once whether you want to recover a particular file. Normally, you recover the most recently deleted version of the file and discard the others.

Occasionally, by the time you realize that you need to recover an accidentally deleted file, other files might have reused some of the file's clusters. In such a case, UNDELETE displays the following message:

```
Only some of the clusters for this file are available.
Do you want to recover this file with only the available clusters? (Y/N)
```

Press Y to recover the available bytes or N to skip the file. If you wait too long before attempting to recover a file, you might not be able to recover the file because other files are using all its clusters. In this case, UNDELETE tells you so and displays this message:

```
Press any key to continue
```

Sometimes, even though most of a file still is on disk, the clusters in the first part of the file might have been reused by another file. In such a case, UNDELETE loses its "map" to the rest of the file and displays the following message:

```
Starting cluster is unavailable. This file cannot be recovered
with the UNDELETE command. Press any key to continue.
```

If you want to know which deleted files you still can recover, type the following command:

```
UNDELETE /LIST
```

UNDELETE displays, from the Delete Sentry directory, the deletion tracking file, the DOS directory, and a list of deleted files from the current directory.

> **Tip**
> If a deletion tracking list is too long to fit in one screen, you can press Ctrl+S to pause the display. Press any key on the keyboard to resume scrolling. Do not use redirection or the MORE filter; these actions create disk files that might overwrite some or all of the data that you want to recover.

> **Caution**
> If you delete all the files in a directory and then delete the directory, you cannot recover any of the deleted files from that directory. UNDELETE cannot recover a deleted directory.

The UNDELETE command is a product of Central Point Software, licensed by Microsoft Corporation for distribution as part of DOS.

Using the DOS Directory to Recover a File

If you were not using the UNDELETE command's resident portion when you accidentally deleted the file that you want to recover, you can try to recover the file by using the information stored in the DOS directory. To do so, type the following command:

```
UNDELETE filename.ext /DOS
```

Substitute for `filename.ext` the name of the file that you want to recover. UNDELETE displays a message similar to the following one:

```
Directory: C:\SPREADSH\QPRODAT
File Specifications: filename.ext

        Delete Sentry Control file not found.
        Deletion-tracking file not found.
        MS-DOS Directory contains 1 deleted files.
        Of those,   1 files may be recovered.

Using the MS-DOS Directory.

    filename     ext      4037    11-29-01     4:58p    ...A
Undelete (Y/N)?
```

Press Y to recover the file or N to skip the file. After you press Y, UNDELETE displays the following prompt:

```
Enter the first character of the filename.
```

Because the DOS directory no longer has any record of this first character, you must supply the letter. Type the letter that you want UNDELETE to use as the beginning letter of the filename. UNDELETE recovers the file and displays the following message:

```
File successfully undeleted.
```

Using the Microsoft Undelete Program for Windows 3.x

If you use Microsoft Windows 3.x, the DOS Setup program probably installed the Windows utilities in their own program group in the Windows Program Manager. The Windows Tools group includes an Undelete program. When you open this program, Windows displays a screen similar to the one shown in Figure 9.20, listing the deleted files in whatever directory was current when you started Windows. The following sections explain how to set up and use Microsoft Undelete for Windows.

> **Note**
>
> Starting with Windows 95, Microsoft no longer includes the DOS-based UNDELETE program. Instead, it offers a new feature called the Recycle Bin, which is located on the desktop and stores the files that are deleted until you empty it.
>
> Because this program is GUI based, if you delete anything from a command prompt, it is gone forever. It is recommended that any file deletion in Windows 9x be done from Explorer.

Figure 9.20
Using the Windows Undelete program.

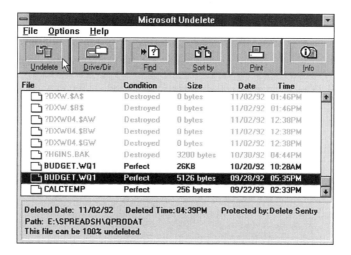

Configuring Microsoft Undelete

If you have installed the DOS version of UNDELETE in your AUTOEXEC.BAT file, you do not need to configure Microsoft Undelete. If you have not installed UNDELETE, however, choose Configure Delete Protection from the Options menu. This command displays a dialog box in which you can choose one of the following options:

- Delete Sentry
- Delete Tracker
- Standard (no delete protection)

You already have seen what each of these options does. If you install Delete Protection through Windows, UNDELETE is automatically installed in your AUTOEXEC.BAT file.

Selecting Files to Recover

If the default directory does not contain the file that you want to recover, click the Drive/Dir button or choose Change Drive/Directory from the File menu. A dialog box appears in which you can type the correct directory path in a text box or choose the directory from a list box. When you click OK, the main window shows the deleted file in your chosen directory (refer to Figure 9.20). When you select a file, Windows displays the following information below the directory window:

- The date and time when the file was deleted, if known (this information is available only if Delete Sentry is used)
- The protection method in use when the file was deleted, if any (if none, Windows displays the message Protected by: DOS)
- The current drive and directory
- The probability that the file can be recovered

If the directory in which the deleted file was stored is not current, click the Find button or choose Find Deleted File from the File menu. The Find Deleted Files dialog box appears (see Figure 9.21).

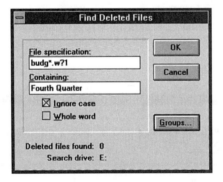

Figure 9.21
The Find Deleted Files dialog box.

In this dialog box, you can type the name of the file that you want to find and also some text from the file; this information helps Undelete locate the correct version of the file. If you want to narrow the search further, click the Groups button to display a list of all the file types whose extensions are associated with a program in Windows. You can narrow the search more by clicking one or more of the listed groups. After you finish specifying what to search for, click OK.

If Undelete finds any matching files, it displays the files in the directory window.

Recovering Files

When you see the file that you want to recover, select it and then perform one of the following actions:

- Click the Undelete button.
- Choose Undelete from the File menu.
- Choose Undelete To from the File menu.

You can select more than one file by clicking each file or by moving the selection bar to each file and pressing the spacebar.

If you use either of the first two methods, Undelete simply recovers the file in its current location. If the prognosis for recovery is not good, however, you might want to use the Undelete To command so that you can recover the file to another drive.

You might have to search the disk to find the data that was in the file. If you're not successful the first time, Undelete To enables you to try again without disturbing the data on the original disk.

If you use the Undelete command and recover the file, the information in the Condition column changes to read Recovered, as shown in Figure 9.22.

Figure 9.22
Successfully undeleting files.

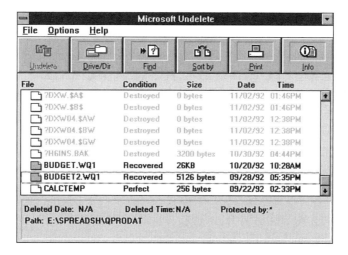

If you try to recover a file whose name is being used by another file, the message `File already exists` appears. Click OK, and you see a dialog box in which you can enter a new name for the file. As you can see in Figure 9.22, both files named BUDGET.WQ1 have been recovered, but one has been renamed.

Using Other Options

Microsoft Undelete includes several other options that are not available when you try to recover a deleted file from the DOS prompt:

- **Sorting**—The Sort By button and the Sort By command (Options menu) enable you to sort the filenames displayed in the Undelete window by name, date, size, directory date and time, deletion date and time, or condition.

- **Printing**—You can group the files in the display by directory and then print them by clicking the Print button or choosing Print List from the File menu.

- **Displaying information**—You can click the Info button or choose File Info from the File menu to display a box in which all the information about a deleted file is conveniently grouped in one place.

- **Selecting files**—The Options menu contains two commands that you can use to select groups of files for recovery. Choose Select by Name to display a dialog box in which you enter a filename. If you include a wildcard pattern in the filename, all matching files are selected. You then can choose the Unselect by Name command to narrow the selection.

- **Deleting files**—If you installed the delete sentry option, you can choose Purge Delete Sentry File from the File menu to get rid of all the files—or selected files—in the Delete Sentry directory. You might want to use this command if you are running low on disk space and need to install a new program.

Project: Developing a Backup Policy

Every PC user should develop a backup policy—a defined method of backing up data regularly. The policy you develop depends on different factors. As you learned earlier in this chapter, you can choose from three different primary backup types: full, differential, and incremental. The decision to be made here is whether to use only full backups every time, or perform incremental or differential backups between full backups.

Deciding on which backups to perform can depend on many factors, such as the amount of data to be backed up, backup capacity and speed, and time constraints. If you have 2GB of data to back up, for example, and your tape drive can back up only 500MB per hour, the full backup will require four hours. But consider what you would do if you had only three hours to perform a backup during the week and six hours on the weekend. Obviously, in this case, you could not perform a full backup every night.

Incremental and differential backups come into play here. After you decide when you will be performing the full backup, you then need to decide whether to perform incremental or differential backups in between. The main difference between these two types is that differential backups do not modify the archive setting for files, so every file changed since the last full backup is backed up. An incremental backup backs up only files that have been added or changed since the last full or incremental backup.

Taking these factors into account, you then need to decide which type of backup works better for you. Obviously, an incremental backup is going to be faster over multiple nights than a differential backup because it is backing up only files changed since the last full or incremental backup. The drawback to this choice is that you must restore the full backup set and then each incremental backup set. If you use differential backups between full backups, you would need to restore only the full backup and then the last differential backup because each differential backup set includes all files changed since the last full backup.

Controlling DOS

10 Working with System Information 275

11 Controlling Your Environment 293

12 Using Peripherals 307

13 Controlling Devices 317

14 Understanding the International Features of DOS 339

CHAPTER 10

WORKING WITH SYSTEM INFORMATION

In this chapter

Changing the Date and Time   276

Displaying the Version Using the VER Command   279

Setting the Version Using the SETVER Command   280

Displaying Memory Statistics   283

Loading a Secondary Command Processor   288

Changing the Date and Time

In Chapter 5, "Understanding Files and Directories," you learned a bit about how DOS stores files using a directory. This directory maintains critical information about each file on your disk, including the filename, its attributes, its size, and where it is stored on the disk. It also contains date and time information that indicates when the file was last updated. This information is often referred to as a *date and time stamp*. This stamp is updated from the system date and time whenever you make changes to the file.

Your computer uses a battery-powered clock to maintain the date and time used by your system. Even when the computer is turned off, power from the battery goes to the chip containing the clock, and the date and time remain current.

Setting the date and time becomes increasingly important as you create more files on your computer. Because the DOS file-naming rules limit you to only eight characters in the root filename and three characters in the file extension (which is generally used to indicate the file type), the names of your files might not be very descriptive. In this situation, you might need to rely on the date and time stamp to tell which file is the most recent. On computers without a clock or with a clock that has a dead battery, however, the date and time are set to the same value each time you turn on the computer. This situation makes it difficult for you—or DOS—to tell the difference between an old file and a revised or new file. In addition, some DOS commands work by comparing file dates. If your system time and date are not correct, these commands will have little value to you.

Occasionally checking your computer's date and time is worthwhile. All batteries eventually fail and need replacing. All clocks in personal computers lose time. How much time your clock loses depends on the programs you run on your computer.

The clock that keeps the date and time in a PC is controlled by an electronic component in the computer—the system timer. This chip is the heartbeat of the computer. Everything the computer does takes a known amount of time. The system timer provides a regular pulse that controls all the functions occurring in the computer.

One of these functions is to update the clock that DOS uses to tell the time (and consequently the date). Commands or other programs that cannot afford to be interrupted while they're working tell DOS not to interrupt them until they finish what they're doing. A typical example is a communications program that waits for a character to be sent from another computer. If DOS is busy performing other tasks, such as updating the clock, the program might miss the character. Consequently, this type of program disables the interrupts; the program tells DOS to do nothing else for the period that it needs full control. During these times, the clock is not updated. These periods are typically only a fraction of a second, but the effect is cumulative, and eventually the time loss is noticeable.

If you do not have an AUTOEXEC.BAT file (see Chapter 2, "Starting DOS"), DOS displays the current date and time when you start your computer and gives you the opportunity to change them. You should take a moment to check these settings. Make sure that you set the date and time correctly whenever you are prompted because both are used in many DOS operations.

Most people, however, use an `AUTOEXEC.BAT` file. This file seldom contains the commands necessary to change the date and time. In these instances, DOS uses its current settings. If you later notice that the date and time are incorrect (for example, a newly created file might contain the wrong date and time), you should change them by using the `DATE` and `TIME` commands.

Issuing the Date Command

`DATE` is an internal command that is simple to use. It has only one possible parameter, as shown in the following syntax:

`DATE` *today*

If you type `DATE` at the DOS prompt and then press Enter, DOS shows you the date currently being used by your system and then prompts you for a new date:

```
Current date is Fri 08-17-2001
Enter new date (mm-dd-yy):
```

The date that is displayed might or might not be correct; you can change it by entering a new date or accept it by pressing Enter. Alternatively, if you don't want to see what the current date setting is, you can enter the `DATE` command followed by the date you want your system to use.

The exact format you should use for entering a date depends on the country code set in your `CONFIG.SYS` file. (Chapter 14, "Understanding the International Features of DOS," includes a discussion of the country code settings.) The date format can be one of the following formats:

Country Code	Format
North America	mm-dd-yy
	mm-dd-yyyy
Europe	dd-mm-yy
	dd-mm-yyyy
East Asia	yy-mm-dd
	yyyy-mm-dd

mm is the month, *dd* is the day, and *yy* and *yyyy* are the year. To set the date to December 23, 2001, on a machine configured for North America, for example, you can enter the following line at the DOS prompt:

`DATE 12-23-2001`

If you use two digits instead of four, DOS will assume that the first two digits should be 19. Rather than the hyphen, you can use periods or slashes as separators. Leading zeros are not required. If the month is January, for example, you can use 1 (instead of typing `01`) for the month.

If you want to change the date, letting DOS prompt you is the best way to use this command because the current date setting appears in the correct format, and you can copy this format rather than remember it. The DOS screen might appear as follows if you let DOS prompt you for the current date:

```
C:\>DATE
Current date is Fri 08-17-2001
Enter new date (mm-dd-yy): 12-23-2001
```

Pressing Enter when DOS prompts you for a new date retains the current setting. If you don't enter the date correctly or if you select a date that is outside the range supported by DOS, you see the error message Invalid date, after which you can again try to enter a date.

ISSUING THE TIME COMMAND

Closely related to the DATE command is the internal TIME command. It also has only one possible parameter:

TIME *now*

As with DATE, if you type only TIME and press Enter at the DOS prompt, DOS shows you the current time setting and prompts you for a new one. You can change the time without being prompted by including the new time on the command line as a parameter.

When you enter a new time setting, you do so using hours, minutes, and seconds. The exact format you should use depends on the country code setting in your CONFIG.SYS file.

You can use either a 12-hour or 24-hour clock. The following line shows the format used for a 24-hour clock:

hrs:*mins*:*secs*.*1/100secs*

hrs is the hour, a number from 0 to 23; *mins* is the minutes, a number from 0 to 59; *secs* is the seconds, a number from 0 to 59; and *1/100secs* is the number of one-hundredth seconds, a number from 0 to 99. The 24-hour clock starts with midnight as 00:00.00. You can use a period rather than a colon when separating the hours, minutes, and seconds, or a comma in place of a period when separating the seconds from the hundredths of a second.

If you decide to enter the time using a 12-hour clock, the format is the same as for the 24-hour clock except that *hrs* is a number from 1 to 12, and you add *a* or *p* to signify a.m. or p.m. If you do not add an *a* or a *p*, DOS assumes a.m.

Just because DOS enables you to enter time to the nearest 1/100 of a second, you don't need to. In fact, you don't need to enter all the parts of the time. DOS sets any missing elements to zero (using the 24-hour clock notation). To set the time to 8:25 p.m., for example, you can enter one of the following lines at the DOS prompt:

TIME 20:25

TIME 8:25p

Either command sets the time to 8:25 p.m. The seconds and hundredths of a second are set to zero. To set the clock to 12:30 a.m., you can enter the following line:

```
TIME :30
```

As with the DATE command, letting DOS prompt you for the time is the easiest way to use this command. When DOS displays the current time, all you need to do is enter a new time using the same format. Following is an example of how the DOS screen might appear if you let DOS prompt you for the current time:

```
C:\>TIME
Current time is 2:35:07.23p
Enter new time: 2:40p
```

You can use the COUNTRY command to change the format DOS uses to display the time (see Chapter 14).

Displaying the Version Using the VER Command

DOS includes an internal command that displays the DOS version currently in use. Knowing how to use the VER command is invaluable if you ever work with an unfamiliar computer. Some commands, such as DISKCOMP, FORMAT, and XCOPY, work differently or are not available with different DOS versions. If you do not know which version of DOS a computer is using, the VER command can tell you.

When you enter the VER command at the DOS prompt, you see a message similar to this one:

```
MS-DOS Version 6.20
```

This is the DOS version used to boot your computer. If a computer with a hard disk is booted from a floppy disk, the version of DOS might not be what you expected. Suppose that your hard disk is formatted for DOS 6.2, but you use a DOS 5.0 floppy disk to boot your computer. The Version 6.2 commands on your hard disk might not work while your computer is running a different version of DOS. In this instance, the following message appears when you try to use one of the DOS 6.22 commands:

```
Incorrect DOS Version
```

Sometimes DOS can be slightly different even within the same version. Some computer manufacturers supply DOS packages specially designed to work with their machines, so you might see a different message if you use a different product. Compaq Computer Corporation's version of DOS, for example, includes Compaq's name with the version number. Because of the differences between these versions, you might be able to track down problems on an unfamiliar computer more easily if you first determine the exact DOS version number and its manufacturer.

Setting the Version Using the SETVER Command

When a new version of DOS is released, some time passes before software manufacturers can upgrade popular applications programs to take full advantage of DOS's new features. Many programs ask the operating system to tell them which version of DOS the computer is running. If a program does not recognize the version of DOS in memory, it might refuse to run. One or more of your applications, therefore, might refuse to run because they have not been certified by the manufacturer to run properly with DOS 6.22.

You can get a reluctant program to run under DOS 6.22 in two ways:

- Contact the software manufacturer or your dealer to find out whether you need a program upgrade.
- Use the SETVER command to add the name of the program to DOS 6.2's version table. The *version table* is a list of programs with DOS version numbers listed next to them. When a program listed in the version table loads into memory and asks DOS for its version number, DOS reports the version number listed in the version table rather than the actual version number—6.2. The application is fooled into running under DOS 6.2.

The first option is the better choice. By checking with the manufacturer, you can determine whether the software has been tested in DOS 6.22.

> **Warning**
> If you use SETVER, you run the risk, however slight, that your program might become corrupted if it is incompatible with DOS 6.2.

The SETVER command operates as both a device driver and an executable command. Before DOS can use the version table, you must load SETVER.EXE as a device driver. Make sure that the command is included in your CONFIG.SYS file so that it executes every time you start your computer. If SETVER.EXE is not in your CONFIG.SYS file, you need to add it. To do so, use the following syntax:

DEVICE=*d:path*\SETVER.EXE

The parameters *d:* and *path*\ are the disk and directory that contain the SETVER.EXE external program file. When you installed DOS, the installation program created a default CONFIG.SYS file for you, which includes the following command:

DEVICE=C:\DOS\SETVER.EXE

After the device driver SETVER.EXE is loaded into memory, DOS can use the version table to report different DOS versions to applications programs listed in the version table.

To see whether a particular program is already in the version table, use SETVER from the DOS command line. To do so, type SETVER at the DOS prompt; do not add switches, filenames, or parameters. DOS displays a two-column listing with program names in the first column and the DOS version number the programs will work with in the second column. Microsoft has already tested the programs listed in the initial version table and determined that they operate properly in DOS 6.22. The version list that appears on your screen should resemble the following list:

```
KERNEL.EXE      5.00
NETX.COM        5.00
NETX.EXE        5.00
NET5.COM        5.00
BNETX.COM       5.00
BNETX.EXE       5.00
EMSNETX.EXE     5.00
EMSNET5.EXE     5.00
XMSNETX.EXE     5.00
XMSNET5.EXE     5.00
DOSOAD.SYS      5.00
REDIR50.EXE     5.00
REDIR5.EXE      5.00
REDIRALL.EXE    5.00
REDIRNP4.EXE    5.00
EDLIN.EXE       5.00
BACKUP.EXE      5.00
ASSIGN.COM      5.00
EXE2BIN.EXE     5.00
JOIN.EXE        5.00
RECOVER.EXE     5.00
GRAFTABL.COM    5.00
LMSETUP.EXE     5.00
STACKER.COM     5.00
NCACHE.EXE      5.00
NCACHE2.EXE     5.00
IBMCACHE.SYS    3.40
XTRADRV.SYS     5.00
2XON.COM        5.00
WINWORD.EXE     4.10
EXCEL.EXE       4.10
LL3.EXE         4.01
REDIR4.EXE      4.00
REDIR40.EXE     4.00
MSREDIR.EXE     4.00
WIN200.BIN      3.40
METRO.EXE       3.31
WIN100.BIN      3.40
HITACHI.SYS     4.00
MSCDEX.EXE      4.00
NET.EXE         4.00
NET.COM         3.30
NETWKSTA.EXE    4.00
DXMA0MOD.SYS    3.30
BAN.EXE         4.00
BAN.COM         4.00
DD.EXE          4.01
DD.BIN          4.01
REDIR.EXE       4.00
SYQ55.SYS       4.00
SSTDRIVE.SYS    4.00
ZDRV.SYS        4.01
ZFMT.SYS        4.01
TOPSRDR.EXE     4.00
```

PART
III

CH
10

When you run one of the programs listed in the first column of the version table, DOS reports to the program the DOS version number listed in the second column.

If you try to run a program and it displays an error message stating that you are using an incompatible version of DOS, you might want to try adding the program to the version table. Enter the SETVER command using the following syntax:

```
SETVER filespec n.nn
```

The *filespec* parameter indicates the full name of the file in question, including a path, a filename, and an extension. The *n.nn* parameter is a DOS version number that the program will recognize. Consult the program's documentation to determine with which versions of DOS the program can run.

You also can use SETVER to delete program names. The syntax for using SETVER to delete programs from the version table is shown in the following line:

```
SETVER filespec /DELETE /QUIET
```

The two switches—/DELETE and /QUIET—can be abbreviated as /D and /Q.

For an example of how you use SETVER, assume that you want to run a program called GOODPROG.EXE, but the program runs only with DOS versions 3.0 to 3.3. To add GOODPROG.EXE to the version table, type the following command at the command prompt and press Enter:

```
SETVER GOODPROG.EXE 3.30
```

DOS displays the following series of messages, including an initial warning:

```
WARNING - The application you are adding to the MS-DOS version table may not
have been verified by Microsoft on this version of MS-DOS. Please contact your
software vendor for information on whether this application will operate
properly under this version of MS-DOS. If you execute this application by
instructing MS-DOS to report a different MS-DOS version number, you may lose or
corrupt data, or cause system instabilities. In that circumstance, Microsoft is
not responsible for any loss or damage.

Version table successfully updated

The version change will take effect the next time you restart your system.
```

To verify that the application has been added to the version table, execute SETVER again without switches or parameters. The added application appears at the end of the list. The modified table takes effect, however, only after you restart or reboot your computer.

If you later decide to delete a program from the version list, use the /D switch and the *filename* parameter. To delete GOODPROG.EXE from the version table, for example, type one of the following commands at the command line and press Enter:

```
SETVER GOODPROG.EXE /DELETE
```

```
SETVER GOODPROG.EXE /D
```

DOS deletes the application name from the version table and displays this message:

```
Version table successfully updated
```

The version change takes effect the next time you start your system.

> **Tip**
> If you are using a batch file to delete a program name from the version table, you might want to suppress the preceding message. To prevent this message from appearing onscreen, add the /QUIET switch in addition to the /DELETE switch.

DISPLAYING MEMORY STATISTICS

One of the handiest DOS commands is MEM. This external command enables you to determine how memory is being used on your system. (For a discussion of the types of memory in your system, see Chapter 1, "DOS and the Personal Computer.")

ISSUING THE MEM COMMAND

The following line shows the syntax for the MEM command:

MEM /DEBUG /CLASSIFY /FREE /MODULE:*programname* /PAGE

All switches are optional, and you will find it handy to abbreviate each switch by typing only the first letter (/D, /C, /F, /M:*programname*, /P). Each switch is independent, meaning that you cannot use them together. The only exception is the /PAGE switch, which tells DOS to pause at the end of each screen it displays. This switch is handy to use because the output generated by MEM can easily run longer than a single screen.

The /DEBUG switch lists all the loaded programs and device drivers. This listing includes the name, size, position, and type of each item.

The /CLASSIFY switch lists the programs loaded into conventional memory as well as in upper memory—the 384KB area of memory between 640KB and 1MB that is usually reserved for use by certain system devices, such as your monitor.

The /FREE switch lists the free areas of conventional and upper memory. The /MODULE: *programname* switch shows the way a program module is currently using memory. You must specify the program name after the /MODULE switch. The MEM /MODULE switch lists the areas of memory the program module is using and shows the address and size of each area.

UNDERSTANDING THE OPERATION OF MEM

To see a "short" version of the memory report that indicates the amount of conventional memory, EMS memory, and XMS memory, just enter MEM at the DOS prompt, without any switches. DOS displays a report similar to this one:

```
Memory Type         Total   =   Used    +   Free
---------------     -------     -------     -------
Conventional         640K          79K        562K
Upper                 71K          33K         38K
Reserved             384K         384K          0K
Extended (XMS)*    7,097K       2,537K      4,560K
```

```
................  .......  .......  .......
Total memory      8,192K   3,033K   5,159K

Total under 1 MB  711K     112K     599K

Total Expanded (EMS)                7,488K (7,667,712 bytes)
Free Expanded (EMS)*                4,800K (4,915,200 bytes)

* EMM386 is using XMS memory to simulate EMS memory as needed.
  Free EMS memory may change as free XMS memory changes.

Largest executable program size     561K (574,752 bytes)
Largest free upper memory block     22K  (22,016 bytes)
MS-DOS is resident in the high memory area.
```

This report gives you three types of information about every type of memory in your system, in three columns: the total amount, the amount currently being used, and the memory available for you to use for programs.

The first line describes the conventional memory: the total amount (generally 640KB; 1KB = 1,024 bytes), the amount of memory currently being used, and the amount of free memory. The next line shows you the amount of upper (reserved) memory and adapter RAM/ROM in the same format. These two amounts total 384KB, which, in addition to the conventional memory, is the total amount of memory that DOS addresses—1,024KB.

The MEM report then tells you the total amount of extended memory that has been mapped (converted) to XMS memory, the amount currently in use, and the amount available for use. In the example, 4,560KB of XMS memory of the original 7,097KB are available.

The next line shows the total amount of memory under 1MB and the amount available to you for running programs. This amount might be misleading because the figure lumps together the amount of free conventional and free reserved memory. Most programs cannot use both of these types of memory as if they were contiguous.

The first two long lines following the totals show the total amount and free amount of expanded memory in your system. A footnote explains that the EMM386.EXE memory manager creates expanded memory from the pool of XMS memory as needed. Finally, MEM indicates whether MS-DOS currently is loaded in the high memory area.

Sometimes, MEM's short report doesn't provide enough information to meet your needs. MEM therefore provides three switches to produce longer versions of the report. Because these reports don't fit on a single screen, you can use the /PAGE switch to display one page of the report at a time.

The reports generated by MEM's /CLASSIFY and /DEBUG switches are highly technical in content. For example, to execute the MEM command with the /DEBUG switch, enter the following line at the DOS prompt:

```
MEM /DEBUG
```

A report similar to this one appears:

```
Conventional Memory Detail:

 Segment           Total           Name        Type
 -------           -----           ----        ----
  00000           1,039   (1K)                 Interrupt Vector
  00040             271   (0K)                 ROM Communication Area
  00050             527   (1K)                 DOS Communication Area
  00070           2,752   (3K)   IO            System Data
                                 CON           System Device Driver
                                 AUX           System Device Driver
                                 PRN           System Device Driver
                                 CLOCK$        System Device Driver
                                 A: - D:       System Device Driver
                                 COM1          System Device Driver
                                 LPT1          System Device Driver
                                 LPT2          System Device Driver
                                 LPT3          System Device Driver
                                 COM2          System Device Driver
                                 COM3          System Device Driver
                                 COM4          System Device Driver
  0011C           5,600   (5K)   MSDOS         System Data
  0027A          49,712  (49K)   IO            System Data
                  1,152   (1K)     XMSXXXX0    Installed Device=HIMEM
                  3,104   (3K)     EMMXXXX0    Installed Device=EMM386
                 37,648  (37K)     DBLSYSH$    Installed Device=DBLSPACE
                  1,600   (2K)                 FILES=32
                    256   (0K)                 FCBS=4
                    512   (1K)                 BUFFERS=10
                  2,288   (2K)                 LASTDRIVE=Z
                  3,008   (3K)                 STACKS=9,256
  00E9D              80   (0K)   MSDOS         System Program
  00EA2           2,656   (3K)   COMMAND       Program
  00F48              80   (0K)   MSDOS         -- Free --
  00F4D             528   (1K)   COMMAND       Environment
  00F6E             128   (0K)   MSDOS         -- Free --
  00F76          17,088  (17K)   MOUSE         Program
  013A2             160   (0K)   MEM           Environment
  013AC          88,992  (87K)   MEM           Program
  02966         485,776 (474K)   MSDOS         -- Free --

Upper Memory Detail:

 Segment  Region      Total          Name       Type
 -------  ------  ---------------   ----------  --------
  0CD4A     1         800   (1K)    IO          System Data
                      768   (1K)      SETVERXX  Installed Device=SETVER
  0CD7C     1       4,224   (4K)    IO          System Data
                    4,192   (4K)      CON       Installed Device=ANSI
  0CE84     1          48   (0K)    MSDOS       -- Free --
  0CE87     1      29,024  (28K)    SMARTDRV    Program
  0D59D     1      16,432  (16K)    MSDOS       -- Free --
  0D9A0     1      22,016  (22K)    MSDOS       -- Free --
```

```
Memory Summary:

    Type of Memory         Total    =     Used    +    Free
    ----------------     ---------      ---------     ---------
    Conventional           655,360         80,384      574,976
    Upper                   72,576         34,080       38,496
    Reserved               393,216        393,216            0
    Extended (XMS)*      7,267,456      2,598,016    4,669,440
    ----------------     ---------      ---------     ---------
    Total memory         8,388,608      3,105,696    5,282,912

    Total under 1 MB       727,936        114,464      613,472


    Handle      EMS Name       Size
    ------      --------       ----
         0                   060000

    Total Expanded (EMS)             7,667,712 (7,488K)
    Free Expanded (EMS)*             4,915,200 (4,800K)

    *  EMM386 is using XMS memory to simulate EMS memory as needed.
       Free EMS memory may change as free XMS memory changes.

    Memory accessible using Int 15h              0     (0K)
    Largest executable program size        574,752   (561K)
    Largest free upper memory block         22,016    (22K)
    MS-DOS is resident in the high memory area.

    XMS version 3.00; driver version 3.16
    EMS version 4.00
```

The first column shows the starting address of each item that MEM found. The address is listed in hexadecimal (base 16) notation. The second column shows the size, in kilobytes, of each program or driver. The third column shows the name of the program or device driver loaded into memory. The final column includes the type of item listed. The types include the system files IO.SYS, MSDOS.SYS, and COMMAND.COM; programs; installed device drivers and system device drivers; environment; and any data areas the programs might need.

To see a listing of programs, drivers, and free space in conventional and upper memory, type the following command and press Enter:

MEM /C

DOS shows you a report similar to this one:

```
Modules using memory below 1 MB:

    Name         Total     =    Conventional   +    Upper Memory
    --------   -------------    --------------      ----------------
    MSDOS      18,029   (18K)    18,029   (18K)         0    (0K)
    HIMEM       1,168    (1K)     1,168    (1K)         0    (0K)
    EMM386      3,120    (3K)     3,120    (3K)         0    (0K)
    DBLSPACE   37,664   (37K)    37,664   (37K)         0    (0K)
    COMMAND     3,184    (3K)     3,184    (3K)         0    (0K)
    MOUSE      17,088   (17K)    17,088   (17K)         0    (0K)
```

```
SETVER         816     (1K)         0    (0K)        816     (1K)
ANSI         4,240     (4K)         0    (0K)      4,240     (4K)
SMARTDRV    29,024    (28K)         0    (0K)     29,024    (28K)
Free       613,472   (599K)   574,976  (562K)     38,496    (38K)

Memory Summary:

   Type of Memory        Total    =    Used    +    Free
   ----------------      -------       -------      -------
   Conventional          655,360        80,384      574,976
   Upper                  72,576        34,080       38,496
   Reserved              393,216       393,216            0
   Extended (XMS)*     7,267,456     2,598,016    4,669,440
   ----------------      -------       -------      -------
   Total memory        8,388,608     3,105,696    5,282,912

   Total under 1 MB      727,936       114,464      613,472

   Total Expanded (EMS)                7,667,712 (7,488K)
   Free Expanded (EMS)*                4,915,200 (4,800K)

   * EMM386 is using XMS memory to simulate EMS memory as needed.
     Free EMS memory may change as free XMS memory changes.

   Largest executable program size     574,752   (561K)
   Largest free upper memory block      22,016    (22K)
   MS-DOS is resident in the high memory area.
```

> **Tip**
>
> Because some of the report scrolls off the screen before you can read it, you might want to use the /P switch to tell DOS to pause after each page. To do so, type the following line:
>
> MEM /C /P
>
> DOS displays the report one page at a time. Press any key when you are ready to display the next page.

The third and fourth columns of the report, titled Conventional and Upper Memory, show you how much memory is allocated to any particular driver or program. Use the Upper Memory column to determine whether any drivers or programs are loaded in upper memory, and use the Memory Summary at the end of the report to see how much upper memory is still free.

Before attempting to move a driver or program from conventional to upper memory (using DEVICEHIGH or LOADHIGH), compare the driver or program's size (in the Conventional memory size column) to the available upper memory block (UMB) size shown at the bottom of the memory summary. The available UMB must be at least as big as the driver or program before you can load the driver or program into upper memory.

A quick way to see a listing of free memory space without searching through one of the longer reports is to use the /FREE switch, as shown in the following line:

MEM /F

If you use this switch, MEM lists the free areas of conventional and upper memory. This report shows you the segment address and size of each free area of conventional memory and the largest free block in each region of upper memory. The switch also summarizes your overall memory use. A sample of the report follows:

```
Free Conventional Memory:

  Segment        Total
  -------    ----------------
   00F48           80   (0K)
   00F6E          128   (0K)
   013A2          160   (0K)
   013AC       88,992  (87K)
   02966      485,776 (474K)

  Total Free: 575,136 (562K)

Free Upper Memory:

  Region  Largest Free    Total Free      Total Size
  ------  ------------    ----------      ----------
     1     22,016 (22K)   38,496 (38K)    72,576 (71K)
```

After you identify a driver or memory-resident program that appears to be the right size to fit in the available UMB, edit CONFIG.SYS or AUTOEXEC.BAT to add DEVICEHIGH or LOADHIGH to the appropriate command or program file. Reboot your computer and issue the MEM /C command again to see whether the driver or program loaded.

To arrive at the best combination of device drivers and memory-resident programs loaded into upper memory, you might have to experiment a little. DOS loads programs into the largest available UMB first, so try loading the largest drivers and programs first by placing their startup commands earliest in CONFIG.SYS or AUTOEXEC.BAT.

LOADING A SECONDARY COMMAND PROCESSOR

The COMMAND command enables you to load a second copy of COMMAND.COM, the system's command processor. Many programs load this processor automatically when they enable you to go to a DOS command prompt without exiting the program. Although you might not have much need to load another command processor in your everyday use of DOS, you might want to do so from within a batch file so that you can run another program in its own environment.

ISSUING THE COMMAND COMMAND

The syntax for COMMAND is shown here:

COMMAND *d:path* /P /MSG /E:*aaaaa* /C *string* /K<*command*>

For this command, *d:path* is the drive and path position of the COMMAND.COM file you are loading. The other parameters are explained briefly in the list that follows and in more detail in the next section:

Parameter	Description
/P	Makes the second copy of the command processor permanent
/MSG	Causes DOS to load DOS messages into memory instead of reading the messages from disk every time they are needed
/E:aaaaa	Enables you to adjust the number of bytes of memory that the command processor reserves for its environment
/C string	Enables you to pass a string of characters to the command processor being started
/Y	Directs COMMAND.COM to step through the batch file specified by the /C or /K switch
/K	Causes the program or named batch file to be run, with the system prompt that belongs to this second iteration of COMMAND.COM being displayed after the program terminates

Understanding the Operation of COMMAND.COM

COMMAND.COM, your command processor, reserves a small amount of memory called the *environment*. It uses this memory space to store variables, such as your PATH, PROMPT, and COMSPEC settings. If you load another copy of COMMAND.COM but omit the *d:path* parameter, the second command processor inherits the contents of the first command processor's environment. If you include the *d:path* parameter, the second command processor does not inherit the old environment and keeps only the COMSPEC path specified by *d:path*.

After you start a secondary command processor, you exit it and return to the first command processor by using the EXIT command. When you leave the second command processor, the first command processor's environment remains unchanged, even if you changed the second command processor's environment while you were working with it.

The optional /P switch makes the second copy of the command processor permanent. The first command processor is no longer available, and DOS runs your AUTOEXEC.BAT file if you have one. Remember, if you use the /P switch, you cannot use the EXIT command to exit the second copy of the command processor and return to the first one. You have to turn off your computer and reboot.

The /MSG switch causes DOS to load DOS messages into memory instead of reading the messages from the disk every time they are needed. Using this switch improves the performance of DOS, but you lose some memory space.

The /E:*aaaaa* switch enables you to adjust the number of bytes of memory that the command processor reserves for its environment. The minimum value for *aaaaa* is 160, and the maximum is 32768. The default is 256 bytes. (The recommended minimum value in a Windows environment is 512 bytes.) Each variable stored in the environment takes up space, and you might find that you run out of room in the environment. If, for example, the environment needs to store long settings (such as the long prompt used in the earlier PROMPT command example), you might have to adjust the size of the environment. If you see the message `Out of environment space`, enlarge the environment.

The /C *string* option enables you to pass a string of characters to the command processor you are starting. This option generally was used in batch files (see Chapter 16, "Understanding Batch Files") in DOS versions before 3.3 but is no longer needed with DOS 3.3 and later versions, in which it has been replaced by the CALL command.

> **Tip**
>
> If you are using DOS 6.22, and you use the /C switch to run a batch file under the new command processor, you also can use the /Y switch to instruct COMMAND.COM to single-step through the batch file. This procedure is similar to the single-stepping of AUTOEXEC.BAT you can do when you first boot DOS. For more information on how single-stepping works, refer to Chapter 2.

USING EXIT TO LEAVE THE CURRENT COPY OF THE COMMAND PROCESSOR

Use the EXIT command to leave the current copy of the command processor and return to the previously loaded copy. The syntax for the EXIT command is as follows:

EXIT

No options or switches exist for this command. You cannot use the EXIT command if the second command processor was started by using the /P switch.

USES FOR A SECONDARY COMMAND PROCESSOR

Used together, the COMMAND and EXIT commands provide two interesting uses. If you have specified an alternative location with the file COMMAND.COM, you use COMMAND to load the second processor. If, for example, the DOS command processor is in the root directory and another command processor is loaded in the OTHER subdirectory, you can enter the following command:

COMMAND C:\OTHER /E:320

This command loads the second COMMAND.COM and assigns it an environment size of 320 bytes. You can use the second command processor to execute commands using the 320-byte environment. When you are finished using the secondary command processor, type EXIT to return to the primary command processor.

You also can use this command pair when you have set up a complex environment and you want to execute a command with a basic environment without changing the existing environment. In this case, you can start the second command processor by using the *d:path* option. If necessary, you can change the environment by using the SET command, covered in Chapter 11, "Controlling Your Environment." Execute the desired commands in the altered environment and then exit the second command processor.

If the command processor is in the root directory of drive C, enter the following command:

COMMAND C:\

This command loads a second copy of the command processor. The new environment includes only a setting for COMSPEC, showing that the command processor is loaded in C:\. The prompt does not have a setting and shows up in the form C>. You then execute any desired commands in the new environment. After you finish issuing the commands, type EXIT to exit the second command processor and return to the first command processor. All the environment settings for the first command processor stay as they were originally.

The principles DOS uses to execute this command are also used by applications programs that enable you to suspend your program temporarily and go to DOS. When you select the DOSSHELL command within your word processor, for example, the program starts a second command processor. All the existing information is kept in memory with the first command processor. You execute DOS commands in the second command processor and type EXIT when the commands are complete. The first command processor is then active, and you return to your application program.

CHAPTER 11

CONTROLLING YOUR ENVIRONMENT

In this chapter

Changing DOS Variables   294

Changing the User Interface   295

Changing Disk Drives   301

Changing DOS Variables

The SET command enables you to adjust the DOS environment by changing the variables that are available to programs running under DOS. This command shows the current settings in the environment, or you can use the command to add or change environment variables.

Issuing the SET Command

The syntax for the SET command is as follows:

SET *name=string*

The variable *name=* is the name of the environment variable. The most frequently used environment variables are COMSPEC, PROMPT, and PATH. You can choose your own variable names in addition to these three, however. Many of the programs that you might use set their own environment variables, or require you to do so, before the program runs. These variables control the way the program works.

The parameter *string* is the value to which you want to set the variable. In the case of PATH, the string can be the list of directories through which you want DOS to search to find program files. If you use the *name=* parameter without a value for *string*, the variable specified is a null value (contains nothing). Using the *name=* parameter this way effectively removes the environment variable, and DOS no longer keeps track of it.

You also can type SET at the command prompt without any variables. The command then lists all the current settings for environment variables.

Changing Environment Variables with SET

Typically, you use the SET command as part of a batch file to set variables to be used within your system. Most often, SET is part of the AUTOEXEC.BAT file, used to set the environment variables before any other programs are run.

If you examine your AUTOEXEC.BAT file, you might see some command lines similar to the following:

```
SET COMSPEC=C:\SYS\COMMAND.COM
PROMPT=$p$g
PATH=C:\;C:\DOS;C:\SYS;
```

These commands, even though they look a bit different from each other, accomplish the same thing: They assign values to system variables. The first command tells DOS that the command processor, COMMAND.COM, is in the SYS subdirectory of drive C. The second command sets the prompt to include the current path and a greater-than sign. The third command defines the root directory, DOS directory, and SYS directory of drive C as the search path for DOS to use.

Notice that the second and third command lines do not explicitly include the SET command. It's not included here because neither of these variables requires the SET command, although you can just as easily use these command lines:

```
SET PROMPT=$p$g
SET PATH=C:\;C:\DOS;C:\SYS;
```

DEFINING YOUR OWN ENVIRONMENTAL VARIABLES WITH SET

You also can use the SET command to set custom variables in the environment. These variables usually are the names of directories or switches that programs use. The programs know to look for particular variables in the environment, take the values assigned to those variables, and use them in the program.

A word processing program, for example, might look for a dictionary file called DICT in the current directory. If you use the SET command, however, a different directory can contain the dictionary file. During installation, the program probably will insert a SET command in the batch file that invokes the program. This command can use the following form:

```
SET DICT=C:\WP\DICT
```

This command enables the program to look in the WP directory for the dictionary file instead of looking in the current directory. Setting a variable in the environment, however, is useful only to programs that know to look for that variable.

> **Tip**
> Each variable stored in the environment occupies space. If a program needs large variables set, you might have to increase the area of memory set aside for the environment when DOS boots. You make this change through the SHELL command in CONFIG.SYS (see Chapter 19, "Configuring Your Computer").

CHANGING THE USER INTERFACE

User interface is a term that is often overused in computer circles. It does describe an integral part of computers, however—how you (the user) interact with the computer. DOS provides what has come to be known as a *text-based* user interface, meaning that you communicate with DOS via a command line. In Chapter 4, "Using the DOS Shell," you learned about the DOS Shell, which provides a different user interface.

If you don't want to use the DOS Shell, you can still modify how you interact with DOS. Primarily, you do so through two commands: PROMPT and MODE. The PROMPT command enables you to change what the DOS command prompt looks like, and the MODE command enables you to define how your system should work in conjunction with your video display.

CHANGING THE COMMAND PROMPT WITH PROMPT

If you have ever booted a plain-vanilla version of DOS (one that does not have a CONFIG.SYS or AUTOEXEC.BAT file), you probably noticed the default command prompt used by DOS. It looks like this:

```
C>
```

This default command prompt shows the current drive and a greater-than sign—that's it. You can, however, create a command prompt that is much more useful. You do so by using the PROMPT command. If you look at your AUTOEXEC.BAT file, for example, you might see a line that looks like this:

```
PROMPT $p$g
```

This line changes the default command-line prompt to the following:

```
C:\>
```

Although this prompt might not look immediately more useful, its value becomes apparent if you switch to another directory on your drive. If you use the CD command, for example, to switch to the DOS subdirectory, your command prompt looks like this:

```
C:\>cd\dos
C:\DOS>
```

It now shows the directory where you are located. This display is of great value whenever you are issuing commands at the DOS prompt. If you use a hard disk, this display is the minimum recommended prompt setting because navigating subdirectories can be difficult if you don't know your current position. For this reason, you will find this use of the PROMPT command in many people's AUTOEXEC.BAT files.

The PROMPT command has many more settings that you can use to further refine your DOS prompt. Used to its fullest, the PROMPT command requires use of the ANSI.SYS device driver (see Chapter 17, "Understanding ANSI.SYS"). Even without using the ANSI.SYS device driver, however, you can choose from many different command prompts.

Issuing the PROMPT Command

The syntax for the PROMPT command is simple:

```
PROMPT string
```

The *string* consists of text that defines how you want the command prompt to appear. This text can contain special pairs of characters, called *meta-strings*, which consist of a dollar sign followed by one of the following characters:

```
b    d    e    g    h    l    n    p    q    t    v    $
```

The string can contain any text or any number of meta-strings in any order. Table 11.1 lists the meaning of the different meta-strings.

TABLE 11.1 META-STRINGS FOR USE WITH THE PROMPT COMMAND

Meta-String	Displayed Information or Result
$_	Carriage return/line feed (moves the cursor to the beginning of the next line)
$b	Vertical bar character (|)
$d	Date
$e	Esc character

TABLE 11.1   CONTINUED

Meta-String	Displayed Information or Result
$g	Greater-than sign (>)
$h	Backspace (moves the cursor one space to the left)
$l	Less-than sign (<)
$n	Current drive
$p	Current path
$q	Equal sign (=)
$t	Time
$v	DOS version
$$	Dollar sign

> **Tip**
> If you don't like the current prompt and you want to reset it to the default originally used by DOS, you can enter the PROMPT command without any parameters. This command causes DOS to reset the prompt to the current drive letter and a greater-than sign.

UNDERSTANDING THE USE OF META-STRINGS

Earlier in this chapter, you saw an example of how to use meta-strings in a PROMPT command:

```
PROMPT $p$g
```

This is just one possible use, albeit the most often used. You also can use other combinations, such as

```
PROMPT Date: $d Time: $t$_$p$g
```

After you issue this command, your command prompt appears as follows:

```
Date: Thu 03-22-2001 Time: 2:35:07.23
C:\WP\MEMOS>
```

Notice that this command creates a two-line command prompt which shows the current date and time, as well as the current directory. You can get as exotic as you want with your command prompt; its appearance is entirely up to you.

Changing the command prompt based on certain configurations you might have within your system is not uncommon. Suppose that you use several different DOS programs, each of which requires its own special setup. You can create a batch file (see Chapter 16, "Understanding Batch Files") that sets up the search paths and system variables necessary for properly using the program. If the name of this program is XYZ Spreadsheet, version 3.7, you might want to add the following line to the batch file that performs the configuration:

```
PROMPT Now using XYZ Spreadsheet, version 3.7$_$p$p
```

When this batch file executes, the command prompt becomes the following:

```
Now using XYZ Spreadsheet, version 3.7
C:\SSDATA>
```

Now you can easily remember what configuration is active within your system. When you run another batch file to change the configuration again, a different prompt command that you have set up can indicate which configuration is in effect. Again, how you set up your command prompt is up to you and how you use your system.

Two of the meta-strings might require further explanation. You use the Esc character ($e) in association with the ANSI.SYS driver (see Chapter 17 for more information). In the same way that you use the dollar sign to indicate to DOS that the next character is a meta-string, you use the Esc character to signal ANSI.SYS that the next few characters are an ANSI.SYS command.

You can :use the Backspace character ($h) to remove characters from the prompt. In the earlier PROMPT example that displayed the date and time, you might find the seconds and hundredths of a second in the displayed prompt are more of a distraction than they are helpful. You can alter the PROMPT command as follows:

```
PROMPT Date: $d Time: $t$h$h$h$h$h$h$_$p$g
```

The result is the following improved prompt, with everything after the minutes erased:

```
Date: Thu 03-22-2001 Time: 2:35
C:\WP\MEMOS>
```

ALTERING THE LOOK OF THE SCREEN WITH MODE

You can use the external MODE command to customize the number of characters per line and the number of lines displayed onscreen. You also can use the MODE command to set the configuration of your computer ports (such as your printer port) and for code page switching.

> **Note:** Certain areas of memory in your system store the character tables for your video screen and your keyboard. By switching tables, you can configure DOS to use alternative character sets to suit your national language and customs. These tables are called *code pages*. For more information about code pages, see Chapter 14, "Understanding the International Features of DOS."

You might already know this fact, but it is possible to attach two types of video displays to your computer. You can use a monochrome adapter and display for your word processing, for example, and a color graphics adapter and display for a graphics program. You can switch between the displays by using the MODE command. When you type at the keyboard on a two-display system, you see the keystrokes only on one of the displays—the *active display*. The keyboard and active display make up the *console*. As you learned in Chapter 5, "Understanding Files and Directories," DOS uses CON as the device name for the console.

Selecting the Display Type

To change display characteristics, you can use two forms of the MODE command (listed in Table 11.2). The following is the simplest form:

MODE dt

The abbreviation *dt* is the display type and mode. Available options are 40, 80, BW40, BW80, CO40, CO80, or MONO, as detailed in Table 11.2. The 40 and 80 refer to the number of text columns displayed. This setting means that you can choose between 40 and 80 characters per line. BW stands for black and white, CO stands for color, and MONO refers to the monochrome display adapter.

TABLE 11.2 MODE SETTINGS FOR DISPLAY TYPE

Command	Meaning
MODE 40	Sets the display to 40 characters per line
MODE 80	Sets the display to 80 characters per line
MODE BW40	Selects the color display in black-and-white mode, 40 characters per line
MODE BW80	Selects the color display in black-and-white mode, 80 characters per line
MODE CO40	Selects the color display, 40 characters per line
MODE CO80	Selects the color display, 80 characters per line
MODE MONO	Selects the monochrome display

Shifting the Screen on a Color Graphics Adapter

The second form of the MODE command is for use on a Color Graphics Adapter (CGA) only. This form, which does not work on an Enhanced Graphics Adapter (EGA) or a Video Graphics Array (VGA), enables you to configure your PC to work with a television instead of a specially designed computer monitor. It moves the horizontal position of the image on your screen. If you cannot see the far-left or far-right character onscreen, the following command corrects the problem:

MODE dt,dir,T

The *dt* parameter is the display type described in the preceding section. The *dir* parameter can have the value R to move the image to the right or L to move the image to the left. If the display is in 80-column mode, MODE moves the image two characters to the right or left. If in 40-column mode, MODE moves the image one character to the right or left.

The optional T parameter, when used, causes MODE to display a test pattern that you can use to align the display. Say you type the following:

MODE CO80,R,T

A line of 80 characters appears across the screen, along with the following prompt:

Do you see the leftmost 0? (y/n)

If you respond N to the prompt, this image moves two positions to the right of its preceding position. If you respond Y to the prompt, the test is completed and the prompt is erased. Using the L option works in the same manner but moves the image to the left.

If you operate your system after shifting the screen, you have a little less memory available for your use. To display the image in an adjusted position, DOS leaves a small portion of the MODE command in memory, occupying about 1KB of memory. This program intercepts all output, adjusts it, and then sends it to the screen.

Using MODE to Adjust the Number of Columns or Lines Onscreen

You also can use MODE to adjust the number of columns or number of lines displayed onscreen. You must install the ANSI.SYS device driver before MODE can adjust your screen, however.

One way you can use MODE to adjust screen size is the following:

MODE CON COLS=a LINES=b

COLS= sets the number of columns displayed onscreen to a, and LINES= sets the number of lines displayed onscreen to b. If you omit a setting for the number of columns or number of lines, the current setting is preserved.

Valid numbers for a are 40 or 80. Valid numbers for b on a VGA screen are 25, 43, or 50; valid numbers for b on an EGA screen are 25 or 43.

If ANSI.SYS is loaded via the CONFIG.SYS file, typing the following command gives you a display mode 80 columns wide and 43 lines high on a computer with an EGA or VGA adapter and monitor:

MODE CON COLS=80 LINES=43

After you set the display mode, you can start your application program. The display mode remains, unless the application resets it. If you use the preceding MODE command on a computer with an EGA screen, for example, you can use WordPerfect in 43-line mode without adjusting any settings in WordPerfect.

> **Note**
> Not all applications can "see" that the extra lines are available. Try some MODE CON commands to determine whether you can use the extra lines. Using MODE CON to set your screen to 43 or 50 lines makes it easier to view long DIR listings, but the type is very small and can be difficult to read.

Another MODE command option enables you to alter the number of lines displayed without specifying that the screen is the console. This form, which is really a variation on the MODE CON format, is handy when you use an auxiliary console instead of CON. Chapter 13, "Controlling Devices," introduces the CTTY command, which establishes another device as the standard input-and-output device. The syntax for this form of the MODE command is as follows:

MODE dt,b

In this syntax, *dt* is the display type, and *b* is the number of lines to be displayed. The acceptable values for *dt* and *b* are as previously described, but not all combinations of values for *dt* and *b* are possible. For example, you cannot adjust the number of lines on a monochrome or CGA monitor. Table 11.3 lists the workable combinations of parameters with the MODE command for setting the display type.

TABLE 11.3 SETTING THE NUMBER OF LINES BY DISPLAY TYPE

Mode Option	MDA	CGA	EGA	VGA
C040,25		4	4	4
C040,43			4	4
C040,50				4
C080,25		4	4	4
C080,43			4	4
C080,50				4
BW40,25		4	4	4
BW40,43			4	4
BW40,50				4
BW80,25		4	4	4
BW80,43			4	4
BW80,50				4
MONO	4			

Using the information in Table 11.3, you can determine that on a VGA system you can alter the display type to color with 40 columns and 50 lines by typing the following command:

MODE C040,50

All forms of the MODE command that adjust the display are similar in syntax and purpose. An incorrect command does not damage anything, and DOS provides reasonably clear error messages. If the ANSI.SYS driver is required and not installed, for example, DOS displays the following error message:

ANSI.SYS must be installed to perform requested function

CHANGING DISK DRIVES

As you configure DOS to the environment you need, you might find times when you need to adjust how DOS treats your disk drives and directories. Three commands enable you to do just that. You use the ASSIGN command to redirect disk requests to different drives, the JOIN command to treat a disk drive as a subdirectory, and the SUBST command to treat a subdirectory as a disk drive.

The ASSIGN Command

You use the external command ASSIGN to redirect all DOS read-and-write (input-and-output) requests from one drive to another. Each drive is a DOS device. When you use the ASSIGN command, DOS can interrogate a different disk from the one actually specified on a command line.

> **Warning:** The FORMAT and DISKCOPY commands ignore any drive ASSIGN commands.

The syntax for the ASSIGN command is as follows:

ASSIGN *d1*=*d2* .../STATUS

d1 is the drive letter for the original disk drive; *d2* is the drive letter for the reassignment. The ellipsis (...) indicates that you can reassign more than one drive on a single command line.

/STATUS, issued with no other parameters, displays a listing of current drive assignments

The JOIN Command

You can use the JOIN command to add a disk drive to the directory structure of another disk. The external command JOIN, for example, enables you to use a floppy disk in such a way that it appears to DOS to be part of a hard disk. You also can use JOIN if you have two hard disks: drive C and drive D. JOIN can attach drive D to a subdirectory on drive C, for instance.

The syntax for JOIN is as follows:

JOIN *d1*: *d2*:*path* /D

The directory structure of disk *d1* is added to the directory structure of hard disk *d2*. *d1*: is a valid disk drive name that becomes the alias or nickname. *d1*: might be a nonexistent disk drive. *d2*:*path* is the valid disk drive name and directory path that will be nicknamed *d1*:. If you use the /D switch, the alias is deleted.

When you use the JOIN command, DOS redirects any access from *d2*:*path* to *d1*:. Thus, if you use the command

JOIN A: C:\SSDATA

any time you access C:\SSDATA, you actually are accessing drive A. This capability is helpful if you have a program that can look only in a specific directory for data and you actually want to keep the data elsewhere.

The SUBST Command

The external command SUBST is the inverse of the JOIN command. Instead of grafting a second disk onto the tree structure of your hard drive, the SUBST command splits a disk's directory structure in two. In effect, the SUBST command creates an alias disk drive name for a subdirectory.

ISSUING THE SUBST COMMAND

You can use the SUBST command to perform different functions. To establish an alias, use the following syntax:

SUBST *d1*: *d2*:*pathname*

To delete an alias, use this form:

SUBST *d1*: /D

To see the current aliases, use the following form:

SUBST

The SUBST command replaces a pathname for a subdirectory with a drive letter. After a SUBST command is in effect, DOS translates all I/O (input/output) requests to a particular drive letter back to the correct pathname. The alias drive created by the SUBST command inherits the directory tree structure of the subdirectory reassigned to a drive letter.

> **Note** As the default, DOS assigns the LASTDRIVE= parameter (used in CONFIG.SYS) a value of E. You can make higher drive designators, however, by inserting a LASTDRIVE= parameter into the CONFIG.SYS file. DOS then establishes as DOS devices each of the drive letters up to and including the specified LASTDRIVE. When you use the SUBST command, DOS understands that you are referring to a device.

USING SUBST TO REFERENCE A PATH WITH A DRIVE LETTER

SUBST is commonly used in two different situations. If you want to run a program that does not support pathnames, you can use the SUBST command to assign a drive letter to a directory. The program then refers to the drive letter, and DOS translates the request into a path. If, for example, the data for a program is stored in C:\WORDPROC, you can use the following command so that you can refer to this subdirectory as drive E:

SUBST E: C:\WORDPROC

After the substitution is made, you can issue the following command:

SUBST

The following message appears:

E: => C:\WORDPROC

To disconnect the substitution of drive E for the C:\WORDPROC directory, type the following command:

SUBST E: /D

The other use for SUBST is to reduce typing long pathnames. When more than one person uses a PC, pathnames can become quite long because each user can use a separate section of the hard disk to store data files and common areas of the disk to store programs. If the paths \USER1\WORDDATA and \USER1\SSDATA exist on drive C, for example, you can reduce the typing required to reach files in the directories by using the following command:

```
SUBST E: C:\USER1
```

Issuing a directory command on drive E produces the following listing:

```
Volume in drive E is HARD DISK C
Volume Serial Number is 1573-0241
Directory of  E:\


 .           <DIR>     05-02-92  12:07p
 ..          <DIR>     05-02-92  12:07p
WORDDATA     <DIR>     05-02-92   1:59p
SSDATA       <DIR>    05-22-01   2:08p
        4 File(s)          0 bytes
                      3477824 bytes free
```

The volume label given is the label from drive C, but the directory itself contains the contents of C:\USER1.

> **Note:** Do not use the following DOS commands in conjunction with drives that you create with the SUBST command: ASSIGN, BACKUP, CHKDSK, DEFRAG, DISKCOMP, DISKCOPY, FDISK, FORMAT, LABEL, MIRROR, RECOVER, RESTORE, SCANFIX, and SYS. Some of these commands might refuse to work, and others might provide unwanted results.

As with JOIN and ASSIGN, you can use the SUBST command to fool software that insists on using an otherwise unusable drive. A friend might have written an applications program, for example, that makes direct reference in its code to a directory on drive C. By using SUBST, you can have your friend's program attach drive D to a subdirectory on your drive C.

Understanding the General Rules for Using SUBST

As you are using the SUBST command, you must keep the following rules in mind:

- *d1:* and *d2:* must be different.
- You cannot specify a networked drive as *d1:* or *d2:*.
- *d1:* cannot be the current drive.
- *d1:* must have a designator less than the value in the LASTDRIVE statement of CONFIG.SYS. (See Chapter 19 for more information on CONFIG.SYS.)
- Do not use SUBST with ASSIGN or JOIN.
- Remove all SUBST settings before you run ASSIGN, BACKUP, DEFRAG, DISKCOMP, DISKCOPY, FDISK, FORMAT, LABEL, MIRROR, PRINT, RECOVER, RESTORE, SCANFIX, or SYS.
- Beware of using APPEND, CHDIR, MKDIR, PATH, and RMDIR with any drives reassigned.

Using the COMSPEC Variable

COMSPEC is a reserved system variable name that defines your command processor's location. Typically, it is set to the complete path and filename for COMMAND.COM. If your command processor is not in the root directory of the boot drive, you must include an appropriate SHELL directive in CONFIG.SYS to inform DOS of the command processor's location. This command, in turn, automatically sets the COMSPEC variable correctly. Thus, you don't need to explicitly set the COMSPEC variable in your AUTOEXEC.BAT file if you use the SHELL directive. If you do not have the COMSPEC variable set on your system, your system might hang when you boot your computer or when you leave an application program that needs to reload the command processor. This failure occurs because the system cannot find the command processor. Refer to Chapter 19 for information on how to use the SHELL directive in CONFIG.SYS to tell the system where to find the command processor.

CHAPTER 12

USING PERIPHERALS

In this chapter

Understanding Device Drivers   308

Setting Up Device Drivers   312

Troubleshooting Device Drivers   314

Understanding Device Drivers

Unlike some operating systems, such as Windows 9x/ME, NT/2000, or OS/2, DOS does not include much built-in support for peripheral devices. Instead, most devices require the addition of device drivers to your DOS configuration in order to access the devices in question.

Virtually every DOS-based computer system needs to work with device drivers at some point, unless it's using an extremely simple hardware configuration. Spending some time familiarizing yourself with this important topic can help you save time when you need to add or manage various device drivers in your system.

DOS contains only rudimentary support for computer hardware. For example, DOS can work with standard VGA video cards, basic IDE hard disks, floppy disk drives, text-mode printers, keyboards, and that's about it. To use other types of hardware usually requires the installation and configuration of a device driver for the device in question. Device drivers enable the following types of devices to work with DOS:

- CD-ROM
- Mouse or trackball
- Tape backup
- Video cards
- Sound cards
- Network cards
- Other nonstandard storage devices, such as Zip and Jaz drives

> **Note**
>
> DOS itself can work with printers in only the simplest possible way: It can send text-only information to a printer that can accept that type of information. This means that, just using DOS, you can print only plain text. Other printer features, such as boldface, underline, or even graphics, require an application that uses an application-specific printer driver that cannot be shared with other applications.
>
> Under DOS, you can direct text output to a printer in several ways. You can press the Print Screen key to send a copy of what's on the screen to the printer. You can copy a text file to the printer by using the command COPY `filename.ext` PRN: and then pressing Enter. You can also use DOS redirection to do the same thing, with the command TYPE `filename.ext` >PRN:.
>
> For serial printers, see Chapter 13, "Controlling Devices," on use of the MODE command, which is usually required with serial-port printers.

You might be wondering why you don't see printers and modems in the preceding list. Note that there are two distinct types of device drivers. The first kind—the kind you usually hear about—enables DOS itself to interact with and manage a particular device, such as a CD-ROM drive. When DOS can access and manage a device through the use of a device driver, applications can then make use of the device, too, through DOS.

The second kind of device driver, an *application-specific device driver*, supports a specific application program that needs to work with a device. For example, WordPerfect for DOS includes its own printer device drivers to allow it to work properly with different printers. The printer device drivers that WordPerfect uses are installed in WordPerfect itself and do not benefit or work with any other application. As another example, most communications programs under DOS either include their own modem device drivers, or they allow fine control of a number of settings that enable them to work with different modems.

To understand device drivers and how they are configured, you first need to understand some basics about standard PC architecture and how DOS works with both application programs and devices to accomplish its work. You also need to understand how the devices themselves interact with the computer because many devices require that you determine and set their hardware interrupt, DMA channel, and memory address manually. The following sections discuss this information.

UNDERSTANDING HARDWARE INTERRUPTS

You have no doubt heard about *hardware interrupts*, also called *IRQs*, inside your computer. All PCs are built so that devices that are part of the computer communicate with the processor through the use of these hardware interrupts. A hardware interrupt enables a device, such as your keyboard, to send a signal to the processor indicating that the device requires the processor's attention. When the processor receives a signal on one of these interrupts, it branches to a region of memory that contains the program that handles the device itself. For example, every time you press a key on your keyboard, an interrupt is generated for your processor. The processor then finds the program that corresponds to the interrupt, which in turn handles whatever the device needs. In the case of a key being pressed, the program reads which key was pressed from the keyboard and then sends the information to DOS so that DOS or a running application program can display the key on the screen or do whatever else was intended.

All PCs have 16 hardware interrupts, and unfortunately this number cannot be expanded. The 16 interrupts are arranged in two banks of 8 interrupts, with the second bank being connected to the first bank through interrupts 2 and 9. Because interrupts 2 and 9 link the two banks together, you generally don't want to use these interrupts for any devices in the system (although there are rare exceptions to this rule).

Hardware interrupts in most PCs are *edge-sensitive*, meaning that the system measures simply whether the interrupt signal is on or off. In some systems, particularly those that use either the EISA or MCA (microchannel) buses, interrupts are *level-sensitive*, meaning that an individual interrupt signal can be set to one of several different levels. The idea behind level-sensitive interrupts is that, in theory, multiple devices can share an interrupt, with each device using a different level for its communication. However, in practice, this doesn't work very well, and so most buses stick with edge-sensitive interrupts.

IRQ assignments can be shared between devices but never between devices that will be used at the same time. For example, if a computer has an interrupt set for one of its communication ports connected to a modem, it also might be capable of using the same interrupt assignment for a tape backup device, provided that the tape backup device is never used while the modem is being used. Another way this works is for systems that have multiple serial devices installed in them. For example, imagine that a computer has a serial mouse connected to COM1 (IRQ 4) and a modem connected to COM2 (IRQ 3). If another serial device is installed as COM3, it is usually assigned to the same IRQ number as COM1. This also means that the additional device can't be used at the same time as the mouse (which probably means that it can never be used because most mouse devices are active all the time). Instead, in this type of circumstance, you are better off placing the modem on COM1, the mouse on COM2, and the third device on COM3, with the understanding that the third device cannot be used while the modem is in use.

You need to be familiar with some standard IRQ assignments. Note that some of them might be different in a particular PC, depending on the extra equipment provided from the manufacturer and which IRQ is assigned to each device. However, for most systems, the interrupt assignments listed in Table 12.1 are correct for the basic hardware devices.

TABLE 12.1 STANDARD HARDWARE INTERRUPT (IRQ) ASSIGNMENTS

IRQ	Assignment
0	System timer
1	Keyboard controller
2	Connected to second bank at IRQ 9
3	Serial port 2 (COM2,4)
4	Serial port 1 (COM1,3)
5	Parallel port 2 (LPT2) (but often used for sound cards because most systems don't have an installed LPT2: port)
6	Disk drive controller
7	Parallel port 1 (LPT1)
8	Real-time clock
9	Connected to first bank at IRQ 2
10	Unused
11	Unused (can often be used for a network card)
12	Mouse controller
13	Math coprocessor
14	Hard disk controller
15	Unused (can often be used for secondary hard disk controller)

What's a Software Interrupt?
Two kinds of interrupts are referred to with PCs and with DOS. You've just learned about hardware interrupts, often abbreviated as IRQs (Interrupt Requests). There are also, however, software interrupts, which are used by applications to communicate with DOS and with the computer's basic input/output system (BIOS).

Software interrupts are used only by software programmers. They provide hundreds of different functions for application programs, from displaying text on the screen to opening a file on a disk drive to getting the current time from the computer's clock for use in the application.

Software interrupts are usually abbreviated with the letters *Int* and usually followed by a hexadecimal number. For instance, the main interrupt used by a program to communicate with DOS is called Int 21H.

You don't need to do anything with software interrupts, but you do need to know what they are so that you don't get them confused with hardware interrupts.

Virtually every card you install in the computer requires that you set its IRQ. Often, add-on cards come with special software that can do this job for you, and they also help you determine which IRQs might be free for the cards to use. Other cards provide only a bank of switches or jumpers on the cards to set this information, and it's up to you to determine which IRQ is free for the cards and to make sure that the system and new device work properly with the chosen IRQ.

UNDERSTANDING DIRECT MEMORY ACCESS (DMA) CHANNELS

Many devices need to transfer large amounts of data to or from the computer's memory. To free the computer's processor from needing to perform these transfers for devices with large data-transfer needs (such as hard disk controllers, video cards, and network cards), the PC architecture includes a chip called a Direct Memory Access Controller, or DMA Controller. The DMA controller can transfer memory from one place in the computer to another memory address, without using the processor to do the work. The DMA controller is told where the source address of the data to be transferred is, where the destination address is, and how much to transfer. The processor is then relieved from doing the actual work, and the DMA controller takes care of moving the data from one place to another. (It also does so more rapidly than the processor usually can.) The PC has a total of eight DMA channels, and these DMA channels cannot be shared among devices that use them. Moreover, different DMA channels have either 8- or 16-bit transfer capabilities, and devices usually require one or the other. Table 12.2 lists the standard DMA channels in a PC and their usual assignments.

TABLE 12.2   STANDARD PC DMA ASSIGNMENTS

DMA	Size	Assignment
0	8-bit	Available
1	8-bit	Available (can be used for network cards)
2	8-bit	Floppy disk controller
3	8-bit	Available (can be used for enhanced parallel ports EPP or ECP)
4		Unavailable (used for memory refresh)
5	16-bit	Available
6	16-bit	Available
7	16-bit	Available (can be used for hard disk controllers)

> **Note:** DMA channels are sometimes abbreviated as *DRQs*.

Four common devices make use of the DMA controller and require that a particular DMA channel be assigned to them. These devices are the floppy disk drive (assigned to DMA channel 2), the hard disk controller, the video card, and any installed network cards. In the last three cases, the devices might or might not use DMAs; it's up to the designers of the cards. In newer PCs, these devices do not use DMAs, whereas older computers (80486-based and earlier) often use versions of these devices that do use DMAs.

Most add-on cards that use a DMA channel offer a default setting that works most often. However, if the device isn't functioning correctly, you might have to try one of the other possible DMA channels available on that particular card.

Understanding Memory Input/Output Addresses

Programs cannot send data to or receive data from devices connected to the computer directly. Instead, small portions of memory are set aside into which programs (and DOS) place information destined for a device, and vice versa. These areas of memory are called I/O port addresses (*I/O* being short for *Input/Output*). These memory spaces cannot be shared, nor can they overlap each other.

Most devices you install into the computer require an I/O port address be assigned to them. Often, the default setting from the manufacturer works, although usually alternative addresses also are provided in case of conflict. Most device drivers also need this information to properly interact with the device itself.

Setting Up Device Drivers

As mentioned at the beginning of the chapter, device drivers are memory-resident programs that enable DOS and application programs to interact with certain devices in the computer. Device drivers are generally set up in DOS through a statement in the system's CONFIG.SYS file. In rare cases, a device driver might be loaded in the AUTOEXEC.BAT file instead. Most device drivers use the .SYS extension.

Device drivers in the CONFIG.SYS file are loaded through either the DEVICE= or DEVICEHIGH= statements. The former loads the device driver into conventional memory, whereas the latter attempts to load the device driver into extended memory. Most device drivers function well either way, although in rare cases, a device driver might work properly only in conventional memory. Aside from this, though, whether they are located in conventional or extended memory is determined by the overall memory tuning for the system, which is discussed in Chapter 19, "Configuring Your Computer."

> **Note:** Device drivers loaded in AUTOEXEC.BAT are placed into conventional memory unless you use the LOADHIGH command to start them.

Two device drivers that most DOS systems load, regardless of what peripherals they have loaded, are HIMEM and EMM386. They are both loaded in the CONFIG.SYS file, and they provide additional memory management services for DOS (in this case, you might think of the system's RAM as a device). Following is an example of how these two lines usually appear in the CONFIG.SYS file:

```
DEVICE=C:\DOS\HIMEM.SYS
DEVICE=C:\DOS\EMM386.EXE RAM
```

As you can see, the actual device driver files can be located anywhere on the computer system, and the DEVICE command accepts drive letters and directories so that they can be located and loaded.

> **Tip**
> Sometimes you need to set up boot disks for different configurations on a system. For instance, some computer games require that only the minimum possible device drivers be loaded to provide the game with enough conventional memory and reduce potential conflicts in the system. If you use boot disks to boot DOS with different configurations, you can dramatically improve your boot time by making sure that any needed device drivers are located on the system's hard disk and that the CONFIG.SYS and AUTOEXEC.BAT files properly reference the device drivers. This way, the system can boot much more quickly than if it had to load the device drivers from the disk itself.

Many device drivers require that the chosen IRQ, DMA, and I/O port addresses be set as part of the device driver load command. A good example is the device driver for supporting a Sound Blaster audio card. The following command is used, for example, for a Sound Blaster 16:

```
DEVICE=C:\SB16\DRV\CTSB16.SYS /UNIT=0 /BLASTER=A:220 I:5 D:1 H:5
```

The first part of the DEVICE= statement simply locates and loads the device driver. The next portion of the statement is the /UNIT parameter, which in this case indicates that this is the first installed Sound Blaster. Next comes the /BLASTER parameter, which indicates what resources in the system the card can use. Each resource is identified with a letter, followed by a colon and the chosen setting. The A parameter sets the memory address for the card, and the I parameter sets the IRQ used (often, IRQ 5 is used for sound cards because most systems don't have an LPT2 port, so that IRQ is available). The D and H parameters set the two DMA channels that the card is to use—1 and 5, respectively (the Sound Blaster 16 uses both an 8- and 16-bit DMA channel).

Unfortunately, every device driver requires different parameters and uses a different syntax to specify any needed options. For each device driver you use, you need to examine the documentation that came with the device for the proper syntax to use when loading the device driver.

Troubleshooting Device Drivers

Generally, you might have problems with a device driver when you install it for the first time, although occasional difficulties can emerge over time if it is incompatible with, say, a new program or an additional device.

If you are having trouble getting a device driver to work initially, you should first suspect a conflict in the device's IRQ, DMA, or I/O memory setting. Depending on the device itself, different conflicts might manifest in different ways. For example, skipping sound coming from a sound card often indicates an IRQ conflict.

If the documentation that came with the device offers no clues on how to determine which resource is conflicting, you will likely have to pursue a trial-and-error approach to changing the settings.

Many versions of DOS come with a program called Microsoft Diagnostics (`MSD.EXE`) that can help you determine which IRQs are free in your computer. Similarly, some utility programs such as Norton Utilities for DOS also can show you this information, as well as information on what I/O port addresses are in use, and sometimes which DMA channels are in use.

Another route you can take when troubleshooting a new device driver is to disable all other device drivers. You do so by editing the `CONFIG.SYS` and `AUTOEXEC.BAT` files from which the system boots. You place the keyword `REM` (followed by a space) in front of any lines in `CONFIG.SYS` or `AUTOEXEC.BAT` that load device drivers. The keyword `REM` stands for *remark* and indicates to DOS that the rest of that particular line is to be ignored. After "remarking out" the other device drivers, you reboot the computer to make the changes take effect. The idea here is to simply see whether you can get the device to function properly with a minimal system. If so, you can proceed in a stepwise fashion to re-enable the other device drivers until you find the one that conflicts, and then you will probably have enough information to resolve the conflict. (You re-enable a device by removing the `REM` from the front of its line in `CONFIG.SYS` or `AUTOEXEC.BAT` and rebooting). If you cannot get a device to work even in a minimal system, even after trying a number of alternative settings, the device might not be working or it might have some kind of hardware incompatibility. In this case, contact the manufacturer of either the device or the computer system for further assistance.

For example, consider the following case: You have a system that contains two COM ports (COM1 and COM2) with a modem on COM1, a mouse on COM2, a sound card, a printer on a parallel port, and a CD-ROM drive. You have just installed a network card into the system, and the first time you try to initialize it, the mouse on COM2 stops working, and the new network card doesn't work at all. How do you go about resolving this (unfortunately all-too-common) problem?

You probably suspect some kind of conflict because not only does the network card not function but neither does the mouse. If just the new network card doesn't work, but everything else is fine, you probably suspect a configuration problem of some kind or a broken network card, but not necessarily a conflict with another device. Because you're dealing with a conflict (and assuming that no troubleshooting tools are available for either device to tell you what the problem is), you then proceed to find out whether you can make the network card work if you disable the mouse. To do so, you look in both `CONFIG.SYS` and `AUTOEXEC.BAT` to find the device driver that controls the mouse (it can be in either place for mouse devices), add REM to the start of its line, and then reboot the computer.

After taking these steps, you discover that the network card starts working. This is good news because you've now proven that the card works, and you've confirmed that you have a conflict with the mouse. If you have any doubt, you can remove the network card or its drivers and see whether the mouse starts working. If so, you've pretty much proven that you have a conflict.

Now the question becomes, what is conflicting? Is it an IRQ, DMA channel, or a memory I/O port? Here, experience really pays off because over time you develop knowledge of the most likely conflict for any given device. However, as a general rule, you should always suspect the IRQ first—that's where most conflicts occur. Looking at the IRQ table (refer to Table 12.1), you see that the COM2 port, which the mouse uses, makes use of IRQ 3. Looking through the documentation for the network card, you find that its default IRQ is also IRQ 3. Eureka!

> **Tip**
> Always remember that manufacturer Web sites can be invaluable resources to troubleshoot and resolve device problems. Usually, they have notes, FAQs, and updated drivers that might resolve your problem. Also, don't forget to check the Web site of the company that made the computer because the manufacturer can also have specific fixes for some devices that, for some reason, conflict only on its computers. For example, when I was beta testing Windows NT 4, I *never* got it to communicate with the serial ports on my main computer. I figured the problem was a bug that would get resolved before NT was released. Well, when I loaded the released version, it had the same problem! Two weeks later, the maker of the computer I was using came up with an update to its BIOS that resolved the problem because Windows NT had changed how it communicated with serial ports in some basic way.

Now that you've guessed that the conflict is on IRQ 3, you can do one of two things:

- You can change the network card's IRQ to another IRQ number.

> **Tip**
> Most network cards work best on IRQs 10, 11, or 12. If those choices aren't available, try IRQ 5.

- You can't easily change the IRQs for COM ports, so you can't change the mouse's COM2 IRQ to something else. However, you might consider changing from a serial mouse that requires a COM port to something called a *bus mouse* that uses its own interface card in the computer (and uses different interrupts from serial mouse devices, too).

You use the same process to work through other types of conflicts, but if changing a device's IRQ doesn't work, you might have to try changing the I/O port address or, if the device uses DMA, its DMA channel.

The following are some general tips for different types of devices that you might have trouble with:

- Some systems have add-on serial port cards instead of (or in addition to) built-in serial ports. These cards usually enable you to change the IRQs used for those add-on serial ports. However, be reluctant in changing them because many application programs don't work properly with a COM port that isn't on a standard COM port IRQ.
- Some video cards use an extra IRQ. The features that require it aren't very important to the functioning of most software, and you can disable a video card's additional IRQ use.
- CD-ROM drives rely on at least two device drivers to function. The first, which is usually part of CONFIG.SYS, initializes the card that connects to the CD-ROM drive. (Often, it is a driver with *ASPI* in its name, but not always.) Secondarily, a device driver called MSCDEX.EXE (Microsoft CD Extensions) is required in the AUTOEXEC.BAT file. The driver in CONFIG.SYS probably requires IRQ, I/O, and DMA assignments, whereas MSCDEX relies on other settings that tell it the name of the device defined in CONFIG.SYS, the drive letter to use, and some other features that can improve CD-ROM performance. Make sure that the parameters to both the CD-ROM device driver and MSCDEX are correct per the manual that came with the CD-ROM and CD-ROM interface card.
- Parallel printers don't rely on DOS device drivers. It is up to each application to work with the printer properly. However, serial-based printers can require that you run the DOS MODE command to properly set the system's COM port to work with the printer. You use the MODE command to set the COM port's baud rate, number of data bits, parity, and number of stop bits, and these settings must correspond to switch-based settings on the printer itself. See Chapter 13 for details on using the MODE command.
- Modems also do not rely on device drivers, but they are subject to IRQ conflicts with other devices that probably use device drivers. If a modem isn't working properly, suspect an IRQ conflict with the COM port that the modem uses. Also, check the specific settings in the communications program you are using, making sure that it's set to use the right COM port and that the baud rate is supported by the modem.

Solving device conflicts can, at times, be a frustrating task, and working through all the possible issues takes patience. However, keep in mind that you need to perform all changes and tests in a controlled, stepwise fashion, and use the information presented in this chapter to help you understand possible sources of trouble and ways of dealing with various device problems that might crop up. If you do so, and remember to involve any appropriate manufacturers or vendors and take advantage of the help they can give, you can sort out device problems in short order.

CHAPTER 13

CONTROLLING DEVICES

In this chapter

Device Commands   318

The CLS Command   319

The GRAPHICS Command   319

The PRINT Command   322

The CTTY Command   325

The MODE Command   326

Using Redirection Commands   332

The MORE Filter   334

The FIND Filter   335

The SORT Filter   337

Device Commands

Devices—hard disks, printers, video displays, keyboards, and modems, for example—can supply input to the computer, receive output from the computer, or both. This chapter discusses the commands that control the devices connected to your computer. You use these commands to redirect input and output, select alternative keyboards, and print graphics and text files.

DOS supplies many different commands to help you interact with devices. With three commands referred to as *filters*, DOS is responsible for channeling information between devices. You can use these filters—MORE, FIND, and SORT—to modify information as it passes from files to the screen. Table 13.1 lists and explains the functions of the commands and filters discussed in this chapter.

TABLE 13.1   DEVICE CONTROL COMMANDS AND FILTERS

Command	Function
CLS	Clears the screen
GRAPHICS	Prints graphics screens
PRINT	Prints in the background
CTTY	Selects a different console; makes the serial port the console
MODE	Controls device operations; redirects a parallel port to a serial port; changes the typematic rate
MORE	Filter to control the display of text
FIND	Filter to find strings of text
SORT	Filter to sort information

Table 13.2 lists and explains the functions of the redirection operators you use in conjunction with the device control commands and filters.

TABLE 13.2   REDIRECTION OPERATORS

Operators	Function
<	Redirects a command's input
>	Redirects a command's output
>>	Redirects a command's output and appends the output to the target, if one exists
|	Passes the output from one command to another as input

The CLS Command

The internal command CLS clears the screen, removing all visible text. CLS then displays the prompt so that you can continue to issue DOS commands. This command clears only the onscreen display. If your system uses two screens, CLS clears only the active display, not both screens.

The CLS command, which has no switches, uses the following syntax:

CLS

Clearing the screen does not change the display mode. If, for example, you used the MODE command to change your screen display to 40 columns, the screen is cleared when you issue the CLS command; CLS then redisplays the DOS prompt in 40-column mode. All other attributes that you set previously—for example, if you defined a background color and foreground color by using ANSI.SYS escape sequences—are also retained.

> **Tip**
> You can frequently use the CLS command in batch files. By inserting a CLS command at the end of the AUTOEXEC.BAT file, for instance, you can remove all the messages that memory-resident programs might display as they load into your system.

The GRAPHICS Command

You might have tried to use the Print Screen key (PrtSc on some keyboards) to print the contents of your screen to a printer. If so, you might have discovered that this key works properly only when your screen is in text mode.

If your monitor is a CGA, EGA, or VGA display, the external command GRAPHICS enables you to use the Print Screen key to print graphics screens, also. When you execute GRAPHICS, a portion of the program remains memory-resident. When you next press Print Screen, all ASCII code characters that would otherwise print as text are converted to graphics before the information is sent to the printer.

Issuing the GRAPHICS Command

Use the following syntax for the GRAPHICS command:

GRAPHICS printer [drive]:path\filename /R /B /LCD /PRINTBOX:STD

printer is the type of printer you are using. Table 13.3 lists the values you can use for the printer parameter. If your printer is not listed, it might be compatible with one of the other printers on the list. Refer to your printer's instruction manual for details. If you do not specify a printer, DOS assumes the GRAPHICS printer type.

Table 13.3 Printer Types and Settings

Printer Type	Model Name
COLOR1	IBM PC Color Printer with black ribbon, which prints in grayscale
COLOR4	IBM PC Color Printer with RGB (red, green, blue) ribbon, which prints four colors (RGB plus black)
COLOR8	IBM PC Color Printer with CMYK (cyan, magenta, yellow, and black) ribbon, which prints eight colors
DESKJET	Hewlett-Packard DeskJet printer
GRAPHICS	IBM Personal Graphics Printer, IBM ProPrinter, or IBM Quietwriter printer
GRAPHICSWIDE	IBM Personal Graphics Printer with an 11-inch carriage, or IBM ProPrinters II and III
HPDEFAULT	Any Hewlett-Packard PCL printer
LASERJET	Hewlett-Packard LaserJet
LASERJETII	Hewlett-Packard LaserJet II
PAINTJET	Hewlett-Packard PaintJet printer
QUIETJET	Hewlett-Packard QuietJet printer
QUIETJETPLUS	Hewlett-Packard QuietJet Plus printer
RUGGEDWRITER	Hewlett-Packard RuggedWriter printer
RUGGEDWRITERWIDE	Hewlett-Packard RuggedWriter wide printer
THERMAL	IBM PC-Convertible thermal printer
THINKJET	Hewlett-Packard ThinkJet printer

[drive]:path\filename is the drive, path, and filename of a printer profile file that can be used by the GRAPHICS command for your printer. This file supports the printers of other manufacturers. If your printer doesn't fit into one of the categories supported by GRAPHICS, you can create a custom printer profile for use with GRAPHICS. The *filename* parameter refers to the profile file, which specifies how graphics are translated for various printers. The profile file is an ASCII text file with two types of information for each printer in the file. A profile can include information about how the printer is controlled, such as selecting printer colors or adjusting the darkness of the printed piece. The second section of the profile lists the translation from the screen to the printer.

/R forces the printer to print a monochrome text screen as you see it—black background and white text. When you use the /R switch with a color screen, the darkest colors (black or blue) print as black, light colors appear as white or light gray, and other colors print as different shades of gray on a grayscale for contrast. If you don't use the /R switch, all onscreen information that is white prints as black, and all black onscreen information (usually the background) prints as white. The paper color in the printer is assumed to be white.

/B prints the background color. Use this switch only if you have a color printer and after you specify COLOR4 or COLOR8 as your printer type. If you try to use the /B switch with a black-and-white printer, DOS displays the following message:

```
The /B switch is invalid with black and white printers.
```

/LCD is a switch designed for use with the IBM PC-Convertible, which comes with a small liquid-crystal display (LCD) screen. /LCD forces the printer to print the screen as it appears, with the size of the screen and characters smaller than on normal monitors. You also can use this switch with any other laptop computer that has an old-style, smaller LCD screen like the IBM PC-Convertible. Most laptops now have a full-sized LCD screen and don't require the use of this switch.

/PRINTBOX:STD sets the printbox size to standard or normal size, as it appears on monochrome and VGA monitors of standard size and shape. You use this setting to print the screen when you work with Quattro Pro, Microsoft Word, or other programs in graphics mode. You also use this setting to print the contents of a narrow LCD screen if you want it to appear as if it were on a standard monitor. By typing /PRINTBOX:LCD, you can use this switch to force the printer to print in LCD mode (a longer form of the /LCD switch, shown earlier). You can abbreviate the /PRINTBOX switch to /PB.

Using GRAPHICS to Print a Screen Image

Suppose that you have an IBM ProPrinter printer. If you use a monochrome system and want to print a screen image with the background as black and the text as white, enter the following command at the DOS prompt:

```
GRAPHICS /R
```

After GRAPHICS loads into memory, you can create the screen of interest and press Print Screen to print to the printer.

To print eight-color images (including the background color) on an IBM PC Color Printer with a CMY ribbon installed, type the following command:

```
GRAPHICS COLOR8 /B
```

On the PC-Convertible with an attached full-sized monitor, you can send the screen image to the IBM PC-Convertible thermal printer by typing the following:

```
GRAPHICS THERMAL /PB:STD
```

Changing the command to either of the following prints the image as it normally appears on the liquid-crystal display:

```
GRAPHICS THERMAL /PB:LCD
```

```
GRAPHICS THERMAL /LCD
```

You should remember the following guidelines when using the GRAPHICS command:

- After you load GRAPHICS, you can press the Print Screen (Shift+PrtSc) key to print graphics screens on listed graphics printers.

- If you omit the /PB and /LCD switches, GRAPHICS uses the previous printbox setting.
- You can print up to eight colors on a color printer.
- You can print up to 19 shades of gray on a black-and-white printer.

THE PRINT COMMAND

In Chapter 8, "Managing Your Files," you learned that the COPY command can transfer information from one device to another. For example, this command copies the file named LETTER.TXT to the device PRN, the printer:

COPY LETTER.TXT PRN

During this copying process, the computer is not available for other use. Copying a large file to the printer can tie up your computer for a great while, depending on the speed of your printer.

You can make better use of your computer if you use the PRINT command. This command enables you to print in the background, thereby freeing up your computer for other tasks while you print a document. Printing occurs during the idle times—while the computer is waiting for you to type at the keyboard, for example. You also can *queue* files, which means send multiple files to the printer, each of which then prints in turn.

ISSUING THE PRINT COMMAND

The external PRINT command uses the following syntax:

PRINT <switches> filename1 /P /T /C filename2 /P /T /C...

You can replace <switches> with any of the switches listed in Table 13.4. *filename1* is the drive, path, and filename of the first file you want to print, and *filename2* is the drive, path, and filename of the next file you want to print. The ellipsis (...) means that you can list more files. You also can use wildcards in the filenames.

TABLE 13.4   SWITCHES FOR THE PRINT COMMAND

Switch	Meaning
/D:*device*	Names the serial or parallel port to which your output device is attached. Acceptable values include all DOS output devices and ports, such as LPT1, LPT2, LPT3, PRN, COM1, COM2, COM3, COM4, or AUX.
/Q:*qsize*	Specifies the maximum number of files—from 4 to 32—that can be queued at a time. If you omit the switch, the default queue size is 10 files.
/B:*size*	Determines the size of buffer used in the printing process. The data for printing is taken from the disk in chunks the size of the specified buffer. Increasing the buffer size causes the PRINT command to read data from the disk in bigger chunks. The minimum buffer size is 512 bytes; the maximum is 16KB. If you don't specify the buffer size, the default size is 512 bytes. Remember that the larger you make the buffer, the less RAM you have for running applications programs.

Table 13.4	Continued
Switch	**Meaning**
/U:*ticks1*	Determines how long (in system clock ticks) the PRINT command waits for the printer to be available. In most cases, the PRINT command sends data to the printer faster than the printer can actually print. When the printer cannot accept any more data, it sends a busy signal to the computer until it is ready to accept more data. The default setting for /U:*ticks1* is 1 clock tick, but you can set it as high as 255. If the printer is busy, PRINT waits the number of clock ticks set by this switch. If the printer is still busy, PRINT immediately transfers control back to DOS for other tasks without using the rest of the clock ticks set aside for it by the /S:*ticks3* switch.
/M:*ticks2*	Specifies the number of system clock ticks that the PRINT command waits for the printer to print a character. You can set *ticks2* to any value between 1 and 255; the default value is 2.
/S:*ticks3*	Determines the number of clock ticks allocated to background printing. Too high a value for this switch causes the computer to respond sluggishly to other commands that you execute while you print in the background. A low value slows the printing process. The range of values is 1 to 255; the default value is 8.

Like GRAPHICS, PRINT leaves a portion of itself in memory after you issue the command, and the switches change how the PRINT command works. You can specify the optional switches in Table 13.4 only when you first issue the PRINT command. The other switches (issued after the filenames) can be issued at any time, however:

- The /P switch places a file in PRINT's queue. The preceding file and all subsequent files on the command line are printed.

- The /C switch cancels the printing of some files. The filename issued before the /C and all files after the /C on the same command line are removed from the print queue. (The printer alarm sounds if you cancel the currently printing file with the /C switch.) You must issue the /P switch to add files to the queue again.

- The /T switch terminates printing. All files are removed from the queue, including the file being printed. The printer alarm sounds, a file cancellation message prints, and the paper advances to the next page.

If you enter filenames without a /P, /C, or /T switch, DOS uses the /P switch as a default so that all files are placed in the queue for printing. If, at the prompt, you type PRINT with no switches, a list of all files in the queue appears. This list includes the name of the file that is currently printing and the order of files yet to print. This command also displays any error messages. If, for example, you forget to turn on the printer, the following error message appears:

```
Errors on list device indicate that it may be off-line. Please check it.
```

Using PRINT to Print Several Files

You do not have to enter the names of all the files to print at one time. You can issue the PRINT command several times to add or remove files from the print queue. You can specify the parameters that affect the way PRINT operates (those in Table 13.4), however, only when you first issue the command. After you first issue the PRINT command, you use the command only to enter filenames for printing or to cancel printing.

If you enter the PRINT command for the first time without specifying a device, PRINT prompts you for a device name. The default, PRN, is the first parallel port (LPT1) on your computer. Pressing Enter at the DOS prompt accepts the default.

If you are in no hurry to collect the printed output of files and want to use the computer while the printer prints your files, you can readjust the default installation settings for PRINT. By changing the /M:*ticks2* or /S:*ticks3* settings, you can give your computer better response time. To alter the default settings, you can type the following when you invoke the PRINT command for the first time:

PRINT /D:PRN /M:1 /S:25

If you are unconcerned about the sluggishness of the keyboard, you can improve the speed of the background printing by altering the buffer size, as well as by adjusting /M:*ticks2* and /S:*ticks3*. You might type the following command, for example:

PRINT /D:PRN /B:16384 /M:1 /S:25

Experiment with these variables until you find a setting that is acceptable. A sluggish keyboard is not always tolerable. If the response time is too slow, you can make errors; for example, you might assume that a program didn't accept your keystrokes and try to retype the command, whereas the program was only waiting to regain control.

By using a combination of the /P, /T, and /C switches, you can adjust the order in which the files print. Suppose, for example, that you want to print four files: LETTER1.TXT, MEMO1.TXT, REPORT1.TXT, and REPORT2.TXT. Type the following on the command line:

PRINT /D:PRN LETTER1.TXT /P MEMO1.TXT REPORT1.TXT REPORT2.TXT

If you then decide that you want to print REPORT2.TXT before REPORT1.TXT, type the following command, which removes REPORT1.TXT from the print queue and adds the file to the end of the queue:

PRINT REPORT1.TXT /C REPORT1.TXT /P

You can cancel all files to be printed by typing the following command:

PRINT /T

General Rules for Using PRINT

As you are using PRINT, you should keep the following guidelines in mind:

- You can specify the /D:*device*, /Q:*qsize*, /B:*size*, /S:*ticks3*, /U:*ticks1*, and /M:*ticks2* optional switches only the first time that you issue the PRINT command.

- If you specify /D:*device*, you must type this switch first, before all other switches.
- If you issue /P, the preceding file and all subsequent files entered on the command line by the PRINT command print until a /T or /C switch is issued.
- If you issue /C, the preceding file and all subsequent files are canceled.
- The files print in the order that you enter them at the command line.
- A page-eject sequence is sent to the printer at the end of each file.
- You cannot use the printer for other purposes while PRINT is in operation. You cannot, for example, use Print Screen when PRINT is in effect.
- The files being printed must be on the same disk drive.
- You cannot alter files that are in the print queue or being printed.
- Specifying a nonexistent device causes unpredictable behavior by the computer.
- Tab characters in the printed file convert to blanks, up to the next 8-column boundary.

> **Note**
>
> GRAPHICS.PRO is the profile file supplied with DOS. If you want to create a custom profile file for your printer, make a copy of the supplied GRAPHICS.PRO file and modify it. This exercise is also useful if you are interested in DOS programming. Modifying the GRAPHICS.PRO file is not necessary for most printers.
>
> If the onscreen colors don't have a sharp enough contrast, the GRAPHICS command can "miss" the difference between colors and produce an all-white or all-black printout. If this problem occurs, try altering your screen colors before you print.

THE CTTY COMMAND

DOS can take information or data from and send it to different kinds of devices. Any device that you can use to give information to DOS is called an *input device*, and any device DOS can send information to is an *output device*. DOS uses your keyboard and screen as the standard input and output devices. Together, these two devices make up the *console*, known to DOS as the CON device. The internal command CTTY enables you to tell DOS that you want to use a different device for input and later enables you to restore the keyboard and screen as the console.

Use one of these syntax lines for the internal command CTTY:

CTTY *device*

CTTY CON

device is the name of a DOS device that you can use for input. CTTY causes DOS to intercept the input/output (I/O) requests that normally come from the keyboard and go to the screen; the command redirects these calls to the device you specify.

By typing the following command, for example, you designate COM1 as the device that sends and receives standard input and output:

CTTY COM1

You use this command in association with specialized programs that need input from a different source from the keyboard. Later, typing the following from the auxiliary device restores the console to the keyboard and display:

CTTY CON

You also can use CTTY if the computer is attached to an intelligent bar-code reader that collects information from packages. This reader, in association with a specialized program, might not need to use the display or keyboard.

You probably will not need to use the CTTY command. DOS usually can gather information through alternative devices without altering the standard input and output devices. Certain applications programs, however, benefit from your use of CTTY. One example is the DOS external program Interlnk, which requires the CTTY command in order to transfer itself to another computer.

→ For more information on the Interlnk program, see Chapter 8, "Managing Your Files."

If you decide that you need to use CTTY, keep the following rules in mind:

- You can use the character-based devices AUX, COM1, COM2, COM3, or COM4 as the alternative console.
- The physical device attached to the relevant AUX, COM1, COM2, COM3, or COM4 must be able to accept input and provide output.
- Programs that do not use DOS function calls cannot make use of the alternative console.

THE MODE COMMAND

MODE is one of the more versatile external commands supplied with DOS. It sets the operational modes of serial and parallel ports and redirects information from parallel ports to serial ports. MODE also can set display modes, and you can use MODE with code pages.

→ For more information about display modes and code pages, **see** Chapter 11, "Controlling Your Environment," **p. 293**, and Chapter 14, "Understanding the International Features of DOS," **p. 339**.

In this chapter, you learn how you can use the MODE command to control the parallel and serial ports, as well as to change how the keyboard acts. To read about all functions of the MODE command, turn to the "Command Reference" later in this book.

USING MODE TO CHANGE PARALLEL PORT SETTINGS

A parallel port transmits data by transferring an entire byte at one time. Because of the way data is transferred, parallel ports are typically used to send information to a printer. To help control your printer, you can use the MODE command to adjust the number of lines per inch and columns per line on your printer and to set the retry feature.

ISSUING THE MODE COMMAND

Use the following syntax for the external MODE command, which changes the parallel printer characteristics:

MODE LPT*n*: *cpl,lpi*, P

LPT*n*: is the parallel port name, such as LPT1 or LPT2. *cpl* is the number of characters per line; the default *cpl* setting is 80. *lpi* is the number of lines per inch; the default setting for *lpi* is 6. P specifies continuous retries on timeout or "busy" errors.

MODE also enables you to use an alternative format, as follows:

MODE LPT*n*: COLS=*wid*, LINES=*lpi*, RETRY=*action*

wid is the number of columns per line, 80 or 132; *lpi* is the number of lines per inch, 6 or 8; and *action* is the message you want DOS to return or the action DOS should take when the printer port is busy.

When you use the MODE command to adjust the parallel port settings, this command alters only two items seen on the printout itself: the characters per line and lines per inch. In general, printing is performed directly from an applications program, which can set many more parameters for a particular printer. The MODE command operates by sending Escape sequences to the printer that can adjust the printed output accordingly.

The RETRY setting is more significant than the other settings. When data is sent to the printer, the port expects to see return signals from the printer indicating that it received the data. If the port doesn't receive any signals within a particular period of time, a timeout error occurs. By default, DOS does not try to send information to the printer again and returns an error message to the screen. If you include the P option, DOS continuously tries to send the data; this action prevents the error message from being displayed. Pressing the Ctrl+Break key combination stops the retry process.

If you use the RETRY switch in the alternative MODE format, various retry options are available. If you don't specify a retry option, DOS doesn't continue trying to send data when a timeout error occurs. When you use the retry option, you can select from several options. The following list explains the various options:

- The B setting returns a busy signal to the device driver when the port is busy. This setting is not available with DOS 6.0.
- The R setting causes a ready signal to be returned from the port—even if the port is busy. Then, when the printer does become ready, the data is ready to send, and an error message does not appear onscreen.
- The E option is most commonly used when the printing is done in the background (by PRINT or a network print queue). The data is not transferred to the printer until the port is not busy.
- The N setting indicates that no retry action is taken.
- The P option causes DOS to try the printer continuously until the busy state ends.

Using MODE to Print a Large File

In some cases, you must use the P option to print a file. Consider a large DOS file that you want to copy to the printer. If the file is larger than the storage capacity of the printer, the printer port will be busy at some point during the data transfer. If the printer remains busy for too long, an error message appears onscreen; DOS thinks the printer is defective, and the printing process aborts. This outcome is a particular concern when you are printing large, complex files such as those created by a PostScript program.

Specifying P in DOS 3.3 and earlier or RETRY=B in DOS 4.0 and 5.0 causes DOS to wait until the printer is ready to receive data. (The B option is not available in DOS 6.0, but you can use the P option for this purpose.) Use the following command for LPT1 in DOS 3.3:

```
MODE LPT1:,,P
```

For DOS 4.0, 4.01, 5.0, and 6.2, use the following command:

```
MODE LPT1 RETRY=B
```

For DOS 6.0 or 6.2, use the following command:

```
MODE LPT1 RETRY=P
```

If the file is large and you want to be able to fit more lines of text on a page, you can print the file with a higher number of lines per inch (8 instead of 6). Also, you can specify 132 columns per line instead of 80. This setting is not a problem for a wide-carriage printer, which accepts wide paper. If you are using a printer that accepts 8 1/2-inch paper, however, you must set the printer to print in a condensed character mode, which can fit 132 columns on a line of 8 1/2-inch paper.

When the printer is attached to LPT2, use the following command to fit as much information as possible on a page:

```
MODE LPT2:132,8
```

General Rules for Using MODE to Change Parallel Port Settings

When you are using the MODE command to change parallel port settings, you should keep the following rules in mind:

- The default values of the port will reset if you reset or initialize the printer.
- If you omit a parameter from the command line, the setting for that parameter does not change.
- Do not use any of the retry options when printers are being shared on an IBM PC network.

Using MODE to Change Serial Port Settings

You can use another option of the MODE command to alter the functions of the serial ports. This command works in a way similar to the parallel port adjustments. DOS changes the parameters that are sent to and from the device driver.

The acceptable serial ports are COM1, COM2, COM3, and COM4. The serial port can receive and transmit data only one bit at a time. The signaling rate (the number of times per second that data is transmitted) is the *baud rate*. The amount of data transferred in a second is referred to as the *bps* (bits per second).

You can use the MODE command to adjust the baud settings and change the amount of data sent in a fixed time. Although it is called a *baud setting*, the numbers used are actually the number of bits transmitted per second. Acceptable baud settings are 110, 150, 300, 600, 1200, 2400, 4800, 9600, and 19200. You need to use only the first two digits of the number to set the baud rate.

The most common devices attached to a serial port that you need to set from DOS are serial printers and plotters. Although modems are serial devices, you usually don't adjust them from DOS. Communications programs, however, use the DOS functions to make adjustments to the serial ports.

Use the following syntax to change the serial port:

```
MODE COMy: baud,parity,databits,stopbits,P
```

The elements of the commands are as follows:

- `COMy:` is the name of the serial port device.
- `baud` is the baud rate. You must specify the baud rate for the serial port.
- `parity` is the parity. Parity is used in error-correction algorithms.
- `databits` is the number of data bits. The default number of data bits is 7.
- `stopbits` is the number of stop bits. Stop bits mark the end of a character being transmitted. The default number of stop bits is 1 for all baud rates except 110, when 2 stop bits are set as the default.
- `P` specifies continuous retries on timeout errors.

You also can use the following syntax:

```
MODE COMy: BAUD=baud PARITY=parity DATA=databits STOP=stopbits RETRY=action
```

All the variables in this version of the MODE command are the same as in the previous version. The only new one is *action*, which is the message you want DOS to return when the port is busy.

With versions of DOS before Version 4.0, the retry feature provided two choices when a timeout error occurred: no retry or continuous retries when you included the P option. When data is sent to the printer, the port expects to see signals from the printer indicating that it received the data. If the port doesn't receive any signals within a particular period of time, a timeout error occurs. By default, DOS does not try again to send information to the printer and returns an error message to the screen. If you include the P option, DOS continuously tries to send the data; this action prevents the error message from being displayed. The Ctrl+Break key combination stops the retry process.

With DOS 4.0 and later, more retry options are available. If you do not specify a retry option, DOS doesn't try again to send data when a timeout error occurs. When you use the retry option, you can select from the following four options:

- The R setting causes a ready signal to be returned from the port even if the port is busy. Then, when the printer does become ready, the data is ready to send, and an error message does not appear onscreen.
- The E option is most commonly used when you are printing in the background (using PRINT or a network print queue). The data is not transferred to the printer until the port is not busy.
- The N option specifies no action; this setting is the default.
- The P action specifies continuous retry.

Using MODE to Set the Serial Port

To set the first serial port to communicate at 2400 bps, with 8 data bits, 1 stop bit, and no parity, you can type one of the following commands:

```
MODE COM1 2400,N,8,1
MODE COM1 24,N,8,1
```

If you are using DOS 3.3 or later, you can type the following instead to get the same settings:

```
MODE COM1 BAUD=24 DATA=8 STOP=1 PARITY=NONE
```

> **Note** The printer or plotter needs to be set to receive data in the same format in which the serial port is sending the data—that is, the same baud rate, parity, and so on.

General Rules for Using MODE with Serial Ports

When you are using the MODE command to change serial port settings, you should keep the following rules in mind:

- If you set a retry option, a portion of MODE remains resident unless you use the DOS 4.0 RETRY=none option.
- The retry option slows the performance of foreground tasks when computers are being shared on an IBM PC network.
- DOS 4.0 and later can include Mark or Space parity settings. All versions of DOS support none, odd, and even parity settings.

Using MODE to Redirect a Parallel Port to a Serial Port

The final MODE setting you can use with ports is the command to redirect a parallel port to a serial port. Typically, you use this setting if you want to redirect printer output to the serial port for use with a plotter or serial printer.

Issuing the MODE Command to Redirect Ports

Use the following syntax for the MODE command that changes the parallel printer to a serial printer:

MODE LPT*n*:=COM*y*:

LPT*n*: is the name of the parallel printer port, and COM*y*: is the name of the serial port.

After you use MODE, DOS channels to the serial port all I/O requests that a program sends to the parallel port. The electronics associated with the port handle automatically the conversion of data from bytewide to bitwide.

Using MODE to Redirect Ports

Some early programs don't directly support serial printers. To use a serial printer, you can set a serial port and redirect a parallel port to that serial port. This process enables you to print when you use a serial printer and also use a program that doesn't directly support the printer.

Earlier in this chapter, you learned how to initialize a serial port by using the MODE command. For example, you initialize a serial port with DOS 3.3 by using a command similar to the following:

MODE COM2 2400,E,7,2

With DOS 4.0 and later, you can type the following command instead:

MODE COM2 BAUD=24 DATA=7 STOP=2 PARITY=EVEN

You then follow the initialization command by typing the following command:

MODE LPT1=COM2

All data that normally goes to LPT1 is transmitted to COM2 at 2400 bps, with 7 data bits, 2 stop bits, and even parity.

General Rules for Using MODE to Redirect Ports

When you are using the MODE command to redirect ports, you should keep the following rules in mind:

- You can redirect any parallel port to any serial port.
- You must initialize the serial port with both speed and data characteristics before the parallel port is redirected.
- The initialization of the serial port must include the retry option if the attached device is a printer.

Using MODE to Change the Typematic Rate

When you press a key on the PC keyboard, a character appears onscreen. If you continue to hold down the key, the pressed character repeats onscreen. The number of times per second the key repeats is known as the *typematic rate*.

The syntax for the MODE command that changes the typematic rate is as follows:

MODE CON RATE=rate DELAY=delay

rate is the number of repetitions per second. The *rate* parameter can have values in the range 1 through 32. These values represent a repeat rate of from 2 to 30 characters per second (the higher the value, the faster the repeat rate). The default value is 20 for an IBM AT and 21 for an IBM PS/2, which is equivalent to approximately 10 characters per second.

The *delay* parameter is the time delay before DOS starts repeating a key. The delay is specified in .25-second intervals. The range for the delay is 1 through 4, making a total possible delay of 1 second.

To set the keyboard so that the delay before the key repeats is 0.75 second and the rate value is 24, type the following:

MODE CON RATE=24 DELAY=3

Using Redirection Commands

DOS uses three standard devices: one for input, one for output, and one for errors. The main input/output device is the console, which is DOS's name for your keyboard and screen. The keyboard is the standard input device, and the display is the standard output and error device. In short, you type commands on the keyboard, and the commands and any error messages appear onscreen.

DOS enables you to choose the devices that you use to input and output information; this process is called *redirection*. (Error messages are always sent to the screen.)

Issuing the Redirection Operators

The redirection symbols are the greater-than and less-than signs. If you think about it, these symbols look like arrows (> or <) that show the input's source and destination. Use the following syntax for redirecting a program or command's input:

command < *inputdevice*

The syntax for redirecting a program or command's output is shown in the following:

command > *outputdevice*

The syntax for redirecting and appending to an existing file is shown in the following:

function command >> *outputdevice*

In each syntax shown here, *inputdevice* is the source of the input, *outputdevice* is the destination of the output, and *command* can specify almost all applications programs or DOS commands. With the redirection command, you can use any DOS output device as an *outputdevice*, and you can use any DOS input device as an *inputdevice*.

Normally, redirected input comes from a file. Some devices, however, such as a mouse or bar-code reader, can also be used as a source of input. You can write a file that consists of the keystrokes used to operate a program, for example, or you can use the output from a mouse as the input for a program.

Most DOS users redirect output more often than they redirect input. The two most common places to redirect output are to the printer or to a disk file. The following command, which redirects the output of a directory to the printer, is a common example of redirection:

```
DIR > PRN
```

When you issue this command, DOS redirects the output (the directory listing itself) to the PRN device instead of sending the listing to the screen. This command produces a hard-copy listing of the directory.

Another common use is redirecting output to a file. To review the statistics of the MEM /C command, for example, type the following command:

```
MEM /C > CLASSIFY.MEM
```

When you use redirection commands with pipes and filters, discussed later in this chapter, the command becomes even more powerful.

> **Warning** Take care when you use the > operator to send output to a file. If you use > and refer to an existing file, DOS overwrites the existing file with the new output—*without warning*.

If you want to redirect to the printer a copy of your disk's directory structure and a list of the files on your hard disk, type the following:

```
TREE C:\ /F >PRN
```

The TREE command does not supply a directory listing that includes file sizes. If you want to create a full listing of all the directories on your hard disk by using redirection to append the output of the command, you specify that each directory be listed and then specify that the output be appended to a file. You then can print the full list. To perform this task, you type a command similar to the following for each directory:

```
DIR C:\ /S >> FULLIST.DIR
```

The DIR command lists the files in all the directories on drive C. The /S switch causes the DIR command to display all subdirectories. You can then substitute the names of other drives for C.

If you are testing programs that require a large amount of user input, the following redirection method is useful. For example, you can type the following:

```
PROGRAM < C:TESTPAT
```

This command results in the file TESTPAT supplying the input to PROGRAM. The redirection process enables you to construct a file that contains the correct keystrokes needed to operate a program. You then can test the program's basic operation before you include the error-trapping sequences. These sequences handle the situations when the user presses an incorrect key.

General Rules for Using Redirection

The following are some helpful rules to know when using redirection:

- Do not use redirection on a DOS batch file command line that includes CALL, FOR, or IF.
- Using > and referring to an existing file cause DOS to overwrite the existing file with the new output.
- Using >> adds the output to an existing file or creates a new file if the file does not exist.

The MORE Filter

DOS uses elements called *filters* to channel information between devices. You can use these filters to modify information as it passes from files to the screen. Filters, which work only on ASCII text files, are often used with the redirection symbols so that input can come from a source other than the keyboard or be sent to a device other than the screen.

Piping is another feature used with these commands. You use the pipe symbol (|) to send output information that normally goes to the screen as input to another program. Piping, a form of redirection, diverts information destined for a device but then makes the information become the input from a device to another program.

The MORE filter buffers information from the input device or file and sends the data to the monitor one screen at a time.

Issuing the MORE Filter

The syntax for the MORE filter, which has no switches, is shown in the following:

MORE

MORE is commonly used in the following way, where *filename* is the input file:

MORE < filename

Or, it is used in the following way, where *command* is any command or program:

command | MORE

MORE collects—and saves in a temporary disk file—information that normally goes to the screen. When a screen of input is obtained, MORE sends that information to the standard output device all at the same time. The text is channeled through the MORE filter until the end-of-file. Press any key when DOS displays the -- More -- prompt; this action displays the next screen. After all the information is displayed onscreen, DOS erases the temporary file created by MORE.

Using MORE to Pause the Screen

When you use MORE to pause directory listings, the filter serves a function similar to the /P switch that is available with the DIR command.

The most common use of MORE, however, is to pause the TYPE command. To read the contents of a README.DOC file one page at a time, for example, type one of the following:

TYPE README.DOC | MORE

MORE <README.DOC

Both syntax forms work identically. To see the contents of a file, you can use the TYPE command. If the output of the file flows off the screen, reissue the command by pressing F3, and add the pipe character (|) and MORE.

GENERAL RULES FOR USING MORE

The following are some helpful rules to know when using MORE:

- Do not use MORE alone. MORE is a filter, which requires input to redirect or pipe.
- To view additional screens full of information, press any key when DOS displays the -- More -- prompt.
- Ctrl+Break (and Ctrl+C) terminates the command without displaying any other screens.

THE FIND FILTER

The FIND filter finds ASCII text in files. This filter often is used in association with redirection and piping.

ISSUING THE FIND FILTER

Use the following syntax for the FIND filter:

FIND /C /N /V /I "*string*" *filename*...

"*string*" specifies the ASCII characters for which you want to search, and *filename* is the full filename of the file to search. The ellipsis (...) indicates that you can specify more than one file to search.

/C causes FIND to count all the lines that contain "*string*". You use the /C switch to count the number of lines with the ASCII string; the text itself isn't passed to the screen.

/N causes FIND to include line numbers of the lines that contain the "*string*". You use the /N switch to locate the line numbers within the text file. The line numbers listed are the line numbers in the original text file, not just sequential numbers. If the third, fifth, and sixth lines in the text file contain the string, for example, the line numbers displayed are 3, 5, and 6—not 1, 2, and 3.

/V causes FIND to search only for lines that do not contain the "*string*". Only these lines are passed on to the screen.

/I makes FIND insensitive to case: Upper- and lowercase letters are considered the same.

> **Note:** You can use /C and /V together. The count displayed is the number of lines that do not contain "`string`". You also can use /V and /N together. The lines that do not contain "`string`" are displayed with their appropriate line numbers.

If you use FIND without options, the filter reads each of the files you specify and displays all lines that contain the ASCII string you are looking for. DOS filters the information that normally goes to the output device. All lines that include the ASCII string are displayed onscreen.

Like the other filter commands, FIND is often used with redirection and piping. If you search a text file for lines that include specific information, redirecting the output to a file might be helpful. You then can use the list as a reference while you look at the whole of the original file.

Using FIND to Find Files on Disk

You can use the FIND command to find all files that have a certain extension. To find all files with the extension .LET, for example, type the following command:

```
DIR /S /B | FIND ".LET"
```

Because the /S switch is used with this DIR command, all files whose names contain LET—either in the root or extension—are listed under the name of the directory containing them. Because the /B switch is used, the filenames are listed in the form FILENAME.EXT, with a period instead of spaces separating the filename and its extension. Therefore, you can search for .LET instead of LET. In this form, each filename is preceded by its directory path.

The DIR command with the /S option lists all the files on a disk. The output for DIR that normally goes to the screen is filtered through the FIND command. The output from FIND then is displayed onscreen.

You also can use the FIND filter with text files as a word-search utility. Suppose, for example, that you forget the name of the memo you sent to your boss, but you know that the file is either MEMO1, MEMO2, or MEMO3. You also know that you always use your boss's title, Supervisor, in memos. You can find the memo you need by typing the following:

```
FIND "Supervisor" MEMO1 MEMO2 MEMO3
```

When you issue this command, each line that contains Supervisor is listed. The listing appears in the following form:

```
---------- MEMO1
---------- MEMO2
Supervisor of Communications
---------- MEMO3
```

General Rules for Using FIND

The following aresome helpful rules to know when using FIND:

- Use FIND only on ASCII text files.
- The "*string*" parameter is normally case sensitive; that is, FIND regards the uppercase string LOOK as different from the lowercase string look. In DOS 5.0 and later, you can use the /I switch to perform a search that is not case sensitive.
- To cause FIND to search for quotation marks in a string, type two quotation marks together (""). FIND then searches for occurrences of ".
- If you do not specify a filename, FIND uses the standard input device.
- You cannot use wildcards in a filename.

The Sort Filter

The third DOS filter is SORT, which sorts the information from an ASCII file before displaying the result onscreen. Like FIND and MORE, SORT often is used with redirection and piping.

Issuing the Sort Filter

Use the following syntax for the SORT filter:

SORT /R /+*n*

/R reverses the sort order, and *n* is the offset column for the sorting process.

The SORT filter processes information that normally goes to your screen or to another output device. The text from the input is analyzed on a line-by-line basis and sorted according to the ASCII binary values of the characters. This order is alphabetical, but SORT doesn't discriminate between upper- and lowercase letters.

When you use SORT with redirection or piping, more sophisticated sorting occurs. The most common use of SORT is to sort a directory listing into a text file, which you then can print.

The offset—the /+*n* option—in the command shows the leftmost column to be sorted. With a directory listing, you can sort by date or file size rather than by root name. Table 13.5 lists the offset values for a directory listing.

TABLE 13.5	Offset Values for Sort
Offset Value	**Sorting By**
1	Root name
10	File extension
14	File size
24	File date
34	File time

The sorted output appears onscreen; the original directory listing itself remains unchanged.

> **Note**
>
> This use of SORT is not as vital as it once was. Beginning with DOS 5.0, you can sort a directory listing by using the /O switch. To sort a directory by name, you can use the following command:
>
> DIR \ /ON
>
> Similarly, you can use /OE to sort by extension, /OS to sort by size, /OD to sort by date and time combined, and /OC to sort by compression ratio (for DoubleSpace volumes). You still need to use SORT if you want to sort the directory by time alone.

Using SORT to Sort Subdirectory Listings

You can use redirection and piping, as well as the FIND and SORT filters, in many ways. In DOS 4.0, 4.01, or 5.0, for example, you can create a sorted list of the subdirectories in the root directory by using the process outlined in the next paragraphs.

To create a sorted list of subdirectories in the root directory, follow these steps:

1. Type the following command:
   TREE C:\ /A | FIND "-" | SORT /+2 >TEMP.LST

   When issued with the /A switch, the TREE command produces a listing that uses the nongraphics character set. The FIND filter then removes all lines that are not subdirectory names. SORT sorts the output from FIND on column 2, and the output is redirected to a temporary file.

2. Use the temporary file as the input to the FIND filter, which removes all directories that are not in the root, by typing the following command:

   FIND /V "|" <TEMP.LST

   The result is an alphabetical list of all subdirectories in the root directory.

General Rules for Using SORT

The following are some helpful rules to know when using SORT:

- If n is not specified, DOS assumes column 1.
- Lines are sorted according to their ASCII binary values, with two exceptions. SORT is not case sensitive; for example, the command sorts *A* and *a* as they occur in the source file. Additionally, SORT sorts characters with values greater than 127 in the order determined by the current COUNTRY code setting. (See Chapter 16, "Understanding Batch Files," for more information.)
- The output filename must be different from the input filename when you use redirection.
- The largest file the SORT program can handle is 64KB.

CHAPTER 14

UNDERSTANDING THE INTERNATIONAL FEATURES OF DOS

In this chapter

- Internationalization 340
- Understanding COUNTRY.SYS 340
- Understanding KEYB.COM 342
- Understanding Code Page Switching 344
- International Country Codes 354

Internationalization

Communication is making the world appear progressively smaller and smaller. Frequent contact among people from many different countries is not unusual. You can use computers to prepare documents and other files to send to all parts of the world.

Anything you work on that has international implications can cause you inconvenience if you do not adapt your computer to handle various languages and national customs. Presumably, most people reading this book and using DOS as their operating system live in the United States and have computers built to operate in the United States. Fortunately, however, Microsoft has built in to DOS the capability to internationalize your computer.

DOS provides three levels of internationalization. These levels involve the use of KEYB.COM and code page switching.

You might consider your standard version of DOS as perfect for most uses. Suppose, however, that you must use a certain national format for expressing the time, the date, and currency symbols. You can learn how to access these formats by reading this chapter and understanding the use of the COUNTRY.SYS configuration driver.

DOS supports 24 national languages or country customs. Each country or language is identified by a country code that corresponds to the country's international telephone code. The International Country Codes section at the end of this chapter lists the countries and languages supported by DOS and their country codes. These country codes are referenced throughout this chapter.

> **Note** When you use the country code or code page number, you must use all three digits, including any leading zeros.

In addition to the American standard version that you can customize for the supported country codes, Microsoft produces special language versions in Arabic, Chinese, Israeli, Japanese, Korean, and Taiwanese.

Understanding COUNTRY.SYS

COUNTRY.SYS is a file that you can use to display alternative currency, date, and time formats on your system without using other language characters. This file contains all the conventions for the supported countries and national formats. Of course, if you have no need to change the default formats for your version of DOS, you have no need to use COUNTRY.SYS.

When you perform a disk directory command (DIR), the date and time stamps for disk files are displayed in the current national format. In the United States, the system date is normally displayed and stamped on files as MM-DD-YY. You can use alternative methods such as YY-MM-DD (French Canadian) or DD/MM/YY (United Kingdom).

Time formats separate hours, minutes, seconds, and hundredths of seconds using colons (HH:MM:SS:HS), periods (HH.MM.SS.HS), or colons and a comma (HH:MM:SS,HS).

In addition to the variety of currency symbols, such as $ and £, differing customs dictate whether the decimal characters are periods or commas—likewise for the thousands separator. The placement of the currency symbol also can vary. In the United States, the dollar sign precedes the amount, but some currency symbols are placed after the amount.

> **Tip**
> COUNTRY.SYS contains information only for the video display, not for keyboards. To provide keyboard support, you must use the KEYB command in your AUTOEXEC.BAT file or from the DOS prompt. For more information, see the next section, "Understanding KEYB.COM."

You load COUNTRY.SYS by entering the COUNTRY command in the CONFIG.SYS file. Use EDIT to enter a statement into the file. Then, enter the command in the following format:

COUNTRY=*xxx*,*yyy*,C:\DOS\COUNTRY.SYS

You must place the three-character numeric country code as the first parameter, as indicated by *xxx*. You cannot omit this code. The second parameter is the code page number for the country, as represented by *yyy*. If you omit this code, DOS uses the default code page number for the country specified by the country code.

> **Note**
> The inclusion of the code page in the COUNTRY command is optional, even if you install code page switching. Be sure to include the code page, however, if you want an alternative code page–rather than the default code page–to be installed for the indicated country.

If you do not specify the second parameter (*yyy*), you still must include the second comma when you include the file specification:

COUNTRY=*xxx*,,C:\DOS\COUNTRY.SYS

The default statement for the United States version is shown in either of the following:

COUNTRY=001

COUNTRY=001,,C:\DOS\COUNTRY.SYS

Figure 14.1 shows a standard directory listing that uses the United States country code formats for the date (MM-DD-YY) and time (12-hour format with a.m. or p.m. indicator).

Figure 14.1
A directory in the United States country code format.

```
Volume in drive C is DSK1_DRVC
Volume Serial Number is 11DA-3B69
Directory of C:\

C-ROOT       <DIR>     02-10-01   2:52p
CHAMPION     <DIR>     02-10-01   3:09p
CHAMPSTA     <DIR>     02-10-01   3:09p
COLLAGE      <DIR>     02-11-01   6:46p
DBASE        <DIR>     02-10-01   3:09p
DOS          <DIR>     02-10-01   1:58p
JOBCST       <DIR>     02-10-01   3:09p
TAPE         <DIR>     02-10-01   2:44p
TEMP         <DIR>     02-10-01   1:58p
UTILS        <DIR>     02-11-01   1:58p
WINA20    386     9349 01-28-01   6:00a
AUTOEXEC  BAT      58 02-11-01   1:47p
DATA      BAT      16 01-27-01   1:39p
NEWDISK   BAT     111 02-10-01   8:33p
COMMAND   COM   52841 01-28-01   6:00a
BEFSETUP  MSD   13996 02-10-01   5:28p
CONFIG    SYS     207 02-11-01   1:51p
       17 file(s)      76578 bytes
                   179462144 bytes free

C:\>
```

If you want to use the United Kingdom currency, date, and time formats, use the following statement in your `CONFIG.SYS` file:

`COUNTRY=044,,C:\DOS\COUNTRY.SYS`

After you use `EDIT` to modify your `CONFIG.SYS` file to contain this statement, save the file to disk and exit the Editor. Then, reboot your computer so that your change takes effect. When you next execute the `DIR` command, a directory listing shows the new format (see Figure 14.2).

Figure 14.2
A directory in the country code format for the United Kingdom.

```
Volume in drive C is DSK1_DRVC
Volume Serial Number is 11DA-3B69
Directory of C:\

C-ROOT       <DIR>     10/02/01   14:52
CHAMPION     <DIR>     10/02/01   15:09
CHAMPSTA     <DIR>     10/02/01   15:09
COLLAGE      <DIR>     11/02/01   18:46
DBASE        <DIR>     10/02/01   15:09
DOS          <DIR>     10/02/01   13:58
JOBCST       <DIR>     10/02/01   15:09
TAPE         <DIR>     10/02/01   14:44
TEMP         <DIR>     10/02/01   13:58
UTILS        <DIR>     11/02/01   13:58
WINA20    386     9349 28/01/01   6:00
AUTOEXEC  BAT      58 11/02/01   13:47
DATA      BAT      16 27/01/01   13:39
NEWDISK   BAT     111 10/02/01   20:33
COMMAND   COM   52841 28/01/01   6:00
BEFSETUP  MSD   13996 10/02/01   17:28
CONFIG    SYS     203 11/02/01   18:53
       17 file(s)      76574 bytes
                   179445760 bytes free

C:\>
```

Notice that the date format has changed to DD/MM/YY, and the time is displayed in 24-hour format.

Understanding KEYB.COM

Whereas the `COUNTRY.SYS` driver provides nondefault formats on the display screen, `KEYB.COM` provides compatible keyboard characters for the selected nationality. For a list of international keyboard codes, refer to the last section in this chapter.

You normally place `KEYB.COM` in the `AUTOEXEC.BAT` file, although you can type the command at the DOS prompt. You also can load `KEYB.COM` through the `CONFIG.SYS` file when you use the `INSTALL=` command.

> **Tip**
> You can use the KEYB command even if you have not installed any country codes through COUNTRY.SYS.

Make sure your DOS subdirectory (normally C:\DOS) is in your system's search path. Then, you do not need to specify the location of KEYB.COM unless you install the utility in the CONFIG.SYS file. The format of this command is as follows:

KEYB *xx*,*yyy*,C:\DOS\KEYBOARD.SYS /E /ID:*nnn*

The *xx* parameter is the two-letter code for the country or language. The *yyy* parameter is the code page number, if used.

→ For country codes and code page numbers, see the "International Country Codes" section at the end of this chapter.

→ For a list of countries with the alternative keyboards and the ID numbers you can use with KEYB, see the "International Country Codes" section at the end of this chapter.

You also can add two options to the KEYB command: /E and /ID. Use /E to tell DOS that you are using an enhanced keyboard (101- or 102-key style) on a computer with an Intel 8086 or compatible processor. The second switch, /ID, tells DOS which keyboard you are using. You can use one of 20 keyboards specially designed for the supported countries. France, Italy, and the United Kingdom each have two keyboard layouts available.

If you set your system to one of these three countries with COUNTRY.SYS and KEYB.COM and you use an alternative keyboard, you might find it useful to add the /ID:*nnn* switch to the KEYB command line (where *nnn* is one of the three-digit ID numbers) to make your keyboard work properly.

If you want to specify the code page to be used, you include it in the command line for KEYB. If the KEYBOARD.SYS file is not in the root directory of the boot drive, you must include that file specification together with its path. The path is normally C:\DOS. If you include the location and name of KEYBOARD.SYS, you must include the second comma, as follows, to hold the place for the code page parameter, even if you do not include the code page number:

KEYB *xx*,,C:\DOS\KEYBOARD.SYS

If you enter the KEYB command without any parameters or switches and you have not yet installed the keyboard utility, DOS responds with the following message:

```
KEYB has not been installed
Active code page not available from CON device
```

At the DOS prompt, type KEYB UK and press Enter to load KEYB with the character set used for the United Kingdom. Then, type KEYB and press Enter. DOS displays the following message:

```
Current keyboard code: UK  code page: 437
Active code page not available from CON device
```

As you can see, DOS assumes the default code page number for the United Kingdom, 437. Because at this point you are not concerned with code page switching, you can ignore the code page message. This subject is discussed later in this chapter (in the section "Understanding Code Page Switching").

To install KEYB when MS-DOS boots and processes the CONFIG.SYS file, use the following format:

INSTALL=C:\DOS\KEYB.COM *xx*,*yyy*,C:\DOS\KEYBOARD.SYS

Because your system search path has not yet been set, you must include the location of the utility. You must include also the full name and extension of the program (C:\DOS\KEYB.COM) before continuing with the parameters for KEYB.

→ For more information on modifying the CONFIG.SYS file, **see** Chapter 2, "Starting DOS," **p. 23**.

DOS provides a way of switching between your hardware default keyboard layout and the layout you loaded with KEYB.COM. Press Ctrl+Alt+F1 (hold down the Ctrl and Alt keys while pressing F1) to switch to the United States keyboard layout. Press Ctrl+Alt+F2 to return to the keyboard layout installed with KEYB.

Understanding Code Page Switching

Certain areas of memory in your system store the character tables for your video screen and your keyboard. By switching tables, you can configure MS-DOS to use alternative character tables to suit your national language and customs. These tables are called *code pages*.

> **Note**
> Changing the character set used in your computer to support another language through code page switching does not change the language that DOS uses. All messages are displayed in the default (English) language in which DOS was written. No translation is made.

You can set your system to use an alternative code page permanently, or you can enable several code pages in memory and switch between them from the command line. These code pages are software prepared; your system's hardware is not changed. Your system already has a built-in hardware code page.

In the previous section that discussed COUNTRY.SYS, you learned that each country or area of the world has a unique country code number borrowed from the international telephone convention. Each country or group of countries also has a code page number. (Many countries share a code page number with another country.)

Each DOS-supported code page includes support for several languages. This feature might simplify international communications so that documents prepared with the same character table might be processed by people in different countries using different languages, with all characters appearing the same to all concerned.

The international code page, code 850, has some graphic limitations to provide room for additional language characters required by some countries. Only 256 codes are available. If you normally use the United States code page (437), for example, you might find that boxes under 850 lose their graphic corners and are replaced with other characters.

> **Note**
> When you install alternative code pages in your computer, the normal keys and their ASCII display characters do not change. Symbol keys are remapped, and by using special keystrokes, you can enter national language characters.

Checking Your Hardware for Code Page Switching

You do need the proper hardware to switch software code pages. All code page information required for loading alternative character sets is contained in disk files with the extension .CPI. Two screen device code page information files are supplied with DOS. EGA.CPI provides support for EGA and VGA displays, and LCD.CPI provides support for LCD screens. You must have an EGA, VGA, or LCD video display. Hercules-type monographic and CGA screens do not support this feature.

> **Note**
> The LCD.CPI, 4201.CPI, 4208.CPI, 5202.CPI, and EGA2.CPI files as well as PRINTER.SYS are no longer automatically supplied as part of DOS. However, these files and others are available from Microsoft on a supplemental disk.
>
> You can download the MS-DOS 6.22 supplemental disks from http://www.microsoft.com/downloads.

If you have an EGA or a VGA display, you can have up to six software code pages. If you have an LCD display, you can have only one software code page. If you have a monochrome or CGA video adapter and monitor, you can use only the built-in hardware code page.

Certain printers, along with others that are 100% compatible with them, also support code page switching. Three code page information files are provided with DOS on the supplemental disks: 4201.CPI, 4208.CPI, and 5202.CPI. Table 14.1 lists the printers supported by these files. Even if your printer emulates one of these printers, it also must have the capability to accept code page switching. (Some printers provide emulation but not code page support.)

TABLE 14.1 NATIONAL CODE PAGE PRINTER FILES

Printer	Code Page File
IBM Proprinter II, III	4201.CPI
IBM Proprinter XL	4201.CPI
IBM Proprinter X24E	4208.CPI
IBM Proprinter XL24E	4208.CPI
IBM QuietWriter III	5202.CPI

Installing Code Page Switching

Assuming that you have the appropriate hardware, you must take a number of steps and load certain programs to enable code page switching, both for your video screen and for your printer. (Use MS-DOS EDIT to make the necessary changes to the CONFIG.SYS and AUTOEXEC.BAT files.)

To enable code page switching for your video display, you add a statement to the CONFIG.SYS file for the DISPLAY.SYS device driver. To enable code page switching for your printer, you add a statement for the PRINTER.SYS device driver. If you want code page switching enabled for both devices, you simply include both statements. (You also must use the COUNTRY.SYS device driver to handle the screen formats for currency, dates, and times.) Then, to provide the national language support, you add the NLSFUNC.EXE command to your AUTOEXEC.BAT file.

The following sections explain how you set up code page switching on your system, including how to use NLSFUNC.EXE to enable the feature, how to use MODE PREPARE to load the code page tables, and how to use CHCP and MODE SELECT to switch the code page.

Using DISPLAY.SYS

You can use the DISPLAY.SYS device driver to enable code page switching for your video display. The DISPLAY.SYS can be used only if you have an EGA, VGA, or LCD monitor and adapter.

The format of the command is either of the following:

```
DEVICE=C:\DOS\DISPLAY.SYS CON=(monitor,hardware,xx)
DEVICE=C:\DOS\DISPLAY.SYS CON=(monitor,hardware,(xx,yy))
```

Unless you move the DISPLAY.SYS file to the root directory of your boot drive, you must specify the location of the file (normally C:\DOS). Enter the *monitor* type as the first parameter for the console device (monitor). EGA is the typical *monitor* entry and stands for both EGA and VGA monitors. Use LCD for LCD screens. No other values are possible.

The second parameter, *hardware*, refers to the built-in hardware code page. In the United States, this code page is 437; if you are not certain of your system's built-in hardware code page, however, do not specify it.

The *xx* variable refers to the number of code pages you want enabled in your system. This parameter tells DOS to set aside memory for the number of additional character tables to be installed in the AUTOEXEC.BAT file or at the DOS prompt.

Enter a number for the *yy* variable to represent the number of subfonts you want. You can specify the number of fonts that DOS is to store in memory. Two subfonts are available for EGA/VGA displays, and only one is available for LCD displays. Normally, all are stored; however, you can lower the number stored to reduce the amount of memory used. If you use this variable, you must place a pair of parentheses around the number of code pages and the number of fonts, as shown in the second example.

Suppose that you want to enable code page switching for your display for French Canada and also to allow for the use of the international code. To do so, you enter the following statement in your CONFIG.SYS file:

```
DEVICE=C:\DOS\DISPLAY.SYS CON=(EGA,,2)
```

No default hardware code page is declared, and DOS is instructed to set aside memory for two code pages for an EGA or VGA adapter and monitor. Do not omit the commas.

You can specify up to six code page tables to be prepared in memory in addition to the hardware code page. Just remember that each code page takes up RAM (about 5,632 bytes for EGA and VGA) and might lower the amount of conventional memory available for your applications. Do not set aside more memory than is required.

→ For further information on memory and memory configuration, **see p. 11** and **p. 441**.

USING PRINTER.SYS

Use the PRINTER.SYS device driver to enable code page switching for your printer if you have one of the supported printers or a compatible. Supported printers can be attached to any or all of the three allowed parallel printer ports: LPT1, LPT2, and LPT3.

The format of the command is as follows:

```
DEVICE=C:\DOS\PRINTER.SYS LPTx=(printer,hardware,yy)
```

Unless you move the PRINTER.SYS file to the root directory of your boot drive, you must specify the location of the file (normally C:\DOS). Replace *x* with the proper parallel port number: 1, 2, or 3.

Replace *printer* with 4201, 4208, or 5202, whichever is appropriate for your printer. The next parameter, *hardware*, refers to the built-in hardware code page. In the United States, this code page is 437, but do not specify it if you are not certain of your printer type.

The variable *yy* refers to the number of additional code pages that your hardware can support and you want prepared. This parameter tells DOS to set aside memory for the number of additional character tables to be installed in the AUTOEXEC.BAT file or at the DOS prompt.

To instruct DOS to set aside memory for two code pages for an IBM QuietWriter III or compatible printer attached to LPT1, for example, enter the following statement in your CONFIG.SYS file:

```
DEVICE=C:\DOS\PRINTER.SYS LPT1=(5202,,2)
```

No default hardware code page is declared.

You can specify up to six code page tables to be prepared in memory. The maximum, however, depends on the printer you are using. Do not set aside more memory than is required because these tables consume memory.

> **Tip:** To enable code page switching on your printer, make sure that your printer is turned on and is online when your system is booted. Otherwise, the control signals cannot be downloaded to the printer.

USING NLSFUNC.EXE

After you take care of the required statements in your CONFIG.SYS file for COUNTRY.SYS and DISPLAY.SYS, move your attention to the AUTOEXEC.BAT file. As discussed in this chapter's "Understanding KEYB.COM" section, make sure that your keyboard is specified for the appropriate national keyboard and code page number. The following command, for example, specifies code page 863 for French Canada:

`KEYB cf,863,C:\DOS\KEYBOARD.SYS`

You then must include NLSFUNC as the next command to provide the National Language Support (NLS) for code page switching. You can type this command at the DOS prompt or place the command in your AUTOEXEC.BAT or CONFIG.SYS file for automatic loading whenever you boot your computer. To enter the NLSFUNC command in your CONFIG.SYS file, use the following format:

`INSTALL=C:\DOS\NLSFUNC.EXE`

Because a path has not yet been established when the command is in your CONFIG.SYS file, you must specify the location of the NLSFUNC file.

Up to this point, you have specified your country code of choice and have prepared your system to use code page switching. The following sections explain how to use the commands that load the specified code pages into the prepared memory areas.

LOADING THE CODE PAGE TABLES

You include the MODE command in the AUTOEXEC.BAT file to load code page information, specifying the code pages to be prepared and the code page file to use for the tables. Use MODE CON: to load the code page information for your video display (the console). Use MODE LPT1: to load the code page information for your printer and download the information to the printer. (Make sure that your printer is turned on and is online to receive the downloaded data.)

In the command, you can list as many code pages as you specified in the CONFIG.SYS file. Do not specify the hardware default code page number because this table is already built in. The format of the command is shown in the following (the parentheses are required):

`MODE device CP PREPARE=((xxx,yyy) filename)`

The *device* parameter indicates that you want to load a character set into your console, keyboard, or parallel printers. The *xxx* and *yyy* parameters indicate the code page numbers to be prepared, and *filename* refers to the CPI file where the table is stored on disk for the device.

Understanding Code Page Switching

Consider the following example:

```
MODE CON: CP PREPARE=((863,850) C:\DOS\EGA.CPI)
```

In this command, MODE is used to PREPARE (or PREP) the console (CON:) for code pages (CP), with code pages 863 for French Canada and 850 for International. EGA.CPI is listed as the table file for EGA and VGA monitors. The location of this file is the C:\DOS subdirectory.

For your printer, use the MODE command for each parallel printer port listed in the CONFIG.SYS file's PRINTER.SYS statement. The following examples prepare the printers at the LPT1 and LPT2 ports:

```
MODE LPT1: CP PREP=((863,850) C:\DOS\5202.CPI)
MODE LPT2: CP PREP=((863,850) C:\DOS\4201.CPI)
```

As with the other AUTOEXEC.BAT commands for code page switching, you also can enter the MODE commands at the DOS prompt.

Switching the Code Page

After you complete all the preparation work—specifying the nationality and code page codes to be used, setting aside the memory for the language tables, and loading the character tables—you are ready to use the new code pages.

In the previous examples, you prepared your system to use the French Canadian character set. To have this character set take effect, you must issue the CHCP command, for *changing the code page*. Use the CHCP command, along with the code page number, as shown in the following:

```
CHCP 863
```

Enter this command in your AUTOEXEC.BAT file or at the DOS prompt. The CHCP command must be listed in AUTOEXEC.BAT after the settings for code switching. The instruction tells DOS to change the current code page to the new code page specified in the command on all devices prepared, including the printer if you have included it in the CONFIG.SYS and AUTOEXEC.BAT files. Make certain that the printer is turned on and is online so that the new code page can take effect.

→ For more information on modifying the CONFIG.SYS and AUTOEXEC.BAT files, **see p. 23**.

You also can selectively change code pages of individual devices by using the MODE SELECT command and pressing Enter. The full format of the command follows:

```
MODE device CODEPAGE SELECT = xxx
```

For *device*, use CON for console or use PRN (which is the same as LPT1), LPT1, LPT2, or LPT3 for the printer ports. After the equal sign (=), enter the code page number (*xxx*).

Suppose, for example, that you want to change the code page in your IBM QuietWriter III printer, but you don't want to affect the monitor display. If your printer is attached to LPT1 and you want to print with the French Canadian character set, issue the following command and press Enter:

```
MODE LPT1 CP SEL=863
```

Tip You can abbreviate CODEPAGE as CP and SELECT as SEL.

Exploring More Uses for MODE and CODEPAGE

To ascertain the currently active code page for any device, issue the following command and press Enter:

MODE *device* CODEPAGE /STATUS

This command works the same with or without the /STATUS option. DOS returns the status of the active code page and all prepared code pages for the specified device, including the hardware code page, as shown in Figure 14.3.

Figure 14.3
Viewing the code page status.

```
C:\>MODE CON CODPAGE /STATUS
Active code page for device CON is 863
Hardware code pages:
code page 437
Prepared code pages:
code page 863
code page 850
MODE status code page function completed
C:\>
```

To check the code page for the display monitor, for example, type this command at the DOS prompt and press Enter:

MODE CON CP

At times, you might need to refresh the code page for a particular device, especially code page printers. The printers do not store the code page fonts when they are turned off and on again. Also, use the following command if the printer was not turned on and online when you enabled code page switching on the printer:

MODE *device* CODEPAGE REFRESH

To refresh the code page for the printer hooked up to LPT1, for example, type the following command at the DOS prompt and press Enter:

MODE LPT1 CP REF

If you issue a code page command for your printer through CHCP, MODE SELECT, or MODE REFRESH, and your printer does not accept code pages or is not turned on and online, an error message appears when you try to print. You might notice a delay before receiving the error message, depending on the length of the timeout period.

> **Tip**
> You can abbreviate REFRESH as REF.

Considering Keyboard Remappings

When you change the default country and keyboard codes on your computer system, you find that certain keys no longer work as labeled. The following information pertains to standard United States keyboards, but changing the country code also might affect systems with national keyboards.

Continuing with the previous examples for COUNTRY.SYS and KEYB.COM, set the country and keyboard codes to 044 and UK for the United Kingdom. Your CONFIG.SYS file should contain the following statement:

```
COUNTRY=044,,C:\DOS\COUNTRY.SYS
```

If necessary, reboot your computer so that this command takes effect. Then, in your AUTOEXEC.BAT file or at the DOS prompt, type the following command and press Enter:

```
KEYB UK,,C:\DOS\KEYBOARD.SYS
```

After your system reboots and KEYB is installed, press the backslash key (\). Notice that instead of displaying the backslash character, your system displays a hash mark (#). Pressing Shift+3 produces the British currency symbol (£). A few other key remappings occur when you use the United Kingdom country and keyboard codes on a standard American keyboard with the American default version of MS-DOS. Table 14.2 lists the remappings for this configuration.

Table 14.2 Remappings for the United Kingdom on a United States Keyboard

Standard Character	Remapped Character
~	/
@	"
#	£
|	~
\	#
"	@

If you require extensive use of an alternative language keyboard, you can save yourself the problem of remembering the key changes. Print the changed characters on address or disk labels, cut out the characters, and paste them to your keyboard in the remapped positions.

Because you lose the backslash key (\) with this remapping of your keyboard, you might have trouble working with subdirectories. To enter the backslash character, hold down the Alt key and, using the numeric keypad on the right side of your keyboard, press the numbers 9 and 2. You also can press Ctrl+Alt+F1 to switch to the United States layout and Ctrl+Alt+F2 to return to the country format you installed.

Using Dead Keys

When you tell DOS to use a different keyboard or character set, your keyboard keys produce different results. In addition to the remapped keyboard, a device called a *dead key* enables you to enter special language characters.

Normally, when you type an alphabetic character on your keyboard, the letter appears without any accents. The use of a dead key enables you to enter an acute accent (´), a grave accent (`), or a circumflex accent (^) with certain vowels and other keys. These marks are used in some languages but are not provided on a standard American keyboard.

When you press the dead key, nothing appears on the screen. When you press the next appropriate letter key, the accented character appears. If you press an inappropriate key, DOS beeps and displays nothing.

Table 14.3 lists the keys on the United States keyboard that are remapped when you enable code page 863 (for French Canada).

TABLE 14.3 LANGUAGE SUPPORT FOR FRENCH CANADA ON UNITED STATES KEYBOARD

Standard Character	Remapped Character
`	#
~	|
@	"
#	/
^	?
\	<
|	>
/	é
?	É

Table 14.4 lists the dead key keyboard mappings for French Canada.

TABLE 14.4 FRENCH CANADA LANGUAGE SUPPORT USING DEAD KEYS

Dead Key	Standard Character	Remapped Character
]	c	ç
Shift+]	C	Ç
Shift+]	e	ë
Shift+]	i	ï
Shift+]	u	ü

Table 14.4 Continued

Dead Key	Standard Character	Remapped Character
Shift+]	E	Ë
Shift+]	I	Ï
Shift+]	U	Ü
[	a	â
[	e	ê
[	i	î
[	o	ô
[	u	û
Shift+[	A	Â
Shift+[	E	Ê
Shift+[	I	Î
Shift+[	O	Ô
Shift+[	U	Û
‘	a	à
‘	e	è
‘	u	ù
‘	A	À
‘	E	È
‘	U	Ù
‘	‘	`

For other national languages on a U.S. or other keyboard, a little testing can give you the capability to use the language-specific characters you require. The four keys you need to test as dead keys are the apostrophe ('), question mark (?), left square bracket ([), and right square bracket (]).

As an alternative to using code page switching to access special language-specific characters, you can load the support for the required language table with the KEYB command and then use the Alt+*nnn* technique. The *nnn* stands for the ASCII code for the specific character and is typed on the numeric keypad of your keyboard (not on the numbers above the typewriter keys of your keyboard).

→ **See** Appendix E for a listing of ASCII codes.

Using Foreign-Language Commands

MS-DOS requires a foreign-language version to be installed in order to use foreign-language keyboard commands and other system functions (such as help screens for commands). Attempting to load an alternative code page—for example, German—and then attempting to issue German commands does not work without using the German version of DOS.

By default, the characters in the default code page are United States English for all versions; DOS uses code pages to convert to the native language.

If you have installed the international version of DOS and are still encountering problems using a code page, first check how you are implementing the KEYB command and then check that the country code you are attempting to use matches the version of DOS you have.

International Country Codes

MS-DOS provides support for a number of different international code pages, which are simply character sets that facilitate the needs of a particular language. The lower ASCII characters (0 to 127) always remain the same, but the characters available in the upper ASCII set (128 to 255) are changed to make certain special characters available. The code page information file included with DOS 6 (EGA.CPI) includes displayable character sets for the following international code pages:

Code Page	Country or Language
437	United States
860	Portuguese
850	Multilingual (Latin I)
863	Canadian-French
852	Slavic (Latin II)
865	Nordic

MS-DOS 6.2 provides an additional file (EGA2.CPI) that supports the following international code pages:

Code Page	Country or Language
437	United States
857	Turkish
850	Multilingual (Latin I)
861	Icelandic
852	Slavic (Latin II)
869	Greek

In the following table, you can find the countries or languages supported by the international features of MS-DOS 6. The country code and the default and alternate code pages (character sets) are specified for each country. DOS's international commands—such as COUNTRY=, CHCP, KEYB, and MODE—use country codes, keyboard codes, and code pages:

Country or Language	Country Code	Default Code Page	Alternate Code Page	First DOS Version
Belgium	032	850	437	2.1
Brazil	055	850	437	5.0
Canada (French)	002	863	850	3.3
Croatia	038	852	850	6.0
Czech Republic	042	852	850	6.0
Denmark	045	850	865	2.1
Finland	358	850	437	2.1
France	033	850	437	2.1
Germany	049	850	437	2.1
Hungary	036	852	850	5.0
International English	061	437	850	2.1
Italy	039	850	437	2.1
Latin America	003	850	437	3.3
Netherlands	031	850	437	2.1
Norway	047	850	865	2.1
Poland	048	852	850	5.0
Portugal	351	850	860	3.3
Serbia/Yugoslavia	038	852	850	6.0
Slovakia	042	852	850	6.0
Slovenia	038	852	850	6.0
Spain	034	850	437	2.1
Sweden	046	850	437	2.1
Switzerland (French)	041	850	437	2.1
Switzerland (German)	041	850	437	2.1
United Kingdom	044	437	850	2.1
United States	001	437	850	2.1

Special versions of MS-DOS that support the following countries and languages also are available: Arabic, Israel, Japan, Korea, People's Republic of China, and Taiwan. Contact

Microsoft for more information about these versions of MS-DOS. (See the "Introduction" for information on contacting Microsoft.)

Each country code has a specific date and time format associated with it. The following table lists those international date and time formats, with an example shown for August 23, 2001, at 2:42 p.m., 10 seconds, 20 hundredths of a second:

Country	Country Code	Date Format	Date Example	Time Format	Time Example
Belgium	032	dd/mm/yyyy	23/08/2001	hh:mm:ss	14:42:10
Brazil	055	dd/mm/yyyy	23/08/2001	hh:mm:ss	14:42:10
Canada (French)	002	yyyy-mm-dd	2001-08-23	hh:mm:ss	14:42:10
Croatia	038	yyyy-mm-dd	2001-08-23	hh:mm:ss	14:42:10
Czech Republic	042	yyyy-mm-dd	2001-08-23	hh:mm:ss	14:42:10
Denmark	045	dd-mm-yyyy	23-08-2001	hh.mm.ss	14.42.10
Finland	358	dd.mm.yyyy	23.08.2001	hh.mm.ss	14.42.10
France	033	dd.mm.yyyy	23.08.2001	hh:mm:ss	14:42:10
Germany	049	dd.mm.yyyy	23.08.2001	hh:mm:ss	14:42:10
Hungary	036	yyyy-mm-dd	2001-08-23	hh:mm:ss	14:42:10
International English	061	dd-mm-yyyy	23-08-2001	hh:mm:ss.00p	2:42:10.20p
Italy	039	dd/mm/yyyy	23/08/2001	hh.mm.ss	14.42.10
Latin America	003	dd/mm/yyyy	23/08/2001	hh:mm:ss.00p	2:42:10.20p
Netherlands	031	dd-mm-yyyy	23-08-2001	hh:mm:ss	14:42:10
Norway	047	dd.mm.yyyy	23.08.2001	hh:mm:ss	14:42:10
Poland	048	yyyy-mm-dd	2001-08-23	hh:mm:ss	14:42:10
Portugal	351	dd-mm-yyyy	23-08-2001	hh:mm:ss	14:42:10
Slovakia	042	yyyy-mm-dd	2001-08-23	hh:mm:ss	14:42:10
Serbia/Yugoslavia	038	yyyy-mm-dd	2001-08-23	hh:mm:ss	14:42:10
Slovenia	038	yyyy-mm-dd	2001-08-23	hh:mm:ss	14:42:10
Spain	034	dd/mm/yyyy	23/08/2001	hh:mm:ss	14:42:10
Sweden	046	yyyy-mm-dd	2001-08-23	hh.mm.ss	14.42.10
Switzerland (French)	041	dd.mm.yyyy	23.08.2001	hh,mm,ss	14,42,10
Switzerland (German)	041	dd.mm.yyyy	23.08.2001	hh,mm,ss	14,42,10
United Kingdom	044	dd/mm/yyyy	23/08/2001	hh:mm:ss.00	14:42:10.20
United States	001	mm-dd-yyyy	08-23-2001	hh:mm:ss.00p	2:42:10.20p

International Country Codes

> **Note:** Microsoft added and/or changed the names for several of the countries in the preceding list for MS-DOS 6.0. In particular, the entry for Yugoslavia has been changed to three separate entries: Serbia/Yugoslavia, Slovenia, and Croatia. Also, the entry for Czechoslovakia is now two separate entries: Czech Republic and Slovakia. These are name changes only; none of the country code assignments have been changed.

MS-DOS 6 supports various alternative keyboard layouts. The following table lists the code(s) and code pages for each country or language. The KEYB command supports international keyboard layouts through the use of the KEYBOARD.SYS information file:

Country or Language	Keyboard Code	Default Code Page	Alternative Code Page	Keyboard ID Code(s)
Belgium	be	850	437	
Brazil	br	850	437	
Canada (French)	cf	863	850	
Croatia	yu	852	850	
Czech Republic	cz	852	850	
Denmark	dk	850	865	
Finland	su	850	437	
France	fr	850	437	120, 189
Germany	gr	850	437	
Hungary	hu	852	850	
Italy	it	850	437	141, 142
Latin America	la	850	437	
Netherlands	nl	850	437	
Norway	no	850	865	
Poland	pl	852	850	
Portugal	po	850	860	
Serbia/Yugoslavia	yu	852	850	
Slovakia	sl	852	850	
Slovenia	yu	852	850	
Spain	sp	850	437	
Sweden	sv	850	437	
Switzerland (French)	sf	850	437	
Switzerland (German)	sg	850	437	
United Kingdom	uk	437	850	166, 168
United States	us	437	85	

MS-DOS 6.2 includes an alternate keyboard layout file, KEYBRD2.SYS, that KEYB can use. KEYBRD2.SYS doesn't support either Switzerland layout, but it adds alternative keyboard layouts for Brazil, Canada, Greece, Iceland, Romania, and Turkey. For information on using the layouts available in KEYBRD2.SYS, see the README.TXT file distributed with MS-DOS 6.2.

PART IV

MAXIMIZING DOS

- **15** Using the DOS Editor   361
- **16** Understanding Batch Files   389
- **17** Understanding `ANSI.SYS`   415
- **18** Mastering DOSKEY and Macros   431
- **19** Configuring Your Computer   441
- **20** Networking DOS   471
- **21** Connecting to the Internet   483
- **22** Third-Party Utilities   493

CHAPTER 15

USING THE DOS EDITOR

In this chapter

Understanding the DOS Editor   362

Navigating the DOS Editor   364

Mastering Fundamental Editing Techniques   368

Learning Special Editing Techniques   371

Block Editing   373

Searching and Replacing   376

Managing Files   379

Starting the DOS Editor with Optional Switches   384

Project: Customizing the DOS Editor Screen   385

Understanding the DOS Editor

The DOS Editor is a text processor, a kind of miniature word processor. It is the perfect tool for creating short text documents and editing text files. When you try the DOS Editor, you are in for a pleasant surprise. The Editor is so easy and intuitive to use that you will likely become a regular user.

The DOS Editor falls into a class of programs known as *text editors*. As the name implies, a text editor works with files that contain pure text (as opposed to binary files, which contain programming instructions or formatted data).

Uses for the DOS Editor

Following are some of the typical tasks for which the DOS Editor is ideally suited:

- Creating, editing, and printing memos (and other text documents)
- Viewing text files whose contents are unknown
- Creating or modifying various system configuration files, such as AUTOEXEC.BAT and CONFIG.SYS
- Writing and modifying batch files

→ For more information about batch files, **see** Chapter 16, "Understanding Batch Files," **p. 389**.

- Writing and saving README files (Many computer users place a README file in a hard disk subdirectory, or on a floppy disk, to explain the contents of other files in the subdirectory or on the disk.)
- Creating and viewing files that are uploaded to or downloaded from electronic bulletin boards, such as CompuServe
- Writing programs for programming language environments that don't include a resident editor

Be aware that document files produced by some word processors aren't pure text files. The files can contain special formatting or printer-control characters. Most word processors can import the pure text files created with the DOS Editor. The Editor, however, might not successfully import word processor document files that contain certain formatting characters.

Files Required to Run the DOS Editor

The Editor is provided with DOS. It is invoked by the external command EDIT, which runs the program EDIT.COM. When you run the Editor, EDIT.COM calls on two other files: QBASIC.EXE and EDIT.HLP. Only QBASIC.EXE is required. EDIT.HLP contains the text of the help messages, but the Editor works without this file.

Using the DOS Editor from a Floppy Disk

Having a bootable floppy disk with the DOS Editor on it can be very useful for troubleshooting computer problems. You can copy the Editor onto a floppy disk in two different ways, depending on the version of DOS you have.

→ To make a floppy disk bootable, **see** "Creating a Floppy Boot Disk," **p. 25**.

If you are using DOS 6.*x*, you must copy the EDIT.COM, EDIT.HLP, and QBASIC.EXE files from the C:\DOS directory to the floppy.

If you are using Windows 9x, you need to copy just the EDIT.COM and EDIT.HLP files from the \Windows\Commands directory. You no longer need to copy the QBASIC.EXE file.

Starting the DOS Editor

You can start the DOS Editor from the DOS Shell or from the command line. To start it, type the following at the DOS prompt and press Enter:

EDIT

A preliminary screen appears (see Figure 15.1).

Figure 15.1
The preliminary DOS Editor screen appears when you first use the EDIT command.

You now must press either Enter or Esc:

- Enter activates the Survival Guide. (The Survival Guide provides help about using the DOS Editor.)
- Esc clears the box in the center of the screen and prepares the Editor for working on a text file.

Press Esc. Now the DOS Editor screen is blank, and you can begin writing a text file. Your screen should look like the one shown in Figure 15.2.

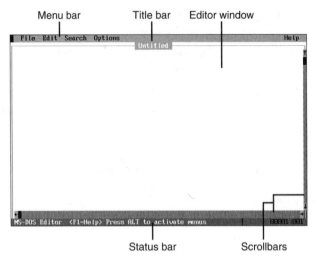

Figure 15.2
The Editor screen, shown with a blank editing area, is ready for you to begin working on a file.

Getting Acquainted with the Initial Editor Screen

Take a moment to look at your screen (or refer to Figure 15.2). The screen consists of several elements:

- The menu bar lists the available menus: File, Edit, Search, Options, and Help. The title bar contains the name of the text file being edited (it is now Untitled).

- The status bar describes the current process and shows certain shortcut key options.

- Scrollbars are a vertical strip along the right edge and a horizontal strip just above the status bar. You use the scrollbars with a mouse to move through the file. (Mouse techniques are described in the section "Using a Mouse" later in this chapter.)

- The Editor window is the large area in which the text of your file appears. The cursor is the flashing underscore character that indicates where typed text will appear.

Navigating the DOS Editor

The DOS Editor provides several ways to perform most commands. The Editor has a user-friendly set of menus from which you can choose options. Many of these options require you to enter further information in an onscreen box known as a *dialog box*, discussed in "Understanding Dialog Boxes" later in the chapter.

The Editor enables you to execute many commands by pressing special shortcut keys. You also can use a mouse to execute commands.

The following sections describe how to use menus, dialog boxes, shortcut keys, and a mouse in the DOS Editor.

Understanding the Menu System

The DOS Editor menu system provides many editing commands. The menu bar contains the following options: File, Edit, Search, Options, and Help. Choosing any of these options displays a pull-down menu. The File option displays a menu that enables you to load, save, and print files. You use the Edit menu to cut and paste text. You can use the Search menu for finding and replacing specified text. The Options menu can be used to reconfigure environment options, and the Help menu provides access to online help.

To activate the menu bar, press Alt. The first letter of each menu name is highlighted. To open a menu, press the first letter of the menu name. To activate the File menu, for example, press Alt and then F (Alt+F). Similarly, press Alt+E to display the Edit menu, Alt+S to display the Search menu, Alt+O to display the Options menu, or Alt+H to display the Help menu.

Every time you open a main menu, the first command on the menu is highlighted. You can move this highlight to the other commands by pressing the up- or down-arrow key. As you move the highlight, notice that the status bar displays a brief description of the highlighted command.

On a menu, one letter of each command is highlighted. On most systems, the highlighted letter appears in high-intensity white. To execute a command, move the highlight to that command and press Enter, or press the key that corresponds to the highlighted letter.

Depending on which editing commands you have executed previously, some commands in a menu might not be available. In such a case, the menu shows the command name in a dull color (usually gray), and no highlighted letter appears in the name. If you try to execute an unavailable command, the DOS Editor sounds a beep and refuses to execute the command.

The Esc key is the "oops" key. Pressing Esc closes the menu system and returns you to the Editor.

In the pull-down menus, an ellipsis (…) following the name of a command indicates that a dialog box opens when you issue that command. (Sometimes, depending on the circumstances, a command without an ellipsis also opens a dialog box.)

Understanding Dialog Boxes

When you execute a menu command, it can start immediately or, depending on the command and the current context, a dialog box might pop up. A dialog box means that the DOS Editor needs more information before it can carry out the command. If, for example, you execute the command to save a new file, the Editor first needs to know what name to give the file. A dialog box prompts you for the necessary information.

If you activate the Search menu, for example, and then choose Change, the DOS Editor displays the Change dialog box (see Figure 15.3).

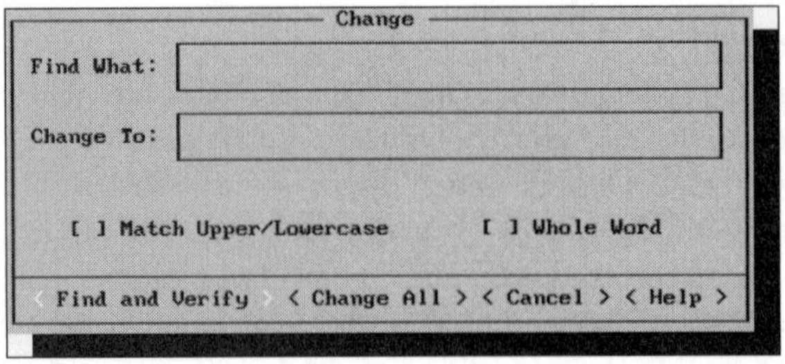

Figure 15.3
In the Change dialog box, you indicate what you want to search and replace.

```
┌─────────────────────── Change ───────────────────────┐
│  Find What:  [                                    ]  │
│                                                      │
│  Change To:  [                                    ]  │
│                                                      │
│     [ ] Match Upper/Lowercase      [ ] Whole Word    │
│                                                      │
│    < Find and Verify > < Change All > < Cancel > < Help > │
└──────────────────────────────────────────────────────┘
```

The DOS Editor uses dialog boxes to get a variety of information. Sometimes you must type something, such as a filename or a search string in a text box. Sometimes you must choose from a list of options. At other times, you select from a series of command buttons.

→ For a discussion of dialog boxes, text boxes, option buttons, and command buttons, **see** Chapter 4, "Using the DOS Shell," **p. 57**.

When a DOS Editor dialog box opens, the following three keys have special significance:

- Tab moves the cursor from one area of the dialog box to the next area. After you specify information in one area, use Tab to move to the next area.

- Esc aborts the menu option and returns you to the Editor. Use Esc when you change your mind and decide against issuing a particular command.

- Enter is the "go ahead" key. Press it when all options in the dialog box are as you want them and you are ready to execute the command. You press Enter only once while you are working inside a dialog box. Use Tab, not Enter, to move the cursor from one area of the dialog box to the next area. (Be careful. Most people tend to press Enter after they type information, such as a filename. Remember that when you need to specify additional information inside the dialog box, press Tab, not Enter.)

In every dialog box, one command button is enclosed in highlighted angle brackets. The highlighted brackets identify the action that takes place when you press Enter.

To highlight the angle brackets of the command button you want, press Tab repeatedly. Be sure not to press Enter until you have specified everything satisfactorily.

> **Tip**
> When you are working with a dialog box, Alt is an "express" key. By pressing Alt and a highlighted letter, you activate an option even if the cursor is in another area.

Using Shortcut Keys

For convenience, many commonly used DOS Editor menu commands have an associated shortcut key. Pressing this shortcut key while you are working with the Editor executes the command directly, bypassing the menu system. Table 15.1 provides a complete list of shortcut keys.

Table 15.1 DOS Editor Keyboard and Mouse Shortcuts

Shortcut Key	Effect	Mouse
F1	View help on menu or command	Click the right button on the desired item
Shift+F1	View help on getting started	Click Getting Started (Help menu)
Ctrl+F1	View the next help topic	Click Next (status bar)
Alt+F1	Review the preceding help screen	Click Back (status bar)
Shift+Ctrl+F1	View the preceding help topic	None
F3	Repeat the last Find	Click Repeat Last Find (Search menu)
F6	Move between help and the desired window	Click in the desired window
Shift+F6	Make the preceding window active	Click in the desired window
Shift+Del	Cut selected text	Click Cut (Edit menu)
Ctrl+Ins	Copy selected text	Click Copy (Edit menu)
Shift+Ins	Paste text from the Clipboard	Click Paste (Edit menu)
Del	Erase selected text	Click Clear (Edit menu)
Ctrl+Q, A	Change text	Click Change (Search menu)
Ctrl+Q, F	Search for a text string	Click Find (Search menu)
Esc	Terminate the Help System	Click Cancel (status bar)
Alt	Enter Menu-selection mode	None
Alt+plus	Enlarge the active window	Drag the title bar up
Alt+minus	Shrink the active window	Drag the title bar down

Using a Mouse

A mouse is an excellent pointing device for computer applications. The DOS Editor supports a mouse. You can execute menu commands and many editing tasks by using a mouse. If your system is mouseless, you can get along fine; if you have a mouse, try it and see what you think.

> **Note**
>
> The DOS Editor works with any Microsoft-compatible mouse and driver. If you have a mouse, you presumably know how to install and activate your mouse driver. Microsoft supplies a generic mouse driver as part of MS-DOS.

When the mouse is active, you see a special mouse cursor onscreen. The mouse cursor is a small rectangle, about the size of one text character, which moves as you move the mouse. Notice that the regular blinking cursor remains active. You can continue to use all the keyboard commands and features. Refer to Table 15.1 for a comprehensive list of mouse techniques.

The following are some additional mouse pointers:

- To open a menu, click the menu name in the menu bar.
- To execute a menu command, click the command name in the menu.
- To set an option in a dialog box, click that option.
- To abort a menu, click a location outside the menu.
- To move the cursor in the file, click at the location you want.
- To select text, drag the mouse cursor over the text. That is, move the mouse cursor to one end of the text you want to select; then press and hold down the mouse button while you move the mouse, across the text, to the other end of the text you want to select.
- To activate the Editor window while a help screen is visible, click anywhere inside the Editor window.
- To expand or shrink the Editor window while a help screen is visible, drag the title bar of the Editor window up or down.
- To scroll the screen horizontally one character, click the left or right arrow at either end of the horizontal scrollbar.
- To scroll the screen vertically one character, click the up or down arrow at either end of the vertical scrollbar.
- To scroll text vertically to a specific position, move the mouse cursor to the scroll box (the inverse-video rectangle inside the vertical scrollbar). Then, drag the scroll box along the scrollbar to the desired position.
- To scroll text one page at a time, click the vertical scrollbar somewhere between the scroll box and the top or bottom of the scrollbar.
- To scroll horizontally several positions at once, click the horizontal scrollbar somewhere between the scroll box and the left or right end of the scrollbar.
- To execute a dialog box action enclosed in angle brackets, click the name between the brackets.
- To execute any keystroke action enclosed in angle brackets in the status bar, click the name inside the angle brackets.

Mastering Fundamental Editing Techniques

Editing is a skill—almost an art. Some editing techniques are simple, others more complex. You can perform many editing tasks in more than one way. The following sections discuss the fundamental editing skills, which include moving the cursor, scrolling, and inserting and deleting text.

Moving the Cursor

When you have text in the DOS Editor window, you can move the cursor around the text in several ways. The Editor provides two alternative cursor-movement interfaces:

- **Keypad interface**—The specialized IBM PC keys—the arrow keys, Ins, Del, and so on—govern most editing activities. To move the cursor up, for example, you use the up-arrow key.

- **Control-key interface**—Ctrl+key combinations can also be used for most editing activities. To move the cursor up, for example, you press Ctrl+E. This interface is used in the word processing program WordStar.

Generally, the DOS Editor accommodates both camps. Most editing techniques are available with both the keypad and Control-key (WordStar-style) sequences. A few techniques, however, can be performed with only one method. This chapter focuses on the keypad style. The Control-key combinations are mentioned only when required by a particular editing technique.

Table 15.2 summarizes the cursor-movement commands.

TABLE 15.2 CURSOR-MOVEMENT COMMANDS

Effect	Keypad	Control-Key Style
Character left	Left arrow	Ctrl+S
Character right	Right arrow	Ctrl+D
Word left	Ctrl+left arrow	Ctrl+A
Word right	Ctrl+right arrow	Ctrl+F
Line up	Up arrow	Ctrl+E
Line down	Down arrow	Ctrl+X
First indentation level	Home	None
Beginning of line	None	Ctrl+Q, S
End of line	End	Ctrl+Q, D
Beginning of next line	Ctrl+Enter	Ctrl+J
Top of window	None	Ctrl+Q, E
Bottom of window	None	Ctrl+Q, X
Beginning of text	Ctrl+Home	Ctrl+Q, R
End of text	Ctrl+End	Ctrl+Q, C
Set marker	None	Ctrl+K, *n* (*n* equals 0–3)
Move to marker	None	Ctrl+Q, *n* (*n* equals 0–3)

Look at the far-right end of the status bar, in the lower-right corner of the DOS Editor screen. You see two numbers, separated by a colon. The two numbers indicate the cursor's current location in your file. The first number is the current row; the second, the current column.

Use the arrow keys to move the cursor, and watch the numbers change. Press Num Lock; an uppercase *N* appears next to the location numbers to indicate that Num Lock is on. Press Num Lock a few more times to toggle the indicator on and off. Press Caps Lock; an uppercase *C* appears next to the location numbers, left of the *N*, to indicate that the Caps Lock key is on.

Scrolling

Scrolling is the movement of text inside the Editor window. When you scroll, you bring into view a portion of the file currently not visible in the Editor window. Scrolling, which can be horizontal as well as vertical, keeps the cursor at the same row and column number but moves the text in the window.

Table 15.3 summarizes the scrolling commands. For large-scale scrolling, you use the PgUp and PgDn keys. Try using these keys by themselves and with the Ctrl key.

TABLE 15.3   SCROLLING TEXT

Effect	Keypad	Control-Key Style
One line up	Ctrl+up arrow	Ctrl+W
One line down	Ctrl+down arrow	Ctrl+Z
Page up	PgUp	Ctrl+R
Page down	PgDn	Ctrl+C
One window left	Ctrl+PgUp	None
One window right	Ctrl+PgDn	None

Inserting Text into a Line

You can insert text into an existing line. To do so, move the cursor to the position at which you want to insert text; then type the text you want to insert. As you type, text to the right of the cursor moves right to accommodate the inserted text. You can move off the line by using any of the cursor-movement keys. Do not press Enter to move off the line. Pressing Enter splits the line in two. If you want to replace, or overwrite, the text instead of inserting, press the Insert key. See the "Overtyping" section later in this chapter.

Deleting Text from a Line

You can use one of the following two methods to delete a few characters from a line:

- Move the cursor to the character you want to delete. Press the Del key. To delete consecutive characters, continue pressing Del.

- Move the cursor to the character immediately to the right of the character you want to delete. Press the Backspace key.

Most people find the first method more natural. Try both methods and make your own choice.

Splitting and Joining Lines

Sometimes you need to split a line of text into two lines. To do so, move the cursor so that it is positioned under the character with which you want to begin the second line of text; then press Enter. The line splits in two, and the second half moves down to form a new line. Succeeding lines are pushed down to accommodate the new line.

Conversely, you can join two lines to form one line. To do so, position the cursor in the second line and press Home to move the cursor to the left end of the line. Then, press Backspace. The second line moves up to the right end of the first line. Lines beneath the split line move up one line.

Inserting and Deleting an Entire Line

To insert a blank line between two lines, move the cursor to column 1 in the lower of the two lines and then press Ctrl+N or Home (to move the cursor to the left end of the current line), and press Enter. Then, move the cursor up to the new blank line.

To delete an entire line, place the cursor anywhere on the line and press Ctrl+Y.

Overtyping

By default, the DOS Editor operates in Insert mode. If you type new text while the cursor is in the middle of a line, the Editor inserts that new text at the cursor location. If you prefer, you can choose Overtype mode, in which the new text replaces the former text.

To activate Overtype mode, press Insert. The cursor changes from a blinking line to a blinking box. The larger cursor signifies Overtype mode, in which any new character you type replaces the character at the cursor location.

> **Note**
> Depending on your keyboard, you might have a key marked either Ins or Insert. Both provide the insert function.

To return to standard Insert mode, press Insert again. The Insert key acts as a toggle switch that alternates between Insert and Overtype modes.

Learning Special Editing Techniques

In addition to the basic editing techniques, the DOS Editor provides several special editing features. The following sections describe how to use the automatic indenting, tab, and place marker features.

Using Automatic Indent

When you type a line and press Enter, the cursor drops down one line but returns to the column where you began the preceding line. This feature is convenient when you want to type a series of indented lines.

For an example, type the following line and press Enter:

```
This line is not indented
```

The cursor moves to the beginning of the next line. Then press the spacebar three times to move the cursor to column 4 and type the following:

```
But this line is
```

Press Enter again. Note that the second time you press Enter, the cursor moves to the next row but remains indented at column 4. Now type this message and press Enter:

```
So is this one
```

The cursor remains indented.

Now press the left-arrow key until the cursor returns to column 1. Type the following and press Enter:

```
Back to no indentation
```

The short text block you typed looks like the following:

```
This line is not indented
   But this line is
   So is this one
Back to no indentation
```

Using Tab

By default, tab stops are set every eight spaces. When you press the Tab key, the cursor moves to the right to the next tab stop. All text to the right of the cursor moves right when you press Tab. Additional tabbing techniques follow:

- To indent an existing line a full tab position, move the cursor to column 1 of the line and press Tab.
- To remove leading spaces and move a line to the left, move the cursor anywhere on the line and then press Shift+Tab.
- To indent or "unindent" an entire block of lines, select the lines by using one of the Shift keystrokes shown in Table 15.4. Then, press Tab to indent the entire block or press Shift+Tab to "unindent" the entire block.
- To change the number of default tab stops, first select Display from the Options menu. In the resulting dialog box, press Tab several times to move the cursor to Tab Stops, type a new value for the number of characters per tab stop, and then press Enter to close the dialog box.

Using Place Markers

A *place marker* designates a specific location—a row and column—in your text. You can set as many as four place markers. After setting a place marker, you can move the cursor instantly from anywhere in the file to that marker's location. The markers are invisible; no character appears in the text to indicate a set marker.

You can set four markers: 0 through 3. To set a place marker, press and release Ctrl+K, and then press a number key from 0 to 3. This action associates the cursor's current position with the marker having the number whose key you pressed. To move the cursor to a previously set place marker, press and release Ctrl+Q, and then press the number of the marker (0 through 3).

You don't turn off markers; they are always set. You can reset them to a different location, but you cannot unset them. They are forgotten when you exit the program.

Block Editing

You can edit blocks of text as a single unit. Block editing requires that you understand two relevant concepts: selecting text and using the Clipboard, which temporarily stores a block of text in a reserved area of memory.

The following sections describe these techniques:

- Selecting text for block operations
- Using the Clipboard
- Cutting and pasting blocks of text

Selecting Text

A block of selected text is always one contiguous group of characters. The block can be one character, a few characters, a line, several lines, a paragraph, or even an entire file. Selected text appears in reverse video.

Follow these steps to select a block of text:

1. Move the cursor to one end of the block.
2. While you hold down the Shift key, use the cursor-movement keys to highlight the block.

Table 15.4 lists the keys used for selecting text. In general, the keys you use to select text are the same as those you use to move the cursor, but you also press Shift when using them to select text.

Table 15.4 Selecting Text

To Select	Use This Key Combination
Character left	Shift+left arrow
Character right	Shift+right arrow
To beginning of line	Shift+Home
To end of line	Shift+End
Current line	Shift+down arrow
Line above	Shift+up arrow
Word left	Shift+Ctrl+left arrow
Word right	Shift+Ctrl+right arrow
Screen up	Shift+PgUp
Screen down	Shift+PgDn
To beginning of text	Shift+Ctrl+Home
To end of text	Shift+Ctrl+End

After you select (highlight) a block, you can deselect it by pressing any arrow key. (Do not use Shift, however; Shift expands or shrinks the selection.) The highlighting disappears, indicating that you have deselected the entire block.

Understanding the Clipboard

The Clipboard is a text storage area in memory; it acts as a kind of halfway house for blocks of text. You can place a block of text into the Clipboard and later retrieve the block. The Clipboard has many uses. Its most common use is to cut and paste—to move or copy a block of text from one place in the file to another.

The Clipboard stores only one block of text at a time. When you place text in the Clipboard, the incoming text completely replaces the previous contents of the Clipboard. Changing the block of text in the Clipboard is always an all-or-nothing affair. You cannot add or subtract incrementally. Similarly, retrieval is all or nothing. You cannot move only part of the Clipboard's contents into your file.

Working with Text Blocks

The DOS Editor supports four block-oriented editing techniques (see Table 15.5). You can access each technique by using the Edit menu or pressing the appropriate shortcut key. (Press Alt+E to activate the Edit menu.)

TABLE 15.5   BLOCK-EDITING TECHNIQUES

Menu Command	Shortcut Key	Description
Cut	Shift+Del	Deletes selected text from a file and places that text in the Clipboard.
Copy	Ctrl+Ins	Places in the Clipboard a copy of selected text from the file; text in the file remains selected.
Paste	Shift+Ins	Inserts the contents of the Clipboard into the file at the cursor location; Clipboard contents remain intact. If the file currently has selected text, Clipboard text replaces the selected text.
Clear	Del	Deletes selected text from the file; the contents of the Clipboard are not affected.

To select the first three lines of text in a file, for example, press Ctrl+Home to return the cursor to the beginning of the file. While you're holding down the Shift key, press the down-arrow key three times to select the first three lines of the file. They now appear in reverse video (highlighted).

After the three lines are selected, you can use one of the block-editing commands. To activate the Edit menu, press Alt+E. The DOS Editor displays the Edit menu shown in Figure 15.4. You can now use one of the menu commands.

> **Tip**
> You can use one of the shortcut keys to operate on the selected block, even without displaying the Edit menu.

Figure 15.4
The Edit menu enables you to cut, copy, paste, and clear text.

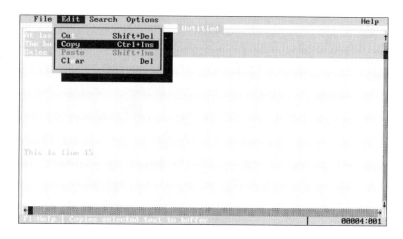

When you perform copy operations, a copy of the selected text moves to the Clipboard but isn't deleted from the original location. If you perform a cut command, however, the DOS Editor removes the highlighted text from its original location and places it in the Clipboard.

After text has been copied or cut to the Clipboard, you can use the paste operation to copy the Clipboard's contents to a new location in the file. To do so, move the cursor to the desired target location and choose Paste from the Edit menu, or press Shift+Ins (the shortcut key for Paste). The Editor inserts a copy of the Clipboard text at the cursor's location.

> **Tip**
> The Clipboard still holds a copy of the pasted text. You can insert additional copies of the Clipboard text at other locations in the file by using the Edit menu or pressing Ctrl+C.

Pressing Del or choosing the Clear command from the Edit menu permanently deletes the selected text from the file without placing a copy of it in the Clipboard.

Searching and Replacing

The Search menu offers several options for searching for and replacing text. These capabilities are most useful in long files.

From the Search menu, you can perform the following actions:

- Find one or more occurrences of a designated text string
- Replace one or more occurrences of a designated text string with a second text string

A *text string* is a sequence of one or more consecutive text characters. These characters can be letters, digits, punctuation, or special symbols—any characters you can type from the keyboard.

Finding or replacing text always involves a search string, which is simply the text string being searched for. A search string can be a single character or, more likely, a word or several consecutive characters.

You cannot search for a string that spans two or more lines. The search string is confined to a group of characters on a single line. You can place some conditions on the search string, however. You can specify, for example, that the search not discriminate between upper- and lowercase letters.

The search begins at the cursor's location and proceeds through the file. If the end of the file is reached before the search string is found, the search continues at the top of the file until the entire file has been traversed. Table 15.6 summarizes the three commands available from the Search menu.

Searching and Replacing

TABLE 15.6 SEARCH MENU COMMANDS

Command	Shortcut Key	Description
Find	None	Opens a dialog box in which you specify the search string; finds the search string in your file
Repeat Last Find	F3	Searches for the text specified in the last Find command
Change	None	Replaces one text string with another

Using the Find Command

To use the Find command, first activate the Search menu by pressing Alt+S. Your screen looks similar to Figure 15.5.

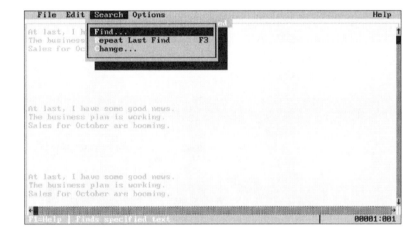

Figure 15.5
Using the Search menu, you can find text, repeat a find, and change text.

Choose Find. The Find dialog box opens, with the cursor on the Find What text box (see Figure 15.6). The word that is at the cursor's current location in the file (or the currently selected text) appears in the text box. If you want to search for this word, press Enter. Otherwise, type the correct search string and then press Enter. The DOS Editor locates the first occurrence of the search string in your file and selects (highlights) the text found.

→ For more information on using wildcards, **see** Chapter 5, "Understanding Files and Directories," **p. 99**.

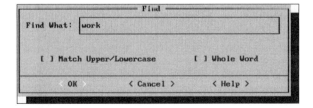

Figure 15.6
The Find dialog box enables you to search for text.

You can press F3 or choose Repeat Last Find from the Search menu. The Editor moves to the next occurrence of the search string (if any).

As you can see in Figure 15.6, you can use the following check boxes in the dialog box to place conditions on the search:

- **Match Upper/Lowercase**—If you select this check box, a successful search occurs only when the upper- and lowercase letters in the text exactly match those in the search string. If this option is not selected, upper- and lowercase letters are considered the same.

- **Whole Word**—If you select this option, the search string must exist as an independent word and cannot be embedded inside a larger word. The character that immediately precedes and immediately follows the search string must be a space, a punctuation character, or one of the special characters (such as <, *, or [).

USING THE CHANGE COMMAND

In addition to just searching for text, you can use the DOS Editor to search for specific text and then replace it with other text.

You activate the Search menu by pressing Alt+S. Then, choose the Change command. The Editor displays the Change dialog box (see Figure 15.7).

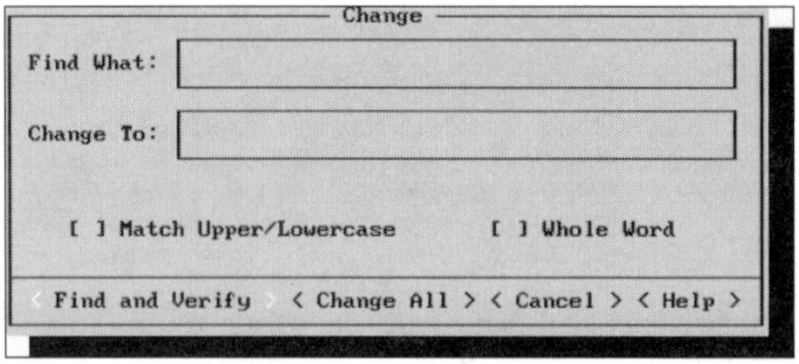

Figure 15.7
The Change dialog box enables you to search and replace text.

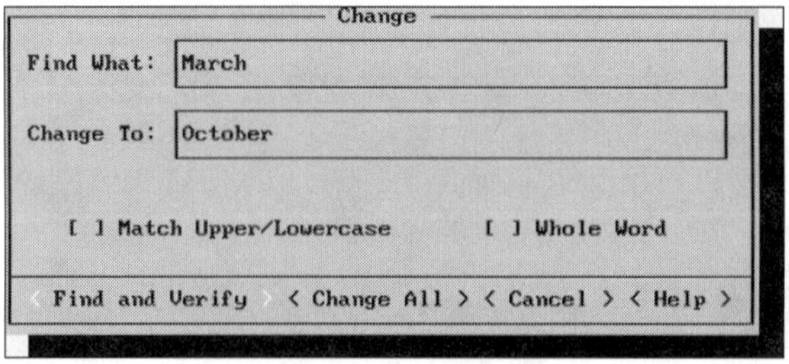

Figure 15.8
The first step in performing a search-and-replace operation is to fill in the Find What and Change To boxes.

The first text box in the Change dialog box is labeled Find What. Type the text you want the Editor to find in this text box (the target text). The second text box is labeled Change To. Type the text you want entered. Figure 15.8 shows a completed Change dialog box.

This dialog box contains two check boxes: Match Upper/Lowercase and Whole Word. Refer to the preceding section for a discussion of these check boxes.

After you make the appropriate entries in the text boxes and select any desired check boxes, choose from among the following three command buttons:

- **Find and Verify**—Select this button to find each occurrence of the target string, one after another. (You specify the target string in the Find What dialog box.) As each occurrence of the target string is found, a second dialog box opens. This second box gives you the choice of making the substitution, skipping to the next occurrence, or canceling the remaining searches. Find and Verify is the default option, which you automatically choose by pressing Enter.

- **Change All**—This button changes all occurrences of the target string to the string specified in the Change To box. The changes occur all at once. A dialog box informs you when the substitutions are complete.

- **Cancel**—This button aborts the Change command, closing the dialog box without making any substitutions. This option is equivalent to pressing Esc.

After the DOS Editor finishes the search-and-replace operation, it displays a second dialog box, which contains the message `Change complete`. If no matching text can be found, the box displays the message `Match not found`. Choose the OK command button to return to the Editor window.

Managing Files

The DOS Editor includes many functions you can use to manage files. These functions, although primitive by the standards of today's full-blown word processors, enable you to perform the basics of file management. The following sections cover, in detail, the file-management operations you can perform using the DOS Editor.

Introducing the File Menu

The File menu is your command center for loading and saving files. Six commands are available on the File menu (see Figure 15.9).

Figure 15.9
The File menu enables you to access the file-management functions of the DOS Editor.

The following list explains the File menu commands:

- **New**—Clears the file currently in the DOS Editor. The result is a clean slate, as though you had just initialized the Editor. This command does not affect other copies of the file. If the file was saved on disk previously, for example, DOS does not erase the disk copy, only the working copy in the Editor.
- **Open**—Loads a file from disk into the DOS Editor environment. You can use this command to see a list of filenames in any directory.
- **Save**—Saves the current file to disk.
- **Save As**—Saves the current file to disk after prompting you for the filename.
- **Print**—Prints all or part of the text in the DOS Editor environment.
- **Exit**—Ends the editing session and returns you to the DOS Shell or the command-line prompt.

> **Note**
>
> When you are working with files, keep in mind these maxims:
> - Until you name a file, the Editor displays the temporary name Untitled in the title bar.
> - When you save a file, the Editor adds the extension TXT to the filename if you don't specify another extension.
> - If you try to exit the Editor or open a new file without first saving a working file in the Editor, a dialog box opens to warn you.

SAVING A FILE

When you save a file for the first time, you should specify two file attributes: the file path (the directory or disk on which to save the file) and the filename.

The DOS Editor stores files on disk in ASCII format. Such files are text files that most text editors and word processors can manipulate. You can view ASCII files directly from the DOS command line by using the TYPE command.

USING THE SAVE AS COMMAND

Follow these steps to save the current Untitled file with a new filename:

1. Choose Save As from the File menu. In the dialog box that opens, the current path is shown below the words File Name (see Figure 15.10). A list box, below the label Dirs/Drives, lists the directories and disk drives available on your system.
2. Type the new filename in the File Name box. You can specify any file extension as part of the filename. Typical file extensions for ASCII text files are TXT and DOC.
3. Press Enter to save the file.

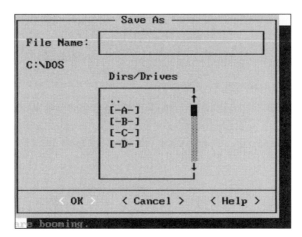

Figure 15.10
The Save As dialog box appears when you first save a file or when you save a file under a new name.

The DOS Editor saves the file to disk in the directory specified by the current path.

Save As is commonly used for storing a file the first time you create it and for saving a second version of a file in a different directory or with a name different from the first version. Assume that you are editing a file named MYWORK.TXT. After making a few changes, you decide to save the new version of the file under the name MEAGAIN.TXT. To do so, display the File menu and choose Save As. The DOS Editor displays the Save As dialog box.

The File Name text box contains the current filename, MYWORK.TXT. Type MEAGAIN.TXT and press Enter. The DOS Editor stores the file on disk as MEAGAIN.TXT, changing the name in the title bar accordingly. The file MYWORK.TXT remains stored on disk. Remember that if you continue editing the file onscreen, you are editing MEAGAIN.TXT (as indicated in the title bar), not MYWORK.TXT.

To store a file in a directory other than that specified by the current path, type the new directory path as part of the filename. If you type the filename \MEMOS\PLAN.BID, for example, the DOS Editor stores the file with the name PLAN.BID in the directory \MEMOS. After you save the file, the name PLAN.BID appears in the title bar. The next time you issue the Save As command, the default directory path is specified in the dialog box as C:\MEMOS. If you save a new file without including an explicit path, DOS saves the file in the C:\MEMOS directory.

You can use this technique to save files on different disk drives. To save a file named MYFILE.TXT in the root directory of the disk in drive A, for example, type the filename as A:\MYFILE.TXT.

Using the Save Command

You use Save to store a file you have already named. No dialog box appears. The current version of the file in the DOS Editor is saved to disk under the existing filename. As you edit a file, use Save periodically to update the file on disk.

Using Save on an unnamed (untitled) file has nearly the same effect as using Save As; the Editor opens a dialog box similar to that shown in Figure 15.10 so that you can enter a filename.

Using the Open Command to Load a File

After text files are stored on disk, you can load a file into the DOS Editor by using the Open command. Because this command lists files in any directory, you also can use Open to search your directories for specific filenames. When you choose Open, the Open dialog box appears (see Figure 15.11).

Figure 15.11
The Open dialog box enables you to load an existing disk file.

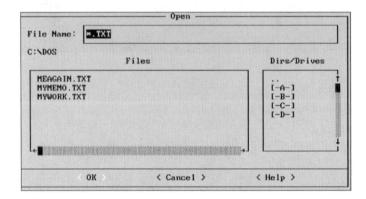

The Open dialog box contains a File Name text box. By default, this box contains *.TXT, the wildcard filename for all files with the extension TXT. The current directory path (C:\DOS in Figure 15.11) appears below the File Name text box. In the File Name text box, type a filename, directory path, or name using the * and ? wildcard characters.

To change the default path, specify a path in the File Name text box and press Enter. Otherwise, the DOS Editor looks in the current directory for files with the extension TXT.

The Files list box contains the names of all files that satisfy the current directory, path, and filename specification. In Figure 15.11, the Files box shows all files that satisfy the path and filename specification C:\DOS*.TXT.

The Dirs/Drives list box lists available directories and disks. You can move the cursor to the Dirs/Drives list box by pressing Tab repeatedly. Then, press the up- and down-arrow keys to move the highlight to one of the directories or drives listed in the box. Press Enter to change the default path.

To load a specific file into the DOS Editor, you can use the File Name box or Files box. To use the File Name box, type in the box the name of the specific file, including a path (or rely on the default path shown below the box). If you don't specify an extension, the Editor assumes the TXT extension. To load the file MYFILE.TXT, which is in the current directory, for example, type MYFILE and press Enter.

You also can select a filename from the Files list box if it contains the filename you want. First, press Tab to move the cursor to the Files list box. Then, use the arrow keys to highlight the target filename. Alternatively, you can press the first letter of the filename to move the highlight. When the name you want is highlighted, press Enter. The DOS Editor loads the file so that you can edit or view it.

Loading a File When You First Start the DOS Editor

You can load a file when you first start the DOS Editor. To do so, use the following syntax:

```
EDIT filename
```

filename is the name of the file you want to edit. Include the path if the file isn't in the current directory. To start the Editor with the file \SALES\MYFILE.TXT loaded, for example, type the following line:

```
EDIT \SALES\MYFILE.TXT
```

The following notes apply when you load a file when you start the DOS Editor:

- The Editor does not assume the extension TXT or any other extension if you don't specify an extension as part of the filename.
- The Editor initializes directly without taking the intermediate step of asking whether you want to see the help material in the onscreen Survival Guide.
- If the Editor cannot locate the specified file, it assumes that you want to create a new file with that name. Accordingly, the Editor initializes with a fresh slate that includes your designated filename in the title bar. After you enter data into the file, you can save it directly by using the Save command. (You don't have to use Save As and specify the filename a second time.)

Using the New Command

Use New when you want to stop work on one file and create a new file. If you haven't saved the old file, the DOS Editor opens a dialog box for confirmation. Otherwise, the old file is cleared, and the screen looks as though you had just initiated the Editor. You see a blank editing area with Untitled in the title bar.

Printing a File

Your computer system probably includes a printer. Whether you have a dot-matrix, inkjet, or laser printer, follow these steps to print a copy of the file currently loaded in the Editor. You can print selected text or the complete file.

1. Activate the File menu.
2. Choose Print to open the Print dialog box (see Figure 15.12).

Figure 15.12
The Print dialog box appears every time you choose the Print command from the File menu.

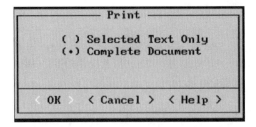

3. Choose one of the following option buttons:

   Selected Text Only—Prints only selected text, which appears in reverse video in the Editor. (Selecting text is explained earlier in this chapter.) This option is the default when a block of text is selected.

   Complete Document—Prints the entire file. This option is the default when no text is selected.

4. Press Enter to begin printing. Make sure that your printer is turned on and is online.

Exiting the DOS Editor

After you finish editing files, you might want to leave the DOS Editor. Just display the File menu and choose the Exit command. If the file already has been saved, the Editor returns to the DOS Shell or to the command line, depending on how you started the program.

If you try to quit without first saving the document you have been editing, the Editor opens a dialog box to ask whether you want to save the file. Choose Yes to save the file and exit the Editor. Choose No to exit from the Editor without saving any changes to the current file. Choose Cancel to close the dialog box and return to the Editor. To get help information about the dialog box, choose Help.

Starting the DOS Editor with Optional Switches

When you start the DOS Editor, four special parameter switches are available. These switches are listed in Table 15.7.

TABLE 15.7	Optional Switches for the EDIT Command
Switch	Description
/B	Displays the DOS Editor in black and white, even when a color graphics adapter is present.
/G	Updates Editor screens as quickly as possible on systems with CGA (Color Graphics Adapter) video. (Note: Some computer systems cannot support this option. If screen flicker occurs when you choose /G, your hardware is not compatible with this option. Also, any system with VGA or better does not need to use this option.)

Table 15.7 Continued

Switch	Description
/H	Displays the maximum number of lines possible with your video hardware. EGA (Enhanced Graphics Adapter) and VGA (Video Graphics Array) systems can produce more than the standard number of lines onscreen.
/NOHI	Effectively displays the Editor on monitors that do not support high intensity.

To display the maximum number of lines when starting the DOS Editor, for example, use the following command:

```
EDIT /H
```

You can specify a filename with one of the command options, as in the following example:

```
EDIT \SALES\MYFILE /H
```

Use the /B switch if you run the DOS Editor on a computer system with a color video adapter but a black-and-white monitor. At the DOS prompt, activate the Editor as follows:

```
EDIT /B
```

Project: Customizing the DOS Editor Screen

Colors on the DOS Editor screen are preset. You can customize most of these colors and other attributes from the Options menu by using the Display command. If you have a color system, you might want different colors for the foreground and background text. If you don't use a mouse with the Editor, you might want to remove the scrollbars.

Changing Colors and Removing Scrollbars

To change screen colors in the DOS Editor, display the Options menu and choose Display. A dialog box similar to the one in Figure 15.13 opens.

Figure 15.13
The Display dialog box enables you to customize how the Editor screen appears.

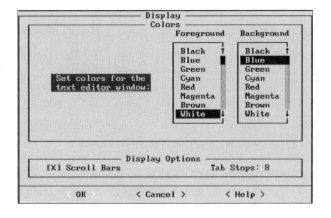

With the cursor on the Foreground box, you can select a new foreground text color by pressing the up- and down-arrow keys. The Foreground box cycles through the colors available with your video hardware. Notice that as you press the arrow keys, the text to the left of the dialog box (Set Colors for the Text Editor Window) shows the current foreground and background colors. Select a new foreground color by moving the highlight to the color you want. Don't press Enter yet. You have more selections to make before closing this dialog box.

Press Tab to move the cursor to the Background box. Select a new background color; the process is similar to the one you followed to select a new foreground color. Now press Enter to return to the Editor screen. The new colors should be in use.

If you don't use a mouse, you might want to consider removing the scrollbars from your screen. Many users think that the screen looks less cluttered without the scrollbars. To see which you prefer, try the following exercise:

1. Reopen the dialog box by displaying the Options menu and choosing Display.
2. Press Tab several times to move the cursor to the Scroll Bars check box. The X inside the brackets indicates that scrollbars are displayed.
3. Press the spacebar or S to deselect the check box. Removing the X indicates that you want to deselect the display of scrollbars.
4. Press Enter, and the scrollbars disappear (see Figure 15.14).

Figure 15.14
The scrollbars have been removed from this Editor screen.

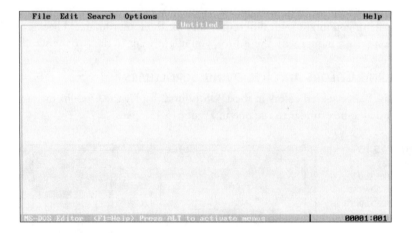

SAVING CUSTOMIZED SETTINGS

If you change one or more display options, the DOS Editor creates a file named QBASIC.INI and stores it in the directory containing the EDIT.COM and QBASIC.EXE files. (For most systems, this directory is \DOS.) The QBASIC.INI file contains a record of the new screen configuration. When you later restart, the Editor uses QBASIC.INI to restore the screen with your customized settings.

Every time you start the Editor, it looks for QBASIC.INI in the default directory or in the directory chain established by the PATH statement in your AUTOEXEC.BAT file. If you restart from a different directory, be sure that the Editor has access to the QBASIC.INI file.

If you want to start the Editor with the original screen configuration, simply erase the QBASIC.INI file.

> **Note**
>
> The DOS Editor "borrows" the programming editor from the QBASIC.EXE file. Thus, the DOS Editor shares the editing environment found in the QBasic programming language. Similarly, the DOS Editor and QBasic share the initial configuration file (QBASIC.INI). Whether you run the DOS Editor or QBasic, the initial configuration is saved in the QBASIC.INI file.

USING THE HELP SYSTEM

The DOS Editor provides online help through the Help menu (see Figure 15.15). Help screens include information about menus and commands, shortcut keys, dialog boxes, keyboard actions, and even about the help system itself.

Figure 15.15
The Help menu helps you learn to use the DOS Editor.

Three categories of information are available from the Help menu:

- **Getting Started**—Provides information about starting the Editor, using the menu and command system, and requesting help
- **Keyboard**—Explains the different editing keystrokes and shortcuts for moving the cursor around your text file
- **About**—Shows the Editor version number and copyright information

The following are general notes on using the Help system:

- To activate the Help system at any time, press Alt+H.
- To move the cursor to the next help topic, press Tab. When the cursor is on the topic you want, press Enter to view the help screen.

- To activate the Getting Started help menu at any time, press Shift+F1.
- To close a help window and exit the help system, press Esc.
- A help screen opens in a separate window. The title bar of this window shows the help topic on display. If you request help on the Save command from the File menu, for example, the title bar of the help window reads HELP: Save command.
- The F1 key provides express help. To get help on any menu, command, or dialog box, press F1 when the cursor or highlight is on the desired item.
- For help when an error message occurs, move the cursor to the Help option in the error message box and press Enter.
- Sometime, at your leisure, consider browsing through all the help screens. To browse, press Shift+F1 and then press Ctrl+F1 repeatedly.
- To scroll any particular help screen, press PgUp or PgDn.
- When help is active, a separate help window opens in addition to the Editor window. You can move the cursor between the help and Editor windows by pressing F6 (or Shift+F6).
- When a help window and Editor window are open simultaneously, you can enlarge or reduce the size of the active window by pressing Alt+plus or Alt+minus. (Here, *plus* and *minus* refer to the + and – keys on the numeric keypad.)
- To cut and paste text from a help screen into your file, first use the normal editing keys to select the text on the help screen. Copy the selected lines to the Clipboard. Press F6 to activate the Editor window and then, using the normal editing keys, paste the help text into your file. Now reactivate the help screen by pressing F6 again.
- When the help system is active, as in all editing contexts, the status bar at the bottom of the screen displays useful keystrokes. If you want to execute a command shown enclosed in angle brackets, press the indicated keystroke or click the mouse when the mouse cursor is on the command name in the status bar.
- The Editor keeps track of the last 20 help screens you have viewed. To cycle back through previously viewed screens, press Alt+F1.
- When you start the Editor, the initial dialog box gives you the option of seeing the Survival Guide. If you press Enter to see the Guide, the help system is activated. A help screen displays information about getting started with the Editor and using the help system.
- The Editor stores the text of the help screens in a file named EDIT.HLP. To display any help screen, the Editor must have access to this file. The Editor searches for EDIT.HLP in the current directory or in directories specified by the PATH statement of your AUTOEXEC.BAT file. Normal DOS installation automatically places this file in the default \DOS directory. If, for some reason, EDIT.HLP is located outside your PATH specifications, however, you can supply the Editor with the path to EDIT.HLP by choosing the Help Path command from the Options menu.

CHAPTER 16

UNDERSTANDING BATCH FILES

In this chapter

Introducing Batch Files   390

Understanding the Contents of Batch Files   391

Creating a Simple Batch File   392

Understanding Replaceable Parameters   393

Using Batch File Commands   397

Pausing for Input in a Batch File   404

Using `FOR..IN..DO`   407

Moving Parameters with `SHIFT`   409

Running Batch Files from Other Batch Files   411

Introducing Batch Files

When you discover that you're repeatedly performing a certain task on your computer, you should look for a way to get the computer to do more of the work. Your computer can perform most tasks faster than you can, and it doesn't make mistakes.

DOS has always enabled you to automate your use of DOS commands by creating *batch files*. A batch file is a text (ASCII) file containing a series of commands that you want DOS to execute. When you type the batch filename, DOS executes these commands in the order they occur within the batch file.

The idea of getting a computer to perform work in convenient, manageable batches pre-dates the personal computer by several years. The earliest computers were large and expensive, and they could do only one job at a time. But even these early machines were fast. Making them wait for keyboard input between jobs was inefficient.

Batch processing was developed to make computers more productive. Collections of tasks to be carried out consecutively were put together offline—that is, without using the computer's resources. The chunks, or batches, of tasks then were fed to the computer at a rate that kept the computer busy and productive.

Today, computers are less expensive than human resources. Batch processing enables computers to carry out a series of tasks automatically so that people don't have to waste time typing frequently used or complex commands.

A batch file is a text file that contains a series of DOS commands. Most commands used in batch files are familiar to you, having been explained in previous chapters of this book. Other commands, which control the flow of action during batch processing are available for use only in batch files. DOS executes the commands in a batch file one line at a time, treating each command as though you issued it individually.

You can use batch files to automate a DOS process. Using a set of commands in a batch file, you actually create a new, more powerful command. After a few experiments, you will find this DOS feature quite handy.

Recognizing a batch file in a directory listing is easy; batch files always have the filename extension BAT. You can execute a batch file by typing the filename at the DOS prompt and then pressing Enter. To execute the batch file SAFE.BAT, for example, you type the following at the DOS prompt and press Enter:

SAFE

COMMAND.COM looks in the current directory for a file named SAFE.COM, then SAFE.EXE, and finally SAFE.BAT. After finding the file, it reads and executes the DOS commands the file contains.

Batch files are useful for issuing frequently used commands whose parameters you have trouble remembering. For example, you can run the Backup program by typing MSBACKUP and then selecting options from the program. But what if you have saved several sets of options in setup files for different circumstances? You can create batch files to run MSBACKUP with the proper setup file when you issue a simple command such as DAILYBAK.

Batch files can echo (display) messages that you designate. This text-display capability is useful for presenting instructions or reminders onscreen. You can compose messages that describe how to execute a command or that contain syntax examples and reminders. Batch files also can use the TYPE command to display text from another file.

In some ways, batch files resemble computer programs. DOS has a host of special commands that are used primarily in batch files. Although you can type some of these commands at the DOS prompt, their main use is in batch files. These commands introduce flow-control and simple decision-making capabilities into a batch file.

Understanding the Contents of Batch Files

Batch files consist entirely of ASCII text characters. You can create batch files in the DOS Editor, in Edlin, and in nearly any other text-editing or word processing program. (If you use a word processing program, you must use a setting that omits the special formatting and control characters that many such programs use for internal purposes.)

The easiest way to create a short batch file, however, is to use the COPY command to redirect input from the keyboard (the CON device) to a file (see Chapter 8, "Managing Your Files," for more information).

When you create batch files, observe the following rules:

- Batch files must be ASCII files. If you use a word processing program, be sure that the program saves the file without formatting characters.
- The name of the batch file, which can be one to eight characters long, must conform to DOS's filename rules. Make batch filenames meaningful so that they are easier to remember.
- The filename must end with the BAT extension.
- The filename cannot be the same as a program filename (a file with an EXE or COM extension).
- The filename cannot be the same as an internal DOS command (such as COPY or DATE).
- The batch file can contain any valid DOS commands that you can enter at the DOS command line (for example – AUTOEXEC.BAT). (Typos cause errors.)
- You can include in the batch file any program name you usually type at the DOS command line. DOS executes the program as though you had entered its name at the command line.
- Use only one command or program name per line in the batch file. DOS executes batch files one line at a time.

You start a batch file by typing its filename (excluding the extension) at the DOS prompt and then pressing Enter. The following list summarizes the rules DOS follows when it executes a batch file:

- When DOS encounters a syntax error in a batch file's command line, DOS displays an error message, skips the incorrect command, and executes the remaining commands in the batch file.

- You can stop a batch file by pressing Ctrl+C or Ctrl+Break. DOS displays the following prompt:
  ```
  Terminate batch job (Y/N)?
  ```
  Type N to skip the current command (the one being carried out) and proceed to the next command in the batch file. Type Y to abort execution of the batch file and return to the DOS prompt.

CREATING A SIMPLE BATCH FILE

Tasks consisting of the same series of commands are ideal candidates for batch files. One task that you might perform repetitively is copying and comparing files.

In this section, you create a simple batch file, using the COPY command to redirect input from the keyboard (the CON device) to create an ASCII text file. (Remember that you also can use the DOS Editor, Edlin, or another text-editing or word processing program to create ASCII text files.)

Suppose that you often work with two spreadsheet files called SALES.WK1 and CUSTOMER.WK1. You frequently update these files and store them in the directory \STORE on drive C. After you update the files, you normally copy them to a disk in drive A and compare the copies on the floppy disk with the originals on the hard disk.

To begin creating a batch file that automates this process, type the following line at the DOS prompt and then press Enter:

```
COPY CON COPYCOMP.BAT
```

This COPY command redirects console (keyboard) input to the file COPYCOMP.BAT. After you press Enter, DOS drops the cursor to the line below the DOS prompt at the left of the screen and then waits for further instructions. Type the following three lines, pressing Enter after each line:

```
@ECHO OFF
COPY C:\STORE A:
FC C:\STORE A:/L
```

After you enter the last line in the file, press F6 or Ctrl+Z (both ways produce the characters ^Z on the screen) to send a signal to DOS that the end of the file has been reached. Then, press Enter. DOS copies the three lines into a file named COPYCOMP.BAT and displays the following message:

```
1 file(s) copied
```

> **Note**
>
> When you use COPY CON to create a text file, check each line before pressing Enter. You can use Backspace and the DOS command-line editing keys (listed in Chapter 3, "Using DOS Commands") to edit the current line. After you press Enter, DOS moves the cursor down to the next line, and you cannot correct any errors in previous lines. You can abort the process without saving the file, however, by pressing Ctrl+C.

The first line of the COPYCOMP batch file, @ECHO OFF, instructs DOS not to display the batch file's commands as they are executed. In other words, when you run the batch file, you do not see the command lines themselves onscreen; you see only the results of their actions. The @ sign, just before the word ECHO, instructs DOS not to display that command line, either. Basically, all you need to remember is that @ stops display of the current line, whereas ECHO OFF stops display of all subsequent lines.

The second line of COPYCOMP.BAT copies the desired files from their source location in C:\STORE to the destination root directory of drive A.

The final line of the batch file uses FC.EXE, an external DOS command that compares the copied files with the originals. Although you can use the /V (verify) switch with COPY, using FC is more thorough.

Now that the COPYCOMP.BAT batch file is complete, you can run the file by typing the following command at the DOS prompt and then pressing Enter:

COPYCOMP

DOS first copies the two files from the C:\STORE directory to drive A and then compares the copies with the original files.

Understanding Replaceable Parameters

The batch files discussed so far in this chapter carry out exactly the same functions every time you use them. You might want a particular batch file to operate on different files each time you use it, even though the commands in the batch file are fixed. When you use replaceable parameters in a batch file, you can use the same commands to perform different tasks.

You already know that a parameter is an additional instruction that defines the task a DOS command will perform. When you type the name of the batch file at the DOS prompt, you can include up to nine parameters. DOS assigns a variable name to each parameter, starting with 1 and going up to 9. (DOS always assigns the variable name 0 to the name of the batch file itself.)

You can use each variable in your batch file by preceding the variable name with the percent sign (%). This combination of the percent sign and variable name is called a *replaceable parameter*.

When used in a batch file, each replaceable parameter, numbered %0 through %9, holds the place for a parameter in one or more commands of a batch file so that you can provide the actual value of the parameter at the time you execute the batch file.

Consider the COPYCOMP.BAT batch file discussed earlier in this chapter:

```
@ECHO OFF
COPY C:\STORE A:
FC C:\STORE A:/L
```

Each time you execute this batch file, it copies all files from the C:\STORE directory to drive A and then compares the files. Suppose that you want to make this batch file more versatile so that you can use it to copy and compare the files in any directory. To do so, revise COPYCOMP.BAT as follows:

```
@ECHO OFF
COPY %1 %2
FC %1 %2 /L
```

Notice that %1 and %2 replace C:\STORE and A:, respectively. These parameters are the replaceable parameters.

After making these changes in COPYCOMP.BAT, you can use the batch file to copy and compare the files from any directory to any disk or directory. To copy and compare the files in the \SPREADSH\QPRO4DAT directory on drive C with the files on a disk in drive B, for example, type the following command and then press Enter:

```
COPYCOMP C:\SPREADSH\QPRO4DAT B:
```

DOS copies all files from C:\SPREADSH\QPRO4DAT to the disk in drive B and then compares the original files with the copies to ensure that the copy procedure was effective.

To see how DOS replaces the parameters, create a batch file called TEST1.BAT that contains the following single line:

```
@ECHO %0 %1 %2 %3 %4 %5 %6 %7 %8 %9
```

After you create this file, type TEST1, followed by one space. Then, type your first name, last name, street address, city, state, ZIP Code, and age, with each entry separated by spaces. Then, press Enter. Your screen should look similar to the following:

```
C\:>TEST1 DAVID SMITH 1234 PINE STREET ANYTOWN IN 46032 39
TEST1 DAVID SMITH 1234 PINE STREET ANYTOWN IN 46032 39
C\:>
```

The batch file command instructs DOS to display the parameters 0 through 9. In the preceding example, these parameters are the following:

Parameter	Word
%0	TEST1
%1	DAVID
%2	SMITH
%3	1234

Parameter	Word
%4	PINE
%5	STREET
%6	ANYTOWN
%7	IN
%8	46032
%9	39

Now try to "shortchange" DOS by not specifying a sufficient number of parameters to fill every variable marker. Run TEST1 again, but this time, type only your first name. Your screen should resemble the following example:

```
C>TEST1 DAVID
TEST1 DAVID
C>
```

DOS displays the batch filename and your first name. No other information is echoed to the screen. You specified fewer parameters, and DOS replaced the unfilled markers with nothing. In this case, the empty markers did no harm.

Some commands you use in a batch file, however, might require that a replaceable parameter contain a value. If you include DEL in a batch file with a replaceable parameter and the parameter is empty, you see the following error message:

```
Invalid number of parameters
```

You can use the IF command (discussed later in this chapter) to avert such errors. In the remainder of this section, you learn how to construct a batch file that takes advantage of replaceable parameters.

Suppose that you use several computers daily, but one of the hard disk systems is your "workhorse," where you store all the files you want to keep. You use floppy disks to move information from computer to computer. After copying a file back to a hard disk, you usually delete the file from the floppy disk. Deleting the file removes it from the process so that the file is not accidentally copied to the hard disk again later. You use the following steps to transfer data from a floppy disk to a hard disk:

1. Copy the file from the floppy disk to the hard disk with the verify switch on.
2. Erase the file from the floppy disk.

To simplify this process, you can create a batch file called C&E.BAT (copy and erase). Type the following commands in the file:

```
COPY A:%1 C:%2 /V
DEL A:%1
```

To use the C&E.BAT file, type the following command at the DOS prompt:

```
C&E oldfilename newfilename
```

The first parameter, *oldfilename*, represents the name of the file you want to copy from the floppy disk to the hard disk; *newfilename* is the new name for the copied file (if you want to change the filename as the file is being copied).

Suppose that you put a disk containing the file NOTES.TXT into drive A and want to copy the file to the hard disk. Type the following command at the DOS prompt:

C&E NOTES.TXT

The screen appears as follows:

```
C>COPY A:NOTES.TXT C: /V
1 file(s) copied
C>DEL A:NOTES.TXT
C>
```

Notice that even though you didn't type the parameter *newfilename*, DOS carried out the batch file, keeping the same filename during the copy. DOS copied NOTES.TXT from drive A to drive C and then deleted the file on the disk in drive A. The %2 parameter was dropped, and the file did not get a new name during the copy operation.

One benefit of creating a batch file that copies a file using parameters is that you can use a pathname as the second parameter. By specifying a pathname, you can copy the file from the floppy disk to a different directory on the hard disk. To copy NOTES.TXT to the WORDS directory, for example, type the following command:

C&E NOTES.TXT \WORDS

The screen display is as follows:

```
C>COPY A:NOTES.TXT C:\WORDS /V
1 file(s) copied
C>DEL A:NOTES.TXT
C>
```

Because \WORDS is a directory name, DOS copies the file NOTES.TXT into the directory \WORDS, following the rules of syntax for the COPY command. The batch file takes advantage of these syntax rules.

Time to Learn

Patience and persistence are important in understanding batch files. Many PC users who tried to avoid using batch files finally experimented with one or two examples; these users picked up the concept rapidly and now produce batch files that anyone would be proud to have created. Give yourself a chance to learn batch files by completing the exercises in this chapter. You can use the sample batch files as templates and apply them to specific situations. When you learn how to compose batch files, you have harnessed one of DOS's most powerful features.

Even if you don't regularly create your own batch files, you can use your knowledge of batch file principles. Many programs are started by batch files rather than by the name of the actual program file. With your knowledge of batch files, you can use the TYPE command to display the contents of any batch file so that you can see what the batch operation is doing.

Many software programs use the commands in an installation batch file to install the main files. You can understand how an installation proceeds if you read the installation batch file. Knowing what the batch file does can help you avert installation conflicts. Suppose that you use drive B to install a program supplied on a 5 1/4-inch disk because your drive A is a 3 1/2-inch drive. Many installation batch files, however, assume that the files are to be installed from drive A. To prevent this conflict, you can modify a version of the installation batch file by changing all instances of A to B. When you run your modified installation batch file, you can install the new software without a hitch.

Working with batch files also can serve as a meaningful introduction to programming. The batch file commands covered in this chapter give batch files the kind of internal flow and decision-making capabilities that programming languages offer. Of course, don't expect batch files to equal the versatility of a full-featured programming environment. But batch files certainly can assume a programming flavor. By using batch files, you can increase DOS's usefulness significantly.

Using Batch File Commands

DOS includes special commands that often are used in batch files. Table 16.1 lists batch file commands.

TABLE 16.1   BATCH FILE COMMANDS

Command	Action
@	Suppresses the display of the command line onscreen
CALL	Runs another batch file and returns to the original batch file
CHOICE	Halts processing until a specified key is pressed (use the IF ERRORLEVEL command to determine which key was pressed)
ECHO	Turns on or off the display of batch commands as they execute; also can display a message onscreen
FOR..IN..DO	Permits the use of the same batch command for several files (the execution "loops")
GOTO	Jumps to the line following the specified label in a batch file
IF	Permits conditional execution of a command
PAUSE	Displays a message and halts processing until a key is pressed
REM	Enables you to insert comments into a batch file that describe the purpose of an operation
SHIFT	Shifts the command-line parameters one parameter to the left

You can use any of the commands listed in Table 16.1 in a batch file; you can use some of them at the DOS system level, as well. For example, you can type ECHO with or without an argument at the DOS prompt. DOS displays the string you type after ECHO or, if you provide no argument, tells you whether echo is on or off. If you type PAUSE at the DOS prompt, DOS displays the following message and waits for a keystroke:

```
Press any key to continue
```

Although these two commands are not very useful at the DOS prompt, the FOR..IN..DO command structure can be quite useful at the operating-system level to carry out repetitive commands (see "Using FOR..IN..DO" later in this chapter).

The following sections explain the batch commands and their uses.

Displaying Messages and Inserting Comments

You already have had an introduction to the ECHO command earlier in this chapter. This command does two things: ECHO ON and ECHO OFF turn on and off the display of lines from batch files as commands are executed, and ECHO also displays messages.

ECHO can display a message up to 122 characters long (the 127-character DOS command-line limit, minus the length of the ECHO command and an additional space).

You can use REM (which stands for *remark*) in a batch file to remind you what the batch file does. When you review a batch file some time after you create it, you might no longer remember why you used certain commands or why you constructed the batch file in a particular way. Leave reminders in your batch file by using REM statements, which don't appear onscreen when echo is off. The REM comments make the batch file self-documenting, a feature that you and other users will appreciate later.

> **Tip**
>
> The REM function is an important feature to use when you're writing batch files. It is a good idea to include remarks with every section in a batch file explaining what the section is doing, such as copying a file from one location to another. These remarks help explain how the batch file works if others need to modify it.
>
> Another important use of the REM function is to comment out a line in a batch file without actually deleting it. This can prove very useful during troubleshooting problems in a batch file.

If you want the batch file to display particular messages, use ECHO. Messages set with ECHO appear onscreen whether or not you set ECHO OFF. To insert a blank line between messages, type a period (but no space) after the ECHO command, as follows:

```
ECHO.
```

Branching with GOTO

When you run a batch file, DOS normally processes commands one line at a time, from the beginning of the batch file to the end. When you use the GOTO command, however, you can change the order in which DOS executes batch commands by instructing DOS to branch to a specific line in the file.

The syntax of GOTO is as follows:

`GOTO label`

The GOTO command uses `label` to specify the place in the file to which DOS should branch. A batch file label is a separate line that is not a command, per se. A label consists of a colon followed by one to eight characters. The label name can be longer than eight characters, but DOS reads only the first eight characters.

When DOS encounters a GOTO command in the batch file, it starts at the beginning of the batch file and searches for a label matching the one specified by GOTO. DOS then branches to the batch file line following the label.

Consider the following batch file, LOOP.BAT. This file is similar to the TEST.BAT batch file you created previously, with the addition of the GOTO and PAUSE commands:

```
@ECHO OFF
:LOOP
   @ECHO Hello, %1
   PAUSE
GOTO LOOP
```

To test the batch file, type the following and press Enter:

`LOOP DAVID`

The screen shows the following message:

```
Hello, DAVID
Press any key to continue_
```

The batch file begins by echoing `Hello, DAVID` and then waits for you to press a key. After you press a key, DOS again displays the following message:

```
Hello, DAVID
Press any key to continue_
```

When you press a key again, DOS executes the GOTO LOOP command, causing execution of the batch file to return to the line labeled :LOOP at the beginning of the file. DOS again displays the message and pauses.

This batch file is an example of what programmers call an *infinite loop*. The program never stops on its own. To abort the batch file, you must press Ctrl+C or Ctrl+Break.

This simple example illustrates the operation of GOTO. You seldom will create infinite loops on purpose, but you should be able to use the GOTO command to control the order in which DOS executes batch file commands.

USING THE IF COMMAND

The IF command is a "test-and-do" command. When a given condition is true, the IF command executes a stated action. When the given condition is false, IF skips the action. If you are familiar with programming languages, such as BASIC, you should recognize the DOS IF command.

The IF command tests the following three conditions:

- The ERRORLEVEL of a program
- Whether a string is equal to another string
- Whether a file exists

The following sections explain these tests.

Using IF to Test ERRORLEVEL

The first condition that IF can test is ERRORLEVEL. The proper syntax for testing the ERRORLEVEL is as follows:

```
IF NOT ERRORLEVEL number command
```

ERRORLEVEL is a code left by a program when it finishes executing. A better name for this condition might be "exit level." This form of the IF command determines whether the value of ERRORLEVEL is greater than or equal to a number specified in the *number* parameter. Conversely, by adding the optional word NOT, you can determine whether the value of ERRORLEVEL is not greater than or equal to the value of the *number* parameter. If the specified condition is true, DOS executes the command specified in the *command* parameter. Otherwise, DOS skips to the next line in the batch file without executing the command.

The only DOS commands that leave an ERRORLEVEL (exit) code are BACKUP, DISKCOMP, DISKCOPY, FORMAT, GRAFTABL, KEYB, REPLACE, RESTORE, and XCOPY. Many other programs generate exit codes, however.

An exit code of zero (0) usually indicates that the command was successful. Any number greater than 0 usually indicates that something went wrong when the program executed. The following exit codes, for example, are generated by the DISKCOPY command:

Code	Meaning
0	The operation was successful.
1	A read/write error that did not terminate the disk-copy operation occurred.
2	The user pressed Ctrl+C.
3	A "fatal" read/write error occurred and terminated the copy procedure before it was completed.
4	An initialization error occurred.

An IF command in a batch file enables you to test for the exit code generated by a DOS command or program to determine whether the command or program worked properly.

When you use ERRORLEVEL to test exit codes, DOS tests whether the code is equal to or greater than the specified number. If the exit code is equal to or greater than the number, DOS executes the *command* parameter. If the code does not meet the condition, DOS skips the *command* parameter and executes the next command in the batch file. You can think of this condition as a BASIC-like statement, as follows:

```
IF exit code >= number THEN do command
```

The `IF ERRORLEVEL` command is most useful with the `CHOICE` command (see "Pausing for Input in a Batch File" later in this chapter). When your batch file uses this utility, the file can pause for keyboard input. The utility puts a value in `ERRORLEVEL` related to the key pressed. You then can make your batch file branch or perform some other task based on the key pressed. A batch file otherwise does not accept keyboard input except when the input is provided on a batch-file command line.

Suppose that you want to create a batch file named `DCOPY.BAT` that makes disk copies in your drive A, using the `DISKCOPY` command and the verify switch. If the disk-copy procedure terminates before completion, you want the batch file to inform you of the cause.

→ For more information about making copies of disks, **see** "Copying Entire Disks with `DISKCOPY`," **p. 210**.

Create a batch file named `DCOPY.BAT` that contains the following lines:

```
@ECHO OFF
DISKCOPY A: A: /V
IF ERRORLEVEL 4 GOTO INIT_ERR
IF ERRORLEVEL 3 GOTO FATL_ERR
IF ERRORLEVEL 2 GOTO CTRL+C
IF ERRORLEVEL 1 GOTO NON_FATL
ECHO DISKCOPY successful and verified!
GOTO END
:INIT_ERR
   ECHO Initialization error!
   GOTO END
:FATL_ERR
   ECHO Fatal error! DISKCOPY stopped!
   GOTO END
:CTRL+C
   ECHO Someone pressed Ctrl+C!
   GOTO END
:NON-FATL
   ECHO A non-fatal error occurred. Check data!
:END
```

To run this batch file, type `DCOPY` at the command line and then press Enter. DOS displays the following message:

```
Insert SOURCE diskette in drive A:
Press any key to continue_
```

When you press a key, DOS begins the disk-copy procedure. After the `DISKCOPY` command in the batch file executes, the batch file runs through a series of `IF ERRORLEVEL` tests. Based on what you already know, these tests are in descending order (4 to 1) because `ERRORLEVEL` considers any number equal to or greater than the specified number to be a match. Thus, if you were to check for 1 first, 4 would also be a match, and you would never get to the proper test.

First, the batch file tests for an initialization error (exit code = 4). If the exit code equals or is greater than 4, DOS skips to the line labeled :INIT_ERR. If the exit code is 3, execution of the batch file skips to the :FATL_ERR label. The batch file branches to the :CTRL_C label if an exit code of 2 is detected, and to the :NON_FATL label when the exit code is 1.

Finally, if no errors are detected by the series of IF ERRORLEVEL commands, the batch file displays the following message:

```
DISKCOPY successful and verified!
```

USING IF TO COMPARE STRINGS

The second use for the IF command is to test whether string 1 equals string 2. The syntax of the batch command is as follows:

```
IF NOT string1==string2 command
```

This form of the IF command determines whether the first character string, *string1*, is the same group of characters as *string2*. Usually, one string is a replaceable parameter. If the two strings are identical, this condition is true and DOS executes the command specified in the command parameter. Otherwise, DOS skips to the next line in the batch file without executing the command. By adding NOT to the IF command, you can test for the condition when the two strings are not the same.

Assume that you want to create a batch file named DAYBACK.BAT that backs up your hard disk each day of the week. On Fridays, you want the batch file to perform a complete backup. On Mondays through Thursdays, you want the batch file to perform an incremental backup. Use the DOS Editor or another text editor to create the following batch file:

```
@ECHO OFF
CLS
IF "%1"=="" GOTO TRY_AGAIN
IF %1==FRI GOTO FULL
IF %1==MON GOTO ADD
IF %1==TUE GOTO ADD
IF %1==WED GOTO ADD
IF %1==THU GOTO ADD
:TRY_AGAIN
    ECHO Try again! Type DAYBACK and day of week (MON-FRI).
    GOTO END
:FULL
    ECHO Insert first disk of backup set.
    PAUSE
    C:
    CD \
    BACKUP C: A: /S
    GOTO END
:ADD
    ECHO Insert last disk of backup set.
    PAUSE
    C:
    CD \
    BACKUP C: A: /S/M/A
:END
```

To run this batch file, type DAYBACK, followed by the three-letter abbreviation for the day of the week (MON, TUE, WED, THU, or FRI), and then press Enter.

The first IF command in DAYBACK.BAT checks to make sure that you have typed the day of the week. If you don't provide enough parameters with the IF command, DOS replaces the replaceable parameter with a null value. (In batch files, null values must be enclosed in quotation marks to prevent a syntax error.)

The remaining IF commands determine whether you typed FRI or another day of the week. If you type FRI, the batch file branches to the :FULL label and performs a full backup. If you typed MON through THU, the file jumps to the :ADD label and performs an additive incremental backup. If you typed anything else, the batch file instructs you to try again.

> **Note**
>
> The :END label often is used to mark the end of the batch file. In the preceding batch file, execution branches to the :END label after a full backup, after an incremental backup, or after you are instructed to try again. When you use this technique, DOS executes only a portion of the batch file each time you run it, skipping the portions of the batch file that don't apply. Because the :END label is the last line in the batch file, the batch file ends at that point.

In the DAYBACK.BAT example, the replaceable parameter in the first IF command is enclosed in quotation marks because programmers commonly use quotation marks to delimit character strings. Actually, a comparison with any letter, number, or symbol can do the job. One common procedure is to use a single period instead of quotation marks, as shown in the following example:

```
IF %1. == . GOTO TRY_AGAIN
```

If you don't enter a parameter for %1, DOS interprets the line as follows:

```
IF . == . GOTO TRY_AGAIN
```

Use the syntax that is easiest for you to remember and understand.

If %1 equals nothing, DOS branches to the line following the label TRY_AGAIN and displays a message. If %1 equals something other than nothing, DOS does not branch to TRY_AGAIN; instead, it executes the second IF command in the batch file, which tests whether you typed DAYBACK FRI, and so on. Notice that GOTO statements are used to jump around the parts of the batch file that DOS should not execute.

When you use the IF command, DOS compares strings literally. Uppercase characters are different from lowercase characters. For example, say you run DAYBACK by typing this command:

```
DAYBACK Fri
```

DOS compares Fri with the uppercase FRI and decides that the two strings are not the same. The IF test fails, and DOS does not perform the backup operation.

Using IF to Look for Files

The third type of `IF` command tests whether a given file is on disk. The syntax for this form of the `IF` command is as follows:

```
IF NOT EXIST filename command
```

This form of the `IF` command determines whether the file specified in the `filename` parameter exists on your computer's disk (or doesn't exist, if you add `NOT`). If the file does exist, the `IF` command executes the command specified in the `command` parameter.

You can use `IF EXIST` when you start a word processing program. Perhaps you use a file called `TEMP.TXT` to store temporary files or write blocks that are to be read into other documents. You can use `IF EXIST` to test for the existence of the file and erase the file if it does exist.

Your batch file, called `WORD.BAT`, would look like the following example:

```
@ECHO OFF
CLS
CD \DOCUMENT
IF EXIST TEMP.TXT DEL TEMP.TXT
CD WORDS
WP
CD \
```

This batch file turns off `ECHO` and clears the screen. The current directory changes to `\DOCUMENT`—the directory where you store your word processing documents.

Next, the `IF` command tests for the existence of `TEMP.TXT`. If the file does exist, DOS deletes the file. Finally, DOS starts your word processing program from the `\WORDS` subdirectory.

Notice the last line of the batch file: `CD \`. When your word processing program starts, the batch file is suspended temporarily. After you quit your word processing program, the batch file regains control. The batch file then executes its last line, `CD \`, which changes back to the root directory. The batch file ends.

Pausing for Input in a Batch File

Before DOS 6.0, the only way to effect the execution of a batch file after the file started was to press Ctrl+C or Ctrl+Break. These key combinations enabled you to cancel a single command or end the entire operation. Starting with DOS 6.0, you are provided a means of temporarily halting the execution of a batch file and accepting limited user input. You can use this feature to decide whether to process certain commands, to branch to a different part of a batch file, or even to present a menu and accept any of a series of choices.

To employ this capability, you use the `CHOICE` command. The command's syntax is as follows:

```
CHOICE /C:choices /N /S /T:c,nn message
```

Following are explanations of the components of this command:

- /C:*choices* lists the keys that can be pressed. If you don't specify choices, the default is YN.
- /N prevents the display of acceptable keys at the end of the prompt.
- /S instructs CHOICE to pay attention to the case of the key pressed; this feature enables you to use Y and y for different choices.
- /T:*c,nn* causes CHOICE to act as though you pressed the key represented by *c* if you don't make a choice within *nn* seconds.
- *message* is the optional prompt to display.

You respond to the key pressed by using a series of IF ERRORLEVEL commands. By default, the choices are Y and N. Y has the ERRORLEVEL code 2, and N has the ERRORLEVEL code 1.

MAKING A TWO-WAY CHOICE

If you don't specify which keys should be pressed, CHOICE assumes Y and N, and adds [Y,N]? to the end of whatever message you choose to include. This feature is extremely useful if you want to decide whether to load a certain program when your computer starts. For example, you might type the following commands near the end of your AUTOEXEC.BAT file:

```
CHOICE Back up hard disk
IF ERRORLEVEL 2 MSBACKUP
```

When the AUTOEXEC.BAT file reaches the first line, DOS displays the following message:

```
Back up hard disk[Y,N]?
```

If you have not yet backed up your hard disk today, you type Y, which generates the ERRORLEVEL code 2. DOS then executes the MSBACKUP program. If you have backed up your hard disk, type N. You need not test for this code, however, because it's the only other alternative. DOS then executes any commands following these lines in AUTOEXEC.BAT, but MSBACKUP doesn't run.

CREATING A SIMPLE MENU

Because you can specify any keys as choices, you can use CHOICE to create a simple menu, using the /C:*choices* parameter to specify the keys to be pressed. You might use a command such as the following:

```
CHOICE /c:swd Load Spreadsheet, Word Processor, or Database Manager
```

DOS displays the following message:

```
Load Spreadsheet, Word Processor, or Database Manager[S,W,D]?
```

The ERRORLEVEL codes for the specified keys read from left to right. Thus, pressing D generates a code 3; pressing W, a code 2; and pressing S, a code 1. These exit codes are then processed by batch file lines such as the following:

```
IF ERRORLEVEL 3 DB
IF ERRORLEVEL 2 WP
IF ERRORLEVEL 1 SS
```

This assumes that your database program is named DB, your word processor is named WP, and your spreadsheet is named SS. There is a problem with this, however. The IF ERRORLEVEL command automatically assumes that all numbers higher than the one specified also are true. If you type D, for example, DOS loads your word processing program as soon as you exit from your database manager and your spreadsheet program as soon as you exit from your word processing program.

You can deal with this situation in either of two ways. One way is to add a second command that changes the flow of execution. Your file would have to resemble the following example:

```
CHOICE /C:swd Load Spreadsheet, Word Processor, or Database Manager
IF ERRORLEVEL 3 DB
IF ERRORLEVEL 3 GOTO END
IF ERRORLEVEL 2 WP
IF ERRORLEVEL 2 GOTO END
IF ERRORLEVEL 1 SS
:END
```

The second way to deal with the limitation of the ERRORLEVEL directive is to have each test execute a batch file instead of a program. (After you pass control to a second batch file, DOS does not return to the original file unless you use CALL or COMMAND /C.) For this command to work properly, the batch files must appear either in the current directory or in a directory in the path that precedes the directories containing the programs.

Always give a user a way to get out of a command without choosing any of the proffered alternatives. The user, of course, can break out of the CHOICE command by pressing Ctrl+C or Ctrl+Break. But you also can include a third alternative, such as Quit, as shown in the following example:

```
CHOICE /C:YNQ Back up hard disk
IF ERRORLEVEL 3   GOTO END
IF ERRORLEVEL 2   GOTO END
IF ERRORLEVEL 1   MSBACKUP
other commands
:END
```

CREATING A SIMPLE DISPLAY MENU

You can use the other switches provided with CHOICE to create a display menu. You create text to explain the choices and suppress the display of characters at the end of the optional message. You might create a batch file called MENU.BAT and type the following commands:

```
@ECHO OFF
CLS
ECHO;
ECHO;
ECHO Press S to load Spreadsheet
ECHO Press W to load Word Processor
ECHO Press D to load Database Manager
ECHO Press Q to quit
ECHO;
CHOICE /C:SWDQ /N /T:Q,10 Your choice?
IF ERRORLEVEL 4 GOTO END
IF ERRORLEVEL 3 GOTO DB
```

```
IF ERRORLEVEL 2 GOTO WP
   ECHO Loading spreadsheet program_
   SS
   GOTO END
:WP
   ECHO Loading word processing program_
   WP
   GOTO END
:DB
   ECHO Loading database management program_
   DB
:END
```

Notice that no ERRORLEVEL choice is available for times the user presses S (the ERRORLEVEL would be 1) because there is no need to branch in this case. Instead, execution of the batch file falls through to the first line after the last ERRORLEVEL statement, which is the command for the spreadsheet section.

When you type the MENU command, DOS clears the screen and displays the following message:

```
Press S to load Spreadsheet
Press W to load Word Processor
Press D to load Database Manager
Press Q to quit
Your choice?
```

If no key is pressed within 10 seconds, the CHOICE command issues a Q, and the DOS prompt returns.

You can construct very elaborate menus by using the ASCII box-drawing characters, ANSI Escape sequences (to establish colors), and the CHOICE command.

→ For a discussion of the uses of ANSI.SYS, **see** Chapter 17, "Understanding ANSI.SYS," **p. 415**.

USING FOR..IN..DO

FOR..IN..DO is an unusual and extremely powerful batch command. The command's syntax is as follows:

`FOR %%variable IN (set) DO command`

variable is a one-letter name that takes on the value of each item in *set*. You can use this command from the DOS prompt as well as within a batch file. When you use the command at the DOS prompt, however, use only one percent sign (%) instead of two (%%) in front of *variable*. You must use two percent signs in a batch file so that DOS does not confuse *variable* with a replaceable parameter.

The *set* parameter is the list of items, commands, or disk files whose value you want variable to take. You can use wildcard filenames with this parameter. You also can use drive names and paths with any filenames you specify. If you have more than one item in the set, use a space or comma between the names.

The *command* parameter is any valid DOS command that you want to perform for each item in *set*.

Using a FOR..IN..DO Batch File

An interesting example of the use of FOR..IN..DO is a batch file that compares filenames found on a disk in drive A with the filenames found on another disk and then produces a list of the files on both disks. Create the batch file CHECKIT.BAT, entering the following lines:

```
@ECHO OFF
CLS
IF "%1"=="" GOTO END
FOR %%a IN (B: C: D: E: b: c: d: e:) DO IF "%%a"=="%1" GOTO COMPARE
ECHO Syntax error: You must specify a disk to compare.
ECHO Be sure to leave a space before directory.
GOTO END
:COMPARE
   %1
   IF "%2"=="" GOTO SKIP
   CD %2
:SKIP
   ECHO The following files are on both disks:
   FOR %%a IN (*.*) DO IF EXIST A:%%a ECHO %%a
:END
```

Insert into drive A the disk that you want to compare and then use the following syntax:

CHECKIT *drive directory*

drive is the drive that contains the other disk that you want to compare, and *directory* is the directory that you want to compare. This batch file substitutes the drive you specify for %1 in the batch file commands and substitutes any directory you specify for %2. The directory is optional; if you specify a drive and directory, separate their names with a space. Otherwise, the batch file treats the drive and directory as one replaceable parameter (%1). If you don't specify a directory name, DOS compares the current directory of the drive with the current directory of the disk in drive A.

Suppose that you want to compare the list of files in drive A with the list of files in the \GAMES directory in drive B. Type the following command at the command line:

CHECKIT B: \GAMES

The batch file determines which files in the \GAMES directory of the disk in drive B also are on the current directory of the disk in drive A.

When the CHECKIT batch file is called, DOS first determines whether %1 is empty. (%1 is empty if you typed no drive letter or directory after CHECKIT in the command line.) If %1 is empty, the batch file displays an error message, branches to the end of the file, and quits without performing a comparison.

If you specify a disk drive, DOS goes to the third line of the batch file and determines whether the drive letter is a valid drive letter. In this batch file, valid drive letters are B, C, D, E, b, c, d, and e. If no valid drive letter is found, or if you don't include a colon (:) and space after the drive letter, the batch file displays a message and branches to the end of the batch file.

If you specified a valid drive, CHECKIT branches to the :COMPARE section of the program. When executing the first line in this section, DOS logs on to the drive you specified in the command line (the drive designation replaces %1 in the batch file). The batch file determines whether you included a directory parameter; if you did include this parameter, DOS changes to that directory.

Finally, the batch file displays a message and then looks at all the filenames in the current directory to see whether a file with the same name exists in drive A. For every match found, the batch file lists the filename.

Using FOR..IN..DO at the DOS Prompt

You might find that you want to issue commands such as the ones in CHECKIT at the DOS prompt. Instead of using the batch file for the preceding example, you can change subdirectories manually and then type the FOR..IN..DO line (the line that does all the work in the batch file) at the DOS prompt. If you do use FOR..IN..DO outside a batch file, DOS requires that you enter only one percent sign.

Using FOR..IN..DO with Other Commands

FOR..IN..DO works as well with commands as with filenames. Instead of naming a set of files, you can name a series of commands that you want DOS to carry out. Consider the following example:

```
FOR %%a IN (COPY DEL) DO %%a C:*.*
```

In a batch file, this line first copies all the files on drive C to the current directory and then erases the files from drive C. Instead of specifying the drive and file, you can use a replaceable parameter in the line, as follows:

```
FOR %%a IN (COPY DEL) DO %%a %1
```

To use this batch file, you first must change to the destination directory (for example, D:\BAK). When you invoke this version of the batch file, you type the names of the files that you want to copy and remove. If you name the batch file MOVER.BAT, you can type the following command to invoke the file:

```
MOVER C:\WP
```

MOVER.BAT copies all the files in the subdirectory C:\WP to D:\BAK and then erases the files in C:\WP. This file works much like the C&E.BAT file you created earlier in this chapter.

Moving Parameters with SHIFT

The SHIFT command moves the parameters in the command line that invoked the batch file; each parameter moves one parameter to the left. SHIFT tricks DOS into accepting more than 9 replaceable parameters (10 if you include the batch filename, which is %0). The diagram of SHIFT is as follows:

```
%0   ←%1   ←%2   ←%3   ←%4   ←%5...
↓
bit bucket
```

In this diagram, parameter 0 is dropped. The old parameter 1 becomes parameter 0. The old parameter 2 becomes parameter 1; parameter 3 becomes 2; parameter 4 becomes 3; and so on. A command-line parameter that previously was 10th in line and not assigned a parameter number now becomes parameter 9.

The following batch file, SHIFTIT.BAT, is a simple example of the use of the SHIFT command:

```
@ECHO OFF
CLS
:START
ECHO %0 %1 %2 %3 %4 %5 %6 %7 %8 %9
SHIFT
PAUSE
IF NOT "%0"=="" GOTO START
```

Suppose that you type the following text:

```
SHIFTIT A B C D E F G H I J K L M N O P Q R S T U V W X Y Z
```

The screen shows the following message:

```
SHIFTIT A B C D E F G H I
Press any key to continue_
```

Notice that the batch filename is displayed because %0 holds the name of the batch file. Press a key to continue; DOS now displays the following message:

```
A B C D E F G H I J
Press any key to continue_
```

In this case, the filename has been dropped into the bit bucket. %0 now equals A. All the parameters have shifted one to the left. Each time you press a key to continue, SHIFT continues moving down the list of parameters you typed. When the leftmost parameter (%0) is empty, the batch file ends.

SHIFT has many uses. You can use it to build a new version of the C&E.BAT file you created earlier in this chapter. The following modified version of the copy-and-erase batch file, called MOVE.BAT, shows a use for SHIFT:

```
@ECHO OFF
CLS
:LOOP
COPY %1 /V
ERASE %1
SHIFT
IF NOT "%1" == "" GOTO LOOP
```

This batch file copies and erases the specified file or files. The batch file assumes nothing about the files to be copied; you can specify a disk drive, path, and filename. The batch file copies the files to the current directory and then erases the files from the original disk or directory.

The last two lines shift the parameters to the left, determine whether any parameters remain, and then repeat the operation if necessary.

Running Batch Files from Other Batch Files

On some occasions, you might want to run a batch file from another batch file. Running batch files from within batch files is particularly useful when you want to create a menu batch file that can start several different programs.

The following sections discuss three ways to run batch files from other batch files. One method is a one-way transfer of control. The other two methods involve running a second batch file and returning control to the first batch file. These techniques are useful if you want to build menus with batch files or use one batch file to set up and start another batch file.

Shifting Control Permanently to Another Batch File

The first method of calling a second batch file is simple: Include the root name of the second batch file as a line in the first batch file. The first batch file runs the second batch file as though you had typed the second batch file's root name at the DOS prompt.

To run BATCH2.BAT, for example, include in BATCH1.BAT the following line:

BATCH2

DOS loads and executes BATCH2.BAT. Control passes in only one direction: from the first batch file to the second. When BATCH2.BAT finishes executing, DOS displays the system prompt. Control goes to the second file but doesn't come back to the first file.

Calling a Batch File and Returning Using CALL

After your batch file is debugged, you can use the CALL statement to run a batch file and then return to the original one. The syntax of the CALL command is as follows:

CALL *filename parameters*

filename is the root name of the batch file. When you type the CALL command, you can specify any parameters that you want to pass to the batch file you are calling. You can place the CALL command anywhere in the first batch file.

When DOS executes a CALL command, DOS temporarily shifts execution to the called batch file. As soon as the called batch file is completed, DOS returns to the first batch file and continues execution with the line immediately following the CALL command.

The following three batch files demonstrate how CALL works:

```
BATCH1.BAT
@ECHO OFF
CLS
REM This file does the setup work for
REM demonstrating the CALL command.
ECHO This is the STARTUP batch file
ECHO The command parameters are %%0-%0 %%1-%1
CALL batch2 second
ECHO MEM from %0
MEM
ECHO Done!
```

BATCH2.BAT

```
ECHO This is the SECOND batch file
ECHO The command parameters are %%0-%0 %%1-%1
CALL batch3 third
ECHO MEM from %0
MEM
```

BATCH3.BAT

```
 ECHO This is the THIRD batch file
ECHO The command parameters are %%0-%0 %%1-%1
ECHO MEM from %0
MEM
```

The first line of BATCH1.BAT sets ECHO OFF. The second line clears the screen. The next two lines in BATCH1 are remarks intended only to document the purpose of the batch file.

The two ECHO lines are similar for all three batch files. The first of the two lines identifies the batch file being used. The second ECHO line shows the %0 parameter (the name by which the batch file was invoked) and the first parameter (the first argument) for the batch file. Notice that to display the strings %0 and %1, you must use two percent signs (%%0 and %%1). If you use a single percent sign, DOS interprets the string as a replaceable parameter and does not display the actual percent symbol.

Each CALL statement in the first and second batch files invokes another batch file. BATCH1.BAT calls BATCH2.BAT, and BATCH2.BAT in turn calls BATCH3.BAT. In each case, a single argument passes to the batch file being called: second to BATCH2.BAT and third to BATCH3.BAT. Each batch file then displays its name (by using the %0 variable) and runs MEM. When DOS reaches the end of each called batch file, DOS returns to the calling batch file.

Check the printout or screen display for the largest executable program size provided by the MEM command (in other words, the largest block of memory available for use by an executable program). This number grows larger after each batch file is executed and removed from memory.

Each time you use the CALL command, DOS temporarily uses 80 bytes of RAM until the called batch file finishes running. Because DOS uses that much memory for each nested CALL command, you can run out of memory. (A nested CALL command is a CALL command from a called batch file.) Not many people nest CALL commands deeply in batch files. The accumulated memory-usage problem does not occur when a single batch file calls multiple other batch files. In that case, you can use the CALL command as many times as you want and use only the same 80 bytes of RAM for each call.

Using COMMAND.COM to Execute a Batch File

In all versions of DOS, you can call a second batch file from the first, execute the second batch file, and return to the first batch file. In DOS 3.0 through 3.2, you use COMMAND /C. In DOS 3.3 and later versions, you use the CALL command, discussed in the following section.

→ For more information on COMMAND /C, **see** "Loading a Secondary Command Processor," **p. 288**.

Although it might appear at first glance that you no longer need to use the COMMAND.COM method of running a batch file, beginning with DOS 6.2 there is a compelling new reason. That is, with DOS 6.2, you can use COMMAND.COM's /Y switch, in conjunction with /C, to single-step through a batch file. Suppose you execute the following command line:

COMMAND /Y /C NEW.BAT

When you do so, DOS loads a copy of the command processor and executes NEW.BAT. As it executes, each line in the batch file is displayed, and you are asked whether you want to execute it. You use this same process when you interactively execute the AUTOEXEC.BAT file, as described in Chapter 2, "Starting DOS."

This interactive execution capability is a great debugging tool for complex batch files. When the entire batch file is through running, DOS exits the command processor and returns to the original batch file.

CHAPTER 17

UNDERSTANDING ANSI.SYS

In this chapter

What Is ANSI.SYS? 416

Installing ANSI.SYS 416

Using ANSI.SYS 416

Controlling Your Screen with ANSI.SYS 419

Customizing Your Keyboard with ANSI.SYS 423

ANSI Control Codes 425

What Is ANSI.SYS?

The term *ANSI* refers to the *American National Standards Institute*. ANSI is one of several sets of computer standards established by the institute to specify the codes that computer manufacturers can use to control video displays and keyboard mapping.

ANSI.SYS is a device driver, which means that it gives DOS additional control of the screen and keyboard devices beyond the control features built into the operating system. You use ANSI.SYS to enhance the functions of your video screen and keyboard. With ANSI.SYS, you can set screen colors, use graphics, and specify other video attributes. You can provide that personal touch to your DOS prompt. You even can change the assignments of keys on your keyboard.

The ANSI.SYS file supplied with MS-DOS contains a subset of the ANSI standards. Third-party suppliers of other ANSI.SYS files might include more features in their versions of this file, but those features are not necessary for most users.

Installing ANSI.SYS

The only way you can install the ANSI.SYS driver is to include it in your CONFIG.SYS file. The format of the line must be one of the following:

```
DEVICE = C:\DOS\ANSI.SYS /X /K /R
DEVICEHIGH = C:\DOS\ANSI.SYS /X /K /R
```

The /X switch enables you to remap extended keys if you are using a 101-key keyboard. The /K switch treats 101-key keyboards as if they were 84-key keyboards, ignoring extended keys. The /R switch slows screen scrolling for improved readability.

> **Tip**
> The /X and /K switches are mutually exclusive because you cannot define a 101-key and 84-key keyboard at the same time.

When you install MS-DOS on your computer, DOS places the ANSI.SYS file in the \DOS subdirectory. If ANSI.SYS is located in the root directory of your boot drive, you don't have to include its drive and directory name in the command line. If you placed the ANSI.SYS file in another directory or on another drive, however, be sure that you specify the exact location of ANSI.SYS in the CONFIG.SYS statement.

In the following sections, you will learn how to use the ANSI.SYS driver and take advantage of its features.

Using ANSI.SYS

You must place the ANSI.SYS command in the CONFIG.SYS file to load the driver and reboot the system so that the new configuration takes effect, you must issue commands that tell DOS to use the ANSI features.

Because some software is written to use ANSI codes, one or more of your programs might require that ANSI.SYS be loaded. The installation procedure for this type of software notifies you of this requirement. (The program might even install the command in the CONFIG.SYS file for you.)

You can activate ANSI.SYS features also by issuing the ANSI commands yourself. However, you cannot simply type the commands at the DOS prompt; you must enter an Escape sequence. All ANSI.SYS sequences begin with the Escape character (ASCII value 27), followed by a left bracket ([). If you type this sequence at the prompt, DOS understands the Escape character to be a command to cancel the current operation; DOS cancels the operation, displays a backslash (\), and moves the cursor down to the next line.

If ANSI.SYS codes are not included in a program, you can send these codes to DOS in three ways: by executing a batch file, by typing a text file (that is, by using the DOS TYPE command), or by including the codes in a PROMPT command. When you embed ANSI codes in Escape sequences, the ANSI.SYS device driver intercepts the codes and executes the appropriate commands, ignoring any characters that are not preceded by the proper codes.

You can create a text file or batch file or set up your PROMPT format in the AUTOEXEC.BAT file by using the MS-DOS editor (EDIT) or another text editor. Whatever utility you use must be capable of entering the Escape character, which is beyond the capability of many word processing programs and older text editors.

To enter the Escape character while using EDIT, hold down the Ctrl key, press P, and then press Esc.

→ For information on using EDIT, **see** Chapter 15, "Using the DOS Editor," **p. 361**.

> **Note**
> Some text editors display the Escape character as ^[. Because the ANSI code sequence requires a left bracket after the Escape character, the ANSI sequence might appear as ^[[.

ISSUING ANSI.SYS CODES IN BATCH FILES

The key to using ANSI.SYS is to have the Escape sequences sent to the display screen. This procedure is the only way to ensure that the device driver properly intercepts and executes the commands. Batch files send these sequences to the screen through the ECHO command, which tells DOS to display all commands on the screen.

→ For more information on batch files, **see** Chapter 16, "Understanding Batch Files," **p. 389**.

> **Note**
> By default, ECHO is set ON unless you explicitly issue an ECHO OFF command. If you do use ECHO OFF, any ANSI code line you enter thereafter must begin with the ECHO command.

Suppose that you want to use a batch file to set up formatting for a double-density disk (360KB) in a 5 1/4-inch high-density (1.2MB) drive. You use EDIT to create the batch file containing the instruction for the special effect, such as changing the color of the screen. Entering the following batch file and giving it the name NEWDISK.BAT do the trick:

```
@ECHO OFF
ECHO <Esc>[37;41m
ECHO THIS FUNCTION FORMATS DOUBLE DENSITY DISKETTES (360K) IN DRIVE A:
FORMAT A:  /F:360
ECHO <Esc>[37;40m
```

The first line in the batch file tells DOS not to display any of the commands in the batch file unless specifically instructed to do so through the ECHO command. The leading character (@) instructs DOS not to display the ECHO OFF command.

The second line is an ANSI.SYS code sequence that sets the color of the screen (red, with white characters). Replace <Esc> with the actual Escape code (ASCII value 27). The ANSI code 37 produces a white foreground; 41 is the ANSI code for a red background. The character m indicates that screen attribute codes are being issued. The last line of the batch file resets the screen to white on black—the default setting. (Make sure that you use the lowercase character m in the ANSI.SYS Escape sequences.)

> **Tip**
>
> If you have a monochrome monitor, you can substitute 7m for 37;41m in the second line of the batch file. The code 7 tells ANSI.SYS to set reverse video. If you use 7m instead of 37;41m, substitute 0m for 37;40m in the last line to set the screen back to normal.

To see why you must use the ECHO command in the ANSI Escape sequence, remove the ECHO command from the last line of the batch file, and then run the file again. The ECHO command is required to pass the codes to the display. If it is not available, DOS informs you that it received a bad command or filename, and the screen color does not change to normal.

Issuing ANSI.SYS Codes in Text Files

Issuing ANSI codes in text files is similar to using the codes in batch files, except that you do not use an ECHO command in a text file. Also, for the commands to take effect, you must use the TYPE command to pass the codes to the display for DOS to execute. To look at a sample text file, create a SCREEN.TXT file that contains the following line:

```
<Esc>[37;41m
```

After you create and save this file, you can change the screen to red with white characters by entering the following command at the DOS prompt:

```
TYPE SCREEN.TXT
```

ANSI.SYS intercepts the characters of the file when being sent to the screen with the TYPE command. The Escape sequence, followed by the bracket, causes the device driver to execute the ANSI commands instead of passing the characters through to DOS. Your screen is now red with white characters.

You can return your screen to normal as follows. In the same way that you created SCREEN.TXT, create NORMAL.TXT with the following single line:

```
<Esc>[37;40m
```

After you enter this line, save the file. At the DOS prompt, enter the following to return your screen to normal:

```
TYPE NORMAL.TXT
```

ISSUING ANSI.SYS CODES WITH THE PROMPT COMMAND

The third way to issue ANSI.SYS instructions is to include these instructions in a PROMPT command. You learned about the PROMPT command in Chapter 11, "Controlling Your Environment." In short, the PROMPT command alters the way the DOS prompt appears. The normal syntax of the command is as follows:

```
PROMPT string
```

The *string* consists of a set of characters that might or might not include an ANSI Escape sequence. The characters you enter tell DOS how you want the DOS prompt to look. For full information on the characters you can use with the command, refer to Chapter 11. This section focuses on using the ANSI sequences with the PROMPT command.

To add more pizzazz to your DOS prompt, you can add color, as outlined in the following examples. If you have a color monitor, enter the following command, using nine spaces for the nine periods:

```
PROMPT $E[1;37;44mTime: $T$H$H$H$H$H$H.........$E[40m$E[K$_$E[1;44mDate:
➥ $D$E[0;40m$E[K$_[DOS 6.2] $P$G
```

The display shows the time and date in bright white text on a blue background, returning to normal white on black for the prompt.

If you have a monochrome monitor, enter the following command, using nine spaces for the nine periods:

```
PROMPT $E[7mTime: $T$H$H$H$H$H$H.........$E[0m$E[K$_$E[7mDate:
➥$D$E[0m$E[K$_[DOS 6.2] $P$G
```

The display now shows the time and date in black characters on a white background, returning to normal white on black for the prompt.

As the inclusion of [DOS 6.2] in these two examples indicates, you also can display a message in the DOS prompt. (The brackets are included for cosmetic purposes only. They are not required.) Be creative. *Beam me up, Scotty*; *The BRAIN*; *USA Forever*; and *BOOM!* are a few examples of DOS users' humor and imagination.

CONTROLLING YOUR SCREEN WITH ANSI.SYS

Now that you understand how to issue ANSI.SYS commands in batch files, in text files, and as part of a PROMPT command, you're ready to use ANSI.SYS commands to control and customize your screen display.

All ANSI screen commands begin with the normal Escape code and a left bracket ([) and end with a letter of the alphabet. The letter depends on the type of command you are asking ANSI.SYS to execute. In all instances, the capitalization of the ending letter is important. As you are working through the examples in this chapter, pay strict attention to the capitalization.

You can use as many ANSI control codes as you require on the same line, as long as the codes are separated by semicolons (;) and no code contradicts another code. The order of the codes is not important.

The following sections detail the general functions that can be performed with ANSI.SYS.

Cursor Movement

If you end the Escape sequence with the uppercase letter *A*, ANSI.SYS assumes you want to move the cursor up a given number of lines on the screen. For instance, the following line moves the cursor up four lines on the screen:

`<Esc>[4A`

The horizontal position of the cursor is not affected; it only moves up. If the cursor is already at the top of the screen, the Escape code is ignored.

If you end the Escape sequence with a *B* (instead of an *A*), the cursor is moved down on the screen. Again, if the cursor is already at the bottom of the screen, the sequence is ignored.

Ending the Escape sequence with a *C* moves the cursor to the right by the number of indicated spaces; a *D* moves the cursor left. For example, the following line moves the cursor 23 spaces to the right:

`<Esc>[23C`

Cursor Positioning

To position the cursor at a given character location on the screen, you can use either the *H* or *f* codes. For instance, either of the following moves the cursor to line 10, column 32:

`<Esc>[10;32H`

`<Esc>[10;32f`

Note that the upper-left corner of the screen is considered position 0,0.

To save the current cursor position (in preparation for moving and later restoring it), you use the *s* code, as shown here:

`<Esc>[s`

There are no other parameters; the cursor position is immediately saved. When you want to restore the cursor to the saved position, use the *u* code:

`<Esc>[u`

Setting the Screen Mode

You can use ANSI.SYS to change the display mode of your system. You do so by providing a screen code and ending the sequence with the *h* code. The screen codes are listed in Table 17.1.

TABLE 17.1 ANSI SCREEN DISPLAY CODES

Code	Screen Type
0	40×25 characters, monochrome
1	40×25 characters, color
2	80×25 characters, monochrome
3	80×25 characters, color
4	320×200 pixels, monochrome
5	320×200 pixels, color
6	640×200 pixels, monochrome
7	Turns word wrap on and off
14	640×200 pixels, color
15	640×360 pixels, monochrome
16	640×360 pixels, color
17	640×480 pixels, monochrome
18	640×480 pixels, color
19	320×200 pixels, color

For example, the following line sets the screen mode to 80×25 color text:

`<Esc>[3h`

You can end the sequence also with a lowercase *l*; the only difference is in how screen code 7 is handled. With the *h* code, line wrap is turned on; with *l*, it is turned off. For instance, the following turns on 80×25 monochrome text with screen wrapping disabled:

`<Esc>[2;7l`

Setting the Text Attributes

Text attributes include color, bold, or reverse video. To set these attributes, list the desired attribute codes, separated by semicolons, and then terminate the Escape sequence with the *m* code. Table 17.2 lists the ANSI codes for setting the character attributes.

Table 17.2 Character Attribute Codes

Code	Effect
0	Normal display (the default)
1	High-intensity text
4	Underlined text (monochrome)
5	Blinking text
7	Reverse video (black on white)
8	Hidden text (black on black)
30	Black foreground (character) color
31	Red foreground (character) color
32	Green foreground (character) color
33	Yellow foreground (character) color
34	Blue foreground (character) color
35	Magenta foreground (character) color
36	Cyan foreground (character) color
37	White foreground (character) color
40	Black background color
41	Red background color
42	Green background color
43	Yellow background color
44	Blue background color
45	Magenta background color
46	Cyan background color
47	White background color

> **Note:** Some screen effects depend on the hardware. Underlined text, for example, cannot be displayed on all monitors.

You can use the codes in Table 17.2 to customize your system. You can, for example, use ANSI codes to set the default screen colors to bright green on black:

```
<Esc>[1;32;40m
```

Screen Control

Besides the functions discussed so far, `ANSI.SYS` also provides functions that you can use to control your screen. You can use the following ANSI code to clear the screen. It is the equivalent of the `CLS` command:

`<Esc>[2J`

If you want to erase only to the end of the current line, the following does the trick:

`<Esc>[K`

Customizing Your Keyboard with ANSI.SYS

Computers use a set of 256 codes to indicate specific characters. These codes make up the *ASCII character set*. (*ASCII* is an acronym for the *American Standard Code for Information Interchange*.) A space, for example, is ASCII code 48; the uppercase *A* is ASCII code 65; and the lowercase *a* is ASCII code 97. You already know that the Escape code used in an ANSI control sequence has an ASCII value of 27. (See Appendix E, "ASCII and Extended ASCII Codes," for a list of ASCII codes.)

Every time you press a key on your keyboard, the system's circuits send a code to DOS. This code interprets the keystroke and displays the appropriate character. Not every code in the ASCII set, however, has a corresponding keyboard key. Moreover, some keys represent more than one character.

Keyboards actually send individual codes to DOS for each key or key combination you press on the keyboard. These codes are known as *scan codes*. Many scan codes correspond to ASCII codes. With the key combinations that involve the Ctrl, Alt, Shift, and Num Lock keys, however, more than 256 keystrokes (the ASCII code limit) are possible. This problem is solved by preceding some scan codes with a 0 entry.

When DOS receives a scan code from the keyboard, the program uses a built-in table to ascertain the proper character. When the `ANSI.SYS` device driver has been loaded through the `CONFIG.SYS` file, the ANSI driver takes over this chore. The driver also enables you to modify the table and assign different characters to the scan codes.

Suppose that you must prepare documents or data files that include fractions. You can assign ASCII codes for some fractions to keys that you normally don't use. ASCII code 171, for example, stands for 1/2, and code 172 stands for 1/4. (See Appendix E for a complete list of ASCII codes.) Using `ANSI.SYS` makes key reassignments easy.

To assign the 1/2 fraction (ASCII 171) to the Shift+6 key combination, which produces the character ^ (ASCII 94), you can use either of the following commands:

`<Esc>["^";"1/2"p`

`<Esc>[94;171p`

The ANSI.SYS keyboard-assignment Escape sequence starts with the standard Escape character, followed by a left bracket ([). The next character is the ASCII code, scan code, or key representation in quotation marks. Then you specify the new ASCII code or key representation in quotation marks. The two characters are separated by a semicolon. The sequence ends with the lowercase *p* code. Thus, in the first example, the key representation ^ is entered with quotation marks ("^") and is changed to "1/2". In the second example, scan code 171 replaces scan code 94.

> **Caution**
>
> Do not use spaces in the ANSI.SYS code sequence. If you use spaces, DOS might not interpret the sequence properly.

Remember that the first specification is for the key to be assigned. To restore the original key assignment, enter the code twice, as in this example:

```
<Esc>[94;94p
```

A key assignment does not need to be a single character. You also can assign a text message to a keystroke. This process is referred to as a *macro substitution*. If you often need to type the same sequence of characters, you can easily set up a macro substitution that enters those characters for you. Don't confuse this with the macro capability of DOSKEY, however. Macros that can be created with DOSKEY are much more powerful than those created with ANSI.SYS.

In the following example, the words *Heigh-Ho, Silver!* are assigned to the F7 key, which has the scan code 0;65:

```
<Esc>[0;65;"Heigh-Ho, Silver!"p
```

After you issue this ANSI.SYS instruction, either in a text file you type or a batch file, DOS (through ANSI.SYS) displays the message Heigh-Ho, Silver! whenever you press F7.

Because no scan code or ASCII code of 0 exists, ANSI.SYS understands that the second number indicates the extended scan code for the F7 key instead of the ASCII code for the uppercase *A*, which is 65. If you want to add a carriage return (ASCII code 13) after the message, include that code in the Escape sequence as follows:

```
<Esc>[0;65;"Heigh-Ho, Silver!";13p
```

You can enter many of the ASCII character codes on your keyboard by holding down the Alt key while you type the ASCII code for the character you want to display. If you reassign keys, however, you no longer can enter certain key characters in this manner. Further, reassigned keys no longer function the same way. If you reassign the backslash key (\), for example, you no longer can use the backslash character to access subdirectories.

REASSIGNING CHARACTER KEYS

ANSI.SYS reassignment of normal character keys on your keyboard is not a good idea. Such a reassignment interferes with the normal operation of DOS and with many, if not all, of your software programs.

> **Caution**
>
> When you use ANSI.SYS to reassign keys, keep in mind that DOS allows a total of 200 characters. If your key reassignments take more than 200 bytes, you overwrite part of the command processor in memory and your system might lock up.

ANSI Control Codes

All ANSI commands are prefixed by two characters: the Escape character (ASCII 27) and the left square bracket (ASCII 91). Because the Escape keypress usually is interpreted as a command, inserting it in a text file might require you to enter a special command, such as Ctrl+P, before your text editor will accept it as text.

Uppercase and lowercase are significant in these commands, so you must type them exactly as indicated. In commands that allow a variable number of codes, separate each code with a semicolon.

ANSI Set and Reset Display Mode Control Codes

Set mode codes end in a lowercase h as shown. Reset mode codes substitute a lowercase l for the h. Not all displays support all screen modes, and other modes might be available for your display:

<Esc>[=0h	Text mode	40×25	Monochrome
<Esc>[=1h	Text mode	40×25	Color
<Esc>[=2h	Text mode	80×25	Monochrome
<Esc>[=3h	Text mode	80×25	Color
<Esc>[=4h	Graphics mode	320×200	4 color
<Esc>[=5h	Graphics mode	320×200	Monochrome
<Esc>[=6h	Graphics mode	640×200	Monochrome
<Esc>[=13h	Graphics mode	320×200	Color
<Esc>[=14h	Graphics mode	640×200	16 color
<Esc>[=15h	Graphics mode	640×350	2 color
<Esc>[=16h	Graphics mode	640×350	16 color
<Esc>[=17h	Graphics mode	640×480	2 color
<Esc>[=18h	Graphics mode	640×480	16 color
<Esc>[=19h	Graphics mode	320×200	256 color

ANSI Display Color and Attribute Control Codes

Background color, foreground color, and screen attribute codes may be combined in a single command. If any of the choices conflict, the rightmost color or attribute in the command is set. Not all colors or attributes are available on all displays:

`<Esc>[code;...;code`m	**Set Display Color/Attribute**
0	All attributes off
1	Bold or bright characters
4	Underlined characters (monochrome display adapter only)
5	Blinking characters
7	Reverse video characters
8	Hidden or invisible characters
30	Foreground color: black
31	Foreground color: red
32	Foreground color: green
33	Foreground color: yellow
34	Foreground color: blue
35	Foreground color: magenta
36	Foreground color: cyan
37	Foreground color: white
40	Background color: black
41	Background color: red
42	Background color: green
43	Background color: yellow
44	Background color: blue
45	Background color: magenta
46	Background color: cyan
47	Background color: white

ANSI Cursor Control Codes

`<Esc>[`*row*`;`*col*`H`	Cursor position. Moves the cursor to the specified *row* and *col* or to home (0;0) if no position is specified.
`<Esc>[`*row*`;`*col*`F`	Cursor position. Same as `<Esc>[`*row*`;`*col*`H`.
`<Esc>[`*num*`A`	Cursor up. Moves the cursor up the specified number of rows or to the first row on the screen.
`<Esc>[`*num*`B`	Cursor down. Moves the cursor down the specified number of rows or to the last row on the screen.
`<Esc>[`*num*`C`	Cursor right. Moves the cursor right the specified number of columns or to the right side of the screen.

`<Esc>[`*num*`D`	Cursor left. Moves the cursor left the specified number of columns or to the left side of the screen.
`<Esc>[s`	Saves current cursor position.
`<Esc>[u`	Returns cursor to saved position.

ANSI Miscellaneous Display Control Codes

`<Esc>[2J`	Clears the entire screen
`<Esc>[K`	Clears from the cursor to the end of the line
`<Esc>[=7h`	Enables line wrapping
`<Esc>[=7l`	Disables line wrapping

ANSI Keyboard Layout Control Codes

By using the following ANSI command, you can redefine the entire keyboard or set simple text macros for use at the command line. Some software application programs ignore keyboard reassignments set this way.

`<Esc>[`*keycode*`;`*keytext*`;...p`

keycode indicates one of the key codes listed in the following table. Some keys use two codes, in which case both must be entered, separated by a semicolon as shown. Keycodes that appear in parentheses might not be available on all keyboards. (Do not include the parentheses.) Also, some keyboards use different codes for certain keys. Check your computer's documentation.

keytext is either the ASCII code for a single character or text enclosed in double quotation marks. For example, both 83 and "S" can be used to represent an uppercase *S*. "Hello" also is allowed; it returns the full word when the key is pressed.

In the following table, keys indicated as (gray) refer to the gray-colored cursor pad area of the keyboard. Keys indicated as *(keypad)* refer to the numeric keypad area. Key codes that appear in parentheses are not available on all keyboards, and ANSI.SYS might not interpret them if the /X switch is not specified in the device command that loaded it. A blank entry indicates that this keyboard combination doesn't return a valid code.

Key	Alone	Shift+Key	Ctrl+Key	Alt+Key
F1	0;59	0;84	0;94	0;104
F2	0;60	0;85	0;95	0;105
F3	0;61	0;86	0;96	0;106
F4	0;62	0;87	0;97	0;107
F5	0;63	0;88	0;98	0;108
F6	0;64	0;89	0;99	0;109
F7	0;65	0;90	0;100	0;110

Key	Alone	Shift+Key	Ctrl+Key	Alt+Key
F8	0;66	0;91	0;101	0;111
F9	0;67	0;92	0;102	0;112
F10	0;68	0;93	0;103	0;113
F11	0;133	0;135	0;137	0;139
F12	0;134	0;136	0;138	0;140
Home	0;71	55	0;119	
Up arrow	0;72	56	(0;141)	
PgUp	0;73	57	0;132	
Left arrow	0;75	52	0;115	
Right arrow	0;77	54	0;116	
End	0;79	49	0;117	
Down arrow	0;80	50	(0;145)	
PgDn	0;81	51	0;118	
Ins	0;82	48	(0;146)	
Del	0;83	46	(0;147)	
PrtSc			0;114	
Pause/Break			0;0	
Backspace	8	8	127	(0)
Enter	13		10	(0;28)
Tab	9	0;15	(0;148)	(0;165)
Home (gray)	(224;71)	(224;71)	(224;119)	(224;151)
Up arrow (gray)	(224;72)	(224;72)	(224;141)	(224;152)
PgUp (gray)	(224;73)	(224;73)	(224;132)	(224;153)
Left arrow (gray)	(224;75)	(224;75)	(224;115)	(224;155)
Right arrow (gray)	(224;77)	(224;77)	(224;116)	(224;157)
End (gray)	(224;79)	(224;79)	(224;117)	(224;159)
Down arrow (gray)	(224;80)	(224;80)	(224;145)	(224;154)
PgDn (gray)	(224;81)	(224;81)	(224;118)	(224;161)
Ins (gray)	(224;82)	(224;82)	(224;146)	(224;162)
Del (gray)	(224;83)	(224;83)	(224;147)	(224;163)
Enter (keypad)	13		10	(0;166)
/ (keypad)	47	47	(0;142)	(0;74)
* (keypad)	42	(0;144)	(0;78)	
- (keypad)	45	45	(0;149)	(0;164)

ANSI Control Codes

Key	Alone	Shift+Key	Ctrl+Key	Alt+Key
+ (keypad)	43	43	(0;150)	(0;55)
5 (keypad)	(0;76)	53	(0;143)	
A	97	65	1	0;30
B	98	66	2	0;48
C	99	67	3	0;46
D	100	68	4	0;32
E	101	69	5	0;18
F	102	70	6	0;33
G	103	71	7	0;34
H	104	72	8	0;35
I	105	73	9	0;23
J	106	74	10	0;36
K	107	75	11	0;37
L	108	76	12	0;38
M	109	77	13	0;50
N	110	78	14	0;49
O	111	79	15	0;24
P	112	80	16	0;25
Q	113	81	17	0;16
R	114	82	18	0;19
S	115	83	19	0;31
T	116	84	20	0;20
U	117	85	21	0;22
V	118	86	22	0;47
W	119	87	23	0;17
X	120	88	24	0;45
Y	121	89	25	0;21
Z	122	90	26	0;44
0	48	41		0;129
1	49	33		0;120
2	50	64	(0) Null	0;121
3	51	35		0;122
4	52	36		0;123
5	53	37		0;124

Key	Alone	Shift+Key	Ctrl+Key	Alt+Key
6	54	94	30	0;125
7	55	38		0;126
8	56	42		0;127
9	57	40		0;128
Spacebar	32	32		
' (single quote)	39	34		0;40
, (comma)	44	60		0;51
- (hyphen)	45	95	31	0;130
. (period)	46	62		0;52
/ (slash)	47	63		0;53
; (semicolon)	59	58		0;39
= (equal)	61	43		0;131
[	91	123	27	0;26
\ (backslash)	92	124	28	0;43
]	93	125	29	0;27
` (accent)	96	126		(0;41)

CHAPTER 18

MASTERING DOSKEY AND MACROS

In this chapter

Using DOSKEY   432

Creating and Using Macros   436

Using DOSKEY

DOSKEY is a program that enables you to edit and reuse DOS commands without retyping them. The program also enables you to create new commands, referred to as *macros*, that can take the place of several DOS commands. Another benefit of DOSKEY is that it occupies only about 4KB of memory when loaded. The following sections explain how to load DOSKEY into your computer's memory and use the program's capabilities.

Loading DOSKEY

DOSKEY is a memory-resident program that was first available in DOS 5.0. This program enables you to easily edit what you enter at the DOS prompt. DOSKEY also maintains a running history of the commands you have entered. DOSKEY then enables you to reuse those commands without retyping them.

Before you can use DOSKEY's features, you must load the program into memory. To load DOSKEY, enter the following command at the DOS prompt:

```
DOSKEY
```

A message appears onscreen, telling you that DOSKEY is installed. After this message appears, all DOSKEY features are available.

> **Tip** The most convenient way to load DOSKEY is to include a command in your AUTOEXEC.BAT file to start the program. In this way, DOSKEY loads every time you start your computer. It is also easier to take advantage of loading DOSKEY in upper memory.

As is true of most DOS commands, DOSKEY has several available switches. The full syntax of the command to install DOSKEY is as follows:

```
DOSKEY /REINSTALL /BUFSIZE=size /MACROS /HISTORY /INSERT /OVERSTRIKE
```

Following are explanations of the components of this command:

- /REINSTALL—Installs another copy of DOSKEY and clears the command-history buffer. This command does not, however, remove existing copies of DOSKEY that already are in memory.
- /BUFSIZE—Sets the size of the command buffer. The *size* parameter represents the number of bytes that the buffer occupies in memory. The default size is 512 bytes; the minimum size is 256 bytes.
- /MACROS—Displays a list of the currently defined DOSKEY macros.
- /HISTORY—Displays the contents of the command-history buffer.
- /INSERT—Instructs DOS to insert new text into the existing text at the cursor position. (You cannot use this switch with /OVERSTRIKE.)
- /OVERSTRIKE—Instructs DOS to insert new text in place of existing text at the cursor position. This condition is the default. (You cannot use this switch with /INSERT

Editing the Command Line

Even before you load DOSKEY, DOS provides some command-line editing capability. Table 18.1 lists the normal DOS command-line editing keys, which are available if DOSKEY is not memory-resident.

Table 18.1 DOS Command-Line Editing Keys

Key	Action
Tab	Moves the cursor to the following tab stop
Esc	Cancels the current line and does not change the buffer
Ins	Enables you to insert characters into the preceding command line
Del	Deletes a character from the preceding command line
F1 or right arrow	Copies one character from the preceding command line
F2	Copies all characters from the preceding command line up to, but not including, the next character you type
F3	Copies all remaining characters from the preceding command line
F4	Deletes all characters from the preceding command line up to, but not including, the next character typed (the opposite of F2)
F5	Moves the current line into the buffer but prevents DOS from executing the line
F6	Produces an end-of-file marker (^Z) when you copy from the console to a disk file

A primary purpose of DOSKEY is to facilitate editing of DOS commands. If you are a typical PC user, you issue the same or similar commands frequently, and you don't always type each command correctly the first time. DOSKEY can save you typing by enabling you to edit commands without typing them from scratch every time you notice an error.

Suppose that you want to see a directory listing of all files with the .WQ1 extension in the \SPREADSH\QPRO2DAT directory in drive C. In haste, however, you type the DIR command as follows:

```
DOR C:\SPREADSH\QPRO2DAT\*.WQ1
```

Before you press Enter, you realize that you mistyped the DIR command, but you don't want to retype it. When DOSKEY is loaded, you can use the following procedure to correct the mistake:

1. Press the Home key to move the cursor to the left end of the command line.
2. Use the right-arrow key to move the cursor to the O in the word DOR.
3. Type I to correct the error.
4. Press Enter.

DOS displays the directory listing as you requested.

> **Tip**
>
> Another quick way to repeat the command is to press the F1 key. Each time it is pressed, it repeats a character of the previous command. Although this technique is more limited, in that it does not enable you to edit a character and then continue repeating, it can be helpful if DOSKEY was not activated before you typed the command.

The keys listed in Table 18.2 supplement the normal DOSKEY command-line editing keys.

TABLE 18.2   ADDITIONAL DOSKEY COMMAND-LINE EDITING KEYS

Key	Action
Left arrow	Moves the cursor one character to the left
Right arrow	Moves the cursor one character to the right
Backspace	Moves the cursor one character to the left; erases the character to the left
Ctrl+left arrow	Moves the cursor one word to the left
Ctrl+right arrow	Moves the cursor one word to the right
Ins	Toggles between Replace mode (the default) and Insert mode
Home	Moves the cursor to the left end of the command line
End	Moves the cursor to the space after the last character in the command line
Esc	Erases the command line

REUSING COMMANDS

In addition to enhancing DOS's command-line editing capabilities, DOSKEY adds a capability that was not previously available in DOS: You can redisplay a command that you issued earlier during the current DOS session. You then can execute the command without changing it, or you can use the DOS and DOSKEY editing keys to make modifications before executing the command.

After you load DOSKEY into memory, the program maintains a buffer in memory that contains a history of DOS commands issued at the command prompt during the current DOS session. DOSKEY enables you to reuse the commands in this command-history buffer.

Suppose that earlier during the current DOS session, you issued the following COPY command:

```
COPY C:\DATABASE\FOXPRO\MAIL.DBF C:\WORDPRO\WP
```

Now you want to issue the following similar command without retyping the entire command:

```
COPY C:\DATABASE\DBASE\MAIL.DBF C:\WORDPRO\WP
```

To edit the earlier command, follow these steps:

1. Press the up-arrow key repeatedly until the original COPY command appears on the command line.
2. Use the DOS and DOSKEY editing keys to change the command.
3. Press Enter.

In addition to the up-arrow key, DOSKEY provides the keys listed in Table 18.3 for use in retrieving commands from the command-history buffer.

TABLE 18.3   DOSKEY COMMAND-HISTORY BUFFER KEYS

Key	Action
Up arrow	Displays] the preceding DOS command.
Down arrow	Displays the DOS command issued after the one currently displayed, or displays a blank line when you are at the end of the list.
Alt+F7	Clears the command-history buffer.
Alt+F10	Clears all macro definitions.
F7	Displays the contents of the command-history buffer in a numbered list.
F8	Searches for the command that most closely matches the characters typed at the command line.
F9	Prompts for a line number, where *line number* refers to the number displayed next to a command in the command-history listing generated by pressing F7. Type the number to display the corresponding command.
PgDn	Displays the last command stored in the DOSKEY command buffer.
PgUp	Displays]the earliest command issued that still is stored in the DOSKEY command buffer.

To view the entire list of commands currently stored in the command-history buffer, press F7. DOSKEY lists all commands contained in the buffer, one on each line, with a number at the left end of each line. The oldest command—the command issued earliest in the current DOS session—is number one. Subsequent commands are listed in the order in which you issued them.

DOSKEY provides another way for you to see the entire list of commands in the command-history buffer. Type the following command and then press Enter:

DOSKEY /HISTORY

DOSKEY generates the same list of commands as the F7 command, but without line numbers.

To create a batch file that contains all the commands in the current command-history buffer, use the following command syntax:

DOSKEY /HISTORY > *filename*.BAT

Substitute for *filename* the name that you want to give the batch file. After you issue this command, the new batch file contains all the commands from the command-history buffer, including the command that created the batch file itself. Use the DOS Editor, Edlin, or some other text editor to delete the last command and any other commands you don't want to include in the batch file.

You can use the up-arrow key to display previously issued commands. Each time you press the up-arrow key, DOSKEY displays the preceding command. After you display one or more previous commands by pressing the up-arrow key, you can use the down-arrow key to move back down through the commands to the most recent command. Sometimes, however, selecting a command from the list generated by pressing F7 is easier. To use this method, press F9. DOSKEY displays the following message:

```
Line number:
```

Type the number that corresponds to the desired command in the list of commands generated by pressing F7. DOSKEY displays the selected command in the command line for you to edit or execute.

When you want to move quickly to the first command in the buffer, press PgUp. To go to the last command in the buffer, press PgDn.

If you want to clear the command-history buffer, press Alt+F7. DOSKEY abandons the contents of the command-history buffer.

DOSKEY also can help you locate a command quickly. Type the first several characters of the command you need to find and then press F8. Suppose that you want to locate the following command:

```
COPY C:\DATABASE\FOXPRO\MAIL.DBF C:\WORDPRO\WP
```

Type COPY and press F8. Each time you press F8, DOSKEY shows you the next command that contains the COPY command. When the desired command is displayed, you easily can edit and reuse the command with minimal typing.

CREATING AND USING MACROS

In addition to providing command-line editing capabilities and the command-history buffer, DOSKEY enables you to create your own DOS commands, referred to as macros. A DOSKEY macro is similar to a batch file but is contained in memory rather than on disk. Each macro can contain one or more DOS commands, up to a maximum of 127 characters.

DOSKEY macros are similar to batch files in the following ways:

- Macros can contain multiple DOS commands.
- You invoke macros by typing a name at the DOS prompt.
- Macros can use replaceable parameters.

Macros differ from batch files in the following ways:

- Macros are stored in memory (RAM); batch files are stored on disk.
- Macros are limited to 127 characters; batch files have unlimited maximum length.
- Ctrl+C or Ctrl+Break stops a single command in a DOSKEY macro; Ctrl+C or Ctrl+Break stops an entire batch file.
- The GOTO command is not available in macros.
- One macro cannot call another macro, and you cannot call a macro from within a batch file.
- Macros can define environment variables but cannot use them.

The following sections explain how to create and run DOSKEY macros.

Creating Macros

DOSKEY enables you to create macros at the command line or through a batch file. The syntax for creating a macro is as follows:

```
DOSKEY macroname=command(s)
```

The *macroname* parameter is the name that you want to give the macro. Use any keyboard characters in the name except <, >, |, or =. Do not include a space in the macro name; use an underscore or hyphen instead if you want the macro name to have the appearance of two words.

The *command* parameter can include any number of DOS commands, subject to the following rules:

- The entire command cannot exceed 127 characters (the DOS command-line limit).
- Each pair of commands must be separated by $t.
- Instead of using the redirection and piping operators <, >, and |, use $l, $g, and $b, respectively.
- The ECHO OFF command is not effective in macros. Commands always appear onscreen.

You can use several special characters when defining your macros. They are shown in Table 18.4.

TABLE 18.4 SPECIAL CHARACTERS FOR USE IN DOSKEY MACROS

Character	Meaning
$G or $g	Redirects output; used in place of the greater-than sign (>)
GG or gg	Redirects and appends output; used in place of the double greater-than sign (>>)
$L or $l	Redirects input; used in place of the less-than sign (<)

Table 18.4 Continued

Character	Meaning
$B or $b	Uses output from one command as input to another; used in place of the vertical bar (|)
$T or $t	Separates commands on the DOSKEY command line
$$	Prints the dollar sign character
$1 through $9	Indicates individual replaceable parameters
$*	Indicates all parameters

Notice that when you want to use replaceable parameters in a macro, you use the codes $1 through $9 rather than %1 through %9. Suppose, for example, that you often use the REPLACE command to keep current copies of particular subdirectory files on floppy disks so that you can take the files with you. To do so, however, you must issue the REPLACE command twice for each subdirectory you want to keep current. An easier method is to create the following macro called UPD:

```
DOSKEY UPD=REPLACE \C:$1\$2 A:\$1 /U $T REPLACE C:\$1\$2 A:\$1 /A
```

In this example, you also see how the $T (or $t) special characters separate commands on the command line.

DOSKEY has a special type of replaceable parameter that is not available in batch files. The characters $* represent not just one parameter, but all the characters you type in the command line to the right of the macro name. This type of replaceable parameter is useful when you don't know ahead of time how many parameters or switches you might type when you execute the macro.

Suppose, for example, that you want to create a macro to help format floppy disks in drive A, a 3 1/2-inch, high-density drive. You want to be able to type FA 720 to format a 720KB disk and FA 1.44 to format a 1.44MB disk. Occasionally, however, you might want to use one or more of FORMAT's switches, such as the /S switch to create a system disk, the /Q Quick Format switch, or the /U unconditional format switch. To create the FA macro, you type the following command:

```
DOSKEY FA=FORMAT A: /F:$*
```

To confirm that DOSKEY has stored the macros you defined, you type the following command and then press Enter:

```
DOSKEY /MACROS
```

DOSKEY lists all macros currently stored in the DOSKEY macro buffer. Assuming you defined the UPD and FA macros, the preceding command displays the following lines:

```
UPD=REPLACE \C:$1\$2 A:\$1 /U $T REPLACE C:\$1\$2 A:\$1 /A
FA=FORMAT A: /F:$*
```

You can easily save a copy of the entire contents of the macro buffer by using redirection. To create a file named MACROS.BAT that contains all the current macros, you type the following command and press Enter:

```
DOSKEY /MACROS > MACROS.BAT
```

If you want to use this batch file later to re-create the macros during a future session, edit the file, adding DOSKEY to the beginning of each line.

Because DOSKEY macros reside in memory rather than on disk, all macros are erased when you turn off or reboot the computer. One disadvantage of using DOSKEY macros is that you need to reenter commonly used macros each time you turn on your computer. You can overcome this drawback, however, by using AUTOEXEC.BAT to define the macros that you use most often. To make the UPD and FA macros routinely available, for example, include the following commands in AUTOEXEC.BAT:

```
DOSKEY UPD=REPLACE \C:$1\$2 A:\$1 /U $T REPLACE C:\$1\$2 A:\$1 /A
DOSKEY FA=FORMAT A: /F:$*
```

Every time you turn on or reboot your computer, the preceding commands create the UPD and FA macros in the DOSKEY macro buffer.

> **Note** The first DOSKEY command in AUTOEXEC.BAT loads the program as memory-resident, even if the command also is defining a macro.

Running Macros

Using a DOSKEY macro is as easy as using any other DOS command. Simply type the macro name at the command line and then press Enter. If the macro has any replaceable parameters, include appropriate values in the command line. Suppose, for example, that you want to use the UPD macro to maintain current copies of files. To do so, just type the following:

```
UPD dirname filespec
```

As with a batch file, *dirname* is the first replaceable parameter, $1, and *filespec* is the second, $2. To keep current all files in C:\PROJECT1, type the following at the DOS prompt:

```
UPD PROJECT1 *.*
```

Perhaps you want to use the FA macro created in the preceding section to format a 1.44MB disk. You want to use Quick Format, make this disk bootable, and assign the volume label BOOT_DISK. You type the following command at the DOS prompt and then press Enter:

```
FA 1.44 /Q /S /V:BOOT_DISK
```

DOS first displays the command in the following format:

```
FORMAT A: /F:1.44 /Q /S /V:BOOT_DISK
```

CHAPTER 18 MASTERING DOSKEY AND MACROS

Then DOS prompts you as follows:

```
Insert new diskette for drive A:
and press ENTER when ready_
```

Press Enter to proceed with the formatting operation. DOS displays messages indicating the progress and successful completion of the procedure. Finally, DOS displays the following message:

```
QuickFormat another (Y/N)?
```

Press Y if you want to use the same switch settings to format another disk or press N to return to the DOS prompt.

DELETING MACROS

You can remove a macro from memory simply by putting nothing to the right of the equal sign when you define the macro. Assume, for example, that you no longer need the FA macro defined earlier. To remove it from memory—thereby freeing more space for other macros—type the following at the DOS prompt:

```
DOSKEY FA=
```

> **Warning**
> If you use a macro name that is the same as an existing DOS command, you effectively replace the DOS command with the macro.

CHAPTER 19

Configuring Your Computer

In this chapter

Getting the Most from Your Computer Resources   442

Understanding Device Drivers   443

Optimizing Your Computer's Memory   445

Providing Memory for Your Applications   460

Increasing Hard Disk Performance   461

Fine-Tuning Your Computer with `CONFIG.SYS` and `AUTOEXEC.BAT`   463

Getting the Most from Your Computer Resources

Computers on the market today have many similarities. They are based on the same family of computer chips, and they have similar components, such as memory, hard disks, and power supplies. Still, the differences between various makes and models of personal computers are greater today than ever before. DOS gives you the tools to fine-tune the operation of every element of your computer system, an exercise often called *configuring* your system. You can adjust a bewildering number of settings; how you manipulate these settings greatly affects how efficiently your PC works. Sadly, the people who do not understand how to configure their PCs greatly outnumber the people who do. By reading this chapter, you can become one of the latter.

Fortunately, the folks at Microsoft realize that configuring a modern PC can be challenging for most users, and perhaps the most important tool that Microsoft includes with DOS is MemMaker, a tool that performs the hardest part of the configuration automatically. If you want to call yourself a PC guru, you need to understand the configuration process; but if you're a novice user, the worst part of working with MS-DOS just disappeared.

The default configuration of DOS, which might be adequate for many users, is designed as a "lowest common denominator," intended to work with the greatest number of systems. As PC technology advances, DOS also must enable users of the most up-to-date systems to take full advantage of their computers' most powerful features. This chapter describes how to use DOS to create the optimal configuration for your computer system, whether your system is a plain vanilla PC or a banana split with all the toppings.

Whether you use your own computer or a computer owned by your employer, someone has invested a significant sum of money in the system. This chapter helps you discover how to configure your computer to operate most efficiently—how to get the "most bang for the buck." You generally can improve the performance of software running on your PC in two ways: You can increase the amount of memory available to the software, and you can increase the speed at which your system or its components operate. You can tackle these efficiency-oriented goals in two general ways:

- Add or replace hardware
- Use software to attain an optimal configuration for your existing hardware resources

DOS fits into the software category. This chapter teaches you how to use DOS to increase the amount of memory available to applications. The chapter also explains how to use special device drivers and utility programs to enhance the performance of your hard disk, which in turn enhances software performance.

Understanding Device Drivers

MS-DOS certain features that every DOS user needs. Regardless of the type of computer you use or the software you run, you must be capable of creating directories, accessing files, and printing to your printer. Many other features, however, might not be important to you, depending on the type of computer you have and how you use it. If you plan to use a mouse with DOS, DOS must load the mouse-handling functions when your computer boots. If you don't plan to use a mouse, loading the mouse-handling functions ties up valuable memory, a sacrifice you don't want to make.

To give you the flexibility of using only the parts of DOS that you need, DOS consists of a base portion (which contains the features that everybody needs) and a series of what you might think of as "plug-in modules" (pieces of programs that give DOS the instructions it needs to perform certain tasks). Because you can decide which of the optional modules to use, you don't waste memory-loading features you don't need.

These plug-in modules are called *device drivers* because they generally give DOS the information needed to access various types of hardware devices. In addition to the device drivers that come with DOS, some add-on hardware comes with a device driver that enables your system to recognize and use the hardware. If, for example, you buy a mouse to use with your computer, you also must load the appropriate device driver so that DOS knows how to control the mouse.

Most device drivers are loaded in your CONFIG.SYS file. One of the most important tasks this file performs is to tell DOS which device drivers to load when the computer boots. The DEVICE command tells DOS to load a device driver and uses the following syntax:

DEVICE = *filespec* /*switches*

filespec is the complete filename (and optional disk and path) for the device driver file, and /*switches* are any switches the device driver software needs.

If you buy a Microsoft mouse, for example, you also get a device driver called MOUSE.SYS that tells DOS how to use the mouse. If you place MOUSE.SYS in the root directory of your C drive, you can load MOUSE.SYS by adding the following command to CONFIG.SYS:

DEVICE = C:\MOUSE.SYS

(The spaces around the equal sign in this syntax are optional.)

You can load as many device drivers as you need, but you must use a separate DEVICE command for each driver you install.

Most users create a special subdirectory called \DRIVERS or \SYS and put the driver files in this directory so that they are out of the way of daily files. If you put the driver files in a separate subdirectory, you must specify the pathname as part of the name of the device driver, as shown in the following examples:

DEVICE = C:\DRIVERS\MOUSE.SYS
DEVICE = C:\SYS\MOUSE.SYS

Table 19.1 lists the device driver files included with DOS 6.22

TABLE 19.1 DOS 6.22 DEVICE DRIVERS

Device Driver	Description
ANSI.SYS	Enables control of the display by using ANSI control sequences.
CHKSTATE.SYS	Used by MemMaker when optimizing your system.
DBLSPACE.BIN	Enables disk compression, greatly increasing the amount of data you can store on your hard disk. The DBLSPACE.SYS file loads this driver in your CONFIG.SYS file.
DISPLAY.SYS	Provides support for code-page switching to the screen.
DMDRVR.BIN	Provides support for Ontrack Disk Manager.
DRIVER.SYS	Sets parameters for physical and logical disk drives.
EGA.SYS	Saves and restores an EGA screen when you're using DOSSHELL and the task swapper.
EMM386.EXE	Uses XMS memory in an 80386 or 80486 computer to emulate EMS memory and provide upper memory blocks.
HIMEM.SYS	Manages extended memory.
INTERLNK.EXE	Provides the Interlnk network client control program and device driver.
MONOUMB.386	Provides a device driver used by Windows that allows EMM386 access to the monochrome video region, treating it as a UMB area.
MOUSE.COM	Provides support for a Microsoft mouse.
POWER.EXE	Provides support for computers utilizing APM (Advanced Power Management) hardware.
PRINTER.SYS	Provides support for international characters and code-page switching on certain printers.
RAMDRIVE.SYS	Uses a portion of random access memory (RAM) to simulate a hard disk—often called a RAM disk.
SETVER.EXE	Establishes a version table that lists the version number DOS reports to named programs.
SMARTDRV.EXE	Uses extended or expanded memory to buffer disk reads.
SSTOR.SYS	Provides support for SpeedStor hard disk compression.
VFINTD.386	Used by Windows to give MWBACKUP access to tape drives.

The most commonly used device drivers are discussed in this chapter. Refer to Appendix F, "Command Reference," for the syntax of the drivers not covered here.

> **Note**
> When you install DOS, you might notice that DOS installs two files that appear to be device drivers because they end in the .SYS extension: COUNTRY.SYS and KEYBOARD.SYS. Despite their extension, these files are not device drivers; they are used internally by other DOS commands, and you cannot use them in your CONFIG.SYS file.

Optimizing Your Computer's Memory

In Chapter 1, "DOS and the Personal Computer," you learned about memory and how it relates to your PC. With that understanding in mind, you are ready to learn how you can make the most of your PC's memory.

→ To learn more about the CONFIG.SYS file and how it works, **see** "Starting DOS," **p. 23**.

Using Extended Memory and HIMEM.SYS

In terms of optimizing your computer, the most significant feature offered by DOS is the capability to load most of the operating system software into extended memory. By doing so, DOS provides more conventional memory for applications, ultimately improving the performance of your system.

Understanding HIMEM.SYS

Before DOS or applications software can use extended memory, you must add a command to your CONFIG.SYS file to load an Extended Memory Manager—a driver that provides a standard way for applications to address extended memory so that no two programs use the same portion of extended memory at the same time. DOS 4.0 and later versions include the Extended Memory Manager HIMEM.SYS.

HIMEM.SYS manages memory according to the rules set out in the Extended Memory Specification (XMS) Version 2.0. According to this specification, three areas of memory above the conventional 640KB barrier can be made available for programs to use:

- **Upper memory area (UMA)**—This area consists of the 384KB of memory above 640KB up to 1MB and is divided into many different-size blocks, called upper memory blocks (UMBs).

- **High memory area (HMA)**—This is a single block of memory essentially consisting of the first 64KB of extended memory. However, the HMA slightly overlaps the upper memory area; the last 16 bytes of the upper memory area are the first 16 bytes of the high memory area. (Most people are not aware of this slight overlap, and it can be a good way to win bar bets.)

- **Extended memory blocks (XMS memory)**—This portion of memory includes all memory above 1,024KB. When extended memory is managed by an Extended Memory Manager, you refer to the memory as XMS memory.

> **Note**
> The terms used to describe DOS memory can be maddening. Try not to confuse high memory with upper memory.

When used on an x86 PC, `HIMEM.SYS` provides HMA and XMS memory to programs that know how to use it. To access upper memory, however, the PC must have at least an 80386 CPU or higher, and you must include one of the following device driver commands in `CONFIG.SYS` after `HIMEM.SYS` is loaded:

`DEVICE=EMM386.EXE RAM`

`DEVICE=EMM386.EXE NOEMS`

Refer to the next section for a full discussion of `EMM386.EXE`.

The syntax for using `HIMEM.SYS` is shown in the following:

`DEVICE=d:path\HIMEM.SYS /A20CONTROL:ON|OFF /NUMHANDLES=n /EISA /HMAMIN=n /INT15=xxxx /MACHINE:xx /SHADOWRAM:ON|OFF /CPUCLOCK:ON|OFF /QUIET`

`d:` is the disk drive where the `HIMEM.SYS` resides, and `path\` is the directory containing the device driver file. If `HIMEM.SYS` is contained in the `\DOS` directory on your C drive, for example, you include the following command in `CONFIG.SYS`:

`DEVICE=C:\DOS\HIMEM.SYS`

In most cases, you need only this command to activate the Extended Memory Manager. In special cases, however, you might need to use one of the available switches described in the following paragraphs. The next section continues the discussion of loading DOS into upper memory.

According to XMS specifications, only one program at a time can use the high memory area. The switch `/HMAMIN=n` sets the minimum amount of memory that must be requested by an application before the application is permitted to use HMA. If you load DOS into HMA, you can omit this switch, as explained in the section "Loading DOS into High Memory" later in this chapter.

When the Extended Memory Manager assigns memory to a particular program, it assigns one or more extended memory block handles to the program. The `/NUMHANDLES=n` switch indicates the maximum number of handles available. The number *n* must be between 1 and 128. The default is 32 handles, usually a sufficient number. Each reserved handle requires an additional 6 bytes of memory. Unless you are running software that complains about not having enough extended memory handles, you probably do not need this option.

Most current versions of commercial software support the XMS specification for addressing extended memory. Some older versions of programs, however, use a different method of addressing extended memory, known as the Interrupt 15h (INT15h) interface. If you work with software that uses the INT15h interface and you want to load DOS into HMA, add the `/INT15=xxxx` switch. The number *xxxx* indicates the amount of extended memory you want `HIMEM.SYS` to assign to the INT15h interface. This number must be from 64 to 65,535 (kilobytes), and the default is 0. If you assign some of your extended memory to the INT15h interface, that memory is not available to programs that expect the XMS interface.

Internally, DOS uses a wire called the A20 memory address line to access the high memory area. What the A20 address line is and how DOS uses it are not important here, but not all brands of PCs handle the A20 line in the same way. Normally, HIMEM.SYS can detect how your computer uses its A20 line, but if it is incorrect, HIMEM.SYS displays the following error message:

```
Unable to control A20
```

If you see this message, use the /MACHINE:*xx* switch in the HIMEM.SYS command to specify which type of A20 handler your machine uses. For *xx* in the /MACHINE switch, insert the code that matches your computer. You can find the text codes in the Code column and the number codes in the Number column in Table 19.2. If you see the error message but your computer is not listed in Table 19.2, try the switch /MACHINE:1.

TABLE 19.2 A20 HANDLER CODES

Code	Number	Computer
at	1	IBM PC/AT
ps2	2	IBM PS/2
pt1cascade	3	Phoenix Cascade BIOS
hpvectra	4	HP Vectra (A and A+)
att6300plus	5	AT&T 6300 Plus
acer1100	6	Acer 1100
toshiba	7	Toshiba 1600 and 1200XE
wyse	8	Wyse 12.5MHz 286
tulip	9	Tulip SX
zenith	10	Zenith ZBIOS
at1	11	IBM PC/AT (alternative delay)
at2	12	IBM PC/AT (alternative delay)
css	12	CSS Labs
at3	13	IBM PC/AT (alternative delay)
philips	13	Philips
fasthp	14	HP Vectra
IBM 7552	15	IBM 7552 Industrial Computer
Bull Mioral	16	Bull Mioral 60
DELL	17	DELL XBios

Before DEVICE=HIMEM.SYS in CONFIG.SYS, you might have listed a device driver that also uses the A20 line. By default, HIMEM.SYS takes control of A20 even though the line is turned on when HIMEM.SYS loads. HIMEM.SYS warns you when this condition occurs by displaying the following message:

```
Warning: The A20 Line was already enabled!
```

Determine see whether you really intend to have both drivers installed at one time. If so, you can prevent `HIMEM.SYS` from taking control of A20 by adding the switch `/A20CONTROL:OFF` (the default setting is `/A20CONTROL:ON`).

All PCs store some of their basic operating instructions in read-only memory (ROM); however, computers usually cannot access instructions from ROM as fast as they can access instructions from RAM. If you have plenty of memory and an 80386 (or better) computer, you can usually increase the performance of your computer by asking the computer to copy the instructions from ROM into an upper memory block (which is RAM). This technique is known as *shadow RAM*.

Shadow RAM uses some of your upper memory blocks. If you prefer to increase the amount of upper memory available for device drivers and memory-resident programs, use the `/SHADOWRAM:OFF` switch. As `HIMEM.SYS` loads, the following message appears:

```
Shadow RAM disabled.
```

In some cases, DOS cannot turn off shadow RAM. Instead, DOS displays a message telling you that shadow RAM is in use and cannot be disabled. (Check your hardware documentation for other methods of disabling shadow RAM.)

The `/CPUCLOCK:ON` switch ensures that `HIMEM.SYS` does not slow your computer's clock speed, the speed at which your computer processes instructions. (Any change in clock speed does not affect your computer's real-time clock, which keeps time of day.) On the front panel of many PCs is an LED or other indicator that indicates the current clock speed. To prevent the clock speed from slowing, add the `/CPUCLOCK:ON` switch to the `DEVICE=HIMEM.SYS` command in `CONFIG.SYS`.

If you are using a machine that uses an Extended Industry Standard Architecture (EISA) bus with more than 16MB of memory, `HIMEM.SYS` does not normally allocate all the extended memory. Use the `/EISA` switch to tell `HIMEM.SYS` to automatically allocate all available extended memory.

When `HIMEM.SYS` loads, it usually prints status messages. If you want `HIMEM.SYS` to load without the usual status messages, add the `/QUIET` switch.

Loading DOS into High Memory

DOS enables you to load most of the operating system into an area of extended memory known as the high memory area (HMA), the first 64KB of extended memory (except the first 16 bytes, which overlap the upper memory area). After the device driver `HIMEM.SYS` is loaded into the computer's memory, the command `DOS=HIGH` in `CONFIG.SYS` loads DOS into high memory.

The next time you boot the computer, DOS uses about 14KB of space in conventional memory and loads the remainder of the operating system into the HMA. If, however, you don't use this command in `CONFIG.SYS` or don't have extended memory installed in your computer, DOS occupies more than 62KB of memory. By loading the operating system into high memory, DOS 6.2 can free about 47KB of conventional memory.

USING EXPANDED MEMORY AND EMM386.EXE

Because expanded memory was introduced before extended memory, many PC applications were written to take advantage of *expanded memory*, not extended memory. Today, however, extended memory is far less expensive and much more common. The DOS device driver EMM386.EXE enables applications to use extended memory as though it were expanded memory, freeing you from the need for the special memory boards and device drivers that expanded memory requires. Thus, EMM386.EXE emulates expanded memory by using extended memory.

> **Note** The device driver HIMEM.SYS, discussed earlier, must be loaded before EMM386.EXE. HIMEM.SYS makes extended memory available, and EMM386.EXE enables you to use some or all extended memory as though it were expanded memory. Do not use EMM386.EXE if you are using another driver from a third-party software vendor as an expanded memory manager.

Some applications today can use either expanded memory or extended memory by accessing whichever is available. If you have a choice, use extended memory, which is faster.

In addition to its role as an expanded memory emulator, EMM386.EXE also is a UMB provider, working with HIMEM.SYS to provide upper memory blocks (UMBs) into which you can load device drivers and memory-resident programs. See the next section, "Loading Device Drivers and TSRs into Upper Memory," for further discussion of providing UMBs.

The syntax of the command for EMM386.EXE, used as a device driver, is shown in the following:

```
DEVICE=EMM386.EXE ON|OFF|AUTO memory W=ON|OFF
    Mx|FRAME=address /Pmmmm Pn=address X=mmmm-nnn
    I=mmmm-nnn B=address L=minxms A=altregs H=handles
    D=nnn RAM NOEMS MIN=n /VERBOSE ROM=mmmm-nnnn NOVCPI
      WIN=mmmm-nnnn NOMOVEXBDA NOHIGHSCAN ALTBOOT NOHI
```

In most cases, one of the following commands is sufficient:

```
DEVICE=EMM386.EXE RAM
```

```
DEVICE=EMM386.EXE NOEMS
```

The first command loads the expanded memory emulator and allocates 256KB of extended memory to be used as expanded memory. The RAM switch enables upper memory. The second command also enables upper memory but tells EMM386 not to allocate extended memory for use as expanded memory.

Sometimes you might need the remaining switches for the EMM386.EXE device driver to customize your computer for use with particularly demanding software or hardware. You can specify ON, OFF, or AUTO in the EMM386.EXE device driver command to indicate whether your computer starts in the `EMM386.EXE` active, inactive, or automatic mode, respectively. By default, the device driver is active, and `EMM386.EXE` makes extended memory available. However, some applications might not run properly when `EMM386.EXE` is active because `EMM386.EXE` places the computer in a mode known as *Virtual 8086 mode*. When you use `EMM386.EXE` as a device driver, the driver loads in memory and remains active (`ON`) unless you specify otherwise by using the `OFF` switch.

The `OFF` switch starts the computer with `EMM386.EXE` loaded in memory but inactive. The XMS memory allocated as EMS memory is unavailable for any purpose. You can activate the driver by entering the following command at the DOS command prompt:

`EMM386 ON`

The `OFF` switch is not compatible, however, with the `RAM` or `NOEMS` switches, discussed later in this section.

Use `AUTO` if you want `EMM386.EXE` to activate only when an application requests EMS memory. This setting provides maximum compatibility with software that might not work properly in Virtual 8086 mode. Like the `OFF` switch, `AUTO` is not compatible with the `RAM` or `NOEMS` switches.

> **Tip**
> Even though `EMM386.EXE` activates when an application requests EMS memory, the driver does not automatically deactivate when the application terminates. To turn off the driver, you must issue the following command at the command prompt:
> `EMM386 OFF`

The *memory* parameter enables you to specify the amount of XMS memory you want `EMM386.EXE` to allocate as EMS memory. Type the number of kilobytes in the range from 16 to 32,768. `EMM386.EXE` rounds any number you type down to the nearest multiple of 16. All unallocated memory remains available as XMS memory. The default EMS memory allocated is 256KB.

As a general rule, allocate only as much EMS memory as is required by your applications. Any memory allocated as EMS memory is no longer available as XMS memory. Most of the newer DOS applications, especially games, require the maximum amount of XMS you can make available. If none of your applications need expanded memory, use the `NOEMS` option so that no memory is allocated as expanded memory.

Use the `L=`*minxms* switch, in which *minxms* is the number of kilobytes, to indicate the minimum XMS memory that `EMM386.EXE` is to allocate. This parameter overrides the *memory* parameter.

If you installed a Weitek math coprocessor chip—a special computer chip that improves the performance of computation-intensive software, such as computer-aided design (CAD) software—use the `W=ON` switch. By default, the device driver does not support this type of coprocessor. You also can turn on or off support for the Weitek coprocessor by entering one of the following commands at the DOS prompt:

EMM386 W=ON

EMM386 W=OFF

In some circumstances, you might want to use upper memory for device drivers and memory-resident programs, but you don't need EMS memory. In this case, use the NOEMS switch with the EMM386.EXE driver to free the maximum amount of upper memory and to provide no EMS memory. You might intend to run Windows 3.1 on your computer, for example. Because Windows can use all your XMS memory, this software doesn't need EMS memory.

The /VERBOSE switch causes EMM386 to print status and error messages when it loads. Normally, EMM386 suppresses these messages. You can abbreviate /VERBOSE as /V.

EMM386 scans the upper memory area (UMA) for all available free memory. Unusual architectures might confuse EMM386, causing trouble when your computer boots or while you use the computer. The NOHIGHSCAN parameter limits EMM386's scanning of the UMA. If you experience problems when you use EMM386, adding the NOHIGHSCAN parameter might solve the problem.

EMM386 loads part of itself into the upper memory area. If one of your programs needs extra upper memory blocks, and you're willing to give up some of your conventional memory, the NOHI parameter causes EMM386 to load all of itself into conventional memory, and does not use any UMA.

The remaining switches available for use with EMM386.EXE are highly technical and beyond the scope of this book. Refer to your DOS User's Guide or the Technical Reference manual for more information.

LOADING DEVICE DRIVERS AND TSRS INTO UPPER MEMORY

In addition to enabling you to run DOS in high memory, DOS provides the capability of loading memory-resident programs and device drivers into upper memory blocks, freeing more conventional memory for other applications. DOS can access this area of memory in 80386 and 80486 PCs (including SXs) that have 1MB or more of memory.

To load device drivers or memory-resident programs, also called *terminate-and-stay-resident (TSR) programs*, into upper memory, the following conditions must be met:

- Your computer has an 80386 or better CPU.
- HIMEM.SYS is loaded as a device driver.
- EMM386.EXE is loaded as a device driver with the RAM or NOEMS switch.
- The command DOS=UMB appears in the CONFIG.SYS file.

If you also want to use the command DOS=HIGH to load DOS into high memory, you can combine the two commands as shown in the following:

DOS=HIGH, UMB

You can load two types of programs into upper memory: device drivers and memory-resident programs (TSRs). You already know that device drivers normally are loaded using the `DEVICE` command. When you want to load a device driver into upper memory, however, you use the `DEVICEHIGH` command. The syntax for this configuration command is as follows:

`DEVICEHIGH=filename.ext /switches`

> **Note**
> The `switches` in the syntax for the preceding command are any switches you use for the file that you are loading, not for the `DEVICEHIGH` command itself.

To load into upper memory the screen driver `ANSI.SYS`, for example, you need the following command in `CONFIG.SYS`:

`DEVICEHIGH=C:\DOS\ANSI.SYS`

When you boot the computer, DOS attempts to load `ANSI.SYS` into the upper memory area.

> **Note**
> `DEVICEHIGH` and `LOADHIGH` recognize two switches: `/L` and `/S`. When you use MemMaker to automatically configure your PC, it might use these switches in the commands it generates. These switches are not intended for use by users.

To load a memory-resident program into upper memory, precede the program's startup command with `LOADHIGH`. (You can use the abbreviation `LH` in place of `LOADHIGH`.) The syntax for the command for `LOADHIGH` is as follows:

`LOADHIGH programname /switches`

As an example, assume that you want to load DOSKEY (discussed in Chapter 18, "Mastering DOSKEY and Macros") into upper memory each time you start your computer. To do so, you add the following command to your `AUTOEXEC.BAT` file:

`LOADHIGH DOSKEY`

The next time you reboot the computer, DOS attempts to load DOSKEY into upper memory. DOS does not load a program into upper memory if the program requests that DOS allocate more memory during initialization than is available in the largest available upper memory block. If DOS is not successful when it tries to load device drivers or TSRs into the upper memory area, it loads the program into conventional memory instead.

> **Tip**
> Use the `MEM` command to determine whether a driver or program has loaded into upper memory.

Displaying the Amount of Free and Used Memory

So that you can make the most efficient use of DOS's memory management utilities, DOS also enables you to display the amount of free and used memory at any point during a DOS session. Use the MEM command for this purpose.

The syntax for the MEM command is as follows:

MEM /CLASSIFY /DEBUG /FREE /MODULE modulename /PAGE

Most of these options (/DEBUG, /FREE, and /MODULE) are primarily of interest to programmers. For any option, you can specify just the first letter, such as /C in place of /CLASSIFY, for example.

With no switches, MEM gives a basic report of how the memory on your machine is being used. The following provides a sample of a basic MEM report from a typical computer with 8MB of memory:

```
Memory Type         Total    =   Used   +   Free
-------------       ------       -----      ------
Conventional         640K         79K        562K
Upper                 71K         33K         38K
Reserved             384K        384K          0K
Extended (XMS)*    7,097K      2,537K      4,560K
-------------       ------       -----      ------
Total memory       8,192K      3,033K      5,159K

Total under 1 MB     711K        112K        599K

Total Expanded (EMS)              7,488K (7,667,712 bytes)
Free Expanded (EMS)*              4,800K (4,915,200 bytes)

* EMM386 is using XMS memory to simulate EMS memory as needed.
  Free EMS memory may change as free XMS memory changes.

Largest executable program size    561K (574,752 bytes)
Largest free upper memory block     22K  (22,016 bytes)
MS-DOS is resident in the high memory area.
```

Even this most basic report includes a wealth of information:

- This computer has 640KB of conventional memory, of which 79KB is currently in use, leaving 562KB free.

- This computer loaded EMM386, which found 71KB available in upper memory blocks; 33KB of the 71KB is currently in use.

- This computer has 7,097KB of extended memory, 2,537KB of which is in use.

- The computer has 599KB of memory available below 1MB, representing the memory available for loading programs and device drivers on this machine.

- The largest program you can load into conventional memory is 561KB.

- The largest free upper memory block is 22KB. Consequently, you cannot load "high" any program or device driver that requires more memory than 22KB.

- Most of DOS has been loaded into the high memory area because the command DOS=HIGH appeared in the CONFIG.SYS file.

With the /CLASSIFY switch, MEM lists all DOS programs and device drivers currently loaded. Along with the information shown previously, MEM lists this additional information if you use /CLASSIFY:

```
Modules using memory below 1 MB:

  Name          Total       =  Conventional  +  Upper Memory
  --------    ---------------  ----------------  ---------------
  MSDOS        18,029  (18K)    18,029  (18K)        0   (0K)
  HIMEM         1,168   (1K)     1,168   (1K)        0   (0K)
  EMM386        3,120   (3K)     3,120   (3K)        0   (0K)
  DBLSPACE     37,664  (37K)    37,664  (37K)        0   (0K)
  COMMAND       3,184   (3K)     3,184   (3K)        0   (0K)
  MOUSE        17,088  (17K)    17,088  (17K)        0   (0K)
  SETVER          816   (1K)         0   (0K)      816   (1K)
  ANSI          4,240   (4K)         0   (0K)    4,240   (4K)
  SMARTDRV     29,024  (28K)         0   (0K)   29,024  (28K)
  Free        613,472 (599K)   574,976 (562K)   38,496  (38K)
```

This sample report shows the programs and device drivers currently loaded and displays the amount of conventional and upper memory used by each:

- MSDOS is the portion of MS-DOS that did not get loaded into the high memory area.
- HIMEM is the HIMEM.SYS device driver.
- EMM386 is the EMM386.EXE device driver.
- DBLSPACE is the DoubleSpace device driver.
- COMMAND is the DOS command interpreter.
- MOUSE is the mouse device driver.
- SETVER is the device driver used to modify how DOS reports version information.
- ANSI is the ANSI.SYS device driver, which this computer loads.
- SMARTDRV is the device driver for caching information going to and from disk drives.

> **Tip** MEM /C often displays more than a screenful of information. The /P option tells MEM to pause after each screenful of data and wait for you to press a key before continuing.

After you identify a driver or memory-resident program that appears to be the right size to fit in the available UMB, edit CONFIG.SYS or AUTOEXEC.BAT to add DEVICEHIGH or LOADHIGH to the appropriate command. Reboot your computer and issue the MEM /C command again to see whether the driver or program loaded.

Arriving at the optimal combination of device drivers and memory-resident programs loaded into upper memory might require some experimentation. DOS loads programs in the largest available UMB first, so try loading the largest drivers and programs first by placing their startup commands earliest in CONFIG.SYS or AUTOEXEC.BAT. To alleviate some of the trial-and-error necessary in arriving at the optimal memory arrangement, DOS now provides the MemMaker utility, which is described in the following section.

Configuring Memory with MemMaker

Understanding and configuring a PC's memory is one of the most challenging activities most users face. Because most users usually configure their computer's memory once, they never really get a chance to build any experience fiddling with the configuration. After several years of watching users stumble at configuring their PCs, Microsoft finally offered help. DOS includes MemMaker, a utility that analyzes your PC and makes the appropriate changes to your CONFIG.SYS and AUTOEXEC.BAT files so that your computer uses its memory most effectively.

> **Tip**
>
> Some people use Windows or a particular application so often that they add a command to the end of their AUTOEXEC.BAT file to start the application automatically every time they boot. If you have added such a command that takes you automatically into Windows or any other program, read this warning carefully. If, on the other hand, you find yourself at the DOS prompt when your computer boots, you can skip this warning.
>
> MemMaker does its work in three phases, and between each phase it reboots your computer. Each time MemMaker causes your computer to reboot, your AUTOEXEC.BAT file starts your application as usual, preventing MemMaker from continuing its work. You must exit these programs for MemMaker to perform the next phase.

You can take Understanding two different paths to configure your memory with MemMaker. One is to follow the Express Setup. The other path you can choose is the Custom Setup.

Express Setup is the easier path to choose. You have little interaction with Express Setup, other than pressing Enter when MemMaker prompts you to do so. MemMaker searches through the upper memory area to find open memory addresses. It then sorts device drivers and TSRs that you load in memory to see the optimum loading order. Finally, it updates your CONFIG.SYS and AUTOEXEC.BAT files for two reasons. MemMaker ensures that HIMEM.SYS and EMM386.EXE load to manage memory and that the DOS=UMB directive is in CONFIG.SYS to provide the link to upper memory blocks. In addition, MemMaker inserts DEVICEHIGH and LOADHIGH before the device drivers and TSRs that load in upper memory.

> **Note**
>
> Although MemMaker adds the device drivers HIMEM.SYS and EMM386.EXE and the upper memory block directive HIGH=UMB, it does not ensure that DOS loads into upper memory with the directive DOS=HIGH. Before you use MemMaker, ensure that your system loads DOS in the high memory area by inserting DOS=HIGH in your CONFIG.SYS file and rebooting your computer. After you are running DOS in the high memory area (the MEM command tells you that DOS is in the high memory area), run MemMaker.

> **Tip**
> If you start an application such as Windows from your `AUTOEXEC.BAT` file, place the word `REM` in front of the startup command (in this case, in front of `WIN`) before using MemMaker. `REM` causes DOS to ignore the rest of the command so that you don't have to exit your application during each MemMaker phase. When MemMaker has completed its work, remove `REM` so that your application again starts automatically each time you boot.

> **Tip**
> An easy way to run MemMaker is to use the `/BATCH` switch. From the command line, type `MEMMAKER /BATCH`. This command runs MemMaker in automatic mode, accepting all the default answers.

Custom Setup is similar to Express Setup in that it scans the upper memory area for open address space, sorts device drivers and TSRs for optimal order, and updates your `AUTOEXEC.BAT` and `CONFIG.SYS` files. As you might expect, however, you can customize how MemMaker performs these tasks. The following list shows the elements you can customize using Custom Setup:

- Specify any TSRs that are not to be included in optimization.
- Aggressively scan the upper memory area.
- Set aside upper memory for Windows use.
- Use an area of upper memory set aside for the Monochrome Display Adapter (MDA) if you are using only an EGA or VGA display (but not SuperVGA).
- Keep any special memory inclusions or exclusions that you specified with `EMM386.EXE`.
- Move the Extended BIOS data area in upper memory blocks.

Now that you understand what MemMaker can do to optimize your computer's memory, you are ready to use MemMaker. The following two sections explain how to use MemMaker with Express Setup and Custom Setup.

Using Express Setup

Follow these steps to run MemMaker using Express Setup:

1. At the DOS prompt, type `MEMMAKER` and press Enter.
2. MemMaker asks whether you want to continue. Press Enter to continue.
3. MemMaker asks whether you want Express or Custom Setup, as shown in Figure 19.1. For most users, an Express Setup does an excellent job. Unless you are very knowledgeable about PCs and want to guide MemMaker's every step, press Enter to select an Express Setup.

Figure 19.1
From this screen, you select the type of setup to be performed.

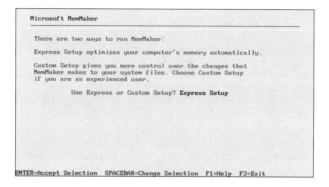

4. MemMaker asks whether you intend to use EMS (expanded) memory, as shown in Figure 19.2. Answer Y or N, and press Enter. (If the answer you want is already showing, just press Enter.)

Figure 19.2
On this screen, you specify use of expanded memory in your system.

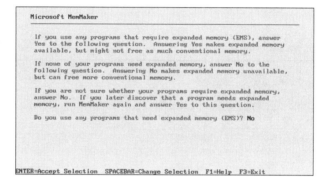

5. When you see a screen indicating that MemMaker must reboot the computer, as shown in Figure 19.3, press Enter to reboot. (If your computer does not start correctly, turning it off and back on reboots it.)

Figure 19.3
If your system does not reboot automatically, you can turn your computer off and then back on.

6. When your computer reboots, MemMaker automatically begins the next phase of its work, telling you that it has calculated the optimal configuration for your computer. MemMaker displays another screen, as shown in Figure 19.4, that asks you to press Enter so that MemMaker can reboot again. Press Enter to continue.

CHAPTER 19 CONFIGURING YOUR COMPUTER

Figure 19.4
After this reboot, your new memory configuration is complete.

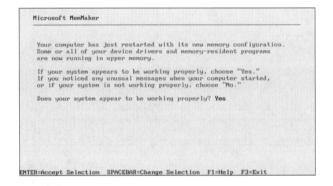

7. During the reboot, your computer executes the CONFIG.SYS and AUTOEXEC.BAT files that MemMaker created. Although MemMaker should do an excellent job of configuring your computer for peak performance, there is always a chance that it can make a mistake. As your computer boots, watch carefully for any errors produced by the device drivers and programs that you load from your CONFIG.SYS and AUTOEXEC.BAT files.

After your computer completes its reboot, MemMaker begins its last phase. MemMaker displays the message shown in Figure 19.5, asking whether you saw any errors during boot. If your computer booted without errors, press Enter.

Figure 19.5
Observe your boot process to see whether it appears normal; if it does, MemMaker is finished.

8. MemMaker displays a table showing how the changes affected your available memory. A sample is shown in Figure 19.6. This report tells you how much of each type of memory you had available before and after MemMaker made its changes. In this example, MemMaker adjusts commands in AUTOEXEC.BAT and CONFIG.SYS so that several device drivers and TSR programs are loaded into upper memory, freeing up about 114KB of conventional memory. MemMaker also tells you that it has saved your original AUTOEXEC.BAT and CONFIG.SYS files as AUTOEXEC.UMB and CONFIG.UMB in case you later discover a problem and want to return to using your original files.

> **Tip**
> After running MemMaker, if you experience problems with any of your programs that you did not have before, issue the MEMMAKER /UNDO command to remove any changes that MemMaker made.

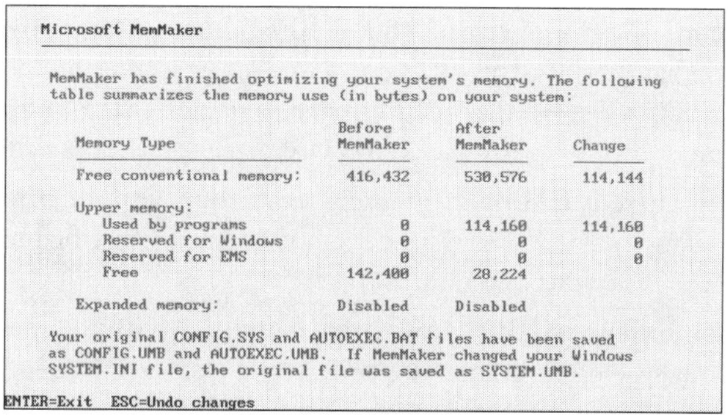

Figure 19.6
In this summary report from MemMaker, the third column indicates how much conventional memory you have saved.

```
Microsoft MemMaker

MemMaker has finished optimizing your system's memory. The following
table summarizes the memory use (in bytes) on your system:

                              Before          After
Memory Type                   MemMaker        MemMaker        Change

Free conventional memory:     416,432         530,576         114,144
Upper memory:
    Used by programs                0         114,160         114,160
    Reserved for Windows            0               0               0
    Reserved for EMS                0               0               0
    Free                      142,400          28,224
Expanded memory:              Disabled        Disabled

Your original CONFIG.SYS and AUTOEXEC.BAT files have been saved
as CONFIG.UMB and AUTOEXEC.UMB. If MemMaker changed your Windows
SYSTEM.INI file, the original file was saved as SYSTEM.UMB.

ENTER=Exit   ESC=Undo changes
```

9. When you finish examining this report, press Enter to exit MemMaker.

USING CUSTOM SETUP

Follow these steps to run MemMaker using Custom Setup:

1. At the DOS Prompt, type MEMMAKER and press Enter.
2. MemMaker asks whether you want to continue. Press Enter.
3. MemMaker asks whether you want Express or Custom Setup (refer to Figure 19.1). Press the spacebar to select Custom Setup and then press Enter to continue.
4. MemMaker asks whether you intend to use EMS memory (refer to Figure 19.2). Press the spacebar to choose Yes or No. After you have made the desired selection, press Enter.
5. MemMaker now displays Advanced Options that enable you to customize the settings used when optimizing memory. Each advanced option requires a Yes or No answer. Use the spacebar to answer. Use the down- and up-arrow keys to move from one option to the next. The following list explains the options that you have to set:
    - **Specify which drivers and TSRs to include in optimization?** Answering Yes enables you to leave out of optimization TSRs that must be loaded into memory in a specific sequence or that give MemMaker trouble during optimization.
    - **Scan the upper memory area aggressively?** If you answer Yes, MemMaker includes the HIGHSCAN parameter in the EMM386.EXE line of CONFIG.SYS. Although EMM386.EXE normally scans the address range C600-EFFF for available upper memory, adding HIGHSCAN instructs EMM386.EXE to scan the address range C600-F7FF.
    - **Optimize upper memory for use with Windows?** If you answer Yes, EMM386.EXE sets aside upper memory for use by Windows. This provides more memory for DOS programs that you run from Windows. If you do not run DOS programs from Windows, choose No.

- **Use monochrome region (B000-BFFF) for running programs?** Answer Yes if you have installed an EGA or VGA display adapter but not a monochrome or SuperVGA display adapter. The address range B000-BFFF can be used as upper memory if you have an EGA or VGA display adapter installed.
- **Keep current EMM386 memory exclusions and inclusions?** If you currently are using `EMM386.EXE` and have specific addresses specified to include or exclude, answer Yes to this question.
- **Move Extended BIOS Data Area from conventional to upper memory?** Normally, `EMM386.EXE` moves the Extended Bios Data Area (EBDA) to upper memory. If any unusual problems occur while you're running MemMaker, however, answer No to this option.

6. After you answer all the Advanced Options correctly, press Enter to continue with MemMaker.
7. MemMaker searches your hard disk for a copy of Windows. If it finds Windows, MemMaker displays the directory in which the copy of Windows resides. If this directory is incorrect, type the correct directory. Press Enter to continue.

From this point, MemMaker behaves exactly as in the Express Setup. Refer to the previous section, picking up with step 5.

Providing Memory for Your Applications

One of the most frustrating problems to encounter using DOS is trying to run a program and discovering that you do not have enough memory available.

If you are trying to run a new application and encounter this problem, you can take some steps to try to resolve it:

- Your `CONFIG.SYS` file loads `HIMEM.SYS` first and then `EMM386.EXE`. Together, these two drivers allow access to extended memory and upper memory blocks.
- Unless you are running applications that need expanded memory, use the `NOEMS` option for `EMM386.EXE` so that all extended memory is available as XMS memory.
- Load DOS into the high memory area and make upper memory available to DOS by entering the command `DOS=HIGH,UMB`.
- Use the `DEVICEHIGH` command for as many drivers as possible in your `CONFIG.SYS` file. You cannot use `DEVICEHIGH` for `HIMEM.SYS` or `EMM386.EXE`, and some other device drivers might not load properly with `DEVICEHIGH`. Experiment and use `MEM/C` to determine whether the drivers loaded properly.
- Use `LOADHIGH` for any TSRs you load in your `AUTOEXEC.BAT` file. Because some TSRs might not work correctly when loaded high, experiment until you determine what TSR you can load high.

- If you own a 386 computer or better, your CONFIG.SYS file begins with the following:

```
DEVICE=C:\DOS\HIMEM.SYS
DEVICE=C:\DOS\EMM386.EXE NOEMS
DOS=HIGH,UMB
```

Using the MEM command is very important in this case to see how much memory is available for programs. Another point to keep in mind is that you need to avoid loading any drivers that are unnecessary. If the application you are trying to run does not require sound, for example, and you have a sound card, try not loading the sound drivers.

> **Tip**
>
> One useful trick is to make multiple start configurations for different uses. If you have a game that requires a lot of memory, for example, and the only way to get it to run is not to load your tape drive driver, make a new startup configuration for it and use the DOS menu function.
>
> To find out more details about creating multiple configurations, refer to Chapter 2, "Starting DOS."

INCREASING HARD DISK PERFORMANCE

If your computer is typical, it spends a lot of its time accessing data and programs on hard disk. Speeding up your hard disk is probably the single most significant change you can make to increase the overall speed of your system. Although most later systems have a fast, IDE-based hard drive, you can configure DOS to make the most of it.

The BUFFERS command in CONFIG.SYS tells DOS how much memory to reserve for file transfers. DOS sets aside an area of RAM called a *buffer* for temporary storage of data being transferred between the disk and an application.

When DOS is asked to retrieve information from a disk, it reads the information in increments of whole sectors (512 bytes). Excess data not required from that sector is left in the buffer. If this data is needed later, DOS does not need to perform another disk access to retrieve the data. Similarly, DOS tries to reduce disk activity when it writes information to the disk. If less than a full sector is to be written to the disk, DOS accumulates the information in a disk buffer. When the buffer is full, DOS writes the information to the disk. This action is called *flushing the buffer*. To make sure that all pertinent information is placed into a file, DOS also flushes the buffers when a program closes a disk file.

Whenever a disk buffer is used, DOS marks it to indicate that it has been used recently. When DOS needs to reuse buffers for new information, it takes the buffer that has not been used for the longest time.

The net effect of DOS's use of buffers is to reduce the number of disk accesses by reading and writing only full sectors. By reusing the least-recently used buffers, DOS retains information more likely to be needed next. Your programs and, therefore, DOS run faster.

You can control the number of buffers available for DOS to use. Each buffer uses up some of your memory but results in faster disk access. The syntax for the BUFFERS command is shown in the following:

BUFFERS = n, m

The n parameter is the number of disk buffers you want DOS to allocate. A single buffer is about 512 bytes long (plus 16 bytes used by DOS). Use a number from 1 to 99. If you do not give the BUFFERS command, DOS uses a default value between 2 and 15, depending on the size of your disk drives, the amount of memory in your system, and the version of DOS you are using. Table 19.3 lists the different default buffer configurations.

TABLE 19.3   DEFAULT NUMBER OF DISK BUFFERS

Buffers	Hardware
2	360KB floppy disk drive
3	Any other hard or floppy disk drive
5	More than 128KB of RAM
10	More than 256KB of RAM
15	More than 512KB of RAM

The m parameter is a number in the range 1 through 8 that specifies the number of sectors DOS reads each time it is instructed to read a file. This feature is sometimes called a *secondary cache* or a *look-ahead buffer*. When files most often are read sequentially, this type of buffer increases performance. Do not use this secondary cache feature if you are using or plan to use a disk caching program such as SMARTDRV.SYS., discussed in Chapter 7, "Preparing and Maintaining Disks."

Increasing the number of buffers generally improves disk performance, up to a point. The recommended number of buffers increases with the size of your hard disk. Consider the suggested buffer numbers listed in Table 19.4 when adding a BUFFERS command to CONFIG.EXE. Using a number higher than the recommended number of buffers probably uses more memory without further improving speed.

TABLE 19.4   SUGGESTED NUMBER OF DISK BUFFERS

Hard Disk Size	Buffers
Less than 40MB	20
40MB to 79MB	30
80MB to 119MB	40
120MB or more	50

If you have an 85MB hard disk and are not using a hard disk caching program, for example, you might include the following BUFFERS command in CONFIG.SYS:

BUFFERS=40,8

Fine-Tuning Your Computer with CONFIG.SYS and AUTOEXEC.BAT

In addition to the commands covered earlier in this chapter, you can use many other commands in CONFIG.SYS or AUTOEXEC.BAT to customize your computer configuration. The following sections discuss other useful commands: FCBS, FILES, LASTDRIVE, SHELL, INSTALL, REM, and SWITCHES.

Accessing Files through FCBS

The FCBS configuration command enables you to use programs written for DOS 1.1; some DOS users find FCBs indispensable. FCB is an acronym for *file control block*. FCBs serve as one way a program can access a file. This method of file access was used by DOS 1.1 to communicate with programs. Later versions of DOS borrow a Unix-like method for controlling files, called *handles* (discussed in "Using the FILES Command" in this chapter). Although FCBs can be used with any version of DOS, only DOS 2.0 and higher can use handles.

The syntax for the FCBS command in the CONFIG.SYS file is as follows:

FCBS = *maxopen*

The *maxopen* parameter is a number between 1 and 255 that sets the maximum number of unique FCBs that programs can open at one time. The default number is four. You don't need to use this command in CONFIG.SYS unless you have a program that was designed to work with DOS 1.1 and the program cannot open all the required files (a message to this effect appears). In this case, use the FCBS command to increase the number of FCBs that can be open at one time.

You pay a small price in RAM to use the FCBS command. For each number greater than four that *maxopen* exceeds, DOS uses about 40 bytes.

Using the FILES Command

FILES is the configuration command used in DOS 2.0 and higher to allow for Unix-like file handling. Unix and later versions of DOS use a file handle (a number corresponding to the filename) instead of file control blocks to access files. You never have to deal with file handles directly. Each application program gives the operating system the name of the file or device you want to use. The operating system gives the program a handle, and the program uses that handle to manipulate the file or device.

To include the FILES command in CONFIG.SYS, use the following syntax:

FILES = *n*

The *n* parameter is a number (8, which is the default, through 255) that determines the number of files that can be open at one time during a DOS session. Each additional file beyond eight increases the size of DOS by 39 bytes.

If you do not specify the `FILES` command, DOS starts with eight file handles and immediately takes five handles for the standard devices, leaving only three handles for your programs. This number is almost never large enough for applications you are likely to run. On most systems, increase the number of handles to 20 or 30.

> **Note** Many installation programs for full-featured applications edit `CONFIG.SYS` for you and increase the number of files when necessary to run the software efficiently.

Using LASTDRIVE to Change the Number of Disk Drives

The `LASTDRIVE` configuration command informs DOS of the maximum number of disk drives on your system. Generally, `LASTDRIVE` is a command used with networked computers or with the pretender commands (such as `SUBST`).

If you do not use the `LASTDRIVE` command, DOS assumes that the last disk drive on your system is one more than the number of physical drives and RAM disks you are using. If your `LASTDRIVE` command specifies a letter corresponding to fewer drives than the number physically attached to your computer or created as RAM disks, DOS ignores the command. The `LASTDRIVE` command enables you to tell DOS how many disk drives, real or apparent, are on your system, including network drives and directories (if any) and drives created with the `SUBST` command.

If you want to use the `LASTDRIVE` command in `CONFIG.SYS`, use the following syntax:

`LASTDRIVE = x`

The *x* parameter is the letter for the last disk drive on your system. The letters *A* through *Z* in upper- or lowercase are acceptable.

Using the SHELL Command

The `SHELL` command was originally implemented to enable programmers to replace the DOS command interpreter (`COMMAND.COM`) with other command interpreters. The `SHELL` command is more commonly used, however, to perform the following two functions:

- Inform DOS that the command interpreter is in another directory, not in the boot disk's root directory.
- Expand the size of the environment—an area of RAM that stores named variables used by DOS and applications. Commands such as `PATH` and `PROMPT` store their current settings as environment variables. To display the contents of the environment, type `SET` at the command prompt and press Enter.

> **Caution**
> SHELL is a tricky command; use it with caution. If used incorrectly, the SHELL command can lock up your system. Keep a bootable floppy disk handy for restarting your computer in case you run into a problem.

The syntax for the SHELL command is as follows:

SHELL = *filespec parameters*

The *filespec* parameter is the path and filename of the command processor and should be COMMAND.COM if you are using the standard DOS command processor. The SHELL command doesn't take any other parameters or switches, but you can add command-line parameters or switches available for use with the command processor. The parameters for COMMAND.COM are explained in the next few paragraphs.

When used from the command line, COMMAND loads a copy of the command processor into memory. A common use of COMMAND is as a parameter of the SHELL command. The syntax for COMMAND is as follows:

COMMAND *d:path\ device* /E:*size* /P /C *string* /K:*filename* /MSG

The *d:path* parameter specifies the disk drive and path that contain the command processor if it is not located in the root directory. Always use this parameter when including COMMAND in the SHELL configuration command. This parameter has the additional effect of setting an environment variable named COMSPEC, which informs DOS and other programs of the location and name of the current command processor.

/E:*size* is an optional switch that sets the environment space. The *size* parameter is a number between 160 and 32,768 that denotes the amount of memory reserved for the environment. (If you do not specify a multiple of 16, DOS rounds the size parameter up to the next highest multiple of 16.) By default, DOS reserves 256 bytes for the environment.

The /P switch instructs DOS to load the command processor permanently. Without the /P switch, DOS loads COMMAND.COM only temporarily into memory. When you are using COMMAND with the SHELL command in CONFIG.SYS, be sure to use the /P switch.

The /C switch and *string* parameter work together. This combination causes DOS to load the command processor, execute any command represented by *string*, and then unload the command processor.

The /MSG switch tells DOS to store all its error messages in memory rather than read them from the disk. This feature can speed operation. More importantly, if you are running a system that has only floppy disks, you sometimes remove the disk that contains COMMAND.COM from the disk drive. Without the /MSG switch, DOS cannot access error messages contained on disk within the COMMAND.COM file itself. Use this switch only if you are running DOS from floppy disks. You also must use the /P switch any time you use the /MSG switch.

The /K parameter tells DOS to run a program or batch file. Use this switch only when you're running COMMAND from the DOS prompt and not as part of the SHELL command in CONFIG.SYS.

The DOS Setup program adds the following command to the default `CONFIG.SYS` file:

```
SHELL=C:\DOS\COMMAND.COM C:\DOS\ /P
```

This configuration command tells DOS that `COMMAND.COM` is the command interpreter and that it is located in the `\DOS` directory on the C drive. The `/P` switch causes the command interpreter to be loaded permanently, not temporarily, in memory.

The preceding `SHELL` command enables you to place a copy of `COMMAND.COM` in `C:\DOS` and delete the copy in the root directory. This practice helps you maintain a clean root directory and protects `COMMAND.COM` from being replaced by an older version that might be on a floppy disk you are copying. If you accidentally copy the disk to the root directory, you don't overwrite the current version of `COMMAND.COM`.

Occasionally, you create such a long `PATH` command in `AUTOEXEC.BAT` that you fill the available environment space, causing DOS to display the following message:

```
Out of environment space
```

If this message appears, use `COMMAND` with the `SHELL` command and the `/E` switch to specify a larger environment space. The following command used in `CONFIG.SYS`, for example, increases the environment to 384 bytes:

```
SHELL=C:\DOS\COMMAND.COM /E:384
```

If you already have a `SHELL` command in `CONFIG.SYS`, you can add the `/E` switch. Combining the two preceding `SHELL` commands, for example, you can include the following command in `CONFIG.SYS`:

```
SHELL=C:\DOS\COMMAND.COM C:\DOS\ /P /E:384
```

> **Tip**
>
> The `SHELL` command itself doesn't use any memory, but by increasing the environment space, you can reduce the amount of free conventional memory by an equal amount. In other words, increasing the environment space from 256 bytes to 384 bytes reduces free memory by 128 bytes.

USING THE INSTALL COMMAND

The `INSTALL` configuration command enables you to load memory-resident programs from within `CONFIG.SYS`. In versions of DOS before 4.0, you had to load these programs from the DOS prompt or through a batch file, such as `AUTOEXEC.BAT`. You can save several kilobytes of memory by loading a program from `CONFIG.SYS` with `INSTALL` rather than from the command line or a batch file as an executable program. DOS 4.0 and later versions support loading any of the following programs by using `INSTALL`:

- `FASTOPEN.EXE`
- `KEYB.COM`
- `NLSFUNC.EXE`
- `SHARE.EXE`

→ For more information about these programs, **see** Appendix F, "Command Reference," **p. 583**.

The following is the syntax for using INSTALL in CONFIG.SYS:

`INSTALL = filespec parameters`

The *filespec* parameter is the path and filename information of the utility you want to load, whereas *parameters* specifies any parameters or switches required by the utility you want DOS to load.

You might be able to use INSTALL with some memory-resident non-DOS programs. Do not use INSTALL, however, to load a memory-resident program that uses environment variables or shortcut keys or that uses COMMAND.COM. The program you install with this command must have the extension .COM or .EXE.

USING THE REM COMMAND

The REM configuration command is equivalent to the REM batch file command. This command enables you to insert remarks into your CONFIG.SYS file. You can leave notes to yourself (or others) explaining what particular lines do. Such documentation in a CONFIG.SYS file is especially helpful if you use non-DOS device drivers for your hardware. You also can temporarily remove a CONFIG.SYS statement by prefacing the statement with a REM command. After you test the new configuration, you can return easily to the old configuration by simply removing the REM command.

The syntax for the REM command is as follows:

`REM remarks`

The *remarks* parameter can be any string of characters that fits on a single line in the CONFIG.SYS file.

USING THE SWITCHES COMMAND

The SWITCHES configuration command enables you to set any of four options that control how four of DOS's features operate. The syntax of the SWITCHES command is as follows:

`SWITCHES = /K /W /N /F`

You can specify one or more of these four switches in a single SWITCHES command.

The /K switch turns off the enhanced keyboard functions. This command works like the ANSI.SYS /K switch. Some software cannot work with the enhanced keyboard. Use this command to disable the enhanced keyboard so that the software functions properly. If you use the SWITCHES=/K command in CONFIG.SYS and also install ANSI.SYS as a device driver, add the /K switch to the DEVICE=ANSI.SYS line as well.

The /W switch specifies that the WINA20.386 file has been moved to a directory other than the root directory. Use this switch if you moved WINA20.386 to another directory and are using Windows in enhanced mode.

Normally, you can use the F5 or F8 keys during the first two seconds of booting to bypass some or all the commands in `CONFIG.SYS` or `AUTOEXEC.BAT`. The `/N` switch tells DOS to ignore F5 or F8 during boot.

Normally, DOS displays this message at the beginning of the boot process and then pauses for two seconds before continuing:

```
Starting MS-DOS
```

The `/F` switch tells DOS to skip the two-second pause.

Telling DOS When to Break

As you already know, Ctrl+Break and Ctrl+C are helpful but not foolproof panic buttons you can use to stop commands. The response to a Ctrl+Break or Ctrl+C is not instantaneous. Although only an "Oh, no" second might pass from the time you press the panic button until DOS responds, you still have time to wonder why DOS takes so long to respond. The reason is that DOS is busy doing other things most of the time and looks for Ctrl+Break only at intervals. You can use the `BREAK` command in `CONFIG.SYS` to tell DOS when to check for this key sequence. `BREAK` does not enable or disable the Break key; the `BREAK` command only controls when DOS checks for the Break key.

The syntax for the `BREAK` command can be either of the following:

`BREAK=ON`

`BREAK=OFF`

The default setting for this command is `OFF`.

If you use the command `BREAK=ON` in `CONFIG.SYS`, DOS checks to see whether you pressed Ctrl+Break whenever a program requests some activity from DOS (performs a DOS function call). If you use the command `BREAK=OFF`, DOS checks for a Ctrl+Break only when DOS is working with the video display, keyboard, printer, or asynchronous serial adapters (the ports at the back of the computer).

> **Tip**
> If you use programs that do a great deal of disk accessing but little keyboard or screen work, you might want to set `BREAK=ON`. This setting enables you to break out of the program quicker when something goes awry or when you simply want to stop DOS.

Using the DOS Pretender Commands

Because DOS manages disks in a logical rather than a strictly physical way, DOS can pretend that a disk's identity is different from the disk's name. DOS provides the following three commands that pretend that a disk's identity has changed:

- `ASSIGN`—Redirects disk operations from one disk to another
- `JOIN`—Attaches an entire disk as a subdirectory to the directory structure of another disk
- `SUBST`—Makes a directory of a disk appear to commands as a separate disk

Using Other Device Control Commands

→ For detailed information on these commands, **see** Chapter 11, "Controlling Your Environment," **p. 293**.

DOS provides other commands to control devices and report system information, which are briefly discussed in this section.

→ These commands are explained in greater detail in Appendix F, "Command Reference," beginning on **p. 583**.

The SET command displays the current environment settings and enables you to make new variable assignments.

The PRINT command enables you to print text files on your printer while you continue to do other PC work. This "background" printing can be a great timesaver if your applications don't have a similar feature.

The MODE command is a multifaceted device-control command. MODE can establish the height and width of your screen's lines and characters and control the speed of your serial ports. MODE can redirect the output from a parallel printer port to a serial port. You also can use MODE in association with code-page support for international character sets on the PC. You might want to browse through the MODE section of the "Command Reference."

CHAPTER 20

NETWORKING DOS

In this chapter

Common Networks for DOS-Based Computers   472

Learning Preinstallation Items   472

Installing the Novell NetWare Client Software   473

Installing the Microsoft Network Client   478

Using the Network   481

Project: Network Client Setup Tips   482

Common Networks for DOS-Based Computers

You might commonly connect a DOS-based computer to two different networks: Novell NetWare and Microsoft Windows NT Server. Both network operating systems (NOSs) provide client software for DOS that enables you to participate in many of the services offered by both networks, such as file sharing, printer sharing, network security for stored files, and so forth. Installing the client software for each network operating system is relatively straightforward. In this chapter, you learn about installing both the NetWare and Microsoft clients.

Learning Preinstallation Items

Before installing either NOS client, you need to perform a few steps. Primarily, they consist of installing an appropriate network card into the PC and making sure that you have the appropriate DOS driver program for that network card for the NOS client you are installing.

Network cards come in many different varieties. You need to have one that is compatible with the following:

- **The computer you are installing it in.** It should fit in an available slot (ISA, EISA, MCA, or PCI), and should be selectable to an available combination of IRQ, memory port address, and (sometimes) DMA channels. See Chapter 12, "Using Peripherals," for more information on these subjects.
- **The network client you are installing.** Often, NetWare and Microsoft clients have separate driver files. To make things trickier, both companies offer different versions of their client software, and the driver must be compatible with the client you are using. For example, Novell has supplied both ODI and VLM clients, whereas Microsoft has supplied both LanManager and Windows NT clients. If in doubt, check the NOS company's Web site for a list of compatible hardware.
- **The network type you have.** Cards are available for Ethernet, Token Ring, and ARCnet, and you need one compatible with the type of network you are accessing.
- **The cabling type you use.** All the different network types can use different types of cabling, and network cards might not have all the available choices built into them. For instance, Ethernet can be cabled with 10BASE-5 cable (Thick Ethernet), 10BASE-2 cable (Thin Ethernet), or Category 3 or 5 twisted-pair cable (10BASE-T and 10BASE-100). Although adapters might be available to make a particular card work with a dissimilar network, it is better to have a card that supports the network cabling directly.
- **What frame type the network uses.** For example, Ethernet networks might use 802.2, 802.3, Ethernet SNAP, or Ethernet II frame types.

You also need to know some details about the network server you are connecting to. You need to know answers to the following questions:

- What protocol is the server using? Novell networks predominantly use IPX/SPX but sometimes can use TCP/IP. Microsoft networks might use NetBEUI, TCP/IP, IPX/SPX, or any combination thereof.
- If you are using TCP/IP, you need to know a host of additional information:
  - The IP address you are to use for the machine
  - The IP mask you are to use for the machine
  - At least one DNS server address you can use (two are better, but only one is required)
  - The address of the gateway through which the network connects to the Internet, if one exists
- What is the username and password of a valid account with which you can log in to the network?
- If using a Novell network, are you going to use a bindery login or a Novell Network Directory Service (NDS) login? Note that even though both usually work, it's also true that only one might work on any given network, depending on how it was set up.

After collecting all the preceding information, you can proceed to install the network client software and make your initial network connection.

INSTALLING THE NOVELL NETWARE CLIENT SOFTWARE

The latest Novell NetWare client for DOS is amazingly large: about 22MB before being installed. It is available on a CD-ROM that comes with the NOS or can be downloaded from Novell's Web site (in a self-extracting zip file). When you download the compressed file, you then execute the file to extract all the installation files. You can then run the INSTALL program, as follows, to begin the actual installation of the client software:

1. When you begin the installation, you first see a license screen (see Figure 20.1). If you agree to the license, press Enter to continue.

Figure 20.1
The Novell license screen.

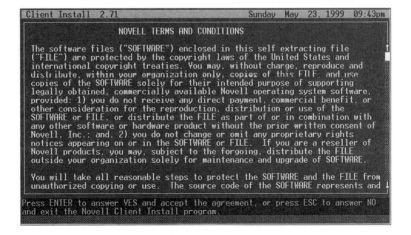

2. You then see a selection screen in which you choose which client options you want to install. This selection screen is shown in Figure 20.2. The choices are detailed in Table 20.1.

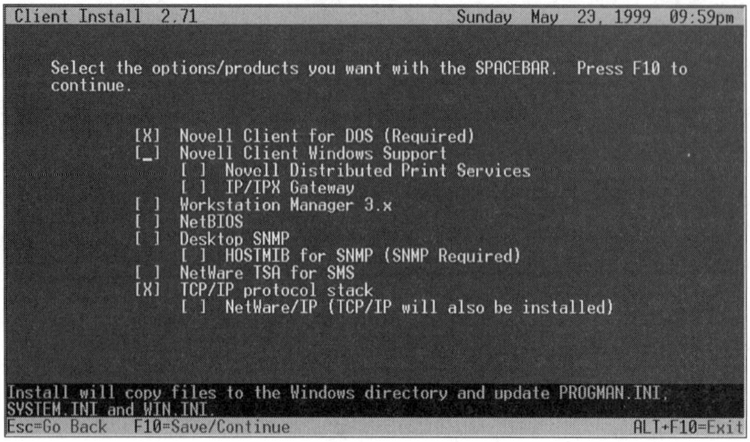

Figure 20.2
The Novell client option selection screen.

```
Client Install  2.71                           Sunday   May  23, 1999  09:59pm

      Select the options/products you want with the SPACEBAR.  Press F10 to
      continue.

                    [X] Novell Client for DOS (Required)
                    [_] Novell Client Windows Support
                        [ ] Novell Distributed Print Services
                        [ ] IP/IPX Gateway
                    [ ] Workstation Manager 3.x
                    [ ] NetBIOS
                    [ ] Desktop SNMP
                        [ ] HOSTMIB for SNMP (SNMP Required)
                    [ ] NetWare TSA for SMS
                    [X] TCP/IP protocol stack
                        [ ] NetWare/IP (TCP/IP will also be installed)



Install will copy files to the Windows directory and update PROGMAN.INI,
SYSTEM.INI and WIN.INI.
Esc=Go Back   F10=Save/Continue                                ALT+F10=Exit
```

TABLE 20.1 NOVELL CLIENT INSTALLATION OPTIONS

Option	Description
Novell Client for DOS	Required; specifies the basic network software with the IPX/SPX protocol
Novell Client Windows Support	Enables additional Windows 3.x support
Novell Distributed Print Services	Provides better print management with Windows 3.x
IP/IPX Gateway	Enables Windows 3.x applications to use a Novell Internet gateway
Workstation Manager 3.x	Adds administrative programs
NetBIOS	Enables NetBIOS support
Desktop SNMP	Enables support for Simple Network Management Protocol
NetWare TSA for SMS	Installs centralized backup support for the client
TCP/IP Protocol Stack	Installs support for TCP/IP
NetWare/IP	Installs support for NetWare/IP

For this example, Novell Client for DOS and TCP/IP Protocol Stack have been chosen. After you select the appropriate check boxes, press F10 to proceed.

3. If you selected TCP/IP, you are asked specific information about your TCP/IP network configuration. The first question prompts you about any DHCP, BOOTP, or RARP hosts on the network, as shown in Figure 20.3. For this example, it is assumed that these hosts do not exist.

Figure 20.3
Select a configuration host for TCP/IP.

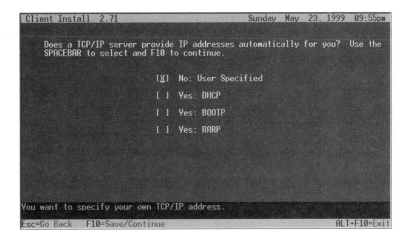

4. Assuming you have chosen to enter your TCP/IP information manually, provide the IP address, router address, subnetwork mask, DNS domain name, and DNS addresses to the configuration. Figure 20.4 shows this screen with some sample values entered.

Figure 20.4
Enter manual TCP/IP information.

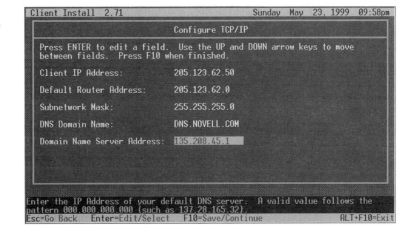

5. You are then prompted for whether you are using a 16- or 32-bit network interface. You have to check the driver files available for your network card. If they have the LAN file extension, they support a 32-bit interface, whereas if they have a COM or EXE extension, they support only a 16-bit interface.

6. You are shown a list of drivers that are included with the Novell client software, as shown in Figure 20.5. Choose your adapter from the list and press F10 to continue.

Figure 20.5
Choose a LAN board.

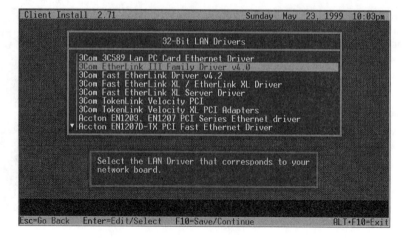

7. You now choose some additional configuration information for your network and network card. Complete the requested information (check with your network administrator if you don't have the answers yet to any of the questions because you must supply the *correct* answers to all the questions so that the network connection can function). Figure 20.6 shows this additional configuration screen.

Figure 20.6
Provide additional configuration information to the setup program.

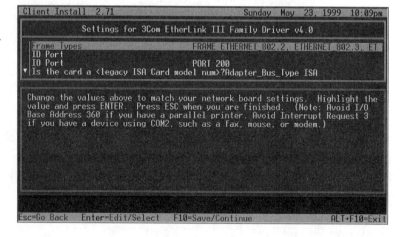

8. After pressing F10, you see the screen shown in Figure 20.7. Here, you choose whether the installation program is to modify your AUTOEXEC.BAT and CONFIG.SYS files (it should), the directory into which the client software is to be installed (accept the default), and you have a chance to confirm the network interface type and card type you plan to use.

Figure 20.7
Check the Installation Configuration Summary screen.

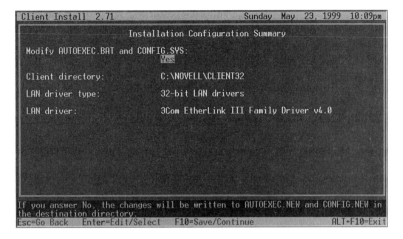

9. After you press F10 a final time, the client software is installed into the computer. As part of this installation, a number of changes take place on the computer's C: drive, including adding two lines to the AUTOEXEC.BAT file. First, the path to the Novell client is added. Second, a reference to another batch file, called (typically) C:\NOVELL\CLIENT32\STARTNET.BAT, is added. The STARTNET.BAT file contains the following lines that actually start the network client when the computer is restarted:

```
SET NWLANGUAGE=ENGLISH
C:\NOVELL\CLIENT32\NIOS.EXE
LOAD C:\NOVELL\CLIENT32\NBIC32.NLM
LOAD C:\NOVELL\CLIENT32\LSLC32.NLM
LOAD C:\NOVELL\CLIENT32\CMSM.NLM
LOAD C:\NOVELL\CLIENT32\ETHERTSM.NLM
LOAD C:\NOVELL\CLIENT32\3C5X9.LAN FRAME=ETHERNET_802.2 PORT=200 ISA RXEARLY=NO
LOAD C:\NOVELL\CLIENT32\3C5X9.LAN FRAME=ETHERNET_802.3 PORT=200 ISA RXEARLY=NO
LOAD C:\NOVELL\CLIENT32\3C5X9.LAN FRAME=ETHERNET_II PORT=200 ISA RXEARLY=NO
LOAD C:\NOVELL\CLIENT32\3C5X9.LAN FRAME=ETHERNET_SNAP PORT=200 ISA RXEARLY=NO
LOAD C:\NOVELL\CLIENT32\TCPIP.NLM
LOAD C:\NOVELL\CLIENT32\TRANNTA.NLM
LOAD C:\NOVELL\CLIENT32\IPX.NLM
LOAD C:\NOVELL\CLIENT32\SPX_SKTS.NLM
LOAD C:\NOVELL\CLIENT32\CLIENT32.NLM
```

For TCP/IP installations, a file called RESOLVE.CFG is created in the C:\NOVELL\CLIENT32\TCP directory; it contains the information about the domain name and DNS server you plan to use.

After you restart the computer, the Novell client starts, and you can log in to a Novell server normally. At this point, if any difficulties arise, consult with a network administrator for your network.

Installing the Microsoft Network Client

Installing the Microsoft network client for MS-DOS is somewhat easier than installing the NetWare client:

1. After you procure the client software (it is available on the Windows NT Server 4.0 CD-ROM or by download from ftp.microsoft.com), extract the component parts into an installation directory. Then, from that directory, use the SETUP program to begin the installation. The introductory screen to the setup program is shown in Figure 20.8.

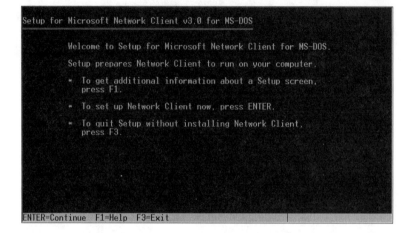

Figure 20.8
The introductory screen for Microsoft Client Setup.

2. Press Enter to be prompted for the directory to which you want to install the Microsoft client. The default is C:\NET. Accept the default and press Enter to continue.
3. You are now prompted for your username on the network. You should have acquired this information from your network administrator. Enter the correct username and press Enter.
4. You now see the master setup screen, as shown in Figure 20.9. Here, you can change your username, change setup options, and set important protocol information.

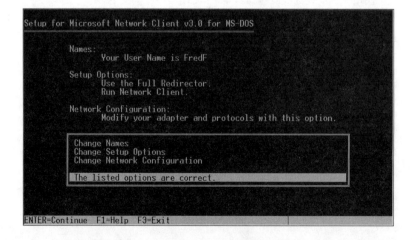

Figure 20.9
The master setup screen.

5. Choose Change Setup Options to see the screen shown in Figure 20.10. You can then set the following options:
   - **Change Redir Options**—Do you use basic or full redirector? The basic redirector supports most functions and uses less memory than the full redirector but cannot log in to a Windows NT domain. Usually, you have to use the full redirector.
   - **Change Startup Options**—You can load the redirector, load the redirector and pop-up, or not load anything. This setting controls which features are started automatically when you boot the computer. Choosing to automatically load the pop-up consumes an additional 29KB of conventional memory but provides you with more network information than otherwise. Usually, you should just choose Load Network Client.
   - **Change Logon Validation**—If your network uses a domain security model, you need to change this option so that you can log in to the domain.
   - **Change Net Pop Hot Key**—Allows you to specify which key to use with Ctrl+Alt to view the pop-up interface.

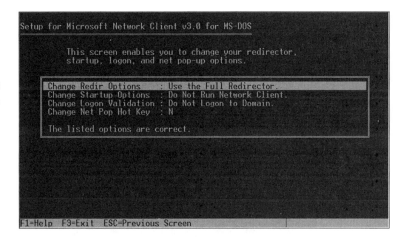

Figure 20.10
You can modify setup options for the Microsoft Network Client during installation using the Change Setup Options screen.

6. Choose the Change Network Configuration option from the master setup screen; you see the screen shown in Figure 20.11. The Change Network Configuration screen is complex and has many possible layers, depending on what networking options you need (and rarely do you need just the default options).

Figure 20.11
The Change Network Configuration screen allows you to make advanced changes to how your client accesses the network.

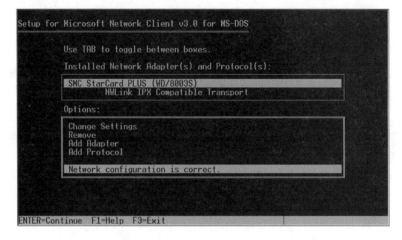

7. The good news is that the installation program detects (if it can) your network card and displays its choice, along with a default protocol selection. If either is incorrect, you can change it by choosing the Change Settings option or the Remove and Add Protocol options. You can also use the Tab key to move between the two boxes and can then choose a different option to change. For example, you can tab to the top box and then choose the IPX/SPX protocol to change any options there. When you choose Change Settings for the network card, you see the detailed settings for your network card, as shown in Figure 20.12. You can select the appropriate IRQ, DMA, and other options for your network card. (You might need to run the setup program for the card itself to get some of these values; you need to do so before you install the network client, if possible.)

Figure 20.12
You can modify your network card hardware and protocol settings during setup.

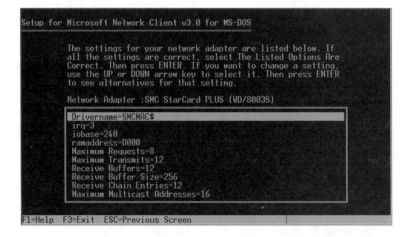

8. If you want to use TCP/IP, use the Add Protocol option and then choose TCP/IP from the following screen. After you return to the Change Network Configuration screen, you can choose the TCP/IP protocol from the list and change its settings. Here, you can set your IP address, subnet mask, and other TCP/IP options gathered at the beginning of this chapter (see Figure 20.13).

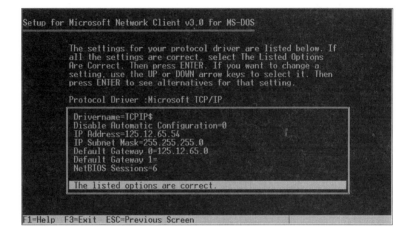

Figure 20.13
You must enter your TCP/IP address settings to use the TCP/IP protocol.

9. After you add the necessary protocols and set all options, choose The Listed Options Are Correct to return to the master setup screen. From there, choose The Listed Options Are Correct to begin the installation, which proceeds without further input from you.

At the completion of the installation, you need to restart the computer to load the appropriate drivers and access the network.

USING THE NETWORK

After you have installed the appropriate DOS client software for your network, you can proceed to use the network. Using the network can be a complex topic; it includes a number of different commands and utilities all unique to the network you are using. For Novell networks, peruse the user manuals that came with the NOS. You will use commands such as LOGIN, MAP, NPRINT, and FILER to accomplish many network tasks, although you should be sure to review the complete list because you might find many commands useful.

For Microsoft networks, you can accomplish most tasks by using the NET command, which is a sort of *hydra* (multiheaded) command that can do many different things, from logging you in to the network to mapping network drives to assigning file permissions to others. Typing NET ? gets you started with these commands (although you need to read the documentation on using the NET command for proper details).

Project: Network Client Setup Tips

Setting up a DOS network client can be difficult if you're not the network administrator and are trying to reinvent the wheel. To make the job go smoothly, make sure you find out any information specific to your network from the network administrator or person who set up the network. If that doesn't work and you're having trouble connecting to the network, you can "dissect" another user's functioning network connection to see what settings might be wrong on your system. Looking at a working computer's setup can be an invaluable aid in quickly spotting the problem with your own connection.

If, for some reason, the preceding two resources don't help you find a quick answer to your connection problem, try the following tips:

- Make sure that the network interface card (NIC) is functioning. Most NICs come with diagnostic software that can perform basic tests. Often, you also can run more comprehensive diagnostic software that sends data between the computer being tested and another running the diagnostic software to confirm that it is fully functioning.

- If you're having a problem with the NIC working properly, the problem is almost certainly the result of a conflict with another device. Chapter 12 provides information on resolving device conflicts.

- Make sure that you have the correct protocol chosen for your network. For Ethernet networks, make sure you've also chosen the correct frame type, which is 802.3, 802.2, Ethernet II, or Ethernet SNAP.

- If your network uses TCP/IP, make sure that you have the correct addresses for your TCP/IP configuration. Also, make sure that you're using a unique address that is not conflicting with another computer. (You might have to rely on a network administrator to help ensure this address because all networks track these things differently.)

- For Novell network clients, watch carefully as the different programs that make up the client load on the screen after the computer is booted. Often, you can see an error message (it might be fleeting) that leads you to the solution.

- Try removing the network startup commands from the AUTOEXEC.BAT file. Boot the system without them and then issue those same commands manually at the DOS prompt. This approach enables you to see error messages or problems more clearly.

The nice thing about networks is that you usually have to solve problems only once, and you then can apply that knowledge to successive installations of the client software. For this reason, I can't emphasize strongly enough that your first course of action if a network client installation isn't working right is to talk to people who have made it work properly and to the administrator of the system who probably will be familiar with whatever problem you are having. In most networks, after the bugs are worked out with a sample client installation or two (or three!), getting the remaining systems up and running then becomes easy.

CHAPTER 21

CONNECTING TO THE INTERNET

In this chapter

Internet Connection Options for DOS-Based Computers   484

Connecting to Your ISP   484

Using Internet Tools   485

A Sample FTP Session   489

Project: Common Problems with DOS Internet Tools   491

Internet Connection Options for DOS-Based Computers

Although you can connect a DOS-based computer directly to the Internet (through an ISP using a PPP connection), this is almost never done. Instead, you can more easily use a terminal emulation program to dial in to what is called a *shell account* with an ISP, such as Netcom. Dialing in this way gives you the appearance of sitting at a Unix-based terminal connected to the Internet. You can use all the Unix tools to perform various tasks on the Internet, such as transferring files from a remote host to your shell account (FTP), opening a terminal session on another computer on the Internet (Telnet), searching for information using Gopher, or getting rudimentary access (text based) to the World Wide Web.

You also need to be aware of another aspect of using DOS with the Internet. Even when you have a Windows-based PC, many of the basic tools for the Internet are text based and work very well in a DOS window. So, you can connect your Windows 9x PC to an ISP; open a DOS window; and run FTP, Telnet, or other DOS-based Internet utilities, for example. In this chapter, you learn about both these DOS-based Internet access methods.

Connecting to Your ISP

Many ISPs offer a type of account called a *shell account*. This account enables you to dial in to the ISP's system using just about any type of computer, provided it has a terminal emulation program that is compatible with the terminal emulation of the shell account (most are). After you have connected, the terminal emulation program gives you a window to a Unix host at the ISP (which means that you'll be using Unix commands), from which you can perform most Internet-related work. Most shell accounts include a certain amount of disk space in which you can store files you've retrieved from other systems or have uploaded from your own computer, and often you can even upload Web pages to the disk space and use the WWW services of your ISP to serve those Web pages up to others.

To connect to an ISP with a shell account, you use a terminal emulation program such as Procomm Plus, SmartTerm, or one of many others. Good shareware terminal emulation programs are also available, such as the top-rated Telix, Qmodem, or SlickTerminal, all of which can be downloaded from a number of Internet sites, including www.zdnet.com.

Usually, connecting to the ISP is relatively easy. Using the information provided by the ISP, follow these steps:

1. Set the terminal emulation program's parameters (COM port, modem type, baud rate, data bits, stop bits, and parity).
2. Set the phone number for the ISP.
3. Dial the number.

After connecting, you see a prompt and can use the basic Unix commands listed in Table 21.1.

TABLE 21.1 BASIC UNIX COMMANDS

Command	Parameters	Description
cd	directory_name	Changes directory. If you don't specify a directory, it displays your current directory.
cp	source_file dest_file	Copies a file.
ls	Optional wildcards	Lists files (very similar to DIR).
mv	source_file dest_file	Moves a file.

> **Note**
>
> Keep in mind that, unlike DOS systems, Unix systems are *case sensitive*. In Unix, you're free to have four files called File, file, FILE, and FiLE, all in the same directory. This also means that your commands don't work correctly unless you match the case of the file you're operating on *exactly*.
>
> Another point to keep in mind is that Unix uses the forward slash (/) for directory separators instead of the DOS backslash (\).

USING INTERNET TOOLS

Whether you are using a shell account or a DOS window on a Windows computer connected to the Internet, you use two key Internet tools. Fortunately, these tools function almost identically either way; Telnet and FTP work similarly under Unix as in a DOS window.

Using the Telnet program is extremely easy. You simply type a command at the shell prompt, followed by the address of the computer to which you want to connect, and press Enter. When you connect to the computer in question, you are prompted for a username and password. After you've logged on to the remote system, you proceed just like you're sitting at a terminal connected to that other system. Working this way can get rather confusing after a while because you can use the remote system to telnet to another system, to yet another system, and so forth.

In some cases, you specify not only the remote system's address, but also a port number. Unix hosts on the Internet can host a number of different services, and often certain services are restricted to certain port numbers. You specify these port numbers after the address, separated by a space.

> **Tip**
>
> Telnet usernames and passwords are case sensitive.

Most publicly available Telnet systems might not require a username and password; you might be able to connect immediately, although in these cases, you are usually restricted to limited actions on the remote system. For example, if you use Telnet to access um-weather.sprl.umich.edu:3000 (note the port number 3000 being used), you quickly connect to a menu system that gives you up-to-date weather conditions for cities all over the U.S. However, you then cannot use Telnet on that computer to connect to another. Instead, you simply disconnect from that host and open a new host (which is actually what you do all the time anyway; anything else is not very productive).

The abbreviation *FTP* stands for two different things; it stands for both *file transfer protocol* as well as *file transfer program*. In fact, the FTP program uses the FTP protocol to do its work; they were developed at the same time and for the same purpose.

FTP enables you to transfer files to and from an *FTP server* over the Internet. For example, you might use Microsoft's FTP server to download a patch for one of its products and use the FTP program to do so. You also might have an FTP server in your organization that you transfer files to and from.

You connect to an FTP server by typing FTP at a command prompt (either DOS window or shell account prompt), followed by the address of the server you want to log in to. You then are prompted for your username and password. Note that many FTP servers are set up to allow anonymous access. For these servers, you type anonymous as the username and your e-mail address as the password.

After you have connected to an FTP server, all the various FTP commands are available to you. Usually, you can get an onscreen list of these commands by typing either ? or HELP and pressing Enter. Figure 21.1 shows the DOS FTP client included with Windows 98 with its help screen displayed. To get a limited amount of help with any particular command, type either ? or HELP, followed by the name of the command.

Note

The commands in the FTP program are not case sensitive. Keep in mind, however, that the file and directory names that you often work with on Unix are.

Figure 21.1
A sample FTP program with its help display.

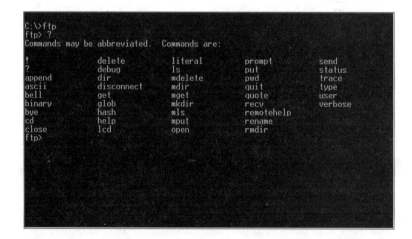

There are a number of important and regularly used commands in the FTP program. Table 21.2 details these FTP commands.

TABLE 21.2 FTP COMMAND SUMMARY

Command	Parameters	Description
ASCII	None	Sets the ASCII file transfer type. Any retrieved or sent files are processed as though they were ASCII files. This is the default mode for FTP but should *not* be used when you're transferring binary files.
BINARY	None	Sets the binary file transfer type, where any received or sent files are sent exactly as they occur, byte by byte. You almost always should issue this command immediately after starting FTP because most file transfers require it for the resulting file to be usable.
BYE	None	Closes the connection and exits the FTP program.
CD	*Directory name*	Changes directory on the remote system.
CLOSE	None	Terminates the FTP session with the remote FTP server but leaves the FTP program open and ready to connect to another server.
DELETE	*Filename*	Deletes a remote file. Note that most FTP servers don't enable you to delete a remote file unless you have complete ownership of the file in question.
DIR	*Directory* or *wildcard*	Lists contents of files on remote systems. This command is identical to ls -l.
DISCONNECT	None	Same as the CLOSE command.
GET	*Filename*	Retrieves a single file from the remote system. Make sure you choose the right file transfer mode first.
LCD	*Directory name*	Changes the local directory name. Use this command before you retrieve a file from the remote system if you don't start FTP from the directory in which you want to store the received file.
LS	*Directory* or *wildcard*	Functions similarly to the DOS DIR command. You also might (on some systems) append different parameters to get different types of listings. For example, try -l and -w. You need not use a directory or wildcard with this command; again, it's just like DIR in this respect. If you leave off the parameter, all files in the current directory are listed.

Table 21.2 Continued

Command	Parameters	Description
MDELETE	Wildcard	Deletes multiple files. You must have permission to delete files on the remote system.
MGET	Wildcard	Gets multiple files from a remote system. For example, MGET *.* gets all the files in the current directory.
MKDIR	Directory name	Creates a directory on the remote system.
MPUT	Wildcard	Sends multiple files to a remote system. You must have file create privileges for the directory to which you are sending the files.
OPEN	FTP Server Name	Opens a connection to the specified FTP server.
PROMPT	None	Toggles on and off the prompt setting. The default is to prompt you for each file when you use MPUT or MGET. Typing PROMPT before using those commands enables them to proceed much faster, without file-by-file confirmation from you.
PUT	Filename	Transfers a file to a remote system. You must have file create privileges on the remote system.
PWD	None	Displays (prints) the working directory on the remote system.
QUIT	None	Closes the FTP connection and exits FTP.
RECV	Filename	Synonymous with GET; works the same.
REMOTEHELP	None	Displays commands accepted by the remote system.
RENAME	Src_file Dest_file	Renames a file on the remote system.
RMDIR	Directory name	Removes a directory on the remote system.
SEND	Filename	Synonymous with PUT.
STATUS	None	Displays current connection status.
!	Various	Placing the exclamation point in front of most of the FTP commands makes them apply to your own computer. For example, !dir lists files in your local directory. Similarly, commands such as !cd, !mkdir, and !rmdir perform those functions on your computer without interrupting your FTP session.

A Sample FTP Session

Now that you know what FTP does, review this section to see how it actually works. For this example, you see how to start FTP, connect to Microsoft's FTP server (used as an example), display and list directories, navigate to a particular directory, and retrieve the files contained there.

> **Tip**
> Start from the directory to which you want to transfer files. Starting from this directory saves time because you don't have to perform the !cd command within the FTP program when you start it.

In this example, the client networking files for MS-DOS will be retrieved from Microsoft's FTP server. The files will be placed in the C:\CLIENT directory, so that directory is chosen before starting the FTP program by simply typing FTP and pressing Enter. Follow these steps:

1. After you start FTP, connect to the site by using the OPEN command, as follows, and then pressing Enter:

   open ftp.microsoft.com

2. After connecting, you are prompted for a username and password. Type anonymous for the username and your e-mail address as the password. Figure 21.2 shows the results of completing these steps.

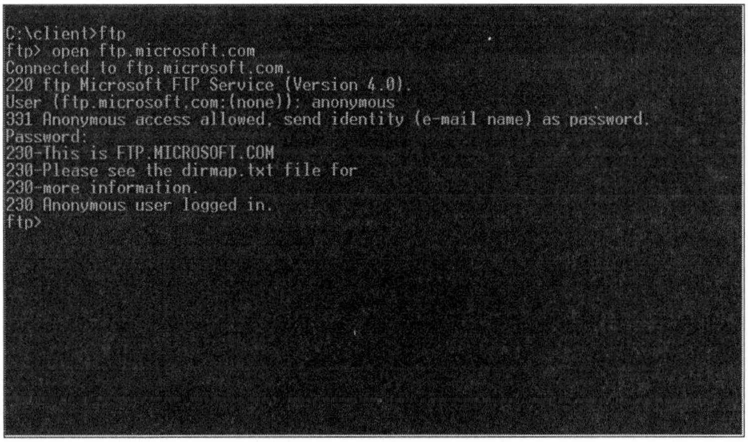

Figure 21.2
Connecting to ftp.microsoft.com.

```
C:\client>ftp
ftp> open ftp.microsoft.com
Connected to ftp.microsoft.com.
220 ftp Microsoft FTP Service (Version 4.0).
User (ftp.microsoft.com:(none)): anonymous
331 Anonymous access allowed, send identity (e-mail name) as password.
Password:
230-This is FTP.MICROSOFT.COM
230-Please see the dirmap.txt file for
230-more information.
230 Anonymous user logged in.
ftp>
```

3. After your password is accepted, you can get your bearings on the remote system by using the ls command. It is preferable to use ls -l because you then can tell the difference between files and directories. Figure 22.3 shows the results of using the ls -l command.

Figure 21.3
Using the `ls -1` command.

```
ftp> ls -l
200 PORT command successful.
150 Opening ASCII mode data connection for /bin/ls.
dr-xr-xr-x   1 owner    group              0 May  4 16:34 bussys
dr-xr-xr-x   1 owner    group              0 Nov  5  1997 deskapps
dr-xr-xr-x   1 owner    group              0 Apr 20 16:41 developr
-r-xr-xr-x   1 owner    group           7983 Jan 28 15:29 dirmap.htm
-r-xr-xr-x   1 owner    group           4333 Jan 28 15:28 dirmap.txt
-r-xr-xr-x   1 owner    group            710 Apr 12  1993 DISCLAIM.TXT
-r-xr-xr-x   1 owner    group            712 Aug 25  1994 disclaimer.txt
-r-xr-xr-x   1 owner    group        1245110 Oct  7  1998 HOMEMM.old
dr-xr-xr-x   1 owner    group              0 Mar 26 18:14 KBHelp
-r-xr-xr-x   1 owner    group       10990633 May 23  3:21 ls-lR.txt
-r-xr-xr-x   1 owner    group        2105460 May 23  3:21 ls-lR.Z
-r-xr-xr-x   1 owner    group        1132501 May 23  3:21 LS-LR.ZIP
dr-xr-xr-x   1 owner    group              0 Oct 11  1995 peropsys
-r-xr-xr-x   1 owner    group           8738 Dec 28  1998 PRODUCT.TBL
dr-xr-xr-x   1 owner    group              0 Apr 12  9:27 Products
dr-xr-xr-x   1 owner    group              0 Mar 24 13:57 ResKit
dr-xr-xr-x   1 owner    group              0 Apr 20 16:59 Services
dr-xr-xr-x   1 owner    group              0 May  3  6:37 Softlib
dr-xr-xr-x   1 owner    group              0 Dec 11  1998 solutions
226 Transfer complete.
ftp: 1325 bytes received in 3.51Seconds 0.38Kbytes/sec.
ftp>
```

Note several important points about the display shown in Figure 21.3. First, the file and directory names are shown at the far right of each line. To their immediate left, you can see the size of the entry. On the extreme left, you can tell whether the entry is a file or directory. If you see the letter d listed in the first column, the entry is a directory; a dash indicates that the entry is a file.

4. Because you're looking for client software for a server product in this example, you deduce that it might be found in the `bussys` subdirectory. Switch to that directory by typing the following command and pressing Enter:

   `cd bussys`

5. Repeat the `ls -1` command to see what's in the `bussys` directory. There, you see a directory called `Clients`. Switch to it by using `cd Clients` (note the case sensitivity) and perform another `ls -1` to see what's there. Voil[ag]a! You see a directory called `MSCLIENT`, which is what you are looking for. You can make one last change to that directory by typing `cd MSCLIENT` and a final `ls -1` to see what files are available. Figure 21.4 shows the results of these steps.

Figure 21.4
Finding the `MSCLIENT` directory.

```
ftp> ls -l
200 PORT command successful.
150 Opening ASCII mode data connection for /bin/ls.
dr-xr-xr-x   1 owner    group              0 Aug 15  1995 LANMAN
dr-xr-xr-x   1 owner    group              0 Aug 15  1995 LANMAN.OS2
-r-xr-xr-x   1 owner    group           2925 Mar 28  1995 LICENSE.TXT
dr-xr-xr-x   1 owner    group              0 Aug 15  1995 MSCLIENT
dr-xr-xr-x   1 owner    group              0 Aug 15  1995 RAS
-r-xr-xr-x   1 owner    group         154795 Mar 28  1995 README.NOW
dr-xr-xr-x   1 owner    group              0 Mar 30  1995 SRVTOOLS
-r-xr-xr-x   1 owner    group            370 Aug 15  1995 update.txt
dr-xr-xr-x   1 owner    group              0 Aug 29  1995 WFW
dr-xr-xr-x   1 owner    group              0 Mar  6  1996 Win95
226 Transfer complete.
ftp: 684 bytes received in 0.22Seconds 3.11Kbytes/sec.
ftp> cd MSCLIENT
250 CWD command successful.
ftp> ls -l
200 PORT command successful.
150 Opening ASCII mode data connection for /bin/ls.
-r-xr-xr-x   1 owner    group         864723 Jul 25  1995 DSK3-1.EXE
-r-xr-xr-x   1 owner    group         288142 Jul 25  1995 DSK3-2.EXE
226 Transfer complete.
ftp: 142 bytes received in 0.11Seconds 1.29Kbytes/sec.
ftp>
```

You see that this directory contains two files: DSK3-1.EXE and DSK3-2.EXE. To retrieve them, follow these additional steps:

1. Type BINARY and press Enter to use a binary file transfer mode. Failing to complete this step renders the files unusable. You see the response Type set to I.

2. Turn off multiple file-prompting by typing PROMPT and pressing Enter. You then see the response Interactive mode Off.

3. Retrieve both files by typing MGET *.* and pressing Enter. You see each file transfer (this response might take a while if you're using a slower modem connection).

Figure 21.5 shows the results of these final steps.

Figure 21.5
Retrieving two files from an FTP site.

After you retrieve the files, simply type QUIT or BYE to terminate the connection and exit FTP. That's it!

PROJECT: COMMON PROBLEMS WITH DOS INTERNET TOOLS

Unfortunately, the full power of the World Wide Web and Internet is not easily available from the world of DOS. However, you still can perform extremely important tasks from DOS on the Internet, including accessing some important information sources with Telnet and transferring files that you might require. In fact, even if you use a Windows-based PC, you might find that you occasionally prefer to open an MS-DOS prompt to use these tools. Not only can they be very productive, but they also can serve to help troubleshoot any Windows-based versions of these tools that you might be using.

If you plan to use a shell account with an ISP, spend some time combing through the ISP's various help files (most have an extensive library of these files). You also can use the Unix man (short for Manual) command to access detailed information on all the Unix commands available to you through a shell account. It wasn't really very long ago, actually, when shell accounts were the only thing that worked on the Internet, and in fact I used them extensively before the Web was truly born. Although often cryptic and confusing, a shell account can also be incredibly productive in a Unix system, although mastering it does require an investment of your time.

Some common problems might crop up as you use these tools. The following are things to watch out for:

- Remember that Unix is case sensitive. Because most PC operating systems (DOS, Windows, OS/2, and so forth) are not case sensitive, you can easily forget this important fact.

- If you are having trouble connecting to a site using Telnet or FTP, make sure the site exists and is operating. Type the command `ping`, followed by the name of the site, to perform a basic connectivity test. The `ping` command reports whether it can connect to the site and can send and receive a small amount of test data. If `ping` can't connect to a site, make sure that you have the correct address and that you're using the right case for the name of the site. You might just need to try again later; sites can often crash and be unavailable until their administrators fix whatever problem they're having.

- Many sites have limits to the number of users they allow at any given time. Sometimes Telnet or FTP reports that there are too many users and that you are being disconnected. The only solution to this problem is to keep trying, perhaps during a time when the site is unlikely to be so busy.

- If a site doesn't allow anonymous access, you need to have a proper username and password to access the site. Some sites require that you send an e-mail to the site's administrator requesting access or take some other steps to secure an account.

- Many sites restrict what commands you can perform on them using Telnet or FTP. For example, some FTP sites enable you to use the command `ls -l`, whereas others enable you to use only the short form, `ls`. Other commands might be similarly restricted, such as commands that move or delete files. Sites that employ such restrictions usually post a notice that you see after you have logged in, or they might include a text file that describes these restrictions in their `/pub` directory.

When you use a shell account and the Unix and Internet tools discussed in this chapter, plan to spend plenty of time learning to use these tools. Most shell account providers have extensive libraries of files describing how to use the tools they make available, in addition to the information you can find by using the Unix `man` command. Also, consider purchasing a basic Unix book, such as Que's *Practical Unix*.

CHAPTER 22

THIRD-PARTY UTILITIES

In this chapter

Enhancing Your Computer with Utility Programs   494

Understanding Freeware, Shareware, and Demoware   494

PKWare's PKZIP and PKUNZIP   495

McAfee VirusScan   496

4DOS   497

Enhancing Your Computer with Utility Programs

Because DOS has been available for so long and has been used on so many computer systems over the years, several utility programs that run under DOS and can accomplish various useful tasks are available. Many of these utilities are available either free or as shareware programs that you can evaluate free and then pay to license if you decide to keep them.

In this chapter, you learn about several such powerful utility programs for DOS; they can help you accomplish more with a DOS-based computer system or even make better use of the DOS command prompt in Windows and OS/2. The following DOS-based utility programs are covered in this chapter:

- PKZIP and PKUNZIP by PKWare
- McAfee VirusScan
- 4DOS by JP Software

Using these programs, you can increase your capability to manage files under DOS; to remain free of computer viruses; to create, manage, and extract compressed file archives; and to make the best use of the DOS command prompt.

Understanding Freeware, Shareware, and Demoware

Programmers write computer programs for many reasons: for fun, for profit, as demonstrations, as self-educational projects, or to solve some computing problem that they have noticed. However, not every program has the commercial appeal of, say, an Intuit Quicken or a Microsoft Word.

Sometimes programmers choose to make their programs available to others free. When they do so, it is understood that the programs are available on an as is basis with no warranty and no support from the programmers if some kind of problem occurs. If the program does something useful for you, that's great. If it doesn't, at least it didn't cost you anything. Note that programs distributed free—often called *freeware*—usually still carry restrictions that you cannot modify the program in any way and that the programmer's original copyright must be left intact. You are typically also free to give copies to others, although you need to examine each program's copyright notice for details because they vary from program to program.

Some software programmers often choose to sell their creations using an electronic version of a "word of mouth" sales approach called *shareware*. In this model, people are free to download and try the software for a limited period of time (usually 30 days or so); and then, if they choose to keep the software, they pay the programmer a reasonable license fee. Users are encouraged to pass along shareware programs they like to other people, who also must pay to license the software if they want to keep it. The basic idea is to make software available for sale with much lower selling and distribution costs than traditional software, with both the programmer and user benefiting from the more efficient transaction: The programmer makes more money on each copy sold, and the user pays much less for useful software. Shareware programs are typically sold with some sort of warranty, with support from the maker, and often with other benefits such as free upgrades to newer versions that become available. Note that all these benefits usually accrue only to buyers of the software, not to those who are simply evaluating the programs.

Another form of program is sometimes called *demoware*. With demoware, the software has been modified so that certain key functions do not work. For instance, a demonstration of a program that generates reports might print only one page of its reports or might print all pages with a prominent notice that the software is unlicensed. (Sometimes software like this is uncharitably called *crippleware* because key functions are deliberately crippled.) Usually, after a user has paid for a license, the crippled functions are restored, or a properly functioning version of the program is sent to the buyer.

The third-party utilities described in this chapter are, for the most part, shareware. All their functions work properly, although continued use requires that you pay for a copy of the program. The nice thing is that all these utilities are very powerful and useful, easy to get, and inexpensive to purchase if you want to continue using them.

> **Note**
> As each program is described, its license terms are noted. However, you should read the appropriate notices for each program—or for any others of this type that you download and use—and comply with them.

PKWare's PKZIP and PKUNZIP

PKZIP and PKUNZIP are programs that can create and read special archive files. These archive files are called *Zip files*, and they invariably end with the .ZIP file extension. Zip files are special archive files that contain compressed copies of one or more normal files. Because of the compression that takes place for Zip files, Zip files are usually many times smaller than the original files themselves. The PKZIP program creates Zip files, whereas the PKUNZIP program reads files from within a Zip file and places copies on your disk. Two other programs included as part of the shareware version of PKZIP are described in Table 22.1.

> **Note**
> You can find PKWare on the Web at http://www.pkware.com/.

TABLE 22.1 PROGRAMS IN PKZIP

Program Name	Description
PKZIP.EXE	Creates Zip files
PKUNZIP.EXE	Extracts files from within Zip files
PKZIPFIX.EXE	Repairs damaged Zip files
ZIP2EXE.EXE	Creates self-extracting Zip files

The PKZIP programs are essential for almost any computer user. They enable you to accomplish many important tasks that you cannot otherwise accomplish with DOS alone, such as the following:

- Save space on your hard disk by putting infrequently used files into Zip files.
- Save much time transmitting files to or from other people. Provided both parties have PKZIP, you can spend as little as one-tenth the time transmitting Zip files to another person than if you were sending the actual uncompressed files.
- Allow large files to fit on a disk when they otherwise do not.
- Access the many Zip files available for download over the Internet. Zip files tend to be the preferred method for distributing sizable documents and program files.

> **Note**
> You can view a quick reference of the parameters for PKZIP.EXE and PKUNZIP.EXE by typing the program names at the command prompt with no parameters.

MCAFEE VIRUSSCAN

McAfee VirusScan is one of the most widely distributed shareware programs in existence. McAfee VirusScan can rapidly scan your computer for viruses, even looking inside documents for macro viruses.

What Is a Computer Virus?

A *computer virus* is a self-replicating program that transmits copies of itself through various methods. Such methods include floppy disks, executable program files, certain types of documents, and some e-mail attachments. Thousands of different computer viruses are around, and their effects range from being relatively innocuous to very serious, including some that can destroy data on your computer and—in very rare cases—can even damage some hardware components (for instance, some older monitors can be set to operate in a mode that damages them).

Computer viruses are almost never transmitted through commercial software programs. If you use only prepackaged programs and work with documents that you generate yourself, you probably don't have to worry too much about computer viruses. However, if you occasionally download programs from the Internet or work with documents (such as Word or Excel documents) that other people also access and use, routinely check your system for computer viruses. Computer viruses are unfortunately common these days; it's better to be safe than sorry.

> **Note**
> You can download McAfee VirusScan for DOS or for other operating systems from the McAfee home page at http://www.mcafee.com.

McAfee VirusScan is downloaded as a single Zip file that, when extracted using PKUNZIP, results in a main program file and a number of support files. The main program file is called either SCAN.EXE or SCANPM.EXE, depending on which of two possible DOS versions you are using. In a pure DOS environment, you use SCAN.EXE. SCANPM.EXE, on the other hand, is a DOS version intended for use with protected-mode versions of DOS, such as the DOS built into Windows 98 or OS/2.

To run a simple scan of a disk drive using VirusScan, type the program name (SCAN or SCANPM), followed by the drive letter to be scanned. The scan starts immediately, and any detected viruses are reported to you, along with a prompt asking whether you want to repair or delete the infected file.

Unless you use your computer disconnected from all other computers, using only your own documents and prepackaged software, you need to regularly scan your system for computer viruses. They are unfortunately common these days, and they can sit dormant on your system for years until the right circumstances trigger them. When triggered, they can wreak havoc on your computer's programs and data, and can require professional assistance for removal—in addition to possibly causing loss of data. Aside from regularly scanning your system for viruses with a program such as McAfee VirusScan, you also need to make regular backups of your important data, which can help protect you from data loss, regardless of whether it is caused by a computer virus or something else.

4DOS

Quite possibly the best utility program for DOS discussed in this chapter is a program called 4DOS, which actually serves to improve upon DOS in virtually every way conceivable. 4DOS is from a company called JP Software, and it replaces DOS's COMMAND.COM with a much more competent version that contains many powerful features not found in MS-DOS or any other DOS. Versions of 4DOS that can run under Windows 9x/ME, Windows NT/2000, and OS/2 also are available.

> **Note**
> On the Web, look for JP Software at `http://www.jpsoft.com/`.

4DOS doesn't change the behavior of any of the DOS commands you have already learned, but it does add more features to all of them. For instance, the DIR command still works in the same way in 4DOS, but it also accepts a larger number of parameters that enable you to format its output much more flexibly than you can with the DIR command in standard DOS. Furthermore, the TYPE command, which cannot accept wildcards or multiple filenames under DOS, easily does so with 4DOS. Table 22.2 shows the major improvements that 4DOS makes to existing DOS commands.

Table 22.2 Important Improvements to Existing DOS Commands with 4DOS

Command	Improvements
CD	Accepts more than two periods to move up more than one directory. For instance, CD .... moves up three directory levels.
CLS	Enables you to specify colors to be used when the screen is cleared.
COPY	Enables you to copy to or from a Clipboard area with the CLIP: device name.
DEL (ERASE)	Accepts multiple filenames (list each one separated by a space); accepts attribute masking; accepts an /S parameter to include subdirectories (use with caution); adds wipe capabilities where deleted files are first overwritten with zeros, making recovery nearly impossible.
DIR	Adds new formatting options.
MD	Adds the capability to create multiple subdirectories at once.
MOVE	Adds new options.
ON	Allows more flexible processing of ON *condition* commands.
PAUSE	Enables you to display a specified message as part of the PAUSE command.
REN	Adds new options.

In addition to extending the functionality of DOS commands, 4DOS adds new commands not available in DOS. For example, you might have been frustrated by the CD command's incapability to change disk drives along with directories. 4DOS contains a command called CDD that enables you to do just that. Or perhaps you have wished for a timed pause for batch files instead of DOS's simple PAUSE command, which waits for a key to be pressed. 4DOS adds a command called DELAY that pauses a batch file for a specified number of seconds. Table 22.3 shows important new commands available in 4DOS that are not generally included with DOS.

Table 22.3 New Commands with 4DOS

Command	Description
BEEP	Sounds the speaker at a specified frequency for a specified number of seconds
CANCEL	Cancels processing of a batch file; returns a specified error code that can be used by ERRORLEVEL processing
CDD	Changes the drive letter and directory with one command
COLOR	Sets new text colors to be used for text displayed after the command is given, such as in a batch file
DELAY	Pauses batch file execution for a specified number of seconds
DESCRIBE	Enables you to store long file descriptions, even for 8.3-character filenames
DIRHISTORY	Displays a list of directories accessed (pressing Ctrl+PgUp displays a list from which you can choose a directory without using this command)

TABLE 22.3 CONTINUED

Command	Description
DRAWBOX	Draws a box on the screen; useful formatting for batch file displays
DRAWHLINE	Draws a horizontal line at specified coordinates
DRAWVLINE	Draws a vertical line at specified coordinates
ESET	Enables you to edit environment variables
EXCEPT	Enables you to exclude files from processing; for instance, you can use COPY *.* EXCEPT *.TXT
FFIND	Searches for specified files
FREE	Displays free space totals for disks
GLOBAL	Executes a specified command for multiple directories
GOSUB	Provides subroutine processing in a batch file
HISTORY	Displays a history of commands used
IFF	Provides IF-THEN-ELSE processing (DOS provides only the IF command)
INKEY	Prompts you for a single key in a batch file
INPUT	Prompts you for input in a batch file
KEYSTACK	Passes keystrokes to an executed program; can often be used to automate processing in a program that otherwise doesn't allow automation
LIST	Displays a scrollable view of a file; far superior to TYPE
LOADBTM	Allows batch files with a .BTM extension to run 2 to 10 times faster than normal .BAT files
LOG	Saves a list of used commands to a log file
MEMORY	Displays the status of system memory
REBOOT	Reboots the computer
SCREEN	Displays a message at certain coordinates on the screen
SCRPUT	Displays text at certain coordinates in a specified color
SELECT	Enables you to tag files to be processed by a command
TEE	Allows a program to display its output to the screen, simultaneously capturing it to a file
TEXT	Enables you to build and display a block of text in a batch file
TIMER	Provides a stopwatch; useful for timing commands or building quick-and-dirty performance tests
TOUCH	Enables you to set the modify and create times and dates for files
TREE	Displays a tree of directories
UNSET	Removes an environment variable
VSCRPUT	Displays text vertically on the screen

> **Tip**
>
> You can use the various 4DOS drawing commands, along with the color commands, to make professional-looking batch files. Add use of the `INKEY` and subroutine processing features, and you can construct a simple menu in 4DOS that beats anything you can do in DOS.

Another powerful feature of 4DOS is extended batch file capabilities, including a built-in batch file debugger that enables you to step through batch files and more easily solve problems within them. Add to this the capability to use `BTM` files that run much more quickly than standard `BAT` files, along with the powerful batch file commands available in 4DOS, and you can see that you can do much, much more with 4DOS batch files than with DOS batch files.

> **Note**
>
> The added batch file capabilities of 4DOS are truly stunning. They almost (but not quite) give DOS batch files the power of a full programming language. The only drawback is that for them to work, any machine using the enhanced batch file must also have 4DOS installed. If you manage a number of machines, you might want to consider a license to use 4DOS on many machines for just this reason.

If you really want to become a DOS wizard, adding 4DOS to your bag of tricks can take you very far, indeed. The nice thing about 4DOS is that you can start using it without knowing much about it because DOS commands still work the same way. As you come across situations in which you wish DOS had some additional feature, you can open the 4DOS help file and see whether it helps you solve a particular problem. Chances are excellent that 4DOS can help you accomplish many tasks you want to perform in DOS.

PART V

APPENDIXES

- **A** Files Supplied with MS-DOS 6.22 503
- **B** DOS Environment Variables 519
- **C** DOS Messages 529
- **D** DOS and DOS Utility Programs' Keyboard Commands 563
- **E** ASCII and Extended ASCII Codes 573
- **F** Command Reference 583
- **G** Glossary 959

APPENDIX

FILES SUPPLIED WITH MS-DOS 6.22

In this appendix

About MS-DOS Files   504

MS-DOS 6.22 Files   504

MS-DOS 6.22 Supplemental Disk Files   512

MS-DOS Utility File Extensions by Version   515

About MS-DOS Files

Microsoft released MS-DOS 6.22 in three versions. When you bought a new computer, you received the OEM version, which might (or might not) include additional utilities specific to your computer system. Two separate upgrade versions also were available. The Microsoft MS-DOS 6.22 Upgrade package could be installed only on a computer running a previous version of DOS, whereas the StepUp version could be installed only on computers running MS-DOS 6.0 because this version simply made changes to the MS-DOS 6.0 files on your disk. In either case, most of the files remain the same, and the descriptions in this appendix apply to either version.

The list of MS-DOS 6.22 files in the following section is arranged alphabetically, with support files grouped under the associated main file. Each is accompanied by a short description of how the file is used.

The files are marked with the following designations where appropriate:

Vital	Files that are required to run MS-DOS
Keep	Files you need to keep handy
Danger!	Dangerous files you might want to move off the path
Remove?	Files few people use or need
International	Files you need only if you use the international features of DOS
80286	Files that require an 80286 or higher processor to use
80386	Files that require an 80386 or higher processor to use
Windows	Files that are useful only if you are running Microsoft Windows

If you decide to remove any of these files from your hard disk, play it safe and copy them to a floppy disk first. That way, you can get them back easily if you make a mistake. Setup places most of these files in the subdirectory you choose, normally C:\DOS. Exceptions are noted.

Most of these files are distributed in a compressed form. Microsoft indicates this fact by replacing the last character of the filename extension with an underscore (_). When Setup installs these files on your system, they are expanded and renamed automatically. If you copy the files from the distribution disks, however, you need to use the Expand utility (located on Setup Disk 1) to make the files usable.

MS-DOS 6.22 Files

The following are the files that are provided with MS-DOS 6.22:

- ANSI.SYS—Keep. ANSI display (CON) device driver. Provides enhanced control of the display, as well as keyboard redefinition support. Used by MODE and certain application programs.
- APPEND.EXE—Append utility (TSR). Defines a search path for data.

- ATTRIB.EXE—File attribute utility. Views or changes file attributes.
- CHKDSK.EXE—Keep. Check-disk utility. Checks a disk's logical file structure for errors and displays useful information about available disk space.
- CHOICE.COM—Command-line choice utility. Displays a prompt and then waits for you to press a key.
- COMMAND.COM—Vital. MS-DOS command-line shell. Normally located in the root directory of the boot disk drive.
- COUNTRY.ICE—International. (DOS 6.0 only) Code page symbol set support for Icelandic keyboards. See the README.TXT file for details.
- COUNTRY.SYS—International. Code page symbol set support file. Loaded with the COUNTRY= command in CONFIG.SYS.
- DBLSPACE.BIN—DoubleSpace device driver loaded into memory by MS-DOS (before CONFIG.SYS processing). Located in the root directory of the startup drive, DBLSPACE.BIN is marked with system, hidden, and read-only attributes.
- DBLSPACE.EXE—DoubleSpace disk compression utility.
- DBLSPACE.HLP—DoubleSpace online help file.
- DBLSPACE.INF—DoubleSpace setup information file.
- DBLSPACE.INI—DoubleSpace configuration information file. Created by DBLSPACE.EXE.
- DBLSPACE.SYS—CONFIG.SYS utility that allows the DBLSPACE.BIN driver to be moved into high memory.
- DBLSPACE.WIN—DoubleSpace uses this file to keep track of Windows during the installation of a compressed volume file (CVF).
- DBLSPACE.00x—DoubleSpace CVF created by DBLSPACE.EXE. You normally do not see these files because they are hidden, but they are your DoubleSpace compressed disk drives.
- DBLWIN.HLP—Windows. Help for the DoubleSpace Info Box in the Windows File Manager Tools menu.
- DEBUG.EXE—Danger! Programmer's debugging utility. A low-level programmer's tool that has almost unrestricted access to your computer. Debug can erase your hard disk with just a few keystrokes. Don't run Debug in a Windows DOS box.
- DEFRAG.EXE—Keep. Disk defragmenting program. Rearranges files to eliminate fragmentation on your disk.
- DEFRAG.HLP—DEFRAG online help file.
- DELOLDOS.EXE—Remove? Deletes OLD_DOS.x subdirectories from your hard disk and then deletes itself. Feel free to delete this file if you've already removed the old DOS files from your system.
- DELTREE.EXE—Delete directory branch utility.
- DISKCOMP.COM—Disk compare utility. Makes an exact comparison of two floppy disks.
- DISKCOPY.COM—Keep. Disk copy utility. Makes a copy of a floppy disk. Use it to make backup copies of the MS-DOS distribution disks.

- DISPLAY.SYS—International. Display device driver with code page symbol set support.
- EGA.CPI—International. Code page information file for EGA and VGA video displays.
- EGA.ICE—International. (DOS 6.0 only) Code page information file for EGA and VGA video displays using an Icelandic symbol set. See the README.TXT file for details.
- EGA2.CPI—International. (DOS 6.2 only) Alternative code page information file for EGA and VGA video displays. See the README.TXT file for details.
- DMDRVR.BIN—On-track disk manager version 5.0 device driver upgrade. Installed by Setup only if an older version is on the disk.
- XBIOS.OVL—On-track disk manager overlay file (AT Software BIOS Extended v1.3). Installed by Setup only if an older version is present on the disk.
- DOSKEY.COM—DOS command-line editing and macro utility (TSR).
- DRIVER.SYS—Remove? Device driver that can assign drive letters to an existing floppy drive or create an alias for a floppy disk drive.
- EDIT.COM—Keep. ASCII text file editor. This file is actually a loader that runs the editor included in QBASIC.EXE. If you delete QBASIC.EXE, you cannot use EDIT.
- EDIT.HLP—ASCII text file editor online help file.
- EGA.SYS—Remove? Device driver that is required by the DOS Shell (and other task swapping software) when running on an EGA display. Without an EGA display, this driver is useless.
- EMM386.EXE—80386 expanded (EMS) and upper (UMB) memory manager. Requires an XMS provider, such as HIMEM, to run. Required by MS-DOS for loadhigh functions.
- EXPAND.EXE—Keep. Utility that expands the files supplied on the MS-DOS distribution disks into a usable form.
- FASTHELP.EXE—Utility that displays syntax help for DOS commands. This is the same help you get when you type the /? switch.
- DOSHELP.HLP—Fasthelp help text file (ASCII text). You can add or edit entries in this file, as long as the entries remain properly formatted in alphabetical order. This file is handy for the shareware utilities you do not remember how to use.
- FASTOPEN.EXE—Danger! Remove? Directory information cache (TSR). FASTOPEN is slower and more dangerous than SMARTDRV. If you can't use SMARTDRV, use the BUFFERS command to optimize disk access on your computer.
- FC.EXE—File compare utility. Useful for both binary and ASCII text files.
- FDISK.EXE—Danger! Disk partitioning utility. Prepares a new hard drive and optionally creates one or more logical drives on it. However, one wrong keystroke can wipe out all the information on your hard disk. Get this program off your path. I strongly advise removing it from your hard disk. Keep it on a bootable floppy disk with other disaster recovery tools.
- FIND.EXE—Find text filter utility. Useful in batch files.
- FORMAT.COM—Keep. Format disk utility.

- GRAPHICS.COM—Enable graphics mode print screen utility (TSR).
- GRAPHICS.PRO—Printer information file used by GRAPHICS.COM (ASCII text).
- HELP.COM—Keep. MS-DOS online hypertext help system. This file is actually a loader that runs QBASIC.EXE. If you delete QBASIC.EXE, you cannot use Help.
- HELP.HLP—Keep. MS-DOS online help system data file.
- HIMEM.SYS—80286. Extended memory (XMS) manager. Required by EMM386 and by MS-DOS for loadhigh support. Required by Windows.
- INTERLNK.EXE—Interlnk network client control program/device driver.
- INTERSVR.EXE—Interlnk network server control program.
- IO.SYS—Vital. One of two files that form the core of the MS-DOS operating system. (The other is MSDOS.SYS.) It must be present in the root directory of the startup drive.
- KEYB.COM—International. Keyboard remapping utility with code page support. Uses the KEYBOARD.SYS file by default.
- KEYBOARD.ICE—International. (DOS 6.0 only) Code page information file for Icelandic keyboards. Loaded by KEYB.COM. See the README.TXT file for details.
- KEYBOARD.SYS—International. Code page information keyboard file. Loaded by KEYB.COM.
- KEYBRD2.SYS—International. (DOS 6.2 only) Alternative code page information keyboard file. Loaded by KEYB.COM. See the README.TXT file for details.
- LABEL.EXE—Disk volume label utility.
- LOADFIX.COM—80286. Patch that fills the first 64KB segment so that programs loaded after it will be in the second 64KB segment of memory. Some programs display a Packed file corrupt message if they are run in the first 64KB segment of RAM.
- MEM.EXE—Keep. Display information on memory usage utility.
- MEMMAKER.EXE—80386. Optimize RAM memory usage program.
- MEMMAKER.HLP—80386. MemMaker help file.
- MEMMAKER.INF—80386. MemMaker configuration file (ASCII text).
- MEMMAKER.STS—80386. MemMaker statistics file (ASCII text). This file is created by MemMaker and can provide insight into the way your system is configured.
- CHKSTATE.SYS—80386. Device driver used by MemMaker to monitor and help optimize memory usage on your system.
- SIZER.EXE—80386. Utility to help MemMaker determine how much memory each device driver and TSR requires.
- MODE.COM—Utility that can control the settings for various standard ports and devices. In some cases, MODE remains resident in memory.
- MONOUMB.386—Windows. Device driver for Windows (SYSTEM.INI) that allows EMM386 to use the B000–B7FFh region of VGA memory as UMB space. See the README.TXT file for details.

- `MORE.COM`—MS-DOS. Filter (pipe) that enables you to view a text file or the screen output of a program one page at a time.
- `MOUSE.COM`—Microsoft Mouse Driver version 8.20. Installed by Setup only if an older version is present on the disk. If you use a Microsoft mouse, keep a close watch on the version you are using. Microsoft distributes updated drivers with most of its software packages, and you can easily end up using an older driver by mistake.
- `MOUSE.INI`—Microsoft Mouse configuration file (ASCII text). This file is created by `MOUSE.COM` in the subdirectory pointed to by the `MOUSE` environment variable if it is defined.
- `MOVE.EXE`—Keep. Move files or rename directories utility.
- `MSAV.EXE`—Microsoft Anti-Virus program.
- `MSAV.HLP`—Microsoft Anti-Virus online help file.
- `MSAV.INI`—Microsoft Anti-Virus configuration file (ASCII text). This file is created by `MSAV` in the same subdirectory as `MSAV.EXE` or in the subdirectory pointed to by the `MSDOSDATA` environment variable if it is defined.
- `MSAVHELP.OVL`—Microsoft Anti-Virus overlay file.
- `MSAVIRUS.LST`—Microsoft Anti-Virus file that contains the list of known virus signatures that `MSAV` uses when scanning your disks.
- `CHKLST.MS`—Microsoft Anti-Virus checksum files. `MSAV` creates these files in every subdirectory it scans, unless you turn off this feature.
- `MSBACKUP.EXE`—Microsoft Backup program.
- `MSBACKUP.LOG`—Microsoft Backup log file. This file is created by `MSBACKUP` or `MWBACKUP` in the same subdirectory as the corresponding executable file or in the subdirectory pointed to by the `MSDOSDATA` environment variable if it is defined. The Windows and DOS versions of Microsoft Backup share this file.
- `MSBACKDB.OVL`—Microsoft Backup overlay file.
- `MSBACKDR.OVL`—Microsoft Backup overlay file.
- `MSBACKFB.OVL`—Microsoft Backup overlay file.
- `MSBACKFR.OVL`—Microsoft Backup overlay file.
- `MSBACKUP.HLP`—Microsoft Backup configuration file (ASCII text). This file is created by `MSBACKUP` in the same subdirectory as `MSBACKUP.EXE` or in the subdirectory pointed to by the `MSDOSDATA` environment variable if it is defined. The Windows version of MS Backup keeps a separate INI file in the Windows directory.
- `MSBACKUP.INI`—Microsoft Backup online help file.
- `MSBACKUP.OVL`—Microsoft Backup overlay file.
- `MSBCONFG.HLP`—Microsoft Backup configuration online help file.
- `MSBCONFG.OVL`—Microsoft Backup configuration overlay file.
- `DEFAULT.SET`—Microsoft Backup default setup file (ASCII text). This file is created by `MSBACKUP` or `MWBACKUP` in the same subdirectory as the corresponding executable file or

in the subdirectory pointed to by the MSDOSDATA environment variable if it is defined. The Windows and DOS versions of Microsoft Backup share this file.

- DEFAULT.SLT—Microsoft Backup default selection file. This file is created by MSBACKUP or MWBACKUP in the same subdirectory as the corresponding executable file or in the subdirectory pointed to by the MSDOSDATA environment variable if it is defined. The Windows and DOS versions of Microsoft Backup share this file.

- *.SET—Microsoft Backup setup files (ASCII text). You create and name these files to save preferred settings for backup sets. These files are created by MSBACKUP or MWBACKUP in the same subdirectory as the corresponding executable file or in the subdirectory pointed to by the MSDOSDATA environment variable if it is defined. The Windows and DOS versions of Microsoft Backup share these files.

- *.SLT—Microsoft Backup selection files. These files contain the file selection information that you've chosen for a particular backup set. These files are created by MSBACKUP or MWBACKUP in the same subdirectory as the corresponding executable file or in the subdirectory pointed to by the MSDOSDATA environment variable if it is defined. The Windows and DOS versions of Microsoft Backup share these files.

- *.FUL, *.INC, *.DIF—Full, incremental, and differential backup catalog files. These files are created by MSBACKUP or MWBACKUP in the same subdirectory as the corresponding executable file or in the subdirectory pointed to by the MSDOSDATA environment variable if it is defined. The Windows and DOS versions of Microsoft Backup share these files.

- MSCDEX.EXE—Utility that assigns drive letters to CD-ROM drives. Installed by Setup only if an older version is present on the disk.

- MSD.EXE—Keep. Microsoft system diagnostics. A handy utility that can tell you how your system is configured. Used by Microsoft Product Support when troubleshooting.

- MSDOS.SYS—Vital. One of two files that form the core of the MS-DOS operating system. (The other is IO.SYS.) It must be present in the root directory of the startup drive.

- MSTOOLS.DLL—Windows. Windows File Manager extension DLL. Provides the File Manager Tools menu.

- MWAV.EXE—Windows. Microsoft Anti-Virus for Windows program.

- MWAV.HLP—Windows. Microsoft Anti-Virus for Windows online help file.

- MWAV.INI—Windows. Microsoft Anti-Virus for Windows configuration file (ASCII text). It is created by MWAV in the same subdirectory as MWAV.EXE or in the subdirectory pointed to by the MSDOSDATA environment variable if it is defined. MSAV and MWAV keep separate configuration files, so options set in one do not affect the other.

- MWAVABSI.DLL—Windows. Microsoft Anti-Virus for Windows absolute disk I/O library.

- MWAVDLG.DLL—Windows. Microsoft Anti-Virus for Windows dialogs library.

- MWAVDOSL.DLL—Windows. Microsoft Anti-Virus for Windows operating system library.

- MWAVDRVL.DLL—Windows. Microsoft Anti-Virus for Windows drive list custom control library.

- MWAVMGR.DLL—Windows. Microsoft Anti-Virus for Windows TSR manager library.

- `MWAVSCAN.DLL`—Windows. Microsoft Anti-Virus for Windows virus scanning support library.
- `MWAVSOS.DLL`—Windows. Microsoft Anti-Virus for Windows context-sensitive help library.
- `MWGRAFIC.DLL`—Windows. Microsoft Anti-Virus for Windows graphics control library.
- `MWAVTSR.EXE`—Windows. `VSAFE` manager program for Windows. Enables `VSAFE` to display warning messages when Windows is running.
- `MWBACKUP.EXE`—Windows. Microsoft Backup for Windows program.
- `MWBACKF.DLL`—Windows. Microsoft Backup for Windows DLL.
- `MWBACKR.DLL`—Windows. Microsoft Backup for Windows DLL.
- `MWBACKUP.HLP`—Windows. Microsoft Backup for Windows online help file.
- `MWBACKUP.INI`—Windows. Microsoft Backup for Windows configuration file (ASCII text). This file is created by `MWBACKUP` in the subdirectory pointed to by the `WINDIR` environment variable. `MSBACKUP` and `MWBACKUP` keep separate configuration files, so options set in one are set in the other.
- `VFINTD.386`—Windows. Windows device driver (`SYSTEM.INI`) that allows `MWBACKUP` to access your tape drive. Setup doesn't check for conflicts with other drivers in your `SYSTEM.INI` file when installing this file. See the `README.TXT` file for details.
- `MWUNDEL.EXE`—Windows. Microsoft Undelete for Windows program.
- `MWUNDEL.HLP`—Windows. Microsoft Undelete for Windows online help file.
- `NETWORKS.TXT`—Remove? ASCII text file containing information about installing and using MS-DOS 6 on various networks.
- `NLSFUNC.EXE`—International. National language support program (TSR). Required to enable code page switching functions in `MODE` and `CHCP`.
- `OS2.TXT`—Remove? ASCII text file describing how to install MS-DOS 6 if you are running OS/2.
- `PACKING.LST`—Remove? ASCII text file listing the contents of the MS-DOS 6 distribution disks. Each file's full name and compressed name are listed.
- `POWER.EXE`—Remove? Power management utility/device driver, with support for Advanced Power Management (APM) hardware.
- `PRINT.EXE`—MS-DOS background print spooler utility (TSR).
- `QBASIC.EXE`—Keep. QuickBasic programming environment. `QBASIC.EXE` is used by `EDIT.COM` and `HELP.COM`, so even if you never plan to do any BASIC programming, you probably should keep this file.
- `QBASIC.HLP`—QuickBasic online help file.
- `QBASIC.INI`—QuickBasic configuration file. `QBASIC.INI` is updated when you make changes to the way QuickBasic is configured on your computer.
- `RAMDRIVE.SYS`—RAM disk device driver.

- README.TXT—Remove? ASCII text file containing last-minute information about MS-DOS 6.22. You would be wise to look for this file in every software package you get and read it before you install the software.
- REPLACE.EXE—Update files utility. With this utility, you can keep two disks or directories full of files in sync.
- RESTORE.EXE—Remove? Restores backup disks created with the old BACKUP utility. If possible, make new backups with MSBACKUP, move RESTORE.EXE to a floppy disk, and forget that the old backup program ever existed.
- SCANDISK.EXE—Keep. ScanDisk disk analysis and repair program. Checks a disk's logical and physical integrity and repairs any errors.
- SCANDISK.INI—Keep. ScanDisk settings information file (ASCII text). Many ScanDisk settings can be customized and controlled from this file.
- SETUP.EXE—MS-DOS installation program.
- BUSETUP.EXE—Bootable upgrade setup utility. If you reboot your computer with distribution disk #1 in drive A, BUSETUP starts, checks whether your computer has an operating system installed, and refuses to continue if it does not. This is Microsoft's way of including a bootable disk in an upgrade-only package. BUSETUP can be run from drive A only.
- DOSSETUP.INI—DOS setup information file (binary).
- SETUP.MSG—DOS setup messages file (ASCII text).
- AUTOEXEC.BAT—DOS setup disk AUTOEXEC.BAT file. Runs BUSETUP.
- CONFIG.SYS—DOS setup disk CONFIG.SYS file.
- UNINSTALL.EXE—Uninstall utility. Placed on the UNINSTALL disk created by Setup during installation of MS-DOS 6.
- SETVER.EXE—DOS version alias program/device driver. This utility fools certain programs into believing they are running under a different version of MS-DOS. Setup installs this program on almost every computer; if you don't need this file, it's a waste of memory.
- SHARE.EXE—Keep. Utility that provides file sharing and locking support for MS-DOS (TSR). Most people need to run SHARE, especially if they use Microsoft Windows. It can save you from some nasty disk errors.
- SMARTDRV.EXE—80286. Disk cache utility (TSR). SMARTDRV can provide a dramatic speedup for your computer.
- SMARTMON.EXE—Windows. Smart monitor, a control program for SMARTDRV that runs under MS Windows. Strangely, this program has no DOS counterpart.
- SMARTMON.HLP—Windows. Smart monitor online help file.
- SMARTMON.LOG—Windows. Smart monitor cache hit log file (ASCII text).
- SORT.EXE—Sort text filter utility. Useful in batch files.

- `SPATCH.BAT`—Batch file that can patch the Windows 3.0 `SWAPFILE.EXE` file to make it compatible with DOS 6. Not required if you are running Windows 3.1. This file is located on distribution disk #3. See the `README.TXT` file for details.
- `SSTOR.SYS`—SpeedStor hard disk device driver version 6.3.1. Installed by Setup only if an older version is on the disk.
- `SUBST.EXE`—Remove? Assign drive alias to a subdirectory utility. Use this utility only when you have to and turn it off when you are finished.
- `SYS.COM`—Keep. Transfer system files utility. Handy for making preformatted disks bootable.
- `TREE.COM`—Display directory structure utility.
- `UNDELETE.EXE`—Keep. Recover deleted files utility. Using the sentry or tracker modes of protection causes `UNDELETE` to stay resident in memory.
- `UNDELETE.INI`—`UNDELETE` and `MWUNDEL` configuration file (ASCII text). It should be located in either the same subdirectory as `UNDELETE.EXE` or the subdirectory pointed to by the `MSDOSDATA` environment variable.
- `UNFORMAT.COM`—Utility for restoring an accidentally formatted disk. Uses the information saved on the disk by `FORMAT` or `MIRROR`.
- `VSAFE.COM`—Memory-resident virus-protection program.
- `WINA20.386`—Windows. Windows A20 line support driver. Setup places this file in the root directory. You can move it, but you must update `SYSTEM.INI` and your `CONFIG.SYS` file if you do so. It is required if you are running Windows in enhanced mode and use any Windows 3.0 device drivers. (This includes most people running Windows and Windows for Workgroups 3.1 and higher.)
- `WNTOOLS.GRP`—Windows. Windows Program Manager group file. Installed by Setup into the Program Manager if you select to install any Windows version of DOS utilities.
- `AV.GRP, BK.GRP, BKAV.GRP, BKUD.GRP, BKUDAV.GRP, UD.GRP, UDAV.GRP`—Depending on which Windows utilities you ask Setup to install, one of these group files is copied and renamed `WNTOOLS.GRP`.
- `XCOPY.EXE`—Keep. Extended copy utility. Copies files and subdirectories.

MS-DOS 6.22 Supplemental Disk Files

Microsoft will send you the MS-DOS 6.22 Supplemental Disk if you request it. This disk contains utilities that provide enhanced support for people with disabilities, updated copies of commands no longer distributed with the standard MS-DOS package, updated drivers for certain networks, and some sample BASIC programs. The disk also contains a batch file (`SETUP.BAT`) that expands the groups of files you select and updates `SETVER`. The contents of the Supplemental Disk often change, so what you receive might be different from the following list. This list is for the DOS 6.0 Supplemental Disk with files dated 4/5/93, 6:00 a.m.

> **Note:** In addition to other files listed in this section, the DOS 6.22 Supplemental Disk includes the DOSSHELL program and its related files. DOSSHELL does not come in the MS-DOS 6.22 package.

The following are the supplemental disk files:

- ADOS.COM—Access DOS program. Provides various utilities designed to assist people with disabilities in using a computer.
- ADOS.CFG—Access DOS configuration file.
- ADOS.OVL—Access DOS overlay file.
- ADOS.TXT—Access DOS instruction manual (ASCII text).
- AREADME.TXT—Access DOS last-minute information (ASCII text).
- FAKEMOUS.COM—IBM PS/2 "No Mouse" utility. See the description of use in ADOS.TXT.
- ASSIGN.COM—DOS 5 disk alias utility. Assigns an alias drive letter to an existing disk drive. Microsoft is encouraging people to use SUBST instead, but ASSIGN is still the best choice for fooling certain older programs.
- BACKUP.EXE—DOS 5 backup utility. Backs up files on your hard disk to a set of floppy disks. This old utility was replaced by the MSBACKUP utility. Avoid the continued use of BACKUP because it is not reliable.
- COMMANDS.TXT—Instructions on how to use the utilities on the DOS 6 Supplemental Disk (ASCII text). This is the manual for this Supplemental Disk.
- COMP.EXE—DOS 5 file compare utility. FC, which is distributed with DOS 6.22, is easier to use and more flexible than COMP.
- CV.COM—Replacement loader for Codeview versions 3.0 to 3.13. Using Codeview versions 3.0 to 3.13 without CV.COM might cause data loss if you are using an 80386 memory manager such as EMM386. See COMMANDS.TXT for details.
- DBLBOOT.BAT—Batch file to aid in creating a bootable DoubleSpace floppy disk.
- DBLBOOT.INI—Prototype INI file used by DBLBOOT.BAT (ASCII text).
- DVORAK.SYS—Alternative keyboard layout. Use with KEYB.COM.
- DVORAK.TXT—Instructions for using DVORAK.SYS (ASCII text).
- EDLIN.EXE—DOS 5 line-oriented text editor. This line editor is old-fashioned and awkward. Instructions on using EDLIN are included in the COMMANDS.TXT file.
- EXE2BIN.EXE—Converts EXE files to binary format. Useful only to programmers who are writing device drivers or COM format utilities and cannot get this service directly from their linker.
- GRAFTABL.COM—Supports international characters and code page switching on a CGA video adapter. Not needed for EGA or VGA.

- JOIN.EXE—DOS 5 utility that makes a disk drive appear to be a subdirectory of another drive. Many DOS commands fail, destroy data, or both when used on a joined drive, so run this utility only if you must.
- KBDBUF.SYS—A device driver that enables you to specify the size of the keyboard type ahead buffer. Cannot be run in high memory.
- LCD.CPI—Code page information file for the IBM PC Convertible's LCD display. Use with DISPLAY.SYS.
- MIRROR.COM—DOS 5 utility that saves information UNDELETE and UNFORMAT use when recovering files. Very useful, but it might interfere with creating DoubleSpace drives.
- MSHERC.COM—TSR that installs support for a Hercules graphics card. Required by some QBasic programs.
- NET.TXT—Supplemental network drivers instruction file (ASCII text). Contains information on when and how to use the following drivers provided on the MS-DOS 6.22 Supplemental Disk. Note that some files must be renamed before they can be used. Their "real" names (what you must rename them to before you can use them) are shown in parentheses.
    - NET.1XE—LAN Manager 2.0 basic version (NET.EXE).
    - NETBEUI.DOS—LAN Manager 2.0 basic and enhanced version driver.
    - NETWKSTA.1XE—LAN Manager 1.x enhanced version (NETWKSTA.EXE).
    - NETWKSTA.2EX—LAN Manager 2.0 enhanced version (NETWKSTA.EXE).
    - REDIR.1XE—LAN Manager 1.x basic version (REDIR.EXE).
    - REDIR.2XE—LAN Manager 2.0 basic version (REDIR.EXE). Microsoft MS-NET (REDIR.EXE). 3COM 3+ Share version 1.6 (MSREDIR.EXE).
- SETNAME.EXE—Microsoft MS-NET utility.
- PRINTER.SYS—Device driver that provides support for international characters and code page switching on certain printers.
- 4201.CPI—Code page information file for IBM Proprinter II and III model 4201 and XL model 4202.
- 4208.CPI—Code page information file for IBM Proprinter X24E model 4207 and XL24E model 4208.
- 5202.CPI—Code page information file for IBM QuietWriter III printer.
- PRINTFIX.COM—Utility that prevents MS-DOS from checking the status of your printer. Use only if problems have developed with your printer since installing MS-DOS 6.
- GORILLA.BAS—QuickBasic sample program (game).
- MONEY.BAS—QuickBasic sample program (personal finance manager).
- NIBBLES.BAS—QuickBasic sample program (game).
- REMLINE.BAS—QuickBasic sample program (remove line numbers).

MS-DOS UTILITY FILE EXTENSIONS BY VERSION

Over the years, Microsoft has changed the name, the extension, or both for many DOS external utilities. Table A.1 lists these changes. The blank entries indicate when Microsoft started or stopped distributing a particular utility. If you are in the habit of entering full pathnames for programs in your batch files, a quick glance at the last few rows shows you which of your batch files you must edit.

APP A

TABLE A.1 FILENAME EXTENSION BY VERSION

File	1.x	2.0	2.1	3.0 3.1	3.2	3.3	4.0	5.0	6.0	6.22
APPEND				EXE	EXE	EXE	EXE	EXE		
ASSIGN	COM	COM	COM	COM	COM	COM	COM			
ATTRIB		EXE	EXE	EXE	EXE	EXE	EXE	EXE		
BACKUP	COM	COM	COM	COM	COM	COM	EXE			
BASIC*	COM	COM	COM	COM	COM					
BASICA*	EXE	EXE	EXE	EXE	EXE					
CHKDSK	COM	COM	COM	COM	COM	COM	COM	EXE	EXE	EXE
CHOICE					COM	COM				
COMMAND	COM	COM	COM	COM	COM	COM	COM	COM	COM	COM
COMP**	COM	COM	COM	COM	COM	COM	COM	EXE		
DBLSPACE					EXE	EXE				
DEBUG	COM	COM	COM	COM	COM	COM	COM	EXE	EXE	EXE
DEFRAG					EXE	EXE				
DELTREE					EXE	EXE				
DELOLDOS				EXE	EXE	EXE				
DISKCOMP	COM	COM	COM	COM	COM	COM	COM	COM	COM	COM
DISKCOPY	COM	COM	COM	COM	COM	COM	COM	COM	COM	COM
DOSKEY					COM	COM	COM			
DOSSHELL					BAT	COM	COM			
EDIT					COM	COM	COM			
EDLIN	COM	COM	COM	COM	COM	COM	COM	EXE		
EMM386					EXE	EXE	EXE			
EXE2BIN	EXE	EXE	EXE	EXE	EXE	EXE	EXE	EXE		
EXPAND					EXE	EXE	EXE			

Appendix A Files Supplied with MS-DOS 6.22

Table A.1 Continued

File	1.x	2.0	2.1	3.0/3.1	3.2	3.3	4.0	5.0	6.0	6.22
FASTHELP					EXE	EXE				
FASTOPEN			EXE	EXE	EXE	EXE	EXE			
FC**			EXE	EXE	EXE	EXE	EXE			
FDISK	COM	COM	COM	COM	COM	EXE	EXE	EXE	EXE	
FILESYS			EXE							
FIND	EXE	EXE	EXE	EXE	EXE	EXE	EXE	EXE	EXE	
FORMAT	COM	COM	COM	COM	COM	COM	COM	COM	COM	COM
GRAFTABL		COM	COM	COM	COM	COM				
GRAPHICS	COM	COM	COM	COM	COM	COM	COM	COM		
GWBASIC*	EXE	EXE								
IFSFUNC				EXE						
INTERLNK							EXE	EXE		
INTERSVR							EXE	EXE		
HELP					EXE	EXE	EXE			
JOIN			EXE	EXE	EXE	EXE	EXE			
KEYB			COM	COM	COM	COM	COM			
KEYBFR		COM	COM							
KEYBGR		COM	COM							
KEYBIT		COM	COM							
KEYBSP		COM	COM							
KEYBUK		COM	COM							
LABEL		COM	COM	COM	COM	EXE	EXE	EXE		
LINK	EXE	EXE	EXE	EXE	EXE	EXE	EXE			
LOADFIX					COM	COM	COM			
MEM					EXE	EXE	EXE	EXE		
MEMMAKER							EXE	EXE		
MIRROR				COM						
MODE	COM	COM	COM	COM	COM	COM	COM	COM	COM	
MORE	COM	COM	COM	COM	COM	COM	COM	COM		
MOVE					EXE	EXE				
MSAV					EXE	EXE				

Table A.1 Continued

File	1.x	2.0	2.1	3.0 3.1	3.2	3.3	4.0	5.0	6.0	6.22
MSBACKUP					EXE	EXE				
MSD					EXE	EXE				
MWAV					EXE	EXE				
MWAVTSR					EXE	EXE				
MWBACKUP					EXE	EXE				
MWUNDEL					EXE	EXE				
NLSFUNC			EXE	EXE	EXE	EXE	EXE			
POWER					EXE	EXE				
PRINT	COM	COM	COM	COM	COM	COM	EXE	EXE	EXE	
QBASIC				EXE	EXE	EXE				
RECOVER	COM	COM	COM	COM	COM	COM	EXE			
REPLACE		EXE	EXE	EXE	EXE	EXE	EXE			
RESTORE	COM	COM	COM	COM	COM	COM	EXE	EXE	EXE	
SCANDISK					EXE					
SELECT		COM	COM	COM	COM					
SETVER				EXE	EXE	EXE				
SHARE		EXE	EXE	EXE	EXE	EXE	EXE	EXE		
SMARTDRV				SYS	SYS	EXE	EXE			
SMARTMON					EXE	EXE				
SORT	EXE	EXE	EXE	EXE	EXE	EXE	EXE	EXE	EXE	
SUBST			EXE	EXE	EXE	EXE	EXE	EXE	EXE	
SYS	COM	COM	COM	COM	COM	COM	COM	COM	COM	COM
TREE	COM	COM	COM	COM	COM	COM	COM	COM		
UNDELETE				EXE	EXE	EXE				
UNFORMAT	COM	COM	COM							
VSAFE					COM	COM				
XCOPY	EXE	EXE	EXE	EXE	EXE					

*BASICA (Advanced BASIC) was often distributed as both an EXE file and a small COM loader program. Also, some OEMs used the GWBASIC name long before Microsoft started calling it that, often including BASIC.COM and BASICA.COM loader files so users could type the same command to start BASIC on any computer. (Industry legend has it that the GW in GWBASIC stands for gee whiz.)

FC and **COMP** have had a confusing journey through the various DOS versions. IBM originally included **COMP** with PC DOS 1.0, and then it disappeared in subsequent IBM releases, reappearing officially in MS-DOS 3.3. During this period, many OEMs added utilities to their versions of MS-DOS. A popular add-on was **COMP**, often under a different name (such as `FILCOM`, `FC`, or `COMPARE`). Even Microsoft's generic MS-DOS often included some type of file compare utility. Mapping all these variations is overly complicated, so the table just indicates that **COMP** has been with DOS since the beginning.

APPENDIX B

DOS Environment Variables

In this appendix

Understanding the DOS Environment   520

APPEND   520

COMSPEC   521

CONFIG   521

COPYCMD   522

DIRCMD   522

MSDOSDATA   523

PATH   524

PROMPT   525

TEMP and TMP   525

windir   526

WINPMT   526

Understanding the DOS Environment

The *environment* is a small area in memory that DOS sets aside for storing text variables. Normally, you set the size of the master environment area with a SHELL = statement in your CONFIG.SYS file. The default size of the environment is 256 bytes, but you almost certainly want to increase this size as you begin to use environment variables to automate your daily tasks.

Each variable in the environment consists of two parts: the name of the variable, which DOS stores in uppercase characters, and the contents of the variable, which is the text associated with the variable. Normally, you view, create, and replace environment variables by using the SET command. The PATH and PROMPT commands store their settings in the environment. MS-DOS automatically creates certain environment variables, such as COMSPEC and CONFIG, when you start up your computer.

Whenever DOS loads a program into memory, it makes a copy of the current environment and passes this copy to the program. This copy is only big enough to include the variables currently defined in the environment, rounded up to an even multiple of 16 bytes. Although this use of memory is efficient, it is inconvenient for people who normally operate from a shell program such as DOS Shell, Norton Commander, or XTree because not much environment space is available, no matter how large an environment area you set aside. If you get an Out of environment space message while you are running a shell program, quit the shell and try the operation again. If you still receive an error message, you must increase the size of the master environment by using the SHELL= statement in your CONFIG.SYS file.

The following sections list the standard environment variables used by MS-DOS. Also noted is the version of DOS in which the variable first appeared, along with the creator of the variable. An *MS-DOS* label indicates that this variable is created automatically when your computer starts up. A *User* label indicates that you must create it by using the SET command or, for certain variables, the PATH, PROMPT, or APPEND command. A *Windows* label indicates that the environment variable is created by Microsoft Windows.

APPEND

The APPEND environment variable is created by DOS if you specify the /E parameter when loading APPEND into memory. With the /E parameter, APPEND stores the appended directory search path in the environment instead of internally.

This variable is stored much like the PATH variable. It is a list of subdirectories to be searched, separated by semicolons. If the APPEND environment variable is created with the SET command, it might appear like this:

```
SET APPEND=C:\DOS;C:\WS
```

When you instruct APPEND to store the appended directory search path in the environment, you can change or replace the search path by using the SET command as well as the APPEND command.

Note that APPEND /E does not work if you are launching programs that must search the appended directory search path from a shell program such as DOS Shell, Norton Commander, or XTree. In such cases, APPEND must store the appended directory search path internally.

COMSPEC

The COMSPEC variable points to the active copy of the command interpreter shell loaded with the SHELL= command in your CONFIG.SYS file. All of COMMAND.COM isn't in memory all the time; when parts of it must be reloaded, the COMSPEC variable is used to find the COMMAND.COM file on disk.

In the following SHELL= command, COMMAND.COM sets the COMSPEC variable using the C:\DOS\ parameter that follows the command interpreter's name:

SHELL=C:\DOS\COMMAND.COM C:\DOS\ /E:512 /P

DOS executes the SHELL= command at the end of CONFIG.SYS processing. When it does, COMMAND.COM sets the COMSPEC variable in the environment as if it had executed SET COMSPEC=C:\DOS\COMMAND.COM. (Note that COMMAND.COM doesn't actually use the SET command.)

Many programs search the environment for the COMSPEC variable when they must locate COMMAND.COM. If you have trouble shelling to a DOS prompt from one of your application programs, check the COMSPEC environment variable and make sure that it's pointing to a valid copy of COMMAND.COM.

CONFIG

When MS-DOS processes a startup menu in CONFIG.SYS, it defines the CONFIG environment variable, setting it equal to the block name of the menu item you selected. You can use the CONFIG environment variable with GOTO and IF in your AUTOEXEC.BAT file to continue making choices based on the configuration chosen in the startup menu.

For example, assume that your CONFIG.SYS file includes the following startup menu:

```
[MENU]
MENUITEM=WIN, Configure for Windows (default)
MENUITEM=DOS, Configure for MS-DOS
MENUITEM=MAINT, Configure for file & disk maintenance
MENUDEFAULT-WIN, 10
```

The CONFIG environment variable is set equal to WIN, DOS, or MAINT, depending on which configuration you select when your computer displays the startup menu. In your AUTOEXEC.BAT file, you can check this value and process different commands for each configuration. For example, you might set up separate sections for each startup configuration and label them with the block names you used in your CONFIG.SYS file, which in this case are :WIN, :DOS, and :MAINT. (For more information on block names, see the [blockname] entry in

Appendix F, "Command Reference.") Then, a simple GOTO statement such as the following might be all you need to jump to the correct section of your AUTOEXEC.BAT file:

```
GOTO %CONFIG%
```

A slightly safer method is to check each value with an IF statement and report an error if an unexpected value for CONFIG is encountered:

```
IF %CONFIG%x==WINx GOTO WIN
IF %CONFIG%x==DOSx GOTO DOS
IF %CONFIG%x==MAINTx GOTO MAINT
GOTO ERROR
```

The use of x prevents the generation of an error message if the CONFIG environment variable is null or undefined. When you use an IF comparison, always include a character (any character will do) that prevents one side of the equation from being empty.

COPYCMD

Starting with MS-DOS 6.2, COPY, MOVE, and XCOPY all prompt for confirmation before overwriting a file. Because this behavior might wreak havoc with your old batch files, this behavior is the default only when these commands are run from the command line. If COPY, MOVE, or XCOPY is run from a batch file, it overwrites files without warning, which is its behavior in previous versions of DOS.

You can change the new default behavior by defining an environment variable named COPYCMD. To force COPY, MOVE, and XCOPY to prompt you before overwriting a file in all cases, even from a batch file, add the following line to your AUTOEXEC.BAT file:

```
SET COPYCMD=/-Y
```

To prevent COPY, MOVE, and XCOPY from prompting before overwriting a file, add the following line to your AUTOEXEC.BAT file:

```
SET COPYCMD=/Y
```

DIRCMD

The DIRCMD environment variable customizes the default options the DIR command uses. When you run the DIR command, the contents of the DIRCMD environment variable—if it exists—are added invisibly to what you type on the command line.

Suppose that you prefer filenames in lowercase letters, sorted by directories and then sorted by date and time. You also want the screen to pause after each page of files is displayed. You can define the DIRCMD variable in your AUTOEXEC.BAT file as follows:

```
SET DIRCMD=/L /O:GD /P
```

Now you don't have to enter those options every time you want to use them. To override these options, specify the switch with a hyphen added before the letter. For example, to turn off the pause option in your customized DIR command, enter the following command:

```
DIR /-P
```

Note that overriding options this way is temporary and changes only the behavior of the command in which the override switch appears.

MSDOSDATA

The MSDOSDATA environment variable defines where certain DOS utility programs look for their data files. Defining this variable can make it easier to keep programs and data separate on your hard disk. Defining the variable can make it easier also to run these utility programs from a network using individual configuration files.

The most convenient place to define the MSDOSDATA variable is in your AUTOEXEC.BAT file with a SET command. Here's an example:

```
SET MSDOSDATA=C:\DOS\DATA
```

This line sets MSDOSDATA to point to the C:\DOS\DATA subdirectory on your hard drive. Note that this subdirectory has to exist first; the SET command does not create it for you.

Table B.1 provides a list of the MS-DOS programs that create data files as well as the locations where the programs look for the data files.

TABLE B.1   DATA FILE SEARCH PATHS

Program	Data File	Primary Location	Secondary Location
DBLSPACE	DBLSPACE.INF	Program directory	
	DBLSPACE.INI	Program directory	
DOSSHELL	DOSSHELL.INI	DOSSHELL	Program directory
MEMMAKER	MEMMAKER.INI	Program directory	
	MEMMAKER.STS	Program directory	
MSAV	CHKLST.MS	All directories	
	MSAV.INI	MSDOSDATA	Program directory
MSBACKUP	MSBACKUP.INI	MSDOSDATA	Program directory
	*.DIF	MSDOSDATA	Program directory
	*.FUL	MSDOSDATA	Program directory
	*.INC	MSDOSDATA	Program directory
	*.SET	MSDOSDATA	Program directory
	*.SLT	MSDOSDATA	Program directory

TABLE B.1 CONTINUED

Program	Data File	Primary Location	Secondary Location
MWAV	MWAV.INI	MSDOSDATA	Program directory
MWBACKUP	MWBACKUP.INI	Windows directory	
	*.DIF	MSDOSDATA	Program directory
	*.FUL	MSDOSDATA	Program directory
	*.INC	MSDOSDATA	Program directory
	*.SET	MSDOSDATA	Program directory
	*.SLT	MSDOSDATA	Program directory
MWUNDEL	UNDELETE.INI	MSDOSDATA	Program directory
SCANDISK	SCANDISK.INI	MSDOSDATA	Program directory
UNDELETE	UNDELETE.INI	MSDOSDATA	Program directory

In Table B.1, *program directory* refers to the directory that the executable program file is located in. Locations shown in all caps are environment variables that point to subdirectories. Programs that list both a primary and secondary location search for the data file in the primary location first.

If you set up a separate data subdirectory for MS-DOS, you might need to move some of these data files from your DOS subdirectory to that subdirectory. See the MOVE command in Appendix F, "Command Reference," for details about how to move a file.

PATH

The PATH command stores its settings in the DOS environment under the PATH variable name. (You can set the path by using either the PATH or SET command.) You probably should set the initial DOS search path in your AUTOEXEC.BAT file. DOS does not define a default PATH automatically, although the Setup program for DOS 6 does insert the PATH command in your AUTOEXEC.BAT file if you don't have one there already.

DOS uses the PATH environment variable to find executable files. Whenever a command is executed, DOS searches for the first word on the command line in the following:

- The DOSKEY macro list, if DOSKEY is loaded
- The COMMAND.COM internal command list
- Files with an extension of COM, then EXE, and then BAT in the current directory
- Files with an extension of COM, then EXE, and then BAT in the first directory listed in the PATH variable

- Files with an extension of COM, then EXE, and then BAT in the second directory listed in the PATH variable

- Files with an extension of COM, then EXE, and then BAT in the next directory listed in the PATH variable, and so on until the last subdirectory in the PATH variable has been searched

You can modify this order depending on what parts of the full pathname you enter with the command name. If you specify a drive or path with the filename, only that drive and path are searched. If you specify an extension, the other extensions are not searched for. The DOSKEY macro and internal command search are skipped if you include a disk drive or path that includes a backslash in the name of the command, but not if you include only an extension.

Other programs might search the PATH variable as well. Programs that require the addition of their subdirectory to the PATH often use the PATH environment variable to find overlay and help files.

PROMPT

The PROMPT environment variable describes the type of command-line prompt you want DOS to use. It is set by the user with either the PROMPT or SET PROMPT= command. The default command-line prompt that DOS uses if the PROMPT environment variable is undefined is the letter of the current drive and >—for example, C>.

If the PROMPT environment variable doesn't exist, the DOS 6.0, 6.2, and 6.22 versions of COMMAND.COM create it automatically with a value of PG. This prompt shows the current directory as well as the current drive; for example, C:\DOS>. The only way to have the PROMPT environment variable undefined is to delete it.

The PROMPT environment variable uses meta-strings to include system information in the command prompt. For a description of which meta-strings are available and how they can be used, see the entry for PROMPT in the "Command Reference."

TEMP AND TMP

Many programs use the TEMP environment variable as the preferred place to create and delete temporary files. This environment variable evolved somewhat informally, which is why it has two popular spellings: TEMP and TMP. TEMP is the more common variation and is the one DOS uses. Typically, if the TEMP environment variable isn't defined, the program creates its temporary files in the root directory of the current drive (or sometimes the startup drive).

DOS creates the following types of files in the directory pointed to by the TEMP environment variable:

- Files required by the use of redirection (< and >) or piping (|)
- Swap files created by the DOS Shell Task Swapper
- Temporary files created by any full-screen application program, such as MSAV, MSBACKUP, and QBASIC
- Temporary disk data storage for DISKCOPY
- Microsoft Windows Print Manager spooling files
- Microsoft Windows swapping files (standard mode only)

Many programs use the TEMP environment variable if it is defined. Temporary files that escape deletion by their parent program are easier to delete when they are gathered in their own subdirectory. Windows recommends at least 2MB in the subdirectory pointed to by the TEMP environment variable. If you point TEMP to a RAM disk, you never have to worry about deleting leftover temporary files. They all disappear whenever you reboot or turn off your computer.

windir

Microsoft Windows adds the windir environment variable whenever you open a DOS window. The windir environment variable always points to the main Windows directory, which is normally C:\WINDOWS. If you issue the SET command to view the variables defined in a DOS window launched from Windows, the list might look like the following:

```
COMSPEC=C:\DOS\COMMAND.COM
PROMPT=$P$G
PATH=C:\BAT;C:\DOS;C:\WINDOWS;C:\UTIL
TEMP=C:\TEMP
TMP=C:\TEMP
windir=C:\WINDOWS
```

Windows adds the windir variable to the environment in lowercase letters to keep you from modifying or deleting it. If you issue a SET windir= command, SET capitalizes the variable name before searching for it, and a new variable named WINDIR is created.

WINPMT

If the WINPMT variable is defined, Microsoft Windows uses it to format the DOS prompt displayed in a DOS window. Using a different DOS prompt from Windows can help you remember that Windows is running and that you need to type EXIT and quit Windows by pressing Alt+F4 before shutting off your computer.

To use the WINPMT environment variable, define WINPMT with the SET command (perhaps in your AUTOEXEC.BAT file) before you start Microsoft Windows. Set WINPMT equal to the prompt you want to use from Windows, using the same formatting you use with the PROMPT command.

For example, you can define the Windows prompt as a simple reminder:

```
SET WINPMT=**Windows** $P$G
```

This results in the following prompt in a DOS window:

```
**Windows** C:\DOS>
```

Use the following if you prefer a more direct reminder of how to close a DOS window:

```
SET  WINPMT=**Type EXIT to return to Windows** $P$G
```

This results in the following prompt in a DOS window:

```
**Type EXIT to return to Windows** C:\DOS>
```

APPENDIX

DOS Messages

In this appendix

General DOS Messages 530

DOS Device Error Messages 537

General DOS Messages

DOS messages can be divided into two groups: general error messages and device error messages. The three types of general DOS messages are as follows:

- **Error messages**—These messages indicate that DOS has encountered a problem with a command or with the syntax you used. Execution stops when DOS displays an error message.
- **Warning messages**—These messages tell you that the next action you take might cause unwanted changes to files or to your system; they often include a prompt, which enables you to select an action.
- **Information messages**—These messages display needed information about your system's operation or your DOS version's performance. Like warning messages, these messages also often include a prompt.

The messages in this section might appear any time during a work session. Messages that can occur when you start DOS are indicated by *(startup)*. With most startup errors, DOS does not start and you must reboot the system:

`d contains n non-contiguous blocks`

> Warning: CHKDSK found noncontiguous blocks on drive *d*. If you like, you can use a defragmenter to eliminate the fragmentation or use COPY or XCOPY to transfer the fragmented files to a freshly formatted floppy disk in a sequential form.

`A BAD UMB number has been specified`

> Error: You have attempted to use LOADHIGH (or LH) with the /L parameter referring to a nonexistent UMB area. The best way to correct this problem is to rerun MemMaker.

`A program was run that took memory that Backup requires`
`The program must be removed from memory before Backup can continue`

> Error: You have installed a terminate-and-stay resident program (TSR) that leaves insufficient memory for BACKUP. Examples are PRINT or some forms of MODE. The resident program must be unloaded before you can continue the backup. Use MEM /C to see which TSR was loaded last.

`Access denied`

> Error: You or a program attempted to change or erase a file that is in use or marked as read-only. You can change the read-only attribute by using the ATTRIB command.

`Active code page: xxx`

> Information: You issued CHCP, which displayed the code page currently in use by the system (represented by *xxx*).

`Active code page for device ddd is xxx`

> Information: You issued MODE, which lists the code page (*xxx*) currently in use for the device (*ddd*). To display a single screen at a time, pipe this command into MORE (MODE|MORE).

```
Active code page not available from CON device
```

Error: You used `KEYB` with a code page not supported on the `CON` device (screen).

```
Add filename? (Y/N)
```

Prompt: You issued `REPLACE /P`. DOS asks whether you want to add the file to the disk.

```
Adding filename
```

Information: `REPLACE` displays this message while adding *filename* to your disk.

```
All available space in the Extended DOS Partition is assigned to logical drives
```

Error: No room remains for logical drives in the extended partition. Use `FDISK` to change the size of the extended partition.

```
All files canceled by operator
```

Information: You issued `PRINT /T`, which removes all files from the print queue.

```
All files in directory will be deleted!
Are you sure (Y/N)?
```

Warning: You issued `DEL` or `ERASE` with the *.* wildcard. To continue, press `Y`; to cancel, press `N`. Then press the Enter key.

```
All logical drives deleted in the Extended DOS Partition
```

Information: While using `FDISK`, you removed all logical drives associated with the extended DOS partition.

```
All specified file(s) are contiguous
```

Information: None of the files you specified (to `CHKDSK`) are fragmented.

```
Allocation error, size adjusted
```

Warning: The contents of a file have been truncated because the size indicated in the directory is inconsistent with the amount of data allocated to the file. Use `SCANDISK` or `CHKDSK /F` to correct the discrepancy.

```
An incompatible DOSKey is already installed
```

Error: The version of DOSKey you are trying to run is incompatible with the one in memory. Make sure you don't mix the `DOSKEY.COM` that comes with DOS 6.0 with the version that comes with DOS 6.2 or another vendor's command-line editor.

```
ANSI.SYS must be installed to perform requested function
```

Warning: While using `MODE`, you requested a screen function that cannot be performed until you load `ANSI.SYS`.

```
APPEND already installed
```

Information: You tried to issue `APPEND` with `/X` or `/E` after previously using `APPEND`. You can use the `/E` switch only the first time you type `APPEND` after starting your system. You can use the `/X` switch only if it was used during initialization.

`APPEND/ASSIGN conflict`

> Warning: You cannot use `APPEND` on an assigned drive. Cancel the drive assignment before using `APPEND` with this drive.

`ATTENTION: A serious disk error has occurred while writing to drive`

> Error: `SMARTDRV` has detected a hard disk error when write caching was enabled. Because the application might have already continued with something else, the usual corrections don't apply. Write caching must be enabled for only reliable media.

`/B invalid with a black and white printer`

> Error: You tried to print the background color by using `GRAPHICS /B`, but you do not have a color printer connected to your computer.

`***Backing up files to drive x:***`

> Information: This message appears while you back up files to the specified drive.

`Bad command or file name`

> Error: You entered an invalid name for invoking a command, program, or batch file. The most frequent causes are misspelling a name, omitting a required disk drive or pathname, or omitting the command name when giving parameters (for example, omitting the WordStar command, `WS`, by typing `MYFILE` instead of `WS MYFILE`).

> Check the spelling on the command line and make sure that the command, program, or batch file is in the location specified. Then, try the command again.

`Bad or missing command interpreter`

> Error (startup): DOS does not start because it cannot find `COMMAND.COM`, the command interpreter.

> If this message appears during startup, `COMMAND.COM` is not on the startup disk or a `COMMAND.COM` file from a previous version of DOS is on the disk. If you used the `SHELL` command in `CONFIG.SYS`, the message means that the `SHELL` command is improperly phrased or that `COMMAND.COM` is not in the location you specified.

> With DOS 6.0 or 6.2, you can override `CONFIG.SYS` by using the F8 or F5 key while booting. This solution works if the correct `COMMAND.COM` is in the root directory. Otherwise, place another disk that contains the operating system (`IO.SYS`, `MSDOS.SYS`, and `COMMAND.COM`) in the floppy disk drive and reset the system. After DOS starts, copy `COMMAND.COM` to the original startup disk so that you can boot DOS in the future.

> Error: If this message appears while you are running DOS, there are several possibilities: `COMMAND.COM` has been erased from the disk and directory you used when starting DOS, a version of `COMMAND.COM` from a previous version of DOS has overwritten the good version, or the `COMSPEC` entry in the environment has been changed. You must restart DOS by resetting the system.

> If resetting the system does not solve your problem, restart the computer from a copy of your DOS master disk. Copy `COMMAND.COM` from this disk to the offending disk.

Bad or missing filename

> Warning (startup): The device driver filename was not found, an error occurred when the device driver was loaded, a break address for the device driver was beyond the RAM available to the computer, or DOS detected an error while loading the driver into memory. DOS continues booting without the device driver filename.
>
> If DOS loads, check your CONFIG.SYS file for the line DEVICE=*filename*. Make sure that the line is typed correctly and that the device driver is at the specified location; then reboot the system. If the message reappears, copy the file from its original disk to the boot disk and try starting DOS again. If the error persists, the device driver is bad; contact the dealer or publisher who sold you the driver.

Bad or missing keyboard definition file

> Warning: DOS cannot find KEYBOARD.SYS as specified by the KEYB command. Solving this problem might take several steps. First, check to make sure that KEYBOARD.SYS exists and is in the correct path; then retype the KEYB command. If you get the same message, KEYB.COM or KEYBOARD.SYS might be corrupted.

Bad partition table

> Error: While using FORMAT, DOS was unable to find a DOS partition on the fixed disk you specified. Run FDISK and create a DOS partition on this fixed-disk drive.

Batch file missing

> Error: DOS could not find the batch file it was processing. The batch file might have been erased or renamed. With DOS 3.0 only, the disk containing the batch file might have been changed, causing DOS to abort processing of the batch file.
>
> If you are using DOS 3.0 and you changed the disk that contains the batch file, restart the batch file without changing the disk. You might need to edit the batch file so that you do not need to change disks. This procedure applies only to DOS 3.0.
>
> If the batch file includes a RENAME command that causes the originating batch filename to change, edit the batch file to prevent renaming when the batch file is processed again. If the file was erased, re-create the batch file from its backup file if possible. Edit the file to ensure that the batch file does not erase itself.

Baud rate required

> Error: When using MODE COMx commands to set any COM port parameters, you must at least indicate the baud rate.

BREAK is off

BREAK is on

> Information: When you use BREAK by itself, one of these messages displays the current BREAK setting. You can set BREAK at the command line or in CONFIG.SYS.

Cannot change BUFSIZE

    Error: When DOSKey has been loaded into memory, you cannot change the buffer size.

Cannot CHDIR to path - tree past this point not processed

    Error: CHKDSK was unable to go to the specified directory. No subdirectories below this directory are verified. Run SCANDISK or CHKDSK /F to correct this error.

Cannot CHDIR to root

    Error: CHKDSK was checking the tree structure of the directory and was unable to return to the root directory. Remaining subdirectories were not checked. Restart DOS. If the message continues to appear, the disk is unusable and must be reformatted.

Cannot CHKDSK a network drive

    Warning: You cannot use CHKDSK to check drives redirected over the network.

Cannot CHKDSK a SUBSTed or ASSIGNed drive

    Warning: You cannot use CHKDSK to check substituted or assigned drives.

Cannot create a zero size partition

    Error: While using FDISK, you tried to create a partition of 0% (0 megabytes). To correct this error, you must allocate 1% (or a minimum of 1MB) of hard disk space to any partition you create.

Cannot create extended DOS partition without primary DOS partition on disk x

    Error: While using FDISK, you tried to create an extended DOS partition before giving your first fixed-disk drive a primary DOS partition. To correct this problem, simply create a DOS partition on your first fixed-disk drive. When this operation is complete, you can create an extended DOS partition if you have room on this disk or if you have a second fixed disk.

Cannot create logical DOS drive without an Extended DOS Partition on the current drive

    Error: When using FDISK, you must create an extended DOS partition before you can create a logical drive.

Cannot DISKCOMP to or from a network drive

    Error: You cannot compare disks on any disk drive that has been reassigned to a network.

Cannot delete Extended DOS Partition while logical drives exist

    Error: When using FDISK to delete an extended DOS partition, you first must remove any logical drives.

`Cannot DISKCOPY to or from a network drive`

> Error: You attempted to copy a floppy disk to a drive that was redirected to a computer network. `DISKCOPY` does not copy disks directly to a networked disk drive. Use `COPY` to copy the disk.

`Cannot do binary reads from a device`

> Error: You tried to copy from a device by using the `/B` switch. To complete the copy process, use the ASCII (`/A`) switch to create an ASCII copy. You also can use the `COPY` command without the `/B` switch.

`Cannot find file QBASIC.EXE`

> Error: `EDIT.COM` or `HELP.COM` cannot find the `QBASIC.EXE` program file. `QBASIC` must be available to edit a file or access the MS-DOS online help system.

`Cannot find GRAPHICS profile`

> Error: You did not give the path of the `GRAPHICS.PRO` file; DOS could not find it in the current directory.

`Cannot find System files`

> Error: While running `FORMAT`, you specified a drive that did not have the system files in the root directory.

`Cannot FORMAT a network drive`

> Error: You tried to format a disk in a drive being used by a network.

`Cannot FORMAT an ASSIGNed or SUBSTed drive`

> Error: You attempted to format a drive that was mapped to another drive with `ASSIGN` or `SUBST`. To perform a successful format, you must run `ASSIGN` or `SUBST` again to clear the drive assignments.

`Cannot LABEL a JOINed, SUBSTed or ASSIGNed drive`

> Error: You attempted to label a drive created with `JOIN`, `SUBST`, or `ASSIGN`.

`Cannot LABEL a network drive`

> Error: You cannot use `LABEL` with drives redirected over the network.

`Cannot load COMMAND, system halted`

> Error: DOS attempted to reload `COMMAND.COM`, but the area where DOS keeps track of memory was destroyed or the command processor was not found in the directory specified by the `COMSPEC=` entry. The system halts.

> This message might indicate that `COMMAND.COM` was erased from the disk and directory you used when starting DOS, or that the `COMSPEC=` entry in the environment has been changed. Restart DOS from your usual startup disk. If DOS does not start, the copy of `COMMAND.COM` has been erased. Restart DOS from the DOS startup or master disk and copy `COMMAND.COM` to your usual startup disk.

Alternatively, an errant program might have corrupted the memory allocation table where DOS tracks available memory. Try running the same program that was in the computer when the system halted. If the problem occurs again, the program is defective. Contact the dealer or publisher who sold you the program.

`Cannot loadhigh batch file`

Warning: The `LOADHIGH` (or `LH`) command is used only for TSR programs. Batch files might not be run this way.

`Cannot move multiple files to a single file`

Error: When using `MOVE` with wildcards for the source file specification, you must specify a directory for the destination. The most common cause of this error is a misspelled name.

`Cannot perform a cyclic copy`

Error: When using `XCOPY /S`, you cannot specify a target that is a subdirectory of the source. You might use a temporary disk or file to bypass this limitation if the directory tree structure allows a temporary disk or file.

`Cannot recover ... entry`
`Entry has a bad attribute (or link or size)`

Error, Warning: The .. entry (the parent directory) is defective and cannot be recovered. If you have specified the `/F` switch, `CHKDSK` tries to correct the error.

`Cannot set up expanded memory`

Error: `FASTOPEN` cannot correctly access expanded memory (EMS).

`Cannot specify default drive`

Error: You specified the default drive as a `SYS` destination. Switch to another drive before issuing the `SYS` command.

`Cannot start COMMAND, exiting`

Error: You or one of your programs directed DOS to load another copy of `COMMAND.COM`, but DOS could not load it. Your `CONFIG.SYS FILES` command is set too low, or you do not have enough free memory for another copy of `COMMAND.COM`.

If your system has 256KB or more and `FILES` is less than 10, edit the `CONFIG.SYS` file on your startup disk, using `FILES=15` or `FILES=20`. Then., restart DOS.

If the problem recurs, you do not have enough memory in your computer, or you have too many resident or background programs competing for memory space. Restart DOS, loading only the essential programs. If necessary, eliminate unneeded device drivers or RAM disk software. You also can obtain additional RAM for your system.

`Cannot SUBST a network drive`

Error: You cannot substitute drives redirected over the network.

```
Cannot SYS a network drive
```
Error: You cannot transfer system files to drives redirected over the network.

```
Cannot use FASTOPEN for drive x
```
Error: You attempted to use `FASTOPEN` over a network, with a floppy disk drive, or with more than four disks at one time.

```
Cannot use PRINT - Use NET PRINT
```
Error: You tried to use `PRINT` over the network. Use `NET PRINT` or consult your system administrator for the correct procedure for printing files over the network.

```
Cannot XCOPY from a reserved device
Cannot XCOPY to a reserved device
```
Error: The specified `XCOPY` source or target is a character device (printer), an asynchronous communication device, or `NULL`. You must specify a file or block device as your source and your target.

```
CHDIR .. failed, trying alternate method
```
Warning: `CHKDSK` was unable to return to a parent directory while checking the tree structure. `CHKDSK` attempts to return to the parent directory by starting over at the root and repeating the search.

```
Code page not prepared
```
Error: While using `MODE`, you selected a code page not yet prepared for the system or without the correct font to support the current video mode. To correct this error, prepare a code page using the `MODE PREPARE` command. If you have installed the `DISPLAY.SYS` installable device driver, make sure that the `DEVICE` command line in your `CONFIG.SYS` file allows additional subfonts.

```
Code page xxx
```
Information: This message displays the code page currently in use by the specified device. If you type `MODE CON`, for example, the message returns the code page in use for your screen.

```
Code page xxx not prepared for all devices
```
Error: While using `CHCP`, you selected a code page not currently supported by a device. To correct this error, first make sure that your device supports code page switching and that it is online. Then issue the `MODE PREPARE` command to ready the device for the code page. You are ready to retry `CHCP`.

```
Code page xxx not prepared for system
```
Error: `CHCP` is unable to select a code page for the system. If `NLSFUNC` is installed and your `CONFIG.SYS` file does not install device drivers, you can retry `CHCP`. If `CONFIG.SYS` installs device drivers, you must issue the `MODE PREPARE` command to prepare the specific code page for each device before retrying the `CHCP` command.

`Code page operation not supported on this device`

> Error: While using MODE, you selected a device and code page combination not recognized by DOS. Make sure that you specified a valid device and code page and that the code page you selected is supported on the device.

`Code page requested (xxx) is not valid for given keyboard code`

> Error: You selected an incompatible keyboard code and code page combination. Re-enter the KEYB command with a valid keyboard code and code page.

`Code page specified has not been prepared`

> Error: You issued the KEYB command with an unrecognized code page. Prepare the code page for your CON (console screen device) by using the MODE PREPARE command; then retry KEYB.

`Code page specified is inconsistent with selected code page`

> Warning: You used KEYB with an option incompatible with the code page for your console screen device. Specify a compatible option or issue the MODE SELECT command to change the code page for your console screen device.

`Code pages cannot be prepared`

> Error: You attempted to use a duplicate code page for the specified device; or with MODE PREPARE, you specified more code pages than DOS supports for that device. Check CONFIG.SYS to see how many prepared code pages your device command line allows or issue MODE /STATUS at the command line to view the code pages already prepared for the device (for example, MODE /STATUS CON).

`Compare error at offset xxxxxxxx`

> Information: The files you are comparing are not the same. The difference occurs *xxxxxxxx* bytes from the beginning of the file. The number of bytes and the values for the differing bytes are given in hexadecimal format (base 16).

`Compare error on side s, track t`

> Information: DISKCOMP has located a difference on the disk in the specified drive on side *s* at track *t*.

`Compare process ended`

> Error: A fatal error occurred during the comparison operation.

`Comparing t tracks n sectors per track, s side(s)`

> Information: This message confirms the format of the disks you are comparing.

`Configuration too large for memory`

> Error (startup): DOS could not load because you set too many files or buffers in your CONFIG.SYS file or specified too large an environment area (/E) with the SHELL command. This problem occurs only on systems with less than 256KB.

Restart DOS with a different configuration; then edit the `CONFIG.SYS` file on your boot disk, lowering the number of files, buffers, or both. You also can edit `CONFIG.SYS` to reduce the size of the environment in addition to or as an alternative to lowering the number of files and buffers. Restart DOS with the edited disk.

Another alternative is to increase the RAM in your system.

`Content of destination lost before copy`

Error: The original contents of the destination file for the `COPY` (concatenation) operation were overwritten because the destination and one of the source files had the same name. You might be able to recover the file by using `UNDELETE`; if not, you can restore the destination file from your backup disk.

`Copy process ended`

Error: The `DISKCOPY` process ended before completion. Test with `SCANDISK` or `CHKDSK` and then copy the remaining files onto the disk with `COPY` or `XCOPY`.

`Current code page settings:`

Information: You issued the `MODE` command and specified a device with code page support. `MODE` displays the active code page, the hardware code page, other prepared code pages, and the space available for additional code pages on the lines that follow the message. If you want to see status information for all devices, type `MODE` without listing a device.

`Current CON code page: xxx`

Information: This message displays the current keyboard code and code page along with the current code page used by the console screen device (`CON`).

`Current drive is no longer valid`

Warning: The system prompt includes the meta-symbol `$p`, to display the current directory, or `$n`, to display the current drive. You tried to change the default drive to an invalid drive. (You tried to make a floppy drive current, for example, without a floppy present.) DOS presented the `Abort, Retry, Fail?` prompt. When you responded by pressing F, DOS temporarily changed the prompt to the `Current drive is no longer valid` message.

The invalid drive error also occurs when a current networked or substituted disk drive is deleted or disconnected. Simply change the current drive to a valid disk drive.

`Current keyboard does not support this code page`

Error: You selected a code page incompatible with the current keyboard code. First, check the selected code page. If the code page is correct, change the keyboard code by using `KEYB`.

`Device n not prepared`

Error: No code page is present for this device.

`Disk boot failure`

> Error (startup): An error occurred when DOS tried to load into memory. The disk contained `IO.SYS` and `MSDOS.SYS`, but one of the two files could not be loaded.
>
> Try starting DOS from the disk again. If the error recurs, try starting DOS from a disk you know is good, such as a copy of your DOS startup or master disk. If DOS still fails to boot, you have a disk drive problem. Contact your dealer.

`Disk full. Edits lost.`

> Error: `EDLIN` cannot save your work to disk because the designated disk is full. Always make sure that you have a disk with plenty of room to save your files.

`Disk unsuitable for system disk`

> Warning: `FORMAT` detected one or more bad sectors on the floppy disk in the area where DOS normally resides. Because the portion of the disk where DOS must reside is unusable, you cannot boot DOS from this disk.
>
> Try reformatting the disk. Some floppy disks format successfully the second time. If `FORMAT` gives this message again, you cannot boot from the disk.

`Divide overflow`

> Error: DOS aborted a program that attempted to divide by zero. The program was incorrectly entered or contains a logic flaw. If you wrote the program, correct the error and try the program again. If you purchased the program, report the problem to the dealer or publisher.
>
> This message also might appear when you attempt to format a RAM disk with DOS 3.0 or 3.1. Make sure that you are formatting the correct disk and try again.

`Do not specify filename(s)`
`Command format: DISKCOMP [drive1: [drive2:]] [/1] [/8]`

> Error: You typed an incorrect switch or added one or more filenames with the `DISKCOMP` command. `DISKCOMP` syntax does not accept filenames on the command line.

`Do not specify filename(s)`
`Command Format: DISKCOPY [drive1: [drive2:]] [/1] [/V]`

> Error: You added an incorrect switch to the command or placed a filename in the command string. Retype the command and press Enter.

`DOS is in HMA`

`DOS is in low memory`

> Information: Most of the DOS system can be optionally loaded above the first megabyte in the high memory area (HMA), if you have at least a 286, have some available extended memory, and use the `DOS=HIGH` parameter in `CONFIG.SYS`. These messages tell you whether DOS is in HMA.

`DOS memory-arena error`

Error: When you are using the DOS editor, this message indicates a serious memory error. If possible, save your work to a different file and reboot your computer.

`Drive assignment syntax error`

Error: `INTERLNK` found a syntax error in its command line. Double-check the syntax by entering `HELP INTERLNK`.

`Drive types or diskette types not compatible`

Error: When using `DISKCOMP` or `DISKCOPY`, you specified two drives of different capacities. You cannot use `DISKCOMP` or `DISKCOPY`, for example, from a 1.2MB drive to a 360KB drive. Retype the command using compatible drives.

`Duplicate filename or file not found`

Error: While using `RENAME` (or `REN`), you attempted to change a filename to a name that already exists, or the file to be renamed did not exist in the directory. Check the directory to make sure that the filename exists and that you have spelled it correctly. Then try again.

`Enter current volume label for drive d:`

Warning: You are attempting to format a hard disk that has a volume label. Enter the exact volume label to proceed with the format; if you do not want to enter a volume label, press Enter and `FORMAT` will quit.

`Error in COUNTRY command`

Warning (startup): The `COUNTRY` command in `CONFIG.SYS` is improperly phrased or has an incorrect country code or code page number. DOS continues to load but uses the default information for the `COUNTRY` command.

After DOS has started, check the `COUNTRY` line in your `CONFIG.SYS` file. Make sure that the command is correctly phrased (with commas between the country code, code page, and `COUNTRY.SYS` file) and that any given information is correct. If you detect an error in the line, edit the line, save the file, and restart DOS.

If you do not find an error, restart DOS. If the same message appears, edit `CONFIG.SYS`. Re-enter the `COUNTRY` command and delete the old `COUNTRY` line. The old line might contain some nonsense characters that DOS can see but that are not apparent to your text-editing program.

`Error in EXE file`

Error: DOS detected an error while attempting to load a program stored in an EXE file. The problem, which is in the relocation information DOS needs to load the program, might occur if the EXE file has been altered.

Restart DOS and try the program again, this time using a backup copy of the program. If the message appears again, the program is flawed. If you are using a purchased program, contact the dealer or publisher. If you wrote the program, issue `LINK` to produce another copy of the program.

`Error loading operating system`

> Error (startup): A disk error occurred when DOS was loading from the hard disk. DOS does not start.
>
> Restart the computer. If the error occurs after several tries, restart DOS from the floppy disk drive. If the hard disk does not respond (that is, you cannot run `DIR` or `CHKDSK` without getting an error), you have a problem with the hard disk. Contact your dealer. If the hard disk does respond, place another copy of DOS on your hard disk by using `SYS`. You also might need to copy `COMMAND.COM` to the hard disk.
>
> Increase to 15 or 20 the number of `FILES` in the `CONFIG.SYS` file of your startup disk. Restart DOS. If the error recurs, you might have a problem with the disk. Try a backup copy of the program. If the backup works, copy the backup over the offending file.
>
> If an error occurs in the copying process, you have a flawed disk. If the problem is a floppy disk, copy the files from the flawed disk to another disk and reformat or discard the original disk. If the problem is the hard disk, immediately back up your files and run `RECOVER` on the offending file. If the problem persists, your hard disk might be damaged.

`Error reading directory`

> Error: During a `FORMAT` procedure, DOS was unable to read the directory; bad sectors might have developed in the file allocation table (FAT) structure.
>
> If the message occurs when DOS is reading a floppy disk, the disk is unusable and should be thrown away. If DOS cannot read your hard disk, however, the problem is more serious, and you might have to reformat your disk. Remember to back up your data files regularly to prevent major losses.

`Error reading (or writing) partition table`

> Error: DOS could not read from (or write to) the disk's partition table during the `FORMAT` operation because the partition table is corrupted. Run `FDISK` on the disk and reformat the disk.

`Error writing to file on remote system`

> Error: `INTERSVR` has detected that the remote system (the one running `INTERLNK`) has a write error. The most likely reason is that the remote disk is full.

`Extended error`

> Error: `COMMAND.COM` has detected an error but cannot tell you the normal error message because the disk containing `COMMAND.COM` is missing. (This error doesn't generally occur on a hard disk system.) To avoid these anonymous errors, use the `/MSG` switch on the `SHELL=` line of `CONFIG.SYS`.

`File allocation table bad, drive d`
`Abort, Retry, Fail?`

> Warning: DOS encountered a problem in the file allocation table of the disk in drive d. Press R to retry several times; if the message recurs, press A to abort.

CHKDSK can't repair this type of error in the file allocation table. If you have DOS 6.2, SCANDISK might be capable of correcting this problem for you. Commercial third-party utility packages often include tools that can repair this problem as well. Otherwise, you will be forced to back up as many files as you can and then reformat the disk. If FORMAT finds no errors, you can safely go back to using the disk.

`File cannot be copied onto itself`

Error: You attempted to copy a file to a disk and directory containing the same filename. This error often occurs when you misspell or omit parts of the source or destination drive, path, or filename. This error might occur also when you are using wildcard characters for filenames or when you use SUBST. Check your spelling and the source and destination names, and then try the command again.

`File creation error`

Error: A program or DOS failed to add a new file to the directory or to replace an existing file.

If the file already exists, issue the ATTRIB command to check whether the file is marked as read-only. If the read-only flag is set and you want to change or erase the file, remove the read-only flag with ATTRIB; then try again. If the problem occurs when the read-only flag is not set, run SCANDISK or CHKDSK without the /F switch to determine whether the directory is full, the disk is full, or some other problem exists with the disk.

`File not found`

Error: DOS could not find the specified file. The file is not on the current disk or directory, or you specified the disk drive name, pathname, or filename incorrectly. Check these possibilities and try the command again.

`Filename device driver cannot be initialized`

Warning (startup): In CONFIG.SYS, the parameters in the device driver filename or the syntax of the DEVICE line is incorrect. Check for incorrect parameters and phrasing errors in the DEVICE line. Edit the DEVICE line in the CONFIG.SYS file, save the file, and restart DOS.

`FIRST diskette bad or incompatible`

`SECOND diskette bad or incompatible`

Error: One of these messages might appear when you issue DISKCOMP. The messages indicate that the FIRST (source) or the SECOND (target) floppy disk is unreadable or that the disks you are attempting to compare have different format densities.

`Format not supported on drive x:`

Error: You cannot use the FORMAT command on the specified drive. If you entered device driver parameters that your computer cannot support, DOS displays this message. Check CONFIG.SYS for bad DEVICE or DRIVPARM commands.

`Formatting while copying`

Information: `DISKCOPY` displays this message as it copies data to an unformatted disk.

`Illegal device name`

Error: DOS does not recognize the device name you entered with the `MODE` command.

`Incorrect DOS version`

Error: The copy of the file holding the command you just entered is from a different version of DOS.

Get a copy of the command from the correct version of DOS (usually from your copy of the DOS startup or master disk) and try the command again. If the disk you are using has been updated to hold new versions of DOS, copy the new versions over the old ones.

`Insert disk with batch file and strike any key when ready`

Prompt: DOS attempted to execute the next command from a batch file, but the disk holding the batch file is not in the disk drive. This message occurs for DOS 3.1 and later versions. DOS 3.0 gives a fatal error when the disk is changed.

`Insert disk with batch file into disk drive, and press a key to continue`

`Insert disk with \COMMAND.COM in drive d and strike any key when ready`

Prompt: DOS needs to reload `COMMAND.COM` but cannot find it on the startup disk. If you are using floppy disks, the disk in drive *d* (usually A) has probably been changed. Place a disk with a good copy of `COMMAND.COM` in drive *d* and press a key.

`Insert diskette for drive x and press any key when ready`

Prompt: On a system with one floppy disk drive or a system in which `DRIVER.SYS` creates more than one logical disk drive from a physical disk drive, you or one of your programs specified a tandem disk drive *x* (such as A or B) that is different from the current disk drive.

If the correct disk is in the disk drive, press a key. Otherwise, insert the correct disk into the floppy disk drive and then press a key.

`Insufficient disk space`

Warning, Error: The disk does not have enough free space to hold the file being written. All DOS programs terminate when this problem occurs, but some non-DOS programs continue.

If you think that the disk should have enough room to hold the file, run `SCANDISK` or `CHKDSK` to determine whether the disk has a problem. When you terminate programs early by pressing Ctrl+Break, DOS might not be capable of doing the necessary cleanup work, leaving some disk space temporarily trapped. `SCANDISK` or `CHKDSK` can free these areas.

If you have simply run out of disk space, free some disk space or insert a different disk; then try the command again.

```
Insufficient memory to store macro. Use the DOSKEY command with the /BUFSIZE
switch to increase available memory.
```

Warning: Your DOSKey macros have filled the total space set aside for them. You must enlarge the memory area for macros (the default is 512 bytes) by using the `BUFSIZE` switch before you can enter any new macros.

```
Intermediate file error during pipe
```

Error: DOS cannot create or write to one or both of the intermediate files it uses when piping information between programs because the disk is full, the root directory of the current disk is full, or the `TEMP` environment variable points to an illegal path. The most frequent cause is insufficient disk space.

Run `DIR` on the root directory of the current disk drive to make sure that you have enough room in the root directory for two additional files. If you do not have enough room, make room by deleting or copying and deleting files. You also can copy the necessary files to a different disk that has sufficient room.

This error also might occur if a program is deleting files, including the temporary files DOS creates. In this case, correct the program, contact the dealer or program publisher, or avoid using the program with piping.

```
Internal stack overflow
System halted
```

Error: Your programs and DOS have exhausted the stack, which is the memory space reserved for temporary use. This problem is usually caused by a rapid succession of hardware devices demanding attention. DOS stops, and the system must be turned off and on again to restart DOS.

The circumstances that cause this message are generally infrequent and erratic, and they might not recur. If you want to prevent this error from occurring, add the `STACKS` command to your `CONFIG.SYS` file. If the command is already in your `CONFIG.SYS` file, increase the number of stacks specified.

```
Invalid /BAUD parameter
```

Warning: You have selected an illegal baud rate for either `INTERLNK` or `INTERSVR`. For example, you have `/BAUD:9200` instead of `/BAUD:9600`.

```
Invalid characters in volume label
```

Error: You attempted to enter more than 11 alphanumeric characters, or you entered illegal characters (+, =, /, \ , and |, for example) when you typed the disk's volume label (the disk name). Retype the volume label with valid characters.

```
Invalid COMMAND.COM in drive d:
```

Warning: DOS tried to reload `COMMAND.COM` from the disk in drive d and found that the file was from a different version of DOS. Follow the instructions for inserting a disk with the correct version.

If you frequently use the disk that generated this warning message, copy the correct version of `COMMAND.COM` to that disk.

`Invalid COMMAND.COM, system halted`

Error: DOS could not find `COMMAND.COM` on the hard disk. DOS halts and must be restarted.

`COMMAND.COM` might have been erased, or the `COMSPEC` variable in the environment might have been changed. Restart the computer from the hard disk. If a message indicates that `COMMAND.COM` is missing, the file was erased. Restart DOS from a floppy disk and copy `COMMAND.COM` to the root directory of the hard disk or to the location your `SHELL` command indicates, if you have placed this command in your `CONFIG.SYS` file.

If you restart DOS and this message appears later, a program or batch file is erasing `COMMAND.COM` or altering the `COMSPEC` variable. If a program is erasing `COMMAND.COM`, contact the dealer or publisher who sold you the program. If a batch file is erasing `COMMAND.COM`, edit the batch file. If `COMSPEC` is being altered, edit the offending batch file or program, or place `COMMAND.COM` in the subdirectory your program or batch file expects.

`Invalid COUNTRY code or code page`

Warning (startup): The `COUNTRY` code number or the code page number given to the `COUNTRY` command in `CONFIG.SYS` is incorrect or incompatible. DOS ignores the `COUNTRY` command and continues the startup process.

Check the `COUNTRY` command in your `CONFIG.SYS` file (see Chapter 14, "Understanding the International Features of DOS") to determine whether the correct and compatible country code and code page numbers are specified. If you detect an error, edit and save the file. Then restart DOS.

`Invalid date`

Error: You gave an impossible date or an invalid character to separate the month, day, and year. This message also appears if you enter the date from the keypad when it is not in numeric mode.

`Invalid device parameters from device driver`

Error: The partition did not fall on a track boundary. You might have set the `DEVICE` drivers incorrectly in `CONFIG.SYS` or attempted to format a hard disk formatted with DOS 2.x so that the total number of hidden sectors is not evenly divisible by the number of sectors on a track. Therefore, the partition might not start on a track boundary.

To correct the error, run `FDISK` before formatting or check `CONFIG.SYS` for a bad `DEVICE` or `DRIVPARM` command.

`Invalid directory`

Error: You specified a directory name that does not exist, you misspelled the directory name, the directory path is on a different disk, you did not give the path character (\) at the beginning of the name, or you did not separate the directory names with the path character. Check your directory names to make sure that the directory exists and try the command again.

`Invalid disk change`
`Abort, Retry, Fail?`

Warning: A floppy disk was changed while a program had open files to be written to the floppy disk. Place the correct disk in the disk drive and press R to retry. Typically, this check is supported on drives larger than 360KB.

`Invalid drive in search path`

Warning: You specified an invalid disk drive name in the PATH command, or a disk drive you named is nonexistent or hidden temporarily by a SUBST or JOIN command.

Use PATH to check the paths you instructed DOS to search. If you gave a nonexistent disk drive name, issue the PATH command again with the correct search paths. If the problem is temporary because of a SUBST or JOIN command, you can run PATH, leaving out or correcting the wrong entry. Or you can just ignore the warning message.

`Invalid drive or file name`

Error: You gave the name of a nonexistent disk drive, or you mistyped the disk drive or filename.

Remember that certain DOS commands (such as SUBST and JOIN) temporarily hide disk drive names while the command is in effect. Check the disk drive name you gave and try the command again.

`Invalid drive specification`

Error: You entered an invalid or nonexistent disk drive as a parameter to a command; you specified the same disk drive for the source and destination; or by not giving a parameter, you defaulted to the same disk drive for the source and the destination.

Remember that some DOS commands (such as SUBST and JOIN) temporarily hide disk drive names while the command is in effect. Check the disk drive names. If the command is objecting to a missing parameter and defaulting to the wrong disk drive, name the correct disk drive explicitly.

`Invalid drive specification`
`Specified drive does not exist or is non-removable`

Error: You gave the name of a nonexistent disk drive, you named the hard disk drive when using commands for only floppy disks, you did not give a disk drive name and defaulted to the hard disk when using commands for only floppy disks, or you named or defaulted to a RAM disk drive when using commands for a floppy disk.

Remember that certain DOS commands (such as SUBST and JOIN) temporarily hide disk drive names while the command is in effect. Check the disk drive name you gave and try the command again.

`Invalid keyboard code specified`

Error: You selected an invalid code. Enter the `KEYB` command again with the correct keyboard code.

`Invalid macro definition`

Error: You entered an illegal character or command with DOSKey or attempted to create a DOSKey macro with an illegal definition. This message appears, for example, if you use a `GOTO` command in a DOSKey macro. Correct any errors and carefully retype the macro.

`Invalid media or Track 0 bad - disk unusable`

Error: A disk you are trying to format might be damaged. A disk might not format the first time. Try to format again; if the same message appears, the disk is bad and should be discarded. With some versions of `FORMAT`, this same symptom can be caused by memory boundary problems. If the symptom occurs for multiple floppy disks, try changing the number or sizes of TSRs to see whether the symptoms change.

`Invalid number of parameters`

Error: You have given too few or too many parameters to a command. One of the following occurred: You omitted required information, you omitted a colon immediately after the disk drive name, you inserted an extra space, you omitted a required space, or you omitted a slash (/) in front of a switch.

`Invalid parameter`

Error: At least one parameter you entered for the command is not valid. One of the following occurred: You omitted required information, you omitted a colon immediately after the disk drive name, you inserted an extra space, you omitted a required space, you omitted a slash (/) in front of a switch, or you used a switch the command does not recognize. For more information, check the explanation of this message in the "Command Reference" for the command you issued.

`Invalid parameter combination`

You typed conflicting parameters with a DOS command. Retype the command with only one of the conflicting switches.

`Invalid partition table`

Error (startup): DOS has detected a problem in the hard disk's partition information. Restart DOS from a floppy disk. Back up all files from the hard disk, if possible, and run `FDISK` to correct the problem. If you change the partition information, you must reformat the hard disk and restore all its files.

`Invalid path`

Error: The pathname contains illegal characters, the pathname has more than 63 characters, or a directory name within the path is misspelled or does not exist.

Check the spelling of the pathname. If necessary, check the disk directory with DIR to make sure that the directory you have specified exists and that you have specified the correct pathname. Make sure that the pathname contains no more than 63 characters. If necessary, change the current directory to a directory closer to the file to shorten the pathname.

`Invalid path or file name`

Error: You gave a directory name or filename that does not exist, specified the wrong directory name (a directory not on the path), or mistyped a name. COPY aborts when it encounters an invalid path or filename. If you specified a wildcard for a filename, COPY transfers all valid files before it issues the error message.

Check to see which files have been transferred. Determine whether the directory and filenames are spelled correctly and whether the path is correct. Then try again.

`Invalid STACK parameters`

Warning (startup): One of the following problems exists with the STACKS command in your CONFIG.SYS file. A comma is missing between the number of stacks and the size of the stack, the number of stack frames is not in the range of 8 to 64, the stack size is not in the range of 32 to 512, you have omitted the number of stack frames or the stack size, or the stack frame or the stack size (but not both) is 0. DOS continues to start but ignores the STACKS command.

Check the STACKS command in your CONFIG.SYS file. Edit and save the file; then restart DOS.

`Invalid time`

Error: You gave an impossible time or invalid character to separate the hours, minutes, and seconds. This message also appears if you enter the time from the keypad when it is not in numeric mode.

`Invalid volume ID`

Error: When formatting a fixed (or hard) disk, you entered an incorrect volume label, and DOS aborted the format attempt. Type VOL at the DOS prompt and press Enter to view the volume label of the disk; then try the command again.

`Memory allocation error`
`Cannot load COMMAND, system halted`

Error. A program destroyed the area where DOS keeps track of memory. You must restart DOS. If this error occurs again with the same program, the program has a flaw. Try a backup copy of the program. If the problem persists, contact the dealer or program publisher.

`Missing operating system`

Error (startup): The DOS hard disk partition entry is marked as bootable (capable of starting DOS), but the DOS partition does not contain a copy of DOS. DOS does not start.

Start DOS from a floppy disk. Issue the SYS C: command to place DOS on the hard disk and then copy COMMAND.COM to the disk. If this command fails to solve the problem, you must back up the existing files, if any, from the hard disk; then issue FORMAT /S to place a copy of the operating system on the hard disk. If necessary, restore the files you backed up.

```
MSBACKUP program files must be located on your hard disk
You cannot start MSBACKUP from a floppy disk
```

Error: MSBACKUP relies on repeated access to its program files during the backup operation. You must start it from a hard disk so that the program files will be available throughout the process. Change the default drive to the hard disk before starting MSBACKUP.

```
Must enter both /T and /N parameters
```

Error: On FORMAT, you must specify /T (number of tracks per side) and /N (number of sectors per disk) on the same command line. If you include the one, you must include the other.

```
Must specify COM1, COM2, COM3, or COM4
```

Error: You must specify COM1, COM2, COM3, or COM4 when using this form of the MODE command.

```
No drive letters redirected
```

Information: INTERLNK isn't currently redirecting any drive letters to the remote system.

```
No free file handles
Cannot start COMMAND, exiting
```

Error: DOS could not load an additional copy of COMMAND.COM because no file handles were available. Edit the CONFIG.SYS file on your startup disk to increase by five the number of file handles (using the FILES command). Restart DOS and try the command again.

```
No printer ports redirected
```

Information: INTERLNK isn't currently redirecting any printer ports to the remote system.

```
No room for system on destination disk
```

Error: This error isn't nearly so prevalent in DOS 6.0 or 6.2 as it was in previous versions. SYS rearranges the files as needed to make a system bootable but issues this error if insufficient room is available or if the root directory is full.

```
No serial ports were found
```

Error: You specified the /COM switch on INTERSVR, but no serial ports are available. This problem could occur if a TSR program has taken control of the available port or if the hardware is configured to an invalid address.

```
No system on default drive
```

Error: `SYS` cannot find the system files. Insert a disk containing the system files, such as the DOS disk, and type the command again. If the system files are available on another drive, issue the other form of the `SYS` command, indicating the location of the system files.

```
Non-System disk or disk error
Replace and strike any key when ready
```

Error (startup): Your disk does not contain `IO.SYS` and `MSDOS.SYS`, or a read error occurred when you started the system. DOS does not start.

If you are using a floppy disk system, insert a bootable disk into drive A and press a key. The most frequent cause of this message on hard disk systems is leaving a non-bootable disk in drive A with the door closed. Open the door to disk drive A and press a key. DOS boots from the hard disk.

```
Not enough memory

Insufficient memory
```

Error: The computer does not have enough free RAM to execute the program or command. If you loaded a resident program, such as `PRINT`, `GRAPHICS`, SideKick, or ProKey, restart DOS and try the command again before loading any resident programs. If this method fails to solve the problem, remove any nonessential device drivers or RAM disk software from `CONFIG.SYS` and restart DOS. If this option also fails, your computer does not have enough memory for this command. You must increase the amount of RAM installed in your computer to run the command.

```
Out of environment space
```

Warning: Not enough room is available in the current environment to add (or change) the variables you have specified with the `SET`, `PATH`, or `PROMPT` command. If you are running `SET`, `PATH`, or `PROMPT` from a shell program such as DOS Shell, quit the shell program and try the command again. If the command still fails, you can increase the size of the environment by increasing the `/E:size` parameter for the `SHELL=` command in your `CONFIG.SYS` file and restarting your computer.

```
Out of memory
```

Error: The amount of memory is insufficient to perform the operation you requested. This error occurs in the DOS 5.0 Editor.

```
Packed file corrupt
```

Error: The program appears to be damaged. A common cause of this symptom is older format-packed executables, which could not load into the first 64KB of conventional memory. With older operating system versions, the resident portion of the system generally used enough memory that this wasn't a problem. In DOS 5.0, 6.0, and 6.2, the `DOS=HIGH`, `DEVICEHIGH`, and `LOADHIGH` features can reduce memory usage enough that this problem occurs with certain programs. Use the `LOADFIX` command to use up enough memory temporarily so that the program is loaded at a location it can manage.

`Parameters not supported`

`Parameters not supported by drive`

> Error: You entered parameters that do not exist, that are not supported by the DOS version you are running, or that are incompatible with the specified disk drive. Run VER to determine whether the current DOS version supports the parameters (or switches) you specified.

`Parameters not compatible with fixed disk`

> Error: A device driver for a hard disk does not support generic IOCtl functions.

`Parse Error`

> Error: COMMAND.COM has detected an error but cannot tell you the normal error message because the floppy disk containing COMMAND.COM is missing. (This error doesn't generally occur on a hard disk system.) To avoid these "anonymous" errors, use the /MSG switch on the SHELL= line of CONFIG.SYS.

`Path not found`

> Error: A specified file or directory path does not exist. You might have misspelled the filename or directory name, or you might have omitted a path character (\) between directory names or between the final directory name and the filename. Another possibility is that the file or directory does not exist in the place specified. Check these possibilities and try again.

`Path too long`

> Error: You have given a pathname that exceeds the DOS 64-character limit, or you omitted a space between filename parameters. Check the command line. If the phrasing is correct, you must change to a directory closer to the file you want and try the command again.

`Program too big to fit in memory`

> Error: The computer does not have enough memory to load the program or command you invoked. If you have any resident programs loaded (such as PRINT, GRAPHICS, or SideKick), restart DOS and try the command again without loading the resident programs. If this message appears again, reduce the number of buffers (BUFFERS) in the CONFIG.SYS file, eliminate nonessential device drivers or RAM disk software, and restart DOS. If the problem persists, your computer does not have enough RAM for the program or command. You must increase the amount of RAM in your computer to run the program.

`Required parameter missing`

> Error: Many DOS commands give this error when you omit part of the parameter list. You might have specified only a single name with the MOVE command, for example.

Same parameter entered twice

> Error: You duplicated a switch when you typed a command. Retype the command using the parameter only once.

Sector size too large in file *filename*

> Error: The device driver *filename* that you are loading in your CONFIG.SYS file with a DEVICE= or DEVICEHIGH= command uses a sector size that is too large. You cannot use this device driver.

SOURCE diskette bad or incompatible

> Error: The disk you attempted to read during a copy process was damaged or in the wrong format (for example, a high-density disk in a double-density disk drive). DOS cannot read the disk.

Specified COM port number not recognized by BIOS

> Error: The port number is legal, but your ROM BIOS doesn't support it. Generally, this problem can happen with an older BIOS that supports only two COM ports. Either replace the computer's ROM BIOS or specify COM1 or COM2.

Syntax error

> Error: You phrased a command improperly by omitting needed information, giving extraneous information, inserting an extra space into a file or pathname, or using an incorrect switch. Check the command line for these possibilities and try the command again.

Target diskette bad or incompatible

Target diskette may be unusable

Target diskette unusable

> Error: A problem exists with the target disk. DOS does not recognize the format of the target disk in the drive, or the disk is defective. Make sure that the target disk is the same density as the source disk, run SCANDISK or CHKDSK on the target disk to determine the problem, or try to reformat the disk before proceeding with the disk copy operation.

Target media has lower capacity than Source
Continue anyway (Y/N)?

> Warning: The target disk can hold fewer bytes of data than the source disk. The most likely cause is bad sectors on the target disk. If you press Y, some data on the source disk might not fit on the target disk.
>
> To avoid the possibility of an incomplete transfer of data, press N and insert a disk with the same capacity as the source disk. If you are not copying "hidden" files, you also can issue the COPY *.* command to transfer files.

```
There are no serial ports or parallel ports available for communication
```

> Error: `INTRSVR` cannot find any serial ports or parallel ports not already in use. Without such a port, `INTRSVR` cannot communicate with `INTRLNK`.

```
There is not enough room to create a restore file
You will not be able to use the unformat utility
Proceed with Format (Y/N)?
```

> Warning: The disk lacks sufficient room to create a restore file. Without this file, you cannot use `UNFORMAT` to reverse the format you are attempting.

```
This program requires Microsoft Windows
```

> Error: At the DOS prompt, you tried to run a program that needs Microsoft Windows to execute. If you are already running Windows, press Alt+Tab to switch to the Program Manager and start it from there. If you haven't started Windows, use `WIN` to do so.

```
Too many block devices
```

> Warning (startup): Your `CONFIG.SYS` file contains too many `DEVICE` commands. DOS continues to start but does not install additional device drivers.
>
> DOS can handle only 26 block devices. The block devices created by the `DEVICE` commands plus the number of block devices automatically created by DOS exceed this number. Remove any unnecessary `DEVICE` commands from your `CONFIG.SYS` file and restart DOS.

```
Too many parallel ports, port ignored
```

> Warning: `INTERLNK` cannot automatically scan this many parallel ports. The earlier ones will be used.

```
Too many serial ports, port ignored
```

> Warning: `INTERLNK` cannot automatically scan this many serial ports. The earlier ones will be used.

```
Top level process aborted, cannot continue
```

> Error (startup): `COMMAND.COM` or another DOS command detected a disk error, and you chose the `A` (abort) option. DOS cannot finish starting itself, and the system halts.
>
> Try to start DOS again. If the error recurs, start DOS from a floppy disk (if starting from the hard disk) or from a different floppy disk (if starting from a floppy disk). After DOS has started, issue the `SYS` command to place another copy of the operating system on the disk and copy `COMMAND.COM` to the disk. If DOS reports an error while copying, the disk is bad. Reformat or discard the floppy disk or back up and reformat the hard disk.

```
Trying to recover allocation unit nnn
```

> Information, Warning: A bad allocation unit was found when the `FORMAT` command executed.

Unable to create destination

> Error: MOVE was unable to create the destination file. Possible reasons are that the destination drive is full or that the destination is the root directory, which lacks room.

Unable to create directory

> Error: You or a program could not create a directory for one of the following reasons. A directory by the same name already exists; a file by the same name already exists; you are adding a directory to the root directory, and the root directory is full; or the directory name has illegal characters or is a device name.
>
> Issue DIR to make sure that no file or directory already exists with the same name. If you are adding the directory to the root directory, remove or move (copy and then erase) any nonessential files or directories. Check the spelling of the directory name and make sure that the command is properly phrased.

Unable to initialize serial port COM*n*

> Error: INTRSVR was unable to initialize the specified serial port. The most common reason is that two devices in the system have the same port address.

Unable to load MS-DOS Shell, Retry (y/n)?

> Error, Prompt: DOSSHELL.COM could not load DOSSHELL.EXE. Normally, this error is caused by not having enough conventional memory. If you are attempting to run DOSSHELL from another program, quit the program and try again.
>
> A less likely cause for this error message is that the DOSSHELL.EXE file is corrupted. If you have plenty of conventional memory available (MEM /FREE), get a fresh copy of DOSSHELL.EXE from a backup disk.

Unable to open source

> Error: MOVE was unable to open the specified source file. This problem could be the result of an illegal character used in the filename, but the more common cause is trying to move a directory to a different place in the disk hierarchy. You can rename a directory by using the MOVE command but not actually move it.

Unable to read source

> Error: A disk problem occurred while transferring the data from the source file to the destination. Use COPY to copy the file, compare it, and then delete the original.

Unable to write BOOT

> Error: FORMAT cannot write to the BOOT track or DOS partition of the disk that is being formatted because one of these areas is bad. Discard the bad disk, insert another unformatted disk, and try the FORMAT command again.

Unable to write destination

> Error: A disk problem occurred while transferring the data from the source file to the destination. Double-check that the destination disk has sufficient room for the file. If the error still occurs, use COPY.

```
Unrecognized command in CONFIG.SYS
Error in CONFIG.SYS line nnn
```

> Warning (startup): DOS detected an improperly phrased command in CONFIG.SYS. The command is ignored, and DOS continues to start. Examine the indicated line in the CONFIG.SYS file, looking for an improperly phrased or incorrect command. Edit the line, save the file, and restart DOS.

```
Unrecognized switch
```

> Error: You tried to use a switch that was illegal for the particular internal command. Type the command followed by /? to find out what options are permitted.

```
Unrecoverable read error on drive x side n, track n
```

> Error: DOS was unable to read the data at the specified location on the disk. DOS makes four attempts before generating this message. Copy all files on the questionable disk to another disk and try the command again, first with a new disk and then with the backup disk. If the original disk cannot be reformatted, discard it.

```
Unrecoverable transmission errors, maximum retries exceeded
```

> Error: INTRSVR is getting excessive errors on the communications cable to INTERLNK. Check that the connections are screwed in tightly and that the cable is not routed too close to electrical interference, such as an arc welder.

```
Unrecoverable write error on drive x side n, track n
```

> Error: DOS was unable to write to a disk at the location specified. Try the command again; if the error recurs, the target disk is damaged at that location. If the damaged disk contains important data, copy the files to an empty, freshly formatted disk and try to reformat the damaged disk. If the disk is bad, discard it.

```
WARNING: Unable to use a disk cache on the specified drive
```

> Warning: You specified a drive that SMARTDRV cannot cache, such as a network drive. The version of SMARTDRV distributed with DOS 6.2 can cache CD-ROM drives, but previous versions cannot. SMARTDRV ignores this drive letter.

```
Write failure, diskette unusable
```

> Error: The disk you are writing to has bad sectors in the boot sector or file allocation table (FAT). Run SCANDISK if you have DOS 6.2 to see whether the error can be corrected. If the disk is a floppy, you should probably discard it.

```
You have started the Interlnk server in a task-switching environment.
Task-switching, key combinations, and some disk-writing operations are
Disabled. To restore these functions, exit the server.
```

> Warning: INTERLNK cannot permit certain operations to occur while it is in control. One of these is the DOSSHELL capability to switch tasks. If INTERLNK was swapped while communicating with INTERSVR, you might lose data. INTERLNK therefore inhibits these operations until it is complete.

```
You must specify the host drive for a DoubleSpace drive
```

Error: SMARTDRV must be given the host drive letter to cache. The compressed drive also is cached, and the effective cache size is increased because of the compression. You cannot separately cache the compressed drive.

DOS Device Error Messages

When DOS detects an error reading or writing to a disk drive or device, one of the error messages in this section is displayed. Most of these messages are followed by this prompt:

```
Abort, Ignore, Retry, Fail?
```

You can enter one of the following characters to indicate the action that you want DOS to take:

A	**Abort**. This option terminates the currently running program and returns you to the DOS prompt. Any unsaved data in an application program is lost.
I	**Ignore**. This option pretends that the error hasn't occurred and returns (successfully) to the program that was running. If you are reading from a file, nonsensical data might be returned to your application program. If you are writing to a file, the application doesn't know that the data hasn't been written to disk, and this message might reappear many times as it keeps writing more data. In most cases, you should avoid choosing Ignore. For most floppy disk errors, the Ignore option is not displayed.
R	**Retry**. This is the safest option to choose. If you can correct the problem (by turning on the printer or closing the disk drive door, for example), do so and then choose Retry. Even if you can't correct the problem, choose Retry a few times to see whether the error message goes away. Bad sectors can often be read if you choose Retry a few times.
F	**Fail**. This option fails the operation and returns to the program that was running. Not all programs notice that the operation they requested has failed, in which case Fail has the same problems as Ignore. Use this option in preference to Ignore, but try Retry first. Versions of DOS before 3.3 never display the Fail option.

Many of the error messages have a similar format, as follows:

error_type reading|writing *drive*|*device*

error_type indicates the type of disk or device error that has occurred. *drive* indicates the disk drive where the error occurred. *device* indicates the device (AUX, CON, PRN, and so on) where the error occurred.

Each type of error can occur when either reading or writing to a disk or device. Rather than list all four possibilities for each error message, only the most common ones are shown in the text:

```
Invalid device request reading drive x:
```
```
Invalid device request writing drive x:
```

> Error: This error message is uncommon. A software program has issued an invalid or unsupported command to the drive or device indicated. The problem might be with the device driver or software program. If either of them is new to your system, contact the manufacturer of the software to see whether an upgrade is available.

```
Invalid device request parameters reading drive x:
```
```
Invalid device request parameters writing drive x:
```

> Error: This error message is uncommon. A software program has issued a command to the indicated drive or device, but the command contains an invalid request header. The problem is usually with the software program. Contact the manufacturer of the software to see whether an upgrade is available.

```
Invalid unit reading drive x:
```

> Error: An invalid subunit number was passed to the device driver. This error is displayed if you try to access one of INTERLNK's drives when the drive letter isn't currently redirected to the INTERLNK server. Use the INTERLNK command to link the drive letter to a drive on the server and try again.

```
Data error reading drive x:
```

> Error: DOS was unable to read some of the data on the disk. When this message appears, choose Retry at least two or three times before giving up. Quit the application you are using and run SCANDISK or CHKDSK to attempt to locate and correct the problem on the disk.

```
Not ready reading drive x:
```
```
Not ready writing drive x:
```

> Error: An error occurred when DOS tried to read or write to the disk drive. For floppy disk drives, the drive door might be open, the floppy disk might not be fully inserted, or the disk might not be formatted. Correct the situation and choose Retry. For hard disk drives, this error might indicate a hardware problem. If you get this error for a device rather than a disk drive, check to see that the device is turned on and ready to read or write.

```
FCB unavailable reading drive x:
```
```
FCB unavailable writing drive x:
```

> Error: A program using file control blocks (FCBs) attempted to open more file control blocks than were specified with the FCBS= command. Usually, you have to choose the Abort option and terminate the program you are using. Increase the value of the FCBS=

command in your `CONFIG.SYS` file by four or five; then reboot the system. If the message appears again, increase the value again and reboot.

This method of opening files dates back to DOS 1 and CP/M and should not be used by any current programs that you work with.

`General failure reading drive x:`

`General failure writing drive x:`

> Error: This message is a catchall for errors not covered elsewhere and can occur with disk drives or other devices. Whenever a device driver is unsure of what to call the error it has just received, it calls the error a general failure. Reading disks formatted for operating systems other than DOS can often result in a general failure message.
>
> If you load the file-sharing SHARE.EXE program into memory, you might see this message more often. SHARE prevents two programs from opening the same file at the same time. Newer programs recognize that SHARE is denying them access, but others might return general failure messages. If you are running Windows and receive this message in a DOS program, don't panic. It probably means that another application has a file open, and you are being denied access.

`Lock violation reading drive x:`

`Lock violation writing drive x:`

> Error: With a file-sharing program such as SHARE.EXE or network software loaded, a program attempted to access a locked file. Your best choice is Retry. If you are on a network, get a cup of coffee and choose Retry again to see whether the other user has released the lock yet. If you just can't seem to get access to the file, choose Fail. The program you are using might notice the failure and ask you what to do about it. The last resort is to choose Abort, but be aware that any unsaved data in memory will be lost when the program is terminated.

`Sharing violation reading drive x:`

`Sharing violation writing drive x:`

> Error: With a file-sharing program such as SHARE.EXE or network software loaded, a program attempted to access a file that is in use by another program. Your best choice is Retry. If you are on a network, get a cup of coffee and then choose Retry again to see whether the file is available yet. If you can't get access to the file, choose Fail. The program you are using might notice the failure and ask you what to do about it. The last resort is to choose Abort, but be aware that any unsaved data in memory will be lost when the program is terminated.

`Printer out of paper error writing device dev`

> Error: The printer is out of paper (or not turned on). Check your printer, add paper, make sure the printer is online, and choose Retry. The message DOS displays stays on the screen waiting for you to make a choice, so you could go across town and buy paper if you need to.

```
Invalid media type reading drive x:
Invalid media type writing drive x:
```

> Error: The boot sector or the file allocation table (FAT) of the disk contains invalid information, making the disk unusable. If you come into contact with computers using operating systems other than DOS, you might be trying to read one of their disks.
>
> When you are sure that the disk is a DOS disk, run SCANDISK or CHKDSK to see whether it can be repaired. Even if the repair is successful, you should back up all the files on the disk and reformat it. If FORMAT finds no errors, you can safely begin using the disk again.

```
Not ready reading drive x:
Not ready writing drive x:
```

> Error: This error message is common. It usually means that you've left open the door to your floppy disk drive. Other common causes are that the drive is empty or the disk isn't seated properly. Check the drive or reinsert the disk, and then choose Retry. If you can't get a floppy disk drive to read any disks that you put in it, you might have a hardware problem.

```
Read fault error reading drive x:
```

> Error: DOS was unable to read data from the drive. Often this problem is caused by a floppy disk that isn't seated properly in the drive, or you might have a bad spot on the disk. Reinsert the disk and choose Retry. Usually, the read operation succeeds after you choose Retry a few times. Check the disk by running SCANDISK to make sure that no errors appear on it, or back up any files and reformat the disk.
>
> If you begin to get several of these errors, your floppy disk drive might be out of alignment. When this problem occurs, people typically start complaining that they can't read your disks. If your drive is out of alignment, your only options are to repair or replace the drive.

```
Sector not found reading drive x:
Sector not found writing drive x:
```

> Error: The disk drive was unable to find the requested sector on the disk. This error is usually the result of a defective spot on the disk. Choose Retry quite a few times before you give up; often the sector will be found if you're persistent. Check the disk by running SCANDISK to make sure that no errors appear on it, or back up any files and reformat the disk.
>
> Some copy-protection schemes use a defective spot to prevent unauthorized duplication of the disk. If you have reason to believe that the disk you are reading or writing to is copy-protected, do not correct the disk by running SCANDISK. Contact the manufacturer of the copy-protected software and ask for a replacement disk.

```
Seek error reading drive x:
Seek error writing drive x:
```

Error: The disk drive could not find the proper track on the disk. Seek errors are often the result of failing drive electronics. If, however, the disk is not properly seated in the drive, reseating it corrects the problem. Choose Retry a few times to see whether the problem goes away. If you are having a hardware problem, you will get more of these errors as time goes on and will eventually have to repair or replace your disk drive.

`Write fault error writing drive x:`

Error: DOS was unable to write data to the drive. Often this problem is caused by a floppy disk that isn't seated properly in the drive, or you might have a bad spot on the disk. Reinsert the disk and choose Retry. The write operation usually succeeds after you choose Retry a few times. Check the disk by running SCANDISK to make sure that no errors appear on it, or back up any files and reformat the disk.

If you begin to get several of these errors, your floppy disk drive might be out of alignment. When this problem occurs, people typically start complaining that they can't read your disks. If your drive is out of alignment, your only options are repair or replacement.

`Write fault error writing device dev`

Error: DOS could not write the data to this device. This error typically is caused by not having your printer turned on or online, although the same thing can happen with an external modem. Check the device and choose Retry. If the problem persists, you might have a faulty cable.

`Write protect error writing drive x:`

Error: DOS attempted to write to a disk that is write-protected. If the disk is a floppy and the write operation is intentional, remove the disk, adjust the write-protect tab, and reinsert the disk. Don't switch floppy disks at this prompt. To allow the write operation to proceed, make sure that the disk is no longer write-protected and choose Retry. If you don't want to allow the program to write to the disk, choose Fail or, as a last resort, Abort. Remember that if you choose Abort, any unsaved data in memory will be lost.

`Invalid disk change reading drive x:`

`Invalid disk change writing drive x:`

Error: You have removed a disk that DOS needs access to. This message can occur only with removable media, such as floppy disks. Unfortunately, DOS doesn't tell you what disk it needs; it tells you only the drive. Think back, put the previous disk back in the drive, and choose Retry. Choosing any other option might mean that the disk that was prematurely removed might be damaged or incomplete. Never choose Fail or Abort at this message without first removing all media from the disk drive because DOS could write the wrong file allocation table (FAT) to that disk and destroy all the data on it.

APPENDIX D

DOS AND DOS UTILITY PROGRAMS' KEYBOARD COMMANDS

In this appendix

DOS Startup Control Keys   564

ROM BIOS Control Keys   564

DOS Control Keys   565

Command-Line Editing Keys Without DOSKEY   565

Command-Line Editing Keys with DOSKEY   567

Edit Keystroke Commands   568

DOS Shell Keystroke Commands   569

DOS Startup Control Keys

When you start your computer and the `Starting MS-DOS...` message appears onscreen, you have about five seconds to press a few special keys to bypass some or all of the commands in your `CONFIG.SYS` and `AUTOEXEC.BAT` files. These keys are available only in MS-DOS 6.0 and later:

- **F5 (Clean Boot).** MS-DOS performs a minimal startup, ignoring any `CONFIG.SYS` and `AUTOEXEC.BAT` files in the root directory of the startup drive. `DBLSPACE.BIN` is still loaded into memory if your system uses compressed drives.

- **Ctrl+F5 (Clean Boot).** Just like F5, except `DBLSPACE.BIN` is not loaded into memory. Any compressed drives are inaccessible.

- **F8 (Interactive Boot).** MS-DOS prompts you for every line in your `CONFIG.SYS` file, enabling you to selectively execute or skip each line. To execute the remaining commands without being prompted, press the Esc key. When the `CONFIG.SYS` file is complete, DOS asks whether you want to execute your `AUTOEXEC.BAT` file.

  Note that `DBLSPACE.BIN` is still loaded into memory if your system uses compressed drives. With F8 (Interactive Boot), you cannot choose whether to load `DBLSPACE.BIN` into memory.

  For MS-DOS 6.2, Microsoft has changed the behavior of the F8 key, and you are now prompted for each line in your `AUTOEXEC.BAT` file as well as in your `CONFIG.SYS` file. To stop being prompted for each line, press the Esc key to execute or press the F5 key to bypass all the remaining lines in your startup files.

- **Ctrl+F8 (Interactive Boot).** This is just like the F8 boot, except `DBLSPACE.BIN` is not loaded into memory. Any compressed drives are inaccessible.

ROM BIOS Control Keys

ROM BIOS commands are available at all times, although an application program can prevent them from working. (All are eliminated or changed when Microsoft Windows is active.) Break and Reboot should be avoided if possible because terminating a program in this way can damage open files, causing lost clusters or data loss. Your computer's ROM BIOS may provide other key combinations as well, such as commands to change processor speed, enter sleep mode, or access the CMOS Setup screen. Some keyboards provide a single key for these services (listed in Table D.1).

TABLE D.1 BIOS CONTROL KEYS AND THEIR FUNCTIONS

Keystroke	Function	Description
Ctrl+Alt+Del	Reboot	Requests the BIOS to perform a system reset (warm boot). Use only at the DOS prompt or when the computer stops responding to normal commands.
Ctrl+Break	Break	Stops (exits) a command or software application program. Use with caution.

Table D.1 Continued

Keystroke	Function	Description
Shift+PrtSc	Print screen	Prints the contents of the video display (text only). Check that your printer is turned on before requesting this service.
SysReq	System request	Requests system services. Does nothing on most PC systems. Not available on older 83-key keyboards.

DOS Control Keys

DOS provides the following functions, listed in Table D.2, although application programs often prevent them from working. (All are eliminated or changed when Microsoft Windows is active.)

Table D.2 DOS Control Keys and Their Functions

Keystroke	Function	Description
Ctrl+C	Break	Stops (exits) a command or software application program. Very useful for halting DOS commands. This DOS-provided Break command is somewhat safer than the Break command provided by the ROM BIOS.
Ctrl+S	Pause	Pauses the system until the next key is pressed. Identical to the ROM BIOS–provided service.
Ctrl+P	Echo to PRN	Echoes all characters to the printer (LPT1) as well as to the screen. Press Ctrl+P a second time to turn off.

Command-Line Editing Keys Without DOSKEY

The following keys listed in Table D.3 enable you to edit text on the command line when DOSKEY is not loaded. When you press Enter, the command line is placed in a template buffer and then executed by DOS. By pressing certain function keys, you can reuse characters from the template buffer in the next command line.

A cursor (current position) is maintained for both the template buffer offscreen and the command line onscreen. Normally, both cursors track each other, but certain function keys can alter this tracking. All actions are performed on the character at the cursor.

Table D.3 MS-DOS Command-Line Editing Keys and Their Functions

Keystroke	Function	Description
Enter	Execute	Executes the current command line and places a copy of it in the template buffer.
Esc	Cancel	Cancels the current command line without changing the template buffer. Resets the template cursor to the beginning of the line.
Backspace or left arrow	Delete	Moves left and one character from the command line. Leaves the template buffer unchanged.
F1 or right arrow	Copy one	Copies one character from the template to the command line.
F2	Copy up to	Copies all remaining characters from the template up to, but not including, the next character you type.
F3	Copy all	Copies all remaining characters from the template to the command line.
Del	Skip one	Skips (deletes) one character in the template buffer. (Complement of F1.)
F4	Skip up to	Skips (deletes) all remaining characters from the template up to, but not including, the next character you type. (Complement of F2.)
Ins	Add in	Toggles insert mode. In insert mode, characters you type at the command line do not cause the template cursor to move. Note that this doesn't enable you to insert characters on the command line by moving the cursor and typing. It enables you only to type without moving the template cursor at the same time.
F5	New template	Copies the current command line into the template buffer but doesn't execute the command line.
F6	EOF	Inserts an end-of-file (EOF) marker (Ctrl+Z) into the command line.

When you use the console like an input file with certain commands (for example, COPY CON filename), some of the previous keystrokes become very useful. Pressing F6 inserts an end-of-file marker (Ctrl+Z) into the file and terminates the copy operation when you press Enter. (Anything you type after the Ctrl+Z is discarded.) Pressing Ctrl+Break or Ctrl+C aborts the copy operation.

COMMAND-LINE EDITING KEYS WITH DOSKEY

If you have DOSKEY loaded, the following keys are available:

Key	Description
Enter	Executes the current command line.
Esc	Clears the current command line.
Left arrow	Moves left one character.
Right arrow	Moves right one character.
Ctrl+left arrow	Moves left one word.
Ctrl+right arrow	Moves right one word.
Home	Moves to the beginning of the command line.
End	Moves to the end of the command line.
Backspace	Moves left one character and deletes that character.
Del	Deletes the character at the cursor.
Ctrl+Home	Deletes all characters from the cursor to the beginning of the command line.
Ctrl+End	Deletes all characters from the cursor to the end of the command line.
Up arrow	Displays the previous DOS command.
Down arrow	Displays the next DOS command; displays a blank line if you are at the end of the list.
PgUp	Displays the first (earliest) command in the command-history buffer.
PgDn	Displays the last command in the command-history buffer.
F7	Displays the contents of the command-history buffer in a numbered list.
Alt+F7	Clears the command-history buffer.
F8	Searches for the command or commands that most closely match the characters on the command line.
F9	Prompts you for the line number of the stored command you want to display. Use F7 to see a numbered list of the commands in the command-history buffer.
Alt+F10	Clears all macro definitions from memory.
Ins	Toggles between overwrite mode (the default) and insert mode. (Note that the cursor changes shape.)
Ctrl+T	Inserts a paragraph mark in the command line. Use Ctrl+T to separate multiple commands typed on one line.

EDIT KEYSTROKE COMMANDS

When you are using the DOS editor (Edit), the following keystroke commands are available.

Key	Alt Key	Description
Enter		Executes the current command line.
Alt		Accesses menus.
Esc		Cancels a menu choice or a dialog box; exits Help.
F1		Opens context-sensitive help.
Shift+F1		Opens the "Getting Started" section of Help.
Left arrow	Ctrl+S	Moves left one character.
Right arrow	Ctrl+D	Moves right one character.
Ctrl+left arrow	Ctrl+A	Moves left one word.
Ctrl+right arrow	Ctrl+F	Moves right one word.
Up arrow	Ctrl+E	Moves up one line.
Down arrow	Ctrl+X	Moves down one line.
	Ctrl+Q,S	Moves to the beginning of the current line.
Home		Moves to the first indent level on the line.
End	Ctrl+Q,D	Moves to the end of the current line.
Ctrl+Enter	Ctrl+J	Moves to the beginning of the next line.
	Ctrl+Q,E	Moves to the top of the window.
	Ctrl+Q,X	Moves to the bottom of the window.
F6		Toggles between the Help window and the Editing window when both are open.
Ctrl+up arrow	Ctrl+W	Scrolls up one line.
Ctrl+down arrow	Ctrl+Z	Scrolls down one line.
PgUp	Ctrl+R	Scrolls up one screen.
PgDn	Ctrl+C	Scrolls down one screen.
Ctrl+PgUp		Scrolls left one window.
Ctrl+PgDn		Scrolls right one window.
Shift+left arrow		Selects the character to the left.
Shift+right arrow		Selects the character to the right.
Ctrl+Shift+left arrow		Selects the word to the left.
Ctrl+Shift+right arrow		Selects the word to the right.
Shift+up arrow		Selects the line above.

Shift+down arrow		Selects one current line.
Shift+PgUp		Selects one screen up.
Shift+PgDn		Selects one screen down.
Ctrl+Shift+Home		Selects to the beginning of the file.
Ctrl+Shift+End		Selects to the end of the file.
Ctrl+Ins		Copies selected text to the Clipboard.
Shift+Ins		Pastes (inserts) text from the Clipboard.
Shift+Del		Cuts selected text to the Clipboard.
Ctrl+Y		Cuts the current line to the Clipboard.
Ctrl+Q,Y		Cuts to the end of the line to the Clipboard.
Backspace	**Ctrl+H**	Deletes the character to the left.
Del	**Ctrl+G**	Deletes the current character.
Del	**Ctrl+G**	Deletes the selected text.
Ctrl+T		Deletes to the end of the current word.
Shift+Tab		Deletes leading spaces from selected lines.
	Home, Ctrl+N	Inserts a line above the cursor.
End+Enter		Inserts a line below the cursor.
	Ctrl+Q,F	Searches for text.
F3	**Ctrl+L**	Repeats the search.
	Ctrl+Q,A	Changes text (search and replace).
Ins	**Ctrl+V**	Toggles between insert mode (the default) and overwrite mode.
Ctrl+P, Ctrl+*key*		Inserts a control character into the text.

DOS SHELL KEYSTROKE COMMANDS

DOS 6.0 assigns special functions to some keys when you use them in the DOS Shell:

Enter	Executes a command or operation.
Esc	Cancels a command or operation; exits Help.
F1	Displays context-sensitive Help.
F3 or **Alt+F4**	Exits the DOS Shell.
Shift+F5	Repaints the screen.
Shift+F9	Goes to the DOS command prompt. You can type EXIT to return to the DOS Shell.
F10 or **Alt**	Accesses the menu bar.

Up arrow	Scrolls up one line.
Down arrow	Scrolls down one line.
PgUp	Scrolls up one screen.
PgDn	Scrolls down one screen.
Letter key	Moves to (finds) the next line in a list that begins with the letter entered.
Home	Moves to the beginning of a line or list.
End	Moves to the end of a line or list.
Ctrl+Home	Moves to the beginning of a list.
Ctrl+End	Moves to the end of a list.
Tab	Moves to the next area or window.
Shift+Tab	Moves to the previous area or window.
F5	Updates (refreshes) the directory tree and file list.
Ctrl+F5	Updates the file list for the current directory.
Ctrl+*drive*	Selects the specified disk drive and displays its directories and files.
F7	Moves the selected files.
F8	Copies the selected files.
F9	Views the contents of the selected file. You can use F9 to toggle between an ASCII view and a hexadecimal view of the file.
Del	Deletes the selected files.
Spacebar	Selects the current file (Add mode).
Shift+up arrow	Selects the previous file.
Shift+down arrow	Selects the next file.
Shift+PgUp	Selects the previous screen of files.
Shift+PgDn	Selects the next screen of files.
Shift+spacebar	Selects all files from the previously selected file to the cursor (Add mode).
Ctrl+/	Selects all files in the list.
Ctrl+	Deselects all files in the list.
Shift+F8	Toggles Add mode on and off.
Minus (–)	Collapses (hides) the current branch of the directory tree.
Plus (+)	Expands (displays) the current branch of the directory tree one level.
Asterisk (*)	Expands (displays) the current branch of the directory tree completely.
Ctrl+*	Expands (displays) all directories in the tree.

When the task list is activated, the following functions are available:

Shift+Enter	Adds a program to the active task list.
Ctrl+Shift+Enter	Adds a program to the active task list. When you run the program, it opens the file specified in the Properties dialog box automatically.
Ctrl+Esc	Suspends a program and returns to the MS-DOS Shell.
Alt+Esc	Switches to the next program in the task list.
Shift+Alt+Esc	Switches to the previous program in the task list.
Alt+Tab	Cycles forward through the active task list.
Ctrl+Alt+Tab	Cycles backward through the active task list.

APPENDIX E

ASCII AND EXTENDED ASCII CODES

ASCII (American Standard Code for Information Interchange) is a widely used standard that defines numeric values for a common set of alphabetic characters. The first 32 characters are reserved for formatting and hardware control codes. Following these codes are 96 "printable" characters. IBM defined symbols for the final 128 ASCII values when it released the IBM PC, and referred to the additional characters as *Extended ASCII codes*. This entire set of 256 characters is often referred to as the *PC-8 character set*, or *code page 437*.

Dec X_{10}	Hex X_{16}	Binary X_2	ASCII Character	Ctrl	Key
000	00	0000 0000	null	NUL	^@
001	01	0000 0001	☺	SOH	^A
002	02	0000 0010	●	STX	^B
003	03	0000 0011	♥	ETX	^C
004	04	0000 0100	♦	EOT	^D
005	05	0000 0101	♣	ENQ	^E
006	06	0000 0110	♠	ACK	^F
007	07	0000 0111	●	BEL	^G
008	08	0000 1000	■	BS	^H
009	09	0000 1001	○	HT	^I

Appendix E ASCII and Extended ASCII Codes

Dec X_{10}	Hex X_{16}	Binary X_2	ASCII Character	Ctrl	Key
010	0A	0000 1010	■	LF	^J
011	0B	0000 1011	♂	VT	^K
012	0C	0000 1100	♀	FF	^L
013	0D	0000 1101	♪	CR	^M
014	0E	0000 1110	♪♪	SO	^N
015	0F	0000 1111	☼	SI	^O
016	10	0001 0000	►	DLE	^P
017	11	0001 0001	◄	DC1	^Q
018	12	0001 0010	↕	DC2	^R
019	13	0001 0011	‼	DC3	^S
020	14	0001 0100	¶	DC4	^T
021	15	0001 0101	§	NAK	^U
022	16	0001 0110	▬	SYN	^V
023	17	0001 0111	↨	ETB	^W
024	18	0001 1000	↑	CAN	^X
025	19	0001 1001	↓	EM	^Y
026	1A	0001 1010	→	SUB	^Z
027	1B	0001 1011	←	ESC	^[
028	1C	0001 1100	∟	FS	^\
029	1D	0001 1101	↔	GS	^]
030	1E	0001 1110	▲	RS	^^
031	1F	0001 1111	▼	US	^_
032	20	0010 0000	Space		
033	21	0010 0001	!		
034	22	0010 0010	"		
035	23	0010 0011	#		
036	24	0010 0100	$		
037	25	0010 0101	%		
038	26	0010 0110	&		
039	27	0010 0111	'		
040	28	0010 1000	(		

Dec X_{10}	Hex X_{16}	Binary X_2	ASCII Character
041	29	0010 1001	)
042	2A	0010 1010	*
043	2B	0010 1011	+
044	2C	0010 1100	,
045	2D	0010 1101	-
046	2E	0010 1110	.
047	2F	0010 1111	/
048	30	0011 0000	0
049	31	0011 0001	1
050	32	0011 0010	2
051	33	0011 0011	3
052	34	0011 0100	4
053	35	0011 0101	5
054	36	0011 0110	6
055	37	0011 0111	7
056	38	0011 1000	8
057	39	0011 1001	9
058	3A	0011 1010	:
059	3B	0011 1011	;
060	3C	0011 1100	<
061	3D	0011 1101	=
062	3E	0011 1110	>
063	3F	0011 1111	?
064	40	0100 0000	@
065	41	0100 0001	A
066	42	0100 0010	B
067	43	0100 0011	C
068	44	0100 0100	D
069	45	0100 0101	E
070	46	0100 0110	F
071	47	0100 0111	G
072	48	0100 1000	H
073	49	0100 1001	I

Appendix E ASCII and Extended ASCII Codes

Dec X_{10}	Hex X_{16}	Binary X_2	ASCII Character
074	4A	0100 1010	J
075	4B	0100 1011	K
076	4C	0100 1100	L
077	4D	0100 1101	M
078	4E	0100 1110	N
079	4F	0100 1111	O
080	50	0101 0000	P
081	51	0101 0001	Q
082	52	0101 0010	R
083	53	0101 0011	S
084	54	0101 0100	T
085	55	0101 0101	U
086	56	0101 0110	V
087	57	0101 0111	W
088	58	0101 1000	X
089	59	0101 1001	Y
090	5A	0101 1010	Z
091	5B	0101 1011	[
092	5C	0101 1100	\
093	5D	0101 1101	]
094	5E	0101 1110	^
095	5F	0101 1111	_
096	60	0110 0000	`
097	61	0110 0001	a
098	62	0110 0010	b
099	63	0110 0011	c
100	64	0110 0100	d
101	65	0110 0101	e
102	66	0110 0110	f
103	67	0110 0111	g
104	68	0110 1000	h
105	69	0110 1001	i

ASCII AND EXTENDED ASCII CODES

Dec X_{10}	Hex X_{16}	Binary X_2	ASCII Character
106	6A	0110 1010	j
107	6B	0110 1011	k
108	6C	0110 1100	l
109	6D	0110 1101	m
110	6E	0110 1110	n
111	6F	0110 1111	o
112	70	0111 0000	p
113	71	0111 0001	q
114	72	0111 0010	r
115	73	0111 0011	s
116	74	0111 0100	t
117	75	0111 0101	u
118	76	0111 0110	v
119	77	0111 0111	w
120	78	0111 1000	x
121	79	0111 1001	y
122	7A	0111 1010	z
123	7B	0111 1011	{
124	7C	0111 1100	¦
125	7D	0111 1101	}
126	7E	0111 1110	~
127	7F	0111 1111	Delete
128	80	1000 0000	Ç
129	81	1000 0001	ü
130	82	1000 0010	é
131	83	1000 0011	â
132	84	1000 0100	ä
133	85	1000 0101	à
134	86	1000 0110	å
135	87	1000 0111	ç
136	88	1000 1000	ê
137	89	1000 1001	ë

Dec X_{10}	Hex X_{16}	Binary X_2	ASCII Character
138	8A	1000 1010	è
139	8B	1000 1011	ï
140	8C	1000 1100	î
141	8D	1000 1101	ì
142	8E	1000 1110	Ä
143	8F	1000 1111	Å
144	90	1001 0000	É
145	91	1001 0001	æ
146	92	1001 0010	Æ
147	93	1001 0011	ô
148	94	1001 0100	ö
149	95	1001 0101	ò
150	96	1001 0110	û
151	97	1001 0111	ù
152	98	1001 1000	ÿ
153	99	1001 1001	Ö
154	9A	1001 1010	Ü
155	9B	1001 1011	¢
156	9C	1001 1100	£
157	9D	1001 1101	¥
158	9E	1001 1110	P$_t$
159	9F	1001 1111	ƒ
160	A0	1010 0000	á
161	A1	1010 0001	í
162	A2	1010 0010	ó
163	A3	1010 0011	ú
164	A4	1010 0100	ñ
165	A5	1010 0101	Ñ
166	A6	1010 0110	ª
167	A7	1010 0111	º
168	A8	1010 1000	¿
169	A9	1010 1001	⌐

Dec X_{10}	Hex X_{16}	Binary X_2	ASCII Character
170	AA	1010 1010	¬
171	AB	1010 1011	½
172	AC	1010 1100	¼
173	AD	1010 1101	¡
174	AE	1010 1110	«
175	AF	1010 1111	»
176	B0	1011 0000	░
177	B1	1011 0001	▒
178	B2	1011 0010	▓
179	B3	1011 0011	│
180	B4	1011 0100	┤
181	B5	1011 0101	╡
182	B6	1011 0110	╢
183	B7	1011 0111	╖
184	B8	1011 1000	╕
185	B9	1011 1001	╣
186	BA	1011 1010	║
187	BB	1011 1011	╗
188	BC	1011 1100	╝
189	BD	1011 1101	╜
190	BE	1011 1110	╛
191	BF	1011 1111	┐
192	C0	1100 0000	└
193	C1	1100 0001	┴
194	C2	1100 0010	┬
195	C3	1100 0011	├
196	C4	1100 0100	─
197	C5	1100 0101	┼
198	C6	1100 0110	╞
199	C7	1100 0111	╟
200	C8	1100 1000	╚
201	C9	1100 1001	╔

Dec X_{10}	Hex X_{16}	Binary X_2	ASCII Character
202	CA	1100 1010	╩
203	CB	1100 1011	╦
204	CC	1100 1100	╠
205	CD	1100 1101	═
206	CE	1100 1110	╬
207	CF	1100 1111	╧
208	D0	1101 0000	╨
209	D1	1101 0001	╤
210	D2	1101 0010	╥
211	D3	1101 0011	╙
212	D4	1101 0100	╘
213	D5	1101 0101	╒
214	D6	1101 0110	╓
215	D7	1101 0111	╫
216	D8	1101 1000	╪
217	D9	1101 1001	┘
218	DA	1101 1010	┌
219	DB	1101 1011	█
220	DC	1101 1100	▄
221	DD	1101 1101	▌
222	DE	1101 1110	▐
223	DF	1101 1111	▀
224	E0	1110 0000	α
225	E1	1110 0001	β
226	E2	1110 0010	Γ
227	E3	1110 0011	π
228	E4	1110 0100	Σ
229	E5	1110 0101	σ
230	E6	1110 0110	μ

Dec X_{10}	Hex X_{16}	Binary X_2	ASCII Character
231	E7	1110 0111	τ
232	E8	1110 1000	Φ
233	E9	1110 1001	θ
234	EA	1110 1010	Ω
235	EB	1110 1011	δ
236	EC	1110 1100	∞
237	ED	1110 1101	ø
238	EE	1110 1110	∈
239	EF	1110 1111	∩
240	F0	1111 0000	≡
241	F1	1111 0001	±
242	F2	1111 0010	≥
243	F3	1111 0011	≤
244	F4	1111 0100	⌠
245	F5	1111 0101	⌡
246	F6	1111 0110	÷
247	F7	1111 0111	≈
248	F8	1111 1000	°
249	F9	1111 1001	•
250	FA	1111 1010	·
251	FB	1111 1011	√
252	FC	1111 1100	η
253	FD	1111 1101	²
254	FE	1111 1110	■
255	FF	1111 1111	

APPENDIX F

COMMAND REFERENCE

With every new release, Microsoft has added features to MS-DOS. MS-DOS 6.22 now contains more than 100 commands, providing configuration support and utilities for the large variety of computers that run MS-DOS. Many commands help you organize the files and subdirectories on your hard disk or enable you to configure your computer system to run more efficiently. Other commands enable you to automate routine tasks that you perform with your computer every day. DOS now includes commands that provide support for the various characters and conventions used in many countries other than the United States.

This command reference describes all the commands that Microsoft provides in the standard MS-DOS 6.22 package. Each command entry includes a description of the command's purpose, its syntax, notes and rules on how to use it, examples of its use, error messages and exit codes when applicable, and a "See Also" section that points you to additional information about using a particular command.

> **Note**
> This command reference also describes commands provided in other common DOS versions, including MS-DOS "7" (in Windows 95), MS-DOS "7.1" (in Windows 98), Caldera DR DOS, and IBM's PC-DOS.

DOS COMMANDS BY FUNCTION

So that you can easily find the command you're looking for, the following lists group the various DOS commands by their functions and contain short descriptions of each command. Many commands have more than one function, so they may appear in more than one group. When you locate the command you want in these function lists, turn to the reference section for much more detailed information about a particular command. The reference section lists the commands in alphabetical order.

In the following function lists, the commands are divided into these categories:

- Batch File Commands
- CONFIG.SYS Commands
- CONFIG.SYS Device Drivers
- Directory Commands
- Disk Commands
- File Commands
- Full-Screen DOS Applications
- Help Commands
- International Commands and Device Drivers
- Memory and System Performance Commands
- Miscellaneous Commands
- Windows Applications

BATCH FILE COMMANDS

CALL	Executes a batch file from within another batch file.
CHOICE	Accepts a single keystroke from the keyboard.
COMMAND	Runs a second copy of the MS-DOS command interpreter.
ECHO	Echoes text to the screen from a batch file.
FOR	FOR-IN-DO loop for batch files.
GOTO	Jumps to a labeled line in a batch file.
IF	IF-THEN decision structure for a batch file.
PAUSE	Waits for a keystroke before continuing.
REM	Inserts a remark into a batch file.
SHIFT	Shifts batch file parameters down one place.

CONFIG.SYS COMMANDS

BREAK=	Turns on or off extended Ctrl+Break checking.
BUFFERS=	Sets the number of disk buffers used by DOS.
COUNTRY=	Sets country information.
DEVICE=	Loads an installable device driver.
DEVICEHIGH=	Loads an installable device driver into high (UMB) memory.

DOS=	Sets whether DOS will use the high memory area (HMA) and upper memory blocks (UMB).
DRIVPARM=	Redefines the physical characteristics of an existing disk drive.
FCBS=	Sets the maximum number of open file control blocks (FCBs) that DOS will allow.
FILES=	Sets the maximum number of open files that DOS will allow.
INCLUDE=	Includes the commands from one CONFIG.SYS block within another.
INSTALL=	Loads TSR programs into memory from CONFIG.SYS.
LASTDRIVE=	Sets the maximum number of drive letters available to DOS.
MENUCOLOR=	Sets the color of the screen for the CONFIG.SYS startup menu.
MENUDEFAULT=	Sets the default menu choice in a CONFIG.SYS menu block.
MENUITEM=	Sets the text and configuration block associated with menu items in CONFIG.SYS.
NUMLOCK=	Sets the state of the NumLock key when the computer starts up.
REM	Inserts a remark into CONFIG.SYS.
SET	Sets environment variables.
SHELL=	Sets the name of the program used as a command-line shell by MS-DOS.
STACKS=	Sets the number of stacks set aside for hardware interrupts.
SUBMENU=	Defines a submenu in CONFIG.SYS.
SWITCHES=	Sets miscellaneous control options for MS-DOS.

CONFIG.SYS DEVICE= DRIVERS

ANSI.SYS	Alternate console driver, which provides ANSI standard control of the display and keyboard.
DBLSPACE.SYS	Dummy drivers that can relocate DBLSPACE.BIN in memory.
DISPLAY.SYS	Device driver for the display with international code page support.
DRIVER.SYS	Driver that sets the DOS drive letter for an existing disk drive or creates an additional drive letter for a disk drive.
EMM386.EXE	Expanded (EMS) Memory Manager with upper memory block (UMB) support.

HIMEM.SYS	Extended (XMS) Memory Manager.
INTERLNK.EXE	Client device driver for an InterLnk network.
POWER.EXE	Advanced Power Management (APM) device driver for portable computers.
RAMDRIVE.SYS	Driver that sets up a disk drive in RAM memory.
SETVER.EXE	DOS version control program that can fool certain programs into running with the "incorrect" version of MS-DOS.
SMARTDRV.EXE	Driver that installs double-buffering to make SMARTDrive compatible with certain hard disk drives.

Directory Commands

CD or CHDIR	Changes the current directory of a disk drive.
DELTREE	Deletes a directory, including all the files and subdirectories it may contain.
MD or MKDIR	Creates a new subdirectory on a disk.
RD or RMDIR	Deletes an empty subdirectory on a disk.
TREE	Displays the subdirectory structure present on a disk.

Disk Commands

CHKDSK	Checks a disk for errors and provides information on the amount of space in use.
DEFRAG	Defragments the files on a disk. Using this command can cut down on the time your computer takes to find files on your hard disk.
DISKCOMP	Compares two floppy disks to see whether they are identical.
DISKCOPY	Makes an exact copy of a floppy disk.
FDISK	Hard disk partitioning program. Prepares a new hard disk to accept DOS or partitions a single drive into two or more logical drives.
FORMAT	Formats a hard or floppy disk for MS-DOS.
LABEL	Creates, edits, or deletes the volume label on a disk.
SCANDISK	Analyzes disks and repairs errors. The ScanDisk utility can repair DoubleSpace-compressed drives as well as normal disks.
SUBST	Creates a disk drive letter that refers to a subdirectory of another drive.

SYS	Installs the MS-DOS system files on another disk.
UNFORMAT	Returns a disk to the state it was in before FORMAT was run.
VERIFY	Controls whether DOS will read everything written to disk to ensure that no errors occurred.
VOL	Displays the volume label of a disk.

File Commands

ATTRIB	Views or changes file attributes.
COPY	Copies or concatenates a file or group of files.
DEL or ERASE	Deletes a file or group of files.
DIR	Displays a listing of the files in a subdirectory.
EXPAND	Expands (uncompresses) files on the MS-DOS 6 distribution disks.
FC	Compares two files for differences.
FIND	Finds matching text in a file.
MOVE	Moves a file from one subdirectory to another or renames a subdirectory.
REN or RENAME	Renames a file or group of files.
REPLACE	Replaces or adds files to a subdirectory.
SHARE	Provides file sharing and locking capabilities for DOS.
TYPE	Displays the contents of a file onscreen.
UNDELETE	Undeletes a file or group of files.
XCOPY	Copies files and subdirectories.

DOS Applications

DBLSPACE	Program that compresses information on a disk, providing up to twice the amount of space you previously had.
DEBUG	Programmer's debugger.
DEFRAG	Program that defragments the files on a disk. Running this program can cut down on the time your computer takes to find files on your hard disk.
DOSSHELL	Graphical shell program for DOS.

EDIT	A full-screen ASCII text file editor.
FDISK	Hard disk partitioning program. Prepares a new hard disk to accept DOS or partitions a single drive into two or more logical drives.
HELP	An online help system that provides descriptions and examples for every DOS command.
MSAV	The Microsoft Anti-Virus program. Checks your computer for viruses.
MSBACKUP	The Microsoft Backup program. Backs up files on your hard disk to a series of floppy disks.
MSD	The Microsoft System Diagnostics program. Provides information about the configuration of your computer system.
QBASIC	Program that provides access to the Microsoft QuickBASIC development environment, which enables you to write and run programs written in the QuickBASIC language.

Help Commands

FASTHELP	Displays a short description of what each DOS command is for and the correct syntax for its use.
HELP	Opens a full-screen, online help system that provides descriptions and examples for every DOS command.
/?	Not an actual command; if you include a /? on the command line with a DOS command, DOS displays a short description of what the command does and how you can use it.

International Commands and Device Drivers

CHCP	Changes the active country code page.
COUNTRY=	Sets country information.
DISPLAY.SYS	Runs a device driver for the display with international code page support.
KEYB	Sets the active keyboard layout.
MODE	Configures standard DOS devices, including changing the active code page for the keyboard, display, and printer.
NLSFUNC	Contains code page switching support required by CHCP and MODE.

Memory and System Performance Commands

BUFFERS=	Sets the number of disk buffers used by DOS.
DEFRAG	Defragments the files on a disk. Using this command can cut down on the time your computer takes to find files on your hard disk.
DEVICEHIGH=	Loads an installable device driver into high (UMB) memory.
DOS=	Determines whether DOS loads itself into conventional memory or into the high memory area (HMA).
EMM386.EXE	Expanded (EMS) Memory Manager with upper memory block (UMB) support.
HIMEM.SYS	Extended (XMS) Memory Manager.
LH or LOADHIGH	Loads a TSR program into high (UMB) memory.
MEM	Displays how memory in your computer system is being used.
MEMMAKER	Utility to optimize memory usage on your computer.
SMARTDRV	Disk cache program that can speed up disk access time.

Miscellaneous Commands

APPEND	Establishes a DOS search path for data files.
BREAK	Turns on or off extended Ctrl+Break checking.
CLS	Clears the screen.
CTTY	Changes the device used for standard input and output.
DATE	Sets or views the system date.
DOSKEY	Provides enhanced command-line editing and macros capability.
EXIT	Exits (terminates) a temporary copy of COMMAND.COM.
GRAPHICS	Provides support for a graphics mode Print Screen function.
INTERLNK	Controls the client device driver in an InterLnk network.
INTERSVR	Controls the server program for an InterLnk network.
LOADFIX	Forces a program to load into the second 64KB of memory.
MODE	Configures standard DOS devices such as serial ports, parallel ports, the display, and the keyboard.
MORE	Pauses display output when the screen is full.
PATH	Establishes a DOS search path for executable files.

PRINT	Controls the print spooler for ASCII text files.
PROMPT	Customizes the prompt used by DOS at the command line.
RESTORE	Restores files backed up with the DOS 5 version of BACKUP.
SET	Sets, clears, or displays environment variables.
SORT	Sorts ASCII text lines into alphabetical order.
TIME	Sets or views the system time.
VER	Displays the version of DOS running on the computer.
VSAFE	Watches for viruses.

Windows Applications

MWAV	The Microsoft Anti-Virus for Windows program. Checks your computer for viruses.
MWAVTSR	A Windows program that enables VSAFE to alert you to trouble when you are running Windows.
MWBACKUP	The Microsoft Backup for Windows program. Backs up files on your hard disk to a series of floppy disks.
MWUNDEL	The Microsoft Undelete for Windows program. Undeletes a file or group of files.
SMARTMON	The SMARTDrive monitoring and configuration program for Windows.

Conventions Used in This Command Reference

The following conventions have been used throughout this reference to make the command descriptions clear and accurate:

Bold	Required literal. Indicates an argument that is required and must be typed as part of the command. For example, the command name always appears in bold because it must be included when you issue the command.
Italic	Optional placeholder. The *placeholder* holds the place for the actual name or value that you would type when you issue the command. In other words, you don't type the word *filename*, you replace *filename* with the actual name of a file.

| `Bold italic` | Required placeholder. Indicates a placeholder argument that is required. When you issue the command, you *must* substitute an appropriate value for an argument that appears in bold italic. |
| `Monospaced type` | Optional literal. Indicates an optional argument that, if included, must be typed as shown. Switches often are optional literal arguments. |

The COPY command, for example, uses all four types of arguments in its syntax:

`COPY` *`source`* `destination` `/V`

- **COPY** is a required literal, so it appears in bold. The command name always has to be typed exactly as it is shown, although you can add a drive and subdirectory path before the command when necessary.
- *source* is a required placeholder, so it appears in bold italic. In this case, you would enter the name of the file or files that you wanted to copy.
- *destination* is an optional placeholder, so it appears in regular italic. If you choose to omit this argument, a default value is assumed. As with all placeholders, if you include this argument, you replace the word *destination* with the filename and path where you want to copy the files.
- /V is an optional literal, so it appears in regular text. Most switches are optional. If you want to include one, you must type it exactly as it is shown.

DOS is not usually sensitive to the case of the characters you use. Normally, you can type command lines in any mixture of upper- or lowercase characters. Some third-party utilities and a few DOS commands, however, do use case-sensitive parameters. When upper- or lowercase is significant in a command's syntax, it is noted in the text.

Pay particular attention to the punctuation used in syntax lines. DOS is often very picky about punctuation; if a semicolon is shown, a comma rarely will do the trick. Spaces are an exception: Where one space is shown, more than one space or tab usually is acceptable. The order of command arguments is usually somewhat flexible, with switches allowed either before or after filename arguments. Exceptions are noted in the text.

Every command line begins the same way—with the name of the command you want to run. *Internal* commands are located inside COMMAND.COM and are always available at the DOS prompt. *External* commands are files with .COM or .EXE extensions that are located on your disk. To run an external command, COMMAND.COM must be able to find the corresponding file on disk. The Setup program for DOS 6 places all the external commands in the C:\DOS subdirectory by default. To help COMMAND.COM find external commands, Setup also adds or edits the PATH statement in your AUTOEXEC.BAT file to include the C:\DOS subdirectory. As long as the subdirectory in which the command is located is included in your DOS PATH, you can simply type the name of the command at the command line and COMMAND.COM finds the executable file. If you move any of the files or if you remove the C:\DOS subdirectory from your

592 APPENDIX F COMMAND REFERENCE

DOS PATH, you have to specify the location of external commands by including the subdirectory in which they are located as part of the name of the command.

ICONS USED IN THIS COMMAND REFERENCE

To help you quickly identify the function of a particular command, this command reference uses the following icons:

Icon	Description
AVOID	You should avoid using this command unless absolutely necessary.
BATCH FILE	This command frequently is used in batch files.
C:\>	You can issue this command from the DOS prompt.
CONFIG.SYS	You can choose to include this command in your CONFIG.SYS file.
DANGER	This command is dangerous; use it with extreme caution.
DEVICE =	This command is used as a device driver and normally is loaded through your CONFIG.SYS file.
(utility)	You use this command to access a full-blown DOS utility.
(globe)	This command enables you to configure your system for use outside the U.S.
NEW MS-DOS 6.2	This command is new in MS-DOS 6.2.
DISK	This command is included on the MS-DOS 6.0 or 6.2 Supplemental Disk.
SYSTEM.INI	You can choose to include this command in your SYSTEM.INI file.
TSR	This terminate-and-stay-resident command loads into memory and may be accessed anytime thereafter.
(windows)	You can use this command with Microsoft Windows.
Windows 9x	This command is specific to the versions of DOS with Windows 95 and Windows 98.
PC-DOS	This command is specific to IBM's PC-DOS.
DR-DOS	This command is specific to Caldera's DR DOS.

Filenames and Pathnames

Filenames and pathnames for MS-DOS consist of a series of standard parts, and DOS makes certain assumptions when these parts are omitted. A fully qualified pathname consists of the following parts:

drive:*path1**path2*\\ ... *filename*.*ext*

drive:	Represents the disk drive letter.
path1, *path2*	Represent the subdirectories.
filename	Represents the one- to eight-character name of the file.
.ext	Represents the optional extension to the filename. When included, the extension can be up to three characters in length.
...	An ellipsis in a syntax line indicates that the preceding argument can be repeated one or more times. The spaces around the ellipsis are added here only for clarity. An actual pathname can never include any spaces.

Note that a disk drive letter, when present, is always followed by a colon. The drive (with colon), all pathnames, and the filename are separated from each other by backslash characters (\\). The filename extension, when present, is always separated from the filename by a period.

If no drive is specified, the current disk drive is assumed. If no path is specified, the current subdirectory of that disk drive is used. Typically, commands that accept wildcard characters in their filename arguments default to "all files" if no filename is specified. Otherwise, no defaults are assumed for the filename portion.

In this command reference, the term *filename* refers to the one- to eight-character name of a file, either with or without a one- to three-character extension. The term *pathname* refers to the complete path to a file (the drive, subdirectory path, and filename).

Legal Filename Characters

DOS allows only certain characters to be included in the name of a file or subdirectory. All the letters A to Z, either upper- or lowercase, and the numbers 0 to 9 are allowed. In addition, the following punctuation characters are acceptable:

& ' @ ^ _ { } $! - # ( ) % ` ~

No other punctuation or special characters are permissible in a filename. (If you are using a non-USA code page, you may have additional legal filename characters, such as accented characters.)

Most of the illegal filename characters have a special meaning on the command line. Spaces, tabs, commas, and semicolons typically are used to separate arguments. The colon (:) indicates a disk drive letter, and the backslash (\\) separates subdirectories or indicates the root directory. The greater-than (>), less-than (<), and pipe (|) characters are used for redirection and piping. Although percent signs (%) are legal, you should avoid using them in your filenames because this character indicates replaceable parameters and can lead to some confusing errors in batch files.

> **Tip:** Consider using an underscore (_) or a hyphen (-) in file or subdirectory names in which you normally would use a space. This naming convention can help make your filenames more readable, as in `MY_FILE.TXT`.

DOS converts all pathname characters to uppercase before searching for the file, so you can enter pathnames in any combination of upper- and lowercase letters that suits you. `MYFILE.TXT`, `myfile.txt`, and `MyFiLe.TxT` all refer to the same file as far as DOS is concerned.

DOS Reserved Names

Although you are free to name your files anything you would like, a few filenames have special meaning to MS-DOS. They refer to specific devices attached to your computer system; when you use them on the command line in place of a filename, they always refer to that device, not a file on the disk.

Name	Device That Name Refers To
NUL	The null device. This is your computer's equivalent of the Black Hole, which accepts (and ignores) anything written to it.
CON	The standard device for input and output. CON normally refers to the keyboard for input and the video display for output.
LPT*x*	The printer (parallel) ports. The *x* represents the port number, as in LPT1.
PRN	The primary printer port, normally the same as LPT1.
COM*x*	The serial ports. The *x* represents the port number, as in COM1.
AUX	The primary serial port, normally the same as COM1.

In some cases, you are required to enter these names followed by a colon (:), as if you were referring to a disk drive. Normally, however, you just use them as though they refer to a file in the current directory. No matter what drive, path, or extension you include with these reserved names, they always refer to that device and never to a file on your disk. (In other words, you cannot have a file named `PRN.TXT` on your disk because this name always refers to the printer and not to a disk file.) If, however, you specify a drive or path that doesn't exist, you do receive an error message.

  ?, *   **1.0 AND LATER—INTERNAL**

With certain commands, you can use wildcard characters in the filename portion of a pathname argument to specify more than one file at a time. You can use the question mark (?) to match any single character and the asterisk (*) to match multiple characters. Wildcards are never allowed in the drive or subdirectory portions of a pathname.

Using the ? Wildcard Character in a Filename or Extension

A question mark (?) can be used to match any single character in a filename or extension. For example, typing MYFILE.T?T matches files named MYFILE.TXT and MYFILE.TOT but not MYFILE.TT or MYFILE.TXB. To match the latter, you have to specify MYFILE.T??. Notice that a question mark placed in the middle of the filename or extension matches any *single* character in that position, whereas a question mark placed at the end also matches zero characters.

Using the * Wildcard Character in a Filename or Extension

An asterisk (*) matches zero or more characters from the position in which it is placed to the end of the filename or extension. For example, MY*.TXT matches MYFILE.TXT and MYHOUSE.TXT but not MYFILE.DOC or YOURFILE.TXT. Any characters following an asterisk in the filename, or following an asterisk in the extension, are ignored. In other words, typing MY*.TXT or MY*FILE.TXT gives you exactly the same result.

For most commands that accept wildcards, if you enter a filename with no extension, all extensions are matched. For example, MYFILE matches MYFILE, MYFILE.TXT, and MYFILE.DOC, whereas MY* matches MYHOUSE.TXT as well. If you type a period after the filename (for example, MYFILE. or MY*.), only files with no extension are matched.

Examples

.	Match any filename.
*	Same as *.* in most cases.
????????.???	Same as *.*
*.	Match any filename that has no extension.
*.??	Match any file that has a zero- to two-letter extension.
?.*	Match any file that has a one-letter filename.
*.BAK	Match all files with a .BAK extension.
MYFILE	Match all files with the filename MYFILE with any (or no) extension.
MY*.*	Match all files that begin with MY.
M?F*.?XT	Match any file that begins with the letter M, has an F as the third character in the filename, and has a three-letter extension that ends in XT.

See Also

"Introducing the DOS File System" in Chapter 5

> AND >>   2.0 AND LATER—INTERNAL

You can use the greater-than redirection symbols (> and >>) on the command line to instruct DOS to take any output that normally would be written to the screen and send it somewhere else. These symbols are handy for sending the output of a command, such as DIR, to the printer (DIR > PRN) or to a file on disk (DIR > MYFILE.TXT). Using two greater-than signs (>>) tells DOS to append the output to the file specified (if it already exists) instead of overwriting the file as it normally would. For example,

```
DIR  C:\DOS  > DIR_LIST.TXT
```

creates (or overwrites if it already exists) the file DIR_LIST.TXT in the current directory and fills it with a list of all the files in the C:\DOS subdirectory. However, the command

```
DIR  C:\WIN  >> DIR_LIST.TXT
```

appends (adds) a list of all the files in the C:\WIN subdirectory to the end of the DIR_LIST.TXT file.

Notice that only the program output normally written to the screen is redirected. For example, the command

```
COPY  MYFILE.TXT  YOURFILE.TXT  >  COPYMSG.TXT
```

still copies MYFILE.TXT to YOURFILE.TXT, but the message 1 file(s) copied is written to the file COPYMSG.TXT.

In batch files, it is fairly common to redirect messages from commands such as COPY to the NUL device, as in the following:

```
COPY  MYFILE.TXT  YOURFILE.TXT  >  NUL
```

This technique can keep the onscreen clutter generated by a batch file to a minimum because anything written to the NUL device is essentially thrown away.

SEE ALSO

<, |, FIND, MORE, and SORT

"Using Redirection Commands" in Chapter 13

<   2.0 AND LATER—INTERNAL

Programs normally expect input from the user to come from the keyboard. If you want to provide this input from a file instead of the keyboard, you can use the less-than redirection symbol (<) to redirect that program's input. DOS includes three commands specifically designed to use with input redirection: MORE, SORT, and FIND.

One common use for input redirection is with the MORE filter program. To display the contents of the file README.TXT one screen at a time, you type the following command:

```
MORE  <  README.TXT
```

To sort all the lines in a text file, you might use the SORT command like this:

```
SORT  <  UNSORTED.TXT  >  SORTED.TXT
```

This command sorts all the lines in UNSORTED.TXT into alphabetical order and writes the sorted output to SORTED.TXT. If you did not include the > SORTED.TXT argument, SORT would write the sorted lines to the display (standard output). If you forgot to redirect the input to the SORT command (that is, if you did not include the < UNSORTED.TXT argument), DOS would wait for you to type the input at the keyboard.

Occasionally, you find a use for input redirection when you are automating the input to a program. Many software patches distributed as batch files use this technique to redirect DEBUG's input to a text file to make changes to a program file. (Indeed, this is just what the SPATCH.BAT file on the DOS 6 distribution disk does.) Just remember that after the input to a program is redirected, control does not return to the keyboard until the program terminates. If you forget to put the keystrokes that exit the program at the end of your input file, you have to reboot your computer to regain control.

SEE ALSO

> and >>, |, FIND, MORE, and SORT

"Using Redirection Commands" in Chapter 13

| 2.0 AND LATER—INTERNAL

You can use the *pipe* character (|) on the command line to tell DOS to use the screen output from one program as the keyboard input to another. (The term *pipe* comes from the Unix operating system, which often uses this method to string together several programs to perform a particular job.) For the pipe character to work, the first program must write output to the screen that the second program expects to get from the keyboard.

In DOS, pipe characters are most often used with the TYPE and MORE commands to display a text file one screen at a time, as in the following:

```
TYPE  README.TXT  |  MORE
```

You also can combine MORE with FIND to look at the results of a text search one screen at a time, as in this example:

```
FIND  "Mr. Merryweather"  BIGTEXT.TXT  |  MORE
```

DOS actually accomplishes piping by writing the output from the first program to a temporary file and then redirecting the input for the second program from that file. When the second program terminates, DOS deletes the temporary file. So, the preceding command accomplishes the same thing as the following three commands:

```
FIND "Mr. Merryweather" BIGTEXT.TXT > TEMP.TXT
MORE < TEMP.TXT
DEL TEMP.TXT
```

Using the pipe character saves you from having to type all three of these commands.

SEE ALSO

> and >>, <, FIND, MORE, and SORT

"Using Redirection Commands" in Chapter 13

  :label   1.0 AND LATER—INTERNAL

In a batch file, you can type a colon (:) in the first column of any line to indicate that the next eight characters on that line should be interpreted as a label. Any additional characters on the line after the label are ignored. Labels are used as the destination for GOTO statements in batch files.

SYNTAX

:*label*

NOTES

1. To define a label, you must use a colon as the first character on the line. Not even a space or tab character can precede it.
2. Only the first eight characters of a label are significant, although the label can be as long as you like. Everything on the line after the eighth character of the label is ignored.
3. Although you can define the same label in more than one place in a batch file, the GOTO command always jumps to the first occurrence.
4. Labels and filenames share the same legal characters with the exception that labels cannot include percent signs (%) or hyphens (-). Batch file labels can be typed in any mixture of upper- and lowercase characters.

EXAMPLES

```
GOTO SKIP_DEL
DEL *.BAK
:SKIP_DEL   This text will be ignored
```

In this example, when DOS executes the line containing the GOTO SKIP_DEL command, DOS searches for the :SKIP_DEL label and continues execution with the line that follows it. The DEL *.BAK command is never executed.

MESSAGES

Label not found

Error: The label specified in a GOTO statement was not found. After displaying this message, the batch file terminates.

See Also

GOTO

"Branching with GOTO" in Chapter 16

 ## %n

1.0 AND LATER—INTERNAL

You can use *replaceable parameters* to represent command-line arguments from within a batch file. DOS replaces these markers with their corresponding command-line arguments when the batch file is executed.

Syntax

%*n*

Notes

1. Ten replaceable parameters are available, %0 through %9.

2. %0 returns the name of the batch file as it was entered on the command line, %1 returns the first argument on the command line, %2 returns the second, and so on. Spaces, tabs, commas, and semicolons all are considered valid argument delimiters. To include a delimiter in a command-line argument, enclose the argument in double quotation marks.

3. DOS can find replaceable parameters almost anywhere in a batch file, including within double quotation marks and embedded in words. For example, the filename MY%1FILE.TXT is a perfectly legal filename for DOS; in a batch file, however, the %1 embedded in the name is replaced with the first argument to the batch file. This can lead to some strange errors.

4. If you want to include a percent sign in a batch file, write it twice. When DOS is parsing the file, it sees the two percent signs (%%) and replaces them with a single percent sign (%). For example, %1 is replaced with the first argument to the batch file, whereas %%1 simply becomes %1.

   This rule explains why the variable markers in a FOR loop must be written as %%a in a batch file, but as %a from the command line. In a batch file, DOS removes the doubled %% signs and replaces them with a single % before the FOR command gets to see it. If you forget and use a single percent sign, DOS removes it and leaves only the a, which results in a syntax error.

5. If you require more than nine arguments in your batch file, you can use the SHIFT command to gain access to them.

6. An empty parameter is replaced with nothing at all. In other words, if you enter MY%2.TXT in your batch file and then forget to enter a second parameter when you run the batch file, DOS looks for the file MY.TXT.

Examples

The following batch file displays a series of files one screen at a time:

```
:START
IF "%1"=="" GOTO END
IF NOT EXIST %1 GOTO END
TYPE %1 | MORE
SHIFT
GOTO START
:END
```

In the first IF statement, the %1 is replaced with the first argument to the batch file. As long as the argument exists, the statement is false and execution continues on the next line. The second IF statement checks to see whether this argument is a valid pathname. If the argument passes this check, execution finally passes to the TYPE command, which types the file to the screen through the MORE filter program. When TYPE finishes, SHIFT moves the arguments down one place, and the next line transfers execution back to the first line in the batch file. The loop continues until the batch file runs out of arguments or finds an invalid pathname.

> **Note** The preceding example isn't quite foolproof. If wildcards are included in the first argument to this batch file, it easily could pass both of the tests you perform with the IF commands. TYPE, however, cannot handle wildcards and would display the message `Invalid filename or file not found` rather than the files you specified.

See Also

%name%, IF, FOR, and SHIFT

"Understanding Replaceable Parameters" in Chapter 16

# %envir%   4.0 AND LATER—INTERNAL

With the addition of the %envir% syntax in MS-DOS 4.0, users finally had access to variables in batch files. Before executing a line in a batch file, DOS replaces every occurrence of %envir% with the contents of the corresponding environment variable. When combined with the capability of the SET command to create and destroy environment variables, this feature can be very powerful.

Syntax

%envir%

Notes

1. The name of the environment variable can be entered in upper- or lowercase characters, but it must be surrounded by percent signs (%) to be recognized by DOS.

2. DOS can find the variable placeholder almost anywhere in a batch file, including enclosed in double quotation marks or embedded within words. Any pair of percent

signs enclosing characters is assumed to be an environment variable. (If the first character following the percent sign is a digit, DOS assumes you are referring to a replaceable parameter, not an environment variable.) The string `with values between 7% and 15% annually` would tell DOS to search for an environment variable named " and 15". When DOS failed to find such a variable, it would change the string to read `with values between 7 annually`.

3. If you want to include a percent sign in a batch file, write it twice. When DOS is parsing the file, it sees the two percent signs (`%%`) and replaces them with a single one (`%`). For example, `%PATH%` is replaced with the contents of the PATH environment variable, whereas `%%PATH%%` becomes `%PATH%`.

4. If no environment variable with that name exists, the `%envir%` placeholder is replaced with an empty string.

EXAMPLES

To add a subdirectory to your PATH, execute a particular program, and then restore your original PATH, you might use a batch file like this:

```
SET OLDPATH=%PATH%
PATH C:\CADD;%PATH%
C:\CADD\CADD.EXE %1
PATH %OLDPATH%
SET OLDPATH=
```

The first line saves the current PATH setting in an environment variable named OLDPATH. Next, the subdirectory C:\CADD is added to the PATH. In the third line, the program is executed, and a single command-line argument is passed to it if one exists. Finally, when the program terminates, PATH is set equal to OLDPATH and the OLDPATH variable is deleted.

You can easily run out of space in the environment while manipulating variables in batch files, especially if you are running them from a Shell program such as DOSSHELL. When this happens, DOS displays the message `Out of environment space` and then continues executing the batch file. To make the preceding example abort if not enough environment space is available, add an IF statement, as follows, to check whether OLDPATH was successfully created:

```
SET OLDPATH=%PATH%
IF "%OLDPATH%"=="" GOTO ERROR
PATH C:\CADD;%PATH%
C:\CADD\CADD.EXE %1
PATH %OLDPATH%
SET OLDPATH=
GOTO END
:ERROR
ECHO Can't start CADD - not enough environment space
:END
```

Now CADD doesn't execute if not enough environment space is available to save OLDPATH. To increase the size of the environment, increase the size of the /E:*size* parameter specified in the SHELL= command in your CONFIG.SYS file.

If you are running batch files from within a Shell program such as DOSSHELL, increasing the /E:size parameter may not help. When DOS runs a program, it gives the program access to a copy of the current environment. This copy is only big enough to hold the environment variables that are currently defined and has very little free space in it. When you run a batch file from within a Shell program, a temporary copy of COMMAND.COM is loaded into memory, and a copy of the shrunken environment the Shell program was using is passed to it. With so little available space in the current environment, batch files often run out of environment space.

One technique to avoid Out of environment space error messages when you run batch files from a Shell program is to define a dummy variable in your AUTOEXEC.BAT file that simply takes up space, as shown in this example:

```
SET DUMMY=XXXXXXXXXXXXXXXXXXXXXXXXXXXXXXXXXXXX
```

When you need space in the environment, simply delete the DUMMY variable, as follows, before you define any new variables that your batch file needs:

```
SET DUMMY=
SET OLDPATH=%PATH%
```

When your batch file terminates, you return to your Shell program, and the copy of the environment that the batch file was using is discarded. Because the DUMMY variable is being thrown away, there is no reason to restore it before the batch file exits.

If you might run this batch file from the DOS prompt when your Shell program isn't running, include a SET statement, such as the following, that restores your DUMMY variable after you delete OLDPATH:

```
SET OLDPATH=
SET DUMMY=XXXXXXXXXXXXXXXXXXXXXXXXXXXXXXXXXXXX
GOTO END
```

SEE ALSO

%n, IF, SET, and SHELL=

Chapter 16, "Understanding Batch Files"

@ 4.0 AND LATER—INTERNAL

Normally, DOS echoes to the screen every line in a batch file before executing it. Although this capability can be handy when you are testing a new batch file, you usually want to use ECHO OFF to turn off the echo feature in a batch file you use every day. With the "at" sign (@), you can turn echo off for each line individually if you want to.

SYNTAX

@command_line

NOTES

1. The @ symbol must be the first character on the line. Don't insert any spaces before or after it.

2. The most common use of the @ symbol is with the ECHO OFF command that begins most batch files. Because the echo feature is on when this command is executed, the ECHO OFF command is echoed to the screen—unless you precede the ECHO OFF command with an @ symbol.

3. Only the display of the command line that DOS executes is suppressed, not screen output generated by a command, which can be rather confusing to some users. To suppress the output generated by a command, you have to redirect the output of the command to the NUL device. For example,

   `@COPY  MYFILE.TXT  YOURFILE.TXT`

   does not echo the command line itself (COPY MYFILE.TXT, and so on) to the screen, but still displays the message `1 file(s) copied` that is generated by COPY. If, in addition, you redirect the screen output of the COPY command to the NUL device

   `@COPY  MYFILE.TXT  YOURFILE.TXT  > NUL`

   nothing is displayed on the screen at all.

SEE ALSO

> and >>, and ECHO

"Using Batch File Commands" in Chapter 16

;   6.0 AND LATER—INTERNAL

When DOS encounters a semicolon as the first character on a line in your CONFIG.SYS file, it ignores the contents of the rest of the line. Using a semicolon in this way is exactly the same as using the REM command. Inserting comments into your CONFIG.SYS file can help you remember what each line is for.

SYNTAX

`;comment text`

NOTES

1. To mark a line in CONFIG.SYS as a comment, you must add the semicolon (;) as the first character on the line. Do not precede it with any spaces.

> **Tip**
>
> The configuration lines necessary for many devices are quite complicated, so using a semicolon to "comment them out" can be a handy way to turn features on and off in your CONFIG.SYS file.

2. Note that this technique for creating a comment line works only in CONFIG.SYS. To insert a comment in a batch file, you either have to use REM or define a dummy label line with a colon.

3. If you find yourself continually commenting and uncommenting DEVICE= lines in your CONFIG.SYS file, consider using the question mark (?) instead so that you can enable or disable that driver interactively each time you boot up. If you insert a question mark (?) between the command name and equal sign, DOS asks you before it executes a command in your CONFIG.SYS file.

EXAMPLES

Comments can help you keep track of what each line in your CONFIG.SYS file is for, as shown in the following:

```
; The old SCSI drive requires double buffering.
; Remember to remove this line when the new drive gets installed!!!
DEVICE=C:\DOS\SMARTDRV.EXE /DOUBLE_BUFFER
```

DOS skips over all lines that start with a semicolon and executes only the DEVICE= line that loads SMARTDrive's double-buffering feature.

SEE ALSO

? and REM

Chapter 2, "Starting DOS"

? 6.0 AND LATER—INTERNAL

In CONFIG.SYS, if you put a question mark (?) between a command and the equal sign (=), DOS prompts you for confirmation before executing that command. This technique works for all CONFIG.SYS commands that use the *command=* form, including the SET command.

SYNTAX

command?=settings

PARAMETERS AND SWITCHES

command   This parameter can be any CONFIG.SYS command that uses the *command=* format.

settings   The settings used with the **command** specified (when you allow it to be run).

NOTES

1. Use the question mark (?) for individual features you want to control. If you find yourself using more than one or two question marks in your CONFIG.SYS file, however, you might want to consider setting up a menu instead. You can easily get confused and select the wrong combination of drivers when you're enabling each line individually.

2. The question mark (?) must come between the command and the equal sign, with no spaces between it and the command name.
3. Each line you have marked for confirmation is displayed followed by [Y,N]?. Enter Y to execute the line and N to skip it.
4. Pressing the F8 key when DOS displays the Starting MS-DOS... message causes DOS to prompt you for confirmation of every line in your CONFIG.SYS file, whether or not the line includes a question mark.
5. DOS doesn't necessarily process the lines in CONFIG.SYS in the order they appear in the file, which can be confusing when you receive a prompt for a line near the end of the file before being prompted for a line at the beginning. In general, DOS processes commands such as DOS=, FILES=, and BUFFERS= before it begins to load any of your device drivers. However, after DOS begins processing the DEVICE= (and DEVICEHIGH=) lines, it loads them in the order they appear in the file.

EXAMPLES

To instruct DOS to prompt you before setting up a 1.4MB RAM disk in extended memory, place a question mark in the line that loads the RAMDRIVE.SYS driver as follows:

```
DEVICEHIGH?=C:\DOS\RAMDRIVE.SYS  1450  512  224  /E
```

If MemMaker has optimized your CONFIG.SYS file, /L and /S switches may appear on the DEVICEHIGH line. Make sure you place the ? directly after the command name, as shown here, not before the equal sign:

```
DEVICEHIGH?  /L:1,1200  /S  =C:\DOS\RAMDRIVE.SYS  1450  512  224  /E
```

MESSAGES

If you place the ? incorrectly in a CONFIG.SYS command, you will receive one of the following error messages when you reboot:

```
Bad command or parameter - ?=
Error in CONFIG.SYS line #
```

or

```
Bad or Missing ?
Error in CONFIG.SYS line #
```

Edit your CONFIG.SYS file and make sure that all your question marks (?) are placed directly after the name of the command, with no intervening spaces.

SEE ALSO

;, [*blockname*], and MENUITEM=

Chapter 2, "Starting DOS"

[blockname]   6.0 AND LATER—INTERNAL

Defining blocks in CONFIG.SYS is part of the multiple configuration feature in DOS 6. By naming blocks of commands, you can choose which blocks to execute from a menu when you start your computer.

SYNTAX

[*blockname*]

NOTES

1. The name for a block can be up to 70 characters long and contain any legal filename characters. You cannot use spaces in block names, so you might want to consider using underscores (_) or hyphens (-) to separate words and make your block names more readable. Upper- and lowercase characters are considered the same. The name must be surrounded by square brackets ([and]) and appear on a line by itself. Any commands that follow the block name are considered to be part of that block until the next [*blockname*] is encountered in the file.

2. Blocks cannot be embedded inside each other. When DOS encounters another block name in the CONFIG.SYS file, it considers the preceding block to be complete.

3. Any block never referred to by a MENUITEM= line is never executed by DOS. Exceptions are the predefined block names [MENU] and [COMMON].

4. The [MENU] block defines entries for the main startup menu and should contain the configuration menu that you want DOS to display when the computer starts up. DOS always executes this block.

5. Commands in a [COMMON] block are always executed by DOS. [COMMON] also is the only block that you are allowed to define more than once in your CONFIG.SYS file. A [COMMON] block located before the [MENU] block is run before the startup menu is displayed. Similarly, a [COMMON] block located at the end of your CONFIG.SYS file is executed after all other blocks.

6. Any commands that you include in CONFIG.SYS before the first block name are considered to be part of a [COMMON] block. As far as DOS is concerned, CONFIG.SYS files that don't use multiple configuration features are simply one big [COMMON] block.

7. Microsoft recommends that you include a [COMMON] block command at the end of your CONFIG.SYS file, even if you don't need to place any commands in it. Many software installation programs modify your CONFIG.SYS file by adding to the end of the file the settings the software requires. With a [COMMON] block defined at the end, these added commands are run when you start your system; without [COMMONBLOCK], these added commands might never run at all.

EXAMPLES

Suppose that you want to set up a menu that enables you to choose among three basic configurations for your computer: Windows, DOS, and Maintenance. Begin by adding a menu block like this at the beginning of your CONFIG.SYS file with the predefined block name [MENU]:

```
[MENU]
MENUITEM=WIN, Configure for Windows (Default)
MENUITEM=DOS, Configure for MS-DOS
MENUITEM=MAINT, Configure for File & Disk Maintenance
```

When these lines are included in your CONFIG.SYS file, DOS searches for blocks named [WIN], [DOS], and [MAINT]. You also might want to include a [COMMON] block that contains any commands that you always want executed, as in this example:

```
[COMMON]
DEVICE=C:\DOS\SETVER.EXE
DEVICE=C:\DOS\HIMEM.SYS
DEVICE=C:\DOS\EMM386.EXE RAM MIN=0
DOS=HIGH,UMB
BREAK=ON
FILES=50
DEVICE=C:\DOS\ANSI.SYS
SHELL=C:\DOS\COMMAND.COM C:\DOS\ /P /E:512

[WIN]
BUFFERS=10

[DOS]
BUFFERS=10
DEVICE=C:\DOS\RAMDRIVE.SYS 1450 512 224 /E

[MAINT]
BUFFERS=30
DEVICE=C:\DOS\RAMDRIVE.SYS 1450 512 224 /E

[COMMON]
```

Include a [COMMON] block at the end of your CONFIG.SYS file. That way, any commands added to the file by software installation programs are executed, no matter what configuration you choose. Without the final [COMMON] block, any commands that are added to the end of the file are executed only when you choose the maintenance configuration because they are part of the [MAINT] block.

DOS displays a startup menu that looks something like this:

```
MS-DOS 6 Startup Menu
=====================

1. Configure for Windows (Default)
2. Configure for MS-DOS
3. Configure for File & Disk Maintenance

Enter a choice: 1
```

Entering 1, 2, or 3 at this menu tells DOS to select the [WIN], [DOS], and [MAINT] blocks, respectively. DOS sets the CONFIG environment variable equal to the name of the configuration block you selected from the startup menu.

In this example, you might be able to better understand the small differences between these three configurations if you look at a few lines from the AUTOEXEC.BAT file:

```
IF "%CONFIG%"=="MAINT" GOTO SET_TEMP
C:\DOS\SMARTDRV

:SET_TEMP
SET TEMP=C:\TEMP
SET TMP=C:\TEMP

IF NOT "%CONFIG%"=="WIN" GOTO THE_REST
MD D:\TEMP
SET TEMP=D:\TEMP
SET TMP=D:\TEMP

:THE_REST
```

The SMARTDrive disk cache is loaded if you are using the DOS or Windows configurations, which is why so few DOS buffers are needed (BUFFERS=10). The Maintenance configuration does not have a disk cache, so the number of DOS buffers is set to 30.

Similarly, the Windows configuration doesn't use a RAM drive; therefore, the TEMP (and TMP) environment variables are set pointing to the C:\TEMP subdirectory, instructing programs to create any temporary files they require in that subdirectory. When a RAM drive is present, temporary files are written to the RAM drive instead.

SEE ALSO

? and MENUITEM=

"Creating Multiple Configurations" in Chapter 2

ANSI.SYS (DEVICE DRIVER) 2.0 AND LATER—EXTERNAL

ANSI.SYS is a device driver that provides a subset of the commands defined by the American National Standards Institute (ANSI) for controlling video displays and keyboards. ANSI.SYS enables you to control cursor positioning, display colors, video modes, and keyboard mapping. To use it, you must load ANSI.SYS with a DEVICE= command in your CONFIG.SYS file. ANSI.SYS replaces the default CON driver provided by the MS-DOS kernel.

SYNTAX

DEVICE=*drive:**path***ANSI.SYS**   /X   /K   /R

or

DEVICEHIGH=*drive:**path***ANSI.SYS**   /X   /K   /R

Parameters and Switches

drive:\path   Indicates the full path to the ANSI.SYS file on your system. Setup places the ANSI.SYS file in the C:\DOS subdirectory by default. If the full path to ANSI.SYS isn't specified, DOS looks for the file in the root directory of the startup drive.

/X   Enables you to remap extended keys if you are using a 101-key keyboard.

/K   Forces ANSI.SYS to treat a 101-key keyboard as if it were an 84-key keyboard, which is a handy feature with older TSR programs that don't recognize the new keycodes properly. Using this switch is the same as specifying SWITCHES=/K. If you are using the SWITCHES=/K switch already, you also should include the /K option in the DEVICE= line that loads ANSI.SYS.

/R   Slows down the line scrolling rate so that lines on the display are more readable. Chances are, you won't notice any difference when you use this switch because the scrolling rate doesn't change that much. Microsoft claims this switch can aid screen-reading programs that make computers more accessible to people with disabilities.

Notes

1. You can load ANSI.SYS with either the /X or /R switch, but not both. These two functions are mutually exclusive.

2. ANSI.SYS occupies about 4KB of memory in your computer and can be loaded into upper memory with the DEVICEHIGH command.

3. Note that all ANSI commands begin with the Escape character and are case sensitive. After it is loaded, ANSI.SYS scans all text that is written to the screen, looking for commands.

4. The MODE command requires ANSI.SYS to be loaded in order to change the number of text lines displayed on your screen. MODE can switch between color and monochrome adapters, however, without ANSI.SYS.

5. When it's loaded, ANSI.SYS resets your screen colors to the default (white on black). If you've set screen colors with the MENUCOLOR= command, they are reset when ANSI.SYS loads into memory. If this is a problem, either insert an ANSI command into your AUTOEXEC.BAT file to reset your screen colors or load ANSI.SYS from a [COMMON] block located before your [MENU] block in CONFIG.SYS.

6. All ANSI commands begin with an Escape character (ASCII 27). When you press the Esc key at the DOS prompt, DOS interprets that as a request to cancel the current command line, so you cannot simply send ANSI commands from the command line by typing them. To get around this problem, people often use PROMPT to send ANSI commands. Another alternative is to place the ANSI commands in a file and then copy the file to the console like this:

    COPY ANSI_CMD.TXT CON

7. Chapter 17, "Understanding ANSI.SYS," provides a list of all the ANSI commands supported by ANSI.SYS.

EXAMPLES

To use the PROMPT command to set your screen colors to blue on white, you would enter the following command:

PROMPT $e[34;47m$p$g

Some people like to create very elaborate DOS prompts with ANSI.SYS. For example, entering the command

PROMPT $e[s$e[Hde[0;68Hte[u"Good morning Mr. Phelps"$_$p$g

changes the DOS prompt to display the current date in the upper-left corner of the screen and the time in the upper-right corner; it also creates a two-line prompt that starts with Good morning Mr. Phelps and then has the familiar C:\> on the following line. Notice that case is significant in ANSI commands, and the preceding command does not work if, for example, you type E rather than e.

SEE ALSO

DEVICE= and PROMPT

Chapter 17, "Understanding ANSI.SYS"

APPEND   3.3 AND LATER—EXTERNAL

You can use the APPEND command to set up a search path that enables DOS to find data files even if they're not in the current directory. The subdirectories in the APPEND path are appended to the current directory when DOS searches for data files. APPEND was developed so that programs requiring you to make their program directories current can be run from the subdirectory that contains their data files rather than the one that contains their program files.

SYNTAX

To load APPEND into memory:

APPEND   /X:*onoff*   /E

or

APPEND   *path1;path2;...*   /X:*onoff*   /PATH:*onoff*

To replace and/or set the appended directory search path:

APPEND   *path1;path2;...*   /X:*onoff*   /PATH:*onoff*

To clear the appended directory search path:

APPEND ;

To display the current appended directory search path:

APPEND

Parameters and Switches

path1;path2;... Each *path* specifies a valid subdirectory that exists on your system. Use full, absolute pathnames that include drive letters for each subdirectory included in your appended directory search path; the current subdirectory and disk drive often change. Separate each subdirectory from the previous one with a semicolon (;).

/E Stores the appended directory search path in an environment variable named APPEND rather than internally. With this switch specified, you can use SET to view or change the appended directory search path. You can specify this option only when you first load APPEND into memory.

/X:*onoff* Specifies whether DOS is to search appended directories (/X or /X:ON) or not (/X:OFF) when executing programs. Directories on the APPEND path are searched before those specified with the PATH command. To use this feature, you must specify it when you load APPEND into memory, after which you can toggle it on (/X or /X:ON) and off (/X:OFF).

/PATH:*onoff* Normally, if you specify a full pathname for a file, DOS searches only that directory. /PATH:ON instructs DOS to search the appended directories even if the full pathname of the file is given. /PATH:OFF turns off this feature.

Notes

1. The first time you run APPEND, it loads itself into memory as a TSR program, occupying about 5KB of memory. APPEND does not remove itself from memory until you restart DOS.

2. After you load APPEND into memory, do not specify the .EXE file extension. At this point, APPEND is resident in memory and will not load more than once.

3. You can use the /E switches only when you first load APPEND into memory, and you cannot specify any search paths on the same line. In other words, if you want the APPEND path to be stored in the environment, you have to run the command twice—once with /E and then again to set your appended directory search path.

4. To use the /X switch, you must specify it in the line that loads APPEND into memory. After APPEND is loaded with this feature enabled, you can toggle it on and off by using /X:ON and /X:OFF.

5. Each path you specify in the appended directory search path must be separated by a semicolon. Don't include any spaces between paths. The total length of the appended directory search path cannot exceed 127 characters.

6. When DOS looks for a data file, it first searches the current directory and then the appended directories in the order you specified them. If DOS encounters an invalid path, it skips that path without displaying any error messages.

7. Do not use APPEND when running Microsoft Windows or Windows Setup.

8. APPEND can't change the environment being used by running applications, so the /E switch does not work with shell programs, such as DOSSHELL, XTree, or Norton Commander. To

work with these types of programs, APPEND must store the appended directory search path internally (in other words, don't specify /E).

9. The DIR command ignores the appended directory search path and never displays files from appended directories.

10. APPEND ignores any drive assignments made with the ASSIGN command. To use both utilities, you must load APPEND into memory before using ASSIGN; otherwise, an error message appears.

11. DOS searches the appended directories when it opens files requested through Interrupt 21h functions 0Fh (Open File), 3Dh (Open File Handle), and 23h (Get File Size). When /X or /X:ON is specified, functions 11h (Find First Entry), 4Eh (Find First File), and 4Bh (Execute Program) search the appended directories as well.

> **Caution**
>
> APPEND is intended for locating and reading files, but not for writing them. Any files written to disk are placed in the current subdirectory, no matter what subdirectory they originally were read from. This capability works out well for program overlay and help files, which are rarely written to, but can be very frustrating if APPEND starts scattering data files all over your hard disk.

EXAMPLES

The following line loads APPEND into memory, enables searching for executable files in appended directories, and stores the active APPEND path in the environment. This line assumes that the file APPEND.EXE is located in the C:\DOS subdirectory:

`C:\DOS\APPEND  /X  /E`

To instruct DOS to search the current directory, C:\BIN, and C:\BIN\OVR when opening data files, enter the following command:

`APPEND  C:\BIN;C:\BIN\OVR`

When the program that needed data file path support terminates, disable APPEND by using the following command:

`APPEND  ;`

To reactivate APPEND, simply specify a new APPEND path.

MESSAGES

`APPEND/ASSIGN conflict`

Error: You tried to load APPEND after reassigning disk drives with ASSIGN. Break any disk drive reassignments you may have set, load APPEND, and then reset your ASSIGN settings.

`APPEND already installed`

Warning: You attempted to load APPEND a second time. Try running the command again, making sure to enter APPEND and not APPEND.EXE on the command line.

`Incorrect APPEND version`

Error: You used a version of APPEND from a different version of DOS. Make sure that you do not use an APPEND version from the IBM local area network (LAN) program. The problem may be that the wrong version of APPEND is loading first from a subdirectory included in your DOS PATH.

No Append

Information: You typed APPEND to display the current appended directory path, and APPEND currently is inactive.

SEE ALSO
PATH

ASSIGN   2.0 TO 5.0—EXTERNAL

ASSIGN was a utility that enabled you to attach an alias drive letter to an existing drive. Microsoft no longer distributes ASSIGN in the standard DOS package and is encouraging everyone to begin using SUBST instead. ASSIGN is included on the DOS 6 Supplemental Disk.

USING SUBST INSTEAD OF ASSIGN

You can use ASSIGN to create an alias of A: for your B: drive if you want to fool an installation program that runs only from drive A:. To accomplish this task with ASSIGN, you use the following command:

ASSIGN B = A

To do the same thing with SUBST, you enter the following command:

SUBST A: B:\

SEE ALSO
SUBST

"Changing Disk Drives" in Chapter 11

ATTRIB   3.0 AND LATER—EXTERNAL

In a file's directory entry on disk, DOS stores information about the file's size, the date and time the file was last modified, and any attributes associated with that file. File attributes flag files that have to be backed up, control whether a file can be written to, and hide files from view. With ATTRIB, you can view or change the attributes associated with a particular file.

Syntax

Use this syntax to display the attributes currently set for a file or group of files:

ATTRIB *pathname* /S

Use this syntax to set or clear attributes for a file or group of files:

ATTRIB +|-A +|-R +|-S +|-H *pathname* /S

Parameters and Switches

+|-A	Sets (+A) or clears (-A) the archive attribute for all files matching the pathname specified. By default, new files always have their archive attribute turned on. DOS sets this attribute each time a file is written to.
+|-R	Sets (+R) or clears (-R) the read-only attribute for all files matching the pathname specified. Marking a file as read-only can prevent COPY from overwriting it, but many programs can override this flag.
+|-S	Sets (+S) or clears (-S) the system attribute for all files matching the pathname specified. Few files use this attribute. It flags the hidden MS-DOS system files that are in the root directory of your startup disk drive.
+|-H	Sets (+H) or clears (-H) the hidden attribute for all files matching the pathname specified. A file with the hidden attribute normally does not show up in a listing of the files in a directory. ATTRIB enables you to set the hidden flag for subdirectories as well as for files.
pathname	Indicates the file or files that you want ATTRIB to display information about. Wildcards are allowed in the filename portion. If no pathname is specified, all files (*.*) in the current directory are displayed. If no filename is specified, ATTRIB displays or changes the attributes of that subdirectory. Notice that the root directory has no attributes and therefore cannot be changed.
/S	Searches for files in the specified subdirectory and all subdirectories below it.

Notes

1. If a file has either the hidden or system attribute set, you must clear that attribute before you can change any other attributes for the file. Otherwise, you are denied access to the file (see the following "Messages" section). If a single file has both the system and hidden attributes set, you must clear both attributes with a single ATTRIB command to avoid being denied access to the file.

2. Normally, ATTRIB only displays or alters the attributes of files. To change the attributes of a subdirectory, you must enter the full pathname for that subdirectory on the command line with ATTRIB. You cannot use wildcards when you are specifying subdirectories.

> **Caution**
>
> Commas can make strange things happen with `ATTRIB`. If you include a comma in an `ATTRIB` command, as shown here, `ATTRIB` clears all the attributes for all the files in the current directory:
>
> `ATTRIB  ,`
>
> If you also include the `/S` switch, as in the following example, `ATTRIB` clears the attributes of all the files on your hard disk, not just the ones below the current directory:
>
> `ATTRIB  ,  /S`
>
> This problem has been confirmed by Microsoft and is present in DOS 5 versions of `ATTRIB` as well.

EXAMPLES

To display the attributes of all the `.TXT` files in the `C:\MYWORK` subdirectory, you would enter the following:

`ATTRIB  C:\MYWORK\*.TXT`

If you want to extend the search to include any subdirectories under the subdirectory, you would include the `/S` switch, as in the following:

`ATTRIB  C:\MYWORK\*.TXT  /S`

To set the archive bit on for all the files you found so that `MSBACKUP` will be sure to back them up the next time you run it, enter the following:

`ATTRIB  +A  C:\MYWORK\*.TXT  /S`

To clear all the attributes of all the files in the root directory of drive C:, including the MS-DOS system files, enter the following:

`ATTRIB  -A  -R  -H  -S  C:\*.*`

To hide the C:\SECRET subdirectory so that it no longer shows up in directory listings, enter the following:

`ATTRIB  +H  C:\SECRET`

MESSAGES

```
Not resetting hidden file
Not resetting system file
```

Error: ATTRIB is unable to set or clear the attributes you've requested because the file has either the hidden or system attribute set. To get around this problem, clear the hidden or system attribute for that file first (for example, use `ATTRIB  -H  -S`); then retry the command.

SEE ALSO

XCOPY

"Understanding File Attributes" in Chapter 5

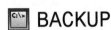 ## BACKUP 2.0 TO 5.0—EXTERNAL

The BACKUP utility has been around for quite a while. You could use it to back up files from your hard disk drive to a series of floppy disks. It created a special file on each backup disk, a file that could be read only by the RESTORE utility. RESTORE, however, would often refuse to restore files if anything went wrong with your disks. With MS-DOS 6.0, Microsoft began distributing the new MSBACKUP program. If you still want to use the old BACKUP utility, Microsoft has included it on the DOS 6 Supplemental Disk.

SEE ALSO

MSBACKUP and RESTORE

 ## BREAK 2.0 AND LATER—INTERNAL
BREAK= 2.0 AND LATER—INTERNAL

When DOS detects a Ctrl+Break (or Ctrl+C), it attempts to stop the program that is currently running. DOS checks for a Ctrl+Break after performing any screen, keyboard, or printer I/O operation. Turning BREAK ON or setting BREAK=ON in your CONFIG.SYS file instructs DOS to check for Ctrl+Break after performing disk I/O operations as well. This way, you can regain control more quickly when you are trying to stop disk-oriented DOS commands.

SYNTAX

In CONFIG.SYS, to set extended Ctrl+Break checking on or off, use the following format:

BREAK=onoff

To turn extended Ctrl+Break checking on or off from the command line, use the following format:

BREAK onoff

PARAMETERS AND SWITCHES

onoff   Specifies whether you want extended Ctrl+Break checking to be turned on or off. The only legal values for the onoff parameter are ON and OFF. In the CONFIG.SYS form of this command, this parameter is required. If you omit the onoff parameter when you run BREAK from the command line, the current state of extended Ctrl+Break checking is displayed.

NOTES

1. When DOS starts, it sets extended Ctrl+Break checking off by default.
2. Set BREAK=ON in your CONFIG.SYS file. The speed penalty is negligible, and if this setting saves just one file from a mistyped COPY command, it is well worthwhile. Most long

operations involve reading or writing to disk. If BREAK is off, you may be unable to stop a lengthy process you would rather not wait for.

3. In most cases, pressing Ctrl+C produces the same effect as pressing Ctrl+Break, but there is a subtle difference. The Ctrl+C key combination is passed through the keyboard buffer. If any other key is pressed before Ctrl+C, it is ignored until the program reads the keyboard. For example, DIR stops if you press Ctrl+C, but not if you press the spacebar and then Ctrl+C. Ctrl+Break is passed directly to DOS without buffering and often gets a quicker response.

4. In theory, turning on extended Ctrl+Break checking should slow down your system. In practice, any slowdown is so insignificant that you probably will never notice it.

5. Programs have complete control over what happens when a Ctrl+Break is detected. The default action is for the running program to be halted, but applications often disable Ctrl+Break so that you can save your work before exiting. Typically, short command-line utilities respond to Ctrl+Break, whereas most full-screen applications do not.

6. The state of the BREAK flag can be changed by a running program. Programming etiquette dictates that when an application finishes running, it should reset all flags to their original states. Still, you may run across applications that forget to reset BREAK. If this causes problems, you can run the application from a batch file that restores the BREAK flag setting when the program terminates.

See Also

VERIFY

"Telling DOS When to Break" in Chapter 19

BUFFERS=   2.0 AND LATER—INTERNAL

DOS stores any information read from or written to disk in memory buffers. With more buffers available, it is more likely that DOS already has in memory the data requested by a program. The BUFFERS= command enables you to fine-tune your system so that DOS can perform disk I/O as efficiently as possible. BUFFERS= can be used only in your CONFIG.SYS file.

Syntax

BUFFERS=*number*,*read_ahead*

Parameters and Switches

number   The number of disk buffers DOS should use, from 1 to 99. The default value varies depending on the amount of memory in your computer. Normally, 15 is used for a computer with at least 512KB of RAM.

read_ahead   The number of buffers in the secondary, read-ahead cache. For DOS 5.0, this value could be from 1 to 8, with a default value of 1. In DOS 6.0, you can specify zero secondary cache buffers, and 0 is the default value.

NOTES

1. Each disk buffer uses approximately 532 bytes of memory. If DOS is loaded HIGH, it attempts to locate these buffers in the HMA as well. About 48 buffers can fit in the HMA with DOS 6. If you have specified more buffers than can fit in the HMA, DOS loads them all into conventional memory.

> **Tip**
> Make sure that you explicitly set the number of DOS buffers in your CONFIG.SYS file. If you aren't using disk-caching software, the default for BUFFERS (usually 15) is too low. You may be slowing down your computer by not requesting more.

2. If you are using disk-caching software, such as SMARTDRV.EXE, you might want to decrease the number of buffers that DOS uses. A dedicated disk cache is much more efficient at optimizing disk access time than the simple memory buffers that DOS uses, and having several DOS buffers can slow your system. In this situation, set the number of buffers fairly low—using only 15 or 20.

3. Although the perfect setting for buffers can be found only through trial and error, a good place to start is to use half the size of your hard disk (in megabytes), adjusted to be in the range of 15 to 55. For example, if you have an 80MB drive, a good setting might be 40. With large drives, you may be tempted to specify a higher number of buffers, but under normal circumstances, using a number higher than 50 hurts rather than helps performance.

4. The secondary read-ahead buffer setting can give you a performance boost if you aren't running any other caching software. Because many programs read files sequentially, DOS can perform fewer disk accesses by reading in more information than was requested. The number of read-ahead buffers you specify is the amount of data that DOS reads from disk in addition to the data requested by a program.

Cache software, such as SMARTDRV.EXE, usually includes much more sophisticated read-ahead capabilities than DOS can provide. If you are using any cache software, you should turn off this feature by letting DOS default to zero read-ahead buffers.

SEE ALSO

DOS=HIGH, FASTOPEN, FILES, HIMEM.SYS, and SMARTDRV.EXE

Chapter 19, "Configuring Your Computer"

CALL   3.3 AND LATER—INTERNAL

You can use the CALL command to execute a second batch file and return control to the first batch file. CALL normally is used to replace the awkward COMMAND /C syntax that was required before DOS 3.3. CALL can be used to run any executable file, but there is no reason to use it for .COM or .EXE files because they return control automatically. If you execute a batch file from a batch file without using CALL, control is never returned.

SYNTAX

CALL *drive:\path***filename** *parameters*

PARAMETERS AND SWITCHES

drive:\path   The drive and/or path to the batch file you want to execute. If no drive or path is specified, the DOS PATH is searched for **filename**.

filename The filename of the batch file you want to execute. This argument is required and wildcards cannot be used. You are not required to enter the .BAT extension, but you can include it if you want to ensure that a batch file, rather than an executable file, is found.

parameters Any parameters that you want passed to the batch file you are executing.

NOTES

1. When you use the CALL command to execute a batch file from within a batch file, control returns to the first batch file when the second one terminates. If you execute a batch file from within a batch file without the CALL command, control never returns to the first batch file.

2. Any *parameters* specified are passed to the called batch file. You can access these *parameters* from within the called batch file by using replaceable parameters (for example, %1) as usual.

3. Avoid using redirection symbols (<, >, and >>) or the pipe character (|) in the *parameters* you pass to the batch file with the CALL command. DOS ignores any redirection operations you specify, which might cause some programs (such as MORE) to lock up or crash.

4. Although the CALL command is very similar to the COMMAND /C command, it has one significant difference: CALL doesn't execute a temporary copy of the command interpreter, whereas COMMAND /C does. For this reason, CALL requires less memory to use.

5. If you use CALL to call a program that returns an exit code, that exit code value will be available after CALL returns. Unfortunately, you can't set the exit code for a batch file, so CALL can't return an exit code from a batch file you have executed. To return status information from a batch file executed with the CALL command, create an environment variable and set it equal to your return status. You then can test this environment variable in the calling batch file.

6. A batch file executed with the CALL command uses the same copy of the command interpreter that its parent is using; therefore, they share access to the same environment area. Any environment variables you set in the called batch file can be read by the parent batch file when it regains control. This is not true when you use COMMAND /C. The environment of a batch file executed with COMMAND /C disappears when the temporary copy of the command interpreter it is running under is removed from memory.

7. If you are going to load any resident software from a called batch file, make sure you use CALL rather than COMMAND /C. When you return from COMMAND /C, the temporary copy of the command interpreter is unloaded from memory. If you load any resident software while this temporary copy is running, the memory occupied by the temporary command interpreter remains unavailable until you reboot your computer. This "memory loss" doesn't happen with the CALL command because no temporary copy of the command interpreter is loaded.

8. A batch file can call itself, but you must be careful to explicitly terminate the batch file at some point to avoid an endless loop. A batch file can be terminated by instructing the user to press Ctrl+Break at a PAUSE or by executing another batch file (without CALL) at some point.

9. Although executing a .COM or .EXE file with the CALL command is perfectly legal, there is little reason to do so. After a .COM or .EXE file is executed, control returns to the batch file with or without using the CALL command. Executing the CALL command from the DOS prompt, although legal, is fairly useless unless it is part of a FOR-IN-DO loop.

EXAMPLES

To call a batch file from another batch file, simply include the name of the batch file in a CALL command, as shown in the following:

```
CALL   OTHER.BAT
```

Note that you can omit the .BAT extension; however, if DOS locates an .EXE or .COM file named OTHER, it executes that program rather than your batch file. DOS searches the current directory as well as any subdirectories listed in your DOS PATH looking for OTHER.BAT. To save time by limiting DOS's search, you can specify the full pathname of the batch file.

Arguments can be passed to the called batch file. Suppose that you previously wrote a batch file named COPYDOC.BAT, which copied all the .DOC files in a subdirectory (%1) to a floppy disk (%2). The project you are working on is stored in five separate subdirectories, and you want to write a batch file, as shown in the following example, that runs COPYDOC once for each subdirectory:

```
@ECHO OFF
CALL COPYDOC.BAT C:\PROJECT\WORK B:
CALL COPYDOC.BAT C:\PROJECT\LTR B:
CALL COPYDOC.BAT C:\PROJECT\EXPN B:
CALL COPYDOC.BAT C:\PROJECT\RES B:
CALL COPYDOC.BAT C:\PROJECT\OLD B:
ECHO *** All Done ***
```

Each CALL command executes COPYDOC with different parameters, backing up all five of the C:\PROJECT subdirectories. After all the copy commands are executed, the message *** All Done *** is displayed onscreen. If you execute the COPYDOC.BAT file without using CALL, the batch file is terminated after backing up one subdirectory because control never returns to this batch file from COPYDOC.BAT.

To eliminate the repetition in the preceding example, you can combine all five CALL commands into a single FOR-IN-DO loop, as shown in the following:

```
@ECHO OFF
FOR %%A IN (WORK LTR EXPN RES OLD) DO CALL COPYDOC.BAT C:\PROJECT\%%A B:
ECHO *** All Done ***
```

Note that you can execute this FOR command from the command line, as long as you remember to substitute single percent signs for the double ones that are required in batch files, like this:

```
FOR %A IN (WORK LTR EXPN RES OLD) DO CALL COPYDOC.BAT C:\PROJECT\%A B:
```

MESSAGES

```
Batch file missing
```

Error: DOS attempted to read the next line from the batch file it was executing and was unable to find the file. This error can happen if you execute a batch file from a floppy disk and change disks before the batch file has finished. The batch file may have renamed or deleted itself, in which case you have to edit it to avoid this behavior.

SEE ALSO

COMMAND

"Running Batch Files from Other Batch Files" in Chapter 16

CD OR CHDIR   2.0 AND LATER—INTERNAL

Each disk drive has one subdirectory that is referred to as the *current* directory. When a pathname contains no subdirectories, DOS assumes the current directory for that drive is being referenced. The CD (or CHDIR) command enables you to display or change the current directory for a disk drive.

SYNTAX

CD *drive:\path*

or

CHDIR *drive:\path*

Parameters and Switches

drive:\path   The subdirectory (*path*) on a particular *drive:* that you want to make current. If only a *path* is specified, it becomes the current directory on the current drive. If only a *drive:* is specified, the name of the current subdirectory on that drive is displayed. If this parameter is omitted, the name of the current directory of the current drive is displayed.

Notes

1. If a backslash (\) is the first (or only) character in a subdirectory path, it is considered an *absolute* path and is specified starting from the root directory. If the subdirectory path begins with a subdirectory name, it is considered a *relative* path, and the current directory is used as the starting point. A drive letter, followed by a colon, can precede either an absolute or relative path.

2. Two periods (..) represent the parent of the current directory. A common shorthand with the CD command is to switch to the parent directory by using a CD .. command. The "double-dot" can be used in any pathname, but it is more useful in relative pathnames than in absolute ones. Notice that the root directory has no parent; attempting to switch to the parent of the root directory (for example, CD \..) causes an error message to be displayed. (See the first item in the following "Messages" section.)

3. Do not specify a filename with the CD (or CHDIR) command; otherwise, DOS interprets the filename as a subdirectory name and displays an error message. (See the first item in the following "Messages" section.)

4. You must include a colon after the drive letter; otherwise, DOS interprets the drive letter as a subdirectory name and displays an error message. (See the first item in the following "Messages" section.)

Examples

To change to the root directory of the current drive, enter CD (or CHDIR) followed by a backslash:

CD   \

To change to the parent or the current directory, enter CD followed by two periods:

CD   ..

If the current directory was the root directory, switching to the parent directory with the preceding command causes an `Invalid directory` message to be displayed (because the root directory has no parent). (See the first item in the following "Messages" section.)

For the next set of examples, assume the following directory tree:

C:\

   DOS

   TEMP

```
WIN
        SYSTEM
WORK
        STEVE
        ALICE
```

Enter the following command to display the current directory on drive C:

`CD  C:`

If you omit the C:, the current directory of the current drive is displayed. Assuming that drive C is the current drive, you enter the following command to change to the C:\WORK\STEVE subdirectory:

`CD  \WORK\STEVE`

Then, if you want to change to the C:\WORK\ALICE subdirectory, you can use either of the following two commands:

`CD  \WORK\ALICE`

or

`CD  ..\ALICE`

The second line uses the "double-dot" directory to specify a relative path to the new subdirectory. It is interpreted as "the subdirectory ALICE of the parent of the current directory."

Relative pathnames can get very convoluted. If C:\WORK\ALICE is the current drive and directory, and you want to change to the C:\WIN\SYSTEM subdirectory, enter one of the following commands:

`CD  ..\..\WIN\SYSTEM`

or

`CD  ..\STEVE\..\..\DOS\..\WIN\SYSTEM`

The preceding examples can help you understand how DOS interprets relative pathnames, but using absolute pathnames is much easier when you want to move to a remote part of the subdirectory structure.

MESSAGES

`Invalid directory`

Error: You have used the *path* argument to specify a directory that doesn't exist. Make sure that you entered the subdirectory path correctly and that you did not include a filename at the end of the *path*.

`Invalid drive specified`

Error: You have specified an invalid drive letter.

See Also

DELTREE, MD (or MKDIR), MOVE, RD (or RMDIR), and TREE

"Changing the Current Directory with CHDIR (CD)" in Chapter 5

CHAIN

You use CHAIN in your CONFIG.SYS file to start another configuration file and process the commands in it.

Syntax

CHAIN *drive:\path\filespec.ext*

Parameters and Switches

drive:\path\filespec.ext   The location and filename of the configuration file to process. If the configuration file is on a different drive, you need to specify the drive and full path for any device commands in the file.

CHCP   3.3 AND LATER—INTERNAL

The CHCP command is a systemwide, code-page (character-set) changer. CHCP simultaneously resets all affected devices to the changed font. MODE works in a similar manner but changes only one device at a time.

Syntax

To change the current code page, use the following format:

CHCP *codepage*

To display the current code page, use the following format:

CHCP

Parameters and Switches

codepage   A valid three-digit code-page number. See "International Country Codes" in Chapter 14, "Understanding the International Features of DOS," for a list of the code pages that MS-DOS supports.

Notes

1. Before using CHCP, you must use the COUNTRY command (to specify the location of the country-information file, normally COUNTRY.SYS), use the NLSFUNC command (to specify a location that overrides that of the COUNTRY command), or place COUNTRY.SYS in the root directory of the current disk. Otherwise, DOS returns the message Cannot open specified country information file.

2. Before using CHCP, you must use the NLSFUNC command.
3. When you select a code page, the new code page becomes the specified code page. If you include CONFIG.SYS directives for devices that use code pages, such as DEVICE=DISPLAY.SYS, CHCP loads the correct code pages for the devices.
4. You can access the COUNTRY.SYS file to get country information. If you do not specify the location of COUNTRY.SYS when you invoke NLSFUNC, COUNTRY.SYS must exist in the current disk's root directory. Otherwise, DOS returns the message `Cannot open specified country information file`.

MESSAGES

`Code page nnn not prepared for device ddd`

Error: CHCP could not select the code page *nnn* because of one of the following errors:

- You did not use MODE to prepare a code page for this device.
- An I/O error occurred while DOS was sending the new font information to the device.
- The device is busy (for example, a printer is in use or offline).
- The device does not support code-page switching.

Check to make sure that the command MODE CODEPAGE PREPARE was issued for the appropriate devices and the devices are online and ready. Then, try CHCP again.

`Invalid code page`

Error: CHCP could not select the code page because of one of the following errors:

- You specified an invalid code page for the country.
- You did not use the MODE command to prepare a code page.

Be sure that you run NLSFUNC and use the command MODE CODEPAGE PREPARE to prepare the code page for the appropriate devices.

`NLSFUNC not installed`

Error: You attempted to change the code page but did not initiate NLSFUNC before using CHCP. If you plan to use code pages and have the correct directives in CONFIG.SYS, add NLSFUNC to your AUTOEXEC.BAT file so that the command is executed when you boot the computer.

SEE ALSO

COUNTRY=, MODE *device* CP, and NLSFUNC

Chapter 14, "Understanding the International Features of DOS"

CHDIR (SEE CD)

CHDIR is an alternative name for the CD command. For information on using the CD or CHDIR command, see the entry for CD earlier in this command reference.

CHECK

The CHECK command checks a Stacker-compressed drive, produces a status report, and fixes any detected problems. The Stacker drive must be installed before using the CHECK command.

SYNTAX

    CHECK *drive:* /b /d /f /n /t /v /wp /?

PARAMETERS AND SWITCHES

drive:	Indicates the Stacker drive to check.
/b	Runs in batch file mode, suppressing pauses.
/d	Displays detailed error and statistics report.
/f	Fixes detected problems.
/n	Prevents new save-header files from being created.
/t	Skips the SmartPack sector check.
/v	Displays the name of each file in every directory as the drive is checked.
/wp	Checks and repairs any write-protected Stacker drives.
/?	Displays the abbreviated online help.

REMARKS

To receive a Stacker drive space report on a compressed drive, use the command check e: /d.

 CHKDSK   1.0 AND LATER—EXTERNAL

The CHKDSK command checks the directory and file allocation table (FAT) of the disk and reports disk and memory status. CHKDSK also can repair errors in the directories or the FAT.

SYNTAX

    CHKDSK *drive:\path\filename.ext* /F /V

PARAMETERS AND SWITCHES

drive:	The disk drive to be analyzed.

`\path\`	The directory path to the files to be analyzed.
`filename.ext`	A valid DOS filename. Wildcards are permitted.
`/F`	Fixes the FAT and other problems if errors are found. (Do not use this switch when you are running under Microsoft Windows or the DOS Task Swapper.)
`/V`	Shows CHKDSK's progress and displays more detailed information about the errors that the program finds. (This switch is known as the *verbose switch*.)

EXIT CODES

ERRORLEVEL Value	Meaning
0	No errors found
255	Errors were found

RULES

1. You must direct CHKDSK to repair the disk by using the /F switch. CHKDSK asks you to confirm that you want the repairs made before it proceeds.
2. CHKDSK cannot process a directory in which you used the JOIN command—that is, a second disk joined to a subdirectory.
3. CHKDSK does not process a disk on which you used a SUBST command.
4. CHKDSK cannot process a disk drive on which you used the ASSIGN command.
5. CHKDSK cannot process a networked (shared) disk.
6. Do not use CHKDSK on disks that contain open files, or have another program running that may access the disk drive while CHKDSK is running.
7. (Not MS-DOS 6.2) After completing its normal checks on a DoubleSpace drive, CHKDSK automatically runs DBLSPACE /CHKDSK on the drive.

NOTES

1. In MS-DOS 6.2, CHKDSK now displays numbers with embedded commas, making them much easier to read.
2. CHKDSK displays the following information:
    - Volume name and creation date (only disks with volume labels)
    - Volume serial number (if it exists)
    - Total disk space
    - Number of files and bytes used for hidden or system files
    - Number of files and bytes used for directories
    - Number of files and bytes used for user (normal) files

- Bytes used by bad sectors (flawed disk space)
- Bytes available on disk (free space)
- Bytes of total conventional memory (RAM)
- Bytes of available conventional memory

> **Tip:** If you are using MS-DOS 6.2, Microsoft advises you to stop using the CHKDSK command and use the new ScanDisk program instead. ScanDisk can identify and fix many more types of errors than CHKDSK. If you use DoubleSpace, ScanDisk can identify and fix any errors it finds on your compressed drives as well.

3. In DOS 4.0 and later, CHKDSK also reports the following information:
   - Total bytes in each allocation unit
   - Total allocation units on the disk
   - Available allocation units on the disk (an allocation unit equates to a cluster)
4. CHKDSK checks the directories and the FAT of a disk. The command also checks the amount of memory in the system and determines how much of that memory is free. If errors are found, CHKDSK reports them onscreen before making a status report.
5. If lost clusters are found, CHKDSK asks whether you want to repair them. You must type Y or N. If you type Y, CHKDSK shows a report onscreen as though the lost clusters were repaired. This report is only a simulation, however. To actually reclaim the lost clusters, you must issue a second command: CHKDSK /F.
6. The CHKDSK filename checks to see whether the specified files are stored contiguously on the disk. DOS reports any noncontiguously stored files and how many different sections store the files. If CHKDSK reports many noncontiguous files, you might want to run DEFRAG on the disk.
7. CHKDSK does not check to see whether your files can be read, nor does CHKDSK test your disk to determine whether new bad spots have appeared.

Messages

```
All specified file(s) are contiguous
```

Information: The files you specified are stored in contiguous sectors on the disk. Disk performance for the files should be optimal.

```
filename
Allocation error, size adjusted
```

Warning: The `filename` has an invalid sector number in the FAT. The file was truncated by CHKDSK at the end of the last valid sector.

Check this file to verify that all information in the file is correct. If you find a problem, use your backup copy of the file. This message usually appears when the problem is in the FAT, not in the file. Your file probably is still good.

```
filename
Contains xxx non-contiguous blocks
```

Information: `filename` is not stored continuously on the disk but in *xxx* number of pieces. This arrangement can diminish the performance of the disk. If you find that many files on a disk are stored in noncontiguous pieces, you might want to run DEFRAG.

```
directoryname
Convert directory to file (Y/N)?
```

Warning: `directoryname` contains so much bad information that the directory no longer is usable. If you type Y, CHKDSK converts the directory into a file so that you can use DEBUG or another tool to repair the directory. If you type N, no action is taken.

The first time you see this message, type N. Try to copy files from this directory to another disk and check the copied files to see whether they are usable. Then, rerun CHKDSK to convert the directory into a file and try to recover the rest of the files.

```
Errors found, F parameter not specified
Corrections will not be written to the disk
```

Information: CHKDSK found an error. This message tells you that CHKDSK will go through the motions of repairing the disk but will not actually change the file because you did not use the /F switch.

```
filename
First allocation unit is invalid, entry truncated
```

Warning: `filename`'s first entry in the FAT refers to a nonexistent portion of the disk. If you used the /F switch, the file becomes a zero-length file (truncated).

Try to copy this file to another floppy disk before CHKDSK truncates the file. You may not get a useful copy, however, and the original file will be lost.

```
. or ..
Entry has a bad attribute
or Entry has a bad size or
Entry has a bad link
```

Warning: The link to the parent directory (..) or the current directory (.) has a problem. If you used the /F switch, CHKDSK attempts to repair the problem. Normally, this procedure is safe, and you do not risk losing files.

```
filename
Has invalid allocation unit, file truncated
```

Information and warning: Part of the chain of FAT entries for `filename` points to a nonexistent part of the disk. The /F switch truncates the file at its last valid sector. If you did not use the /F switch, DOS takes no corrective action. Try to copy this file to a different disk and then rerun CHKDSK with the /F switch. (You may lose part of the file.)

```
filename1
Is cross linked on allocation unit x
filename2
Is cross linked on allocation unit x
```

Warning: Two files—`filename1` and `filename2`—had entries in the FAT that point to the same area (cluster) of the disk. In other words, the two files believe that they own the same piece of the disk.

CHKDSK takes no action. To handle the problem, copy both files to another floppy disk, delete the files from the original disk, and edit the files as necessary. (The files may contain garbage.)

```
Insufficient room in root directory
Erase files from root and repeat CHKDSK
```

Error: CHKDSK recovered so many "lost" clusters from the disk that the root directory is full. CHKDSK aborts at this point.

Examine the FILE*xxxx*.CHK files. If you find nothing useful, delete them. Rerun CHKDSK with the /F switch to continue recovering lost clusters.

```
xxxxxxxxx bytes disk space freed
```

Information: CHKDSK regained some disk space that was improperly marked as "in use." *xxxxxxxxx* tells you how many additional bytes are now available. To free this disk space, review and delete any FILE*xxxx*.CHK file that does not contain useful information.

```
xxx lost allocation units found in yyy chains
Convert lost chains to files (Y/N)?
```

Information: Although CHKDSK found *xxx* blocks of data allocated in the FAT, no file on the disk is using these blocks. The blocks are lost clusters, which CHKDSK normally can free if no other error or warning message appears.

If you use the /F switch and type Y, CHKDSK joins each set of lost chains into a file placed in the root directory of the disk. That file is called FILE*xxxx*.CHK, in which *xxxx* is a consecutive number between 0000 and 9999. Examine this file and delete any clusters that contain no useful information.

If you use the /F switch and type N, CHKDSK simply frees the lost chains so that other files can reuse the disk space. No files are created. If you type Y and omit /F, CHKDSK displays the actions that you can take but takes no action itself.

SEE ALSO

DEFRAG, DOUBLESPACE/CHKDSK, and SCANDISK

"Analyzing a Disk with CHKDSK" in Chapter 7

CHKSTATE.SYS (SEE MEMMAKER)

The CHKSTATE.SYS device driver helps MemMaker optimize memory use on your computer. MemMaker requires this driver only while optimizing your system; it's not needed at any other time. You should not attempt to use this device driver yourself.

Very few details about CHKSTATE.SYS's operation are documented. It's loaded into memory by MemMaker with a DEVICE= line in your CONFIG.SYS file during the optimization process. Presumably, CHKSTATE.SYS communicates with MEMMAKER about the state of your computer, verifying that system integrity is not violated as different combinations of drivers are loaded. When optimization is complete, MemMaker removes this driver from the CONFIG.SYS file.

SEE ALSO

MEMMAKER and SIZER

CHOICE   6.0 AND LATER—EXTERNAL

The CHOICE command suspends batch-file processing and prompts the user to make a choice before processing resumes. You can specify which keystrokes are accepted and what default choices are made if no keys are pressed.

SYNTAX

CHOICE   /C:keys   /N   /S   /T:choice,seconds   prompt

PARAMETERS AND SWITCHES

/C:keys   Specifies which *keys* are displayed in the prompt. The colon (:) is optional. If /C is not specified, CHOICE acts as though you specified /C:YN.

/N Suppresses the key list and question mark that DOS normally adds to the *prompt* (see the first item in the following "Notes" section).

/S Enables case sensitivity for the keys. That is, if /S is specified, the uppercase key represents a different response from the lowercase key. If /S is not specified, the uppercase key is the same as the lowercase key.

/T:*choice,seconds*   Specifies a default key and the number of seconds to wait for the user to press a key before the default is used. The colon (:) is optional. *choice* must be one of the keys specified by /C:*keys*, and *seconds* must be from 0 to 99 (0 means no pause before *choice* is used).

prompt   Specifies the prompt line that is displayed to inform the user about the choice that has to be made. To the end of the *prompt* you specify, DOS adds a bracketed list of allowable keys and a question mark. Quotation marks (") can be used around text, but you don't have to use them unless the *prompt* contains a switch character (/), redirection symbols, or trailing blank spaces. If no *prompt* is specified, DOS does not display any prompt at all.

Exit Codes

ERRORLEVEL Value	Meaning
0	CHOICE terminated by user (Ctrl+Break or Ctrl+C)
1	User picked the first key in /C:*keys* parameter
2	User picked the second key in /C:*keys* parameter
3	User picked the third key in /C:*keys* parameter
4 up	… and so on …
255	Terminated by illegal syntax or other error conditions

Notes

1. When a CHOICE command is executed, the user sees the command's *prompt*, followed by a prompt. The prompt is a left bracket ([), followed by the first key in /C:*keys*, followed by a comma, followed by any other keys in *keys* (separated by commas), followed by a right bracket (]), followed by a question mark (?). /C:YN, for example, produces the prompt [Y,N]?
2. CHOICE returns different exit code values to the batch file, depending on which of the keys in /C:*keys* is pressed in response to the prompt. Pressing the first key returns 1, pressing the second returns 2, and so on.
3. If the user presses Ctrl+Break and then does not terminate the batch job, a value of 0 is returned. If DOS detects an error, a value of 255 is returned.
4. If the user presses a key that is not one of the keys in /C:*keys*, the computer beeps.

Examples

To ask the user whether to continue with the batch file, issue the following commands:

```
CHOICE /C:YN "Yes to continue and No to exit "
IF ERRORLEVEL 2 GOTO EXIT
```

You then see the following line:

```
Yes to continue and No to exit [Y,N]?
```

Notice the trailing space at the end of the prompt text specified in the CHOICE command. CHOICE adds the [Y,N]? text to the end of the prompt you specify. Adding a trailing space to your prompt text can make the final prompt more readable onscreen.

To load the mouse driver from your AUTOEXEC.BAT file unless told otherwise within three seconds, issue the following commands:

```
CHOICE /C:YN /T:3,Y "Load the mouse driver "
IF ERRORLEVEL 2 GOTO NOMOUSE
```

To provide a menu of choices, enter the following:

```
@ECHO OFF
CLS
ECHO.
ECHO F First action
ECHO S Second action
ECHO T Third action
ECHO.
CHOICE /C:FST "Choose an action "
IF ERRORLEVEL 255 GOTO ERROR
IF ERRORLEVEL 3 GOTO THIRD
IF ERRORLEVEL 2 GOTO SECOND
IF ERRORLEVEL 1 GOTO FIRST

:ERROR
ECHO GOT AN ERROR OR BREAK
GOTO END

:THIRD
ECHO PRESSED T
GOTO END

:SECOND
ECHO PRESSED S
GOTO END

:FIRST
ECHO PRESSED F
GOTO END

:END
```

SEE ALSO

IF

"Making a Two-Way Choice" in Chapter 16

CLS   2.0 AND LATER—INTERNAL

The CLS command clears a text screen and returns the cursor to the upper-left corner. It's very useful for clearing away messages left by other commands or batch files. Normally, CLS is limited to clearing 25-line text mode screens, but if ANSI.SYS is loaded, CLS clears 43- and 50-line text modes as well.

SYNTAX

CLS

NOTES

1. This command clears all information from the screen and places the cursor at the home position in the upper-left corner.

634　Appendix F　Command Reference

2. This command affects only the active video display, not memory.
3. If you used the ANSI control codes to set the foreground and background, the color settings remain in effect.
4. If you did not set the foreground/background color, the screen reverts to light characters on a dark background.

SEE ALSO

ANSI.SYS

"The CLS Command" in Chapter 13

CMOSCLK.SYS

CMOSCLK.SYS replaces the default DOS clock so that any request for the current date and time accesses this device driver instead of the DOS system clock.

SYNTAX

DEVICE=*drive:\path* **CMOSCLK.SYS**

PARAMETERS AND SWITCHES

drive:\path　　Location of the CMOSCLK.SYS file.

NOTES

This device driver must be loaded by either a DEVICE= or DEVICEHIGH= statement in the CONFIG.SYS file.

CNFIGNAM.EXE

PCM Plus uses CNFIGNAM.EXE to specify configuration parameters for a specified setup configuration. The PCM Plus setup utility adds CNFIGNAM to the CONFIG.SYS file.

This device driver must be loaded by a DEVICE= statement in the CONFIG.SYS file. It cannot be loaded high.

SYNTAX

DEVICE=cnfignam.exe /*config_name*

PARAMETERS AND SWITCHES

config_name　　PCM Plus configuration to use. PCM Plus can have multiple setup configurations in the PCM.INI file.

NOTES

The CNFIGNAM statement in the CONFIG.SYS file is inserted automatically through the PCMSET-UP program. Multiple configurations are identified and handled without user intervention.

COMMAND 2.0 AND LATER—EXTERNAL

COMMAND invokes another copy of COMMAND.COM, the command processor. If you write complicated batch files, this command may be useful. Normally, a user gets involved with this command when setting up the SHELL= line in the CONFIG.SYS file.

SYNTAX

COMMAND *path\\ cttydevice* /E:*size* /K *filename* /P /MSG /C *string*

In your CONFIG.SYS file, use the following format:

SHELL=*drive:\path***COMMAND.COM** *path\\ condevice* /E:*size* /P /MSG

PARAMETERS AND SWITCHES

drive:\path
Indicates the DOS drive and path to the copy of COMMAND.COM that the SHELL= command should load.

path
Indicates the drive and directory location of COMMAND.COM. This path is assigned to the COMSPEC environment variable.

condevice
Indicates the device used for input and output. The default is CON:. The colon is optional. This parameter rarely is used.

/E:*size*
Sets the size of the environment. *size* is a decimal number from 160 to 32,768 bytes, rounded up to the nearest multiple of 16 (refer to the SHELL command). The default is 256.

/K *filename*
Runs *filename* (a program or batch file) and then displays the DOS command prompt.

/P
Keeps this copy permanently in memory (until the next system reset). Generally used only as part of the SHELL command. Do not use the /P parameter from a batch file.

/MSG
Loads all error messages into memory. Must be used with /P. Generally useful only if you are running DOS from floppy disks.

/C *string*
Passes the command and parameters represented by *string* to the new copy of COMMAND.COM and returns to the primary command processor.

Rules

1. The string in the /C option is interpreted by the additional copy of COMMAND.COM, just as though you typed the string at the system level. /C must be the last switch used in the line. Do not use the form COMMAND/C *string* /P.
2. You can exit from the second copy of the command processor by issuing the command EXIT, unless you used the /P option (permanent).
3. If you issue the /P and /C switches together, /P is ignored.
4. Do not use the /K switch in the SHELL command line in your CONFIG.SYS file. This switch can cause problems with applications and installation programs that alter your AUTOEXEC.BAT file.

Notes

1. COMMAND often is used with the SHELL directive to enable COMMAND.COM to reside in a subdirectory rather than in the root directory.
2. You can use COMMAND with all versions of DOS to call a second batch file from an originating batch file. Suppose that a batch file named BATCH1.BAT contains the following line:

    COMMAND   /C   BATCH2

    BATCH1 calls BATCH2.BAT. BATCH2.BAT executes and, after completing the last line of the batch file, returns to BATCH1 to complete the originating batch file. This method of calling a batch file is similar to the CALL batch subcommand available in DOS version 3.3 and later.
3. If you use DOS 5.0 or 6.0 with a floppy-disk–only system, you can specify the /MSG switch in the SHELL directive of CONFIG.SYS. This switch loads all error messages in memory. If an error occurs, you do not need a disk with COMMAND.COM in the drive. (The switch uses an additional 1KB of RAM.)
4. You can use the /K *filename* switch to specify that the DOS prompt in Microsoft Windows should use a startup file other than AUTOEXEC.BAT. Open the DOSPRMPT.PIF file (using the PIF Editor) and type /K *filename* in the Optional Parameters box.

See Also

CALL and SHELL=

"Loading a Secondary Command Processor" in Chapter 10

COMP 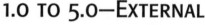 1.0 TO 5.0—EXTERNAL

You can use COMP to compare two sets of disk files of the same name and length. The FC command, which is discussed later in this command reference, provides many of the same capabilities as COMP. COMP is included on the DOS 6 Supplemental Disk, not in the standard DOS 6.0 package.

Syntax

COMP *pathname1 pathname2* /D /A /L /N=x /C

Parameters and Switches

pathname1	Indicates the drive, path, and filename for the primary set of files. Wildcards are allowed. If no filename is specified, all files (*.*) are assumed.
pathname2	Indicates the drive, path, and filename for the secondary set of files. Wildcards are allowed. If no filename is specified, all files (*.*) are assumed.
/D	Displays differences in hexadecimal format.
/A	Displays differences as alphanumeric characters.
/L	Displays the line number in which the difference occurred.
/N=x	Compares the first *x* number of lines of a file.
/C	Performs a non–case-sensitive comparison of files.

Notes

1. If you do not enter a filename, all files for that set, whether primary or secondary, are compared (which is the same as typing *.*). However, only the files in the secondary set with names that match filenames in the primary set are compared.

2. If you do not enter a drive, path, or filename, COMP prompts you for the primary and secondary file sets to compare. Otherwise, the correct disks must be in the correct drive if you are comparing files on disks. COMP does not wait for you to insert disks if you use both primary and secondary filenames.

3. After 10 mismatches (unequal comparisons) between the contents of two compared files, COMP ends the comparison and aborts.

4. A more versatile utility for file comparison is FC, discussed later in this command reference. COMP no longer is distributed with the standard DOS package.

Messages

```
Compare error at offset xxxxxxxx
```

Information: The files that you are comparing are not the same. The difference occurs at *xxxxxxxx* bytes from the start of the file. The number provided is in hexadecimal format, base 16. The values of the differing bytes in the files also are displayed in hexadecimal format.

```
Files are different sizes
```

638 APPENDIX F COMMAND REFERENCE

Warning: You asked COMP to compare two files of different lengths. Because COMP compares only files of the same size, COMP skips the comparison.

```
10 Mismatches - ending compare
```

Warning: COMP found 10 mismatches between the two files you compared. COMP, therefore, assumes that no reason exists to continue, and the comparison is aborted.

SEE ALSO

FC

CONFIG

CONFIG re-creates the STACKER.INI file. It searches for all the STACVOL files on all the Stacker drives, disables the current STACKER.INI file, and creates a new one.

SYNTAX

CONFIG *drive*: [-]*drivelist* /a=*drivelist* /c=*filename* /i=*filename* /s=*dirname* /a /a- /d /d- /?

PARAMETERS AND SWITCHES

drive:	Specifies the drive in which to update the configuration files.
[-]*drivelist*	Specifies a list of removable drives with no colons. A minus sign in front of the drive letter removes the automount specification for the drive.
/a=*drivelist*	Updates automount specifications for these removable drives in the configuration file.
/c=*filename*	Updates the named file instead of CONFIG.SYS.
/i=*filename*	Updates the named file instead of STACKER.INI.
/s=*dirname*	Uses *dirname* as the Stacker directory in the new configuration file.
/a	Updates configuration files to turn on automount for removable drives.
/a-	Updates configuration files to turn off automount for removable drives.
/d	Adds the Stacker DPMS (DOS Protected Mode Services) driver to configuration files.
/d-	Removes the Stacker DPMS driver from configuration files.
/?	Displays the abbreviated online help.

COPY   **1.0 AND LATER—INTERNAL**

You can use the COPY command to copy files between disk drives or between drives and devices. COPY enables you to keep or change the filenames and also enables you to combine (concatenate) files.

SYNTAX

The syntax used to copy files from one place to another is very simple:

`COPY source destination /V /Y /Y-`

You can tell DOS what kinds of files you are copying by using the /A (ASCII) and /B (BINARY) parameters:

`COPY /A /B source /A /B destination /A /B /V /Y /Y-`

By adding plus signs, you can specify more than one source file and have them all combined (concatenated) into one destination file:

`COPY /A /B source /A /B +source2 /A /B +... /A /B destination /A /B /V /Y /Y-`

PARAMETERS AND SWITCHES

source	Specifies the file or files that you want to copy. A full pathname (for example, `drive:\path\ ... \filename.ext`) can be specified, and wildcards are allowed. This parameter is required and must include a filename (`*.*` is not assumed). To combine files, specify more than one *source* pathname and separate them with plus signs (+).
destination	Specifies the location and optionally the filename you want to copy to. A full pathname can be specified, although normally only a drive and/or path is included. Wildcards are allowed when a filename is specified. If this parameter is omitted, the current drive and subdirectory are used as the destination.
/V	Verifies that the copy was recorded correctly. Similar to setting VERIFY ON for this COPY operation.
/Y	Specifies that you want COPY to overwrite files without prompting you for confirmation. Including this parameter overrides any setting specified with the COPYCMD environment variable.
/-Y	Specifies that you want COPY to prompt you for confirmation before overwriting any files, even if the command is run from within a batch file. Including this parameter overrides any setting specified with the COPYCMD environment variable.

The /A and /B switches create different effects on the source and destination files. Normally, you don't have to specify these switches because DOS's default assumptions are correct.

For the source file:

/A   Treats the file as an ASCII (text) file. The command copies all the information in the file up to, but not including, the end-of-file marker (Ctrl+Z). Data after the end-of-file marker is ignored. This is the default for copy operations that combine multiple files.

/B   Copies the entire file (based on size, as listed in the directory) as though the file were a program file (*binary1*). All end-of-file markers (Ctrl+Z) are treated as normal characters, and EOF characters are copied. This is the default for copy operations that do not combine multiple files.

For the destination file:

/A   Adds an end-of-file marker (Ctrl+Z) to the end of the ASCII text file at the conclusion of the copying process. This is the default for copy operations that combine multiple files.

/B   Does not add the end-of-file marker to this binary file. This is the default for copy operations that do not combine multiple files.

RULES

Adhere to the following rules when you are copying files for which both the source and the destination are given:

1. These rules apply to the filename:
   - You must provide either a pathname or a filename. Wildcards are allowed in the source filename. If you do not provide a filename but provide a pathname for the source, DOS assumes *.*.
   - If you do not provide a destination filename, the copied file has the same name, creation date, and creation time as the source file.
2. You can substitute a device name for the complete source or destination name.
3. When you copy between disk drives, COPY assumes that binary files are copied (as though you used the /B switch).
4. When you copy to or from a device other than a disk drive, COPY assumes that ASCII files are copied (as though you used the /A switch).
5. An /A or /B switch overrides the default settings for COPY.

Adhere to the following rules when you are copying files and only one file is specified:

1. The file specification you use (*d1:path1****filename1.ext1**) is the source. This specification must have one or both of these items:

- A valid filename. Wildcards are allowed.
- A drive name, pathname, or both. If you provide only one name, that name must differ from the current drive name or pathname. If you provide both names, at least one name must differ from the current drive name or pathname.

2. The source cannot be a device name.
3. The destination is the current drive and current directory.
4. The copied files use the same names as the source files.
5. COPY assumes that binary files are copied (as though you used the /B switch).

Adhere to these rules when you concatenate files:

1. The destination file is the last file in the list unless you add a plus sign (+) before that filename. If you do not specify a destination filename, the first source name becomes the destination name.
2. If you do not provide a drive name, DOS uses the current drive.
3. If you do not provide a path, DOS uses the current directory.
4. These rules apply to source files:
   - You must provide a valid filename. Wildcards are allowed, but using them can be dangerous. If you do not provide a destination filename, DOS uses the first filename as the destination filename.
   - After the first filename, any additional source file specifications must be preceded by a plus sign (+).
5. These rules apply to the destination file:
   - You can use only one destination file specification. If you provide a destination without wildcards, DOS uses that name for the destination file. If you provide a destination filename with wildcards, DOS uses the first source filename for the destination file.
   - If you do not provide a destination, DOS uses the first source file as the destination. The first file that matches the wildcard filename is used as the destination file if you used a wildcard as part of the first source filename, and the files to be joined are appended to the first source file.

Notes

1. The COPY command, when run from the command line, now prompts you for confirmation before overwriting files. However, to avoid forcing you to rewrite all your batch files, COPY does not prompt you before overwriting a file when it is run from a batch file.

   If you don't like the way COPY now behaves, you can change it by defining an environment variable named COPYCMD. Setting COPYCMD equal to /Y forces COPY to act as it has in all previous versions of DOS, never prompting for confirmation before overwriting a file. If you set COPYCMD equal to /-Y, COPY always prompts for confirmation—even when it is run from within a batch file.

2. The meanings of the /A and /B switches depend on their positions in the line. The /A or /B switch affects the file that immediately precedes the switch and all files that follow the switch until DOS encounters another /A or /B switch. When you use one of these switches before a filename, the switch affects all following files until DOS encounters another /A or /B switch that contradicts the earlier switch.
3. Use XCOPY to copy zero-length files and all of a directory's files and subdirectories.
4. To change the time and date of a file to the current time and date, enter the following command:
   COPY /B filename.ext+,,
5. You can create a text file by copying what you type to a file. To do so, use the following format:
   COPY CON filename.ext
   Everything you type is then copied to `filename.ext` until you press Ctrl+Z or F6.

MESSAGES

Cannot do binary reads from a device

Error: If you specify a device name such as CON or COM1 as the *source* in a COPY command, you cannot include the /B switch. These devices operate in character mode only. Try the command again without specifying the /B switch.

Content of destination lost before copy

Error: You may see this message when you are combining files with the COPY command. If the destination file has the same name as any of the source files (except the first) that you've specified, COPY overwrites that source file before it has a chance to read it. When this message appears, at least one of your source files has been overwritten, and the file is gone for good. Be very careful combining files with the COPY command, especially if you are using wildcards in the *source* or *destination* parameters.

File cannot be copied onto itself

Error: COPY tried to copy a file onto itself. The destination file must have a different filename or be in a different subdirectory than the source file. Change the *destination* parameter you specified and try the COPY command again.

SEE ALSO

MOVE, REN or RENAME, and VERIFY

"Copying Files" in Chapter 8

 COUNTRY=   3.0 AND LATER—INTERNAL

You can use the COUNTRY= command to instruct DOS to use certain country-specific conventions when it displays or accepts dates, times, numbers, currency, sort ordering, and case conversions. So that transitions from one set of conventions to another can be as painless for the user as possible, application programs are encouraged to use this country-specific information. You can use COUNTRY= only in your CONFIG.SYS file.

SYNTAX

COUNTRY=*country_code*,*code_page*,*path\filename*

PARAMETERS AND SWITCHES

country_code A three-digit number that indicates the country whose conventions you want to use. Typically, the number is the international long-distance telephone code for that country. (See Chapter 14, "Understanding the International Features of DOS.")

code_page The code page (character set) to use for the country that you are specifying. If no code page is specified, the default code page for that country is used. You can switch between the default and alternative code pages by using MODE or CHCP.

path\filename The full path and filename of the file that contains country-specific information; it is usually COUNTRY.SYS. If no filename is specified, COUNTRY= looks for COUNTRY.SYS in the root directory of the startup drive.

NOTES

1. COUNTRY= affects the following items:

   - Date and time formats, both for display and input. DOS commands that use the country setting for date and time include DATE, TIME, RESTORE, DIR, PROMPT, and XCOPY.
   - The thousands separator and decimal character used in numbers. In the U.S., they are a comma and period, respectively (for example, 1,024.45).
   - The location and symbol used for currency.
   - Upper- to lowercase conversions. For each character set (code page), a table of case conversions is maintained by DOS.
   - Alphabetical sorting order for characters in the set. This allows accented characters to sort into their proper places.

> **Tip**
> Always include the full path to the COUNTRY.SYS file when you use the COUNTRY= command. In this way, you can keep the COUNTRY.SYS file in a more logical place, such as in your C:\DOS directory (which is the place Setup puts it, anyway).

2. The default country code is 001 (United States), code page 437, for versions of MS-DOS sold in the U.S.

3. Not all application programs are written to support the international features of DOS, and many ignore the COUNTRY= settings.
4. The MS-DOS distribution disks include a special version of COUNTRY.SYS named COUNTRY.ICE (COUNTRY.IC_ in its compressed form) that contains information supporting an Icelandic keyboard and character set. For details, see the README.TXT file distributed with DOS 6.
5. Microsoft has special versions of MS-DOS available for other languages and countries not listed in the country codes table, such as Arabic, Israel, Japan, Korea, the People's Republic of China, and Taiwan.
6. It is often best to leave out the code page argument in the COUNTRY= line and let DOS use the default code page. To do so, just type two commas before you enter the location and name of the COUNTRY.SYS file. (See the first example that follows.)

EXAMPLES

To set the country to France, insert the following line in your CONFIG.SYS file:

COUNTRY=033,,C:\DOS\COUNTRY.SYS

Notice that two commas are used so that DOS selects the default code page, which in this case is code page 850. Later, you could change to code page 437 by using the CHCP command.

The following line sets the country to the United States with code page 437 active:

COUNTRY=001,437,C:\DOS\COUNTRY.SYS

In the U.S., this example is almost the same as not using the COUNTRY= command at all, except that you now have the ability to switch to code page 850 if you want to.

SEE ALSO

MODE *device* CP, CHCP, NLSFUNC, and KEYB

Chapter 14, "Understanding the International Features of DOS"

COUNTRY.SYS (SEE COUNTRY=)

Despite the .SYS extension, COUNTRY.SYS is not a device driver. It is a file that contains country information—such as code page symbol sets—used by the COUNTRY= command. A similar file, containing information needed for an Icelandic configuration, is located in the file COUNTRY.ICE on the MS-DOS 6 distribution disks. (For details on setting up an Icelandic configuration, see the README.TXT file distributed with DOS 6.)

> **Note** Do not attempt to load COUNTRY.SYS into memory by placing it in a DEVICE= or DEVICEHIGH= command in your CONFIG.SYS file. Your computer will lock up, and you will have to reboot from a floppy disk.

SEE ALSO

COUNTRY= and NLSFUNC

Chapter 14, "Understanding the International Features of DOS"

CPBACKUP

CPBACKUP makes a backup copy of data to disks, tape, or a network drive using full, incremental, differential, or unattended methods. Data can be compressed, encrypted, and checked for viruses as it is backed up.

SYNTAX

```
CPBACKUP d: setname filespec... /date=mmddyy-mddyy   /exattr=hsr /full|/inc|
/sep|/copy|/fullerase|/dif /drive=tape |/drive=d:n /addr=base-i-d /rate=rate
/no /r setupfilename|filespec /ecc|/noecc /save|/nosave /sf|/nonsf /mtask /?
   /video /video options
```

PARAMETERS AND SWITCHES

d:	Specifies the drive to back up or restore to. This setting overrides any drive that is specified in the CPBACKUP.CFG file and the setup file.
setname	Loads the specified setup file. When CPBACKUP is started with a setup file, the directory tree and file list are always visible.
filespec...	Accepts any valid DOS filespec.
/date=mmddyy-mmddyy	Specifies dates of files to back up.
/exattr=hsr	Excludes (h)idden, (s)ystem, and (r)ead-only attributes.
/full	Marks full backup as being backed up.
/copy	Does not mark full backup as backed up.
/fullerase	Specifies a full backup after the tape is erased.
/inc	Specifies an incremental backup and appends to the full backup.
/sep	Specifies a separate incremental backup.
/dif	Specifies a differential backup.
/drive=tape | /drive=d:n	Specifies media as tape and drive size to back up to (360, 720, 1200, or 1400).

Option	Description
`/addr=base-i-d`	Specifies I/O addresses for a tape drive.
`base`	Hexadecimal base address.
`i`	Interrupt request (IRQ).
`d`	Direct memory access (DMA) channel.
`/rate=rate`	Sets the data rate (rate=1000KB per second, 500KB per second or 250KB per second) that the controller must support.
`/no`	Specifies not to use overlapped input and output. Use of this switch turns off the use of simultaneous hard disk and disk DMA.
`/r`	Specifies that the restore mode is to start automatically using the specifications in the .CFG file.
`/r setupfilename`	Starts backup in restore mode and loads the settings saved in the setup file. This parameter must be specified before any others.
`/r filespec`	Restores specific files based on the `filespec` parameter with `/r`.
`/save`	Saves history to the hard disk.
`/nosave`	Does not save history to the hard disk.
`/ecc`	Uses error correction.
`/noecc`	Does not use error correction.
`/sf`	Uses standard formatting.
`/nonsf`	Uses nonstandard formatting.
`/mtask`	Protects files from being changed in multitasking modes.
`/?`	Displays help for the DOS command prompt options.
`/video options`	Displays help for the following video and mouse selections:
`/in`	Uses the default color scheme.
`/bw`	Uses black and white.
`/mono`	Uses monochrome color scheme (IBM monochrome).
`/lcd`	Uses an LCD color scheme (for laptops).
`/ff`	Speeds up the display.
`/bf`	Specifies a BIOS font.
`/nf`	Indicates no fonts; graphics characters are not to be used.

/ngm	Indicates that a character mouse pointer is used.
/le	Specifies a left-handed mouse.
/im	Ignores mouse.
/ps2	Resets the mouse hardware on a PS/2.

NOTES

Commands used to back up data require a compatible command to restore the data.

SEE ALSO

CPSCHED, SCHEDULE

CPBDIR

CPBDIR determines the number of disks and the correct order of a high-speed or medium-speed disk backup and gives information about how the backup was made.

SYNTAX

CPBDIR *drive*: /x /v /?]

PARAMETERS AND SWITCHES

drive:	Specifies the drive containing the CPBACKUP disk to view.
/x	Displays extended information about the disk.
/v	Specifies that the disk is to be verified.
/?	Displays the abbreviated online help.

SEE ALSO

CPBACKUP

CPSCHED

CPSCHED activates CPSCHED.EXE, which is the memory-resident portion of the Scheduler program. The Scheduler program schedules other DOS programs to run automatically at a preset date and time.

SYNTAX

CPSCHED /u /low /?

CRC

The CRC command gives a Cyclic Redundancy Check (CRC) number for a filename. This number uniquely identifies a file. CRC ensures that a file transfer has been completed without error. It also can be applied to disk copy operations, periodic checks for file corruption, and more.

Syntax

CRC *drive:\path filespec* /s /p /?

Parameters and Switches

drive:\path filespec	Specifies the location and name of the file for which the CRC number is required.
/s	Processes files in all directories in the specified path.
/p	Pauses after each screen of information.
/?	Displays the abbreviated online help.

CREATE

The CREATE command creates an empty Stacker drive using available disk space or a RAM drive.

Syntax

CREATE *drive:\stacvol.xxx* /c=*n* /r=*n.n* /s=*sss.s* /m /?

Parameters and Switches

drive:	Specifies the drive letter of the uncompressed drive.
\stacvol.xxx	Indicates the name of the *stacvol* file to create. The default is STACVOL.DSK.

Earlier section:

Parameters and Switches

/u	Removes the currently loaded resident version of CPSCHED from memory.
/low	Specifies that CPSCHED not be loaded into the upper memory blocks.
/?	Displays the abbreviated online help.

See Also

SCHEDULE

/c=n	Sets cluster size, in kilobytes, for the Stacker drive. *n* can be 4, 8, 16, or 32.
/r=n.n	Sets the maximum size of the Stacker drive by using an estimated compression ratio of *n.n* to 1.
/s=sss.s	Allocates the amount of space in megabytes for the *stacvol* file.
/m	Specifies monochrome display mode be used.
/?	Displays the abbreviated online help.

SEE ALSO

RAMDRIVE.SYS

CSCRIPT

The CSCRIPT command-line tool starts the Windows Scripting Host. It runs batch files written in the Visual Basic Scripting Edition or JScript languages. These batch files can be used to automate common tasks or create macros.

SYNTAX

CSCRIPT /*filename* //i //b //h:cscript //:wscript //logo //nologo //s //t:*nn* /arguments //?

PARAMETERS AND SWITCHES

/*filename*	Specifies the name of the VBScript or JScript file to run.
//i	Sets interactive mode so that the user can respond to any prompts in the script.
//b	Sets batch mode, which doesn't display errors or script prompts.
//h:cscript and //h:wscript	Changes the default scripting host to cscript or wscript (the Windows version), respectively.
//logo and //nologo	Displays the scripting host logo or suppresses it from displaying, respectively.
//s	Saves the CSCRIPT command-line options for the current Windows user.
//t:*nn*	Limits script running time to *nn* seconds.
//?	Displays abbreviated online help.

Notes

CSCRIPT was unavailable with the first Windows 95 release. It first appeared with Windows 95 OSR2.

CTTY 2.0 AND LATER—INTERNAL

You can use the CTTY command to change the standard input and output devices to an auxiliary console or to change the input and output devices back from an auxiliary console to the keyboard and video display.

Syntax

CTTY *device*

Parameters and Switches

device   The device you want to use as the new standard input and output device. This name must refer to a valid DOS character device. Normally, CON is the standard input and output device, which allows you to enter standard input from the keyboard and view standard output on the display. This parameter is required.

Notes

1. The device must be a character-oriented device capable of both input and output. DOS supplies several such devices, including AUX, COM1, COM2, COM3, COM4, CON, LPT1, LPT2, LPT3, and PRN.

2. Typing a colon (:) after the device name is optional. If you don't include a *device* in the command line for CTTY, an Invalid device message is displayed.

3. CTTY does not affect any other form of redirected I/O or piping. For example, the < (redirect input symbol), > (redirect output symbol), and | (pipe-between-programs character) work as usual.

4. The CTTY command is designed so that you can use a terminal or teleprinter—rather than the normal keyboard and video display—for console input and output. This versatility has little effect on most PC users.

5. To return control to the standard console, type CTTY CON on the auxiliary console. If the auxiliary console isn't working or you don't have one connected to your computer, you must reboot to re-enable the standard console.

6. The CTTY command does not affect programs that input and output directly to hardware. Most major software applications fall into this category, so the CTTY command is rarely useful with them.

7. COMMAND also can be used to change the device that DOS uses for standard input and output.

8. Do not attempt to reconfigure Windows with the CTTY command. Windows can be configured to use devices other than the keyboard and video display, but not with the CTTY command.

SEE ALSO

COMMAND

"The CTTY Command" in Chapter 13

CURSOR.EXE

CURSOR.EXE makes a large cursor that is easier to see on LCD screens. You can even change the blink rate.

SYNTAX

CURSOR /S*nn* /C OFF /H

PARAMETERS AND SWITCHES

/S*nn* Sets the cursor blink interval to *nn*/20th of a second, where *nn* can be from 1 to 20.

/C Ensures compatibility with some CGA screens.

OFF Returns to using the built-in hardware cursor.

/H Displays abbreviated help.

CVT.EXE

In Windows 95 OSR2 and Windows 98, CVT.EXE converts a drive from FAT16 format to FAT32. The minimum drive size to convert to FAT32 is 512MB.

SYNTAX

CVT *driveletter:* /cvt32

PARAMETERS AND SWITCHES

driveletter The letter of the drive to be converted.

/cvt32 As a safety measure, this parameter must be included to convert a drive. It helps prevent unintentional conversions.

NOTES

When a drive has been converted to FAT32, Windows and DOS cannot convert it back. Some third-party utilities, such as PartitionMagic, can convert from FAT32 to FAT16. In DOS, the only way to do so is to reformat the drive, destroying all the data in the process.

If you use this drive with other operating systems that are not FAT32-compatible, they cannot read the converted drive.

DATAMON

DATAMON provides protection against accidental file deletion. You can choose from two options to track deleted files: Delete Tracker or Delete Sentry. Delete Tracker saves the name of each deleted file and a list of the cluster numbers it occupied in a hidden file called PCTRACKR.DEL. Delete Sentry saves each deleted file in a hidden directory called \SENTRY.

Syntax

DATAMON /load /low /u /s /sentry+ /sentry- /tracker+ /tracker- /?

Parameters and Switches

/load	Loads the Data Monitor program using the options in the DATAMON.INI file.
/low	Loads the Data Monitor program into conventional memory even if upper memory is available.
/u	Removes the Data Monitor program from the computer's memory.
/s	Indicates which tracking option is active in the Data Monitor program.
/sentry+	Activates the Delete Sentry option.
/sentry-	Deactivates the Delete Sentry option.
/tracker+	Activates the Delete Tracker option.
/tracker-	Deactivates the Delete Tracker option.
/?	Displays the abbreviated online help.

Notes

Either the Delete Sentry or Delete Tracker option can be used at a time. DATAMON has to be added with one of the options to the AUTOEXEC.BAT file.

To disable the option temporarily, use the following commands:

datamon /sentry-

datamon /tracker-

DATAMON should be turned off before starting the Stacker compression program and before running Stacker uncompression.

DATE 1.0 AND LATER—INTERNAL

The DATE command can display and set the current date for your computer. Normally, DOS and your computer's hardware keep the date set properly for you. If you don't have an AUTOEXEC.BAT file, DOS prompts you to enter the current date each time your computer reboots.

SYNTAX

DATE *mon-day-year*

PARAMETERS AND SWITCHES

mon-day-year   The current date in a format consistent with the COUNTRY= setting in your CONFIG.SYS file. *mon* can be any number from 1 to 12. *day* can be any number from 1 to 31. *year* can be any number from 80 to 99 or from 1980 to 2099. In the United States, legal delimiters are the hyphen, period, or slash (/). If this parameter is omitted, the current date is displayed, and you are prompted to enter a new date.

NOTES

1. The date entry and display correspond to the COUNTRY setting in your CONFIG.SYS file. If you are unsure of what format to use for the date, enter the DATE command with no parameters. DOS displays the current date in an appropriate format, and you can use it as a guide when entering a new date at the prompt.

2. When you boot the computer, DOS issues the DATE and TIME commands to set the system clock. If you placed an AUTOEXEC.BAT file on the boot disk, DOS does not display a prompt for the date or time. You can include the DATE or TIME commands in the AUTOEXEC.BAT file to have these functions set when DOS boots.

3. Most computers contain a real-time clock running on a battery. The date should stay set properly as you turn your computer on and off, but it's a good idea to check the date occasionally.

4. When you create or update a file, DOS updates the directory using the current date in the computer. This date shows which copy is the latest revision of the file. Several DOS commands (such as XCOPY) can use the date in selecting files.

5. The day-of-year calendar uses the time-of-day clock. If you leave your system on overnight, the day advances by one at midnight. DOS makes appropriate calendar adjustments for leap years.

SEE ALSO

COUNTRY= and TIME

"Changing the Date and Time" in Chapter 10

DBLSPACE 6.0 AND LATER—EXTERNAL

DBLSPACE starts the full-screen interface to the DoubleSpace disk-compression utility. DoubleSpace automatically compresses information on hard disks or floppy disks and configures many aspects of the compression process. Compression enables you to put more programs and information on a disk.

With switches and parameters, you can control each aspect of DoubleSpace from the DOS command line. The many combinations are covered in the sections that deal with specific DoubleSpace commands.

MS-DOS 6.2 brought a number of new features to DoubleSpace. DoubleSpace can now share the HMA with MS-DOS, thereby decreasing DoubleSpace's size in memory from 43KB to 33KB (or 37KB if the new automount feature is enabled). A DoubleGuard feature verifies the integrity of your data before writing it to disk. Also added is the Uncompress command, which enables you to uncompress a DoubleSpace drive easily. Finally, removable disks can now be automounted, enabling you to work with compressed floppy and cartridge disks from Windows.

SYNTAX

DBLSPACE

NOTES

1. The first time you use the DBLSPACE command, DoubleSpace Setup starts. The setup program enables you to compress one or more hard disks and loads DBLSPACE.BIN into memory. (DBLSPACE.BIN is the device driver that provides access to compressed drives.) Subsequent uses of the DBLSPACE command start the full-screen interface. The full-screen interface and the DBLSPACE switches and parameters give you control of all DoubleSpace operations.

2. DoubleSpace creates a large hidden file, called a *compressed volume file* (*CVF*), on one of your drives, called the *host drive*, and presents that drive as a new drive, called a *compressed drive*. For example, you might make a CVF on your drive D that results in a compressed drive E; you and your programs then can use the files on the compressed drive without taking any special action.

3. CVF names use the format DBLSPACE.*xxx*, where *xxx* is a number (such as 000 or 001).

 4. Normally, after you have started using DoubleSpace on your computer, it automatically loads into memory every time you start your computer. To start your computer without loading DoubleSpace into memory, press Ctrl+F5 (Clean) or Ctrl+F8 (Interactive) when the Starting MS-DOS... message appears on your screen. Because DBLSPACE.BIN will not be loaded, you may not be able to access any of your compressed drives. For more information, see Appendix D, "DOS and DOS Utility Programs' Keyboard Commands."

See Also

"Understanding DoubleSpace" in Chapter 6

DBLSPACE / AUTOMOUNT   6.2—External

The DBLSPACE /AUTOMOUNT command enables or disables automatic mounting of removable drives such as floppy and cartridge disks. This command changes the automount settings saved in the DBLSPACE.INI file. The default setting is for DoubleSpace to automatically mount removable drives.

Automounting makes it possible for you to change compressed floppy and cartridge disks from Microsoft Windows. You cannot use the DBLSPACE /AUTOMOUNT command while Windows is running.

Syntax

DBLSPACE   /AUTOMOUNT=drives

Parameters and Switches

drives   The removable drives that you want DoubleSpace to automatically mount. Enter each drive letter—without a colon—and with no spaces in between. You also can specify 0 to disable automatic mounting or 1 to automatically mount all removable drives. The default setting is 1.

Notes

1. For the automount setting to take effect, you must restart your computer.
2. Specifying 0 decreases the size of DoubleSpace in memory by approximately 4KB.
3. The parameters you specify are written to the AUTOMOUNT= line of the DBLSPACE.INI file.

Examples

To enable automounting of only two floppy drives A and B, enter the following command:

DBLSPACE   /AUTOMOUNT=AB

To disable automounting of all removable drives (and save a little memory), enter the following command:

DBLSPACE   /AUTOMOUNT=0

See Also

"Understanding DoubleSpace" in Chapter 6

DBLSPACE / CHKDSK   6.0 ONLY—EXTERNAL

DBLSPACE /CHKDSK checks the structure of a compressed drive. The command reports errors (such as lost clusters and cross-linked files) and can correct some errors. If you are running DOS 6.2, this command is not available; you should use the SCANDISK utility instead.

SYNTAX

DBLSPACE   **/CHKDSK**   /F   *drive:*

or

DBLSPACE   **/CHK**   /F   *drive:*

PARAMETERS AND SWITCHES

/F   DoubleSpace attempts to repair any errors it finds rather than simply report them.

drive: The letter of the compressed drive you want to check. The default is the current drive.

NOTES

If you run CHKDSK on a compressed drive, DBLSPACE /CHKDSK is invoked automatically after CHKDSK finishes checking the integrity of the drive's file allocation table (FAT).

SEE ALSO

CHKDSK and SCANDISK

"Understanding DoubleSpace" in Chapter 6

DBLSPACE / COMPRESS   6.0 AND LATER—EXTERNAL

DBLSPACE /COMPRESS compresses the files on an existing hard disk, floppy disk, or other removable disk, making more space available.

SYNTAX

DBLSPACE   **/COMPRESS**   *drive:*   /NEWDRIVE=*host:*   /RESERVE=*size*   /F

or

DBLSPACE   **/COM**   *drive:*   /NEW=*host:*   /RES=*size*   /F

PARAMETERS AND SWITCHES

drive: The uncompressed (host) drive that you want to compress.

/NEWDRIVE=*host:*   The uncompressed (host) drive after compression. This parameter can be abbreviated to /NEW=*host:*. If you omit the /NEWDRIVE=*host:* parameter, DoubleSpace uses the next available drive letter. Enter DBLSPACE /LIST to see a list of drive assignments.

| /RESERVE=size | The amount of space (in megabytes) to be left uncompressed on the host drive. This parameter can be abbreviated to /RES=size. The default is 2MB for hard disks and 0 for floppy disks. |
| [ic:C9]/F | DoubleSpace doesn't display the compression statistics screen when compression is complete but simply returns to the DOS command prompt. Use this switch when you are running DBLSPACE /COMPRESS from a batch file. |

NOTES

1. A drive must contain some free space before DoubleSpace can compress it. If you want to compress your boot drive, for example, it must have at least 1.2MB of free space. Other hard disks and floppy disks must have at least 1.1MB of free space (650KB for DOS 6.0).
2. DoubleSpace cannot compress 360KB floppy disks because they do not have enough free space.
3. A compressed floppy disk must be mounted before you can use it. (For more information, see the DBLSPACE /MOUNT command.)
4. If you want to read a compressed floppy disk on another computer, that computer must be running DoubleSpace as well.
5. Your system probably needs some uncompressed disk space because some files (such as Windows permanent swap files) do not work properly if you store them on a compressed drive.

EXAMPLES

To compress drive D so that the compressed part is known as D and the uncompressed (host) part is known as E, and contains 3MB of uncompressed free space, use the following:

DBLSPACE /COMPRESS D: /NEWDRIVE=E: /RESERVE=3

SEE ALSO

DBLSPACE /CREATE, DBLSPACE /LIST, and DBLSPACE /MOUNT

"Understanding DoubleSpace" in Chapter 6

DBLSPACE / CREATE   6.0 AND LATER—EXTERNAL

DBLSPACE /CREATE creates a new compressed drive by using free space on an uncompressed drive. DBLSPACE /CREATE can be used only on nonremovable media, such as a hard drive.

Syntax

DBLSPACE /CREATE *drive:* /NEWDRIVE=*host:* /RESERVE=*size* /SIZE=*size*

or

DBLSPACE /CR *drive:* /N=*host:* /RE=*size* /SI=*size*

Parameters and Switches

drive:	The uncompressed (host) drive that contains the free space from which the new compressed drive will be created.
/NEWDRIVE=*host:*	The new compressed drive. The default is the next available drive letter. This parameter can be abbreviated to /N=*host:*.
/RESERVE=*size*	The amount of space (in megabytes) to be left uncompressed on the host drive. This parameter can be abbreviated to /RE=*size*. To make the compressed drive as large as possible, specify a *size* of 0. If you omit both the /RESERVE and /SIZE parameters, DoubleSpace reserves 1MB of uncompressed space on your disk. You cannot specify /RESERVE if you specify /SIZE.
/SIZE=*size*	The size (in megabytes) of the compressed volume file (CVF) that will be created on the host drive. This parameter can be abbreviated to /SI=*size*. Depending on how well your files compress, the CVF can hold approximately twice as much information as you specify for *size*. You cannot specify /SIZE if you specify /RESERVE.

Notes

1. The DBLSPACE /CREATE command creates a compressed volume file (CVF) with the name DBLSPACE.001 on the drive specified with the *drive:* parameter. If this file already exists, the 002 extension is added, and then the 003 extension is added, and so on.

2. When you use the DBLSPACE /CREATE command, unlike the DBLSPACE /COMPRESS command, the letter with which you refer to the host drive does not change.

3. You can use the DBLSPACE /CREATE command to create additional CVF files on the host drive of a disk compressed with the DBLSPACE /COMPRESS command. However, after you have created a CVF on a disk drive with the DBLSPACE /CREATE command, you cannot use the DBLSPACE /COMPRESS command on that drive without first deleting the existing CVF files. DBLSPACE /COMPRESS reassigns the drive letter you will use when accessing the host drive; it cannot do so if the host drive contains compressed drives.

4. You cannot use DBLSPACE /CREATE on removable media such as floppy disk drives or cartridge hard drives. To compress a floppy disk or cartridge hard disk, use the DBLSPACE /COMPRESS command.

5. Microsoft recommends that you use DBLSPACE /CREATE rather than DBLSPACE /COMPRESS to create a compressed drive on a RAM disk.

6. Your system probably needs some uncompressed disk space because some files (such as Windows permanent swap files) do not work properly when you store them on a compressed drive.

EXAMPLES

To create a compressed drive that has the next available drive letter as its name and uses all the available free space on the uncompressed drive D, use the following:

DBLSPACE   /CREATE   D: /RESERVE=0

To create a new compressed drive F that uses 20MB of free space on the uncompressed drive D, enter this command:

DBLSPACE   /CREATE   D: /NEWDRIVE=F: /SIZE=20

SEE ALSO

DBLSPACE /COMPRESS, DBLSPACE /LIST, and DBLSPACE /MOUNT

"Understanding DoubleSpace" in Chapter 6

DBLSPACE / DEFRAGMENT   6.0 AND LATER—EXTERNAL

DBLSPACE /DEFRAGMENT defragments a compressed drive by moving all the drive's free space to the end of the drive. This command enables you to get the maximum reduction in the size of the drive when you issue the DBLSPACE /SIZE command.

SYNTAX

DBLSPACE   /DEFRAGMENT   drive: /F

or

DBLSPACE   /DEF   drive: /F

PARAMETERS AND SWITCHES

drive: Specifies the compressed drive that you want to defragment. The default is the current drive.

/F   Specifies that you would like the DoubleSpace drive defragmented more fully.

NOTES

1. Unlike defragmenting an uncompressed hard disk, defragmenting a DoubleSpace disk does not improve the disk's performance. Defragmenting only moves the free space to the end of the compressed drive so that DBLSPACE /SIZE can be most effective.

2. You cannot tell how badly fragmented a compressed drive is before you decide to defragment it.

3. How long defragmenting takes depends on many factors, including the speed of your computer, the size of your compressed drive, and the speed of your disk drive. The process can take a long time—perhaps several hours.

4. You can stop the defragmentation process at any time by pressing Esc.

5. To thoroughly defragment a compressed drive, perform the following steps. First, correct any errors on the host and compressed drives by using the ScanDisk utility. Next, defragment the host drive by using the DEFRAG command. Then, defragment the compressed drive by using the DBLSPACE /DEFRAGMENT /F command. Finally, collect all the free space at the end of the compressed drive by entering the DBLSPACE /DEFRAGMENT command. (Don't specify the /F switch.)

SEE ALSO

CHKDSK and SCANDISK

"Understanding DoubleSpace" in Chapter 6

DBLSPACE/DELETE   6.0 AND LATER—EXTERNAL

The DBLSPACE /DELETE command unmounts a compressed drive and deletes its compressed volume file (CVF) from the host drive. If you simply want to delete all the files on a compressed drive, use the DBLSPACE /FORMAT command.

SYNTAX

DBLSPACE /DELETE *drive:*

or

DBLSPACE /DEL *drive:*

PARAMETERS AND SWITCHES

drive: The compressed drive that you want to delete. Note that you should specify the compressed drive, not the host drive.

NOTES

1. Deleting a compressed drive deletes all the files in that drive.

2. If you accidentally delete a compressed drive, you may be able to restore it by using UNDELETE because a compressed drive is a file on one of your uncompressed disks (its host drive). The files corresponding to compressed drives are hidden and have names in the format DBLSPACE.*xxx*, where *xxx* is a number such as 000 or 001. If you can undelete the associated file, you can remount it by entering DBLSPACE /MOUNT.

3. DoubleSpace does not allow you to delete a compressed drive C.

See Also

DBLSPACE /FORMAT and UNDELETE

"Understanding DoubleSpace" in Chapter 6

DBLSPACE / DOUBLEGUARD   6.2—External

DoubleGuard is a safety feature that monitors the integrity of the memory that DoubleSpace is using to minimize damage by a runaway program. This setting is stored on the DOUBLEGUARD= line in the DBLSPACE.INI file.

Syntax

DBLSPACE /DOUBLEGUARD=zero_one

Parameters and Switches

zero_one   Enables (1) or disables (0) the DoubleGuard feature.

Notes

1. If DoubleGuard is enabled and memory corruption is detected, DoubleSpace halts your computer to minimize damage to data on the disk. DoubleGuard is enabled by default.
2. Disabling DoubleGuard (/DOUBLEGUARD=0) may speed up your system a little but could lead to a loss of data if an errant program overwrites DoubleSpace's memory.
3. You must restart your computer for this setting to take effect.

Examples

To turn on DoubleGuard integrity checking, enter the following command and reboot your computer:

DBLSPACE /DOUBLEGUARD=0

To turn on DoubleGuard integrity checking again, enter the following command and reboot your computer:

DBLSPACE /DOUBLEGUARD=1

See Also

"Understanding DoubleSpace" in Chapter 6

DBLSPACE / FORMAT   6.0 and later—External

The DBLSPACE /FORMAT command deletes all the files and subdirectories on a compressed drive but leaves the drive itself intact. UNFORMAT cannot restore the files deleted with this command, so be careful when you use it. To delete the drive as well, use the DBLSPACE /DELETE command.

> **Note**
>
> DBLSPACE /FORMAT is a dangerous command. Formatting a compressed drive is a quick operation, and after you have given DoubleSpace the go-ahead, you cannot turn back. You cannot use the UNFORMAT command to recover a formatted compressed drive. Make absolutely sure you don't need anything on the drive before formatting it.

Syntax

    DBLSPACE /FORMAT *drive:*

or

    DBLSPACE /F *drive:*

Parameters and Switches

    drive: The compressed drive that you want to format. Note that you should specify the compressed drive, not the host drive.

Notes

1. Formatting a compressed drive deletes all the files on that drive.
2. You cannot unformat a compressed drive after performing a /FORMAT operation on it.
3. DoubleSpace does not allow you to format drive C.

See Also

    DBLSPACE /DELETE

    "Understanding DoubleSpace" in Chapter 6

DBLSPACE / INFO   6.0 AND LATER—EXTERNAL

The DBLSPACE /INFO command displays the following information about the specified compressed drive: its host drive, used and free space, actual and estimated compression ratio, and total size. DBLSPACE /INFO can be handy for monitoring the compression ratio on the drive.

Syntax

    DBLSPACE /INFO *drive:*

Parameters and Switches

    /INFO   This parameter can be omitted. If /INFO is included and *drive:* is omitted, information about the current drive is displayed. If both /INFO and *drive:* are omitted, the full-screen DoubleSpace program is run.

drive: The compressed drive that you want information about. Note that you should specify the compressed drive, not the host drive. If *drive:* is omitted and /INFO is specified, information about the current drive is displayed.

SEE ALSO

DBLSPACE /LIST

"Understanding DoubleSpace" in Chapter 6

DBLSPACE /LIST   6.0 AND LATER—EXTERNAL

The DBLSPACE /LIST command displays information about all the local drives connected to your computer, whether or not they are compressed drives. For each drive, the letter, type, free space, total size, and compressed volume file (CVF) filename are displayed. DBLSPACE /LIST can be handy for finding out the host drive for a compressed drive because the host drive is included in the CVF filename. DBLSPACE /LIST cannot display information about network or CD-ROM drives attached to your computer.

SYNTAX

DBLSPACE /LIST

or

DBLSPACE /L

SEE ALSO

DBLSPACE /INFO

"Understanding DoubleSpace" in Chapter 6

DBLSPACE /MOUNT   6.0 AND LATER—EXTERNAL

The DBLSPACE /MOUNT command associates a drive letter with a compressed volume file (CVF) so that you can access the files in the CVF as though they were on a disk. Normally, DoubleSpace mounts CVFs for you, so you must mount a CVF only if you have explicitly unmounted it or if the CVF is on a removable (floppy) disk.

SYNTAX

DBLSPACE /MOUNT=*nnn*   *host:*   /NEWDRIVE=*drive:*

or

DBLSPACE /MO=*nnn*   *host:*   /NEW=*drive:*

Parameters and Switches

=nnn
Mounts the CVF named DBLSPACE.*nnn* on *host:*. This parameter can be abbreviated to /MO=*nnn*. If *nnn* is not specified, DBLSPACE.000 is assumed.

host:
The uncompressed (host) drive containing the CVF that you want mounted.

/NEWDRIVE=*drive:*
If you are mounting a CVF file created with the /COMPRESS parameter (*nnn*=000), *drive:* specifies the drive letter you want to use for the host drive after the CVF is mounted. If you are mounting a CVF file created with the /CREATE parameter (*nnn*>000), *drive:* specifies the drive letter you want to use for the compressed drive after the CVF is mounted. This parameter can be abbreviated to /NEW=*drive:*. The default is the next available drive letter.

Notes

You cannot mount a compressed drive from Microsoft Windows. If you are running MS-DOS 6.2, you can get around this restriction by using the new automount feature, which works while Windows is running. If you are using MS-DOS 6.0, you must exit Windows before mounting a compressed floppy or removable cartridge disk.

Examples

To mount CVF D:\DBLSPACE.001 as the next available drive letter, use the following:

DBLSPACE   /MOUNT=001   D:

To mount a DoubleSpace compressed floppy disk in A as the next available drive letter, enter the following:

DBLSPACE   /MOUNT   A:

See Also

DBLSPACE   /UNMOUNT

"Understanding DoubleSpace" in Chapter 6

DBLSPACE /RATIO   6.0 AND LATER—EXTERNAL

DoubleSpace uses the estimated compression ratio to estimate how much free space a compressed drive contains. By using the DBLSPACE /RATIO command, you can change the estimated compression ratio that DoubleSpace is using for a compressed drive. You might want to change the estimated ratio if you are about to copy to the compressed drive files that differ significantly from those that already are on the drive.

Syntax

DBLSPACE /**RATIO**=*ratio* *drive:* /ALL

or

DBLSPACE /**RA**=*ratio* *drive:* /ALL

Parameters and Switches

=*ratio*	Specifies the new estimated compression ratio from 1.0 to 16.0. *ratio* must be entered with one decimal place (for example, 2.0, not 2). The default is the actual compression ratio for the drive.
drive:	Specifies the compressed drive for which you want to change the estimated compression ratio. DOS uses the current drive unless you specify /ALL. You cannot specify both *drive:* and /ALL.
/ALL	Changes the estimated compression ratios for all mounted compressed drives. You cannot specify both *drive:* and /ALL.

Notes

To view the actual compression ratio for a compressed drive, use the DBLSPACE /INFO command.

Examples

To change all your mounted compressed drives so that their estimated compression ratios equal their actual compression ratios, use the following:

DBLSPACE /RATIO D: /ALL

To change the estimated compression ratio of compressed drive E to 1.7, enter the following:

DBLSPACE /RATIO=1.7 E:

See Also

DBLSPACE /INFO

"Understanding DoubleSpace" in Chapter 6

DBLSPACE/SIZE 6.0 and later—External

The DBLSPACE /SIZE command changes the size of a compressed drive. You might want to make a compressed drive smaller if you need more free space on its host drive. Alternatively, you might want to make a compressed drive larger if its host drive has a great deal of free space.

Syntax

DBLSPACE **/SIZE**=*size* **/RESERVE**=*size* ***drive:***

or

DBLSPACE **/SI**=*size* **/RES**=*size* ***drive:***

Parameters and Switches

=size   The space (in megabytes) that the CVF on *drive:* should take up on its host (uncompressed) drive. You cannot specify both *=size* and /RESERVE=*size*. The default is to make the host drive as small as possible.

/RESERVE=*size*   The space (in megabytes) to be left free on the host (uncompressed) drive after *drive:* is resized. This parameter can be abbreviated to /RES=*size*. You cannot specify both *=size* and /RESERVE=*size*. The default is to make the host drive as small as possible.

drive: The compressed drive that you want to make larger or smaller.

Examples

To change the size of compressed drive E so that its CVF takes up 30MB on its host (uncompressed) drive, use the following:

DBLSPACE /SIZE=30 E:

To make compressed drive E as large as possible so that its host drive contains no uncompressed free space, enter the following:

DBLSPACE /SIZE /RESERVE=0 E:

Notice that when you specify the amount of space to reserve with the /RESERVE=0 parameter, you cannot specify a *size* with the /SIZE parameter.

See Also

"Understanding DoubleSpace" in Chapter 6

DBLSPACE / UNCOMPRESS   6.2—External

The DBLSPACE /UNCOMPRESS command uncompresses a compressed DoubleSpace drive. If you uncompress all the compressed drives in your system, DoubleSpace removes itself from memory.

Syntax

DBLSPACE **/UNCOMPRESS** ***drive:***

Parameters and Switches

drive: The compressed drive that you want to uncompress.

Notes

1. You should always back up all the files on a compressed drive before uncompresssing it. (If anything can go wrong, it will.)
2. You can uncompress a drive only if the files in the compressed drive will fit on the host drive in their uncompressed state.
3. If files in the root directories of both the host and compressed drives have the same names, DoubleSpace cannot uncompress the drive. When this happens, DoubleSpace displays an error message and saves to the DBLSPACE.LOG file a list of the duplicate files involved. After you have resolved all the duplicate root directory filenames by renaming, moving, or deleting the files listed in DBLSPACE.LOG, you can try to uncompress the drive again.
4. After the last compressed drive in your system has been uncompressed, DoubleSpace removes DBLSPACE.BIN from memory. Removing this file can free 40KB to 50KB of memory in your system. The next time you mount a compressed volume file, DBLSPACE.BIN must be loaded back into memory before you can access the compressed drive.

See Also

DBLSPACE /COMPRESS and DBLSPACE /CREATE

"Understanding DoubleSpace" in Chapter 6

DBLSPACE / UNMOUNT   6.0 AND LATER—EXTERNAL

The DBLSPACE /UNMOUNT command breaks the association between a drive letter and a compressed volume file (CVF), temporarily making a compressed drive unavailable.

Syntax

DBLSPACE /UNMOUNT *drive:*

or

DBLSPACE /U *drive:*

Parameters and Switches

drive: The compressed drive that you want to unmount. The default is the current drive.

NOTES

1. You cannot unmount drive C.
2. Use DBLSPACE /MOUNT to regain access to the compressed drive.

SEE ALSO

DBLSPACE /MOUNT

"Understanding DoubleSpace" in Chapter 6

DBLSPACE.SYS (DEVICE DRIVER)   6.0 AND LATER— EXTERNAL

To allow DoubleSpace to perform its compression magic, DOS loads the DBLSPACE.BIN file into memory early in the boot process. Initially, DBLSPACE.BIN is placed at the top of conventional memory. The DBLSPACE.SYS device driver enables you to move DBLSPACE.BIN to its final location in conventional or upper memory. Moving DBLSPACE.BIN to upper memory can save as much as 43KB of conventional memory for your DOS programs to use. To move DBLSPACE.BIN, DBLSPACE.SYS must be loaded in a DEVICE= or DEVICEHIGH= statement in your CONFIG.SYS file.

In MS-DOS 6.2, DoubleSpace can share the high memory area (HMA) with DOS, decreasing the size of DoubleSpace in upper or lower memory to 33KB or to 37KB if the auto-mounting feature is enabled.

SYNTAX

To relocate the DBLSPACE.BIN driver to the bottom of conventional memory, load the DBLSPACE.SYS device driver by using the DEVICE= command as follows:

DEVICE=*drive:\path***DBLSPACE.SYS**   **/MOVE**   /NOHMA

To relocate the DBLSPACE.BIN driver into upper memory, load the DBLSPACE.SYS device driver by using the DEVICEHIGH= command like this:

DEVICEHIGH=*drive:\path***DBLSPACE.SYS**   **/MOVE**   /NOHMA

PARAMETERS AND SWITCHES

drive:\path	Specifies the full path to the DBLSPACE.SYS file on your system. Setup places the DBLSPACE.SYS file in the C:\DOS subdirectory by default. If the full path to DBLSPACE.SYS isn't specified, DOS looks for the file in the root directory of the startup drive.
/MOVE	Makes DBLSPACE.SYS move the DBLSPACE.BIN driver in memory. This parameter is required.
/NOHMA	Prevents DoubleSpace from locating a portion of itself in the HMA with DOS.

NOTES

1. When DBLSPACE.BIN is first loaded into memory, it locates itself at the top of conventional memory. If you let DBLSPACE.BIN remain in that position, a device driver that requires access to this area in memory may overwrite it, crashing your computer. If you are using DoubleSpace, you should always use the DBLSPACE.SYS device driver to relocate DBLSPACE.BIN to a more permanent, safe location.

2. To relocate DBLSPACE.BIN to the bottom of conventional memory, load DBLSPACE.SYS by using the DEVICE= command. To relocate DBLSPACE.BIN to upper memory, load DBLSPACE.SYS by using the DEVICEHIGH= command. Note that you must specify the /MOVE parameter either way. If you do not load the DBLSPACE.SYS driver, DBLSPACE.BIN is moved to the bottom of conventional memory after all other CONFIG.SYS processing is complete.

3. Moving DBLSPACE.BIN to upper memory by using DEVICEHIGH= frees approximately 43KB of conventional memory. If not enough room is available in upper memory, DBLSPACE.BIN is moved to the bottom of conventional memory instead.

4. (DOS 6.2 only) DoubleSpace can share the HMA with DOS, thereby decreasing the amount of upper or lower memory it requires to 33KB or to 37KB if the automounting feature is enabled. You can prevent DoubleSpace from loading into the HMA by using the /NOHMA parameter.

5. If DOS and DoubleSpace are sharing space in the HMA and you are using a disk cache (for example, SMARTDrive), you might want to decrease the BUFFERS= setting to 10. With DoubleSpace in the HMA, there is room for about 10 buffers, so specifying more than this number may cause DOS to locate all its buffers in conventional memory instead.

6. MemMaker optimizes the placement of DBLSPACE.BIN in memory if it finds the DBLSPACE.SYS driver being loaded in CONFIG.SYS. Specifying the /L and /S options with DEVICEHIGH= causes DBLSPACE.SYS to move DBLSPACE.BIN to the specified region(s). Therefore, to MemMaker, optimization for this device driver works just like any other.

7. Unlike most device drivers, DBLSPACE.SYS doesn't remain in memory. After it has moved DBLSPACE.BIN into upper or lower memory, it unloads itself. Therefore, you can install DBLSPACE.SYS more than once in your CONFIG.SYS file without wasting memory. DoubleSpace may insert more than one DEVICE=DBLSPACE.SYS statement in your CONFIG.SYS file to avoid certain problems with network device drivers.

8. You should load DBLSPACE.SYS before loading INTERLNK.EXE in your CONFIG.SYS file. If you load INTERLNK.EXE first, you might not be able to access all the drives on the client computer. In general, INTERLNK.EXE should be the last block device driver loaded in CONFIG.SYS.

9. If DBLSPACE.BIN is relocated after certain network drivers are loaded in memory, your system may begin rebooting when certain DBLSPACE commands are run. If this happens, make sure that the device line for DBLSPACE.SYS comes before all network drivers loaded from CONFIG.SYS.

10. The placement of the `DEVICE=DBLSPACE.SYS` line in your `CONFIG.SYS` file may affect the drive letters used in your system. In general, to allow device drivers to allocate letters that follow the physical drives in the system, load them before the `DBLSPACE.SYS` driver. After `DBLSPACE.BIN` has been moved, it allocates extra drive letters for host drives. Any device drivers loaded after this are assigned drive letters that follow DoubleSpace's drive letters.

> **Caution**
>
> Having drive letters change simply because you added a device driver to your `CONFIG.SYS` file can result in time-consuming chores. Batch files often have to be edited to reflect the new drive letters. All references to drives that have changed must be corrected in your `CONFIG.SYS` and `AUTOEXEC.BAT` files. Microsoft Windows is sensitive to drive letter changes, and some Windows applications will fail if they are suddenly located on a different drive.
>
> Before you add or rearrange `DEVICE=` lines in your `CONFIG.SYS` file, think through the changes you may be making to drive letter assignments. You often can accomplish what you need without changing drive letter assignments.

EXAMPLES

The following lines install a RAM disk and relocate the `DBLSPACE.BIN` driver in upper memory if enough space is available:

```
DEVICEHIGH=C:\DOS\RAMDRIVE.SYS   1450   512   224   /E
DEVICEHIGH=C:\DOS\DBLSPACE.SYS   /MOVE
```

Because the RAM drive was loaded before `DBLSPACE.BIN` was moved, `RAMDRIVE.SYS` allocates drive letters before DoubleSpace. In a typical system with one or two floppy drives and a hard disk (with a CVF), the RAM drive would be D, and DoubleSpace, which normally saves four letters for later use, would use I as the host drive for C.

In the next example, the order is reversed, and the `DEVICE=` command is used to relocate `DBLSPACE.BIN` to the bottom of conventional memory instead of upper memory:

```
DEVICE=C:\DOS\DBLSPACE.SYS   /MOVE
DEVICEHIGH=C:\DOS\RAMDRIVE.SYS   1450   512   224   /E
```

This time, DoubleSpace uses H for the host drive, and the RAM drive will become drive I.

SEE ALSO

DBLSPACE, DEVICE=, and DEVICEHIGH=

"Understanding DoubleSpace" in Chapter 6

DCONVERT

Converts a DoubleSpace- or SuperStor/DS-compressed removable or unmounted disk to a Stacker drive.

SYNTAX

DCONVERT *source target* /c *compressed-volume-name* /g *compressed-volume-name stacvol-filename* /m /?

PARAMETERS AND SWITCHES

source	Indicates the name of the DBL/DRVSPACE to convert.
target	Indicates the name of the STACVOL file to create when using the /g switch.
/c *compressed-volume-name*	Converts the named compressed DoubleSpace volume to the new Stacker format.
/g *compressed-volume-name stacvol-filename*	Generates a STACVOL file in the new format by copying the named compressed volume as a Stacker volume.
/m	Use with either /c or /g on a monochrome monitor.
/?	Displays the abbreviated online help.

NOTES

DCONVERT needs some working space on a disk to convert it, as much as 1MB depending on the situation. If it runs out of space and a WRITE ERROR is displayed, use /g instead to make a converted copy of the compressed volume file on a different disk. Then, use COPY to transfer the resulting STACVOL file to the disk needed.

The attributes of the original file must be changed in order to delete it.

SEE ALSO

ATTRIB

DEBUG 1.0 AND LATER—EXTERNAL

The DEBUG utility tests and edits programs. You can use DEBUG to view and change the state of your computer at the hardware level. Be very careful when using DEBUG because, with just a few keystrokes, you can wipe out your hard drive, destroy files, disable your mouse, lock up the keyboard, and cause all sorts of nasty problems. However, you can also learn a lot about your computer by poking around with DEBUG. This program is a programmer's tool and is rarely used by anyone else.

SYNTAX

DEBUG *pathname parameters*

PARAMETERS AND SWITCHES

pathname The program file that you would like DEBUG to load into memory. If this parameter is omitted, DEBUG starts with no file loaded.

parameters Any parameters that you want to pass to the program file you specified with the *pathname* parameter. You cannot specify *parameters* if you do not specify *pathname*. This parameter is useful only if you are loading program files that accept arguments on their command line.

NOTES

1. The DEBUG utility enables you to load a program into memory and then edit, test, and save the edited program back to the disk. You also can use DEBUG to create small assembly language programs.

2. Most people come in contact with DEBUG only when they are given explicit instructions on patching a particular file. In most cases, this involves creating a text file and then redirecting the input to DEBUG. The SPATCH.BAT file on the DOS 6 distribution disks uses this technique to patch (change) the Windows SWAPFILE.EXE program.

3. Details on using the DEBUG program are beyond the scope of this book. If you want to learn about using DEBUG, check the MS-DOS online help system or the DOS 6 Technical Reference manual.

EXAMPLES

To start DEBUG, simply enter the following:

DEBUG

To start DEBUG and load PROGRAM.EXE from C:\UTILS for editing, enter this:

DEBUG C:\UTILS\PROGRAM.EXE

After you start the DEBUG program, it displays its prompt (the hyphen) and waits for you to enter commands. To quit DEBUG, enter the Q (quit) command.

DEFRAG   6.0 AND LATER—EXTERNAL

Files become fragmented because of the way MS-DOS stores them on the disk. If parts of a single file are scattered over the disk, your disk drive requires more time to find and load all the pieces into memory. DEFRAG rearranges the files on your disk so that each is located in a series of contiguous clusters. Rearranging the files this way makes file access more efficient.

SYNTAX

DEFRAG *drive:* /F /Q /U /S:*order* /B /H /SKIPHIGH /LCD /BW /G0

Parameters and Switches

drive: Specifies the drive to be optimized. If this parameter is omitted, DEFRAG assumes that you want to defragment the current drive.

/F Performs the *full* optimization method, which provides the best optimization but takes the most time. It defragments all your files, moves them to the front of the disk, and puts all the empty space at the end of the disk. You cannot specify the /U or /Q parameters with /F.

/Q (Undocumented) Performs the *quick* optimization method. This method moves all your files to the beginning of the disk and maximizes the amount of contiguous free space on the disk, but your files are still fragmented. You cannot specify the /F, /U, or /S parameters with /Q. This parameter is not documented by Microsoft and may not be available in all versions.

/U Performs the *unfragment-only* optimization method. This method defragments all your files but does not rearrange them on the disk. The empty space is left spread over the disk. You cannot specify the /F, /Q, or /S parameters with /U.

/S:*order* Controls the order of files in their directories. If you omit this switch, the current order of files on your disk is unchanged. The colon (:) is optional. Use any combination of the following values for *order*, without separating them with spaces:

N	Sorts in alphabetical order by name (A to Z)
N-	Sorts in reverse alphabetical order by name (Z to A)
E	Sorts in alphabetical order by extension (A to Z)
E-	Sorts in reverse alphabetical order by extension (Z to A)
D	Sorts by date and time (newest to oldest)
D-	Sorts by date and time (oldest to newest)
S	Sorts by size (smallest to largest)
S-	Sorts by size (largest to smallest)

/B Restarts (reboots) your computer after the files have been reorganized. Make sure you use this switch if you use the FASTOPEN utility.

/H Allows DEFRAG to move a file even if it has the hidden attribute set. (Normally, DEFRAG does not move files with hidden attributes.) Note that even when /H is specified, DEFRAG still does not move files with the system attribute.

/SKIPHIGH Normally, DEFRAG uses upper memory if it is available. Specifying the /SKIPHIGH switch forces DEFRAG not to use any upper memory.

/LCD   Uses screen colors suited to a liquid crystal display. You cannot specify the /BW parameter with /LCD.

/BW   Uses screen colors suited to a monochrome display. You cannot specify the /LCD parameter with /BW.

/G0   Disables the graphic mouse and graphic character set on EGA and VGA screens. (Note that this switch is G and a zero.) By combining /G0 with the /BW or /LCD parameter, you should be able to run DEFRAG on any DOS display.

Exit Codes

ERRORLEVEL Value	Meaning
0	Disk was defragmented successfully
1	An internal error occurred
2	No free clusters (DEFRAG requires at least one)
3	Operation halted by the user (Ctrl+C)
4	Operation halted by a general error
5	Operation halted by a disk read error
6	Operation halted by a disk write error
7	Operation halted by an error in the FAT; use CHKDSK /F
8	Operation halted by a memory allocation error
9	Not enough free memory to defragment this disk

Notes

1. DOS starts DEFRAG in interactive mode if you omit one or more required parameters from the command line.
2. DEFRAG takes over the entire screen to show what it is doing.
3. By default, DEFRAG is loaded into upper memory if enough memory is free.
4. Do not use DEFRAG to optimize network drives or drives created with INTERLNK.
5. If you are using FASTOPEN when you defragment, specify DEFRAG /B so that out-of-date buffers kept by FASTOPEN are not used after the defragmenting operation.
6. Do not run DEFRAG when any other program is running, including Microsoft Windows. If you have any programs resident in memory that might try to access the disk being defragmented, you should disable or remove them from memory before running DEFRAG. An exception is the SMARTDRV disk cache. (You don't have to remove it because DEFRAG disables it for you automatically.) If a program accesses a disk while it is being defragmented, data may be lost.
7. It is a good idea to run a utility such as CHKDSK or SCANDISK before running DEFRAG to correct any logical errors on the drive before defragmenting its files.

See Also

CHKDSK and SCANDISK

"Defragmenting Your Disk" in Chapter 7

DEL OR ERASE   1.0 AND LATER—INTERNAL

The DEL command deletes one or more files from the drive and directory you specify. ERASE is an alternative name for this command. Many times, you can restore an accidentally deleted file by using the UNDELETE command—if you use the command soon enough.

Syntax

DEL *pathname* /P

or

ERASE *pathname* /P

Parameters and Switches

pathname   The file or files that you want to delete. If no drive is specified, the current drive is used. If no subdirectory path is specified, the current subdirectory is used. If only a path (with or without a drive) is specified, all files (*.*) are assumed. Wildcards are allowed.

/P   DOS prompts you before deleting each file. This can make it easier to delete a group of files that are difficult to specify with wildcards.

Notes

1. If you provide a drive name, pathname, or both, and specify either *.* or no name for the filename, the DEL command prepares to delete all the files in the specified directory. Before it deletes them, DOS displays the following message:

   ```
   All files in directory will be deleted. Are you sure (Y/N)?
   ```

   If you type Y, DOS erases all files in the specified directory (but not in the subdirectories). If you type N, no files are erased.

2. If you specify the /P parameter, DEL prompts you before deleting each file by displaying a line such as the following:

   ```
   MYFILE.TXT    Delete (Y/N)?
   ```

   If you type Y, DOS erases the file. If you type N, the file is skipped.

3. You may be able to recover an erased file by using the special DOS 5.0 and 6.0 UNDELETE utility program. Use UNDELETE immediately after accidentally erasing a file.

4. The DOS RECOVER utility does not recover erased files. RECOVER is designed only to repair a file that contains bad sectors or that has a bad directory entry.

Appendix F Command Reference

MESSAGES

```
Access denied
```

Error: You attempted to erase a file that is marked as read-only or that is being used by another program or computer and is temporarily marked as read-only. If the file that you intend to erase has the read-only, system, or hidden attribute set, use the ATTRIB command to turn off these attributes before attempting to erase the file again.

SEE ALSO

DELTREE and UNDELETE

"Deleting Files" in Chapter 8

DELOLDOS   5.0 AND LATER—EXTERNAL

DELOLDOS deletes from the hard disk all files from a previous version of DOS after a DOS 5.0 or 6.0 installation.

SYNTAX

DELOLDOS /B

PARAMETERS AND SWITCHES

/B Forces DELOLDOS to use black-and-white screen mode. You might want to use this switch if you have an LCD display screen or a one-color monitor attached to a CGA adapter.

NOTES

1. When you upgrade to DOS 5.0 or 6.0, the old version of DOS is preserved in part on your hard disk in the directory OLD_DOS.1 and on the Uninstall disks that the DOS Setup program creates. After you are sure that the upgrade works correctly and is compatible with the programs that you normally use, you can delete the old DOS from the hard disk, thereby freeing additional storage space.

2. After you start DELOLDOS, you can exit without deleting the old version of DOS by pressing any key except Y.

3. Be sure that all your programs are compatible with the new DOS before you delete the old version.

4. After running DELOLDOS, you cannot use the Uninstall disks created by DOS 5.0 or 6.0 Setup to restore your previous DOS version.

5. After DELOLDOS deletes the previous version of DOS from your disk, it deletes itself. It really is a one-shot utility.

SEE ALSO

SETUP

DELPURGE.EXE

DELPURGE.EXE permanently deletes deleted files being saved by DELWATCH.

Syntax

DELPURGE *drive:\path\filespec* /A /D:*mm-dd-yy* /T:*hh:mm:ss* /D:-*nnn* /L /P /S /H

Parameters and Switches

drive:\path\filespec	Indicates the drive and directory to delete files from according to *filespec* filename parameters.
/A	Purges matching files without prompting.
/D:*mm-dd-yy*	Purges only files deleted before specified date.
/T:*hh:mm:ss*	Purges only files deleted before specified time.
/D:-*nnn*	Purges only files deleted more than *nnn* days ago.
/L	Lists matching files without purging.
/P	Pauses after each page is displayed.
/S	Includes files in subdirectories.
/H	Displays abbreviated help.

DELWATCH.EXE

DELWATCH is a TSR that monitors file deletions on a drive and saves information about them to allow the UNDELETE command to function in restoring deleted files.

Syntax

DELWATCH /MP*memtype* /MR*memtype* /MBX- /U *drive:..* /B:*nnn* /E:*ext...* /F:*nnn*|All /MB*memtype* /0:*ext...* /D /S /H /HI /HD

Parameters and Switches

/MP*memtype*	Specifies the type of memory that the TSR is to be loaded into, where *memtype* can be X for extended DPMS memory, U for upper memory, or C for conventional memory. /MP*memtype*- specifies that DELWATCH must not use the specified memory type.
/MR*memtype*	Specifies the type of memory that the real mode code is to be loaded into, where *memtype* can be the same options listed for /MP*memtype*. /MR*memtype*- specifies that DELWATCH real mode code must not use the specified memory type.
/MBX-	Specifies not to use XMS memory.
/U	Uninstalls DELWATCH. Allowed only if no drives are enabled.

`drive:...`	Specifies the drive or drives to use.
`/B:nnn`	Specifies how many files in the same directory with the same name can be saved, where *nnn* can be from 1 to 65,535.
`/E:ext...`	Excludes saving files with the extension *ext* for up to 10 *ext*.
`/F:nnn`	Specifies the maximum number of files to save. `ALL` saves all files until the disk is full and overrides the `/B` setting.
`/MBmemtype`	Specifies the type of memory to be used for drive data, where *memtype* can be `X` for extended DPMS memory, `U` for upper memory, or `C` for conventional. `/MBmemtype-` specifies that the specified memory type cannot be used for drive data buffers. Extended memory may not be used if `/MBX-` is specified.
`/O:ext...`	Saves only files with the extension *ext* for up to 10 *ext*.
`/D`	Disables `DELWATCH` on the specified drive or drives.
`/S`	Shows the status of `DELWATCH`.
`/H`	Displays an abbreviated help message.
`/HI`	Displays an abbreviated help message on install switches.
`/HD`	Displays an abbreviated help message on drive-enabled switches.

SEE ALSO

UNDELETE and DELPURGE

DELQ OR ERAQ

DELQ or ERAQ deletes a file or files but prompts you before deleting each file.

SYNTAX

DELQ *drive:\path\filespec* /S /?

ERAQ *drive:\path\filespec* /S /?

PARAMETERS AND SWITCHES

`drive:\path\filespec`	Specifies the drive, path, and filename or file specification using standard wildcards to be deleted.
`/S`	Includes system files if they match the *filespec* to be deleted.
`/?`	Displays abbreviated help.

DELTREE   6.0 AND LATER—EXTERNAL

By using DELTREE, you can delete an entire branch of your subdirectory tree. Unlike RD (or RMDIR), DELTREE deletes subdirectories that contain files. Because you can delete so many files so quickly with this command, you should always be careful when using it.

SYNTAX

DELTREE   *drive:\path*   /Y

PARAMETERS AND SWITCHES

drive: Specifies the drive that contains the subdirectory you want to delete.

path   Specifies the subdirectory to be deleted. All subdirectories and files contained in the specified subdirectory are deleted as well. You are allowed to use wildcards in the *path* parameter, but you must use extreme caution if you do.

/Y   Suppresses prompting for permission to delete each directory specified by *path*. Do not use this switch. A typographical error could wipe out too many files.

EXIT CODES

ERRORLEVEL Value	Meaning
0	Subdirectory was successfully deleted

NOTES

1. This command deletes all files, including hidden, read-only, and system files.
2. DOS prompts you for permission to delete each directory specified by *path*, unless you specify /Y.

Caution   Use great care with the DELTREE command, particularly if you specify wildcards. You easily can delete more files than you intend.

SEE ALSO

DEL or DELETE, and RD or RMDIR

"Using DELTREE to Delete Directories" in Chapter 5

DEVICE=   2.0 AND LATER—INTERNAL

The DEVICE= command loads device drivers into conventional memory. Through the use of installable device drivers, DOS can be expanded to support many features and devices that aren't supported in the DOS kernel. Installation programs often add device drivers to your CONFIG.SYS file for you. DEVICE= can be used only in your CONFIG.SYS file.

Syntax

DEVICE=*drive:\path***filename** *parameters*

Parameters and Switches

drive:\path Although this parameter is optional, you should always include the full drive and path to the device driver file. If you omit it, the device driver file is assumed to be in the root directory of the startup drive.

filename The full filename, with extension, of the device driver to be loaded. Although many device drivers use a SYS extension, this isn't assumed, and the driver file's extension must always be specified. No wildcards are allowed. This parameter is required.

parameters Any parameters that the device driver may require are included after its name. DOS passes these parameters directly to the driver when it is loaded into memory. Some device drivers use case-sensitive or position-sensitive parameters. See the instructions provided with the device driver for details.

Notes

1. If MS-DOS cannot find the specified device driver file, it displays a Bad or missing filename message and continues processing CONFIG.SYS. (See the first message in the "Messages" section for the DEVICE= command.)

2. Device drivers are often sensitive to the order in which they are loaded. DOS executes each DEVICE= or DEVICEHIGH= command in the order in which it appears in CONFIG.SYS.

3. The following device drivers are provided with MS-DOS:

    ANSI.SYS
    CHKSTATE.SYS*
    DBLSPACE.SYS
    DISPLAY.SYS
    DRIVER.SYS
    EGA.SYS
    EMM386.EXE
    HIMEM.SYS
    INTERLNK.EXE
    POWER.EXE
    PRINTER.SYS**
    RAMDRIVE.SYS
    SETVER.EXE
    SMARTDRV.EXE
    SMARTDRV.SYS***

    * CHKSTATE.SYS is used by MemMaker and shouldn't be installed in your CONFIG.SYS file.
    ** PRINTER.SYS is not distributed with DOS 6 but is available on the supplemental disk.

*** SMARTDRV.SYS was replaced by SMARTDRV.EXE in MS-DOS version 6.

All the device drivers in this list can be installed with the DEVICE= command.

> **Caution**
>
> DOS 6 includes two files with the SYS extension that are not device drivers: COUNTRY.SYS and KEYBOARD.SYS. If you attempt to load these files by using the DEVICE= or DEVICEHIGH= commands, your computer may lock up, forcing you to reboot. COUNTRY.SYS and KEYBOARD.SYS are data files used by COUNTRY= and KEYB, respectively.

4. You cannot load normal executable files into memory by using the DEVICE= command. Entering CHKDSK.EXE or even DOSKEY.COM on a DEVICE= line generates an error message (see the first message in the "Messages" section) or lock up your computer. Device drivers are in a special format, and only files conforming to that format can be successfully loaded with the DEVICE= command. If an executable program can be loaded during the processing of the CONFIG.SYS file (not all can), it can be placed in memory by the INSTALL= command.

External commands that load in a DEVICE= command line and run from the DOS prompt as well (such as EMM386, INTERLNK, POWER, and SETVER) are hybrid files that conform to both formats. When loaded from a DEVICE= command in CONFIG.SYS, the device driver portion of the file is loaded into memory. Executing the same command from the DOS prompt runs the executable portion of the file, which typically sets operating parameters or displays the status of the device driver already in memory.

EXAMPLES

Normally, the following two DEVICE= lines appear in CONFIG.SYS somewhere near the beginning of the file:

```
DEVICE=C:\DOS\HIMEM.SYS
DEVICE=C:\DOS\EMM386.EXE   RAM   MIN=0
DOS=HIGH,UMB
```

The DEVICE= lines load HIMEM.SYS and EMM386.EXE into memory, and provide the services necessary for DOS to load into the HMA with the DOS=HIGH,UMB command. Note that the DEVICE= line for HIMEM.SYS must appear before the line for EMM386.EXE because EMM386 requires memory provided by HIMEM to operate.

MESSAGES

```
Bad or missing filename

Error in CONFIG.SYS line number
```

Warning: DOS displays this message if it can't find the file you specified in the DEVICE=, DEVICEHIGH=, or INSTALL= command in your CONFIG.SYS file. *filename* is the name of the file that DOS was looking for, and *number* is the line in CONFIG.SYS where the command is located. Edit the line so that the path and filename are correct and then restart your computer.

```
Unrecognized command in CONFIG.SYS
Error in CONFIG.SYS line number
```

Warning: A line in your `CONFIG.SYS` file contains an illegal command. Usually, this message indicates that you have mistyped the name of a `CONFIG.SYS` command or have placed the ? in an illegal position.

SEE ALSO

`DEVICEHIGH=` and `INSTALL=`

Chapter 19, "Configuring Your Computer"

DEVICEHIGH=   5.0 AND LATER—INTERNAL

With the `DEVICEHIGH=` command, DOS can load device drivers into upper memory space, saving conventional memory for your application programs. To do so, DOS must have a UMB provider, such as `EMM386`, available. Also, the driver must be small enough to fit into the available UMB space. If DOS cannot load a driver specified with the `DEVICEHIGH=` command into upper memory, it loads the driver into conventional memory instead. Not all device drivers can run in upper memory. `DEVICEHIGH=` can be used only in your `CONFIG.SYS` file.

> **Caution**
> Before you begin inserting `DEVICEHIGH=` commands in `CONFIG.SYS`, you should have a bootable floppy disk available. That way, you can always start DOS from a floppy disk if changes you make in `CONFIG.SYS` prevent DOS from booting. Alternatively, with DOS 6, you can press the F5 (Clean boot) key to bypass `CONFIG.SYS` completely or F8 (Interactive) to choose which lines in `CONFIG.SYS` to execute when problems arise.

SYNTAX

In its simplest form, which follows, the `DEVICEHIGH=` command works just like the `DEVICE=` command:

DEVICEHIGH=drive:\path***filename*** parameters

(DOS 6 only) `DEVICEHIGH=` has two additional switches that MemMaker uses to specify the placement and size of the device driver in memory:

DEVICE /L:*region,min;region,min;*... /S =*drive:\path**filename** parameters*

The following alternative syntax is used with DOS 5. Although the following is supported under DOS 6, you are advised to switch to the new syntax whenever possible:

DEVICE   SIZE=*hexsize*   *drive:\path**filename** parameters*

Parameters and Switches

drive:\path Although this parameter is optional, you should always include the full drive and path to the device driver file. If you omit it, the device driver file is assumed to be in the root directory of the startup drive.

filename The full filename, with extension, of the device driver to be loaded. Although many device drivers use a SYS extension, this isn't assumed, and the driver file's extension must always be specified. No wildcards are allowed. This parameter is required.

parameters Any parameters that the device driver may need are included after its name. DOS passes these parameters directly to the driver when it is loaded into memory. Some device drivers use case-sensitive or position-sensitive parameters. See the instructions provided with the device driver for details.

/L:region,min (DOS 6 only) The region in upper memory, and optionally the minimum size in bytes, that the device driver should be loaded into. You can specify more than one region by separating each region from the previous one with a semicolon. For instance, /L:1;2 gives the driver access to UMB regions 1 and 2. /L:1,4096;2,512 further specifies that the minimum size of regions 1 and 2 should be 4,096 bytes and 512 bytes, respectively. This parameter must precede the device driver *filename*. MemMaker sets these values for you.

/S (DOS 6 only) If the /L parameter is specified with a minimum size, /S instructs DOS to shrink the UMB to the specified size and create a new UMB from the remainder. /S must precede the device driver *filename*. This switch is best left to MemMaker's use.

SIZE=*hexsize* (DOS 5) The minimum size block, in hexadecimal notation, into which DOS should attempt to load the driver. (MEM /D can provide the hexadecimal value needed for this syntax.) This parameter must precede the device driver *filename*.

Notes

1. Before using the DEVICEHIGH= command, you must install a UMB provider and then execute a DOS=UMB command. Typically, this means that you must load HIMEM.SYS and EMM386.EXE with UMB support enabled and then specify DOS=UMB (or DOS=HIGH,UMB) before using the DEVICEHIGH= command.

Caution You must install a UMB provider and add the DOS=UMB command before using the DEVICEHIGH= command in your CONFIG.SYS file. That way, you can always start DOS from a floppy disk if changes you make in CONFIG.SYS prevent DOS from booting. Alternatively, with DOS 6, you can press the F5 (Clean) and F8 (Interactive) boot keys to bypass completely or choose which lines in CONFIG.SYS to execute when problems arise.

> **Caution**
>
> If you use other memory managers, such as 386MAX, BLUEMAX, QEMM, or CEMM, use their versions of DEVICEHIGH= and LOADHIGH may be better than using the ones DOS provides. Sometimes, simply specifying DOS=UMB is a mistake. Follow the instructions and recommendations that came with the product you purchased.

2. If DOS is unable to load the device driver into upper memory, it loads the driver into conventional memory instead. No error messages are displayed when this happens. To see what device drivers have been loaded into upper memory, use the MEM /C command.
3. If MS-DOS cannot find the specified device driver file, it displays a Bad or missing filename message and continues processing CONFIG.SYS. (See the first message in the DEVICEHIGH= command's "Messages" section.)
4. Device drivers are often sensitive to the order in which they are loaded. DOS executes each DEVICE= or DEVICEHIGH= command in the order in which it appears in CONFIG.SYS.
5. The following device drivers provided with MS-DOS can be loaded into UMB space with the DEVICEHIGH= command:

   ANSI.SYS
   DBLSPACE.SYS
   DISPLAY.SYS
   DRIVER.SYS
   EGA.SYS
   PRINTER.SYS*
   RAMDRIVE.SYS
   SETVER.EXE

   *PRINTER.SYS is not distributed with DOS 6 but is available on the supplemental disk.

   INTERLNK.EXE, POWER.EXE, and SMARTDRV.EXE all use UMB space automatically if it is available, so you don't need to load them with a DEVICEHIGH= command. CHKSTATE.SYS is best left for MemMaker to handle. HIMEM.SYS and EMM386.EXE minimize their use of conventional memory when they load.

> **Caution**
>
> DOS 6 includes two files with the .SYS extension that are not device drivers: COUNTRY.SYS and KEYBOARD.SYS. If you attempt to load these files with the DEVICE= or DEVICEHIGH= command, your computer may lock up, forcing you to reboot. COUNTRY.SYS and KEYBOARD.SYS are data files used by COUNTRY= and KEYB, respectively.

6. MemMaker can optimize your CONFIG.SYS file for you, inserting DEVICEHIGH= and LOADHIGH commands as needed to load as many device drivers and resident programs into upper memory space as possible. MemMaker also takes care of specifying the correct parameters for EMM386.EXE, ensuring that you have the maximum amount of UMB space available. This can be a big timesaver.
7. Before you start optimizing memory in your system, look at the resident software you're loading to see whether you need it all. For instance, the setup program for DOS

6 installs SETVER.EXE whether or not you use any software that needs to be fooled into working with DOS 6. The cardinal rule is Less is More. Fewer drivers and TSRs mean fewer complicated interactions and fewer problems with load orders and "RAM cram." Look for the balance of features and free memory that enables you to use your system efficiently. Trim your system to the essentials and then let MemMaker optimize it.

8. By default, DOS loads a driver into the largest free UMB and makes the other UMBs available to that driver. The /L switch can be used to fine-tune your configuration by forcing small drivers to be loaded into small UMBs. However, loading a driver with the /L switch gives the driver access to only the UMB specified. Therefore, if the driver requires more than one UMB, you must specify multiple regions by using the /L switch (for example, /L:1;2). To see how a driver uses memory and get a better idea of what values to use with the /L switch, use the MEM /M *driver_name* command.

9. MEM can be an enormous help when you're trying to understand memory usage in your computer. If you redirect the output of MEM to a file with the line

    /C > MEM_USE.TXT

    and then load that file into EDIT, you can page back and forth through MEM's report. With the information MEM supplies, you can easily see how your computer's memory has been divided and which drivers and TSRs are responsible for your "RAM cram" problems.

10. DOS doesn't load a driver in a UMB if the UMB is smaller than the driver's load size. (Usually, the device driver's file size is equal to its load size.) If the driver requires more memory to run, you must specify one or more *min* parameters, which are the sizes of the UMBs that the driver requires when it runs. This procedure forces DOS to load the driver into a larger than normal UMB. Specify *min* in bytes after the corresponding *region* parameter, with a comma between (for example, /L:1,4096;2,512).

11. In DR DOS, HIDEVICE is an alternative command that functions the same as DEVICEHIGH.

EXAMPLES

Before you can use the DEVICEHIGH= command to load device drivers into upper memory, UMB space must be available to DOS. The following lines set the stage for using DEVICEHIGH= on a typical 80386 or 80486 computer system:

```
DEVICE-C:\DOS\HIMEM.SYS
DEVICE=C:\DOS\EMM386.EXE  RAM
DOS=HIGH,UMB
```

First, the DEVICE= lines load HIMEM.SYS and EMM386.EXE into memory. These drivers provide the services necessary for the DOS=HIGH,UMB command, which comes next. Without these three lines at the beginning of your CONFIG.SYS file, the DEVICEHIGH= and LOADHIGH commands cannot access upper memory, so they use conventional memory instead. Note that the DEVICE= line for HIMEM.SYS must come before the line for EMM386.EXE because EMM386 requires memory provided by HIMEM. Neither of these device drivers can be loaded with the

`DEVICEHIGH=` command, but both drivers do attempt to minimize their impact on conventional memory when they load.

Now that everything is ready, use the `DEVICEHIGH=` command to load device drivers into upper memory just as you would use the `DEVICE=` command to load them into conventional memory. For instance, the following lines load the `ANSI.SYS` and `SETVER.EXE` device drivers into UMBs:

```
DEVICEHIGH=C:\DOS\ANSI.SYS
DEVICEHIGH=C:\DOS\SETVER.EXE
```

When MemMaker optimizes your `CONFIG.SYS` file for you, the `DEVICEHIGH=` command lines start looking more complicated with the inclusion of the `/L` and `/S` switches:

```
DEVICEHIGH   /L:1,4096   /S=C:\DOS\ANSI.SYS
DEVICEHIGH   /L:1,1024   /S=C:\DOS\SETVER.EXE
```

At this point, if you want DOS to prompt you before loading `ANSI.SYS` and `SETVER.EXE`, add question marks directly after `DEVICEHIGH` on each command line:

```
DEVICEHIGH?   /L:1,4096   /S=C:\DOS\ANSI.SYS
DEVICEHIGH?   /L:1,1024   /S=C:\DOS\SETVER.EXE
```

Note that making these drivers optional defeats the purpose of optimizing their placement in memory, but it does clearly show that the question mark must be placed directly after the command name, not with the equal sign.

MESSAGES

```
Bad or missing filename
Error in CONFIG.SYS line number
```

Warning: DOS displays this message if it can't find the file you specified in a `DEVICE=`, `DEVICEHIGH=`, or `INSTALL=` command in your `CONFIG.SYS` file. *filename* is the name of the file that DOS is looking for, and *number* is the line in `CONFIG.SYS` where the command is located. Edit the line so that the path and filename are correct and then restart your computer.

```
Unrecognized command in CONFIG.SYS
Error in CONFIG.SYS line number
```

Warning: A line in your `CONFIG.SYS` file contains an illegal command. Usually, this message indicates that you have mistyped the name of a `CONFIG.SYS` command or have placed ? in an illegal position.

SEE ALSO

`DEVICE=`, `DOS=`, `EMM386.EXE`, `HIMEM.SYS`, `LH` or `LOADHIGH`, `MEM`, and `MEMMAKER`

"Loading Device Drivers and TSRs into Upper Memory" in Chapter 19

DEVLOAD

The DEVLOAD command can be used outside CONFIG.SYS to load some device drivers that should usually be loaded in CONFIG.SYS. Not all device drives can be loaded from the command line with this command.

SYNTAX

DEVLOAD *drive:\path\driver.ext arguments*

PARAMETERS AND SWITCHES

drive:\path\driver.ext	The full drive, path, and filename for the device driver to be loaded.
arguments	Any arguments or parameters specific to the device driver being loaded.

DIR   1.0 AND LATER—INTERNAL

The DIR command displays information about files on your disks. It is one of the most commonly used DOS commands. DIR is very handy for trying out complicated pathnames with wildcards to see whether they match the files you wanted.

SYNTAX

DIR *pathname* /P /W /A:*attributes* /O:*sortorder* /S /B /L /C /CH

PARAMETERS AND SWITCHES

pathname	Specifies the file or group of files that you want to display information about. Wildcards are permitted in the filename portion. If no drive is specified, the current drive is used. If no subdirectory path is specified, the current subdirectory is used. If no filename is specified, all files (*.*) are assumed.
/P	Pauses when the screen is full and waits for you to press any key.
/W	Generates a wide (80-column) display of the filenames; the file size, date, and time are not displayed.
/A:*attributes*	(DOS 5 and later) Displays only files with the attributes you specify. If the /A:*attributes* parameter is omitted, DOS displays all files except hidden and system files. The colon is optional. For *attributes*, you can use any combination of the following, but do not separate them with spaces:

	A	Displays files that are ready for archiving (backup)
	-A	Displays files that have not changed since the last backup

	D	Displays only directories (no files)
	-D	Displays only files (no directories)
	H	Displays hidden files
	-H	Displays all files that are not hidden
	R	Displays read-only files
	-R	Displays files that are not read-only
	S	Displays only system files
	-S	Displays all files except system files

/O:*sortorder* (DOS 5 and later) Controls the order in which DOS displays the information about the files and directories. If you omit the /O:*sortorder* parameter, DOS displays directories and files in the order in which they occur on the disk. The colon is optional. *sortorder* can be any combination of the following, but do not separate them with any spaces:

	N	Sorts alphabetically by name (A to Z)
	-N	Sorts by name in reverse alphabetical order (Z to A)
	E	Sorts alphabetically by extension (A to Z)
	-E	Sorts by extension in reverse alphabetical order (Z to A)
	D	Sorts by date and time (earliest to latest)
	-D	Sorts by date and time in reverse order (latest to earliest)
	S	Sorts by size (smallest to largest)
	-S	Sorts by size (largest to smallest)
	C	(DOS 6.0 only) Sorts by DoubleSpace compression ratio (lowest to highest)
	-C	(DOS 6.0 only) Sorts by DoubleSpace compression ratio (highest to lowest)
	G	Groups directories before files
	-G	Groups directories after files

/S (DOS 5 and later) Lists all the specified files in the specified directory and any subdirectories below it.

/B (DOS 5 and later) Lists only filenames with no header or trailer information. This switch overrides /W. When it is combined with /S, the drive and path are included with each filename, but no date, time, or size information is displayed.

/L (DOS 5 and later) Displays directory names and filenames in lowercase.

/C (DOS 6.0 and later) Displays the compression ratios of files on a DoubleSpace volume, assuming an 8KB cluster size. /C is suppressed by /W or /B. This parameter cannot be combined with the /CH parameter.

/CH   (DOS 6.0 and later) Displays the compression ratios of files on a DoubleSpace volume, assuming the cluster size of the host drive. /CH is suppressed by /W or /B. This parameter cannot be combined with the /C parameter.

NOTES

1. DIR now displays numbers with embedded commas, making them much easier to read.
2. By default, the list displayed by the DIR command includes the following information:

   Volume label and serial number

   One directory or filename per line

   File size (in bytes)

   Date and time of the last modification

   Number of files listed

   Total bytes listed

   Number of available bytes remaining on the disk

3. When more than one *sortorder* value is specified, the filenames are sorted from the left value to the right value.
4. You cannot use the DIR command for a drive in which you used the ASSIGN or JOIN command. You must break the assignment before you view the directory for a drive in which you used ASSIGN. You cannot use the DIR command on the guest disk drive involved in a JOIN command.
5. DIR does not report statistics for disk drives in which you used the ASSIGN or JOIN command. For disk drives in which you used JOIN, DIR reports the free space of the host disk drive (the disk drive to which the second disk drive is joined) but does not report the total of the two disk drives. You can remove ASSIGN or JOIN from the drive to find its amount of free space.
6. In DOS 5.0 or 6.0, you can use SET DIRCMD to set DIR switches in the AUTOEXEC.BAT file. If you want DIR to display files and directories a page at a time, enter the following command in your AUTOEXEC.BAT file:

   SET   DIRCMD=/P

   To override the preset switch, use the following format:

   DIR   /-P

   To view the options set with the DIRCMD variable, type the following command:

   SET

SEE ALSO

SET

Appendix B, "DOS Environment Variables," and "Searching for Files with the DIR Command" in Chapter 8

DISKCOMP 1.0 AND LATER—EXTERNAL

DISKCOMP compares two floppy disks on a track-for-track, sector-for-sector basis to see whether their contents are identical.

SYNTAX

DISKCOMP source: destination: /1 /8

PARAMETERS AND SWITCHES

- *source:*   Indicates the source drive to use for the comparison. If this parameter is omitted, the current drive is used. The *source* drive must be a DOS floppy disk drive.

- *destination:*   Indicates the destination drive to use for the comparison. If this parameter is omitted, the current drive is used. The *destination* drive must be a DOS floppy disk drive and can be the same as the *source* drive.

- /1   Compares only the first side of the floppy disk, even if the disk or disk drive is double-sided.

- /8   Compares only eight sectors per track, even if the first disk has a different number of sectors per track.

EXIT CODES

ERRORLEVEL Value	Meaning
0	Disks are the same (success)
1	Disks are not the same
2	Operation halted by the user (Ctrl+C)
3	Operation halted by a fatal disk error
4	Operation halted by an internal error

NOTES

1. If you provide only one valid floppy drive name, DOS uses the current drive for the comparison.
2. If *source:* and *destination:* are the same, DISKCOMP prompts you when disks must be swapped.
3. Compare only compatible floppy disks formatted with the same number of tracks, sectors, and sides. Other types of comparisons will fail or give misleading results.
4. Do not use DISKCOMP for a network drive or a drive in which you used the ASSIGN, JOIN, or SUBST command.
5. Two disks containing the same files do not compare the same with DISKCOMP if the information in the files is arranged differently. For that reason, DISKCOMP is useful only when you're comparing floppy disks that were duplicated with the DISKCOPY command.

Messages

```
Compare error on
Track track, side side
```

Warning: The disks you are comparing are different at the indicated track and side. DISKCOMP does not specify which sectors are different. If you just used DISKCOPY on these disks and DOS reported no problem, the second disk probably has a flaw. Reformat the disk and try DISKCOPY again. Otherwise, assume that the disks are different.

```
Compare OK
```

Information: DISKCOMP compared the two floppy disks and found that they match.

```
Drive types or diskette types not compatible
```

or

```
Incompatible disks
```

Error: The disk drives are of different types (3 1/2- or 5 1/4-inch disks), or the floppy disks are different. The first disk was successfully read on both sides. DOS noticed the discrepancy when it tried to read the second disk.

```
Unrecoverable read error on drive x
Track track, side side
```

Warning: DOS made four attempts to read the data from the floppy disk in the specified drive. The error is on the indicated track and side. If drive *x* is the disk that holds the destination (copied) disk, the copy probably is bad. (The disk has a hard, or unrecoverable, read error.) If drive *x* holds the original disk, a flaw existed when the disk was formatted, or a flaw developed during use.

Run CHKDSK on the original disk and look for the line `bytes in bad sectors`. Even if this line is displayed, the original disk and copy may be good. (The bad sectors may not be used by any of the files on the disk.) When you format a disk, FORMAT detects bad sectors and "hides" them. DISKCOMP, however, does not check for bad sectors; it tries to compare the tracks, even if bad sectors exist. For safety's sake, retire the original disk soon.

```
Invalid drive specification
Specified drive does not exist or is non-removable
```

Error: One (or both) of the specified drives does not exist or is a hard disk. This error can result if you specify only one drive to DISKCOMP and the current drive is a hard disk.

See Also

DISKCOPY

"Comparing Disks with DISKCOMP" in Chapter 8

 **DISKCOPY** 1.0 AND LATER—EXTERNAL

DISKCOPY copies the contents of one floppy disk to another on a track-for-track basis, making an exact copy. DISKCOPY works only with floppy disks.

SYNTAX

DISKCOPY *source:* *destination:* /1 /8 /V

PARAMETERS AND SWITCHES

source: Indicates the source drive to use for the copy. If this parameter is omitted, the current drive is used. The *source* drive must be a DOS floppy disk drive.

destination: Indicates the destination drive on which the copy will be made. If this parameter is omitted, the current drive is used. The *destination* drive must be a DOS floppy disk drive and can be the same as the *source* drive.

/1 Compares only the first side of the floppy disk, even if the disk or disk drive is double-sided.

/8 (DOS 1.0 to 5.0 only) Compares only eight sectors per track, even if the first disk has a different number of sectors per track.

/V Verifies that the copy is correct by reading back all information written to the destination disk. This verification slows the copy process. The /V switch is similar to VERIFY set ON.

EXIT CODES

ERRORLEVEL Value	Meaning
0	DISKCOPY operation successful
1	Operation halted by a nonfatal disk read/write error
2	Operation halted by the user (Ctrl+C)
3	Operation halted by a fatal disk error
4	Operation halted by an internal error

NOTES

1. DISKCOPY now uses the directory that the TEMP environment variable points to if it runs out of memory while reading the source disk. Therefore, if you make single drive copies (for example, DISKCOPY A: A:), you no longer have to swap disks two or three times to make those copies. As long as your hard drive has enough space, DISKCOPY reads the entire source disk before asking for the destination disk.

2. The source and destination disk drives must be floppy disk drives—not hard or networked disk drives, RAM disks, or disk drives in which you used the JOIN or SUBST command. Defaulting to or specifying a nonreal source or destination disk drive causes DOS to return an error message and abort the copy operation.

3. If you do not provide a source disk drive name, DISKCOPY uses the default disk drive. If you provide an improper source disk drive, DISKCOPY issues an error message and aborts.

4. If your system has a single floppy disk drive and you provide only one valid floppy disk drive name, DOS uses that drive as both the source and destination disk drive for the copy. If your system uses two floppy disk drives and you provide only one valid disk drive name, DOS displays the `Invalid drive specification` error message.

5. DISKCOPY destroys any information recorded on the destination disk. Do not use as the destination disk one that contains information you want to keep.

6. To ensure that the copy is correct, run DISKCOMP on the two disks.

7. DISKCOPY ignores the effects of an ASSIGN command.

8. DISKCOPY recognizes unformatted destination disks and automatically formats them as part of the copying process.

9. Write-protecting the source disk is important when you use only one floppy disk drive to make a copy of a disk. DOS periodically prompts you to change the disk. You cannot damage a write-protected source disk if you inadvertently insert that disk when DOS asks for the destination disk.

10. When you use DISKCOPY, DOS reads into memory as much information as possible from the source disk. DOS then copies this information to the destination disk and reads the next batch of information from the source disk. The more free memory is available, the less time you need to copy a disk.

11. DISKCOPY copies whatever level of file fragmentation is on the source disk to the destination disk. To avert this problem, you might want to run DEFRAG on the source disk before copying it or use FORMAT on the destination disk and then use XCOPY to copy files to it.

MESSAGES

```
Drive types or diskette types not compatible
```

Error: The drive types or disk capacities that you tried to use are different and cannot handle the operation, or the destination disk is the wrong capacity. DOS read the first disk, but the drive specified as the destination is not the right type. DISKCOPY cannot create a high-density copy in a double- or single-density disk drive, or a double-sided copy in a single-sided disk drive. Additionally, most high-density drives cannot make a high-density copy using double-density disks.

```
Read error on drive d:
Write error on drive d:
```

Warning: DISKCOPY cannot accurately read or write the disk in drive *d*. The disk is not properly inserted, the source disk is not formatted (or is a non-DOS disk), or the drive door is open. Check these possibilities.

```
SOURCE diskette bad or incompatible
TARGET diskette bad or incompatible
```

Warning: DISKCOPY detected errors while reading the source disk (first message) or writing to the destination, or target, disk (second message). Bad sectors may exist on either disk, or the disk may be in the wrong type of drive.

Determine whether either floppy disk has bad sectors. If so, do not use DISKCOPY on either disk. If the source disk is bad, use COPY *.* to copy files from the source disk. If the destination disk is bad, try a different disk or try to reformat the disk and then use DISKCOPY.

```
Invalid drive specification
Specified drive does not exist or is non-removable
```

Error: One or both of the two specified drives do not exist or are hard disks.

SEE ALSO

DISKCOMP and VERIFY

"Copying Entire Disks with DISKCOPY" in Chapter 8

DISKMAP.EXE

DISKMAP.EXE creates a backup FAT that may aid UNDELETE in restoring deleted files. It is not as reliable as DELWATCH, but it uses less memory.

SYNTAX

DISKMAP *drive:...* /D

PARAMETERS AND SWITCHES

drive:...   Indicates the drive or drives to run DISKMAP on. Specifying a drive overwrites any existing DISKMAP file. Without this switch, the existing file is updated.

/D   Overwrites any existing DISKMAP file with a new one.

DISKOPT.EXE

DISKOPT.EXE optimizes drive performance by defragmenting files and free space and organizing files in a directory in contiguous space.

SYNTAX

DISKOPT *drive:* /S*x* /M*x* /B /O /N /RESTORE=*drive:*\STACVOL.EXT

Parameters and Switches

drive:	Indicates the drive to optimize.
/S*x*	Selects directory sort order, where *x* can be any of the following:

        a Sort by name
        e Sort by extension
        d Sort by date
        s Sort by file size
        n No sort

/M*x*	Selects the disk optimization method, where *x* can be any of the following:

        1 Full Optimization
        2 Full with File Reordering
        3 File Defragment Only
        4 Free Space Defragment Only
        5 Sort Directories Only
        6 Full Optimization with Restack

/B	Uses a monochrome display.
/O	Starts optimization immediately without user intervention.
/N	Does not redefine characters of EGA or VGA systems.
/RESTORE=*drive:*\STACVOL.EXT	Restores an unmounted Stacker drive if optimization was interrupted.

DISPLAY.SYS (DEVICE DRIVER)   3.3 AND LATER—EXTERNAL

The DISPLAY.SYS device driver adds international code page switching to the DOS console device. When combined with the other international utilities that DOS provides, it enables you to display one of six international character sets (code pages) on your EGA, VGA, or LCD screen. DISPLAY.SYS must be loaded in a DEVICE= or DEVICEHIGH= statement in your CONFIG.SYS file.

Syntax

    DEVICE=*drive:**path***DISPLAY.SYS**   **CON:**=(***type***,*hard_cp*,*num_cp*)

    DEVICEHIGH=*drive:**path***DISPLAY.SYS CON:**=(***type***,*hard_cp*,*num_cp*)

To specify the number of subfonts that the display hardware can support, use the following format:

DEVICE=*drive:\path***DISPLAY.SYS CON:=(***type*,*hard_cp*,(*num_cp*,*subfonts*)**)**

DEVICEHIGH=*drive:\path***DISPLAY.SYS CON:=(***type*,*hard_cp*,(*num_cp*,*subfonts*)**)**

PARAMETERS AND SWITCHES

drive:\path — Specifies the full path to the DISPLAY.SYS file on your system. Setup places the DISPLAY.SYS file in the C:\DOS subdirectory by default. If the full path to DISPLAY.SYS isn't specified, DOS looks for the file in the root directory of the startup drive.

CON:= — Specifies that the CON device is being described. The colon is optional, but the parameter itself is required.

type — Indicates the type of display being used. It must be one of the type codes from the following display type table. This parameter must be enclosed in parentheses.

Display Type	type	num_cp	subfonts
Color Graphics Adapter	CGA	0	0
Monochrome Display Adapter	MONO	0	0
EGA, VGA, or Super VGA	EGA	0 to 6	2
IBM PC Convertible LCD	LCD	0 to 1	1

Note that although CGA and MONO display types are allowed, neither of these displays supports code page switching. Loading DISPLAY.SYS for a CGA or MDA display is a waste of memory.

hard_cp — Specifies the hardware code page built into the display, normally 437 in the United States. As long as you specify this parameter, you can always switch back to the default hardware code page built into your display adapter. See Chapter 14, "Understanding the International Features of DOS," for a list of the code pages that MS-DOS supports.

num_cp — Specifies the number of software code pages to allow space for in memory. Valid values for *num_cp* are shown in the previous display type table. If this parameter is omitted, a default value of 1 is used. Specifying 0 reserves no memory for display code pages, which effectively disables code page switching.

subfonts — Indicates the number of subfonts that your display hardware supports for each code page. The default values for this parameter are shown in the previous display type table. If *subfonts* is specified, it and the *num_cp* parameter must be enclosed in a second set of parentheses.

NOTES

1. Load the DISPLAY.SYS driver after any other device drivers that affect the DOS console device. For instance, you should load DISPLAY.SYS after you load ANSI.SYS in your CONFIG.SYS file. Otherwise, the other console driver is likely to disable DISPLAY.SYS.
2. When DISPLAY.SYS is loaded, it reserves memory for itself and for *num_cp* code pages. DISPLAY.SYS itself uses about 5KB of memory, the first code page adds 13KB, and each additional code page requires about another 10KB. In total, DISPLAY.SYS needs 18KB of RAM for one code page, 28KB of RAM for two code pages, and so on.
3. If you do not specify the hardware code page that the display supports, you cannot switch back to it after you activate an alternative software code page. For this reason, you should always specify a value for *hard_cp*.
4. Although you are allowed to specify *num_cp* equal to zero, doing so defeats the purpose of loading DISPLAY.SYS. With no additional code pages in memory, you can't switch to a different one, which is the only reason for using DISPLAY.SYS in the first place. CGA and MDA displays do not support code page switching, so the maximum *num_cp* you can specify for these displays is zero, which once again is a pointless configuration.
5. To display a software code page, you need to perform a number of additional steps. You use the MODE command to prepare and load the code page information into the memory set aside by DISPLAY.SYS. Then, you can use MODE to select the display code page, or you can load NLSFUNC and use the CHCP command to change the active code page for all your devices at once. Additionally, you might want to add the COUNTRY= command to your CONFIG.SYS file to make case conversion and sort order information available.
6. The KEYB utility provides code page support for the input side of the DOS console device. By using KEYB, you can remap your keyboard to conform with various international conventions.
7. PRINTER.SYS performs a similar function for certain IBM printers that support code page switching. It is available on the DOS 6 Supplemental disk.

EXAMPLES

The following line enables an EGA or a VGA display, which uses hardware code page 437, to load and switch to an alternative code page:

DEVICE=C:\DOS\DISPLAY.SYS CON:=(EGA,437,1)

If you want to load DISPLAY.SYS into upper memory with room for two code pages, use the following line:

DEVICEHIGH=C:\DOS\DISPLAY.SYS CON=(EGA,437,2)

Notice that you can use the CON= or the CON:= format. Two subfonts are available in both of these examples because a display type of EGA defaults to two subfonts.

If you have an IBM Convertible LCD display that uses hardware code page 865 (Nordic) and you want to enable code page switching on it, add the following line to your CONFIG.SYS file:

```
DEVICE=C:\DOS\DISPLAY.SYS  CON=(LCD,865,1)
```

Only one subfont is available because that is the default (and maximum) for LCD displays.

SEE ALSO

CHCP, COUNTRY=, MODE *device* CP, NLSFUNC, and PRINTER.SYS

Chapter 14, "Understanding the International Features of DOS"

DOS=   5.0 AND LATER—INTERNAL

The DOS= command offers two options that enable you to adjust the way DOS loads and uses upper memory. If you specify DOS=HIGH, DOS attempts to load itself into the high memory area (HMA). The DOS=UMB command enables DOS to load resident programs into upper memory blocks (UMBs) with the DEVICEHIGH= and LOADHIGH commands. DOS= can be used only in your CONFIG.SYS file.

SYNTAX

DOS=*high_low,umb_noumb*

PARAMETERS AND SWITCHES

high_low   Specifies whether DOS should attempt to load itself in the high memory area (DOS=HIGH) or in conventional memory (DOS=LOW). To load HIGH, DOS requires an extended memory (XMS) manager such as HIMEM.SYS. The default value is LOW.

umb_noumb   Specifies whether DOS should manage upper memory blocks created by a UMB provider such as EMM386.EXE (DOS=UMB) or not (DOS=NOUMB). The default value is NOUMB.

NOTES

1. If you include a DOS= command in your CONFIG.SYS file, you must include at least one parameter with it. To include more than one parameter, separate them with commas (for example, DOS=HIGH,UMB).

> **Tip**
>
> Always specify DOS=HIGH in CONFIG.SYS if your computer supports it. Few programs use the HMA, and loading DOS high can easily free 45KB to 55KB of conventional memory. This is a rare opportunity to get something valuable without losing anything.

2. Although you can enter more than one DOS= line in your CONFIG.SYS file, it's better not to do so. In general, if the combination of parameters specified with more than one DOS= line would be legal on the first DOS= line in the file, you are okay. Sometimes you can specify DOS=UMB after using the DEVICEHIGH= command, but you should avoid doing so when possible. All the load order interactions are too confusing and aren't guaranteed to remain the same from one version of DOS to the next. Use one DOS= line, located directly after the line that loads your memory manager software.

3. You must load HIMEM.SYS (or another extended memory manager) before specifying DOS=HIGH in your CONFIG.SYS file. DOS loads itself into the HMA after all other CONFIG.SYS processing is complete. If the HMA is unavailable or in use at that time, DOS displays an error message (see the first message in the "Messages" section) and loads itself into conventional memory. The HMA is not available on 8088 and 8086 processors, but is available on 80286 computers with A20 line support and at least 1MB of RAM.

4. To allow DOS to load resident programs into upper memory blocks, you must load a UMB provider (such as EMM386.EXE) and specify DOS=UMB in your CONFIG.SYS file. No error message is displayed if DOS is unable to access the upper memory blocks.

EXAMPLES

A typical entry for DOS= in your CONFIG.SYS file follows:

```
DEVICE=C:\DOS\HIMEM.SYS
DEVICE=C:\DOS\EMM386.EXE   RAM
DOS=HIGH,UMB
```

This entry loads DOS into the HMA and enables the use of the LOADHIGH and DEVICEHIGH= commands. Note that HIMEM.SYS and EMM386.EXE must be loaded before the DOS=HIGH,UMB command. The following series of commands uses an alternative syntax to do the same thing:

```
DEVICE=C:\DOS\HIMEM.SYS
DEVICE=C:\DOS\EMM386.EXE   RAM
DOS=HIGH
DOS=UMB
```

Because you can split the DOS=HIGH and DOS=UMB commands, you may be tempted to add other commands between them. The following series of commands is legal, but you should avoid chaotic arrangements like this in your CONFIG.SYS file:

```
DEVICE=C:\DOS\HIMEM.SYS
DOS=HIGH
FILES=50
BUFFERS=20
DEVICE=C:\DOS\EMM386.EXE   RAM
LASTDRIVE=Z
SWITCHES=/W
DEVICEHIGH=C:\DOS\ANSI.SYS
DEVICEHIGH=C:\DOS\RAMDRIVE.SYS
DOS=UMB
```

The use of DEVICEHIGH= before the DOS=UMB command is misleading. Also, if a future version of DOS executes the UMB portion of the DOS= command with the first DOS=HIGH line, UMB support may not be present yet, and the command could fail without displaying an error message. Although this particular series of commands seems to work, other arrangements and commands may cause problems. Because you gain nothing from this type of arrangement, avoid it. Use one DOS= line in your CONFIG.SYS file, located directly after the lines that load HIMEM.SYS and EMM386.EXE, and insert blank lines to make logical groups of commands stand out, as shown here:

```
DEVICE=C:\DOS\HIMEM.SYS
DEVICE=C:\DOS\EMM386.EXE   RAM
DOS=HIGH,UMB

BUFFERS=20
FILES=50
LASTDRIVE=Z
SWITCHES=/W

DEVICEHIGH=C:\DOS\ANSI.SYS
DEVICEHIGH=C:\DOS\RAMDRIVE.SYS
```

You probably will agree that this example is much easier to read and understand than the one before it.

MESSAGES

```
HMA not available: Loading DOS low
```

Warning: You specified DOS=HIGH, but DOS was unable to load into the HMA. Typically, it cannot load into this area because the DEVICE=C:\DOS\HIMEM.SYS line in your CONFIG.SYS file is not present or is after the DOS=HIGH line. Less likely causes are that the HMA is already in use or that HIMEM was unable to gain control of the A20 line.

SEE ALSO

DEVICEHIGH=, EMM386.EXE, HIMEM.SYS, and LH (or LOADHIGH)

Chapter 19, "Configuring Your Computer"

DOSBOOK

DOSBOOK starts the full-screen help utility and online documentation for DR DOS. Normally, you would just enter DOSBOOK at the command line and choose from topics in the menu system. However, you can jump directly to topics using the following syntax.

SYNTAX

DOSBOOK *topic*

PARAMETERS AND SWITCHES

topic   The name of a DR DOS command

DOSDATA

DOSDATA loads the system tables into upper memory or conventional memory.

Syntax

DOSDATA=umb | noumb

Parameters and Switches

umb | noumb   Specifies whether the system tables are loaded into upper memory or conventional memory. The umb parameter loads the system tables (FILES, FCBS, BUFFERS, LASTDRIVE, STACKS) into upper memory if available. The noumb parameter loads the system tables into conventional memory. The default setting is noumb.

DOSDOCK

DOSDOCK enables mobile computer users to use hot or warm docking. The command specified must be any DOS executable format (for example, .EXE, .COM, or .BAT files).

DOSDOCK loads and remains resident waiting for a DOCK or UNDOCK event. You can set the DOCK or UNDOCK environment variable in the AUTOEXEC.BAT file by using the SET command. DOSDOCK can run the SET DOCK= or SET UNDOCK= command only when no other applications, including Windows, are running.

Syntax

DOSDOCK /?

Parameters and Switches

/?   Displays the abbreviated online help.

DOSKEY   5.0 AND LATER—EXTERNAL

DOSKEY enhances the usability of the DOS command line. It adds standard editing capabilities and the capability to recall recently used command lines. It also has fairly extensive macro capabilities, with which you can create command aliases or fast batch files. When DOSKEY is first run, it loads itself into memory and remains there until you reboot your computer.

Syntax

DOSKEY /REINSTALL /BUFSIZE=*size* /MACROS /HISTORY /INSERT /OVERSTRIKE *macroname=text* ...

or

DOSKEY /REINSTALL /BUFSIZE=*size* /M /H /INSERT /OVERSTRIKE *macroname=text* ...

Parameters and Switches

/REINSTALL	Installs a new copy of DOSKEY even if a copy already is installed. This is the only way to resize the DOSKEY buffer without restarting your computer, but the memory used by the previous copy of DOSKEY will be wasted. This clears the DOSKEY buffer.
/BUFSIZE=*size*	Indicates the size of the buffer, in bytes, that DOSKEY uses to store macros and command lines. The default is 512, and the minimum is 256. Increasing or decreasing the buffer size affects how much memory DOSKEY requires when loaded.
/MACROS	Displays a list of the DOSKEY macros you have defined. You can redirect output by using the redirection symbol, >. This switch can be abbreviated as /M.
/HISTORY	Displays a list of all commands currently stored by DOSKEY. You can redirect output by using the redirection symbol, >. This switch can be abbreviated as /H.
/INSERT	Inserts new text into the command line (insert mode on). The default is /OVERSTRIKE. Pressing the Insert key toggles between insert and overstrike modes.
/OVERSTRIKE	Makes new text overwrite old text on the command line (overstrike mode on). This is the default setting. Pressing the Insert key toggles between insert and overstrike modes.
macroname	Specifies the name of the macro that you want to define.
text	Specifies the commands that you want DOS to execute when you type *macroname* at a DOS command prompt. If *text* is null, the definition of *macroname* is deleted.
...	Indicates that you can enter as many *macroname*=*text* definitions as will fit into the current command line. (DOS is limited to 127 characters in a single command line.)

Notes

1. Ordinarily, DOS remembers the last command you typed at the command line. With DOSKEY, however, DOS can store a history of commands in memory. The number of commands retained in memory depends on the size of the buffer (normally 512 bytes). When the buffer is full, DOSKEY eliminates the oldest command to make room for the new command. The buffer contains macros and the history of commands.

2. You can press several keys to recall a command in the history. In addition, you can use many keys and key combinations to edit a command on the command line. These keys and their functions are listed in Appendix D, "DOS and DOS Utility Programs' Keyboard Commands."

3. DOSKEY enables you to create macros. A macro, like a batch file, performs one or more DOS commands assigned to a specific name. After you type the name of a macro and press Enter, the macro executes the commands assigned to the macro name. When you create a macro, you can use the following special symbols:

Code	Description
$g or $G	Redirects output; use instead of >
gg or GG	Adds to an output file; use instead of >>
$l or $L	Redirects input; use instead of <
$b or $B	Indicates piping; use instead of |
$t or $T	Separates macro commands
$$	Places the dollar sign in the command line
$1 through $9	Replaceable parameters; same as %1 through %9 in a batch file
$*	Replaceable parameter that represents everything typed in the command line after the macro name

When you create a macro, you can include any valid DOS command, including the name of a batch file. You can start a batch file from a macro, but you cannot start a macro from a batch file.

EXAMPLES

With DOSKEY installed, you can easily turn the last few DOS commands that you typed into a batch file. Simply ask DOSKEY to display the contents of the command-line history buffer and redirect the output to a file as follows:

```
DOSKEY /HISTORY > MYHIST.BAT
```

Next, load MYHIST.BAT into an ASCII editor such as EDIT and remove any command lines that you don't need.

To define a macro, enter the name of the macro followed by the commands you want executed. Separate the macro name from the commands with an equal sign. For example, the following creates a macro named CDD that changes the current drive and current directory:

```
DOSKEY CDD=$1: $T CD $2
```

After the CDD macro is defined, you could enter the following command at the DOS prompt to make drive D the current drive and \MYSTUFF the current directory on drive D:

```
C:\>CDD D \MYSTUFF
```

When the preceding command is executed, the CDD macro runs and executes the following DOS commands:

```
C:\>D:
D:\>CD \MYSTUFF
D:\MYSTUFF>
```

Messages

```
Cannot change BUFSIZE
```

Error: You cannot change the DOSKEY buffer unless you also use the /REINSTALL switch, which clears the buffer.

```
Insufficient memory to store macro.
Use the DOSKEY command with the /BUFSIZE switch to increase available memory.
```

Warning: Your DOSKEY macros have filled the total space set aside for them. You must enlarge the memory area for macros (the default is 512 bytes) by using the BUFSIZE switch (and the /REINSTALL switch) before you can enter any new macros. Using REINSTALL clears the buffer.

```
Invalid macro definition
```

Error: You entered an illegal character or command with DOSKEY or attempted to create a DOSKEY macro with an illegal definition. This message appears, for example, if you use a GOTO command in a DOSKEY macro. Correct any errors and carefully retype the macro.

See Also

Chapter 18, "Mastering DOSKEY and Macros" and Appendix D, "DOS and DOS Utility Programs' Keyboard Commands"

DOSSHELL   4.0 to 6.0—External

The DOSSHELL command starts the DOS Shell program, which is a full-screen graphical shell program that provides an alternative to using the traditional DOS command line. DOSSHELL is not included in the standard DOS 6.22 package but is available on the DOS 6.22 Supplemental disk.

Syntax

DOSSHELL /B /T:*screen* /G:*screen*

Parameters and Switches

/B	Starts the DOS Shell in black-and-white mode rather than in color.
/T:*screen*	Displays the DOS Shell in text mode, using the resolution described by *screen*. (See the screen table below.) You cannot specify /T:*screen* with /G:*screen*.
/G:*screen*	Displays the DOS Shell in graphics mode, using the resolution described by *screen*. (See the following table.) You cannot specify /G:*screen* with /T:*screen*.

Switch	Monochrome or CGA	EGA	VGA
/T:L	25 lines	25 lines	25 lines
/T:M		43 lines	43 lines

/T:M1		43 lines	43 lines
/T:M2		43 lines	50 lines
/T:H		43 lines	43 lines
/T:H1		43 lines	43 lines
/T:H2		43 lines	50 lines
/G:L	25 lines	25 lines	25 lines
/G:M		43 lines	30 lines
/G:M1		43 lines	30 lines
/G:M2		43 lines	34 lines
/G:H		43 lines	43 lines
/G:H1		43 lines	43 lines
/G:H2		43 lines	60 lines

NOTES

1. When you start the DOS Shell without parameters, it uses the display and color settings from the last time DOSSHELL was run. To use a different display mode, specify a /T:*screen* or /G:*screen* parameter when you start the program. DOS Shell records these settings in the DOSSHELL.INI file.

2. At least 384KB of free conventional memory are required to start the DOS Shell.

3. Each time you start the DOS Shell, it searches the disk for directories and files to display up-to-date listings in file and tree windows. If you have a large hard disk or a complicated directory structure, this search may take a few seconds.

4. Do not start Microsoft Windows from the DOS Shell. If you need to run both programs, start Microsoft Windows first and then run the DOS Shell from Windows.

5. Your DOSSHELL settings are preserved in your DOSSHELL.INI file. The DOS 6.0 installation does not overwrite or modify this file if it exists, which may produce inconsistencies on your system (references to BACKUP rather than to MSBACKUP, for example). You can avoid these inconsistencies by renaming DOSSHELL.INI before you install DOS 6.0 and then manually editing changes from the renamed DOSSHELL.INI into the new DOSSHELL.INI.

   When the DOS 6.0 Setup program installs DOSSHELL, it expands one of three files (CGA.IN_ for CGA monitors, EGA.IN_ for EGA and VGA monitors, or MONO.IN_ for monochrome monitors) from the DOS 6.0 distribution disks and renames it DOSSHELL.INI. To restore your DOS Shell configuration to its defaults, you can expand one of these three files (by using EXPAND) and replace your present copy of DOSSHELL.INI with it.

6. By defining an environment variable named DOSSHELL, you can specify where you would like DOSSHELL.INI to be located. For instance, to store the DOSSHELL.INI file in the C:\DOS\MSDOSDATA subdirectory, you could add the following SET command to your

AUTOEXEC.BAT file.

```
SET DOSSHELL=C:\DOS\MSDOSDATA
```

If no environment variable named DOSSHELL is defined, DOS Shell searches for its settings file in the directory that contains DOSSHELL.EXE. If DOSSHELL.INI cannot be found, a new one is created.

7. DOS Shell creates any temporary files, including task swapping files, in the subdirectory pointed to by the TEMP environment variable if it is defined. If TEMP isn't defined, temporary files are created in the subdirectory that contains DOSSHELL.EXE.

8. If you are running POWER, the clock displayed in the DOS Shell program may slow down or stop completely. DOS Shell uses a timer to update the onscreen clock, and POWER slows down the timer. Note that only the onscreen clock displayed by DOS Shell is affected. The MS-DOS system clock continues to reflect the correct time.

9. In DOS 4.0, DOS Shell was started by a batch file that recorded all the configuration information needed to run DOS Shell on your system. This version of the DOS Shell was very different from later versions, and most of the information presented here doesn't apply to it.

EXAMPLES

To start the DOS Shell in the default screen mode, enter the following:

```
DOSSHELL
```

To start the DOS Shell in black-and-white mode, enter the following:

```
DOSSHELL /B
```

Use this command if you have a black-and-white monitor or a laptop or notebook computer with an LCD screen.

MESSAGES

```
Not enough memory to run DOSSHELL
```

Error: Not enough conventional memory is available to start DOSSHELL. The DOS Shell program requires 384KB of free conventional RAM to load into memory. You may have too many resident programs (TSRs) loaded into memory, in which case you should attempt to remove any that you don't need. You may be trying to start DOSSHELL from a secondary copy of the command processor launched from another program, in which case you should type EXIT to return to your program, quit the program, and then run DOSSHELL.

```
Not enough free conventional memory to run program
```

or

```
Not enough free extended memory to run program
```

Either of these messages can appear when you try to start a program from the DOS Shell without sufficient available memory. Remove TSRs from memory to free conventional memory. If you are short of extended memory, use MEM /C to see what programs are using extended memory in your computer. Often you can make more extended memory available by decreasing the size of your SMARTDRV disk cache or by allocating less memory to use as expanded memory with EMM386.

```
Unable to run specified program.
Too many tasks running.
```

Error: You have already opened the maximum number of tasks for your configuration. Close one or more of the open tasks.

```
Unable to run specified program.
```

Error: The program that you tried to start cannot be started correctly. You may have specified the program name incorrectly.

```
You cannot quit MS-DOS Shell with programs in the Active Task List; quit those
programs first.
```

Error: You tried to exit the DOS Shell while at least one program was switched. Exit the switched program and then quit the DOS Shell.

SEE ALSO

Chapter 4, "Using the DOS Shell"

DPMI

DPMI temporarily loads or unloads DOS Protected Mode Interface support for the EMM memory manager. DPMI is normally handled through a switch on the EMM386 drive in the CONFIG.SYS file. This enables you to unload or load it from the command line.

SYNTAX

DPMI ON|OFF /H

PARAMETERS AND SWITCHES

ON|OFF   ON loads DPMI support; OFF unloads it.

/H   Displays abbreviated help.

DPMS.EXE

DPMS.EXE allows most of the Stacker driver to be stored in extended memory, freeing conventional and upper memory for other programs.

SYNTAX

DEVICE=c:\stacker\dpms.exe /?

Parameters and Switches

/?   Displays the abbreviated online help.

Notes

DPMS requires at least a 386 computer with more than 1MB of RAM and a memory manager that provides Virtual Control Program Interface (VCPI) services.

DPMS does not work unless the DPMS.EXE file is stored on the hard disk and referenced by a DEVICE= line in the CONFIG.SYS file.

Examining the CONFIG.SYS file and messages shown when the computer is started helps determine whether DPMS is used.

Stacker Setup automatically uses DPMS when possible. However, if STACKER.INI contains an /EMS, /UM, or /-DPMS switch, Stacker does not use DPMS. Stacker Setup adds the EMS switch only if DPMS cannot be used and if a large drive (more than 400MB) is compressed.

To use EMS, delete any switches that enable DPMS. Using expanded memory (EMS) requires a special memory manager, such as EMM386.

DRIVER.SYS (DEVICE DRIVER)   3.2 AND LATER— EXTERNAL

The DRIVER.SYS device driver can be used to create an additional drive letter for a floppy disk drive or set the characteristics of a floppy disk drive. For instance, if an external floppy drive is attached to your computer, you can use DRIVER.SYS (or DRIVPARM=) to tell DOS to assign a drive letter to the drive. A more common use is to create a new drive letter— perhaps one with different characteristics—for a drive.

Syntax

DEVICE=drive:\path**DRIVER.SYS**   **/D:**num   /C   /F:type   /H:heads   /S:sectors   /T:tracks

or

DEVICEHIGH=drive:\path**DRIVER.SYS**   **/D:**num   /C   /F:type   /H:heads   /S:sectors   /T:tracks

Parameters and Switches

drive:\path\   Specifies the full path to the DRIVER.SYS file on your system. Setup places the DRIVER.SYS file in the C:\DOS subdirectory by default. If the full path to DRIVER.SYS isn't specified, DOS looks for the file in the root directory of the startup drive.

/D:num   Specifies the physical drive number (num). Valid numbers are 0 to 127. DOS assigns floppy drive numbers sequentially, with the first floppy drive as 0, the second as 1, the third as 2, and so on. Note that if you have only one floppy disk drive installed, DOS assigns it both letters A and B, but it is still drive 0, not drive 1. This parameter is required, and must be the first parameter specified after the name and location of the DRIVER.SYS file.

/C Specifies that the drive has change line support. This means that the drive can signal DOS that the medium in it may have been changed. Most newer floppy disk drives have change line support built in. Specifying the /C parameter can speed up access to your floppy drive.

/F:*type* Indicates the type of drive that is being accessed, where *type* is one of the values in the following table. If you omit this value, a default value of 2 (720KB 3 1/2-inch) is assumed.

type	Floppy Drive Specifications	Heads (Sides)	Sectors per Track	Tracks per Head (Side)
0	Double-density 360KB 5 1/4-inch floppy disk drive; includes 160KB, 180KB, 320KB, and 360KB formatted media sizes	2	9	40
1	High-density 1.2MB 5 1/4-inch floppy disk drive	2	15	80
2	Double-density 720KB 3 1/2-inch floppy disk drive	2	9	80
7	High-density 1.44MB 3 1/2-inch floppy disk drive	2	18	80
9	Super high-density 2.88MB 3 1/2-inch floppy disk drive	2	36	80

/H:*heads* Specifies the number of read/write heads (sides) that the drive has. Valid values are 1 to 99. The default value is 2.

/S:*sectors* Specifies the number of sectors per track for the drive's media. Valid values are 1 to 99. The default value depends on the /F:*type* setting or is 9 if /F:*type* is omitted. See the preceding table.

/T:*tracks* Specifies the number of tracks per side (head) for the drive's media. Valid values are 1 to 999. The default value depends on the /F:*type* setting or is 80 if /F:*type* is omitted. See the preceding table.

Notes

1. DOS assigns drive letters in a specific order. A and B always refer to the first one or two floppy drives in the system. If the system has a hard disk, the primary partition is assigned the letter C. Next, any remaining hard disk partitions are assigned letters. After that, each DOS-accessible block device driver listed in CONFIG.SYS is assigned a letter on a first-come, first-served basis. (If DoubleSpace is loaded, it modifies this assignment order by skipping four letters and then working backward. See DBLSPACE for more information.)

   For instance, if you have two floppy drives and one hard disk (with a single partition) and you include a single DRIVER.SYS line in your CONFIG.SYS file, the letter D would be assigned. DRIVER.SYS displays a message informing you of the letter assigned when it is installed. (See the first message in the "Messages" section.)

2. Most newer floppy disk drives can signal the computer when their drive door has been opened. Because opening the door implies that the disk in the drive may have been changed, this feature is referred to as *change line support*. Unless you are installing a 360KB 5 1/4-inch disk drive, the chances are good that your new floppy drive has change line support built in. Specifying the /C parameter can speed up DOS access to the drive.

3. MS-DOS 6 seems to have problems recognizing that the medium in a drive has changed when the medium does not have a volume serial number. Disks most likely to not have serial numbers are ones formatted by DOS versions before 4.0, preformatted disks, and disks formatted with some third-party utilities. This is a good reason to make sure that the hardware change line is working for your disk drive. If DOS is unaware that you have changed the disk in a floppy disk drive, it may write the wrong file allocation table (FAT) to the disk, destroying any data that was previously stored on it.

4. If you specify the /F:*type* parameter, you can omit the /H:*heads*, /S:*sectors*, and /T:*tracks* parameters, and vice versa. You can use any combination of these parameters; the last ones entered have precedence.

5. Many times, the DRIVER.SYS device driver is simpler and more flexible to use than DRIVPARM=, although both often achieve the same results. They can both configure logical drives, but only DRIVER.SYS can create a new one. DRIVPARM=, however, uses no additional memory in your system.

6. You cannot use DRIVER.SYS to reconfigure an existing drive to support a format it was not made for. For instance, DRIVER.SYS cannot be used to allow an older 360KB 5 1/2-inch disk drive to read the newer 1.2MB disks. DRIVER.SYS can instruct DOS to make use of only the capabilities that both DOS and the drive support.

Examples

Suppose that your system has two 5 1/4-inch disk drives and a hard disk. To configure an external 1.44MB 3 1/2-inch floppy disk drive that you have attached to your system, enter a line such as the following in your CONFIG.SYS file:

DEVICE=C:\DOS\DRIVER.SYS /D:2 /F:7

After loading, DRIVER.SYS displays the following message: Loaded External Disk Driver for Drive D.

Or, if your system has a single 1.44MB 3 1/2-inch floppy and a hard drive, you might want to create an alias for the floppy drive so that you can format 720KB disks without specifying any switches for FORMAT. To create a 720KB alias for it, you might enter the following line in your CONFIG.SYS file:

DEVICEHIGH=C:\DOS\DRIVER.SYS /D:0 /F:2

As far as DOS is concerned, drive D refers to a 720KB 3 1/2-inch floppy drive. Drives A and B are unchanged and refer to a 1.44MB 3 1/2-inch floppy drive. All three drive letters refer to the same physical drive, but D has different characteristics from A and B.

Messages

Loaded External Disk Driver for Drive *letter*

Information: After installing DRIVER.SYS, DOS displays this message to tell you which drive letter has been assigned.

See Also

DRIVPARM=

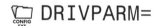

DRIVPARM=   3.2 AND LATER—INTERNAL

DRIVPARM is an advanced command that defines the characteristics of an existing block device, such as a disk drive, and associates a drive letter with it. Normally, you use this command only when instructed to do so by the manufacturer of the drive you are installing. DRIVPARM= can be used only in your CONFIG.SYS file.

Syntax

DRIVPARM=/D:*num*   /C   /F:*type*   /H:*heads*   /I   /N   /S:*sectors*   /T:*tracks*

Parameters and Switches

/D:*num*   Specifies the physical drive number (*num*). Valid numbers are 0 to 255, where drive A is 0, drive B is 1, drive C is 2, and so on. This parameter is required and must be the first parameter on the command line.

Switch	Description
/C	Specifies that the drive has change line support. This means that the drive can signal DOS that the medium in it may have been changed. Most newer floppy disk drives have change line support built in. Specifying the /C parameter can speed up access to your floppy drive.
/F:*type*	Indicates the type of drive that is being accessed, where *type* is one of the values in the following table. If you omit this value, a default value of 2 (720KB 3 1/2-inch) is used.

type	Drive Specifications
0	A double-density 360KB 5 1/4-inch floppy disk drive; includes 160KB, 180KB, 320KB, and 360KB formatted media sizes
1	A high-density 1.2MB 5 1/4-inch floppy disk drive
2	A double-density 720KB 3 1/2-inch floppy disk drive
5	A hard disk
6	A tape drive
7	A high-density 1.44MB 3 1/2-inch floppy disk drive
8	A read-write optical disk drive
9	A super high-density 2.88MB 3 1/2-inch floppy disk drive

Note that types 3 and 4, which formerly specified single-density and double-density 8-inch floppy disk drives, respectively, are no longer supported by MS-DOS.

Switch	Description
/H:*heads*	Specifies the number of read/write heads (sides) that the drive has. Valid values are 1 to 99. The default value depends on the /F:*type* setting.
/I	Indicates that a 3 1/2-inch disk drive, which the ROM BIOS doesn't support, is attached to a standard floppy disk drive controller.
/N	Indicates that this drive uses nonremovable media. This switch is assumed if /F:5 (hard disk) is specified.
/S:*sectors*	Specifies the number of sectors per track for the drive's media. Valid values are 1 to 99. The default value depends on the /F:*type* setting.
/T:*tracks*	Specifies the number of tracks per side (head) for the drive's media. Valid values are 1 to 999. The default value depends on the /F:*type* setting.

NOTES

1. In many cases, the DRIVER.SYS device driver is simpler and more flexible to use than DRIVPARM=, although both often achieve the same results. They can both configure logical drives, but only DRIVER.SYS can create a new one. However, DRIVPARM= uses no additional memory in your system.

2. In most cases, the DRIVPARM= line should come immediately after the line that loads the device driver for the drive you are configuring. Normally, the instructions for installing the drive's device driver tell you which parameters to use with DRIVPARM=. An exception occurs when you are adding support for a 3 1/2-inch floppy drive attached to a standard floppy controller, which requires no device driver.

3. Most newer floppy disk drives can signal the computer when their drive door has been opened. Because opening the door implies that the disk in the drive may have been changed, this feature is referred to as *change line support.* Unless you are installing a 360KB 5 1/4-inch disk drive, the chances are good that your new floppy drive has change line support built in. Specifying the /C parameter can speed up DOS access to the drive.

4. MS-DOS 6 seems to have problems recognizing that the medium in a drive has changed when the medium does not have a volume serial number. Disks most likely to not have serial numbers are ones formatted by DOS versions before 4.0, preformatted disks, and disks formatted with some third-party utilities. This is a good reason to make sure that the hardware change line is working for your disk drive. If DOS is unaware that you have changed the disk in a floppy disk drive, it may write the wrong file allocation table (FAT) to the disk, destroying any data that was previously stored on it.

5. Do not use DRIVPARM= unless the installation instructions for the hardware or software you are installing in your system tells you to do so. Normally, DRIVPARM= can be used only to support additions to your system rather than reconfigure existing hardware or software.

6. You cannot use DRIVER.SYS to reconfigure an existing drive to support a format it was not made for. For instance, DRIVER.SYS cannot be used to allow an older 360KB 5 1/2-inch disk drive to read the newer 1.2MB disks. DRIVER.SYS can instruct DOS to make use of only the capabilities that both DOS and the drive support.

EXAMPLES

Probably the most common use of the DRIVPARM= command is to create a drive letter for a 3 1/2-inch floppy disk drive that is not supported by the ROM BIOS in that computer. The following line defines the 3 1/2-inch 1.44MB floppy disk drive as drive D (3), using the default values for heads, sectors, and tracks:

```
DRIVPARM=/D:3  /F:7  /I
```

If the floppy disk drive were the second one in your system and supported only 720KB media, you would use the following line:

```
DRIVPARM=/D:1  /I
```

Note that you can omit the /F:2 because, in this case, the default value is correct. If you run the preceding command on a system in which the second floppy drive is a 1.44MB 3 1/2-inch drive, you can read only 720KB disks; you cannot read 1.44MB disks.

SEE ALSO

DRIVER.SYS

DRMOUSE

The DRMOUSE driver detects a serial or PS2 mouse and loads support for it.

SYNTAX

DRMOUSE /P /C /L /R*nm* /U /H

PARAMETERS AND SWITCHES

/P	Forces PS2 port.
/C	Forces the COM port to automatically detect the mouse.
/L	Changes the mouse direction for left-hand use instead of the right-hand default.
/R*nm*	Sets the resolution manually, where *n* and *m* are the horizontal and vertical resolution in numbers from 1 to 9. /R0 specifies to use the hardware's default resolution.
/U	Unloads the mouse driver.
/H	Displays abbreviated help.

DRVLOCK

DRVLOCK locks or unlocks the specified drive or socket. When used to lock a drive, it secures the medium. When used to lock a socket, it prevents PCMCIA PC Card removal.

SYNTAX

DRVLOCK *drive:*|*socket:* /on |/off /?

PARAMETERS AND SWITCHES

drive:	Specifies a drive to lock or unlock. If no drive or socket is specified, DRVLOCK defaults to the current drive.
socket:	Specifies a PCMCIA socket to be locked or unlocked. If no drive or socket is specified, DRVLOCK defaults to the current drive.
/on	Turns lock on.
/off	Turns lock off.
/?	Displays the abbreviated online help.

DYNALOAD

DYNALOAD enables you to dynamically load a device driver from the DOS command prompt.

SYNTAX

To load the device driver into low memory, use the following syntax:

DYNALOAD *device_driver* *parm1 parm2* ...   /?]

To load the device driver into high memory, use the following syntax:

LOADHIGH DYNALOAD *device_driver* *parm1 parm2* ...   /?]

PARAMETERS AND SWITCHES

device_driver   Specifies the drive, path, and filename of the device driver to be loaded.

parm1 parm2 ....   Specifies any command-line parameters required by the device driver for proper execution.

/?   Displays the abbreviated online help.

NOTES

DYNALOAD cannot be run in a Windows Virtual DOS Machine (VDM) when task swapping is active or when DESQview is active.

DYNALOAD works with the following DOS device drivers:

ANSI.SYS	SETVER.EXE
CMOSCLK.SYS	SMARTDRV.EXE
CNFIGNAM.EXE	STACHIGH.SYS
DISPLAY.SYS	UMBCGA.SYS
DRIVER.SYS	UMBEMS.SYS
EMM386.EXE	UMBHERC.SYS
HIMEM.SYS	UMBMONO.SYS
SCREATE.SYS	

E

The E command starts the PC DOS E Editor, a full-screen editor used to create, edit, save, and print ASCII text files.

SYNTAX

E /q /b /s /d /i /c /a /dm /80|/132 *drive:\path\filename* =*filename* /?

Parameters and Switches

`drive:\path\filename`	Specifies the drive, directory, and file to edit. Multiple files can be edited at one time. Each file requires its drive and path specification.
`/q`	Turns off the display of the `Loading...` message.
`/b`	Displays files in browse (read-only) mode.
`/s`	Uses EMS (or hardfile if no EMS is available) to edit files too large for conventional memory.
`/d`	Forces a file to be loaded from disk.
`/i`	Opens the `STACKER.INI` file for editing.
`/c`	Opens the `CONFIG.SYS` file for editing.
`/a`	Opens the `AUTOEXEC.BAT` file for editing.
`/dm`	Disables the mouse.
`/80`	Enables 80-column, 16-color text video (CGA/EGA/MCGA/VGA/SVGA/XGA).
`/132`	Enables 132-column, 16-color text video (XGA). Using this switch disables the mouse.
`=filename`	Specifies use of the same path as last specified at the DOS command prompt or "same as current file's" at the editor command line.
`/?`	Displays the abbreviated online help.

Notes

The four switches `/s`, `/dm`, `/80`, and `/132` can be preset in the `E` environment variable. You type them on the same line in the `AUTOEXEC.BAT` file as follows:

`SET E=/s /dm /80`

ECHO   2.0 AND LATER—INTERNAL

The ECHO command has two functions. First, you can use it to display messages onscreen from a batch file. Second, you can use ECHO to control whether DOS displays onscreen each command line from the batch file before executing the command line.

Syntax

To display a message, use the following format:

ECHO *message*

To turn on or off the display of commands and other batch-command messages, use the following format:

ECHO *onoff*

To see the status of ECHO, use the following format:

ECHO

Parameters and Switches

message Specifies the text of the message to be displayed onscreen.

onoff Specifies whether or not each command line in the batch file is displayed before being executed. ECHO ON turns on the display of command lines. ECHO OFF turns off the display of command lines. Note that this setting has no effect on the output generated by a command, only on the display of the command line that DOS is about to execute.

Notes

1. Setting ECHO ON or OFF controls only the display of command lines from the batch file before they are executed. It has no effect on the output generated by a DOS command. The message generated by the PAUSE command, Press any key to continue..., and the message generated by the COPY command, 1 file(s) copied, are examples of output generated by a command. They are not suppressed by ECHO OFF.

2. When ECHO is ON, DOS displays each command line before executing it. This capability can be handy when you are debugging a batch file. After the batch file is working correctly, you generally want to include an ECHO OFF command at the beginning of the batch file to suppress echoing command lines. Using ECHO OFF can speed up the batch file a little as well.

3. You can suppress the display of a single batch file line by typing @ as the first character in the line. The command itself is executed, but the command line is not displayed. For example, when you type the line @ECHO OFF, the command line ECHO OFF is not displayed, but the ECHO flag is set to OFF.

4. To display a blank line onscreen, enter the command ECHO followed by a period (with no intervening spaces) in your batch file. This is a special use for the ECHO command and can make your batch file screen output more attractive and readable.

5. You cannot display pipe characters (|) or redirection symbols (< or >) in an ECHO message. Redirection symbols are intercepted by the parser and are acted on.

6. DOS starts every batch file with ECHO ON. The ECHO setting (ON or OFF) remains in effect until DOS completes batch processing or encounters another ECHO ON or ECHO OFF command. If one batch file invokes another, the ECHO setting from the first batch file remains in effect. When DOS returns control to the command line, ECHO is restored to the ON state.

7. If you issue an ECHO OFF command at the DOS prompt, the DOS prompt is not displayed. You can still see the commands you are entering, however. To restore the DOS prompt, enter ECHO ON.

8. You can use ECHO to send ANSI commands to your screen. If ANSI.SYS is active in memory and the message displayed by ECHO contains legal ANSI commands, they are acted on rather than displayed. You can use this technique to display very complex, multicolored screens from a batch file. To enter ANSI commands into your batch file, you need an editor that enables you to enter Escape characters (ASCII 27) into the text.

9. To suppress the output of a command, use I/O redirection to the null device (NUL). For example, to suppress the 1 file(s) copied message generated by the COPY command, use the following format:

```
COPY  file1.ext  file2.ext  >  NUL
```

The command output is sent to the null device instead of to the console, so it is not displayed onscreen.

> **Caution**
>
> If you redirect the output of a program that is going to remain resident in memory (TSR), you may waste one of the file handles that DOS has available for programs to use. When you redirect the output of a program to the NUL device, the NUL device is assigned a file handle that isn't released until the program terminates. In the case of resident programs, this file handle often remains unavailable until you restart DOS. This can cause problems if you are in the habit of suppressing the output of resident programs loaded in your AUTOEXEC.BAT file.

EXAMPLES

Batch files commonly begin with the following line:

```
@ECHO OFF
```

This command turns ECHO OFF at the beginning of the batch file, and the at sign (@) tells DOS not to display the ECHO OFF command itself. If you start a batch file with this command, no unnecessary screen output is displayed.

Another very common use for ECHO is to explain the inclusion of a PAUSE command in a batch file. For example, to instruct the user to insert a particular floppy disk in drive B, include the following lines in a batch file:

```
ECHO Insert the Working Backup disk in drive B:
ECHO.
ECHO Press Ctrl-Break to abort the backup, or
PAUSE
```

Assuming that ECHO is OFF when these commands are executed, the following messages are displayed:

```
Insert the Working Backup disk in drive B:

Press Ctrl-Break to abort the backup, or
Press any key to continue...
```

Note that the PAUSE message is anticipated in the ECHO messages. If you use the CHOICE command instead, you can control all the text that is displayed onscreen.

To display a menu, you can use ECHO to display a screenful of messages. Then, you can let the user pick an item from the list by using the CHOICE command, as the following lines demonstrate:

```
@ECHO OFF
CLS
ECHO.
ECHO F  First action
ECHO S  Second action
ECHO T  Third action
ECHO.
CHOICE /C:FST "Choose an action "
```

The CLS command is often used with ECHO to control the amount of distracting information that is left behind on the screen by other commands. Note that the ECHO. (ECHO period) command is used to display blank lines. (Blank lines included in a batch file are ignored by DOS and are not displayed onscreen.)

SEE ALSO

@, ANSI.SYS, CHOICE, CLS, and PAUSE

Chapter 16, "Understanding Batch Files"

EDIT   5.0 AND LATER—EXTERNAL

The EDIT command activates the DOS full-screen ASCII text-file editor. EDIT is very handy for writing batch files or making changes to your AUTOEXEC.BAT or CONFIG.SYS file. Although limited to working on one file at a time, EDIT offers block copy and move operations as well as search and replace features. EDIT uses the editor built into QBASIC.EXE; so to use EDIT, QBASIC.EXE must be in one of the subdirectories listed in your PATH variable.

SYNTAX

EDIT *pathname* /B /G /H /NOHI

PARAMETERS AND SWITCHES

pathname   Specifies the file you want EDIT to load. If no drive is specified, the current drive is assumed. If no subdirectory path is specified, the current directory is assumed. Wildcards are not allowed.

/B   Specifies that EDIT should use colors more appropriate for a black-and-white (monochrome) or LCD display.

/G   Specifies that EDIT should use the fastest screen-updating method for a CGA monitor. Don't specify the /G switch if you see "snow" on your monitor.

/H	Specifies that EDIT should display 43 lines on an EGA monitor or 50 lines on a VGA monitor.
/NOHI	Specifies that EDIT should limit itself to 8 colors rather than 16.

SEE ALSO

Chapter 15, "Using the DOS Editor"

EDLIN　　　　　　　　　　　　　　　　1.0 TO 5.0—EXTERNAL

EDLIN is an old-fashioned, line-oriented text editor that is much more awkward to use than EDIT. If you have anything else to use for editing ASCII text files, you probably should avoid using EDLIN. The only good thing about EDLIN is that the program file is small. EDLIN is no longer distributed with the standard DOS package but is available on the DOS 6 Supplemental Disk. Instructions for using EDLIN are in the COMMANDS.TXT file included on the Supplemental Disk.

SEE ALSO

EDIT

EGA.SYS (DEVICE DRIVER)　　　5.0 AND LATER—EXTERNAL

Because of the way EGA display adapters are made, they present certain problems for task-switching software. EGA.SYS attempts to solve these problems. If you have an EGA display and use the task-switching functions of the DOS Shell program, you need to load EGA.SYS. You must load EGA.SYS in either a DEVICE= or DEVICEHIGH= statement in your CONFIG.SYS file.

SYNTAX

DEVICE=drive:\path**EGA.SYS**

or

DEVICEHIGH=drive:\path**EGA.SYS**

PARAMETERS AND SWITCHES

drive:\path\	The full path to the EGA.SYS file on your system. Setup places the EGA.SYS file in the C:\DOS subdirectory by default. If the full path to EGA.SYS isn't specified, DOS looks for the file in the root directory of the startup drive.

NOTES

1. You can use EGA.SYS only if your system uses an EGA display. With any other type of display, EGA.SYS does not load into memory.

2. In addition to being required by the task swapper in DOS Shell, EGA.SYS may be required by Microsoft Windows. Third-party task-switching software often requires the assistance of EGA.SYS or a similar driver that it provides. You can have (and need) only one EGA.SYS type driver loaded at a time.

3. If you have an EGA display and you use the Microsoft Mouse driver, you may be able to save some memory by loading EGA.SYS before loading your mouse driver into memory. Many of the functions in EGA.SYS are duplicated in the Microsoft Mouse driver, and if it finds EGA support already in place, the mouse driver doesn't load those functions.

EXAMPLES

To load the EGA.SYS device driver into upper memory, you might add the following line to your CONFIG.SYS file:

DEVICEHIGH=C:\DOS\EGA.SYS

SEE ALSO

DOSSHELL and MOUSE

EJECT

The EJECT command ejects the medium from a drive. If no drive is specified, the medium is ejected from the current drive.

SYNTAX

EJECT *drive:* /?

PARAMETERS AND SWITCHES

drive: Specifies the drive letter of the drive from which to eject the medium.

/?   Displays the abbreviated online help.

REMARKS

The medium cannot be ejected from the drive specified when the drive is locked.

EMM386   5.0 AND LATER—EXTERNAL

The EMM386 command enables you to control the use of expanded memory (EMS) and upper memory blocks (UMBs) in a computer with an 80386SX or higher CPU. Before you can run EMM386 from the DOS command line, you must load the EMM386.EXE device driver into memory by adding a DEVICE= statement in your CONFIG.SYS file. After the EMM386.EXE device driver is loaded into memory, you can use EMM386 from the DOS command line to view the status of EMS and UMB memory and turn various features on and off.

Syntax

EMM386 *onoffauto* W=*onoff*

Parameters and Switches

onoffauto   Enables EMM386.EXE (ON), disables it (OFF), or enables it to provide expanded memory and upper memory block support only when a program requests it (AUTO). The default is ON.

W=*onoff*   Enables (W=ON) or disables (W=OFF) support for the Weitek coprocessor. The default is W=OFF.

Notes

1. Before you can use EMM386.EXE from the command line, you must install EMM386 as a device driver in CONFIG.SYS.
2. Entering EMM386 with no parameters causes a status report of EMS and UMB memory use to be displayed.
3. EMM386 honors a request to be turned off only when no EMS or UMB memory is in use. In other words, you can't use the OFF parameter if you are loading any programs into upper memory.
4. The high memory area (HMA) must be available to enable a Weitek coprocessor. If DOS is loaded into HMA by a DOS=HIGH statement in your CONFIG.SYS file, you might not be able to enable the Weitek coprocessor.

See Also

EMM386.EXE

"Using Expanded Memory and EMM386.EXE" in Chapter 19

EMM386.EXE (Device Driver) 5.0 and Later—External

The EMM386.EXE device driver can convert extended memory (XMS) into LIM 4.0–compatible expanded memory (EMS) on a computer with an 80386SX or higher CPU. EMM386.EXE can also create upper memory blocks (UMBs), which DOS can use to load other device drivers and programs into when you add the DEVICEHIGH= and LOADHIGH commands, respectively. EMM386.EXE requires that an XMS-compatible memory manager, such as HIMEM.SYS, be present before EMM386.EXE will load into memory. EMM386.EXE must be loaded in a DEVICE= statement in your CONFIG.SYS file.

Syntax

```
DEVICE=drive:\path\EMM386.EXE  onoffauto  ramval  MIN=size  W=onoff  Ms
FRAME=xxxx  /Pyyyy  /Pn=yyyy  X=mmmm-nnnn  I=mmmm-nnnn  B=zzzz  L=xmsmem
A=regs  H=hhh  D=nnn  RAM=mmmm-nnnn  NOEMS  NOVCPI  HIGHSCAN  VERBOSE
WIN=mmmm-nnnn  NOHI  ROM=mmmm-nnnn  NOMOVEXBDA  ALTBOOT
```

Parameters and Switches

drive:\path Specifies the full path to the EMM386.EXE file on your system. By default, Setup places the EMM386.EXE file in the C:\DOS subdirectory. If the full path to EMM386.EXE isn't specified, DOS looks for the file in the root directory of the startup drive.

onoffauto Enables EMM386.EXE (ON), disables it (OFF), or enables it to provide expanded memory and upper memory block support only when a program requests it (AUTO). The default is ON.

ramval Represents the maximum amount of RAM, in kilobytes, to be assigned as EMS 4.0/Virtual Control Program Interface (VCPI) memory. Enter a value ranging from 64 to 32768 or the amount of extended memory available when EMM386.EXE is loaded. Any number that you enter is rounded down to the nearest multiple of 16. The default is 0 if NOEMS is specified. Otherwise, all available extended memory is used as EMS/VCPI memory.

MIN=*size* (DOS 6 and later) Specifies the minimum amount of RAM (in kilobytes) that EMM386 is guaranteed to provide. Enter a value ranging from 0 to the value of *ramval*. The default is 0 if NOEMS is specified; otherwise, it is 256. If *size* is greater than *ramval*, *size* is used.

W=*onoff* Enables (W=ON) or disables (W=OFF) support for the Weitek coprocessor. The default is W=OFF.

M*s* Indicates the beginning address of the EMS page frame. *s* is a number that represents the beginning address. You cannot combine the M*s* parameter with the /FRAME=*xxxx* or /P*yyyy* parameters. The numbers and associated hexadecimal addresses are as follows:

M*s*	Memory Address	M*s*	Memory Address
M1	C000	M8	DC00
M2	C400	M9	E000
M3	C800	M10*	8000

M*s*	Memory Address	M*s*	Memory Address
M4	CC00	M11*	8400
M5	D000	M12*	8800
M6	D400	M13*	8C00

*Use only in computers with at least 512KB of memory.

FRAME=*xxxx*	Specifies a hexadecimal address from 8000 through 9000, and C000 through E000 in increments of 400 hexadecimal or NONE. The latter disables the page frame and may cause programs that require expanded memory to fail. You cannot combine the FRAME=*xxxx* parameter with the Ms or /P*yyyy* parameters.
/P*yyyy*	Specifies a hexadecimal address from 8000 through 9000, and C000 through E000 in increments of 400 hexadecimal. You cannot combine the /P*yyyy* parameter with the Ms or FRAME=*xxxx* parameters.
P*n*=*yyyy*	Defines an address for a page segment. *n* represents the page and can have a value of 0 through 255. *yyyy* is a hexadecimal address from 8000 through 9000, and C000 through E000 in increments of 400 hexadecimal. To remain compatible with EMS 3.2, P0 through P3 must be contiguous addresses. You cannot specify P0 through P3 with this option if you use the Ms, FRAME=*xxxx*, or /P*yyyy* parameters.
X=*mmmm*-*nnnn*	Specifies a range of memory that should not be used for an EMS page frame or UMB space. *mmmm* and *nnnn* can have values ranging from A000H through FFFFH and are rounded down to the nearest 4KB boundary. The X switch overrides the I switch if their ranges overlap.
I=*mmmm*-*nnnn*	Specifies a range of memory that can be used for an EMS page frame or UMB space. *mmmm* and *nnnn* can have values ranging from A000H through FFFFH and are rounded down to the nearest 4KB boundary. The X switch overrides the I switch if their ranges overlap.
B=*zzzz*	Indicates the lowest address to use for bank switching (swapping of 16KB pages). *zzzz* can have a value from 1000H through 4000H. The default is 4000H.
L=*xmsmem*	Specifies the number of kilobytes that must remain as extended memory instead of being converted to EMS memory. The default is 0. For 1MB of memory to remain as extended memory, use L=1024.
A=*regs*	Allocates the number of fast alternative register sets that EMM386.EXE may use (for multitasking). *regs* can have a value from 0 through 254. The default is 7. Each alternative register set adds about 200 bytes to the size of EMM386.EXE in memory.
H=*hhh*	Enables you to change the number of handles EMM386.EXE can use. *hhh* can have a value from 2 to 255. The default is 64.
D=*nnn*	Specifies the amount of memory (in kilobytes) reserved for DMA (buffered direct-memory access). This value should cover the largest nonfloppy transfer. *nnn* can have a value from 16 through 256. The default is 32.

RAM=*mmmm*-*nnnn*	Specifies a range of memory to be used for UMBs. If you specify RAM without a value, EMM386.EXE allocates all available extended memory, an EMS page frame is established in upper memory, and all remaining upper memory space is converted to UMBs.
NOEMS	Specifies that access to UMBs be provided, but not for expanded memory; that is, an EMS page frame is prohibited.
NOVCPI	(DOS 6.0 and later) Disables support for VCPI applications. Must be used with NOEMS, in which case *ramval* and MIN are ignored.
HIGHSCAN	(DOS 6.0 and later) Causes EMM386.EXE to be more aggressive in scanning upper memory for UMBs. Your computer may stop responding if you use this switch.
VERBOSE	(DOS 6.0 and later) Directs EMM386.EXE to display status and error messages when DOS boots. This switch can be abbreviated as V. (You can also get status and error messages by holding down the Alt key while DOS boots.)
V	(DOS 6.0 and later) Same as VERBOSE (see preceding entry).
WIN=*mmmm*-*nnnn*	(DOS 6.0 and later) Reserves the specified memory address range for Microsoft Windows and prevents EMM386.EXE from using that area of memory. *mmmm* and *nnnn* can have values ranging from A000H through FFFFH and are rounded down to the nearest 4KB boundary. The X switch overrides the WIN switch if their ranges overlap. The WIN switch overrides the RAM, ROM, and I switches if their ranges overlap.
NOHI	(DOS 6.0 and later) Prevents EMM386.EXE from loading any part of itself into upper memory. Normally, EMM386.EXE uses about 5KB of upper memory for itself. Specifying this switch makes more UMB space available but increases the size of EMM386.EXE in conventional memory.
ROM=*mmmm*-*nnnn*	(DOS 6.0 and later) Specifies a range of memory for shadow RAM, which is read-only memory (ROM) copied into faster RAM. *mmmm* and *nnnn* can have values ranging from A000H through FFFFH and are rounded down to the nearest 4KB boundary.
NOMOVEXBDA	(DOS 6.0 and later) Prevents EMM386.EXE from moving the extended BIOS data from conventional memory to upper memory.
ALTBOOT	(DOS 6 and later) Directs EMM386.EXE to use a different method of restarting your computer when you press Ctrl+Alt+Del. Specify this parameter only if your computer stops responding or exhibits other unusual behavior when EMM386.EXE is loaded into memory and you press Ctrl+Alt+Del.

Notes

1. `EMM386.EXE` works only on 80386, 80386SX, and higher systems.
2. `HIMEM.SYS` must be installed as a device driver in `CONFIG.SYS` before `EMM386.EXE`.
3. You cannot use the `DEVICEHIGH=` command to load `EMM386.EXE` into memory. `EMM386.EXE` is required to provide the UMBs that the `DEVICEHIGH=` command loads device drivers into. `EMM386.EXE` does attempt to minimize its impact on conventional memory when it loads, using only about 3KB in most cases. To prevent `EMM386.EXE` from loading parts of itself into upper memory, specify the `NOHI` parameter.
4. To create UMBs, you must include the `RAM` or `NOEMS` parameters, and you must include at least `DOS=UMB` in `CONFIG.SYS`.
5. Before you can use `EMM386` from the command line, you must install `EMM386.EXE` as a device driver in `CONFIG.SYS`.
6. Any `DEVICEHIGH=` commands in `CONFIG.SYS` must come after the `DEVICE=HIMEM.SYS` and `DEVICE=EMM386.EXE RAM` (or `NOEMS`) commands.
7. When `EMM386.EXE` is used with Microsoft Windows 3.1, the `I`, `X`, `NOEMS`, `Ms`, `FRAME`, and `Pyyyy` switches override the `EMMINCLUDE`, `EMMEXCLUDE`, and `EMMPAGEFRAME` settings in the Windows `SYSTEM.INI` file.
8. `SMARTDRV` double-buffering may be required before `DEVICEHIGH=` commands, which load installable device drivers that use expanded memory.
9. When `EMM386.EXE` is not supplying expanded memory, non–VCPI-compliant programs can run (for example, Microsoft Windows 3.0 in Standard mode).
10. The high memory area (HMA) must be available to enable a Weitek coprocessor. If DOS is loaded into HMA by a `DOS=HIGH` statement in your `CONFIG.SYS` file, you might not be able to enable the Weitek coprocessor.

See Also

`DEVICE=` and `HIMEM.SYS`

"Using Expanded Memory and `EMM386.EXE`" in Chapter 19

ERASE (SEE DEL)

ERASE is an alternative name for the DEL command. For information on using the DEL or ERASE command, see the entry for DEL in this command reference.

ERAQ (SEE DELQ)

ERAQ is an alternative command for the DR DOS DELQ command. See the detailed description under DELQ.

EXE2BIN 1.1 TO 5.0—EXTERNAL

The EXE2BIN command changes appropriately formatted .EXE files to .BIN or .COM files. EXE2BIN is a programmer's utility; it is provided as a courtesy for those who have compilers that cannot create a memory-image file directly. Most people never find an occasion to use this program. EXE2BIN is included with the DOS 6.0 Supplemental Disk, not in the standard DOS 6.0 package.

SYNTAX
   EXE2BIN *exe_file* *binary_file*

PARAMETERS AND SWITCHES

exe_file The .EXE file to be converted into a memory-image file. If no drive is specified, the current drive is assumed. If no subdirectory path is specified, the current subdirectory is assumed. A filename is required, but if you don't specify an extension, .EXE is assumed. Wildcards are not allowed.

binary_file The name of the memory-image file to be created. If no drive is specified, the current drive is assumed. If no subdirectory path is specified, the current subdirectory is assumed. If no filename is specified, the filename designated in *exe_file* is used. If no extension is specified, a .BIN extension is added.

NOTES

1. EXE2BIN is a programming utility that converts .EXE (executable) program files to .COM or .BIN (memory-image) files. The resulting program consumes less disk space and loads slightly faster. Unless you use a compiler-based programming language, you probably will never use this command.

2. Before EXE2BIN converts an .EXE file to memory-image format, a number of requirements have to be met. In most cases, a program has to be written with this transformation in mind. You cannot convert the typical .EXE program file by using EXE2BIN.

EXIT 2.0 AND LATER—INTERNAL

You can use EXIT to remove a temporary copy of COMMAND.COM from memory. Typically, you use this command to return to an application program that gives you access to the DOS prompt while it's running. EXIT can remove only temporary copies of COMMAND.COM; it cannot accidentally remove the permanent copy that is loaded when your computer starts up.

SYNTAX
   EXIT

Notes

1. EXIT has no effect on a copy of COMMAND.COM loaded with the /P switch. Normally, you load COMMAND.COM with the /P switch only in the SHELL= command in your CONFIG.SYS file. Any additional copies that you run (from a batch file, for example) can be removed from memory with the EXIT command.
2. EXIT is used to close a DOS window in Microsoft Windows. It terminates the temporary copy of COMMAND.COM that Windows launched to create the DOS window.

See Also

COMMAND

"Using EXIT to Leave the Current Copy of the Command Processor" in Chapter 10

EXPAND   5.0 AND LATER—EXTERNAL

You can use the EXPAND command to copy a compressed, unusable file from the DOS distribution disks to an uncompressed, usable form.

Syntax

EXPAND *source1 source2 ... destination*

Parameters and Switches

source1   The name of the compressed source file. If no drive is provided, the current drive is assumed. If no subdirectory path is provided, the current subdirectory is assumed. If this parameter is omitted, you are prompted for the source and destination. Wildcards are not allowed.

source2   Additional compressed source files. You can designate as many as can fit in the 127-character limit for a DOS command line. You cannot specify additional *source* parameters without also specifying a *destination* parameter.

destination   If only one source file is specified, *destination* can be the full name and location of the destination file, with normal default assumptions. If more than one source file is specified, only a drive and/or path can be specified for the destination. If *destination* is omitted, DOS prompts you for the name and location to use for expanded files.

Rules

1. You can use EXPAND to decompress files from the DOS distribution disks only.
2. If you specify more than one compressed file, you can specify only a destination drive or path (not a filename).

3. If you don't specify a compressed file or a destination, EXPAND prompts you for the missing information.
4. If you use EXPAND on a file that is not compressed, an error message appears (see the first item in the following "Messages" section). Despite the error message, the file is still copied to the destination; it just isn't expanded.

NOTES

1. Files stored on the original DOS 5.0 and 6.0 disks are compressed files. This compression enables more data to be stored on fewer disks. Before you can use a file on these disks, however, you must decompress the file.
2. When you use SETUP to install DOS, the files are decompressed as they are transferred to the subdirectory you chose to install DOS into. If you delete a file accidentally or if a file becomes corrupted, you must retrieve the file again from the original DOS disk. EXPAND transfers the file and decompresses it in the process. Consider EXPAND to be a kind of "one-way" COPY command.
3. Refer to the file PACKING.LST for a list of which files are included on each of the DOS distribution disks. Microsoft marks the compressed files by replacing the last letter of the extension with an underscore (_). Setup copies the PACKING.LST file into your DOS subdirectory when it installs MS-DOS 6.

EXAMPLES

To expand MOVE.EXE from DOS distribution disk #1 to the C:\DOS subdirectory, enter the following line:

```
EXPAND  A:MOVE.EX_  C:\DOS\MOVE.EXE
```

MESSAGES

```
Input file 'filename' already in expanded format
```

Error: You attempted to expand an uncompressed file. Verify that you specified the correct compressed file.

```
Error in compressed input file format: filename
```

Error: The compressed file was corrupted. Use a different copy of the compressed file.

SEE ALSO

SETUP

EXTRACT

EXTRACT extracts files from compressed cabinet, or .CAB, files. Microsoft uses .CAB files to compress all the installation files for Windows 95 and Windows 98.

Syntax

EXTRACT /Y /A /D|/E /L drive:\path cabinet filename ...

EXTRACT /Y source newname

EXTRACT /Y /C source destination

Parameters and Switches

cabinet	Specifies the name of the cabinet, or .CAB, file to extract files from.
filename	Specifies the filename of the file or files to be extracted. Standard wildcards can be used.
source	Extracts a compressed file consisting of a cabinet file with only one file in it.
newname	Specifies a newname to give the extracted file a name other than the original name.
/A	Extracts all cabinet files in the set beginning with the specified file.
/C	Copies a source file from Microsoft's proprietary DMF format disks to destination.
/D	Displays a cabinet directory.
/E	Extracts all files.
/L drive:\path	Specifies the location to place extracted files.
/Y	Does not prompt before overwriting an existing file.

FASTHELP   6.0 AND LATER—External

The FASTHELP command provides a brief description and the syntax of a DOS command. This is the same help you get by including the /? switch when you issue a DOS command.

Syntax

FASTHELP command

Parameters and Switches

command	The DOS command for which you want help. If you do not provide a command name, DOS provides short, one-line descriptions of all DOS commands.

Notes

The information FASTHELP provides about a command is the same as that provided by the following:

command /?

For more extensive information on DOS commands, type HELP command.

See Also

HELP

"Getting Help" in Chapter 3

FASTOPEN   3.3 AND LATER—EXTERNAL

FASTOPEN keeps directory information in memory so that DOS can quickly find and open the files you use most. FASTOPEN remains in memory (TSR), so be careful not to run it more than once. If you use FASTOPEN, you should add it to your AUTOEXEC.BAT file.

Syntax

FASTOPEN *drive:*=num ... /X

Parameters and Switches

drive: Specifies the name of the drive for which directory information should be held in memory.

=num   Specifies the number of directory entries to be held in memory (10 to 999). The default is 48. The equal sign is optional.

...   Specifies the number of additional *drive:*=num parameters you need.

/X   Tells DOS to use expanded memory to store the information buffered by FASTOPEN.

Rules

1. You must specify the name of at least one drive for which entries are to be kept in memory. The drive cannot be a floppy drive.
2. You can use FASTOPEN for up to 24 nonfloppy drives, for a total of 999 files. In the command line, simply type the additional drive names, separated by spaces.
3. Do not use FASTOPEN from the DOS Shell or when you are running Windows or a disk defragmentation program, such as DEFRAG.
4. If you provide *nnn*, the value must be between 10 and 999, inclusive. The minimum value for FASTOPEN is 10, or the maximum level of your deepest directory plus 1— whichever is greater.

5. You cannot run more than one copy of FASTOPEN. If you want to change FASTOPEN settings, you must reboot your computer.

6. Each FASTOPEN entry you specify increases the size of FASTOPEN by approximately 48 bytes.

NOTES

1. FASTOPEN works by keeping directory information in memory. Because disk buffers already hold FAT information, FASTOPEN enables DOS to search memory for a file or subdirectory entry, to locate the corresponding FAT entry quickly, and to open the file. If you have many files and use FASTOPEN effectively, you can increase DOS's performance.

2. As is true of BUFFERS, no predetermined best number exists. The default value of 48 works well in many installations. If your subdirectories run many levels deep or if you use many files, specifying a larger number can improve performance. Using too large a value for *nnn* (greater than 200), however, slows the system. DOS spends more time examining in-memory directory entries than rereading the entries from the disk.

3. Alternatively, FASTOPEN can be loaded from your CONFIG.SYS file with the INSTALL= command rather than in your AUTOEXEC.BAT file. With DOS 6, there is no advantage to either placement. Just make sure that you do not attempt to load FASTOPEN from both your CONFIG.SYS and your AUTOEXEC.BAT files.

4. In most cases, you should use the SMARTDRV disk cache instead of FASTOPEN. SMARTDRV has fewer dangerous interactions with other programs and can speed up your computer even more than FASTOPEN. If you don't have enough memory to use SMARTDRV effectively, consider using the BUFFERS= command to optimize disk-access time.

SEE ALSO

BUFFERS= and SMARTDRV

"Using FASTOPEN" in Chapter 7

FC — 3.3 AND LATER—EXTERNAL

The FC command enables you to compare files for differences. Using the FC switches, you can configure it to do a strict byte-for-byte comparison (as COMP does) or to attempt to resynchronize after differences are detected.

SYNTAX

For ASCII text files, use the following syntax:

FC *pathname1* *pathname2* /A /C /L /LB*buffer* /N /T /W /resync

For binary files, use the following syntax:

FC *pathname1* *pathname2* /B

Parameters and Switches

pathname1 Specifies a file or group of files to compare. Normal drive and subdirectory defaults apply, and wildcards are permitted. This parameter must match at least one existing file.

pathname2 Specifies the file or group of files that should be compared to **pathname1**. Normal drive and subdirectory defaults apply, and wildcards are permitted. Wildcards used with FC are interpreted the same way they are with COPY and REN:. Missing characters in the filename are replaced with the corresponding characters in **pathname1**. If this file isn't found, FC moves on to the next set of files.

/A Abbreviates the display of an ASCII comparison to the first and last lines of each group of differences.

/B Forces a binary file comparison, which involves a byte-by-byte comparison with no synchronization after a mismatch. This switch is the default for files with .EXE, .COM, .SYS, .OBJ, .LIB, and .BIN extensions.

/C Causes DOS to ignore the case of letters.

/L Compares files in ASCII mode, which involves a line-by-line comparison with resynchronization attempted after a mismatch. This switch is the default for files without .EXE, .COM, .SYS, .OBJ, .LIB, and .BIN extensions.

/LB*buffer* Sets the internal buffer to the number of lines specified by *buffer*. A comparison is terminated if the files have more than this number of consecutive differing lines.

/N Displays line numbers for ASCII comparisons.

/T Suppresses expansion of tabs to spaces.

/W Compresses tabs and spaces to a single space and causes tabs and spaces to be ignored if those characters are at the beginning or end of a line.

/*resync* Sets the number of lines (1 through 9) that must match before the files are considered to be resynchronized. The default is 2.

Notes

1. A difference in a binary file comparison is displayed as follows:

   aaaaaaaa: *xx yy*

   aaaaaaaa represents the hexadecimal address of a mismatching pair of bytes, *xx* is the mismatching hexadecimal byte from the first file, and *yy* is the mismatching hexadecimal byte from the second file.

2. If you use a wildcard in the first filename, DOS compares all the specified files with the second filename. If you use a wildcard in the second filename, DOS uses the corresponding value from the first filename in the second filename.

EXAMPLES

To compare every text file in the current directory with C:\README.TXT, use the following command:

`FC   *.TXT   C:\README.TXT`

To compare README.TXT in the current directory with C:\README.TXT, use the following command:

`FC   README.TXT   C:\*.TXT`

To compare every text file in the current directory with the file of the same name in C:\, use this command:

`FC   *.TXT   C:\*.TXT`

SEE ALSO

DISKCOMP

"Comparing Files with FC" in Chapter 8

FCBS=   3.1 AND LATER—INTERNAL

File handles were added in DOS 2.0. Most programs written since that time use file handles, not file control blocks (FCBs), to open files. The FCBS= command sets the maximum number of open files a program using DOS 1.0 FCBs can have. With newer programs, you usually don't need this command. FCBS= can be used only in your CONFIG.SYS file.

SYNTAX

FCBS=*maxopen*

PARAMETERS AND SWITCHES

maxopen   The maximum number of open FCBs that a program can use. Any value in the range of 1 to 255 is allowed. The default value is 4.

NOTES

1. Not many programs use FCBs anymore. Include the FCBS= command in your CONFIG.SYS file only if a program asks you to, or if an old utility starts mysteriously failing. Otherwise, accept DOS's default setting of four FCBs. If you set *maxopen* to 1, you might find that certain small command-line utilities begin to fail.

2. Be aware that FCBs are ancient history. If you depend on any programs that require them, you are living on borrowed time, and you should start looking for replacements. If you receive a new program that asks you to use the FCBS= command, complain (loudly) to the manufacturer. Microsoft has carried this legacy from CP/M for several years

now, and with every release of DOS comes the chance that FCBs will no longer be supported.

3. If a program attempts to open more than *maxopen* FCBs, DOS automatically closes some of them.
4. Each FCB that is available to programs increases the size of DOS by approximately 60 bytes.
5. For newer programs, set the maximum number of open files by using the `FILES=` command.
6. Some older versions of DOS supported a second argument, *neverclose*, for `FCBS=`. DOS 5 and 6 have no need for the *neverclose* argument and will ignore it.

SEE ALSO

`FILES=`

"Accessing Files through FCBS" in Chapter 19

FDISK   2.0 AND LATER—EXTERNAL

FDISK is a full-screen program that prepares a hard disk to accept an operating system, such as DOS. It sets up partitions on a hard disk as well as designates which partitions are used to start up the computer if no floppy disk is in drive A. On a new hard drive, you must run FDISK before you can use the FORMAT command on the drive.

> **Caution** FDISK is an extremely dangerous command. Making any changes with FDISK effectively deletes all the information on your hard drive. MS-DOS 6 does not include any utilities with which you can recover information lost through the use of FDISK.

SYNTAX

FDISK   /STATUS

PARAMETERS AND SWITCHES

/STATUS   (DOS 6.0 and later) Displays some partition information without starting FDISK.

RULES

1. You must use FDISK to create a partition on a hard disk before you can use FORMAT to format the hard disk.
2. You can change the size of a partition only by deleting existing partitions and creating new ones. This procedure deletes all data in the partitions.

3. FDISK does not work with SUBST aliases, Interlnk drives, network drives, CD-ROM drives, or removable drives of any kind. FDISK works only with hard drives that are supported by the ROM BIOS in your computer. FDISK does not work with hard drives that require you to load a device driver in your CONFIG.SYS file to operate.

NOTES

1. Although Setup places FDISK in the C:\DOS subdirectory by default, consider copying FDISK.EXE to a floppy disk and deleting it from your hard drive. If FDISK.EXE isn't on your hard disk, no one can run it, thus avoiding the possible data loss that could result from someone's curiosity.

2. If you need to use FDISK, back up your hard disk; make sure that you have a bootable floppy disk with at least the FORMAT command and your backup software on it. After FDISK has finished with your hard drive, you cannot boot from it (or even read it) until you have reformatted the drive.

3. The MIRROR command can save partition information into a file, which can be used by the UNFORMAT command to restore a damaged partition table. Although this capability is still a part of UNFORMAT, the MIRROR command is no longer distributed with DOS and is available only on the Supplemental Disk. Before you use FDISK, you might want to get a copy of MIRROR and save your partition information so that you can restore it if you have problems.

4. Starting with DOS 3.3, you can use FDISK to create multiple logical partitions on a single drive. In DOS 4.0, FDISK and DOS were upgraded to handle partitions larger than 32MB. The maximum size of a single partition for the DOS 6 version of FDISK is 2GB.

5. If you plan to use more than one operating system, use FDISK to partition part of the hard disk for DOS and another part of the hard disk for the other operating system.

SEE ALSO

MIRROR, UNDELETE, and UNFORMAT

"Dividing a Hard Disk with FDISK" in Chapter 7

FILELINK

FILELINK is a utility to transfer files between two computers via a serial or parallel port connection. The FILELINK command with no parameters starts the FILELINK utility in full-screen mode. This command has so many command-line parameters that it is highly recommended you run it without any parameters to start the full-screen utility rather than use it via the command line.

 FILES=   2.0 AND LATER—INTERNAL

When a program tries to open a file, DOS assigns that file a handle, which is just a fancy name for an ID number. The FILES= command sets the maximum number of file handles that DOS has available for programs to use. FILES= can be used only in your CONFIG.SYS file.

SYNTAX

FILES=*maxopen*

PARAMETERS AND SWITCHES

maxopen   The maximum number of open file handles that DOS allows. Any value in the range of 8 to 255 is allowed. The default value is 8.

NOTES

1. Always specify a value for FILES= in your CONFIG.SYS file. DOS's default value of 8 is much too low for today's software programs. You typically need around 30 to 40 file handles, perhaps more if you are running programs such as Microsoft Windows. A good minimum setting is 20.

2. If a program attempts to open a file when DOS has no more file handles available, it is denied access to the file. DOS does not close open file handles, unlike FCBs, while a program is running.

> **Tip**
> If you are in the habit of redirecting the output to the NUL device when you load resident software in your AUTOEXEC.BAT file, you may be wasting file handles. Each such redirection unnecessarily ties up one file handle until you restart your computer.

3. Each file handle available to programs increases the size of DOS by approximately 60 bytes.

4. Most programs display a meaningful message if they run out of file handles. If this happens, increase the FILES= setting in your CONFIG.SYS file by 5 and restart your computer.

5. Many software installation programs inspect the setting you are using for FILES= and may even increase it without telling you. Always look through your CONFIG.SYS and AUTOEXEC.BAT files after installing new software, and make sure that any modifications they've made are acceptable to you.

EXAMPLES

The following line sets the maximum number of open file handles to 30:

FILES=30

SEE ALSO

FCBS=

"Using the FILES Command" in Chapter 19

FILEUP

FILEUP starts the File Update System application to maintain duplicate files in two locations.

SYNTAX

FILEUP /?

PARAMETERS AND SWITCHES

/? Displays the abbreviated online help.

NOTES

Using the File Update program with floppies requires that the File Update program reside on both systems. For INTERLNK or a LAN, the File Update program files need to reside in only one system.

SEE ALSO

INTERLNK

FIND   2.0 AND LATER—EXTERNAL

The FIND command displays all the lines of the designated files that match (or do not match, depending on the switches used) the specified string.

SYNTAX

FIND /V /C /N /I "*string*" *pathname* ...

PARAMETERS AND SWITCHES

"*string*"	Represents the characters you want to find. The characters must be enclosed in quotation marks.
pathname	Indicates the file that you want to search. All the normal drive and subdirectory defaults apply, but you cannot use wildcards. If you omit *pathname*, FIND acts as a filter, searching input that has been redirected to it.
...	Indicates that you can enter as many *pathname* parameters as necessary.
/C	Displays a count of the total number of lines that contain "*string*".

/I	Specifies that the search is not case sensitive (DOS 5.0 and later versions).
/N	Displays lines that contain "*string*", preceded by the file line number.
/V	Displays lines that do not contain "*string*".

Exit Codes

ERRORLEVEL Value	Meaning
0	FIND completed successfully and found at least one match.
1	FIND completed successfully but found no matches.
2	FIND aborted due to an error and cannot report whether any matches were found.

Rules

1. You can use more than one file specification. All file specifications must appear after the string and must be separated by spaces.
2. If you do not provide any file specifications, FIND expects information from the keyboard (standard input).
3. If you use switches with FIND, you must place them between FIND and the string. Most DOS commands require that you place switches at the end of the command line.
4. You must enclose the string in double quotation marks. To use the double-quotation mark character itself in the string, use two double quotation marks in a row.
5. Wildcards are not allowed in file specifications. You can get the effect of wildcards by using FIND in a FOR command.

Notes

1. FIND is one of several filters provided with DOS 3.0 and later versions. The command can find lines that contain strings and those that do not. FIND also can number and count lines of text, instead of simply displaying them.
2. This filter is useful when it is combined with DOS I/O redirection. You can redirect the FIND command's output to a file by using the > redirection symbol. Because FIND accepts a sequence of files to search, you do not have to redirect the input to FIND.

Examples

To search README.TXT for "Microsoft", use the following command:

```
FIND "Microsoft" C:\DOS\README.TXT
```

To search all batch files in the current directory for "default", use the following command:

```
FOR %%A IN (*.BAT) DO FIND "default" %%A
```

To determine the path and filenames for all batch files on the current disk, use this command:

```
DIR \ /S /B | FIND ".BAT"
```

SEE ALSO

MORE and SORT

"The FIND Filter" in Chapter 13

FOR   2.0 AND LATER—INTERNAL

You can use the FOR command to repeat a single command, executing it once for each member of a list or group of files. Unlike most of the other batch commands, FOR can be very useful from both the command line as well as in a batch file.

SYNTAX

When used in a batch file, the syntax is as follows:

FOR *%%variable* **IN** *(set)* **DO** *command parameters*

When used on the DOS command line, the syntax is as follows:

FOR *%variable* **IN** *(set)* **DO** *command parameters*

PARAMETERS AND SWITCHES

variable Specifies a single character DOS uses to represent the current value of **set**. You can use any character for **variable** except the digits 0 through 9, the redirection symbols (<, >, and |), and the slash (/). In a batch file, **variable** must be preceded by two percent signs (%%), but on the DOS command line only one is used.

set Specifies one or more words or pathnames separated by spaces or commas. Wildcards are allowed in the *filename.ext* portion of any pathname specified. None of the members of **set** can include embedded spaces. The enclosing parentheses are required.

command Represents the DOS command to be executed for each word or file in the **set**. Almost all DOS internal or external commands can be used, with the notable exception of the FOR command itself.

parameters Represents any parameters you would like to pass to the **command** being executed. Normally, one or more occurrences of **variable** are used in the command parameters to pass the current value of **set** to the **command**.

Notes

1. You can use more than one word or file pathname in the *set*. Use spaces or commas to separate each word or file pathname from the next. Any or all parts of a pathname may be used, but wildcards are allowed only in the filename and extension portions.

2. No member of the *set* can include embedded spaces. In other words, you can't use *variable* to replace more than a single "word."

3. You must precede every occurrence of *variable* with two percent signs in a batch file and one percent sign at the DOS prompt. The reason for this difference is that each line in a batch file is passed through a routine called a parser, which fills in any replaceable parameters before DOS executes each command. The parser removes any single percent signs it finds; if two percent signs in a row are encountered, however, one will remain after the parser is finished. By the time DOS executes the command, only one of the two percent signs you typed remains. When you execute the FOR command from the DOS prompt, the line isn't parsed, and no percent signs are removed.

4. *variable* becomes each literal word or filename in *set*. If wildcards are used, each file matched becomes a member of the set. The DO command executes once for each value in the set.

5. *variable* can be used in the *command* portion of the FOR command as well as in the *parameters* portion. This capability can be useful if you want to execute a series of commands. You can use the *variable* as many times as you need to after the DO keyword. It will be replaced with the current member of *set* every time it appears.

6. You cannot nest FOR..IN..DO commands. That is, you cannot use FOR as the command executed in the DO portion of a FOR..IN..DO loop. All other DOS internal and external commands are legal.

7. If you execute a batch file directly in the DO portion of the FOR loop, batch file processing ends when that batch file terminates, and control never is returned to the FOR loop. To avoid this situation, use the CALL or COMMAND /C commands to execute batch files in FOR..IN..DO loops.

8. If you use a variable name that is more than one character long or if you omit IN, the parentheses around *set*, or DO, DOS displays a syntax error message.

9. Avoid using redirection symbols (<, >, and |) with the FOR command. In general, DOS ignores output redirection, and most redirected input will fail.

10. Do not attempt to use the "at" sign (@) to suppress the display of the command in the DO loop. DOS does not interpret the @ correctly and searches for an executable file that begins with an "at" sign. To accomplish the same thing, use ECHO OFF before executing the FOR command.

11. Although doing so is legal, you can't use the GOTO command to jump to a series of labels in a batch file from the DO portion of a FOR command. The GOTO command works just fine, but there is no mechanism available that enables you to return to the FOR loop when the section of the batch file that you jumped to is finished. To accomplish this task, you have to use the CALL command to call separate batch files instead of jumping to sections in the same batch file.

12. Be very careful if you are using destructive commands such as DEL or DELTREE in a FOR loop. Although you are debugging the FOR command, you might want to substitute the DIR command, which does not do any harm if anything goes wrong. Make sure that you think through every possible situation. Also, make sure that the wrong files won't be deleted before putting any batch file with a destructive FOR loop into use.

Examples

Suppose that you want to back up all settings files that Windows uses from a batch file. By combining the COPY command with FOR, you could accomplish this with the following line in your batch file:

```
FOR %%A IN (INI GRP PAR DAT) DO COPY C:\WINDOWS\*.%%A A:\
```

Assuming that you had previously prompted to insert the backup disk in drive A, the FOR command would execute the COPY command once for each type of file (.INI, .GRP, .PAR, and .DAT) in which Windows typically saves configuration information.

To execute the same command from the DOS prompt, use single percent signs rather than double ones, as shown here:

```
FOR %A IN (INI GRP PAR DAT) DO COPY C:\WINDOWS\*.%A A:\
```

You can use the FOR command to execute a command a specific number of times. For example, to display five blank lines from a batch file, you could include the following command:

```
FOR %%A IN (1 2 3 4 5) DO ECHO.
```

After all, there is no rule that says you have to use the %%A variable in the DO portion of the command. The preceding FOR loop repeats the ECHO. (ECHO period) command once for each member in the set, displaying five blank lines onscreen.

You can use FOR to enable a command that doesn't support wildcards to process a pathname specified with wildcards. A classic example of this technique involves the TYPE command. To display multiple files with TYPE, you could enter the following command in a batch file:

```
FOR %%A IN (%1) DO TYPE %%A
```

If you specified a pathname that included wildcards as the first parameter to the batch file, TYPE would be executed once for each file that matched the pathname. The only thing wrong with this is that TYPE would display all the files without pausing; so, to see a particular file, you would have to hover over the pause key. Despite this drawback, this example illustrates how you can use the FOR command to overcome this limitation in a command.

See Also

"Using FOR..IN..DO" in Chapter 16

FORMAT   1.0 AND LATER—EXTERNAL

The FORMAT command initializes a disk to accept DOS information and files. FORMAT also checks the disk for defective tracks and (optionally) places DOS on the floppy disk or hard disk.

SYNTAX

FORMAT *drive:* /V /V:*label* /Q /U /F:*size* /N:*sectors* /T:*tracks* /S /B /1 /4 /8

PARAMETERS AND SWITCHES

drive:	Specifies a valid drive letter to be formatted, followed by a colon (:).
/V	Prompts for a volume label for the disk.
/V:*label*	Makes *label* (which can be up to 11 characters long) the disk's volume label.
/Q	Performs a quick format by clearing only the FAT and root directory on the disk; this switch does not check the disk for bad sectors.
/U	Performs an unconditional format for a floppy disk. Unconditional formatting destroys all data on a floppy disk, which means that you cannot unformat the disk. (For more information on unformatting, see UNFORMAT later in this command reference.)
/F:*size*	Specifies the size to which a disk should be formatted, which can be less than the drive's maximum. Generally, you should use this switch in preference to a combination of /N and /T. The following table lists the possible values for *size*:

Drive Capacity	Allowable Values for *size*
160KB, 180KB	160, 160K, 160KB, 180, 180K, and 180KB
320KB, 360KB	All preceding, plus 320, 320K, 320KB, 360, 360K, and 360KB
1.2MB	All preceding, plus 1200, 1200K, 1200KB, 1.2, 1.2M, and 1.2MB
720KB	720, 720K, and 720KB
1.44MB	All for 720KB, plus 1440, 1440K, 1440KB, 1.44, 1.44M, and 1.44MB
2.88MB	All for 1.44MB, plus 2880, 2880K, 2880KB, 2.88, 2.88M, and 2.88MB

/N:*sectors*	Formats the disk with the number of sectors (*sectors* ranges from 1 to 99). This switch must be used with /T. Generally, you should use /F instead of this switch.

/T:*tracks*		Formats the disk with the number of tracks per side (*tracks* ranges from 1 to 999). This switch must be used with /N. Generally, you should use /F instead of this switch.
/S		Places copies of the operating system files on the disk so that DOS can boot from the disk. For MS-DOS, those files are the command-line interpreter pointed to by the environment variable COMSPEC (generally COMMAND.COM), the hidden files IO.SYS and MSDOS.SYS, and, if necessary, DBLSPACE.BIN.
/B		Leaves space for the system version but does not place the operating system files on the disk. (See the section on the SYS command later in this command reference.) This switch is not necessary in DOS 6.0.
/1		Formats only the first side of the floppy disk.
/4		Formats a floppy disk in a 1.2MB drive for double-density (320KB/360KB) use. Some systems, however, cannot reliably read the resulting disk.
/8		Formats an eight-sector 5 1/4-inch floppy disk (for compatibility with DOS 1.0).

Exit Codes

ERRORLEVEL Value	Meaning
0	Format operation successful
3	Halted by user (Ctrl+C)
4	Halted by a fatal disk error
5	Halted by user at the Proceed with Format (Y/N)? prompt

Rules

1. If you do not provide a drive name, DOS uses the current drive.
2. Unless otherwise directed through a switch, DOS formats the disk to the DOS maximum capacity for the drive.
3. Some switches do not work together. For example, you cannot use the following switch combinations:

    /V with /8

    /1, /4, /8, or /B with the hard disk

    /F with /N and /T

4. In DOS 5.0 and later versions, if you do not specify /U, FORMAT performs a "safe" format. DOS creates a file containing file information and saves the file to a safe place on disk where the UNFORMAT command can find it if you need to unformat the disk. FORMAT then clears the FAT and root directory of the disk but does not erase any data. Therefore, the UNFORMAT command enables you to restore a disk if you did not intend to format it.

5. If you are formatting a hard disk, FORMAT displays the following message:
   ```
   WARNING, ALL DATA ON NON-REMOVABLE DISK
   DRIVE d: WILL BE LOST!
   Proceed with Format (Y/N)?
   ```
   Type Y to format the hard disk or N to abort the formatting operation.

Notes

1. FORMAT now displays numbers with embedded commas, making them much easier to read.

2. Do not try to format any type of virtual disk; a disk that is part of an ASSIGN, SUBST, or JOIN command; or a networked or Interlnk disk.

3. Never try to format a RAM disk. Under some circumstances, FORMAT acts erratically when you use it to format a RAM disk, particularly RAMDRIVE (the DOS RAM disk program). The responses can range from a `Divide overflow` message to a lockup of your computer. If the computer locks up, turn off the system and then turn it on again. Obviously, you lose the RAM disk's contents, but no hard or floppy disks are damaged.

4. In pre-5.0 versions of DOS, FORMAT destroys the information recorded on a floppy or hard disk. Do not use the command on any disk—floppy or hard—that contains useful information.

5. In DOS 5.0 and later versions, FORMAT performs a safe format. When you use the command to format a previously formatted disk, DOS copies the FAT and root directory before clearing them and then checks the disk. The existing data is not cleared. If you accidentally format a safely formatted disk, you can unformat the disk. To erase all data from a previously used floppy disk, use the /U switch. An unconditional format takes about 27 percent longer than the default safe format.

6. The /Q switch, another feature of DOS 5.0 and later, enables you to format a disk quickly. The /Q switch clears the FAT and root directory but does not check the disk for bad sectors. To reuse a disk that you know is good, use the /Q switch. The quick format is nearly 80 percent faster than the default safe format.

7. The 160KB and 180KB disks are known as single-sided, double-density, 5 1/4-inch disks.

   The 320KB and 360KB disks are known as double-sided, double-density, 5 1/4-inch disks.

   The 1.2MB disks are known as double-sided, quadruple or high-density, 5 1/4-inch disks.

   The 720KB disks are known as double-sided, double-density, 3 1/2-inch disks.

   The 1.44MB disks are known as double-sided, quadruple or high-density, 3 1/2-inch disks.

   The 2.88MB disks are known as double-sided, extra-high-density, 3 1/2-inch disks.

Messages

```
Checking existing disk format
```

Information: FORMAT is checking the disk to see whether it has been formatted previously.

```
Saving UNFORMAT information
```

Information: If the disk has been formatted, the directory and FAT are saved on the disk, and a safe format is performed. A safely formatted disk can be unformatted.

```
Drive A error. Insufficient space for the MIRROR image file.
There was an error creating the format recovery file.
```

Warning: The previously formatted disk doesn't have room for the mirror-image file (the file that contains a copy of the FAT and root directory). The disk doesn't have enough room to save a copy of the root directory and FAT. Be sure that you want to format the disk that is located in the drive.

```
This disk cannot be unformatted.
```

Warning: FORMAT displays this message when it is prevented from saving information on the disk for UNFORMAT to use. You most likely will see this message when the disk is too full and not enough free space exists for the UNFORMAT information to be saved.

```
Invalid media or track 0 bad
disk unusable
```

Warning: Track 0 holds the boot record, FAT, and directory. This track is bad, and the floppy disk is unusable. Try reformatting the floppy disk. If the error reoccurs, you cannot use the floppy disk.

This error can occur when you format 720KB floppy disks as 1.44MB floppy disks (if you forget to use the /N:9 or /F:720 switch when you format the disk in a 1.44MB drive), or when you format 360KB floppy disks as 1.2MB floppy disks (if you forget the /4 or /F:360 switch).

This error also can occur when you format 1.2MB floppy disks at lower capacities (such as 360KB) and use the /4 switch. In this case, try using a floppy disk rated for double-sided, double-density use.

```
WARNING, ALL DATA ON NON-REMOVABLE DISK
DRIVE d: WILL BE LOST!
Proceed with Format (Y/N)?
```

Warning: FORMAT is warning you that you are about to format a hard disk. To format the hard disk, type Y and press Enter. If you do not want to format the hard disk, type N and press Enter.

See Also

SYS and UNFORMAT

Chapter 6, "Understanding Disks and Disk Drives"

GOTO   2.0 AND LATER—INTERNAL

GOTO transfers control to the line following a labeled line in the batch file and continues executing the batch file from that line. GOTO is an unconditional jump and always transfers control whenever the command is encountered.

SYNTAX

GOTO *label*

PARAMETERS AND SWITCHES

label   The label that DOS should jump to. *label* transfers execution to the batch file line following *label*.

NOTES

1. To define a label, enter it at the beginning of a line, preceded by a colon (:). Only the first eight characters of a label are significant, although you can enter as many characters as you want without generating an error. All characters on a line past the eighth character of a label are ignored. Spaces are not allowed in labels.

2. When the command GOTO *label* is executed, DOS jumps to the line following the label and continues executing the batch file. The label can be placed before or after the GOTO statement in the batch file.

3. If a batch file does not contain the label specified by GOTO, the batch file stops and DOS displays a Label not found error message.

4. Adding a colon as the first character of a line in a batch file effectively "comments out" the line by causing DOS to treat it as a label rather than as a line to be executed. DOS interprets it as a label, however, so using REM is safer.

5. Although GOTO doesn't generate an error message when you use it from the DOS command line, neither does it serve any purpose. Labels have no meaning on the command line, so the GOTO command has no place to jump to.

SEE ALSO

:*label* and REM

"Branching with GOTO" in Chapter 16

GRAFTABL   3.0 TO 5.0—EXTERNAL

GRAFTABL loads into memory the tables of additional character sets to be displayed on the Color Graphics Adapter (CGA). GRAFTABL is included on the DOS 6.0 Supplemental Disk, not in the standard DOS 6.0 package.

SYNTAX

GRAFTABL *codepage* /STATUS

Parameters and Switches

codepage   Represents the three-digit number of the code page for the display. The default value is 437, the code page for the U.S. See Chapter 14, "Understanding the International Features of DOS," for a list of the code pages that DOS supports.

/STATUS   Displays the code page selected for use by GRAFTABL. You cannot specify a *codepage* and request /STATUS information in the same command. This parameter can be abbreviated as /STA.

Exit Codes

ERRORLEVEL Value	Meaning
0	New character set loaded; no set was loaded previously
1	New character set loaded; previous set replaced
2	Disk error prevented loading new character set
3	Command line invalid; no action taken
4	Incorrect DOS version running

Notes

1. Load GRAFTABL to display legible characters in the ASCII range 128 to 255 when you are in graphics mode on the Color Graphics Adapter (CGA).
2. GRAFTABL increases the size of DOS by 1,360 bytes.
3. If you do not specify a *codepage*, DOS uses code page 437 in the USA.
4. After you invoke GRAFTABL, the only way to deactivate the command is to restart DOS.
5. The IBM CGA in graphics mode produces low-quality ASCII characters in the 128-to-255 range.
6. GRAFTABL is useful only when your system is equipped with the CGA and when you use the CGA in medium- or high-resolution graphics mode.

See Also

DISPLAY.SYS and CHCP

GRAPHICS   2.0 AND LATER—EXTERNAL

GRAPHICS enables the Print Screen key to print the contents of a graphics screen on a suitable printer. When you first run GRAPHICS, it loads itself into memory and remains there until you restart your computer.

Syntax

GRAPHICS *printer pathname.pro* /R /B /PRINTBOX:STD /PRINTBOX:LCD /LCD

Parameters and Switches

printer Specifies the type of printer you are using. *printer* can be one of the following values:

Printer	Description
COLOR1	IBM Personal Color Printer with a black ribbon
COLOR4	IBM Personal Color Printer with an RGB (red, green, blue, and black) ribbon, which produces four colors
COLOR8	IBM Personal Color Printer with a CMYK (cyan, magenta, yellow, and black) ribbon, which produces eight colors
GRAPHICS	IBM Personal Graphics Printer, IBM ProPrinter, or IBM Quietwriter
THERMAL	IBM PC-Convertible thermal printer
GRAPHICSWIDE	IBM Personal Graphics Printer with an 11-inch-wide carriage
HPDEFAULT	Any Hewlett-Packard PCL printer
DESKJET	A Hewlett-Packard DeskJet printer
LASERJET	A Hewlett-Packard LaserJet printer
LASERJETII	A Hewlett-Packard LaserJet II printer
PAINTJET	A Hewlett-Packard PaintJet printer
QUIETJET	A Hewlett-Packard QuietJet printer
QUIETJETPLUS	A Hewlett-Packard QuietJet Plus printer
RUGGEDWRITER	A Hewlett-Packard RuggedWriter printer
RUGGEDWRITERWIDE	A Hewlett-Packard RuggedWriter wide printer
THINKJET	A Hewlett-Packard ThinkJet printer

pathname.pro Specifies the file that contains printer information. Normal drive and subdirectory defaults apply, but wildcards are not allowed. If you do not specify a printer information file, DOS looks for the file GRAPHICS.PRO in the current directory or the directory containing the GRAPHICS.COM program file (normally C:\DOS).

/R Reverses the colors so that the image on the paper matches the image onscreen (a white image on a black background).

/B Prints the background in the color displayed onscreen. You can use this switch only when the printer type is COLOR4 or COLOR8.

/PRINTBOX:STD or /PRINTBOX:LCD   Indicates the printbox size, or aspect ratio, to use when converting the image onscreen. This parameter must match the first Printbox statement in the printer profile. You can abbreviate /PRINTBOX as /PB.

/LCD   Prints the image as displayed on the PC Convertible's LCD display. This switch is the equivalent of /PRINTBOX:LCD.

SEE ALSO

"The GRAPHICS Command" in Chapter 13

HCONVERT

HCONVERT updates an earlier Stacker drive that was not mounted during Stacker Setup or a removable Stacker drive that needs to be updated.

SYNTAX

HCONVERT *drive*: ***source target*** /c *source*|/g /m /?

PARAMETERS AND SWITCHES

Drive   Specifies the drive letter to be converted.

source   Specifies the name of the STACVOL file to update.

target   Indicates the STACVOL file to create when using the /g switch.

/c *source*   Updates the named STACVOL file to the new Stacker format.

/g *source target*   Generates a STACVOL file in the new storage format by copying the named old STACVOL file as a new Stacker volume. It does not change the existing STACVOL file. If you omit the drive letter in either volume name, the current disk is used.

/m   Use with either /c or /g on a monochrome monitor.

/?   Displays the abbreviated online help.

REMARKS

Do not interrupt the HCONVERT program and run it only from the DOS command prompt.

HELP   5.0 AND LATER—EXTERNAL

HELP is a full-screen, online help system that includes information about every DOS command. HELP contains the entire text of the "MS-DOS 6 Command Reference" section from the Technical Reference manual published by Microsoft. In addition, it provides hypertext links and a searchable index that can help you move quickly from one topic to the next.

DOS version 5.0 included a HELP command as well, but it bore more resemblance to the DOS 6 FASTHELP command than to the DOS 6 online help system.

SYNTAX

HELP *command* /B /G /H /NOHI

PARAMETERS AND SWITCHES

command   Indicates the command that you want information about. If this parameter is omitted, HELP displays its table of contents screen.

/B   Specifies that HELP should use colors more appropriate for a black-and-white (monochrome) or LCD display.

/G   Specifies that HELP should use the fastest screen-updating method for a CGA monitor. Don't specify the /G switch if you see "snow" on your monitor.

/H   Specifies that HELP should display 43 lines on an EGA monitor or 50 lines on a VGA monitor.

/NOHI   Specifies that HELP should limit itself to 8 colors rather than 16.

NOTES

1. For HELP to work, QBASIC.EXE must be in the current directory, in your search path, or in the same directory as HELP.COM.
2. Help is available for many topics other than DOS commands (for example, CONFIG.SYS commands). See HELP'S table of contents for a complete list.
3. In addition to extensive syntax help, HELP displays usage notes, examples, and links-related material by hypertext links.
4. You can get simple syntax help for DOS commands from FASTHELP or by typing the following command:
   command /?

SEE ALSO

FASTHELP

"Getting Help" in Chapter 3

HIINSTALL OR INSTALLHIGH

HIINSTALL (or INSTALLHIGH) executes a program from the CONFIG.SYS file and loads it into upper memory.

SYNTAX

HIINSTALL *drive:\path\filename arguments*

Parameters and Switches

drive:\path\filename   The drive, path, and filename for the program to execute.

arguments   Any optional or required arguments for the program being executed by HIINSTALL.

HILOAD (SEE LOADHIGH)

HILOAD is a DR DOS alternative command for the LOADHIGH command. See the detailed description under LOADHIGH.

HIMEM.SYS (DEVICE DRIVER) 4.0 AND LATER— EXTERNAL

If your computer has more than 1MB of RAM installed, you should load HIMEM.SYS in your CONFIG.SYS file. HIMEM.SYS is an XMS v3.0-compatible extended memory manager. Its services are required in order for DOS to use the extended memory your computer has installed. HIMEM.SYS should be one of the first device drivers loaded with the DEVICE= command in your CONFIG.SYS file.

Syntax

For most people, the DEVICE= line that loads HIMEM.SYS can be very simple:

`DEVICE=`*drive:\path*`HIMEM.SYS`

The full syntax for HIMEM.SYS can seem intimidating, but all the optional parameters have appropriate defaults:

`DEVICE=`*drive:\path*`HIMEM.SYS   /A20CONTROL:`*onoff*`   /CPUCLOCK:`*onoff*`   /EISA`
`/HMAMIN=`*min*`   /INT15=`*size*`   /NOTEST   /NUMHANDLES=`*num*`   /MACHINE:`*machcode*
`/SHADOWRAM:`*onoff*`   /VERBOSE   /V`

Parameters and Switches

drive:\path   The full path to the HIMEM.SYS file on your system. Setup places the HIMEM.SYS file in the C:\DOS subdirectory by default. If the full path to HIMEM.SYS isn't specified, DOS looks for the file in the root directory of the startup drive.

/A20CONTROL:*onoff*   The A20 line is the address line that controls access to extended memory, including the high memory area (HMA). Specifying /A20CONTROL:OFF instructs HIMEM.SYS to take control of the A20 line only if it's off when HIMEM.SYS loads into memory. The default value is /A20CONTROL:ON, which allows HIMEM.SYS to take control of the A20 address line no matter what state it is in. As long as HIMEM.SYS is the first program to access extended memory when you reboot your computer, you should never need this parameter.

HIMEM.SYS (DEVICE DRIVER)   4.0 AND LATER—EXTERNAL

/CPUCLOCK:*onoff*   On certain computers, HIMEM.SYS may change the CPU clock speed when it loads. If this happens to you, specify the /CPUCLOCK:ON parameter to prevent HIMEM.SYS from changing the CPU clock speed. The default value is /CPUCLOCK:OFF, which allows HIMEM.SYS to load a little faster on most computers.

/EISA   You need to include this parameter only if you have an EISA (Extended Industry Standard Architecture) computer with more than 16MB of RAM installed. Including this parameter allows HIMEM.SYS to control all the available extended memory in such a system.

> **Note**
>
> HIMEM.SYS versions 3.07 through 3.09 (v3.09 is distributed with DOS 6) may fail to recognize more than 64MB of memory on an EISA computer even with the /EISA parameter specified. If you have this problem, contact Microsoft and ask for document number Q98111 as well as any other available material that can help you get around this limitation.

/HMAMIN=*min*   Only one application can use the HMA at a time. The /HMAMIN=*min* parameter specifies the minimum amount of RAM (in kilobytes) that an application must request to be granted access to the HMA. Valid values for *min* are in the range 0 through 63. If this parameter is omitted, a value of 0 is assumed, and the HMA is granted to the first program that requests it.

Normally, you want to load DOS into the HMA to save 43KB of conventional memory. However, DOS does not allocate the HMA until after all other device drivers and programs in your CONFIG.SYS file are loaded. To prevent them from allocating the HMA before DOS can get to it, try specifying /HMAMIN=40 in the line that loads HIMEM.SYS.

/INT15=*size*   Certain older applications use the Interrupt 15h interface to allocate extended memory. If you are using a program that requires this type of memory, you can set some aside for it by using the /INT15=*size* parameter. *size* is specified in kilobytes and can be any value in the range 64 to 65,535, or the amount of extended memory you have in your system—whichever is lower. Note that you should specify 64KB more than your application requires because the HMA is allocated from this memory as well. Any memory you set aside with the /INT15 parameter is unavailable to programs using the standard XMS interface. If you do not specify the /INT15 parameter, no memory is set aside (except the HMA).

/NOTEST *(NEW MS-DOS 6.2)*   This parameter specifies that you do not want HIMEM.SYS to scan extended memory when it loads. Normally, HIMEM.SYS attempts to identify weak and unreliable RAM chips by scanning all extended memory.

/NUMHANDLES=*num*   When programs request extended memory, they are given a handle to an extended memory block by HIMEM.SYS. The /NUMHANDLES=*num* parameter specifies how many handles HIMEM.SYS should have available. *num* can be any value in the range 1 to 128. If this parameter is omitted, 32 handles will be available. Each handle increases the size of HIMEM in memory by approximately 6 bytes. If the /VERBOSE (or /V) parameter is specified, HIMEM.SYS displays the number of handles available when it finishes loading into memory. (See the message `num extended memory handles available` in the following "Messages" section.)

/MACHINE:*machcode*   This parameter is required only if HIMEM.SYS is unable to gain control of the A20 address line for your computer. When this happens, HIMEM.SYS stops loading and displays an error message. (See the message `ERROR: Unable to control A20 line!` in the following "Messages" section.) To enable HIMEM.SYS to work with your computer, you might have to specify one of the machine codes from the following table. The default value for this parameter is /MACHINE:1 or /MACHINE:AT.

machcode can be the number in the Code column or the abbreviation shown, whichever you find easier to type and remember. Note that more than one computer type can use the same code number.

Computer Type	Code	Abbreviation
IBM AT or 100% compatible	1	AT
CompuAdd 386 systems	1 or 8	AT
JDR 386/33	1	AT
Phoenix BIOS	1 or 8	AT or WYSE
IBM PS/2	2	PS2
Datamedia 386/486	2	PS2
UNISYS PowerPort	2	PS2
Phoenix Cascade BIOS	3	PTLCASCADE
HP Vectra (A and A+)	4	HPVECTRA
AT&T 6300 Plus	5	ATT6300PLUS
Acer 1100	6	ACER1100
Toshiba 1600, 1200XE, and 5100	7	TOSHIBA
Wyse 12.5MHz 286	8	WYSE
Hitachi HL500C	8	WYSE
Intel 301z or 302	8	WYSE

Tulip SX	9	TULIP
Zenith ZBIOS	10	ZENITH
IBM PC / AT (alternative delay)	11	AT1
IBM PC / AT (alternative delay)	12	AT2
CSS Labs	12	CSS
IBM PC / AT (alternative delay)	13	AT3
Philips	13	PHILIPS
HP Vectra	14	FASTHP
IBM 7552 Industrial Computer *	15	IBM7552
Bull Micral 60 *	16	BULLMICRAL
Dell XBIOS *	17	DELL

*Not available in the version of HIMEM.SYS distributed with DOS 5.

You might have to specify 1 or AT as the machine type for your computer, despite the fact that 1 is the default value for the /MACHINE parameter. HIMEM.SYS tries to determine what type of computer you have when it loads into memory; if it gets confused, it may select the wrong method for controlling the A20 line. In these cases, you might have to explicitly set the machine type to 1.

For the version of HIMEM.SYS that is distributed with DOS 6 (v3.09), the only systems that should require the use of the /MACHINE parameter to operate are the Acer 1100 (code 6), the Wyse 12.5MHz 286 (code 8), and the IBM 7552 Industrial Computer (code 15). Systems that have the same code value as these systems are likely to require this parameter as well.

/SHADOWRAM:onoff This parameter is useful only on computer systems with less than 2MB of RAM. On such systems, if HIMEM.SYS detects that the ROM BIOS is running from shadow RAM, it attempts to reclaim that memory and turn it into available XMS memory. If you don't want HIMEM.SYS to do this, specify the /SHADOWRAM:ON parameter.

Note that specifying /SHADOWRAM:ON allows only the ROM BIOS to continue to run from RAM. HIMEM.SYS cannot set up shadow RAM on a system that doesn't already have it.

/VERBOSE This parameter specifies that HIMEM.SYS should display status messages while it loads. By default, HIMEM.SYS doesn't display any messages unless an error occurs. You also can turn on the display of messages while HIMEM.SYS is loading by pressing the Alt key.

/V This switch is an abbreviated form of the /VERBOSE parameter.

Notes

1. HIMEM.SYS now automatically performs a memory scan to identify RAM chips that are becoming unreliable. An unreliable RAM chip can halt your computer in the middle of a critical operation and could lead to a serious loss of data. If you don't want HIMEM.SYS to perform this memory scan, include the new /NOTEST switch.

2. HIMEM.SYS requires at least an 80286-based computer with more than 1MB of RAM installed in order to run. Computers with less than 1MB of RAM have no extended memory to manage.

3. You cannot load HIMEM.SYS with a DEVICEHIGH= command. HIMEM.SYS is one of the programs that enables you to load other device drivers or programs into upper memory with the DEVICEHIGH= or LOADHIGH commands. HIMEM.SYS does attempt to minimize its use of conventional memory; after HIMEM.SYS is loaded, it uses only about 1KB of conventional memory.

4. The line that loads HIMEM.SYS should be one of the very first DEVICE= lines in your CONFIG.SYS file. If any other driver using extended memory is loaded before HIMEM.SYS, the chances are very good that HIMEM.SYS will refuse to load.

5. The DOS 6 Setup program inserts the DEVICE= line, which loads SETVER.EXE before the line for HIMEM.SYS. This doesn't cause any problems, but it does prevent you from loading SETVER.EXE into upper memory with the DEVICEHIGH= command. To gain a little conventional memory, move the DEVICE= line for SETVER.EXE after the lines that load HIMEM.SYS and EMM386.EXE and change the DEVICE= command into a DEVICEHIGH= command.

6. HIMEM.SYS (or another XMS-compatible memory manager) must be loaded before you can use any of the following commands or drivers in your CONFIG.SYS file:
   DEVICEHIGH=
   DOS=HIGH
   DOS=UMB
   EMM386.EXE

   The DOS=UMB and DEVICEHIGH= commands actually depend on a UMB provider such as EMM386.EXE. Because most UMB providers require the use of XMS memory, however, they all indirectly depend on HIMEM.SYS.

7. If HIMEM.SYS is unable to gain control of the A20 address line, it aborts with an error message. (See the message ERROR: Unable to control A20 line! in the following "Messages" section.) Unless your computer's hardware is incompatible, HIMEM.SYS should be able to gain control; its failure to do so usually means that another program is preventing HIMEM.SYS from doing its job. Two programs cannot share control of extended memory, so you have to remove one of them from your CONFIG.SYS file. Check to see whether you are loading any third-party memory managers before the line that loads HIMEM.SYS. (If HIMEM.SYS were loading first, your third-party memory manager would be the one displaying the error message, probably telling you to remove HIMEM.SYS.)

   If no other memory managers are loading before HIMEM.SYS, it might be baffled by the method used to control the A20 address line in your computer. In these cases, you have to specify a /MACHINE:*machcode* parameter to tell HIMEM how to control the A20 address line. Look for your computer in the table of machine codes. (See the table of machine codes in the preceding "Parameters and Switches" section.) If you find your computer listed, add a /MACHINE:*machcode* parameter to the line that loads HIMEM.SYS in your CONFIG.SYS file.

EXAMPLES

The first few lines in most people's CONFIG.SYS files look something like this:

```
DEVICE=C:\DOS\HIMEM.SYS
DEVICE=C:\DOS\EMM386.EXE RAM MIN=0
DOS=HIGH,UMB
```

First, HIMEM.SYS is loaded into memory to provide access to the HMA and XMS-compatible memory. Then, EMM386.EXE is loaded, which provides upper memory block (UMB) support for DOS as well as EMS-compatible memory for those programs that use it. (The RAM switch enables UMB and EMS support, and MIN=0 lets EMM386.EXE release back into the memory pool EMS memory that's not in use.) Finally, DOS is instructed to load itself into the high memory area (HMA) provided by HIMEM.SYS and to establish connections with the UMBs provided by EMM386.EXE.

If you own an Acer 1100 computer, you might have to include a /MACHINE parameter to let HIMEM.SYS know how to control the A20 line in your computer, as shown in the following example:

```
DEVICE=C:\DOS\HIMEM.SYS   /MACHINE:ACER1100   /V
```

When you include the /V (or /VERBOSE) parameter, HIMEM.SYS displays all messages while it loads into memory, so you can keep track of how it is doing. Notice that you can enter the machine code parameter as /MACHINE:ACER1100 or /MACHINE:6, but not as /ACER1100.

MESSAGES

```
64K High Memory Area is available
```

Information: If you have specified the /VERBOSE parameter, HIMEM.SYS displays this message after successfully gaining control of the A20 line.

```
ERROR: An Extended Memory Manager is already installed
```

Error: Another XMS memory manager was installed before HIMEM.SYS. If you are using a third-party memory manager, remove the line that loads HIMEM.SYS from your CONFIG.SYS file. If you want to use HIMEM.SYS, remove the other memory manager instead.

```
ERROR: HIMEM.SYS requires an 80x86-based machine
```

Error: HIMEM.SYS can't run on 8088- and 8086-based computers. The only function of HIMEM.SYS is to control and regulate the use of extended memory, and these types of computers don't have any.

```
ERROR: HIMEM.SYS requires DOS 3.00 or higher
```

Error: Version 3.09 of HIMEM.SYS, which is the version distributed with MS-DOS 6.0, requires at least DOS 3 to run. If you know that you're running DOS 5 or 6 (to find out, use the VER command), check your SETVER.EXE version table to make sure that no one has entered HIMEM.SYS into it as a practical joke.

```
ERROR: No available extended memory was found
```

Error: HIMEM.SYS can't find any extended memory in your system. You may not have enough RAM installed to run HIMEM.SYS.

```
ERROR: Unable to control A20 line!
```

Error: HIMEM.SYS displays this message if it is unable to gain control of the A20 line in your computer. Normally, this message means that you must specify a /MACHINE:*machcode* parameter on the line that loads HIMEM.SYS in your CONFIG.SYS file.

```
ERROR: VDISK memory allocator already installed
XMS Driver not installed
```

Error: A device driver that loaded before HIMEM.SYS allocated some extended memory with the Interrupt 15h interface. To get HIMEM.SYS to load, make sure that the DEVICE= line for HIMEM.SYS precedes the driver using Interrupt 15h. To reserve memory for this other driver, specify an /INT15=*size* parameter on the line for HIMEM.SYS.

```
Installed A20 handler number num
```

Information: HIMEM.SYS has gained control of the A20 line using machine handler number *num*. Check the table shown earlier in the "Parameters and Switches" section to see what computer system *num* corresponds to.

```
Minimum HMA size set to minK
```

Information: Programs that attempt to allocate less than *min*K RAM in the HMA are denied. If *min* is greater than zero, you've probably set the /HMAMIN=*min* parameter to prevent another program from grabbing the HMA before DOS can get to it.

```
num extended memory handles available
```

Information: HIMEM.SYS has created *num* extended memory block handles, either by default or through the use of the /NUMHANDLES=*num* parameter.

```
Shadow RAM disabled
```

Information: On computers with less than 2MB of RAM, HIMEM.SYS often disables shadow RAM to make more extended memory available. If you don't want HIMEM.SYS to disable shadow RAM, specify the /SHADOWRAM:ON parameter.

```
WARNING: Invalid parameter ignored
```

Warning: An invalid parameter was specified on the line that loaded HIMEM.SYS. Check the line in CONFIG.SYS carefully and look any for mistyped options.

```
WARNING: Shadow RAM disable not supported on this system
```

Warning: `HIMEM.SYS` is unable to disable shadow RAM for your computer. If you want to turn off shadow RAM, you have to use your computer's CMOS Setup program or set jumpers on the motherboard.

```
WARNING: Shadow RAM is in use and can't be disabled
```

Warning: You have specified `/SHADOWRAM:OFF`, but it's already in use and `HIMEM.SYS` can't disable it. You might have to use your CMOS Setup program if you want to turn off shadow RAM on your computer.

```
WARNING: The A20 Line was already enabled
```

Warning: Another program has enabled your computer's `A20` line, and `HIMEM.SYS` is unsure what to make of it. Usually, `HIMEM.SYS` still assumes control of extended memory. To avoid this warning, make sure that `HIMEM.SYS` is loaded before any other drivers that use extended memory. If you have another device driver that needs to control the `A20` line, you might have to specify the `/A20CONTROL:OFF` parameter to get `HIMEM.SYS` to cooperate with the other device driver.

```
WARNING: The High Memory Area is unavailable
```

Warning: This message may appear if you have only 1MB of RAM or if another program has taken over the HMA. Make sure that `HIMEM.SYS` is loaded before any other drivers that use extended memory.

SEE ALSO

`DEVICE=`, `DOS=`, and `EMM386.EXE`

"Using Extended Memory and `HIMEM.SYS`" in Chapter 19

IBMAVD

`IBMAVD` opens the IBM AntiVirus/DOS full-screen utility program.

SYNTAX

IBMAVD

IBMAVSP

You use the `IBMAVSP` command to start IBMAVSP, the IBM AntiVirus standalone program. This program can help find and remove a virus when the system is too badly infected to use the full-screen IBM AntiVirus program. It can also be incorporated into `.BAT` files. If no options are specified, `IBMAVSP` operates interactively.

SYNTAX

IBMAVSP * *n *drive*... -mem -allfiles -programs -oneflop -log*logfilename* -vlog -nlog -nb -copenerr -cerr -nrep -nwipe -nfscan -yrep -ywipe -yfscan /?

Parameters and Switches

`*`	Scans all local fixed drives for viruses.
`*n`	Scans all network drives.
`drive:...`	Scans the drive specified. One or more drive letters can be specified on the command-line statement.
`-mem`	Scans memory. This parameter can be used when only memory (not drives) needs to be checked.
`-allfiles`	Scans all files on the specified drives for viruses.
`-programs`	Scans only programs on the specified drives for viruses.
`-oneflop`	Prevents the IBMAVSP program from asking for a second disk to scan.
`-loglogfilename`	Specifies where IBMAVSP is to place the log file. If `logfilename` is not specified, the log is written to the file IBMAVSP.LOG in the current directory.
`-vlog`	Specifies that the names of all scanned files and boot sectors be placed into the log file, whether an object was infected or not.
`-nlog`	Specifies that no log file is to be created.
`-nb`	Specifies no beep when a virus is found.
`-copenerr`	Continues checking for viruses without asking, even if a file cannot be opened for scanning.
`-cerr`	Continues checking for viruses without asking, even if a nonfatal error is encountered.
`-nrep`	Specifies that infected files or boot sectors should not be repaired.
`-nwipe`	Specifies that infected files should not be erased and infected boot sectors should not be replaced if they cannot be repaired.
`-nfscan`	Specifies not to offer to perform a final, thorough scan if viruses are found.
`-yrep`	Specifies that infected files or boot sectors be repaired.
`-ywipe`	Specifies that infected files should be erased and infected boot sectors should be replaced if they cannot be repaired.
`-yfscan`	Specifies that a final, thorough scan should be performed automatically if viruses are found.
`/?`	Displays the abbreviated online help.

IEXTRACT

The IEXTRACT command extracts a file from an Internet Explorer backup information file with the .DAT extension.

SYNTAX

    IEXTRACT /W /L dir drive:\path filename ...

PARAMETERS AND SWITCHES

/W	Generates a warning before overwriting a file.
/L dir	Saves extracted files in the location specified by *dir*.
drive:\path	Specifies the drive and path location of the .DAT file.
filename	Specifies the name of the file or files to extract from the backup information file. If no *filename* is specified, all files in the .DAT file will be extracted.

IF   2.0 AND LATER—INTERNAL

You can use the IF command to add conditional execution of a DOS command to your batch files. You can test for three types of conditions with the IF command: the value of an exit code returned by a program, the equivalence of two alphanumeric strings, and the existence of a file or subdirectory.

SYNTAX

To test the exit code returned by a program, use the following form of the IF command:

    IF NOT ERRORLEVEL number command parameters

To compare two alphanumeric strings, use the following form of the IF command:

    IF NOT string1==string2 command parameters

To check for the existence of a file or files, use the following form of the IF command:

    IF NOT EXIST pathname command parameters

PARAMETERS AND SWITCHES

NOT	Tests for the opposite of the condition. In other words, IF NOT executes the *command* if the condition is false.
ERRORLEVEL number	Tests the exit code (0 to 255) that a program returns when it terminates. If the exit code is greater than or equal to the *number*, the condition is true.
string1==string2	Compares two alphanumeric strings to determine whether they are identical. This comparison is case sensitive, so upper- and lowercase

characters are not considered equal. The strings can include literals, batch file replaceable parameters (such as %1), environment variables (such as %COMSPEC%), or any combination of the three.

EXIST *pathname*   Tests whether the file specified by *pathname* exists. If no drive or path is included in *pathname*, the current drive or directory is assumed. The filename portion is required. Wildcards are allowed in the filename and extension portions of *pathname*.

command   Represents the DOS command that is executed if the condition is true (or false if NOT is specified). If you want to run a batch file, use the CALL or COMMAND /C command instead of executing the batch file directly.

parameters   Represents any parameters you want to pass to the *command* being executed.

NOTES

1. For the IF command, if the condition is true, the *command* is executed. If the condition is false, DOS skips the *command* and immediately executes the next line of the batch file.

2. For the IF NOT subcommand, if the condition is false, the *command* is executed. If the condition is true, DOS skips the *command* and immediately executes the next line of the batch file.

3. If you want to run a batch file from the command portion of an IF command, use the CALL or COMMAND /C command instead of executing it directly. Without CALL or COMMAND /C, control never returns to your batch file.

4. IF commands can be nested. That is, you can use the IF command in the *command* portion of an IF command. This can be a handy way to test for a range of exit code values, freeing you from the tyranny of descending order IF ERRORLEVEL statements. (See the following "Examples" section.)

5. Do not attempt to use the "at" sign (@) to suppress the display of the command specified in the command portion of an IF command. DOS will not interpret the @ correctly and will search for an executable file that begins with an "at" sign. To accomplish the same thing, enter ECHO OFF before executing the IF statement.

6. IF ERRORLEVEL *number* returns true if the number you specified is less than or equal to the exit code returned by the previous program. For this reason, IF ERRORLEVEL commands usually have to be arranged in descending order to get the desired results. You must test for this value immediately after the program terminates. Executing any other command, even if it doesn't return an exit code, may clear the previous exit code from memory.

7. Not all programs return exit codes. If a program doesn't return an exit code, an IF ERRORLEVEL 0 command evaluates to true, but any other number causes the IF statement to be false. Presently, no DOS internal commands return exit codes, and,

unfortunately, you can't set the exit code for a batch file either. The following DOS external commands return exit codes:

BACKUP	DISKCOPY	MSAV
CHKDSK	FIND	REPLACE
CHOICE	FORMAT	RESTORE
DEFRAG	GRAFTABL	SCANDISK
DELTREE	KEYB	SETVER
DISKCOMP	MOVE	XCOPY

8. If you use CALL to call a program that returns an exit code, that exit code value is available after CALL returns. Unfortunately, you can't set the exit code for a batch file, so CALL can't return an exit code from a batch file you have executed. To return status information from a batch file executed with the CALL command, create an environment variable and set it equal to your return status. Then, you can test this environment variable in the calling batch file.

9. For *string1==string2*, DOS makes a literal, character-by-character comparison of the two strings. Neither string can contain embedded spaces or equal signs. If you want to include a percent sign (%) in either string, include it twice if this IF command is executed from a batch file. The comparison IF performs is case sensitive; that is, uppercase and lowercase characters are considered to be different.

10. When you include environment variables (such as %COMSPEC%) or replaceable parameters (such as %0 through %9) in either string argument in a batch file, they are replaced with the value of the environment variable or replaceable parameter when DOS parses the line. DOS does not parse commands you enter at the DOS prompt, so you can't include either type of variable in a command that you execute from the DOS prompt.

11. When IF is performing *string1==string2* comparisons, each string must have at least one character in it; otherwise, a syntax error will result, and DOS will abort the batch file. In DOS 6 and later, *string2* can be empty without causing an error. This problem often happens in IF statements that test replaceable parameters or environment variables and typically is solved by adding dummy characters to both strings. For instance, test %1x==ERNIEx or "%1"=="ERNIE" instead of %1==ERNIE.

12. Including only one equal sign in an IF string comparison results in a syntax error. Interestingly enough, you can use more than two equal signs without causing an error.

13. The EXIST *pathname* form of the IF command returns true if at least one file matches the pathname specified. If an invalid subdirectory or drive is specified, the condition is false. DOS does not search the DOS PATH for *pathname*; DOS searches only the drive and subdirectory specified. If *pathname* is omitted, DOS searches the current drive and directory.

14. Although the EXIST *pathname* form of the IF command is intended to test for the existence of files, you can use it to test for the existence of a subdirectory by specifying the NUL device as the filename. The NUL device (or any other valid DOS device) exists in every subdirectory; so if the specified subdirectory exists, the IF EXIST *path*\NUL command is true.

Examples

Notice that because of the way the `IF ERRORLEVEL` command works—testing whether an exit code is greater than or equal to the number specified—the following statement always executes the `GOTO` statement:

```
IF  ERRORLEVEL  0  GOTO  ALWAYS_JUMP
```

When you're testing an `ERRORLEVEL` number, be sure to test for the highest possible number first. Consider the following example:

```
IF  ERRORLEVEL  1  GOTO  ONE_OR_GREATER
IF  ERRORLEVEL  2  GOTO  TWO_OR_GREATER
```

The preceding example always goes to `ONE_OR_GREATER`, even if an `ERRORLEVEL` of 2 is returned because 2 is greater than or equal to 1. Make sure that when you use `IF ERRORLEVEL` commands, you include them in descending order.

You can get around the limitation just noted by nesting `IF ERRORLEVEL` commands, checking for ranges of values with upper and lower bounds. Test for the lowest value; then test for `NOT` the highest value plus one in an embedded `IF` command. For example, consider the following `IF` commands:

```
IF  ERRORLEVEL  1  IF  NOT  ERRORLEVEL  4  GOTO  ONE_TO_THREE
```

In English, if the exit code returned by the program is greater than or equal to the first value (1) and less than the second value (not greater than or equal to 4), execute the command. Notice that this form of the `IF ERRORLEVEL` command executes the proper `GOTO` command, no matter what order they are executed in. To test for a single value, simply embed a negative test for one more than the value you want, like this:

```
IF  ERRORLEVEL  2  IF  NOT  ERRORLEVEL  3  GOTO  ONLY_TWO
```

`IF` string comparisons are often used to make sure that at least one parameter is specified when the batch file is executed, as shown in these examples:

```
IF  "%1"==""  GOTO  HELP_MESSAGE
IF  "%1"=="/?"  GOTO  HELP_MESSAGE
```

If no parameters to the batch file are specified, the first `IF` condition is true, and the `GOTO` command jumps to a section of the batch file where you can display a help message. The second `IF` statement tests for the `/?` help switch, enabling this batch file to honor a request for help from the user as well.

Sometimes this technique is combined with the `SHIFT` command to enable a batch file to loop through a variable number of parameters, as shown in the following:

```
:LOOP
IF  "%1"==""  GOTO  END
TYPE  %1  |  MORE
SHIFT
GOTO  LOOP

:END
```

You could specify as many text files as you wanted to when executing this batch file, and the TYPE command would display each one in turn. After the last file had been displayed, the IF command would execute the GOTO END command, and the batch file would terminate. When you combine IF and GOTO in this way, you can create a multiline loop in a batch file.

To jump around part of a batch file if the network menu choice was not chosen from a DOS 6.0 startup menu, use the following line:

```
IF NOT "%CONFIG%"=="NETWORK" GOTO FINISH
```

Notice that in all the preceding examples, quotation marks are used to ensure that the string comparisons never try to evaluate a null string. For example, in the preceding command, if the CONFIG environment variable turns out to be undefined, DOS evaluates the following statement after the parser makes substitutions:

```
IF NOT ""=="NETWORK" GOTO FINISH
```

Without the quotation marks, one side of the comparison would be empty, and the batch file would be aborted with a syntax error message. With the quotation marks included, DOS simply finds "" not equal to "NETWORK".

Suppose that you want to copy all the .DOC files in your C:\WORK subdirectory to a backup disk. You could use the IF EXIST command, as follows, to make sure that at least one .DOC file existed before executing the COPY command:

```
IF EXIST C:\WORK\*.DOC COPY C:\WORK\*.DOC A:
```

The IF EXIST command can be used to check for the existence of a subdirectory if you specify the NUL device as the filename. You can use this technique to create a subdirectory if it doesn't already exist:

```
IF NOT EXIST C:\WORK\NUL MD C:\WORK
```

By nesting IF EXIST commands, you also can check to make sure that a file doesn't exist:

```
IF EXIST C:\WORK\NUL IF NOT EXIST C:\WORK\MYFILE.TXT GOTO NOFILE
```

Notice that simply checking for the file with IF NOT EXIST can return true if the subdirectory or drive is invalid, which might lead to errors later in your batch file. By testing for the existence of the path and then checking that the file doesn't exist, you can be sure that creating MYFILE.TXT in the C:\WORK subdirectory will succeed without overwriting another file.

SEE ALSO

:label, %envir%, %n, and GOTO

"Using the IF Command" in Chapter 16

INCLUDE= 6.0 AND LATER—INTERNAL

After you set up a startup menu, you might find that in certain configuration blocks, you are entering the same commands over and over. Instead of retyping them, you can gather them all together in a block of their own and use the INCLUDE= command to include that block within the others. The [COMMON] block performs a similar function for commands that you want to include in all your configuration blocks. INCLUDE= can be used only in your CONFIG.SYS file.

SYNTAX

INCLUDE=*blockname*

PARAMETERS AND SWITCHES

blockname   The name of the configuration block that you want to include when the active configuration block is processed. *blockname* must match a configuration block you have defined elsewhere in your CONFIG.SYS file, and it also can contain INCLUDE= commands. This argument is required.

NOTES

1. The INCLUDE= command can appear only inside configuration blocks in CONFIG.SYS and can refer only to another configuration block. You cannot use INCLUDE= to include the selections from one menu block within another.

2. CONFIG.SYS allows two types of blocks: menu blocks and configuration blocks. Each block begins with a [*blockname*] and includes all the lines that follow up to the next [*blockname*]. Menu blocks, which are blocks named [MENU] or defined with a SUBMENU= command, can include only menu-related commands. All other CONFIG.SYS commands belong in configuration blocks.

   The [COMMON] block is a special kind of configuration block, and certain special rules apply to it. It is the only block name that you can have more than once in your CONFIG.SYS file. All commands included in a [COMMON] block are always executed. Any commands in CONFIG.SYS that are not included in any block (that is, they appear before the first [*blockname*]) are assumed to be in a [COMMON] block.

   [COMMON] blocks are an alternative to using the INCLUDE= command. If you are using INCLUDE= to include a single block of commands in all your configuration blocks, consider using a [COMMON] block instead.

3. You are allowed to nest INCLUDE= commands. That is, a block included with the INCLUDE= command can have another INCLUDE= command within it. Although there is no clear limit to how deep this nesting can go, for the sake of clarity, you should limit yourself to no more than one or two levels of INCLUDE= commands.

> **Caution**
> Because nesting is allowed, there is the possibility of creating an endless loop. Make sure that an included block never includes any block that included it (that is, A includes B, which includes A).

4. The INCLUDE command is meant to help you eliminate repetition in your CONFIG.SYS file. Its use, however, often makes your CONFIG.SYS file harder to understand. Weigh these factors carefully when you decide whether to use an INCLUDE block. When software you are installing makes a mess of your menu system, a clear, simple CONFIG.SYS file is easier to repair than a complicated one.

EXAMPLES

The following sample CONFIG.SYS file illustrates the use of INCLUDE= blocks and [COMMON] blocks:

```
[MENU]
MENUITEM=MINIMUM, Minimal Configuration
MENUITEM=NORMAL, Normal Configuration (Default)
MENUITEM=NORM_EMS, Normal Configuration with EMS Available
MENUITEM=MAXIMUM, All the Bells and Whistles
MENUDEFAULT=NORMAL, 30

[COMMON]
DEVICE=C:\DOS\HIMEM.SYS
DOS=HIGH
BREAK=ON
NUMLOCK=OFF

[MINIMUM]
BUFFERS=30
LASTDRIVE=H
STACKS=9,256

[NORMAL]
INCLUDE=MINIMUM
DEVICE=C:\DOS\EMM386.EXE NOEMS
DOS=UMB

[NORM_EMS]
INCLUDE=MINIMUM
DEVICE=C:\DOS\EMM386.EXE RAM
DOS=UMB

[MAXIMUM]
INCLUDE=NORM_EMS
DEVICEHIGH=C:\DOS\RAMDRIVE.SYS 1450 512 224 /E
DEVICEHIGH=C:\DOS\ANSI.SYS

[COMMON]
SHELL=C:\DOS\COMMAND.COM C:\DOS\ /P /E:512
```

Notice that the MAXIMUM configuration includes the NORM_EMS configuration, which in turn includes the MINIMUM configuration. All the configuration choices automatically "include" the commands in the two COMMON blocks. As you can see, this kind of nesting can quickly become confusing. Don't use this example as a model for your own CONFIG.SYS file; it is only meant to illustrate the use of the INCLUDE= command and is much more complicated than it needs to be.

As it turns out, all the commands in the MINIMUM block could be placed in the COMMON block preceding it, leaving the MINIMUM block empty. (No matter what configuration you choose, the MINIMUM block is included.) However, if you removed the MINIMUM block completely, the corresponding menu line would not be displayed, and you would need to remove the INCLUDE=MINIMUM commands from the other blocks as well.

SEE ALSO

[*blockname*] and MENUITEM=

"Creating Multiple Configurations" in Chapter 2

INSTALL=   4.0 AND LATER—INTERNAL

INSTALL= can load resident software (TSRs) from your CONFIG.SYS file into conventional memory. Programs loaded with INSTALL= are executed after all other CONFIG.SYS lines have been processed and just before the command-line interpreter (COMMAND.COM) is loaded into memory. INSTALL= can be used only in your CONFIG.SYS file.

SYNTAX

    INSTALL=*drive:\path***filename**   *parameters*

PARAMETERS AND SWITCHES

drive:\path   Although this parameter is optional, you should always include the full drive and path to the resident program file. If they are omitted, the file is assumed to be in the root directory of the startup drive.

filename   The full filename, with extension, of the resident program to be loaded. No extension is assumed, and wildcards are not allowed. This parameter is required.

parameters   Any parameters that the resident program requires are included after its name. DOS passes these parameters directly to the program when it's loaded into memory. For more information, see the instructions for loading the resident program.

NOTES

1. If MS-DOS cannot find the program file you have specified, it displays a Bad or missing filename message and continues processing CONFIG.SYS. (See the first item in the following "Messages" section.)

2. Resident programs included with DOS that can be safely loaded with the INSTALL= command include FASTOPEN.EXE, KEYB.COM, NLSFUNC.EXE, and SHARE.EXE.

3. In versions of DOS earlier than DOS 6, many resident programs could not be loaded with INSTALL= because no environment was available to them. Starting with DOS 6, an environment is available to installed programs, and most resident software can now be successfully loaded this way.

4. With DOS 6, there is little reason to use INSTALL= anymore. In the past, one of the main reasons to use INSTALL= was to save the small amount of memory wasted on environments for resident software. But with DOS 6, you save little or nothing. Also, INSTALL= is limited to loading software into conventional memory, and you can't include LOADHIGH in an INSTALL= command to get around this limitation. All in all, you usually are better off avoiding INSTALL= entirely; instead, load your resident software from your AUTOEXEC.BAT file.

5. DOS executes all other lines in CONFIG.SYS, including any SET commands, before executing any INSTALL= lines. When all the INSTALL= lines have been processed, the command interpreter (COMMAND.COM) is loaded and begins to process your AUTOEXEC.BAT file.

6. Only resident software should be loaded with an INSTALL= command. DOS waits until the program terminates before continuing, and if a normal program is run, neither COMMAND.COM nor your AUTOEXEC.BAT file is loaded until you quit the program. Although this setup might be interesting, it could make your system very unstable and should be avoided.

EXAMPLES

To load SHARE.EXE from your CONFIG.SYS file, you would include the following line:

```
INCLUDE=C:\DOS\SHARE.EXE   /L:50
```

This line assumes that SHARE.EXE is located in the C:\DOS subdirectory and sets the number of file locks to 50. For DOS to find SHARE.EXE, the file extension must always be included with the filename because no default extensions are assumed with INSTALL=.

MESSAGES

```
Bad or missing filename
Error in CONFIG.SYS line number
```

Warning: DOS displays this message if it can't find the file you specified in a DEVICE=, DEVICEHIGH=, or INSTALL= command in your CONFIG.SYS file. *filename* is the name of the file that DOS was looking for, and *number* is the line in CONFIG.SYS where the command is located. Edit the line so that the path and filename are correct and then restart your computer.

SEE ALSO

DEVICE= and LOADHIGH

"Using the INSTALL Command" in Chapter 19

INSTALLHIGH (SEE HIINSTALL)

INSTALLHIGH is a DR DOS alternative command for the HIINSTALL command. See the detailed description under HIINSTALL.

INTERLNK   6.0 AND LATER—EXTERNAL

When you run INTERLNK from the DOS command line, it communicates with the INTERLNK.EXE device driver in memory, allowing you to view or change the server drives you have access to. If the connection to the server hasn't been established, INTERLNK attempts to connect with the server, using the parameters you specified when you loaded the INTERLNK.EXE device driver. Before you can run INTERLNK from the DOS command line, you must load the INTERLNK.EXE device driver into memory by adding a DEVICE= statement in your CONFIG.SYS file.

SYNTAX

INTERLNK *client:*=*server:* ...

PARAMETERS AND SWITCHES

client: The client drive letter that you want to use to access a disk drive on the Interlnk server. *client:* must be one of the drive letters that the INTERLNK.EXE device driver reserved when it loaded into memory. The trailing colon is optional.

server: The server drive that you want *client:* to refer to. *server:* must be a drive on the Interlnk server that is available for redirection. The trailing colon is optional. If this parameter is omitted, the *client:* drive letter is disconnected from the Interlnk server.

NOTES

1. The INTERLNK.EXE device driver must be installed before you can run INTERLNK from the command line. If you try to run INTERLNK without installing the device driver, an error message is displayed. (See the following "Messages" section.)

2. INTERLNK.EXE actually is two files: a device driver and an executable program. The device driver portion does all the real work and has to be loaded into memory with a DEVICE= command in your CONFIG.SYS file. After this device driver has been loaded into memory, the executable portion of the file communicates with the device driver to reassign drive letters and display status information.

3. To display Interlnk's status, type INTERLNK at the DOS prompt. Interlnk displays a list of client drive letters on the left, with the server drives they are connected to on the right. If any of the server drives have volume labels, they are displayed as well.

4. You can include as many *client:*=*server:* parameters as you need in a single INTERLNK command. Separate each *client:*=*server:* assignment with spaces.

5. To disconnect an Interlnk drive, specify the *client:*= parameter but omit the *server:* drive letter. A disconnected *client:* drive letter is immediately available for use connecting to another server drive. You can perform a mixture of drive assignments and disconnections in a single INTERLNK command by separating each one with spaces.

6. The drives that `INTERLNK.EXE` reserves when it loads into memory are private; they can't be used by other programs even if Interlnk isn't using them. For example, you cannot use an inactive Interlnk drive letter as a network drive or a `SUBST` alias. `INTERLNK.EXE` displays the drive letters it has reserved when it is loading into memory.

7. To use a printer on an Interlnk server from within Windows, you first have to access the Printer dialog box in Control Panel. Next, click the Connect button. In the Connect dialog box, either clear the Fast Printing Direct To Port check box, or specify the port as `LPT1.DOS` or `LPT2.DOS` rather than `LPT1` or `LPT2`. Normally, Windows prints directly to the hardware and bypasses Interlnk's printer redirection. However, when you disable Fast Printing or print to a filename rather than the port name, Windows prints through DOS, and Interlnk can redirect the data to the server's printer port.

8. All disk drives redirected by Interlnk are considered removable drives because the connection to them can be lost at any time. DoubleSpace refers to Interlnk drives as normal, removable local drives. MSD reports that Interlnk drives are floppy drives with one cylinder. SMARTDrive defaults to read-caching Interlnk drives, as it does with local floppy disk drives. Windows File Manager represents Interlnk drives with a "floppy icon."

9. An Interlnk client cannot access CD-ROM drives on the server. Interlnk can recognize only standard DOS drives, not network drives. CD-ROM drives use the network interface, so Interlnk cannot be used to give the client computer access to CD-ROM drives on the server.

10. Redirected Interlnk drives do not support disk-level operations, and the following DOS commands should not be used on redirected drives:

CHKDSK	FORMAT
DEFRAG	MIRROR
DEBUG	SCANDISK
DISKCOMP	SYS
DISKCOPY	UNDELETE
FDISK	UNFORMAT

    Third-party utilities that require low-level disk access also should be avoided.

11. To be able to run, `INTERLNK` requires DOS 3.0 or later. You can run different versions of DOS on the client and server computers, although the limitations of each version must be respected. For example, disk partitions greater than 32MB on an Interlnk server are not accessible on an Interlnk client running DOS 3.0. (The Microsoft MS DOS 6 license agreement requires at least one of the two computers involved to be running a licensed copy of MS-DOS 6.)

12. An appropriate cable is required to connect two computers with Interlnk. If you are using serial ports for the Interlnk connection, a 3-wire or 7-wire null-modem serial cable is required. If you are using parallel ports, an 11-wire parallel cable is required. These cables often are referred to as LapLink cables, in honor of the product that popularized this simple type of network. Check the two computers to see what type of connectors

you need. Microsoft includes detailed wiring charts for these cables in the entry for INTERLNK in the DOS 6 online help system (that is, type HELP INTERLNK at the DOS prompt and click the Notes entry).

EXAMPLES

Assuming that Interlnk is running and you have successfully connected with the server, redirect the client drive letter D: to access drive C: on the server by entering the following command.

```
INTERLNK  D=C
```

Notice that you are not required to enter colons with the drive letters, although colons are acceptable.

To break the relationship (cancel the redirection) between the client's D drive and the server drive, enter this command:

```
INTERLNK  D=
```

You can make more than one assignment in a single command by separating them with spaces like this:

```
INTERLNK  D=A  E=B  F=C
```

This command would connect you to three server drives. Drive D on the client computer would refer to drive A on the server, drive E to drive B on the server, and drive F to drive C on the server.

If you ever get lost and want to see what assignments you have, type the INTERLNK command with no parameters as follows:

```
INTERLNK
```

INTERLNK displays a status screen that looks something like this:

```
This Computer        Other Computer
  (Client)             (Server)
-------------        ----------------------
   D:    equals      A:
   E:    equals      B:
   F:    equals      C: (120Mb)   CONNER 120
   LPT2: equals      LPT1:
```

This screen reflects the assignments made earlier with the INTERLNK D=A E=B F=C command. You can't control the assignment of printer ports from the command line, but the display does show you what drive assignments Interlnk has made. To print to the server's printer, you would print to LPT2 on the client computer.

Interlnk shows the size of any server hard drives in parentheses after the drive letter in the right column. Notice that if any of the server drives have volume labels, they're displayed as well (CONNER 120 is the volume label for the server's C: drive in the example). Volume labels can make a confusing assignment display a bit easier to understand.

Messages

```
Connection NOT Established
Make sure that a serial or parallel cable connects the server and client
computers, and that INTERSVR.EXE is running on the server computer.
```

Error: Interlnk was unable to establish a connection with the server program. Before you try to establish this connection from the client computer, make sure that the cable is connected at both ends and that INTERSVR is running on the server computer.

```
Drive assignment syntax error.
```

Error: You have made a syntax error while attempting to assign drive letters to remote drives on the Interlnk server. This message is often caused by trying to assign drive letters that weren't reserved by INTERLNK.EXE. The only drive letters you can use to access drives on the Interlnk server are the ones that INTERLNK.EXE displays when it is loaded into memory from your CONFIG.SYS file.

```
Driver NOT installed
To install Interlnk, add the following line to your CONFIG.SYS file and reboot:
    DEVICE=drive:\path\INTERLNK.EXE
```

Information: You have attempted to run the INTERLNK program without first installing the INTERLNK.EXE device driver. *drive:\path* in the preceding message reflects the current location of INTERLNK.EXE on your system. You can run INTERLNK from the command line only when the client device driver is in memory, so you must load INTERLNK.EXE from your CONFIG.SYS file before you can access the executable portion of the program.

```
Invalid unit reading drive drive
Abort, Retry, Fail
```

Error: You've tried to access an Interlnk drive that isn't assigned to a drive on the Interlnk server. Press A to abort, R to Retry, and F to Fail. The safest choice is to fail the operation by pressing F. In most cases, Retry simply redisplays the error message. After you clear the error message, you can assign this drive letter to a server drive by using the INTERLNK *client:=server:* command.

```
Not ready reading drive drive
Abort, Retry, Fail
```

Error: You have tried to access an Interlnk drive (or another reserved drive letter), but the connection to the Interlnk server hasn't been made yet. Press A to abort, R to Retry, and F to Fail. Normally, you should fail the operation by pressing F. You can establish the connection to the server by running INTERLNK from the command line.

```
The version number of Interlnk in memory does not match the version
number in the file: pathname
```

Error: The version of Interlnk you ran from the DOS command line doesn't match the version of the device driver that is being loaded in your CONFIG.SYS file. Somehow, you have ended up with two different copies of INTERLNK.EXE on your disk. Locate the newer copy of INTERLNK.EXE and make sure that you are loading that copy in your CONFIG.SYS file. You might want to remove the old copy of INTERLNK.EXE from your disk so that you do not run it by accident.

SEE ALSO

INTERLNK.EXE and INTERSVR

"Using Interlnk to Share Another Computer's Resources" in Chapter 8

INTERLNK.EXE (DEVICE DRIVER)   6.0 AND LATER— EXTERNAL

The INTERLNK.EXE device driver establishes a link by way of a serial or parallel cable with another computer that is running the INTERSVR program. INTERLNK.EXE provides the client side of this relationship and usually is installed on a laptop computer (the client) from which you want to access files or printers on a desktop computer (the server). INTERLNK.EXE must be loaded in a DEVICE= statement in your CONFIG.SYS file.

SYNTAX

DEVICE=*drive:\path***INTERLNK.EXE**   /DRIVES:*num*   /NOPRINTER   /COM
/COM:*num*   /COM:*addr*   /LPT   /LPT:*num*   /LPT:*addr*   /AUTO   /NOSCAN   /LOW
/BAUD:*rate*   /V

PARAMETERS AND SWITCHES

drive:\path — The full path to the INTERLNK.EXE file on your system. Setup places the INTERLNK.EXE file in the C:\DOS subdirectory by default. If the full path to INTERLNK.EXE isn't specified, DOS looks for the file in the root directory of the startup drive.

/DRIVES:*num* — The number of drive letters to reserve for redirected drives on the client computer. *Num* can be any value from 0 to the number of drive letters still available when INTERLNK.EXE is loaded. (DOS can allocate 26 drive letters, from A to Z.) If this parameter is omitted, 3 drive letters are reserved. Specifying /DRIVES:0 disables drive redirection, and only printers are redirected.

/NOPRINTER — This parameter specifies that no printers should be redirected. Normally, Interlnk redirects all available printers. Specifying this parameter can reduce the size of INTERLNK.EXE in memory.

/COM — This parameter specifies that Interlnk should scan all serial ports when it's looking for a connection with the server. This is the default setting. If you have a serial mouse, you might want to use a /COM:*num* or /LPT:*num* parameter to specify the port that Interlnk should use.

/COM:*num* — The serial port (by DOS number) that Interlnk should use to connect with the server. This parameter can be entered as /COM:1 or as /COM1; the colon is optional. Typical values are /COM1, /COM2, /COM3, and /COM4.

/COM:*addr*	The serial port (by hexadecimal port address) that Interlnk should use to connect with the server. Typical addresses for serial ports are 3F8 and 2F8. Unless you have a particular reason to specify the serial port by address, you should use the more familiar port numbers.
/LPT	This parameter specifies that Interlnk should scan all parallel ports when it's looking for a connection with the server. This is the default setting.
/LPT:*num*	The parallel port (by DOS number) that Interlnk should use to connect with the server. This parameter can be entered as /LPT:1 or as /LPT1; the colon is optional. Typical values are /LPT1, /LPT2, and /LPT3. This parameter has nothing to do with redirected printers. It specifies the port being used to connect the two computers together.
/LPT:*addr*	The parallel port (by hexadecimal port address) that Interlnk should use to connect with the server. Typical addresses for parallel ports are 3BC, 378, and 278. Unless you have a particular reason to specify the parallel port by address, you should use the more familiar port numbers instead.
/AUTO	Specifying this parameter instructs INTERLNK.EXE not to remain in memory if the server is unavailable. By using this parameter, you can leave in your CONFIG.SYS file the DEVICE= line that loads INTERLNK.EXE. With /AUTO specified, Interlnk loads into memory only if you are connected to a server when you start up your computer.
/NOSCAN	Specifying this parameter stops INTERLNK.EXE from trying to establish a connection with the server when INTERLNK.EXE loads into memory. You have to establish the connection later by running INTERLNK from the DOS command line.
/LOW	If upper memory is available, INTERLNK.EXE normally tries to load itself high. If you want to make sure that INTERLNK.EXE loads into conventional memory instead, specify the /LOW parameter.
/BAUD:*rate*	The maximum baud rate you want Interlnk to use for serial communications. *rate* can be one of the following values: 9600, 19200, 38400, 57600, and 115200. If no maximum rate is specified, 115200 is assumed. Note that *rate* limits only the maximum data transfer rate that can be used between the client and server for a serial connection. If you are using a parallel connection, the /BAUD:*rate* parameter has no effect.
/V	If either the client or the server computer freezes while accessing Interlnk drives, try specifying the /V parameter on one or both computers. This parameter attempts to correct problems that arise from conflicts with the system timers on connected computers.

Notes

1. The `INTERLNK.EXE` device driver must be installed before you can run `INTERLNK` from the command line. If you try to run `INTERLNK` without installing the device driver, an error message is displayed. (See the first item in the following "Messages" section.)

> **Caution**
> When Interlnk scans serial ports looking for a server connection, it interferes with the operation of any mouse drivers that are servicing those ports. If your mouse is attached to a serial port, be sure to use a `/COM:num` or `/LPT:num` parameter to specify the port that Interlnk should use.

2. `INTERLNK.EXE` actually is two files: a device driver and an executable program. The device driver portion does all the real work and has to be loaded into memory with a `DEVICE=` command in your `CONFIG.SYS` file. After this device driver is loaded into memory, the executable portion of the file communicates with the device driver to reassign drive letters and display status information.

3. If you regularly use Interlnk to connect your laptop to a desktop computer, make sure that you specify the `/AUTO` parameter. Then, when you're on the road, `INTERLNK.EXE` will fail to find the server and not waste memory by loading anyway. Whenever you want to use Interlnk, simply connect the cable to a server and reboot the laptop.

4. `INTERLNK.EXE` automatically loads into upper memory if it's available. You don't need to use the `DEVICEHIGH=` command with `INTERLNK.EXE`.

5. By default, all the client's serial ports and then all the client's parallel ports are scanned when Interlnk looks for a connection with the server. As soon as the server is found, scanning stops. If `/COM` is specified without `/LPT`, only the client's serial ports are scanned. Similarly, if `/LPT` is specified without `/COM`, only the client's parallel ports are scanned. Interlnk's default behavior is equivalent to specifying both the `/COM` and `/LPT` parameters.

6. Under normal circumstances, `INTERLNK.EXE` requires about 15KB of memory. You can decrease this amount by specifying certain parameters. When you specify the `/NOPRINTER` parameter, Interlnk does not load the routines required to redirect printer output. If you specify the `/DRIVES:0` parameter, Interlnk does not load the routines required to redirect disk drives. If you specify either the `/COM` or `/LPT` parameter (but not both), Interlnk does not load the routines required to access the type of port you are not using. Depending on what combination of Interlnk services you need, you might be able to slim Interlnk's memory use significantly.

7. The drives that `INTERLNK.EXE` reserves when it loads into memory are private and can't be claimed by other programs even if Interlnk isn't using them. For example, you cannot use an inactive Interlnk drive letter as a network drive or a `SUBST` alias.

8. If `INTERLNK.EXE` fails to connect with a server when it loads or the `/NOSCAN` parameter prevents it from connecting, the drives it reserves will be empty. To establish a connection with the server, you have to run `INTERLNK` from the command line and redirect the server drives manually.

9. Because `INTERLNK.EXE` allocates drive letters, you should be very careful about where you locate it in your `CONFIG.SYS` file. In most cases, you will want to load `INTERLNK.EXE` last so that any drives it allocates leave other drive assignments in `CONFIG.SYS` unchanged.

> **Caution**
>
> Having your drive letters change simply because you added a device driver to your `CONFIG.SYS` file can be painful. Often, you have to edit batch files to reflect the new drive letters. All references to drives that have changed have to be corrected in your `CONFIG.SYS` and `AUTOEXEC.BAT` files. Microsoft Windows is very sensitive to drive-letter changes, and some Windows' applications fail if they are suddenly located on a different drive.
>
> Before you add or rearrange `DEVICE=` lines in your `CONFIG.SYS` file, think through the changes you may be making to drive-letter assignments and the impact the changes will have on your system. If you are careful, you can often accomplish your task without changing any drive-letter assignments, or at least keep the changes to a minimum. Doing so can save you a great deal of work.

10. If you use DoubleSpace, always load the `DBLSPACE.SYS` driver before you load `INTERLNK.EXE`. If you load `INTERLNK.EXE` first, the DoubleSpace host (uncompressed) drives may become unavailable on the client computer.

11. To use a printer on an Interlnk server from within Windows, you first have to access the Printer dialog box in Control Panel. Next, click the Connect button. In the Connect dialog box, either clear the Fast Printing Direct To Port check box, or specify the port as `LPT1.DOS` or `LPT2.DOS` rather than `LPT1` or `LPT2`. Normally, Windows prints directly to the hardware and bypasses Interlnk's printer redirection. However, when you disable Fast Printing or print to a filename instead of the port name, Windows prints through DOS, and Interlnk can redirect the data to the server's printer port.

12. All disk drives redirected by Interlnk are considered removable drives because the connection to them can be lost at any time. DoubleSpace refers to Interlnk drives as normal, removable local drives. MSD reports that Interlnk drives are floppy drives with one cylinder. SMARTDrive defaults to read-caching Interlnk drives, as it does with local floppy disk drives. Windows File Manager represents Interlnk drives with a "floppy icon."

13. An Interlnk client cannot access CD-ROM drives on the server. Interlnk can recognize only standard DOS drives, not network drives. Because CD-ROM drives use the network interface, Interlnk cannot be used to give the client computer access to CD-ROM drives on the server.

14. Redirected Interlnk drives do not support disk-level operations, and the following DOS commands should not be used on redirected drives:

CHKDSK	FORMAT
DEFRAG	MIRROR
DEBUG	SCANDISK
DISKCOMP	SYS
DISKCOPY	UNDELETE
FDISK	UNFORMAT

    Third-party utilities that require low-level disk access also should be avoided.

15. `INTERLNK.EXE` requires DOS 3.0 or later to run. You can run different versions of DOS on the client and server computers, although the limitations of each version must be respected. For example, disk partitions greater than 32MB on an Interlnk server are not accessible on an Interlnk client running DOS 3.0. (The Microsoft MS-DOS 6 license agreement requires at least one of the two computers involved to be running a licensed copy of MS-DOS 6.)

16. An appropriate cable is required to connect two computers with Interlnk. If you are using serial ports for the Interlnk connection, a 3-wire or 7-wire null-modem serial cable is required. If you are using parallel ports, an 11-wire parallel cable is required. These cables often are referred to as LapLink cables, in honor of the product that popularized this simple type of network. Check the two computers to see what type of connectors you need. Microsoft includes detailed wiring charts for these cables in the entry for `INTERLNK` in the DOS 6 online help system (that is, type `HELP INTERLNK` at the DOS prompt and click the Notes entry).

EXAMPLES

A typical line that loads `INTERLNK.EXE` in the `CONFIG.SYS` file of your Laptop computer might look like this:

`DEVICE=C:\DOS\INTERLNK.EXE   /COM2   /AUTO`

As long as the connection with the Interlnk server is established (on `COM2`), the Interlnk client device driver will load into memory and reserve three drive letters (the default is three) with which it can access drives on the server. Any printers attached to the server will be available on the client computer as well. Because of the `/AUTO` parameter, if `INTERSVR` isn't running on the server when this `DEVICE=` line is executed, `INTERLNK.EXE` won't load into memory.

If memory is tight, and you don't need access to more than one disk drive or any printers on the Interlnk server, you could add the `/NOPRINTER` parameter, like this:

`DEVICE=C:\DOS\INTERLNK.EXE   /COM2   /AUTO   /DRIVES:1   /NOPRINTER`

Note that in both of the preceding examples, `INTERLNK.EXE` loads into upper memory if it's available. To force `INTERLNK.EXE` to load into conventional memory, specify the `/LOW` parameter, as in the following:

`DEVICE=C:\DOS\INTERLNK.EXE   /COM2   /AUTO   /LOW`

If you used a parallel cable to connect the two computers instead of a serial cable, you would specify a parallel port rather than a serial port:

`DEVICE=C:\DOS\INTERLNK.EXE   /LPT1   /AUTO`

Note that you must use the same type of port on both computers. You can't use a serial port on one computer and a parallel port on the other. The cables you need aren't interchangeable, either.

After `INTERLNK.EXE` has successfully established a connection with the Interlnk server, it automatically assigns the drive letters it has reserved to disk drives on the Interlnk server. To see what assignments have been made, run `INTERLNK` from the DOS command line.

Messages

```
*** Bad /COM argument parameter
```

Error: Interlnk was unable to initialize the serial port you specified with a /COM:*num* parameter. Check to make sure that you specified /COM1, /COM2, /COM3, or /COM4, and that your computer has that port installed. If you can't get this parameter to work, you may be forced to use the /COM:*addr* parameter.

```
*** Bad /DRIVES parameter ignored (/DRIVES:n, n = 0 - 24).
```

Error: You have specified an invalid /DRIVES:*num* parameter. Legal values for *num* are in the range 0 to 24, as indicated in the message. You may get this message if you have embedded any spaces in the parameter or if you have specified a letter instead of a digit.

```
*** Bad /LPT argument parameter
```

Error: Interlnk was unable to initialize the parallel port you specified with an /LPT:*num* parameter. Check to make sure that you specified /LPT1, /LPT2, or /LPT3, and that your computer has that port installed. If you can't get this parameter to work, you may be forced to use the /LPT:*addr* parameter.

```
*** Bad parallel port address: addr
```

or

```
*** Bad serial port address: addr
```

Error: Interlnk was unable to initialize the parallel or serial port you specified with an /LPT:*num* or /COM:*num* parameter. Make sure that you are specifying the correct value for *addr* and that the value is entered in hexadecimal notation.

```
*** Invalid /BAUD parameter ignored.
```

Warning: You have specified an invalid /BAUD:*rate* parameter, and Interlnk has used the default value of 115200. Check to make sure that the value you specified for *rate* is 9600, 19200, 38400, 57600, or 115200. You can't embed commas in these values.

```
*** Specified COM port number not recognized by BIOS: COM#
```

or

```
*** Specified LPT port number not recognized by BIOS: LPT#
```

Error: You have specified a port with the /LPT:*num* or /COM:*num* parameter, which isn't supported by the ROM BIOS in your computer. You may get this message if you specify a port that doesn't exist in your computer, or if your ports are using nonstandard port addresses. If the problem is nonstandard port addresses, you still might be able to use this port by specifying its address with an /LPT:*addr* or /COM:*addr* parameter.

```
Connection NOT Established
Make sure that a serial or parallel cable connects the server and client
computers, and that INTERSVR.EXE is running on the server computer.
```

Error: Interlnk was unable to establish a connection with the server program. Before you try to establish this connection from the client computer, make sure that the cable is connected at both ends and that INTERSVR is running on the server computer.

```
Drive letters redirected: num (drive: through drive:)
```

Information: INTERLNK.EXE displays this message when it loads into memory. You might want to write down the drive letters that the INTERLNK.EXE device driver has reserved. They are the only letters you can use to access drives on the Interlnk server.

```
Driver NOT installed
To install Interlnk, add the following line to your CONFIG.SYS file and reboot:
    DEVICE=drive:\path\INTERLNK.EXE
```

Information: You have attempted to run the INTERLNK program without first installing the INTERLNK.EXE device driver. The *drive:\path* in the preceding message reflects the current location of INTERLNK.EXE on your system. You can run INTERLNK only from the command line when the client device driver is in memory; therefore, you must load INTERLNK.EXE from your CONFIG.SYS file before you can access the executable portion of the program.

```
Invalid switch - parameter
```

Error: You have specified an invalid parameter on the DEVICE= line for INTERLNK.EXE in your CONFIG.SYS file. The *parameter* displayed in the message is the one that's confusing INTERLNK.EXE. Correct this entry and try the command again.

```
No drive letters redirected
```

Information: You have loaded the INTERLNK.EXE device driver with a /DRIVES:0 parameter. You cannot access any disk drives on the Interlnk server.

```
No printer ports redirected
```

Information: You have loaded the INTERLNK.EXE device driver with a /NOPRINTER parameter. You cannot access any printers on the Interlnk server.

```
The Interlnk device driver requires version 3.0 or later of DOS.
```

Error: INTERLNK.EXE requires that you be running at least DOS 3.0. If you know that the computer is running a later version of DOS than 3.0 (type VER), you may have a bad entry for INTERLNK.EXE in your SETVER table.

```
Too many block devices
```

Warning: DOS has run out of drive letters and cannot load any more block devices from your CONFIG.SYS file. DOS will continue to start up, but some of your device drivers may not be loaded. DOS can handle up to 26 accessible block devices.

Certain device drivers allocate more than one letter when they are loaded. DoubleSpace allocates at least one letter for each compressed drive you have in your system, plus some spares. INTERLNK.EXE allocates the number requested with the /DRIVES:*num* parameter, or three if a number isn't specified. RAMDRIVE.SYS and DRIVER.SYS allocate one letter each time they are loaded. Check your CONFIG.SYS file and eliminate any DEVICE= lines you don't need, or decrease the number of drives set aside for Interlnk.

See Also

DEVICE=, INTERLNK, and INTERSVR

"Using Interlnk to Share Another Computer's Resources" in Chapter 8

INTERSVR   6.0 AND LATER—EXTERNAL

INTERSVR provides server services for an Interlnk network. The server in an Interlnk network is the computer that is making its drives and printers available for use on another computer (the client). INTERSVR monopolizes the server computer while it is running, preventing you from using the server computer for anything else. You have to have an appropriate serial or parallel cable to connect the two computers.

Syntax

INTERSVR *drive:* ... /X=*drive:* ... /COM /COM:*num* /COM:*addr* /LPT /LPT:*num* /LPT:*addr* /BAUD:*rate* /V /B

To copy the Interlnk files to a connected computer that is not running Interlnk, use the following format:

INTERSVR /RCOPY

Parameters and Switches

drive: ...	Specifies the letter of a drive that can be redirected. The ellipsis (...) indicates that more than one drive can be redirected by a single INTERSVR command. By default, all drives are available for redirection.
/X=*drive:* ...	Specifies the letter of a drive that will not be redirected. The ellipsis (...) indicates that more than one drive can be excluded by a single INTERSVR command. By default, no drives are excluded.
/COM	Specifies that INTERSVR should scan all serial ports when it's looking for a connection with the client. This is the default setting. If you have a serial mouse, you might want to use a /COM:*num* or /LPT:*num* parameter to specify the port Interlnk should use.
/COM:*num*	Indicates the serial port (by DOS number) that INTERSVR should use to connect with the client. This parameter can be entered as /COM:1 or as /COM1; the colon is optional. Typical values are /COM1, /COM2, /COM3, and /COM4.
/COM:*addr*	Indicates the serial port (by hexadecimal port address) that INTERSVR should use to connect with the client. Typical addresses for serial ports are 3F8 and 2F8. Unless you have a particular reason to specify the serial port by address, you should use the more familiar port numbers instead.

/LPT	Specifies that INTERSVR should scan all parallel ports when it's looking for a connection with the client. This is the default setting.
/LPT:*num*	Specifies the parallel port (by DOS number) that INTERSVR should use to connect with the client. This parameter can be entered as /LPT:1 or as /LPT1; the colon is optional. Typical values are /LPT1, /LPT2, and /LPT3. Note that this parameter has nothing to do with redirected printers; it specifies the port being used to connect the two computers together.
/LPT:*addr*	Indicates the parallel port (by hexadecimal port address) that INTERSVR should use to connect with the client. Typical addresses for parallel ports are 3BC, 378, and 278. Unless you have a particular reason to specify the parallel port by address, you should use the more familiar port numbers instead.
/BAUD:*rate*	Indicates the maximum baud rate you want Interlnk to use for serial communications. *rate* can be one of the following values: 9600, 19200, 38400, 57600, and 115200. If no maximum rate is specified, 115200 is assumed.
	rate limits only the maximum data transfer rate that can be used between the client and server for a serial connection. If you are using a parallel connection, the /BAUD:*rate* parameter has no effect.
/V	If either the client or server computer freezes while accessing Interlnk drives, try specifying the /V parameter on one or both computers. This parameter attempts to correct problems that arise from conflicts with the system timers on connected computers.
/B	Forces the use of a color scheme appropriate for a black-and-white (monochrome) monitor or LCD display.
/RCOPY	Copies the Interlnk files INTERLNK.EXE and INTERSVR.EXE to another computer. If your laptop computer doesn't have a floppy disk drive, use this parameter to set up an Interlnk connection. The two computers must be connected by a 7-wire, null-modem serial cable (sometimes referred to as a LapLink cable). The MODE command must be available on the target computer for this transfer to work. You can't specify any other parameters when you're using the /RCOPY feature.

NOTES

1. When INTERSVR scans serial ports looking for a client connection, it interferes with the operation of any mouse drivers that are servicing those ports. If your mouse is attached to a serial port, be sure to use a /COM:*num* or /LPT:*num* parameter to specify the port that Interlnk should use.

2. By default, all the server's serial ports and then all the server's parallel ports are scanned when Interlnk searches for a connection with the client computer. As soon as the client is found, scanning stops. If /COM is specified without /LPT, only the server's serial ports are scanned. Similarly, if /LPT is specified without /COM, only the server's parallel ports are scanned. INTERSVR's default behavior is equivalent to specifying both the /COM and /LPT parameters.

3. INTERSVR is unable to make network or CD-ROM drives available to the client computer. Network and CD-ROM drives are not considered local drives because DOS uses the network redirector interface to access them.

4. While INTERSVR is running, it displays a list of redirected drives and printers onscreen. The left column lists the disk drives and printers on the server that are being shared, and the right column lists the letters and/or ports that are being used on the client computer to access the server drives. To exit INTERSVR and disconnect the Interlnk network, press Alt+F4.

5. You can't use the computer for anything else while INTERSVR is running. If you start INTERSVR in a task-switching environment such as Windows, it doesn't allow you to switch to another task without first exiting the INTERSVR program. Don't try to access any memory-resident programs; serious data loss could result. To be safe, you might want to disable or remove memory-resident programs before running INTERSVR.

6. Redirected Interlnk drives do not support disk-level operations, and the following DOS commands should not be used on redirected drives:

    ```
    CHKDSK        FORMAT
    DEFRAG        MIRROR
    DEBUG         SCANDISK
    DISKCOMP      SYS
    DISKCOPY      UNDELETE
    FDISK         UNFORMAT
    ```

    Third-party utilities that require low-level disk access also should be avoided.

7. INTERSVR.EXE requires DOS 3.0 or later to run. You can run different versions of DOS on the client and server computers, although the limitations of each version must be respected. For example, disk partitions greater than 32MB on an Interlnk server are accessible on an Interlnk client running DOS 3.0. (The Microsoft MS-DOS 6 license agreement requires at least one of the two computers involved to be running a licensed copy of MS-DOS 6.)

8. An appropriate cable is required to connect two computers with Interlnk. If you're using serial ports for the Interlnk connection, a 3-wire or 7-wire null-modem serial cable is required. If you are using parallel ports, an 11-wire parallel cable is required. These cables often are referred to as LapLink cables in honor of the product that popularized this simple type of network. Check the two computers to see what type of connectors you need. Microsoft includes detailed wiring charts for these cables in the entry for INTERLNK in the DOS 6 online help system (that is, type HELP INTERLNK at the DOS prompt and click the Notes entry).

EXAMPLES

Before you start the Interlnk server program, connect the two computers you want to link by using an appropriate serial or parallel cable. You also might want to remove or disable any resident programs you are running. You don't have to quit Windows or the DOS Shell, but you cannot switch to another task while the Interlnk server program is running.

To start the Interlnk server program, type the following command:

```
INTERSVR
```

INTERSVR scans your ports looking for an Interlnk connection. After it finds one, INTERSVR makes all local drives and printers on the server computer available to the Interlnk client.

If you are using a serial mouse, you should specify the port Interlnk should use. For example, if your mouse is attached to COM1 and you want to use COM2 on the server for the Interlnk connection, add the /COM2 parameter as follows:

```
INTERSVR   /COM2
```

If you don't need access to either of the server's floppy disk drives (A: and B:, in this example) from the client computer, you can exclude them by adding an /X=drive: parameter like this:

```
INTERSVR   /COM2   /X=A:   B:
```

If either computer stops responding when you access a remote drive or printer, you might have to specify the /V parameter for INTERSVR as follows:

```
INTERSVR   /COM2   /V
```

To use the remote copy feature, you must first connect the two computers with a 7-wire null-modem serial cable. (These cables often are referred to as LapLink cables, in honor of the company that made this sort of connection popular.) You cannot use parallel ports for this operation. Next, make sure that the computer which is to receive the Interlnk files is running DOS 3.0 or later and that the MODE command is available. Finally, on the computer containing the Interlnk files, start the Interlnk server by using the /RCOPY parameter as follows:

```
INTERSVR   /RCOPY
```

INTERSVR leads you through the copy operation, prompting you at each step. After the files INTERLNK.EXE and INTERSVR.EXE have been successfully transferred, you can start up the Interlnk network by running INTERSVR on the server computer, adding the INTERLNK.EXE device driver to the CONFIG.SYS file on the client computer, and rebooting the client computer.

MESSAGES

```
Error initializing port port at address addr
```

Error: INTERSVR found your Interlnk port but was unable to initialize it. This error can be caused by INTERSVR finding the wrong port when it scans your system. Specify the port that you want to use with the /COM:*num* or /LPT:*num* parameter and try the command again.

```
File allocation error in: pathname, run chkdsk /f to correct.
```

Error: INTERSVR encountered a problem in the file allocation table (FAT) while it was accessing the file in *pathname*. Quit INTERSVR, and run SCANDISK or CHKDSK /F to identify and fix the problem.

```
If SHARE.EXE is loaded on the remote computer the remote install cannot be
performed on COM2. Please use COM1 or insure that SHARE.EXE is not loaded on
the remote computer before attempting a remote install.
```

Warning: You are performing a remote copy operation using COM2 on the remote computer. Interlnk is warning you that the operation may fail if SHARE.EXE is running on the remote computer. If SHARE.EXE is running on the remote computer, you might want to choose a different serial port or restart the remote computer without loading SHARE.EXE.

```
Invalid /BAUD parameter - rate
```

Error: You have specified an invalid /BAUD:*rate* parameter. Check to make sure that the value you specified for *rate* is 9600, 19200, 38400, 57600, or 115200. You can't embed commas in these values.

```
Invalid parallel port address LPT#: addr
```

Error: You have specified a parallel port address with the /LPT:*addr* parameter, but Interlnk is unable to communicate with it. Make sure that you are specifying the correct value for *addr* and that the value is entered in hexadecimal notation.

```
Invalid serial port address COM#: addr
```

Error: You have specified a serial port address with the /COM:*addr* parameter, but Interlnk is unable to communicate with it. Make sure that you are specifying the correct value for *addr*, and that the value is entered in hexadecimal notation.

```
Invalid server drive letter - drive
```

Error: You have specified a server drive letter that either doesn't exist or Interlnk is unable to redirect. You cannot redirect any network or CD-ROM drives connected to the server computer. Check your entry to make sure that all the drive letters you have specified are valid, local disk drives.

```
Invalid switch - parameter
```

Error: You have specified an invalid parameter on the command line for INTERSVR. The *parameter* displayed in the message is the one that is confusing INTERSVR. Correct this entry and try the command again.

```
There are no serial or parallel ports available for communication.
```

Error: When INTERSVR scanned your computer's ports, it couldn't find the port you are using for the Interlnk connection. Specify the port that you want to use with the /COM:*num* or /LPT:*num* parameter and try the command again.

```
Unable to initialize serial port COM#
```

Error: `INTERSVR` found your Interlnk port but was unable to initialize it. This error can be caused by specifying the wrong port. Correct your entry for the `/COM:num` or `/LPT:num` parameter and try the command again.

```
Unrecoverable transmission error, maximum retries exceeded.
```

Error: Your Interlnk connection has failed. Make sure that the cable you are using hasn't become unplugged at one or both ends. If you continue to see this error message, you may have to purchase a new cable.

```
You have started the Interlnk server in a task-switching environment. Task-
switching, key combinations, and some disk-writing operations are disabled. To
restore these functions, exit the server.
```

Information: `INTERSVR` displays this message if you start the server program while a task-switching environment such as Windows is active. You cannot switch tasks until you exit `INTERSVR` by using the Alt+F4 command.

SEE ALSO

`INTERLNK` and `INTERLNK.EXE`

"Using Interlnk to Share Another Computer's Resources" in Chapter 8

JOIN   3.1 TO 5.0—EXTERNAL

The JOIN command produces a directory structure by connecting one drive to a subdirectory of another drive. JOIN is included on the DOS 6.0 Supplemental Disk, not in the standard DOS 6.0 package.

SYNTAX

To connect disk drives, use the following format:

JOIN *drive:* *drive2:\dirname*

To disconnect disk drives, use the following format:

JOIN *drive:* **/D**

To show currently connected drives, use the following format:

JOIN

PARAMETERS AND SWITCHES

drive: Specifies the drive that you want to refer to as a subdirectory on another drive. DOS calls *drive:* the *guest disk drive*.

drive2: Specifies the drive to which *drive:* is to be connected. DOS calls *drive2:* the *host disk drive*. If *drive2:* isn't specified, the current drive is assumed.

\dirname	Specifies a subdirectory on *drive2:* (the host drive). DOS calls \dirname the *host subdirectory*. \dirname holds the connection to *drive:* (the guest drive), and should be empty. If \dirname doesn't exist, DOS creates it.
/D	Disconnects the specified guest drive from the host drive.

Rules

1. You must specify the guest drive when you make or change assignments.
2. If you do not name a host drive, DOS uses the current drive.
3. You must specify the host subdirectory. The host subdirectory cannot be the root directory of any drive.
4. The host and guest drives must not be network or CD-ROM drives.
5. The host and guest drives must not be part of a SUBST or ASSIGN command.
6. You cannot use the current drive as the guest drive.
7. If the host subdirectory does not exist, JOIN creates one. The subdirectory, if it exists, must be empty (DIR must show only the . and .. entries).
8. When the drives are joined, the guest drive's root directory and entire directory tree are added to the host subdirectory. All subdirectories of the guest's root directory become subdirectories of the host subdirectory.
9. A guest drive, when joined to the host drive, appears to be part of the host subdirectory. You can access this drive only through the host drive and subdirectory.
10. To break the connection, specify the guest drive's normal name with the /D switch. You can use the guest drive's normal name only when you disconnect the drives.
11. To see all the current drive connections, type JOIN with no parameters. If no connections exist, JOIN does not display any message, and the system prompt appears.
12. Do not use the BACKUP, CHKDSK, DISKCOMP, DISKCOPY, FDISK, RESTORE, or FORMAT command in the guest or host drive.
13. When JOIN is in effect, the DIR command works normally but reports the bytes free only for the host drive.
14. While JOIN is in effect, CHKDSK processes the host drive but does not process or report information on the guest portion of the drive. To run CHKDSK on the guest drive, you first must disconnect the guest drive from the host drive.

Notes

1. You can use JOIN to connect a RAM disk to a real disk so that you can use the RAM disk as though it were part of a floppy disk or hard disk drive. You also can use JOIN to connect two hard drives.
2. Some programs allow only one drive to hold data or certain parts of the program. Programs written for DOS 2.0 and later, however, enable you to specify subdirectory

names. If you use such a program, you can invoke the JOIN command to trick the program into using multiple drives as though the drives were one large drive.

3. JOIN does not affect the guest drive. Rather, JOIN affects only the way you access the files in that drive. You cannot exceed the maximum number of files in the guest drive's root directory. In the host subdirectory, a file's size cannot exceed the guest drive's size.

MESSAGES

```
Directory not empty
```

Error: You tried to use a host subdirectory that is not empty; the subdirectory contains files other than the . and .. entries. Perform any one of the following actions before you try the command again:

- Delete all files in the host subdirectory.
- Specify an empty subdirectory.
- Create a new subdirectory.
- Name a nonexistent host subdirectory.

SEE ALSO

ASSIGN and SUBST

"The JOIN Command" in Chapter 11

KBDBUF.SYS (DEVICE DRIVER) EXTERNAL

The keyboard buffer set aside by the ROM BIOS is normally 16 bytes long. If a program fails to read the keyboard before the 17th character arrives, characters are lost. If you're a fast typist, you might want to increase the size of the keyboard buffer with KBDBUF.SYS to avoid losing keystrokes. KBDBUF.SYS isn't distributed with the standard DOS 6 package but is available from Microsoft on the MS-DOS 6 Supplemental Disk. You must load KBDBUF.SYS in a DEVICE= statement in your CONFIG.SYS file.

SYNTAX

DEVICE=*drive:\path***KBDBUF.SYS** *bufsize*

PARAMETERS AND SWITCHES

drive:\path   The full path to the KBDBUF.SYS file on your system. KBDBUF.SYS is available on the DOS 6.22 Supplemental Disk. If you do not specify the full path to KBDBUF.SYS, DOS looks for the file in the root directory of the startup drive.

bufsize   The new keyboard buffer size, in bytes. Acceptable values are in the range of 16 to 1024. This parameter is required.

Notes

1. Some programs read keystrokes directly from the keyboard, bypassing the keyboard buffer that the ROM BIOS maintains. KBDBUF.SYS does not affect programs that read the keyboard directly.

2. Do not attempt to load KBDBUF.SYS into upper memory by using the DEVICEHIGH= command. The ROM BIOS can't use a keyboard buffer located in upper memory.

3. You should load the KBDBUF.SYS device driver as early as you can in CONFIG.SYS to avoid troublesome interactions with other device drivers and resident programs.

4. Requesting a very large keyboard buffer is not normally a very good idea. If you have increased it to 50 or 100 characters and your software is still losing keystrokes, the program is probably not using the keyboard buffer at all. A large keyboard buffer might be useful when you are injecting keystrokes into it from another source that can't wait when the buffer is full.

Examples

To increase the size of the keyboard buffer to 32 characters, enter the following line in your CONFIG.SYS file:

```
DEVICE=C:\DOS\KBDBUF.SYS  32
```

This line assumes that you have copied the KBDBUF.SYS file from the DOS 6 Supplemental Disk to your C:\DOS subdirectory.

Messages

```
Part of the new keyboard buffer is beyond the range of the ROM BIOS data
segment. Load this driver earlier in CONFIG.SYS, do not load it into high
memory, or decrease the size of the buffer.
```

Error: KBDBUF.SYS couldn't create the keyboard buffer you requested, usually because you tried to load it with the DEVICEHIGH= command. Use the DEVICE= command to load KBDBUF.SYS into conventional memory instead.

```
Requested buffer size is too large.
```

Error: You have specified a keyboard buffer size larger than 1,024 characters, which is the maximum size allowed by KBDBUF.SYS.

```
Requested buffer size is too small.
```

Error: You have specified a keyboard buffer size under 16 characters, which is the minimum size allowed by KBDBUF.SYS.

See Also

DEVICE=

KEYB 3.3 AND LATER—EXTERNAL

The KEYB command changes the keyboard layout and characters from American English to another language/country.

SYNTAX

To change the current keyboard layout, use the following format:

KEYB *keycode*, *codepage*, *drive:\path*\KEYBOARD.SYS /ID:*code* /E

To display the current values for KEYB, use the following format:

KEYB

PARAMETERS AND SWITCHES

keycode	Specifies the two-character keyboard code for the keyboard layout that you want to use. See Chapter 14, "Understanding the International Features of DOS," for a list of keyboard codes that MS-DOS supports.
codepage	Specifies the three-digit code page that you want to use. *codepage* must be one of the code pages available for use with the *keycode* specified. If you omit *codepage*, DOS assumes the default code page for the *keycode* specified. See Chapter 14 for a list of the code pages that MS-DOS supports.
drive:\path\KEYBOARD.SYS	Specifies the drive and path to KEYBOARD.SYS or an equivalent file that contains keyboard layout information. Setup places this file in the C:\DOS subdirectory by default.
/E	Informs KEYB that an enhanced keyboard is being used. This switch is necessary only on 8088- and 8086-based systems that use enhanced keyboards.
/ID:*code*	Specifies the type of enhanced keyboard that you want to use. This switch is only for countries that have more than one keyboard for the same language (for example, France, Italy, and the United Kingdom). See Chapter 14 for a list of the keyboard ID codes that MS-DOS supports.

EXIT CODES

ERRORLEVEL Value	Meaning
0	New keyboard template loaded successfully
1	Invalid keyboard code, code page, or command-line syntax
2	Keyboard definition file is bad or missing
4	Halted by console (CON) error
5	Requested code page not prepared

Notes

1. To use one of the foreign-language character sets, load the KEYB program and type the appropriate two-letter code for your country.
2. If you do not specify a code page, DOS uses the default code page for your country. The default code page is established by the COUNTRY directive in CONFIG.SYS or by the DOS default code page if the COUNTRY directive is not used.
3. You must specify a code page that is compatible with your keyboard code selection.
4. If you do not specify the keyboard definition file, it defaults to KEYBOARD.SYS. DOS looks for this file in the current disk's root directory. Otherwise, DOS uses the full filename to search for the file. If you do not specify a disk drive, DOS searches the current disk drive. If you do not specify a path, DOS searches the current directory.
5. After loading, the program reconfigures the keyboard into the appropriate layout for the specified language.
6. To use the American English layout after you issue the KEYB command, press Ctrl+Alt+F1. To return to the foreign-language layout, press Ctrl+Alt+F2. To switch to "typewriter mode," press Ctrl+Alt+F7.
7. When you use KEYB command for the first time, it increases the size of DOS by approximately 10KB. After that, you can use KEYB as often as you want without further enlarging DOS. You can load KEYB into upper memory by using the LOADHIGH command.
8. To display the active keyboard and the code pages, type KEYB without any parameters.
9. You can use KEYB with INSTALL in your CONFIG.SYS file.

Messages

```
Active code page not available from CON device
```

Information: You issued the KEYB command to display the current setting, but the command could not determine what code page was in use. The DEVICE=DISPLAY.SYS directive is not in CONFIG.SYS, or no currently loaded CON code page is active.

If the DISPLAY.SYS line was included in your CONFIG.SYS file, you must give the MODE CON CODEPAGE PREPARE command to load the font files into memory.

```
Bad or missing Keyboard Definition File
```

Error: The keyboard definition file (usually KEYBOARD.SYS) is corrupted, or KEYB cannot find the file. If you did not specify a drive and pathname, KEYB looks for the file in the current drive's root directory.

Copy the file to the root directory, or provide the full drive and pathname for the file to KEYB.

```
Code page requested (codepage) is not valid for given keyboard code
```

Error: You provided a keyboard code but not a code page, or the specified keyboard code does not match the currently active code page for the console. KEYB does not alter the current keyboard or code page. Choose a new console code page that matches the keyboard code (by using the MODE CON CODEPAGE SELECT command) or specify the appropriate matching code page when you reissue the KEYB command.

```
Code page specified is inconsistent with the selected code page
```

Warning: You specified a keyboard code and a code page, but a different code page is active for the console (CON). The code page specified to KEYB is now active for the keyboard but not for the video display.

Use the MODE CON CODEPAGE SELECT command to activate the correct code page (the one specified to KEYB) for the video screen.

```
Code page specified has not been prepared
```

Error: The DEVICE=DISPLAY.SYS directive was included in your CONFIG.SYS file, but your KEYB command specified a keyboard code that needs a code page that is not prepared. Use the MODE CON CODEPAGE PREPARE command to prepare the code page for the keyboard code that you want to use.

```
Current CON code page: codepage
```

Information: The console's current code page is designated by the number *codepage*.

```
Current keyboard code: keycode
code page: codepage
```

Information: The current keyboard code is a two-character *keycode*, and the code page used by the keyboard is a three-digit *codepage*. A list of the legal keyboard codes and their corresponding code pages is included in Chapter 14, "Understanding the International Features of DOS."

```
One or more CON code pages invalid for given keyboard code
```

Warning: You used the MODE command to prepare several code pages for the console (CON), but you specified a keyboard code that is not compatible with one or more console code pages. KEYB creates the necessary information to work with those keyboard and code pages that are compatible. DOS ignores the incompatible keyboard and code page combinations.

SEE ALSO

CHCP, COUNTRY=, DISPLAY.SYS, MODE *device* CP, and NLSFUNC

"Understanding KEYB.COM" in Chapter 14, "Understanding the International Features of DOS"

KEYBOARD.SYS (SEE KEYB)

Despite the .SYS extension, KEYBOARD.SYS is not a device driver. KEYBOARD.SYS is a data file that contains information about the various keyboard layouts that are used in different countries. The KEYB command uses this file.

> **Caution** Do not attempt to load KEYBOARD.SYS (or DVORAK.SYS) into memory by using a DEVICE= or DEVICEHIGH= command in CONFIG.SYS. If you do, your computer will lock up, and you will need to reboot from a floppy disk.

A similar file, containing information needed for an Icelandic keyboard layout, is the file KEYBOARD.ICE on the MS-DOS 6 distribution disks. (For details on setting up an Icelandic configuration, see the README.TXT file distributed with DOS 6.) If you prefer a Dvorak keyboard, you can use the DVORAK.SYS file on the DOS 6 Supplemental Disk; it supports two-handed, left-handed, and right-handed Dvorak layouts.

DOS 6.22 includes an alternative keyboard layout information file named KEYBRD2.SYS, which contains a few additional keyboard layouts. For details, see Chapter 14, "Understanding the International Features of DOS," or the README.TXT file included with MS-DOS 6.22.

SEE ALSO

KEYB

"Understanding KEYB.COM" in Chapter 14, "Understanding the International Features of DOS"

LABEL 3.0 AND LATER—INTERNAL

Each disk can have a volume label as well as a volume serial number. The volume label is text and can be up to 11 characters long. The LABEL command enables you to display, add, delete, or change the volume label for a disk.

SYNTAX

LABEL *drive:volume_label*

PARAMETERS AND SWITCHES

drive: The disk whose label you want to change or display. (The colon is required.)

volume_label The disk's new volume label.

RULES

1. A valid volume label immediately becomes the volume label for the specified drive.
2. If you do not specify a volume label, DOS prompts you to enter a new one. You can perform one of the following actions:
    - Type a valid volume name and then press Enter. DOS makes this name the new volume label. If a volume label already exists, DOS replaces the old volume label with the new.

- Press Enter to delete the current label without specifying a replacement label. DOS asks you to confirm the deletion.

3. If you enter an invalid volume label, DOS responds with a warning message and asks again for the new volume label.

4. Do not use LABEL in a networked disk drive (one that belongs to another computer). If you try to label a networked drive, DOS displays an error message and ignores the command.

5. Do not use LABEL on a disk in any drive that is affected by the SUBST, JOIN, or ASSIGN commands because DOS labels the "real" disk in the drive instead.

   Suppose that you use the command ASSIGN A=C. If you then enter the command LABEL A:, DOS actually changes the volume label of the disk in drive C.

6. A label consists of up to 11 printing characters and may include spaces but not tabs or any of the following characters:

   * ? / \ | . , ; : + = [ ] ( ) & ^ < >

   Lowercase ASCII characters are mapped to uppercase.

Notes

1. When you format a disk in DOS 4.0 and later versions, DOS prompts you to enter a volume label. Whether or not you assign a label, DOS gives the disk a serial number. The serial number is not part of the volume label. Remember that a space is a valid character in a volume label.

2. Spaces and underscores can increase the readability of a volume label. DOS 3.0 and 3.1, however, reject a space in a volume name when the name is typed in the command line (for example, LABEL MY DISK). To put a space in a volume label, type LABEL, press the spacebar, type the drive name (if needed), and then press Enter. Do not type a volume label in the command line. When LABEL asks for a new volume label, you can type the label with spaces.

Messages

```
Delete current volume label (Y/N)?
```

Information and Warning: You did not enter a volume label when DOS prompted you. DOS is asking whether to delete the current label or to leave it unaltered. To delete the current label, press Y; to keep the label intact, press N.

See Also

FORMAT and VOL

"Naming Disks with LABEL" in Chapter 7

LASTDRIVE=   3.0 AND LATER—INTERNAL

If you're connected to a network, running MSCDEX for access to a CD-ROM drive, or using the SUBST command to create drive aliases, you might need the LASTDRIVE= command to tell DOS to save space for the additional drive letters you'll need. You can use LASTDRIVE= only in your CONFIG.SYS file.

SYNTAX

LASTDRIVE=*drive*

PARAMETERS AND SWITCHES

drive   The letter of the last disk drive that you want to have available. Note that *drive* is entered without a trailing colon. Valid letters are A to Z. The default value is either E or the last drive letter allocated during the processing of your CONFIG.SYS file, whichever is higher.

NOTES

1. If you specify a letter lower than the number of letters needed for your system, DOS overrides it and allocates space for the drives your system has. For instance, if you have one floppy and one hard drive and you specify LASTDRIVE=A, DOS allocates space in the current directory data structure for drives A, B, and C (as if you had specified LASTDRIVE=C). DOS does not display an error message if it overrides your LASTDRIVE= parameter. Notice that DOS allocates two floppy drive letters (A and B) even if you have only one floppy disk drive installed in the system.

2. Each additional drive letter (above E) you have available increases the size of DOS in memory. If you aren't attached to a network, running a CD-ROM drive, or using SUBST drive aliases, you have little reason to waste memory on extra drive letters.

3. You never need LASTDRIVE= for a device that is assigned a drive letter when its driver is loaded in CONFIG.SYS. This includes drives assigned by DoubleSpace, RAMDRIVE.SYS, INTERLNK.EXE, or DRIVER.SYS. LASTDRIVE= is needed only to reserve space for drive letters created after the processing of your CONFIG.SYS file is complete.

EXAMPLES

If you are attached to a network, you usually want the following line in your CONFIG.SYS file:

LASTDRIVE=Z

This line allows room for the maximum number of drive letters, leaving plenty of room to attach network drives. On the other hand, if you have two floppy drives (A and B), a hard disk with two partitions (C and D), a RAM disk (E), and have run DBLSPACE to compress both partitions (hosts assigned to I and J), your highest drive letter is J. To leave room for two additional drives after J, you can enter the following command:

LASTDRIVE=L

Notice that in the preceding example, drive letters F, G, H, K, and L would be available for network, CD-ROM, or SUBST drives. If you had included no LASTDRIVE= command, drive letters F, G, and H would still be available.

MESSAGES

```
Bad command or parameters Error in CONFIG.SYS line number
```

Warning: If you specify an invalid parameter for LASTDRIVE=, you get this error message. A very common mistake is to enter a colon after the drive letter in the LASTDRIVE= command.

SEE ALSO

SUBST

"Using LASTDRIVE to Change the Available Disk Drives" in Chapter 19

LH   (SEE LOADHIGH)

LH is an alternative name for the LOADHIGH command. For information on using the LOADHIGH or LH command, see the entry for LOADHIGH in this command reference.

LOADER

By using LOADER, you can have more than one operating system installed on your computer. You can choose from a menu of installed operating systems to be started at boot time. If you install DR DOS on a computer with Windows 95, for example, the setup installs LOADER and sets up the correct files for it to run.

SYNTAX

LOADER *bootfile.ext num* /Q /S /U

Parameters and Switches

/Q or /S	Specifies the quiet mode to run LOADER without any onscreen feedback.
/U	Uninstalls LOADER from the hard disk.
bootfile.ext	Specifies a text file that must be in the root directory. Each line (up to 20 lines are allowed) lists the parameters for loading a different operating system at bootup. Use the following syntax for each line:

`filename.ext x num text...`

The parameters for this syntax are as follows:

filename.ext	Specifies the name of the boot file for the operating system, such as MSDOS.SYS.
x	Specifies the type of operating system. These types are listed in the description of LOADER in DOSBOOK.
num	Specifies a timeout value that loads the operating system in this line after *num* seconds if no other choice is made. Only one line can include a *num* statement.
text...	Displays an optional comment of your choosing on bootup.

LOADFIX   5.0 AND LATER—EXTERNAL

Some programs may have trouble running if they are loaded in the first segment of memory. When this happens, they often display a `Packed file corrupt` message and abort. LOADFIX can help a program with this problem to run by making sure that it's loaded in the second 64KB segment of memory.

Syntax

LOADFIX *program parameters*

PARAMETERS AND SWITCHES

program   The program file that you want to load into the second 64KB segment of memory. A drive and path can be specified. If they are omitted, the current directory and all directories on the DOS PATH are searched for the executable file. This parameter is required.

parameters   The parameters you want passed to *program* when it's loaded into memory.

NOTES

If you are using DOS 5.0 or a later version to load DOS into the high memory area (HMA), a packed file may be loaded into the first 64KB of RAM and may fail to work. In such a case, DOS may display the error message `Packed file corrupt`, and the computer then returns to the DOS prompt.

Use LOADFIX only to start a program when DOS displays the message `Packed file corrupt`.

LOADHIGH OR LH   5.0 AND LATER—INTERNAL

You can use the LOADHIGH command to load programs into upper memory. By loading resident software into upper memory, you can leave more conventional memory available for application programs to use. LOADHIGH is typically used in your AUTOEXEC.BAT file.

SYNTAX

LOADHIGH *program* *parameters*

or

LH *program* *parameters*

In DOS 6, LOADHIGH has two additional switches that MemMaker uses to specify the placement and size of the program in memory:

LOADHIGH /L:*region,min;region,min;...* /S *program* *parameters*

or

LH /L:*region,min;region,min;...* /S *program* *parameters*

PARAMETERS AND SWITCHES

program   Specifies the program file that you want to load into upper memory. You can specify a drive and path. If you omit them, DOS searches the current directory and all directories on the DOS PATH for the executable file. This parameter is required.

parameters   Specifies any parameters you want passed to *program* when it's loaded into memory.

/L:region,min   (DOS 6) Specifies the region in upper memory, and optionally the minimum size in bytes, into which the program should be loaded. You can specify more than one region by separating each region from the preceding one with a semicolon. For instance, /L:1;2 allows the program access to UMB regions 1 and 2, and /L:1,4096;2,512 further specifies that the minimum size of regions 1 and 2 should be 4,096 and 512 bytes, respectively. This parameter must precede the program's filename on the line. MemMaker sets these values for you.

/S   (DOS 6) If you specify the /L parameter with a minimum size, /S instructs DOS to shrink the UMB to the specified size and create a new UMB from the remainder. /S must precede the program's filename on the line. This switch is best left to MemMaker's use.

NOTES

In DR DOS, HILOAD is an alternative to the LOADHIGH command that performs the same function.

RULES

1. You must use an upper memory manager. For a computer equipped with an 80386SX or higher microprocessor and at least 1MB of RAM, DOS provides EMM386.EXE.

2. Your CONFIG.SYS file must contain at least the following statements (or the equivalent third-party memory-management routines):
   ```
   DEVICE=HIMEM.SYS
   DEVICE=EMM386.EXE  RAM  (or NOEMS)
   DOS=UMB
   ```

3. If not enough upper memory is available to accommodate a program, DOS loads the program into conventional memory without warning.

4. When a program is loaded by default into the largest free UMB, that program automatically gains access to all other UMBs. If you use /L, you have to explicitly grant the program access to other upper memory regions by specifying other /L parameters.

5. /S normally is used only by MemMaker, which analyzes a program's memory usage to determine whether /S is safe.

6. You can use /S only when you also include an /L switch that specifies a minimum size.

7. Use *min* when a program is larger when it runs than when it loads.

8. Use MEM /F to determine the size of free regions.

EXAMPLES

To load the driver into upper memory regions 1 and 3, use the following format:
```
LOADHIGH  /L:1;3  C:\BIN\MYDRV.COM
```

See Also

`DEVICEHIGH=`, `MEM`, and `MEMMAKER`

"Loading Device Drivers and TSRs into Upper Memory" in Chapter 19

MD OR MKDIR   2.0 AND LATER—INTERNAL

The MD (or MKDIR) command can create new subdirectories on your disks. Storing files in various subdirectories helps you to keep them organized, and with MD, you can create as many as you need.

Syntax

    MD   *drive:\path*

    MKDIR   *drive:\path*

Parameters and Switches

drive: The *drive:* on which you want to create a new subdirectory. If you omit *drive:*, DOS assumes the current drive.

path   The subdirectory on *drive:* that you want to create. *path* can be either absolute or relative—that is, specified from the root directory or specified from the current directory (see Note 7 in the following section). If you specify only the name, DOS creates the new subdirectory in the current directory. You cannot create a subdirectory with the same name as a file in its parent directory.

Notes

1. Separate each subdirectory in *path* with a backslash (\) character. The last subdirectory name in *path* is the subdirectory created.

2. You must specify the new subdirectory name (1 to 8 characters); specifying an extension is optional. The name must conform to the rules for creating directory names.

> **Tip**
>
> Avoid using extensions with subdirectory names. Although doing so is perfectly legal, having them "extensionless" makes them easier to pick out from the filenames in a directory listing. This practice has become so pervasive that certain programs have difficulties using subdirectories with extensions because they are rather uncommon and rarely tested for in new software.

> **Tip**
>
> Keep your subdirectory names as short as you can. Doing so can help with DOS's 63-character pathname limit and 127-character command-line limit, and it saves typing as well.

3. You cannot use a directory name that is identical to a filename in the parent directory. If you have a file named MYFILE in the current directory, for example, you cannot create the subdirectory MYFILE in this directory. If the file is named MYFILE.TXT, however, the names do not conflict, and you can create the MYFILE subdirectory.

4. The maximum length of a path (from the root directory to the final directory) is 63 characters, including the backslashes.

5. You are not restricted to creating subdirectories in the current directory. If you add a pathname, DOS establishes a new subdirectory in the directory that you specify.

6. You must put a colon after the drive letter if it is included. If you don't include the colon, DOS interprets the drive letter as a subdirectory name, which is probably not what you wanted.

7. If a backslash (\) is the first (or only) character in a subdirectory path, it's considered absolute and specified starting from the root directory. If the subdirectory path begins with a subdirectory name, it's considered relative, and the current directory is used as its starting point. A drive letter, followed by a colon, can precede either an absolute or a relative path.

MESSAGES

```
Unable to create directory
```

Error: One of the following errors occurred:

- You tried to create a directory that already exists.
- You provided an incorrect pathname.
- The disk's directory is full.
- The disk is full.
- A file with the same name already exists.

Check the directory in which the new subdirectory was to be created. If a conflicting name exists, either change the filename or use a new directory name. If the disk or the root directory is full, delete some files, create the subdirectory in a different directory, or use a different disk.

```
Invalid drive specified
```

Error: You have specified an invalid drive letter.

SEE ALSO

CD or CHDIR, MOVE, and RD or RMDIR

"Creating Directories with MKDIR (MD)" in Chapter 5

MEM   4.0 AND LATER—EXTERNAL

MEM is a utility that displays the amount of used and unused memory, allocated and open memory areas, and all programs currently in the system. MEM can be enormously useful when you want to see just how your memory is being used, and whether you have enough space left for another resident program to be loaded high.

SYNTAX

For DOS 6, the following parameters are available for MEM:

MEM   /CLASSIFY   /DEBUG   /FREE   /MODULE *name*   /PAGE

or

MEM   /C   /D   /F   /M *name*   /P

For DOS 5.0, the following parameters are available for MEM:

MEM   /CLASSIFY   /DEBUG   /PROGRAM

or

MEM   /C   /D   /P

PARAMETERS AND SWITCHES

/CLASSIFY or /C — Displays programs that are in conventional and upper memory, their location in memory, and their size. Also displays a summary of the total free bytes of conventional and upper memory and the size of the largest executable program. You cannot use this switch with /DEBUG, /FREE, or /MODULE *name*.

/DEBUG or /D — Displays detailed information about the programs and driver in memory, including the address, name, size, and type of each segment for every program. Also displays a summary of the total free bytes of conventional and upper memory and the size of the largest executable program. You cannot use this switch with /CLASSIFY, /FREE, or /MODULE *name*.

/FREE or /F — (DOS 6) Displays the free areas of conventional and upper memory in decimal and hexadecimal format. You cannot use this switch with /CLASSIFY, /DEBUG, or /MODULE *name*.

/MODULE *name* or **/M *name*** — (DOS 6) Displays the memory usage of the *name* program or driver, including the segment address, UMB region number, name, and type of each segment. You cannot use this switch with /CLASSIFY, /DEBUG, or /FREE.

/PAGE or /P — (DOS 6) Pauses after each screen of output. You can use this switch with any of the other switches.

/PROGRAM or /P — (DOS 4.0 and 5.0 only) Displays the status of programs that are loaded into memory. You cannot use this switch with /CLASSIFY or /DEBUG.

Rules

1. You must specify /CLASSIFY, /DEBUG, /FREE, and /MODULE one at a time. You cannot combine any of these parameters. You can combine the /PAGE parameter with any of them, however.
2. MEM displays the status of extended memory only if you have more than 1MB of memory in your computer. If you have only 1MB or less, you don't have any extended memory.
3. The status of expanded memory is displayed only if you have expanded memory that conforms to Version 4.0 of the Lotus/Intel/Microsoft Expanded Memory Specification (LIM EMS). Loading EMM386.EXE in your CONFIG.SYS file can provide expanded memory for 80386 or better computer systems with more than 1MB of memory installed.
4. MEM displays the status of upper memory only if a UMB provider (for example, EMM386) is installed and DOS=UMB is included in your CONFIG.SYS file.
5. MEM does not display the status of upper memory if you are running DOS under Microsoft Windows 3.0.

Notes

1. Starting with DOS 6.2, MEM displays numbers with embedded commas, making them much easier to read.
2. A good way to determine a module name for MEM /MODULE *name* is first to issue the command MEM /C.
3. If your PC has UMBs, you can use MEM /C or MEM /D extensively as you begin to load device drivers and TSRs into upper memory. MEM displays the location and size of each program in memory. This information can help you determine the order in which device drivers and TSRs load so that you can determine how best to use UMBs.

See Also

DEVICEHIGH=, EMM386.EXE, HIMEM.SYS, LOADHIGH or LH, and MEMMAKER

"Displaying the Amount of Free and Used Memory" in Chapter 10

MEMMAKER   6.0 AND LATER—EXTERNAL

MemMaker is a full-screen program that attempts to maximize the amount of free conventional memory you have in your computer by moving device drivers and memory-resident programs (TSRs) into upper memory blocks (UMBs). To use MemMaker, you must have an 80386SX or higher computer with more than 1MB of memory installed. MemMaker relies on the services provided by HIMEM.SYS, EMM386.EXE and DOS. (If you are using third-party memory management software, you should use its memory optimization program instead of MemMaker.)

Syntax

MEMMAKER /B /BATCH /SESSION /SWAP:*drive* /T /UNDO /W:*size1,size2*

Parameters and Switches

/B
: Causes MemMaker to display correctly on a monochrome (black-and-white) monitor or LCD screen.

/BATCH
: Runs MemMaker in batch (unattended) mode. When you use this switch, DOS takes only the default actions and, if an error occurs, restores your CONFIG.SYS, AUTOEXEC.BAT, and (if necessary) Microsoft Windows SYSTEM.INI files. You can determine what was done by looking in the MEMMAKER.STS file.

/SESSION
: Used only by MemMaker during its optimization process. Do not specify this parameter.

/SWAP:*drive*
: Specifies your boot drive's original disk letter, the one that refers to the drive when your CONFIG.SYS file begins. You need this switch only in rare cases (for example, when disk-compression software, such as Stacker 1.0, swaps drive letters). Unless MemMaker knows your boot disk drive, it cannot find your startup files. You do not need this switch if you are using DoubleSpace, Stacker 2.0 or later, or SuperStor.

/T
: Disables IBM Token Ring detection. Use this switch only if you are connected to a Token Ring network and have trouble running MemMaker.

/UNDO
: Undoes changes in the CONFIG.SYS, AUTOEXEC.BAT, and (if necessary) Microsoft Windows SYSTEM.INI files from a previous use of MemMaker. Use this switch if your system does not work after you run MemMaker or if you are dissatisfied with the new configuration.

/W:*size1,size2*
: Specifies how much upper memory (in kilobytes) to reserve for Microsoft Windows translation buffers. Windows needs two such buffers in either upper or conventional memory. *size1* is the size of the first, and *size2* is the size of the second. You might need to increase these values if Windows begins to run slowly after optimizing with MemMaker. The default is /W:0,0; MemMaker reserves no upper memory for Windows translation buffers.

See Also

DEVICEHIGH=, EMM386.EXE, HIMEM.SYS, LOADHIGH or LH, and MEM

"Configuring Memory with MemMaker" in Chapter 19

MEMMAX

You can use MEMMAX to enable or disable sections of memory. You can run it from the system prompt or in AUTOEXEC.BAT. MEMMAX is useful if programs you run have trouble attempting to load into memory and you need to disable an area to prevent the program from loading there.

Syntax

MEMMAX +|-U +|-L +|-V /U /L /V /?

Parameters and Switches

+|-U	Enables or disables upper memory.
+|-L	Enables or disables lower memory.
+|-V	Allows or disallows loading programs into video memory area.
/U	Displays upper memory status.
/L	Displays lower memory status.
/V	Displays video memory status.
/?	Displays abbreviated help.

MENUCOLOR= 6.0 AND LATER—INTERNAL

Normally, DOS displays a startup menu in white text on a black background. When you use the MENUCOLOR= command, you can choose the screen colors that DOS uses. This command affects all text that DOS displays onscreen, not just the startup menu. You can use MENUCOLOR= only inside a menu block in your CONFIG.SYS file.

Syntax

MENUCOLOR=*textcolor*,*background*

Parameters and Switches

textcolor The color to use for foreground text. Legal values are 0 through 15 (see the following table of color values). This parameter is required.

background The color to use for the background. Legal values are 0 through 15 (see the following table of color numbers). On some displays, using background colors with values higher than 7 causes the screen to blink. Do not include a space after the comma, or DOS ignores the entire MENUCOLOR= command. If no value is entered, DOS assumes Black (0).

Value	Color	Value	Color
0	Black	8	Gray
1	Blue	9	Bright Blue

Value	Color	Value	Color
2	Green	10	Bright Green
3	Cyan	11	Bright Cyan
4	Red	12	Bright Red
5	Magenta	13	Bright Magenta
6	Brown	14	Yellow
7	White	15	Bright White

Notes

1. The MENUCOLOR= command can appear only once inside each menu block in CONFIG.SYS.

2. CONFIG.SYS allows two types of blocks: *menu blocks* and *configuration blocks*. Each block begins with a [blockname] and includes all the lines that follow, up to the next [blockname]. Menu blocks, which are blocks named [MENU] or defined with a SUBMENU= command, can include only menu-related commands. All other CONFIG.SYS commands belong in configuration blocks.

3. If you do not specify a MENUCOLOR= command, the menu is displayed in white (7) on black (0). If only a foreground text color is specified, the background remains black (0). You cannot set the background color without also setting the foreground text color.

4. Color choices set with this command remain in effect until another command or program resets them. Running CLS or loading the ANSI.SYS device driver resets the screen to its default colors.

> **Caution**
>
> Unlike many other commands, the MENUCOLOR= command does not allow a space after the comma between its parameters. If you include a space, DOS ignores the MENUCOLOR= command and does not set your color choices.

5. If you select a bright background color (values higher than 7), some displays set the blink attribute for the foreground text, and all the text onscreen starts to blink. Although blinking text may be annoying, it does no harm, and you can turn it off by using the CLS or MODE CO80 command. To fix the problem, choose a background color between 0 and 7, and restart your computer.

6. A really nasty mistake is to set the foreground color the same as the background color. Because you can't read any of the prompts when the colors are the same, you might need to reboot and use the F5 Clean key to bypass your CONFIG.SYS file. Alternatively, you can select a menu choice blind (press 1 and then press Enter), wait for all the drive activity to stop, and then type CLS and press Enter.

Examples

Suppose that you want to set up a menu that enables you to choose from three basic configurations for your computer: Windows, DOS, and Maintenance. To jazz it up a bit, you want to set the screen colors to bright blue text on a white background. To do so, add the following lines to your CONFIG.SYS file:

```
[MENU]
MENUITEM=WIN, Configure for Windows (Default)
MENUITEM=DOS, Configure for MS-DOS
MENUITEM=MAINT, Configure for File & Disk Maintenance
MENUDEFAULT=WIN, 30
MENUCOLOR=9,7
```

The MENUCOLOR= command sets the foreground color to bright blue (9) and the background color to white (7). These colors remain in effect until another program resets them.

See Also

[*blockname*], MENUDEFAULT=, MENUITEM=, and SUBMENU=

"Creating Multiple Configurations" in Chapter 2

MENUDEFAULT=   6.0 AND LATER—INTERNAL

Using the MENUDEFAULT= command, you can select which startup configuration DOS executes if no keys are pressed within the timeout period you specify. Without this command, DOS chooses menu item #1 and waits for you to press the Enter key. If you specify a default configuration and timeout period, DOS can continue booting without you. You can use MENUDEFAULT= only inside a menu block in your CONFIG.SYS file.

Syntax

MENUDEFAULT=*blockname, timeout*

Parameters and Switches

blockname   The menu line that DOS should highlight when the menu is displayed. If you specify a *timeout* value, DOS executes this configuration block automatically after *timeout* seconds. *blockname* must match the corresponding entry in a MENUITEM= or SUBMENU= command. This argument is required.

timeout   The number of seconds, from 0 to 90, that DOS should wait before executing the *blockname* configuration block. If you do not specify a *timeout* value, DOS waits until you press the Enter key before executing the selected configuration. A *timeout* value of 0 executes the *blockname* configuration block without displaying the menu onscreen at all.

Notes

1. The `MENUDEFAULT=` command can appear only once inside each menu block in `CONFIG.SYS`.

2. `CONFIG.SYS` allows two types of blocks: *menu blocks* and *configuration blocks*. Each block begins with a `[blockname]` and includes all the lines that follow, up to the next `[blockname]`. Menu blocks, which are blocks named `[MENU]` or defined with a `SUBMENU=` command, can include only menu-related commands. All other `CONFIG.SYS` commands belong in configuration blocks.

3. The menu item selected with the `MENUDEFAULT=` command displays highlighted onscreen. You can move the highlight with the arrow keys or type the line number to select a different menu line. The `Enter a Choice:` prompt displays the number of the selected menu item.

4. When you specify a `timeout` value, DOS displays a countdown onscreen as it waits for you to override the default choice. If you press any key before the `timeout` period has elapsed, the timer stops, and DOS waits for you to make a menu selection and press the Enter key.

> **Caution** If the `timeout` parameter contains an illegal value, DOS assigns a timeout of zero, and the menu isn't displayed at all. Not having a menu display can be troublesome when you are debugging a new menu. To determine whether an incorrectly set `timeout` value is causing the problem, press the F8 Interactive key when the `Starting MS-DOS...` message appears onscreen. If the menu appears, the `timeout` value is defaulting to zero. If the menu still doesn't appear, look for undefined or misspelled blocknames.

Examples

Suppose that you want to set up a menu that enables you to choose from three basic configurations for your computer: Windows, DOS, and Maintenance. Because you normally work with Windows programs, you want the default choice to be the WIN configuration. To do so, add the following lines to your `CONFIG.SYS` file:

```
[MENU]
MENUITEM=WIN, Configure for Windows (Default)
MENUITEM=DOS, Configure for MS-DOS
MENUITEM=MAINT, Configure for File & Disk Maintenance
MENUDEFAULT=WIN, 30
```

When you include these lines in your `CONFIG.SYS` file, DOS searches for blocks named `[WIN]`, `[DOS]`, and `[MAINT]`. As long as those blocks exist in the file, the menu that DOS displays looks something like this:

```
MS-DOS 6 Startup Menu
=====================

1. Configure for Windows (Default)
2. Configure for MS-DOS
```

```
3. Configure for File & Disk Maintenance

Enter a choice: 1
```

Entering 1, 2, or 3 at this menu instructs DOS to select the [WIN], [DOS], or [MAINT] block, respectively. If you don't make an entry within about 30 seconds, DOS chooses the [WIN] configuration by default.

SEE ALSO

[*blockname*], MENUCOLOR=, MENUITEM=, and SUBMENU=

"Creating Multiple Configurations" in Chapter 2

MENUITEM= 6.0 AND LATER—INTERNAL

New with DOS 6 is the capability to define a startup menu from which you can choose the group of CONFIG.SYS commands to process when you reboot. You use the MENUITEM= command to define the text of a menu line, as well as the configuration block that DOS should process when that menu line is chosen. You can use MENUITEM= only inside a menu block in your CONFIG.SYS file.

SYNTAX

MENUITEM=*blockname*, *menutext*

PARAMETERS AND SWITCHES

blockname   The name of the configuration block that you want to execute when this menu item is chosen. ***blockname*** can be up to 70 characters long, but it can't contain any spaces or the following special characters:

\ / , ; = [ ]

(For more details, see [*blockname*] in this command reference.) The CONFIG environment variable is set to the value of the ***blockname*** selected. This argument is required.

menutext   The text you want DOS to display for this menu line. *menutext* can be up to 70 characters long and contain any text you want, including spaces. Separate *menutext* from ***blockname*** with a comma. If you do not provide *menutext*, DOS displays the ***blockname*** in the menu.

NOTES

1. The MENUITEM= command can appear only inside menu blocks in CONFIG.SYS.
2. CONFIG.SYS allows two types of blocks: *menu blocks* and *configuration blocks*. Each block begins with a [*blockname*], and includes all the lines that follow, up to the next

[*blockname*]. Menu blocks, which are blocks named [MENU] or defined with a SUBMENU= command, can include only menu-related commands. All other CONFIG.SYS commands belong in configuration blocks.

3. The top-level (first) menu block must be named [MENU] so that DOS can recognize it. You can name additional menu blocks that you define with the SUBMENU= command anything you like.

4. Up to nine choices can be displayed in a menu, so you are limited to nine MENUITEM= and/or SUBMENU= commands in a menu block. The menu items are displayed onscreen in the order that they appear in the menu block, numbered from 1 to 9.

5. If DOS cannot find the block referred to by a MENUITEM= command in your CONFIG.SYS file, it doesn't display that choice in the menu. To get around this limitation, add a [*blockname*] line to your CONFIG.SYS file, but don't include any commands in it.

6. DOS sets the CONFIG environment variable equal to the name of the configuration block selected from the startup menu. You can use the CONFIG variable in your AUTOEXEC.BAT file to continue customizing your system's configuration based on the choice you made at the startup menu.

> **Caution**
>
> If you intend to use the CONFIG variable in GOTO statements in your AUTOEXEC.BAT file, try to keep your blocknames short. Only the first eight characters in a batch file label are significant, so if any of your blocknames start with the same eight characters, one or more of the GOTO labels you set up will never be reached. You can get around this limitation by using the IF command to make comparisons or by simply using shorter blocknames.

EXAMPLES

Suppose that you want to set up a menu that enables you choose from three basic configurations for your computer: Windows, DOS, and Maintenance. To do so, add the following lines to your CONFIG.SYS file:

```
[MENU]
MENUITEM=WIN, Configure for Windows (Default)
MENUITEM=DOS, Configure for MS-DOS
MENUITEM=MAINT, Configure for File & Disk Maintenance
MENUDEFAULT=WIN, 30
```

When you include these lines in your CONFIG.SYS file, DOS searches for blocks named [WIN], [DOS], and [MAINT]. As long as those blocks exist in the file, the menu that DOS displays looks something like this:

```
MS-DOS 6 Startup Menu
=====================

1. Configure for Windows (Default)
2. Configure for MS-DOS
```

```
3. Configure for File & Disk Maintenance

Enter a choice: 1
```

Entering 1, 2, or 3 at this menu instructs DOS to select the [WIN], [DOS], or [MAINT] block, respectively. If you don't make an entry within about 30 seconds, DOS chooses the [WIN] configuration by default.

SEE ALSO

[*blockname*], MENUCOLOR=, MENUDEFAULT=, and SUBMENU=

"Creating Multiple Configurations" in Chapter 2

MIRROR   5.0—EXTERNAL

MIRROR is a utility that can record information about the file allocation table (FAT) and root directory to enable you to use the UNFORMAT and UNDELETE commands. MIRROR also can save partition table information to a file that UNFORMAT can use if your partition table becomes corrupted.

MIRROR is included on the DOS 6.0 Supplemental Disk, but not in the standard DOS 6 package. For information about similar capabilities in DOS 6, see the section on the UNDELETE command later in this command reference.

SYNTAX

MIRROR *drive:* ... /T*drive*-*entries* /1

To save information about a drive partition, use the following format:

MIRROR /PARTN

To quit tracking deleted files, use the following format:

MIRROR /U

PARAMETERS AND SWITCHES

drive: ...	Specifies the drive(s) for which you want MIRROR to record FAT and root directory information. You can specify as many drive letters (with colons) as you want; just separate each one from the others with a space.
/T*drive*-*entries*	Loads a memory-resident tracking program that records information about deleted files. The *drive* specifies the drive where MIRROR saves information about deleted files. -*entries* is an optional value (ranging from 1 to 999) that specifies the maximum number of deleted files to be tracked. Default values are listed in the table in following the Notes section.

/1	Keeps MIRROR from creating a backup of the mirror file when the FAT and root directory information are updated.
/PARTN	Makes a copy of the drive's partition table.
/U	Removes the deleted-file tracking program from memory. You might not be able to unload MIRROR if you've loaded other resident software into memory after MIRROR.

Rules

1. Do not use the /T switch with drives that use JOIN or SUBST.
2. If you use ASSIGN, you must place this command before the MIRROR command. If possible, don't use any "pretender" programs while Mirror's deleted-file tracking program is active.
3. DOS saves information about deleted files in the file PCTRACKR.DEL. The UNDELETE command uses this file. With DOS 6, UNDELETE has Delete Tracker and Delete Sentry options of its own, and you should use them in preference to Mirror's deleted-file tracking features.
4. DOS saves system information, the FAT, and the root directory in the file MIRROR.FIL. The UNFORMAT command uses this file. FORMAT saves information for UNFORMAT as well.
5. DOS saves information about the hard drive partition in the file PARTNSAV.FIL. The UNFORMAT command uses this file. In DOS 6, no utility in the standard package can save this information for UNFORMAT to use.

Notes

> **Caution**
> The MIRROR and UNFORMAT commands are not replacements for proper backups of your hard disk. Although the information that MIRROR saves can be very handy, full and regular backups are a much safer and more reliable means of ensuring that you do not lose data.

1. When you track deleted files, you can specify how many files are contained in the PCTRACKR.DEL file (1 to 999) by using the /T*drive-entries* parameter. The default values, however, probably are satisfactory. Those values are as follows:

Size of Disk	Entries Stored
360KB	25
720KB	50
1.2MB/1.44MB	75
20MB	101
32MB	202
Larger than 32MB	303

2. Using the /PARTN switch with MIRROR creates the file PARTNSAV.FIL, which contains information from the drive's partition table. The partition initially is created with FDISK. You are instructed to place a floppy disk in drive A rather than save PARTNSAV.FIL on the hard disk. The file is saved on the disk. Label and store the disk in a safe place.

3. UNFORMAT, a companion command to MIRROR, uses these files. If you lose information, if you accidentally format a disk, or if the partition table is damaged, you can recover the lost information by using UNFORMAT if you previously used MIRROR.

MESSAGES

```
Creates an image of the system area. Drive C being processed.
The MIRROR process was successful.
```

Information: These messages appear when you issue the command MIRROR while drive C is the current drive. The messages indicate that MIRROR performed successfully.

```
Deletion-tracking software being installed.
The following drives are supported:
Drive C - Default files saved.
Installation complete.
```

Information: These messages appear when you install MIRROR with delete tracking. The messages indicate that delete tracking for drive C is installed correctly.

```
WARNING! Unrecognized DOS INT 25h/26h handler. Some other TSR
programs may behave erratically while deletion-tracking software is resident
Try installing MIRROR program before your other resident programs.
```

Warning: Some other TSR conflicted with delete tracking. Experiment with loading TSRs and delete tracking in a different order. As suggested in the message, you might have to install MIRROR before any other resident software you use. When you find the correct order, modify AUTOEXEC.BAT so that the TSRs and delete tracking are loaded in the correct sequence.

SEE ALSO

FDISK, UNDELETE, and UNFORMAT

MKDIR (SEE MD)

MKDIR is an alternative name for the MD command. For information on using the MD or MKDIR command, see the entry for MD in this command reference.

MODE   1.1 AND LATER—EXTERNAL

The MODE command generally configures system devices. The details of the command's functions, however, are so varied that the syntax quickly becomes quite complex. Therefore, the following sections cover each of the MODE command's functions separately:

To set serial ports, see the entry for MODE COM#.

To configure the keyboard and display, see the entry for MODE CON.

To use MODE's code page functions, see the entry for MODE *device* CP.

To set the display device and mode, see the entry for MODE *display*.

To set parallel (printer) ports, see the entry for MODE LPT#.

DISPLAY DEVICE STATUS INFORMATION

To display the status of any or all the devices that MODE can control, use the following command format:

MODE *device* /STATUS

PARAMETERS AND SWITCHES

device   The DOS device for which you want to see status information. *device* can be any one of the following:

Device Name	Description
COM1 through COM4	Serial communication ports
CON	The console, which is your keyboard and display
LPT1 through LPT3	Parallel printer ports
PRN	The primary printer port, normally LPT1

If you omit this parameter, MODE displays information about the status of all the devices attached to your system.

/STATUS   Including this parameter requests the status of any redirected parallel ports you may have set without canceling the redirection. If you omit the /STATUS parameter and you are redirecting any parallel ports, the redirection is canceled when the information about that port is displayed. You can abbreviate /STATUS as /STA.

NOTES

1. If you ask for the status of the PRN device (for example, MODE PRN), MODE displays information about the code page status of the primary printer port. If you ask for the status of LPT1, however, it reports on the retry setting currently in effect.
2. You can include a colon after the device name or leave it off; its use is optional.
3. The AUX device, which is normally the same as COM1, is not recognized by the MODE command.
4. Status information has been available from the MODE command since DOS 4.0.

MESSAGES

```
Illegal device name - device
```

Error: You have specified a device name that is not present in your computer. *device* is the name of the device that you entered in the MODE command.

Invalid parameter - *parameter*

Error: You have specified the name of a device that MODE doesn't recognize or have included an unsupported parameter. Check the command to make sure that you have entered it correctly.

SEE ALSO

ANSI.SYS, CHCP, COUNTRY=, DISPLAY.SYS, KEYB, and NLSFUNC

"Altering the Look of the Screen with MODE" in Chapter 11, "The MODE Command" in Chapter 13, and "Understanding Code Page Switching" in Chapter 14

MODE COM#   1.1 AND LATER—EXTERNAL

You use the MODE COM# form of the MODE command to initialize serial ports connected to your computer. Many programs initialize the ports themselves, but in case they don't, DOS provides this functionality in the MODE COM# command. The INTERSVR /RCOPY remote copy operation depends on the services of MODE COM# to make the remote copy operation succeed, for instance.

SYNTAX

The old syntax, which is simple but not very intuitive, is as follows:

MODE COM#: *baud, parity, databits, stopbits, retry*

If you are running DOS 4.0 or later, you can use the following format:

MODE COM#:   BAUD=*baud*   PARITY=*parity*   DATA=*databits*   STOP=*stopbits*   RETRY=*retry*

PARAMETERS AND SWITCHES

- **#:** Specifies the serial port that you want to initialize. DOS supports COM ports 1, 2, 3, and 4, but they may not all be installed in your computer. The colon after the number is optional.

- *baud*   Specifies the baud rate to use. Legal values for *baud* are 110, 150, 300, 600, 1200, 2400, 4800, 9600, or 19200. You need to enter only the first two digits—for instance, 24 instead of 2400. (Baud equals bits per second for rates higher than 300.) Not all computers can support 19200-baud serial transmissions.

- *parity*   Indicates the parity checking setting. Legal values are N for None, O for Odd, E for Even, M for Mark, or S for Space. Not all computers support the Mark and Space parity settings. The default setting is E.

- *databits*   Specifies the number of data bits. Legal values are 5 through 8. The default value is 7. Not all computers support 5 and 6 data bits.

stopbits Specifies the number of stop bits. Legal values are 1, 1.5, and 2. If *baud* is 110, the default is 2; otherwise, the default is 1. Not all computers support 1.5 stop bits.

retry Instructs DOS about how to handle timeout errors. Using this parameter causes part of MODE to remain resident in memory. You can choose one of the following options:

retry	Action
B	Return busy when the port is busy
E	Return error when the port is busy
P	Retry until output is accepted
R	Return ready when the port is busy (infinite retry)
N or NONE	Take no action (the default)

NOTES

1. For DOS versions before 5.0, you must enter the adapter's number, followed by a space and baud rate. If you type the optional colon, you must type the adapter number immediately before the colon. All other parameters are optional.

2. Note that with the older, unlabeled syntax, MODE interprets each parameter by position alone, and you must enter them in the order shown. If you do not want to enter a value for a particular parameter, enter a comma for that value, or use the newer syntax where relative position on the command line is unimportant.

3. If you enter an invalid parameter, DOS responds with an invalid-parameter message and takes no further action.

4. You can abbreviate the baud rate parameter by using only the first two digits of the baud rate. For example, you can specify 11 for 110 baud, or 96 for 9600 baud.

5. If you want continuous retries after a timeout, you must enter RETRY=B (or P for versions of DOS before 5.0) every time you use the MODE COM#: command. Other settings remain in effect if you do not specify new values for them.

6. If the adapter is set for continuous retries (RETRY=B) and the device is not ready, the computer may appear to hang up when it's really just waiting for the port. You can abort this loop by pressing Ctrl+Break.

7. If you use a networked printer, do not specify any of the RETRY values.

8. To display the current status of a serial port, enter the MODE COM# command without any parameters. To display the status of all the DOS devices attached to your computer, enter the MODE command alone.

SEE ALSO

MODE LPT# and MODE *device* /STATUS

"Using MODE to Change Serial Port Settings" in Chapter 13

MODE CON 4.0 AND LATER—EXTERNAL

MODE can configure various aspects of the console device, which refers to your keyboard and display. For the keyboard, MODE can set the keyboard repeat rate and delay. For the monitor, MODE can, with the help of the ANSI.SYS device driver, control the number of lines and columns displayed in text mode.

SYNTAX

To configure the keyboard, use the following format:

MODE CON: RATE=rate **DELAY=**delay

To configure the monitor, use the following format:

MODE CON: COLS=columns **LINES=**lines

PARAMETERS AND SWITCHES

CON: Specifies the console device. The colon is optional.

rate Specifies the rate at which a character repeats when you hold down a key. Legal values are in the range of 1 to 32, which represents approximately 2 to 30 characters per second. The default is 20 for most keyboards and 21 for IBM PS/2 keyboards. To set the *rate*, you also must set the *delay*.

delay Specifies the length of the delay between the initial pressing of the key and the start of automatic character repetition. This value can be 1, 2, 3, or 4, which represent delays of 1/4 second, 1/2 second, 3/4 second, and one full second, respectively. The default is 2. To set the *delay*, you also must set the *rate*.

columns Indicates the number of columns to display onscreen. Legal values are 40 and 80. Most computers start up in an 80-column screen mode. If you omit this parameter, the display keeps its present column setting.

lines Indicates the number of lines to display onscreen. Legal values are different for different types of monitors. CGA and MDA monitors support 25-line text modes only. EGA monitors support 25- and 43-line text modes. VGA monitors support 25-, 43-, and 50-line text modes. Most computers start up in a 25-line screen mode. If you omit this parameter, the display keeps its present lines setting.

NOTES

1. To set the keyboard repeat rate, you must specify both *rate* and *delay* settings. You cannot use these parameters individually.
2. The CapsLock, ScrollLock, NumLock, and Insert keys never repeat, no matter how long you hold them down.
3. Only enhanced keyboards support having their repeat rate changed. The original 84-key keyboards supplied with the IBM PC use a fixed repeat rate and ignore the MODE CON command.

4. Using the MODE CON command to change the number of lines and columns displayed on your screen requires the assistance of the ANSI.SYS device driver. If ANSI.SYS isn't in memory when the command executes, an error message is displayed, and the requested screen mode change does not take place. (See the first message in the "Messages" section.)

EXAMPLES

To set the keyboard to repeat as quickly as possible but increase the delay before repeating to 3/4 of a second, you enter the following command:

```
MODE   COM   RATE=32   DELAY=3
```

To reset the keyboard to its default values, you enter the following command:

```
MODE   COM   RATE=20   DELAY=2
```

To set an EGA or VGA monitor to a 43-line text mode, you enter the following command:

```
MODE   CON   LINES=43
```

MESSAGES

```
ANSI.SYS must be installed to perform requested function
```

Error: MODE requires the assistance of the ANSI.SYS device driver to perform the requested operation, but it isn't loaded. To use this MODE command, you have to add a DEVICE= line loading the ANSI.SYS device driver to your CONFIG.SYS file and restart your computer.

```
Rate and delay must be specified together
```

Error: MODE CON requires that you specify both the *rate* and *delay* settings in order to change the keyboard settings for these parameters. Make sure that you specified both parameters on the command line.

SEE ALSO

ANSI.SYS and MODE display

"Using MODE to Change the Typematic Rate" in Chapter 13

MODE *device* CP   3.3 AND LATER—EXTERNAL

The MODE command offers four subfunctions that you can use to prepare and manipulate code pages on your computer. You use these commands in conjunction with the other international commands to configure your computer to use standards popular in various countries.

SYNTAX

To prepare and load a code page into the DISPLAY.SYS and/or PRINTER.SYS device drivers, use the following format:

MODE *device* **CODEPAGE PREPARE=((***codepage*...**)** *cpi_file***)**

or

MODE *device* **CP PREP=((***codepage*...**)** *cpi_file***)**

To switch to a code page that has been previously prepared, use the following format:

MODE *device* **CODEPAGE SELECT=***codepage*

or

MODE *device* **CP SEL=***codepage*

To reload the current code page into the hardware, use the following format:

MODE *device* **CODEPAGE REFRESH**

or

MODE *device* **CP REF**

To display code page status information, use the following format:

MODE *device* **CODEPAGE /STATUS**

or

MODE *device* **CP /STA**

Parameters and Switches

device — Specifies the DOS device that you want to use. This parameter is required. *device* can be any one of the following:

Device Name	Description
CON	The console, which is your keyboard and display
LPT1 through LPT3	Parallel printer ports
PRN	The primary printer port, normally LPT1

CODEPAGE PREPARE or **CP PREP** — Prepares code pages (character sets), which simply means that it loads the specified code page into the device driver in memory (DISPLAY.SYS or PRINTER.SYS). You must prepare a code page before you can use it with the CHCP or the MODE *device* CODEPAGE SELECT commands. **CODEPAGE** can be abbreviated as **CP**, and **PREPARE** can be abbreviated as **PREP**.

CODEPAGE SELECT or **CP SEL** — Switches the current code page to the one specified. The code page you switch to must have been previously loaded with the MODE *device* CODEPAGE PREPARE command, or be permanently available from the hardware. **CODEPAGE** can be abbreviated as **CP**, and **SELECT** can be abbreviated as **SEL**.

CODEPAGE REFRESH or **CP REF** — Reloads the current code page. You need to use this command if your printer loses the code page information loaded into it by being turned off. The code page you refresh must have been previously loaded with the MODE *device* CODEPAGE PREPARE command. **CODEPAGE** can be abbreviated as **CP**, and **REFRESH** can be abbreviated as **REF**.

codepage   Specifies the code page (character set) that you want to prepare or select. You can enter more than one *codepage* in the PREPARE command. For a list of the code pages supported by MS-DOS, see Chapter 14, "Understanding the International Features of DOS."

cpi_file   Specifies the name and location of the file that contains code page information for the specified device. If you don't specify a drive, DOS assumes the current drive. If you don't specify a subdirectory path, DOS assumes the current directory. The filename is required. MS-DOS 6 provides the following code page information files for use with DISPLAY.SYS and PRINTER.SYS:

CPI File	Description
EGA.CPI	Code pages for EGA and VGA displays
EGA.ICE	(DOS 6.0 only) Icelandic code pages for EGA and VGA displays
EGA2.CPI *(NEW MS-DOS 6.2)*	An alternative set of code pages for EGA and VGA displays
LCD.CPI	(Supplemental Disk) Code pages for an IBM Convertible's LCD display
4201.CPI	(Supplemental Disk) Code pages for IBM Proprinters II and III Model 4201 and IBM Proprinters II and III XL Model 4202
4208.CPI	(Supplemental Disk) Code pages for IBM Proprinters X24E Model 4207 and IBM Proprinters XL24E Model 4208
5202.CPI	(Supplemental Disk) Code pages for IBM Quietwriter III printer

Setup places these files in the C:\DOS subdirectory by default.

/STATUS   Displays the number of code pages prepared or selected for the specified *device*. You can include this parameter or leave it out; it makes no difference. Microsoft states that you can abbreviate it as /STA, but because you can abbreviate it to nothing, it hardly matters.

NOTES

1. You must specify a valid device. The options are CON:, PRN:, LPT1:, LPT2:, and LPT3:. The colon after the device name is optional.

2. MODE *device* CODEPAGE PREPARE prepares code pages (character sets) for the console (keyboard and display) and printers. Issue this subcommand before issuing the MODE *device* CODEPAGE SELECT subcommand, unless you use the IBM Quietwriter III printer, whose font information is contained in cartridges. If the code page that you need is in a cartridge, you do not need to use the PREPARE command.

3. For the PREPARE command, you must specify one or more code pages. You can use commas or spaces to separate the numbers if you specify more than one. You must enclose the entire list of code pages in parentheses.

4. When you add or replace code pages by using a PREPARE command, enter a comma for any code page that you do not want to change.

5. For the SELECT command, you must specify a single code page. The code page must be either part of a MODE *device* CODEPAGE PREPARE command for the device or the hardware code page specified to the appropriate device driver.

6. MODE *device* CODEPAGE SELECT activates a currently prepared code page or reactivates a hardware code page. You can use MODE *device* CODEPAGE SELECT only on these two types of code pages.

7. MODE *device* CODEPAGE SELECT usually downloads any software font to the device, except for the Quietwriter III printer, which uses cartridges.

8. MODE *device* CODEPAGE SELECT activates code pages for individual devices. You can use the CHCP command to activate the code pages for all available devices.

9. MODE *device* CODEPAGE REFRESH downloads, if necessary, and reactivates the currently selected code page on a device. Use this command after you turn on your printer, or after a program changes the video display and leaves the console code page in ruins.

10. MODE *device* CODEPAGE /STATUS displays the following information about the device:
    - The selected (active) code page, if one is selected
    - The hardware code page(s)
    - Any prepared code page(s)
    - Any available positions for additional prepared code pages

EXAMPLES

To prepare the first parallel port with the multilingual (Latin 1) code page found in the file C:\DOS\4201.CPI, enter the following:

MODE   LPT1   CP   PREP=((850) C:\DOS\4201.CPI)

SEE ALSO

CHCP, COUNTRY=, DISPLAY.SYS, KEYB, NLSFUNC, and PRINTER.SYS

"Understanding Code Page Switching" in Chapter 14

MODE *display* 2.0 AND LATER—EXTERNAL

The MODE *display* form of the MODE command can switch the active display adapter between the monochrome display (MDA) and a graphics display adapter (Color Graphics Adapter (CGA), Enhanced Color Graphics Adapter (EGA), or Video Graphics Array (VGA)) on a two-display system.

Syntax

MODE *display_mode*, *lines*

For systems with CGA monitors, you can use the following syntax to shift the display on your screen:

MODE *display_mode*, **shift**, T

Parameters and Switches

display_mode Indicates the display adapter to activate if you have more than one installed in your computer. This parameter also specifies the text mode to be used, so it's handy even with only one monitor installed. Legal values for *display_mode* are listed in the following table.

Display Mode	Description
40	Sets the graphics display to 40 characters per line
80	Sets the graphics display to 80 characters per line
BW40	Makes the graphics display the active display and sets the mode to 40 characters per line, black and white (color disabled)
BW80	Makes the graphics display the active display and sets the mode to 80 characters per line, black and white (color disabled)
CO40	Makes the graphics display the active display and sets the mode to 40 characters per line (color enabled)
CO80	Makes the graphics display the active display and sets the mode to 80 characters per line (color enabled)
MONO	Makes the monochrome display the active display

If your computer has an MDA adapter (monochrome or Hercules Mono), it starts up in MONO mode. All other display adapters start up in CO80 mode.

lines Specifies the number of lines to display onscreen. Legal values are different for different types of monitors. CGA and MDA monitors support 25-line text modes only. EGA monitors support 25- and 43-line text modes. VGA monitors support 25-, 43-, and 50-line text modes. Most computers start up in a 25-line screen mode. If you omit this parameter, the display keeps its current lines setting.

shift (CGA displays only) Enables you to shift the onscreen image left or right. Legal values are L to shift left and R to shift right. In an 80-column mode, the screen shifts two characters at a time, and in a 40-column mode, one character at a time.

T (CGA displays only) Displays a test pattern. This parameter can help you when you are using the left and right shift parameter to get the screen centered.

NOTES

1. The MODE CO80 command can be very handy for resetting your screen when it's left in an unknown state by an inconsiderate program. It also restores the cursor to its normal size and position. If your screen goes black when you exit a graphics utility program, for example, try typing in this command, even if you can't see what you're typing.
2. For the first form of the command, you must enter the *display_mode*. All other parameters are optional.
3. The second form of this command is legal to use only with displays that use a Color Graphics Adapter (CGA). On any other type of display, this form of the command does nothing. To adjust a CGA display, you must enter the *shift* parameter (L or R), but you can avoid resetting the *display_mode* by typing a comma before the *shift* parameter. Depending on whether you are in a 40- or an 80-column screen mode, the screen shifts one or two characters to the right or left. Including the T parameter displays a test pattern onscreen and prompts you to type Y if the screen is centered or N to shift the display further left or right.
4. Using the MODE CON command to change the number of *lines* displayed on your screen requires the assistance of the ANSI.SYS device driver. (You can change the *display_mode* without ANSI.SYS, however.) If ANSI.SYS isn't in memory when the command executes, an error message is displayed, and the requested screen mode change does not take place. (See the first message in the "Messages" section.)

EXAMPLES

If you have a CGA, EGA, or VGA display and you want to reset the screen to normal, including the shape of the cursor, enter the following command:

```
MODE  CO80
```

MODE CO80 can be a lifesaver when a program leaves your screen in limbo. Even if you can't see what you're typing, DOS resets the screen mode to its normal mode when you enter these commands.

MESSAGES

```
ANSI.SYS must be installed to perform requested function
```

Error: MODE requires the assistance of the ANSI.SYS device driver to perform the requested operation, but it isn't loaded. To use this MODE command, you have to add a DEVICE= line that loads the ANSI.SYS device driver to your CONFIG.SYS file and restart your computer.

See Also

`CLS` and `MODE CON`

"Altering the Look of the Screen with MODE" in Chapter 11

MODE LPT#   3.2 and later—External

You can use the `MODE LPT#` form of the `MODE` command to set the operating characteristics of your printer or to redirect printer output to a serial port. You can set the lines and columns only for IBM- and Epson-compatible printers.

Syntax

    `MODE LPT#: columns, lines, retry`

or

    `MODE LPT#: COLS=columns LINES=lines RETRY=retry`

To force DOS to print to a serial printer instead of a parallel printer, use the following format:

    `MODE LPT#:=COM#`

Parameters and Switches

LPT#:   Specifies the parallel printer port you want to configure. DOS supports LPT ports 1, 2, and 3, but they may not all be installed in your computer. The colon after the number is optional.

COM#:   Specifies the serial port to which you want to redirect printer output. DOS supports COM ports 1, 2, 3, and 4, but they may not all be installed in your computer. The colon after the number is optional.

columns   (IBM- and Epson-compatible printers only) Indicates the number of characters per line to print on the printer. Legal values are 80 and 132. Most printers start up in an 80-column mode. If you omit this parameter, the printer keeps its current characters-per-line setting.

lines   (IBM- and Epson-compatible printers only) Specifies the number of lines per inch to print on the printer. Legal values are 6 and 8. Most printers start up in a 6-line-per-inch mode. If you omit this parameter, the printer keeps its current lines-per-inch setting.

retry   Instructs DOS about how to handle timeout errors. Using this parameter causes part of MODE to remain resident in memory. You can choose one of the following options:

retry	Action
B	Return busy when the port is busy
E	Return error when the port is busy

retry	Action
P	Retry until output is accepted
R	Return ready when the port is busy (infinite retry)
N or NONE	Take no action (the default)

Rules

1. When configuring a parallel port, you must specify a printer number, but all other parameters are optional, including the colon after the printer number.
2. If you do not want to change a configuration parameter, enter a comma for that parameter.
3. The MODE LPT#:=COM#: command cancels the effect of the MODE LPT#: command.
4. A parameter does not change if you skip that parameter or use an invalid parameter. The printer number, however, must be entered correctly.
5. In DOS 3.3 and earlier versions, if you specify P for continuous retries, you can cancel P only by reentering the MODE command without P. In later versions of DOS, the RETRY=B option has the same effect as the P option of previous DOS versions.
6. If you use a networked printer, do not use any of the RETRY values.
7. The characters-per-line and lines-per-inch portions of the command affect only IBM printers, Epson printers, and other printers that use Epson-compatible control codes.
8. When you are redirecting printer output, the ports you specify for both the parallel printer port and serial printer port must be valid. In other words, you cannot redirect printer output to a serial printer if you don't have a parallel port, and you can't use a nonexistent parallel port to get around this problem.
9. After you issue the redirection command, all printing that normally goes to the parallel printer goes to the designated serial printer. Programs that write directly to the hardware, such as Microsoft Windows, are not affected by this redirection. For such programs, try printing to a file named LPT1.TXT, substituting whatever parallel port you've redirected.
10. If you are using a serial printer, you usually have to use the MODE COM# command to set the parameters on your serial port to match the printer. Check your printer's documentation to find out the correct settings to use.
11. You can cancel or undo the redirection command by issuing the MODE LPT#: command.

Notes

This command controls IBM dot-matrix and graphics printers, all Epson printers, and Epson-compatible printers. The command may work partially or not at all on other printers.

When you change the column width, MODE sends the special printer-control code that specifies the normal font (80) or the condensed font (132). When you change the lines-per-inch setting, MODE sends the correct printer-control code for printing 6 or 8 lines per inch. MODE also sets the printer to 88 lines per page for an 8-lines-per-inch setting and to 66 lines per page for a 6-lines-per-inch setting.

If you use the P option of DOS 3.3 or earlier versions or the B retry option of later versions of DOS and attempt to print on a deselected printer, the computer does not issue a timeout error. Rather, the computer internally loops until the printer is ready (turned on, connected to the PC, and selected). For about a minute, the computer appears to be locked up. To abort the continuous retry, press Ctrl+Break.

The redirection capabilities of MODE are useful for systems that are connected to a serial printer. When you type the following command, the serial printer receives all the output that usually is sent to the system printer (assuming that the serial printer is connected to the first Asynchronous Communications Adapter):

MODE LPT1: = COM1:

This output includes the print-screen (Shift+PrtSc) function. Before you issue the MODE LPT=COM*y* command, use the MODE COM*n*: command to set up the serial adapter used for the serial printer.

SEE ALSO

MODE COM#

"Using MODE to Change Parallel Port Settings" and "Using MODE to Redirect a Parallel Port to a Serial Port" in Chapter 13

MONOUMB.386   6.0 AND LATER—WINDOWS

If you have a VGA display, you might be able to increase the amount of upper memory space by instructing MemMaker to include the monochrome display region (B000h to B7FFh) in its search for available UMB space. If you run Windows, and you're using this region as UMB space, you need to add a device line for the MONOUMB.386 driver to the [386Enh] section of SYSTEM.INI so that Windows knows what you're up to.

SYNTAX

To use the monochrome region as UMB space, include the following line in the [386Enh] section of SYSTEM.INI:

DEVICE=*drive:\path***MONOUMB.386**

PARAMETERS AND SWITCHES

drive:\path   Specifies the full path to the MONOUMB.386 file on your system. The setup program for DOS 6 places this file in the C:\DOS subdirectory by default.

Notes

1. There are a few good reasons why you might not want to use the monochrome region as upper memory space on a VGA system. If you or one of your software programs switches the VGA to monochrome mode (perhaps with the MODE MONO command), the display overwrites whatever resident software you have loaded there. Also, some Super VGA adapters use this memory region when they are in high-resolution graphics modes.
2. To instruct MemMaker to include this region in its search for upper memory space, choose Custom Setup and answer yes to the question Use monochrome region (B000-B7FF) for running programs?.

See Also

MEMMAKER

MORE   2.0 AND LATER—EXTERNAL

MORE displays one screen of information from the standard input device, pauses, and then displays the message -More-. When you press any key, MORE displays the next screen of information. MORE is one of the filter programs that MS-DOS provides and normally is used with input redirection or pipes from the command line.

Syntax

MORE < pathname

or

command | MORE

Parameters and Switches

   < pathname   Indicates the name of a file that you want MORE to display one page at a time on your screen. All the normal defaults for drives and subdirectories apply. Wildcards are not allowed.

   command | Pipes the screen output from a command into the MORE program, which displays it one screen at a time. *command* can be any legal DOS command that writes its output to the standard output device (normally the screen).

Rules

1. MORE displays one screen of information on a standard screen.
2. After displaying a screen of information, MORE waits for a keystroke before filling the screen with new information. This process repeats until all output has been displayed.
3. MORE is useful with input and output redirection and piping.

NOTES

1. MORE is a DOS filter that enables you to display information without manually pausing the screen.
2. MORE, when used with redirection or piping, is similar to the TYPE command, but MORE pauses after each screen of information.
3. MORE intelligently handles two aspects of displaying text. The command pauses after displaying a screenful of lines, as you define by using the MODE command. The command also wraps lines that are longer than the width of your screen and reduces the number of lines that appear so that unread lines do not scroll off the screen.

SEE ALSO

FIND and SORT

"The MORE Filter" in Chapter 13

MOVE   6.0 AND LATER—EXTERNAL

You can use MOVE to move a file or group of files from one location to another or to rename subdirectories.

SYNTAX

To move a file or group of files, use the following format:

MOVE *source*, *source*, ... *destination* /Y /-Y

To rename a subdirectory, use the following format:

MOVE *old_dirname* *new_dirname*

PARAMETERS AND SWITCHES

source Specifies the file or files that you want to move. You can specify a full pathname—that is, *drive:\path\...\filename.ext*)—and wildcards are allowed. You can enter additional *source* parameters by separating them with commas. This parameter is required and must include a filename (*.* is not assumed).

destination Specifies the location to which you want to move the *source* file(s). Normally, just a drive and/or path is included, although you can enter a destination filename (to rename it) if you are moving only one file. If you omit parts of this parameter, DOS assumes the current drive and subdirectory as necessary.

old_dirname Indicates the name of the subdirectory that you want to rename. You can include a disk drive and subdirectory path if you want. If *old_dirname* refers to a file, DOS moves the file instead.

new_dirname   Indicates the new name that you want to give the **old_dirname** subdirectory. If **new_dirname** isn't in the current directory, you must specify the same drive and/or path you specified with **old_dirname**; otherwise, DOS thinks you are trying to move the subdirectory, which isn't allowed.

 /Y   Specifies that you want MOVE to overwrite files without prompting you for confirmation. Including this parameter overrides any setting specified with the COPYCMD environment variable.

 /-Y   Specifies that you want MOVE to prompt you for confirmation before overwriting any files, even if the command is run from within a batch file. Including this parameter overrides any setting specified with the COPYCMD environment variable.

Exit Codes

ERRORLEVEL Value	Meaning
0	Files were moved successfully.
1	Files weren't moved due to errors or user abort.

Notes

1. Starting with DOS 6.2, the MOVE command, when run from the command line, prompts you for confirmation before overwriting files. However, to avoid forcing you to rewrite all of your batch files, when you run MOVE from a batch file, it does not prompt you before overwriting a file.

   If you don't like MOVE's new behavior, you can change it by defining an environment variable named COPYCMD. Setting COPYCMD equal to /Y forces MOVE to act as it did in all previous versions of DOS, never prompting for confirmation before overwriting a file. If you set COPYCMD equal to /-Y, MOVE always prompts for confirmation, even when it's run from within a batch file.

2. If you move a file to a directory that already includes a file with that name, DOS overwrites the file in the destination directory without warning.

3. You cannot rename a directory that you are moving to a different disk or to a different relative position on a disk. The drive and path in front of both *old_dirname* and *new_dirname* have to be the same.

4. If the destination directory does not exist, DOS can create it automatically.

5. If you specify several files to be moved and a filename rather than a directory as the destination, DOS displays the message Cannot move multiple files to a single file.

6. If a MOVE operation is successful, DOS returns an ERRORLEVEL of 0. If an error occurs, DOS returns a value of 1.

EXAMPLES

To move the file README.TXT in the current directory and the file C:\BIN\SETUP.EXE to the directory C:\TEMP (the files are not renamed), enter the following:

```
MOVE  README.TXT, C:\BIN\SETUP.EXE  C:\TEMP
```

To change the name of the file README.TXT in the current directory to README.1ST, enter the following:

```
MOVE  README.TXT  README.1ST
```

To move and rename C:\INFO\README.TXT to C:\TEMP\README.BAK, enter the following:

```
MOVE  C:\INFO\README.TXT  C:\TEMP\README.BAK
```

To change the name of the directory C:\BIN to C:\OLDBIN, enter the following:

```
MOVE  C:\BIN  C:\OLDBIN
```

SEE ALSO

COPY, REN or RENAME, and XCOPY

"Using the MOVE Command" in Chapter 8

MSAV   6.0 AND LATER—EXTERNAL

Microsoft Anti-Virus (MSAV) is a full-screen program that can help you to detect and clean any computer viruses found in your system. You can adapt it to be run from a batch file, so you can automate routine scans of your system or floppy disk drives.

SYNTAX

To interact with MSAV's full-screen interface, use the following format:

MSAV /R /*video* /*mouse*

To immediately start scanning one or more disks, directories, and/or files using MSAV's full-screen interface to show progress, use the following format:

MSAV *pathname drive:* ... /S /C /R /A /L /*video* /*mouse*

To immediately start scanning one or more disks, directories, and/or files using a command-line interface to show progress, include the /N or the /P switch as follows:

MSAV *pathname drive:* ... /S /C /R /A /L /N /P /F /*video* /*mouse*

To get online help for MSAV's video and mouse options, use the following format:

MSAV /**VIDEO**

Parameters and Switches

pathname   Specifies the drive, subdirectory, or file to limit the virus scan to. All normal drive and subdirectory defaults apply. If you specify a subdirectory, Anti-Virus also scans all subdirectories below the one specified. Do not specify additional drives when you are specifying a pathname as the scan target.

drive: ...   Specifies one or more drives that you want MSAV to scan.

/S   Specifies that you want to scan for viruses but not remove any that are found. This is the default setting. Using this switch causes MSAV to start scanning immediately.

/C   Specifies that you want MSAV to remove (clean) any viruses it finds. Using this switch causes MSAV to start scanning immediately.

/R   Specifies that MSAV should record the results of each scan in a file (MSAV.RPT) that is created in the root directory of each drive scanned.

/A   Causes MSAV to scan all your drives, including network and CD-ROM drives, but not floppy disk drives. If you have a CD-ROM drive or are connected to a network, you should probably avoid this switch.

/L   Causes MSAV to scan all your local drives, including any floppy disk drives, but not network and CD-ROM drives.

/N   Specifies that MSAV should not display anything at all while it's working. It displays the contents of the MSAV.TXT file if it exists in the same subdirectory as MSAV.EXE (normally C:\DOS). If a virus is found, an exit code of 86 is returned instead of a warning message. When the specified scanning operation is completed, MSAV terminates automatically, making it suitable for use in a batch file. You cannot specify both the /P and /N switches.

/P   Activates MSAV's command-line interface instead of the full-screen interface it normally uses. When the specified scanning operation is completed, MSAV terminates automatically, making it suitable for use in a batch file. You cannot specify both the /P and /N switches.

/F   Specifies that you do not want MSAV to display a list of the files it's scanning. You can use this switch only with the /N or /P switch.

/*video*   MSAV provides quite a few video-related options. Legal values for *video* are listed in the following table:

video	Description
25	Sets the display to 25 lines (the default)
28	Sets the display to 28 lines (VGA only)
43	Sets the display to 43 lines (EGA and VGA)
50	Sets the display to 50 lines (VGA only)

video	Description
60	Sets the display to 60 lines (Video 7 video adapters only)
IN	Forces the display to use color
BW	Forces the display to use shades of gray
MONO	Forces the display to use black and white only (monochrome)
LCD	Forces the display to use a liquid-crystal display (LCD) color scheme
FF	Uses the fastest screen updating for CGA (may cause "snow")
BF	Uses your computer's BIOS fonts (use only if the default graphics characters in the full-screen display are not displayed properly)
NF	No fonts (no graphics characters should be used in the full-screen display)
BT	Allows the use of a graphics mouse in Microsoft Windows and graphics fonts in DESQview and UltraVision

/mouse   MSAV provides three mouse-related options. Legal values for *mouse* are listed in the following table:

mouse	Description
NGM	No graphics mouse; uses the default mouse character rather than a graphics cursor in the full-screen display
LE	Switches the left and right mouse buttons
PS2	Resets the mouse if the cursor disappears or freezes

/VIDEO   Specifying this option alone on the command line requests MSAV to display a list of the available video and mouse options.

EXIT CODES

When you run MSAV with the /N switch, it generates the following exit codes, which can be read by the IF ERRORLEVEL command in a batch file.

ERRORLEVEL Value	Meaning
0	No viruses were detected.
86	One or more viruses were found.

NOTES

1. Different options are available from the full-screen display and from the command line.
2. The options you choose while in full-screen mode are recorded in the file MSAV.INI.

SEE ALSO

MWAV and VSAFE

"Understanding Computer Viruses" in Chapter 9

MSBACKUP   6.0 AND LATER—EXTERNAL

Microsoft Backup (MSBACKUP) is a full-screen program that can back up the contents of your hard disk to a series of floppy disks (or another DOS-accessible drive). You can define setup files that record your preferences and enable you to quickly perform different backup chores. No matter how careful you are, you should periodically back up the contents of your hard disk.

SYNTAX

MSBACKUP *setupfile* /BW /LCD /MDA

PARAMETERS AND SWITCHES

setupfile   Specifies the file that holds your saved settings, the names of the files to be backed up, and the type of backup you want. This file must have an .SET extension. The default is DEFAULT.SET. DOS searches for this file in the subdirectory pointed to by the MSDOSDATA environment variable if you do not specify drive or subdirectory information in the pathname.

/BW   Specifies that MSBACKUP should use colors appropriate for a black-and-white display.

/LCD   Specifies that MSBACKUP should use colors appropriate for a liquid-crystal display.

/MDA   Specifies that MSBACKUP should use colors appropriate for a monochrome display adapter.

RULES

1. You do not explicitly create a setup file. MSBACKUP creates a setup file (or updates it, if you specified one in the MSBACKUP command line) when you save your program settings and file selections.

2. You cannot start MSBACKUP from a floppy disk. This utility and its other program files must be on your hard disk.

3. When looking for its configuration information, backup sets, and catalogs, MSBACKUP first looks in the directory specified by the MSDOSDATA environment variable, then in the directory from which it was started, and then in the current directory. You can use MSDOSDATA to point to your own configuration if you share MSBACKUP with other people.

4. DOS 6.0 includes a Microsoft Windows version of MSBACKUP.

Notes

1. When it performs a backup, MSBACKUP creates a catalog file that contains information about the files that it backs up. When you need to restore a file, you can search the catalog files to determine which one contains the files you want.

   Catalog files encode information in their names. Decoding CD10401A.FUL, for example, yields the following characters:

Character	Meaning
C	The first drive backed up in this set.
D	The last drive backed up in this set. (Had C been the only drive, the catalog file's name would have been CC10401A.FUL.)
3	The last digit of the year of the backup (here, 2001).
04	The month of the backup (here, April).
01	The day of the backup (here, the first).
A	The ID of the backup on that day. If more than one backup of the same drive(s) is performed on the same day and the Keep Old Backup Catalogs options is set, MSBACKUP assigns a letter, from A through Z, to indicate the order in which the otherwise identically named catalog files were created. A is the first, B is the second, and so on. If the Keep Old Backup Catalogs option is not set, the ID alternates between A and B.
FUL	The backup type (here, FULL). The other possibilities are INC (incremental) and DIF (differential).

2. When you perform a full backup, MSBACKUP creates a master catalog file, which keeps track of all the backup catalogs that are made during a backup cycle. When you need to restore a file, loading the master catalog automatically merges all the catalogs of the backup cycle, so you can select the latest version of a file easily (although you can choose to restore an earlier version).

   MSBACKUP puts one copy of the backup catalog on your hard disk and a second copy on the disk or network drive that contains your backup set.

3. If DOS displays the message Insufficient memory while you are using MSBACKUP, follow these steps:

   a. Make sure that your computer has at least 512KB of conventional memory.

   b. Quit MSBACKUP, remove all memory-resident programs (TSRs) from memory, and try again.

   c. In MSBACKUP, turn off the Compress Backup Data option (in the Disk Backup Options dialog box).

See Also

MWBACKUP

"Understanding Microsoft Backup" in Chapter 9

MSCDEX 6.0 AND LATER—EXTERNAL

MSCDEX provides DOS access to CD-ROM drives. CD-ROM drives usually have their own device drivers, but these drivers aren't directly accessible to DOS. MSCDEX uses the network redirector interface to assign a drive letter to a CD-ROM drive. To be able to use MSCDEX, you must have one or more drive letters available and often have to include the LASTDRIVE= command in your CONFIG.SYS file to set them aside.

SYNTAX

MSCDEX /**D:***driversig* ... /E /K /S /V /L:*letter* /M:*number*

PARAMETERS AND SWITCHES

/**D:***driversig* ...   For each CD-ROM drive to which you want to assign a drive letter, you need to specify the driver signature (*driversig*) that you assigned to its device driver with the /D switch when you loaded it in your CONFIG.SYS file. You must specify at least one driver signature.

/E   Enables the CD-ROM driver to use available expanded memory to store its sector buffers, thus conserving conventional memory for application programs.

/K   Enables recognition of Kanji (Japanese) CD-ROM labels. Normally, MSCDEX cannot recognize Japanese CD-ROM disks.

/S   Enables sharing of CD-ROM drives on an MS-NET or Windows for Workgroups network server.

/V   Displays memory statistics when MSCDEX starts (Verbose).

/L:*letter*   Specifies the drive letter to be assigned to the first CD-ROM. Additional CD-ROMs are assigned letters in sequence. These drive letters must be available for use. The default is to use the next available drive letter(s).

/M:*number*   Specifies the number of sector buffers MSCDEX should use to buffer CD-ROM reads. More buffers can increase the speed of your CD-ROM drive, but they also use more memory. You can put these buffers in expanded memory by using the /E switch.

NOTES

1. Your CD-ROM's device driver must be loaded by your CONFIG.SYS file. It should include a /D parameter to assign a driver signature (also called a *driver name*) to the driver.
2. Your CONFIG.SYS file must include a LASTDRIVE command that provides enough device letters for your network, SUBST, and MSCDEX needs.
3. MSCDEX can be invoked by your AUTOEXEC.BAT file or from the DOS command line.
4. You need to invoke MSCDEX before you start Microsoft Windows.

EXAMPLES

Following is a typical `CONFIG.SYS` line that loads a device driver to access a CD-ROM drive. Notice that the driver signature is assigned with the /D switch:

```
DEVICE=C:\DEVICES\CDROMDRV.SYS   /D:MSCD000
```

The following line would most likely be included in your `AUTOEXEC.BAT` file and would enable the MSCD000 CD-ROM drive as drive E:

```
C:\DOS\MSCDEX   /D:MSCD000   /L:E
```

SEE ALSO

```
LASTDRIVE=
```

MSD   6.0 AND LATER—EXTERNAL

MSD, which stands for Microsoft System Diagnostics, is a handy tool for checking what is going on in a computer system. Via certain command-line options, you can instruct MSD to generate text files that record the state of your computer. These reports can be very useful when you are troubleshooting.

SYNTAX

To use MSD interactively with a full-screen display, use the following format:

MSD   /B   /I

To use MSD to generate a report to a file, use the following format:

MSD   /I   /F*pathname*   /P*pathname*   /S*pathname*

PARAMETERS AND SWITCHES

/B   Forces the display to black and white for monochrome or LCD displays.

/I   Prevents MSD from detecting hardware when it starts. Use this switch if MSD does not start or run properly on your computer.

/F*pathname*   Specifies that you want a full report generated. MSD prompts you for certain information (your name, company, address, country, telephone number, and comments) and then incorporates that information into a report that it writes to the specified file. You can specify a full pathname with drive and/or path information, but wildcards are not allowed. If you do not include *pathname*, MSD writes the report to the screen.

/P*pathname*   Specifies that you want a partial report generated. A partial report contains all the detailed system information but none of the identifying information that /F prompts you for. You can specify a full pathname with drive and/or path information, but wildcards are not allowed. If you do not include *pathname*, MSD writes the report to the screen.

*/S*pathname   Specifies that you want a summary report generated. A summary report provides a shorter listing that highlights the key features of your computer's configuration. You can specify a full pathname with drive and/or path information, but wildcards are not allowed. If you do not include *pathname*, MSD writes the report to the screen.

NOTES

MSD provides information about your computer (for example, its manufacturer, bus type, and ROM BIOS manufacturer) and about its upper memory use, video display, network, operating system, mouse, other adapters, disk drives, LPT ports, COM ports, IRQ stations, TSR programs, and device drivers. This information can be valuable when you are correcting problems or installing new hardware.

SEE ALSO

MEM

MSHERC

Because the Hercules Monochrome Graphics Adapter had no support built into the ROM BIOS of the computer, to use the display, programmers had to write their own drivers. The MSHERC program, when run, installs itself in memory and provides BIOS-like services for a Hercules Graphics Adapter. Certain QBasic programs require the use of this program to run. If you do not use a Hercules Graphics Adapter, you will have no use for this command. MSHERC is not distributed in the standard DOS 6 package but is available on the DOS 6 Supplemental Disk.

SYNTAX

MSHERC /HALF

PARAMETERS AND SWITCHES

/HALF   Specifying this parameter enables you to use a Hercules Graphics Adapter and a Color Graphics Adapter (CGA) in the same system. It limits the driver to using only the memory on the Hercules card, which does not conflict with standard CGA memory space.

NOTES

Hercules has stopped making these graphics cards for sale. If you need to set up a two-monitor system and need both monitors to be graphics capable, look into setting up two VGA monitors or a VGA monitor with an 8514 display.

MWAV   6.0 AND LATER—WINDOWS

Microsoft Anti-Virus for Windows (MWAV) is a Windows program that can help you to detect and clean any computer viruses found in your system. This program is the Windows counterpart 0201620 to the MSAV program.

You cannot run MWAV from the DOS command line; you need to start it from within Windows, for example, by opening Program Manager's File menu and choosing the Run command. For instruction on using the program, run MWAV and press F1, or choose Help from the menu.

MWAV keeps its settings information in a separate file from MSAV, so the settings you make in one program are not honored in the other program. MWAV stores its settings in the MWAV.INI file, which it creates in the main Windows directory. MSAV stores its settings in the MSAV.INI file, which it creates in either the subdirectory that contains MSAV.EXE or the one pointed to by the MSDOSDATA environment variable.

SEE ALSO

MSAV, MWAVTSR, and VSAFE

"Using the Windows Version of Microsoft Anti-Virus" in Chapter 9

 ## MWAVTSR   6.0 AND LATER—WINDOWS

When Windows is running, VSAFE cannot display its messages when a forbidden system activity arises. MWAVTSR provides a channel through which VSAFE can contact you if it needs your attention while Windows is running. If you are using both Windows and VSAFE, you should add MWAVTSR to your startup group or include it in the LOAD= line in WIN.INI so that it starts up automatically every time you start Windows.

You cannot run MWAVTSR from the DOS command line; you need to start it from within Windows, for example, by opening the Program Manager's File menu and choosing the Run command.

SEE ALSO

MSAV, MWAV, and VSAFE

"Guarding Against Infection" in Chapter 9

 ## MWBACKUP   6.0 AND LATER—WINDOWS

Microsoft Backup for Windows (MWBACKUP) is a Windows program that can back up the contents of your hard disk to a series of floppy disks (or another DOS-accessible drive). You can define setup files that record your preferences and enable you to quickly perform different backup chores. No matter how careful you are, you should periodically back up the contents of your hard disk. This program is the Windows counterpart to the MSBACKUP program.

You cannot run MWBACKUP from the DOS command line; you need to start it from within Windows, for example, by opening Program Manager's File menu and choosing the Run command. For instruction on using the program, run MWBACKUP and press F1 or choose Help from the menu.

MWBACKUP keeps its settings information in a separate file from MSBACKUP, so the settings you make in one program are not honored in the other program. MWBACKUP stores its settings in the MWBACKUP.INI file, which it creates in the main Windows directory. MSBACKUP stores its settings in the MSBACKUP.INI file, which it creates in either the subdirectory that contains MSBACKUP.EXE or the one pointed to by the MSDOSDATA environment variable.

MWBACKUP and MSBACKUP can share catalog files and backup set files. If the MSDOSDATA environment variable is defined, both programs look for these files in the subdirectory it points to. If MSDOSDATA is not defined, they create and look for these files in the subdirectory where the corresponding executable file is located.

SEE ALSO

MSBACKUP

"Understanding Microsoft Backup" in Chapter 9

MWUNDEL 6.0 AND LATER—WINDOWS

Microsoft Undelete for Windows (MWUNDEL) is a Windows program that enables you to recover files that you have deleted accidentally. This program is the Windows counterpart to the UNDELETE program. If you are running Windows, you should use this program in preference to the DOS version. You can control various aspects of the "tracking" and "sentry" options of UNDELETE from within Windows by using MWUNDEL, but the resident portions of UNDELETE need to be loaded into memory before you start Windows.

You cannot run MWUNDEL from the DOS command line; you need to start it from within Windows, for example, by opening Program Manager's File menu and then choosing the Run command. For instruction on using the program, run MWUNDEL and press F1 or choose Help from the menu.

MWUNDEL shares its settings file with UNDELETE. Both programs look for the UNDELETE.INI file in the subdirectory pointed to by the MSDOSDATA environment variable. If MSDOSDATA is not defined, they create and look for UNDELETE.INI in the subdirectory where their executable files are located, which is C:\DOS by default.

SEE ALSO

UNDELETE

"Using the Microsoft Undelete Program for Windows" in Chapter 9

NLSFUNC 3.3 AND LATER—EXTERNAL

NLSFUNC is a resident program that provides support for code page switching on your computer. If you use code pages, you usually have to load NLSFUNC. You can load NLSFUNC from your CONFIG.SYS file by adding the INSTALL= command. Do not attempt to load NLSFUNC if Windows is running on your computer.

SYNTAX

NLSFUNC *drive:\path\COUNTRY.SYS*

PARAMETERS AND SWITCHES

drive:\path\COUNTRY.SYS   The name and location of the country information file you want to use. It normally is COUNTRY.SYS, which Setup places in the C:\DOS subdirectory by default. You don't have to include this parameter if you have included the full pathname of the country file in the COUNTRY= command in your CONFIG.SYS file. If you don't specify this parameter, either here or in the COUNTRY= command, DOS searches for COUNTRY.SYS in the root directory of the startup drive.

NOTES

1. If you provide a drive or pathname, you also must provide the name of the information file (usually COUNTRY.SYS).
2. If you omit the full filename, DOS searches for the file COUNTRY.SYS in the root directory of the current disk.
3. After NLSFUNC is loaded, it remains active until you restart DOS.
4. You can load NLSFUNC into upper memory by using the LOADHIGH command if you have upper memory available on your computer.
5. You can load NLSFUNC from your CONFIG.SYS file by adding the INSTALL= command. If you use INSTALL=, remember that you must include the full pathname (with the extension) of the NLSFUNC.EXE file on your system. Setup places the NLSFUNC.EXE file in the C:\DOS subdirectory by default.

SEE ALSO

CHCP, COUNTRY=, DISPLAY.SYS, KEYB, MODE *device* CP, and PRINTER.SYS

Chapter 14, "Understanding the International Features of DOS"

NUMLOCK= 6.0 AND LATER—INTERNAL

NUMLOCK= was introduced with DOS 6. It enables you to choose the state of the NumLock key (ON or OFF) when the system starts up. If your computer toggles the NumLock key the "wrong" way when you reboot, the NUMLOCK= command is just what you need. NUMLOCK= can be used only in your CONFIG.SYS file.

SYNTAX

To have NumLock turned on (numbers on the keypad active) when you reboot your computer, include the following line in your CONFIG.SYS file:

NUMLOCK=ON

To have NumLock turned off (cursor keys on the keypad active) when you reboot your computer, include the following line in your CONFIG.SYS file:

NUMLOCK=OFF

NOTES

1. Although you may read information to the contrary, you can use NUMLOCK= anywhere in your CONFIG.SYS file. You don't have to set up menus in CONFIG.SYS to use the NUMLOCK= command. In its documentation, Microsoft erroneously implied that NUMLOCK= could be used only in a menu block, and this mistake has been duplicated in virtually every description of this command since then.

2. The CMOS Setup program in certain computers has a setting for controlling the state of NumLock as well. If your computer has such a setting, you can either use it to set NumLock or use the NUMLOCK= command. If the settings disagree, no harm is done, but the setting in CONFIG.SYS overrides the CMOS Setup because it is executed after the ROM BIOS startup routines are complete.

3. If you are using an older computer, you might find that using the NUMLOCK= command causes the NumLock light on your keyboard to get out of sync with the state the key is in. In the design of the original IBM PC, there was no way for the computer to tell the keyboard to toggle the lights. IBM fixed this problem when it introduced the enhanced 101-key keyboard with the IBM AT. If your computer still uses the old-style interface, however, you might have to either ignore the light or avoid using the NUMLOCK= command.

EXAMPLES

If your computer normally sets the NumLock key on at startup, and you want it turned off, include the following line anywhere in your CONFIG.SYS file:

NUMLOCK=OFF

If you want DOS to ask you whether to turn off the NumLock key at startup, insert a ? into the NUMLOCK= command, like this:

NUMLOCK?=OFF

When DOS processes your CONFIG.SYS file, it prompts you with NUMLOCK=OFF [Y,N]? before executing the NUMLOCK= command. Type Y to turn off the NumLock key or N to leave it on.

NWCACHE

NWCACHE is a disk-caching program to speed up disk performance. The syntax and parameters are different depending on whether you are initially loading the cache program or it is already started.

Syntax for Loading NWCACHE

NWCACHE *MaxSize MinSize drive*: +|- *MaxSize MinSize* /L /X=*address* /E /ML /MU /MLX /MUX /BL,/BU,/BE=*size* /LEND=ON|OFF /DELAY=ON|OFF|*time* /W=*size* /CHECK /A20

Parameters for Loading NWCACHE

MaxSize	Specifies a maximum amount of memory in kilobytes to use for the cache—up to 7,670KB.
MinSize	Specifies a minimum amount of memory in kilobytes to use for the cache.
drive:	Enables write-through cache for the drive.
drive:+	Enables write-delay cache for the drive.
drive:-	Disables caching of the drive.
/L	Uses conventional memory for the cache.
/X=*address*	Uses extended memory for the cache. If EMM386.EXE is not loaded, you need to specify the *address* for the cache in kilobytes.
/E	Uses expanded memory (EMS) for the cache.
/ML,/MU,/MLX,/MUX	Loads NWCACHE into one of the following:
	/ML Conventional memory
	/MU Upper memory
	/MLX Conventional and XMS memory using DPMS
	/MUX Upper and XMS memory using DPMS
/BL,/BU,/BE=*size*	Specifies a lookahead buffer memory type and size from 4KB to 16KB:
	/BL Uses conventional memory
	/BU Uses upper memory
	/BE Uses EMS memory
/LEND=ON|OFF	Enables or disables lending extended or EMS cache memory to other applications.
/DELAY=ON|OFF|*time*	Enables write delay (ON) or disables it (OFF). *time* is a value from 50 to 5,000 milliseconds that writes are collected in the cache before being written to disk.

/W=size	Sets delayed write data limit in kilobytes.
/CHECK	Verifies that memory is performing correctly at startup time of the cache program.
/A20	If an XMS memory manager is not loaded and you are having compatibility problems, you might need to use this setting to suppress enhanced line A20 handling.

SYNTAX FOR NWCACHE AFTER IT IS LOADED

NWCACHE +|- *drive:*+|- /SIZE=MIN|MAX /DELAY=ON|OFF|*time* /S /U /?

PARAMETERS FOR NWCACHE AFTER IT IS LOADED

+|-	Flushes and reenables or disables caching for all drives.
drive:	Reenables write-through cache for the drive.
drive:+|-	Reenables (+) write delay cache for the drive or disables the cache (-).
/SIZE=MIN|MAX	Completes writing anything in the cache if write delay is enabled, clears everything from the cache, and either resets the cache to the minimum allowable size or resets it to the maximum size if enough memory is available.
/DELAY=ON|OFF|*time*	Enables write delay (ON) or disables it (OFF). *time* is a value from 50 to 5,000 milliseconds that writes are collected in cache before being written to disk.
/S	Shows cache status.
/Q or /U	Terminates and unloads the cache.
/?	Displays abbreviated help.

NWCDEX

You can use NWCDEX to enable access to CD-ROM drives.

SYNTAX

NWCDEX /**D:***filename* /E /K /N /V /F:*handles* /L:*letter* /M:*buffers* /?

PARAMETERS AND SWITCHES

/**D:***filename*	Specifies the filename for the CD-ROM driver.
/E	Uses expanded memory if DPMS is not available.
/K	Enables recognition of Kanji (Japanese) CD-ROM labels.

	/N	Disables use of DPMS memory.
	/V	Prints debug information during initialization.
	/F:*handles*	Specifies the number of file handles to allocate.
	/L:*letter*	Specifies the drive letter to assign to the drive.
	/M:*buffers*	Specifies the number of buffers to allocate.

NOTES

CONFIG.SYS must contain a DEVICE or DEVICEHIGH statement to load the appropriate driver for the CD-ROM drive. The driver loaded here is the same one specified in the **D:*filename*** parameter.

SEE ALSO

Files, Buffers

PASSWD

You can use PASSWD to set a read/write and read-only password for Stacker drives.

SYNTAX

PASSWD *drive*: ***oldpassword*** *newpassword* /ro /?

PARAMETERS AND SWITCHES

drive:	Indicates the Stacker drive for which to set a password.
oldpassword	Identifies the old password.
newpassword	Identifies the new password.
/ro	Changes the read-only password.
/?	Displays the abbreviated online help.

NOTES

The first time a password is assigned to a Stacker drive, it must be a read/write password.

PASSWORD

PASSWORD assigns passwords to files or directories.

SYNTAX

PASSWORD *d:\path\filespec*... /R|W|D|P|G:*password* /N /S /H

Parameters and Switches

`d:\path\filespec`	Specifies the drive, path, and filename (or file specification using wildcards) of the file (or files or directory) to be protected. More than one filename can be specified.
`/R:password`	Sets a password for reading, writing, or deleting files.
`/W:password`	Sets a password for writing or deleting files.
`/D:password`	Sets a password required to delete files.
`/P:password`	Sets a password for reading, writing, or deleting subdirectories.
`/G:password`	Sets a global default password used by DR DOS to try to open any files you access. This setting is useful if you set the same password for many files.
`/N`	Removes password protection from files.
`/NP`	Removes password protection from directories.
`/NG`	Removes a global default password.
`/S`	Applies the specified password to files and subdirectories matching the `filespec` in the current directory.
`/H`	Applies the specified password to hidden files and subdirectories matching the `filespec` in the current directory.

Notes

If you run the PASSWORD command with no parameters, it displays the password status for the files in the directory.

PATH 2.0 AND LATER—INTERNAL

The PATH command can be used to change or display the PATH environment variable. When DOS cannot find an executable program in the current directory, it searches through each directory listed in the PATH environment variable. Executable programs are files that end in .COM, .EXE, or .BAT, and DOS searches each directory on the search path, in that order, for each type. By specifying a PATH, you can save yourself from having to enter the full pathname for each command you want to execute. The Setup program for DOS 6 places a PATH command in your AUTOEXEC.BAT file that places the C:\DOS subdirectory (or whatever install directory you specified) on your search path.

Syntax

To specify an executable file search path, use the following format:

PATH *path1;path2;path3;...*

To display the current PATH, use the following format:

PATH

To clear the current PATH, use the following format:

PATH ;

PARAMETERS AND SWITCHES

path1;path2;path3;... — Each path listed must specify a valid subdirectory that exists on your system. The current subdirectory often changes, so it is a good idea to use full, absolute pathnames—including drive letters—for each subdirectory included in your PATH statement. Separate each subdirectory from the previous one by adding a semicolon (;).

NOTES

1. If you specify more than one set of paths, the following rules apply:
   - The path sets must be separated by semicolons.
   - The order in which you list the path sets is the order DOS looks for the programs or batch files. First, DOS searches the current directory; then DOS searches the first *path* specified, then the second *path* specified, and so on, until the command or batch file is found.

2. The maximum length of PATH is 127 characters. This is one of the most compelling reasons to use short subdirectory names whenever you can.

3. The PATH command establishes the value of an environment variable named PATH. You can view, set, or delete the PATH by using the SET command, as well as the PATH command. The PATH command is simply shorthand for SET PATH=.

4. When you type the name of a program or batch file, DOS searches the current directory. If the program or batch file is not found, DOS searches each path in sequence. If the program or batch file is not found in any of the paths, DOS displays the error message `Bad command or filename`.

5. You can shorten PATH by using the SUBST command to substitute drive letters for deeply nested paths. Another technique is to remove a path that is included only to start one program. Then, you can make a batch file that uses CD to change directory to that path and invokes the program, and place the batch file in a directory that is still included in PATH.

MESSAGES

```
Invalid drive in search path
```

Warning: You specified a nonexistent drive name in one of the paths. This message appears when DOS searches for a program or batch file, not when you give the PATH command.

Use PATH or SET to see the current path. If the drive temporarily is invalid because of a JOIN or SUBST command, you can ignore this message. If you specified the wrong disk drive, issue the PATH command again and provide the complete set of directory paths that you want to use.

SEE ALSO

SET

"Helping DOS Find Files with PATH" in Chapter 5

PAUSE   1.0 AND LATER—INTERNAL

The PAUSE command displays a `Press any key to continue...` message and waits for the user before continuing to execute the batch file. This command is useful if you want the user to be able to abort a batch file, using Ctrl+C or Ctrl+Break, before some action is taken. You also can use PAUSE to give the user time to read a screen of messages displayed with the ECHO command.

SYNTAX

PAUSE

NOTES

1. The PAUSE command simply displays the `Press any key to continue...` message when it is executed. The next key you press (except Ctrl+C or Ctrl+Break; see Note #2) releases the pause, and execution of the batch file continues.

2. Pressing Ctrl+C or Ctrl+Break in response to the `Press any key to continue...` message displays the `Terminate batch job (Y/N)?` message. Pressing Y aborts the batch file, returning you to the DOS prompt. Pressing N skips the line that was executing and continues with the next line in the batch file.

3. If you are running the batch file from within a Shell program, such as DOS Shell, the `Terminate batch job (Y/N)?` message is not displayed. When you press Ctrl+C or Ctrl+Break in these circumstances, the batch file is always aborted.

4. If you want to wait for a keypress but don't want PAUSE to display the `Press any key to continue...` message, you can redirect the output of the PAUSE command to the NUL device. DOS still waits for a keypress, but no message is displayed.

5. The CHOICE command included with DOS 6 gives you much more flexibility in choosing allowable keys and making decisions than PAUSE. If you are using DOS 6, consider using CHOICE instead of PAUSE in your batch files.

Examples

One very common use for PAUSE is to give the user time to do something. For example, if you want to make certain that a floppy disk had been placed in drive B, you might include the following lines in a batch file:

```
ECHO Insert the Working Backup disk in drive B:
ECHO.
ECHO Press Ctrl+Break to abort the backup, or
PAUSE
```

When these commands are executed, the following messages are displayed:

```
Insert the Working Backup disk in drive B:

Press Ctrl+Break to abort the backup, or
Press any key to continue...
```

Note that the PAUSE message is anticipated in the ECHO messages. If you redirect the output from PAUSE to the NUL device, you can control all the text displayed onscreen, as shown in the following:

```
ECHO  Insert the Working Backup disk in drive B:
ECHO.
ECHO  Press Ctrl+Break to abort the backup, or any
ECHO  other key to update the Working Backup disk.
PAUSE  >  NUL
```

When these commands are executed, the following messages are displayed:

```
Insert the Working Backup disk in drive B:

Press Ctrl+Break to abort the backup, or any
other key to update the Working Backup disk.
```

If you press Ctrl+C or Ctrl+Break at the pause, the following message is displayed (as long as you aren't running this batch file from within a Shell program):

```
Terminate batch job (Y/N)?
```

Type Y to abort the batch file; type N to continue with the next line.

Messages

```
Press any key to continue...
```

Prompt: PAUSE displays this message any time it is executed. DOS waits for a key to be pressed before continuing execution of the batch file. Entering Ctrl+C or Ctrl+Break when this message is displayed enables you to terminate the batch file rather than continuing.

```
Terminate Batch Job (Y/N)?
```

Prompt: When you press Ctrl+C or Ctrl+Break while a batch file is running, DOS displays this message. Typing Y aborts the batch file, returning you to the DOS prompt. Typing N skips the line that was executing and continues with the next line in the batch file. Note that if you run the batch file from within a Shell program, such as DOS Shell, this message isn't displayed, and the batch file is aborted.

SEE ALSO

CHOICE and ECHO

"Pausing for Input in a Batch File" in Chapter 16

PCM

PCM enables the DOS version of the online PCMCIA configuration program shipped with PC DOS 7. You use this program to configure input/output (I/O) cards such as fax/modem, LAN, and other I/O cards.

SYNTAX
PCM

NOTES

If you want to use the PCM command, the computer must be loaded with the version of PCMCIA support provided with PC DOS 7.

PCMATA.SYS

PCMATA.SYS enables the system to access ATA-configured PCMCIA cards as IDE hard drive devices using an IDE partition table. It acts as an I/O client to Card Services.

With the PCMCIA version shipped with PC DOS 7, PCMATA settings are recorded in the PCM.INI file. This file is editable.

PCMCS

PCMCS.EXE functions as an extension to the operating system. It must be loaded directly after Socket Services. It coordinates access to the PCMCIA cards and allocates system resources among client drivers. PCMCS runs as a driver loaded from CONFIG.SYS.

The parameters affecting the way PCMCS operates are added to the PCMCS= line in the PCM.INI file.

PCMDINST

PCMDINST enables the PCMCIA support provided with PC DOS 7. The PCMDINST command initiates a program that backs up the current system PC DOS and Windows files as .PCM files. Common command-line statements for prior versions of PCMCIA are commented out of the current configuration files.

SYNTAX
PCMDINST

PCMFDISK

PCMFDISK, like the DOS FDISK utility, sets the partition table for ATA rotating disk and solid-state mass-storage PCMCIA cards. PCMFDISK is a full-screen interface available to PCMCIA users who have installed the PCMCIA version shipped with PC DOS 7.

Syntax

PCMFDISK

Notes

The PCMFDISK command should be used with extreme caution.

PCMRMAN (Standalone Utility)

The PCMCIA Resource Management Utility (PCMRMAN), which is a standalone utility, manages and displays the resources used by PCM Plus, such as memory, I/O addresses, and interrupts. It is full-screen interface available to PCMCIA users who have installed the PCMCIA version shipped with PC DOS 7.

Syntax

PCMRMAN

Notes

The PCMRMAN program should be used with extreme caution. When used improperly, it can adversely affect the way the computer operates with PCMCIA cards.

PCMRMAN (Command-Line Utility)

The PCMRMAN command-line utility temporarily changes the current runtime values for the allocation of some system resources. The changes take effect when they are invoked and last only for the duration of the current session.

Syntax

PCMRMAN /mem=xx-yy /xmem=xx-yy /io=xxxx-yyyy /xio=xxxx-yyyy /irq=x-y /xirq=x-y /map /?

Parameters and Switches

/mem=xx-yy — Permits PCM Plus to use the memory range xx00:0000 to yyFF:0000 in hexadecimal. The argument range is C0 to EF in hexadecimal.

/xmem=xx-yy — Excludes PCM Plus from using the memory range xx00:0000 to yyFF:0000 in hexadecimal.

/io=xxxx-yyyy	Permits PCM Plus to use the I/O range specified. Argument ranges must be between 100 and 3FF in hexadecimal.
/xio= xxxx-yyyy	Excludes PCM Plus from using the I/O range specified. Argument ranges must be between 100 and 3FF in hexadecimal.
/irq=x-y	Permits PCM Plus to use IRQ in the range x to y. The argument range is between 0 and F in hexadecimal (0 to 15 in decimal).
/xirq=x-y	Excludes PCM Plus from using IRQ in the range x to y. The argument range is between 0 and F in hexadecimal (0 to 15 in decimal).
/map	Displays a map of card services and system resources.
/?	Displays the abbreviated online help.

NOTES

The PCMRMAN command should be used with caution. When used improperly, it can adversely affect the way the computer operates with PCMCIA cards.

PCMSCD

The Phoenix Super Client Driver, PCMSCD, is a Card Services client that increases the efficiency of resource acquisition by requesting system resources from Card Services, such as memory, I/O, and IRQ. When requested in this way, they appear to the system as resident for use by software.

SYNTAX
PCMSCD

NOTES

PCMSCD must reside in the same directory as the active PCM.INI. PCMSCD reads its boot options as well as configuration information used to enable PCMCIA cards from PCM.INI.

PCMSETUP

PCMSETUP enables the online configuration part of Phoenix Card Manager Plus Version 3.01. This is the PCMCIA support supplied with PC DOS 7.

SYNTAX
PCMSETUP

POWER 6.0 AND LATER—EXTERNAL

For laptop computers that conform to the Advanced Power Management (APM) specification, the POWER command enables you to control the trade-off between extended battery life and maximum performance from your computer. You also can use POWER to switch back and forth between the power-management system built into your laptop and the APM-style idle detection methods. Before you can run POWER from the command line, you must use a DEVICE= command to load the POWER.EXE device driver into memory from your CONFIG.SYS file.

SYNTAX

POWER *setting*

PARAMETERS AND SWITCHES

setting   This value determines how aggressive you want the power-management features to be. *setting* can be one of the values listed in the following table. You can specify only one setting at a time. If no value is included for *setting*, POWER displays a short report on the current power settings in your computer. (See item #2 in the following "Notes" section.)

setting Value	Description
ADV:MAX	Enables the most aggressive power setting. Power savings can be as much as 25%, but performance may suffer.
ADV:REG	Enables the default setting.
ADV:MIN	Enables the most conservative power setting. You can use this setting when you are running programs that slow down too much when the ADV:REG setting is used.
ADV	Performs the same as specifying ADV:REG.
STD	Uses the computer's built-in power-management features for computers that conform to the APM specification. For computers that don't support the APM specification, this setting is the same as OFF.
OFF	Disables the power-management features. You might want to use this setting (or STD) when you are running communications software.

NOTES

1. You must install the POWER.EXE device driver before you can run POWER from the command line. If you try to run POWER without installing the device driver, an error message appears. (See the following "Messages" section.)

2. POWER.EXE is actually two files: a device driver and an executable program. The device driver portion does all the real work. You have to load it into memory by adding a

`DEVICE=` command in your `CONFIG.SYS` file for the DOS power-management features to be enabled. After this device driver has been loaded into memory, the executable portion of `POWER.EXE` communicates with the device driver to adjust settings and display status information.

3. If you enter the `POWER` command without specifying a new setting, you see a status report that summarizes the active settings and current power use in your system. On non–APM-compliant systems, `POWER` displays the following report:

```
Power Management Status
-----------------------
Setting = ADV:REG
CPU: idle 75% of the time
```

If your system supports the APM specification, a more detailed report, like the following, is displayed:

```
Power Management Status
-----------------------
Setting = ADV:REG
CPU: idle 75% of time
AC Line Status : OFFLINE
Battery status : High
Battery life (%) : 90
```

The computer's ROM BIOS provides the additional information in this report. This information is not displayed on non–APM-compliant computers.

4. When you are running communications software, CPU-intensive applications, or other applications that don't access your hard disk very often, you might want to turn off power-management features. With an `ADV:MAX` setting, `POWER` may think your computer was idle when it was actually busy handling serial communications or recalculating a large spreadsheet. To minimize the possibility of false idle-time detection but still keep power-management features active, use a setting of `ADV:MIN`. To disable APM features and regain maximum performance from your computer, use a setting of `OFF` or `STD`.

5. `POWER.EXE` detects idle time with a variety of methods. It monitors hard disk activity, video functions, and MS-DOS service requests to determine whether your system is busy. In addition, `POWER.EXE` monitors the keyboard polling and application-idle interrupts to sense idle time in active programs. When idle time is detected, a `CPU HALT` instruction is executed, causing the CPU to sleep until the next hardware interrupt arrives. (The timer interrupt occurs 18.2 times per second, so the CPU sleeps for only 55 milliseconds or less.)

If a busy program routinely polls the keyboard, such as communication programs often do, `POWER.EXE` may think your computer is idle when it isn't. False idle detection can interfere with a program's operation, unnecessarily slowing it down. The `ADV:MAX`, `REG`, and `MIN` settings control the level of keyboard polling detection that `POWER.EXE` uses. If you are having performance problems with an application, try turning down keyboard polling detection by using an `ADV:REG` setting or disabling it by using `ADV:MIN`.

6. Even if your system doesn't support the APM specification, you still may get some benefit from `POWER.EXE`. Microsoft's testing indicates that, on the average, a 5% reduction

in power consumption can be realized by using POWER.EXE on non–APM-compliant computers. Of course, the power-management features built into your laptop might surpass this savings, in which case you are better off not using POWER.EXE at all.

EXAMPLES

Assuming the POWER.EXE device driver has been loaded from your CONFIG.SYS file, entering the following command requests maximum power savings:

POWER   ADV:MAX

If you want to fax some work back to the office, you might want to turn down your power-management features to avoid interfering with your communications software. You could enter the following line:

POWER   ADV:MIN

Back in your hotel room, working on deadline, you want to disable the power-management system entirely so that you can get maximum performance out of your laptop computer. After all, you don't need to extend battery life when you are plugged into an AC outlet. In this case, just enter the following command:

POWER   OFF

MESSAGES

Power Manager (POWER.EXE) not installed

Information: You have attempted to run the POWER program without first installing the POWER.EXE device driver. POWER can adjust the settings of the device driver in memory only, so you must load POWER.EXE by adding a DEVICE= command in your CONFIG.SYS file before you can use any of its features.

SEE ALSO

POWER.EXE

POWER.EXE (DEVICE DRIVER)

6.0 AND LATER— EXTERNAL

For laptop computers that conform to the Advanced Power Management (APM) specification, POWER.EXE enables you to control the trade-off between extended battery life and maximum performance from your computer. You must load POWER.EXE by adding a DEVICE= statement in your CONFIG.SYS file before you can use it from the command line.

SYNTAX

DEVICE=drive:\path**POWER.EXE**   setting   /LOW

Parameters and Switches

drive:\path The full path to the POWER.EXE file on your system. Setup places the POWER.EXE file in the C:\DOS subdirectory by default. If the full path to POWER.EXE isn't specified, DOS looks for the file in the root directory of the startup drive.

setting This value determines how aggressive you want the power-management features to be. *setting* can be one of the values listed in the table below. You cannot specify more than one setting at a time. If no value is included, the ADV:REG setting is assumed.

Value	Description
ADV:MAX	Enables the most aggressive power setting. Power savings can be as much as 25%, but performance may suffer.
ADV:REG	Enables the default setting.
ADV:MIN	Enables the most conservative power setting. You can use this setting when you are running programs that slow down too much when the ADV:REG setting is used.
ADV	Performs the same as specifying ADV:REG.
STD	Uses your computer's built-in power-management features for computers that conform to the APM specification. For computers that don't support the APM specification, this setting is the same as OFF.
OFF	Disables the power-management features. You might want to use this setting (or STD) when you are running communications software.

/LOW Instructs POWER.EXE to load itself into conventional memory. Normally, POWER.EXE loads into upper memory if it is available.

Notes

1. You must install the POWER.EXE device driver before you can run POWER from the command line. If you try to run POWER without installing the device driver, an error message appears. (See the following "Messages" section.)

2. POWER.EXE is actually two files: a device driver and an executable program. The device driver portion does all the real work. You have to load it into memory by adding a DEVICE= command in your CONFIG.SYS file for the DOS power-management features to be enabled. After this device driver has been loaded into memory, the executable portion of POWER.EXE communicates with the device driver to adjust settings and display status information.

3. POWER.EXE automatically loads into upper memory if it is available. You do not need to use the DEVICEHIGH= command with POWER.EXE.

4. When you are running communications software, CPU-intensive applications, or other applications that don't access your hard disk very often, you might want to turn off the power-management features. With an ADV:MAX setting, POWER might think your computer was idle when it was actually busy handling serial communications or recalculating a large spreadsheet. To minimize the chance of false idle-time detection but keep power-management features active, use a setting of ADV:MIN. To disable APM features and regain maximum performance from your computer, use a setting of OFF or STD.

5. POWER.EXE detects idle time with a variety of methods. It monitors hard disk activity, video functions, and MS-DOS service requests to determine whether your system is busy. In addition, POWER.EXE monitors the keyboard polling and application-idle interrupts to sense idle time in active programs. When idle time is detected, a CPU HALT instruction is executed, causing the CPU to sleep until the next hardware interrupt arrives. (The timer interrupt occurs 18.2 times per second, so the CPU sleeps for only 55 milliseconds or less.)

   If a busy program routinely polls the keyboard, as communications programs often do, POWER.EXE may think your computer is idle when it isn't. False idle detection can interfere with a program's operation, unnecessarily slowing it down. The ADV:MAX, REG, and MIN settings control the level of keyboard polling detection that POWER.EXE uses. If you are having performance problems with an application, try turning down keyboard polling detection by using an ADV:REG setting or disabling it by using ADV:MIN.

6. Even if your system doesn't support the APM specification, you still may get some benefit from POWER.EXE. Microsoft's testing indicates that, on the average, a 5% reduction in power consumption can be realized by using POWER.EXE on non–APM-compliant computers. Of course, the power-management features built into your laptop might surpass this savings, in which case you are better off not using POWER.EXE at all.

7. POWER.EXE is fully compatible with Windows. If you are running Windows 3.1 on a system with an APM-compliant ROM BIOS, you should select MS-DOS System with APM in Windows's Setup as the type of computer you are using. When you do so, Windows can cooperate and control the power-management features supplied by POWER.EXE. On non–APM-compliant computer systems, you can use POWER.EXE without selecting a special computer type.

EXAMPLES

To load the POWER.EXE device driver and enable the ADV:REG (default) level of power management, you could add the following line to your CONFIG.SYS file:

DEVICE=C:\DOS\POWER.EXE

If you want to enable the maximum level of power management, specify the ADV:MAX setting instead of using the default, as shown in the following line:

DEVICE=C:\DOS\POWER.EXE   ADV:MAX

As long as enough upper memory is available, POWER.EXE loads high without using the DEVICEHIGH= command. If you want to force it to load into conventional memory instead, add the /LOW parameter, as shown here:

```
DEVICE=C:\DOS\POWER.EXE    /LOW
```

MESSAGES

```
Power Manager (POWER.EXE) not installed
```

Information: You have attempted to run the POWER program without first installing the POWER.EXE device driver. POWER can adjust the settings of the device driver in memory only, so you must load POWER.EXE from your CONFIG.SYS file before you can use any of its features.

SEE ALSO

POWER

PRINT   2.0 AND LATER—EXTERNAL

The PRINT command is a memory-resident utility that enables you to print files in the background on your computer. Unfortunately, PRINT is limited to printing text files; you can't use it as a general-purpose print spooler.

SYNTAX

To load PRINT into memory, use the following format:

PRINT /D:*device*   /B:*bufsiz*   /M:*maxticks*   /Q:*maxfiles*   /S:*timeslice*
/U:*busyticks* /T *textfile* /P /C

To add or delete files in the queue, use the following format:

PRINT /T /P /C *textfile1* /P /C *textfile2* /P /C ...

PARAMETERS AND SWITCHES

When you first use the PRINT command after turning on or rebooting your computer, you can specify any of the following switches:

/B:*bufsiz*	The size (in bytes) of the memory buffer to be used while the files are printing. *bufsiz* can be any number from 512 to 16,384. The default is 512 bytes. You don't have to increase this value unless you have a very fast printer.
/D:*device*	The device to be used for printing. Legal values are PRN, LPT1, LPT2, LPT3, COM1, COM2, COM3, or COM4. The default is PRN. This parameter must precede any *textfile* included on the command line.
/M:*maxticks*	The maximum amount of time (in clock ticks) that PRINT uses to send characters to the printer every time PRINT gets a turn. *maxtick* can be any number from 1 to 255. The default is 2.

/Q:*maxfiles*	The number of files that can be held in the queue for printing. *maxfiles* can be any number from 4 to 32. The default is 10.
/S:*timeslice*	The number of clock ticks allocated for PRINT. *timeslice* can be a number from 1 to 255. The default is 8. Increasing *timeslice* speeds printing and slows other tasks.
/U:*busyticks*	The maximum amount of time (in clock ticks) PRINT should wait for a busy or unavailable printer before releasing its timeslice. PRINT tries again the next time it gets control. *busytick* can be any number from 1 to 255. The default is 1.

You can specify any of these switches whenever you use PRINT:

/C	Cancels the background printing of files. (See item #3 in the following "Notes" section.)
/P	Queues files for printing. (See item #3 in the following "Notes" section.)
/T	Terminates the background printing of all files, including any file that currently is printing (clears the queue).

Rules

1. If you do not provide a filename, DOS displays the background printing status.
2. You can specify the switches /B, /D, /M, /Q, /S, and /U only when you first use PRINT. If you use the /D switch, you must type this switch first in the line. You can list the remaining five switches in any order before you specify a filename.
3. The /D switch specifies the print device that you want to use (LPT1, LPT2, LPT3, COM1, COM2, COM3, or COM4). If you omit /D the first time you use PRINT, DOS displays the following prompt:
   `Name of list device [PRN]:`
   You can respond in either of two ways:
   - Press Enter to send the files to PRN (normally LPT1:). If LPT1: is redirected (refer to the MODE command entry earlier in this command reference), the files are rerouted.
   - Enter a valid DOS device name. Printing is directed to this device. If you enter a device that is not connected to your system, PRINT accepts files in the queue. The files are not processed, however, and you lose processing speed.

   After you choose the print device that you want PRINT to use, you cannot change it without restarting DOS.
4. If you name a file with no switch, DOS assumes that you want to use the /P (print) switch.
5. Files print in the order in which you list their names. If you use wildcards, files are printed in the order in which they are listed in the directory.

6. The command PRINT /C has no effect if you do not specify a filename.

7. The first time you invoke PRINT, DOS increases in size by approximately 5,500 bytes. When you increase or decrease certain default settings, you proportionally change the size of DOS. To regain this memory space, however, you must restart DOS.

8. If you use PRINT to print files to a serial printer, you might need to configure the serial port by using the MODE COM# command.

9. PRINT expands tab characters in the files it prints the same way the TYPE command does. Also, PRINT stops printing a file when it encounters an end-of-file marker (Ctrl+Z). For these two reasons, you should print only straight ASCII files with PRINT. Any other type of file is likely to be garbled by tab expansion and truncated when it encounters a Ctrl+Z character and terminates prematurely.

Notes

1. The /B switch acts like a disk buffer. PRINT reads into memory a portion of the document to be printed. As you increase the value of *bufsiz*, you decrease the number of times PRINT must read the file from the disk, thereby increasing printing speed. Always use a multiple of 512 (1,024, 2,048, and so on) as the value of *bufsiz*. The default size (512 bytes) is adequate for most printers.

2. When the default values are assumed, PRINT gets 22 percent of the computer's time.

3. The positions of the /P, /C, and /T switches in the command line are important. Each switch affects the file immediately preceding it in the command line, and all subsequent files, until DOS encounters another switch. The following command, for example, uses the /P switch to place the files LETTER.TXT and PROGRAM.DOC in the queue to be printed. The /C switch cancels the background printing of MYFILE.TXT and TEST.DOC:

    PRINT LETTER.TXT /P PROGRAM.DOC MYFILE.TXT /C TEST.DOC

    In this example, the /P switch affects the preceding file (LETTER.TXT) and the following file (PROGRAM.DOC). Similarly, the /C switch affects the preceding file (MYFILE.TXT) and the following file (TEXT.DOC).

4. If you use the /T switch, background printing is canceled for all files in the queue, including the file that is currently printing, and any files listed in the command line.

5. If a disk error occurs during background printing, DOS cancels the current print job and places a disk-error message on the printout. The printer then performs a form feed, the bell rings, and DOS prints all remaining files in the queue.

Messages

    filename is currently being printed
    filename is in queue

Information: This message tells you which file is printing and names the files that are in line to be printed. This message appears when you use PRINT with no parameters or when you queue additional files.

```
PRINT queue is empty
```

Information: No files are in line to be printed by PRINT.

```
PRINT queue is full
```

Warning: You attempted to place too many files in the PRINT queue. The request to add more files fails for each file past the limit. You must wait until PRINT processes a file before you can add another file to the queue.

```
Resident part of PRINT installed
```

Information: The first time you use PRINT, this message indicates that PRINT installed itself in DOS and increased the size of DOS by about 5,500 bytes.

SEE ALSO

MODE COM#

"The PRINT Command" in Chapter 13

PRINTER.SYS (DEVICE DRIVER)   3.3 TO 5.0— EXTERNAL

The PRINTER.SYS device driver provides international code page support for certain IBM printers or close compatibles. When combined with the other international utilities DOS provides, PRINTER.SYS enables you to use various international character sets with your printer. You must load PRINTER.SYS by using a DEVICE= or DEVICEHIGH= statement in your CONFIG.SYS file. Microsoft no longer distributes PRINTER.SYS with MS-DOS, but it is available on the MS-DOS 6 Supplemental Disk.

SYNTAX

DEVICE=*drive:\path***PRINTER.SYS**   **LPT***x***=(***type***,***hard_cp***,***num_cp***)**

DEVICEHIGH=*drive:\path***PRINTER.SYS**   **LPT***x***=(***type***,***hard_cp***,***num_cp***)**

PARAMETERS AND SWITCHES

drive:\path   The full path to the PRINTER.SYS file on your system. If the full path to PRINTER.SYS isn't specified, DOS looks for the file in the root directory of the startup drive. The PRINTER.SYS file is included on the MS-DOS 6 Supplemental Disk.

LPT*x*=   The printer port (LPT1=, LPT2=, or LPT3=) your printer is attached to. You can enter a colon between the port name and equal sign (for example, LPT1:=). This parameter is required.

type	The type code for the printer being used. You must use a type code from the following table, and you must enclose the parameter in parentheses.

type Code	Printer
4201	IBM Proprinters II and III, Model 4201 IBM Proprinters II XL and III XL, Model 4202
4208	IBM Proprinter X24E, Model 4207 IBM Proprinter XL24E, Model 4208
5202	IBM Quietwriter III, Model 5202

hard_cp	The hardware code page built into the printer. See Chapter 14, "Understanding the International Features of DOS," for a list of the code pages that MS-DOS supports.
num_cp	The number of software code pages you want to use with the printer. Valid entries for *num_cp* are 1 and 2.

NOTES

1. PRINTER.SYS no longer is distributed with MS-DOS, but it is available on the MS-DOS 6 Supplemental Disk. Three printer code page information files are included as well: 4201.CPI, 4208.CPI, and 5202.CPI. The MODE command requires these files when it is preparing to download code page information to your printer.

2. When PRINTER.SYS is loaded, it uses about 11KB of memory.

3. Although you can have up to three printers attached to your computer, PRINTER.SYS can support international code pages on only one of them at a time. To change to a different printer or printer port, you have to edit the DEVICE= line for PRINTER.SYS and reboot your computer.

4. You should always specify a value for *hard_cp*. IBM printers often use a hardware code page of 850, but you should check your printer manual to be sure.

5. Even if you don't own one of the printers listed in the table, your printer may be compatible with one of them. To find out whether you can use PRINTER.SYS, check your printer's documentation or call the manufacturer.

6. To print with a software code page, you must perform a number of additional steps. You use the MODE command to prepare and download code page information to your printer. After you do so, you can use MODE to select the downloaded code page, or you can load NLSFUNC and use the CHCP command to change the active code page for all your devices at once. Additionally, you might want to add the COUNTRY= command to your CONFIG.SYS file to make case conversion and sort order information available.

7. DISPLAY.SYS performs a similar function for EGA, VGA, Super VGA, and LCD screens.

EXAMPLES

You can add the following line to your CONFIG.SYS file to set up an IBM Proprinter X24E, attached to LPT1, for use with two additional code pages. The hardware code page for the X24E is 850, Multilingual (Latin I):

```
DEVICE=C:\DOS\PRINTER.SYS  LPT1=(4208,850,2)
```

If an IBM Quietwriter is attached to LPT2, and you want to load PRINTER.SYS into upper memory, you would use the following command:

```
DEVICEHIGH=C:\DOS\PRINTER.SYS  LPT2=(5202,850,2)
```

SEE ALSO

CHCP, COUNTRY=, DISPLAY.SYS, MODE *device* CP, and NLSFUNC

Chapter 14, "Understanding the International Features of DOS"

PROMPT   2.0 AND LATER—INTERNAL

You can customize the prompt that MS-DOS displays by using the PROMPT command. PROMPT, like PATH, saves its settings in the DOS environment. People often use ANSI control codes in their prompt strings, in which case ANSI.SYS has to be loaded into memory from the CONFIG.SYS file.

SYNTAX

PROMPT *promptstring*

PARAMETERS AND SWITCHES

promptstring The text of the DOS command-line prompt. It can include any of the meta-strings defined for use in the PROMPT command (see the following table).

NOTES

1. If you do not enter the *promptstring*, the standard system prompt, which is equivalent to PROMPT NG (C>), reappears.

2. A very popular prompt string, and the one that the Setup program for MS-DOS 6 inserts into your AUTOEXEC.BAT file, is PROMPT PG (C:\DOS>). Beginning with DOS 6.0, COMMAND.COM inserts the value PG in PROMPT if it finds the PROMPT environment variable undefined when the system starts up.

3. The new system prompt stays in effect until you restart DOS or reissue the PROMPT command.

4. The PROMPT command establishes the value of an environment variable named PROMPT. You can view, set, or delete the PROMPT environment variable by using the SET command, as well as the PROMPT command. The PROMPT command is simply shorthand for SET PROMPT=.

5. Any text you type for *promptstring* becomes the new system prompt. You can include special characters by using the meta-strings.

A *meta-string* is a group of characters transformed into another character or group of characters. All meta-strings begin with the dollar-sign symbol ($) and have two characters, including the $. The case of the characters isn't significant in a prompt meta-string, but it is significant in ANSI commands. The following table contains the meta-string characters and their meanings:

Meta-String	Example	Description
$$	$	Dollar sign
$B			Vertical bar (pipe) character
$D	Tue 09-11-2001	The current date
$G	>	Greater-than symbol
$L	<	Less-than symbol
$N	C	The current drive letter
$P	C:\DOS	The current drive and path, including the current directory
$Q	=	Equal sign
$T	12:19:12.45	The current time (Note that the time is not updated as the time changes, only when a new prompt line is displayed.)
$V	MS-DOS Version 6.0	The DOS version number

The following meta-strings do not display characters onscreen, but they are useful when you want to make a fancier DOS prompt.

Meta-String	Description
$_ (underscore)	Carriage return and line feed—moves the cursor to the first position of the following line
$E	The Escape character (ASCII 27)—useful for sending ANSI control codes

Meta-String	Description
$H	The Backspace character (ASCII 8)—erases the preceding character
$ (any other)	Nothing or null character—DOS ignores

Note To include a dollar sign in a prompt string, you have to enter it twice.

6. When you open a DOS window within Windows, the prompt is changed to the value of the WINPMT environment variable if it has been defined. If you want to have a different prompt under Windows, use the SET command to define an environment variable named WINPMT and set it equal to the prompt you want to use. For example, the line
SET WINPMT=**Windows** PG

gives you the following prompt in a DOS window within Windows:
Windows C:\DOS>

This is a handy prompt to remind you that Windows is running.

EXAMPLES

To use the current drive and path as the prompt, followed by >, use this command:
PROMPT PG

Assuming that your CONFIG.SYS file loads ANSI.SYS and that you have white text (foreground) on a blue background, the following command changes the prompt to a blinking red HI, followed by >:
PROMPT &E[5; 3/mHI$E[0; 37; 44m$G

SEE ALSO

ANSI.SYS and SET

"Changing the Command Prompt with PROMPT" in Chapter 11.

QBASIC 5.0 AND LATER—EXTERNAL

QBasic is the Microsoft QuickBasic programming environment, a full-screen, interactive programming tool for writing programs in BASIC. Traditionally, all operating system software came with a simple set of programming tools. Few microcomputer users have an interest in these programs anymore, but it is nice that Microsoft keeps providing them free for those who want them. QBasic also is the "behind the scenes" program that EDIT and HELP require; so whether or not you actually write any BASIC programs, it's likely that you will be running QBasic on your computer.

SYNTAX

QBASIC   /RUN *pathname*   /EDITOR *pathname*   /B   /G   /H   /NOHI   /MBF

PARAMETERS AND SWITCHES

/RUN *pathname*   Specifies the BASIC file that you want QBASIC to load into memory and run. If no drive is specified, the current drive is assumed. If no subdirectory path is specified, the current directory is assumed. Wildcards are not allowed. You cannot specify the /EDITOR parameter with the /RUN parameter.

/EDITOR pathname	Specifies the ASCII file that you want QBASIC to load into the full-screen text editor (EDIT). If no drive is specified, the current drive is assumed. If no subdirectory path is specified, the current directory is assumed. Wildcards are not allowed. If you don't specify a *pathname*, the editor starts without a file. You cannot specify the /RUN parameter with the /EDITOR parameter.
/B	Specifies that QBASIC should use colors more appropriate for a black-and-white (monochrome) or LCD screen.
/G	Specifies that QBASIC should use the fastest screen-updating method for a CGA monitor. Don't specify the /G switch if you see "snow" on your monitor.
/H	Specifies that QBASIC should display 43 lines on an EGA monitor or 50 lines on a VGA monitor.
/NOHI	Specifies that QBASIC should limit itself to 8 colors rather than 16.
/MBF	Specifies that QBASIC should use the Microsoft Binary Format for floating-point numbers. Specifically, the /MBF switch converts CVS, CVD, MKS$, and MKD$ so that they act like CVSMBF, CVDMBF, MKSMBF$, and MKDMBF$, respectively.

NOTES

1. QBasic is a comprehensive development environment for interpreted BASIC and a subset of Microsoft QuickBasic. BASIC, BASICA, and GWBASIC are no longer provided with MS-DOS.
2. QBASIC.EXE is required to run EDIT and HELP.
3. The use and operation of QBasic is beyond the scope of this book. If you want to learn to write BASIC programs with QBasic, you can either try to find your way with the QBasic help system, or you can get a book on programming with QBasic.

QCONFIG

QCONFIG displays detailed technical information about the computer.

SYNTAX

QCONFIG /a /c /d /e /i /o /o *filename* /p /q /? key="*text*"

PARAMETERS AND SWITCHES

/a	Lists all the Micro Channel adapters supported by the QConfig program.
/c	Provides specific details on asynchronous ports.

/d	Generates a detailed listing of hardware. This list also provides volume label and file system reporting.
/i	Displays CONFIG.SYS and AUTOEXEC.BAT files.
/o	Redirects output to the file QCONFIG.OUT.
/o filename	Redirects output.
/p	Pauses the output between screens.
/q	Indicates that the redirected message is not to be displayed.
key="text"	Defines key with text to appear in output. This option must be the last option.
/?	Provides online help for the QCONFIG command.

RAMBOOST

The RAMBOOST command monitors for any changes that take place in the system. It optimizes memory and then maintains DOS memory on an ongoing basis. This command is a terminate-and-stay-resident (TSR) utility that resides in memory.

SYNTAX

RAMBOOST active disable learn mode pif sync track *filename* id /?

PARAMETERS AND SWITCHES

active	Forces RAMBoost to remain fully active and reoptimizes memory the next time the computer is restarted or any time it detects a change to a tracked file. Active mode is the default.
disable	Disables RAMBoost by preventing it from loading.
learn	Forces RAMBoost to enter learn mode the next time you restart the computer, even if no tracked file has changed.
mode	Returns a value, indicating the current status of RAMBoost as not resident (0), in active mode (1), or in learn mode (2).
pif	Displays a table listing of network drivers, TSRs, DOS tables, and any other files loaded into memory and indicates what block of memory they are loaded into.
sync	Updates the signatures for all tracked files in the RAMBOOST.INI file. It should be used only after a change is made to a tracked file that does not affect memory such as a SET command, PATH adjustment, and so on.

RAMDRIVE.SYS (DEVICE DRIVER)   3.2 AND LATER—EXTERNAL   867

track *filename* /d	Displays the names and signatures of the files that RAMBoost currently tracks. The *filename* variable specifies a device driver or TSR to add (or delete if /d is specified) to the list of tracked files. The files in the list are tracked for possible changes that would affect memory usage.
/?	Displays the online abbreviated help.

RAMBOOST.EXE

RAMBOOST.EXE increases the available conventional memory of the computer and reduces the complexity of using the DOS memory manager EMM386.EXE.

SYNTAX

DEVICE=*drive:\path***ramboost.exe** load /p=*profile*

PARAMETERS AND SWITCHES

drive:\path	Specifies the location of the device driver file.
load	Installs RAMBoost resident in memory.
/p=*profile*	Indicates the name of the alternative configuration profile.

NOTES

The RAMBOOST.INI file is an ASCII text file that can be edited.

RAMDRIVE.SYS (DEVICE DRIVER)   3.2 AND LATER— EXTERNAL

A RAM disk is a simulated drive that uses RAM, rather than a magnetic disk, to store files. Because it has no moving parts, a RAM disk is much faster than a hard drive or floppy disk. Unfortunately, whenever you shut down or restart your computer, the contents of a RAM disk are lost. Using RAMDRIVE.SYS, you can create a RAM disk in extended, expanded, or conventional memory. You must load RAMDRIVE.SYS by adding a DEVICE= or DEVICEHIGH= statement in your CONFIG.SYS file.

SYNTAX

DEVICE=*drive:\path***RAMDRIVE.SYS** *disksize   sectorsize   dir_entries*   /E /A

To load the RAMDRIVE.SYS device driver into upper memory, use the DEVICEHIGH= command to specify the placement in memory of the driver, not the RAM disk:

DEVICEHIGH=*drive:\path***RAMDRIVE.SYS** *disksize   sectorsize   dir_entries*   /E /A

Parameters and Switches

drive:\path Specifies the full path to the RAMDRIVE.SYS file on your system. Setup places the RAMDRIVE.SYS file in the C:\DOS subdirectory by default. If the full path to RAMDRIVE.SYS isn't specified, DOS looks for the file in the root directory of the startup drive.

disksize Indicates the size, in kilobytes, of the RAM disk you want to create. *disksize* can be from 4KB to 32,767KB. (For DOS 5, the limits were 16KB to 4,096KB.) If no *disksize* is specified, a 64KB RAM disk is created.

sectorsize Indicates the sector size the RAM disk should use. *sectorsize* can be 128, 256, or 512. If this parameter is omitted, a *sectorsize* of 512 is assumed. (You should have a very good reason before setting *sectorsize* to a different value. All DOS disks use a sector size of 512, and many disk utilities fail if a different sector size is used.) To specify *sectorsize*, you also must specify *disksize*.

dir_entries Specifies the maximum number of root directory entries that the RAM disk can hold (in other words, the size of the root directory). *dir_entries* can be in the range 2 to 1024 and are rounded up to the nearest multiple that fits evenly in *sectorsize*. Each directory entry takes 32 bytes of disk space. If this parameter is omitted, a root directory with room for 64 entries is created (four 512-byte sectors in size). To specify *dir_entries*, you also must specify *disksize* and *sectorsize*.

dir_entries limits only the size of the root directory, not any subdirectories you create on the RAM disk. Subdirectories grow as needed to accommodate an unlimited number of directory entries.

/E Creates the RAM disk in extended memory. An XMS-compatible memory manager, such as HIMEM.SYS, must be available.

/A Creates the RAM disk in expanded memory. A LIM EMS-compatible memory manager, such as EMM386.EXE, must be available.

Notes

1. DEVICEHIGH= loads the RAMDRIVE.SYS device driver into upper memory, but the RAM disk still is created in the memory area you have specified with the command's parameters. RAMDRIVE.SYS uses about 1KB of memory for the device driver.

2. If not enough room is available in memory for the RAM disk you have specified, RAMDRIVE.SYS decreases the size of the root directory to 16 entries and tries again. If the RAM disk still doesn't fit, the driver aborts with an error message. (See the third item in the following "Messages" section.)

3. A RAM disk runs more efficiently from extended memory than from the simulated expanded memory provided by EMM386.EXE. Unless you have a hardware EMS board in your computer, always create RAM disks in extended memory.

4. Normally, you don't want to create RAM disks in conventional memory. Although they run efficiently there, they also use up memory that is required to run your application programs. This memory trade-off might be worthwhile only when you are working on a floppy-disk–only system. The increased speed from a RAM disk could be worth the loss of memory for certain operations.

5. Although RAM disks are very fast, SMARTDrive can provide similar speed increases for all your programs—not just those that use the RAM disk. For many people, committing memory into a disk cache such as SMARTDRV.EXE makes more sense than creating a RAM drive. Of course, if you have a lot of RAM that you don't use, you can always do both.

> **Caution**
> If you use a RAM disk to store data files, remember to copy them to your hard drive before shutting off your system or rebooting. Whenever you restart your computer, everything on a RAM disk is lost.

6. One popular use of a RAM disk is to store temporary files generated by programs. When you set the TEMP and TMP environment variables to point to a RAM disk, many programs create their temporary files on the RAM disk. (See Appendix B, "DOS Environment Variables," for a description of the DOS programs that use the TEMP environment variable.) Not only can this technique speed up your applications, but it also can eliminate the need to periodically delete temporary files that, for one reason or another, have escaped automatic deletion by their parent programs.

7. If you run Windows and set the TEMP variable to point to a RAM disk, Microsoft advises that the RAM disk be at least 2MB (2,048KB) in size to avoid possible printing problems.

8. You can load RAMDRIVE.SYS as many times as memory allows from CONFIG.SYS. Each time you load it, another RAM disk is created. When created, a RAM disk is assigned the next available drive letter by DOS.

9. If RAMDRIVE.SYS is loaded after DBLSPACE.SYS, it receives a drive letter that follows the letters allocated by DoubleSpace. To avoid having your RAM disk drive letter change as you create and destroy DoubleSpace drives, always place the DEVICE= line for RAMDRIVE.SYS before the line for DBLSPACE.SYS in your CONFIG.SYS file.

10. You can use DoubleSpace to compress a RAM disk, but the compressed volume file (CVF) that DoubleSpace creates is lost each time you reboot your computer. To keep from having to create a new CVF file each time you start up, you could clear its attributes with the ATTRIB command and copy it from the RAM disk to your hard disk. Your AUTOEXEC.BAT file could then copy the CVF file back to the RAM disk; restore the system, hidden, and read-only attributes; and mount it for you each time you reboot.

EXAMPLES

For the following examples, assume that the computer you are using has 8MB of RAM, `HIMEM.SYS` loaded, `EMM386.EXE` loaded, and UMB support enabled. To create a 64KB RAM disk in conventional memory, you can load `RAMDRIVE.SYS` with no parameters, as shown here:

`DEVICEHIGH=C:\DOS\RAMDRIVE.SYS`

The `DEVICEHIGH=` command locates the `RAMDRIVE.SYS` driver in upper memory, but the RAM disk itself still is created in conventional memory. To increase the size of the RAM disk to 1MB (1,024KB) and place it in extended memory, you add the *disksize* and /E parameters, as the following line shows:

`DEVICEHIGH=C:\DOS\RAMDRIVE.SYS   1024   /E`

Because other values are not specified, the sector size is 512, and the root directory has room for 64 directory entries. If you want to create a RAM disk that is about the same size as a 1.44MB 3 1/2-inch floppy disk, you can use the following line in your `CONFIG.SYS` file:

`DEVICEHIGH=C:\DOS\RAMDRIVE.SYS   1450   512   224   /E`

To increase the number of root directory entries to 224, you have to specify a sector size of 512, despite the fact that 512 is the default value for sector size.

MESSAGES

Messages from the `RAMDRIVE.SYS` device driver all begin with the word `RAMDrive:`. You are most likely to encounter the messages listed here.

`RAMDrive: Expanded memory manager not present`

Error: You have specified the /A switch to create a RAM drive in expanded memory; however, expanded memory is not available, and the RAM disk was not created. Make sure that you have loaded `EMM386.EXE` (or another EMS provider), with EMS enabled, before the `DEVICE=` line in the `CONFIG.SYS` file that loads `RAMDRIVE.SYS`.

`RAMDrive: Extended memory manager not present`

Error: You have specified the /E switch to create a RAM drive in extended memory; however, extended memory is not available, and the RAM disk was not created. Make sure that you have loaded `HIMEM.SYS` (or another XMS provider) before the `DEVICE=` line in the `CONFIG.SYS` file that loads `RAMDRIVE.SYS`.

`RAMDrive: Insufficient memory`

Error: Not enough memory was available to create the RAM drive you specified. Typically, this problem is caused by forgetting to specify the /E or /A switch, in which case `RAMDRIVE.SYS` attempts to create the RAM disk in conventional memory. You also may receive this message if you specify the *disksize* in bytes rather than kilobytes. Edit the `DEVICE=` line for `RAMDRIVE.SYS` in your `CONFIG.SYS` file to correct any errors; then restart your computer.

```
RAMDrive: No extended memory available
```

Error: You have specified the `/E` switch to create a RAM drive in extended memory, but no extended memory is available. Usually, this error is caused when `EMM386.EXE` claims all available XMS memory to use for EMS memory. With the DOS 6 version of `EMM386.EXE`, you can include a `MIN` parameter so that `EMM386.EXE` returns unused EMS memory to the memory pool when another program, such as `RAMDRIVE.SYS`, requests extended memory.

SEE ALSO

`DEVICE=`, `DEVICEHIGH=`, `DBLSPACE.SYS`, and `SMARTDRV.EXE`

"Using a RAM Disk" in Chapter 7 and Appendix B, "DOS Environment Variables"

RAMSETUP

The `RAMSETUP` command starts the RAMBoost Setup program. The RAMBoost Setup program installs the `RAMBOOST` device driver in the `CONFIG.SYS` file and then reboots the system.

SYNTAX

```
RAMSETUP /25 /28 /43 /50 /60 /in /bw /mono /lcd /ff /bf /nf /bt /ngm /le /im /ps2 /?
```

PARAMETERS AND SWITCHES

/25	Sets screen display to 25 lines (the default).
/28	Sets screen display to 28 lines (VGA only).
/43	Sets screen display to 43 lines (VGA and EGA).
/50	Sets screen display to 50 lines (VGA only).
/60	Sets screen display to 60 lines (Video 7 only).
/in	Runs the program in color mode even if a color display device is not detected.
/bw	Uses the black-and-white color scheme.
/mono	Uses the monochrome color scheme (IBM monochrome).
/lcd	Uses the LCD color scheme (for laptops).
/ff	Speeds up display (CGA only). Can cause a "snow" effect on some display devices.
/bf	Uses the BIOS font (use if graphics are not displayed properly).
/nf	Does not use fonts (does not use graphics characters).
/bt	Allows graphics mouse in Windows, and graphics fonts with DESQview or UltraVision.

/ngm	Does not use the graphics mouse pointer.
/le	Uses the left-handed mouse.
/im	Disables the mouse.
/ps2	Resets the mouse hardware.
/?	Displays the abbreviated online help.

NOTES

RAMSETUP strips all DEVICEHIGH= statements from the CONFIG.SYS file and converts them into DEVICE= statements. It also strips out all LOADHIGH= or LH= statements in the AUTOEXEC.BAT file. The DOS LOADHIGH, DEVICEHIGH, and DOS=UMB functions are built into RAMBOOST and are no longer required.

RAMSETUP does not edit nested or called batch files.

SEE ALSO

RAMBOOST.EXE

RD OR RMDIR   2.0 AND LATER—INTERNAL

You can use the RD (or RMDIR) command to delete empty subdirectories. If the subdirectory still contains any files, RD aborts and displays an error message. To delete a subdirectory and all its files, use the DELTREE command.

SYNTAX

```
RD    drive:\path
RMDIR drive:\path
```

PARAMETERS AND SWITCHES

drive: The drive containing the subdirectory you want to delete. If *drive:* is omitted, the current drive is assumed.

path   The subdirectory you want to delete on *drive:*. *path* can either be absolute or relative—that is, specified from the root directory or specified from the current directory (see item #4 in the following "Notes" section). If only the subdirectory name is specified with no path information, the subdirectory in the current directory with that name is deleted. You cannot delete the current directory.

NOTES

1. You must explicitly name the subdirectory you want to delete.
2. The subdirectory you want to delete must be empty of all files, including hidden files.

3. You cannot delete the current directory of any drive.
4. If a backslash (\) is the first (or only) character in a subdirectory path, it is considered absolute and is specified starting from the root directory. If the subdirectory path begins with a subdirectory name, it is considered relative, and the current directory is used as its starting point. A drive letter, followed by a colon, can precede either an absolute or a relative path.

MESSAGES

```
Invalid path, not directory
or directory not empty
```

Error: RMDIR did not remove the specified directory because one of the following errors occurred:

- You listed an invalid directory in the path.
- Files other than the . and .. entries still exist.
- You misspelled the path or directory name.

Check each possibility and try again.

You can delete all the files in a directory and remove the directory in one step by using DELTREE.

```
Attempt to remove current directory - drive:path
```

Error: RMDIR did not remove the specified directory for one of the following reasons:

- The directory is the current directory of the current drive.
- The directory is the current directory of another drive.
- The directory is redirected with the SUBST command.

For the first two cases, perform a CHDIR operation on a directory that is not a subdirectory of the directory that you want to delete and then attempt the RMDIR operation again. For the third case, perform an RMDIR operation on the actual directory affected by the SUBST command.

SEE ALSO

CD (or CHDIR), DELTREE, and MD (or MKDIR)

"Deleting Directories with RMDIR (RD)" in Chapter 5

RECOVER 2.0–5.0—EXTERNAL

RECOVER is a dangerous utility that can do more harm than good. If a disk develops a bad sector within a file, DOS is unable to copy any part of the file. If the root directory of a disk becomes damaged, DOS may not be able to read the disk at all. RECOVER is supposed to help you in these situations, but at times it is a case of a little help being worse than no help at all. With DOS 6, Microsoft stopped distributing RECOVER, and it's not even available on the Supplemental Disk. If you have a copy of RECOVER on your disk, you might want to delete it to keep from running it accidentally.

Situations like the ones that RECOVER was supposed to address do arise. DOS 6.22 includes the ScanDisk utility, which can repair many of the problems that can arise on your disks. If ScanDisk can't fix the problem, or if you aren't running DOS 6.22 when disaster strikes, reach for a good third-party utility package. The Norton Utilities, PC Tools, and the Mace Utilities are just a few of the packages that offer excellent tools to help you recover damaged files and disks. Any one of these packages will pay for itself many times over the first time you lose access to your hard disk due to a runaway program overwriting your root directory.

SEE ALSO

SCANDISK

"Analyzing a Disk with SCANDISK" in Chapter 7

REM   1.0 AND LATER—INTERNAL

You can use the REM command to insert comments into batch files or your CONFIG.SYS file. Any text on the line after REM (with a few exceptions in batch files) is ignored when DOS is processing that line in the file. Using this command can be extremely handy for documenting or temporarily "commenting out" lines in the file.

SYNTAX

REM *comment*

PARAMETERS AND SWITCHES

comment Can be any text. DOS truncates any line longer than 127 characters, but this usually doesn't matter in a comment line. In batch files, comments are read by the parser, so the pipe character (|) and redirection symbols (< and >) should be avoided.

NOTES

1. REM should be placed at the beginning of a line, with only spaces or tabs preceding it. A legal delimiter of some sort (for example, a space) needs to follow the REM so that DOS can recognize it.

2. In batch files, the pipe (|) and redirection symbols (< and >) should be avoided in comments because the parser may see and act on them. Including a greater-than sign in a comment line may cause an empty file to be created with the next eight characters as its name.

3. DOS has a maximum line length of 127 characters; any line longer than that is truncated. Still, as long as you are not depending on the comment line being displayed, it really doesn't matter whether DOS cuts it off. Comments are for you to read when you are working on the file, and the length of the line is really limited by your editing software, not DOS.
4. In CONFIG.SYS, you can use a semicolon rather than REM as an easier and somewhat cleaner way to mark comments. The semicolon comment isn't valid in batch files or versions of DOS before MS-DOS 6.
5. Blank lines can make your batch files and CONFIG.SYS file much easier to understand. DOS ignores any blank lines in these files, so you don't need to mark them as comments with REM.
6. Although REM is legal at the DOS prompt, it serves no purpose. REM is useful only for inserting comments in batch files and CONFIG.SYS.

EXAMPLES

If you want to document why a particular environment variable is being created in your AUTOEXEC.BAT file, you might include something like this:

```
REM  I set DIRCMD here to avoid always telling DIR that I prefer my
REM  filenames in lowercase letters with screen pauses.
SET  DIRCMD=/L /P
```

Or perhaps you want to "comment out" the line that loads the driver for your tape drive until the replacement driver arrives in the mail:

```
REM  DEVICE=C:\DOS\TAPE\SQ55.SYS
```

You also could use a semicolon to comment out the preceding line, like this:

```
;DEVICE=C:\DOS\TAPE\SQ55.SYS
```

SEE ALSO

;

Chapter 16, "Understanding Batch Files," and Chapter 19, "Configuring Your Computer"

REMOVDRV

REMOVDRV deletes the Stacker stacvol file and all the data from the specified Stacker drive.

SYNTAX

REMOVDRV *drive*: /?

PARAMETERS AND SWITCHES

drive: Indicates the Stacker drive from which you want to delete all data.

/?   Displays the abbreviated online help.

NOTES

The drive must be a mounted Stacker drive.

REN OR RENAME   1.0 AND LATER—INTERNAL

REN (or RENAME) is a utility you can use to rename files. Unlike many third-party utilities, REN cannot move files from one subdirectory to another, and it cannot rename subdirectories. To rename subdirectories, see the MOVE command.

SYNTAX

REN *old_name new_name*

or

RENAME *old_name new_name*

PARAMETERS AND SWITCHES

old_name The file, or files, that you want to rename. A full pathname (such as *drive:\path\...\filename.ext*) can be specified, and wildcards are allowed. This parameter is required and must include a filename (*.* is not assumed).

new_name The new filename, or names, you want to use. Only a filename and extension can be specified; you can't include any drive or path information. Wildcards are allowed; if they are used, they are filled in with the corresponding characters from *old_name*. This parameter is required.

NOTES

1. REN (or the long form, RENAME) changes the name of a file on the disk. The command does not rename directories. You can use the MOVE command to rename a directory.

2. Because you are renaming an established disk file, the file's drive or path designation goes with the old name so that DOS knows which file to rename.

3. Wildcard characters are acceptable in either the old or new name.

MESSAGES

`Duplicate filename or File not found`

Error: You attempted to change a filename to a name that already exists, or you asked DOS to rename a file that does not exist in the directory. Check the directory for conflicting names, make sure that the filename exists and that you spelled the name correctly, and then reissue the command.

SEE ALSO

MOVE

"Renaming Files" in Chapter 8

RENDIR

You can use the RENDIR command to rename a directory or subdirectory.

Syntax

RENDIR *drive:\path***oldname** *drive:\path***newname** /?

Parameters and Switches

drive:\path	Specifies the full path to the subdirectory that is to be renamed. This path cannot change when you are renaming the subdirectory.
oldname	Specifies the name of the subdirectory to be changed.
newname	Specifies the new name of the renamed subdirectory.
/?	Displays abbreviated help.

REPLACE   3.2 and later—External

The REPLACE command enables you to selectively update files on one disk from matching files on another disk, thereby overwriting old copies of files. REPLACE has other options that can help you maintain backup floppy disks, such as adding new files only or prompting you for confirmation before copying each file.

Syntax

REPLACE *source_files destination_path* /A /S /U /P /R /W

Parameters and Switches

source_files	Specifies the file, or files, that you want to selectively copy. A full pathname (such as *drive:\path\...\filename.ext*) can be specified, and wildcards are allowed. The filename portion of this parameter is required.
destination_path	Specifies the location you want to selectively copy the *source_files* to. You can include a drive and a path, but you cannot specify a filename. If this parameter is omitted, the current drive and subdirectory are used as the destination.
/A	Adds all the files specified by *source_files* that do not exist on the *destination_path*. You cannot combine the /A switch with the /S or /U switches.
/S	Replaces all the files specified by *source_files* that are found in *destination_path* or any subdirectories below it. You cannot combine the /S switch with the /A switch.

/U	Updates (replaces) all the files specified by *source_files* that are found in *destination_path* with dates and times preceding the source file's date and time. You cannot combine the /U switch with the /A switch.
/P	Prompts you as each file is replaced or added to *destination_path*.
/R	Enables REPLACE to overwrite read-only files on the *destination_path*. Normally, REPLACE terminates with an error if it attempts to overwrite a read-only file.
/W	Tells REPLACE to display the Press any key to continue... message and wait for a keystroke before beginning the replace operation. Using this switch gives you time to switch floppy disks if necessary.

Exit Codes

ERRORLEVEL Value	Meaning
0	Replace operation successful
1	Incorrect DOS version running (6.0 and later)
1	Invalid command-line syntax (3.2 and 3.3)
2	Source file(s) not found
3	Source or destination path not found
5	Unable to replace files—access denied
8	Insufficient memory to complete replace operation
11	Invalid command-line syntax (4.0 and later)
15	Source or destination drive invalid (undocumented)

Rules

1. If you do not name the source drive, DOS uses the current drive.
2. If you do not name the source path, DOS uses the current directory.
3. You must specify a source filename. Wildcards are allowed.
4. If you do not name the destination drive, DOS adds files to, or replaces files in, the current drive.
5. If you do not name the destination path, DOS adds files to, or replaces files in, the current directory.

Notes

1. Use REPLACE with caution because this command's speedy find-and-replace capability can have the effect of an unrelenting search-and-destroy mission on your data. Be careful when you unleash REPLACE on several subdirectories at a time, particularly when you

use REPLACE /S on the entire disk. Because REPLACE updates a file based only on the filename, you could accidentally replace a file somewhere on the disk that you intended to save.

2. To prevent such unwanted replacements, limit the destination pathname to cover only the directories that hold the files you want replaced. Check the source and destination directories for matching filenames. If you find conflicts or have doubts, use the /P switch; REPLACE asks for approval before replacing files.

3. If you use DOS 4.0 or later, the /U switch can help you avoid replacing wrong files. /U compares the files' date and time stamps. The destination file is replaced only if the file is older than the source file.

Messages

```
File cannot be copied onto itself filename
```

Warning: The source and destination disk and directories are identical. You probably did not specify a destination, so the source disk and directory are the current disk and directory. Otherwise, you specified the same drive and directory twice. REPLACE does not process *filename*.

Check the command line to ensure that you specified the correct source and destination for REPLACE and then try the command again.

nnn file(s) added

or

nnn file(s) replaced

Information: REPLACE indicates how many files are added or replaced. The first message appears when you use the /A switch; the second message appears if you do not use the /A switch. The message does not indicate that potential files are added or replaced; rather, the message appears when at least one file is added or replaced, regardless of errors that occur later.

```
No files found filename
```

Error: REPLACE could not find any files that matched the source filename. One of the following errors probably occurred:

- You misspelled the source filename.
- You provided the drive and directory names but omitted the filename.
- You provided the wrong drive or directory name for the source.
- You inserted the wrong floppy disk into the drive.

Check the command line to ensure that the correct disk is in the drive and then retry the command.

```
Invalid parameter combination
```

Error: You used both the /A and /S switches or the /A and /U switches, which you cannot use together in a REPLACE command. To replace files, omit /A. Because you cannot add files to more than one directory at a time, you cannot use /S with /A. To add files to more than one directory, issue separate REPLACE commands, each time specifying a different directory to which files are to be added.

SEE ALSO

COPY and XCOPY

"Combining Copying and Directory Management with XCOPY" and "Using the COPY Command" in Chapter 8

REPORT

The REPORT command reports statistics for Stacker drives. Typing REPORT at the DOS command prompt displays an online interface window that enables you to examine how the files are compressed.

SYNTAX

REPORT *drive:* /m /?

PARAMETERS AND SWITCHES

drive: Specifies the Stacker drive for which you want to see statistics.

/m   Specifies a monochrome display.

/?   Displays the online help screen for this command.

SEE ALSO

SDIR

RESIZE

The RESIZE command resizes a Stacker drive.

SYNTAX

RESIZE *drive:* /h /b /lcd /bw /?

PARAMETERS AND SWITCHES

drive: Specifies the drive to resize. The current drive is the default.

/h   Specifies hidden files to be moved.

/b   Restarts the computer after resizing the drive.

/lcd	Specifies an LCD color scheme (for laptops).
/bw	Specifies a monochrome display.
/?	Displays the abbreviated online help.

RESTORE   2.0 AND LATER—EXTERNAL

You can use the RESTORE command to restore from one disk to another disk one or more backup files created with the BACKUP command. If your backup file was created by MSBACKUP, you must use MSBACKUP to restore data from that file.

SYNTAX

RESTORE *drive1*: *drive2:path**filename.ext* /S /P /M /N /B:*date* /A:*date* /L:*time* /E:*time* /D

PARAMETERS AND SWITCHES

drive1:	Indicates the drive that holds the backup files.
drive2:	Indicates the drive that is to receive the restored files.
path	Specifies the path to the directory that is to receive the restored files. This parameter must be the same as the directory from which the files were backed up.
filename.ext	Indicates the file, or files, that you want to restore. Wildcards are allowed.
/A:*date*	Restores all files that were created or modified on or after the date you specify. The format of *date* depends on the COUNTRY in your CONFIG.SYS file.
/B:*date*	Restores all files that were created or modified on or before the date you specify. The format of *date* depends on the COUNTRY in your CONFIG.SYS file.
/D	(DOS 5.0 and later) Lists files to be restored without actually performing the restoration. You must specify *drive2:*.
/E:*time*	Restores all files that were created or modified either at the time or earlier than the time you specify. The format of *time* depends on the COUNTRY in your CONFIG.SYS file.
/L:*time*	Restores all files that were created or modified either at the time or later than the time you specify. The format of *time* depends on the COUNTRY in your CONFIG.SYS file.
/M	Restores all files that were modified or deleted since the backup set was made.
/N	Restores all files that no longer exist in the destination directory.

/P	Prompts you before restoring a file that was changed since the last backup or before restoring a file marked as read-only.
/S	Restores files in the current directory and all subdirectories. When you use this switch, RESTORE re-creates all necessary subdirectories that were removed and then restores the files in the re-created subdirectories.

Exit Codes

ERRORLEVEL Value	Meaning
0	Restore operation successful
1	No files found to restore
2	Halted by file-sharing violation (undocumented)
3	Halted by user (Ctrl+C)
4	Halted by fatal disk error

Rules

1. You must provide the name of the drive that holds the backup files. If the current disk is to receive the restored files, you do not have to specify the destination drive.
2. If you do not name a path, RESTORE uses the current directory of the receiving disk.
3. If you do not provide a filename, RESTORE restores all backup files from the directory. Omitting the filename is the same as using *.*.
4. RESTORE prompts you to insert the backup disks in order. If you insert a disk out of order, RESTORE prompts you to insert the correct disk.
5. Do not combine the /B, /A, and /N switches in the same RESTORE command.
6. Be cautious when you restore files that were backed up while an ASSIGN, SUBST, or JOIN command was in effect. When you use RESTORE, clear any existing APPEND, ASSIGN, SUBST, or JOIN commands. Do not use RESTORE /M or RESTORE /N while APPEND /X is in effect. RESTORE attempts to search the directories for modified or missing files. APPEND tricks RESTORE into finding files in the paths specified to the APPEND command. RESTORE may then restore files that should not be restored, and not restore files that should be restored. To disable APPEND, issue the APPEND ; command.
7. RESTORE cannot restore DOS system files (for example, IO.SYS and MSDOS.SYS) to the appropriate positions in the file structure so that the disk is bootable.

Notes

BACKUP and RESTORE in DOS 3.3 and later are radically different from the corresponding commands in previous versions. These commands place all backed-up files in one larger file and maintain a separate information file on the same disk. In DOS 3.3 and later, RESTORE handles the new and old backup-file formats, which means that these newer versions of RESTORE can restore backups created by any version of BACKUP.

Messages

```
Insert backup diskette nn in drive d:
Strike any key when ready
```

Information: RESTORE wants the next disk in sequence. This message appears when you are restoring files that were backed up onto floppy disks. Insert the next floppy disk (in the proper sequence) into drive *d:* and then press any key.

```
Insert restore target in drive d:
Strike any key when ready
```

Information: RESTORE is asking you to insert the floppy disk that is to receive the restored files. This message appears only when you restore files onto floppy disks. Insert the target disk into drive *d:* and then press any key.

```
***Listing files on drive A:***
```

Information: You used the /D switch with RESTORE, and the files that *would be* restored are displayed. The listed files follow the file specification that you used for restoration.

```
Source does not contain backup files
```

Error: RESTORE found no files that were backed up with the BACKUP command. BACKUP may have malfunctioned when backing up files, or you may have inserted the wrong disk.

```
Source and target drives are the same
```

Error: RESTORE determined that the drive that holds the backup files is the same as the drive that you designated to receive the restored files. You may have forgotten to specify the drive that holds the backup files or the target disk. If your system has one floppy drive and you tried to restore files onto a floppy disk, specify drives A and B.

```
System files restored
Target disk may not be bootable
```

Warning: You restored the three system files (IO.SYS, MSDOS.SYS, and COMMAND.COM) from the backup floppy disks. These files may not have been restored to the proper location on the disk, and you cannot use them to start DOS.

```
Warning! Diskette is out of sequence
Replace the diskette or continue if okay
Strike any key when ready
```

Warning: You inserted a backup floppy disk out of order. Place the correct disk in the drive and continue.

```
Warning! File filename
was changed after it was backed up
or is a read-only file
Replace the file (Y/N)?
```

Warning: This message appears when you use the /P switch. Either the file *filename* already exists on the hard disk and is marked as read-only, or the date of the file on the target disk is more recent than that of the backup copy (which may mean that the backup copy is obsolete). Type Y to replace the existing file with the backup copy or N to skip the file.

```
Warning! No files were found to restore
```

Warning: The files you wanted to restore are not on the disk from which you tried to restore them. Try again with another disk or another file specification. If you did not create a log file when you created the BACKUP floppy disk, you can determine which directories and files are on the floppy disk by using the TYPE command to display the floppy disk's binary CONTROL.*xxx* file and then interpreting what you see. The *xxx* in the filename reflects the backup disk's number. For example, the first disk in the backup set would have the file CONTROL.001 on it.

RMDIR (SEE RD)

RMDIR is the alternative name for the RD command. For information on using the RD or RMDIR command, see the entry for RD in this command reference.

SCANDISK

6.22—EXTERNAL

The ScanDisk program can locate and fix errors on disks. It works on most local drives, including DoubleSpace compressed drives. ScanDisk also can perform a surface scan, which reads every sector on the disk to make sure that it is error free and readable.

SYNTAX

To check one or more disk drives for errors, use the following format:

SCANDISK *drive:* ... /ALL /CHECKONLY /AUTOFIX /NOSAVE /CUSTOM /SURFACE /MONO /NOSUMMARY

To check an unmounted DoubleSpace volume file for errors, use the following format:

SCANDISK *cvf_file* /CHECKONLY /AUTOFIX /NOSAVE /CUSTOM /MONO /NOSUMMARY

To check the degree of fragmentation in a group of files, use the following format:

SCANDISK /FRAGMENT *pathname*

To undo the changes ScanDisk previously made fixing files, use the following format:

SCANDISK /UNDO *undo:* /MONO

PARAMETERS AND SWITCHES

drive: ...   Specifies the disk drive, or drives, you want to scan for errors. You can specify as many drive letters as you want. If *drive:* is omitted, the current drive is assumed. The colon following the drive letter is optional. You can't combine this parameter with the /ALL parameter.

cvf_file   Specifies the name of an unmounted DoubleSpace volume file you want to scan for errors. You should include the drive letter and the full name of the compressed volume file (CVF), such as C:\DBLSPACE.000.

pathname	Specifies the file, or files, you want to check for fragmentation. A full pathname is allowed, and all the normal defaults for drives and/or paths apply. Wildcards are allowed in the filename portion of the pathname.
undo:	Specifies the disk drive containing the undo disk that ScanDisk previously created. The colon following the drive letter is optional.
/ALL	Requests that ScanDisk check all local disk drives. If you specify this switch, you should not include any *drive:* parameters.
/CHECKONLY	Requests that ScanDisk check the drive for errors but not repair any errors it finds. You must specify this parameter if you want to run ScanDisk while other programs are running, such as Windows. You can't combine this parameter with the /AUTOFIX, /NOSAVE, or /CUSTOM parameters.
/AUTOFIX	Requests that ScanDisk fix any errors it finds without prompting you first. Any lost clusters that are found are saved as files in the root directory of the drive. If you specify the /NOSAVE parameter with /AUTOFIX, any lost clusters are deleted. You can't combine this parameter with the /CHECKONLY or /CUSTOM parameters.
/NOSAVE	Requests that ScanDisk delete any lost clusters it finds on the disk. You can use this parameter only if you also specify the /AUTOFIX parameter.
/CUSTOM	Requests that ScanDisk follow the settings in the [CUSTOM] section of the SCANDISK.INI file. If you intend to run ScanDisk from a batch file, you might want to use this parameter. For information about setting options in the SCANDISK.INI file, read the comments included in the file itself. You can't combine this parameter with the /AUTOFIX, /NOSAVE, or /CHECKONLY parameters.
/SURFACE	Requests that ScanDisk automatically perform a surface scan after checking the disk for errors. Surface scans can take time, but they do verify that all the data on your disk is error free and readable.
/MONO	Configures ScanDisk to use display colors more appropriate for a monochrome monitor or LCD screen.
/NOSUMMARY	Prevents ScanDisk from displaying a full-screen summary after scanning each drive.
/FRAGMENT	Requests that ScanDisk check all files specified with the *pathname* parameter to see how fragmented they are. You can't specify any other parameters except *pathname* when you are requesting a fragmentation report.
/UNDO	Requests that ScanDisk reverse the changes it made to your disk. The drive specified with this parameter must be the drive containing the undo disk that ScanDisk created. Note that you should not undo the changes ScanDisk made if you have made any changes to the disk since fixing the errors.

Exit Codes

ERRORLEVEL Value	Meaning
0	ScanDisk found no errors
1	Command-line syntax error
2	Terminated due to an internal error or lack of memory
3	ScanDisk halted by user during integrity checks
4	ScanDisk halted by user during surface scan
254	ScanDisk found errors, but they were all corrected
255	ScanDisk found errors, and they were not all corrected

Notes

1. If you enter SCANDISK with no parameters, ScanDisk scans the current drive.
2. Normally, if any errors are found, a dialog box appears with information explaining what the error is. You can choose to have ScanDisk fix the error or leave it alone. If you have specified the /AUTOFIX parameter, these dialog boxes are skipped.
3. After the disk has been checked for errors in its logical structure, ScanDisk asks whether you want to perform a surface scan. If you have specified the /SURFACE parameter, the surface scan takes place automatically. If you have specified the /CHECKONLY parameter, no surface scan is done.
4. ScanDisk can find and repair errors on most hard disk drives, floppy disk drives, DoubleSpace drives, RAM disk drives, and memory card drives.
5. ScanDisk can check only local disk drives. Do not attempt to run ScanDisk on any network, CD-ROM, or Interlnk drives attached to your system. You also shouldn't run ScanDisk on any alias drives created by the ASSIGN, JOIN, or SUBST commands.
6. If you try to run ScanDisk when other programs are running, ScanDisk refuses to fix any problems it encounters because the other programs might try to access the disk while ScanDisk is working, and more serious problems could be created. If Windows is running and you try to start ScanDisk, you see the message shown in the third item in the following "Messages" section.

   If you run ScanDisk with the /CHECKONLY parameter, it checks your disks for errors while other software, such as Windows, is running. If ScanDisk finds any errors, quit all your active programs, including Windows, and run ScanDisk again. In multitasking situations, ScanDisk might find errors when none really exist. By running ScanDisk again with no outside interference, you can find out for sure.
7. If you ask ScanDisk to check a mounted or unmounted DoubleSpace drive, it asks whether it should first check the host drive for errors. Normally, you should answer Yes. It is best to fix the host drive and then the DoubleSpace volume if errors exist in either of them. Answer No only if you have just finished checking the host drive and are sure that no errors exist.

8. After ScanDisk repairs errors on a drive, it asks whether you want to create an undo disk. It is usually a good idea to make an undo disk. You must have a blank, formatted floppy disk that you can place in drive A or B for the undo information to be written to. After you have exited ScanDisk, try not to write anything to the disk until you are sure that you don't want to undo the changes ScanDisk has made. Do not undo changes after writing to the disk; otherwise, serious damage could result.

9. ScanDisk can find and repair the following types of problems on your drives:
    - Bad sectors on the disk
    - Boot sector errors
    - Crosslinked files
    - Directory tree structural errors
    - DoubleSpace compression structure errors
    - DoubleSpace volume file allocation errors
    - DoubleSpace volume header structure errors
    - DoubleSpace volume signature errors
    - File allocation table (FAT) errors
    - Lost clusters

10. You can customize many of ScanDisk's settings by editing the SCANDISK.INI file. Setup places this file in the C:\DOS subdirectory by default. By setting the features you want to use in SCANDISK.INI and using the /CUSTOM parameter, you can automate a ScanDisk session and run it all from a batch file. For instructions on editing the SCANDISK.INI file, see the comments included in the SCANDISK.INI file itself.

EXAMPLES

To scan drives C and D for errors, you enter the following command:

SCANDISK C: D:

If you want to perform a surface scan as well, and not be prompted about fixing errors, you include the /SURFACE and /AUTOFIX options as follows:

SCANDISK C: D: /AUTOFIX   /SURFACE

If Windows is running, you have to do the surface scan later and for now specify the /CHECKONLY parameter, as in the following:

SCANDISK C: D: /CHECKONLY

To find out if it is time to run DEFRAG, you can check on the fragmentation level of the files in your correspondence subdirectory, like this:

SCANDISK C:\LETTERS*.*   /FRAGMENT

MESSAGES

```
Invalid switch: parameter
```

Error: The *parameter* you specified is unknown to ScanDisk. Check the command line for typing errors. To see a list of legal parameters for ScanDisk, enter the SCANDISK /? command.

```
parameter is not a valid name for a DoubleSpace volume file
```

Error: You have entered an incorrect parameter for ScanDisk. You see this message if you omit one of the slashes (/), which begin most of ScanDisk's parameters. Of course, you may have mistyped the name of a DoubleSpace CVF file as well.

```
You cannot use ScanDisk to fix problems while Windows is running.

To check for disk problems without fixing them, type SCANDISK /CHECKONLY at
the command prompt.
```

Error: You have attempted to run ScanDisk without the /CHECKONLY parameter while Microsoft Windows is running. Specify the /CHECKONLY parameter and try again.

SEE ALSO

CHKDSK and DEFRAG

SCANREG

SCANREG, which is a Windows 98 tool (not available with Windows 95), can back up, restore, or fix the data files that make up the Windows Registry.

SYNTAX

SCANREG /backup /restore /fix /scanonly /autoscan /comment="*comment*" /opt *filename* /?

PARAMETERS AND SWITCHES

/backup	Backs up the Registry data files to .CAB files.
/restore	Displays a list of available backup files that can be used to restore the Registry.
/fix	Repairs any damaged Registry settings and optimizes the Registry by removing unused space.
/opt	Optimizes the Registry by removing unused space.
/scanonly	Scans the Registry and displays any error messages but does not back it up.
/autoscan	Scans the Registry and backs it up without prompting if there are no backups already on the same date.

/comment="*comment*"	Adds the "*comment*" to the .CAB file created by /backup.
filename	Scans the specified Registry file and displays messages about any errors without backing up the Registry. The allowable files are as follows: SYSTEM.DAT USER.DAT
/?	Displays the abbreviated online help.

NOTES

SCANREG requires extended memory to run and does not run anything except the /restore option from the Windows Safe Mode command prompt.

If you restore an older backup, you lose any customizations and configurations you have made since that backup. This can cause your system to be unstable if you have installed new software or hardware since the backup.

When Windows is first installed, Setup creates an original Registry file named SYSTEM.1ST in the root directory. You can use it to restore the original Registry if the Registry is ever damaged.

SCHEDULE

The SCHEDULE command starts the Schedule program, which is a full-screen utility program to specify a future date and time to automatically run DOS programs.

The CPSCHED terminate-and-stay resident program must be loaded for scheduled events to run at the preset date and time.

SYNTAX

SCHEDULE *filename* /25 /28 /43 /50 /60 /in /bw /mono /lcd /ff /bf /nf /bt /ngm /le /im /ps2 /?

PARAMETERS AND SWITCHES

filename	Displays events for the specified file.
/25	Sets the screen display to 25 lines (default).
/28	Sets the screen display to 28 lines (VGA only).
/43	Sets the screen display to 43 lines (VGA and EGA).
/50	Sets the screen display to 50 lines (VGA only).
/60	Sets the screen display to 60 lines (Video 7 only).
/in	Runs the program in color even if a color display device is not detected.
/bw	Uses the black-and-white color scheme.

/mono	Uses the monochrome color scheme (IBM monochrome).
/lcd	Uses the LCD color scheme (for laptops).
/ff	Speeds up display (CGA only).
/bf	Uses the BIOS font.
/nf	Does not use fonts.
/bt	Allows a graphics mouse in Windows, allow graphics fonts with DESQview or UltraVision.
/ngm	Does not use the graphics mouse pointer. Uses a text-character mouse pointer.
/le	Uses the left-handed mouse.
/im	Disables the mouse.
/ps2	Resets the mouse hardware.
/?	Displays the abbreviated online help.

SEE ALSO

CPSCHED

SCREATE.SYS

SCREATE.SYS compresses RAM drives. It is one of the installable device drivers provided with PC DOS 7 and must be loaded by a DEVICE= statement in the CONFIG.SYS file.

SYNTAX

DEVICE=*drive:\path***screate.sys** *drive:* /c=*cluster size*

PARAMETERS AND SWITCHES

drive:\path	Location of the SCREATE.SYS file.
drive	Drive letter of the RAM drive.
/c=*cluster size*	Cluster size.

SEE ALSO

RAMDRIVE.SYS and STACHIGH.SYS

SCRIPT

SCRIPT is a command-line utility for printing PostScript files. It also can be used to redirect output from the result of other commands to a PostScript file or output device.

SYNTAX

SCRIPT /O=P|L /T=*size* /L=*size* /P=*size* /TI=*time* /U /R *drive:\path\filename device* /?

PARAMETERS AND SWITCHES

/O=P|L	Sets the page orientation to portrait or landscape.
/T=*size*	Sets the top margin to *size* inches.
/L=*size*	Sets the left margin to *size* inches.
/P=*size*	Sets the font to *size* in points.
/TI=*time*	Defines a printer timeout of *time* seconds.
/R	Resets the printer.
/U	Uninstalls the utility from memory.
drive:\path\filename	Specifies the source file to be printed. Specifying no source sends all output to the specified device until the utility is unloaded from memory.
device	Specifies the device to print to, such as LPT1. Can also be a filename.
/?	Displays abbreviated help.

NOTES

To send the result of commands to the SCRIPT utility, use this syntax:

command | **script**

SDEFRAG

The SDEFRAG command runs the Stacker Optimizer to defragment or recompress a Stacker drive. It also can change the size of a Stacker drive, resulting in a corresponding change to its uncompressed drive.

SYNTAX

SDEFRAG *drive:* /r /p=*n* /f /d /u /b /gl /gp /sorder /batch /skiphigh /noxms /lcd /bw /h /v /buffer=*nnnn* /restore=*drive:stacvol.ext*: /?

PARAMETERS AND SWITCHES

drive:	Specifies the Stacker drive to optimize; the current drive is the default.
/r	Recompresses data to complete conversion or maximize the available space.

/p=n	Recompresses data using level *n* (n is from 1 to 9).
/f	Specifies a full optimization.
/d	Optimizes directories only.
/u	Specifies a Quick optimization.
/b	Restarts the computer after optimization.
/gl	Changes the expected compression ratio for the Stacker drive.
/gp	Increases Stacker drive size or gets more uncompressed space.
/sorder	Sorts file information in the following order:
	n By filename; this is the default
	e By file extension
	d By time of creation
	s By file size
	u No sort
	- Following any of the above order, reverse the order
/batch	Runs in batch mode.
/skiphigh	Skips loading data in high memory.
/noxms	Prevents SDEFRAG from using extended memory during processing.
/lcd	Uses the monochrome display color setting.
/bw	Uses the monochrome display color setting.
/h	Moves hidden files.
/v	Verifies all writes.
/buffer=nnnn	Runs the optimizer with reduced memory requirements (where *nnnn* is between 256 and 4096). The default is 4096.
/restore=drive:stacvol.ext	Restores the Stacker drive if optimization was interrupted by a restart or power failure.
/?	Displays the abbreviated online help.

SDIR

The SDIR command displays the compression ratio for a list of files and directories. It should be used only for Stacker-compressed drives.

Syntax
SDIR *drive:\path filename* /p /w /a:*attributes* /o:*attributes* /s /b /l /ch /n /?

Parameters and Switches

drive:\path	Specifies the Stacker drive and directory for which the listing is needed.
filename	Specifies the file or group of files for which the listing is needed.
/p	Displays one screen of the listing at a time.
/w	Displays the listing in wide format, with as many as five filenames or directory names on each line.
/a:*attributes*	Displays only the names of those directories and files with the attributes specified. The options are as follows:

h	Hidden files
-h	Files that are not hidden
s	System files
-s	Files other than system files
d	Directories
-d	Files only (not directories)
a	Files ready for archiving (backup)
-a	Files that have not changed since the last backup
r	Read-only files
-r	Files that are not read-only

/o:*attributes*	Controls the order in which directory names and filenames are sorted and displayed. The options are as follows:

n	In alphabetical order by name
-n	In reverse alphabetical order
e	In alphabetical order by extension
-e	In reverse alphabetical order by extension
d	By date and time, earliest first
-d	By date and time, latest first
s	By size, smallest first
-s	By size, largest first
g	With directories grouped before files
-g	With directories grouped after files
c	By compression ratio (smallest first)

/s   Displays files in the specified directory and all subdirectories. You can use this switch with the /p switch to see the file listing one screen at a time.

/b   Lists each directory name or filename, one per line (including the filename extension). This switch displays no heading information and no summary. The /b switch overrides the /w switch.

/l   Displays unsorted directory names and filenames in lowercase. This switch does not convert extended characters to lowercase.

/ch   Displays the file compression ratio for Stacker-compressed files. /ch uses the host allocation size.

/n   Specifies no switches. Resets SDIR to the defaults.

/?   Displays the abbreviated online help.

SEE ALSO

REPORT

SET   2.0 AND LATER—INTERNAL

The SET command enables you to view, add, delete, or change variables contained in the DOS environment. Starting with DOS 6.0, you can use the SET command in your CONFIG.SYS file. MS-DOS uses several environment variables to control different aspects of its operation.

SYNTAX

To display all the variables defined in the environment, use the following format:

SET

To add or replace an environment variable, use the following format:

SET *name*=*string*

PARAMETERS AND SWITCHES

name   The string that you want to add to the environment. DOS converts these characters to uppercase before storing the variable in the environment.

string   The text that you want associated with *name*. *string* is stored in the environment exactly as you enter it—with upper- and lowercase characters and including any spaces you specify.

NOTES

1. The environment is an area of memory that DOS sets aside to store a series of text strings in the form *name*=*string*. The *name* portion is converted to uppercase before being stored in memory, but the *string* portion is stored as is.

2. If SET is executed with no parameters, the current contents of the DOS environment are displayed. (Don't use this form of the SET command in your CONFIG.SYS file.) To display the value of a single environment variable, pipe the output from SET through the FIND filter. (See the following "Examples" section.)

3. Entering SET with the *name* of the variable and an equal sign but no *string* deletes the specified variable from the environment. Note that if no variable with the *name* you've specified is found, nothing happens, and no error message is displayed.

4. When SET is executed with both *name* and *string* parameters, DOS searches the current environment looking for a variable that matches *name*. If a match is found, DOS replaces the variable with the new value specified in *string*. If no match is found, a new variable is defined in the current environment.

5. The total length of an environment variable, including the name and equal sign, cannot exceed the DOS 127-character limit. When you use SET to create environment variables, the limit is actually 123 because the SET command itself uses 3 characters and a space.

6. Spaces are legal in both the *name* and *string* portion of an environment variable. In fact, spaces are not ignored when searching for environment variables; so any trailing spaces you include after the *name*, but before the equal sign, become a significant portion of that variable's name. Keep this point in mind when you define new environment variables.

7. Avoid using redirection symbols (<, >, and |) and equal signs (=) in environment variables. Although you can use them in some cases, they can cause strange, hard-to-predict side effects when you use these variables in a batch file.

8. The DOS environment is limited to the size specified by the /E:*size* parameter specified in the SHELL= statement that names the command interpreter (usually COMMAND.COM) in your CONFIG.SYS file. If you haven't specified an /E:*size* parameter, it defaults to 256 characters. When a program is run, it is passed a copy of the current environment that has been shrunk to the smallest multiple of 16, which is big enough to hold all the variables currently defined.

    One annoying side effect of this behavior is that, if you normally run DOS from a Shell program, you will never have much environment space available—no matter how big you make it in your CONFIG.SYS file. To avoid the Out of environment space error messages, you might have to define a DUMMY variable that you can delete from a batch file whenever you need more environment space. (See the following "Examples" section.)

9. Several DOS commands use the environment to store their current values. PATH and PROMPT both store their settings in the environment. If you are running APPEND with the /E parameter, it stores its settings in the environment as well.

10. DOS defines a number of environment variables when you start up your computer, and certain commands modify their behavior if certain variables are defined. For more information about the environment variables DOS uses, refer to Appendix B, "DOS Environment Variables."

EXAMPLES

To display the contents of the current DOS environment, enter SET with no parameters, as shown here:

```
SET
```

A series of definitions similar to the following is then displayed on your screen:

```
CONFIG=WIN
COMSPEC=C:\DOS\COMMAND.COM
MOUSE=C:\DOS
TEMP=C:\TEMP
TMP=C:\TEMP
DIRCMD=/L
PATH=C:\BAT;C:\NORTON;C:\DOS;C:\UTIL
PROMPT=*Windows* $p$g
windir=d:\win
```

You can tell many interesting things from this list. First of all, the computer uses a startup menu, and the configuration that was chosen is named WIN (CONFIG=WIN). Also, notice that the WINDIR environment variable is shown in lowercase. Microsoft Windows inserts this variable into the environment as a flag to indicate that it is active. Inserting it in lowercase is a trick that prevents you from changing or deleting it with the SET command.

If you want to see how a particular environment variable is defined, pipe the output of the SET command through the FIND filter, like this:

```
SET | FIND "COMSPEC"
```

Only the lines that contain "COMSPEC" are displayed. Note that FIND is case sensitive by default, so make sure that you enter the name of the variable you are looking for in all uppercase (or specify the /I switch).

To change the defaults for the DIR command to lowercase filenames (/L) five columns wide (/W), sorted by date with directories first (/OGD), you can define (or replace) the DIRCMD environment variable by using the following SET command:

```
SET DIRCMD=/L /W /OGD
```

Note that you can't include any spaces before the equal sign; otherwise, a new variable (DIRCMD<space>) that the DIR command does not recognize is defined. To delete the DIRCMD variable entirely and let DIR use its built-in defaults, use the following command.

```
SET DIRCMD=
```

If you want to make sure that an environment variable you define in a batch file was successfully created, add an IF command after the SET command that defines the new variable:

```
SET NEWVAR=Do we have space for this?
IF "%NEWVAR%"=="" GOTO OUT_OF_SPACE
```

One technique to help you avoid Out of environment space error messages when you run batch files from a Shell program is to define a DUMMY variable in your AUTOEXEC.BAT file to simply take up space:

```
SET DUMMY=XXXXXXXXXXXXXXXXXXXXXXXXXXXXXXXXXXXXX
```

When you need space in the environment, simply delete the DUMMY variable, as follows, before you define any new variables that your batch file needs:

```
SET   DUMMY=
SET   NEWVAR=Now we have space for this
```

When your batch file terminates, returning you to your Shell program, the copy of the environment that the batch file was using is discarded. Because it is being thrown away, there is no reason to restore the DUMMY variable before the batch file ends.

If you might run this batch file when your Shell program is not running, you should reset the DUMMY variable and delete the NEWVAR variable before exiting the batch file like this:

```
SET   NEWVAR=
SET   DUMMY=XXXXXXXXXXXXXXXXXXXXXXXXXXXXXXXXXXXX
```

Otherwise, the next time you need the DUMMY variable, it might not be there.

MESSAGES

```
Out of environment space
```

Error: You see this message if the environment is not large enough to hold the string you want to add with the PATH, PROMPT, or SET command. To increase the size of the environment, use the /E:*size* parameter in the SHELL= statement in your CONFIG.SYS file.

```
Syntax error
```

Error: SET displays a syntax error message if you forget to include the equal sign. This error most often happens after you have been using the PATH and PROMPT commands, which get you out of the habit of including an equal sign between the variable name and its value.

SEE ALSO

COMMAND, PATH, PROMPT, and SHELL=

"Changing DOS Variables" in Chapter 11 and Appendix B, "DOS Environment Variables"

SETUP (STACKER)

SETUP activates the Stacker online interface after running SSETUP.

SYNTAX

SETUP /m /t=*drive* /?

PARAMETERS AND SWITCHES

/m   Specifies the monochrome display mode to be used.

/t=*drive*   Specifies the drive's temporary installation location.

/?   Displays the abbreviated online help.

SETVER 5.0 AND LATER—EXTERNAL

When programmers write software, they often add code to check the version of DOS that is running. To be on the safe side, they may prevent their program from running if the preliminary check reveals the presence of a version of DOS that they didn't test. In many cases, this paranoia is unnecessary, and lying to the program about which version of DOS is running enables the software to operate safely. The SETVER.EXE device driver maintains in memory a version table that tells it exactly which programs to lie to and what version of DOS to tell the program it is running. When you run SETVER from the command line, you can view, add, change, or delete entries in SETVER.EXE's version table. These changes take effect the next time SETVER.EXE is loaded into memory.

SYNTAX

SETVER *drive:\path filename n.nn*

SETVER *drive:\path filename* /DELETE /D /QUIET

PARAMETERS AND SWITCHES

drive:\path Specifies the drive and path to the SETVER.EXE file. Setup places the SETVER.EXE file in the C:\DOS subdirectory by default. If *drive:\path* is not specified, SETVER searches the current directory and along the DOS PATH to find the SETVER.EXE file. You usually can omit this parameter.

filename Specifies the full name of the program you want SETVER to locate in the version table. Include the filename and extension, but do not include any path information. No default extensions are assumed, and wildcards are not allowed. If you include this parameter, you also must include either an *n.nn*, /DELETE, or /D parameter.

n.nn Specifies the DOS version number that SETVER.EXE reports to the program specified by the *filename* parameter. Valid entries are in the range 2.11 to 9.99. You are required to enter the period delimiting the major and minor version numbers, and you should always enter the value with two decimal places (that is, 2.00, not 2.0 or 2). If you specify this parameter, you cannot specify the /DELETE, /D, or /QUIET parameters.

/DELETE Deletes the version table entry for the program file specified by *filename*. If you specify /DELETE, you cannot specify the *n.nn* parameter.

/D Same as /DELETE.

/QUIET Suppresses the two-line successful update message that appears after an entry is deleted from the version table. (Refer to the actual message in the following "Messages" section.) You can specify /QUIET only with /DELETE or /D.

Exit Codes

ERRORLEVEL Value	Meaning
0	SETVER operation successful
1	Invalid command-line switch specified
2	Invalid filename specified
3	Insufficient memory to complete the requested operation
4	Invalid version number format used
5	Entry not found in the version table
6	SETVER.EXE not found
7	Invalid drive letter specified
8	Too many command-line parameters specified
9	Required command-line parameter missing
10	Error reading from SETVER.EXE
11	Version table in SETVER.EXE is corrupt
12	SETVER.EXE file specified doesn't support a version table
13	Version table full
14	Error writing to SETVER.EXE

Notes

1. If you enter SETVER without any parameters, DOS displays all entries it comes across from the version table contained in the first copy of SETVER.EXE. DOS searches the current directory for the SETVER.EXE file, followed by all the subdirectories specified in your DOS PATH. If you enter SETVER *drive:\path*, the entries in the version table contained in the *drive:\path*\SETVER.EXE file are displayed. In this case, no other directories are searched if SETVER.EXE isn't found in the *drive:\path* subdirectory.

2. Microsoft ships SETVER.EXE with a version table that lists programs known to work safely with MS-DOS 6, but which have to be fooled in order to run.

Microsoft's SETVER.EXE Version Table for MS-DOS 6

filename	n.nn	filename	n.nn
KERNEL.EXE	5.00	JOIN.EXE	5.00
NETX.COM	5.00	RECOVER.EXE	5.00
NETX.EXE	5.00*	GRAFTABL.COM	5.00
NET5.COM	5.00	LMSETUP.EXE	5.00
BNETX.COM	5.00	STACKER.COM	5.00
BNETX.EXE	5.00*	NCACHE.EXE	5.00
EMSNETX.EXE	5.00*	NCACHE2.EXE	5.00

EMSNET5.EXE	5.00	IBMCACHE.SYS	5.00
XMSNETX.EXE	5.00*	XTRADRV.SYS	5.00
XMSNET5.EXE	5.00	2XON.COM	5.00
DOSOAD.SYS	5.00	WINWORD.EXE	4.10
REDIR50.EXE	5.00	EXCEL.EXE	4.10
REDIR5.EXE	5.00	LL3.EXE	4.01
REDIRALL.EXE	5.00	REDIR4.EXE	4.00
REDIRNP4.EXE	5.00	REDIR40.EXE	4.00
EDLIN.EXE	5.00	MSREDIR.EXE	4.00
BACKUP.EXE	5.00	WIN200.BIN	3.40
ASSIGN.COM	5.00	METRO.EXE	3.31
EXE2BIN.EXE	5.00		

The n.nn entry for these files was changed to 6.00 in MS-DOS 6.22.

> **Note**
>
> If you look through the version table provided by Microsoft, you see that WINWORD.EXE and EXCEL.EXE are listed as requiring DOS version 4.10. However, Word for Windows 2.0 and Excel 4.0 can run under DOS 6.22 without SETVER. These entries are for older versions of these programs. If your Windows software is up to date, you don't have to worry about using SETVER to fool these two programs.
>
> In the version table, you also see entries for the DOS utilities that were not distributed with DOS 6. When you use the DOS 5 versions of these utilities, they have to be included in the version table for SETVER; otherwise, they do not run. Instead, an Incorrect DOS version message is displayed. If you install updated versions of these utilities with the DOS 6 Supplemental Disk Setup program, their version table entries are deleted.

3. Do not specify the DOS version number with the filename if you are trying to delete an entry in the version table. Doing so causes this error message to be displayed: Too many command line parameters. (Read more about this message in the following "Messages" section.)

4. Don't add a program to the SETVER.EXE version table unless you are sure that it can run safely with DOS 6. There is a chance that an incompatible program might appear to run and still cause system instabilities or data loss. This is the reason Microsoft displays the WARNING paragraph whenever you add or update an entry in the version table. (Read more about this message in the following "Messages" section.) To be safe, contact the manufacturer of the software program in question to find out whether the version you have can be run safely under DOS 6.

5. Any changes you make to the version table with SETVER are written to the SETVER.EXE file on disk, not to the device driver in memory. These changes do not take effect until you reload the SETVER.EXE device driver into memory by restarting your computer.

6. Specify the drive and path to the SETVER.EXE file you want to update and not the drive and path to the program you are looking for in the version table. If you don't specify the drive and path correctly, SETVER usually fails to find SETVER.EXE, and an error message is displayed (see the second item in the following "Messages" section). Normally, SETVER.EXE is located on your DOS PATH, and you can omit the *drive:\path* parameter to avoid this confusing syntax.

7. Remember to specify only the filename (with extension) of the program file you want to add, update, or delete from the SETVER version table. No path information is stored in the table, so only the filename is needed to locate the entry. The extension is included in the table, so you must specify it as well. No default extensions are assumed, and wildcards are not allowed.

8. Device drivers, as well as executable programs, can be included in the version table. If SETVER.EXE is already in memory when the device driver loads in your CONFIG.SYS file, SETVER.EXE can lie to it about the version of DOS that is running.

EXAMPLES

To display the contents of the version table in the SETVER.EXE file located on your DOS PATH, enter SETVER on the command line as follows:

```
SETVER
```

You don't use the METRO.EXE program, and you want to delete the entry from the version table. To do so, enter the following command:

```
SETVER   METRO.EXE   /DELETE
```

You can abbreviate the /DELETE switch as /D if you want to. To add METRO.EXE back into the version table and restore its setting to DOS 3.31, you enter the following command:

```
SETVER   METRO.EXE   3.31
```

If all goes well, you see the WARNING paragraph. (See the last item in the following "Messages" section.)

MESSAGES

```
An invalid path to SETVER.EXE was specified
```

Error: A subdirectory you specified in the path to SETVER.EXE is invalid.

```
Could not find the file SETVER.EXE
```

Error: SETVER.EXE was not found along the DOS search path or in the subdirectory you specified. (ERRORLEVEL value 6 returned)

```
ERROR: Reading SETVER.EXE file
```

Error: A disk error occurred while the SETVER.EXE file was being read. This problem could be the result of file-sharing violations, errors in the disk's FAT, corrupted formatting information, or bad sectors on the disk. The SETVER.EXE file may be corrupted. (ERROR-LEVEL value 10 returned)

```
ERROR: Writing SETVER.EXE file
```

Error: A disk error occurred while the SETVER.EXE file was being written to. This problem can happen if the disk fills up or a bad sector is encountered. The SETVER.EXE file may be corrupted. (ERRORLEVEL value 14 returned)

```
Insuffient memory
```

Error: Not enough memory is available to run SETVER. (*Note:* The spelling error is Microsoft's, not ours.) (ERRORLEVEL value 3 returned)

```
Invalid drive specifier
```

Error: The disk drive you specified in the path to SETVER.EXE isn't a valid DOS drive. (ERRORLEVEL value 7 returned)

```
Invalid filename
```

Error: An invalid filename was specified on the command line, or the specified file doesn't exist. (ERRORLEVEL value 2 returned)

```
Invalid switch
```

Error: On the command line, you have specified a switch that SETVER doesn't understand. (ERRORLEVEL value 1 returned)

```
Invalid version number, format must be 2.11 - 9.99
```

Error: The version number you specified is invalid. You can report DOS versions 2.11 through 9.99 only. You also may see this message if you specify DELETE or D without the slash (/R). (ERRORLEVEL value 4 returned)

```
Missing parameter
```

Error: You specified a filename, but you have not included either a version number (to add or update an entry) or /D (to delete an entry). (ERRORLEVEL value 9 returned)

```
No entries found in version table
```

Information: You asked SETVER to display the version table, but the copy of SETVER.EXE it found has no entries in the version table. This can happen if you delete all the entries (one by one) in SETVER.EXE by using the SETVER /D command.

```
NOTE: SETVER device not loaded. To activate SETVER version reporting you must
load the SETVER.EXE device in your CONFIG.SYS.
```

Warning: When you use SETVER without loading the SETVER.EXE device, it displays this message to remind you that the version table is active only when the SETVER.EXE device driver is loaded.

```
Specified entry was not found in the version table
```

Warning: You have tried to delete an entry that is not in the version table. Check to see whether you mistyped the name of the program or included the wrong extension. If everything looks correct, type SETVER and take another look at the current version table to make sure that the program you are trying to delete is indeed included in it. (ERRORLEVEL value 5 returned)

```
There is no more space in version table new entries
```

Error: The version table in SETVER.EXE is full. You must delete one or two entries before you can add any more. (Microsoft seems to have misplaced the *for* in this message.) (ERRORLEVEL value 13 returned)

```
Too many command line parameters
```

Error: Too many command-line parameters were specified, and SETVER doesn't know what to do with them all. (ERRORLEVEL value 8 returned)

```
Version table is corrupt
```

Error: The version table stored within SETVER.EXE has become damaged. You need to delete the damaged file and replace it with a fresh copy from your MS-DOS 6 distribution disks. SETVER.EXE is compressed on the distribution disks, and you must use the EXPAND command to expand it so that you can use it. (ERRORLEVEL value 11 returned)

```
Version table successfully updated
The version change will take effect the next time you restart your system
```

Information: You have successfully deleted an entry in the version table. This is the message you can suppress by using the /QUIET parameter. (ERRORLEVEL value 0 returned)

```
WARNING - Contact your software vendor for information about whether a
specific program works with MS-DOS version 6.0. It is possible that
Microsoft has not verified whether the program will successfully run if
you use the SETVER command to change the program version number and
version table. If you run the program after changing the version table
in MS-DOS version 6.0, you may lose or corrupt data or introduce system
instabilities. Microsoft is not responsible for any loss or damage, or
for lost or corrupted data.

Version table successfully updated
The version change will take effect the next time you restart your system
```

Information: You have successfully updated the version table. The warning paragraph is a reminder that lying to software programs can be a risky business, and you do so at your own risk. To be safe, contact the manufacturer of the program you are trying to fool and ask whether it's safe to run that software under DOS 6. (ERRORLEVEL value 0 returned)

SEE ALSO

SETVER.EXE

"Setting the Version Using the SETVER Command" in Chapter 10

SETVER.EXE (DEVICE DRIVER)   5.0 AND LATER— EXTERNAL

When programmers write software, they often add code to check the version of DOS that is running. To be on the safe side, they may prevent their program from running if the preliminary check reveals the presence of a version of DOS that they didn't test. In many cases, this paranoia is unnecessary, and lying to the program about which version of DOS is running enables the software to operate safely. The SETVER.EXE device driver maintains in memory a version table that tells it exactly which programs to lie to and what version of DOS to tell the program it is running. SETVER.EXE must be loaded in a DEVICE= or DEVICEHIGH= statement in your CONFIG.SYS file.

SYNTAX

DEVICE=*drive:\path***SETVER.EXE**

or

DEVICEHIGH=*drive:\path***SETVER.EXE**

PARAMETERS AND SWITCHES

drive:\path   The drive and path to the SETVER.EXE file on your system. Setup places the SETVER.EXE file in the C:\DOS subdirectory by default. If the full path to SETVER.EXE isn't specified, DOS looks for the file in the root directory of the startup drive.

NOTES

1. Microsoft ships SETVER.EXE with a version table that lists programs known to work safely with MS-DOS 6, but which need to be fooled in order to run. You can add or subtract programs from the version table by running SETVER from the command line. To activate any changes you make, you must reboot your computer.

Microsoft's SETVER.EXE Version Table for MS-DOS 6

filename	n.nn	filename	n.nn
KERNEL.EXE	5.00	JOIN.EXE	5.00
NETX.COM	5.00	RECOVER.EXE	5.00
NETX.EXE	5.00*	GRAFTABL.COM	5.00
NET5.COM	5.00	LMSETUP.EXE	5.00
BNETX.COM	5.00	STACKER.COM	5.00
BNETX.EXE	5.00*	NCACHE.EXE	5.00
EMSNETX.EXE	5.00*	NCACHE2.EXE	5.00
EMSNET5.EXE	5.00	IBMCACHE.SYS	5.00
XMSNETX.EXE	5.00*	XTRADRV.SYS	5.00

filename	n.nn	filename	n.nn
XMSNET5.EXE	5.00	2XON.COM	5.00
DOSOAD.SYS	5.00	WINWORD.EXE	4.10
REDIR50.EXE	5.00	EXCEL.EXE	4.10
REDIR5.EXE	5.00	LL3.EXE	4.01
REDIRALL.EXE	5.00	REDIR4.EXE	4.00
REDIRNP4.EXE	5.00	REDIR40.EXE	4.00
EDLIN.EXE	5.00	MSREDIR.EXE	4.00
BACKUP.EXE	5.00	WIN200.BIN	3.40
ASSIGN.COM	5.00	METRO.EXE	3.31
EXE2BIN.EXE	5.00		

The n.nn entry for these files was changed to 6.00 in MS-DOS 6.22.

> **Note**
>
> If you look through the version table provided by Microsoft, you see that WINWORD.EXE and EXCEL.EXE are listed as requiring DOS version 4.10. However, Word for Windows 2.0 and Excel 4.0 can run under DOS 6.22 without SETVER. These entries are for older versions of these programs. If your Windows software is up-to-date, you don't have to worry about using SETVER to fool these two programs.
>
> In the version table, you also see entries for the DOS utilities that were not distributed with DOS 6. When you use the DOS 5 versions of these utilities, they have to be included in the version table for SETVER; otherwise, they do not run. Instead, an Incorrect DOS version message is displayed. If you install updated versions of these utilities with the DOS 6 Supplemental Disk Setup program, their version table entries are deleted.

2. If upper memory is available on your computer, SETVER.EXE can be loaded there with the DEVICEHIGH= command. SETVER.EXE requires about 500 bytes of memory with its original version table.

3. The Setup program for DOS 6 automatically includes a DEVICE= line loading SETVER.EXE in your CONFIG.SYS file. You might want to look over the contents of the version table to see whether you are using any of the programs listed in it. If you are not using any of the programs and the rest of your software is happy running under DOS 6, you can safely delete the SETVER.EXE device driver from your CONFIG.SYS file.

4. Besides lying to programs, SETVER.EXE can also lie to device drivers. Just make sure that SETVER.EXE is loaded before the device driver loads and that the name of that device driver is included in the version table.

EXAMPLES

To load the DOS version table driver into memory, include the following line in your CON-FIG.SYS file:

DEVICE=C:\DOS\SETVER.EXE

This line assumes that the SETVER.EXE file is in the C:\DOS subdirectory. If your computer has upper memory available, you might want to load SETVER.EXE into upper memory by using the following command:

DEVICEHIGH=C:\DOS\SETVER.EXE

MESSAGES

Version table is corrupt

Error: The version table stored within SETVER.EXE has become damaged. You must delete the damaged file and replace it with a fresh copy from your MS-DOS 6 distribution disks. SETVER.EXE is compressed on the distribution disks, so you must use the EXPAND command to expand it before you can use it.

SEE ALSO

DEVICE=, DEVICEHIGH=, and SETVER

"Setting the Version with SETVER" in Chapter 10

SHARE 3.0 AND LATER—EXTERNAL

The SHARE program enables DOS support for file and record locking. When you run SHARE, it remains resident in memory, becoming a part of DOS. If you use any multitasking software, such as Microsoft Windows, you should run SHARE in your AUTOEXEC.BAT file. You can load SHARE into upper memory by using the LOADHIGH command on systems that have upper memory available.

SYNTAX

SHARE   /F:*name_space*   /L:*numlocks*

PARAMETERS AND SWITCHES

/F:*name_space*   The amount of memory space in bytes to use for file sharing. The default is 2,048.

/L:*numlocks*   The maximum number of file/record locks that are available to programs. The default is 20.

RULES

1. When SHARE is loaded, DOS checks for file and record locks as each file is opened, read, and written.

2. SHARE normally enlarges DOS by approximately 6,192 bytes in DOS 5.0 and approximately 5,248 bytes in DOS 6.0. If the number of locks (/L switch) or memory space (/F switch) increases or decreases, DOS also increases or decreases proportionately. You can load SHARE into upper memory by using the LOADHIGH command.
3. The only way to remove SHARE is to restart DOS.
4. In DOS 4.0, use SHARE if your hard disk is formatted with partitions larger than 32MB. SHARE is not required to use large partitions in DOS 5.0 and later versions.
5. You can load SHARE by using INSTALL= in your CONFIG.SYS file (DOS 4.0 and later versions).
6. You should be running SHARE if you use any multitasking software on your computer. In a multitasking environment, two programs might attempt to update the same file. If that happens, data can be lost. Examples of multitasking environments include the DOS Shell's Task Swapper, Microsoft Windows, and DESQview.

NOTES

1. Use SHARE when two or more programs or processes share a computer's files. After SHARE is loaded, DOS checks each file for locks whenever the file is opened, read, or written. If a file is open for exclusive use, an error message results from subsequent attempts to open the file. If one program locks a portion of a file, an error message results if another program tries to read or write the locked portion.
2. SHARE is most effective when all file-sharing programs can handle the DOS functions for locking files and records (DOS 3.0 and later versions). SHARE is either partially or completely ineffective with programs that do not use the DOS file- and record-locking features.
3. SHARE affects two or more programs running on the same computer, not two or more computers using the same file (networked computers). For networks, record- and file-locking are made possible by software provided with the network.
4. You must use SHARE if you use DOS 4.0 or 4.01 and if your hard disk is formatted larger than 32MB. For convenience, you can use INSTALL= in the CONFIG.SYS file to activate SHARE. In the CONFIG.SYS file, for example, the following command activates SHARE if SHARE.EXE is located in the \DOS subdirectory of drive C:
   INSTALL=C:\DOS\SHARE.EXE

SEE ALSO

INSTALL= and LOADHIGH

 **SHELL=**   **2.0 AND LATER—INTERNAL**

You use SHELL= to specify the name and location of the command interpreter that MS-DOS should use. Normally, you use COMMAND.COM, but other third-party shells, such as 4DOS and NDOS, can use SHELL= to gain control of the command line. Another common use of the

SHELL= command is to change the size of the environment. SHELL= can be used only in your CONFIG.SYS file.

SYNTAX

SHELL=*drive:\path***filename** *parameters*

PARAMETERS AND SWITCHES

drive:\path   The drive and path to the command interpreter must be specified here if the command interpreter isn't located in the root directory of the startup drive.

filename   The name of the program to use as the command interpreter for DOS. Normally, it is COMMAND.COM.

parameters   Any parameters or switches that the specified command interpreter requires. (For the parameters and switches that COMMAND.COM uses, see the description for COMMAND earlier in this command reference.)

NOTES

1. Be careful when you experiment with the SHELL= command and be sure that you have a bootable floppy disk handy. If you set something incorrectly, chances are you either will have to reboot from a floppy disk or perform a "clean boot" by pressing F5.

2. If no SHELL= command exists in CONFIG.SYS, DOS attempts to load COMMAND.COM from the root directory of the startup drive. If COMMAND.COM cannot be found or is from a different version of DOS, an error message is displayed (see the following "Messages" section). When you receive this error message, you must either enter the full pathname of a valid copy of COMMAND.COM or reboot the computer from a bootable floppy disk.

3. Do not confuse the SHELL= command with the DOSSHELL program. SHELL= is a CONFIG.SYS command that designates the program to be used as the command-line interface to MS-DOS. DOSSHELL is a program that provides a graphical interface from which you can operate your computer if you choose. The DOSSHELL program and SHELL= command have nothing to do with each other.

4. MemMaker "comments out" the SHELL= line in your CONFIG.SYS file if the SHELL= line specifies a command interpreter other than COMMAND.COM. If you are using a third-party shell program, be sure that COMMAND.COM is in the root directory of the startup drive before you run MemMaker. After MemMaker is done, you must manually "uncomment" the SHELL= line that loads your command-line interpreter to restore the use of your third-party shell.

5. Many third-party shell programs do not require the /P switch to tell them that they should install themselves permanently in memory. Instead, they look for a valid environment. If one is present, they assume that they have already been run, do not install

themselves permanently, and do not execute the AUTOEXEC.BAT file. In DOS 6, an environment already may be present when the shell programs are loaded from the SHELL= line in CONFIG.SYS, which can lead to problems.

If you find yourself in the situation just described, try including the /P switch on the SHELL= line that loads your command-line interpreter. Also, you should contact the manufacturer of your shell program to see whether an upgrade that is more compatible with MS-DOS 6 is available.

EXAMPLES

The setup program for DOS 6 may insert a SHELL= line in your CONFIG.SYS file that looks something like this:

```
SHELL=C:\DOS\COMMAND.COM   C:\DOS\   /E:512   /P
```

It sets the command interpreter to COMMAND.COM, located in the C:\DOS subdirectory, with a reload path of C:\DOS and an environment size of 512 bytes. The final /P switch tells COMMAND.COM to remain in memory permanently. Never specify the /P switch for COMMAND.COM except in the SHELL= line in your CONFIG.SYS file.

MESSAGES

```
Bad or missing Command Interpreter
Enter correct name of Command Interpreter (eg, C:\COMMAND.COM)
```

Error: If the SHELL= command in your CONFIG.SYS file does not point to a valid command interpreter, and the copy of COMMAND.COM in the root directory of your startup drive is missing or invalid, this message is displayed. To continue, you have to enter the full path to a valid (DOS 6) copy of COMMAND.COM so that DOS can load it into memory. DOS has already checked the copy of COMMAND.COM in your root directory, so entering C:\COMMAND.COM as suggested in the error message usually does not work. You can try entering C:\DOS\COMMAND.COM because Setup places a copy of COMMAND.COM in the subdirectory in which DOS was installed. If a valid copy of COMMAND.COM can't be found, you must reboot from a floppy disk.

Even if you locate a valid copy of COMMAND.COM and load it into memory, this copy of COMMAND.COM is only temporary; so typing EXIT brings this error message right back onscreen. Also, your AUTOEXEC.BAT file is not executed by temporary copies of COMMAND.COM, so none of the settings or resident software you typically use will be available. Use the COPY command to transfer a new copy of COMMAND.COM to the root directory of your startup disk (usually C:\) and reboot by pressing Ctrl+Alt+Del to set things back to the way they should be.

SEE ALSO

COMMAND

"Using the SHELL Command" in Chapter 19

SHIFT   2.0 AND LATER—INTERNAL

The SHIFT command shifts a batch file's command-line parameters one position to the left. You have to use the SHIFT command if your batch file requires more than nine parameters. SHIFT also is handy for batch files that repeat an operation for each command-line parameter. SHIFT is useful only when used in a batch file.

SYNTAX
SHIFT

NOTES

1. When you use SHIFT, DOS moves the command-line parameters one position to the left. That is, the parameter %1 becomes %0, %2 becomes %1, %3 becomes %2, and so on.
2. DOS discards the former first parameter (%0). Any parameter shifted off the left end is gone for good.
3. DOS shifts parameter 10, if it exists, into %9, parameter 11 into parameter 10, and so on. Using SHIFT is the only way to access more than nine command-line parameters from within a batch file.

SEE ALSO

"Moving Parameters with SHIFT" in Chapter 16

SIZER   (SEE MEMMAKER)

MemMaker uses the SIZER program to help it optimize memory use on your computer. MemMaker requires this program while optimizing your system, but it is not necessary at any other time. You cannot use this program yourself. SIZER aborts if MemMaker (and possibly CHKSTATE.SYS) is not in control when it is run, displaying the following message:

```
SIZER.EXE is used by MemMaker during the memory-optimization process
and is not intended to be started from the command prompt.
```

Very few details about SIZER's operation are documented. When MemMaker is optimizing, it adds a SIZER.EXE command to the beginning of every command that loads device drivers or resident programs in your CONFIG.SYS and AUTOEXEC.BAT files. Load size information about these drivers and programs is written to the MEMMAKER.STS file by SIZER. When optimization is complete, MemMaker removes all references to the SIZER program from your startup files.

SEE ALSO

CHKSTATE.SYS and MEMMAKER

SMARTDRV 6.0 AND LATER—EXTERNAL

When used from the command line, SMARTDRV loads or configures SMARTDrive, a disk-caching utility that can speed disk operations significantly. The first time you run SMARTDRV, it loads itself into memory (upper memory if space is available) and establishes the disk cache. To unload SMARTDRV from memory, you have to reboot your computer.

SYNTAX

To start SMARTDrive from your AUTOEXEC.BAT file or from a command prompt, use the following format:

SMARTDRV /X *drive* ± ... *initsize winsize* /U /C /R /F /N /V /Q /S /L /E:*esize* /B:*bsize*

After SMARTDrive is running, use the following format:

SMARTDRV *drive* +|- ... /C /R /Q /S

With DOS version 6.22, you also can use the /X, /F, and /N parameters after SMARTDrive is running:

SMARTDRV /X *drive* +|- ... /C /R /F /N /Q /S

PARAMETERS AND SWITCHES

/X		Specifies that you want to disable write-behind caching for all drives by default. You can then enable or disable individual drives by using the *drive* ± parameter.
drive ± ...		Specifies one or more drives for which you want to enable or disable disk caching. *drive* enables read caching and disables write caching. *drive*+ enables read and write caching. *drive*- disables caching.
		If you start SMARTDrive but do not specify a drive, floppy and Interlnk drives are read cached only; hard drives are read and write cached; and CD-ROM, network, compressed, and Microsoft Flash memory card drives are not cached.
		CD-ROM drives are read cached by default.
initsize		Specifies the size (in kilobytes) of the cache when SMARTDrive starts. The following table shows the default values for this parameter:

Extended Memory	initsize	winsize
Up to 1MB	All	0 (no caching)
Up to 2MB	1024KB	256KB
Up to 4MB	1024KB	512KB
Up to 6MB	2048KB	1024KB
More than 6MB	2048KB	2048KB

	`winsize`	Specifies the size (in kilobytes) by which SMARTDrive reduces its cache when Microsoft Windows starts, freeing that memory for Windows to use. When you quit Windows, that memory is returned to SMARTDrive and defaults to the values listed in the preceding table. If `winsize` is larger than `initsize`, SMARTDrive acts as though the two parameters were the same.
NEW MS-DOS 6.2	/U	Specifies that you do not want SMARTDrive to load the CD-ROM caching module. If you specify this switch, SMARTDrive cannot cache any CD-ROM drives. If you don't specify /U, you can enable or disable CD-ROM caching at any time by using the `drive` ± parameter.
	/C	Clears SMARTDrive by writing all write buffers to disk.
NEW MS-DOS 6.2	/R	Resets SMARTDrive by clearing all caches and restarting SMARTDrive.
	/F	Writes cached data to the disk after each command finishes, before the DOS command prompt reappears. This is the default behavior.
NEW MS-DOS 6.2	/N	Writes cached data to the disk whenever the system is idle. To ensure that all data is written to disk, use the /C (Clear) switch.
	/N	(Not DOS 6.22) Forces "verbose" mode, so status messages appear when SMARTDrive starts. In DOS 6.22, this switch has been renamed to /V. You cannot use this switch with /Q.
NEW MS-DOS 6.2	/V	Forces "verbose" mode, so status messages appear when SMARTDrive starts. You cannot use this switch with /Q.
	/Q	Forces "quiet" mode, so status messages do not appear when SMARTDrive starts. (Error messages always appear.) /Q is the default. You cannot use this switch with /N.
	/S	Displays SMARTDrive's status, including what and how drives are cached and a cache hit statistic.
	/L	Forces SMARTDrive to load into low (conventional) memory even if room exists in upper memory.
	/E:`esize`	The element size (in bytes), which is the amount of cache data that SMARTDrive moves in one operation. Values can be 1024, 2048, 4096, and 8192. The default is 8192. The smaller the number, the less memory SMARTDrive takes and the slower the performance.
	/B:`bsize`	The size of the read-ahead buffer (in bytes that are a multiple of `esize`), which is how much SMARTDrive reads beyond a disk request. The default is 16384. The smaller the number, the less memory SMARTDrive takes and the slower the performance.

NOTES

1. Before you turn off or reset your computer, you must perform a SMARTDRV /C operation to guarantee that no data is lost from SMARTDrive's write buffers. SMARTDrive performs the operation automatically if you press Ctrl+Alt+Del.

    SMARTDrive now flushes all write buffers to disk before allowing COMMAND.COM to display the DOS command-line prompt. As long as you haven't turned off this option, you can safely turn off your computer as soon as you see the DOS prompt.

2. For SMARTDrive to use extended memory, you must load HIMEM.SYS or some other extended memory manager.

3. By default, SMARTDRV.EXE tries to load into upper memory. You do not need to use the LOADHIGH command.

4. If you are using double buffering and your system runs slowly, try loading SMARTDrive with the /L switch.

5. Double buffering is required only by some ESDI and SCSI hard disk interfaces.

6. If you have a compressed disk drive, use SMARTDrive on the underlying uncompressed (host) drive.

 7. If you want SMARTDrive to cache a CD-ROM drive, you have to load MSCDEX into memory before SMARTDrive. MSCDEX creates the link that DOS needs to access a CD-ROM drive. If SMARTDrive is loaded before the drive letter is allocated, it will never know that the drive exists. You can enable or disable CD-ROM read caching by using the *drive* ± parameter, or you can disable it completely by using the /U switch. Using the /U switch decreases SMARTDrive's memory use a little.

8. If you are using a third-party CONFIG.SYS and AUTOEXEC.BAT file manager, that utility needs to be set up to perform a SMARTDRV /C operation before it reboots your computer.

9. DOS 6.0 comes with SMARTMON.EXE, a Windows program for monitoring and adjusting SMARTDrive.

EXAMPLES

To start SMARTDrive with all the defaults (a good fit for most systems), use the following command:

```
C:\DOS\SMARTDRV
```

To enable read caching for drive C, read and write caching for drive D, and using a 4MB cache for DOS that can get no smaller than 2MB when Microsoft Windows is running, issue the following command:

```
C:\DOS\SMARTDRV   C   D+ 4096 2048
```

SEE ALSO

BUFFERS=, EMM386.EXE, HIMEM.SYS, SMARTDRV.EXE, and SMARTMON

"Using a Disk Cache (SMARTDrive)" in Chapter 7

SMARTDRV.EXE (DEVICE DRIVER) 6.0 AND LATER— EXTERNAL

When used as a device driver, SMARTDRV.EXE enables double buffering, which is required by certain types of hard disk controllers that cannot work with the memory provided by EMM386.EXE.

SYNTAX

DEVICE=*drive:\path***SMARTDRV.EXE**   /DOUBLE_BUFFER

PARAMETERS AND SWITCHES

drive:\path   Specifies the full path to the SMARTDRV.EXE file on your system. Setup places the SMARTDRV.EXE file in the C:\DOS subdirectory by default. If the full path to SMARTDRV.EXE isn't specified, DOS looks for the file in the root directory of the startup drive.

/DOUBLE_BUFFER   Enables double buffering. Inserting this switch into your CONFIG.SYS file does not hurt if your system does not need it, but it does take up memory. You can remove the switch if all the entries in the buffering column of the SMARTDRV /S display are no. (It may take a while for - entries to turn into no entries.)

NOTES

1. Double buffering is required only by some ESDI and SCSI hard disk interfaces when used on a computer that provides upper memory blocks for DOS to use.

2. If you are using double buffering and your system runs slowly, try loading SMARTDrive with the /L switch.

EXAMPLES

To load the SMARTDrive double-buffering feature, add the following line to your CONFIG.SYS file:

DEVICE=C:\DOS\SMARTDRV.EXE   /DOUBLE_BUFFER

SEE ALSO

DEVICE= and SMARTDRV

"Using a Disk Cache (SMARTDrive)" in Chapter 7

SMARTMON 6.0 AND LATER—WINDOWS

The SMARTDrive Monitor (SMARTMON) is a Windows program that can display the status of the SMARTDrive disk cache and adjust its settings. SMARTMON can even help you update the setting you use to load SMARTDRV in your AUTOEXEC.BAT file. For SMARTMON to be useful, you must be running the SMARTDrive disk cache on your computer.

SMARTMON cannot be run from the DOS command line. You can start SMARTMON from within Windows, for example, by opening the Program Manager's File menu and choosing the Run command. For instructions on using the program, run SMARTMON and press F1 or choose Help from the menu.

SEE ALSO

SMARTDRV

SORT   2.0 AND LATER—EXTERNAL

SORT is a program that reads lines from the standard input device, performs an ASCII sort on those lines, and then writes them to the standard output device. The sort can be in ascending or descending order and can start at any column in the line. SORT is one of the filter programs provided by MS-DOS for use with redirection symbols from the command line.

SYNTAX

SORT /R /+*column* < *source_file* > *dest_file*

or

command | **SORT** /R /+*column*

PARAMETERS AND SWITCHES

< *source_file*   Specifies the name of a file that you want SORT to sort. All the normal defaults for drives and subdirectories apply. Wildcards are not allowed.

> *dest_file*   Specifies the name of a file that you want SORT to write the sorted output to. All the normal defaults for drives and subdirectories apply. Wildcards are not allowed. If the output of SORT is not redirected, it is written to the screen.

command | Pipes the screen output from a command into the SORT program, which displays it sorted. *command* can be any legal DOS command that writes its output to the standard output device (normally the screen).

/+*column*   Starts sorting with the characters in column number *column*. *column* needs to be a positive integer. The default is 1.

/R   Sorts in descending order. Thus, the letter Z comes first and the letter A comes last, followed by the numbers 9 to 0. The default sort order is ascending.

Notes

1. If you do not redirect the input or output, all input is from the keyboard (standard input), and all output is to the video display (standard output). If you redirect input and output, use different names for the input and output files.
2. SORT can handle a maximum file size of 64KB (65,535 characters).
3. SORT sorts text files and discards any information after, and including, the end-of-file marker (Ctrl+Z).
4. SORT uses the collating sequence appropriate to your country code and code-page settings if you are using them.
5. SORT is not case sensitive; that is, the command treats *b* and *B* alike.
6. You cannot set the maximum column that SORT can use to resolve equalities. SORT starts at the /+*column* specified and continues the comparison until the lines are proven unequal or the end of the line is reached. Because of this sorting method, you cannot use SORT to perform a multikey sort by sorting the file more than once.

Examples

To sort the lines in the file WORDS.TXT and display the sorted lines onscreen, use the following command:

```
SORT  <  WORDS.TXT
```

To sort, in reverse order, the lines in the file WORDS.TXT and display the lines onscreen, use this command:

```
SORT  <  WORDS.TXT  /R
```

To start sorting at the eighth character of each line in WORDS.TXT and display the output onscreen, use this command:

```
SORT  /+8  <  WORDS.TXT
```

To display directory information, sorted by file size, use the following command:

```
DIR  |  SORT  /+14
```

(The file size starts in the 14th column.) Unfortunately, other lines, such as the volume label, also are sorted, starting in the 14th column. DIR /O provides a more direct and elaborate way of sorting directory information.

See Also

FIND and MORE

"The SORT Filter" in Chapter 13

SSETUP

SSETUP sets up Stacker software for use by moving the Stacker files from the C:\DOS directory to the C:\Stacker directory.

Syntax

SSETUP /m /t=*drive:* /?

Parameters and Switches

drive:	Specifies the Stacker drive for the temporary installation location.
/m	Specifies that the monochrome display mode be used.
/t=*drive*	Identifies the temporary installation location.
/?	Displays the abbreviated online help.

STAC

STAC accesses the Stacker toolbox to use the DOS Stacker tools.

Syntax

STAC /m /?

Parameters and Switches

/m	Specifies that the monochrome display mode be used.
/?	Displays the abbreviated online help.

STACHIGH.SYS

STACHIGH.SYS loads Stacker high. You must load this device driver by inserting a DEVICE= statement in the CONFIG.SYS file.

Syntax

DEVICE=*drive:\path***stachigh.sys**

Parameters and Switches

drive:\path	Locations of the STACHIGH.SYS file.

STACKER

STACKER mounts or unmounts Stacker drives or displays the Stacker drive map.

Syntax

STACKER *-drive1:* */?*

or

STACKER *drive2:=drive3:\stacvol.xxx*

or

STACKER *@drive4:=\stacvol.xxx*

Parameters and Switches

drive1:	Specifies the Stacker drive for an installation location.
-drive1:	Unmounts the Stacker drive.
drive2:=drive3:\stacvol.xxx	Mounts *drive3\stacvol.xxx* as drive d2.
@drive4:\stacvol.xxx	Mounts *drive4\stacvol.xxx* as drive d4.
/?	Displays the abbreviated online help.

STACKS=   3.2 and later—Internal

Whenever a device needs the computer's attention, it generates an interrupt. Before switching to the appropriate interrupt service routine, DOS stores the information it needs to resume the interrupted task in an area called a *stack*. You can use the STACKS= command to determine how many stacks DOS sets aside for this purpose and how big each stack is. You can use STACKS= only in your CONFIG.SYS file.

Syntax

STACKS=*numstacks,size*

Parameters and Switches

numstacks	The number of stacks to set aside for hardware interrupts. Legal values are 0 and 8 through 64. The default value is 0 for 8088- and 8086-based computers and 9 for all others.
size	The size of each stack in bytes. Legal values are 0 (only if you specify 0 stacks as well) and 32 through 512. The default value is 0 for 8088- and 8086-based computers and 128 for all others.

Notes

1. Both parameters for the STACKS= command are required. Note that a *size* of 0 is allowed only if you are using 0 *numstacks* as well.

2. There is considerable controversy over whether separate hardware stacks are needed for the average computer system, but in general, using at least MS-DOS's default values is a good idea. This uses some memory, but if it saves you from losing your work, it's worthwhile. Almost all the devices attached to your computer generate interrupts and if they all want attention at once, they can quickly exhaust a low STACKS= setting. When the internal DOS stacks overflow, an error message appears (see the first item, Internal Stack Overflow, in the following "Messages" section), and the system halts. MemMaker often increases the STACKS= setting to 9,256.

   STACKS=0,0 forces DOS to use the active program's stack space when servicing hardware interrupts. Many people run their computers with this setting and never experience any problems. But be warned that STACKS=0,0 may work for months and then, without warning, overflow a program's stack space, crashing your computer. If you are using this setting and see a Stack Overflow error message, increase the STACKS= setting to at least 9,128 or 9,256.

3. If you are not using the STACKS=0,0 setting, try to limit your choices for the *size* parameter to 128, 256, or 512. Using these settings isn't required, but specifying a *size* that is an even power of two makes the stacks easier for DOS to manage. Also, except when you're using the STACKS=0,0 setting, avoid *size* values less than 128. A small stack is much more likely to overflow, and you are just asking for trouble if you set the size of DOS's hardware stacks to anything less than 128.

Examples

To use the default number of stacks but increase their size to 256 bytes each, use the following line in your CONFIG.SYS file. (This setting has virtually become the standard for people who are not disabling internal stacks in their computers.)

```
STACKS=9,256
```

To instruct DOS not to set up any internal stacks, and use the active program's stack space for servicing interrupts, include the following line in your CONFIG.SYS file:

```
STACKS=0,0
```

Messages

```
Internal stack overflow
System halted
```

Error: The stack that MS-DOS was using to service interrupts has overflowed, and the system has been halted. You need to restart your computer. If you have this problem, increase the *numstacks* and/or *size* setting for the STACKS= command in your CONFIG.SYS file.

Exception Error 12

Error: Same as the preceding message, except that this message is displayed when you are running in protected mode (for example, under Windows).

Invalid STACK parameters

Warning: You have specified an invalid parameter on the STACKS= line in your CONFIG.SYS file. Check the entry to make sure that you have specified values for both *numstacks* and *size* and that these values are within the legal range for the STACKS= command.

 ## SUBMENU=   6.0 AND LATER—INTERNAL

SUBMENU= is one of the new CONFIG.SYS menu commands. With it, you can create a multi-level menu from which to choose your startup configuration. You can use SUBMENU= only inside a menu block in your CONFIG.SYS file.

SYNTAX

SUBMENU=*blockname, menutext*

PARAMETERS AND SWITCHES

blockname The name of the menu block that you want to display when this menu item is chosen. ***blockname*** can be up to 70 characters long, but it can't contain any spaces or the following special characters:

\   /   ,   ;   =   [   ]

(For more details, see the entry for [*blockname*] in this command reference.) This argument is required.

menutext The text you want DOS to display for this menu line. *menutext* can be up to 70 characters long and contain any text you want, including spaces. Separate *menutext* from ***blockname*** with a comma. If no *menutext* is provided, DOS displays the ***blockname*** in the menu.

NOTES

1. The SUBMENU= command can appear only inside menu blocks in CONFIG.SYS.

> **Note**
>
> CONFIG.SYS allows two types of blocks: menu blocks and configuration blocks. Each block begins with a [*blockname*], and includes all the lines that follow, up to the next [*blockname*]. Menu blocks, which are blocks named [MENU] or defined with a SUBMENU= command, can include only menu-related commands. All other CONFIG.SYS commands belong in configuration blocks.

2. Up to nine choices can be displayed in a menu, so you are limited to nine MENUITEM= and SUBMENU= commands in each menu block. Each menu item appears onscreen in the order that it appears in the menu block, numbered from 1 to 9.

> **Tip**
> Before you construct an extensive menu system in CONFIG.SYS, remember that you will have to wade through it each time you reboot your computer. A simple startup menu, with a handful of options and perhaps one submenu, works best.

3. If DOS cannot find the block referred to by a SUBMENU= command in your CONFIG.SYS file, it doesn't display that choice in the menu. Your startup menu may fail if SUBMENU= doesn't refer to a valid menu block.
4. In a multiconfiguration submenu, you can return to the previous menu by pressing the Backspace key.

EXAMPLES

Suppose that you're using a main menu that enables you to choose from three basic configurations for your computer: Windows, DOS, and Maintenance. For the DOS configuration, you want to add a submenu with two variations: One configures memory for normal DOS programs, and the other provides your CADD program with the special memory interface it requires. To do so, add the following lines to your CONFIG.SYS file:

```
[MENU]
MENUITEM=WIN, Configure for Windows (Default)
SUBMENU=DOS, Configure for MS-DOS
MENUITEM=MAINT, Configure for File & Disk Maintenance
MENUDEFAULT=WIN, 30
[DOS]
MENUITEM=NORMAL, Configure for Normal MS-DOS Programs
MENUITEM=CADD, Configure for CADD with INT15 Interface
MENUDEFAULT=NORMAL, 30
```

When you include these lines in your CONFIG.SYS file, DOS searches for blocks named [WIN], [DOS], and [MAINT]. If those blocks exist in the file, the main menu that DOS displays looks something like the following:

```
MS-DOS 6 Startup Menu
=====================

1. Configure for Windows (Default)
2. Configure for MS-DOS
3. Configure for File & Disk Maintenance

Enter a choice: 1
```

Entering 1, 2, or 3 at this menu instructs DOS to execute the [WIN], [DOS], or [MAINT] block, respectively. If no entry is made within about 30 seconds, DOS chooses the [WIN] configuration by default. As long as the [NORMAL] and [CADD] blocks exist in CONFIG.SYS, choosing 2 brings up the following submenu.

```
MS-DOS 6 Startup Menu
=====================

1. Configure for Normal MS-DOS Programs
2. Configure for CADD with INT15 Interface

Enter a choice: 1
```

Entering 1 or 2 at this menu instructs DOS to execute the [NORMAL] or [CADD] configuration block, respectively. If you do not make an entry within about 30 seconds, DOS chooses the [NORMAL] configuration by default. To return to the first menu, press the Backspace key.

SEE ALSO

[*blockname*], MENUCOLOR=, MENUDEFAULT=, and MENUITEM=

"Creating Multiple Configurations" in Chapter 2

SUBST   3.1 AND LATER—EXTERNAL

SUBST is one of the pretender commands. It can create a drive alias for a subdirectory and fool many (but not all) programs. You might need to use SUBST to get older programs that don't understand subdirectories to run. Unless you have a specific use for SUBST, however, avoid it. You can easily make a mistake and lose data when you are pretending.

SYNTAX

SUBST *alias: drive:path* /D

PARAMETERS AND SWITCHES

alias: Specifies a valid drive name that becomes the alias, or nickname. *alias:* may be a nonexistent drive, but it must be available for use and less than or equal to the value specified by the LASTDRIVE= command in your CONFIG.SYS file.

drive:path   Specifies the drive name and directory path to be nicknamed *alias:*. The default for *drive:* is the current drive. You cannot specify the /D parameter when you create an alias by using *drive:path*.

/D   Deletes the alias drive. Do not specify a *drive:path* parameter when you are deleting an alias drive.

NOTES

1. Entering SUBST with no parameters displays a list of all the drive substitutions currently defined.

2. The drive letter you use as the alias drive must be available and within the range specified with the LASTDRIVE= command in your CONFIG.SYS file. You cannot use drive letters reserved by Interlnk as SUBST drive aliases. If a drive letter is already in use as a SUBST drive alias, you must delete the previous assignment before assigning that drive letter to another *drive:path*.

3. You cannot create SUBST alias drives that refer to subdirectories on a drive that is not local to your computer. Network, CD-ROM, and Interlnk drives are all redirected drives and cannot be used with SUBST.

4. When you delete an alias drive created by the SUBST command, include the drive letter of the alias drive, not the subdirectory that the alias refers to. For example, to delete the alias drive E, enter the following line at the DOS prompt:
   ```
   SUBST  E:  /D
   ```

5. You can't use any of the following DOS commands on an alias drive created by the SUBST command:

ASSIGN	FORMAT
BACKUP	JOIN
CHKDSK	LABEL
DEFRAG	MIRROR
DISKCOMP	RECOVER
DISKCOPY	RESTORE
FDISK	SYS

   The preceding commands refuse to work on an alias drive created by SUBST, so if you do try to use them, no harm will be done.

6. Do not create or delete any SUBST alias drives while Microsoft Windows is running. If you create the SUBST aliases before starting Microsoft Windows, you can use the alias drives from within a DOS session in Windows.

MESSAGES

```
Cannot SUBST a network drive
```

Error: You tried to use a nonlocal drive as the alias drive. You cannot use network, Interlnk, or CD-ROM drives with SUBST.

```
Drive already SUBSTed
```

Error: You are trying to create a new SUBST drive alias using a drive letter that already is a SUBST drive alias. Delete the previous assignment by entering SUBST *drive:* /D and try again.

```
Invalid parameter
```

Error: The value that you specified for the alias drive (*alias:*) is invalid. You might need to increase the value specified by the LASTDRIVE= command in your CONFIG.SYS file. This message is also displayed if you try to create an alias for a subdirectory on an alias drive. The *drive:path* parameter for the SUBST command must refer to a real local disk drive.

See Also

ASSIGN and JOIN

"The SUBST Command" in Chapter 11

SWITCH

You can use the SWITCH command to enable several different optional subroutines in a CONFIG.SYS file.

Syntax

SWITCH *label1, label2, ...*

Parameters and Switches

label1, label2, ...   The names of up to nine subroutines in the CONFIG.SYS file. The subroutine names are preceded by a colon (:) at the beginning of the line in the CONFIG.SYS file and subroutine blocks end with RETURN.

SWITCHES=   5.0 and later—Internal

The SWITCHES= command is a collection of options that configure DOS for certain circumstances. Options enable you to move the WINA20.386 file out of the root directory, cause an enhanced keyboard to behave like a standard keyboard, and disable DOS 6's new startup keys. You can use SWITCHES= only in your CONFIG.SYS file.

Syntax

SWITCHES=/K   /F   /N   /W

Parameters and Switches

/K   Forces an enhanced keyboard to behave as though it were an older, standard keyboard.

/F   (DOS 6 only) Eliminates the two-second pause that occurs when the Starting MS-DOS... message appears onscreen.

/N   (DOS 6 only) Disables the F5 Clean and F8 Interactive boot keys.

/W   Enables you to move the WINA20.386 file out of the root directory of your startup drive.

Notes

1. The SWITCHES= command can be located anywhere in your CONFIG.SYS file. DOS scans the file looking for it before displaying the Starting MS-DOS... message.

2. If you are having problems with an older application incorrectly interpreting your enhanced keyboard, the /K switch might solve your problems. Enhanced keyboards normally generate certain key codes that were not available on the older 84-key keyboards. Specifying /K forces DOS to translate these new key codes into their equivalent 84-key keyboard codes.

   The /K switch affects only programs that get their keyboard input from DOS. Many programs bypass DOS, getting keyboard input from the BIOS or, in some cases, directly from the keyboard. For these programs, the /K switch has no effect.

3. If you are using both the /K switch and ANSI.SYS device driver, make sure to include a /K switch on the line that loads ANSI.SYS as well.

4. By disabling DOS 6.22's F5 Clean and F8 Interactive boot keys with the /N switch, you force your computer to always start up with the CONFIG.SYS and AUTOEXEC.BAT files that are present in your root directory. If security is a concern, and you load security features in these files, you might want to specify this switch. To truly secure your computer, however, you might need to lock your floppy drives, protect your startup files, and take other precautions as well. This switch is only a minor obstacle to a determined user and is meant as a simple means to perhaps "user-proof" a menu system.

Note Before you specify the /N switch, be sure that you have a bootable floppy disk that starts up your system in a usable condition. (You need access to your hard drive and at least a text editor such as EDIT to fix your startup files.) Never specify this switch until you have completely debugged your CONFIG.SYS and AUTOEXEC.BAT files.

5. The /F switch is intended to be used with the /N switch. After you have disabled the F5 and F8 keys, you don't need a two-second pause at startup so that you can press them.

6. Windows 3.0 in enhanced mode requires the WINA20.386 driver file to be available before it loads. (See the first message in the following "Messages" section.) If you want to move the WINA20.386 file out of your root directory, you need to specify the /W switch in CONFIG.SYS and add the following line to the [386Enh] section of your SYSTEM.INI file:

   DEVICE=*drive:**path*\WINA20.386

   You should specify the full drive and path to WINA20.386 in the device line in SYSTEM.INI.

Note Windows 3.1 can load successfully in enhanced mode without access to the WINA20.386 driver, but any version 3.0 drivers that you're using may still require the services of the WINA20.386 driver. If they do and that driver is unavailable, Windows may become unstable or crash. Because enhanced-mode drivers for Windows are distributed with many software packages, most people are running Windows 3.1 with Windows 3.0 drivers without knowing it. To be safe, be sure that the WINA20.386 driver is available, either in the root directory or through the /W switch and a device line in SYSTEM.INI.

Examples

You depend on an older application that doesn't respond to the right-side Shift and Ctrl keys properly. To force your enhanced keyboard to return the same keycodes for both the left and right Shift and Ctrl keys, you include the following line in your CONFIG.SYS file:

```
SWITCHES=/K
```

If you use ANSI.SYS, remember to add the /K switch to the DEVICE= line that loads ANSI.SYS as well.

Perhaps you have set up a menu system that you want everyone who uses your computer to use. To avoid having people bypass it, you might want to disable the new DOS 6 interactive startup features by adding the following line in your CONFIG.SYS file:

```
SWITCHES=/F /N
```

Although you use Windows 3.1, you're not sure whether all your Windows enhanced-mode drivers have been updated yet and want to make sure that the WINA20.386 driver is available, just in case. Because you've moved the WINA20.386 file into the C:\DOS subdirectory with your other DOS 6.x files, you need to include the following line in your CONFIG.SYS file:

```
SWITCHES=/W
```

Now that DOS knows you've moved WINA20.386, you need to tell Windows where you put it. To do so, add the following line to the [386Enh] section of your SYSTEM.INI file, which is located in your main Windows subdirectory:

```
DEVICE=C:\DOS\WINA20.386
```

Messages

```
You must have the file WINA20.386 in the root directory of your boot drive to
run Windows in Enhanced Mode
```

Error: This message is displayed only if you are running Windows 3.0 in enhanced mode and the WINA20.386 file is not present in your root directory. To enable Windows 3.0 to run in enhanced mode with the WINA20.386 driver located somewhere else, specify the SWITCHES=/W command in your CONFIG.SYS file and enter a DEVICE=*drive:\path*\WINA20.386 line in the [386Enh] section of SYSTEM.INI.

See Also

ANSI.SYS and WINA20.386

"Using the SWITCHES Command" in Chapter 19

SYS   1.0 AND LATER—EXTERNAL

SYS can make a floppy disk bootable without reformatting the disk. It places a copy of DOS (the hidden system files IO.SYS, MSDOS.SYS, and COMMAND.COM for MS-DOS; the files IBMBIO.COM, IBMDOS.COM, and COMMAND.COM for IBM DOS) on the specified disk. In DOS 6, DBLSPACE.BIN also can be copied.

Syntax

SYS *source* *drive*:

Parameters and Switches

source   The source drive and path for the system files. This parameter defaults to the root directory of the current drive for the system files and to the file pointed to by the environment variable COMSPEC for the command-line interpreter (generally, COMMAND.COM).

drive: The drive that is to receive the copies of the DOS files from the root directory of the current drive. The trailing colon (*:*) is required.

Notes

1. You must specify the drive that will receive a copy of DOS.

2. In pre-4.0 versions of DOS, the disk that was to receive the DOS operating system files was required to have sufficient contiguous free space for the files IO.SYS and MSDOS.SYS (IBMBIO.COM and IBMDOS.COM in IBM DOS). Subsequent versions of DOS require only that enough free space exist, not that the space be contiguous.

3. SYS copies the DOS system files from the root directory of the current disk (or *source* if it was specified) to the destination *drive:*. If the DOS system files (IO.SYS and MSDOS.SYS) are not found and the source drive is a floppy disk drive, you are prompted to insert a system disk into the drive. If the source disk is a hard drive, reenter the SYS command and specify where the DOS system files are located by adding the *source* parameter.

4. You cannot use SYS in a networked drive; in a drive formed by ASSIGN, JOIN, or SUBST; or in an Interlnk drive.

5. In pre-5.0 versions of DOS, you have to copy COMMAND.COM to the target disk in a separate step.

6. SYS looks for a copy of COMMAND.COM either in the root directory of the current drive or in the subdirectory specified by the *source* parameter if one is specified. If COMMAND.COM is not found, a warning message is displayed. When you see this message, use the COPY command to add a copy of COMMAND.COM to the disk.

7. With DOS 6, SYS copies the DBLSPACE.BIN file to the system disk you are creating even if you do not use DoubleSpace. If SYS is unable to find the DBLSPACE.BIN file, no error message is displayed. SYS searches the DOS PATH for DBLSPACE.BIN if the file isn't found in the same location as the other system files.

Messages

```
Could not copy COMMAND.COM onto target disk
```

Warning: SYS was unable to find the file COMMAND.COM in the root directory of the current drive or, if you specified a *source* parameter, in the *source* subdirectory. To make the disk bootable, use the COPY command to copy COMMAND.COM to the disk.

```
Insert system disk in drive d:
and strike any key when ready
```

Prompt: SYS cannot find the DOS system files (IO.SYS and MSDOS.SYS) on the floppy drive that you specified with the *source* parameter (or the root directory of the current drive if you didn't specify a *source* parameter). Insert a floppy disk that contains the DOS system files.

```
Invalid path or System files not found
```

Error: You executed the SYS command with a *source* parameter, but SYS cannot find the DOS system files in the subdirectory you specified. This message is displayed if the *source* subdirectory is invalid or does not contain the files IO.SYS and MSDOS.SYS. Correct your *source* parameter entry and retry the command.

```
No room for system on destination disk
```

Error: The disk you are trying to make bootable with SYS doesn't have enough free space for the system files. Delete some of the files on the disk and try the SYS command again.

```
No system on default disk drive
```

Error: You executed the SYS command without specifying a *source* parameter, but SYS cannot find the DOS system files (IO.SYS and MSDOS.SYS) on the current hard drive. Reenter the SYS command, specifying the location of the DOS system files by adding the *source* parameter.

```
SYS cannot operate on target drive
```

Error: SYS cannot transfer the system files (IO.SYS and MSDOS.SYS) to the target drive. You may get this message if you try to use SYS to make a DoubleSpace-compressed drive bootable. SYS can transfer the DOS system files to the host drive but not to the DoubleSpace-compressed drive. SYS is unable to transfer the DOS system files to network and Interlnk drives as well.

```
System transferred
```

Information: SYS has placed the files IO.SYS, MSDOS.SYS, COMMAND.COM, and possibly DBLSPACE.BIN on the target disk.

SEE ALSO

FORMAT

SYSINFO

SYSINFO gathers and displays information about the computer system. This information is gathered in a file called SYSINFO.TXT or a filename designated. You can view it in browse mode by using the E editor.

Syntax

SYSINFO /e=filename /h /n=filename /r /q /s /w /wr: /f /t /?

Parameters and Switches

/e=filename	Uses the specified program for editing.
/h	Gathers and displays hardware information only.
/n=filename	Writes output to a specified file (rather than to SYSINFO.TXT).
/r	Displays preexisting SYSINFO.TXT (or a file specified by /n).
/q	Gathers and displays a Quick Info string only.
/s	Gathers and displays software information only.
/w	Gathers and displays Windows information only.
/wr:	Gathers Windows information from all drives.
/f	Gathers and displays Stacker volume information only.
/t	Uses the TMP or TEMP directory for the output file.
/?	Displays the abbreviated online help.

TASKMGR

TASKMGR is a menu-driven utility to load more than one DOS program simultaneously and switch between them. The following syntax and parameters are valid for systems with a 386 or higher processor and at least 2MB of memory. Background programs continue to run when in multitasking mode.

Syntax

TASKMGR /M /S /? /S?

Parameters and Switches

/M	Allows you to switch with the numbers on the main keyboard. Normally, you switch between tasks in TASKMGR by using the keys on the numeric keypad.
/S	Loads TASKMGR in task-switching mode instead of multitasking. In task-switching mode, background applications are suspended.
/?	Displays abbreviated help for multitasking.
/S?	Displays abbreviated help for task switching.

NOTES

Use the DR DOS setup utility to configure and load TASKMGR permanently.

TIME   1.0 AND LATER—INTERNAL

The TIME command can display and set the current time for your computer. Normally, DOS and your computer's hardware attempt to keep the time set properly. If you don't have an AUTOEXEC.BAT file, DOS prompts you to enter the current date each time your computer reboots.

SYNTAX

TIME *hh:mm:ss.xx* A|P

To display the time and have DOS prompt you to enter a new time, use the following format:

TIME

PARAMETERS AND SWITCHES

hh   The one- or two-digit number that represents hours (0 to 23). To set the time, this parameter is required.

mm   The one- or two-digit number that represents minutes (0 to 59). This parameter is optional.

ss   The one- or two-digit number that represents seconds (0 to 59). This parameter is optional.

xx   The one- or two-digit number that represents hundredths of a second (0 to 99). This parameter is optional.

A|P   Entering an A or a P can designate a.m. or p.m., respectively. You can use upper- or lowercase letters. If you do not use A or P, you must enter the time in 24-hour (military) format.

NOTES

1. Depending on the country code setting in your CONFIG.SYS file, a comma may be the separator between seconds and hundredths of seconds. (Refer to the section on the COUNTRY command earlier in this command reference.)

2. The TIME command sets the computer's internal 24-hour clock. The time and date are recorded in the directory when you create or change a file. This information can help you find the most recent version of a file when you check your directory.

3. Most PCs use an internal clock, backed up by a battery, that is accurate to about one minute a month, so you rarely have to set the time after you set it initially. If your system does not retain the time after you turn off your computer, however, put TIME and

DATE commands in your AUTOEXEC.BAT file so that DOS does not default to a nonsense time and date when you turn on your computer.

4. If you press Enter after the time prompt, DOS does not change the current time.

SEE ALSO

COUNTRY= and DATE

"Issuing the TIME Command" in Chapter 10

TIMEOUT

 TIMEOUT specifies how long to wait for a user response to a SWITCH or ? statement in a CONFIG.SYS file. In the case of SWITCH, after the specified TIMEOUT period, the first option is executed. In the case of ?, the command that ? applies to is skipped. TIMEOUT should precede the SWITCH or ? statement in the CONFIG.SYS file.

SYNTAX

TIMEOUT=*n*

PARAMETERS AND SWITCHES

=*n* Time to wait in seconds.

SEE ALSO

? and SWITCH

TOUCH

TOUCH modifies the date and time DOS lists for a file or set of files.

SYNTAX

TOUCH *drive:\path\filespec* /T:*hh:mm:ss* /D:*date* /F:E|J|U /P /R /S /?

PARAMETERS AND SWITCHES

drive:\path\filespec	The path and filename or file specification for which to change the date or time.
/T:*hh:mm:ss*	Sets the file time in hours *hh* starting at 00 for midnight and running to 23, minutes *mm* from 0 to 59, and seconds *ss* from 0 to 59.

/D:*date*	Sets the file date. The date format is determined by your system country code.
	Europe date format is *dd-mm-yyyy*
	Japan date format is *yyyy-mm-dd*
	U.S. date format is *mm-dd-yyyy*
/F:E|J|U	Overrides the system country code and uses European, Japanese, or U.S. date format.
/P	Prompts before changing the date or time of each file.
/R	Includes read-only files when changing the date and time.
/S	Includes files in subdirectories when changing files according to a filespec.
/?	Displays abbreviated help.

TREE 2.0 AND LATER—EXTERNAL

The TREE command displays a visual representation of the subdirectory structure on your disk, which is often referred to as the *directory tree*. TREE can be useful for printing a map of your hard drive if you redirect its output to your printer.

SYNTAX

TREE *drive:path*   /F   /A

PARAMETERS AND SWITCHES

drive:	Specifies the drive that holds the disk for which you want to display the directory structure. If you omit *drive:*, DOS assumes the current drive.
path	Specifies the subdirectory in which you want the examination to start. If you omit *path*, DOS displays a directory tree that starts with the current directory.
/F	Displays all files in each directory. Using the /F switch can make the output generated by TREE rather lengthy.
/A	Uses ASCII characters rather than the default graphics characters to display the connection of subdirectories. If you are redirecting the output of TREE to your printer, you might want to use this switch. Not all printers can print the block graphics characters that TREE uses in its display.

SEE ALSO

CD or CHDIR, DELTREE, MD or MKDIR, MOVE, and RD or RMDIR

"Listing Directories with TREE" in Chapter 5

TUNER

TUNER displays the Stacker online tuner interface, allowing the choice of compression speed for the system.

SYNTAX

TUNER /m /?

PARAMETERS AND SWITCHES

/m   Uses the monochrome display mode.

/?   Displays the abbreviated online help.

TYPE   1.0 AND LATER—INTERNAL

The TYPE command displays the contents of a file onscreen. If the file is an ASCII text file, you are able to read it. If it's a binary file, however, the screen may seem to fill up with gibberish while beeping, and you may think you've broken your computer. No harm has been done, but displaying binary files onscreen is a fairly useless operation. The CLS command cleans up the mess for you.

SYNTAX

TYPE *pathname*

PARAMETERS AND SWITCHES

pathname   The file that you want TYPE to display. If you do not specify a drive, DOS assumes the current drive. If you do not specify a subdirectory path, DOS assumes the current directory. The filename portion of this parameter is required. Wildcards are not allowed.

NOTES

1. The TYPE command displays a file's characters onscreen. You can use TYPE to see a file's contents.

2. Strange characters appear onscreen when you use TYPE for some data files and most program files because TYPE tries to display the machine-language instructions as ASCII characters.

3. As you can with most other DOS commands, you can redirect the output of TYPE to the printer by adding > PRN to the command line or by pressing Ctrl+PrtSc. Don't forget to press Ctrl+PrtSc again to turn off the printing instruction.

4. To keep the contents of a long file from scrolling off the screen before you can read them, you can pipe the output of TYPE through MORE. Alternatively, you can press Ctrl+S to stop the display and Ctrl+Q to restart it.

EXAMPLES

To display the contents of the DOS README.TXT file one screen at a time, use the following command:

```
TYPE  C:\DOS\README.TXT   |   MORE
```

SEE ALSO

MORE

"Viewing Files" in Chapter 8

UMBCGA.SYS

UMBCGA.SYS maps the video memory of a color adapter as upper memory blocks (UMBs) that are used for loading programs with the LOADHIGH command if a CGA, EGA, or VGA adapter also is present in combination with a monochrome adapter.

UMBCGA.SYS is one of the installable device drivers provided with DOS. You must load it by using either a DEVICE= or DEVICEHIGH= command in the CONFIG.SYS file.

SYNTAX

DEVICE=*drive:\path***umbcga.sys**

PARAMETERS AND SWITCHES

drive:\path   Location of the device driver file.

NOTES

Programs that directly write into color adapter memory are likely to crash the computer. UMBCGA.SYS includes defense mechanisms, but they are not foolproof.

UMBEMS.SYS

UMBEMS.SYS maps a 64KB block of EMS memory as upper memory blocks (UMBs) that are used for loading programs with the LOADHIGH command if an EMS card with at least 64KB of EMS also is present in a computer.

UMBEMS.SYS is one of the installable device drivers provided with DOS. You must load it by using either a DEVICE= or DEVICEHIGH= command in the CONFIG.SYS file.

SYNTAX

DEVICE=*drive:\path***umbems.sys**

PARAMETERS AND SWITCHES

drive:\path   Location of the device driver file.

UMBHERC.SYS

UMBHERC.SYS maps the video memory of a Hercules adapter as upper memory blocks (UMBs) that are used for loading programs with the LOADHIGH command if a Hercules graphics adapter or Hercules Graphics Adapter Plus also is present.

UMBHERC.SYS is one of the installable device drivers provided with DOS. You must load it by using either a DEVICE= or DEVICEHIGH= command in the CONFIG.SYS file.

Syntax

DEVICE=*drive:\path*umbherc.sys /x

Parameters and Switches

drive:\path   Specifies the location of the device driver file.

/x   Omits the video memory DMA test during startup. This switch should be used only after an adapter has successfully passed the test. Adapters that fail this test are not compatible with UMBHERC.SYS.

Notes

Programs that use the Hercules card in its graphics modes are incompatible with this device driver. If the Hercules card is one of the RAMFONT type, any program that uses the RAMFONT capability also is incompatible with this device driver.

UMBMONO.SYS

UMBMONO.SYS maps the video memory of the monochrome adapter as upper memory blocks (UMBs) that are used for loading programs with the LOADHIGH command if a CGA, EGA, or VGA adapter also is present.

UMBMONO.SYS is one of the installable device drivers provided with DOS. You must load it by using either a DEVICE= or DEVICEHIGH= command in the CONFIG.SYS file.

Syntax

DEVICE=*drive:\path*umbmono.sys

Parameters and Switches

drive:\path   Location of the device driver file.

Notes

Programs that directly write into monochrome adapter memory are likely to crash the computer. UMBMONO.SYS includes defense mechanisms, but they are not foolproof.

UNCOMP

UNCOMP uncompresses all the data stored in the Stacker drive, storing it on the original uncompressed disk. The `stacvol` file is deleted.

Syntax

UNCOMP *drive:* /?

Parameters and Switches

drive: Indicates the Stacker drive to decompress.

/? Displays the abbreviated online help.

UNDELETE   5.0 AND LATER—EXTERNAL

UNDELETE recovers files that were deleted with the DEL command. In DOS 5.0, UNDELETE uses MIRROR's delete tracking file (if available) to restore a deleted file. In DOS 6, UNDELETE uses a delete sentry file or a delete tracking file (if either exists) to restore a deleted file. Either version may be able to restore a deleted file without any special files if the file was deleted recently and little disk activity has occurred since the deletion.

Syntax

In DOS 5.0, use the following format:

UNDELETE *pathname* /LIST /DT /DOS /ALL

In DOS 6, to load the memory-resident program that UNDELETE uses for delete sentry and delete tracking protection, use the following format:

UNDELETE /LOAD /S*drive* /T*drive-entries*

In DOS 6, to manipulate UNDELETE, use the following format:

UNDELETE /LIST /ALL /PURGE*drive* /STATUS /UNLOAD

In DOS 6, to undelete one or more files, use the following format:

UNDELETE *pathname* /DT /DS /DOS /LIST /ALL

Parameters and Switches

pathname Specifies the file or files that you want to undelete. If you do not specify a drive, DOS assumes the current drive. If you do not specify a subdirectory path, DOS assumes the current directory. Wildcards are allowed. If you omit this parameter, DOS undeletes all deleted files in the current directory.

Switch	Description
/ALL	Restores files without prompting. The Delete Sentry method is used if it is available. Otherwise, the Delete Tracker method is used, if it is available. If neither method is available, the normal DOS directory method is used (see the "Notes" section for this command). You can use /ALL with any of the other switches.
/DOS	Restores files that DOS lists as deleted. UNDELETE prompts you before each file is restored.
/DS	Recovers only the files listed in the SENTRY directory. UNDELETE prompts you before each file is restored.
/DT	Restores only the files listed in the delete tracking file. UNDELETE prompts you before each file is restored.
/LIST	Provides a list of deleted files but does not undelete them. The type of list produced varies with the use of the /DT, /DS, and /DOS switches.
/LOAD	Loads the Undelete memory-resident program into conventional memory, using the UNDELETE.INI file. If that file does not exist, UNDELETE creates a default UNDELETE.INI file.
/PURGE*drive*	Deletes the contents of the SENTRY directory created by Delete Sentry protection. *drive* defaults to the current drive.
/S*drive*	Enables Delete Sentry protection and loads the Undelete memory-resident program into memory, using the UNDELETE.INI file. *drive* defaults to the current drive.
/STATUS	Displays the type of protection in effect for each drive.
/T*drive-entries*	Enables Delete Tracker protection and loads the Undelete memory-resident program into memory, using the UNDELETE.INI file. The *drive* parameter is the drive for which you want Delete Tracker protection. *entries* is a number (ranging from 1 through 999) that specifies the maximum number of entries in the delete tracking file, PCTRACKR.DEL. DOS determines the default value by the factors in the following list:

Disk Size	Entries	PCTRACKR.DEL Size
360KB	25	5KB
720KB	50	9KB
1.2MB	75	14KB
1.44MB	75	14KB
20MB	101	18KB
32MB	202	36KB
Larger than 32MB	303	55KB

/UNLOAD   Unloads the Undelete memory-resident program from memory, disabling Delete Tracker or Delete Sentry protection if either was active. UNDELETE is unable to release the memory it was using if any other memory-resident software has been loaded after it.

Rules

1. UNDELETE cannot restore deleted subdirectories.
2. UNDELETE cannot restore a file if you deleted the subdirectory that contained the file.
3. Do not use Delete Tracker for any drive that has been redirected with JOIN or SUBST.

Notes

1. UNDELETE restores deleted files, using the delete tracking or delete sentry file (if either exists), or the standard DOS directory.
2. Delete Sentry provides the highest level of protection by saving deleted files in a SENTRY directory. The size of the SENTRY directory (including the files that it contains) is limited to approximately 7 percent of your disk. DOS purges old files to make room for new ones.
3. Delete Tracker provides an intermediate level of protection by maintaining a hidden file called PCTRACKR.DEL that records the locations of a file's allocation units (clusters). You can recover a deleted file until its freed allocation units are allocated to a new file. Delete Tracker takes the same amount of memory as Delete Sentry.
4. When you delete a file, DOS removes the first character in the filename. If you use UNDELETE with the /DOS switch, you are prompted for a character to replace the missing first character. If you use the /ALL switch, and if a delete tracking or delete sentry file does not exist, UNDELETE restores each deleted file without prompts, using the character # as the first character of the filename. A deleted file named BETTER.TXT, for example, is undeleted as #ETTER.TXT.

    If BETTER.TXT and LETTER.TXT are deleted, DOS restores BETTER.TXT as #ETTER.TXT and LETTER.TXT as %ETTER.TXT. UNDELETE tries the following replacement characters for the first letter of the filename, in the order shown, until a unique filename is found:

    The pound sign (#)

    The percentage sign (%)

    The ampersand (&)

    The digits 0 through 9

    The characters *A* through *Z*

5. Although UNDELETE enables you to recover files that you deleted accidentally, do not use this command as a substitute for backing up data. Be sure to keep up to date backups of your data.

EXAMPLES

For the following examples, assume that the DOS commands are stored in a directory that is in your PATH.

To restore all deleted files in the root directory of drive C without prompting for confirmation on each file, use this command:

`C:\UNDELETE /ALL`

To provide a list of all currently deleted files, use the following command:

`UNDELETE /LIST`

To create `C:\PCTRACKR.DEL` to track up to 200 deleted files on drive C and load the memory-resident portion of UNDELETE, use this command:

`UNDELETE /TC-200`

SEE ALSO

MWUNDEL and UNFORMAT

"Recovering Deleted Files with UNDELETE" in Chapter 9

UNFORMAT   5.0 AND LATER—EXTERNAL

The UNFORMAT utility can recover a disk that was inadvertently reformatted. In DOS 5.0, UNFORMAT uses the files produced by the MIRROR command (if those files are available) to restore the disk to its condition before reformatting. In DOS 5.0 and 6, you probably can unformat disks if they were not formatted with FORMAT /U. The UNFORMAT command works on both hard disks and floppy disks.

SYNTAX

UNFORMAT *drive***:** /J /L /P /U /TEST /PARTN

PARAMETERS AND SWITCHES

*drive***:**	Specifies the drive where the deleted file resides. This parameter is required.
/J	Confirms that the MIRROR command contains the necessary information to restore the disk. This switch does not unformat the disk.
/L	Lists all files and directory names found. If used with the /PARTN switch, /L displays current partition tables. The default (no /L) is to list only subdirectories and fragmented files.
/P	Directs all output to the printer connected to LPT1.
/PARTN	Restores the partition table of a hard disk. You must use the PARTNSAV.FIL file created by the MIRROR /PARTN command.

/TEST	Shows how UNFORMAT will re-create the information on the disk. Like the /J switch, this switch does not actually unformat the disk.
/U	Unformats without using the mirror files.

Rules

1. To unformat your hard disk, you first must reboot from drive A, using a specially prepared floppy disk (see the "Notes" section for this command).
2. If you format a floppy disk by using the FORMAT /U switch, UNFORMAT cannot restore the disk.
3. UNFORMAT works only on disks that use sector sizes of 512, 1024, or 2048 bytes.
4. The /J, /U, and /PARTN parameters for UNFORMAT were omitted from the documentation for MS-DOS 6, but UNFORMAT still supports them. They are included in the FASTHELP that you display by entering UNDELETE /? at the DOS command prompt.

Notes

1. UNFORMAT attempts to recover a formatted disk by using the MIRROR.FIL and MIRORSAV.FIL files created by the MIRROR command or by using information in the disk's root directory and file allocation table. The second process is slower and less reliable than the first.
2. To prepare for the eventuality that you may need to use UNFORMAT, format a floppy disk (using the /S switch to make the disk bootable) and then transfer the UNFORMAT.EXE file to that disk. Also, transfer the CONFIG.SYS files, the AUTOEXEC.BAT files, and any device drivers needed for the computer's operation. Thereafter, if you accidentally format the hard disk, you can boot from the floppy disk and perform an UNFORMAT operation.

    Before you use UNFORMAT to recover the disk, use the command with the /J or /TEST switches to determine whether your mirror files are up to date or whether the UNFORMAT command can recover files in the way that you want.
3. In DOS 6, UNFORMAT cannot recover fragmented files. DOS asks you whether you want to recover such files by truncating them at the end of their contiguous sectors.

See Also

MIRROR and UNDELETE

"Unformatting a Disk" in Chapter 9

UNINSTALL

If you install DR DOS on a system that already contains an operating system, UNINSTALL removes DR DOS and restores the previous operating system if you saved the OS during

DR DOS setup. UNINSTALL also is used to delete the saved old OS files if you determine that you no longer need them. When you do that, you cannot uninstall DR DOS and restore the old OS by using this command.

SYNTAX
UNINSTALL /C /?

PARAMETERS AND SWITCHES

/C	Removes the old operating system files.
/?	Displays abbreviated help.

UNPACK2

UNPACK2 unpacks bundled files from PC DOS disks.

SYNTAX
UNPACK2 *drive:\path source_drive:\destination_path* /v /p /c /n:*specific_file* /?

or

UNPACK2 *drive:\path source_ drive:\destination_path* /show /sizes /?

PARAMETERS AND SWITCHES

drive:\path	Indicates the location of the UNPACK2 file.
source	Specifies the name of the bundle from which to unpack files.
destination_path	Specifies the directory to unpack to.
/v	Writes with VERIFY.
/p	Prepends the command-line path to the packed file path.
/c	Creates a target directory if it does not exist.
/n:*specific_file*	Unpacks a designated file from a bundle.
/show	Shows all packed files in a bundle.
/sizes	Shows the size of packed files in a bundle.
/?	Displays the abbreviated online help.

NOTES
The /sizes switch must be used with the /show switch. It cannot be used by itself.

UNSTACK

UNSTACK uncompresses a compressed Stacker drive and writes the data to an uncompressed drive.

SYNTAX

UNSTACK *drive:* /M /?

PARAMETERS AND SWITCHES

drive: Specifies the compressed drive to be unstacked.

/M   Displays the unstack screen on a monochrome monitor.

/?   Displays abbreviated help.

VER   2.0 AND LATER—INTERNAL

VER is a simple command that displays the version number of MS-DOS onscreen. If you ever wonder what version of DOS is running on the computer you are using, type VER at the DOS command prompt.

SYNTAX

VER

NOTES

1. The VER command displays a one-digit DOS version number, followed by a two-digit revision number, reminding you which DOS version the computer is using.

2. If a computer is running a customized OEM version of MS-DOS, the name of that company is normally included in the line that VER displays. For instance, Compaq computers usually display the name COMPAQ along with the DOS version number. IBM versions normally display PC DOS instead of MS-DOS.

3. VER is unaffected by the SETVER program. VER always displays the actual version of DOS that the computer is running.

EXAMPLES

To display the version of MS-DOS that's running on a computer, enter the VER command at the DOS prompt as follows:

VER

For MS-DOS 6.22, the following line is displayed onscreen:

MS-DOS Version 6.22

See Also

"Displaying the Version with VER" in Chapter 10

VERIFY   2.0 AND LATER—INTERNAL

Normally, when DOS writes information to a disk, it trusts the disk hardware to make sure that the data was stored safely. If you want to be absolutely sure, you can enter VERIFY ON; DOS then reads back all the data written to disk and compares it to make sure that it was stored safely. Using VERIFY ON, however, slows down disk-write operations substantially, so this additional level of protection doesn't come without a price.

Syntax

VERIFY *onoff*

Parameters and Switches

onoff   Specifies whether you want to turn on (VERIFY ON) or off (VERIFY OFF) this command. If you omit this parameter, the current state of the verify flag is displayed.

Notes

1. By default, when DOS starts up, VERIFY is OFF.
2. VERIFY accepts only the parameters ON and OFF.
3. VERIFY works by instructing the disk controller to read back all data written to disk, calculate a new CRC (error checking) value from the data read, and compare it to the CRC value stored on the disk. (The disk controller normally does this every time data is read from the disk, which is how DOS discovers bad sectors when copying files.) Any differences between the two CRC values indicates that an error has occurred. Setting VERIFY ON doesn't compare the data on disk to the data that DOS was requested to write; it only makes sure that the data written to the disk is readable.
4. If VERIFY is set ON, you have more assurance that your data is being safely stored on disk. If VERIFY is set OFF, writing data to disk takes less time. When deciding which setting to use, you have to choose between data integrity and speed.
5. Specifying the /V parameter for COPY, DISKCOPY, or XCOPY sets VERIFY ON for the duration of the command. When the copy operation is finished, these commands set VERIFY back to the state it was in before the command executed.
6. The VERIFY state can be changed by a running program. Programming etiquette dictates that, when done, an application should reset any flag, such as VERIFY, to the state in which it was found. Still, you might run across applications that forget to reset VERIFY. If this causes problems, run the application from a batch file to restore the VERIFY state when the program terminates.

EXAMPLES

If you are about to update your company's accounts receivables, you might want to turn on the verify flag, as follows, before starting your accounting software:

```
VERIFY ON
```

After you are finished, you might set the verify flag off again, as follows, so that your routine computer tasks aren't unnecessarily slowed down:

```
VERIFY OFF
```

If you ever want to know whether the verify flag is off or on, enter the VERIFY command with no parameters at the DOS prompt like this:

```
VERIFY
```

MESSAGES

```
Must specify ON or OFF
```

Error: The only parameters that the VERIFY command accepts are ON or OFF. Entering anything else displays the preceding error message.

```
VERIFY is on
```

or

```
VERIFY is off
```

Information: If you enter VERIFY with no parameters, one of the preceding messages is displayed, informing you of the current state of the verify flag.

VFINTD.386   6.0 AND LATER—WINDOWS

Setup installs the VFINTD.386 device driver in the [386Enh] section of SYSTEM.INI to allow Microsoft Backup for Windows access to your floppy disk drives. If you have any other Windows backup software installed, this driver often conflicts with the drivers installed for that software.

SYNTAX

To use Microsoft Backup for Windows, you must include the following line in the [386Enh] section of the SYSTEM.INI file:

DEVICE=*drive:\path***VFINTD.386**

PARAMETERS AND SWITCHES

drive:\path   The full path to the VFINTD.386 file on your system. The setup program for DOS 6 places this file in the C:\DOS subdirectory by default.

NOTES

1. Almost all backup software for Windows adds a device driver to SYSTEM.INI that allows access to your tape drives and floppy disk drives. Unfortunately, few of these drivers can get along with each other, and you're usually forced to remove all but one driver before any of them will work. The following list includes some of the more common third-party drivers to look for in SYSTEM.INI:

Driver Filename	Backup Program
VFINTD.386	Microsoft Backup for Windows (with DOS 6) and Norton Backup for Windows
CMSDTAPE.386	Colorado Tape Backup
MYABU.386	My Advanced Backup
FASTBACK.386	Fastback for Windows
VFD.386	Central Point Backup for Windows
CPBVXD.386	Central Point Backup for Windows

2. Microsoft suggests that you disable any third-party drivers you find in SYSTEM.INI by adding a semicolon to the front of the DEVICE= line that loads them. Be aware that doing so may cause your other backup software to stop working.

3. If your computer fails the compatibility test that Microsoft Backup for Windows runs, you are probably having a driver conflict in SYSTEM.INI. If this happens, quit Windows, "comment out" any lines in SYSTEM.INI that load third-party backup drivers (see the preceding Driver table), restart Windows, and try the test again. As long as you comment out the driver lines (by placing a semicolon at the beginning of the line) instead of deleting them, you can easily restore them when you want to use your other backup software.

4. Be aware that Windows does not recognize any changes you make in SYSTEM.INI until you quit Windows completely and restart it from the DOS prompt.

EXAMPLES

Setup for DOS 6 adds the following line to the [386Enh] section of your SYSTEM.INI file when it installs Microsoft Backup for Windows on your computer:

DEVICE=C:\DOS\VFINTD.386

Setup does not, however, comment out third-party drivers in SYSTEM.INI that are known to cause conflicts with the VFINTD.386 driver.

VIEW

You can use VIEW to view an online document.

SYNTAX

VIEW *drive:\path\filename.inf* /?

PARAMETERS AND SWITCHES

`drive:\path\filename.inf` Specifies the location and name of the file to view. The following three online documents are available:

`CMDREF.INF`	PC DOS 7 Command Reference
`DOSREXX.INF`	PC DOS 7 REXX Reference
`DOSERROR.INF`	PC DOS 7 Error Messages

`/?` Displays the abbreviated online help.

VOL   2.0 AND LATER—INTERNAL

VOL displays the volume label and serial number of a disk if they exist. The volume label is simply a name that you can assign when you format a disk or later when you use the LABEL command. DOS began adding serial numbers to disks with DOS 4.0.

SYNTAX

VOL `drive:`

PARAMETERS AND SWITCHES

`drive:` The drive whose label and serial number you want to display. If you omit this parameter, DOS assumes the current drive.

NOTES

1. You can add a label to a disk when you format it by using the FORMAT /V command or later by using the LABEL command.
2. The serial number is a unique identifier assigned to the disk when it's formatted. DOS uses the serial number to verify that a disk hasn't been changed in disk drives that don't have change line support. Preformatted disks often do not have serial numbers on them, and some third-party formatting utilities neglect to add them, as well. DOS may be unable to tell whether you have changed a floppy disk if it has no serial number and your drive doesn't have change line support.
3. DOS can assign serial numbers to a disk only with the FORMAT command. You can't add or change the serial number of a disk without reformatting it.

EXAMPLES

To display the volume label of a floppy disk in drive B:, enter the following command at the DOS prompt:

`VOL B:`

If you omit the `drive:` parameter (B:), DOS assumes the current disk.

VOL displays the following messages if the disk specified has both a volume label and a serial number:

```
Volume in drive B: is NEW WORK
Volume Serial Number is 4EF7-9C30
```

If the disk has no serial number, the second line is omitted. If the disk has no volume label, the following message is displayed:

```
Volume in drive B: has no label
```

MESSAGES

```
Invalid drive specification
```

Error: You specified an invalid drive letter in the *drive:* parameter.

```
Invalid switch - switch
```

Error: You specified an invalid *switch* parameter. The only parameter that VOL accepts is a single disk drive.

```
Too many parameters - parameter
```

Error: You've specified more than one parameter on the command line. The only parameter that VOL accepts is a single disk drive.

SEE ALSO

FORMAT and LABEL

"Examining Volume Labels with VOL" in Chapter 7

VSAFE 6.0 AND LATER—EXTERNAL

VSAFE is a memory-resident utility that can monitor the activity in your computer. If any program is acting suspiciously, VSAFE can halt the process and request guidance from you as to what to do about it.

SYNTAX

VSAFE /option+|- ... /NE /NX /Akey /Ckey /N /D /U

PARAMETERS AND SWITCHES

/Akey	Sets the hot key as Alt plus the key specified by *key*.
/Ckey	Sets the hot key as Ctrl plus the key specified by *key*.
/D	Turns off checksumming.
/N	Instructs VSAFE to monitor network drives.
/NE	Prevents VSAFE from loading into expanded memory.

/NX		Prevents VSAFE from loading into extended memory.
/option+|- ...		Specifies how VSAFE checks for viruses. Use a plus sign (+) after *option* to enable the switch; use a minus sign (-) after *option* to disable it. Choose *option* from the following list:
	1	Warns of low-level formatting that could erase your hard disk (default: on)
	2	Warns of a program's attempt to stay resident in memory (default: off)
	3	Prevents programs from writing to any of your disks (default: off)
	4	Checks executable files that DOS opens for viruses (default: on)
	5	Checks all disks for boot sector viruses (default: on)
	6	Warns of attempts to write to the boot sector or to the partition table of the hard disk (default: on)
	7	Warns of attempts to write to the boot sector of a floppy disk (default: off)
	8	Warns of attempts to modify executable files (default: on)
/U		Disables and unloads VSAFE from memory. If VSAFE wasn't the last resident program loaded, the memory it was using will not be released.

Rules

1. Turn off VSAFE before you install Microsoft Windows.
2. Do not use VSAFE after you start Microsoft Windows.
3. If you use VSAFE with Microsoft Windows, run the MWAVTSR.EXE memory-resident program by adding the following line to your WIN.INI file:
   LOAD=C:\DOS\MWAVTSR.EXE

   MWAVTSR.EXE enables VSAFE messages to be displayed in Windows.
4. The default hot key is Alt+V.

Notes

VSAFE is a memory-resident program that takes up a varying amount of conventional, extended, and expanded memory. In DOS 6.0 and higher, VSAFE takes up 44KB of conventional memory, 23KB of conventional and 23KB of extended memory, or 7KB of conventional and 64KB of expanded memory.

Examples

To turn on warnings about programs' attempts to stay in memory, to turn off checks for boot sector viruses, and to make Alt+Q the hot key, use the following command:

VSAFE /2+ /5- /AQ

See Also

MSAV, MWAV, and MWAVTSR

"Guarding Against Infection" in Chapter 9

WINA20.386   5.0 AND LATER—WINDOWS

Windows 3.0 enhanced-mode drivers often require the help of the WINA20.386 driver to perform their duties. Setup for MS-DOS 6 places this driver in the root directory if it finds Windows installed on your system. If you move the WINA20.386 file to another subdirectory, you need to tell Windows where it is and add a SWITCHES=/W line to your CONFIG.SYS file.

Syntax

To tell Windows where you have located the WINA20.386 driver, include the following line in the [386Enh] section of SYSTEM.INI:

DEVICE=*drive:\path***WINA20.386**

Parameters and Switches

drive:\path   The full path to the WINA20.386 file on your system. The setup program for DOS 6 places this file in the root directory of the startup drive by default.

Notes

Windows 3.0 in enhanced mode requires the WINA20.386 driver file to be available before it can load. (See the first message in the following "Messages" section.) If you want to move the WINA20.386 file out of your root directory, you need to specify the /W switch in CONFIG.SYS and add a DEVICE=*drive:\path*WINA20.386 line to the [386Enh] section of your SYSTEM.INI file. You should specify the full drive and path to WINA20.386 in the device line in SYSTEM.INI.

> **Note**
> Windows 3.1 will load successfully in enhanced mode without access to the WINA20.386 driver, but any version 3.0 drivers that you're using may still require the services of the WINA20.386 driver. If they do and that driver is unavailable, Windows may become unstable or crash. Because enhanced-mode drivers for Windows are distributed with many software packages, most people are running Windows 3.1 with Windows 3.0 drivers without knowing it. To be safe, be sure that the WINA20.386 driver is available, either in the root directory or through the /W switch and a device line in SYSTEM.INI.

EXAMPLES

Although you use Windows version 3.1, you're not sure whether all your Windows enhanced-mode drivers have been updated yet and want to make sure that the WINA20.386 driver is available, just in case. Because you've moved the WINA20.386 file into the C:\DOS subdirectory with your other DOS 6 files, you need to include the following line in your CONFIG.SYS file:

SWITCHES=/W

Now that DOS knows you've moved WINA20.386, you need to tell Windows where you put it. To do so, add the following line to the [386Enh] section of your SYSTEM.INI file, which is in your main Windows subdirectory:

DEVICE=C:\DOS\WINA20.386

MESSAGES

```
You must have the file WINA20.386 in the root directory of your boot drive to
run Windows in Enhanced Mode
```

Error: This message is displayed only if you are running Windows 3.0 in enhanced mode and the WINA20.386 file is not present in your root directory. To allow Windows 3.0 to run in enhanced mode with the WINA20.386 driver located somewhere else, specify the SWITCHES=/W command in your CONFIG.SYS file and enter a DEVICE=*drive:**path*\WINA20.386 line in the [386Enh] section of SYSTEM.INI.

SEE ALSO

SWITCHES=

XCOPY   3.2 AND LATER—EXTERNAL

XCOPY can copy groups of files and subdirectories from one disk to another. When copying large groups of files, XCOPY is somewhat faster than COPY because it reads more than one file at a time into memory.

SYNTAX

XCOPY *source* *destination* /A /D:*date* /E /M /P /S /V /W /Y /-Y

PARAMETERS AND SWITCHES

source   Specifies the file or files that you want to copy. You can specify a full pathname (that is *drive:**path*\...*filename.ext*), and wildcards are allowed. This parameter is required. If you include a drive and/or path but no filename, DOS assumes all files (*.*).

destination   Specifies the location and optionally the filename or names to which you want to copy. You can specify a full pathname, although normally just a

		drive and/or path is included. Wildcards are allowed when a filename is specified. If you omit this parameter, DOS uses the current drive and subdirectory as the destination.
	/A	Copies only files whose archive attribute is on (modified files) but doesn't turn off the archive attribute. /A is similar to /M, except that /A does not reset the archive attribute.
	/D:*date*	Copies only files that were changed or created on or after the date you specify. The date's form depends on the setting of the COUNTRY= command in CONFIG.SYS.
	/E	Creates parallel subdirectories on the destination disk, even if the original subdirectory is empty.
	/M	Copies only files whose archive attribute is on (modified files) and turns off the archive attribute. /M is similar to /A, except /M resets the archive attribute.
	/P	Causes XCOPY to prompt you for approval before copying each file.
	/S	Copies all directories and subdirectories below *source* that contain files.
	/V	Verifies that the copy was written correctly.
	/W	Causes XCOPY to prompt you and wait for your response before starting the copy operation. You can use this switch to give yourself time to insert the source floppy disk, for example.
NEW MS-DOS 6.2	/Y	Specifies that you want XCOPY to overwrite files without prompting you for confirmation. Including this parameter overrides any setting specified with the COPYCMD environment variable.
NEW MS-DOS 6.2	/-Y	Specifies that you want XCOPY to prompt you for confirmation before overwriting any files, even if the command is run from within a batch file. Including this parameter overrides any setting specified with the COPYCMD environment variable.

Exit Codes

ERRORLEVEL Value	Meaning
0	Extended copy operation successful
1	No files found to copy
2	Halted by user (Ctrl+C)
4	Copy operation failed—Invalid drive letter, invalid switches or parameters, not enough memory, or not enough disk space
5	Halted by fatal error writing to disk

Rules

1. You must specify the source drive, path, and filename first, and then the destination drive, path, and filename.
2. Do not use a device name other than a drive for *source* or *destination*. For example, you cannot use LPT1: or COM1:.
3. The source file specified must include one or both of the following:
   - A valid filename. Wildcards are permitted.
   - A drive name, a pathname, or both.
4. If you do not specify the source drive name, DOS uses the current drive.
5. If you do not specify the source path, DOS uses the drive's current directory.
6. If you specify a drive or path for the source but do not specify a source filename, DOS assumes all files (*.*).
7. If you omit a new name for the destination file, the copied file has the same name as the source file.
8. If you do not specify a *destination* parameter, the *source* parameter must include one or both of the following:
   - A drive name other than the current drive.
   - A pathname other than the current disk's current directory.
9. XCOPY sets the archive bit on for the files it creates.

Notes

1. Starting with DOS 6.22, the XCOPY command, when run from the command line, prompts you for confirmation before overwriting files. However, to avoid forcing you to rewrite all your batch files, XCOPY does not prompt you before overwriting a file when run from a batch file.

   If you don't like XCOPY's new behavior, you can change it by defining an environment variable named COPYCMD. Setting COPYCMD equal to /Y forces XCOPY to act as it did in all previous versions of DOS, never prompting for confirmation before overwriting a file. If you set COPYCMD equal to /-Y, XCOPY always prompts for confirmation, even when it's run from within a batch file.

2. To use XCOPY to copy more files than fit on one destination disk, make sure that the files' archive attribute is on. You can use the ATTRIB command to perform this step. Then use the XCOPY command repeatedly with the /M or /M /S switches.

   When the destination floppy disk is full, change floppy disks and reissue the command. The files that were copied now have their archive attribute turned off, so XCOPY skips these files. XCOPY copies the files not already copied—those files that have the archive attribute turned on.

3. XCOPY and APPEND /X are a troublesome combination. To use XCOPY on a disk that is involved in an APPEND command, disconnect APPEND before you execute the XCOPY command.

4. Use XCOPY, rather than DISKCOPY, to copy files to a device that is not the same format as the source.

Messages

```
Cannot perform a cyclic copy
```

Error: You used the /S switch, and at least one of the destination directories is a subdirectory of the source directories. When you use /S, XCOPY cannot copy files to destination directories that are part of the source directories. If you must copy files from more than one directory, issue individual XCOPY commands to copy the directories one at a time.

```
Cannot XCOPY from a reserved device
```

Error: You specified one of DOS's reserved device names (for example, LPT1) as the source of the files to be copied. Reissue XCOPY, using a disk path and directory.

```
Does pathname specify a filename
or directory name on the target
(F = file, D = directory)?
```

Information: You specified a destination filename in which the final name does not exist as a directory. XCOPY does not know whether the final name in the destination is a filename or a directory.

If the destination name is a directory name, press D. XCOPY creates the needed directory and begins copying files. If the destination name is a filename, press F. XCOPY copies files to this file.

```
nnn File(s) copied
```

Information: XCOPY copied *nnn* files to the destination disk. This message appears regardless of any errors that occur.

```
Insufficient disk space
```

Error: The destination disk ran out of space. The file that you were copying when the error occurred was erased from the destination. Delete any unneeded files from the destination disk, or use a different disk and then retry the command.

```
Reading source file(s)...
```

Information: XCOPY is reading the source directories for filenames.

```
Unable to create directory
```

Error: XCOPY cannot create a subdirectory on the destination disk for one of the following reasons:

- Part of the destination pathname is wrong or misspelled.
- The disk's root directory is full.

- The disk is full.
- A file with the same name as the created directory already exists.
- You used a directory name that actually is a device name.

Be sure that the destination name is correct. Use the DIR command to check the destination disk. If the disk or the root directory is full, erase files or use another destination disk. If a file that uses the same name as the intended directory already exists, rename the file or change the directory's name when you reissue the XCOPY command.

SEE ALSO

COPY and REPLACE

"Management with XCOPY" in Chapter 8

XCOPY32

XCOPY32 is functionally equal to XCOPY, but it is the 32-bit version for use with long filenames and 32-bit Windows 95 and Windows 98. All the syntax and parameters used with XCOPY are also used with XCOPY32. The following additional parameters also are available with XCOPY32:

/C	Forces XCOPY32 to continue copying even if errors occur.
/I	Makes *destination* a directory if *destination* does not exist and you're copying more than one file.
/Q	Copies in quiet mode without displaying filenames onscreen.
/F	Displays full source and destination filenames while copying.
/L	Displays files that would be copied.
/H	Copies hidden and system files also.
/R	Overwrites read-only files.
/T	Creates directory structure but does not copy files. Does not include empty directories or subdirectories. /T /E includes empty directories and subdirectories.
/U	Updates any files that already exist in destination.
/K	Copies attributes. XCOPY resets read-only attributes.
/N	Copies using the 8.3 DOS filename versions of long filenames.

XDEL

XDEL is a utility to delete multiple files across subdirectories and delete empty subdirectories.

Syntax

XDEL *drive:\path\filespec* /D /N /O /R /P /S /?

Parameters and Switches

drive:\path\filespec	Specifies the drive, path, and filename or file specification using wildcards to be deleted.
/D	Deletes empty subdirectories.
/N	Deletes files with no prompts or confirmation warnings.
/O	Overwrites the file with other data before deleting it, making the deletion more secure and difficult to undelete.
/R	Deletes read-only files.
/P	Prompts you before overwriting each file.
/S	Deletes files in subdirectories.
/?	Displays abbreviated help.

XDF

Using the XDF command starts the XDF program, a terminate-and-stay-resident (TSR) program that supports XDF-formatted disks.

Syntax

XDF /u /?

Parameters and Switches

/u	Unloads the XDF TSR.
/?	Displays the abbreviated online help.

Notes

You can use the DIR command with XDF-formatted disks to view the entire contents of the disk when the XDF program is loaded.

XDFCOPY

XDFCOPY copies the contents of an eXtended Density Format (XDF) disk.

XDFCOPY creates a temporary file on drive C during the copy process. When copying to a disk, XDFCOPY automatically formats (prepares) the target disk during the copy process. The target disk must be the same size and type as the source disk.

Syntax

XDFCOPY *source_drive* *target_drive* /y /nv /?

Parameters and Switches

source_drive	Specifies the drive that contains the disk to be copied. On systems with only one disk drive, use XDFCOPY by specifying the same drive as the source and target.
target_drive	Specifies the drive where you want to copy the disk to. If the disk to be used is not empty, any existing information is overwritten.
/y	Starts without waiting for a disk change.
/nv	Turns off read-after-write verify.
/?	Displays the abbreviated online help.

XDIR

XDIR is an enhanced version of the standard DIR command.

Syntax

XDIR +|-*attributes* *d:\path\filespec* /B /C /L /N /P /S /T /W /X /Y /Z /R

Parameters and Switches

+|-*attributes*	Displays only files that have (+) or do not have (-) the specified attributes. See the DIR command for each of the attributes.
d:\path\filespec	Specifies the drive and directory for which to list files. A *filespec* that includes wildcards limits the listing to matching files.
/B	Displays only the file path and name.
/C	Computes and displays checksum for each file that you can use to verify that two files are identical.
/L	Displays the long display format with full information about each file and subdirectory.
/N	Displays files in the order they appear on the drive.

/P	Pauses after each page is displayed.
/S	Includes files in subdirectories in the listing.
/T	Displays files sorted by date and time.
/W	Displays only filenames in wide format.
/X	Displays files sorted by extension.
/Y	Displays files sorted by Stacker compression ratio for files on Stacker drives.
/Z	Displays files sorted by file size.
/R	Displays the files in reverse sort order when used with /T, /X, /Y, or /Z.

SEE ALSO

DIR

APPENDIX

GLOSSARY

In this appendix

This glossary is designed to provide short, quick definitions of some of the more common terms used in this book. If you require more in-depth information, refer to a computing dictionary such as *Que's Computer and Internet Dictionary, Sixth Edition*.

Absolute path The path named from the root directory, including all intervening subdirectories.

Attribute A directory-based indicator of a file's status. Attributes include read-only, archive, system, hidden, and volume label.

AUTOEXEC.BAT A special batch file that DOS automatically executes during the booting process. This file, usually placed in the root directory, is an ideal place to include commands that initialize the operation of a PC.

Batch file A text file containing commands that DOS executes as though the commands were entered at the DOS prompt. Batch files always have the .BAT extension.

Binary file A file containing instructions or data that has meaning to the PC but cannot be displayed or printed as ASCII characters.

Boot sector A special area in track 0 of each DOS disk. DOS uses this area to record important information about a disk's format to reference later when working with the disk.

Buffer A portion of memory reserved for storing data.

Character string A series of ASCII characters.

Clipboard An area of memory where text can be stored temporarily.

Cluster A unit of one, four, or eight sectors. This is the smallest amount of disk space that DOS allocates to a file.

Cold boot To start a PC from a power-off condition.

Command A directive you type at the DOS prompt or include in a batch file to instruct DOS to perform an action.

Compare To make a byte-by-byte comparison of the contents of a file or an entire disk to ensure that they are accurate copies of each other.

CONFIG.SYS A special text file that DOS reads during booting to find and execute configuration commands.

Cylinder A unit of storage consisting of the set of *tracks* that occupy the same position on opposite sides of the same disk platter.

Default A condition or value that is used when you do not supply one.

Delimiter A character that separates the "words" in a command. Common delimiters are the space and the slash (/).

Device driver A special program file, usually with a .SYS extension, that DOS can load through a configuration command. Device drivers control how DOS and applications programs interact with specific items of hardware.

Dialog box A window that pops open when a program needs more information before executing a command.

Directory A disk-based table of filenames and other file-related information that DOS uses with the file allocation table (FAT) to access a file's data content.

Disk A magnetic storage medium and the predominant means of file storage for DOS.

Disk drive The electromechanical components that record and play back data from the magnetic surfaces of a disk.

Disk partition A division of a hard disk that DOS views as a separate disk.

Diskette Another term for a 5 1/4-inch or 3 1/2-inch disk.

DOS prompt The characters that COMMAND.COM displays to inform you that you can enter a DOS command.

End-of-file (EOF) marker In a text file, a Ctrl+Z (^Z) ASCII character, which tells DOS that the end of the usable portion of a file has been reached.

Expanded memory Also referred to as EMS, or Expanded Memory Specification. Special RAM that DOS accesses as a device. Expanded memory conforms to the Lotus/Intel/Microsoft (LIM) EMS 3.2 or 4.0 standards.

Extended memory Memory at addresses above 1MB on 80286, 80386, and 80486 PCs. DOS can load most of the operating system into the first 64KB of extended memory.

External command A DOS command whose instructions are stored in a file other than COMMAND.COM.

File A variable-length collection of related information referenced by a name.

File system The predefined organizational method that a disk operating system uses to read and write to data files on disks.

Filter A program that modifies information coming from a program before the information reaches the screen or is piped to another program.

Floppy disk Any disk with a lower capacity than the hard drive that you can remove from your PC's drive.

Flow control The capability to control the order in which DOS processes lines of a batch file.

Format The initial preparation of a disk for data storage.

Full backup A special series of disks containing all the data stored on a hard disk, along with information about the previous location of the data files.

Graphics mode A screen mode available to users of PCs equipped with graphics adapters. In graphics mode, the screen presentation uses bitmapped graphics.

Ground An electrical path directly to the earth. Grounds can dissipate static discharges safely. A PC chassis normally is grounded, but this grounding is not always adequate to stop a static discharge.

Hard disk A high-capacity, typically nonremovable disk drive.

High memory area (HMA) The first 64KB of extended memory. DOS can load part of the operating system files into this area of memory.

Highlighted option A command or option that appears in reverse video. The highlighted option executes when you press Enter.

Insert mode The editing mode in which a typed character is inserted into the existing text at the current cursor position.

Intermediate backup A series of disks containing copies of all files modified since the most recent full backup.

Internal command A DOS command built into `COMMAND.COM`.

Keyword A word that specifically identifies the action you want DOS to perform.

LCD A liquid-crystal display. This type of screen is found on most laptop and notebook computers.

Location counter The two numbers at the right end of the status bar that indicate the cursor's current row and column.

Logical drive A partitioned section of a hard disk that DOS views as an additional hard disk.

Macro A series of DOS commands stored in memory under a single name. You execute a macro by typing its name.

Meta-string A series of characters for which DOS applies a meaning different from the string's literal meaning. DOS displays substitute text when the program finds meta-strings in the `PROMPT` command.

Mouse pointer The block- or arrow-shaped screen icon that indicates where the mouse action occurs.

Name The first portion of a filename, consisting of up to eight characters. It usually describes the contents of a file.

Overtype mode The editing mode in which a typed character replaces the character at the current cursor position.

Parameter Additional information given with a command to more precisely control its actions.

Parser A portion of a computer program that translates a command line into specific commands that the program can act on.

Pipe To send information that normally goes to the screen to another program by using the pipe symbol (|).

Platter Synonymous with disk.

Pull-down menu   A menu interface used in many programs that is characterized by a vertical list of main menu choices. When you use a mouse to select one of the choices, additional choices appear below the main menu choices.

Queue   A list of files to be printed.

Redirection   The act of sending the output from a command or program to a device other than the one expected (usually the screen); sending input to a command or program from a point other than the one expected (usually the keyboard).

Relative path   A path specified with the current directory—as opposed to the root directory—as the starting point.

Root directory   A master directory created on each disk by FORMAT.

Scrollbar   An area of the screen containing arrows and icons that move (or scroll) text or graphics through the window.

Sector   A section of a track that is the disk's smallest possible storage unit.

Selected text   A block of text you highlight with various Shift+key combinations. Selected text can be deleted, moved, or edited as a single block.

Selection cursor   An area of highlighted text that shows where the selected action occurs.

Shell   A program that provides the user interface to the features and capabilities of an operating system.

Shortcut key   A keystroke combination that immediately activates an editing command, bypassing the menu system.

Sorting   Ordering a list of items.

Source   A filename expression that identifies the file(s) to be copied or the device that will serve as the source for a copy operation.

Static electricity   A high-voltage charge that builds on objects (including people) and can be discharged when another object is touched. Static electricity discharges can damage electronic circuits.

Subdirectory   A directory within another directory.

Surge protector   A protective device inserted between a power outlet and a computer's power plug. By acting as a circuit breaker, a surge protector helps block power surges that can damage the computer's circuits.

Switch   A slash followed by one or more characters that are used to enable a command's optional functions. (Similar to a *parameter*.)

Syntax   A specific set of rules you follow when issuing commands.

Target   A filename expression that identifies the disk location of the files(s) to be created as a result of a copy operation. A target also can be a DOS device other than a file.

Task A program that DOS has loaded into memory.

Text file A file that contains only ASCII text characters (without special formatting characters). The DOS Editor works only with text files.

Text mode The screen mode available to all PC users. In text mode, all screen presentation is composed of ASCII characters.

Track A circular section of a disk's surface that holds data.

Undelete To restore the FAT and directory entries of a file to undo a deletion.

Upper memory area A 386KB area of memory between 640KB and 1MB, usually reserved for use by certain system devices, such as a monitor. DOS can use a portion of this upper memory area, referred to as *upper memory blocks*, for memory-resident programs and device drivers.

Voltage regulator An electrical device that keeps voltage fluctuations from reaching an electrical device. Regulators usually don't stop all power surges.

Volume label A name that identifies a particular disk.

Warm boot To restart a PC while the power is on.

Wildcard A character in a command that represents one or more characters. In DOS, the ? wildcard presents any single character. The * wildcard represents any remaining characters in the command.

XMS The Lotus/Intel/Microsoft/AST Extended Memory Specification. This standard specifies a set of rules by which several programs can use extended memory cooperatively by means of a device driver.

INDEX

Symbols

* (asterisk) wildcard
  commands, 54-55
  character, 595
/1 switch, DISKCOPY command, 211
/4 switch, FORMAT command, 157
/8 switch, FORMAT command, 157
/? (help switch) on command line, 46
? (question mark), 604-605
  wildcard commands, 54-55, 595
| (pipe character), 201, 597-598
@ (at symbol), 602-603
@ command, batch files, 397
3 1/2" disks, capacities, 153
4DOS utility, 497
  batch file debugger, 500
  commands
    BEEP, 498
    CANCEL, 498
    CDD, 498
    COLOR, 498
    DELAY, 498
    DESCRIBE, 498
    DIRHISTORY, 498
    DRAWBOX, 499
    DRAWHLINE, 499
    DRAWVLINE, 499
    ESET, 499
    EXCEPT, 499
    FFIND, 499
    FREE, 499
    GLOBAL, 499
    GOSUB, 499
    HISTORY, 499
    IFF, 499
    improvements, 497-498
    INKEY, 499
    INPUT, 499
    KEYSTACK, 499
    LIST, 499
    LOADBTM, 499
    LOG, 499
    MEMORY, 499
    REBOOT, 499
    SCREEN, 499
    SCRPUT, 499
    SELECT, 499
    TEE, 499
    TEXT, 499
    TIMER, 499
    TOUCH, 499
    TREE, 499
    UNSET, 499
    VSCRPUT, 499
5 1/4" disks, capacities, 153
10BASE-2 cabling, 472
10BASE-5 cabling, 472
10BASE-100 cabling, 472
10BASE-T cabling, 472
4201.CPI file, 514
4208.CPI file, 514
5202.CPI file, 514
80286 file designation, 504
80386 chips (Intel), 18
80386 file designation, 504
80486 chips (Intel), 18

A

/A switch
  COPY command, 203
  DIR command, 194-196
  FC command, 216
  FORMAT command, 157
  XCOPY command, 207
abort (A) option, device error messages, 557
About command (Help menu-DOS Editor), 387
accessing
  CD-ROM drives, 835-836, 843-844
  CVFs (compressed volume files), 663-664
  files (FCBS command), 463
  online help commands, 46-47
  PCMCIA cards, 849
  servers, 770-773
activating
  Help system (DOS Editor), 387-388
  menu bar (DOS Editor), 365
active display, 298
adapters (display), 720-721
Add Group dialog box, 79
Add Program dialog box, 82
adding
  disk drives to other disk directories (JOIN command), 302
  environment variables, 894-897
  program groups (DOS Shell), 78-80
  program items to program (DOS Shell), 81-82

ADOS.CFG FILE

ADOS.CFG file, 513
ADOS.COM file, 513
ADOS.OVL file, 513
ADOS.TXT file, 513
Advanced Power Management (APM), 852-857
aliases, disk drives, 613
  creating, 922-923
/ALL switch
  SCANDISK command, 189
  UNDELETE command, 263
ALL command, batch files, 397
All Files view (DOS Shell), 74
allocating system resources among client drivers, 849
allocation units (FORMAT command), 155
Alt shortcut key (DOS Editor), 367
Alt+B (Previous Topic), online help command key, 49-50
Alt+C (Contents), online help command key, 49-50
Alt+Esc key, DOS Shell hotkey, 66
Alt+F keystroke (help system exit), 51
Alt+F1 shortcut key (DOS Editor), 367
Alt+F4 key, DOS Shell hotkey, 66
Alt+minus shortcut key (DOS Editor), 367
Alt+N (New Topic), online help command key, 49-50
Alt+Tab key, DOS Shell hotkey, 66
American National Standards Institute. *See* ANSI

analyzing disks
  CHKDSK command, 184-188
  SCANDISK utility, 188-189
ANSI (American National Standards Institute), 416, 608
  attribute control codes, 425-426
  cursor control codes, 426-427
  display color codes, 425-426
  keyboard layout control codes, 427-430
  reset mode controls, 425
  set mode controls, 425
ANSI.SYS (device driver), 444, 504
  activating, 417
  character keys, reassigning, 424
  codes
    issuing in batch files, 417-418
    issuing in text files, 418-419
    issuing with PROMPT command, 419
    sending to DOS, 417
  commands
    ECHO, 417-418
    parameters/switches, 609
    PROMPT, 419
    TYPE, 418-419
  escape character, command activation, 417
  installing, 416
  keyboards
    controls, 416
    customizing, 423-424
  screen controls, 419-420
    clearing (CLS command), 423
    cursor movement, 420
    cursor positioning, 420
    display codes, 421
    text attributes, 421-422

switches
  /K, 416
  /R, 416
  /X, 416
  third-party features, 416
  video controls, 416
antivirus programs
  Microsoft Anti-Virus, 253-255
    checklists, 255
    virus list, 256
  Norton Antivirus, 253
APM (Advanced Power Management), 852-857
APPEND command, 610-613
APPEND environment variable, 520-521
APPEND.EXE file, 504
application-specific device drivers, 308
applications
  dedicated directories, 193
  defined, 192
  memory, troubleshooting, 460-461
  overlays, 192
  versus utilities, 192-193
ARC (Archive) filename extension, 105, 108
archiving files for disk space maximization, 183
area (DOS Shell)
  moving, 63-64
  selecting, 62
AREADME.TXT file, 513
ASC (ASCII text) filename extension, 105
ASCII (American Standard Code for Information Interchange), 14, 574-581
  code sets, 423-424
  DOS Shell, file displays, 59
  Extended character set, 14
  files, 200
    combining (COPY command), 204-205
    viewing (TYPE command), 200-201

scan codes, 423
text files, editing, 719-720
ASCII command (FTP), 487
ASM (Assembler source file) filename extension, 105
ASSIGN command, 468-469, 613
   disk drive requests, assigning, 302
ASSIGN.COM file, 513
Associate command (File menu), 93
Associate File dialog box, 93
associating files with programs (DOS Shell), 92-93
asterisk (*) wildcard commands, 54-55
AT processors, 17
at symbol (@), 602-603
ATA rotating disk, partitioning, 850
ATTRIB command, 108, 613-615
   file attributes, changing, 109-110
   parameters/switches, 614
ATTRIB.EXE file, 505
attributes (files), 107-108
   Archive, 108
   Hidden, 108
   modifying (ATTRIB command), 109-110
   Read-only, 108, 110
   Subdirectory, 108
   System, 108
   viewing (DIR command), 195-196, 613-615
   Volume Label, 108
audio tape recorders, magnetic disk storage comparison, 129
AUTOEXEC.BAT file, 511
   boot disk, 24-25
   boot process, 17
      modifying, 38-39

dates/times, 276
defining macros from bootup (DOSKEY), 439
device drivers
   directory location, 312-313
   troubleshooting, 314-315
editing (EDIT command), 32
function of, 30
line-by-line examination, 31-32
mouse drivers, 59
SET command, 30
system configuration, 26, 30-32
UNDELETE command, 264
/AUTOFIX switch, SCANDISK command, 189
automatic indenting (DOS Editor), 372
auxiliary consoles, I/O devices, 650-651

B

/B switch
   COPY command, 203
   DIR command, 194, 197
   FC command, 216
   FORMAT command, 157
background printing, 857-860
backing up
   data, 645-647
   disks (XCOPY command), 208-209
   files, 616, 833-834
   hard disks, 833-834, 838 839
   high-speed/medium-speed, 647
backslashes (\), command syntax, 45
backspace meta-string, 297
BACKUP command, 616
backup files, restoring, 881-884

Backup Options dialog box, 247-248
BACKUP.EXE file, 513
backups (data), 233-234
   differential, 238
   files
      selecting manually, 243-245
      selection criteria, 245-246
   frequency of, 238
   full, 238
   incremental, 238
   Microsoft Backup, 233
      Backup function, 236-238
      Compare function, 236-238
      comparison with original files, 241
      configuring, 235-236
      features, 233-234
      full, performing, 239-241
      MSBACKUP command, 239
      Options dialog box, 247-248
      Quit function, 236-238
      Restore function, 236-238
   Microsoft Backup for Windows 3.x, 233
      Backup function, 236-238
      Compare function, 236-238
      configuring, 235-236
      differential, performing, 242
      features, 233-234
      full, performing, 242
      incremental, performing, 242
      Options dialog box, 247-248
      Quit function, 236, 238
      Restore function, 236-238
   policy development, 270-271
   restoring, 248-251
   selective restoration, 251
   virus protection tactics, 497

BAK (Backup) filename
  extension, 105
BAS (BASIC program file)
  filename extension, 105
BAT (Batch) filename extension, 105, 390
batch files, 390-391
  %envir%, 600-602
  @ (at symbol), 602-603
  ANSI.SYS codes, issuing in,
    417-418
  as templates, 396
  automation features, 390
  branching to specific lines
    (GOTO command),
    398-399
  calling/returning (CALL
    command), 411-412
  CHECKIT.BAT, 408
  CHOICE command
    *display menu creation,
      406-407*
    *simple menu creation,
      405-406*
  command-history
    (DOSKEY), creating,
    435-436
  commands, 390
    @, 397
    CALL, 397
    CHOICE, 397
    ECHO, 397
    FOR..IN..DO, 397
    GOTO, 397
    IF, 397
    PAUSE, 397
    REM, 397
    SHIFT, 397
  comments, 874-875
    inserting, 398
  conditional execution,
    761-765
  contents, 391
  COPYCOMP, 393
  copying files, 395-396
  creating
    COPY command, 392-393
    DOS Editor, 391
    Edlin, 391
    guidelines, 391

DCOPY.BAT, 401-402
debugging (4DOS utility),
  500
displaying contents, 396
echo messaging, 391
executing, 412
FOR..IN..DO command,
  407-409
  command interaction, 409
  DOS prompt, 409
frequently used commands,
  390
IF command, 399-400
  *comparing strings,
    402-403*
  *ERRORLEVEL testing,
    400-402*
  finding files, 404
installation types, 397
messages, displaying, 398
modifying (DOS Editor),
  362
on-screen messages,
  716-719
pausing, 847-848
  *CHOICE command,
    404-405*
processing, 390
replaceable parameters,
  393-397, 599-600
running, 619-621
running other batch files,
  411
  *calling/returning (CALL
    command), 411-412*
  shifting control, 411
SHIFT command, moving
  parameters, 409-411
starting, 392
suspending, 631-633
versus macros, 437
batch processing, 390
**baud settings on serial ports
  (MODE command),
  328-330**
**BEEP command (4DOS util-
  ity), 498**
**BGI (Borland Graphics
  Interface) filename extension, 105**

BIN (Binary prgram file)
  filename extension, 105
  converting .EXE files to,
    727
BINARY command (FTP),
  487
binary files, editing
  (DEBUG command), 200
binary mode, FC command,
  217-218
bindery logins (Novell
  NetWare), 473
bit buckets, 104
bits (binary digits), 13
block editing
  fundamentals, 373
  text
    changing, 378-379
    Clipboard, 374-376
    finding, 377-378
    *search and replace feature,
      376-377*
    selecting, 373-374
blocks (commands), 606-608
**BMP (Windows bitmap) file-
  name extension, 105**
boot disk
  AUTOEXEC.BAT file,
    24-25
  COMMAND.COM file,
    24-25
  CONFIG.SYS file, 24-25
  creating, 167-168, 926-928
  floppy, creating, 25-26
  FORMAT command, 25
  IO.SYS file, 24-25
  MSDOS.SYS file, 24-25
  SYS command, 25
booting
  cold, 24
  from floppy disk, damaged
    hard drive
    (COMMAND.COM file),
    25-26
  PCs, reboot commands,
    809-811
  possible data loss, 24
  warm, 24

booting process, 15
    AUTOEXEC.BAT file, 17
        modifying, 38-39
    bootstrap loader, 16
    CMOS chip check, 16
    COMMAND.COM file, 17
    CONFIG.SYS file, 17
        modifying, 38-39
    IO.SYS file, 16
    MSDOS.SYS file, 17
    Power On Self Test (POST), 16

bootstrap loader, 16

boundaries (sectors), 136

branches (directories)
    collapsing (DOS Shell), 84-86
    copying (XCOPY command), 209-210
    deleting, 679
    expanding (DOS Shell), 84-86

BRB (Big Red Button Time), 24

BREAK command, 616-617
    CONFIG.SYS file, 27
    parameters/switches, 616
    syntax, 468

Break key (Ctrl+Break keystroke), ROM BIOS controls, 564

BREAK= command, 616-617

buffers, keyboard, 788-789

BUFFERS command, 461-462, 617-618
    parameters/switches, 617

bulletin board files, viewing (DOS Editor), 362

bundled files, unpacking, 941

BUSETUP.EXE file, 511

BYE command (FTP), 487

bytes, 13
    ASCII code, 14
    data storage, 138
    file storage, 199

C

/C string parameter (COMMAND command), 289

/C switch
    DIR command, 194
    FC command, 216
    FORMAT command, 157

C&E.BAT file, 395

CAB (compressed cabinet) files, extracting, 730

cabling
    10BASE-2, 472
    10BASE-5, 472
    10BASE-100, 472
    10BASE-T, 472
    Interlnk configurations, 223-224
    network cards, installation considerations, 472

caching
    directory information (FAST OPEN program), 173-174
    disks, 842-843
        SMARTDrive, 911-913
    hard disks, 169-172

CALL command, 619-621
    calling/returning batch files, 411-412
    parameters/switches, 619

calling batch files (CALL command), 411-412

Canadian-French code page, 354

CANCEL command (4DOS), 498

canceling commands (Ctrl+C keystroke), 52

carriage return/line feed meta-string, 296

CBL (COBOL source file) filename extension, 105

CD command, 487, 621-623

cd command (Unix), 485

CD-ROM drives
    accessing, 835-836, 843-844
    device drivers, troubleshooting, 316

CD-Rs (write-once CDs), 128

CD-RWs (rewritable CDs), 128

CDD command (4DOS), 498

central processing units. *See* **CPUs**

CFG (program configuration information), filename extension, 105

CGA (Color Graphics Adapter), 299-300, 821

/CH switch, DIR command, 194

CHAIN command, 624

Change Compression Ratio dialog box, 144

Change dialog box, 365-366, 378-379
    change all option, 379
    find and verify option, 379

Change Size dialog box, 143

changing text, block editing (DOS Editor), 378-379

character attribute codes (ANSI.SYS), 421-422

character sets
    changing, 624-625
    international, 860-862
    loading into memory, 747-748

character tables, code page switching, 344-345

characters
    filenames, 593-594
    keyboards
        ASCII code sets, 423-424
        changing to other languages, 790-792
        dead keys, 352-353

*international settings
(KEYB.COM file),*
342-344
macro substitutions, 424
reassigning (ANSI.SYS),
424
remapping, 351-353
wildcard, filenames,
594-596
characters per line (screen display), 298
CHCP command, 624-625
code page switching, loading, 349-350
parameters/switches, 624
CHDIR command, 621-623
directory modifications, 119-120
CHECK command, 626
CHECKIT.BAT file, 408
/CHECKONLY switch, SCANDISK command, 189
CHKDSK command, 108, 626-630
directory problems, 184
disk analysis, 184-188
FAT problems, 184
parameters/switches, 626-627
report display, 185-186
switches, 185
CHKDSK.EXE file, 505
CHKLST.MS file, 508
CHKSTATE.SYS (device driver), 444, 507, 631
CHOICE command, 631-633
batch files, 397, 401
pausing for input, 404-405
display menus, creating, 406-407
parameters/switches, 631
simple menus, creating, 405-406
CHOICE.COM file, 505
CHP (Chapter) filename extension, 105

CHR (Character) filename extension, 105
/CLASSIFY switch, MEM command, 283
Clean Boot, F5 startup control key, 564
cleaning floppy drive read/write heads, 156
clearing
command-history buffer (DOSKEY), 436
screen display (ANSI.SYS), 423
clients, 781-786
network cards, installation considerations, 472
network software configuration tips, 482
Clipboard, text
block editing (DOS Editor), 374-376
copying, 375
cutting, 375
deleting, 375
pasting, 375
clock
CMOSCLK.SYS command, 634
DATE command, 277-278
setting, 276-277, 930-932
TIME command, 278-279
CLOCK$ devices, 104
CLOSE command (FTP), 487
CLS command, 633-634
ANSI.SYS, screen clears, 423
uses, 319
clusters, 150-151
FAT, 112-113
hard disks, 195
CMOS (Complementary Metal Oxide Semiconductor) chips, 16
CMOSCLK.SYS command, 634

CNF (Program configuration information), filename extension, 105
CNFIGNAM.EXE device driver, 634-635
code page switching, internationalization, 340, 344-345
hardware requirements, 345
installing (CHCP command), 349-350
installing (DISPLAY.SYS), 346-347
installing (MODE command), 348-349
installing (NLSFUNC.EXE), 348
installing (PRINTER.SYS), 347-348
code pages, 298
changing, 624-625
configuring, 818-821
international support, 860-862
international switching, 695-698
cold booting versus warm booting, 24
COLOR command (4DOS), 498
Color Graphics Adapter (CGA), 299-300, 747, 821
colors
menus, displaying (CONFIG.SYS file [menu] section), 34-35
screen
changing (DOS Editor), 385-386
selecting, 805-807
columns, screen, adjusting, 300-301
COM (Program) filename extension, 105
COM files, converting .EXE files to, 727
combining ASCII files (COPY command), 204-205

COMMAND command,
  635-636
  parameters, 289
  secondary command
    processor, 288-291
  switches, 635
command interpreter, specifying, 907-909
command line
  DOS Editor, launching, 363
  editing capabilities, 701-704
  editing keys, 52-54,
    433-434
    with DOSKEY, 434, 567
    without DOSKEY,
      565-566
  files, deleting from (ERASE
    command), 221-222
  help switch (/?), 46
  versus DOS Shell, 59
**command processor,
  289-290**
  COMSPEC variable, 304
  copying, 635-636
  deleting temporary copy,
    727-728
  exiting, 290
  secondary, 289
**command prompt, changing,
  295-296**
command reference
  conventions, 590-592
  icons, 592
command-history buffer
  batch files, creating
    (DOSKEY), 435-436
  clearing (DOSKEY), 436
  viewing (DOSKEY), 435
**COMMAND.COM file,
  289-290, 505**
  batch file execution, 412
  boot disk, 24-25
  booting process, 17
  copying, 635-636
  damaged, troubleshooting,
    25-26
  deleting temporary copy,
    727-728

  exiting, 290
  second copy, 290-291
    loading, 288-289
commands
  4DOS
    BEEP, 498
    CANCEL, 498
    CDD, 498
    COLOR, 498
    DELAY, 498
    DESCRIBE, 498
    DIRHISTORY, 498
    DRAWBOX, 499
    DRAWHLINE, 499
    DRAWVLINE, 499
    ESET, 499
    EXCEPT, 499
    FFIND, 499
    FREE, 499
    GLOBAL, 499
    GOSUB, 499
    HISTORY, 499
    IFF, 499
    INKEY, 499
    INPUT, 499
    KEYSTACK, 499
    LIST, 499
    LOADBTM, 499
    LOG, 499
    MEMORY, 499
    REBOOT, 499
    SCREEN, 499
    SCRPUT, 499
    SELECT, 499
    TEE, 499
    TEXT, 499
    TIMER, 499
    TOUCH, 499
    TREE, 499
    UNSET, 499
    VSCRPUT, 499
    ? (question mark), 604-605
    @ (at symbol), 602-603
      batch files, 397
  ANSI.SYS, 608-610
    ECHO, 417-418
    Escape character, 417
    parameters/switches, 609
    PROMPT, 419
    TYPE, 418-419

  APPEND, 610-613
  ASSIGN, 613
    disk drive requests, 302
  ATTRIB, 108-110, 613-615
  AUTOEXEC.BAT file,
    line-by-line examination,
    31-32
  BACKUP, 616
  batch files, 390, 397-398,
    584
  blocks, 606-608
  BREAK, 616-617
    parameters/switches, 616
    syntax, 468
  BREAK=, 616-617
  BUFFERS, 461-462,
    617-618
    parameters/switches, 617
  CALL, 619-621
    batch files, 397
    *calling/returning batch
      files, 411-412*
    parameters/switches, 619
  canceling (Ctrl+C), 52
  CD, 621-623
    parameters/switches, 622
  CHAIN, 624
  CHCP, 624-625
    *code page switching,
      349-350*
    parameters/switches, 624
  CHDIR, 621-623
    *directory modifications,
      119-120*
  CHECK, 626
  CHKDSK, 108, 184-188,
    626-630
    *parameters/switches,
      626-627*
  CHOICE, 631-633
    batch files, 397, 401
    *display menu creation,
      406-407*
    parameters/switches, 631
    *pausing batch files for
      input, 404-405*
    *simple menu creation,
      405-406*
  CLS, 633-634
  CMOSCLK.SYS, 634

COMMANDS

COMMAND, 635-636
  parameters, 289, 635
  secondary command processor, 288-291
COMP, 636-638
Compress menu
  Create new drive, 146
  Existing drive, 145
CONFIG, 638
CONFIG.SYS DEVICE
  drivers, 585-586
CONFIG.SYS file, 584-585
  BREAK, 27
  BUFFERS, 27
  COUNTRY, 27
  DEVICE, 27
  DEVICEHIGH, 27
  DOS, 27
  DRIVPARM, 27
  FCBS, 27
  FILE, 27
  INCLUDE, 27
  INSTALL, 27
  LASTDRIVE, 27
  line-by-line examination, 28-29
  MENUCOLOR, 27
  MENUDEFAULT, 27
  MENUITEM, 27
  NUMLOCK, 27
  REM, 27
  SET, 27
  SHELL, 27
  STACKS, 28
  SUBMENU, 28
  SWITCHES, 28
COPY, 108, 203, 639-642
  batch file creation, 392-393
  combining ASCII files, 204-205
  copying files, 202-203
  copying files from console devices, 205-206
  defaults, 214
  groups of files, copying, 204
  parameters/switches, 639-640
  redirecting input to COPYCOMP.BAT file, 392
  renaming files, 205
  switches, 203
  use guidelines, 202-203
COUNTRY=, 642-644
CPBACKUP, 645-647
CPBDIR, 647
CPSCHED, 647-648
CRC, 648
CREATE, 648-649
CSCRIPT, 649-650
CTTY, 650-651
CURSOR.EXE, 651
CVT.EXE, 651-652
DATAMON, 652
DATE, 277-278, 653
DBLSPACE, 654
DBLSPACE/
  AUTOMOUNT, 655
DBLSPACE/CHKDSK, 656
DBLSPACE/COMPRESS, 656-657
DBLSPACE/CREATE, 657-659
DBLSPACE/
  DEFRAGMENT, 659-660
DBLSPACE/DELETE, 660
DBLSPACE/
  DOUBLEGUARD, 661
DBLSPACE/FORMAT, 661-662
DBLSPACE/INFO, 662-663
DBLSPACE/LIST, 663
DBLSPACE/MOUNT, 663-664
DBLSPACE/RATIO, 664-665
DBLSPACE/SIZE, 665-666
DBLSPACE/
  UNCOMPRESS, 666-667
DBLSPACE/UNMOUNT, 667-668
DCONVERT, 671
DEBUG, 200, 671-672
DEFRAG, 136, 672-674

DEL, 675-676
  deleting files, 135
  parameters/switches, 675
DELOLDOS, 676
DELPURGE, 677
DELQ, 678
DELTREE, 679
  directory deletions, 120-121
  parameters/switches, 679
DELWATCH, 677-678
DEVICE, 223, 443-444
  device drivers, loading, 313
device controls
  MODE, 469
  PRINT, 469
  SET, 469
device drivers, 588
DEVICE=, 679-682
DEVICEHIGH=, 19, 682-686
  parameters/switches, 683
devices, 318
  CLS, 319
  CTTY, 325-326
  GRAPHICS, 319-322
  MODE, 326-332
  PRINT, 322-325
DEVLOAD, 687
DIR, 108, 687-689
  customizing, 199
  directory entry views, 111-112
  finding files, 198
  issuing, 193-194
  listing files, 193-195
  parameters/switches, 687-689
  switches, 193
  viewing screen information, 195
directory, 586
disk, 586-587
DISKCOMP, 690-691
  comparing disks, 219-220
  parameters/switches, 690
DISKCOPY, 692-694
  copying disks, 210-212
  exit codes, 400
  parameters/switches, 692
  switches, 211

DISKMAP.EXE, 694
DISKOPT.EXE, 694-695
DOS Editor, shortcut keys,
 366, 568-569
DOS Shell hotkeys
 + key, 66
 Alt key, 66
 Alt+Esc key, 66
 Alt+F4 key, 66
 Alt+Tab key, 66
 Ctrl+* key, 66
 Ctrl+/ key, 67
 Ctrl+F5 key, 67
 Ctrl+\ key, 67
 Del key, 66
 Esc key, 67
 F1 key, 66
 F3 key, 66
 F5 key, 66
 F7 key, 66
 F8 key, 66
 F9 key, 66
 F10 key, 66
 Shift+down arrow key, 66
 Shift+F5 key, 66
 Shift+F8 key, 66
 Shift+F9 key, 66
 Shift+left arrow key, 67
 Shift+right arrow key, 67
 Shift+Tab key, 67
 Shift+up arrow key, 66
 Tab key, 67
DOS=, 698-700
DOSBOOK, 700
DOSDATA, 701
DOSDOCK, 701
DOSKEY, 701-704
 parameters, 432
 parameters/switches, 702
 reusing, 434-435
DOSSHELL, 705-707
 *parameters/switches,
 704-705*
DPMI, 707
DPMS.EXE, 707-708
DRIVPARM=, 711-713
 *parameters/switches,
 711-712*
DRLOCK, 714
DRMOUSE, 714
DRVLOCK, 714

DYNLOAD, 715
E, 715-716
ECHO, 397, 716-719
 batch files, 397-398
 parameters/switches, 717
EDIT, 187, 719-720
 parameters/switches, 719
EDLIN, 720
EJECT, 721
EMM386, 721-722
environment variables
 PATH, 520
 PROMPT, 520
 SET, 520
ERAQ, 678
ERASE, 675-676
 deleting files, 221-222
EXE2BIN, 727
executing (DOS Editor),
 364
EXIT, 727-728
 command processor, 290
 secondary command processor, 290-291
EXPAND, 728-729
external, 42, 192
EXTRACT, 730
FASTHELP, 730-731
FASTOPEN, 731-732
FC, 217, 732-734
 ASCII mode, 217
 binary mode, 217-218
 *comparing copied files to
 originals, 218*
 *comparing text files,
 218-219*
 *file integrity comparisons,
 215-216*
 parameters/switches, 733
 switches, 216
FCBS (file control blocks),
 463, 734-735
FDISK, 735-736
 parameters/switches, 735
 *partitioning hard disks,
 159-163*
 read-only files, 110
 *repartitioning hard disks,
 164-165*
 */STATUS switch,
 163-164*

File menu
 Associate, 93
 Copy, 91
 Create Directory, 86-87
 Deselect All, 89
 Find Deleted File, 268
 Move, 91
 Select All, 89
 Undelete, 269
 Undelete To, 269
 View File Contents, 91-92
File menu (DOS Editor)
 Exit, 380
 New, 379
 Open, 380-383
 Print, 380, 383-384
 Save, 380-381
 Save As, 380-381
FILELINK, 736
FILES, 463-464, 737
FILEUP, 738
FIND, 738-740
finding (DOSKEY), 436
FOR, 740-742
FOR..IN..DO, 407-409
 batch files, 397
 command interaction, 409
 DOS prompt, 409
FORMAT, 111, 140,
 150-151, 259, 743-746
 /1 switch, 157
 /4 switch, 157
 /8 switch, 157
 /B switch, 157
 boot disk, 25
 /C switch, 157
 /F switch, 153
 *formatting floppy disks,
 151-158*
 formatting hard disks, 166
 /N switch, 157
 *parameters/switches,
 743-744*
 /Q switch, 157
 *quick formatting floppy
 disks, 157*
 read-only files, 110
 /S switch, 157
 switches, 156-157
 /T switch, 157

/U switch, 157
unconditional formatting
 floppy disks, 158
/V switch, 157
FTP
 !, 488
 ASCII, 487
 BINARY, 487
 BYE, 487
 CD, 487
 CLOSE, 487
 DELETE, 487
 DIR, 487
 DISCONNECT, 487
 GET, 487
 LCD, 487
 LS, 487
 MDELETE, 488
 MGET, 488
 MKDIR, 488
 MPUT, 488
 OPEN, 488
 PROMPT, 488
 PUT, 488
 PWD, 488
 QUIT, 488
 RECV, 488
 REMOTEHELP, 488
 RENAME, 488
 RMDIR, 488
 SEND, 488
 STATUS, 488
GOTO, 747
 batch files, 397
 batch files, branching,
  398-399
GRAFTABL, 747-748
GRAPHICS, 748-750
grouping in blocks, 765-768
HCONVERT, 750
HELP, 588, 730-731,
 750-751
Help menu (DOS Editor)
 About, 387
 activating, 387-388
 Getting Started, 387
 Keyboard, 387
HIINSTALL, 751-752
IBAVD, 759
IBMAVSP, 759-760
IEXTRACT, 761

IF, 761-765
 batch files, 397-400
 comparing strings,
  402-403
 ERRORLEVEL testing,
  400-402
 finding files, 404
 parameters/switches, 761
INCLUDE=, 765-768
 parameters/switches, 766
input buffer, editing keys,
 52-54
INSTALL
 parameters, 466-467
 switches, 466-467
INSTALL=, 768-769
INSTALLHIGH, 751-752,
 769
INTERLNK, 223, 770-780
 parameters/switches, 770
internal, 42
international, 588
INTERSVR, 223, 781-786
 parameters/switches,
  781-782
JOIN, 786-788
 adding disk drives to other
  disk directories, 302
 parameters/switches, 786
KBDBUF.SYS, 788-789
KEYB, 790-792
KEYBOARD.SYS, 792-793
keywords, 42-43
LABEL, 166-167, 793-794
 parameters/switches, 793
LASTDRIVE, 464,
 795-796
LOADER, 796-797
LOADFIX, 797-798
LOADHIGH, 19, 798-799
MEM, 283-288, 802-803
 free/used displays, 453-454
 parameters/switches, 802
MEMMAKER, 803-804
MEMMAX, 805
memory, 589
menu bar (DOS Editor),
 365
MENUCOLOR=, 805-807
MENUDEFAULT=,
 807-809

MENUITEM=, 809-811
MIRROR, 811-813
miscellaneous, 589-590
MKDIR, 800-801
 directory creation,
  117-119
 parameters/switches, 800
MODE, 813-815
 code page configuration,
  818-821
 code page switching,
  348-349
 Color Graphics Adapter
  (CGA), 299-300
 parameters/switches, 814,
  819-823
 screen appearance, 298
 screen columns/lines,
  300-301
 screen type, 299
 video adapters, 821-823
MODE COM#, 815-816
MODE CON, 300,
 817-818
MODE LPT#, 824-826
MONOUMB.386, 826-827
MORE, 827-828
 parameters/switches, 827
 viewing ASCII files, 201
mouse, cursor movement
 (DOS Editor), 369-370
MOVE, 828-830
 defaults, 214
 directories, 214
 directory movement,
  121-122, 213
 files, 212-213
 parameters/switches, 828
 switches, 212
MSAV, 830-832
MSBACKUP (Microsoft
 Backup), 108, 239,
 833-834
MSCDEX, 835-836
MSD, 836-837
MSHERC, 837
MWA, 838
MWAVTSR, 838
MWBACKUP, 838-839
MWUNDEL, 839
NLSFUNC, 840

Novell networks
  FILER, 481
  LOGIN, 481
  MAP, 481
NUMLOCK=, 840-841
NWCACHE, 842-843
NWCDEX, 843-844
online help
  accessing, 46-47
  Alt+B (Previous Topic), 49-50
  Alt+C (Contents), 49-50
  Alt+N (Next Topic), 49-50
  exiting, 51
  jump words, 48-49
  menu options, 49
  navigating, 47-50
  topics, printing, 50-51
  topics, searching, 51
Optimize Menu
  (DEFRAG), 179
parameters, 42-44
  filespec, 45
  overriding, 51-52
PASSWD, 844
PASSWORD, 844-845
PATH, 845-847
  finding files, 122-123
  parameters/switches, 846
PAUSE, 398, 847-848
  batch files, 397
PCM, 849
PCMATA.SYS, 849
PCMCS, 849
PCMDINST, 849
PCMFIDISK, 850
PCMRMAN, 850-851
PCMSCD, 851
PCMSETUP, 851
POWER, 852-854
pretender
  ASSIGN, 168-169
  JOIN, 468-469
  SUBST, 468-469
PRINT, 857-860
processing when rebooting, 809-811
PROMPT, 295-297, 862-864
  meta-strings, 296-298
  parameters/switches, 862

QBASIC, 864-865
QCONFIG, 865
RAMBOOST, 866-867
RAMSETUP, 871-872
RD, 872-873
RECOVER, 259, 873
REM, 874-875
  batch files, 397-398
  parameters, 467
REMOVDRV, 875
REN, 876
RENAME, 214-215, 876
RENDIR, 877
repeating for group of files, 740-742
REPLACE, 877-880
replaceable parameters, 599-600
REPORT, 880
reserved names, 594
RESIZE, 880
RESTORE, 881-884
reusing, 434-435
RMDIR, 872-873
  directory deletions, 120
  parameters/switches, 872
SCANDISK, 884-888
  /ALL switch, 189
  /AUTOFIX switch, 189
  /CHECKONLY switch, 189
  /CUSTOM switch, 189
  /FRAGMENT switch, 189
  /MONO switch, 189
  /NOSAVE switch, 189
  /NOSUMMARY switch, 189
  parameters/switches, 884-885
  /SURFACE switch, 189
  /UNDO switch, 189
SCANREG, 888-889
SCHEDULE, 889-890
SCRIPT, 890-891
scrolling (DOS Editor), 370
SDEFRAG, 891-892
SDIR, 892-894

SET, 294, 894-897
  AUTOEXEC.BAT file, 30
  environment variables, 294-295
  parameters/switches, 894
SETUP, 897
SETVER, 898-903
  DOS versions, 280-283
  parameters/switches, 898
SHARE, 906-907
SHELL, 464
  environment size, 26
  parameters, 465-466
  switches, 465-466
SHELL=, 907-909
SHIFT, 910
  batch files, 397
  moving batch file parameters, 409-410
SIZER, 910
SMARTDRV, 911-913
SMARTMON, 914
SORT, 915-916
SSETUP, 917
STAC, 917
STACHIGH, 917
STACKER, 918
STACKS=, 918-920
SUBMENU=, 920-922
SUBST, 302-303, 922-923
  parameters/switches, 922
  referencing drive paths, 303-304
  rules for use, 304
SWITCH, 924
switches, 44-45
  overriding, 51-52
SWITCHES, 467-468, 924-926
syntax, 42-43
  backslashes (\), 45
  Drive\Files format, 43-44
  paradigm, 44
  slashes (/), 45
  SourceFiles format, 43-44
SYS, 167-168, 926-928
  boot disk, 25
  parameters/switches, 927
SYSINFO, 928-929
system performance, 589
TASKMGR, 929

TIME, 278-279, 930-931
    parameters/switches, 930
TIMEOUT, 931
TOUCH, 931-932
TREE, 113-114, 932
    listing directories, 123-124
    parameters/switches, 932
TUNER, 933
TYPE, 187, 933-934
    displaying batch file contents, 396
    parameters/switches, 933
    use guidelines, 201
    viewing ASCII files, 200-201
UNCOMP, 936
UNDELETE, 221, 936-939
    parameters/switches, 936-938
    recovering files, 262-266
UNFORMAT, 939-940
    parameters/switches, 939
    recovering partition tables, 261
    unformatting disks, 257-261
UNINSTALL, 940
UNPACK2, 941
UNSTACK, 942
VER, 942
    DOS versions, 279
VERIFY, 943-944
VFINDTD, 944
VIEW, 945-946
View menu
    Program List, 74
    Refresh, 71
VOL, 167, 946-947
VSAFE, 947-948
wildcards
    asterisk (*), 54-55
    characters, 594-596
    question mark (?), 54-55
    Windows programs, 590
XCOPY, 950-954
    backing up disks, 208-209
    copying directories, 206-207
    copying directory branches, 209-210
    copying disks, 209
    defaults, 214
    parameters/switches, 950-951
    switches, 206
    use guidelines, 207-208
XCOPY32, 954
XDEL, 955
XDF, 955
XDFCOPY, 956
XDIR, 956-957

COMMANDS.TXT file, 513

comments, batch files, 874-875
    inserting, 398

COMP command, 636-638

COMP.EXE file, 513

comparing
    backups against original files (Microsoft Backup), 241
    disks (DISKCOMP command), 219-220
    files, 217, 636-638
        copied to originals (FC command), 218
        integrity (FC command), 215-216
        with FC command, 732-734
    floppy disks, 690-691
    strings (IF command), 402-403
    text files (FC command), 218-219

Complementary Metal Oxide Semiconductor chips. *See* **CMOS chips**

Compress menu commands
    Create new drive, 146
    Existing drive, 145

compressed disk drives, 656
    changing sizes, 665-666
    defragmenting, 659-660
    deleting (DoubleSpace), 145
    files and subdirectories, deleting, 661-662
    formatting (DoubleSpace), 145
    free space, 657-659, 664-665
    information, viewing, 662-663
    uncompressing, 666-667
    unmounting, 660

Compressed Drive Information dialog box, 143

compressed files, copying, 728-729

compressed volume files. *See* **CVFs**

compressing
    disks (DoubleSpace), 140-141, 145-146, 654-657
    files for disk space maximization, 183
    RAM drives, 890
    Stacker drives, 936, 942

compression ratio, 664-665
    DoubleSpace utility, 143-144
    files/directories, 892-894

compression utilities, download sites, 183

computer viruses
    McAfee VirusScan, 496
        disk scanning, 497
        downloading, 496
        frequency of scans, 497
    potential damage, 496
    prevention, 496
    transmission of, 496

computers, linking, 774-786

COMSPEC variable, 304, 521

CON devices, 104

CONFIG command, 638

CONFIG environment variable, 521-522

CONFIG.SYS DEVICE driver command, 584-586

CONFIG.SYS file, 511
  ANSI.SYS driver, locating, 416
  blocks (commands), 606-608
  boot disk, 24-25
  boot process, modifying, 17, 38-39
  commands
    BREAK, 27, 468
    BUFFERS, 27
    COUNTRY, 27
    DEVICE, 27
    DEVICEHIGH, 27
    DOS, 27
    DRIVPARM, 27
    FCBS, 27
    FILE, 27
    INCLUDE, 27
    INSTALL, 27
    LASTDRIVE, 27
    MENUCOLOR, 27
    MENUDEFAULT, 27
    MENUITEM, 27
    NUMLOCK, 27
    REM, 27
    SET, 27
    SHELL, 27
    STACKS, 28
    SUBMENU, 28
    SWITCHES, 28
  [common] section, 33
  configuration menu, using as system menu, 36-38
  default configuration, 34
  device drivers, 443-444
    directory location, 312-313
    troubleshooting, 314-315
  FCBS command, 463
  FILES command, 463-464
  LASTDRIVE command, 464
  line-by-line examination, 28-29
  [menu] section, 33
    menu color selection, 34-35
  multiple configurations, 32-33
  subroutines, 924
  system configuration, 26-29

configuration files
  modifying (DOS Editor), 362
  starting, 624

configuring
  backup utilities
    Microsoft Backup, 235-236
    Microsoft Backup for Windows 3.x, 235-236
  cables (Interlnk), 223-224
  code pages, 818-821
  console devices, 817-818
  device drivers, 312-313
  DOS, 924-926
  DOS versions, 280-283
  Interlnk, 223-224
  keyboards, 817-818
  memory (MemMaker), 455-460
  Microsoft Undelete (Windows), 267
  monitors, 817-818
  startup menu, 920-922
  system devices, 813-815

connecting
  Interlnk, 227
  Internet
    FTP, 485-486, 489-491
    Gopher, 484
    ISP shell account, 484-485
    Telnet, 484-485
    troubleshooting guidelines, 491-492

consoles, 298
  auxiliary, I/O devices, 650-651
  configuring, 817-818
  copying files from (COPY command), 205-206
  CTTY command, 325-326

Contents command (Alt+C keystroke), online help, 49-50

Control Program for Microcomputers (CP/M), forerunner of DOS, 15

controlling
  DoubleSpace, 142
  screen display (ANSI.SYS), 419-423

conventional memory, 283-288
  increasing, 867
  listing contents, 286-287
  loading
    device drivers, 679-682
    TSRs, 768-769
  maximizing, 803-804

conventional memory (RAM), 18-19

conventions
  command reference, 590-592
  country-specific, 642-644
  filenames, 104-107

converting
  drives from FAT16 to FAT32, 651-652
  EXE files to .BIN/.COM files, 727
  XMS (extended memory) to LIM expanded memory (EMS), 722-726

COPY command, 108, 203, 639-642
  batch files, creating, 392-393
  combining ASCII files, 204-205
  copying files from console devices, 205-206
  defaults, 214
  files
    copying, 202-203
    group copying, 204
  parameters/switches, 639-640
  redirecting input to COPYCOMP.BAT file, 392
  renaming files, 205
  switches, 203
    /A, 203
    /B, 203
    /V, 203
    /Y, 203
  use guidelines, 202-203

Copy command (File menu), 91
Copy File dialog box, 67, 91
COPYCMD environment variable, 522
COPYCOMP.BAT file, redirecting input with COPY command, 392
copying
  command processor (COMMAND.COM), 635-636
  directories, 950-954
    XCOPY command, 206-207
    directory branches (XCOPY command), 209-210
  disks
    DISKCOPY command, 210-212
    XCOPY command, 209
  DOS Editor to floppy disks, 363
  environment, program loading, 520
  eXtended Density Format (XDF) disk contents, 956
  files, 639-642, 950-954
    compressed, 728-729
    COPY command, 202-203
    DOS Shell, 89-91
    from console devices (COPY command), 205-206
    groups of (COPY command), 204
    with batch files, 395-396
  floppy disks, 692-694
  subdirectories, 950-954
  text (Clipboard), 375
country codes, internationalization settings, 354-355
COUNTRY command (CONFIG.SYS file), 27
country-specific conventions, 642-644
COUNTRY.ICE file, 505
COUNTRY.SYS file, 505, 644

COUNTRY= command, 642-644
cp command (Unix), 485
CP/M (Control Program for Microcomputers), 15
CPBACKUP command, 645-647
CPBDIR command, 647
CPI (Code page information), 105
CPP (C++ source file) filename extension, 105
CPSCHED command, 647-648
CPUs (central processing units), 13
  early versions
    AT computers, 17
    XT computers, 17
  expanded memory, 19
  Intel
    80386 chips, 18
    80486 chips, 18
  memory, real mode versus protected mode, 17
  motherboards, 13
  system buses, communication functions, 13
CRC (Cyclic Redundancy Check) numbers, 648
CRC command, 648
CREATE command, 648-649
Create Directory command (File menu), 86-87
Create Directory dialog box, 86-87
Create new drive command (Compress menu), 146
creating
  batch files
    COPY command, 392-393
    DOS Editor, 391
    Edlin, 391
    guidelines, 391

  directories
    DOS Shell, 86-87
    MKDIR command, 117-119
  floppy boot disk, 25-26
  macros (DOSKEY), 436-439
  memos (DOS Editor), 362
crippleware, 495
CSCRIPT command, 649-650
Ctrl+* key, DOS Shell hotkey, 66
Ctrl+/ key, DOS Shell hotkey, 67
Ctrl+Alt+Del key combination (warm booting), 24
  ROM BIOS controls, 564
Ctrl+Break keystroke, Break, 564
Ctrl+C keystroke
  Break, 565
  commands, canceling, 52
Ctrl+F1 shortcut key (DOS Editor), 367
Ctrl+F5 key
  Clean Boot startup, 564
  DOS Shell hotkey, 67
Ctrl+F8 key (Interactive Boot), startup control key, 564
Ctrl+Ins shortcut key (DOS Editor), 367
Ctrl+P keystroke, Echo to PRN, 565
Ctrl+Q shortcut key (DOS Editor), 367
Ctrl+S keystroke, Pause, 565
Ctrl+\ key, DOS Shell hotkey, 67
CTTY command, 650-651
  guidelines for use, 326
  I/O devices, 325-326
  parameters/switches, 650
  syntax, 325

currencies (COUNTRY.SYS file), 340-342
current directory, changing, 621-623
current drive meta-string, 297
current path meta-string, 297
CURSOR.EXE command, 651
cursors
  ANSI control codes, 426-427
  LCD screens, 651
  mouse (DOS Editor), 368-370
  movement controls (ANSI.SYS), 420
  positioning controls (ANSI.SYS), 420
/CUSTOM switch, SCANDISK command, 189
Custom setup (DoubleSpace), 142
Custom Setup (MemMaker), 456-460
customizing
  DIR command, 199
  environment variables (SET command), 294, 894-897
  keyboards (ANSI.SYS), 423-424
  prompt, 862-864
  screen appearance (MODE command), 298
  screen display (ANSI.SYS), 421-422
  upper memory, 698-700
cutting text (Clipboard), 375
CV.COM file, 513
CVFs (compressed volume files)
  accessing, 663-664
  deleting, 660
  unmounting, 667-668

CVT.EXE command, 651-652
Cyclic Redundancy Check (CRC) numbers, 648
cylinders (disks), 134-136
  disks, 151
  hard disks, 139

D

/D switch
  SETVER command, 282
  XCOPY command, 207
danger! file designation, 504
DAT files, 105
  extracting files from, 761
data
  byte storage, 138
  loss
    hardware causes, 232-233
    preventing, 232-233
    restoring from backups, 248-251
    software causes, 232-233
DATAMON command, 652
date, setting, 931-932
date and time stamp, 276-277
DATE command, 277-278, 653
date meta-string, 296
dates
  COUNTRY.SYS file, 340-342
  DATE command, 277-278
  international formats, 356-357
  setting, 276-277, 653
  TIME command, 278-279
DAYBACK.BAT file, 402
DB (Database, Paradox) filename extension, 105
DBF (Database, dBASE) filename extension, 105
DBLBOOT.BAT file, 513

DBLBOOT.INI file, 513
DBLSPACE/AUTOMOUNT command, 655
DBLSPACE/CHKDSK command, 656
DBLSPACE/COMPRESS command, 656-657
DBLSPACE/CREATE command, 657-659
DBLSPACE/DEFRAGMENT command, 659-660
DBLSPACE/DELETE command, 660
DBLSPACE/DOUBLEGUARD command, 661
DBLSPACE/FORMAT command, 661-662
DBLSPACE/INFO command, 662-663
DBLSPACE/LIST command, 663
DBLSPACE/MOUNT command, 663-664
DBLSPACE/RATIO command, 664-665
DBLSPACE/SIZE command, 665-666
DBLSPACE/UNCOMPRESS command, 666-667
DBLSPACE/UNMOUNT command, 667-668
DBLSPACE command, 654
DBLSPACE.00x file, 505
DBLSPACE.BIN file (device driver), 444, 505
DBLSPACE.EXE file, 505
DBLSPACE.HLP file, 505
DBLSPACE.INF file, 505
DBLSPACE.INI file, 505
DBLSPACE.SYS device driver, 668-670
DBLSPACE.SYS file, 505
DBLSPACE.WIN file, 505

DBLWIN.HLP file, 505
DCONVERT command, 671
DCOPY.BAT file, 401-402
DCT (Dictionary) filename extension, 105
dead keys, 352-353
/DEBUG switch, MEM command, 283
DEBUG command, 200, 671-672
DEBUG program, 671-672
DEBUG.EXE file, 505
default system configurations, creating, 34
DEFAULT.SET file, 508
DEFAULT.SLT file, 509
defining environment variables (SET command), 295
DEFRAG command, 136, 672-674
DEFRAG program, 177-181
    Optimize menu commands, 179
    parameters, 180-181
    switches, 180-181
    use guidelines, 181
DEFRAG.EXE file, 505
DEFRAG.HLP file, 505
Defragment option (DoubleSpace), 146
defragmenting
    compressed disk drives, 659-660
    files, 672-674
    hard disks, 177-181
    (DEFRAG program)
    Stacker drives, 891-892
DEL command, 675-676
    deleting files, 135
    parameters/switches, 675
Del shortcut key (DOS Editor), 66, 367
DELAY command (4DOS), 498

DELETE command (FTP), 487
Delete Item dialog box, 80-81
delete sentry, 262
    installing, 264
delete tracker, 262
    installing, 264
deleted files, recovering, 694, 839, 936-939
deleting
    compressed drives (DoubleSpace), 145
    CVFs (compressed volume files), 660
    directories
        DELTREE command, 120-121
        RMDIR command, 120
    directories/subdirectories branches, 679
    empty subdirectories, 955
    environment variables, 894-897
    files, 222
        being saved by DELWATCH, 677
        from command line (ERASE command), 221-222
        compressed drives, 661-662
        from disks, 135
        from drives and directories, 675-676
        ERASE command, 221-222
        maximizing hard disk space, 182-183
        multiple, 955
        previous versions of DOS, 676
        prompting before, 678
    macros (DOSKEY), 440
    partitions, 161
    program groups (DOS Shell), 80-81
    program items to program (DOS Shell), 82-83

    Stacker stacvol file, 875
    subdirectories, 872-873
        compressed drives, 661-662
    temporary copy of COMMAND.COM file, 727-728
    text
        Clipboard, 375
        DOS Editor, 370-371
DELOLDOS command, 676
DELOLDOS.EXE file, 505
DELPURGE command, 677
DELQ command, 678
DELTREE command, 505, 679
    directory deletions, 120-121
    parameters/switches, 679
DELWATCH, 677-678
DELWATCH.EXE command, 677-678
demoware, 495
DESCRIBE command (4DOS), 498
Deselect All command (File menu), 89
deselecting all files (DOS Shell), 89
Desktop SNMP (Novell NetWare Client), 474
DEV (Program device driver) filename extension, 105
DEVICE command, 223, 443-444
    CONFIG.SYS file, 27
    device drivers, loading, 313
device drivers
    ANSI.SYS, 444
        commands, 608-610
        installing, 416
    CHKSTATE.SYS, 444, 631
    CNFIGNAM.EXE, 634-635
    commands, 443-444, 588
    CONFIG.SYS file, 443-444

DIALOG BOXES 981

configuring, 312-313
DBLSPACE.BIN, 444
DBLSPACE.SYS, 668-670
defined, 443
DISPLAY.SYS, 444,
  695-698
DMA channels, assignments, 311-312
DMDRVR.BIN, 444
DRIVER.SYS, 444,
  708-711
EGA.SYS, 444, 720-721
EMM386.EXE, 444,
  722-726
  expanded memory,
    449-451
  parameters/switches,
    723-725
floppy disk drives, 708-711
hardware interrupts,
  309-310
  IRQ assignments, 310-311
HIMEM.SYS, 444, 752-759
  Extended Memory
    Manager, 445-448
  parameters/switches,
    752-755
  syntax, 446
INTERLNK.EXE, 444,
  770-780
KBDBUF.SYS, 788-789
loading, 687
  from DOS command
    prompt, 715
  into conventional memory,
    679-682
  into upper memory, 803
  into upper memory area,
    682-686
MONOUMB.386, 444
MOUSE.COM, 444
peripherals, 308-309
POWER.EXE, 444,
  854-857
PRINTER.SYS, 444,
  860-862
RAMDRIVE.SYS, 444,
  867-871
SCREATE.SYS, 890
SETVER.EXE, 444,
  904-906

SMARTDRV.EXE, 444,
  914
SSTOR.SYS, 444
STACHIGH.SYS, 917
system configuration, 444
troubleshooting scenarios
  AUTOEXEC.BAT file,
    editing, 314-315
  CD-ROM drives, 316
  CONFIG.SYS file, editing, 314-315
  conflicts, 314
  IRQ conflicts, 314-315
  modems, 316
  parallel printers, 316
  serial port cards, 316
  video cards, 316
UMBCGA.SYS, 934
UMBEMS.SYS, 934
UMBHERC.SYS, 935
UMBMONO.SYS, 935
upper memory area (UMA),
  loading, 451-452
VFINTD.386, 444,
  944-945
WINA20.386, 949-950
device error messages
  abort (A) option, 557
  alphabetical listing, 557-561
  fail (F) option, 557
  ignore (I) option, 557
  retry (R) option, 557
device filters
  FIND, 335-337
  MORE, 334-335
  SORT, 337-338
DEVICEHIGH command,
  19, 682-686
  CONFIG.SYS file, 27
  upper memory area (UMA),
    452
devices
  code pages, status viewing,
    350
  commands, 318
    CLS, 319
    CTTY, 325-326
    GRAPHICS, 319-322
    MODE, 326-332
    PRINT, 322-325

control commands
  MODE, 469
  PRINT, 469
  SET, 469
filters, 334-335
logical, 103-104
memory, I/O addresses, 312
names
  CLOCK$, 104
  COM, 104
  CON, 104
  LPT, 104
  NUL, 104
redirection operators, 332
  guidelines for use, 334
  issuing, 332-333
DEVLOAD command, 687
dialog boxes
  Add Group, 79
  Add Program, 82
  Associate File, 93
  Backup Options, 247-248
  Change, 365-366, 378-379
    change all option, 379
    find and verify option, 379
  Change Compression Ratio,
    144
  Change Size, 143
  Compressed Drive
    Information, 143
  Copy File, 91
  Create Directory, 86-87
  Delete Item, 80-81
  DOS Backup, 236
  DOS Shell
    command buttons, 70
    Copy File, 67
    File Display Options,
      68-69
    list box entries, 68
    option buttons, 68-69
    option check boxes, 69
    text box entries, 67-68
  Find, 51, 377-378
    match upper/lowercase
      option, 378
    whole word option, 378
  Find Deleted Files, 268
  function of, 364
  Move File, 91

New Program Object, 79
Open, 382-383
Print, 50-51, 383
  Complete Document option, 384
  Selected Text Only option, 384
Program Group Properties, 80
Screen Display Mode, 75-76
DIF (Data Interchange Format), 105
differential backups
  executing (Microsoft Backup for Windows 3.x), 242
  frequency of, 238
  Microsoft Backup, 238
DIR (Program data file, directory) filename extension, 105
DIR command, 108, 687-689
  customizing, 199
  DIRCMD environment variable, 199
  directory entries, viewing, 111-112
  finding files, 198
  issuing, 193-194
  listing files, 193-195
  parameters/switches, 687-689
  switches, 193
    /A, 195-196
    /B, 197
    /L, 197
    /O, 197
    /P, 195
    /W, 195
  syntax, 193
  viewing screen information, 195
DIR command (FTP), 487
DIRCMD environment variable, 199, 522-523

directories, 102, 110
  adding disk drives (JOIN command), 302
  branches
    copying (XCOPY command), 209-210
    deleting, 679
  changing, 621-623
  checking, 626-630
  compression ratio, 892-894
  copying (XCOPY command), 206-207, 950-954
  creating (MKDIR command), 117-119, 800-801
  dedicated for applications, 193
  deleting
    empty, 955
    DELTREE command, 120-121
    RMDIR command, 120
  DOS Shell
    branches, collapsing, 84-86
    branches, expanding, 84-86
    creating, 86-87
    hierarchical structure, 83
    tree structure, 83
    views, modifying, 70-74
  entries, viewing (DIR command), 111-112
  files
    deleting, 675-676
    information, 687-689
    recovery of, 266
    selecting (DOS Shell), 89
  FTP
    displaying, 490-491
    retrieving, 491
  information
    caching (FASTOPEN), 173-174
    columns, 194
  listing (TREE command), 123-124
  modifying (CHDIR command), 119-120
  moving (MOVE command), 213

  passwords, 844-845
  pathname expressions, 115-117
  renaming (MOVE command), 121-122, 214
  sorting (DEFRAG program), 179-180
  splitting (SUBST command), 302-303
  temporary, 124-125
  trees, 932
  troubleshooting (CHKDSK command), 184
  Unix, filename case sensitivity, 485
  view options in DOS Shell, 61
  viewing (DIR command), 194-195
DIRHISTORY command (4DOS), 498
disabling memory, 805
DISCONNECT command (FTP), 487
disk buffers
  BUFFERS command, 461-462
  default number of, 462
  flushing, 461
  look-ahead buffers, 462
  secondary caches, 462
  suggested number of, 462
disk caching (SMARTDrive), 169-172
disk commands, 586-587
disk drives
  adding to directory of other disks (JOIN command), 302
  aliases, 613
  compressed, 656
    changing size, 665-666
    defragmenting, 659-660
    files and subdirectories, deleting, 661-662
    free space, 664-665
    information, 662-663
    uncompressing, 666-667
    unmounting, 660

current directories, changing, 621-623
cylinders, 134-136
directories, splitting (SUBST command), 302-303
free space, 657-659
information, 663
installing, 711-713
mounting removable, 655
names, 176
networks, drive letters, 795-796
number of, changing (LASTDRIVE command), 464
read/write heads, 133
requests, redirecting (ASSIGN command), 302
sectors, 136-137
tracks, 134

disk errors (ScanDisk), 884-888

disk failures, files, restoring, 250-251

disk-based memory, 14
floppy disks, 14
hard disks, 14
media, 20-21

disk-compression programs, 654-657

DISKCOMP command, 505, 690-691
comparing disks, 219-220
parameters/switches, 690

DISKCOPY command, 505, 692-694
copying disks, 210-212
exit codes, 400
parameters/switches, 692
switches, 211
/1, 211
/M, 211
/V, 211

DISKMAP.EXE command, 694

DISKOPT.EXE command, 694-695

disks
3 1/2" capacities, 153
5 1/4" capacities, 153
analyzing (CHKDSK command), 184-188
analyzing (SCANDISK utility), 188-189
backing up (XCOPY command), 208-209
bootable, creating, 167-168
byte storage, 138
caching, 842-843
SMARTDrive, 911-913
capacity, 153
clusters, 150-151
comparing (DISKCOMP command), 219-220, 690-691
compressing (DoubleSpace), 140-141, 145-146
copying
directories to (XCOPY command), 206-207
DISKCOPY command, 210-212, 692-694
XCOPY command, 209
cylinders, 151
DOS Shell, logging to different disk, 70-71
eXtended Density Format (XDF), contents, copying, 956
floppy
bootable, creating, 926-928
formats, 138
formatting (FORMAT command), 150-151
raw/usable capacity, 139
SSDD (single-sided, double density), 138
formats, 137
formatting, 136
fragmentation effects, 177
hard
cylinders, 139
formats, 139-140
recovering partition tables, 261

naming (LABEL command), 166-167
RAM, 174-176
reformatted, recovering, 939-940
sectors, 134, 150-151
serial numbers, 154-156
displaying, 946-947
storage systems, evolution of, 128
system files, transferring to, 167-168
tracks, 150
unformatting, 257-258
recovering from accidental formats, 258-261
volume labels, 154-156, 793-794
displaying, 946-947
VOL command, 167

display adapters
Color Graphics Adapter (CGA), 747
EGA, 720-721

display menus, creating (CHOICE command), 406-407

DISPLAY.SYS (device driver), 444, 695-698
code page switching, loading, 346-347

displaying
batch file contents, 396
compressed information (DoubleSpace), 142-143
compression ratio for files/directories, 892-894
DOS versions, 279, 942
file contents, 933-934
FTP directories, 490-491
memory, free/used (MEM command), 453-454, 802-803
messages, batch files, 398
online documents, 945
PC's techinal information, 865
serial numbers (disks), 946-947
volume labels, 946-947

DLL (Windows Dynamic Link Library) filename extension, 105
DMA (direct memory access) channels, 311-312
large data-transfer functions, 311-312
DMDRVR.BIN (device driver), 444, 506
DOC (Document) filename extension, 106
docking laptops, 701
documents, on-line, displaying, 945
dollar sign meta-string, 297
DOS (DIsk Operating System)
introduction of, 15
starting, timeout periods, 807-809
versions
displaying, 279
setting, 280-283
DOS Backup dialog box, 236
DOS control keys
Ctrl+C (Break), 565
Ctrl+P (Echo to PRN), 565
Ctrl+S (Pause), 565
DOS Editor, 362
batch files
creating, 391
modifying, 362
block editing
Clipboard, 374-376
fundamentals, 373
text, changing, 378-379
text, finding, 377-378
text searching and replacing, 376-377
text selection, 373-374
bulletin board files, viewing, 362
commands
executing, 364
shortcut keys, 366
configuration files, modifying, 362

cursor movement interfaces
control keys, 369-370
keypad, 369-370
dialog boxes
Change, 365-366
Enter key, 366
Esc key, 366
Tab key, 366
EDIT command
/B switch, 384
/G switch, 384
/H switch, 385
/NOHI switch, 385
exiting, 384
File menu commands, 379-384
files, loading when launching, 383
floppy disks, using with, 363
Help menu commands, 387-388
Insert mode, 371
keystroke commands, 568-569
launching, 363
memos, creating, 362
menu bar, 364
activating, 365
command options, 365
Edit menu, 365
ellipsis indicator, 365
Esc key, 365
File menu, 365
Help menu, 365
highlighted commands, 365
Search menu, 365
mouse
actions list, 368
cursor movement, 369-370
Microsoft-compatible, 367
Overtype mode, 371
QBASIC.INI file, 386-387
README files, writing, 362
required files
EDIT.COM, 362
EDIT.HLP, 362
QBASIC.EXE, 362

screen
appearance, 363
colors, changing, 385-386
saving custom options, 386-387
scrollbars, removing, 386
scrollbars, 364
scrolling commands, 370
status bar, 364
text
automatic indenting, 372
overtyping, 371
place markers, 373
tab stops, 372
unknown text files, viewing, 362
window appearance, 364
DOS Protected Mode Interface support, loading/unloading, 707
DOS Shell
advantages/disadvantages, 58
All Files view, 74
dialog boxes
command buttons, 70
Copy File, 67
File Display Options, 68-69
list box entries, 68
option buttons, 68-69
option check boxes, 69
text box entries, 67-68
types, 67
directories
branches, collapsing, 84-86
branches, expanding, 84-86
creating, 86-87
hierarchical structure, 83
tree structure, 83
views, modifying, 70-74
disks, logging to different disk, 70-71
DOS Editor, launching, 363
file lists, switching between, 72-73
files
ASCII display, 59
associating with programs, 92-93

copying, 89-91
entire deselection, 89
entire selection, 89
hexadecimal display, 59
moving, 91
multiple selection, 87-88
select across directories option, 89
single selection, 87
viewing, 91-92
views, modifying, 70-74
graphics mode, 58
GUI simulation, 58
help screen
　commands, 94-95
　contextual, 94-95
hotkey commands
　+ key, 66
　Alt key, 66
　Alt+Esc key, 66
　Alt+F4 key, 66
　Alt+Tab key, 66
　Ctrl+ key, 66*
　Ctrl+/ key, 67
　Ctrl+F5 key, 67
　Ctrl+\ key, 67
　Del key, 66
　Esc key, 67
　F1 key, 66
　F3 key, 66
　F5 key, 66
　F7 key, 66
　F8 key, 66
　F9 key, 66
　F10 key, 66
　Shift+down arrow key, 66
　Shift+F5 key, 66
　Shift+F8 key, 66
　Shift+F9 key, 66
　Shift+left arrow key, 67
　Shift+right arrow key, 67
　Shift+Tab key, 67
　Shift+up arrow key, 66
　Tab key, 67
installation of, 59
introduction of, 58
keystroke commands, 569-571
launching, 59, 704-707

menus
　menu bar, 64
　pull-down, 64-65
mouse requirements, 59
multitasking features, 59
point-and-click usage, 58
program groups
　adding, 78-80
　deleting, 80-81
　examples, 77-78
　hierarchy, 77-78
　naming guidelines, 79
　passwords, 80
　program items, adding, 81-82
　program items, deleting, 82-83
　program items, modifying, 82
　properties, modifying, 80
　reordering, 81
program list, viewing, 74
screen modes, 75-76
scrollbars, 63
scrollboxes, 63
selection cursor, 63-64
shortcut keys, launching programs, 83
similarity to Windows interface, 58
Supplemental Programs Disk inclusion, 58
Task Swapper, activating, 93-94
text-based interface, 58
versus DOS command line, 58-59
video modes, 75-76
window
　appearance, 59
　area title bar, 61
　area, moving, 63-64
　area, selecting, 62
　directory views, 61
　drive area, 61
　menu bar, 60
　program groups, 62
　scrollbars, 61
　status line, 60
　task list area, 62
　title bar, 60

DOS version meta-string, 297
DOS= command, 698-700
DOSBOOK command, 700
DOSDATA command, 701
DOSDOCK command, 701
DOSHELP.HLP file, 506
DOSKEY
　benefits, 432
　command-history buffer keys, 435-436
　command-line editing keys, 433-434, 565-567
　commands, locating, 436
　loading, 432
　macros
　　creating, 436-439
　　defining from bootup, 439
　　deleting, 440
　　naming, 440
　　replaceable parameters, 438
　　running, 439-440
　　special characters, 437-438
　parameters, 432
　　command, 437
　　macroname, 437
　reusing commands, 434-435
DOSKEY command, 506, 701-704
DOSSETUP.INI file, 511
DOSSHELL command, 704-707
DOT (Word for Windows template) filename extension, 106
double buffering, enabling, 914
double-density disks, 138, 153
DoubleGuard, 661
DoubleSpace, 656-659
　automounting, 655
　compressed disk drives, 145-146
　　free space, 664-665
　　information, 662-663
　　size, 665-666

DOUBLESPACE

compression ratio, changing, 143-144
controlling, 142
CVF access, 663-664
Defragment option, 146
deleting
compressed disk drive files and subdirectories, 661-662
compressed drives, 145
device driver, 668-670
disk compression program, 140-141
disk drive information, 663
displaying compressed information, 142-143
DoubleGuard, 661
drive sizes, changing, 143
formatting compressed drives, 145
installing, 141-142
SCANDISK, 147
starting, 654
uncompressing disk drives, 147, 666-667
unmounting
CVFs, 667-668
drives, 660

downloading
compression utilities, Web site resources, 183
Novell NetWare Client, 473

Downloads.com Web site, 183

DPMI command, 707

DPMS.EXE command, 707-708

DR-DOS
help, starting, 700
uninstalling, 940

DRAWBOX command (4DOS), 499

DRAWHLINE command (4DOS), 499

DRAWVLINE command (4DOS), 499

drifting (hard disks), 148

drive area (DOS Shell), 61

drive letters for networks, 795-796

DRIVER.SYS (device driver), 444, 506, 708-711

drivers
device
ANSI.SYS, 608-610
CHKSTATE.SYS, 631
CNFIGNAM.EXE, 634-635
commands, 588
DBLSPACE.SYS, 668-670
DISPLAY.SYS, 695-698
DRIVER.SYS, 708-711
EGA.SYS, 720-721
EMM386.EXE, 722-726
floppy disk drives, 708-711
HIMEM.SYS, 752-759
INTERLINK.EXE, 770-773
INTERLNK.EXE, 774-780
KBDBUF.SYS, 788-789
loading, 679-687
loading from DOS command prompt, 715
POWER.EXE, 854-857
PRINTER.SYS, 860-862
RAMDRIVE.SYS, 867-871
SCREATE.SYS, 890
SETVER.EXE, 904-906
SMARTDRV.EXE, 914
STACHIGH.SYS, 917
UMBCGA.SYS, 934
UMBEMS.SYS, 934
UMBHERC.SYS, 935
UMBMONO.SYS, 935
VFINTD.386, 944-945
WINA20.386, 949-950
DRMOUSE, 714
Novell NetWare Client, configuring, 475
Phoenix Super Client, 851
Stacker, storing in extended memory, 707-708

drives (disk)
aliases, creating, 922-923
CD-ROM, accessing, 835-836, 843-844
converting from FAT16 to FAT32, 651-652
disk
cylinders, 134-136
read/write heads, 133
sectors, 136-137
tracks, 134
ejecting medium, 721
fixed, 130
floppy disk
components, 129-130
size evolution, 131-132
versus hard disks, 131
hard disk, 130
advantages/disadvantages, 131
components diagram, 130
future of, 131
platters, 130
locking/unlocking, 714
machine components, 130
mounting removable, 655
pathname expressions, 115-117
performance, optimizing, 694-695
RAM, compressing, 890
removable, 130
Stacker
checking, 626
creating, 648-649
defragmenting/recompressing, 891-892
mounting/unmounting, 918
read/write, read-only passwords, 844
resizing, 880
statistics, 880
uncompressing, 936, 942
updating, 750
subdirectories, joining, 786-788

Drive\Files command syntax, 43-44
DRIVPARM command, CONFIG.SYS file, 27, 711-713
DRMOUSE command, 714
DRV (program device driver) filename extension, 106
DRVLOCK command, 714
/DS switch, UNDELETE command, 263
/DT switch, UNDELETE command, 263
DTA (Data) filename extension, 106
dual file lists, switching from single type (DOS Shell), 72-73
DVD-ROMs, storage evolution, 128
DVORAK.SYS file, 513

E

/E switch, XCOPY command, 206
E command, 715-716
ECHO command, 397, 716-719
   ANSI.SYS, 417-418
   batch files, 397-398
   parameters/switches, 717
Echo to PRN key (Ctrl+P keystroke), 565
EDIT command, 187, 719-720
   AUTOEXEC.BAT file, editing, 32
   parameters/switches, 719
   switches
      /B (DOS Editor), 384
      /G (DOS Editor), 384
      /H (DOS Editor), 385
      /NOHI (DOS Editor), 385

Edit menu (DOS Editor), 365
EDIT.COM file (DOS Editor), 362, 506
EDIT.HLP file (DOS Editor), 362, 506
editing
   binary files (DEBUG command), 200
   command line capabilities, 433-434, 701-704
   command line keys, 52-54
      with DOSKEY, 566-567
      without DOSKEY, 565-566
   files
      ASCII text, 719-720
      troubleshooting, 229
   mouse, cursor-movement commands (DOS Editor), 369-370
   programs, 671-672
   scrolling commands (DOS Editor), 370
   text
      automatic indenting (DOS Editor), 372
      line deletion, 370-371
      line insertion, 370-371
      line joining, 371
      line splitting, 371
      place markers (DOS Editor), 373
      tab stops (DOS Editor), 372
Editor. *See* DOS Editor
Edlin, batch files, creating (EDLIN command), 391, 720
EDLIN.EXE file, 513
EEMS (Enhanced Expanded Memory Specification), 19
EGA (Enhanced Color Graphics Adapter), 821
   display adapters, 720-721
EGA.CGI file, 506
EGA.ICE file, 506

EGA.SYS device driver, 444, 506, 720-721
EGA2.CPI file, 506
EISA (Extended Industry Standard Architecture) bus, 448
EJECT command, 721
ejecting media from drives, 721
ellipsis indicator on menu bar (DOS Editor), 365
EMM (Expanded Memory Manager), 20
   DOS Protected Mode Interface support, loading/unloading, 707
EMM386 command, 721-722
EMM386.EXE (device driver), 19, 444, 506, 722-726
   expanded memory, 449-451
   switches, 449-451
   upper memory area (UMA), 449
empty subdirectories, deleting, 955
EMS (Expanded Memory Specification), 19
   controlling, 721-722
   converting XMS (extended memory) into, 722-726
   mapping as upper memory blocks, 934
   memory, 283-288
enabling
   double buffering, 914
   memory, 805
   PCMCIA configuration program (DOS version), 849
END label (batch files), 403
Enhanced Color Graphics Adapter (EGA), 821
Enhanced Expanded Memory Specification (EEMS), 19

environment
    copying, 520
    default size, 26
    Out of environment space message, 520
    size, setting (SHELL= statement), 520
environment variables
    adding, 894-897
    APPEND, 520-521
    changing (SET command), 294
    commands
        PATH, 520
        PROMPT, 520
        SET, 520
    COMSPEC, 521
    CONFIG.SYS file, 521-522
        using configuration menu as system menu, 36-38
    COPYCMD, 522
    customizing, 894-897
    defining (SET command), 295
    deleting, 894-897
    DIRCMD, 522-523
    MS-DOS label, 520
    MSDOSDATA, 523-524
    PATH, 524-525, 845-847
    PROMPT, 525
    TEMP, 525-526
    TMP, 525-526
    User label, 520
    windir, 526
    Windows label, 520
    WINPMT, 526-527
EPS (Encapsulated PostScript) filename extension, 106
equal meta-string, 297
ERAQ command, 678
ERASE command, 675-676
    deleting files, 221-222
    deleting files from command line, 221-222
    /P switch, 221
    use guidelines, 221

error messages
    alphabetical listing, 530-557
    device/drive
        abort (A) option, 557
        alphabetical listing, 557-561
        fail (F) option, 557
        ignore (I) option, 557
        retry (R) option, 557
    Invalid number of parameters, 395
    Out of environment space, 520
ERRORLEVEL, testing, 400-402
Esc key
    dialog boxes (DOS Editor), 366
    DOS Shell hotkey, 67
    menu bar (DOS Editor), 365-367
Escape character, ANSI.SYS commands, 417
escape meta-string, 296
ESET command (4DOS), 499
EXCEPT command (4DOS), 499
EXE (Executable program) filename extension, 106
EXE files, converting to .BIN or .COM files, 727
EXE2BIN command, 727
EXEBIN.EXE file, 513
executing
    batch files, 392, 412
        from other batch files, 411
    commands (DOS Editor), 364
    DEFRAG program, 177-181
    differential backups (Microsoft Backup for Windows 3.x), 242

    full backups
        Microsoft Backup, 239-241
        Microsoft Backup for Windows 3.x, 242
    incremental backups (Microsoft Backup for Windows 3.x), 242
    programs remotely with Interlnk, 229
Existing drive command (Compress menu), 145
exit codes
    DISKCOPY command, 400
    programs, 400
EXIT command, 727-728
    command processor, 290
    secondary command processor, 290-291
Exit command (Alt+F), online help system, 51
Exit command (File menu-DOS Editor), 380
exiting
    command processor, 290
    DOS Editor, 384
    online help, 51
EXPAND command, 728-729
EXPAND.EXE file, 506
expanded memory (EMS), 19
    controlling, 721-722
    converting XMS (extended memory) into, 722-726
    EEMS specification, 19
    EMM386.EXE, 449-451
    LIM 3.2 specification, 19
    RAM, 18
Expanded Memory Manager (EMM386), 20
Express Setup (DoubleSpace), 141
Express Setup (MemMaker), 455-458

Extended ASCII codes, 574-581

eXtended Density Format (XDF) disks, 956

Extended Industry Standard Architecture (EISA) bus, 448

extended memory (Extended Memory Specification), 20
  converting to LIM expanded memory (EMS), 722-726
  storing Stacker drivers, 707-708

extended memory blocks (XMS), 445

Extended Memory Manager (HIMEM.SYS), 445-448

Extended Memory Specification (XMS), 20

extended partitions, 160-162

extended-memory managers, 752-759

extensions
  filenames, 101-107
  utility files, 515-517

external commands, 42, 192

EXTRACT command, 730

extracting files
  from .CAB (compressed cabinet) files, 730
  from Interent Explorer backup files (DAT), 761

F

/F switch, FORMAT command, 153, 157

F1 key
  DOS Editor, 367
  DOS Shell hotkey, 66

F3 key
  DOS Editor, 367
  DOS Shell hotkey, 66

F5 key
  Clean Boot, 564
  DOS Shell hotkey, 66

F6 shortcut key (DOS Editor), 367

F7 key, DOS Shell hotkey, 66

F8 key
  DOS Shell hotkey, 66
  Interactive Boot, startup control key, 564

F9 key, DOS Shell hotkey, 66

F10 key, DOS Shell hotkey, 66

fail (F) option, device error messages, 557

FAKEMOUS.COM file, 513

FASTHELP command, 506, 730-731

FASTOPEN command, 506, 731-732
  hard disks, directory caching, 173-174

FATs (File Allocation Tables), 101, 135, 626
  checking, 626-630
  CHKDSK command, 184
  clusters, 112-113, 150-151
  file fragmentation, 136
  information, recording, 811-813

FC command, 217, 506, 732-734
  ASCII mode, 217
  binary mode, 217-218
  comparing
    copied files to originals, 218
    text files, 218-219
  files, integrity comparisons, 215-216
  parameters/switches, 733
  switches
    /A, 216
    /B, 216
    /C, 216
    /L, 216
    /M, 217
    /T, 217
    /W, 217

FCBS (file control blocks), 463
  command, 734-735
  CONFIG.SYS file, 27
  files, accessing, 463
  number of open files, 734-735

FDISK command, 735-736
  hard disks
    formatting, 158-159
    partitioning, 159-163
  parameters/switches, 735
  read-only files, 110
  repartitioning hard disks, 164-165
  /STATUS switch, 163-164

FDISK program, 506, 735-736

FFIND command (4DOS), 499

File Allocation Tables. *See* FATs

FILE command, CONFIG.SYS file, 27

file control blocks (FCBs), number of open files, 734-735

File Display Options dialog box (DOS Shell), 68-69

file fragmentation, 136

file handles, 463-464
  maximum number, 737

file lists (DOS Shell), dual versus single, switching between, 72-73

File menu commands
  Associate, 93
  Copy, 91
  Create Directory, 86-87
  Deselect All, 89
  Find Deleted File, 268
  Move, 91
  Select All, 89
  Undelete, 269
  Undelete To, 269
  View File Contents, 91-92

File menu commands (DOS Editor)
   Exit, 380
   menu bar (DOS Editor), 365
   New, 379
   Open, 380-383
   Print, 380, 383-384
   Save, 380-381
   Save As, 380-381

file systems, organization of, 100

File Transfer Protocol. *See* **FTP**

File Update System program, starting, 738

FILELINK command, 736

filenames, 101, 593
   character guidelines, 101
   characters, 593-594
   conventions, 104-107
   CRC, 648
   creating, rules for, 102-103
   extensions, listing of common, 105-107
   File Allocation Table (FAT), 101
   illegal characters, 102
   parsing, 103
   reserved names, logical devices, 103-104
   troubleshooting, 125-126
   utility file extensions, 515-517
   wildcard characters, 594-596

FILER command (Novell networks), 481

files
   accessing (FCBS command), 463
   ANSI.SYS, 504
   APPEND.EXE, 504
   archiving for disk space maximization, 183
   ASCII, 200
      combining (COPY command), 204-205
      viewing (TYPE command), 200-201

ATTRIB.EXE, 505
attributes, 107-108
   Archive, 108
   Hidden, 108
   modifying (ATTRIB command), 109-110
   Read-only, 108-110
   Subdirectory, 108
   System, 108
   viewing (DIR command), 195-196, 613-615
   Volume Label, 108
AUTOEXEC.BAT, 511
   dates/times, 276
   defining macros from bootup (DOSKEY), 439
backups, 616. 833-834
   restoring from, 248-251, 881-884
   selecting, 243
   selecting manually, 243-245
   selection criteria, 245-246
   selective restoration, 251
bare listings (DIR command), 197
batch. *See* batch files
binary, 200
bundled, unpacking, 941
BUSETUP.EXE, 511
byte storage, 199
C&E.BAT, 395
CAB (compressed cabinet), extracting, 730
CHECKIT.BAT, 408
CHKDSK.EXE, 505
CHKLST.MS, 508
CHKSTATE.SYS, 507
CHOICE.COM, 505
COMMAND.COM, 289-290, 505
   deleting temporary copy, 727-728
   exiting, 290
   second copy, 288-291
comparing, 217, 636-638, 732-734
   copied to originals (FC command), 218

compressed disk drives, deleting, 661-662
compressing, 656-657
   for disk space maximization, 183
compression ratios, 892-894
compression/decompression utilities, 495-496
CONFIG.SYS, 511
   subroutines, 924
contents, 100-101
   displaying, 933-934
COPYCOMP.BAT, redirecting input with COPY command, 392
copying, 202-203, 639-642, 950-954
   compressed, 728-729
   from console devices (COPY command), 205-206
   with batch files, 395-396
COUNTRY.ICE, 505
COUNTRY.SYS, 505, 644
DAT, extracting files from, 761
date and time stamp, 276-277
   DATE command, 277-278
   TIME command, 278-279
DAYBACK.BAT, 402
DBLSPACE.00x, 505
DBLSPACE.BIN, 505
DBLSPACE.EXE, 505
DBLSPACE.HLP, 505
DBLSPACE.INF, 505
DBLSPACE.INI, 505
DBLSPACE.SYS, 505
DBLSPACE.WIN, 505
DBLWIN.HLP, 505
DCOPY.BAT, 401-402
DEBUG.EXE, 505
DEFAULT.SET, 508
DEFAULT.SLT, 509
DEFRAG.EXE, 505
DEFRAG.HLP, 505
defragmenting, 672-674
delete sentry, 262
delete tracker, 262
deleted
   recovering, 839, 936-939
   restoring, 694

FILES

deleting, 222
   being saved by DELWATCH, 677
   from command line (ERASE command), 221-222
   from disks, 135
   from drives and directories, 675-676
   maximizing hard disk space, 182-183
   multiple, 955
   previous versions of DOS, 676
   prompting before, 678
deletion-tracking, 265
DELOLDOS.EXE, 505
DELTREE.EXE, 505
designations
   80286, 504
   80386, 504
   danger!, 504
   international, 504
   keep, 504
   remove?, 504
   vital, 504
   Windows, 504
DISKCOMP.COM, 505
DISKCOPY.COM, 505
DISPLAY.SYS, 506
DMDRVR.BIN, 506
DOS Shell
   All Files view, 74
   ASCII display, 59
   associating with programs, 92-93
   copying, 89-91
   entire deselection, 89
   entire selection, 89
   hexadecimal display, 59
   moving, 91
   multiple selection, 87-88
   select across directories option, 89
   single selection, 87
   viewing, 91-92
   views, modifying, 70-74
DOSHELP.HLP, 506
DOSKEY.COM, 506
DOSSETUP.INI, 511
DRIVER.SYS, 506

EDIT.COM, 506
EDIT.HLP, 506
editing
   ASCII text, 719-720
   troubleshooting, 229
EGA.CGI, 506
EGA.ICE, 506
EGA.SYS, 506
EGA2.CPI, 506
EMM386.EXE, 506
EXE, converting to .BIN or .COM files, 727
EXPAND.EXE, 506
extensions, 101
FASTHELP.EXE, 506
FASTOPEN.EXE, 506
FAT clusters, 112-113
FC.EXE, 506
FDISK.EXE, 506
filenames, character guidelines, 101
FIND.EXE, 506
finding, 738-740
   APPEND command, 610-613
   DIR command, 198
   IF command, 404
   PATH command, 122-123
FORMAT.COM, 506
formats, 100
GRAPHICS.COM, 507
GRAPHICS.PRO, 507
groups, copying (COPY command), 204
headers, 229
HELP.COM, 507
HELP.HLP, 507
HIMEM.SYS, 507
Include/Exclude list
   editing (Microsoft Backup for Windows 3.x), 246
   editing (Microsoft Backup), 245-246
included with MS-DOS 6.22, 505-510, 512
information, viewing, 687-689
integrity comparisons (FC command), 215-216
INTERLNK.EXE, loading, 225-226, 507

INTERSVR.EXE, loading, 226, 507
IO.SYS, 507
KEYB.COM, 507
KEYBOARD.ICE, 507
KEYBOARD.SYS, 507
KEYBRD2.SYS, 507
LABEL.EXE, 507
listing (DIR command), 193-195
LOADFIX.COM, 507
loading when launching DOS Editor, 383
locating (FIND filter), 336
locking, 906-907
lower-case listings (DIR command), 197
MACROS.BAT, 439
MEM.EXE, 507
MEMMAKER.EXE, 507
MEMMAKER.HLP, 507
MEMMAKER.INF, 507
MEMMAKER.STS, 507
MIRROR image, 258
   recovering data from accidental formats, 258-259
MODE.COM, 507
MONOUMB.386, 507
MORE.COM, 508
MOUSE.COM, 508
MOUSE.INI, 508
MOVE.EXE, 508
moving (MOVE command), 212-213, 828-830
MSAV.EXE, 508
MSAV.HLP, 508
MSAV.INI, 508
MSAVHELP.OVL, 508
MSAVIRUS.LST, 508
MSBACKDB.OVL, 508
MSBACKDR.OVL, 508
MSBACKFB.OVL, 508
MSBACKFR.OVL, 508
MSBACKUP.EXE, 508
MSBACKUP.HLP, 508
MSBACKUP.INI, 508
MSBACKUP.LOG, 508
MSBACKUP.OVL, 508
MSCDEX.EXE, 509
MSCONFG.HLP, 508

MSCONFG.OVL, 508
MSD.EXE, 509
MSDOS.SYS, 509
MSTOOLS.DLL, 509
MWAV.EXE, 509
MWAV.HLP, 509
MWAV.INI, 509
MWAVABSI.DLL, 509
MWAVDLG.DLL, 509
MWAVDOSL.DLL, 509
MWAVDRVL.DLL, 509
MWAVMGR.DLL, 509
MWAVSCAN.DLL, 510
MWAVSOS.DLL, 510
MWAVTSR.EXE, 510
MWBACKF.DLL, 510
MWBACKR.DLL, 510
MWBACKUP.EXE, 510
MWBACKUP.HLP, 510
MWBACKUP.INI, 510
MWGRAFIC.DLL, 510
MWUNDEL.EXE, 510
MWUNDEL.HLP, 510
naming, 101
   conventions, 21, 104-107
   reserved names, 103-104
   rules, 102-103
   troubleshooting, 125-126
NETWORKS.TXT, 510
NLSFUNC.EXE, 510
opening, 731-732
   FCBs, 734-735
   Open command (DOS Editor), 382-383
OS2.TXT, 510
PACKING.LST, 510
passwords, 844-845
pathname expressions, 115-117
PostScript, printing, 890-891
POWER.EXE, 510
PRINT.EXE, 510
printing, 201
   DOS Editor, 383-384
   in background, 857-860
protecting from accidental deletions, 652
QBASIC.EXE, 510
QBASIC.HLP, 510

QBASIC.INI, 510
RAMDRIVE.SYS, 510
README.TXT, 511
recovering, 262
   DOS directory method, 266
   Microsoft Undelete (Windows), 269-270
   selecting, 268
   UNDELETE command, 262-266
   Undelete program (Windows), 267
renaming (COPY command), 205
renaming (RENAME command), 214-215
REPLACE.EXE, 511
replacing, 877-880
RESTORE.EXE, 511
saving
   Save As command (DOS Editor), 380-381
   Save command (DOS Editor), 381
SCANDISK.EXE, 511
SCANDISK.INI, 511
scratchpad, temporary directories, 124-125
selecting to recover (Microsoft Undelete), 268
SERVER.EXE, 511
SETUP.EXE, 511
SETUP.MSG, 511
SHARE.EXE, 511
SIZER.EXE, 507
SMARTDRV.EXE, 511
SMARTMON.EXE, 511
SMARTMON.HLP, 511
SMARTMON.LOG, 511
software-dependent, 100
SORT.EXE, 511
sorting (DIR command), 197
SPATCH.BAT, 512
SSTOR.SYS, 512
Stacker stacvol, deleting, 875
STACKER.INI, re-creating, 638

storage
   floppy disks, 101
   hard disks, 101
SUBST.EXE, 512
supplemental disk
   4201.CPI, 514
   4208.CPI, 514
   5202.CPI, 514
   ADOS.CFG, 513
   ADOS.COM, 513
   ADOS.OVL, 513
   ADOS.TXT, 513
   AREADME.TXT, 513
   ASSIGN.COM, 513
   BACKUP.EXE, 513
   COMMANDS.TXT, 513
   COMP.EXE, 513
   CV.COM, 513
   DBLBOOT.BAT, 513
   DBLBOOT.INI, 513
   DVORAK.SYS, 513
   DVORAK.TXT, 513
   EDLIN.EXE, 513
   EXE2BIN.EXE, 513
   FAKEMOUS.COM, 513
   GORILLA.BAS, 514
   GRAFTABL.COM, 513
   JOIN.EXE, 514
   KBDBUF.SYS, 514
   LCD.CPI, 514
   MIRROR.COM, 514
   MONEY.BAS, 514
   MSHERC.COM, 514
   NET.1XE, 514
   NETBEUI.DOS, 514
   NETWKSTA.1XE, 514
   NETWKSTA.2XE, 514
   NIBBLES.BAS, 514
   NXT.TXT, 514
   PRINTER.SYS, 514
   PRINTFIX.COM, 514
   REDIR.1XE, 514
   REDIR.2XE, 514
   REMLINE.BAS, 514
   SETNAME.EXE, 514
SYS.CO, 512
system
   formatting disks, 158
   transferring to disks, 167-168

text files, comparing (FC command), 218-219
transferring
  between two computers, 736
  via Interlnk, 228
TREE.COM, 512
UNDELETE.EXE, 512
UNDELETE.INI, 512
undeleting, 221
UNFORMAT.COM, 512
UNINSTALL.EXE, 511
VFINTD.386, 510
VSAFE.COM, 512
WINA20.386, 512
WNTOOLS.GRP, 512
XBIOS.OVL, 506
XCOPY.EXE, 512

FILES command, CONFIG.SYS file, 463-464, 737

filespec parameters (commands), 45

FILEUP command, 738

filter programs, 827-828

filters, devices
  FIND, 335-337
  MORE, 334-335
  SORT, 337-338

FIND command, 738-740

Find Deleted File command (File menu), 268

Find Deleted Files dialog box, 268

Find dialog box, 377-378
  match upper/lowercase option, 378
  online help, 51
  whole word option, 378

FIND filter
  files, locating, 336
  guidelines for use, 337
  switches, 335-336
  syntax, 335-336

FIND.EXE file, 506

finding
  commands (DOSKEY), 436
  files, 738-740
    APPEND command, 610-613
    DIR command, 198
    IF command, 404
    PATH command, 122-123
  text, block editing (DOS Editor), 377-378

fixed disks. *See* **hard disks**

floppy disk drives
  cleaning, 156
  components, 129-130
  device drivers, 708-711
  versus hard disk drives, 131

floppy disks
  analyzing (CHKDSK command), 184-188
  analyzing (SCANDISK utility), 188-189
  bootable, creating, 25-26, 926-928
  comparing, 690-691
  compressing files, 656-657
  copying, 692-694
  disk-based storage, 20-21
  DOS Editor, using with, 363
  evolution of, 21
  files, storing, 101
  formats, 138-139
  formatting, 155-156, 743-746
    grinding noises, 155
    preparation (FORMAT command), 151-154
    quick, 157
    system files on, 158
    unconditional, 158
  LS-120, 21
  naming (LABEL command), 166-167
  proper care, 232
  raw/usable capacity, 139
  rotational speeds, 134
  serial numbers, 154-156
  size evolution, 131-132

storage evolution, 128
system files, transferring to, 167-168
tracks, 150
uses, 21
volume labels, 154-156
  VOL command, 167
write-protecting, 132

flushing disk buffers, 461

FNT (Font) filename extension, 106

FOR command, 740-742

FOR..IN..DO command, 407-409
  batch files, 397
  command interaction, 409
  DOS prompt, 409

foreign countries. *See* **internationalization**

FORMAT command, 111, 140, 150-151, 259, 743-746
  /1 switch, 157
  /4 switch, 157
  /8 switch, 157
  allocation units, 155
  /B switch, 157
  boot disk, 25
  /C switch, 157
  /F switch, 153, 157
  formatting floppy disks, 151-156
  formatting hard disks, 166
  /N switch, 157
  parameters/switches, 743-744
  /Q switch, 157
  quick formatting floppy disks, 157-158
  read-only files, 110
  /S switch, 157
  serial numbers, 154-156
  switches, 156-157
  /T switch, 157
  /U switch, 157
  unconditional formatting floppy disks, 158
  /V switch, 157
  volume labels, 154-156

FORMAT.COM file, 506
formatting
  compressed drives (DoubleSpace), 145
  disks, 136, 743-746
  floppy disks, 138-139, 155-156
    FORMAT command, 152-154
    grinding noises, 155
    preparation (FORMAT command), 151-152
    quick, 157
    system files on, 158
    unconditional, 158
  hard disks, 139-140, 166
    FDISK command, 158-159
/FRAGMENT switch, SCANDISK command, 189
fragmentation (disks), 136, 177
frames, network cards, installation considerations, 472
/FREE switch, MEM command, 283
FREE command (4DOS), 499
freeware, 494
FTP (File Transfer Protocol), 486
  commands
    !, 488
    ASCII, 487
    BINARY, 487
    BYE, 487
    CD, 487
    CLOSE, 487
    DELETE, 487
    DIR, 487
    DISCONNECT, 487
    GET, 487
    LCD, 487
    LS, 487
    MDELETE, 488
    MGET, 488
    MKDIR, 488
    MPUT, 488
    OPEN, 488
    PROMPT, 488
    PUT, 488
    PWD, 488
    QUIT, 488
    RECV, 488
    REMOTEHELP, 488
    RENAME, 488
    RMDIR, 488
    SEND, 488
    STATUS, 488
  directories
    displaying, 490-491
    retrieving, 491
  Internet connections, 485-486, 489-491
    troubleshooting, 491-492
  sessions
    launching, 489
    sample, 489-491
full backups
  executing (Microsoft Backup for Windows 3.x), 242
  executing (Microsoft Backup), 239-241
  frequency of, 238
  Microsoft Backup, 238

G

GET command (FTP), 487
Getting Started command (Help menu-DOS Editor), 387
GIF (Graphics Interchange Format) filename extension, 106
GLOBAL command (4DOS), 499
Gopher, Internet connection option, 484
GORILLA.BAS file, 514
GOSUB command (4DOS), 499
GOTO command, 747
  batch files, 397
    branching to specific lines, 398-399
  parameters/switches, 747
GRAFTABL command, 747-748
GRAFTABL.COM file, 513
graphics, printing, 748-750
GRAPHICS command, 748-750
  printer types, 320-321
  screen images, printing, 321-322
  syntax, 319
  uses, 319
graphics display adapter (Color Graphics Adapter), 821
GRAPHICS.COM file, 507
GRAPHICS.PRO file, 507
greater-than meta-string, 297
Greek code page, 354
grouping commands in blocks, 765-768
groups of files, copying (COPY command), 204
GRP (Windows Program Group) filename extension, 106
GUI (graphical user interface), DOS Shell, ASCII drawing characters, 58

H

handler codes (memory), 447-448
handles (files), 463-464
hard disks, 130
  advantages/disadvantages, 131
  analyzing (CHKDSK command), 184-188

analyzing (SCANDISK
  utility), 188-189
backup files, 616, 833-839
  restoring from, 248-251
  selective restoration, 251
buffers, 617-618
clusters, 195
components diagram, 13
compressing, 656-657
  DoubleSpace, 140-141
cylinders, 139
damaged state, booting
  from floppy disks, 25-26
defragmenting (DEFRAG
  program), 177-181
directories, splitting
  (SUBST command),
  302-303
disk buffers, suggested
  number of, 462
disk caching, 169-172
disk-based storage, 20-21
DoubleSpace
  compression ratio, 143-144
  controlling, 142
  Defragment option, 146
  *deleting compressed drives,
    145*
  *displaying compressed
    information, 142-143*
  drive size changes, 143
  *formatting compressed
    drives, 145*
  installing, 141-142
  SCANDISK, 147
  Uncompress option, 147
drifting, 148
errors (ScanDisk), 884-888
failures, restoring from
  backup files, 250-251
FASTOPEN program,
  directory caching,
  173-174
files
  deleting, 677-678
  *deleting previous versions
    of DOS, 676*
  information, 687-689
  storing, 101

formats, 139-140
formatting, 139-140,
  158-159, 166, 743-746
future of, 131
maximizing space, 181-182
  archiving, 183
  compression, 183
  deleting files, 182-183
naming (LABEL com-
  mand), 166-167
partitioning (FDISK com-
  mand), 159-164, 735-736
partitions
  extended, 160
  primary, 160
performance optimization,
  168-169, 461-462
platter stacking, 21
RAM disks, 174-176
recovering partition tables,
  261
repartitioning (FDISK
  command), 164-165
rotational speeds, 134
sector interleaving, 134
status, 626
storage evolution, 128
subdirectories, creating,
  800-801
system files, transferring to,
  167-168
volume labels (VOL com-
  mand), 167

hardware
  code pages, viewing status,
    350
  CPUs, 13
  data loss, troubleshooting,
    232-233
  device drivers, 308-309
    application specific, 308
    *CONFIG.SYS file,
      443-444*
    configuring, 312-313
    defined, 443
    *DMA channel assign-
      ments, 311-312*
    memory I/O addresses, 312
    *troubleshooting scenarios,
      314-316*

  DOS communication func-
    tions, 13
  logical devices, reserved
    names, 103-104
  memory
    bits, 13
    bytes, 13
  motherboards, 13
  overheating, 232
  peripherals, 13
    *diverse proprietary stan-
      dards, 15*
    examples, 14
  requirements for code page
    switching, 345

**hardware interrupts (IRQs),
309**
  edge-sensitive, 309-310
  IRQ assignments, 310-311
  level-sensitive, 309-310
  versus software interrupts,
    310

**HCONVERT command,
750**

headers (files), 229

help
  commands, 730-731
  DR-DOS, starting, 700

**HELP command, 46,
750-751**
  summary listing, 47-50,
    750-751

**Help menu commands (DOS
Editor), 365**
  About, 387
  activating, 387-388
  Getting Started, 387
  Keyboard, 387

help screen (DOS Shell)
  commands, 94-95
  contextual, 94-95

**help switch (/?), command
line, 46**

HELP.COM file, 507

HELP.HLP file, 507

Hercules Monochrome
  Graphics Adapter, 837
   video memory, mapping as
    upper memory blocks, 935
hexadecimal format, file displays (DOS Shell), 59
Hidden file attribute, 108
high memory area (HMA),
  19, 445, 698
   loading, 446-448
high-density disks, 153
highlighted commands on
  menu bar (DOS Editor),
  365
HIINSTALL command,
  751-752
HIMEM.SYS (device driver),
  444, 507, 752-759
   extended memory blocks
    (XMS), 445
   high memory area (HMA),
    445
   syntax, 446
   upper memory area (UMA),
    445
HISTORY command
  (4DOS), 499
HLP (Help) filename extension, 106
hotkeys (DOS Shell)
   + key, 66
   Alt key, 66
   Alt+Esc key, 66
   Alt+F4 key, 66
   Alt+Tab key, 66
   Ctrl+* key, 66
   Ctrl+/ key, 67
   Ctrl+F5 key, 67
   Ctrl+\ key, 67
   Del key, 66
   Esc key, 67
   F1 key, 66
   F3 key, 66
   F5 key, 66
   F7 key, 66
   F8 key, 66
   F9 key, 66
   F10 key, 66
   Shift+down arrow key, 66
   Shift+F5 key, 66
   Shift+F8 key, 66
   Shift+F9 key, 66
   Shift+left arrow key, 67
   Shift+right arrow key, 67
   Shift+Tab key, 67
   Shift+up arrow key, 66
   Tab key, 67

I

I/O (input/output) devices,
  312
   auxiliary consoles, 650-651
   consoles (CTTY command), 325-326
   device addresses, 312
IBM AntiVirus program,
  759-760
IBM PC
   introduction of, 12
   introduction of DOS, 15
IBMAVD command, 759
IBMAVSP command,
  759-760
Icelandic code page, 354
icons, command reference,
  592
IDX (Index file), 106
IEXTRACT command, 761
IF command, 761-765
   batch files, 397-400
   comparing strings, 402-403
   ERRORLEVEL testing,
    400-402
   finding files, 404
   parameters/switches, 761
IFF command (4DOS), 499
ignore (I) option, device
  error messages, 557
illegal characters (filenames),
  102
images (screen), printing
  (GRAPHICS command),
  321-322
IMG (GEM image) filename
  extension, 106
INCLUDE command,
  CONFIG.SYS file, 27
Include/Exclude list
   editing (Microsoft Backup
    for Windows 3.x), 246
   editing (Microsoft Backup),
    245-246
INCLUDE= command,
  765-768
incremental backups
   executing (Microsoft
    Backup for Windows 3.x),
    242
   frequency of, 238
   Microsoft Backup, 238
indenting text (DOS Editor),
  372
INF (Information) filename
  extension, 106
infinite loops, 399
information messages,
  alphabetical listing,
  530-557
INI (Initialization) filename
  extension, 106
initializing serial ports,
  815-816
INKEY command (4DOS),
  499
INPUT command (4DOS),
  499
Insert mode (DOS Editor),
  371
inserting
   comments in batch files,
    398
   text (DOS Editor), 370-371
INSTALL command,
  768-769
   CONFIG.SYS file, 27
   parameters, 466-467
   switches, 466-467

installation batch files, 397
INSTALLHIGH command, 751-752, 769
installing
  ANSI.SYS, 416
  code page switching, 346
    CHCP command, 349-350
    DISPLAY.SYS file, 346-347
    MODE command, 348-349
    NLSFUNC.EXE file, 348
    PRINTER.SYS file, 347-348
  disk drives, 711-713
  DOS Shell, 59
  DoubleSpace, 141-142
  DR-DOS, 940
  Interlnk remotely, 228-229
  network cards
    cabling considerations, 472
    client considerations, 472
    frame type considerations, 472
    network type considerations, 472
    server protocols, 473
    slot availability, 472
    TCP/IP considerations, 473
  UNDELETE command in AUTOEXEC.BAT, 264
Intel, Pentium chips, evolution of, 18
Interactive Boot
  Ctrl+F8 startup control key, 564
  F8 startup control key, 564
interfaces, Stacker online, 897, 933
Interlnk, 222-223
  cable configurations, 223-224
  client, loading, 225-226
  configuring, 223-224
  connecting, 227
  files, transferring, 228
  programs, remote execution, 229

  remote installations, 228-229
  remote printing, 228
  server, loading, 226
INTERLNK command, 223, 770-780
INTERLNK.EXE (device driver), 444, 503, 770-780
  loading, 224-226
internal commands, 42
internationalization
  character sets, 860-862
  code page switching, 340, 344-345, 695-698, 860-862
    hardware requirements, 345
    installing (CHCP command), 349-350
    installing (DISPLAY.SYS file), 346-347
    installing (MODE command), 348-349
    installing (NLSFUNC.EXE file), 348
    installing (PRINTER.SYS file), 347-348
  country codes, 354-355
  COUNTRY.SYS file settings, 340-342
  date formats, 356-357
  file designation, 504
  KEYB.COM file, 340
    settings, 342-344
  keyboards
    dead keys, 352-353
    layouts, 357-358
    remapping, 351-353
  number of countries supported, 340
  time formats, 356-357
Internet
  connection options
    FTP, 485-486, 489-491
    Gopher, 484
    ISP shell accounts, 484-485
    Telnet, 484-485
    troubleshooting, 491-492

  interrupts, 918-920
INTERSVR command, 223, 507, 781-786
  loading, 226
  parameters/switches, 781-782
  /RCOPY switch, 224
Invalid number of parameters error message, 395
IO.SYS file, 507
  boot disk, 24-25
  booting process, 16
Iomega Zip drives, 21
IP/IPX Gateway (Novell NetWare Client), 474
IRQs (hardware interrupts), 309
  assignments, 310-311
  device drivers, troubleshooting, 314-315
  edge-sensitive, 309-310
  level-sensitive, 309-310
  utilities, MSD.EXE (Microsoft Diagnostics), 314
ISPs (Internet service providers), shell accounts, terminal emulation, 484-485
issuing
  ANSI.SYS codes
    in batch files, 417-418
    in text files, 418-419
    with PROMPT command, 419
  DIR command, 193-194

J - K

/J switch, UNFORMAT command, 258
Jaz drives, 21
JOIN command, 514, 786-788
  adding disk drives to other disk directories, 302
  parameters/switches, 786
  pretender, 468-469

joining text (DOS Editor), 371

JP Software Web site, 4DOS utility, downloading, 497

/K switch (ANSI.SYS), 416

KBDBUF.SYS command, 514, 788-789

keep file designation, 504

KEYB.COM file, 507
  command, 790-792
  international keyboard settings, 340-344
  keyboards, remapping, 351-353

Keyboard command (Help menu-DOS Editor), 387

KEYBOARD.ICE file, 507

KEYBOARD.SYS file, 507

keyboards
  ANSI.SYS, 416
    character keys, reassigning, 424
    customizing, 423-424
    layout control codes, 427-430
    switch options, 416
  buffers, 788-789
  command, 792-793
  configuring, 817-818
  copying files from (COPY command), 205-206
  dead keys, 352-353
  international layouts, 357-358
  international settings, remapping, 351-353
  KEYB.COM file, international characters, 342-344
  layout/characters
    changing to other languages, 790-792
    data files for other countries, 792-793
  macro substitutions, 424
  typematic rates, changing (MODE command), 331-332

KEYBRD2.SYS file, 507

keys
  DOS controls
    Ctrl+C (Break), 565
    Ctrl+P (Echo to PRN), 565
    Ctrl+S (Pause), 565
    Print Screen, 748
  ROM BIOS controls
    Ctrl+Alt+Del (Reboot), 564
    Ctrl+Break (Break), 564
    Shift+PrtSc (Print screen), 565
    SysReq (System request), 565
  startup control
    Ctrl+F5 (Clean Boot), 564
    Ctrl+F8 (Interactive Boot), 564

KEYSTACK command (4DOS), 499

keystroke commmands
  DOS Editor, 568-569
  DOS Shell, 569-571

L

/L switch
  DIR command, 194, 197
  FC command, 216
  UNFORMAT command, 258

LABEL command, 166-167, 793-794

LABEL.EXE file, 507

labels (batch files)
  END, 403
  TRY_AGAIN, 403
  volume, displaying, 946-947

laptops
  docking, 701
  extended battery life/maximum performance control, 852-857

LASTDRIVE command, CONFIG.SYS file, 27, 464, 795-796

launching
  applications via shortcut keys (DOS Shell), 83
  DOS Editor, 363, 383
  DOS Shell, 59
  FTP sessions, 489

layouts (keyboards)
  changing to other languages, 790-792
  data files for other countries, 792-793

LCD command (FTP), 487

LCD.CPI file, 514

less-than meta-string, 297

LET (Letter) filename extension, 106

LH command, 796, 799

LHA (Compressed) filename extension, 106

LIB (Program library) filename extension, 106

LIM 3.2 specification (expanded memory), 19

line feed/carriage return meta-string, 296

lines, screen, adjusting, 300-301

linking computers, 774-786

/LIST switch, UNDELETE command, 263

LIST command (4DOS), 499

listing
  directories (TREE command), 123-124
  files (DIR command), 193-195

/LOAD switch, UNDELETE command, 263

LOADBTM command (4DOS), 499

LOADER command, 796-797

LOADFIX command, 507, 797-798

LOADHIGH command, 19, 798-799
parameters/switches, 798
upper memory area (UMA), 452

loading. *See also* installing
character sets into memory, 747-748
device drivers, 687
DEVICE command, 313
from DOS command prompt, 715
TSRs, 451-452
upper memory area (UMA), 451-452
device drivers
into conventional memory, 679-682
into upper memory, 682-686
DOS in high memory area (HMA), 446-448
DOS Protected Mode Interface support, 707
DOSKEY, 432
files, Open command (DOS Editor), 382-383
INTERLNK.EXE file (client), 225-226
INTERSVR.EXE file (server), 226
multiple programs, 929
programs into upper memory, 798-799
secondary command processor, 288-289
system tables in conventional/upper memory, 701
TSRs into conventional memory, 768-769

locking
drives/sockets, 714
files, 906-907
records, 906-907

LOG (File logging actions) filename extension, 106

LOG command (4DOS), 499

logging disks (DOS Shell), 70-71

logical devices, 103-104

LOGIN command (Novell networks), 481

look-ahead disk buffers, 462

LPT devices, 104

LS command (FTP), 487

ls command (Unix), 485

LS-120 floppy disks, 21

LST (Program listing) filename extension, 106

M

/M switch
DISKCOPY command, 211
XCOPY command, 207

macros (DOSKEY)
benefits, 432
creating, 436-439
defining from bootup, 439
deleting 440
naming, 440
replaceable parameters, 438
running, 439-440
special characters, 437-438
substitutions (keystrokes), 424
syntax, 437-439
versus batch files, 437

MACROS.BAT file, 439

magnetic disk storage
audio tape recorder comparison, 129
evolution of, 128

MAK (Programmer's make file) filename extension, 106

MAP (Linker map) filename extension, 106

MAP command (Novell networks), 481

maximizing
conventional memory, 803-804
hard disk space, 181-182
archiving, 183
compression, 183
deleting files, 182-183

McAfee VirusScan, 496
disk scans
frequency of, 497
launching, 497
downloading, 496

MDA (monochrome display adapter), 821

MDELETE command (FTP), 488

MEBACKR.DLL file, 510

MEM command, 283-288, 802-803
free/used memory displays, 453-454
parameters/switches, 802
sample report, 453-454
syntax, 453

MEM.EXE file, 507

MemMaker
Custom Setup, 456, 459-460
Express Setup, 455-458
memory configuration, 455-460
system configuration tool, 442

MEMMAKER command, 803-804

MEMMAKER.EXE file, 507
MEMMAKER.HLP file, 507
MEMMAKER.INF file, 507
MEMMAKER.STS file, 507

MEMMAX command, 805

memory
applications, troubleshooting, 460-461
bits, 13
buffers, 617-618
bytes, 13-14

MEMORY

configuring (MemMaker), 455-460
conventional, 283-288
  increasing, 867
  listing contents, 286-287
  loading TSRs, 768-769
  maximizing, 803-804
CPUs, real mode versus protected mode, 17
disk-based storage
  floppy disks, 14
  hard disks, 14
  media, 20-21
EMM386.EXE, 19
EMS (expanded), 283-288
  controlling, 721-722
  mapping as upper memory blocks, 934
enabling/disabling, 805
expanded (EMM386.EXE), 19, 449-451
extended memory blocks (XMS), 445
  storing Stacker drivers, 707-708
extended-memory managers, 752-759
free/used, displaying (MEM command), 453-454
handler codes, 447-448
high memory area (HMA), loading, 445-448
HIMEM.SYS, 19, 445-448
loading character sets, 747-748
loading device drivers
  conventional, 679-682
  upper memory, 682-686
loading system tables into, 701
MEM command, 283-288
monitoring integrity, 661
optimizing, 631, 910
overlays, 174
programs loaded in first segment, 797-798
RAM, 14
  conventional, 18-19
  disks, 174-176, 867-871
  early versions, 17
  volatility of, 14
ROM, 14
shadow RAM, 448
status, 626
system configuration, optimizing, 445-451
Task Swapper, 93-94
UMAs (upper memory areas), 445
UMBs (upper memory blocks), creating, 722-726
upper
  customizing, 698-700
  listing contents, 286-287
  loading programs, 798-799
  VGA display, 826-827
used/unused amounts, displaying, 802-803
video
  Hercules adapters, mapping as upper memory blocks, 935
  mapping as upper memory blocks, 934
  monochrome adapters, mapping as upper memory blocks, 935
XMS (extended memory), 283-288
  converting to LIM expanded memory (EMS), 722-726

MEMORY command (4DOS), 499

memory I/O addresses (devices), 312

memory resident portion (Scheduler program), activating, 647-648

memos, creating (DOS Editor), 362

menu bar (DOS Editor), 364
  activating, 365
  command options, 365
  Edit menu, 365
  Esc key, 365
  File menu, 365
  Help menu, 365
  highlighted commands, 365
  Search menu, 365

menu bar (DOS Shell), 60, 64
  File menu, 64
  Help menu, 64
  point-and-shoot method, 64
  Tree menu, 64
  View menu, 64

MENUCOLOR command, CONFIG.SYS file, 27, 805-807

MENUDEFAULT command, CONFIG.SYS file, 27, 807-809

MENUITEM command, CONFIG.SYS file, 27, 809-811

menus
  colors, displaying (CONFIG.SYS file [menu] section), 34-35
  display, creating (CHOICE command), 406-407
  DOS Shell
    menu bar, 64
    pull-down, 64-65
  simple, creating (CHOICE command), 405-406

messages
  batch files, displaying, 398
  error, alphabetical listing, 530-557
  information, alphabetical listing, 530-557
  warning, alphabetical listing, 530-557

meta-strings, PROMPT command, 296-298

MGET command (FTP), 488

microprocessor chips. *See* CPUs

Microsoft Anti-Virus (MSAV), 253-255, 830-832
  checklists, 255
  virus list, 256

Microsoft Anti-Virus for Windows (MWAV), 253-257, 838

Microsoft Backup, 233, 833-834
  Backup function, 236-238
  backup types
    differential, 238
    full, 238
    incremental, 238
  backups, comparing against original files, 241
  Compare function, 236-238
  configuring, 235-236
  features, 233-234
  file restoration, 248-251
  full backups, executing, 239-241
  MSBACKUP command
    switches, 239
    syntax, 239
  options, setting, 247-248
  Quit function, 236-238
  Restore function, 236-238
  selection criteria
    Display, 245
    Include/Exclude, 245-246
    Special, 245

Microsoft Backup for Windows, 838-839

Microsoft Backup for Windows 3.x, 233
  Backup function, 236-238
  Compare function, 236-238
  configuring, 235-236
  differential backups, executing, 242
  features, 233-234
  file restoration, 248-251
  files, manual selection, 243-245
  full backups, executing, 242
  incremental backups, executing, 242
  options, setting, 247-248
  Quit function, 236-238
  Restore function, 236-238
  selection criteria
    Display, 245
    Include/Exclude, 245-246
    Legend, 245
    Print, 245
    Special, 245

Microsoft Diagnostics (MSD.EXE), 314

Microsoft Network Client
  basic redirector option, 479
  full redirector option, 479
  installing, 478-481
  logon validation, 479
  network card settings, 481
  network configuration, 479
  setup screen, 478-479
  startup options, 479

Microsoft QuickBASIC programming environment. *See* QBASIC

Microsoft System Diagnostics, 836-837

Microsoft Undelete for Windows, 267-270, 839
  configuring, 267
  file selection, 268
  recovering files, 269

Microsoft Windows NT Server
  client software, installing, 478-481
  NET commands, 481
  networking features, 472

MIRROR command, 811-813

MIRROR image files, recovering data from accidental formats, 258-259

MIRROR.COM file, 514

MKDIR command, 800-801
  directories, creating, 117-119
  parameters/switches, 800

MKDIR command (FTP), 488

mobile computers, docking, 701

MODE command, 469, 813-815
  code pages
    configuration, 818-821
    switching, loading, 348-349
  Color Graphics Adapter (CGA), 299-300
  guidelines for use, 330-331
  keyboards, typematic rates, changing, 331-332
  large files, printing, 328
  parallel ports, changing settings, 326-328
  parameters/switches, 814, 819-823
  ports, redirecting, 331
  printer characteristics, 327
  screen appearance, 298
  screen columns/lines, 300-301
  screen type, 299
  serial ports, changing settings, 328-330
  syntax, 327-332
  video adapters, 821-823

MODE CON command, 300, 817-818

MODE LPT# command, 824-826

MODE.COM file, 507

modems, drivers, troubleshooting, 316

modifying
  batch files (DOS Editor), 362
  boot process
    AUTOEXEC.BAT file, 38-39
    CONFIG.SYS file, 38-39
  configuration files (DOS Editor), 362
  directories (CHDIR command), 119-120
  DOS Shell
    directory views, 70-74
    files views, 70-74
  file attributes (ATTRIB command), 109-110
  international settings, COUNTRY.SYS file, 340-342
  program group properties (DOS Shell), 80
  program items to program (DOS Shell), 82

MONEY.BAS file, 514
monitoring system changes, 866-867
monitors
    configuring, 817-818
    GRAPHICS command, 319
        images, printing, 321-322
        printer types, 320-321
        syntax, 319
    screen colors, selecting, 805-807
    screen mode, ANSI.SYS controls, 421
    text attributes, ANSI.SYS controls, 421-422
/MONO switch, SCANDISK command, 189
monochrome display adapters (MDA), 821
    mapping as UMB space, 826-827, 935
MONOUMB.386 (device driver), 444, 507, 826-827
MORE command, 827-828
    viewing ASCII files, 201
MORE filter
    guidelines for use, 335
    piping (|) feature, 334
    screen pauses, 334-335
    syntax, 334
MORE.COM file, 508
motherboards, 13
mounting
    removable drives, 655
    Stacker drives, 918
mouse
    cursor, movement commands (DOS Editor), 369-370
    DOS Editor
        actions list, 368
        cursor, 368
        Microsoft-compatible, 367
    DOS Shell requirements, 59

MOUSE.COM (device driver), 444, 508
MOUSE.INI file, 508
MOVE command, 828-830
    defaults, 214
    directories
        moving, 213
        renaming, 121-122, 214
    files, 212-213
    parameters/switches, 828
    /Y switch, 212
Move command (File menu), 91
Move File dialog box, 91
MOVE.EXE file, 508
moving
    directories (MOVE command), 213
    DOS Shell area, 63-64
    files, 828-830
        DOS Shell, 91
        MOVE command, 212-213
    parameters of batch files (SHIFT command), 409-410
MPUT command (FTP), 488
MS-DOS
    age of, 12
    files included with version 6.22, 505-512
    introduction of, 15
    PC DOS 2000 incarnation, 12
    PC platforms, statistical usage, 12
MSAV command, 830-832
MSAV.EXE file, 508
MSAV.HLP file, 508
MSAV.INI file, 508
MSAVHELP.OVL file, 508
MSAVIRUS.LST file, 508
MSBACKDB.OVL file, 508
MSBACKDR.OVL file, 508

MSBACKFB.OVL file, 508
MSBACKFR.OVL file, 508
MSBACKUP command, 108, 833-834
    parameters/switches, 833
    switches, 239
    syntax, 239
MSBACKUP.EXE file, 233-234, 508
MSBACKUP.HLP file, 508
MSBACKUP.INI file, 508
MSBACKUP.LOG file, 508
MSBACKUP.OVL file, 508
MSCDEX command, 835-836
MSCDEX.EXE file, 509
MSCONFG.HLP file, 508
MSCONFG.OVL file, 508
MSD command, 836-837
MSD.EXE (Microsoft Diagnostics) utility, 314, 509
MSDOS.SYS file, 509
    boot disk, 24-25
    booting process, 17
MSDOSDATA environment variable, 523-524
MSG (Program message) filename extension, 106
MSHERC command, 837
MSHERC.COM file, 514, 837
MSTOOLS.DLL file, 509
Multilingual (Latin I) code page, 354
multiple files
    DOS Shell, selecting, 87-88
    printing (PRINT command), 324
multiple system configurations, creating, 32-33
mv command (Unix), 485
MWA command, 838

MWAV.EXE file, 509
MWAV.HLP file, 509
MWAV.INI file, 509
MWAVABSI.DLL file, 509
MWAVDLG.DLL file, 509
MWAVDOSL.DLL file, 509
MWAVDRVL.DLL file, 509
MWAVMRG.DLL file, 509
MWAVSCAN.DLL file, 510
MWAVSOS.DLL file, 510
MWAVTSR command, 838
MWAVTSR.EXE file, 510
MWBACKF.DLL file, 510
MWBACKUP command, 838-839
MWBACKUP.EXE file, 233-234, 510
MWBACKUP.HLP file, 510
MWBACKUP.INI file, 510
MWGRAFIC.DLL file, 510
MWUNDEL command, 839
MWUNDEL.EXE file, 510
MWUNDEL.HLP file, 510

N

/N switch
   FC command, 217
   FORMAT command, 157
names
   directories, 877
   files, 593, 876
      characters, 593-594
      CRC, 648
      wildcard characters, 594-596
   paths, 593
   reserved, 594
   subdirectories, 877
naming
   directories (MOVE command), 214
   disk drives, 176
   disks (LABEL command), 166-167

files, 101
   conventions, 21, 104-107
   RENAME command, 214-215
   reserved names, 103-104
   rules, 102-103
   troubleshooting, 125-126
macros (DOSKEY), 440
program groups (DOS Shell), 79

navigating online help commands, 47-50
NDS (Novell Network Directory Service), 473
NDX (Index) filename extension, 106
NET command (Microsoft networks), 481
NET1XE file, 514
NETBEUI.DOS file, 514
NetBIOS (Novell NetWare Client), 474
NetWare TSA for SMS, 474
NETWKSTA.1XE file, 514
NETWKSTA.2XE file, 514
network cards
   Microsoft Network Client, configuring, 481
   requirements
      cabling considerations, 472
      client considerations, 472
      frame type considerations, 472
      network type, 472
      slot availability, 472
      TCP/IP considerations, 473
network operating systems (NOSs), 472
networks
   cards
      cabling considerations, 472
      client considerations, 472
      frame type considerations, 472
      network type considerations, 472
      slot availability, 472

clients, software setup tips, 482
commands
   FILER (Novell NetWare), 481
   LOGIN (Novell NetWare), 481
   MAP (Novell NetWare), 481
   NET (Microsoft Windows NT Server), 481
drive letters, 795-796
Microsoft Network Client, installing, 478-481
Novell NetWare Client, installing, 473-477
servers
   protocol considerations, 473
   TCP/IP considerations, 473
types
   Microsoft Windows NT Server, 472
   Novell NetWare, 472

NETWORKS.TXT file, 510
New command (File menu-DOS Editor), 379
New Program Object dialog box, 79
New Topic command (Alt+N keystroke), online help, 49-50
NIBBLES.BAS file, 514
NLSFUNC command, 840
NLSFUNC.EXE file, 510
   code page switching, loading, 348
Nordic code page, 354
Norton Antivirus, 253
/NOSAVE switch, SCANDISK command, 189
NOSs (network operating systems), 472
/NOSUMMARY switch, SCANDISK command, 189
Novell Client for DOS, 474
Novell Client Windows Support, 474

Novell Distributed Print Services, 474

Novell NetWare
bindery logins, 473
client software, installing, 473-477
commands
FILER, 481
LOGIN, 481
MAP, 481
NDS logins, 473
networking features, 472

Novell NetWare Client
downloading, 473
driver settings, configuring, 475
installing, 473-477
options
Desktop SNMP, 474
IP/IPX Gateway, 474
NetBIOS, 474
NetWare TSA for SMS, 474
Novell Client for DOS, 474
Novell Client Windows Support, 474
Novell Distributed Print Services, 474
Workstation Manager 3.x, 474
TCP/IP settings, configuring, 475

NUL devices, 104

NUMLOCK command, CONFIG.SYS file, 27

NumLock key, turning on/off, 840-841

NWCACHE command, 842-843

NWCDEX command, 843-844

NXT.TXT file, 514

O

/O switch, DIR command, 194, 197

OBJ (Intermediate object code), filename extension, 106

OLD (Backup) filename extension, 106

online documents, displaying, 945

online help, 750-751
commands
accessing, 46-47
Alt+B (Previous Topic), 49-50
Alt+C (Contents), 49-50
Alt+N (New Topic), 49-50
exiting, 51
jump words, 48-49
menu options, 49
navigating, 47, 49-50
topics, printing, 50-51
topics, searching, 51

onscreen messages, batch files, 716-719

Open command (File menu-DOS Editor), 380-383

OPEN command (FTP), 488

Open dialog box, 382-383

opening files, 731-732
FCBs, 734-735
Open command (DOS Editor), 382-383

operating characteristics (printers), 824-826

Optimize menu commands (DEFRAG), 179

optimizing
drive performance, 694-695
memory, 631, 910
system configuration, 445-451

option buttons, DOS Shell dialog boxes, 68-69

option check boxes, DOS Shell dialog boxes, 69

original files, comparing with backups (Microsoft Backup), 241

OS2.TXT file, 510

Out of environment space message, 520

overheated hardware and data loss, 232

overlays
applications, 192
RAM disks, 174

Overtype mode (DOS Editor), 371

overtyping text in DOS Editor, 371

OVL (Program overlay) filename extension, 106

OVR (Program overlay) filename extension, 106

P

/P switch
COMMAND command, 289
DIR command, 194-195
ERASE command, 221
XCOPY command, 206
UNFORMAT command, 258

PACKING.LST file, 510

PAK (Packed archive) filename extension, 106

paradigm
command syntax, 44

parallel ports (printers), 326
device drivers, troubleshooting, 316
MODE command, 326
changing settings, 326-328
redirection to serial ports, 331

parameters
ANSI.SYS command, 609
APPEND command, 611
ATTRIB command, 614

PARAMETERS

batch files, moving (SHIFT command), 409-410
BREAK command, 616
BUFFERS= command, 617
CALL command, 619
CD command, 622
CHAIN command, 624
CHCP command, 624
CHKDSK command, 626-627
CHOICE command, 631
CMOSCLK.SYS command, 634
CNFIGNAM.EXE device driver, 634
COMMAND command, 635
commands, 42-44
  filespec, 45
  overriding, 51-52
COMP command, 637
CONFIG command, 638
COPY command, 639-640
COUNTRY= command, 643
CPBACKUP command, 645-647
CPBDIR command, 647
CPSCHED command, 648
CRC command, 648
CREATE command, 648
CSCRIPT command, 649
CTTY command, 650
CURSOR.EXE command, 651
CVT.EXE command, 651
DATAMON command, 652
DATE command, 653
DBLSPACE/AUTOMOUNT command, 655
DBLSPACE/CHKDSK command, 656
DBLSPACE/COMPRESS command, 656
DBLSPACE/CREATE command, 658
DBLSPACE/DEFRAGMENT command, 659
DBLSPACE/DELETE command, 660

DBLSPACE/DOUBLEGUARD command, 661
DBLSPACE/FORMAT command, 662
DBLSPACE/INFO command, 662
DBLSPACE/MOUNT command, 664
DBLSPACE/RATIO command, 665
DBLSPACE/SIZE command, 666
DBLSPACE/UNCOMPRESS command, 667
DBLSPACE/UNMOUNT command, 667
DBLSPACE.SYS device driver, 668
DEBUG command, 672
DEFRAG command, 673-674
DEL command, 675
DELOLDOS command, 676
DELPURGE.EXE command, 677
DELQ command, 678
DELTREE command, 679
DELWATCH.EXE command, 677-678
DEVICE= command, 680
DEVICEHIGH= command, 683
DEVLOAD command, 687
DIR command, 687-689
DISKCOMP command, 690
DISKCOPY command, 692
DISKMAP.EXE command, 694
DISKOPT.EXE command, 695
DISPLAY.SYS device driver, 696
DOS= command, 698
DOSBOOK command, 700
DOSDATA command, 701
DOSDOCK command, 701
DOSKEY command, 702
DOSSHELL command, 704-705

DPMI command, 707
DPMS.EXE command, 708
DRIVER.SYS device driver, 708-709
DRIVPARM= command, 711-712
DRMOUSE command, 714
DRVLOCK command, 714
DYNALOAD command, 715
E command, 716
ECHO command, 717
EDIT command, 719
EGA.SYS device driver, 720
EJECT command, 721
EMM386 command, 722
EMM386.EXE device driver, 723-725
EXE2BIN command, 727
EXPAND command, 728
EXTRACT command, 730
FASTHELP command, 730
FASTOPEN command, 731
FC command, 733
FCBS= command, 734
FDISK command, 735
FILES= command, 737
FILEUP command, 738
FIND command, 738
FOR command, 740
FOR..IN..DO command, 407
FORMAT command, 743-744
GOTO command, 747
GRAFTABL command, 748
GRAPHICS command, 749-750
HCONVERT command, 750
HELP command, 751
HIINSTALL/INSTALLHIGH command, 752
HIMEM.SYS device driver, 752-755
IBMAVSP command, 760
IEXTRACT command, 761
IF command, 761

INCLUDE= command, 766
INSTALL= command, 768
INTERLNK command, 770
INTERLNK.EXE command, 774-775
INTERSVR command, 781-782
JOIN command, 786
KBDBUF.SYS device driver, 788
KEYB command, 790
LABEL command, 793
LASTDRIVE= command, 795
LOADER command, 796-797
LOADFIX command, 798
MEM command, 802
MEMMAKER command, 804
MEMMAX command, 805
MENUCOLOR= command, 805
MENUDEFAULT= command, 807
MENUITEM= command, 809
MIRROR command, 811
MKDIR command, 800
MODE COM# command, 815
MODE command, 814, 819-823
MODE CON command, 817
MODE LPT# command, 824
MONOUMB.386 command, 826
MORE command, 827
MOVE command, 828
MSAV command, 831-832
MSBACKUP command, 833
MSCDEX command, 835
MSD command, 836
MSHERC command, 837
NLSFUNC command, 840

NWCACHE command, 842-843
NWCDEX command, 843
PASSWD command, 844
PASSWORD command, 845
PATH command, 846
PCMRMAN command, 850
POWER command, 852
POWER.EXE device driver, 855
PRINT command, 857
PRINTER.SYS device driver, 860
PROMPT command, 862
QBASIC command, 864
QCONFIG command, 865
RAMBOOST command, 866
RAMBOOST.EXT command, 867
RAMDRIVE.SYS device driver, 868
RAMSETUP command, 871
REM command, 874
REMOVDRV command, 875
RENAME command, 876
RENDIR command, 877
REPLACE command, 877
replaceable, 599-600
replaceable (batch files), 393-397
REPORT command, 880
RESIZE command, 880
RESTORE command, 881
RMDIR command, 872
SCANDISK command, 884-885
SCANREG command, 888
SCHEDULE command, 889
SCREATE.SYS device driver, 890
SCRIPT command, 891
SDEFRAG command, 891-892
SDIR command, 893-894

SET command, 894
SETUP command, 897
SETVER command, 898
SETVER.EXE device driver, 904
SHARE command, 906
SHELL= command, 908
SMARTDRV command, 911-912
SMARTDRV.EXE device driver, 914
SORT command, 915
SSETUP command, 917
STAC command, 917
STACHIGH command, 917
STACKER command, 918
STACKS= command, 918
SUBMENU= command, 920
SUBST command, 922
SWITCH command, 924
SYS command, 927
SYSINFO command, 929
TASKMGR command, 929
TIME command, 930
TIMEOUT command, 931
TOUCH command, 931
TREE command, 932
TUNER command, 933
TYPE command, 933
UMBCGA.SYS device driver, 934
UMBEMS.SYS device driver, 934
UMBHERC.SYS device driver, 935
UMBMONO.SYS device driver, 935
UNCOMP command, 936
UNDELETE command, 936-938
UNFORMAT command, 939
UNINSTALL command, 941
UNPACK2 command, 941
UNSTACK command, 942
VERIFY command, 943
VFINDTD command, 944

VIEW command, 946
VOL command, 946
VSAFE command, 947
WINA20.386 device driver, 949
XCOPY command, 950-951
XCOPY32 command, 954
XDEL command, 955
XDF command, 955
XDFCOPY command, 956
XDIR command, 956-957

parse, 103

partitioning
ATA rotating disk, 850
hard disks, 735-736
FDISK command, 159-163
status (FDISK command), 163-164
PCMCIA cards, 850

partitions
deleting, 161
extended, 160-162
primary, 160
tables
information, saving, 811-813
recovering, 261

/PARTN switch, UNFORMAT command, 258, 261

PAS (Pascal source) filename extension, 106

PASSWD command, 844

PASSWORD command, 844-845

passwords
files/directories, 844-845
program groups (DOS Shell), 80
Stacker drives, 844

pasting text (Clipboard), 375

PATH command, 845-847
environment variables, managing, 520
finding files, 122-123
parameters/switches, 846

PATH environment variable, 524-525, 845-847

pathname expressions, 115-117, 593
absolute path, 116
relative path, 116

paths, drives, referencing (SUBST command), 303-304

PAUSE command, 398, 847-848
batch files, 397

Pause key (Ctrl+S keystroke), DOS controls, 565

pausing
batch files, 847-848
for input (CHOICE command), 404-405
screen output (MORE filter), 334-335

PCM command, 849

PCMATA.SYS command, 849

PCMCIA cards
access, 849
enabling, 849
partitioning, 850
Resource Management Utility command-line utility, 850-851
Resource Management Utility standalone utility, 850

PCMCS.EXE command, 849

PCMDINST command, 849

PCMFDISK command, 850

PCMRMAN command, 850-851

PCMSCD command, 851

PCMSETUP command, 851

PCs (personal computers)
booting process, 15
AUTOEXEC.BAT file, 17
bootstrap loader, 16
CMOS chip check, 16
COMMAND.COM file, 17
CONFIG.SYS file, 17
IO.SYS file, 16
MSDOS.SYS file, 17
Power On Self Test (POST), 16
reboot commands, 809-811
hardware
CPUs, 13
DOS communication functions, 13
memory, 13
motherboards, 13
peripherals, 13-15
technical information, displaying, 865
troubleshooting with Microsoft System Diagnostics, 836-837

PCX (Picture, PC Paintbrush) filename extension, 106

Pentium chip family evolution, 18

performance
hard disks, 168-169, 461-462
disk caching, 169-172
FASTOPEN program, 173-174
RAM disks, 174-176

peripherals, 13
device drivers, 308-309
application-specific, 308
hardware interrupts, 309-311
diverse proprietary standards, 15
DOS communication functions, 13
examples, 14

Phoenix Card Manager Plus, 851

Phoenix Super Client Driver, 851

PIF (Program Information File), filename extension, 106

pipe symbol (|), 201, 597-598

piping (|) feature (MORE filter), 334
PKUNZIP utility, 495-496
PKWare Web site, Zip utilities, 495
PKZIP utility, 495-496
place markers in text (DOS Editor), 373
platters, hard disk drives, 130
PM4 (PageMaker 4 data) filename extension, 107
PM5 (PageMaker 5 data) filename extension, 107
ports
   parallel to serial, output redirection (MODE command), 331
   serial, initializing, 815-816
Portuguese code page, 354
POST (Power On Self Test), booting process, 16
PostScript files, printing, 890-891
POWER command, 852-854
Power On Self Test (POST), booting process, 16
POWER.EXE device driver, 444, 510, 854-857
Practical Unix, 492
preparing floppy disks for formatting (FORMAT command), 151-152
Press any key to continue... message, 847
pretender commands
   ASSIGN, 468-469
   JOIN, 468-469
   SUBST, 468-469
preventing
   data loss, 232-233
   viruses, protection guidelines, 257

Previous Topic command (Alt+B keystroke), online help, 49-50
primary partitions, 160
PRINT command, 322, 469, 857-860
   guidelines for use, 324-325
   issuing, 322-323
   multiple files, printing, 324
   parameters/switches, 857
   switches, 322-323
   syntax, 322-323
Print command (File menu-DOS Editor), 380, 383-384
Print dialog box, 383
   Complete Document option, 384
   online help, 50-51
   Selected Text Only option, 384
Print screen key (Shift+PrtSc keystroke), 565, 748
PRINT.EXE file, 510
PRINTER.SYS file, 444, 514, 860-862
   code page switching, loading, 347-348
printers
   device drivers, troubleshooting, 316
   GRAPHICS command
      images, printing, 321-322
      settings, 320-321
   MODE command
      large files, printing, 328
      settings, 327
   operating characteristics, 824-826
PRINTFIX.COM file, 514
printing
   background printing, 857-860
   files, 201
      Print command (DOS Editor), 383-384

   graphics, 748-750
   multiple files (PRINT command), 324
   online help topics, 50-51
   PostScript files, 890-891
   remote, 228
   text file contents, 201
PRN (Program listing, printing), filename extension, 107
PRO (Profile) filename extension, 107
Procomm Plus, terminal emulation, 484
Program Group Properties dialog box, 80
program groups (DOS Shell)
   adding, 78-80
   deleting, 80-81
   examples, 77-78
   naming guidelines, 79
   passwords, 80
   program items, adding, 81-82
   program items, deleting, 82-83
   program items, modifying, 82
   properties, modifying, 80
   reordering, 81
Program List command (View menu), 74
programs
   BACKUP, 616
   bootstrap loader, 16
   DEBUG, 671-672
   DEFRAG, 177-181
   DELWATCH, 677-678
   demoware, 495
   disk-compression, 654-657
   DOS commands, 587-588
   DOSKEY
      command-history buffer keys, 435
      command-line editing, 433-434
      finding commands, 436
      loading, 432
      reusing commands, 434-435

DOS Shell, starting,
  704-707
DoubleSpace, 140-141,
  656-659
  automounting, 655
  *compressed disk drive free
    space, 664-665*
  *compressed disk drive size,
    665-666*
  *compressed drive information,
    662-663*
  *compressing drives,
    145-146*
  *compression ratios,
    143-144*
  controlling, 142
  CVF access, 663-664
  Defragment option, 146
  *deleting compressed disk
    drive files and subdirectories,
    661-662*
  *deleting compressed drives,
    145*
  device driver, 668-670
  *disk drive information,
    663*
  *displaying compressed
    information, 142-143*
  DoubleGuard, 661
  drive size changes, 143
  *formatting compressed
    drives, 145*
  installing, 141-142
  SCANDISK, 147
  starting, 654
  *uncompressing disk drives,
    147, 666-667*
  *unmounting CVFs,
    667-668*
  unmounting drives, 660
  editing, 671-672
EXE2BIN, 727
FASTOPEN, 731-732
  directory caching, 173-174
FDISK, 735-736
File Update System, starting, 738
FILELINK, 736
files, associating (DOS
  Shell), 92-93

filter, 827-828
freeware, 494
HIMEM.SYS, 752-759
IBM AntiVirus standalone,
  759-760
IBM AntiVirus/DOS full-
  screen, starting, 759
INTERSVR, 774, 781-786
loading
  *in first segment of memory,
    797-798*
  *into upper memory,
    798-799*
  multiple, 929
Microsoft Anti-Virus,
  830-832
Microsoft Anti-Virus for
  Windows, 838
Microsoft Backup, 833-834
Microsoft Backup for
  Windows, 838-839
Microsoft System
  Diagnostics, 836-837
Microsoft Undelete for
  Windows, 267-270, 839
  configuring, 267
  file selection, 268
  recovering files, 269
MSHERC, 837
MWAVTSR, 838
NWCACHE, 842-843
PC DOS E Editor, starting,
  715-716
PCMCIA configuration
  (DOS version), 849
Phoenix Card Manager
  Plus, 851
QBASIC, 864-865
RAMBoost Setup, 871-872
remote execution (Interlnk),
  229
ScanDisk, 884-888
Schedule, 889-890
shareware, 494
SIZER, 910
SMARTDrive Monitor, 914
Stacker Optimizer, 891-892
stopping, 616-617
Task Swapper, switching
  features, 93-94

testing, 671-672
troubleshooting, running
  from C\ prompt, 55
TSRs (Interlnk), 223
VSAFE, running, 838
Windows commands, 590
XDF, starting, 955
projects
  boot process, modifying,
    38-39
  networks, client software
    configuration tips, 482
**prompt, customizing,
  862-864**
**PROMPT command,
  295-297, 862-864**
  ANSI.SYS codes, issuing
    with, 419
  environment variables,
    managing, 520
  meta-strings, 296-298
  parameters/switches, 862
**PROMPT command (FTP),
  488**
PROMPT environment variable, 525
protected mode, CPU memory, 17
protecting files against accidental deletion, 652
**protocols, network cards,
  installation considerations,
  473**
**PS (PostScript program)
  filename extension, 107**
**pull-down menus, DOS
  Shell item selection, 64-65**
**/PURGE switch,
  UNDELETE command,
  263**
PUT command (FTP), 488
PWD command (FTP), 488

Q

/Q switch
  FORMAT command, 157
  SETVER command, 282
QBASIC command, 864-865
QBASIC.EXE file (DOS Editor), 362, 510
QBASIC.HLP file, 510
QBASIC.INI file (DOS Editor), 386-387, 510
QCONFIG command, 865
Que's Computer and Internet Dictionary, Sixth Edition, 959
question marks (?), 604-605
  wildcard commands, 54-55
quick formatting of disks, 157
QUIT command (FTP), 488

R

/R switch (ANSI.SYS), 416
/RCOPY switch, INTERSVR command, 224
RAM (random access memory), 14
  conventional memory, 18-19
  disk buffers, 461-462
  expanded memory, 18-19
  extended memory, 20
  high memory area, 19
  non-volatile nature, 14
  shadow RAM, 448
  Task Swapper, 93-94
  upper memory area, 19
  volatile nature, 14
RAM disks, 174-176, 867-871
  overlays, 174
  RAMDRIVE.SYS, 175-176
  TEMP environment variable, 176

RAM drives, compressing, 890
RAMBOOST command, 866-867
  Setup program, 871-872
RAMBOOST.EXE command, 867
RAMDRIVE.SYS (device driver), 444, 510, 867-871
  RAM disks, 175-176
RAMSETUP command, 871-872
random access memory. *See* **RAM**
raw capacity (disks), 139
RD command, 872-873
read only memory. *See* **ROM**
read-caching, 170
read-only file attribute, 108-110
read-only passwords (Stacker drives), 844
read/write heads, 133
  cleaning, 156
read/write passwords (Stacker drives), 844
README.TXT file, 511
  writing (DOS Editor), 362
real mode, CPU memory, 17
reassigning character keys on keyboards (ANSI.SYS), 424
REBOOT command (4DOS), 499
Reboot key (Ctrl+Alt+Del keystroke), ROM BIOS controls, 564
recompressing Stacker drives, 891-892
recording FAT information, 811-813
records, locking, 906-907
RECOVER command, 259, 873

recovering. *See also* **restoring**
  data, accidental formats, 258-261
  deleted files, 839, 936-939
  files, 262
    DOS directory method, 266
    Microsoft Undelete (Windows), 269-270
    selecting, 268
    UNDELETE *command,* 262-266
    Undelete program (Windows), 267
  partition tables, 261
  reformatted disks, 939-940
RECV command (FTP), 488
REDIR.1XE file, 514
REDIR.2XE file, 514
redirecting
  disk drive requests (ASSIGN command), 302
  output, parallel port to serial port (MODE command), 331
redirection operators
  devices, 332
  guidelines for use, 334
  issuing, 332-333
  syntax, 332-333
referencing drive paths (SUBST command), 303-304
reformatted disks, recovering, 939-940
Refresh command (View menu), 71
REM command, 874-875
  batch files, 397-398
  CONFIG.SYS file, 27
  parameters, 467, 874
remapping keyboards for international settings, 351-353
REMLINE.BAS file, 514
remote installations (Interlnk), 228-229

remote printing, Interlnk connections, 228
REMOTEHELP command (FTP), 488
removable disk media
   Iomega Zip drives, 21
   Jaz drives, 21
   mounting, 655
REMOVDRV command, 875
remove? file designation, 504
REN command, 876
RENAME command, 214-215, 876
RENAME command (FTP), 488
renaming
   directories, 877
      MOVE command, 121-122, 214
   files, 876
      COPY command, 205
      RENAME command, 214-215
   subdirectories, 828-830, 877
RENDIR command, 877
reordering program groups in DOS Shell, 81
repartitioning hard disks (FDISK command), 164-165
repeating commands for groups of files, 740-742
REPLACE command, 877-880
REPLACE.EXE file, 511
replaceable parameters, 599-600
   batch files, 393-397
   macros (DOSKEY), 438
REPORT command, 880
reports (CHKDSK command), 185-186

reserved names, 594
   logical devices, 103-104
RESIZE command, 880
resizing Stacker drives, 880
RESTORE command, 881-884
RESTORE.EXE file, 511
restoring. *See also* recovering
   backup files, 248-251, 881-884
   deleted files, 694
retrieving FTP directories, 491
retry (R) option, device error messages, 557
returning batch files (CALL command), 411-412
reusing commands, 434-435
REXX programming language, 12
RFT (Revisable Form Text) filename extension, 107
RMDIR command, 872-873
   directory deletions, 120
   parameters/switches, 872
RMDIR command (FTP), 488
ROM (read only memory), 14
ROM BIOS control keys
   Ctrl+Alt+Del (Reboot), 564
   Ctrl+Break (Break), 564
   Shift+PrtSc (Print Screen), 565
   SysReq (System request), 565
root directories, subdirectories, branching, 113-114
RPT (Report) filename extension, 107
RTF (Rich Text Format, Microsoft), filename extension, 107

running. *See also* executing; launching
   batch files, 619-621
      calling/returning (CALL command), 411-412
      shifting control, 411
   macros (DOSKEY), 439-440
   programs remotely with Interlnk, 229
   VSAFE, 838

S

/S switch
   DIR command, 194
   FORMAT command, 157
   UNDELETE command, 263
   XCOPY command, 206
SAM (Ami-Pro) filename extension, 107
SAV (Backup) filename extension, 107
Save As command (File menu-DOS Editor), 380-381
Save command (File menu-DOS Editor), 380-381
saving
   files
      Save As command (DOS Editor), 380-381
      Save command (DOS Editor), 381
   partition table information, 811-813
scan codes, keyboards, 423
SCANDISK command, 884-888
   /ALL switch, 189
   /AUTOFIX switch, 189
   /CHECKONLY switch, 189
   /CUSTOM switch, 189
   /FRAGMENT switch, 189
   /MONO switch, 189
   /NOSAVE switch, 189

/NOSUMMARY switch, 189
parameters/switches, 884-885
/SURFACE switch, 189
/UNDO switch, 189

SCANDISK utility, 147, 511, 884-888
disk analysis, 188-189
DoubleSpace, 147
switches, 188-189

SCANDISK.INI file, 511

SCANREG command, 888-889

SCHEDULE command, 889-890

Scheduler program, 889-890
memory resident portion, activating, 647-648

scratchpad files, temporary directories, 124-125

SCREATE.SYS device driver, 890

screen
  ANSI display controls
    attribute control codes, 425-426
    color codes, 425-426
    cursors, 426-427
    reset mode, 425
    set mode, 425
  ANSI.SYS controls, 416, 419-420
    clearing (CLS command), 423
    cursor movement, 420
    cursor positioning, 420
    modes, setting, 421
    text attributes, 421-422
  appearance, customizing (MODE command), 298
  CLS command, 319
  Color Graphics Adapter, 299-300
  colors, changing (DOS Editor), 385-386, 805-807
  columns/lines, adjusting, 300-301

custom options, saving (DOS Editor), 386-387
GRAPHICS command, 319
  images, printing, 321-322
  printer types, 320-321
  syntax, 319
information output, pausing (MORE filter), 334-335
scroll control, 54
scrollbars, removing (DOS Editor), 386
text, clearing, 633-634
type, selecting (MODE command), 299

SCREEN command (4DOS), 499

Screen Display Mode display box, 75-76

screen modes (DOS Shell), 75-76

SCRIPT command, 890-891

scrollbars, 364
  controlling screen displays, 54
  DOS Shell, 61-63
  screen, removing (DOS Editor), 386

scrollboxes (DOS Shell), 63

SCRPUT command (4DOS), 499

SDEFRAG command, 891-892

SDIR command, 892-894

search and replace feature, block editing (DOS Editor), 376-377

Search menu bar (DOS Editor), 365

searching
  lost files (FIND filter), 336
  online help topics, 51

secondary caches, disk buffers, 462

secondary command processor, 290-291
  loading, 288-289

sector boundaries, 136
sector interleaving, 134
sectors (disks), 134-137, 150-151

Select All command (File menu), 89

SELECT command (4DOS), 499

selecting
  all files (DOS Shell), 89
  DOS Shell area, 62
  files
    across directories (DOS Shell), 89
    for backups, 243-245
    for recovery, 268
  multiple files (DOS Shell), 87-88
  screen colors, 805-807
  screen type (MODE command), 299
  single files (DOS Shell), 87
  text, block editing (DOS Editor), 373-374

selection cursor (DOS Shell), 63-64

selective restores (backups), 251

SEND command (FTP), 488

sending ANSI.SYS codes, 417
serial numbers (disks), displaying, 154-156, 946-947
serial port cards
  device drivers, troubleshooting, 316
  initializing, 815-816
  MODE command, changing settings, 328-330

SERVER.EXE file, 511

servers, 781-786
  accessing, 770-773
  Interlnk, loading, 226
  protocols, considerations, 473

SET command, 294, 469, 894-897
    AUTOEXEC.BAT file, 30
    CONFIG.SYS file, 27
    environment variables
        changing, 294
        defining, 295
        managing, 520
    parameters/switches, 894
.SET file extension, 509
SETNAME.EXE file, 514
setting environment size (SHELL= statement), 520
SETUP command, 897
SETUP.EXE file, 511
SETUP.MSG file, 511
SETVER command, 898-903
    DOS versions, 280-283
    parameters/switches, 898
SETVER.EXE (device driver), 444, 904-906
shadow RAM, 448
SHARE command, 906-907
SHARE.EXE file, 511
shareware, 494
sharing computers. *See* Interlnk
shell accounts (ISPs)
    Internet connections, 484-485
        troubleshooting, 491-492
    terminal emulation programs, 484-485
SHELL command, 464
    CONFIG.SYS file, 27
    environment size, 26
    parameters, 465-466
    switches, 465-466
SHELL= command, 907-909
SHELL= statement, environment size, setting, 520
SHIFT command, 910
    batch files, 397
    moving batch file parameters, 409-410

Shift+Ctrl+F1 shortcut key (DOS Editor), 367
Shift+Del shortcut key (DOS Editor), 367
Shift+down arrow key, DOS Shell hotkey, 66
Shift+F1 shortcut key (DOS Editor), 367
Shift+F5 key, DOS Shell hotkey, 66
Shift+F6 shortcut key (DOS Editor), 367
Shift+F9 key, DOS Shell hotkey, 66
Shift+Ins shortcut key (DOS Editor), 367
Shift+left arrow key, DOS Shell hotkey, 67
Shift+PrtSc keystroke, Print screen, ROM BIOS controls, 565
Shift+right arrow key, DOS Shell hotkey, 67
Shift+Tab key, DOS Shell hotkey, 67
Shift+up arrow key, DOS Shell hotkey, 66
shortcut keys (DOS Editor), 366
    Alt, 367
    Alt+F1, 367
    Alt+minus, 367
    Alt+plus, 367
    Ctrl+F1, 367
    Ctrl+Ins, 367
    Ctrl+Q, 367
    Del, 367
    Esc, 367
    F1, 367
    F3, 367
    F6, 367
    Shift+Ctrl+F1, 367
    Shift+Del, 367
    Shift+F1, 367
    Shift+F6, 367
    Shift+Ins, 367

shortcut keys (DOS Shell), 83
simple menus, creating (CHOICE command), 405-406
single files, selecting (DOS Shell), 87
single-sided, double density floppy disks (SSDD), 138
SIZER command, 910
SIZER.EXE file, 507, 910
sizing Stacker drives, 880
slashes (/), command syntax, 45
Slavic (Latin II) code page, 354
SlickTerminal, terminal emulation, 484
.SLT file extension, 509
SMARTDrive Monitor program, 914
SMARTDrive utility, 911-913
    disk caching, 169-172
SMARTDRV command, 911-913
    parameters/switches, 911-912
SMARTDRV.EXE device driver, 444, 511, 914
SMARTMON command, 914
SMARTMON.EXE file, 511
SMARTMON.HLP file, 511
SMARTMON.LOG file, 511
SmartTerm, terminal emulation, 484
sockets, locking/unlocking, 714
software
    data loss, troubleshooting, 232-233
    interrupts versus hardware interrupts, 310

SORT command, 915-916
SORT filter
 guidelines for use, 338
 offset values, 337-338
 subdirectory listings, sorting, 338
 syntax, 337-338
SORT.EXE file, 511
sorting
 directories (DEFRAG program), 179-180
 files (DIR command), 197
 subdirectory lists (SORT filter), 338
source code, 163
SourceFiles command syntax, 43-44
SPATCH.BAT file, 512
special characters, DOSKEY macros, 437-438
specifying shortcut key combinations (DOS Shell), 83
splitting
 directories (SUBST command), 302-303
 text (DOS Editor), 371
SSDD floppy disks (single-sided, double density), 138
SSETUP command, 917
SSTOR.SYS file (device driver), 444, 512
STAC command, 917
STACHIGH command, 917
STACKER command, 918
Stacker drives
 checking compressed drives, 626
 creating, 648-649
 defragmenting/recompressing, 891-892
 mounting/unmounting, 918
 online interface, 897, 933
 read/write, read-only passwords, 844
 resizing, 880
 stacvol file, deleting, 875

 statistics, 880
 storing in extended memory, 707-708
 uncompressing, 936, 942
 updating, 750
Stacker Optimizer, 891-892
Stacker Toolbox, 917
STACKER.INI file, re-creating, 638
STACKS= command, 918-920
starting. *See also* executing; launching
 batch files, 392
 configuration files, 624
 DOS after timeout periods, 807-809
 DOS Shell program, 704-707
 DoubleSpace, 654
 DR-DOS help, 700
 File Update System program, 738
 IBM AntiVirus/DOS full-screen program, 759
 PC DOS E Editor, 715-716
 Schedule program, 889-890
 Windows Scripting Host, 649-650
 XDF program, 955
startup control keys
 Ctrl+F5 (Clean Boot), 564
 Ctrl+F8 (Interactive Boot), 564
startup menus
 configuration, 920-922
 defining, 809-811
static electricity and data loss, 232
status bar (DOS Editor), 364
STATUS command (FTP), 488
/STATUS switch
 FDISK command, 163-164
 UNDELETE command, 263

stopping programs, 616-617
storing
 files
  floppy disks, 101
  hard disks, 101
 Stacker driver, extended memory, 707-708
strings, comparing (IF command), 402-403
STY (Stylesheet) filename extension, 107
subdirectories
 branches, deleting, 679
 compressed disk drives, deleting, 661-662
 copying, 950-954
 creating (TREE command), 113-114, 800-801
 deleting, 872-873
  empty, 955
 directory tree, 932
 joining to other drives, 786-788
 renaming, 828-830, 877
 viewing (DIR command), 194-195
Subdirectory file attribute, 108
subdirectory lists, sorting (SORT filter), 338
SUBMENU command, CONFIG.SYS file, 28
SUBMENU= command, 920-922
SUBST command, 302-303, 922-923
 parameters/switches, 922
 pretender, 468-469
 referencing drive paths, 303-304
 rules for use, 304
SUBST.EXE file, 512
supplemental disk files, 512
 4201.CPI, 514
 4208.CPI, 514
 5202.CPI, 514
 ADOS.CFG, 513

SWITCHES   1015

ADOS.COM, 513
ADOS.OVL, 513
ADOS.TXT, 513
AREADME.TXT, 513
ASSIGN.COM, 513
BACKUP.EXE, 513
COMMANDS.TXT, 513
COMP.EXE, 513
CV.COM, 513
DBLBOOT.BAT, 513
DBLBOOT.INI, 513
DVORAK.SYS, 513
DVORAK.TXT, 513
EDLIN.EXE, 513
EXE2BIN.EXE, 513
FAKEMOUS.COM, 513
GORILLA.BAS, 514
GRAFTABL.COM, 513
JOIN.EXE, 514
KBDBUF.SYS, 514
LCD.CPI, 514
MIRROR.COM, 514
MONEY.BAS, 514
MSHERC.COM, 514
NET.1XE, 514
NETWKSTA.1XE, 514
NETWKSTA.2XE, 514
NEUBEUI.DOS, 514
NIBBLES.BAS, 514
NXT.TXT, 514
PRINTER.SYS, 514
PRINTFIX.COM, 514
REDIR.1XE, 514
REDIR.2XE, 514
REMLINE.BAS, 514
SETNAME.EXE, 514
/SURFACE switch, SCANDISK command, 189
suspending batch files, 631-633
SWITCH command, 924
switches
/1
  DISKCOPY command, 211
  FORMAT command, 157
/4, FORMAT command, 157
/8, FORMAT command, 157

/? (help), 46
/A
  COPY command, 203
  DIR command, 194-196
  FC command, 216
  XCOPY command, 207
/ALL
  SCANDISK command, 189
  UNDELETE command, 263
/AUTOFIX, SCANDISK command, 189
/B
  COPY command, 203
  DIR command, 194, 197
  FC command, 216
  FORMAT command, 157
/C
  DIR command, 194
  FC command, 216
  FORMAT command, 157
/CH, DIR command, 194
/CHECKONLY, SCANDISK command, 189
/CLASSIFY, MEM command, 283
/CUSTOM, SCANDISK command, 189
/D
  SETVER command, 282
  XCOPY command, 207
/DEBUG, MEM command, 283
/DOS, UNDELETE command, 263
/DS, UNDELETE command, 263
/DT, UNDELETE command, 263
/E, XCOPY command, 206
/F, FORMAT command, 153, 157
/FRAGMENT, SCANDISK command, 189
/FREE, MEM command, 283
/J, UNFORMAT command, 258

/L
  DIR command, 194, 197
  FC command, 216
  UNFORMAT command, 258
/LIST, UNDELETE command, 263
/LOAD, UNDELETE command, 263
/M
  DISKCOPY command, 211
  XCOPY command, 207
/MODULE, MEM command, 283
/MONO, SCANDISK command, 189
/N
  FC command, 217
  FORMAT command, 157
/NOSAVE, SCANDISK command, 189
/NOSUMMARY, SCANDISK command, 189
/O, DIR command, 194, 197
/P
  DIR command, 194-195
  ERASE command, 221
  UNFORMAT command, 258
  XCOPY command, 206
/PARTN, UNFORMAT command, 258, 261
/PURGE, UNDELETE command, 263
/Q
  FORMAT command, 157
  SETVER command, 282
/RCOPY, INTERSVR command, 224
/S
  DIR command, 194
  FORMAT command, 157
  UNDELETE command, 263
  XCOPY command, 206
/STATUS
  FDISK command, 163-164
  UNDELETE command, 263

/SURFACE, SCANDISK
  command, 189
/T
  FC command, 217
  FORMAT command, 157
  UNDELETE command,
    263
/TEST, UNFORMAT
  command, 258
/U
  FORMAT command, 157
  UNFORMAT command,
    258
/UNDO, SCANDISK
  command, 189
/UNLOAD, UNDELETE
  command, 263
/V
  COPY command, 203
  DISKCOPY command,
    211
  EMM386.EXE, 451
  FORMAT command, 157
  XCOPY command, 206
/W
  DIR command, 194-195
  FC command, 217
  XCOPY command, 206
/Y
  COPY command, 203
  MOVE command, 212
  XCOPY command, 207
ANSI.SYS
  /K, 416
  /R, 416
  /X, 416
ANSI.SYS command, 609
APPEND command, 611
ATTRIB command, 614
BREAK command, 616
BUFFERS= command, 617
CALL command, 619
CD command, 622
CHCP command, 624
CHKDSK command, 185,
  626-627
CHOICE command, 631
COMMAND command,
  635
COMP command, 637
COPY command, 639-640
COUNTRY= command,
  643

CTTY command, 650
DATE command, 653
DBLSPACE/
  AUTOMOUNT command, 655
DBLSPACE/CHKDSK
  command, 656
DBLSPACE/COMPRESS
  command, 656
DBLSPACE/CREATE
  command, 658
DBLSPACE/
  DEFRAGMENT command, 659
DBLSPACE/DELETE
  command, 660
DBLSPACE/
  DOUBLEGUARD command, 661
DBLSPACE/FORMAT
  command, 662
DBLSPACE/INFO command, 662
DBLSPACE/MOUNT
  command, 664
DBLSPACE/RATIO command, 665
DBLSPACE/SIZE command, 666
DBLSPACE/
  UNCOMPRESS command, 667
DBLSPACE/UNMOUNT
  command, 667
DBLSPACE.SYS device
  driver, 668
DEBUG command, 672
DEFRAG command,
  673-674
DEL command, 675
DELOLDOS command,
  676
DELTREE command, 679
DEVICE= command, 680
DEVICEHIGH= command, 683
DIR command, 193,
  687-689
DISKCOMP command,
  690
DISKCOPY command, 692
DISPLAY.SYS device driver, 696

DOS= command, 698
DOSKEY command, 702
DOSSHELL command,
  704-705
DRIVER.SYS device driver,
  708-709
DRIVPARM= command,
  711-712
ECHO command, 717
EDIT command, 719
  /B (DOS Editor), 384
  /G (DOS Editor), 384
  /H (DOS Editor), 385
  /NOHI (DOS Editor),
    385
EGA.SYS device driver, 720
EMM386 command, 722
EMM386.EXE, 449-451,
  723-725
EXE2BIN command, 727
EXPAND command, 728
FASTHELP command, 730
FASTOPEN command,
  731
FC command, 733
FCBS= command, 734
FDISK command, 735
FILES= command, 737
FIND command, 738
FIND filter, 335-336
FOR command, 740
FORMAT command,
  743-744
GOTO command, 747
GRAFTABL command,
  748
GRAPHICS command,
  749-750
HCONVERT command,
  750
HELP command, 751
HIMEM.SYS device driver,
  752-755
IF command, 761
INCLUDE= command,
  766
INSTALL command,
  466-467
INSTALL= command, 768
INTERLNK command,
  770-775

INTERSVR command, 781-782
JOIN command, 786
KBDBUF.SYS device driver, 788
KEYB command, 790
LABEL command, 793
LASTDRIVE= command, 795
LOADFIX command, 798
LOADHIGH command, 798
MEM command, 283, 802
MEMMAKER command, 804
MENUCOLOR= command, 805
MENUDEFAULT= command, 807
MENUITEM= command, 809
MIRROR command, 811
MKDIR command, 800
MODE COM# command, 815
MODE command, 814, 819-823
MODE CON command, 817
MODE LPT# command, 824
MONOUMB.386 command, 826
MORE command, 827
MOVE command, 212, 828
MSAV command, 831-832
MSBACKUP command, 833
MSCDEX command, 835
MSD command, 836
MSHERC command, 837
NLSFUNC command, 840
PATH command, 846
POWER command, 852
POWER.EXE device driver, 855
PRINT command, 322-323, 857
PRINTER.SYS device driver, 860

PROMPT command, 862
QBASIC command, 864
RAMDRIVE.SYS device driver, 868
REM command, 874
RENAME command, 876
REPLACE command, 877
RESTORE command, 881
RMDIR command, 872
SCANDISK command, 189, 884-885
SCANDISK utility, 188-189
SET command, 894
SETVER command, 898, 904
SHARE command, 906
SHELL command, 465-466
SHELL= command, 908
SMARTDRV command, 911-914
SORT command, 915
STACKS= command, 918
SUBMENU= command, 920
SUBST command, 922
SWITCHES= command, 924
SYS command, 927
TIME command, 930
TREE command, 932
TYPE command, 933
UNDELETE command, 936-938
UNFORMAT command, 258, 939
VERIFY command, 943
VFINDTD command, 944
VOL command, 946
VSAFE command, 947
WINA20.386 device driver, 949
XCOPY command, 206, 950-951
SWITCHES command
CONFIG.SYS file, 28
parameters, 467-468
switches, 467-468

SWITCHES= command, 924-926
switching file lists, dual versus single (DOS Shell), 72-73
Symantec Web site, Norton Antivirus information, 253
syntax (commands)
  backslash (\) usage, 45
  Drive\Files format, 43-44
  paradigm, 44
  slash (/) usage, 45
  SourceFiles format, 43-44
SYS (System or device driver) filename extension, 107
SYS command, 167-168, 926-928
  boot disk, 25
  parameters/switches, 927
SYS.COM file, 512
SYSINFO command, 928-929
SysReq keystroke, ROM BIOS controls, 565
system buses, CPU communication, 13
system configuration, 442
  AUTOEXEC.BAT file, 26, 30-32
  changes, monitoring, 866-867
  CONFIG.SYS file, 26-29
  default, 442
    creating, 34
  device drivers, 444
    configuring, 813-815
  hard disks, optimizing, 461-462
  information, gathering, 928-929
  memory
    free/used, displaying, 453-454
    MemMaker, 455-460
    optimizing, 445-451

multiple, creating, 32-33
performance commands, 589
tool (MemMaker), 442
system files
   attribute, 108
   formatting disks, 158
   transferring to disks, 167-168
system resources, allocating among client drivers, 849
system tables, loading into conventional/upper memory, 701

T

/T switch
   FC command, 217
   FORMAT command, 157
   UNDELETE command, 263
Tab key
   dialog boxes (DOS Editor), 366
   DOS Shell hotkey, 67
tab stops in text, setting (DOS Editor), 372
task list area (DOS Shell), 62
Task Swapper (DOS Shell), activating, 93-94
TASKMGR command, 929
TCP/IP (Transmission Control Protocol/Internet Protocol)
   Novell NetWare Client, configuring, 475
   required information, 473
technical information (PCs), displaying, 865
TEE command (4DOS), 499
Telix, terminal emulation, 484
Telnet
   Internet connections, 484-485
      troubleshooting, 491-492

   passwords, 485
   usernames, 485
TEMP environment variable, 525-526
   RAM disks, 176
templates, batch files as, 396
temporary directories, 124-125
terminal emulation
   Procomm Plus, 484
   SlickTerminal, 484
   SmartTerm, 484
   Telix, 484
   Unix commands
      cd, 485
      cp, 485
      ls, 485
      mv, 485
terminate-and-stay-ready (TSR) programs (Interlnk), 223
/TEST switch, UNFORMAT command, 258
testing
   ERRORLEVEL command, 400-402
   programs, 671-672
text
   attributes, screen display (ANSI.SYS controls), 421-422
   automatic indenting (DOS Editor), 372
   block editing
      Clipboard, 374-376
      fundamentals, 373
      text, changing, 378-379
      text, finding, 377-378
      text searching and replacing, 376-377
      text selection, 373-374
   copying (Clipboard), 375
   cutting (Clipboard), 375
   deleting (Clipboard), 375
   deleting from line (DOS Editor), 370-371
   inserting into line (DOS Editor), 370-371

   joining in line (DOS Editor), 371
   overtyping (DOS Editor), 371
   pasting (Clipboard), 375
   place markers (DOS Editor), 373
   splitting in line (DOS Editor), 371
   tab stops (DOS Editor), 372
text boxes, DOS Shell dialog boxes, 67-68
TEXT command (4DOS), 499
text editors. *See* **DOS Editor**
text files
   ANSI.SYS codes, issuing in, 418-419
   ASCII
      editing, 719-720
      viewing (TYPE command), 200-201
   combining (COPY command), 204-205
   comparing (FC command), 218-219
   printing, 201
text screens, clearing, 633-634
text strings
   changing (DOS Editor), 378-379
   finding (DOS Editor), 377-378
   searching and replacing, 376-377
text-based user interfaces
   changing, 295
   Color Graphics Adapter (CGA), 299-300
   command prompt, modifying (PROMPT command), 295-296
   screen
      appearance, customizing (MODE command), 298
      columns/lines adjustments, 300-301
      type, selecting (MODE command), 299

Thick Ethernet, 472
Thin Ethernet, 472
TIF (Tagged Image File Format) filename extension, 107
time, setting, 930-932
TIME command, 278-279, 930-931
time meta-string, 297
TIMEOUT command, 931
timeout periods
    startup configuration, 807-809
    user response time, 931
TIMER command (4DOS), 499
times
    COUNTRY.SYS file, 340-342
    international formats, 356-357
    setting, 276-277
title bar (DOS Shell), 60
TMP (Temporary) filename extension, 107
TMP environment variable, 525-526
topics (online help)
    printing, 50-51
    searching, 51
TOUCH command, 931-932
TOUCH command (4DOS), 499
tracks
    disk drives, 134
    floppy disks, 150
transferring files
    between two computers, 736
    Interlnk, 228
transmitting viruses, 252-253
TREE command, 932
    listing directories, 123-124
    parameters/switches, 932
    subdirectories, creating, 113-114

TREE command (4DOS), 499
TREE.COM file, 512
troubleshooting
    data loss
        hardware causes, 232-233
        software causes, 232-233
    device drivers
        AUTOEXEC.BAT file, editing, 314-315
        CD-ROM drives, 316
        CONFIG.SYS file, editing, 314-315
        conflicts, 314
        IRQ conflicts, 314-315
        modems, 316
        parallel printers, 316
        serial port cards, 316
        video cards, 316
    file editing, 229
    filenames, 125-126
    hard disks, drifting, 148
    Internet connections
        FTP sessions, 491-492
        shell accounts (ISPs), 491-492
        Telnet, 491-492
    memory problems, 460-461
    networks, client software setup, 482
    PCs, Microsoft System Diagnostics, 836-837
    programs, running from C\ prompt, 55
TRY_AGAIN label (batch files), 403
TSRs (terminate-and-stay resident programs), 451
    DELWATCH, 677-678
    device drivers, loading, 451-452
    FASTOPEN, 731-732
    Interlnk, 223
    loading
        into conventional memory, 768-769
        into upper memory, 451-452, 803

TST (Test) filename extension, 107
TUNER command, 933
Turkish code page, 354
turning on/off NumLock key, 840-841
TXT (Text) filename extension, 107
TYPE command, 187, 933-934
    ANSI.SYS, 418-419
    displaying batch file contents, 396
    parameters/switches, 933
    use guidelines, 201
    viewing ASCII files, 200-201
typematic rates, keyboards, changing (MODE command), 331-332

U

/U switch
    FORMAT command, 157
    UNFORMAT command, 258
UMBCGA.SYS device driver, 934
UMBEMS.SYS device driver, 934
UMBHERC.SYS device driver, 935
UMBMONO.SYS device driver, 935
UMBs (upper memory blocks)
    controlling, 721-722
    creating, 722-726
    EMS memory mapping, 934
    video memory, mapping, 934
        Hercules adapters, 935
        monochrome adapters, 935

UNCOMP command, 936
Uncompress option (DoubleSpace), 147
uncompressing
    disk drives, 147, 666-667
    Stacker drives, 936, 942
unconditional formatting of disks, 158
UNDELETE command, 221, 936-939
    parameters/switches, 936-938
    recovering files, 262-266
Undelete command (File menu), 269
Undelete To command (File menu), 269
UNDELETE.EXE file, 512
UNDELETE.INI file, 512
undeleting files, 221
/UNDO switch, SCANDISK command, 189
UNFORMAT command, 939-940
    parameters/switches, 939
    recovering partition tables, 261
    unformatting disks, 257-261
UNFORMAT.COM file, 512
unformatting disks, 257-258
    recovering from accidental formats, 258-261
UNINSTALL command, 940-941
UNINSTALL.EXE file, 511
uninstalling DR-DOS, 940
United States code page, 354
Unix
    filenames, case sensitivity, 485
    Practical Unix, 492
    terminal emulation, 484-485
        cd command, 485
        cp command, 485
        ls command, 485
        mv command, 485

unknown text files, viewing (DOS Editor), 362
/UNLOAD switch, UNDELETE command, 263
unloading DOS Protected Mode Interface support, 707
unlocking drives/sockets, 714
unmounting
    compressed disk drives, 660
    CVFs, 667-668
    Stacker drives, 918
UNPACK2 command, 941
unpacking bundled files, 941
UNSET command (4DOS), 499
UNSTACK command, 942
unused memory, displaying amount of, 802-803
updating
    files, 877-880
    Stacker drives, 750
upper memory
    customizing, 698-700
    listing contents, 286-287
    loading device drivers, 682-686
    loading programs, 798-799
    VGA display, 826-827
upper memory area (UMA), 445
    device drivers, loading, 451-452
    DEVICEHIGH command, 452
    EMM386.EXE, 449
    LOADHIGH command, 452
    RAM, 19
upper memory blocks (UMBs)
    controlling, 721-722
    creating, 722-726
    loading
        device drivers, 803
        TSRs, 803

usable capacity (disks), 139
used memory, displaying amount of, 802-803
user interface
    Color Graphics Adapter (CGA), 299-300
    command prompt, modifying (PROMPT command), 295-296
    screen
        appearance, customizing (MODE command), 298
        columns/lines adjustments, 300-301
        type, selecting (MODE command), 299
    text-based, changing, 295
User label, environment variables, 520
user response time (timeout periods), 931
utilities
    4DOS, 497
        batch file debugger, 500
        command improvements, 497-498
        commands, 498-499
    COM files, 192
    defined, 192
    demoware, 495
    EXE files, 192
    freeware, 494
    McAfee VirusScan, 496-497
    MemMaker, 442
    MSD.EXE (Microsoft Diagnostics), 314
    PCMCIA Resource Management command-line, 850-851
    PKUNZIP, 495-496
    PKZIP, 495-496
    SCANDISK, 188-189
    shareware, 494
    SMARTDrive, 911-913
    versus applications, 192-193

V

/V switch
COPY command, 203
DISKCOPY command, 211
EMM386.EXE, 451
FORMAT command, 157
XCOPY command, 206

variables
environment, 294
APPEND, 520-521
changing (SET command), 294
COMSPEC, 521
CONFIG, 521-522
COPYCMD, 522
defining (SET command), 295
DIRCMD, 522-523
MSDOSDATA, 523-524
PATH, 524-525
PROMPT, 525
TEMP, 525-526
TMP, 525-526
windir, 526
WINPMT, 526-527
system, 304

VER command, 279, 942

VERIFY command, 943-944

version numbers (DOS)
displaying, 279, 942
setting, 280-283

vertical bar meta-string, 296

VFINDTD command, 944

VFINTD.386 device driver, 444, 944-945

VFINTD.386 file, 510

VGA (Video Graphics Array) display, 821
upper memory, increasing, 826-827

video cards
ANSI.SYS controls, 416
device drivers, troubleshooting, 316

video displays. *See also* screen
Hercules Monochrome Graphics Adapter, 837
switching between, 821-823
VGA, upper memory space, increasing, 826-827

Video Graphics Array (VGA), 821
upper memory, increasing, 826-827

video memory, mapping as upper memory blocks, 935
Hercules adapters, 934
monochrome adapters, 935

video modes (DOS Shell), 75-76

VIEW command, 945-946

View File Contents command (File menu), 91-92

View menu commands
Program List, 74
Refresh, 71

viewing
ASCII files (TYPE command), 200-201
bulletin board files (DOS Editor), 362
command-history buffer (DOSKEY), 435
compressed disk drive information, 662-663
directories (DIR command), 194-195
disk drive information, 663
DOS Shell
directories, modifying, 70-74
files, modifying, 70-74
program list, 74
file attributes, 613-615
file information, 687-689
files (DOS Shell), 91-92
subdirectories (DIR command), 194-195
unknown text files (DOS Editor), 362

virtual disks. *See* RAM disks

viruses
data loss, 232
Microsoft Anti-Virus (MSAV), 253-255, 830-832, 838
checklists, 255
virus list, 256
Microsoft Anti-Virus for Windows (MWAV), 253-257
Norton Antivirus, 253
number of, 252-253
potential damage, 252-253
protection guidelines, 257
transmission, 252-253
variations, 252-253

vital file designation, 504

VOL command, 167, 946-947

Volume Label file attribute, 108

volume labels
disks, 793-794
VOL command, 167
displaying, 946-947
floppy disks, 154-156

VSAFE command, 947-948

VSAFE.COM file, 512
running, 838

VSCRPUT command (4DOS), 499

W

/W switch
DIR command, 194-195
FC command, 217
XCOPY command, 206

warm booting
BRB (Big Red Button Time), 24
Ctrl+Alt+Del key combination, 24
effect of, 24
versus cold booting, 24

warning messages, alphabetical listing, 530-557
Web sites
  Downloads.com, 183
  JP Software, 4DOS utility, 497
  PKWare, Zip utilities, 495
  Symantec, 253
  ZDNet, 183
    terminal emulation programs, 484
wildcards
  commands
    asterisk (*), 54-55
    question mark (?), 54-55
  filenames, 594-596
WINA20.386 device driver, 512, 949-950
windir environment variable, 526
window appearance (DOS Editor), 364
Windows 98, SCANREG tool, 888-889
Windows file designation, 504
Windows label, environment variables, 520
Windows Scripting Host, starting, 649-650
WINPMT environment variable, 526-527
WK1 (Worksheet) filename extension, 107
WK2 (Quattro Pro 5.0 spreadsheet) filename extension, 107
WK3 (Worksheet) filename extension, 107
WKQ (Quattro) filename extension, 107
WKS (Worksheet) filename extension, 107
WNTOOLS.GRP file, 512

Workstation Manager 3.x (Novell NetWare Client), 474
WQ1 (Quattro Pro spreadsheet) filename extension, 107
write-caching, 170
write-protecting floppy disks, 132
write/read heads, 133
write/read passwords (Stacker drives), 844
writing README files (DOS Editor), 362

X - Y - Z

/X switch (ANSI.SYS), 416
XBIOS.OVL file, 506
XCOPY command, 950-954
  backing up disks, 208-209
  copying
    directories, 206-207
    directory branches, 209-210
    disks, 209
  defaults, 214
  parameters/switches, 950-951
  switches, 206
    /A, 207
    /D, 207
    /E, 206
    /M, 207
    /P, 206
    /S, 206
    /V, 206
    /W, 206
    /Y, 207
  use guidelines, 207-208
XCOPY.EXE file, 512
XCOPY32 command, 954
XDEL command, 955
XDF command, 955
XDF program, starting, 955

XDFCOPY command, 956
XDIR command, 956-957
XLM (Excel macro) filename extension, 107
XLS (Excel spreadsheet) filename extension, 107
XMS (Extended Memory Specification), 20, 283-288
  converting to LIM expanded memory (EMS), 722-726
XT processors, 17

/Y switch
  COPY command, 203
  MOVE command, 212
  XCOPY command, 207

ZDNet Web site, 183
  terminal emulation programs, 484
Zip drives, 21
Zip files
  filename extension, 107
  utilities
    PKUNZIP, 495-496
    PKZIP, 495-496

Hey, you've got enough worries.
Don't let IT training be one of them.

Get on the fast track to IT training at InformIT,
your total Information Technology training network.

 | **www.informit.com** |

- Hundreds of timely articles on dozens of topics ■ Discounts on IT books from all our publishing partners, including Que Publishing ■ Free, unabridged books from the InformIT Free Library ■ "Expert Q&A"—our live, online chat with IT experts ■ Faster, easier certification and training from our Web- or classroom-based training programs ■ Current IT news ■ Software downloads
- Career-enhancing resources

InformIT is a registered trademark of Pearson. Copyright ©2001 by Pearson.
Copyright ©2001 by Que Corporation.